CATHEDRAL PREP BASKETBALL CHRONICLES
1924-2017

Daniel J. Brabender, Jr.

Erie, Pennyslvania
2017

Address all correspondence to:
Daniel J. Brabender, Jr.
411 Cherokee Drive
Erie, Pennsylvania 16505

Publishing Management:
Printing Concepts, Inc.
4982 Pacific Avenue
Erie, Pennsylvania 16506
(814) 833-8080

Printed in the United States of America.

ISBN No. 978-0-692-97554-1

Dedication

This book is written so that the basketball players and coaches, who by their athletic prowess and achievements have done so much for the sports-loving people of Erie, Pennsylvania, may not be forgotten.

To those named herein, this book is dedicated.

This book is also dedicated to Rambler students and fans—past, present and future.

Contents

Foreword

Dan Brabender previously set down Cathedral Prep's celebrated football history and now has faithfully chronicled its glorious basketball history.

The *Cathedral Prep Basketball Chronicles* reflects diligent research drawing from innumerable sources. It presents Prep and Erie area basketball objectively and makes a solid contribution to Erie's sports antiquity.

Danny brings the Rambler spirit to his book and this worthwhile work will always hold a prominent position in our school's archives.

Father Scott Jabo
President, Cathedral Preparatory School

Preface

I am confident that the *Cathedral Prep Basketball Chronicles* is the most comprehensive high school basketball history ever assembled.

Over a dozen years of intense research went into the compilation and writing of this book. Innumerable sources were hunted down in search of information that simply is not readily available. There is a wealth of trivia, detail and statistical matter put together in a year-by-year format. The charts and records presented in this book are all completely original and cannot be found anywhere else.

Many thanks to Jodie Farbotnik of Ever After Images for her expert advice and assistance on the cover art and on hundreds of photographs, most which have never been published before. Further photographic assistance was provided by Chris Millette of the *Erie Times-News*. Many contributed photos, including Ron Sertz, Jim Hamilton, Jim Spoden, Grant Miller, Tim Maloney, Keith Hardner, Vern Gambill, Jim Stevenson, Mary Mehl, Mike Fetzner, Denis O'Brien, Pam Hampy, Margaret Piotrowicz, Natalie Sweny, Ray Fiorelli, Todd Filipkowski, Sue Dipre, Julia Fetzner, Bobby Achille, Danny Achille, Rick Bordonaro, Tim Fox, Marty Orzechowski, Mickey McMahon, Andy Sisinni, Dave Wenrick, Pat Flaherty, Julie Kuhar, Jim Fetzner, Joanne Kubinski and, of course, the *Erie Times-News*.

Many thanks to Michael P. Martin and Shannon Lutz of Printing Concepts, Inc. for their patience and expert advice in the production of this book.

In an effort to keep this material as complete and accurate as possible, readers are encouraged to send further information and corrections to the author. Please include verification, such as newspaper accounts, scorebooks, etc.

We now have a permanent record of Cathedral Prep and Erie area high school basketball.

Daniel J. Brabender, Jr.

Introduction

The honorable game of "Basket Ball" was invented in Springfield (MA) in 1891 by Canadian Dr. James Naismith, who was trying to keep his gym class active on a rainy day. He devised basic rules and nailed a peach basket onto a 10-foot elevated track. The peach basket retained its bottom, and balls had to be retrieved manually after each "basket" or point scored. This proved inefficient, however, so the bottom of the basket was removed. Metal rims with backboards did not come into effect until 1906.

Dr. James Naismith

Originally played with 9-man teams divided into three sections, games were rough and tumble affairs, with few rules and few infractions called by mustachioed referees wearing tall hats. Basketball was originally played with soccer balls that were eventually replaced by dark brown "basket-balls." The orange-colored balls did not come into prominence until the 1950's.

Basketball's early adherents were dispatched to YMCAs throughout the United States, and it quickly spread through the USA and Canada. The game was well established at several high schools by 1895 when it became a five-man sport.

Before widespread school district consolidation, most American high schools were far smaller than their present-day counterparts. During the first decades of the 20th century, basketball quickly became the ideal interscholastic sport due to its modest equipment and personnel requirements. In the days before widespread television coverage of professional and college sports, the popularity of high school basketball was unrivaled in many parts of America. Today nearly every high school in America has a basketball team.

Prior to the 1919-20 school year, the City of Erie, Pennsylvania had one secondary school—Erie High School (1891-1920), which was well regarded for fielding excellent football squads and basketball fives. With the opening of brand new Academy High on upper State Street in 1919, the city had two high schools competing at a "Class A", or large school, level. The new East High on Atkins Street opened in 1920 and Erie then had three city public secondary "Class A" schools. Hence began the "City Series," a sports league consisting of East, Academy and what was called Central High School (1920-1930), the outgrowth of old Erie High. Central was located in the same building on the southeast corner of West

Erie High School 1918

Tenth and Sassafras Streets. That building later became Technical High School (1931-1959), after Central's entire student body and faculty was moved to the new school on West Eighth Street called Strong Vincent in 1930.

Central High was the early power in City Series basketball, winning the league title four straight years, from 1920 (as Erie High, 11-4) to 1923. Central's final records from 1921 to 1923 were 13-3, 14-4 and 16-8. The city's big stars early in the decade were **Ted Meier**, **Augie Newcamp** and **Dallas Butler** of East; **"Flip" Hershey**, **Byron Bauer**, **Sam Roberts**, **Johnnie Brace**, **Joe Schilling** and **Edmund L. Thomas** of Academy; and Central's **Ottomer Deck**, **"String" Nash** and **Robin Bell**, a transfer from West Virginia. East dominated the mid-20's with coach Gus Anderson, winning in 1924 (15-6), 1925 (21-2) and 1926 (25-2). The 1926 East team made it all the way to the PIAA state championship game where it lost to Nanticoke, 44-25. Central was again on top in 1927 (15-5) and 1928 (17-7) under coach **Jim Hyde**, while Academy, coached by **Darby Mannix**, won its first title in 1929 (20-2). Academy won again in 1931 (21-4) under coach **Howard Kelly**.

East again dominated in the next decade, regaining the crown in 1930 (19-5), then winning every title from 1933 to 1938, except for 1936. Hyde was the East mentor from 1929 to 1934, whereupon **"Jack" Komora** took over the East reins for the next 11 years. The East records its championship years: 19-5, 13-6, 15-6, 21-6, 15-9 and 13-7. Strong Vincent won the City Series and made it to the PIAA state final in 1932 (24-3-1) under coach H**arold "Sam" Kramer**, where it lost to Old Forge, 24-19. SV also won the city diadem in 1936 (21-5) under Kramer. Academy regained its form under coach **Edmund L. "Pee Wee" Thomas** in 1939 (15-8-1) and 1940 (14-2-2). Coach Komora also won city titles at East from 1941 through 1944 (18-6-1, 14-5, 16-6 and 20-9). Technical finally won its first city championships in 1945 (17-3) and 1946 (17-7) under coach **"Ted" Robb**.

Erie Cathedral Preparatory School for Boys, with its campus covering nearly an entire city block between Sassafras and Myrtle Streets and West Ninth and West Tenth Streets, was founded in 1921 by sports-loving **Bishop John Mark Gannon**. The first headmaster was **Monsignor Joseph "Doc" Wehrle** (1921-41), a remarkable academician who nevertheless did have an interest in his boys engaging in athletics. "The Prep school" sponsored its first basketball team in 1924-25 and played mostly an independent "Class B" schedule for several years. The 1942-43 season marked Prep's initial

Bishop John Mark Gannon   *Monsignor Joseph Wehrle*

entry into the Erie City Series basketball league. For the first time in basketball the "Ramblers" competed as an official league member against Strong Vincent, Technical, East and Academy. This affiliation was a direct result of the World War II-inspired travel restrictions caused by gasoline and tire rationing and the need for the public schools to schedule local contests to comply. Though Prep was in the City Series in football from 1934-38, from 1943 on the Ramblers would compete against its city rivals in league competition in all sports. Cathedral Prep basketball first earned the title "City Champion" in 1947 (19-6) under coach **Walt Strosser**. Though Strosser is famous for coaching Prep football to its first City Series crown in 1949, most don't realize he was the first Prep basketball coach to win a city championship.

All of the city public schools at one time or another had been considered Prep's "archrival," particularly Strong Vincent and Technical, primarily because of locality. Tech remained a rival when it became Tech Memorial (1959-1992) and moved from being "kiddie corner" from Prep to upper Cherry Street in the late 1950's. Tech became a different school called Central Tech (1993-2017) and once-great Academy (1919-1992) is now non-athletic Collegiate Academy (1994-present).

Brand new Erie High School, a consolidation of Vincent, East and Central Tech, will be housed in the Cherry Street facility, beginning with the 2017-18 school year. Vincent and East will be converted to middle schools.

Prep's main rival since the late 1960's is, without a doubt, McDowell High School. For decades the "Trojans" have offered stiff competition for Prep in every sport which they compete. Located in Erie's important suburb of Millcreek Township, McDowell was originally called "West Millcreek High," and later simply "Millcreek High," and was located on West Ridge Road near the township's present school administration building. The new school, opened in 1954, was built on West 38th Street near Caughey Road and christened "McDowell High School," in honor of the McDowell sisters who willed their family farm to the school district. As "West Millcreek" and "Millcreek," the Trojans toiled mostly with "Class B" competition in the Erie County League. McDowell entered "Class A" circles for good in the 1950's when the school's enrollment grew steadily and Millcreek Township became fully suburbanized.

Though most high schools may be fortunate to have had one so-called "Golden Era" in basketball, Cathedral Prep has had many, witness the regimes of **Richard "Dick" Detzel** (1948-57), **Richard "Dick" Fox** (1967-71), **William "Bill" Flaherty** (1971-84), **Marcel Arribi** (1987-99), **Brian Flanagan** (2004-08) and currently **Mark Majewski** (2008-present). All of Prep's local rivals have had golden years, but no secondary school in the Erie area has come close to achieving the success Prep has had in basketball, despite a rather slow start. The Ramblers now have no less than 45 league championships, 21 District 10 titles, 9 state final appearances and 6 state crowns.

The Pennsylvania Interscholastic Athletic Association (PIAA) is the voluntary membership organization that consists of almost all of the public high schools and many of the charter and private high schools in the Commonwealth of Pennsylvania. Generally stated, the function of the PIAA is to develop and enforce rules regulating interscholastic athletic competition, which are authorized or adopted by the member schools. The PIAA was formed in Pittsburgh on December 29, 1913, by a group of high school principals who wanted to eliminate abuses, establish uniform rules, and place interscholastic athletics in the overall context of secondary education. There are currently 12 "districts" within the PIAA, of which Northwestern Pennsylvania is represented by "District 10." Cathedral Prep was not granted membership in the PIAA District 10 until 1973.

The PIAA had a long history of discrimination and bigotry against private, Catholic schools. Cathedral Prep made application to join the PIAA on various occasions since 1928, but had always been refused on one pretext or another. The PIAA always ruled Catholic schools couldn't possibly belong because they didn't follow "the rules" as set down by the PIAA, such as having full-time coaches that taught within the schools and an "8-semester" rule. When many parochial schools adopted and strictly followed the PIAA rules, as Prep did from 1928 on, the answer was still "no."

Prep had been a charter member of an offshoot called the Pennsylvania Catholic Interscholastic Athletic Association (PCIAA) since 1943. Championship teams were determined from each of the six dioceses in the state, with the winners meeting in inter-diocesan play along the same lines as the PIAA district competition. Prep won Class A (large school) state championships in 1953 (23-4), 1954 (22-3), 1968 (19-5) and 1971 (21-3). The final PCIAA Class A tourney was held in 1973, but it was a shadow of itself because many Catholic schools had already joined the PIAA, Prep included. The final PCIAA Class B and Class C tourneys were held in 1974.

Many times over the decades legislators had risen in the chamber at Harrisburg to demand that the PIAA be investigated, that it clean house, rid itself of bigotry and open the door to athletes of all the secondary schools, no matter what the race, color or creed. Somehow, however, the PIAA had slyly weathered all attacks and went its wretched way. That was until October, 1972, when **Governor Milton Shapp** signed a bill into law that allowed private and Catholic schools to join the then-1,100 member organization. Under the old rules, private and parochial schools could only compete with public schools during the regular season, but not in post-season playoffs. Prep athletes then became eligible to compete in section, district, regional and state playoffs. Headmaster **Father John Dollinger** (1972-84) oversaw Prep's transition into the PIAA and within a short time he became a power within the District 10 committee. Prep has won PIAA state basketball championships in 1980 (33-1) and 1993 (21-7); and has finished runners-up in 1984 (27-6), 1994 (24-7) and 1996 (24-8).

Cathedral Prep now competes under the PIAA banner in 12 different sports. Over the years the school, the teams and individuals have made solid athletic reputations locally, state-wide and nationally. There is currently great excitement as Prep embarks on a new era with the opening of the Cathedral Prep-Villa Maria Events Center (PVEC), with its brand new gymnasium and natatorium.

Headmaster **Monsignor Robert McDonald** (1944-72) maintained high spiritual, scholastic and athletic standards at Prep, and further set an example for all of his students with his motto of "Aim High." Monsignor McDonald, though stern and demanding, wanted nothing but the best for his students and he wanted them to give nothing less than their best in return. All of the Prep headmasters, right down to current Prep-Villa president **Father Scott Jabo** (2000-present), have done a tremendous job of keeping with Prep's mission of developing men of vision in spirit, mind, and body. For that this author is thankful.

Monsignor Robert McDonald   *Father Scott Jabo*

Legend:

Date—Exact Date Game was Played
Dec.—Won or Lost
Loc.—Site Where a Game was Played
Pos.—Usual Position
F—Forward
C—Center
G—Guard
Prior School—School Attended before Prep
Class—Year in School
Sr.—Senior
Jr.—Junior
Soph.—Sophomore
Fr.—Freshman
Ht.—Height

G(GS)—Games Played In (Games Started)
FG(3)—Field Goals (3-point Field Goals)
FT—Free Throws
Total—Total Points in a Season
Career—Total Points in a Career
PPG—Average Points Per Game
(0-0)—Usually an Opponent's Season Record
W—Won
L—Lost
H—Home
A—Away
N—Neutral
[College]—College Played At or Pro Team
*—Record High or Most
**—Record Low or Least

CATHEDRAL PREP BASKETBALL CHRONICLES
1924-2017

Daniel J. Brabender, Jr.

The 1920's

Cathedral Prep's first varsity basketball team (1924-25). Front row, L to R: Kenny Sechrist, Captain Walter McCallion, Lester Hahn, Harrison Clemens; Back Row: George Murphy, Nelson "Fat" Schumacher, Frank Kaltenbach, Ralph Cochrane, Manager Walter White.

Watch the Prep!

1924-25 (5-12)

Coach: Wilmot G. Quillman
Captain: Walter McCallion
Manager: Walter "One Shot" White

Wilmot Quillman, Prep's first basketball coach.

Date	PREP		Dec.	Loc.	High Scorer	Opponent
1/6		East (CANCELLED)		A		
1/16	19	Central High Seconds	30	L	H	Murphy (7)	Hamm (7)
2/4	29	Sharon Sacred Heart	47	L	A	Murphy (12)	Conlon (13)
2/6	13**	Cleveland (OH) Cathedral Latin	41	L	A	UNREPORTED	
2/11	13**	Phillips Fruits	21	L	H	Murphy (6)	Metz & Jordano (8)
2/13	36*	Greenville St. Michael's	11**	W	H	UNREPORTED	
2/14	15	Central High Seconds	12	W	A	Clemens (6)	Haggerty (4)
2/17	27	"L" Club	25	W	H	Kaltenbach (12)	Wallace (9)
2/20	22	Sharon Sacred Heart	25	L	H	Kaltenbach (11)	Conlon (10)
2/21	27	Schaller Morticians	58*	L	H	Hahn (16)*	Laprice (27)*
2/28	27	Union City	44	L	H	McCallion (7)	Brooks (10)
3/4	27	Wayne M.E.	30	L	A	Clemens (13)	C. Texter (13)
3/5	18	Carlton Druggists	27	L	H	Hahn (10)	J. Heintzel (10)
3/6	31	Greenville St. Michael's	24	W	A	Sechrist (7)	Bresnan (10)
3/10	17	Carlton Druggists	19	L	A	Cochrane (5)	Birk (5)
3/13	21	Wayne M. E.	26	L	H	Kaltenbach (10)	Schwindt (11)
3/25	28	Harlock Pentagons	25	W	H	Hahn (12)	Wurst (8)
3/28	15	Sharrer's Elites	31	L	H	Hahn (6)	Matts (17)
	385* (22.6*)		**496* (29.2*)**			

Pos.	Player	Prior School	Class	G(GS)	FG	FT	Total	PPG
C	Frank "Spike" Kaltenbach	St. Joseph	Jr.	12(11)	27	10*	64*	5.3
F	Lester Hahn	St. Patrick's	Jr.	15*(12)	31*	0	62	4.1
F	Walter McCallion	Gridley	Sr.	10(9)	23	5	51	5.1
F-G	Harrison Clemens	Central HS	Soph.	7(7)	21	6	48	6.9*
G	George "Uncle" Murphy	Gridley	Sr.	6(5)	13	6	32	5.3
G	Nelson "Fat" Schumacher	St. Peter's	Jr.	15*(14*)	9	1	19	1.3
G	Ralph Cochrane	St. John's	Sr.	8(5)	7	5	19	2.4
F	Kenneth "Ribs" Sechrist	St. Patrick's	Soph.	6(2)	9	1	19	3.2
G	Joe "Flash" Gorny	St. Stan's	Soph.	7(6)	4	6	14	2.0
G	Harry "Hic" Roland	Emerson	Sr.	3(1)	2	0	4	1.3
C	Joe Szczepanski	St. Stan's	Soph.	1(1)	1	0	2	2.0
F	Bill Brown	St. John's	Sr.	1	1	0	2	2.0
C	Richard "Dick" Schumacher	St. Peter's	Fr.	1(1)	0	0	0	0.0

HIGHLIGHTS:

- Cathedral Prep was founded by **Archbishop John Mark Gannon** in 1921. Prep's first headmaster was **Father Joseph J. Wehrle**, D.D., who served from 1921 to 1941. A remarkable academian, "Doc" Wehrle was impressed with how well the Prep boys comported themselves in the school's first football season (1924) and he gave the OK for the inauguration of a basketball program.

- 1924-1925 was Cathedral Prep's first basketball season, and all home games were played at St. Joseph's Orphanage on "the West Lake Road" (now West Sixth Street), near Delaware Avenue. Practice sessions were also held at the orphanage's gymnasium, built in 1912.

- Thirteen boys made the cut for Prep's first basketball team out of 30 that reported for tryouts. On the night before the season opener, the players voted for team captain in a secret ballot. Senior **Walter McCallion** was chosen to be the captain of Prep's first basketball team. His first duty was to pass out the new orange and black suits to the team. That same day during practice Bishop Gannon came by and gave words of encouragement and advice to the squad. The boys later stated "it was worth more than a million dollars" to know the Bishop had confidence in his Prep boys.

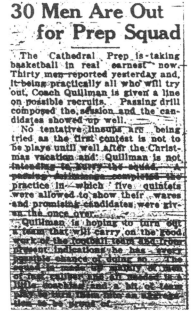

30 Men Are Out for Prep Squad

The Cathedral Prep is taking basketball in real earnest now. Thirty men reported yesterday and, it being practically all who will try out, Coach Quillman is given a line on possible recruits. Passing drill composed the session and the candidates showed up well.

No tentative lineups are being tried as the first contest is not to be played until well after the Christmas vacation and Quillman is not intending to hurry the squad. A passing scrimmage completed the practice in which five quintets were allowed to show their wares and promising candidates were given the once over.

Quillman is hoping to turn out a team that will carry on the good work of the football team and from present indications he has every possible chance of doing so...

- In the local newspapers the team was referred to as "Cathedral High," or adding a nickname the "Cathedral Preps" or simply the "Preps." The first team's motto as it aspired to great things in the future: "Watch the Prep!"

- Although Prep was a regular opponent of the city schools throughout the years of the Great Depression, it mostly competed with smaller, "Class B" schools. It was not until the 1942-43 school year that Prep became an official City Series member in all available sports. Prior to that year, Prep was a league member on occasion in the "minor" sports of golf and tennis, and in football from 1935 to 1938.

- Prep was supposed to play Erie Central in a December 19 opener, but the squad was simply not ready and a gloom was cast over the pre-season when captain **Walter McCallion**, according to the *Erie Daily Times*, was "seized with an attack of appendicitis" and unable to perform.

- Another Prep contest was scheduled for January 6, 1925 vs. defending Erie city champion East High (21-2), but coach **Wilmot Quillman** "deemed it

Walter McCallion, the captain of Prep's first basketball team.

advisable to cancel." One reason was that the Prep netters had a long break over Christmas vacation, and East, though only in existence for five years, was already considered a regional power. East, District 8 champion, reached the PIAA Western Final where it lost to eventual state champion Uniontown, 30-20. East had won the D-8 title in 1923 and finished runner-up to Greenville Penn in 1924.

- Coach Quillman, a former Gridley Junior High and Erie Central High star, was also the head coach of Prep's first football team (also 1924). Prep authorities were so impressed with the value of Quillman's work on the gridiron that he was sought out for the roundball mentor position as well.

- City public schools Erie East High, Erie Central and Erie Academy were members of District III of the Northwest Pennsylvania Interscholastic Athletic League (NWPIAL), one of three districts in the state's ruling body, the Pennsylvania Interscholastic Athletic Association (PIAA). Other NWPIAL D-III member schools included Franklin, Meadville, Oil City, Titusville and Warren. The PIAA reorganized into eight districts for the 1923-24 season, with District 8 covering the same area as the NWPIAL. The counties in D-8 included Erie, Crawford, Venango, Warren, McKean, Potter, Cameron, Elk, Forest, Jefferson, Clarion and Mercer.

- Prep's first game ever was a 30-19 loss to the Central High Seconds on January 16, 1925 on the Orphanage court. It was noted in the newspapers that both teams were "ragged and erratic" and that "over-confidence did as much to spoil the chances of the Prep as any other factor." Prep's first field goal ever was scored by senior **George Murphy** in that game, while **Ralph Cochrane** made Prep's first foul shot. Bishop Gannon paid a visit to the team the next day and told them what a good game they played. Prep avenged that defeat four weeks later on the Downtown YMCA court, 15-12. The "Preps" did not play another Erie city school for the rest of the 1920's decade.

PREPS DROPPED FIRST COURT GAME

Displaying a loose and somewhat slow game, the Cathedral Preps yesterday afternoon on their court bowed in defeat to the Central Seconds, 30 to 19. In every department of play there was a looseness on the part of the Prep team that spelled defeat for them before the final whistle decided the fact. Neither team scored consistently, both being ragged and erratic - with Central caging enough more to vanquish their rivals.

It may be said that over-confidence did as much to spoil the chances of the Prep as any other factor. They, at the outset, were confident as to the final score and when they saw the need of a scoring spurt that would put them in the lead, they were either too careless of their own chances or were too closely guarded by Andy Fletcher's proteges. With the ball in their possession, the Prepites seemed incapable of handling it to their own advantage, and many times assisted their opponents to count up field goals by their unaimed and careless passing. Central, aided by these small, but almost consistent breaks, kept ringing in from the hands of Felbinger, Hamm, and Rice, sufficient baskets enough to clinch the game for the Red and Black...

- Prep's second battle was its first road trip and a 47-29 loss to Sharon Sacred Heart (12-7). Ahead by just two at the start of the 4th quarter, Sacred Heart went on a 23-7 run in the final period to bury the Preps. SH also won a close rematch at the Orphanage court. Prep never played Sharon Sacred Heart again, most likely because it became an all-girls' school shortly thereafter! Sacred Heart star **Joe Conlon**, just a 9th-grader, transferred to Sharon High where he was team captain of the 1928 District 8 champions. He also started the previous season for Sharon (1926-27), a team that finished 25-2 and made it to the state final.

- Prep opened with four straight losses, including one at Cathedral Latin (10-7), the defending Cleveland city champions. Cathedral Latin went on to play in the second annual National

Catholic Interscholastic Basketball Tournament (NCIBT) in Chicago after defeating St. Ignatius for the Cleveland Catholic title. Latin won its first round matchup over Rockford (IL) St. Thomas Academy, 30-12, before losing to eventual runner-up Milwaukee (WI) Marquette, 21-11.

- Prep finally recorded its first-ever basketball victory over Greenville St. Mike's on February 13, 1925. Later was a 5-game consecutive loss string (tied in 1931, 1935, 1936 and 1943), which lasted as a Prep record until 1943, when the Ramblers lost 8 straight.

- **George Murphy** was Prep's leading scorer until mid-season, when sickness forced him to miss the remainder of the campaign. He did play for the Cathedral Prep College team in the 1926-27 season.

George Murphy scored the first field goal ever for Prep.

- Cathedral Prep and opponents Sharon Sacred Heart and Greenville St. Michael's, as well as Titusville St. Titus, became members of what was called the Catholic School League of Northwestern Pennsylvania. Other schools considered for the new circuit included Punxsutawney Sts. Cosmas and Damien, DuBois St. Catherine's, Franklin St. Patrick's and Erie St. Stanislaus, but their participation never came to fruition. At season's end, St. Titus, for which contests with Prep never materialized, claimed the Catholic championship of Northwestern PA by virtue of its 26-25 overtime victory over Sacred Heart, which defeated Prep twice. The final standings of Prep's initial venture into league play:

	W	L
Titusville St. Titus	2	1
Sharon Sacred Heart	3	2
CATHEDRAL PREP	2	2
Greenville St. Michael's	2	4

- Opponents Phillips Fruits and Schaller Morticians were local Erie club teams from the City Junior League. Other teams in the league included Neighborhood House, St. Mary's Gems, Pennants, Times Seniors, Academy Crescents and the 8th Street Boys' Club Alerts, more commonly known as the "Pebocs."

- Prep's poorest showing was against the Schaller Morticians "being the result of inaccurate shooting, poor passing and the inability to stop several of their opponents' advances," according to the *Erie Dispatch-Herald*.

- Wayne Methodist Episcopal (Wayne M. E.) was an independent church team that played a notch above the local Sunday School League fives. Wayne M. E. finished the 1924-25 season with a 30-3 record!

- The Harlock Pentagons were an independent team composed of players from Simpson M. E. of the Sunday School League along with some members of the Academy High School varsity.

- Opponents Carlton Druggists and "L" Club (formerly called the "YMCA Leaders") were local Erie independent club teams.

- Sharrer's Elites was a strong independent team sponsored by a clothes shop located on Parade Street. They were sometimes called the "Parade Street Merchants."

- Early Prep records included **Lester Hahn's** 8 field goals against Schaller Morticians and **Frank Kaltenbach's** (later **Monsignor Frank Kaltenbach**) 4 successful free throws versus the "L" Club. Leading scorer **Harrison Clemens** (6.9 PPG), only a sophomore, simply left school after the first semester.

- The length of the quarters in a game was set at 10 minutes.

- There was no "10-second rule" in effect until 1933. Oftentimes a team would "freeze" the ball in its own backcourt, thus resulting in several low-scoring games.

- Rules at the time provided for jump balls at center court after every field goal. The time clock continued during these stoppages of play, taking an average of 12 minutes per game away from each contest. The rule providing possession of the ball to the opposition after a field goal did not come into effect until 1937.

- Defenders were allowed to "goal-tend" until 1944. A tall player would often position himself beneath the hoop and knock the ball out of the net and rim, thus making it difficult to score.

- The American Basketball Association professional league formed in 1925 and added 3 major rules: mandatory backboards, a 3- second violation in the lane and a "5 fouls and you're out" rule.

- Passaic (NJ) High School was considered the foremost schoolboy basketball program at the time with a world's record 159-game winning skein and outscoring opponents by an average of 59-20 since the 1919-20 season. The streak came to an end on February 6, 1925, when Hackensack (NJ) defeated the Indians, 39-35. Passaic's seasons' records during the streak: 1919-20—26-0; 1920-21—31-0; 1921-22—33-0; 1922-23—28-0; 1923-24—29-0; and before the loss in 1924-25—12-0!

1925 All-Opponent Team:

Al Hamm, Central Seconds
Joseph Conlon, Sharon Sacred Heart
Ed Buckley, Sharon Sacred Heart
Francis McCann, Cathedral Latin
Mike Cannavino, Phillips Fruits
William Carney, Sharon Sacred Heart
Ed Kinney, Sharon Sacred Heart
Chester Laprice, Schaller Morticians
Ed Allen, Schaller Morticians
Harold Brooks, Union City
Frank Wolfe, Union City
Clifford Texter, Wayne M. E.
Ralph Texter, Wayne M. E.
Joe Heintzel, Carlton Druggists
Bruno Heintzel, Carlton Druggists
Tom Bresnan, Greenville St. Mike's

Ralph Cochrane was the first Prepster to convert a foul shot.

Walter White, Prep's first basketball manager.

The "Preps" Win Silver Loving Cup! East High Goes All the Way to State Final!

1925-26 (7-7)

Coach: James V. ("Jim" or "Gyp" or "Gipe") Sullivan
Captain: Nelson "Fat" Schumacher
Manager: Henry Francisco

Nelson "Fat" Schumacher, team captain. He went on to star in football at St. Bonaventure.

Date	PREP			Dec.	Loc.	High Scorer	Opponent
1/8	14	Greenville St. Michael's	12	W	H	Hahn (8)	LaSalle (5)
1/15	20	Titusville St. Titus	28	L	A	Gorny (13)	Teege (14)
1/18	9**	Alliance Academy	55	L	A	Gorny (5)	Miller (17)
1/22	19	Alumni	17	W	H	Gorny (7)	Murphy (6)
2/5		Union City (CANCELLED)		H			
2/5	11	St. Mary's Gems	18	L	H	Hahn (7)	N. Haft (10)
2/19	20	Titusville St. Titus	19	W	H	Sechrist (7)	Foley (7)
2/26	28	Brocton (NY) Central	30	L	A	Hahn & Gorny (10)	Lathrop (14)
2/27	13	Meadville	27	L	A	Sechrist (6)	Anselmo (13)
		BROCTON (NY) INVITATIONAL TOURNAMENT					
3/5	9**	Silver Creek (NY) Central	14	L	N	Sechrist & Gorny (4)	C. Millet (6)
3/6	17	Ripley (NY) Central	4**	W	N	Kaltenbach (11)	Ottoway & Atkins (2)
3/6	30	Falconer (NY) Central	16	W	N	Hahn & Sechrist (8)	Lawson (8)
3/12	42*	Brocton (NY) Central	17	W	H	Gorny (12)	L. Skinner (5)
3/20	23	Greenville St. Michael's	16	W	A	Gorny (11)	Driscoll (8)
3/27	11	Alliance Academy	25	L	H	Gorny (5)	Furtik & Kurzawski (10)
	266 (19.0**)**		**298** (21.3**)**				

Pos.	Player	Prior School	Class	G(GS)	FG	FT	Total	PPG	Career
G-F	Joe "Flash" Gorny	St. Stan's	Jr.	14(14*)	33*	18*	84*	6.0	98
F	Kenneth "Ribs" Sechrist	St. Patrick's	Jr.	14(14*)	27	4	58	4.1	77
F	Lester Hahn	St. Patrick's	Sr.	13(13)	21	8	50	3.8	112*
C	Frank "Spike" Kaltenbach	St. Joseph	Sr.	13(13)	17	8	42	3.2	106
G	Nelson "Fat" Schumacher	St. Peter's	Sr.	14(14*)	9	7	25	1.8	44
C-F	John "Damon" Daly	St. Mary's	Fr.	9(1)	4	1	9	1.0	9
G	Richard "Dick" Schumacher	St. Peter's	Soph.	8(1)	0	1	1	0.1	1
F	Joe McGrath	St. Peter's	Soph.	3	0	0	0	0.0	0
G	Frank Richards	St. Peter's	Soph.	1	0	0	0	0.0	0
G	Joe Krotoszynski[Kroto]	Holy Rosary	Soph.	1	0	0	0	0.0	0

HIGHLIGHTS:

- Cathedral Prep's first basketball coach, **Wilmot Quillman**, left the position to attend and compete at Grove City College, where he became a star. Prep retained a new coach for its second season, **James ("Jim" or "Gyp" or "Gipe") Sullivan**, who kept 10 boys out of the 25 that tried out. Sullivan, a Homestead native, played for the Central Stars of the City League and was attending classes at Villa Maria College. He was also a star lineman on Prep's 1926 and 1927 football teams that played mostly a college freshmen and prep school schedule.

- Prep's first two home games of the season were played at St. Mary's Parish gym at East 9th and German Streets, while the remainder were played at St. Joseph's Orphanage. Some practice sessions were held at Columbus School at West 17th and Poplar Streets in Erie's Little Italy section.

- Alliance Academy's (5-1) 47-point victory margin stayed as a Prep record largest losing spread for 47 years until the Ramblers lost to Cleveland St. Joe's, 85-38, in 1972-73.

- Polish National Alliance (PNA) College in Cambridge Springs, Crawford County, was founded as Alliance Academy in 1912. As a junior college, Alliance Academy competed with area high schools in athletics until a 1938 PIAA ruling which forbade high schools from competing with junior colleges or college freshmen teams. Alliance Academy became four-year Alliance College in 1948, eventually closing its doors in 1988.

- It was common in the early era for a high school athletic team to play against an alumni squad from its school. An alumni team would usually fall just short of the regular school team, and the results were always made part of the regular season statistics. Prep basketball teams played 18 times against alumni fives, the last time during the 1960-61 season. Prep's all-time record against the Prep Alumni: 18-0!

- Prep was originally scheduled to host Union City on February 5, but the Bears cancelled the contest when it interfered with its Erie County Interscholastic League (ECIL) schedule. St. Mary's Gems, heralded as one of the best Junior League teams in Erie, agreed to replace Union City as part of a three-game series with Prep. Only the first game was played however, and Prep was left idle for a two-week period.

- Prep's most exciting win was the 20-19 rematch verdict over St. Titus (7-4), with **Kenny Sechrist** sinking the winning field goal "on a pretty heave from the side" in the closing moments. The Orange & Black connected on all six free throw attempts to provide the winning margin. From the *Titusville Herald*: "The game was hard-fought all the way. The Preps, defeated here earlier in the season, have had a two-week layoff previous to the game and seemingly gained confidence with a familiar floor underfoot and a friendly crowd behind them."

- Prep and Crawford County opponent Meadville High (10-7), coached by **Waldo S. Tippin**, did not renew their basketball rivalry until 1963.

- Prep won its first athletic trophy ever, winning a silver loving cup for taking consolation honors at the 1st annual 8-team Brocton (NY) Invitational Tournament on March 5 & 6, 1926. According to *The Brocton Mirror*: "The Silver Loving Cup was donated through the generosity of the Welch Estate, Westfield, NY." The basketball tourney was the first Prep ever participated in and the cup, presented by Brocton High principal **Florence McCarty,** was proudly displayed in the Downing Building at 225 West Ninth Street, where Prep's administration was housed.

- Prep replaced Sherman at the Brocton Invitational, while other entrants included Brocton, Mayville, Westfield Academy and Forestville, as well as opponents Silver Creek (8-4), Ripley (1-11) and Falconer. "Cathedral's fast passing attack was one of the features of the entire tournament," declared the *Erie Daily Times*. Mayville won the tourney and the Welch Cup by defeating Westfield in the final, 15-7. Prep never played any of its Western New York opponents from the 1925-26 season again.

- The participants at the Brocton Invitational Tournament were all members of the Chautauqua (NY) County League, which consisted of the following: Northern League—Fredonia, Westfield, Silver Creek, Forestville, Ripley and Brocton; and Southern League—league champion Chautauqua, Mayville, Lakewood, Frewsburg and Sherman. A theory for little Chautauqua High's success in this season and others was, as reported by the *Westfield Republican*, "that the Chautauqua school allows no boy to enter into athletic contests who smokes cigarettes."

- Many games during this era took on the aspects of a football contest with rough play and inconsistent foul calling by usually one referee. There were also many fights, but few ejections. Leading scorer **Joe Gorny** played a good portion of the season with a pair of black eyes received in the ballgames. The *Lake Shore Visitor* referred to Prep's loss at Brocton Central (7-11) on February 26 as "a good exhibition of football, with but two fouls called the entire game."

- Prep's first booster event was staged on a Thursday night at the Orphanage court, and it was somewhat of a freakish affair. Students with the least knowledge of the roundball sport were picked to play, and the players actually wore football togs and played the game with a football. Enough money was realized to purchase sweaters for the basketball team's letter winners.

- On a local level, PIAA District 8 champ East High (25-2) became the first Erie team to make it to the state final, losing the PIAA State Championship game to undefeated Nanticoke High School, 44-25, at the Penn State Armory in State College.

PREP TOSSERS PUT AN END TO LOSING STREAK

Kenny Sechrist's Timely Goal in Closing Seconds Beats St. Titus'

CLOSE THROUGHOUT

By DONALD HAYES

[newspaper article text]

PREPS CARRY OFF TROPHY IN BROCTON GAMES

Cathedral Fives Captures Two Games to Win Consolation Cup

RIPLEY IS SWAMPED

[newspaper article text]

East stars included **Tommy Dowler** (later of Colgate fame and the NFL's Brooklyn Dodgers), **Charlie "Bus" Downing, Syl Gromacki, Eddie Clouser, Ed Williams, Ernie Watts, Joe Weber, Jerome "Pug" Mahoney** and **Cyril "Blubber" Sullivan** (Colgate). The Scarlet Warriors were coached by Gus Anderson, formerly the Central High coach, who later became the legendary mentor at Millcreek High School (1929-1950). Aside from the City Series, East, along with Central and Academy, were also members of the Northwest Pennsylvania Interscholastic Athletic Association (NWPIAA), which also included Oil City, Titusville, Warren, Franklin and Meadville.

- Pennsylvania state champion Nanticoke moved on to the National Invitational Basketball Tournament at the University of Chicago, gaining victories in the first three rounds before losing to Fitchburg (MA) in the quarterfinals, 22-14.

- **Damon Daly** was a promising freshman center for Prep, but transferred to East High where he starred for the next three seasons in basketball and football and was team captain of the Warrior hoopsters in 1928-29.

- A sophomore (JV) team that called themselves the "Prep Phantoms" had a successful season with a 12-7 record. The Phantoms participated in the St. Mary's Junior League, which also consisted of St. Mary's Orioles, Holy Rosary Gems and Cadet Reserves. Other opponents of the Phantoms included parish teams from St. Joseph's and St. John's; the Gridley "Seconds"; and other teams with names like Giants, Rovers, Quakers, Irish Aces, Invaders, Cardinals, Globe Trotters, Boys' Club Whirlwinds and Kuhn's Cleaners.

- A Prep team of underclassmen called the "Cathedral Lites" engaged the GE Techs on February 4, only to get clobbered 41-6. Erie's General Electric Company sponsored athletic teams consisting of young employees or apprentices that competed against high schools locally and throughout the state, usually on a varsity level, from the early 1920's well into the 1940's.

- **Nels "Fat" Schumacher**, Prep's first all-scholastic athlete ever (in football), played for the Cathedral Prep College team in 1926-27 and later played the gridiron sport at St. Bonaventure. He starred at the right tackle spot for the Brown Indians. "Fat" was inducted posthumously into the Cathedral Prep Athletic Hall of Fame in 2005.

1926 All-Opponent Team:

    James Teege, St. Titus
    Pat Foley, St. Titus
    Miller, Alliance Academy
    Sadlowski, Alliance Academy
    Norman "Doughnut" Haft, St. Mary's Gems
    Clyde Lathrop, Brocton
    Sam Anselmo, Meadville
    Cosmos Miletello, Silver Creek
    Elliot Lawson, Falconer
    John LaSalle, Greenville St. Mike's
    Stanley Furtik, Alliance Academy
    Kurzawski, Alliance Academy

The Scarlet Warriors of East High were the first local team to reach the PIAA state final. Front Row, L to R: "Blubber" Sullivan, Syl Gromacki, Tommy Dowler, Charlie "Bus" Downing, Eddie Clouser; Back Row: Coach Gus Anderson, Joe Weber, "Pug" Mahoney, Ed Williams, manager Art Arrowsmith. Missing: Ernie Watts.

Prep's First Winning Season!

1926-27 (12-7)

Coach: James V. ("Jim" or "Gyp" or "Gipe") Sullivan
Captain: Kenny "Ribs" Sechrist
Managers: George "Jerry" Stout, Joe Ponzer

Kenny Sechrist. He, along with Joe Gorny, were Prep's first 3-year letter winners.

Date	PREP			Dec.	Loc.	High Scorer	Opponent
12/15	26	Alumni	19	W	H	Gorny (9)	Murphy (8)
1/8	25	Albion	13	W	H	Kress (11)	Renick (5)
1/12	22	Erie Business College	16	W	A	Gorny (6)	Tower (7)
1/21	15	Titusville St. Titus	16	L	H	Sechrist (5)	Foley (9)
1/24	26	Ridgway St. Leo's	13	W	A	Gorny (12)	Lawler (8)
1/29	31	Edinboro	36	L	A	Kress (7)	Proud (9)
2/2	23	Albion	21	W	A	Gorny (8)	Bayer (11)
2/4	25	Erie St. Stanislaus	17	W	H	Gorny (13)	Wilkos (8)
2/5	17	Bradford St. Bernard's	12	W	A	Gorny (7)	Foster & Clark (5)
2/10	20	Greenville St. Michael's	16	W	H	several w/ (4)	Baker (6)
2/11	19	Titusville St. Titus	24	L	A	Schumacher (6)	Foley & Johnson (11)
2/16	28	Erie St. Stanislaus	26	W	A	Gorny (11)	Wilkos (8)
2/19	17	Ridgway St. Leo's	8	W	H	Gorny (8)	Eagen (3)
2/25	30	Greenville St. Michael's	31	L	A	Gorny (11)	Driscoll (14)
3/2	23	West Millcreek	21	W	A	Sechrist (11)	Bolkey (8)
3/11	20	Kanty College	23	L	H	Gorny (13)	Waskiewicz (14)
3/12	22	Bradford St. Bernard's	16	W	A	Jones (11)	Dailey & Reagan (6)
3/16	31	Erie Business College	32	L	H	Sechrist (11)	Phillips (14)
3/23	26	West Millcreek	28	L	H	Gorny (12)	Davis (11)
	446* (23.4*)		**388 (20.4**)**				

Pos.	Player	Prior School	Class	G(GS)	FG	FT	Total	PPG	Career
G-F	Joe "Flash" Gorny	St. Stan's	Sr.	19(19*)	63*	31*	157*	8.3*	255*
F	Kenneth "Ribs" Sechrist	St. Patrick's	Sr.	19(18)	35	24	94	4.9	171
F	Maurice "Casey" Jones	St. Patrick's	Fr.	18(14)	23	23	69	3.8	69
C	Richard "Dick" Schumacher	St. Peter's	Jr.	19(19*)	26	12	64	3.4	65
G	William "Todd" Kress	St. Patrick's	Fr.	14(8)	18	7	43	3.1	43
G	James "Horse" Cavanaugh	St. Patrick's	Sr.	13(11)	3	1	7	0.6	7
F	Francis "Buddy" Flanagan	St. Patrick's	Soph.	5(2)	3	1	7	1.4	7
G	Joe McGrath	St. Peter's	Jr.	12(5)	3	0	6	0.5	6
G	Tommy Doyle	Central HS	Sr.	1	0	1	1	1.0	1
F	Robert Seus	St. Mary's	Soph.	1	0	0	0	0.0	0
F	Norman "Dick" Blissell	Oil City St. Joe's	Fr.	1	0	0	0	0.0	0
G	Thomas Manning	St. Joseph's	Fr.	1	0	0	0	0.0	0

Prep's first winning team. Front row, L to R: Flanagan, Gorny, Jones, Kress; Back row: manager Stout, Cavanaugh, captain Sechrist, Shumacher, manager Ponzer.

HIGHLIGHTS:

- **Jim "Gyp" Sullivan** was kept on board as Cathedral Prep coach for a second season, since "he was the first coach to offer his services gratis." Sullivan was also playing for the Cathedral College basketball team at the time. He later moved to Cincinnati (OH) and became a salesman in the food business.

- At one point pre-season school officials called off the entire basketball program, with financial hardship to support both a prep school team and a high school team given as the reason. Prep officials later stated to the local newspapers: "There would be no curtailment of the winter schedule mapped out. Finances of the high school team are in excellent condition. The team has already been equipped with new uniforms and playing paraphernalia for the season."

- All Cathedral Prep's home games were played at St. Joseph's Orphanage, with the exception of the St. Leo's contest, which was played at Gridley Junior High on Park Avenue North, across from Gridley Park.

- 1926-27 was Prep's first winning season, with a record number of victories. Three of Prep's losses were by a single point, and Prep's seven losses were by a combined total of only 18 points. Merely a dozen field goals kept this Prep team from an undefeated season!

- **Joe Gorny** started every contest in the 1925-26 and 1926-27 seasons, as did **Ken Sechrist**, save one. They were the first three-time letter winners and the early all-time leading scorers for the Prep school.

- The seniors and sophomores at St. Benedict Academy furnished the preliminary matchup to the Prep opener against the Alumni.

- Prep's two losses to Titusville St. Titus (10-5) may have cost it a chance to be invited to the 32-team National Catholic Interscholastic Basketball Tournament at Loyola University of Chicago. St. Titus proclaimed itself Northwest Pennsylvania Catholic champs by virtue of it victories over Prep, but nevertheless was disappointed not to get the NCIBT invite. Joliet (IL) De La Salle won the 1927 NCIBT, defeating Philadelphia Roman Catholic in the final, 26-11.

- After 12 years of consecutive losses to Titusville High, St. Titus final won the Titusville city championship by defeating THS twice in a three-game series by the scores of 30-24, 23-25 and 21-17.

- The premier national high school tournament in the country in the 1920's was the National Interscholastic Basketball Tournament (NIBT) conducted by **Amos Alonzo Stagg** and sponsored by the University of Chicago. The tourney existed as an avenue whereby Stagg could recruit basketball talent to the University of Chicago, which is why he invited public school state champions only. In 1923, Chicago (IL) Loyola Academy specifically asked Stagg to include Catholic and private schools into the tournament, but was rebuffed, as Stagg did not see the Catholic schools as potential feeders into the university's athletic program. Loyola Academy AD **Rev. Joseph Thorning** then proposed to Loyola University that it establish a national Catholic tournament patterned after that of Stagg's. Tremendous support was immediately received and the tournament began in 1924. The National Catholic Interscholastic Basketball Tournament thrived, while Stagg's tournament came under fire until it foundered and was cancelled in 1930. The NCIBT became a catalyst for state tournaments across the nation and featured as participants such luminaries as **Ed "Moose" Krause, Ray Meyer** and **George Ireland**, all of later collegiate fame. The tournament lasted until 1941, cancelled once the United States entered World War II after the bombing of Pearl Harbor.

- Erie Business College (5-5), founded in 1884, later became Erie Business Center. It was located at 246 West 9th Street, directly across from Cathedral Prep. EBC was known for excellent junior college level basketball teams in the late 1960's and early 1970's. It finally closed its doors in 2015 after educating Erieites for 131 years.

- In Prep's first loss of the season, a one-pointer to St. Titus, "W. McDonald's long heave in the last 20 seconds of play was responsible for Cathedral High's initial defeat of the season…" **Walter "Wad" McDonald**, incidentally, was the younger brother of **Monsignor Robert McDonald**, Prep's future headmaster (1944-72), and also a good athlete and graduate of St. Titus. Walter later became head coach at St. Titus.

- **"Casey" Jones** and **"Todd" Kress** were declared "ineligible" for the game at Albion, most likely because of headmaster **Father "Doc" Wehrle's** academic guidelines. A pair of promising freshmen, Jones was later expelled for truancy and Kress merely flunked out.

- After finishing 14-2 in 1925-26, Erie St. Stanislaus gained a pair of contests with Prep for the 1926-27 season. In the second St. Stanislaus (2-4) game, played on the YMCA court, Prep abruptly terminated the game "taking exception to the officiating of **'Maggy' Okonski** in the last two minutes of play." The officiating must have been poor, because the contest was nevertheless counted as a 28-26 victory for Prep! St. Stan's High School was a parish school located at 521 East 12th near Wallace Street in Erie, and served students of Polish descent. It was in existence from 1920 to 1938.

- **"Todd" Kress** fractured his shoulder after "colliding with the side wall following a fierce scrimmage" in the Kanty College (6-4) game at the Orphanage court. Taken to St. Vincent Hospital, he was forced to miss the final three games of the campaign because of the injury. The Kanty squad which defeated Prep by three was the same team which lost two close games to the Cathedral Prep College team.

- Originally founded as St. John Kanty College and High School in 1912, Kanty was a boarding school largely for students of Polish extraction. The school was located on "Mill Road" (now East 38th Street), near Shannon Road in Wesleyville. The college section was discontinued in 1943 as World War II caused a decline in enrollment. From that point on school authorities concentrated on the preparatory high school until it closed for good in 1980, at a time when Kanty's enrollment (202) was its highest ever.

- Opponents Albion (10-10, later Northwestern), Edinboro (7-5, later General McLane) and West Millcreek (16-10, later McDowell) were part of the rural Erie County Interscholastic League (ECIL), forerunner of the Erie County League (ECL). The ECIL divisions at the time included: West—Girard (formally Rice Avenue Union High), North Girard, West Millcreek and Albion; East—Union City, Waterford (later Fort LeBoeuf) and Edinboro. North East was kicked out of the Eastern division for the season as its gymnasium was judged as "unsafe" and no games were permitted there. West Millcreek was ECIL basketball champ three years running: 1924, 1925 (17-3) and 1926 (27-3). One of the Trojan victories in 1925 was over Waterford by the score of 84-2! Girard won the crown in 1927.

- West Millcreek High School, often referred to as "Westminster" and later simply called Millcreek High, was the forerunner of McDowell High School, built in 1953. Millcreek Township, Erie's most important suburb, had three high schools that played basketball early in the 20th century. The others were called East Millcreek High, located on Buffalo Road at the present site of Burton School; and Glenwood High, before that area was incorporated into the City of Erie proper.

- St. Francis College in Loretto sponsored the first Catholic state championship tournament at the season's end. Any Catholic high school in Pennsylvania was invited to participate if it so desired. The tourney was staged under PIAA regulations "with competent officials in charge." Six teams had entered, but Johnstown Central Catholic and Williamsport St. Mary's withdrew before competing. Semifinals action saw Altoona Catholic defeat Clearfield St. Francis, 26-5; while Renovo St. Joseph's triumphed over DuBois St. Catherine's, 32-17. St. Francis beat St. Catherine's in the consolation game, 11-9; while Altoona Catholic was crowned the first Catholic state champion with a 29-19 victory over Renovo St. Joseph's in the title clash. The winner received a trophy cup while members of the victorious team were awarded golden basketball charms.

- St. Francis College also sponsored a public school "Class B" state tournament in conjunction with the state Catholic tourney. Twelve schools with enrollments of less than 250 students entered the bracket, including Lilly, Portage, Beaverdale, Nanty-Glo, Gallitzin, Conemaugh, Bellwood, Reade Township, Dale, Ferndale, St. Marys and Spangler.

- Cathedral Prep also presented a team of underclassmen called the "St. Mark's Fraternity" team, consisting of Prep underclassmen who were residing at St. Mark's Hall on East Third Street. Team members included such stars as **Johnny Mehler** and **Ray Meier** (later **Monsignor Ray Meier**) of Sharon; **Gene McGarry** and **Jim Madden** of Warren; **Dick Blissell** of Oil City; **"Irish" Carroll** of Uniontown; **Ted Wayne** of Osceola; and **"Fat" Wiley** of Erie. The squad was coached by varsity mentor **Jim Sullivan**. The main rival of the fraternity boys was the Wolverines, a group of Prep freshmen which included **Mike Figula, Richard Cooney** and **John Shalkham**. Another rival was the "Mysterious Five," another team of Prepsters which included guys like **Marino Phillips, Albert Phillips** and **Jim Maloney**.

- **James "Horse" Cavanaugh**, Prep's first three-year letterman in football, went on to star for the St. Bonaventure gridiron team at the right end position.

James "Horse" Cavanaugh. He later starred in football at St. Bonaventure.

1927 All-Opponent Team:

Pat Foley, St. Titus
Jim Lawler, Ridgway St. Leo's
Ralph Proud, Edinboro
Frank "Jerry" Wilkos, St. Stan's
Wladislaus (Walter) Zawadzski, St. Stan's
Edward "Krush" Kruszewski, St. Stan's
John Driscoll, Greenville St. Mike's
Roy Bolkey, West Millcreek [Edinboro Normal School]
Waszkiewicz, Kanty College
Phillips, EBC
John Caughey, EBC
Gerald Davis, West Millcreek

Cathedral Prep College Team (5-5)

Coach: Andy Fletcher

Captain: John "Bunk" McGeever

Managers: Tommy Lehan, Fred Geisler

Date		COLLEGE		Dec.	Loc.	High Scorer	Opponent
12/18	32	Hammermill Paper Co.	44	L	A	Randolph (13)	Gromacki (11)
1/21	25	Kanty College	21	W	A	Giesler (7)	Szczygiel (8)
1/22	32	MTI (Mechanical Trades Institute)	33	L	A	Giesler (12)	Torzynski (12)
1/28	32	Franklin YMCA	40(OT)	L	A	Nash & Doyle (10)	Way (12)
2/4	37	Clarion Normal School	33	W	A	Giesler (24)	Scherntal (20)
2/5	13	Indiana Normal School	26	L	A	Giesler (5)	Lahr & Bishop (8)
2/18	28	MTI (Mechanical Trades Institute)	25	W	H	McGeever (15)	Tarta (6)
2/19	23	Franklin YMCA	22	W	H	McGeever (9)	Shuffstall (8)
2/26	26	PNA College (Alliance)	43	L	A	Giesler & McGeever (8)	Galica (13)
3/4	19	Kanty College	17	W	H	McGeever (8)	Szczygiel (6)
	267 (26.7)		**304 (30.4)**				

Pos.	Player	Class	High School	G(GS)	FG	FT	Total	PPG
C-F	Fred "Red" Giesler	PG	Academy	10(10)	33	19	85	8.5
C	John "Bunk" McGeever	PG	Homestead	9(8)	23	14	60	6.7
G-F	Art Weindorf	Sr.	Central	9(7)	14	3	31	3.4
F	William "String" Nash	PG	Central	3(3)	9	6	24	8.0
G-F	Tommy Doyle	Sr.	Central	6(6)	6	5	18	3.0
F	George Murphy	PG	Prep	8(8)	6	4	16	2.0
F	Harry Randolph	PG	Central	1(1)	6	1	13	13.0
G	Nelson "Fat" Schumacher	PG	Prep	7(3)	4	0	8	1.1
G	Jim "Gyp" Sullivan	Sr.	Homestead	8(4)	2	1	5	0.6
F	Eddie Williams	PG	East	1	1	2	4	4.0
G	Leonard Pasqual [Pasqualicchio]	PG	Academy	1(1)	1	1	3	3.0

HIGHLIGHTS:

- The Cathedral Prep college team was formed from boys attending Prep as older seniors and post-graduates or "P.G.'s". All, with the exception of leading scorer **Fred "Red" Geisler,** were star football players for the Orange & Black. These students took classes at the Prep or at then co-ed Villa Maria College at West 8th and Liberty Streets as college freshmen. This basketball team had a similar setup as the Prep football squad which played college freshmen/prep school schedules in 1926 and 1927.

- **Andy Fletcher**, former Erie High star, Central High coach and coach of Prep's excellent 1926 football team, was tabbed as coach for this unit as well.

- The opener against Hammermill Paper Company, played on the Downtown YMCA court, was the first time Hammermill president **Ernst Behrend** witnessed his team win a basketball game. Every previous occasion Behrend was in attendance his squad came up on the short end. Hammermill stars included former East High luminaries **Charlie "Bus" Downing, Syl Gromacki** and **Augie Newcamp**. Another in the Hammermill lineup was **Thomas "Boody" Sullivan**, who later became the legendary mentor at all-girls St. Benedict Academy, where he coached for 33 years, from 1933 through 1966.

- The college squad had difficulty scheduling games because of a lack of finances and because few local courts of appropriate size were available for use because of the abundance of high school and city recreation league games. After just one game the squad disbanded, with Coach Fletcher agreeing with Prep athletic officials that there appeared to be no other course

to take. "The prospects for a brilliant season were more than ordinarily good," stated Fletcher to the *Erie Dispatch-Herald*. "The boys who have been drilling for the past five or six weeks will be greatly disappointed. Prep has some of the best basketball talent in this section of the state, including Nash, McGeever, **Tommy Doyle**, Pasqual, Weindorf, Sullivan, **[Johnny] Grasberger** and several others."

- A few days later it was reported that the Cathedral Prep team reorganized and would finish the season on a much smaller plane than first contemplated. **Fred Geisler**, the former Academy star, was appointed manager, while **John "Bunk" McGeever** was named captain and would direct the squad with help from some veteran members of the team. According to the *Erie Dispatch-Herald*, ""McGeever, well over six feet tall and typically built for the position he plays, appears well-qualified to lead his team." **Andy Fletcher** was no longer at the helm. All further home games were staged at Gridley Junior High.

- Opponent Mechanical Trades Institute was affiliated with PNA College (Alliance) in Cambridge Springs. MTI's one-point win over Cathedral was a thriller, with the Preps erasing a 14-point halftime deficit, but failing to tie the score in the closing moments when McGeever missed a free throw.

- Opponents Clarion Normal School and Indiana Normal School later became Clarion State Teachers College and Indiana State Teachers College, and are now known as Clarion University of Pennsylvania and Indiana University of Pennsylvania (IUP), respectively.

- Prep College's most exciting win was the 23-22 victory over the Franklin "Y" on the Gridley Junior High court, outscoring its opponent 9-0 in the final quarter to gain the triumph. **"Bunk" McGeever** got the winning bucket in the closing moments.

- **John "Bunk" McGeever** was a prominent player on Homestead's WPIAL and PIAA state championship team in 1924. Homestead defeated Nanticoke, 32-21, in that title game held at the Penn State Armory in State College. McGeever went on to star at Duquesne University under coach **Chick Davies**, where he was team captain in 1932 and 1933. He became head basketball coach at Allegheny College, then later at Linesville High School, where one of his stars was future Prep head coach **Richard "Dick" Fox**.

- **Jim "Gyp" Sullivan** served as Prep coach for two seasons, while **"String" Nash** became Technical's head basketball coach for three seasons (1941-44). Sullivan also saw service with the University of Pittsburgh freshmen team.

- At 6'0", 180 pounds, **Tom Doyle** went on to star at guard in football at Colgate. Doyle played in the sixth annual East-West Shrine Game on December 27, 1930, won by the West All-Stars, 3-0. He thereafter became the line coach at Colgate.

- **Nelson Schumacher** starred at St. Bonaventure at the right tackle position. **Fred Giesler** played basketball at Edinboro Normal School, now known as Edinboro University of Pennsylvania.

Fred "Red" Giesler, leading scorer of the Cathedral Prep College team. His little brother, George "Whitey" Giesler, was the long-time teacher and track coach at Academy.

The Erie Diocesan League

1927-28 (4-7)

Coach: Nelson "Fat" Schumacher
Captain: Richard "Dick" Schumacher
Manager: John Walsh

Team captain Dick Schumacher, later Monsignor Richard Schumacher, was the first Prep boy to play college basketball.

Date	PREP			Dec.	Loc.	High Scorer	Opponent
1/4	31	Alumni	25	W	H	Hayes (10)	Sechrist (10)
1/13	55*	Corry St. Edward's	13	W	H	Hayes (20*)	J. Maloney (9)
1/18	41	Meadville St. Agatha's	11	W	A	Hayes (18)	Berry (5)
1/20	19	Erie St. Stanislaus	20	L	A	Hayes (8)	Zawadzski (7)
1/21	27	Corry	30	L	A	Hayes (10)	Brown (13)
1/31	13	Titusville St. Titus	37	L	A	Mullen (6)	Prenatt (10)
2/7	9**	Kanty Prep	35	L	H	Flanagan (5)	Pawlina (15)
2/10	52	Corry St. Edward's	12	W	A	Hayes (16)	J. W. Maloney (5)
2/17	19	Erie St. Stanislaus	20	L	A	Hayes (8)	Zawadski & Kruszewski (5)
2/24	15	Kanty Prep	33	L	A	Henry (4)	Kozlowski (8)
3/15	22	Oil City St. Joseph's	28(OT)	L	A	Hayes (14)	Harkins (9)
	303 (27.5*)		**264** (24.0)				

Pos.	Player	Prior School	Class	G(GS)	FG	FT	Total	PPG	Career
F-C	Don Hayes	St. Patrick's	Sr.	11(10)	49	16	114	10.4*	114
F	Jim Mullen	St. Patrick's	Sr.	10(9)	20	5	45	4.5	45
C	Alois "Alloy" Skonieczka	East HS	Sr.	8(7)	16	6	38	4.8	38
G	Joe McGrath	St. Peter's	Sr.	10(9)	11	9	31	3.1	37
F	Francis "Buddy" Flanagan	St. Patrick's	Jr.	10(3)	13	3	29	2.9	36
C-G-F	Frank "Yosko" Henry	St. Peter's	Sr.	11(4)	10	1	21	1.9	21
G-C	Richard "Dick" Schumacher	St. Peter's	Sr.	11(11)	4	3	11	1.0	76
F	Marino Phillips	St. Michael's	Sr.	9(2)	4	3	11	1.2	11
G	Frank Richards	Central HS	Sr.	7	1	1	3	0.4	3
F	Patrick O'Neill	St. Jos. Home	Jr.	2	0	0	0	0.0	0
C	Bill Kneib	St. Mary's	Soph.	1	0	0	0	0.0	0
G	Richard Sertz	St. Joseph's	Soph.	1	0	0	0	0.0	0
G	Ted Amann	East HS	Sr.	0	0	0	0	0.0	0

HIGHLIGHTS:

- Cathedral Prep's home games with the Alumni and Corry St. Ed's were played at St. Mary's Parish Gymnasium. The first Kanty Prep contest was played on the St. Joseph's Orphanage court, while both St. Stan's battles were played at the CYMA [East Side Boys Club] at 12ᵗʰ and Wallace Streets.

- Former Prep star **Nelson "Fat" Schumacher**, a student at St. Bonaventure on a football scholarship, started coaching the Prep basketball team while on his Christmas vacation from college. His younger brother, team captain **Dick Schumacher**, was chief organizer of the squad. "Fat" Schumacher was able to coach the boys for most of the season, therefore, even though he could not be present for most games beginning in February, the entire 1927-28 record of games is credited to him.

- The 1927-28 edition of the Prep team showed practically all new faces. The only returning players were seniors **Dick Schumacher** and **Joe McGrath** and junior **"Buddy" Flanagan**.

- A record-breaking 55-point performance against Corry St. Edward's and the consistent scoring punch of senior forward **Don Hayes** were the high points of the season. Hayes scored 20 against St. Ed's, the first Prepster to ever reach that plateau. Hayes was also the first Rambler to average in double digits per game.

- Corry St. Ed's (0-6) was routed in every game it played for the season, as its team consisted entirely of underclassmen and it was not to become a four-year institution until the 1928-29 school year.

- Cathedral mounted a furious 4ᵗʰ quarter rally only to fall short by three at Corry (13-8), the public school in Erie County's second city, located some 45 miles southeast of Erie.

- Prep's first overtime contest ever was the season-ending, 28-22 loss to Oil City St. Joseph's (7-12). The Irish outscored the Preps, 8-2, in the extra 5-minute session.

- Biggest disappointments were a pair of one-point (both 20-19) losses to St. Stanislaus (7-3) and the relatively poor showing in the Erie Diocesan League Section 1, Prep's next venture into organized league play. After the first St. Stan's win, the *Erie Dispatch-Herald* noted that Prep appeared overconfident and further that: "If there ever was a thoroughly surprised and dumbfounded basketball team it was the Cathedral High combination that stepped off the CYMA Friday night following a 40-minute tilt with St. Stanislaus."

- Prep headmaster **Father Joseph "Doc" Wehrle**, also the Superintendant of Schools in the Erie Diocese, was named president of the Erie Diocesan League, while **John Fahey** served as secretary. The motto for the new league formed for the 1927-28 season was "Chicago or quits," referring to the annual National Catholic Interscholastic Basketball Tournament (NCIBT) played in Chicago. Every school in this version of the Diocesan league is now closed, with the exception of Cathedral Prep.

- The final standings of the Erie Diocesan League:

Section 1

Kanty High	6-0
Erie St. Stanislaus	4-2
CATHEDRAL HIGH	**2-4**
Corry St. Edward's	0-6

Section 2

Greenville St. Michael's	5-1
Titusville St. Titus	5-1
Oil City St. Joseph's	2-4
Meadville St. Agatha's	0-6

Section 3

DuBois St. Catherine's	5-1
Bradford St. Bernard's	4-2
Ridgway St. Leo's	2-4
Clearfield St. Francis	1-5

- Kanty Prep (18-4), though it finished the league campaign undefeated, was involved in an eligibility dispute, according to the *Oil City Derrick*. The argument was that many of the Kantians were beyond high school age, deeming competition unfair. Kanty was given time, according to the *Erie Dispatch-Herald*, to submit in writing proof of the scholastic standings of its players. Kanty instead, through coach John Kolasa, resigned from the loop; its resignation was unanimously accepted; and it therefore did not participate in the post-season playoffs for the Diocesan crown.

- St. Michael's first beat St. Titus in a hard-fought battle, 16-14, for the right to represent Section 2; and in an elimination contest defeated St. Catherine's, 28-17. St. Mike's then won the Erie Diocesan championship, defeating St. Stan's, 43-33, in the title game played in Oil City. The entire tournament was refereed by **Joe Hart** of Erie. League president Father Wehrle presented the winners with the championship trophy and the runner-up with the game ball. The St. Mike's Irish were led by team captain **Ed Baker** with 11 points. Another star for St. Mike's was **Joe Conners**, who was later hired by Prep headmaster **Father Robert McDonald** in 1945 to coach the Rambler five. Several weeks later, however, Conners asked to be released from his contract, and Father McDonald granted his request. Conners went back to coach with success at Oil City St. Joseph's.

- St. Mike's next went to St. Francis College in Loretto for the 2ⁿᵈ annual state Catholic tournament, only to lose to Duquesne Prep in the title game, 21-18, while Johnstown Central Catholic forfeited to Loretto St. Francis Prep in the consolation. Another participant was Clearfield St. Francis, while Altoona Catholic, Williamsport St. Mary's and Oil City St. Joseph's simply dropped out of the tourney.

- Though St. Titus (7-4), coached by Father McDonald's brother **Walter McDonald**, lost to St. Mike's, it still went on to the NCIBT in Chicago. There it suffered a first round defeat to Chicago (IL) St. Philip's, 35-11.

- Parish schools that were casualties of the Great Depression were Titusville St. Titus (closed in 1932, though Titusville St. Joseph's Academy opened in 1932) and Erie St. Stanislaus (1920-1938). Corry St. Edward's (1924-1949) facility and gymnasium served St. Thomas Parish grade school until 2015. The 1960's ushered the closure of aging parish schools DuBois St. Catherines's (1915-1961); Bradford St. Bernard's (1885-1962); Oil City St. Joseph's (1930-1962); Greenville St. Michael's (1906-1965); Ridgway St. Leo's (1900-1962) and Meadville St. Agatha's (1899-1969). In their places came new regional high schools, including DuBois Central Christian (founded in 1961); Oil City Venango Christian (1962-2016); Bradford Central Christian (1962-2000) and Hermitage Kennedy Christian (founded in 1965). Kanty Prep (1912-1980) and Clearfield St. Francis (1893-1985) held on several years longer.

- Other Erie Diocesan schools which fostered basketball teams over the years, but were not in the original Diocesan League, include St. Marys Central Catholic (1925-1962), later served by Elk County Christian (founded in 1962); Clarion Immaculate Conception (1912-1965); DeLancey St. Adrian's (1900-1955); DuBois St. Joseph's (1931-1957); Lucinda St. Joseph's (1896-1976); Punxsutawney Sts. Cosmas and Damien (1891-1967); Franklin St. Patrick's (1894-1952); North East St. Gregory's (1948-1968); St. Mark's Seminary (founded in 1958, quit having basketball teams in the 1980's) and Titusville St. Joseph's Academy (1932-1969). Divine Word Seminary (1912-1966), formerly called the Sacred Heart Mission House, would also occasionally sponsor football and basketball teams and hosted Cathedral Prep's football camps from 1946 to 1959.

- Another Erie Catholic school that sponsored basketball was St. Mary's Commercial High (1903-1932), a two-year school affiliated with St. Mary's parish at 9th and German Streets. The difficulty for St. Mary's was that it was forced to schedule four-year institutions in order to fill out a schedule and often ended on the losing side.

- Senior center **Al Skonieczka** was a transfer from East, while sophomore center **Bill Kneib** transferred to a boarding school at the conclusion of the 1927-28 school year.

- Kanty Prep star **Ben Pawlina** played football at Duquesne under **Elmer Layden**, then in the 1940's became head football coach, head basketball coach and athletic director at Alliance College.

- Prep star **Dick Schumacher**, later **Monsignor Richard Schumacher**, became Prep's first collegiate basketball player at a four-year school, toiling for Saint Vincent College in Latrobe. A Bearcat press release two years later noted: "Schumacher is the alternate center on the five and his height gives him an advantage on the jump."

1928 All-Opponent Team:

John Maloney, Corry St. Ed's
John W. Maloney, Corry St. Ed's
Wilson Brown, Corry
Jim Prenatt, St. Titus
Ernest Jackson, St. Titus
Ben "Rookie" Pawlina, Kanty [Duquesne, football]
Eddie Kruszewski, St. Stan's
Wladislaus (Walter) "Bully" Zawadzki, St. Stan's
Francis Harkins, Oil City St. Joe's

Father Conway era begins!

1928-29 (14-6)

Coach: Rev. Walter Conway
Assistants: Ed Williams, Bob McCollum
Captain: Francis "Buddy" Flanagan
Manager: Jim Gannon

Father Walter Conway, Prep's Depression-era coach.

Date	PREP			Dec.	Loc.	High Scorer	Opponent
12/18	20	Wesleyville	19	W	H	Schrenk (6)	Burch & DerManuel (6)
1/8	21	Ridgway St. Leo's	14	W	H	Perry (10)	Whitaker (8)
1/11	39	Fairview	21	W	A	Perry (19)	Hauck & Ponde (7)
1/15	27	Corry St. Edward's	10	W	H	Perry & Mehler (7)	Nichols (6)
1/15	22	Alumni	19	W	H	Perry (11)	Hayes (10)
1/22	29	Fairview	5	W	H	Perry (12)	E. Miller (3)
1/24	35	Corry St. Edward's	21	W	A	Blissell (12)	Burkhardt (9)
1/29	16	Girard	18	L	H	Perry (9)	Morton (7)
2/1	16	Titusville St. Titus	26	L	A	Perry (8)	Prenatt (13)
2/5	25	Bradford St. Bernard's	14	W	H	Schrenk (11)	Grant (8)
2/9	11	Girard	25	L	A	Schrenk (4)	Andrews (14)
2/12	33	North East	18	W	H	Blissell (11)	Gilmore (15)
2/16	33	North East	32	W	A	Perry (23*)	Gilmore (17)
2/19	28	Titusville St. Titus	8	W	H	Perry (17)	Prenatt (4)
2/23	11	Bradford St. Bernard's	18	L	A	Perry (7)	Zias & Hobday (6)
2/26	40	Youngsville	24	W	H	Perry (18)	Hendrickson (14)
3/2	12	Ridgway St. Leo's	21	L	A	Perry (7)	Steis (10)
3/5	26	Wesleyville	14	W	H	Davis (7)	McShea (4)
		PENNSYLVANIA STATE CATHOLIC H. S. TOURNAMENT @ DUQUESNE UNIVERSITY					
3/7	15	Altoona Catholic	26	L	N	Blissell (6)	Conlon (10)
3/8		Youngsville (POSTPONED—STATE TOURNEY)			A		
3/15	47	Youngsville	34	W	A	Schrenk (22)	Hendrickson (8)
	506* (25.3)		**342 (17.1**)**				

Pos.	Player	Prior School	Class	G(GS)	FG	FT	Total	PPG	Career
C-G	Herbert "Joe" Perry (#6)	W. Phila. HS	Soph.	19(15)	65*	54*	184*	9.7	184
F-C-G	Robert Schrenk (#7)	St. Mary's	Soph.	19(15)	53	21	127	6.7	127
G	Norman "Dick" Blissell (#5)	Oil City St. Joe's	Jr.	18(11)	23	8	54	3.0	54
F-G	Mike Figula (#3)	St. Jos. Home	Jr.	20*(14)	14	10	38	1.9	38
G	Joe Earley (#10)	St. Peter's	Soph.	19(15)	5	10	20	1.0	20
F	Francis "Buddy" Flanagan (#4)	St. Patrick's	Sr.	15(8)	5	4	14	0.9	50
F-G-C	Hubert Davis (#14)	Sharon St. Joe's	Sr.	15(6)	10	9	29	1.9	29
G-C	Harry Liebel (#15)	St. Peter's	Fr.	10(3)	5	2	12	1.2	12
F	John Mehler (#16)	Sharon St. Joe's	Sr.	6(2)	4	2	10	1.7	10
C-G	John Young (#9)	St. Mary's	Soph.	11(9)	2	4	8	0.7	8
G-F	John Lyons (#12)	Stoneboro HS	Sr.	9(1)	4	0	8	0.9	8
C	George Wozniak (#8)	St. Stan's	Sr.	2(1)	1	0	2	1.0	2
F	Edward Mayer	St. Peter's	Sr.	1	0	0	0	0.0	0
F	Henry Pluskota (#11)	St. Jos. Home	Jr.	1	0	0	0	0.0	0
G	John Zelonish	St. Jos. Home	Sr.	1	0	0	0	0.0	0

HIGHLIGHTS:

- After Cathedral Prep played half of the previous season without a coach, **Father Walter "Plunger" Conway**, a former Holy Cross College football star, was appointed head coach of the Prep football and basketball teams. A graduate of Christ the King Seminary at St. Bonaventure (NY), Father Conway was a professor at St. Mary's College in Kansas for two years where he also coached the baseball, basketball and football teams. He had already been named athletic director at Prep by the school's founder, **Bishop John Mark Gannon**, in 1927.

- All Prep's home games were played at the Academy High School gymnasium at 29th and State Streets.

- Rather than automatically playing 10-minute quarters, teams were allowed to agree whether or not to play 8, 9 or 10-minute periods. Often it was different within the course of a game—in other words, for example, quarters might be set at 8 minutes for the 1st and 3rd periods, and 10 minutes for the 2nd and 4th periods.

- Father Conway took over a green team that won only 4 games the year before, opened with a couple of come-from-behind wins and reeled off a record 7 straight victories before losing in the final seconds to Girard. It was the best start (7-0) in Prep history until tied in 1941-42 and bested in 1946-47 (9-0).

- Prep was no longer in the "Northern Division" of the Erie Diocesan League, which consisted of smaller "Class B" schools Erie St. Stan's, Greenville St. Mike's, Meadville St. Agatha's, Oil City St. Joseph's and Corry St. Edward's. Prep was then considered as the only "Class A" school in the Diocese.

- Prep opened and closed the regular season against Wesleyville (1-17), Erie's important southeast suburb. The Bulldogs opened with 17 consecutive losses before defeating Union City in their season finale, 11-8. At the time Wesleyville would compete with Prep and West Millcreek for "Class B" championships in football.

- The first Corry St. Edward's (1-12) and the Alumni games were played back-to-back on the same evening, January 15, on the Academy floor. St. Ed's requested a date change to that evening and Prep officials did not want to cancel the Alumni game which had already been scheduled. In the absence of Coach Father Conway, who was ill, assistants **Ed Williams** and **Bob McCollum** coached Prep for the doubleheader. St. Ed's went its entire season without a victory until it defeated a Corry Area all-star team at a booster event for the last game of the season.

- Prep's public school opponents from rural Erie County, including Wesleyville, Girard and North East, were part of the class B Erie County Interscholastic League (ECIL), formed in 1921-22. Other county schools in the loop at the time included West Millcreek, Albion, Corry, Edinboro and Union City. This league was the forerunner to the Erie County League (ECL). The ECL football league began in 1932.

- Prep was leading 23-0 entering the 4th quarter of the second Fairview (5-8) contest. The Tigers, who were not in the County League at the time, escaped a whitewash by scoring in the last two minutes of play. As a result, the Tigers never agreed to play Prep again after 1928-29.

- Prep came back from a 15-0 deficit in the second North East (8-12) game. **Herb Perry**, "leaving a sick bed to take his place in the Cathedral lineup," entered early in the 2nd quarter, and scored in the final seconds to win the exciting battle. Perry battled with the Grapepickers' **Robert Gilmore** and finished with a Prep record 23 points.

- **Herb Perry** was a transfer student from West Philadelphia High School. A non-Catholic, Perry was big and tough and shattered Prep's scoring records in his first season with the Orange & Black.

Star sophomore Herb Perry transferred to Prep from West Philadelphia HS.

- The home loss by two points to two-time defending ECIL champion Girard (16-10) looked to be a game that might go into overtime. According to the *Erie Dispatch-Herald*: "**Art Jacobsen**, center of the Girard aggregation, pegged one from the side that swished through the hoop. Cathedral still might have won, but missed three fairly open shots in the remaining 50 seconds."

- Prep gave up exactly no field goals in the entire second St. Titus (13-2) contest, a nice 20-point revenge win after losing by 10 in Titusville earlier in the season. Perry and particularly sophomore **John Young** played exceptional defense in the contest. It was St. Titus' only loss in the regular season.

- A preliminary to Prep's loss at Bradford St. Bernard's (6-5) on February 23 featured a girls' contest between Villa Maria Academy and St. Bernard's. Though the VMA "Chicks" were trounced, 22-2, it was noted they "entertained with the Prep boys" following the games. The *Bradford Evening and Daily Record* noted that a party was given in honor of the Prep boys

CATHEDRAL ACCEPTS INVITATION TO PLAY IN STATE TOURNEY

By ART MONAHAN

TWO high schools in the Erie Diocese will compete for the state Catholic scholastic basketball championship and the right to enter the national tournament in Pittsburgh on March 7, 8 and 9, according to the invitation received by Cathedral high from Duquesne university, which will sponsor the state series.

Father Conway, coach of the Orange and Black team, said last night that Cathedral would accept the invitation and enter the tournament at Pittsburgh. Whether the second Erie Diocese team has already been picked is not known, but it is believed that Duquesne officials will wait until the league season is completed.

Two teams from the Erie, Pittsburgh, Harrisburg, Scranton, Philadelphia and Altoona Dioceses will compete at Pittsburgh. Duquesne university will provide rooms and meals for eight players, manager and coach of each team.

Cathedral's invitation at this early stage was probably due to the fact that it is not entered in the Erie Diocese league. The record of the Orange and Black, however, has apparently met favor with the Pittsburgh authorities.

The state champion will have all expenses paid to Chicago, where the national tournament will be held on March 20, 21, 22, 23 and 24. A one-year cup, a permanent trophy and gold basketballs will be awarded to each individual of the winning team at Duquesne.

A consolation tournament will also be staged, with permanent trophies going to the two teams in the finals. An all-star team will also be selected, with awards to the men picked.

and Villa girls and "sponsored by the combined basketball outfits of the girls and boys at St. Bernard's."

- A real incentive was offered to the teams of the Cathedral Prep inter-class basketball league, when AD Father Conway announced that Palace Hardware would donate a 14" loving cup to the winner. According to the *Erie Dispatch-Herald*: "The cup, now on display, is an exceptional piece of workmanship and beauty."

- Prep received a bid to the first annual Pennsylvania State Catholic High School Tournament at Duquesne University in Pittsburgh, featuring Diocesan champions and top teams from across the state. In charge of the event was none other than **Elmer Layden**, the Duquesne football coach and a former member of the famed "Four Horsemen" of Notre Dame. The teams that went to Pittsburgh from other parts of the state had their expenses paid by the university and the Pennsylvania champion was to be sent to Chicago for the National Catholic Interscholastic Basketball Tournament (NCIBT), with all expenses paid. The theme for the state Catholic tourney: "On to Chicago!"

- Prep lost in the first round of the state tourney to Altoona Catholic (23-10), a team that made it to the final of the 13-team bracket, only to bow to tournament favorite Philadelphia Northeast Catholic (closed in 2010) in the title game, 10-8. According to Pittsburgh Post-Gazette reports: "The Preps fought desperately but they hardly got a chance to get in position for a shot"; and "Altoona High showed amazing power to crush the highly touted Erie Prep…" Altoona Catholic, founded in 1922, won the state Catholic titles in 1927, with a 29-19 win over Renovo St. Joseph's; and again in 1930 (19-8) with a 16-15 victory over Duquesne Prep. The Yellow Jackets' best team in that span was in 1928 (24-5), when they did not enter a state tourney. Altoona Catholic moved to a new building and was renamed Bishop Guilfoyle High School in 1960. In the 1920's Monsignor (named Bishop in 1936) **Richard Guilfoyle** was an administrator at Cathedral Prep.

- The winner of the State Catholic Tourney, Philadelphia Northeast Catholic (21-1), suffered its only loss of the season in the first round of the NCIBT to Peoria (IL) Spalding Institute, 23-13.

- Other participants in the State Catholic tourney included Greenville St. Michael's, Titusville St. Titus, Oil City St. Joseph's, Pittsburgh (Shadyside) Sacred Heart, Williamsport St. Joseph's, Loretto St. Francis Prep, Duquesne Prep, Pittsburgh Central Catholic, Hazleton St. Gabriel's, Bethlehem Catholic and Erie St. Stanislaus. Oil City St. Joe's was tossed in the first round but nevertheless was awarded the best sportsmanship cup by the Notre Dame Club of Pittsburgh. The Joes, a last-minute substitution for St. Marys Central Catholic which withdrew from the affair, drove five hours through a blizzard and reached the court 10 minutes before game time. Though they lost, according to the *Pittsburgh Press*: "they outscored and outplayed Pittsburgh Sacred Heart in the second half."

- **Johnny Mehler,** a native of St. Joseph's Parish in Sharon, sadly died of typhoid fever in the summer of 1930.

1929 All-Opponent Team:

Eugene Der Manuel, Wesleyville
Leyman Burch, Wesleyville
Homer Whitaker, Ridgway St. Leo's
Howard "Duck" Ponde, Fairview
William Nichols, Corry St. Ed's
Charles Burkhardt, Corry St. Ed's
Burdette Morton, Girard
Art "Swede" Jacobsen, Girard
Jim Prenatt, St. Titus
Hugh Grant, Bradford St. Bernard's
Jimmy Andrews, Girard
Frank "Hank" Foye, Girard
Robert Gilmore, North East
Ed Zias, Bradford St. Bernard's
Jack Hobday, Bradford St. Bernard's
Roger Hendrickson, Youngsville
Bernard Steis, Ridgway St. Leo's
Jack McShea, Wesleyville
Ray "Ramie" Conlon, Altoona Catholic
Tommy Irwin, Altoona Catholic
   [North Carolina; MLB Cleveland Indians]

Hubert Davis came to Prep from Sharon St. Joe's.

The 1930's

Prep Halts Oiler St. Joe's Sensational Win Streak

20 Game Victory March Broken By Ramblers

By Howard Parsons

Launching a long-range barrage to capture an early lead and resorting to the same style of attack after their opponents' tight shifting zone defense proved impregnable, Cathedral Prep's Ramblers scored a surprise 24-17 victory over St. Joseph's high, of Oil City, Monday night at Vincent and broke the invaders' season 20-game win streak.

Holding St. Joseph's to a pair of foul points in the first period while they were pumping in a trio of action shots and a foul, the Ramblers snatched a 7-2 lead, and left the court at intermission boasting a 10-7 advantage.

Bob Carrick, capable guard, led the Rambler attack, cutting the net four times with long shots. He started Prep on its victory drive with two baskets in the early minutes to present the winners with a four-point lead. His second two goals came in the third chapter when Prep tallied 10 points to enjoy its greatest scoring opportunity.

While the Ramblers were playing their finest ball, even though Coach Father Walter Conway was not present, having turned his duties over to "Bidge" Weindorf, St. Joseph's was having constant trouble, particularly with its shooting.

Not until seven minutes had elapsed in the second quarter were the invaders able to cage an action shot, Joe Cunningham scoring from near the hoop. Two goals were tallied in each of the two succeeding chapters.

St. Joseph's missed numerous shots under the basket, and its long-range shooting was unsuccessful, being forced to shoot off balance.

Weindorf did not make a substitution in Prep's lineup, Hughes, Razanoski, Quinn, Carrick and Pasqualicchio performing the entire game. They played smart ball, holding the pellet out of play in the final period when the invaders showed a determination to wipe away their disadvantage. Razanoski and Hughes were invaluable as floor men, keeping the ball moving and taking advantage of opportunities. Summary:

Prep (24)	Fd	Fl	T	St. Josephs (17)	Fd	Fl	T
Hughes,f	2	0	4	O'Connor,r	1	3	5
Razanoski,f	1	3	5	Driscoll,f	0	3	3
Quinn,c	1	3	5	Heber,c	0	1	1
Carrick,g	4	0	8	Schwakoff,g	3	0	6
Pasqual'hio	1	0	2	Cun'gham,g	3	0	6
				Flaherty,f	0	0	0
				Eagan,g	1	0	2
Totals	9	6	24	Totals	5	7	17

Referee: Pitting.
Halftime: 10-7, Prep.

One of Cathedral Prep's biggest moments of the decade was the 1936 victory over Oil City St. Joseph's.

CATHEDRAL HIGH CAGERS SWAMP WESLEYVILLE HI

Bulldogs Hopelessly Outclassed; Beaten by 52-5 Score

HERB PERRY STARS

COMBINING a beautifully executed passing game that invariably resulted in easy tries under the net, with an airtight defense, the Orange and Black cagers of Cathedral high opened their campaign auspiciously by trouncing Wesleyville high, 52 to 5 on the Academy high girls' court last night.

Coach Father Conway's machine slipped into high gear at the start and seemed to function smoother as the game progressed. By their splendid performance the Ramblers demonstrated that they are not only the Class B champions of the city, but a combination that compares with the best ever turned out at Cathedral.

Apparently still smarting under the stigma of the setback suffered at the hands of the Suburbanites on the gridiron the past season, the Cathedral tossers put all their pep and energy into the fray, with the result that the Eichart aggregation was limited to a lone field goal, a true indication of the Orange and Black's stellar defensive work.

Herb Perry, Cathedral grid star, was the major factor in his team's triumph, scoring 13 field goals and a pair of fouls for 28 points, a most notable feat. Perry was in the thick of the fight at all stages, and dashed through the porous Wesleyville defense time and again to locate the net with one or more men dangling at his body. It was the brilliant work of Perry that virtually disrupted the Suburbanite forces.

For the first few minutes it was a real tussle, but after that it could hardly be called such. Lacking a co-ordinated attack, and wild in their shooting when they did get an opportunity to tally, the Eichert lads were simply outclassed, and their feeble efforts to keep the score down were thrust aside.

Although Perry was the galloping ghost of the hardwood, he was given fine support by his mates, especially by Schrenks, Captain Blissell and Early, who accounted for 19 points between them. Joe Figula, the other regular, failed to register a field goal, but his performance in the rear court was all that could be asked.

Flashing their way through the Wesleyville defense with the speed of a locomotive, the Ramblers piled up a 16 to 0 lead at the end of the first period, and increased it 35 to 2 at intermission. From then on it became a question of how high the score would mount before the final whistle.

With the game in the cooler, Coach Father Conway sent in nine reserve players at various times during the late stages. Against the scrubs, Wesleyville offered stronger resistance defensively, but failed to improve its scoring tactics. Eichler and Burch were responsible for all of their team's points. Lineup:

Prep (52)	F.	Fl.	T.	Wesleyville (5)	F.	Fl.	T.
Schrenk,f	2	1	5	Eichler,f	1	0	2
Blissell,f	2	2	6	Dudley,f	0	0	0
Young,c	1	0	2	McShea,c,f	0	0	0
Perry,g	13	2	28	Burch,g	0	2	2
Figula,g	0	1	1	Steiner,g	0	0	0
Early,g	4	0	8	McQuiston,f	0	0	0
Nash,g	0	0	0	Hankoske,c	0	1	1
T.Flatley,f	0	0	0	Cook,g	0	0	0
Holland,c	1	0	2	Lewis,c	0	0	0
Skelly,g	0	0	0	Ripley,f	0	0	0
W.Flatley,f	0	0	0				
Weindorf,f	0	0	0				
Smith,g	0	0	0				
Totals	23	6	52	Totals	1	3	5

Cathedral Prep began the 1930's with a 52-5 win over Wesleyville.

Early Records Set!

Mike Figula, 1930 team captain. Coming to Prep from the Orphanage, he was also a fierce little running back.

1929-**30** (15-7)

Coach: Rev. Walter Conway
Captains: Norman "Dick" Blissell, Mike Figula
Managers: Jim Gannon, Anthony Brown (asst.)

Date	PREP			Dec.	Loc.	High Scorer	Opponent
12/17	52	Wesleyville	5	W	H	Perry (28*)	Eichler & Burch (2)
1/7	15	North East	20	L	H	Schrenk (5)	Reid (7)
1/14	26	Cleveland (OH) St. Ignatius	27(OT)	L	H	Perry (10)	Daoust (12)
1/18	18	Girard	30	L	A	Perry (19)	Burr & Andrews (8)
1/21	34	Bradford St. Bernard's	9	W	H	Perry (14)	Steckmeyer (6)
1/25	41	Ridgway St. Leo's	26	W	A	Schrenk (13)	Feleshifter (8)
1/28	35	Wesleyville	12	W	A	Perry (7)	Eichler (6)
1/31	17	North East	27	L	A	Perry (11)	Powers (12)
2/5	22	Buffalo (NY) Canisius	20	W	H	Lyons (8)	DePerro (12)
2/8	34	Youngsville	17	W	H	Perry (12)	Hendrickson (5)
2/11	54	Alumni	34	W	H	Perry (22)	Hayes (15)
2/15	27	Cleveland (OH) St. Ignatius	28	L	A	Perry (14)	Daoust (8)
2/18	37	Youngsville	18	W	A	Perry (15)	Root (7)
2/20		Titusville St. Titus (CANCELLED)			A		
2/22	48	Corry St. Edward's	21	W	A	Lyons (19)	Maloney (8)
2/25	14	Girard	16	L	H	Perry (9)	Andrews (7)
3/1	18	Buffalo (NY) Canisius	16	W	A	Lyons (8)	Hilligas (6)
3/4	40	Corry St. Edward's	22	W	H	Perry (15)	Maloney (12)
3/8	32	Bradford St. Bernard's	22	W	A	Perry (20)	Matthews (13)
3/11	45	Ridgway St. Leo's	20	W	H	Schrenk (17)	Fileshifter (6)
3/14	40	Silver Creek (NY) St. Columban's	16	W	A	Perry (16)	Stacks & Degnor (6)

LAKE ERIE TRI-STATE BASKETBALL TOURNAMENT @ EAST HIGH

Date	PREP			Dec.	Loc.	High Scorer	Opponent
3/19	24	East High Reserves	16	W	A	Perry (16)	Arrowsmith & Weber(4)
3/21	16	West Millcreek	17	L	N	Earley & Perry (6)	Waldo (8)
	641*(30.5*)		**418* (19.9)**				

Richard Sertz, father of three outstanding Prep coaches, including Rick Sertz and Hall-of-Famers Ron Sertz and Jim Sertz.

Leading scorer John Young started all 40 games as a junior and a senior.

Pos.	Player	Prior School	Class	G(GS)	FG	FT	Total	PPG	Career
C-G	Herbert "Joe" Perry (#6)	W. Phila. HS	Jr.	22*(22*)	109*	42	260*	11.8*	444*
F	Robert Schrenk (#7)	St. Mary's	Jr.	21(20)	49	26	124	6.2	251
G	James "Jay" Lyons	Central HS	Sr.	10(9)	29	10	68	6.8	68
C	John Young (#9)	St. Mary's	Jr.	21(21)	29	4	62	3.0	70
G	Joe Earley (#10)	St. Peter's	Jr.	20(10)	26	8	60	3.0	80
G-F	Mike Figula (#3)	St. Jos. Home	Sr.	22*(20)	26	8	60	2.7	98
F	Tom Flatley (#12)	St. Ann's	Sr.	18(4)	10	7	27	1.5	27
C-G	Richard "Dick" Sertz (#4)	St. Joseph's	Sr.	12(1)	4	2	10	0.8	10
F	Norman "Dick" Blissell	Oil City St. Joe's	Sr.	1(1)	2	2	6	6.0	60
C	William "Bill" Holland (#5)	St. Patrick's	Jr.	9	2	0	4	0.4	4
F	Henry Pluskota (#11)	St. Jos. Home	Sr.	8	2	2	6	0.6	6
G	Robert Applebee (#8)	St. Joseph's	Jr.	4	0	0	0	0.0	0
G	Harold Nash (#15)	St. Mary's	Soph.	4	0	0	0	0.0	0
F	Harry "Bidge" Weindorff (#14)	St. Patrick's	Fr.	4	0	0	0	0.0	0
G	Francis "Irish" Carroll	Gridley	Sr.	3	0	0	0	0.0	0
G-F	John Scully (#16)	St. Patrick's	Jr.	3	0	0	0	0.0	0
F-G	Willard "Bud" Flatley	St. Ann's	Soph.	2	0	0	0	0.0	0
G	James Smith	St. Joseph's	Jr.	1	0	0	0	0.0	0
G	John "Dinny" O'Brien	St. Ann's	Soph.	1	0	0	0	0.0	0

HIGHLIGHTS:

- **Father Walter Conway's** second season as Cathedral Prep's head coach produced a record 15-win season, which remained a school record until topped by Prep's first city champs in 1947 under coach **Walt Strosser**.

- To this point newspapers occasionally referred to "Cathedral High" with nicknames such as the "Fighting Irish," the "Preps" or simply the "Catholics." Beginning with the 1929 football season, the *Erie Daily Times* referred to Prep as the "Terriers," which was then the mascot at the University of Notre Dame, while the *Erie Dispatch-Herald* referred to the Cathedral team as the "Ramblers," a send-up to ND's "Rockne's Ramblers."

- All Cathedral Prep's home games were played at the Academy High School gymnasium, as they were the previous season.

- One disappointment was the absence of senior **Dick Blissell**, who was named team captain prior to the season opener. He was taken ill after the first game and was out for the remainder of the season.

- A special rules change in 1929-30 was that two referees could be used in a basketball game.

The 1929-30 Prep squad notched 15 wins, a team record that stood until 1947. First row, L to R: Flatley, Earley, Figula, Schrenk, Perry; Second Row: Mgr. Gannon, Sertz, Young, Lyons, Mgr. Brown; Third row: Scully, Holland, Weindorff.

- Apparently still smarting from the stigma of the setback to Wesleyville (1-14) on the gridiron in 1929, and further prodded by Coach Father Conway, the Prepsters clobbered the Bulldogs, 52-5, in the season opener. It was 35-2 at intermission before Father Conway started putting in reserves. A record 13 FGs and 28 points were scored by **Herb Perry** in that game against the Bulldogs. That point total lasted as a Prep record for 22 years, until broken by **Al Hatkevich** against Technical in 1951-52.

- Prep missed 8 of 9 free throw attempts in its first loss of the season, at home, 20-15, to North East (12-13). The Grapepickers won the rematch by 10 in North East.

- Prep suffered a pair of losses to Erie County Interscholastic League titlist Girard (24-4). The Yellow Jackets finished 12-0 in the ECIL.

- After Prep's two victories over Bradford St. Bernard's (3-10), the two did not compete again until the 1945-46 season.

- Huge were a pair of two-point victories over a good Buffalo Canisius squad, while the biggest disappointments of the season were a pair of one-point losses to St. Ignatius. Canisius and St. Ignatius are both Jesuit high schools. Canisius, founded in 1870, is located in downtown Buffalo and St. Ignatius, founded in 1886, is on the west side of Cleveland in a neighborhood known as Ohio City. Canisius is closely affiliated with Canisius College, while St. Ignatius was the forerunner of John Carroll University.

- **Walter Daoust** of St. Ignatius (13-3) led the entire city of Cleveland in scoring in 1929-30 with 192 points. The Golden Tornado (later, "Wildcats") made it to the sectional semifinals of the Ohio state tournament, where it lost to Akron North, 26-14.

- Titusville St. Titus cancelled its February 20 date with Prep, notifying Orange & Black coach Father Conway that it could not secure a floor for the contest.

- St. Columban's Seminary, whom Prep defeated in the regular season finale, was a minor seminary school for young men interested in becoming missionary priests, founded by the Columban Fathers in Silver Creek (NY), a small town on the south shore of Lake Erie about 40 miles from the city of Buffalo. In 1968 the seminary was handed over to the Columban Sisters who transformed the property into St. Columban's-on the-Lake Retirement Home the well-aged.

- Prep participated in the16-team Class "B" division of the "first annual" Lake Erie Tri-State Basketball Tournament held at East High, which also had another 13-team Class "A" bracket and an 8-team junior high playdown. Prep's opening game victory over the East Reserves was satisfying, though it was the East varsity (19-5) that was Erie's city champions, dethroning defending titlist Academy (15-4). Neither the Warriors nor the Lions participated in this tourney. The Ramblers then suffered a quarterfinal loss to West Millcreek (16-7). The Trojans then lost to Allegany (NY) High, which went on to defeat Girard, 26-24, to capture the Class "B" title. New Castle defeated Sharpsville, 26-15, in the final of the "A" division. Prep did not play in another tournament until the PCIAA's began in 1943.

- Other schools participating in the Class "B" division included Fairview, Kanty Prep, Corry, Hickory, Brocton (NY), North East, Marienville, Sharpsburg, West Middlesex, Oil City JV's and Central Reserves. Other "A" teams were Westfield (NY), Meadville, Cochranton, Kittanning, Jamestown (NY), Erie Central, Aliquippa, Franklin, Hollidaysburg, Warren and Ford City. Hotel accomodations were provided by the tournament committee and meals were served each day of the event in the East cafeteria.

- Several awards were presented at the Tri-State Tourney, mostly for the winners and runners-up. The award for the one player who was the "MVP to his team—a shirt by Mulvihill and Koch"—was given to Prep's **Herb Perry**!

- The junior high schools playing in the Lake Erie Tri-State Basketball Tournament were Academy, West Millcreek, Warren, Gridley, Corry, Allegany (NY) and finalists Roosevelt and Wilson. In a classic east side of Erie (Wilson) versus west side (Roosevelt), Wilson's "brilliant brand of ball was too much for Roosevelt," as the Presidents defeated the Teddies, 35-13. Some of Wilson's stars: Gorniak, Scolio, Wright, Karznia, Schreckengost. Some of Roosevelt's stars: Calabrese, Cargioli, DiTullio, Gambatese, DeFazio, Agresti, Bellomini, and Rosenthal.

- Though Prep went 6-0 against Erie Diocesan opponents, it did not receive a bid to the second annual Pennsylvania State Catholic tournament. Prep was not part of the Erie Diocesan League which at the time consisted of: District I—Oil City St. Joseph's, Titusville St. Titus, Corry St. Edward's, Erie St. Stanislaus, Meadville St. Agatha's and Greenville St. Michael's; District II—Bradford St. Bernard's, Clearfield St. Francis, DuBois St. Catherine's, Ridgway St. Leo's and St. Marys St. Mary's. St. Stan's won the Diocesan title for 1930. The Eagles moved on to the State Catholic Tournament at Duquesne and came away with an impressive third place finish, defeating Pittsburgh Central Catholic, 31-20, in the consolation game. To get there, St. Stan's beat Clearfield St. Francis, 38-18, but lost to Duquesne Prep in the semifinals, 29-22. The "Duke Preps" then lost in the state title game to Altoona Catholic, a 16-15 thriller. St. Stan's star forward, **Stephen Sczeszny**, made the all-tournament team. Another noted member of the Eagles was Joseph Radzisiewski (later **Father Joe Radzisiewski**), who was to become Prep's first regular JV basketball coach in the 1940's.

- In PIAA action, Sharon High became the first District 8 (now District 10) team to win the state championship. The Tigers defeated Lower Merion, 18-14, in the final at the Palestra in Philadelphia. Sharon was coached by **A. Warner "Pop" Dickerson**, rated as one of Pennsylvania's outstanding coaches after four of his teams reached the finals of state championship tournaments and his 1930 quintet won the crown. Under Dickerson's tutelage, the Tigers won more than 20 different titles from 1919 to 1935 when he retired because of poor health. He died in 1941 at age 50 from pneumonia after a brief illness.

- Seniors **Mike Figula, Dick Sertz, Henry Pluskota, Jay Lyons** and **"Irish" Carroll** were all gridiron stars for Father Conway's Prep football team that finished 6-2 in 1929.

- **Richard "Dick" Sertz** was the father of future Prep coaches Jim Sertz, Ron Sertz and Rick Sertz. Ron was inducted into the Prep Athletic Hall of Fame in 2003, while Jim was inducted in 2015.

- **Herbert "Joe" Perry**, also a star fullback for the Ramblers, finished the season as Prep's all-time leader in FGs, FTs and points. He was the first Rambler to score over 200 points in a season and 400 for a career. Only one other Prepster in the next 15 years averaged in double figures per game, and Perry's record of 12.0 *PPG* lasted until broken by **Al Hatkevich** in 1951.

- At a post-season banquet it was announced that **Herb Perry**, "the Galloping Ghost of the Hardwood," was chosen as captain of the 1930-31 hoop team. Unfortunately for Prep, Perry, who had been staying for two years with his aunt and uncle in Erie, did not return for his senior season. His transcripts were sent to The Perkiomen School near his native Philadelphia.

1930 All-Opponent Team:

Dick Reid, North East
Robert Gilmore, North East
Jimmy Andrews, Girard
Art "Swede" Jacobsen, Girard
Walter Daoust, St. Ignatius
Louis DePerro, Canisius [Canisius]
Roger Hendrickson, Youngsville
John Maloney, Corry St. Ed's
Bob Matthews, Bradford St. Bernard's
Tom Fileshifter, Ridgway St. Leo's
Lew Waldo, West Millcreek

Prep Plays Erie City Series Teams!

1930-31 (8-11)

Coach: Rev. Walter Conway
Captain: John Young
Manager: Anthony Brown

Three-year starter Bob Schrenk was only the second Prepster to record 300 career points.

Date	PREP			Dec.	Loc.	High Scorer	Opponent
12/15	18	Wesleyville	3**	W	H	Earley (8)	several (1)
12/19	27	Wesleyville	6	W	A	Young (8)	McShea (4)
1/6	15	Strong Vincent	25	L	A	Young (6)	R. Calabrese (7)
1/9	13	Corry	29	L	A	Schrenk (4)	Paulson (8)
1/12	10	Titusville St. Titus	28	L	H	Nash (4)	Hettrick (10)
1/17	25	Niagara Falls (NY) St. Mary's	17	W	A	Coleman (9)	Gallagher (6)
1/19	10	Corry	11	L	H	Earley & Young (4)	several (3)
1/23	25	Corry St. Edward's	11	W	A	Coleman (8)	Nichols & Hovey (4)
1/26	19	Erie DeMolay	24	L	H	Earley (10)	Cohen & Lee (7)
1/29	23	West Millcreek	12	W	A	Young (10)	Waldo (5)
2/3	14	Academy	36	L	H	Coleman & Earley (4)	Tell (9)
2/10	16	East	26	L	H	Schrenk (5)	Prizinsky (11)
2/14	17	Academy	38	L	A	Coleman (7)	Spath (11)
2/16	18	West Millcreek	21	L	H	Young (8)	Wilkins (8)
2/20	11	Erie DeMolay	13	L	A	Holland (6)	Siegel (8)
2/23	22	Niagara Falls (NY) St. Mary's	15	W	H	Young (10)	Siedlekt (7)
2/28	20	East	26	L	A	Young & Holland (7)	Prizinsky (11)
3/2	41	Corry St. Edward's	14	W	H	Young (12)	Crum (7)
3/8	28	Silver Creek (NY) St. Columban's	19	W	H	Earley & Holland (10)	McMahon (8)
	372 (19.5)		**374 (19.7)**				

Pos.	Player	Prior School	Class	G(GS)	FG	FT	Total	PPG	Career
C	John Young (#9)	St. Mary's	Sr.	19(19)	33	27	93	4.9	163
G-F	Joe Earley (#10)	St. Peter's	Sr.	18(18)	38	15	91	5.1	171
F	Eugene "Dog" Coleman	Sacred Heart	Soph.	14(8)	17	20	54	3.9	54
F	Robert Schrenk (#7)	St. Mary's	Sr.	18(16)	19	11	49	2.7	300
G	William "Bill" Holland (#5)	St. Patrick's	Sr.	17(12)	22	4	48	2.8	52
F	John Scully (#16)	St. Patrick's	Sr.	10(5)	4	4	12	1.2	12
F	Harold Nash (#15)	St. Mary's	Jr.	5(1)	4	0	8	1.6	8
F	Harrison Rogers	Albion	Sr.	15	2	3	7	0.5	7
G	Willard "Bud" Flatley	St. Ann's	Jr.	14(5)	1	4	6	0.4	6
G	Robert Applebee (#8)	St. Joseph's	Sr.	16(10)	1	1	3	0.2	3
F-G	James Smith	St. Joseph's	Sr.	3	0	2	2	0.7	2
F	James Ward	St. Stan's	Sr.	3	0	0	0	0.0	0
G	John "Dinny" O'Brien	St. Ann's	Jr.	2	0	0	0	0.0	0
F	Robert Alexander	St. Peter's	Jr.	2	0	0	0	0.0	0
G	Richard "Red" McBride	St. Patrick's	Fr.	1	0	0	0	0.0	0

1930-31 Prep Team. Front, L to R: Schrenk, Holland, Young, Earley, Applebee; Back: O'Brien, Flatley, Scully, Rogers, Coleman, Alexander, Mgr. Brown.

HIGHLIGHTS:

- After two years of success, Cathedral Prep coach **Father Walter Conway** made a serious effort to upgrade the schedule of the Orange & Black. 1931 marked Prep's first basketball competition ever against City Series rivals Vincent, Academy and East (all losses). Academy (21-4) ousted defending champion East (18-3) to win the 1931 City Series crown.

- The 1930-31 Ramblers were hurt by the absence of all-time scoring leader **Herbert "Joe" Perry**, who was chosen as team captain but transferred to The Perkiomen School before his senior campaign. Perry had also been a star fullback on the Orange & Black football squad.

- Prep gave up a total of one FG combined in its first two games of the season, both victories over Wesleyville (7-10). The December 19 contest was the first ever staged in Wesleyville's brand new gymnasium.

- Erie High School ceased to exist after its 1920 graduation exercises, and for the next decade the school's building located on the southeast corner of 10th and Sassafras Streets was known as Central High School. The City of Erie then had three high schools, as both East High (1920) and Academy (1919) had been recently founded. In 1930 the entire faculty and student body at Central was shifted to the huge new school of Strong Vincent located on the far west side of town between Weschler Avenue and Washington Place on West 8th Street. All of Cathedral Prep's home games were played at the new Vincent High School gymnasium.

- Strong Vincent (12-12) defeated Prep by 10 before the first capacity crowd ever in the new SV gym. The Colonels' leading scorer was star **Ralph "Baron" Calabrese**, who succeeded **Father Walter Conway** as Prep's head basketball coach in 1937-38. SV star **Chuck Bauder's** son, **Chuck Bauder, Jr.**, became a Prep star in the late 1950's. Chuck, Sr. played baseball in the minors for eight seasons, including with Little Rock of the Southern Association and Wilkes-Barre of the Eastern League.

- In Prep's hard-fought 11-10 road loss to Corry (16-6), two technical fouls were called on the Ramblers in the game's final moments. The first was for "delaying the game," while the second was called while time was out, presumably for Father Conway giving Referee Burns "a piece of his mind." Though the first free throw was missed, the second one was made to provide for the Beavers' margin of victory. Corry had a huge upset win over Vincent earlier in the season.

- Prep won twice over the Erie Diocesan League's cellar dwellers, Corry St. Edward's (2-9). Others in the EDL included Titusville St. Titus, Erie St. Stanislaus, Greenville St. Michael's and Meadville St. Agatha's.

- New opponent Erie DeMolay (4-6) was part of a world-wide Masonic organization that sponsored athletics, among other things, for boys and men 12-21 years of age. DeMolay bases its approach on timeless principles and practical hands-on experience to develop civic awareness, personal responsibility and leadership skills. It was common for the Erie chapter to compete against the local high schools in basketball.

- New opponent Niagara Falls St. Mary's was founded in 1927 and was the only Catholic High School in Niagara County (NY) at the time. It closed in 1959, eventually evolving with Bishop Duffy (all boys) and Madonna (all girls) to form Niagara Catholic High School in 1975.

- Prep played on even terms in both battles with powerful East High, only to be overtaken both times by 4th quarter Warrior surges. East star **Jack Laraway** became a World War II casualty with the U. S. Marines in 1944.

- In a preliminary to the varsity game, a Prep JV team, led by **Wally Coleman's** 12 points, defeated the St. Columban's JV's, 17-15.

- St. Titus (9-2), which easily handled Prep early in the season, earned a bid the State Catholic Tournament at Duquesne University by virtue of its 28-13 Erie Diocesan League playoff victory over Erie St. Stanislaus (8-3). Both squads had finished atop the loop standings with 7-1 records. St. Titus then lost in the first round to Philadelphia West Catholic, 40-27. Duquesne Prep won the crown with a 39-11 romp over Pittsburgh St. Mary of the Mount in the state final. Philadelphia West Catholic defeated Pittsburgh Central Catholic for consolation honors, 36-19.

- 6'4" **Bill Holland** came on strong at the end of the campaign. He then became a full star at Edinboro State Teachers College and later became the first Prepster to become a professional football player, toiling for the Warren Red Jackets in the mid-1930's. In 1983 Holland was inducted into Edinboro's Athletic Hall of Fame, having been the school's first dominating center on a college team noted to be one of the first in the country to average more than 50 points per game.

1931 All-Opponent Team:

Ralph Calabrese, Vincent [Findlay]
Chuck Bauder, Vincent [Allentown Prep;
    Class A baseball, Indians & Red Sox]
Richard Paulson, Corry
Richard Bachofner, Corry
William Burns, St. Titus
Abe Cohen, DeMolay
Abe Lee, DeMolay
Robert Tell, Academy
Paul Prizinsky, East
Ed "Muckles" Hiller, East
Chester Spath, Academy
Murel Schreckengost, Academy
George Wilkins, West Millcreek
Bill Siegel, DeMolay
Jack Laraway, East

Joe Earley started every game and was Prep's second leading scorer.

Bob Applebee was a defensive specialist.

Rival Strong Vincent Goes to the PIAA State Final!

1931-32 (7-12)

Coach: Rev. Walter Conway
Captains: Harold Nash, Willard Flatley
Manager: Edgar Jones

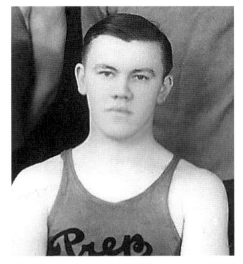

Three-year starter Gene "Dog" Coleman was a colorful athlete, later known as "Father Eugene Coleman."

Date	PREP			Dec.	Loc.	High Scorer	Opponent
12/14	34	Corry St. Edward's	10	W	H	Kuziora (12)	Burkett (6)
12/16	14	Wesleyville	18	L	A	Nash (8)	McQuiston (11)
1/9	18	Buffalo (NY) Canisius	31	L	A	Coleman (13)	Francis (9)
1/11	21	Wesleyville	23	L	H	Kuziora (10)	Dudley (7)
1/16	26	West Millcreek	28	L	A	Coleman (8)	Wilkins (10)
1/18	34	Alumni	21	W	H	Nash (9)	Earley (7)
1/22	12	Strong Vincent	35	L	A	Sinnott & Kuziora (3)	Bell & Sickafus (6)
1/25	16	Erie DeMolay	26	L	H	Coleman & Nash (5)	Forest (18)
1/29	12	Oil City St. Joseph's	11	W	A	Nash (5)	Driscoll (5)
2/1	15	Strong Vincent	36	L	A	Coleman (7)	Bauder (8)
2/8	15	Girard	31	L	H	Coleman (5)	Andrews (10)
2/13	24	Buffalo (NY) Canisius	30(OT)	L	H	Coleman & Kuziora (9)	Fornes (12)
2/15	21	West Millcreek	20	W	H	Nash (8)	Waldo (10)
2/22	11	Technical	34	L	H	Kuziora (5)	Calabrese & Gorniak (9)
2/25	11	Erie DeMolay	22	L	A	Coleman (7)	Todd & Mink (6)
2/27	27	Titusville St. Titus	17	W	A	Kuziora (10)	Geary (11)
2/29	21	Lawrence Park	19	W	H	Coleman (7)	Holmes (8)
3/4	36	Corry St. Edward's	22	W	A	Coleman (24)	Burkett (8)
3/7		Oil City St. Joseph's (POSTPONED—WEATHER)			H		
3/9	23	Oil City St. Joseph's	26	L	H	Kuziora (8)	Hall & Carroll (8)
	391 (20.6)			**460 (24.2)**			

Pos.	Player	Prior School	Class	G(GS)	FG	FT	Total	PPG	Career
F	Eugene "Dog" Coleman	Sacred Heart	Jr.	19(19)	49	37	135	7.1	189
C	Len "Lefty" Kuziora	St. John's	Jr.	17(17)	38	13	89	5.2	89
F	Harold Nash	St. Mary's	Sr.	19(18)	28	12	68	3.6	76
G	Willard "Bud" Flatley	St. Ann's	Sr.	17(14)	10	7	27	1.6	33
G	Stanley Pickett	Holy Rosary	Soph.	16(11)	10	4	24	1.5	24
G	Carl Maya	Academy HS	Jr.	18(7)	7	3	17	0.9	17
G	Tom Flatley	St. Ann's	PG	5(3)	8	3	19	3.8	46
G	Robert Crotty	St. Mary's	Jr.	7	2	0	4	0.6	4
F	Joe Sinnott	St. Patrick's	Jr.	6	1	1	3	0.5	3
G	Richard McCarthy	Gridley	Sr.	1(1)	1	0	2	2.0	2
C	James Walrath	Mohawk HS	Sr.	3	0	1	1	0.3	1
G	Francis Fetzner	St. Ann's	Sr.	4	0	1	1	0.3	1
G	William Lee	North East	Sr.	7	0	1	1	0.1	1
G	John "Dinny" O'Brien	St. Ann's	Sr.	7(2)	0	0	0	0.0	0
G	John Straub	Rouseville	Jr.	4(1)	0	0	0	0.0	0
F	Robert Alexander	St. Peter's	Sr.	4	0	0	0	0.0	0
C	Bob Joyce	St. Peter's	Soph.	2	0	0	0	0.0	0
G	Leo Downey	Albion	Jr.	1	0	0	0	0.0	0
G	Harry "Bidge" Weindorff	St. Patrick's	Jr.	1	0	0	0	0.0	0

HIGHLIGHTS:

- All Cathedral Prep's home games were played at the Strong Vincent High School gymnasium.

- City Series and District 10 champion Strong Vincent (24-3-1) was 1932 PIAA State runner-up, losing to unbeaten Old Forge in the final at the Penn State Armory in State College, 24-19. Legendary Vincent coach **Harold "Sam" Kramer's** men were handicapped by the new glass bank boards installed at the Armory, a type which the Colonel hoopsters had never run up against before. SV stars included **Ralph Calabrese, Vince Bell, Lou Sickafus, Rich Hetico, Chuck Bauder, Ken Bossart, George Suesser and Al Calabrese**. Two of Vincent's three regular season blemishes were to East High (11-5-1), coached by legendary **Jim Hyde**: a 26-26 draw (3 overtimes was the limit then); and a loss, 26-25. SV's other loss was at Jamestown (17-1), 30-26, in Vincent's third game of the season.

- The PIAA went from eight to ten districts beginning with the 1931-32 season. Northwest Pennsylvania's designation then changed from "District 8" to "District 10." Vincent defeated Oil City, 24-18, and Girard, 23-21, to gain the D-10 crown; then beat DuBois, 28-9, and Pittsburgh Fifth Avenue, 41-25, to win the Western Pennsylvania title.

- Two of Vincent's stars later became head basketball coaches at Cathedral Prep: **Ralph Calabrese** in 1937-38; and his cousin, **Al Calabrese**, in 1941-42.

- Though Academy (17-2) did compete with Prep the previous season, the Golden Lions were not on the Ramblers' 1931-32 calendar. Academy, under coach **Howard Kelly**, presented a

1931-32

THE CATHEDRAL Prep Basketball Team of 1932 included, first row, l to r, Stanley Pichett, John O'Brien, Bud Flatley, Harold Nash and Fr. Eugene Coleman. Standing, l to r, Edgar Jones, Carl Maya, Father Leonard Kuziora, Robert Alexander and Jack Straub. This weeks photo was sent to the LSV by Harold Nash.

talented squad, including **Frank Lugo** and **Bob Tell**, and lost only to—Strong Vincent, twice!

- High school basketball games were officially set with 8-minute quarters. No longer were teams using the option to play 9- or 10-minute quarters.

- When the entire faculty and student body from Central High was shifted to the new Strong Vincent school on Erie's west side in 1930, the old Central building sat vacant for a year. Technical High School (7-8) then opened in the old building for the 1931-32 school year and hence became Prep's biggest rival. Although the basketball competition between the two took a three-year hiatus after the initial game, the schools resumed hoop hostilities and played every year thereafter.

- No less than a dozen of the Prep hoopsters played on the outstanding 9-2 Rambler football squad, including star senior quarterback **John "Dinny" O'Brien** and senior linemen **Willard "Bud" Flatley, Francis Fetzner** and **Bob Alexander**.

- Prep opened with an easy win over Corry St. Edward's (11-7). Despite the Ramblers defeating them again later in the season, the 1931-32 Shamrocks were considered their best team to date. One of their victories was a 2-0 forfeit win over Erie St. Stanislaus, when the Eagles' coach **John "Rink" Stanczak** walked his team off the floor at the start of the fourth quarter as he was extremely upset with the officiating. St. Stan's was ahead, 9-8, at the time. It was the Eagles only loss of the regular season. Invited to the Pennsylvania State Catholic Basketball Tourney at Duquesne University, St. Stan's was beaten by Scranton St. Thomas in the first round, 25-10. St. Thomas made it to the championship final where it lost to Philadelphia Northeastern Catholic, coached by legendary Philadelphia sports figure **John "Jocko" Collins**, 33-28. 1932 was the last year of the Duquesne

Strong Vincent's 1932 PIAA state finalists. Two boys on this team later became head coaches at Prep. Front row, L to R: Leet, Hetico, Bell, Captain R. Calabrese, Bauder, Bossart, Chimenti; Middle: Jones, A. Calabrese, Rosenthal, White, Sisson, Gillespie, Markowitz; Back: Asst. Coach Bert Gustavson, De-Fazio, Suesser, Mgr. Conti, Donatucci, Quillman, Coach Sam Kramer.

CATHEDRAL RALLIES IN LAST 20 SECONDS TO BEAT MILLCREEK HI

state Catholic tourney, a victim of the Great Depression.

- One of Prep's biggest victories was the mid-season one-point success at Oil City St. Joe's (23-3). It was the first time ever that St. Joe's lost on its home court. The Hilltoppers only other losses of the season were to Oil City High and Mercer.

- Prep took a sound beating from Girard (19-3), the Erie County League champion. The Yellow Jackets, behind superstar **Jimmy Andrews**, crushed Bloomfield, 50-22, and Sharpsville, 49-18, in D-10 play, but lost to Strong Vincent in the D-10 final, 23-21.

- Prep's second loss to Canisius was the only overtime game played by the Ramblers in the 1930's decade. Canisius, Buffalo city Catholic champions, went on to the National Catholic Interscholastic Basketball Tournament (NCIBT) in Chicago. It lost in the first round, however, to Peoria (IL) Spalding Institute, 26-21.

- Another big Prep win was over West Millcreek (12-5), when the Ramblers were down 20-13 early in the 4th quarter, then rallied to score 8 unanswered points, including 4 in the last 20 seconds (FGs by **Len Kuziora** and **Eugene Coleman**), to win 21-20. The Ramblers held Trojan star **George Wilkins** to one point, this after Wilkins had burned Prep with 10 in Millcreek's 2-point win over Prep earlier in the season.

- Erie DeMolay (7-6) defeated Prep twice for the second year in a row. The pair never competed again.

- Prep's win at the Titusville YMCA against St. Titus (2-9-1) was the last time the two played, as St. Titus closed following the 1931-32 school year. After the Prep game, St. Titus' last game ever was a 14-8 victory over Punxsutawney Sts. Cosmas and Damien. Titusville St. Joseph's Academy opened the following school year, and most of the St. Titus athletes and their coach, **Leo Robie** of Erie, transferred to the new school. It was noted for Coach Robie that it was "the first time a Catholic school in Titusville had a regular paid coach." St. Joe's was nicknamed the "Robots," a send-up of the last name of Coach Robie.

- St. Titus' only other non-losses were an opening game victory over Erie St. Mary's Commercial High (1-11) and a three-overtime, 22-22 tie with Greenville St. Michael's. The St. Mary's team was handicapped by the fact it was a two-year school with an enrollment of only 35 boys and it was necessary to take on teams from four-year institutions in order to round out a schedule. As for the St. Titus-St. Mike's draw, national rules at the time specified there were to be no more than three OT's in high school games.

- In a preliminary to the Prep-St. Titus battle, the Erie Boy Scouts defeated the Titusville Boy Scouts, 24-20. Future Prep star **Bob Carrick** led the Erie Boy Scouts with 10 points.

SINK TWO GOALS TO REGISTER BY POINT, 21 TO 20

Kuziora and Coleman in Hero Roles As Prep Takes Battle

played 2-15-32 @SV

FIELD goals by Kuziora and Coleman in the last 20 seconds of play enabled Cathedral high to take a 21-29 victory over West Millcreek last night on the Vincent floor. Trailing by three points, Kuziora sank a shot and then Eugene Coleman took one off the board and sank the winning goal.

Millcreek took the lead at the outset of the game and held it up to the last half-minute. Waldo and Bolte dropped in charity throws to give Millcreek its start and then Bolte sank a nice shot from the side court to put Millcreek four points in the lead. Nash gave Prep its first count in the last minute.

Millcreek continued to hold the lead during the second chapter and was leading eight to six at half time. Prep took new life as the second half got under way and tied it up at 10 all and again at 12. They couldn't get enough power to take the lead.

The last quarter was fast and furious, with Coleman starting it off and again tieing up the score at 13-13. Millcreek then went on a scoring spree and went ahead seven points, 20-13. Prep then took a page from a novel and field goals by Kuziora and Nash put it in the running, while the two baskets by Kuziora and Coleman gave Cathedral the game. Score:

- Wesleyville (2-10) hung two early season losses on Prep and unbelievably didn't win another game the rest of the season, finishing last in the Erie County League.

- **Tom Flatley, Sr.**, father of Prep stars **Willard Flatley** and **Tom Flatley, Jr.**, later became mayor of the City of Erie (1952-54), while junior **Joe Sinnott's** grandson, **Attorney Joe Sinnott**, also became Erie's mayor (2006-present).

1932 All-Opponent Team:

Clayton Burkett, Corry St. Ed's
Bob McQuiston, Wesleyville
Ralph Dudley, Wesleyville
Billy Voight, Wesleyville
George Wilkins, West Millcreek
Robert Bolte, West Millcreek
Vince Bell, Vincent [Muskingum, basketball & football]
Lou Sickafus, Vincent
Chuck Bauder, Vincent [Allentown Prep; Class A baseball, Indians & Red Sox]
Ernest Forest, DeMolay
Tom Driscoll, Oil City St. Joe's
Jimmy Andrews, Girard
Donald Fornes, Canisius
Lew Waldo, West Millcreek
Ray Calabrese, Technical
Ed Gorniak, Technical
William Holmes, Lawrence Park
Phil Hall, Oil City St. Joe's
Francis "Cootie" Carroll, Oil City St. Joe's [Xavier (OH)]

Seniors Get Ramblers Back to Winning Form!

1932-33 (10-7)

Coach: Rev. Walter Conway
Captain: Len Kuziora
Manager: Tommy Meagher

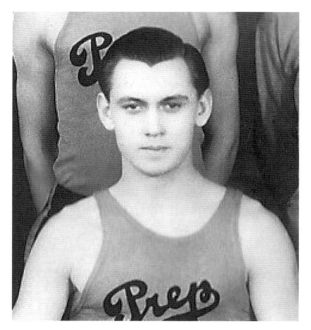

Len Kuziora went on to star in the backfield for Holy Cross. Later "Father Len Kuziora," he was Prep's football and basketball coach during the war years.

Date	PREP			Dec.	Loc.	High Scorer	Opponent
12/12	28	Alumni	15	W	H	Coleman (17)	Flatley & Earley (5)
12/16	28	Corry St Edward's	19	W	A	Coleman (13)	McGrath (8)
1/9	22	West Millcreek	31	L	H	Kuziora (9)	Lange (11)
1/16	36	Lawrence Park	20	W	H	Coleman (15)	Kahl (7)
1/20	24	Edinboro	17	W	A	Kuziora (14)	Miller (8)
1/27	18	Oil City St. Joseph's	22	L	H	Kuziora (6)	Hall (8)
1/31	25	Wesleyville	32	L	A	Coleman (8)	Zill (10)
2/3	16	Cleveland (OH) St. Ignatius	28	L	A	Coleman (8)	Dodson (8)
2/6	25	Lawrence Park	17	W	H	Coleman (14)	Jackson (8)
2/10	21	Corry	16	W	A	Coleman (7)	Daye (12)
2/13	26	Edinboro	29	L	H	Coleman (10)	Case (13)
2/17	30	Cleveland (OH) St. Ignatius	27	W	H	Kuziora (15)	Meszaros (8)
2/20	39	Wesleyville	12	W	H	Kuziora (14)	Russ (6)
2/22	22	West Millcreek	24	L	A	Coleman (11)	Lange (7)
2/27	28	Corry St. Edward's	16	W	H	Kuziora (8)	McGrath (10)
3/3	25	Oil City St. Joseph's	34	L	A	Crotty (12)	Carroll (12)
3/6	45	Corry	23	W	H	Coleman (15)	Daye (11)
	458 (26.9)		**382 (22.5)**				

Pos.	Player	Prior School	Class	G(GS)	FG	FT	Total	*PPG*	Career
F	Eugene "Dog" Coleman	Sacred Heart	Sr.	17(15)	59	29	147	8.6	337
C	Leonard "Lefty" Kuziora	St. John's	Sr.	15(15)	57	19	133	8.7	222
G	Robert "Bob" Crotty	St. Mary's	Sr.	17(17)	36	11	83	4.9	87
C-G	Harry "Bidge" Weindorff	St. Patrick's	Sr.	16(15)	20	5	45	2.8	45
F-G	Bob "Mickey" McLaughlin (#10)	St. Ann's	Soph.	14(8)	5	2	12	0.9	12
F	John "Jack" Straub	Rouseville	Sr.	5(5)	6	0	12	2.4	12
F-G-C	Leo "Morton" Downey	Albion	Sr.	10(4)	2	2	6	0.6	6
G-F	Bill Griskey (#6)	St. Peter's	Fr.	11	1	3	5	0.5	5
G	Stanley Pickett	Holy Rosary	Jr.	7(3)	2	1	5	0.7	29
G-F	Jim Stroker	Madera (CA) HS	Sr.	4	1	0	2	0.5	2
F	Robert Almeda	St. Mary's	Soph.	5	0	2	2	0.4	2
F	Walter "Wally" Coleman (#4)	Sacred Heart	Jr.	5	1	0	2	0.4	2
G	Bernard "Chub" Reiser	St. Joseph's	Sr.	6(3)	1	0	2	0.3	2
F-C-G	Joe LeCorchick (#9)	St. Joseph's	Jr.	8	0	0	0	0.0	0
F-G	Jim Sperry	St. Peter's	Sr.	5	0	0	0	0.0	0
G-C	Bob Joyce	St. Peter's	Jr.	2	0	0	0	0.0	0
C	Frank "Bud" Raid (#8)	St. Joseph's	Jr.	2	0	0	0	0.0	0
G	Robert "Bob" Dailey	St. Ann's	Soph.	1	0	0	0	0.0	0

1932-33 Prep Ramblers. Front, L to R: Crotty, E. Coleman, Kuziora, Weindorff, Straub; Back: LeCorchick, Pickett, Sperry, McLaughlin, Griskey, Downey, W. Coleman.

HIGHLIGHTS:

- **Father Walter Conway's** fifth season as Cathedral Prep mentor was successful as the senior leadership of **Gene Coleman, Len Kuziora, Bob Crotty** and **Harry "Bidge" Weindorff** put the Ramblers back on the winning side after two straight losing seasons.

- Coach Father Conway was faced with a great handicap when only 9 candidates initially came out for the team. It was difficult to encourage some to participate as it was the worst year of the Great Depression and many boys were forced to try to earn money or do needed chores to help the family and home. The addition of several more players, including the return of **Len Kuziora** after the first two games, brought needed strength to the Ramblers. Kuziora had been out of action since the middle of the previous football season when he broke his leg in the Girard game.

- All Cathedral Prep's home games were played at the Strong Vincent High School gymnasium.

- The season's biggest disappointments were the pairs of losses to tough Oil City St. Joe's (24-3) and to coach **Gus Anderson's** crack West Millcreek Trojans (13-5) with 6'4" **Tyco Lange**; as well as the home game loss to Edinboro High School (6-9), after handily defeating the Turtles in the 'Boro.

- Oil City St. Joe's win over Prep on January 27 was the 25th consecutive victory for the Hilltoppers.

- Prep's game at Cleveland St. Ignatius (3-10) was held up for an hour at the end of the third quarter, when coach Father Conway, dissatisfied with the officiating of Referee Murphy, refused to continue until a new official was substituted! The Ramblers were forced to start the contest without the services of **"Bidge" Weindorff, Gene Coleman** and **Stanley Pickett,** who got lost on the way to Cleveland and did not arrive until the second quarter had started. The Golden Tornadoes were the only Class "A" squad on the Prep schedule.

- Prep gained sweet revenge against St. Ignatius in Erie, after trailing for three quarters and being down 24-20 entering the 4th period. The Ramblers, led by **Len Kuziora** and **Leo Downey,** outscored the Golden Tornado 10-3 in the final session for a 30-27 conquest. It was the best effort of the season for the Orange & Black.

- The season's biggest turnaround came with Prep's 27-point shellacking of Wesleyville (4-14), after the Bulldogs had upset the Ramblers by a 7-point margin just three weeks before. Wesleyville's only other victories for the season were a pair over Albion and its season finale versus Ripley (NY).

- Prep's two victories over Lawrence Park (3-9) were the last time the two competed. The Ramblers won the short series over the Tigers, 3-0. Lawrence Park and fellow East Erie suburban opponent Wesleyville merged in 1965 to form Iroquois High School. Prep has never played Iroquois, an Erie County League member until that loop's demise, in basketball.

- Opponents Wesleyville, West Millcreek and Lawrence Park were part of the Erie County League's Northern Division, along with Girard, North Girard and Albion. Opponent Edinboro was in the ECL's Southern Division, along with Cambridge Springs, Fairview, Waterford, McKean and Union City.

- On the local level, city champion East High (13-6) won its first district title since 1926, then defeated Oil City, 30-17, before losing to DuBois, 35-34, in PIAA competition. Warrior stars included **Lawrence Thomas, Leo Kaminski** and **George Kopec.**

- Corry High (8-13) officials complained about playing on a certain Monday night for the last game of the season. Apparently the Beavers, according to the *Corry Evening Journal*, "were handicapped due to the fact they were sent through a tough workout Monday afternoon at Corry, figuring they were to play in Erie on Tuesday."

- A highly competitive intramural league operated at Prep, with the following final standings:

	W	**L**
Sophomores	4	0
Seniors	2	2
Juniors	2	2
Freshmen	0	4

- A Prep junior varsity squad played one game, losing to St. Mary's Gaels of the parish league, 20-17, in overtime.

- **"Bidge" Weindorff, "Chub" Reiser** and **"Lefty" Kuziora** (later **Father Len Kuziora**) were three of Prep's famous 1932 "Four Horsemen" backfield that led the Ramblers to their first undefeated season (9-0) in 1932. Weindorff and Kuziora went on to star in football at Holy Cross, while **"Dog" Coleman** (later **Father Eugene Coleman**), a star lineman, competed at St. Bonaventure. Kuziora later became Prep's head basketball and head football coach (1942-44). He was inducted posthumously into the Cathedral Prep Athletic Hall of Fame in 2005.

- Senior **Jim Sperry** (later **Monsignor James Sperry**) became a legendary Erie Parochial League coach at St. Joseph's Orphanage and at Harborcreek Training School.

1933 All-Opponent Team:

Tyco Lange, West Millcreek
Howard Kahl, Lawrence Park
Phil Hall, Oil City St. Joe's
Matthew Zill, Wesleyville
Sam Russ, Wesleyville
Bobby Stanton, St. Ignatius
Joe Jackson, Lawrence Park
Motio Chiricuzio, Corry
Klahr Daye, Corry
Fred Case, Edinboro [Edinboro St.]
Jim Harrison, Edinboro
Frankie Meszaros, St. Ignatius
Robert Osterberg, West Millcreek
Joe McGrath, Corry St. Edward's
Joe Eagan, Oil City St. Joe's
Francis "Cootie" Carroll, Oil City St. Joe's
    [Xavier (OH)]

Coleman, McLaughlin Lead Ramblers!

Wally Coleman came on strong as a senior and led the Ramblers in scoring. He was sadly killed in an auto accident in 1936 at age 20.

1933-34 (10-6)

Coach: Rev. Walter Conway
Captain: Bob "Mickey" McLaughlin
Managers: Tommy Meagher, Lou Curran (asst.)

Date	PREP	Dec.			Loc.	High Scorer	Opponent
12/15	19	Corry St. Edward's	13	W	A	Razanoski (7)	Swan (7)
12/18	22	Wesleyville	11	W	H	Coleman & McLaughlin (7)	Adams (4)
1/9	10	North East	30	L	A	Coleman (5)	Stebbins (10)
1/16	12	Wesleyville	17	L	A	UNREPORTED	
1/19	26	Oil City St. Joseph's	27	L	H	McLaughlin (11)	Cunningham (11)
1/22	22	Alliance Academy	20	W	H	McLaughlin (13)	Sienicki (9)
1/24	24	West Millcreek	18	W	A	McLaughlin (12)	Tracy (6)
1/30	14	Edinboro	15	L	H	Coleman (7)	Crawford (8)
2/1	25	Titusville St. Joseph's Academy	16	W	A	McLaughlin (11)	Prenatt (7)
2/5	58*	Corry St. Edward's	18	W	H	McLaughlin (22)	Prugar (10)
2/13	31	Edinboro	22	W	A	McLaughlin (11)	Crawford (8)
2/17	19	North East	10	W	H	Coleman (9)	Stebbins (4)
2/19	35	West Millcreek	13	W	H	Coleman (17)	Fails (5)
2/23	10	Oil City St. Joseph's	17	L	A	Coleman (5)	Haas & Ham'cher (5)
2/26		Titusville St. Joseph's Academy (POSTPONED—SNOW)			H		
3/2	17	Alliance Academy	35	L	A	UNREPORTED	
3/5	31	Titusville St. Joseph's Academy	16	W	H	Coleman (13)	Ciaiola (8)
	375 (23.4)		**298** (18.6)				

Pos.	Player	Prior School	Class	G(GS)	FG	FT	Total	*PPG*	Career
F	Wally Coleman (#4)	Sacred Heart	Sr.	14(14)	45	39	129	9.2	131
C	Bob "Mickey" McLaughlin (#10)	St. Ann's	Jr.	14(14)	48	26	122	8.7	134
F	Willy "Razz" Razanoski (#3)	St. Hedwig's	Soph.	12(11)	15	4	34	2.8	34
G	Frank "Bud" Raid (#8)	St. Joseph's	Sr.	12(10)	8	5	21	1.8	21
F-G	Joe LeCorchick (#9)	St. Joseph's	Sr.	13(10)	2	5	9	0.7	9
G	Stanley Pickett	Holy Rosary	Sr.	6(3)	3	2	8	1.3	37
G	Lou Tullio (#12)	Holy Rosary	Jr.	9(5)	2	2	6	0.7	6
F	Bernie Quinn (#5)	St. Mary's	Soph.	6	3	0	6	1.0	6
F	Bill Griskey (#6)	St. Peter's	Soph.	9	2	0	4	0.4	4
F	Abe Louch (#7)	St. Andrew's	Jr.	6(1)	1	2	4	0.7	4
C-G	Tom Clancey (#11)	Sacred Heart	Sr.	10(2)	1	1	3	0.3	3
G	Francis "Yutz" Hughes (#0)	St. Patrick's	Soph.	2	0	0	0	0.0	0
G	John Flanagan	St. Joseph's	Jr.	1	0	0	0	0.0	0
F	Joe Causgrove	St. Patrick's	Jr.	1	0	0	0	0.0	0

1933-34 Prep Team. Front, L to R: Razanoski, LeCorchick, McLaughlin, Raid, Coleman; Back: Hughes, Griskey, Louch, Quinn, Tullio, Clancey, Manager Meagher.

HIGHLIGHTS:

- Cathedral Prep coach **Father Walter Conway**, in his sixth season as Rambler coach, was also appointed to the position of Director of Youth Activities for the Erie Diocese. One of his early projects was starting the Boy Scout chapters in the Erie area; another was launching the Erie Parochial Grade School Basketball League which is still in existence to this day. The first league champion (1934) was St. Joseph's Home, coached by **Claren Griffin**. Following the Orphans in the initial standings were the other charter member schools: St. Mary's, St. Andrew's, Harborcreek Training School, St. Peter's and St. Stanislaus.

- All Cathedral Prep's home games were played at the Strong Vincent High School gymnasium, with the exception of the Oil City St. Joe's game, which was played at the Niagara Athletic Association gym. The NAA court was actually at the Erie Police Department, at 27 South Perry Square, downtown Erie. In that game, Prep blew 22-6 halftime and 25-14 third quarter leads in its 27-26 loss to the Hilltoppers.

- The "10-second rule" came into effect in 1933, requiring the team with possession of the basketball to cross the mid-court line within 10 seconds.

- Edinboro High School (14-5) was christened with the nickname the "Turtles" specifically because of its extremely slow style of play in its first game against the Ramblers. In that contest, **"Windy" Crawford** sank a half-court shot with one second remaining to enable Edinboro to beat Prep, 15-14, for its ninth straight victory. (As a side note, Crawford later coached at Sharon High School and was in the 1960's the highly respected athletic director at UC-Riverside and UC-Irvine.) Prep gained

- revenge just two weeks later in Edinboro, 31-22. The nickname "Turtles" remained until Edinboro merged with McKean Joint to form General McLane "Lancers" in the late 1950's.

- In a preliminary to the Prep-Edinboro contest, a group of Prep Sophomores defeated a Rambler Freshmen team in an inter-class league game, 18-15. **Bernie Quinn** led the Sophs with 8 points, while **John Wilson** chipped in 6 and **Don Rowbottom** 4. **Joey Barabas** led the Frosh with 7 markers.

- Edinboro won the Southern Division of the Erie County League, which also included Waterford, Albion, Union City, McKean and Corry.

- North East (21-8) was undefeated at 9-0 when Prep dumped the Grapepickers, 19-10. Prep had lost by 20 in the teams' first encounter. North East finished as champion of the Northern Division of the Erie County League, which also included Millcreek, Fairview, Girard, Wesleyville and Lawrence Park. North East then defeated Southern champ Edinboro, 33-24, to win the ECL title.

- Nicknamed the "Fox Twins", **Wally Coleman** and **"Mickey" McLaughlin** carried the brunt of Prep's attack the entire season. In the second St. Ed's (2-9) game, the pair combined for 37 of the Ramblers' record-breaking 58 points. In the sweet victory over Alliance Academy (8-3), the pair combined for all 22 points scored. It was the first time the Ramblers and Eagles competed since 1926. (**Walter Coleman, Gene Coleman's** younger brother, was sadly killed in an automobile accident on West Lake Road in April, 1936, at age 20.)

- Of note were Prep's two victories over West Millcreek (10-9), which had broken Girard's 44-game win streak during the season. A preliminary to the West Millcreek game played on the Vincent hardcourt saw Harborcreek Training School, coached by former Prep footballer **Camillus "Lou" Cipalla**, defeat St. Stan's Grade School, 17-9.

- Oil City St. Joe's (21-2) hung a pair of losses on Prep and was invited to the National Catholic Interscholastic Basketball Tournament in Chicago, where it defeated Iowa City (IA) St. Mary's, 18-17, in the first round. In the second round the Hilltoppers were beaten by the eventual tourney runner-up, Stockton (CA) St. Mary's, 23-11.

- In a situation somewhat similar to the previous season's finale against Corry, Titusville St. Joe's (8-10) quickly arranged its Monday night trip to Erie. From the *Titusville Herald*: "The Robots didn't know they were supposed to play at Erie until Monday afternoon, when word was received from Erie that the game had been arranged. Hurried preparations were necessary. Because of the conditions of the roads, the players didn't get back until very late."

1934 All-Opponent Team:

> Jack Stebbins, North East
> Ross Hollister, North East
> Lloyd Bemiss, North East
> Henry "Hank" Langer, Wesleyville
> Joe Cunningham, Oil City St. Joe's
> Francis "Cootie" Carroll, Oil City St. Joe's
>   [Xavier (OH)]
> Sienicki, Alliance Academy
> Wayne "Windy" Crawford, Edinboro [Illinois, football
>   and baseball]
> Art Prenatt, Titusville St. Joe's
> Stanley Prugar, Corry St. Ed's
> Fred Case, Edinboro [Edinboro St.]
> Bob Tracy, West Millcreek
> Johnny Fails, West Millcreek

PREP-MILLCREEK BATTLE TONIGHT

A bitter Class B basketball feud will be renewed Wednesday night on the Millcreek court when Cathedral Prep comes to grips with Gus Anderson's Trojans. Prep will be seeking its fourth victory in seven starts this season.

The teams have met six times in the past three years, with Millcreek winning four games. An indication of the spirited rivalry which has developed between the schools is the fact that three of the six games have been decided by only two points, while two others were settled by a single point.

Things have not changed much over the decades!

Close Losses Mean Losing Season

1934-35 (8-10)

Coach: Rev. Walter Conway
Captain: Bob "Mickey" McLaughlin
Manager: Tommy Meagher

Three-year star Bob "Mickey" McLaughlin was the first Rambler to twice serve as team captain.

Date	PREP	Dec.		Loc.	High Scorer	Opponent
12/14	26	Corry St Edward's	9 W	A	Hughes (9)	Hyatt (5)
12/21	16	Dunkirk (NY) St. Mary	19 L	A	Louch (7)	F. Dougherty (7)
1/7	14	Dunkirk (NY) St. Mary	24 L	H	McLaughlin (6)	F. Dougherty (10)
1/11	15	Millcreek	29 L	A	McLaughlin (12)	Tracy (14)
1/14	17	East	29 L	H	McLaughlin (10)	Kaminski (10)
1/18	16	North East	22 L	A	McLaughlin (9)	J. Reid & Meyer (6)
1/21	44	Kanty Prep	7 W	H	McLaughlin (24)	Gnias'ski (4)
1/25	20	East	39 L	A	McLaughlin (14)	Barney (9)
1/29	24	Wesleyville	23 W	H	McLaughlin (12)	Bellingham (8)
2/1	24	Technical	22 W	A	Culhane (7)	Cantoni (9)
2/4	43	Corry St. Edward's	17 W	H	Grabowski (10)	Hyatt (7)
2/8	15	Strong Vincent	19 L	A	McLaughlin & Culhane (4)	Ross (8)
2/12	22	Technical	29 L	H	Razanoski (6)	Cantoni (10)
2/15	24	Cleveland (OH) Cathedral Latin	27 L	A	UNREPORTED	
2/19	21	North East	16 W	H	Culhane (10)	Stebbins (9)
2/22	17	Cleveland (OH) Cathedral Latin	19 L	H	Culhane (8)	Andrews (9)
2/26	36	Wesleyville	21 W	A	McLaughlin & Grabowski (10)	Adams (11)
3/1	43	Millcreek	26 W	H	McLaughlin (22)	Freeburg (9)
3/8		Titusville St. Joseph Academy (CANCELLED)		A		
	437 (24.3)		**397 (22.1)**			

Pos.	Player	Prior School	Class	G(GS)	FG	FT	Total	*PPG*	Career
F	Bob "Mickey" McLaughlin (#10)	St. Ann's	Sr.	17(17)	64	36	164	9.6	298
G-F	Robert Culhane (#9)	St. John's/Academy	Sr.	15(12)	26	8	60	4.0	60
G	Abe Louch (#7)	St. Andrew's	Sr.	17(17)	17	12	46	2.7	50
F	Bill Razanoski (#3)	St. Hedwig's	Jr.	17(13)	15	10	40	2.4	74
F	Francis Hughes (#4)	St. Patrick's	Jr.	17(10)	17	5	39	2.3	39
C	Charlie Grabowski (#11)	St. Stan's/East JH	Fr.	8(8)	14	11	39	4.9	39
G-F	Lou Tullio	Holy Rosary	Sr.	10(6)	4	8	16	1.6	22
G	Edward Franz	Sacred Heart	Jr.	3	1	2	4	1.3	4
F	Bernie Quinn (#6)	St. Mary's	Jr.	10(2)	1	1	3	0.3	9
G	Joe Causgrove	St. Patrick's	Sr.	3	1	0	2	0.7	2
G	Tom Meagher (#8)	St. Patrick's	Sr.	7(1)	0	0	0	0.0	0
G	Eddie Pasqualicchio (#5)	Sacred Heart	Jr.	6	0	0	0	0.0	0
F	John Wilson	St. Patrick's	Jr.	2	0	0	0	0.0	0
G	Harry Gannon (#12)	St. Peter's	Soph.	2	0	0	0	0.0	0
G	James Griffin	Gridley	Soph.	1	0	0	0	0.0	0
G	George Behringer	St. Peter's	Jr.	1	0	0	0	0.0	0
F	Bill Griskey	St. Peter's	Jr.	0	0	0	0	0.0	4
G	Carl Spiesman	St. Joe's Home	Fr.	0	0	0	0	0.0	0
F	Walter "Fudge" Kuziora	St. Ann's	Fr.	0	0	0	0	0.0	0
F	Joseph "Bud" Healy	Sacred Heart	Fr.	0	0	0	0	0.0	0
G	Gene Carmosino	Sacred Heart	Fr.	0	0	0	0	0.0	0

1934-35 Prep Ramblers. Front, L to R: Culhane, Grabowski, McLaughlin, Louch, Razanoski; Back: Pasqualicchio, Hughes, Quinn, Gannon, Meagher, Causgrove.

HIGHLIGHTS:

- All Cathedral Prep's home games were played at the Strong Vincent High School gymnasium, with the exception of the Cathedral Latin contest, which was played at the Niagara Athletic Association court.

- The 1934-35 edition of the Prep Ramblers was better than its final record indicated, noting several close losses. Only East High had its own way, and four Orange & Black losses were by the margin of 4 points or less. By season's end the Ramblers reversed losses to North East and Millcreek; soundly defeated Wesleyville; and came close in a pair of thrillers versus St. Ignatius. The most prominent feature of the season was the scoring capabilities of star senior **Bob "Mickey" McLaughlin**, Prep's first two-time team captain.

- Early-season opponent Dunkirk St. Mary's (17-9) was a co-educational parish school that closed in 1954. Cardinal Mindszenty then served the Dunkirk area Catholic students until its closure in 1979.

- In Prep's early season loss to Millcreek (5-10), the Ramblers scored but 3 points in the first half and only 6 points in the first three quarters. Prep had little trouble putting together one of their highest scoring games in the season finale rematch.

- **Paul Meyer** was one of the leading scorers for North East (8-13) when the Grapepickers defeated Prep by six. Only a 9th-grader at the time, Meyer later transferred to Prep and starred on the Ramblers' 1936-37 and 1937-38 editions. He finished second in points scored as a junior and as team captain led the Orange & Black in scoring as a senior.

- Prep's most thrilling victory was its 24-23 win over Wesleyville (8-7). With the Ramblers on the short end of a 23-19 score with only 1:30 left to play, **Bob Culhane** broke through for a couple of baskets and **"Mickey" McLaughlin** scored the winning free throw with only seconds remaining.

- In the rematch at Wesleyville, a fistfight between Culhane and feisty Bulldog guard **Tom McMahon** led to a five-year severance of relations between the bitter rivals. At the time Prep was staving off a furious Wesleyville rally when the rough play got out of control. According to the *Erie Dispatch-Herald*: "the two combatants were rolling around on the floor, swapping punches, with other players and a few spectators joining in the jamboree." The

A wild fistfight between Bob Culhane and an opposing player led to a five-year severance of athletic relations between Prep and Wesleyville.

newspaper further noted: "threats of severance of relations in all branches of sport were forthcoming from the suburban school's officials." Prep and Wesleyville only competed once more, in 1940, and the two never met again in any sport through Wesleyville's closing in 1966.

- Prep's 22-20 win over Technical (13-7) was the Ramblers' first-ever victory over a City Series opponent. McLaughlin stood out for the Ramblers, as did 6'2" freshman center **Charlie Grabowski**, seeing his first varsity action. Unfortunately for the Orange & Black, Grabowski transferred to rival Tech for his sophomore year. In a preliminary matchup, the Tech Reserves defeated the Prep Reserves, 16-13. In the second Tech varsity clash, Prep blew an 18-4 lead before bowing, 29-22. The Tech Reserves beat the Prep Reserves in the preliminary to that one as well, 16-14.

- The Erie Tech basketball team, according to its head coach **Eddie Abramoski**, boasted the tallest high school basketball player in the nation—**Joe Karwowski**! At 6'8", he was about a half-inch taller than another Prep opponent—Wesleyville's **"Moose" Bellingham**. Karwowski, a 17-year old freshman, was playing at 6'7 ½" just the year before at Wilson Junior High. It was noted in the newspapers, however, that "unlike most tall lads of his age, Karwowski is well-proportioned and is not awkward."

- Cathedral Latin (14-4), an eastside Cleveland all-male school run by the Brothers of the Society of Mary (Marianists) from Dayton (OH), had an excellent athletic history until it closed in 1979. Its closure was forced by a declining neighborhood, declining enrollment and rising costs. In 1988, with support of the disgruntled alumni association trying to revive the Latin spirit, the school merged with all-female Notre Dame Academy in Chardon (OH) and became known as Notre Dame-Cathedral Latin School.

Abe Louch was also a star gridder for the Ramblers. He later led the Cathedral College basketball team in scoring.

- East High (21-6) won its third consecutive City Series and PIAA District 10 titles. Warrior mainstays included **Johnny Kaminski, Dominic Mando, Joe Lisek, Ivan Barney** and **Joe Amendola.** The Sunrisers would not achieve their fourth D-10 crown until 1968.

- **"Mickey" McLaughlin** and **Abe Louch** both performed for the Cathedral College team in 1936-37. Cathedral College was the forerunner of Gannon College, chartered in 1941.

- **Lou Tullio** went on to play football at **Father Walter Conway's** alma mater, Holy Cross, and later became head football coach for the Erie Vets semi-pro team, Gannon College and Academy High

Lou Tullio later became Erie's six-term mayor.

School. He was also a head basketball coach at Gannon and later became Erie's six-term mayor (1966-1989). He was inducted to the Metro Erie Sports Hall of Fame in 1988.

1935 All-Opponent Team:

- Fred Dougherty, Dunkirk St. Mary's
- Bob Tracy, Millcreek
- Johnny Kaminski, East
- Joe Lisek, East [Drake, basketball & football]
- Johnny Reid, North East
- Paul Meyer, North East
- Ivan Barney, East
- Billy Ross, Vincent
- Donald "Dubs" Cantoni, Tech
- Joe Logue, Tech
- Mike Leone, Tech
- Ray "Moose" Bellingham, Wesleyville [Westminster]
- Ken Connare, Cathedral Latin
- Chuck "Red" Lavelle, Cathedral Latin [Xavier (OH), football]
- John Andrews, Cathedral Latin
- Dencil Adams, Wesleyville
- Elton Bock, West Millcreek

Ramblers Break Even

Carrick

Quinn

Razanoski

Hughes

Pasqualicchio

"Prep's Five Iron-Men"

1935-36 (9-9)

Coach: Rev. Walter Conway
Captain: Francis Hughes
Manager: Donald Trabold

Date	PREP				Dec.	Loc.	High Scorer	Opponent
12/13	16	Alumni		11	W	H	Quinn (6)	Louch (5)
12/16	11	East		45	L	H	Hughes & Pratt (3)	Malinowski (12)
12/20	29	Millcreek		41	L	A	Carrick (10)	Freeburg (13)
1/6	32	Titusville St. Joseph Academy		11	W	H	Quinn, Pratt & Carrick (8)	several (2)
1/8	22	East		34	L	A	Quinn (8)	Malinowski (11)
1/13	19	Strong Vincent		59*	L	H	Hughes (5)	Klemm (21)
1/17	35	Titusville St. Joseph Academy		15	W	A	Pratt (18)	Madden (8)
1/21	17	Strong Vincent		45	L	A	Pratt & Carrick (4)	Klemm (13)
1/24		Oil City St. Joseph's (CANCELLED--SNOW)				A		
1/27		Corry St. Edward's (CANCELLED--SNOW)				H		
1/31	19	Dunkirk (NY) St. Mary		39	L	A	Razanoski (9)	Draves (15)
2/3	20	Technical		25	L	H	Quinn (7)	Cardamone (12)
2/7	15	Oil City St. Joseph's		31	L	A	Razanoski & Carrick (5)	Cunningham (10)
2/10	11	Dunkirk (NY) St. Mary		28	L	H	Razanoski (4)	Ganey (12)
2/14	35	Kanty Prep		15	W	A	Carrick (12)	Janowski (6)
2/18	50	Meadville St. Agatha's		18	W	A	Carrick (13)	Scullion (6)
2/24	24	Oil City St. Joseph's		17	W	H	Carrick (8)	Cunningham (6)
2/26	37	Meadville St. Agatha's		14	W	H	Razanoski (17)	several (4)
2/28	38	Kanty Prep		22	W	H	Carrick (14)	Zalewski (13)
3/5	31	Alliance Academy		30	W	A	Razanoski (13)	Musial (11)
	461 (25.6)			**500* (27.8)**				

Pos.	Player	Prior School	Class	G(GS)	FG	FT	Total	*PPG*	Career
G	Bob Carrick (#6)	Gridley/Vincent	Jr.	18(18)	52	13	117	6.5	117
F-G	Bill Razanoski (#11)	St. Hedwig's	Sr.	18(18)	40	35	115	6.4	189
F-C	Bernie Quinn (#8)	St. Mary's	Sr.	17(17)	39	13	91	5.4	100
F-C-G	Francis Hughes (#12)	St. Patrick's	Sr.	16(16)	21	11	53	3.3	92
C	Louis Pratt	Wilson	Sr.	9(8)	17	7	41	4.6	41
F-G-C	John Wilson (#4)	St. Patrick's	Sr.	16(4)	12	6	30	1.9	30
G	Ed Pasqualicchio (#9)	Sacred Heart	Sr.	14(7)	3	0	6	0.4	6
G	Harry Gannon (#5)	St. Peter's	Jr.	9	1	0	2	0.2	2
G-F	Fred Meiser (#3)	Gridley	Jr.	6	0	2	2	0.3	2
C	Robert Rooney	St. Peter's	Fr.	4	1	0	2	0.5	2
F	Walter "Fudge" Kuziora	St. Ann's	Soph.	2(2)	1	0	2	1.0	2
G	Johnny Sunda [Pietrasanta] (#10)	St. Peter's	Jr.	10	0	0	0	0.0	0
C	Ed Franz	Sacred Heart	Sr.	4	0	0	0	0.0	4
F	Fred Yochim	St. John's	Sr.	4	0	0	0	0.0	0
G-F	James Griffin	Gridley	Jr.	3	0	0	0	0.0	0
F	Bill Nies (#7)	St. John's	Sr.	3	0	0	0	0.0	0
G	Michael Sullivan	St. Peter's	Soph.	2	0	0	0	0.0	0
G	Gerald Connell	St. Peter's	Fr.	2	0	0	0	0.0	0
G	Andy Sanders	Sacred Heart	Jr.	1	0	0	0	0.0	0
F	William "Bill" Laws	Osceola Mills	Soph.	1	0	0	0	0.0	0
F	Joseph "Bud" Healy	Sacred Heart	Soph.	1	0	0	0	0.0	0
F	John Latimer	St. Peter's	Fr.	1	0	0	0	0.0	0
F	James Opdyke	Lawrence Park	Jr.	1	0	0	0	0.0	0
G	Vincent McBride	St. Peter's	Jr.	1	0	0	0	0.0	0

Prep Basketball Team Makes Fine Showing

Handing St. Joseph's quintet of Oil City its first defeat in 20 games, the Ramblers of Erie Cathedral Prep have won their last six consecutive games in one of the best seasons of recent years.
Members of the squad are: front row, left to right, Edward Pasqualicchio, Bernard Quinn, Francis Hughes, Robert Carrick, William Razanoski; back row, left to right, William Neis, Robert Sunda, Harry Gannon, Frederick Meiser, John Wilson and Manager Donald Trabold.

HIGHLIGHTS:

- Despite a senior-laden squad, the Ramblers could only finish even at .500, in what was coach **Father Walter Conway's** 8th season as mentor. Though Prep tied a team record with five consecutive losses, the Ramblers closed the season with six straight victories, including the one-point thriller at Alliance Academy (5-3) in Cambridge Springs.

- All Cathedral Prep's home games were played at the Strong Vincent High School gymnasium.

- Games against Oil City St. Joe's on January 24 and Corry St. Ed's on January 27 were cancelled due to snow. The St. Joe's game was played on February 7 when a scheduled game with Cleveland Holy Name never materialized, while the St. Ed's contest was not able to be rescheduled.

- Prep was 0-5 against Erie teams, which included a record 59-point onslaught by City Series champ Strong Vincent (21-5). East (20-5) and Tech (17-5) also made for a very strong city league. SV ended its season losing to Sharon in the District 10 playoffs, 42-37. Colonel stars included **Herb Klemm, "Ziggy" Markowitz** and **Frank Soscia**.

- In a preliminary to the Vincent game, the Prep Freshmen defeated a team of Prep Juniors, 21-2. **Johnny Sunda** scored a first quarter field goal for the Juniors, but the team was unable to score thereafter. **Bob Rooney** led the Frosh with 8.

- Though unknown at the time, Prep's opening-game victory over the Alumni on December 13 was the 100th triumph in Rambler history.

- Prep's game at Oil City St. Joe's (22-2) was delayed until after 10:00 pm due to a breakdown of the Prep bus near Riceville in Crawford County. From the *Titusville Herald*: "Two Joe drivers set out posthaste for the scene of the accident and brought the team and the coach, **Father Walter Conway**, to town where they were greeted by a rousing welcome by an SRO throng that wouldn't go home despite the delay and who amused themselves by watching the play of two preliminaries." In that game the Ramblers had a stretch of 19 minutes, 37 seconds without scoring and lost handily, 31-15. Though unknown at the time, the loss at St. Joe's was the 100th defeat in Prep basketball history.

- One of Prep's great moments was its rematch win over Oil City St. Joe's, which had entered the contest with a record of 20-0. St. Joe's record since 1931-32 to that point was 120-12, for a winning percentage of .900. In the absence of head coach Father Conway, former Prep athlete **Harry "Bidge" Weindorff** led the Ramblers. It was the only time all season Prep did not use substitutions, instead using, according to writer **Wes Driscoll** of the *Erie Dispatch-Herald*: "five iron-men: Hughes, Razanoski, Quinn, 'rugged' Carrick and Pasqualicchio."

- Prep had two stars finish in the top 10 in the city in scoring— **Bob Carrick** finished 7th and **Bill Razanoski** finished 9th. East's **Mike Malinowski (Mallin)** led the entire city with 256 points.

- Prep's starting center **Lou Pratt**, a transfer from Harborcreek and also a fine lineman on the Rambler eleven, left school at the start of the second semester and didn't finish the season.

- St. Benedict's Academy and Mercyhurst Seminary agreed to play a best-of-five series in an effort to win the Father Conway Trophy and bragging rights of Erie's girls' basketball. The first two battles ended in draws—29-29 and 20-20. St. Ben's broke the jinx and scored a 30-18 win in game three. The fourth contest unbelievably ended in another tie—29-29! If the 'Hurst would win the final game—the series would start over again! The Lassies game through in game five, though, to win the trophy, 26-14. Forwards **Jean Kraus** and **Winifred Rettger** were the St. Ben's stars, while center **Katherine Beattie** was the big noise for Mercyhurst.

- Three of the Prep seniors continued their athletic careers in college—in football: **Franny Hughes** at Niagara; **Eddie Pasqualicchio** at Duquesne (and tennis); and **Bernie Quinn** at Holy Cross.

- Basketball was first included in the Olympic games in 1936, with 21 nations entering the competition.

1936 All-Opponent Team:

Mike "Lefty" Malinowski (Mallin), East
Wesley Freeburg, Millcreek [Clarion St.]
Frank Bolte, Millcreek
Herb Klemm, Vincent
Frank Soscia, Vincent [Edinboro St.]
James "Ziggy" Markowitz, Vincent [Corry Pros]
Harold Arkwright, Vincent [Edinboro St.]
Eddie Draves, Dunkirk St. Mary's [Fredonia St.]
Frank Dougherty, Dunkirk St. Mary's
Bill "Wee Willie" Ganey, Dunkirk St. Mary's
Frank "Red" Cardamone, Tech
Johnny Alex, Tech
John Cunningham, Oil City St. Joe's
Eddie Orleski, Alliance Academy
Ed "Turk" Musial, Alliance Academy

Father Conway's Final Year at the Helm!

1936-37 (6-8)

Coach: Rev. Walter Conway
Captain: Bob Carrick
Manager: Harry Belding

Father Walter Conway, Prep's Depression-era coach. He retired as Rambler mentor in 1937, but stayed on as Prep A.D. through 1943.

Date	PREP			Dec.	Loc.	High Scorer	Opponent
12/14	30	Titusville St. Joseph's Academy	22	W	H	Renz (11)	Madden (8)
1/4	18	Millcreek	32	L	H	Meyer (10)	Tracy (13)
1/11	31	Corry St. Edward's	19	W	H	Carrick (14)	J. Mead (6)
1/14	18	Millcreek	41	L	A	Barabas (6)	Tracy (12)
1/18	13	East	34	L	H	Carrick (7)	Malinowski & Klein (6)
1/21	28	Corry St. Edward's	32	L	A	Barabas (11)	Hudock (20)
1/25	41	Meadville St. Agatha's	7	W	H	Murphy (13)	Linz (4)
2/1	25	Oil City St. Joseph's	21	W	H	Carrick (9)	Kelley (10)
2/5	31	Titusville St. Joseph's Academy	39	L	A	Barabas (9)	Madden (13)
2/9	14	Strong Vincent	40	L	A	Carrick & Meyer (5)	Kuch (8)
2/12	23	Kanty Prep	33	L	A	Carrick (11)	Chodicki (12)
2/15	19	Technical	24	L	H	Carrick (11)	Lipchick (10)
2/19	12	Oil City St. Joseph's	10	W	A	Meyer (5)	Seyler (4)
3/1	30	Kanty Prep	17	W	H	Carrick (10)	Torka (7)
	333 (23.8)		**371 (26.5)**				

Pos.	Player	Prior School	Class	G(GS)	FG	FT	Total	*PPG*	Career
G-C	Robert "Bob" Carrick	Gridley/Vincent	Sr.	14(14)	43	19	105	*7.5*	222
G-F	Paul Meyer	North East	Jr.	14(14)	31	17	79	*5.6*	79
F-G	Joey Barabas	St. Jos. Home	Sr.	14(13)	25	6	56	*4.0*	56
C	Joe Cecho	Holy Rosary	Sr.	13(9)	11	7	29	*2.2*	29
F	Fred Nies	St. John's	Jr.	13(8)	12	5	29	*2.2*	29
F-G	John "Jack" Murphy	St. Peter's	Jr.	13(8)	8	7	23	*1.9*	23
F	Jimmy Renz	Academy HS	Sr.	6(2)	5	2	12	*2.0*	12
F	Bill Laws	Osceola Mills	Jr.	5(1)	0	0	0	*0.0*	0
F	Frank Radziszewski	St. Stan's	Sr.	3	0	0	0	*0.0*	0
C-G	James White	Coudersport	Sr.	3	0	0	0	*0.0*	0
C	Johnny Sunda [Pietrasanta]	St. Peter's	Sr.	1(1)	0	0	0	*0.0*	0
G	Harold Pfister	Holy Rosary	Fr.	1	0	0	0	*0.0*	0
G	Tom Fuhrman	St. Ann's	Soph.	1	0	0	0	*0.0*	0
G	Jamie McCarthy	St. Andrew's	Fr.	1	0	0	0	*0.0*	0
G	Bob Mangan	St. Andrew's	Fr.	1	0	0	0	*0.0*	0
G	Lawrence Reilly	St. Andrew's	Fr.	1	0	0	0	*0.0*	0
G	James Griffin	Gridley	Sr.	0	0	0	0	*0.0*	0

HIGHLIGHTS

- This was the last of nine seasons that **Father Walter Conway** coached the Rambler hoopsters. He finished with a career record of 86-76, for a .531 winning percentage. Father Conway, who was also Prep football coach from 1928-36 and athletic director from 1927-1942, was inducted posthumously into the Cathedral Prep Athletic Hall of Fame in 2003. He stayed on as Prep AD until 1943, when he was appointed pastor of Erie's Holy Rosary Parish.

- All Cathedral Prep's home games were played at the Strong Vincent High School gymnasium.

- The center jump was eliminated after each basket beginning with the 1936-37 season. Previously, teams lined up after each basket for a jump ball. The rule eliminating the center jump was intended to de-emphasize the advantage of height!

- Officially called "Millcreek" High rather than "West Millcreek", the Trojans (18-5) twice pasted Prep. The Ramblers were also 0-3 vs. city competition, including East (16-9), which won its fourth City Series title in five years. Opponents Vincent (16-9) and Technical (13-9) also had solid teams.

- Prep blew a 12-point 4th quarter lead in its only loss ever to Corry St. Edward's (6-11). Though the Ramblers outscored St. Ed's 9-0 in the first period, they were outscored by a whopping 17-1 margin in the final session! **Johnny Hudock**, the Shamrocks' flashy forward, scored 13 of his 20 points in the final frame, including this bucket, according to the *Corry Evening Journal*, to tie the score: "Hudock stood in the middle of the court and let a long fly that swished the net to tie the tally."

- Corry St. Ed's victory over Prep was its first in 18 tries. The series ended in 1941, with the Ramblers on the heavy end of a 23-1 series ledger.

- Titusville St. Joseph's (9-6) win over Prep was also its first in 6 attempts. After the last game between the two was played in 1965, the Ramblers won the series, 18-1.

- The season's highlight was the pair of close, upset wins over Oil City St. Joseph's (18-9). In the first battle, Prep was down 21-20 before **Fred Nies** and **Joey Barabas** scored buckets in the final moments. Though the Ramblers only shot 2 for 17 from the floor in the second contest (baskets by **Paul Meyer** and **Bob Carrick**), they were aided by the fact that the Hilltoppers could only muster 4 of 60 attempts! St. Joe's fell to 13-3 after that second loss to Prep!

- Team captain **Bob Carrick** was in the starting lineup every game his junior and senior years—32 straight games. He was given a round of applause by Prep students and fans following the season-ending Kanty Prep (5-2) victory.

- Cathedral College, operating under the St. Vincent's Latrobe charter and the forerunner of Gannon College, presented a basketball team that finished with a record of 4-4. Victories were achieved over Weil-McLain, 39-29, Kanty College, 31-20, and a pair over Erie DeMolay, 50-35 and 33-30. Losses were to the Academy Reserves, 37-31, Weil-McLain, 25-24, and a pair to the Ohio College of Chiropody, 55-33 and 40-30. Former Prep star **Robert Culhane** was the manager of the squad, which included former Prepsters **Bob "Mickey" McLaughlin, Joseph Haughney, Bill Baptist** and the College's leading scorer, **Abe Louch**. Some other team members included **Ralph Van Stone** of Central, **Charlie Grabowski** of Tech, **Bob Camp** of West Millcreek, and **Nick Tate** and **Billy Ross** of Strong Vincent.

- 1937 was the first year for the **Bishop William J. Hafey** Trophy, awarded to Altoona Catholic, the winner of the Pennsylvania Catholic State Basketball Tournament, played in Williamsport. The tourney was sponsored by the Williamsport Knights of Columbus chapter. Altoona Catholic defeated Renovo St. Joseph's, Scranton St. Mary's and Williamsport St. Joseph's, before defeating Johnstown Central Catholic in the final, 25-23.

- Cathedral Prep's first sacrifice at the altar of World War II was **Joe Cecho** '37, killed in a bomber crash in Brazil in 1942.

1937 All-Opponent Team:

Jack Madden, Titusville St. Joe's
Bob Tracy, Millcreek
Wesley Freeburg, Millcreek [Clarion St.]
Sam Willis, Millcreek
Mike "Lefty" Malinowski [Mallin], East
Bob Klein, East
Johnny Hudock, Corry St. Ed's
George "Blaze" Kelly, Oil City St. Joe's
Bob Reagan, Titusville St. Joe's
Jackson "Jackie" Kuch, Vincent
Al DiVecchio, Vincent
Steve Lipchick, Tech
Henry "Hank" Galla, Tech

Joe Cecho was Prep's first sacrifice at the altar of World War II, killed in a bomber crash in 1942.

The "Baron" Takes Over!

1937-38 (8-9)

Coach: Ralph "Baron" Calabrese
Captain: Paul Meyer
Manager: Harry Belding

Prep Coach Ralph "Baron" Calabrese later became the esteemed Hall of Fame mentor at Strong Vincent.

Date	PREP			Dec.	Loc.	High Scorer	Opponent
12/20	21	Edinboro	17	W	H	Meyer (8)	Stevenson (9)
1/7	15	Corry	32	L	H	Kuziora (7)	Lundy (12)
1/10	34	Corry St. Edward's	12	W	H	Meyer (12)	Crane (5)
1/14	39	Kanty Prep	36	W	H	Kuziora (16)	Dzubanski (24)
1/17	21	Alumni	18	W	H	Murphy (5)	Carrick (6)
1/24	16	Millcreek	36	L	H	Meyer (9)	Flanagan (11)
1/27	15	Edinboro	32	L	A	Kuziora (5)	Hall (18)
2/2	33	Meadville St. Agatha	12	W	H	Nies (16)	Barickman (7)
2/4	28	Kanty Prep	42	L	A	Kuziora (12)	Wasik (13)
2/7	14	Technical	39	L	H	Meyer (8)	Cardamone (9)
2/10	19	Millcreek	38	L	A	Meyer (10)	Freeburg (11)
2/14	24	East	48	L	H	Pfister (7)	Amendola (11)
2/17	30	Meadville St. Agatha	15	W	A	Meyer (9)	Linz (10)
2/22	12	Strong Vincent	45	L	A	Meyer (5)	Reinecke (15)
2/25	34	Corry St. Edward's	32	W	A	Meyer (12)	Crane (11)
3/1	16	Corry	37	L	A	Meyer (6)	Lundy (11)
3/4	34	Union City	28	W	A	Meyer (11)	Smith (10)
	405 (23.8)		**519* (30.5*)**				

Pos.	Player	Prior School	Class	G(GS)	FG	FT	Total	*PPG*	Career
F	Paul Meyer	North East	Sr.	15(15)	45	16	106	*7.1*	185
G-F	Walter "Fudge" Kuziora	St. Ann's	Sr.	15(14)	37	8	82	*5.5*	84
C	Fred Nies	St. John's	Sr.	17(17)	22	16	60	*3.6*	89
G-C	John "Jack" Murphy	St. Peter's	Sr.	17(14)	20	7	47	*2.8*	70
G	John Latimer	St. Peter's	Jr.	15(10)	19	4	42	*2.8*	42
G	Harold Pfister	Holy Rosary	Soph.	10(7)	10	5	25	*2.5*	25
F-G	Joe McCafferty	St. Peter's	Fr.	9(6)	8	2	18	*2.0*	18
F-C	George Jepson	St. Joseph's	Sr.	10(2)	5	3	13	*1.3*	13
C	Johnny Melvin	St. Mary's	Soph.	2	2	0	4	*2.0*	4
G	Edmund "Brub" Mehl	St. Andrew's	Fr.	1	1	0	2	*2.0*	2
F	Robert "Bob" Formaini	Sacred Heart	Soph.	3	0	0	0	*0.0*	0
G	Leo Davis	St. John's	Soph.	1	0	0	0	*0.0*	0

HIGHLIGHTS:

- All Cathedral Prep's home games were played at the Strong Vincent High School gymnasium, with the exception of the St. Agatha's (4-10) game, which was played at the East Side Boys Club.

- Prep football coach **Larry Danbom** (1937-38), a former Notre Dame gridiron all-star, guided the Ramblers through the first two weeks of practice, but found that his duties as cage mentor conflicted with those of his postion as athletic director of St. Andrew's parish. He then informed athletic director **Father Walter Conway** he would be unable to continue as coach of the Orange & Black.

- Coach **Ralph "Baron" Calabrese** was hired by athletic director Father Conway to coach the Ramblers after successfully piloting St. Paul's to the parochial grade school championship the year before. Calabrese, a former Strong Vincent and Findlay College star, later became the venerated coach at Vincent (1952-70), guiding the Colonels to 14 consecutive winning seasons, 5 City Series championships, 9 Section One titles, 7 District 10 crowns and a record of 254-120. Coach Calabrese was universally respected as a true gentleman and class act, and forever remembered as "The Baron." He was inducted into the Metropolitan Erie Sports Hall of Fame in 1988.

- Coach Calabrese was handicapped by the return of just three lettermen: **Paul Meyer, Fred Nies** and **Jack Murphy**. Twenty boys tried out for the squad, though only 12 were selected.

- The best wins for Prep were the season opener and season finale against Erie County foes Edinboro (7-13) and Union City (11-19). Prep sent a junior varsity team out to Union City for a preliminary game, only to see the Baby Ramblers go down to defeat, 50-9. This is believed to be the worst pasting of a JV team in Prep history.

- The biggest disappointments were the Ramblers' inability to make good showings against city rivals Tech (12-6), Vincent (12-14) and city champ East (16-7, 5th title in 6 years); and the two losses each to Corry (10-12) and to Millcreek (12-7), the latter before a capacity crowd on the Trojan floor. Academy (16-10-1) was the only local five not on the Rambler schedule.

- Some of the city's stars included **Harry "Horse" Ganza** of Tech; **Fausto Addessi** and **Bob Stephenson** of Vincent; **Dave Wiley, Naz Servidio** and **Frank Liebel** of Academy; and **Chester Herdzik, Larry Karuba, Art Amendola, Clark Tyzinski** and **George Demyanovich** of East.

- In a preliminary to the Corry home game, the Prep Sophomores defeated the Prep Freshmen, 20-12. In a preliminary to the Kanty Prep home game, a group of Prep seniors beat the Frosh, 25-5.

- Johnstown Central Catholic (20-1) captured the 1938 **Bishop William J. Hafey** Trophy for winning the Pennsylvania Catholic State Basketball Tourney in Williamsport. The Crimson Crushers defeated Pittsburgh St. Basil in the title game, 47-35.

- A Prep Reserve team finished with a record of 0-5, averaging but 9.6 *PPG*.

- **Johnny Melvin** left for Technical at the start of his junior year, but came back to coach the Prep JV's in football in 1944-45.

- **Walter Kuziora**, younger brother of former Prep star and future Prep coach **Father Len Kuziora**, was a World War II casualty, killed in a plane crash over the North Sea, near Holland, in 1943.

- The professional National Basketball League was established for the 1937-38 season. After its twelfth season in 1948-49, the NBL merged with the Basketball Association of America to form the National Basketball Association.

1938 All-Opponent Team:

Vic Fuller, Edinboro
James Lundy, Corry
Tony Dzubanski, Kanty Prep
Art Amendola, East
Larry Karuba, East
Harry Borowy, East
Merle Hall, Edinboro
"Bud" Stevenson, Edinboro
Leo Barickman, St. Agatha's
Harry "Horse" Ganza, Tech
Wesley Freeburg, Millcreek [Clarion St.]
Albert Linz, St. Agatha's
Bill Reinecke, Vincent
Richard Karle, Vincent
Tom Crane, Corry St. Ed's
Paul Sutton, Corry
Bill Smith, Union City
Sam Mineo, Union City

Two-year starter John Latimer.

Second-leading scorer Walter "Fudge" Kuziora became a World War II casualty, killed in a plane crash near Holland in 1943.

Frosh Spark Ramblers!

1938-39 (9-6)

Coach: George Williams
Captain: John Latimer
Manager: Paul Causgrove

Head coach George Williams, a former East High and Prep football star.

Date	PREP			Dec.	Loc.	High Scorer	Opponent
12/12	49	Corry St. Edward's	23	W	H	Fuhrman (17)	Ressler (8)
12/16	27	Conneaut (OH) Rowe	25	W	A	Fuhrman (8)	Hicks (7)
12/19	28	Kanty Prep	19	W	H	Morasky (11)	Wasik (8)
1/5	30	Meadville St. Agatha's	7	W	A	Tupek (11)	Angaun (3)
1/9	55	Alumni	27	W	H	Latimer (16)	Carrick (7)
1/13	22	Titusville St. Joseph's Academy	21	W	A	Morasky (8)	Fulton (10)
1/16	20	East	49	L	A	Fuhrman & Roscher (6)	Guzak (15)
1/23	32	Titusville St. Joseph's Academy	22	W	H	Fuhrman (10)	Fulton (12)
1/27	18	Oil City St. Joseph's	36	L	A	Fuhrman (6)	Kelly, Hall & Feeney (6)
2/3	29	Kanty Prep	31	L	A	Morasky (14)	Kielczewski (11)
2/6	33	Conneaut (OH) Rowe	27	W	H	Morasky (13)	Bittler (12)
2/13	14	Technical	29	L	H	Tupek & Fuhrman (4)	Fetzner (12)
2/20	24	Strong Vincent	50	L	A	Fuhrman (10)	DiBacco (10)
2/27	30	Oil City St. Joseph's	31	L	H	Morasky (7)	Eckert (10)
3/2	51	Corry St. Edward's	22	W	A	Fuhrman (18)	Ressler (9)
3/6		Meadville St. Agatha (CANCELLED)			H		
	462 (30.8)		**419 (27.9)**				

Pos.	Player	Prior School	Class	G(GS)	FG	FT	Total	PPG	Career
C-F	Tom Fuhrman (#4)	St. Ann's	Sr.	15(15)	61	9	131	8.7	131
F-G	Ted Morasky (#5)	Harborcreek Training	Fr.	15(15)	43	19	105	7.0	105
F	Robert "Bob" Formaini (#6)	Sacred Heart	Jr.	15(14)	25	5	55	3.7	55
G-F	Joseph Tupek (#3)	Harborcreek Training	Fr.	14(11)	21	10	52	3.7	52
G-F-C	John Roscher (#8)	Sacred Heart	Jr.	12(5)	22	8	52	4.3	52
G	John Latimer (#11)	St. Peter's	Sr.	15(14)	20	6	46	3.1	88
G	Edmund "Brub" Mehl (#12)	St. Andrew's	Soph.	10(1)	3	1	7	0.7	9
C	Tom Carrick (#7)	St. Andrew's	Soph.	5	3	0	6	1.2	6
G	Rodger Lamb (#10)	St. Peter's	Soph.	7	1	3	5	0.7	5
F	John "Jack" Goodill (#9)	St. Patrick's	Jr.	8	1	0	2	0.3	2
F	Wilfred Lohse	Holy Rosary	Jr.	3	1	0	2	0.7	2
G	Gerald Connell	St. Peter's	Sr.	2	1	0	2	2.0	2
C-F	Buckley Hubbard	Ashtabula	Soph.	5	0	0	0	0.0	0
F	Jack Quinn	St. Andrew's	Fr.	1	0	0	0	0.0	0
C	Paul Clancey	Sacred Heart	Sr.	1	0	0	0	0.0	0

1938-39 Ramblers. Front, L to R: Roscher, Formaini, Latimer, Morasky, Fuhrman; Back: Coach Williams, Mehl, Goodill, Lamb, Carrick, Tupek, Mgr. Causgrove.

HIGHLIGHTS:

Tom Fuhrman started every game and led Prep in scoring.

- Prep opened with six straight wins under first-year coach **George Williams**, the former East High and Cathedral Prep football star (1927). Only coaching the Ramblers for two seasons, Williams coached Erie's professional Post Jewelers team, later called St. Mary's Auditoriums, in 1944-45.

- All Cathedral Prep's home games were played at the Strong Vincent High School gymnasium, just as they had been throughout the entire 1930's.

- Prep fared well in Coach Williams' first campaign, particularly with a young team that included two freshmen in the starting lineup. Only senior captain **John Latimer** had any appreciable experience. The team's leading scorer, senior **Tom Fuhrman**, did not play as a junior.

- 1938-39 was the Ramblers' first winning season in five years, since 1933-34. The six-game winning streak actually gave the Orange & Black a record-tying win string of seven, counting the 1937-38 season finale at Union City.

- The two promising freshmen in Prep's starting lineup both came from Harborcreek Training School where they led HTS to the Erie Parochial Grade School League championship in 1938. **Teddy Morasky** went on to become Prep's all-time leading scorer in basketball as well as the finest quarterback Erie had seen in years. **Joe Tupek**, unfortunately for Prep, returned to Oil City after his three-year stay at Harborcreek was complete.

- In between Prep's two fine victories over Conneaut Rowe (18-7), the Vikings ran up a 10-game winning streak. Rowe also suffered a loss to Technical High. Rowe opened in 1936-37 and its first basketball team went 10-2. The Vikings fared well in just their third season in 1938-39, winning Ashtabula County's Class B championship.

- Academy High School (14-9-1), which the Ramblers had not played since 1931, won its first City Series title in a decade and the PIAA

District 10 championship. The Lions' big star was **Dave Wiley**, named First Team All-State by the Associated Press (AP), the first Erieite to be so honored. Other big names included leading scorer **Naz Servidio** and **Frank Liebel**. Academy had three close big wins over strong arch-rival East High (14-5). The Lions would not win another D-10 title until 1974, a span of 35 years.

- Academy's **Naz Servidio** later became head basketball coach at Millcreek High (1952-53) and later a well-known high school, college and Olympic games referee.

Promising freshman Joe Tupek may have helped the Ramblers further had his stay at Harborcreek Training School not been lifted.

- Biggest disappointments were Prep's inability to make good showings against city rivals, including Tech (7-8) and Vincent (9-12-1); the two-point loss at Kanty Prep (6-2); and the one-point loss to rival Oil City St. Joe's (23-4), which went on to win the 1939 Pennsylvania State Catholic title, defeating Pittsburgh Central Catholic in Williamsport, 26-22.

1939 All-Opponent Team:

Orel Hicks, Conneaut Rowe
Warren Fulton, Titusville St. Joe's
Steve Guzak, East
George Demyanovich, East
Forrest Hall, Oil City St. Joe's [Duquesne, San Francisco, football; NFL San Francisco 49'ers]
Lou Kielczewski, Kanty Prep
Wally Bittler, Conneaut Rowe
Len Fetzner, Tech
Lou DiBacco, Vincent [Gannon]
Dick DiTullio, Vincent
Tom Martin, Vincent
George "Blaze" Kelly, Oil City St. Joe's
Bill Eckert, Oil City St. Joe's
Don Feeney, Oil City St. Joe's (1st team Catholic all-state)

The 1940's

Prep Quint Beats Vincent to Win City Title

PIAA, PCIAA AGREE ON UNIFORM CODE

Ramblers Rally for 39 to 35 Verdict

By DICK MARATINE

The Ramblers of Cathedral Prep wear Erie's scholastic basketball crown for the first time in history.

Flashing a last half defensive that held Strong Vincent scoreless from the field until the final minute, the charges of Coach Wally Strosser took the climbing battle, 39-35, Thursday night.

Prep rooters, strewn densely through the capacity gallery of 1,100 at East High Auditorium, gave

Standings

the Ramblers voluminous support as they came blazing from behind a 20-26 count at halftime to score 16 points during the third period, while limiting the Colonels to a pair of free throws.

VINCENT YELL-LEADERS, meanwhile, were helpless to achieve any respectable decible rating as the count continued to mount against the Colonels until it stood at 39-26 with a minute remaining.

Prep slackened its pace at that time and the Colonels broke through with a triplet of fielders and a free throw that proved too little and were obviously too late.

Prep had taken the lead twice during the first half—but only for moments; at Vincent displayed a mastery on the floor. The Colonels led by five points at two instances during the first 16 minutes.

ART HILINSKI scoring from the floor and Chuck Genck's throwing from the charity line kept Prep in the game during the first half. Hilinski was the game's high scorer with 15 points, dropping through one-handed counters from all angles.

But the third period scoring rash that gave the Ramblers 16, while their tight defensive was holding Vincent to two free throws, was spread through the ranks. Genck opened the firing. Eddie Hyziewicz scored twice, Don Laird dropped in a pair of free tosses and Hilinski added a field goal.

Vincent's attack stopped at midfloor up to the final minute and what shots flew at the board were

Cath. Prep Captures First City Basketball Crown

22 THE ERIE DAILY TIMES, Friday, February 21, 1947

CITY COURT CHAMPIONS—Cathedral Prep last night captured its first city basketball championship by defeating Vincent, 39-35. The squad includes: Front row, left to right, Dick Trombetta, Don Laird, Ed Hyziewicz, Captain Jim White, Charles Genck, Art Hilinski and Manager Raymond Hooper; second row, Joe Luteran, Henry Glowacki, Bill DiPlacido, Adam Gorski, Jack Flanagan, Paul Murosky, Gary Orr, John Harabedian, and Coach Walter Strosser. (Times Photo).

Ramblers In 39-35 Win Over Vincent

Colonels Falter In Final Periods

By Dick Stone

CATHEDRAL PREP won the first major scholastic championship in the school's history last night, winning the basketball crown with a 39-35 victory over Strong Vincent on the East high hardwood.

Approximately 1,100 fans saw the Ramblers take complete charge of

TEAM STANDINGS

	W	L	Pct.
Prep			.750
Vincent	5	3	.625
Tech	4	3	.571
East	3	4	.429
Academy	1	7	.138

the contest in the final half after a closely-played first two periods.

THE COLONELS were in a semi-helpless state during that period failing to connect with a single field goal until the last 45 seconds of the ball game.

And by then it was too late as Prep had built up a 39-26 advantage, sparked by the scoring of Art Hilinski, who wound up with a game high aggregate of 15 markers.

The Red and Black, stubbornly refusing to quit, even with defeat staring it in the face, quickly rang up five markers but the final whistle ended the valiant effort four points short of the number required for a deadlock.

PREP'S BRILLIANT zone defense limited the Vincent squad to 11 shots at the basket, of which only 11 were successful.

The Ramblers' percentage was ess impressive as they converted only 12 of 26 tries, but the latter figure indicates the Orange and Black's more efficient control of both the ball and the boards.

Prep also had less success from the foul stripe as it made only 15 of 30 tries, while the Detzelmen were successful on 18 out of 27 attempts.

The entire contest was excellently patrolled by referees Charles Bauder and Tony Curti who never once allowed the ball game to get out of hand.

TWENTY FOULS were called against the Colonels while 17 rule infractions, which caused the departure of both Don Laird and Ed Hyziewicz in the last canto, were declared against the Ramblers.

The first two quarters were almost evenly contested with Vincent emerging with 13-9 and 25-20 leads at end of-the first two periods.

Then came the fatal third canto when Prep racked on 10 markers, while Vincent, passing and shooting wildly, was able to add only two points to its side of the scoring ledger, both on fouls.

HILINSKI AND Chuck Genck, who compiled an 11 point aggregate, each contributed two fielders in the final quarter which saw the Colonels unable to work the ball to within a decent point under the Prep basket.

Despite a sprained ankle Laird managed to remain through most of the game, while teammate Dick Trombetta saw brief action after having been released from a sick bed early Thursday morning.

Vincent's two scoring twins, Jake Williams and Jack Busch, again paced the Colonel attack, the former sinking 10 points and the latter adding nine markers.

BESIDES WINNING the game and the championship, Prep also

Coach Walt Strosser receives Prep's first City Championship trophy from Tech coach Ted Robb (1947).

Close Losses Doom Season

1939-40 (5-10)

Coach: George Williams
Captain: Jack Goodill
Manager: Richard Buseck

Jack Goodill, 1939-40 team captain.

Date	PREP			Dec.	Loc.	High Scorer	Opponent
12/11	29	Corry St. Edward's	21	W	H	Formaini (10)	Ressler (8)
12/18	20	Kanty Prep	22	L	H	Goodill (6)	Zielinski (11)
1/5	28	Conneaut (OH) Rowe	30	L	A	Morasky (9)	Palagyi (12)
1/8	18	Girard	14	W	H	Morasky (10)	Yuhas & Daggett (4)
1/12	20	Wesleyville	21	L	A	Roscher (7)	Pratt (8)
1/17	25	Millcreek	28	L	A	Roscher (8)	Willis (18)
1/19		Corry St. Edward's (CANCELLED)			A		
1/22	38	Technical	41	L	H	Roscher (14)	Spirito (8)
1/26	36	Titusville St. Joseph's Academy	14	W	A	Formaini (11)	Dowling (11)
2/6	11	Strong Vincent	30	L	A	Morasky (3)	Burton (7)
2/9	13	Buffalo (NY) Canisius	31	L	H	Lamb (6)	Trimboli (12)
2/12	33	Millcreek	15	W	H	Morasky (11)	Willis (9)
2/16	23	Kanty Prep	25	L	A	Morasky (12)	Zielinski (10)
2/19	21	Oil City St. Joseph's	27	L	H	Lamb (10)	Kelly (10)
2/27	45	Girard	28	W	A	Roscher (12)	Weidler (8)
3/1	26	Oil City St. Joseph's	52	L	A	Roscher (8)	Kelly & Eckert (16)
3/4		Titusville St. Joseph's Academy (CANCELLED)			H		
3/8		Buffalo (NY) Canisius (CANCELLED)			A		
	356 (23.7)		**399 (26.7)**				

Pos.	Player	Prior School	Class	G(GS)	FG	FT	Total	*PPG*	Career
F-C	Teddy Morasky (#8)	Harborcreek Training	Soph.	13(12)	36	20	92	7.1	197
G	Bob Formaini (#6)	Sacred Heart	Sr.	14(14)	32	16	80	5.7	135
C-G	John Roscher (#7)	Sacred Heart	Sr.	9(8)	27	10	64	7.1	116
G-F	Harold Pfister (#11)	Holy Rosary	Sr.	13(12)	16	12	48	3.7	48
C-G	Rodger Lamb (#10)	St. Peter's	Jr.	13(9)	14	12	40	3.1	45
G-F	Jack Goodill (#3)	St. Patrick's	Sr.	15(14)	10	4	24	1.7	26
G-F	Jack Lalley (#5)	St. Andrew's	Jr.	5	8	1	17	3.4	17
F-G	George Shickler (#12)	St. Patrick's	Soph.	10(4)	3	3	8	0.8	8
G-F	Edmund "Brub" Mehl (#4)	St. Andrew's	Jr.	11(2)	0	6	6	0.6	15
G	Wilfred Lohse (#10)	Holy Rosary	Sr.	7	2	0	4	0.6	6
F-G	Tim O'Hara (#9)	St. Patrick's	Fr.	4	1	0	2	0.5	2
G-C	Jack Erb (#5)	St. John's	Jr.	5	0	0	0	0.0	0
G	Richard Ankiel	St. Peter's	Jr.	1	0	0	0	0.0	0
G	Harold Marshall	St. John's	Soph.	1	0	0	0	0.0	0
F	John McMahon	St. Patrick's	Sr.	0	0	0	0	0.0	0
F	Richard Wolfram	St. John's	Sr.	0	0	0	0	0.0	0
G	Ray Quinlan	St. John's	Jr.	0	0	0	0	0.0	0
G	Bob Sensor	St. Peter's	Jr.	0	0	0	0	0.0	0

The hard-luck 1940 Prep Ramblers. Front, L to R: Roscher, Goodill, Formaini, Pfister, Morasky; Back: Coach Williams, Lalley, Lamb, Lohse, Schickler, O'Hara, Erb, Mehl, Manager Buseck.

HIGHLIGHTS:

- The PIAA District 10 member schools, 67 in all at the time, all public, voted to reject the 19-year age limit proposed by the statewide PIAA organization. Of the City of Erie coaches, only **Sam Kramer** of Vincent favored lowering the age limit from 20 to 19. Academy's **Lowell Drake**, East's **Jim Hyde** and Technical's **Eddie Abramoski** favored keeping the age limit at 20, as did nearly every rural area school in the district. All were in agreement, though, to adopt an amendment calling for a maximum of 8 semesters of eligibility past the 8th grade.

- Cathedral Prep's pre-season workouts were held at the Erie Boys' Club, while home games were played at the Strong Vincent High School gymnasium.

- Star sophomore **Ted Morasky**, who started all 15 games as a freshman, missed the first two games while still recuperating from a broken leg received while playing quarterback on the Rambler football squad.

- Aside from Morasky, nearly every Prep hoopster, including senior stars **Bob Formaini, Harold Pfister, Jack Goodill, Wilfred Lohse, Johnny McMahon** and **Dick Wolfram**, were members of the fine Rambler football squad that finished 6-2 under new coach **Salvatore "Jimmy" Foti**. Foti became Prep's head basketball coach for the 1940-41 season.

Bob Formaini, a rugged competitor in football and basketball.

- The 1939-40 Prep team lost many close games, including its first five setbacks by a total of 11 points. The last of those five was a bitterly fought and rough battle against arch-rival Technical High (8-9).

Harold Pfister, one tough customer on the hardcourt and the gridiron.

- Prep opened the campaign with a victory over Corry St. Edward's (1-14), but St. Ed's simply cancelled the return contest, with no particular reason given. The Shamrocks opened their own season with a 38-32 win over Spartansburg, but were unable to gain another triumph for the balance of the season.

- Rival Kanty Prep (11-6) defeated the Ramblers twice, both by two-point margins.

- On December 12, as a preliminary to the East-Oil City contest, a Prep reserve team lost to the East Reserves, 44-23. As a prelim to the Prep-Girard game, the Rambler Reserves defeated the Yellow Jacket Reserves, 25-15.

- Prep's 2-point loss to eventual Ashtabula County Class B champ Conneaut Rowe (19-3) was the last the two competed until the 1954-55 season. The Vikings won every Class B title in Ashtabula County from 1939 through 1946 with the following records: 1938-39: 18-7; 1939-40: 19-3; 1940-41: 16-2; 1941-42: 19-3; 1942-43: 21-3, with first team all-stater **Fred Hirsimaki**; 1943-44: 20-3, with first team all-stater **Bob Puffer**; 1944-45: 15-4; and Rowe's greatest team, featuring all-around athlete and two-time second team all-stater **Jerry Puffer**, 1945-46: 27-2.

- Rowe's **Lou Palagyi** pitched for the Dayton Indians of the Class D Ohio State League in 1947. Lou was also the younger brother of **Mike Palagyi**, who caused a sensation in Conneaut when he was called up from the minors to pitch for the Washington Senators in August, 1939. Entering in a 9th inning relief appearance against the vaunted Boston Red Sox, Palagyi faced but four batters, promptly hitting the first and walking the next three—ending with 3 earned runs. Palagyi never pitched in the majors again and entered the military. But who were the four batters he faced? Wow, in order: great Hall of Famers **Jimmie Foxx, Ted Williams** and **Joe Cronin**; and Ohio Hall of Famer **Joe Vosmik**!

- The one-point Wesleyville (4-14) defeat was particularly annoying and the direct result of referee **Nord Cofini's** discretion. With only seconds remaining to be played and the score tied 20-20, Prep's Jack Goodill was at the foul line. The ref then decided Goodill was taking too long in shooting the free throw and called a technical foul. The Bulldogs' **Jim Pratt** promptly went to the charity stripe and sank the technical, handing the Orange & Black its close loss. This was the first time Prep and Wesleyville competed since the famous 1935 brawl and the last time there was any athletic relations between the two.

- A capacity crowd saw Strong Vincent (9-12) crush Prep. According to the *Erie Daily Times*: "The proceedings were enlivened at the opening of the 4th quarter when **Rodger Lamb**, Cathedral Prep center, tossed a punch at **Dick DiTullio** of the Colonels. Referee **Paul Fitting** banished Lamb from the game."

- Prep's best game was the 18-point upset over Millcreek (18-4), avenging an earlier 3-point loss to the Trojans. It was the Ramblers' first win over Millcreek since 1935.

- Despite Prep's lopsided win over Titusville St. Joseph's (7-9), the contest was filled with tension. According to the *Titusville Herald*: "The game was by far the roughest from a Robot standpoint of any they have had in a long time and there were several threatened fisticuffs." The Joes' **Jim McDonald** was ejected from the battle when he went after a pair of Ramblers on their way to the locker room. The *Herald* noted: "McDonald lost his cool, which he normally doesn't do."

- Prep missed an opportunity for another victory when Titusville St. Joe's cancelled the March 4th contest. According to the *Titusville Herald*: the Robots "decided it was best to close the books on the season without further competition as at least three of their players were deemed academically ineligible."

- Though not a Prep opponent, Academy (14-2-2) won its second consecutive City Series title. Stars on the hilltop included **Phil Haendler** and **Kenny Longnecker**.

- Girard's **Ronald "Bud" McCoy** later became McDowell High School's first head basketball coach (1953-1956).

- **Rodger Lamb** was lost for the season after twisting his ankle badly on a jump ball in the Oil City St. Joe's contest.

- Oil City St. Joseph's (19-11) again made it to the Bishop Hafey/ K. of C. Pennsylvania State Catholic championship final, only to lose to Johnstown Central Catholic, 32-26. Preliminaries to the Rambler-Irish contests saw St. Peter's Cathedral Sodality girls defeat the St. Joe's girls in Erie, 27-4; while later in Oil City the St. Joe's girls defeated the St. Pete's girls, 19-16.

- Oil City St. Joe's star **Sgt. George "Blaze" Kelly** was sadly pronounced dead by the U. S. War Department, one year after he was reported missing in action in Germany after his plane crashed into a hillside on April 13, 1945.

1940 All-Opponent Team:
- W. "Shadow" Zielinski, Kanty Prep
- Lou Kielczewski, Kanty Prep
- Lou Palagyi, Conneaut Rowe [Indians Class D baseball]
- Bob Childs, Conneaut Rowe
- Adolph Kultti, Conneaut Rowe (2nd team all-state, OH, 1941)
- Ronald "Bud" McCoy, Girard
- Jim Pratt, Wesleyville
- Bob Nelson, Wesleyville
- Ted Willis, Millcreek [Clarion St.]
- Mickey Ford, Millcreek
- Jim Coursey, Millcreek
- Mike Spirito, Tech
- Bernie Dowling, Titusville St. Joe's
- Bill Burton, Vincent
- Tom Martin, Vincent
- Joe Trimboli, Canisius [Canisius]
- Jack Connolly, Canisius
- Dick Weidler, Girard
- Dave Daggett, Girard
- George "Blaze" Kelly, Oil City St. Joe's (1st team Catholic all-state)
- Bill Eckert, Oil City St. Joe's (1st team Catholic all-state)
- Don Feeney, Oil City St. Joe's

Ramblers Bounce Back!

1940-41 (11-5)

Coach: Salvatore J. "Jimmy" Foti
Captains: Rodger Lamb, Edmund Mehl
Manager: Richard Buseck

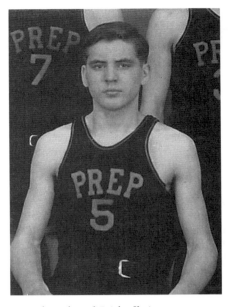

One of Prep's and Erie's all-time greatest all-around athletes–Ted Morasky.

Date	PREP			Dec.	Loc.	High Scorer	Opponent
12/16	71*	Corry St. Edward's	17	W	H	Morasky & Lamb (16)	Sarnicki (13)
12/18	32	Millcreek	37	L	A	Morasky (15)	Bricker (20)
12/20	26	Albion	17	W	A	Morasky (9)	Somerville (9)
12/27	30	Dunkirk (NY) St. Mary's	23	W	A	Morasky (9)	J. Reilly (9)
1/6	78*	Meadville St. Agatha's	12	W	H	Morasky & Schickler (20)	Thomas (4)
1/10	68	Titusville St. Joseph's Academy	14	W	A	Lamb (21)	Hall & Madden (6)
1/13	39	Greenville St. Michael's	18	W	H	Morasky (11)	Strosser & Moynihan (4)
1/20	13	Oil City St. Joseph's	39	L	H	Morasky (10)	Eckert (9)
1/23	75	Meadville St. Agatha's	16	W	A	Morasky (14)	Thomas (6)
1/24		Dunkirk (NY) St. Mary's (CANCELLED--SNOW)			H		
1/27	20	Technical	24	L	H	Mahon (5)	Flowers (9)
1/31		Corry St. Edward's (CANCELLED--SNOW)			A		
2/4	27	Strong Vincent	33	L	A	Morasky (10)	Fabian (11)
2/14	44	Kanty Prep	30	W	A	Morasky (18)	Plonski (8)
2/17	2 (20)	Buffalo (NY) Canisius (FFT)	0 (20)	W	H	Lamb (9)	Wardynski (7)
2/20	41	Greenville St. Michael's	30	W	A	Lamb (16)	McKay (10)
2/24	35	Kanty Prep	24	W	H	Schickler (14)	Momieski (8)
3/7	35	Oil City St. Joseph's	37 (OT)	L	A	Schickler (14)	Hall (17)
	654* (40.8*)		391 (24.4)				

Pos.	Player	Prior School	Class	G(GS)	FG	FT	Total	PPG	Career
F	Ted Morasky (#5)	Harborcreek Training	Jr.	13(11)	69	14	152	11.7	349
C-G	Rodger Lamb (#10)	St. Peter's	Sr.	14(14)	55	21	131	9.4	176
F-G	George Schickler (#12)	St. Patrick's	Jr.	14(8)	41	7	89	6.4	97
G	Joe McCafferty (#7)	St. Peter's	Jr.	13(11)	26	6	58	4.5	58
G-F	Ed "Brub" Mehl (#4)	St. Andrew's	Sr.	14(12)	24	7	55	3.9	70
G-C	Jack Erb (#11)	St. John's	Sr.	15(10)	19	9	47	3.1	47
C-F-G	Ed Driscoll (#9)	St. Patrick's	Fr.	15(6)	12	6	30	2.0	30
C-F-G	Richard "Red" Doyle (#8)	St. Patrick's	Fr.	8(1)	13	3	29	3.6	29
G-F	Ray Laughlin (#3)	St. Patrick's	Jr.	7(3)	10	0	20	2.9	20
F-G	Joe or Jim Miller	St. Pat's/Pete's	Soph.	5	7	3	17	3.4	17
F-G	Robert Nies	St. John's	Soph.	7(1)	3	1	7	1.0	7
F-G	Joe Flatley	St. Ann's	Sr.	2	2	0	4	2.0	4
G-F-C	Ed "Sonny" Mead	St. Peter's	Fr.	4	2	0	4	1.0	4
F	Johnny Flanigan (#6)	St. John's	Soph.	4(2)	1	1	3	0.8	3
F	Bob Ankiel	St. Peter's	Fr.	2(1)	1	0	2	2.0	2
F	Bill Latimer	St. Peter's	Soph.	1	1	0	2	2.0	2
F	Frank Mannarino	St. Patrick's	Soph.	1	1	0	2	2.0	2
F	John "Hump" Sullivan	St. Peter's	Fr.	1	0	0	0	0.0	0

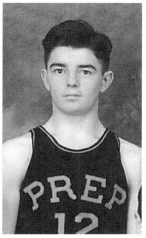

Ed "Brub" Mehl, considered to be Prep's oldest living basketball star.

Joe McCafferty, Rambler all-star.

HIGHLIGHTS:

- Coach **Salvatore J. "Jimmy" Foti**, a Jamestown (NY) native, was hired as Cathedral Prep's basketball mentor after two years of success coaching the Rambler football squad. Foti had played college basketball at St. Bonaventure and coached the freshmen cage team at John Carroll, where he had also played his senior year. At the conclusion of the 1940-41 campaign, Foti left Prep to take a coaching position at Wheeling (WV) Central. He went on to have a tremendous coaching career in West Virginia, and was eventually inducted into that state's Athletic Hall of Fame.

- All Cathedral Prep's home games were played at the Strong Vincent High School gymnasium.

- The 1940-41 Prep hoop squad was the first to average more than 40 points per game, twice breaking the school record for most points in a game. Losses were only to Erie teams Millcreek (11-7), Tech (12-7) and Vincent (5-14), and twice to state champ Oil City St. Joseph's (26-6). The first St. Joe's loss was the only blowout. East (18-6-1) and Academy (9-11) were not scheduled. Stars for the rugged city champion East squad included **Walt Hatkevich, "Chuck" Kuhl, "Vinnie" Marchant, Mark Karuba** and **Al Oldach**.

- Fan-shaped backboards were made legal beginning with the 1940-41 season.

- Highlight of the season was the consistent play of classy junior forward **Ted Morasky**, already an acknowledged football star for the Ramblers. Morasky was the first Prepster to average in double figures (11.7 *PPG*) since 1930, when **Herb Perry** averaged 12.0 per game.

- Prep's victorious opener over Corry St. Edwards's (6-14) put the Ramblers on the long side of a 23-1 series ledger. The *Corry Evening Journal* reported the final score as 56-17; the *Erie Daily Times* reported the final score as 68-17; and what appears to be a more competent account by the *Erie Dispatch-Herald* put the final count at 71-17. Despite the one-sided triumph, Coach Foti said following the game that he was "still dissatisfied with the play of some of the boys," and further claimed "there is room for plenty of improvement." Prep and St. Ed's never played again, and St. Ed's closed in 1949.

- Prep's early season victory over Albion (10-10) was impressive, as the Redskins were a three-time defending Erie County League champion. Albion won the Class B crown in 1940 and the Class A titles in 1938 and 1939. Albion High's first casualty of World War II was star athlete and student **Jack Somerville**,

who was lost with the torpedo-sinking of the U.S. Destroyer Jacob Jones on March 5, 1942. Somerville was the leading scorer for the Redskins against the Ramblers and was well-known for his All-County skills in baseball, basketball and football and for his magnetic personality.

- Prep's forfeit win over Canisius (11-6, 11-7 including Prep game) came when Crusader coach **Johnny Barnes** pulled his team from the floor after referee **Chuck Bauder** refused to reverse his ejection of Canisius team captain **Jack "Bucky" Connelly**, who "kneed" Rambler **Rodger Lamb** after a jump ball call. Some reports have Canisius ahead at the time, 22-18 in the 2nd quarter, while other accounts state the game was tied at that moment, 20-20. Canisius records ignore that the game was played at all. East High coach **Jack Komora** had also complained about rough play from Canisius earlier in the season. Komora stated that the Canisius players were "unnecessarily rough and their fouling could hardly come under the heading of good basketball." Komora was also at a loss to explain "the attitude of Coach Barnes."

- Prep had scheduled a return game with Canisius in Buffalo, but Coach Foti said "future relations with the school were in the hands of athletic director **Father Walter Conway**." Prep did not play that return game, nor did the Ramblers and Crusaders compete again in basketball for the next dozen years.

- Prep registered two good victories over Kanty Prep (13-11), the start of an 8-game win streak over the Eagles.

- Several Ramblers were ruled ineligible near the season's end by headmaster **Monsignor Joseph "Doc" Wehrle**, for academic deficiencies. At least two or three various starters and several others were forced to miss some of the final five games. Prep was only able to take six players to the St. Mike's game in Greenville!

- Prep's best effort was the overtime loss to Oil City St. Joseph's. This was actually the nightcap of a doubleheader played by the Hilltoppers on its home floor! In the first game, St. Joe's defeated Apollo High, 35-33, on a long heave in the last second by **"Forrey" Hall**; they then bested the Ramblers by two in overtime.

- Oil City St. Joe's, for the third straight year, made it to the Bishop Hafey/ K. of C. Pennsylvania State Catholic championship final, this time smashing Hazelton St. Gabriel's to win all the marbles, 36-33. It was St. Joe's second Catholic state title in three years and the final was considered the greatest upset in the history of the tourney. The Hilltoppers then accepted a bid to the National Catholic Interscholastic Basketball Tournament in Chicago, capturing the imagination of the fans with a 46-35 upset over LaCrosse (WI) Aquinas. St. Joe's then lost a 39-37 heartbreaker to Lynn (MS) St. Mary's. Unfortunately it was

Prep Scores Via Forfeit

Canisius High Team Walks Off The Court

BUFFALO CANISIUS HIGH cagers went home from Strong Vincent in a huff last night before the game was half over and Cathedral Prep won by a forfeit. According to Coach Jim Foti, of Prep, it happened like this:

It was straight basketball in the first quarter, with the invaders seeping through the Ramblers' defense to pile up a 12-5 lead. Going into the second frame, however, the Foti machine began to click and two minutes before intermission Canisius had but a four point lead, 22-18.

In a bit of scrimmage under the basket, Referee Bauder called Lamb and Connolly, opposing centers for a jump ball. While walking into position to jump, Lamb was kneed by Connolly, who was ordered out of the game by Bauder, referee.

Coach John Barnees of Canisius, said he would take his team from the floor if the decision held. It held, and he did, and Prep was awarded the game by a forfeit.

Canisius (22)	F.	Fl.	T.	Prep (18)	F.	Fl.	T.
McArtemy, f	1	0	2	Morasky, f.	2	1	5
Waldyiski, f	3	1	7	Laughlin, f.	1	0	2
Connolly, c.	2	2	6	R.Lamb, c.	4	1	9
Trinboli, g.	2	1	5	Driscoll, g.	0	0	0
Ralickt, g.	1	0	2	Erb, g.	0	0	0
Leiser, g.	0	0	0	McCaffty, g	1	0	2
				Mehl, g.	0	0	0
Totals	9	4	22	Totals	8	2	18

the last of the NCIBT tourneys, cancelled once the United States entered World War II after the bombing of Pearl Harbor. Chicago (IL) Leo won the last NCIBT, defeating St. Francis (SD) Mission in the title game, 49-41, in overtime. Mission was an all-American Sioux Indian team that participated in several NCIBTs and was always a crowd favorite.

- **Ed Mead** transferred during his junior year to Phillips Academy Andover (MA) where he became a full star in football and later as well at Princeton University.

- When coach **"Jimmy" Foti** was asked by a reporter if he'd like to see Prep get into City Series competition, for the next season, he stated: "Our aggregation might be handicapped for practice facilities and equipment. Otherwise the idea is not distasteful to me." The Ramblers were eventually forced into city competition in 1942-43 by the rationing of WW II; and Prep would finally get its own facility in 1944.

Rodger Lamb never backed down from a good fistfight. He died fighting for his country in World War II.

- **Rodger Lamb**, also a rugged gridiron star for the Ramblers, was sadly killed in action in the Pacific fighting for his country in World War II.

1941 All-Opponent Team:

Pete Bricker, Millcreek
Jack Somerville, Albion
Jim Reilly, Dunkirk St. Mary's
Richard Strosser, Greenville St. Mike's
Bill Eckert, Oil City St. Joe's
Ed "Red" McGurn, Oil City St. Joe's
"Moose" McNerney, Oil City St. Joe's
Don Fabian, Vincent
Lou DiBacco, Vincent [Gannon]
Stan Flowers, Tech [Redlands, football]
Johnny Lipchick, Tech [Gannon]
Ernie Spirito, Tech
Ray "Jambers" Wisniewski, Tech
Jack "Bucky" Connelly, Canisius
Forrest Hall, Oil City St. Joe's [Duquesne, San Francisco, football; NFL San Francisco 49'ers]

Al Calabrese Leads Prep to Best Record!

1941-42 (12-2)

Coach: Albert R. "Al" Calabrese
Captain: Ted Morasky
Manager: Richard Buseck

Coach Al Calabrese, who later became Tech's Hall of Fame basketball mentor.

Date	PREP	Dec.	Loc.			High Scorer	Opponent
12/8	31	Albion	17	W	H	Schickler (14)	Orr (6)
12/15	31	Millcreek	22	W	H	Schickler (11)	Lossie (12)
12/19	26	Greenville St. Michael's	17	W	A	Flanigan (11)	McKay (6)
1/5	36	Alumni	20	W	H	McCafferty (9)	Goodill (5)
1/12	35	Greenville St. Michael's	23	W	H	Morasky (10)	McKay (6)
1/16	34	Niagara Falls (NY) St. Mary's	27	W	A	Schickler (11)	Noonan (7)
1/19	35	Kanty Prep	27	W	H	Schickler (10)	Porembski (16)
1/26	12	East	31	L	H	Morasky (5)	Oldach (9)
1/30	19	Millcreek	14	W	A	Morasky (6)	Stadler (4)
2/6	21	Oil City St. Joseph's	22	L	H	Laughlin (11)	Flaherty (7)
2/10	36	Strong Vincent	34(2OT)	W	A	Morasky (9)	Robinson (15)
2/16	30	Technical	26	W	H	Laughlin (12)	Dombrowski (10)
2/20	42	Kanty Prep	20	W	A	Morasky & Schickler (12)	Porembski (10)
2/27	29	Oil City St. Joseph's	26	W	A	Morasky & Schickler (9)	McGurn (13)
	417 (29.8)		**326 (23.2)**				

Pos.	Player	Prior School	Class	G(GS)	FG	FT	Total	*PPG*	Career
F-G	Ted "Moe" Morasky (#5)	Harborcreek Training	Sr.	14(14)	41	16	98	7.0	447*
G-C	George Schickler (#12)	St. Patrick's	Sr.	14(14)	43	8	94	6.7	191
F-C	Ray Laughlin (#3)	St. Patrick's	Sr.	14(11)	32	9	73	5.2	93
F-G-C	Johnny Flanigan (#11)	St. John's	Jr.	14(5)	18	9	45	3.2	48
F-C-G	Silvio Mannarino (#10)	St. Patrick's	Fr.	10(4)	11	8	30	3.0	30
G-C	Joe McCafferty (#7)	St. Peter's	Sr.	9(7)	12	6	30	3.3	88
C-G	Ed Driscoll (#9)	St. Patrick's	Soph.	13(9)	7	8	22	1.7	52
G	Richard "Red" Doyle (#8)	St. Patrick's	Soph.	8(2)	6	1	13	1.6	42
F-G-C	Bob Bellomini	Roosevelt	Soph.	8(4)	4	1	9	1.1	9
G	Joe Weschler (#6)	St. Peter's/SV	Jr.	4	1	0	2	2.0	2
G-C	Ray Oldakowski (#4)	St. Patrick's	Fr.	9	0	1	1	0.1	1
F-G	Robert Nies	St. John's	Jr.	4	0	0	0	0.0	9
F	Paul Downey	Albion	Sr.	1	0	0	0	0.0	0

The outstanding 1942 Prep Ramblers. Front, L to R: McCafferty, Schickler, Morasky, Driscoll, Laughlin; Back: Headmaster Father Miller, Mannarino, Oldach, Coach Calabrese, Manager Buseck, Doyle, Weschler, Athletic Director Father Conway.

HIGHLIGHTS:

- **Father Victor Miller** became Prep's second headmaster in 1941, succeeding **Monsignor Joseph "Doc" Wehrle**, who then became president of the new Gannon College. "Doc" Wehrle served with aplomb as Prep leader for the school's first two decades (1921-1941) and is credited with setting the tone for Prep's excellent academic reputation.

After 20 years as Prep headmaster, Msgr. "Doc" Wehrle became the first president of Gannon College.

- Coach **Al Calabrese**, a former Strong Vincent and Findlay College star, was hired as Prep's basketball mentor after coaching the Rambler football squad to a fine record of 7-2 in 1941. Calabrese was the head basketball coach at Tech the previous season (1940-41), where he compiled a record of 12-7. After coaching the Ramblers but one season, Calabrese eventually went back to Tech (1948). He coached the Centaurs all the way through 1976, save a few seasons in the late 1950's when he was Tech's head football coach, compiling a hoop record of 313-219. Calabrese was inducted into the Metropolitan Erie Sports Hall of Fame in 1990.

- All Cathedral Prep's home games were played at the Strong Vincent High School gymnasium.

- The Orange & Black began the season with a record-tying seven straight wins behind the scoring of **George Schickler**, including an easy victory in the opener over Albion (6-11). That contest saw the late appearance of senior **Paul Downey**, a resident of Albion Borough whose hometown friends all played for the Redskins.

- Prep had a pair of impressive triumphs over Greenville St. Michael's (13-6), which finished the season with the best record of any of Mercer County's Class B schools. In the first contest on the Greenville Penn High floor, the Ramblers held a slim 2-1 margin after the 1st period. Junior **John Flanigan** was inserted in the 2nd quarter and he immediately blasted the nets for 9 points and a 16-4 Prep halftime lead. In game two, the *Greenville Record-Argus* noted that "The defensive play of **Joe McCafferty** and the work of **Ray Laughlin** on offense featured for the Erieites."

- In a preliminary to the Alumni game, Prep Seniors defeated the Sophomores, 13-6.

- Prep's greatest victory in school history to this point was its 36-34 double overtime conquest of heavily favored Strong Vincent (11-11). It was the first Rambler victory over the Colonels ever, after 10

George Schickler. This Rambler hoop and gridiron star played basketball at Gannon.

Ray Laughlin was the third leading scorer behind Morasky and Schickler.

Prep Nips Vincent, 36-34; Academy Tops Hickory

consecutive losses. Floor leader **Teddy Morasky** starred in the battle, but **Johnny Flanigan** was the eventual hero. Flanigan not only nailed a free throw to put the game into OT, but also sunk the game-winner from the side of the foul circle 1:32 into the second OT, which was played under "sudden death" rules.

- Other big Rambler wins included the pair over an excellent Millcreek (20-3) squad; the first win over Tech (4-15) since 1935; the upset road successes against powerful Niagara Falls St. Mary's and defending state Catholic champ Oil City St. Joseph's (18-9), after seven straight losses to the Hilltoppers. Prep baffled St. Joe's by alternating man-to-man and zone defenses and by "freezing" the ball in the 4th quarter to protect a slim lead.

- The only time Prep was overmatched was against city champion East High (14-5), which won its second in a string of four straight City Series and Section One crowns.

- Oil City St. Joe's, coached by Erieite **Bernard "Babe" Harkins**, was invited to Williamsport to defend its K. of C. State Catholic championship, only to lose to Philadelphia LaSalle in the first round. LaSalle ended winning the state crown by defeating Pittsburgh North Catholic in the title game by a 59-37 margin.

- Prep's victories over Millcreek were the start of a 20-game winning string against the Trojans, a skein that didn't end until 1958. The two Rambler-Trojan battles were the most physical of the season. Millcreek won the 1941-42 Erie County League championship, its first of six consecutive ECL crowns.

- The .857 winning percentage by the Orange & Black was the school's best to this point. This team record wasn't broken until 1954, when **Dick Detzel's** squad won its second straight PCIAA state championship with a 22-3 record and .880 winning percentage.

- A post-season City-County All-Star game was played at the Downtown YMCA in observance of the Golden Jubilee of basketball, the game founded by **James Naismith** 50 years before in 1891. Academy's **Jack Komora** and Strong Vincent's **Sam Kramer** selected the 11-man City roster, including one from Tech, four from Academy and six from Vincent. East High's players had to decline invitations as they were still engaged in District 10 playoff action, while no Cathedral Prep players were picked because "Prep has concluded its

Ted Morasky, Prep's first four-year letter winner in basketball. Later an All-East QB at Holy Cross, he was sadly killed in an auto accident at age 25.

season and all equipment has been turned in." This last reason seemed dubious as three Prepsters participated in an East-West game nine days later.

- The City's All-Stars included Tech's **Ray Dombrowski;** Academy's **Dick Shuffstall, Neil Mangold** and **Tom Franzkowski;** and Vincent's **Giocondo "Chick" Rufini, Bill Robinson, Sam Talarico, Ed Casella, Bob Gensheimer** and **Bill Kelly**. The City, behind Shuffstall's 14 points, defeated the County, 51-26. The County squad was coached by Millcreek's **Gus Anderson** and Edinboro's **Ken Westlake**. In a preliminary battle, St. Benedict Academy's Lassies defeated Pittsburgh St. Rosalia in a thriller, 42-36.

- Vincent star **"Chick" Rufini** was killed in 1944, fighting in the Pacific in World War II.

- Seniors **Joe McCafferty** (ineligible after the 9th game because of the 8-semester rule), **Ray Laughlin** and **Ted Morasky** all participated in the first East-West all-star game, sponsored by the East Side Federation of Clubs for the benefit of the Red Cross. They are considered Prep's first basketball "All-Stars." Though Laughlin was scoreless for the East, Morasky for the East and McCafferty for the West each scored six. The West, behind SV's **Sam Talarico's** 19 points, won the contest, 49-42.

- **George Schickler**, Prep's second leading scorer for the season, went on to play at Gannon College.

- **Ted Morasky**, star Prep captain and the first four-year starter in the history of Rambler basketball, finished his career as

Headmaster Father Miller breaks ground for the new Cathedral Prep school.

Prep's all-time leading scorer with 447 points, surpassing **Herb Perry** who scored 444 from 1928-30. Though unknown at the time, Morasky broke Perry's mark in the second Oil City St. Joe's game, the last game of "Moe's" great career. Morasky, the boy who led Harborcreek Training School to the Erie Parochial League championship in 1938, went on to star at quarterback at Holy Cross, where he earned *Associated Press* All-East honors in 1944. He was sadly killed in an automobile accident in 1947 at the age of 25. He was inducted posthumously into the Cathedral Prep Athletic Hall of Fame in 2006.

• On January 18, **Fr. Edward Maher**, director of the National Catholic Interscholastic Basketball Tournament (NCIBT), announced cancellation of the event, which had been held continuously since 1924. The principal reason given was because of the "national emergency" arising from the United States' entrance into World War II.

1942 All-Opponent Team:

Bobby Orr, Albion
Bob "Monk" Cryder, Albion
William "Jeep" Lossie, Millcreek
Tommy McKay, Greenville St. Mike's
Carlos Noonan, Niagara Falls St. Mary's
Anthony Porembski, Kanty Prep
Al Oldach (Oldakowski), East
Mark Karuba, East
Roy Stadler, Millcreek
Bobby "Ducky" Hall, Oil City St. Joe's
Bill Robinson, Vincent
Sam Talarico, Vincent [Gannon]
Giocondo "Chick" Rufini, Vincent
Ray Dombrowski, Tech [Lock Haven, football]
George "Ace" Flaherty, Oil City St. Joe's
Ed "Red" McGurn, Oil City St. Joe's

Some rough and tumble action on the Vincent court.

Driscoll wins the tip at the SV gymnasium.

Prep's War-Time Schedule: the City Series and PCIAA!

1942-43 (4-15)

Coach: Rev. Leonard "Len" Kuziora
Assistant: Rev. Joseph Radziszewski
Captain: John Flanigan
Managers: Richard Buseck, Richard Mantz

Johnny Flanigan will always be remembered as "the boy that hit that shot that beat Vincent."

Date	PREP			Dec.	Loc.	High Scorer	Opponent
12/8	22	East	38	L	H	Mannarino (8)	Demyanovich (14)
12/14	18	Academy	36	L	H	Mannarino (8)	Klein (10)
12/19	29	Technical	46	L	A	DeLuca (11)	Krepcho (12)
1/7	31	Strong Vincent	51	L	A	Doyle (12)	Fabian (11)
1/12	37	East	48	L	A	Doyle (11)	Jablonski & Hatkevich (15)
1/15	38	Kanty Prep	35	W	H	Oldach (12)	Porembski (17)
1/19	23	Academy	40	L	A	Flanigan (7)	Yawger (11)
1/21	36	Technical	47	L	H	Doyle (15)	Krepcho (14)
1/25	32	Strong Vincent	50	L	A	Doyle (12	Blood & Surace (11)
2/2	32	East	52	L	N	Doyle (12)	Bilecki (17)
2/6	45	Academy	47	L	N	Mannarino (18)	Schwindt (17)
2/13	25	Technical	33	L	N	Doyle (7)	Bernardini (10)
2/16	35	Strong Vincent	45	L	N	Doyle (12)	Fabian (15)
2/20	38	East	48	L	N	DeLuca (11)	Becker (14)
2/23	40	Academy	23	W	N	DeLuca (14)	Schwindt (17)
2/26	51	Kanty Prep	31	W	A	Mannarino (17)	Skrypczak (9)
3/2	37	Technical	50	L	N	Driscoll (8)	Krepcho (15)
3/4	48	Strong Vincent	40	W	N	DeLuca & Oldach (13)	Fabian (9)

P.C.I.A.A. STATE CATHOLIC H.S. TOURNAMENT

Date	PREP			Dec.	Loc.	High Scorer	Opponent
3/19	25	Johnstown Central Catholic	35	L	H	Driscoll (8)	Pavlick (12)
	642 (33.8)		**795* (41.8*)**				

Pos.	Player	Prior School	Class	G(GS)	FG	FT	Total	PPG	Career
F	Richard "Red" Doyle (#7)	St. Patrick's	Jr.	19(18)	60	31	151	7.9	193
G	Johnny DeLuca (#4)	St. Patrick's	Soph.	19(17)	47	32	126	6.6	126
F	Silvio "Sil" Mannarino	St. Patrick's	Soph.	19(19)	49	25	123	6.8	153
G	Ray Oldakowski (Oldach)(#9)	St. Patrick's	Soph.	19(17)	39	16	94	4.9	95
C	Johnny "Smiley" Flanigan(#5)	St. John's	Sr.	18(11)	30	13	73	4.1	121
C-G	Ed Driscoll (#6)	St. Patrick's	Jr.	14(9)	20	12	52	3.7	104
F-C	Joe Weschler	St. Peter's/SV	Sr.	13(3)	7	1	15	1.2	17
F	Cheslaus "Cooper" Kupniewski (#10)	St. Stan's	Fr.	4	2	1	5	1.3	5
C	Robert "Bob" Borczon	Holy Trinity	Jr.	6(1)	1	0	2	0.3	2
F	Tom Mangan	St. Andrew's	Sr.	4	1	0	2	0.5	2
C	Jim Mahoney (#12)	Sacred Heart	Soph.	0	0	0	0	0.0	0

HIGHLIGHTS:

- The new coach was **Father Len Kuziora**, the former Cathedral Prep and Holy Cross football star from the Prep Class of 1933. Father Kuziora, who had just been ordained on May 14, 1942, also coached the Rambler gridders from 1942-44.

- **Father Joe Radziszewski**, Prep's first junior varsity coach , also became the first regular varsity basketball assistant coach in school history.

- 1942-43 marked Prep's initial entry into the Erie City Series basketball league. For the first time in basketball the Ramblers would compete as an official league member against Strong Vincent, Technical, East and Academy. This affiliation was a direct result of the World War II-inspired travel restrictions caused by gasoline and tire rationing. Though Prep was in the City Series in football from 1934-38, from this point on the Ramblers would compete against its city rivals in league competition in all sports.

The 1943 Ramblers, Prep's first City Series entrant. Front, L to R: Manager Mantz, Flanigan, Oldach, Doyle, DeLuca, Driscoll, Manager Buseck; Back: Assistant Coach Father Radzizsewski, Kupniewski, Wagner, Carideo, Mahoney, Mannarino, Coach Father Kuziora.

- The 1942-43 and 1943-44 seasons presented Erie's war time schedule, in which the City Series schools competed four times against each other. Kanty Prep was the lone independent opponent in 1942-43, while in 1943-44 the Ramblers added Oil City St. Joe's, Conneaut (OH) and St. Marys Central Catholic, along with Kanty, to its roster of independent games.

- Prep actually replaced Sharon and Farrell high schools which agreed to compete with Erie's four public schools in a conference that was to be called the "Big Six". WW II restrictions foiled that concept and Prep lobbied for entry.

- Lineups for the Erie public schools were constantly changing with February graduations and others leaving for World War II military service. Promising 9th-grader **Chet Kupniewski** left Prep in May, 1943 to join the Coast Guard. Senior **Tom Mangan** left the squad to start school at Gannon College.

- All Cathedral Prep's home games were played at the Strong Vincent High School gymnasium. The "second half" City Series games were played as parts of doubleheaders at St. Mary's Auditorium on East 10th Street, between German and Parade Streets. The PCIAA playoff encounter was held at SV.

Pre-season drills at the Strong Vincent gym.

- Prep went from its best season ever in 1941-42 to its worst, percentage-wise, in 1942-43. The Orange & Black's 15 losses broke the record of 11 set in 1931. Included were a record 8 straight losses. A strong regular season finish and three sophomores and a junior in the starting lineup gave the Ramblers hope for the future. The win over Academy (12-8) was not only Prep's first ever against the Lions (although they hadn't played since 1931), but also its first ever in actual City Series play.

Johnny DeLuca lets one fly.

- Prep won three of its last four regular season games, including the season finale against Strong Vincent (8-11). Sophomores **Johnny DeLuca** and **Ray Oldach** were the big guns in the upset over the Colonels, a game which gave East (16-6) the city crown before it had to square off against Tech (9-9) in the nightcap of the sold-out doubleheader at St. Mary's.

- The final standings of Prep's first foray in City Series basketball were as follows:

First Half	W	L	Second Half	W	L
*East	8	1	East	7	1
Academy	7	2	Vincent	5	3
Tech	3	5	Tech	4	4
Vincent	3	5	Academy	2	6
Prep	0	8	Prep	2	6

won 1st half in playoff & City Series title for winning both halves.

- Travel restrictions and gasoline rationing also eliminated nearly every independent game, save the two with Kanty Prep (1-11) of Wesleyville. There were 41 fouls called in the second Kanty contest at Wesleyville.

- The Ramblers played in their first Pennsylvania State Catholic High School Basketball Tournament since 1929. Under a new setup and organization called the Pennsylvania Catholic Interscholastic Athletic Association (PCIAA), championship teams were determined from each of the six dioceses in the state, with the winners meeting in inter-diocesan play along the same lines as the PIAA district competition. Prep was the Class A representative of the Erie Diocese (its only "A" team), while Kanty Prep was the entrant in Class B. Both lost first round matchups, the Ramblers to Johnstown Central Catholic (15-7), now known as Bishop McCort High School. Pittsburgh North Catholic won the first PCIAA A state crown with a 30-29 victory over Philadelphia Roman Catholic in the title clash. Pittsburgh (Mount Oliver) St. Joseph's won the first B title over Tamaqua St. Jerome's, 37-26.

- What is interesting about the Johnstown Central Catholic team is that it was coached by "Nat" Hickey, the famous multi-sport professional athlete and coach. Hickey played from the 1920's through the 1940's with multiple early professional basketball teams, including the New York Original Celtics and the Cleveland Rosenblums of the American Basketball League; and the Pittsburgh Raiders, Indianapolis Kautskys and Tri-Cities Blackhawks of the National Basketball League. Hickey also played and managed several seasons of minor league baseball and is known for being Stan "the Man" Musial's first manager with the Williamson Colts in 1938. After coaching at Johnstown CC, Hickey coached the Providence Steamrollers of the Basketball Association of America (forerunner of the NBA) during the 1947-48 season. Hickey activated himself as a player with the Steamrollers for one game, scoring 2 points. Thus, at two days shy of age 46, Hickey is revered as the oldest player in NBA history.

- Prep's top four scorers, and five out of the top six, "Red" Doyle, Johnny DeLuca, Sil Mannarino, Ray Oldakowski and Ed Driscoll, were all members of St. Patrick's Parish. They were members of St. Pat's first grade school championship teams of 1939, 1940 and 1941. The Shamrocks went on to capture 14 more Erie Parochial League crowns, as well as Pennsylvania state titles in 1963 and 1964 and a runner-up finish in 1961.

Mannarino gets loose underneath.

- The Erie Basketball Writers Association, consisting of the sportswriters from the *Erie Daily Times* and the *Erie Dispatch-Herald*, chose 10 players—by agreement two from each City team—to battle the Erie Coaches Association in a post-season contest game pitting city stars against a squad of local coaches. Prepsters named the 1943 City Scholastic All-Star Team were sophomore Johnny DeLuca, named First Team by the *Dispatch* and Second Team by the *Times*; and Dick "Red" Doyle, named Second Team by both papers. In this regard, DeLuca and Doyle are considered Prep's first All-City selections.

- A preliminary attraction to the first Coaches All-Star Game was an East-West JV All-Star game, won by the East, 36-28. East High's **Billy Biletnikoff** and **Artie Arkelian** scored 8 and 7 for the winners, while Vincent twins **Billy** and **Bobby Brabender** played scrappy defense for the West. Prep JV's **Jim Mahoney** and **Jimmy Mead** toiled for the East, while Ramblers **Jimmy Carideo** and **Bob Ferretti** played for the West.

- **Johnny DeLuca** led all scorers with 13 points though the City All-Stars were defeated by the Coaches, 58-54. **"Red" Doyle** scored 5 for the Stars. **Bill "String" Nash** led the coaches with 11 and a quintet of city school mentors, including **Bob Arrowsmith, Reno Strand, Ken "Red" Cochrane, Marion "Bimp" Lewis** and **Othmar Wuenschel**, each had 8. Wuenschel, an Academy graduate, had previously been head coach at Conemaugh, where in 1940 his squad lost in the PIAA state title game to Lebanon, 37-32.

- DeLuca and Doyle also played in the 2nd annual City-County All-Star game for the benefit of the Red Cross. DeLuca scored 7 points in the contest and Doyle 2 in a 35-32 victory for the County over the City.

- **John Flanigan**, captain of the Ramblers, went on to play at Gannon College.

1943 All-Opponent Team:

Mike Demyanovich, East
Dave Krepcho, Tech
Sumner "Summy" Nichols, Vincent [Allegheny]
Don Fabian, Vincent
Joe Jablonski, East
Walt Hatkevich, East [Penn State, Temple]
Anthony Porembski, Kanty
Dick Yawger, Academy
Kal Schonthaler, Academy
Jerry Blakeslee, Academy
Richard "Woody" Drzewiecki, Tech
Jimmy Blood, Vincent
Dominick Surace, Vincent
Jimmy D'Aurora, Vincent
Ray Bilecki, East (hm, all-state)
Mark Karuba, East (4th team, all-state)
Ray Bernardini, Tech [Gannon]
Cal Neithamer, Academy [Allegheny]
Mike Pavlick, Johnstown Central Catholic

Ramblers Lose Many Battles!

1943-44 (7-17)

Coach: Rev. Leonard "Len" Kuziora
Asst. Coach: Rev. Joseph Radziszewski
Captain: Richard "Red" Doyle
Manager: Tom Heubel

Richard "Red" Doyle, team captain and four-year letter winner.

Date	PREP			Dec.	Loc.	High Scorer	Opponent
12/3	46	Kanty Prep	19	W	A	DeLuca (14)	Skrzypczak (10)
12/7	13	Academy	29	L	A	Doyle & Oldach (3)	Roach & Klein (6)
12/9	30	East	34	L	H	Doyle (9)	Andrews (10)
12/13	29	Oil City St. Joseph's	27	W	H	DeLuca (17)	Kenniston (14)
12/18	31	Technical	29	W	A	Doyle (14)	Tevis (8)
12/21	42	Strong Vincent	24	W	A	Mannarino (17)	Cerami (8)
1/3	25	Academy	39	L	H	Oldach (9)	Schwindt (18)
1/6	14	East	31	L	A	DeLuca (5)	Biletnikoff (12)
1/10	46	Kanty Prep	21	W	H	Doyle (15)	Porembski (8)
1/12	22	Technical	20	W	H	Doyle (9)	Zuravleff (7)
1/14	18	Oil City St. Joseph's	25	L	A	DeLuca & Oldach (6)	Flaherty (10)
1/18	27	Strong Vincent	30	L	A	Doyle (11)	Horn (10)
1/20	23	Academy	49	L	A	Mannarino (8)	Grabill (12)
1/25	24	East	46	L	H	Oldach (13)	Swanson (17)
1/28	32	Conneaut (OH)	30	W	H	Doyle (12)	four w/ (6)
2/1	37	Technical	40	L	H	Mannarino (11)	Tevis (11)
2/3	24	Strong Vincent	34	L	A	Mannarino (11)	McIntyre (8)
2/7	26	Academy	38	L	H	Mannarino (10)	Coyne (12)
2/10	25	East	51	L	A	Doyle (13)	Zygai (9)
2/15	23	Conneaut (OH)	25	L	A	Mannarino (8)	Smith (9)
2/18	38	Technical	39	L	A	Mannarino (17)	Zuravleff & Tevis (12)
2/22	31	Strong Vincent	44	L	A	DeLuca (10)	Cerami (12)
2/27	37	St. Marys Central Catholic	40	L	A	Mannarino (14)	Simbeck (16)
3/7	24	East (EXHIBITION GAME)	51	L	A	Doyle (8)	Biletnikoff (17)
		P.C.I.A.A. STATE CATHOLIC H.S. TOURNAMENT					
3/9	19	Johnstown Central Catholic	20	L	A	Mannarino (8)	Seman & Wildner (5)
	660* (27.6)		**784 (32.7)**				

Pos.	Player	Prior School	Class	G(GS)	FG	FT	Total	PPG	Career
F	Silvio "Sil" Mannarino (#10)	St. Patrick's	Jr.	24(24)*	71	33	175	7.3	328
F	Richard "Red" Doyle (#7)	St. Patrick's	Sr.	23(23)	68	33	169	7.0	362
C-G	Johnny DeLuca (#4)	St. Patrick's	Jr.	24(24)*	68	29	165	6.9	291
G	Ray Oldakowski (Oldach) (#9)	St. Patrick's	Jr.	21(20)	43	28	114	5.4	209
G-C	Robert "Bob" Borczon (#5)	Holy Trinity	Sr.	16(8)	7	6	20	1.3	22
G	Charlie Colvin (#6)	St. Peter's	Soph.	20(19)	3	10	16	0.8	16
F-C-G	Jim Carideo (#11)	Sacred Heart	Soph.	17(3)	6	3	15	0.9	15
F	Bob Ferretti	Holy Rosary	Soph.	2	1	1	3	1.5	3
F	Jim White (#3)	St. Patrick's	Fr.	4	1	0	2	0.5	2
F	Richard "Dick" Rettger (#3)	Sacred Heart	Soph.	2	1	0	2	2.0	2
G	Jim Trost	Sacred Heart	Jr.	1	0	1	1	1.0	1
G-C	John Larson (#8)	Millcreek	Jr.	9(1)	0	0	0	0.0	0
C	Jim Mahoney (#12)	Sacred Heart	Jr.	2	0	0	0	0.0	0
G	Jimmy Mead	St. Peter's	Soph.	1	0	0	0	0.0	0

The 1944 Prep Squad. Front, L to R: Colvin, Manager Heubel, Rettger; Middle: Larson, Doyle, Mannarino; Assistant Coach Father Radzizsewski, DeLuca, Borczon, Carideo, Coach Father Kuziora.

HIGHLIGHTS:

- For the fourteenth consecutive and final year, all Cathedral Prep's home games were played at the Strong Vincent High School gymnasium.

- **Father William R. Hastings** replaced **Father Walter J. Conway** as Prep athletic director in 1943. Father Conway had served in the AD post since 1926. He was rewarded for his good work by being appointed pastor of Holy Rosary Parish on Erie's eastside. Father Conway passed away in 1979 and was inducted posthumously into the Cathedral Prep Athletic Hall of Fame in 2003.

Father William Hastings succeeded Father Conway as Prep AD.

- For the second consecutive year Prep broke its record for most losses in a season, as well as most consecutive losses (9). The 9-game losing streak is a Rambler record to this day.

The Orange & Black might have fared better if it weren't for the loss of star center **Ed Driscoll**, a senior, who had joined the U. S. Navy at the conclusion of his junior year. The Ramblers were left with but two seniors, **Richard "Red" Doyle** and **Bob Borczon**, and had to rely on a pair of talented sophomores, **Charlie Colvin** and **Jimmy Carideo**.

Senior Bob Borczon was a defensive ace.

Rugged center Ed Driscoll would have been a four-year letter winner had he not left for the U.S. Navy.

- The Ramblers were 6-4 to start the season, but lost 13 of last 14, including 9 straight City Series contests. While seven of the 17 losses were by 4 points or less, four of the victories were by a margin of only two points.

- Prep's balanced scoring attack set a team record for most points in a season.

- The ending of Prep's victory at Oil City St. Joe's (13-4) was not without controversy. With Prep down, 27-25, **Johnny DeLuca** was fouled underneath the hoop with four seconds remaining. Irish coach **Father Charles Hurley** vehemently disputed the call and drew a technical foul. DeLuca made two of three free throws to knot the score, with Prep retaining possession underneath. Regaining the leather on a pass from a teammate, DeLuca let go from the sidecourt and the final buzzer sounded as the ball was in the air. The sphere swished through the net, referee **Jack Komora** called it "good" and the Ramblers won, 29-27. The Venango County boys thought the final whistle had blown before DeLuca took his game-winning shot, causing some minor mayhem on the Strong Vincent hardwood.

- In the rematch, St. Joe's was determined to square accounts with the Ramblers, as it was the Hilltoppers' only loss of the season to that point. Prep could convert only 7 of 47 shots, while St. Joe's hit 10 of 41 in its 7-point triumph.

- Prep's only victory in the last 14 games was the 2-point squeaker over Conneaut (OH) (7-9). It was Prep's first meeting ever with the Trojans, though the schools had battled once in football to that point, in 1940. Conneaut won the rematch by 2 later in the season on the Trojan hardcourt.

- The Prep-Vincent game on January 18 raised $10.12 for the local infantile paralysis (polio) fund.

- In the one-point loss to Tech (6-11) on February 18, the Centaurs' **Ed Maras** sank two free throws with only 5 seconds remaining after being fouled in the act of shooting by **"Red" Doyle**.

- St. Marys Central Catholic's (20-5) win over Prep sealed an invitation for the Crusaders in the 8th annual Bishop Hafey/ K. of C. State Catholic Invitational Tournament in Williamsport. There St. Marys CC defeated Wilkes-Barre St. Mary's, but lost to Pittsburgh St. Basil's, 39-33, in a semifinal. St. Basil's then lost the state title game to Easton Catholic, 43-26. St. Marys also was the Erie Diocese' Class B entrant in the PCIAA tourney, where it defeated Renovo St. Joseph's, 48-29, then lost to Pittsburgh St. Joseph's, 37-22, in a Western regional.

- St. Marys Central Catholic was located in St. Marys, PA, and was a Class B Erie Diocesan entrant. The Crusaders entered Class A competition in 1956-57, giving Prep an annual PCIAA first round game. St. Marys CC closed following the 1962 season and that city's Catholic students were then served by Elk County Christian, now known as Elk County Catholic.

- **Sil Mannarino**, who thrilled crowds with many uncanny buckets, was the high scorer in the City Series basketball race for the entire season. He bested Academy's **Joe Pizzat** by 3 points and East's **Bill Biletnikoff** by 5.

- The final standings in City Series basketball were as follows:

First Half	W	L	Second Half	W	L
*East	8	1	*East	7	2
Academy	7	2	Academy	6	3
Prep	3	5	Tech	4	4
Vincent	2	6	Vincent	4	4
Tech	1	7	Prep	0	8

won both halves in playoffs for City Series title

- The March 7 game with East (20-9) was a tune-up for playoff competition for both squads, considered an exhibition, and, therefore, not counted in regular statistics. The Warriors ended losing to Sharon in the District 10 final, 48-34.

- East and Academy (19-7) tied for first in both halves. The Warriors clipped the Lions in playoff games for both titles, 32-31, and 51-40. Thus the two competed six times throughout the season, with three of the contests decided by one-point margins. East accounted for four of Academy's losses for the season.

- Cathedral Prep's two victories over Kanty Prep (2-4) marked the last time the rivals played, with the Ramblers holding a 14-8 series edge over the Eagles.

- At the season's conclusion junior **John Larson** transferred to Vincent, while **Jimmy Mead** followed his brother Ed's footsteps and transferred to Phillips Academy Andover (MA).

- After the one-point win over the heart-broken Ramblers in a first round PCIAA playoff battle, Johnstown Central Catholic (21-11) eliminated Pittsburgh North Catholic in the Western Final, 23-14, only to lose to Philadelphia Southeastern Catholic in the Class A Final, 38-20, before a crowd of 6,000 at Convention Hall in Philadelphia.

- **"Red" Doyle** and **Sil Mannarino** completed their careers as Prep's 3rd & 4th all-time leading scorers at the time. Doyle, just the second Rambler four-year letterman, entered the U. S. Army immediately upon graduation from Prep. Mannarino, who started every game as a sophomore and junior, would most likely have graduated as the Ramblers' all-time leading scorer had he not joined the Army Air Corps at the conclusion of the 1943-44 school year.

Three-year star Silvio Mannarino would have been Prep's all-time leading scorer had he not left for the Army AirCorps at the end of his junior year.

- Doyle and Mannarino played in the 2nd annual Coaches All-Star game held for the benefit of the Red Cross. The contest was won by the Coaches, 46-35, as **"Red" Cochrane** and **"PeeWee" Thomas** led the way with 12 and 11 points respectively. Mannarino and Doyle each scored two. Prepsters that played in the preliminary JV All-Star Game included **Jim White** and **Don Malmberg** for the East; and **Dick Roberts** and **Dick Rettger** for the West. The East won, 36-18.

- **Jim Mahoney** was an acknowledged football star who was named Prep's first 1st team Associated Press all-state athlete in 1944. He went on to play the gridiron sport at the University of Notre Dame. Mahoney was inducted into the Metro Erie Sports Hall of Fame in 1997 and the Cathedral Prep Athletic Hall of Fame in 2003.

- Following the 1944 football season, it was announced that head coach **Father Len Kuziora** had been appointed only to the teaching staff at Cathedral Prep. Father Kuziora had done a creditable job coaching the Rambler athletic teams, but as a priest with so many other more important responsibilities, he could not devote all his time to coaching as the mentors in the public schools could. Father Kuziora cheerfully carried the burden at Prep, though the going was rough and the results often disappointing. As much as "Father Len" enjoyed athletics, it was safe to say that it was a great relief to him to be relieved of his coaching duties at Prep. Also a stellar athlete at Prep and Holy Cross, Father Kuziora was inducted posthumously into the Cathedral Prep Athletic Hall of Fame in 2005.

1944 All-Opponent Team:

Pete Lipchick, Tech [Miami (FL), football]
Alex Litowkin, Tech [SMU, football]
Art "Deco" Schwindt, Academy
Joe Pizzat, Academy [Gannon]
Bill Biletnikoff, East [Slippery Rock, Gannon]
Jack "Kenny" Kenniston, Oil City St. Joe's
George "Ace" Flaherty, Oil City St. Joe's
Bob Horn, Vincent
Les Grabill, Academy
Al Klein, Academy
Tom Andrews, East
Bob Tevis, Tech
Joe Cerami, Vincent [Gannon, basketball & football]
Tom Coyne, Academy
Joe Zuravleff, Tech [Northwestern, football]
Bob Swanson, East
Joe Jablonski, East
Ed Maras, Tech
Bob Smith, Conneaut
Bill Manniko, Conneaut
Bobby Simbeck, St. Marys Central Catholic
Herb Straub, St. Marys Central Catholic
Eddie Seman, Johnstown Central Catholic

New Building, New Headmaster, New Coach, New Era!

1944-45 (13-8)

Coach: Florian "Sam" Yezerski
Asst. Coach: Rev. Leonard "Len" Kuziora
Captain: Johnny DeLuca
Manager: Jerry Kearney

Head coach Florian "Sam" Yezerski a former Notre Dame basketball star.

Date	PREP	Dec.			Loc.	High Scorer	Opponent
12/2	20	Lackawanna (NY) Our Lady of Victory	7	W	H	three w/ (5)	three w/ (2)
12/4	34	Corry	16	W	A	Horn & Oldach (6)	Darnofal (6)
12/19	17	East	31	L	H	Horn & Oldach (4)	Biletnikoff (10)
12/29	20	Academy	27	L	H	Oldach (11)	Coyne (12)
1/6	17	Technical	31	L	A	Trombetta (7)	Zuravleff (13)
1/11	24	Strong Vincent	32	L	H	Horn (8)	Herbstritt (12)
1/16	31	East	41	L	A	DeLuca (11)	Brasington (13)
1/18	32	Technical	29	W	H	Oldach (11)	Karuba (9)
1/25	36	Academy	24	W	A	DeLuca (16)	Coyne (10)
2/1	39	Strong Vincent	36	W	A	DeLuca & Oldach (15)	Horn (13)
2/3	33	St. Marys Central Catholic	21	W	H	DeLuca (14)	Straub (7)
2/6	33	East	23	W	N	DeLuca & Oldach (12)	Swanson (10)
2/8	22	Technical	31	L	N	Oldach (9)	Zuravleff & Ekimoff (9)
2/10	37	Corry	23	W	H	DeLuca (14)	Darnofal (9)
2/15	29	Academy	28	W	N	DeLuca (9)	Roach (11)
2/20	39	Strong Vincent	29	W	N	DeLuca (13)	Smart (10)
2/22	30	Alumni	28	W	H	Horn (12)	McCafferty (8)
2/24	33	Lackawanna (NY) Our Lady of Victory	31	W	A	DeLuca (17)	Dover (10)
3/2	29	St. Marys Central Catholic	35	L	A	White (9)	Mulcahy (14)
		P.C.I.A.A. STATE CATHOLIC H.S. TOURNAMENT					
3/12	37	Johnstown Central Catholic	22	W	H	DeLuca (18)	Pavlick & Seman (7)
3/17	22	Pittsburgh Central Catholic	30	L	A	DeLuca (13)	Haus (13)
	614 (29.2)		**575 (27.4)**				

Pos.	Player	Prior School	Class	G(GS)	FG	FT	Total	PPG	Career
C-G	Johnny DeLuca (#4)	St. Patrick's	Sr.	21(21)	74	59*	207	9.9	498*
G	Ray Oldakowski (Oldach) (#9)	St. Patrick's	Sr.	21(21)	60	26	146	7.0	355
F-C	Charlie Horn (#12)	Sacred Heart	Sr.	21(19)	39	16	94	4.5	94
F	Dick Trombetta (#8)	St. Andrew's	Soph.	18(15)	34	9	77	4.3	77
F-G	Jim White (#3)	St. Patrick's	Soph.	21(8)	19	11	49	2.3	51
G	Charlie Colvin (#6)	St. Peter's	Jr.	19(13)	5	5	15	0.8	31
F	Jim Carideo (#11)	Sacred Heart	Jr.	7(5)	3	4	10	1.4	25
F	Bob Ferretti (#7)	Holy Rosary	Jr.	10	3	3	9	0.9	12
G	Donald Malmberg	St. John's	Jr.	5(2)	1	1	3	0.6	3
G	Chuck Genck	St. Patrick's	Fr.	2	1	0	2	1.0	2
G	Jerry Bechtold (#5)	St. Peter's	Jr.	7(1)	0	0	0	0.0	0
C	Jim Minton (#10)	St. Peter's	Jr.	7	0	0	0	0.0	0
F	Ron Carroll (#11)	Sacred Heart	Sr.	3	0	0	0	0.0	0
C	John "Jack" Doyle	St. Patrick's	Jr.	2	0	0	0	0.0	0
F	Carmen "Joe" Romeo (#10)	St. Andrew's	Jr.	2	0	0	0	0.0	0
G	John Burger	St. Ann's	Jr.	1	0	0	0	0.0	0
C	Donald "Willie" Ester	St. Patrick's	Jr.	1	0	0	0	0.0	0

1945, the beginning of a new era for Prep. Front, L to R: Trombetta, Mgr. Kearney, Ferretti; Middle: White, Oldach, Horn, DeLuca; Back: Coach Yezerski, Bechtold, Colvin, Carroll, Romeo Asst. Coach Father Kuziora.

HIGHLIGHTS:

- New Cathedral Prep headmaster **Father Robert McDonald**, who stayed in the position from 1944 through 1972, announced the launching of an athletic program that will grow "slowly, sanely and wisely". The 1944-45 school year saw the opening of the beautiful new Prep school and the signaling of a new era.

Prep's star captains: Bob Knox (football) and John DeLuca (basketball).

- Father McDonald, a first generation Irishman, was a native of Titusville St. Titus Parish. A fine athlete in his own right, Father McDonald was 38 years old at the time and had been the Superintendant of Erie Diocesan Schools the previous three years. Thus began his long and distinguished 28-year reign as headmaster, with "Black Mac" being the determined and demanding leader of what was to become one of the leading educational and athletic schools in the nation.

- New head coach **Florian "Sam" Yezerski** was a native of Shamokin (PA). He received a basketball scholarship to the University of Notre Dame, and started for the Fighting Irish. Upon his graduation from ND, Yezerski played professionally in Lewistown (PA). Prior to coming to Prep, he taught and coached at Madrid (NY) High School and Lafayette College for the Army.

- Coach Yezerski led Prep to its first winning season in three years. The Ramblers were a mix of cagy veterans, with **John DeLuca** and **Ray Oldach**, blended with youth, including flashy sophomores **Jim White** and **Dick "Bomber" Trombetta**. Oldach was

also Prep's rugged First Team All-Scholastic fullback.

- Prep's 13 victories were the most for a Rambler squad since the 1929-30 season, when 15 were achieved under coach **Father Walter Conway**. Help came with the addition of senior transfer student **Charlie Horn**.

- Both **Charlie Horn** and junior **Charlie Colvin** were transfers from Pontifical College Josephinum, a seminary located on the outskirts of Columbus (OH).

- For the first time in the school's history, Prep actually played its home games at home. The brand new, "spacious" Cathedral Center court was inaugurated in Prep's season opener, the 20-7 football-like score over Lackawanna Our Lady of Victory. OLV was later named Father Baker High School after Buffalo's venerated **Father Nelson Baker**, and then later renamed Baker-Victory School. The two schools did not compete again until the 1969-70 season.

John DeLuca about to let a perfect hook shot fly as curly-haired Charlie Horn looks to help.

- Two of Prep's triumphs were over Corry (16-11), which joined Class A basketball and became a member of Section One beginning with the 1944-45 campaign. The Ramblers and the Beavers had not played since 1938.

- City Series play was reduced from two rounds of 8 games each to one round of 12. The third meeting with teams was always played on a neutral court. After 5 straight City losses, Prep countered with four straight wins, eventually capturing a surprising third place finish. Prep did beat rival Tech (17-3) once, though the Centaurs won the city championship, their first outright title in any sport.

- In Prep's 32-29 upset over eventual city champion Tech, the Ramblers came from a 15-2 deficit early in the second quarter. **Johnny DeLuca** scored the go-ahead bucket early in the fourth quarter, then **Ray Oldach** followed with a 2-pointer to extend the lead. Tech's 6'4" superstar **Joe Zuravleff** was held to three buckets and neither team scored in the final, frantic seven minutes. The Centaurs were 5-0 in city play at the time, while the Ramblers were 0-5.

- Prep's win over East (10-6) on February 6 was its first over the Warriors in 20 attempts.

- The final standings in City Series basketball were as follows:

	W	L
Tech	11	1
East	7	5
Prep	6	6
Academy	4	8
Vincent	2	10

- Prep's victory over St. Marys Central Catholic (29-4) was one of only two regular season losses hung on the Crusaders. St. Marys was 14-0 at the time. The Crusaders, the Class B champs of the Erie Diocese for the second straight season, made it to the Class B Western Final, where it bowed to Pittsburgh St. Casimir's, 43-32, at Duquesne University. St. Marys also finished third at the Knights of Columbus State Catholic Invitational in Williamsport.

- Prep's upset win over Johnstown Central Catholic (18-5) on the home floor in the PCIAA tourney was the first post-season triumph in the school's history. The Ramblers then lost in the Class A Western Final to Pittsburgh Central Catholic (27-4), a large all-male school in the Oakland section of Pittsburgh, its first loss in a string of 15 straight to a Pittsburgh team in the PCIAA's. That game was played at Pittsburgh's Southside Recreation Center. The Vikings then lost a 41-38 heartbreaker to Allentown Central Catholic in the Class A final at the Duquesne University gym.

- **Johnny DeLuca** broke **Herb Perry's** 15-year old Prep record for most free throws made in a season.

- Seniors **Johnny DeLuca** and **Ray Oldach** finished 2nd and 3rd respectively in City Series scoring, only behind Tech's Zuravleff. DeLuca and Oldach were

Johnny DeLuca, Prep's first First Team All-City performer. He went on to a stellar career at Canisius.

both selected to participate in the 3rd annual Coaches All-Star Game, but neither played because PCIAA action was still pending. Coach Yezerski did play in the contest and led all scorers with 19 in a losing cause, as the coaches were defeated by the city high school stars, 53-50.

- What was interesting about the all-star game is that it was the first time Tech coach **Ed Abramoski's** 3-point play idea was put in effect. Yezerski nailed one 3-pointer, thus making him the first person affiliated with Prep to score a "trey." Other coaches scoring 3-pointers included Academy's **Edmund "Pee-Wee" Thomas** and **Marion Lewis**; and Vincent's **"Red" Cochrane** and **Johnny Grasberger**, who nailed two. All-Stars tossing in 3-pointers included Academy's **Bill Roach** and East High's **Billy Biletnikoff** and **Pete Bechtos**.

- The city's coaches also played in a benefit game for the Red Cross, that a 38-35 victory over the Cathedral Prep Alumni. SV's **Vince Bell** led the coaches with 13 points while **Sil Mannarino** with 13 and **Sam Yezerski** with 9 led the Rambler old-timers. **Father Jim Sperry** and **Father Len Kuziora** only scored two points between them, but were reported to have played some solid defense and do some good rebounding for Prep.

- Three-year star **Johnny DeLuca** finished as Prep's all-time leading scorer (although just one bucket shy of being Prep's first to score 500 career points), then went on to star at Canisius College under coach **Joe Niland**. There he was team captain in 1950-51. DeLuca was inducted into the Metro Erie Sports Hall of Fame in 2005 and into the Cathedral Prep Hall of Fame posthumously in 2017.

- **Ray Oldach** finished as Prep's 5th all-time leading scorer and went on to star in football at Northwestern.

- 1945 was the first year the PIAA had "Class A" and "Class B" championships. The new ruling dictated that "Class B" teams were those with school enrollments of 400 or less. "Class A" schools included Erie's four public schools as well as new "A" classifications for Millcreek and Corry. Allentown won the state "Class A" title with a 40-38 verdict over Donora, while McAdoo won the "B" crown with a 52-28 win over District 10's Conneautville.

All-around athlete Ray Oldach. A rugged competitor, he went on to star in football at Northwestern.

1945 All-Opponent Team:

Bill Biletnikoff, East [Slippery Rock, Gannon]
Lee Kontis, East
Tom Coyne, Academy
Bill Roach, Academy
Joe Zuravleff, Tech [Northwestern, football]
Don Earl, Tech
Don Herbstritt, Vincent
Joe Cerami, Vincent [Gannon, basketball & football]
Chuck Brasington, East
Pete Karuba, Tech [Kentucky, Gannon, football]

Bob Swanson, East
Bob Horn, Vincent
Herb Straub, St. Marys Central Catholic
Joe Darnofal, Corry
Allan "Allie" Mulcahy, St. Marys Central Catholic
Eddie Seman, Johnstown Central Catholic
Bill Pavlick, Johnstown Central Catholic [Giants Class
    AA baseball, Erie Sailors]
George Jacobs, Pittsburgh Central Catholic
Francis "Fanny" Haus, Pgh. Central
    Catholic [Cardinals Class AAA baseball]

The beautiful, brand new Cathedral Preparatory School for Boys opened its doors in Fall, 1944.

Bishop Gannon with Prep's varsity and junior varsity basketball lettermen.

Yezerski Given the Axe by "Black Mac"!
1945-46 (14-9)

Coach: Florian "Sam" Yezerski
Captain: Charles "Charlie" Colvin
Manager: Jerry Kearney

Don "Dummer" Laird, Prep's popular 3-year star.

Date	PREP	Dec.		Loc.		High Scorer	Opponent
12/8	33	Alumni	11	W	H	Laird (14)	Carrick (6)
12/11	19	Academy	11	W	H	Hyziewicz & Trombetta (6)	Carr (5)
12/14	38	Bradford St. Bernard's	11	W	H	Laird (10)	Dwyer (5)
12/19	32	North East	7	W	H	Ferretti (9)	Grabowski (2)
12/21	31	Millcreek	20	W	A	Ferretti (7)	Davis & R. Hedderick (9)
12/29	32	Millcreek	27	W	H	Trombetta (11)	R. Hedderick (9)
1/3	29	Strong Vincent	36	L	H	Laird (11)	Smart (13)
1/5	21	St. Marys Central Catholic	19	W	H	Laird (9)	Nissell (8)
1/10	19	East	27	L	A	Trombetta (7)	Matulevich (9)
1/15	38	Technical	44	L	H	Laird (13)	Zuravleff (17)
1/19	26	Academy	22	W	A	UNREPORTED	
1/23	40	North East	22	W	A	Genck (13)	Greider (8)
1/25	48	Bradford St. Bernard's	21	W	A	Carideo (22)	Frisina & Camarco (6)
1/31	31	East	25	W	H	Trombetta (12)	Vommaro (11)
2/2	35	Technical	38	L	A	Carideo (12)	Ekimoff (15)
2/5	22	Strong Vincent	24	L	A	Laird (9)	Williams (7)
2/7	41	Technical	33	W	N	Trombetta (15)	Ekimoff (12)
2/14	47	Academy	31	W	N	Carideo (14)	Kehl & Carr (8)
2/19	24	East	30	L	N	White (10)	Bechtos (12)
2/21	39	Strong Vincent	43	L	N	Carideo (15)	Peterson (15)
3/1	24	St. Marys Central Catholic	44	L	A	White (11)	Nissell (18)
		P.C.I.A.A. STATE CATHOLIC H.S. TOURNAMENT					
3/7	33	Johnstown Central Catholic	32	W	A	Laird (9)	Seman (15)
3/14	33	Pittsburgh North Catholic	34	L	N	Laird & White (8)	Brennan (16)
	735* (32.0)		**612 (26.6)**				

Pos.	Player	Prior School	Class	G(GS)	FG	FT	Total	*PPG*	Career
F	Don Laird (#4)	St. Andrew	Soph.	23(23)	60	38	158	6.9	158
F	Dick "Dead Eye" Trombetta (#8)	St. Andrew	Jr.	23(23)	54	24	132	5.7	209
F-C	Jim "Cards" Carideo (#11)	Sacred Heart	Sr.	17(14)	50	19	119	7.0	144
G	Chuck Genck (#9)	St. Patrick's	Soph.	23(23)	40	33	113	4.9	115
G	Jim White (#3)	St. Patrick's	Jr.	23(23)	37	18	92	4.0	143
F	Bob "Emmett" Ferretti (#7)	Holy Rosary	Sr.	22	20	7	47	2.1	59
G	Charlie Colvin (#6)	St. Peter's	Sr.	17(2)	11	9	31	1.8	62
C-G	Ed Hyziewicz (Hunter) (#12)	St. Stan's	Jr.	12(7)	7	7	21	1.8	21
F	Dick Esser (#10)	St. Mary's	Jr.	5	2	1	5	1.0	5
G-F	Garrett "Gary" Orr (#17)	St. Peter's	Jr.	2	2	0	4	2.0	4
G	Jim Fuhrman	Sacred Heart	Jr.	3	2	0	4	1.3	4
F	Richard Roberts	Sacred Heart	Sr.	2	1	1	3	1.5	3
G	Bill DiPlacido	Sacred Heart	Soph.	1	1	0	2	2.0	2
F	Richard Regotti	Brockway	Jr.	1	1	0	2	2.0	2
F-C	Paul Murosky (#14)	St. John's	Jr.	2	0	0	0	0.0	0
G	Jack Earley	Sacred Heart	Jr.	1	0	0	0	0.0	0
G	Art Hilinski	St. Stan's	Fr.	1	0	0	0	0.0	0

1946 Prep Ramblers. Front, L to R: Trombetta, Fuhrman, Colvin, Murosky, Ferretti; Back: Carideo, Laird, White, Hyziewicz, Genck, Esser.

HIGHLIGHTS:

- **John J. "Joe" Connors**, highly successful mentor in both football and basketball at Oil City St. Joseph's, was named Cathedral Prep's new basketball coach. Several weeks later, however, he asked to be released from his contract, and headmaster **Father Robert McDonald** granted his request. **"Sam" Yezerski** stayed on for a second season as head coach.

- Prep's 14 victories was the most since the Ramblers recorded 15 wins in the 1929-30 season under coach **Father Walter Conway**. This was despite what was considered a poor fourth place finish in city competition. The Ramblers were considered young with juniors **Dick Trombetta** and **Jim White**; and sophomores **Chuck Genck** and leading scorer **Don Laird**. All four underclassmen started every game for the season. The lone senior starter was **Jim Carideo**, who often thrilled crowds with his "trick" shots.

Jim "Cards" Carideo thrilled crowds with fancy moves and trick shots.

- Prep renewed a rivalry that laid dormant since 1930 with two easy wins over Bradford St. Bernard's (17-11). The Bernies went on to win the 1946 Erie Diocesan Class B championship with a 34-30 playoff triumph over Clearfield St. Francis. St. Bernard's then defeated Loretto St. Francis Prep, 40-35, to gain a spot in the PCIAA Class B Western Final. There they lost, 39-23, to Pittsburgh St. Casimir, which won the state crown with a 38-34 verdict over Easton Catholic. Prep and St. Bernard's agreed to a home-and-home series through the 1950-51 campaign.

- Prep held North East to no field goals on December 19, the first time in nearly a dozen years in Erie, when Tech held Academy

to no field goals on February 20, 1934.

- City Series play was again one round of 12. The third meeting with teams was again played on a neutral court.

- The best wins of the season for Prep's young squad were a pair over Erie County League Class A champion and Section One champ Millcreek (15-7), and the 41-33 upset over repeat City Series champion Technical (17-7). Millcreek upset Tech, 35-27, in the S-I championship playoff, then lost to Warren (22-4) in the District 10 final, 39-27, before a sold out crowd of 1,200 at Edinboro State Teachers' College. The Dragons then ousted Pittsburgh Peabody before being humbled in the PIAA Western Final by Homestead, 44-13.

- Another nice win for Prep was the 2-point verdict over St. Marys Central Catholic (24-3). The Crusaders only other regular season loss was to Kane by one point, 27-26. St. Marys 20-point win over the Ramblers at season's end gave the Crusaders a bid to the 8-team Knights of Columbus State Catholic Invitational in Williamsport. There the Crusaders defeated Hazleton St. Gabriel's in first round action, but lost to eventual state runner-up Chester St. James, 41-25, in the semifinals.

- **Jim White** also sank a half-court desperation shot, presumably to tie the game, on February 5 at Vincent (13-8). Time, however, had officially elapsed, but the bedlam of noise in the Colonel gym made it impossible for any of the players to hear the final buzzer which sounded just seconds before White's shot. The shot was ruled "no good", and the Ramblers lost by two.

- The final standings in City Series basketball were as follows:

	W	**L**
Tech	10	2
East	7	5
Vincent	6	6
Prep	5	7
Academy	2	10

- The biggest play of the season was **Jimmy White's** looping set shot field goal just outside the foul circle with just four seconds left to play, before over 1,000 fans, at Johnstown in the PCIAA playoffs. That shot gave Prep a thrilling one-point victory over Central Catholic's Crimson Crushers (15-4). The Ramblers were then edged by one in the Western Final before 1,400 fans at East High on a hook shot from the foul line by North Catholic's **Dick Rauluk** with less than a minute remaining. That shot, the only bucket scored by Rauluk all evening, spoiled a great comeback by the Orange & Black, who were down by 12 midway in the third quarter. The Trojans considered that victory as the greatest in its school's history to that point. North Catholic (25-6), coached by legendary **Joe Thomas**, went on to win its second of six PCIAA Class A state titles with a 45-42 triumph over Allentown Central Catholic. The Trojans won it again in 1947, defeating Philadelphia St. Joseph's Prep, 43-37. Coach Thomas then moved onto Mineola (NY) Chaminade, where he coached football from 1948 to 1969, compiling a record of 120-47-7.

Charlie Colvin, team captain and three-year varsity man.

- North Catholic was located in a German neighborhood in the Troy Hill section of Pittsburgh, hence the nickname "Trojans." Founded in 1939 as a boys' school by the Marianist brothers, in conjunction with the Diocese of Pittsburgh, the school became co-educational in 1974. North Catholic won four more PCIAA playoff games against Prep and finished 5-1 against Prep in PCIAA play, the Ramblers finally defeating the Trojans in 1970. North Catholic moved further north to Cranberry Township in 2013 and is now known as "Bishop Wuerl North Catholic High School."

- No Ramblers were picked by the local sportswriters to participate in the 4th annual Coaches All-Star Game, as Prep was still in the PCIAA playoff hunt when the game contested. Freshman **Art Hilinski** and sophomores **Joe Luteran, Bill DiPlacido** and **Johnny Harabedian** all played in a preliminary East-West JV All-Star contest, won by the East, 24-20.

- Coach **"Sam" Yezerski** was suddenly dismissed after a two-year record of 27-17, with school officials citing that "a coach must be a 'multi-sport' coach and Yezerski showed no promise in football." **Monsignor Robert McDonald** gave Yezerski his pink slip on April 12, in the morning after the school's all-sports banquet. Petitions for reinstatement were discussed, but Yezerski moved on to Kanty Prep where he became the successful head coach in football, basketball and baseball.

1946 All-Opponent Team:

Ray Hedderick, Millcreek [Penn State, football]
Jerry Kohl, Millcreek
Art Patterson, Millcreek
Ford Smart, Vincent
Melvin "Sam" Nissell, St. Marys Central Catholic [Providence]
Joe Matulevich, East
Chuck Detzel, East
Joe Zuravleff, Tech [Northwestern, football]
Len Ekimoff, Tech [South Carolina]
George Greider, North East
Herbie Tufts, Vincent
Len Vommaro, East
Len Kubiak, Tech [Duquesne, football]
Pete Bechtos, East
Ron Peterson, Vincent
Jim Mullard, Vincent
Allan "Allie" Mulcahy, St. Marys Central Catholic
"Slim" Jim Schlimm, St. Marys Central Catholic [Providence]
Eddie "Sam" Seman, Johnstown Central Catholic
Jimmy Brennan, North Catholic
Dick Rauluk, North Catholic

Team captain Charlie Colvin passing the torch to 1946-47 captain Jim White.

Ramblers Win First City Series Championship!
1946-47 (19-6)

Coach: Walter C. "Walt" Strosser
Captain: Jim White
Manager: Ray Hooper

Walt Strosser, coach of Prep's first basketball and football city champions. He was a charter inductee to the Prep Hall of Fame.

Date	PREP			Dec.	Loc.	High Scorer	Opponent
12/10	35	Dunkirk (NY)	18	W	H	Genck (11)	Formanowicz (8)
12/13	40	Cleveland (OH) St. Ignatius	23	W	H	Genck (15)	Dilling (12)
12/19	42	Millcreek	26	W	H	Genck (9)	Lytle (9)
12/21	42	Dunkirk (NY) St. Mary's	16	W	A	Laird & Hyziewicz (10)	Panowicz (6)
12/28	47	Millcreek	33	W	A	White (12)	Lytle (9)
1/2	32	Technical	24	W	H	Laird (10)	Zuravleff (8)
1/3	44	Cleveland (OH) Cathedral Latin	31	W	H	Laird (15)	Hasselo (10)
1/9	38	Academy	25	W	H	Genck (12)	Kehl (8)
1/10	48	Bradford St. Bernard's	30	W	A	Genck (10)	Gleason (10)
1/11	25	St. Marys Central Catholic	27	L	A	Genck (11)	Straub (9)
1/16	31	East	28	W	H	Laird (8)	Ohman (8)
1/23	26	Strong Vincent	35	L	N	Laird (7)	Busch & Tufts (10)
1/24	54	Dunkirk (NY) St. Mary's	19	W	H	Hilinski (12)	Panowicz (11)
1/28	52	Youngstown (OH) Ursuline	38	W	H	Laird (20)	Rossi (17)
2/1	46	Rochester (NY) Aquinas	36	W	H	Trombetta (15)	Dimino (11)
2/4	48	Academy	36	W	A	Trombetta (20)	Kehl (12)
2/8	38	St. Marys Central Catholic	44	L	H	Genck (12)	Nissel (12)
2/13	35	East	52	L	A	Genck (13)	Detzel (20)
2/14	51	Bradford St. Bernard's	26	W	H	Hilinski (11)	Pecora (14)
2/18	39	Technical	34	W	A	Hilinski (15)	Zuravleff & Ruggiero (13)
2/20	39	Strong Vincent	35	W	N	Hilinski (15)	Williams (10)
2/21	29	Sharpsville	45	L	A	White (8)	Weber (19)
2/25	38	Ashtabula (OH)	35	W	A	Genck (16)	DeChurch (10)
2/28	43	Alumni	33	W	H	Hilinski (11)	Schickler (10)
		P.C.I.A.A. STATE CATHOLIC H.S. TOURNAMENT					
3/6	38	Johnstown Central Catholic	47	L	N	Hilinski (11)	Leslie (14)
	1000* (40.0)		**796* (31.8)**				

Pos.	Player	Prior School	Class	G(GS)	FG	FT	Total	PPG	Career
C	Chuck Genck (#9)	St. Patrick's	Jr.	25*(25*)	75	54	204	8.2	319
G	Jim White (#13)	St. Patrick's	Sr.	25*(25*)	48	42	138	5.5	281
F	Art Hilinski (#7)	St. Stan's	Soph.	24 (9)	64	37	135	5.6	135
F	Don Laird (#5)	St. Andrew's	Jr.	25*(24)	44	44	132	5.3	290
G-F	Ed Hyziewicz (Hunter) (#4)	St. Stan's	Sr.	25*(17)	47	36	130	5.2	151
F	Dick Trombetta (#8)	St. Andrew's	Sr.	23 (18)	48	9	105	4.6	314
G-F	Joe Luteran (#12)	St. Jos. Home	Jr.	18 (5)	18	4	40	2.2	40
G	Paul Murosky (#14)	St. John's	Sr.	5	8	5	21	4.2	21
F	John Harabedian (#3)	St. Peter's	Jr.	12 (2)	8	5	21	1.8	21
C	Jack Flanagan (#15)	Sacred Heart	Jr.	6	5	2	12	2.0	12
G-C	Bill DiPlacido (#11)	Sacred Heart	Jr.	7	3	3	9	1.3	11
G	Hank Glowacki (#6)	St. Stan's	Jr.	5	2	4	8	1.6	8
G-C	Garrett "Gary" Orr (#17)	St. Peter's	Sr.	3	3	1	7	2.3	11
C-G	Dick Esser (#10)	St. Mary's	Sr.	2	0	2	2	1.0	7

Cathedral Prep's first City Champions (1947). Front, L to R: Trombetta, Laird, Hyziewicz, Mgr. Hooper; Back: Luteran, Glowacki, DiPlacido, Esser, Flanagan, Murosky, Orr, Harabedian, Coach Strosser.

HIGHLIGHTS:

- **Walter "Walt" Strosser**, assistant football and basketball coach, was named Cathedral Prep's new hoop coach. Strosser was the former Greenville St. Michael's and St. Vincent College all-around athlete who went on to become one of Erie's greatest football coaches at Prep (1948-56) and Tech Memorial (1959-65).

Bishop John Mark Gannon enjoys another Prep victory, as his nephew, Father Jim Gannon, grins with approval.

- **Father James Gannon**, a nephew of **Bishop John Mark Gannon**, succeeded **Father William Hastings** and began a long and colorful tenure as athletic director at Cathedral Prep. Father Jim was a 1930 graduate of Prep and played on **Father Walter Conway's** first two football teams. He had been recently discharged as a full lieutenant and chaplain with the U. S. Marines. Later **"Monsignor" Jim Gannon**, he remained as Prep A.D. through 1961.

- Father Hastings, later **"Monsignor" William Hastings**, later became Vicar General of the Erie Diocese

Father Jim Gannon, Prep's colorful athletic director (1946-61).

as well as pastor at Oil City St. Stephen's and pastor at Holy Rosary Parish in Erie, succeeding Father Conway.

- Prep started the season with a nice win over first-time opponent Dunkirk (10-5), a team that had just swamped Academy, 35-25. The Ramblers proceeded to a school record 9 straight victories before losing to St. Marys Central Catholic.

- Prep used balanced scoring to win its first City Series basketball championship ever, the Ramblers' first city crown in a major sport. As a result the Ninth Street school received two awards for its accomplishments: the Exchange Club trophy, presented to the annual winner; and the Board of Education Trophy, which would be retired by the first school to receive it three times. **Walt Strosser** later coached the Rambler football squad to its first city crown in 1949.

- The 19 Rambler victories broke an all-time team record of 15 set in the 1929-30 season under coach **Father Walter Conway**. This was also the first Prep team to reach 1,000 points in a year. The season's 25 games was also a team record for most played. **Jim White** and big **Chuck Genck** started every contest for the Orange & Black.

Junior big man Chuck Genck led the city scoring.

- City Series play was reduced to one double-round robin of 8 games. Games were played on the home team's floors, with the exception of both Prep-Vincent

Prep's starting five: Hilinski, Genck, White, Laird, Harabedian; with Coach Strosser.

contests, which were played at neutral East to accommodate turn-away crowds. Over 1200 packed into East's auditorium for the first Prep-SV battle, with another 1,000 being turned away at the door.

- Prep's battles with arch-rival Technical (10-9) were always sold-out, action-packed, heated affairs with plenty of rough play. The intense, second Ramblers-Centaurs clash had a total of 38 personal fouls, with a pair of Prepsters fouling out and with four Techsters finishing with four fouls apiece. Even before that Prep's **Chuck Genck** and Tech's **Ed Palkovic** were ejected in the first quarter by referee **Gene Munson**, for "throwing hips at one another."

- The final standings in City Series basketball were as follows:

	W	L
Prep	6	2
Tech	5	3
Vincent	5	3
East	3	5
Academy	1	7

- Other than Prep's showing in city strife, its best wins of the season were a pair over Erie County League champion Millcreek (17-4), and the victories over Catholic school rivals St. Ignatius (8-7), Cathedral Latin (5-9), St. Bernard's (15-7), Ursuline (14-5) and Aquinas (8-8).

- Prep renewed the rivalry with Cathedral Latin which laid dormant for a dozen years, as well as the St. Ignatius series which hadn't been played since 1933. Of note is that Latin was coached by **Al Hook**, who later coached Gannon College to a record of 12-13 in 1950-51.

- Youngstown Ursuline, founded in 1905 and located on the North Side near Youngstown State, was an all-female academy until 1930 when it became co-ed. Ursuline operated in the Youngstown City Series, which also included Woodrow Wilson, Chaney, Rayen, North, South and East. Ursuline and Prep competed just four more times in basketball, ending the series in 1954. The series was renewed in 2015-16 after a 62-year lapse.

- Rochester Aquinas Institute was at the time an all-male school known as the "Little Notre Dame of the East" in athletics, particularly football. Founded in 1902, Aquinas opened its doors to female students in 1982. The Lil' Irish and Prep competed consistently in basketball through the 1950's and in football through the 1960's.

- One of Prep's best wins of the year was the three-point thriller at Lake Shore League champion Ashtabula (17-8). The Ramblers,

down 19-9 at the half, outscored the Panthers, 29-16, in the final two frames to take the verdict. Ashtabula, which finished its regular season at just 11-7 (including 0-5 versus Erie teams), breezed through four foes to win its sectional title, including a 40-32 upset over Cleveland Heights in the final. The Panthers then shocked Barberton, 46-32, and Cuyahoga Falls, 32-27, to reach Ohio's Class A (large school) final four (of 213) in Columbus. Midnight fell on Ashtabula with a 36-32 semifinal loss to Middletown, which then defeated East Liverpool, 47-29, to win Ohio's 1947 state title.

- Another new opponent was powerful Section III champion Sharpsville, which would never agree to play the Ramblers anywhere but on its own home court.

- The biggest disappointments were a pair of close losses to St. Marys Central Catholic (27-3) and the first round PCIAA ouster to Johnstown Central Catholic (18-6), led by **LeRoy Leslie**, later of Notre Dame fame and Johnstown CC's head coach from 1959 through 1964. Johnstown then lost to the eventual state champ, Pittsburgh North Catholic, 35-23. St. Marys CC opted for the 11th (and last) annual K. of C. /Bishop William J. Hafey state tournament in Williamsport, suffering its only loss of the

Sophomore Art Hilinski came on strong the second half of the season.

season to a high school team (its other two losses were to a college combine) in the final to Pittsburgh Central Catholic (18-4), 43-34. The Crusaders upset two-time defending champ Reading Central Catholic, 37-28, then defeated Ambridge St. Veronica's, 39-34, to get to the championship tilt.

- Prep and St. Marys Central Catholic halted regular season relations because of what was considered "bad blood" between them. Fistfights between players and fans of the two rivals had become commonplace. The Ramblers and Crusaders did not meet again for another decade, until the 1956-57 season.

- The Ramblers went 12-1 on their home floor at the Cathedral Center, losing only to St. Marys Central Catholic.

- Team captain **Jim White**, Prep's mainspring in its successful drive for the city crown, was honored as a First Team All-Scholastic choice by the *Erie Dispatch-Herald*. **Chuck Genck**, who led the City Series in scoring, and **Art Hilinski** (5th in city scoring, only

Dick Trombetta, nicknamed "Bomber" or "Dead-Eye" for his uncanny outside shooting ability.

a sophomore), who came on strong at the end, were Second Team choices. The *Erie Daily Times* named White, Genck and Hilinski to its 10-man Scholastic All-Star Team.

- **Jim White** (12 points), **Dick Trombetta** and **Ed Hyziewicz** all participated in the 5th annual Coaches All-Star Game, which again pitted the city's high school stars against various coaches from the city schools.

- **Dick Trombetta**, also known as "Bomber" or "Dead Eye" because of his long-range shooting ability, went on to star at Alliance College.

- **Jim White**, another in a line of Rambler stars from St. Patrick's grade school, went on to star at Gannon College. He was the first Gannon cager to start every game (99) in his four-year career and was named the Golden Knights' "Athlete of the Year" in 1951. He was enshrined into the Gannon Hall of Fame in 1984 and the Cathedral Prep Athletic Hall of Fame, posthumously, in 2015.

- **Ed Hyziewicz**, the "speedy blond forward" according to the *Ashtabula (OH) Beacon*, also went on to play at Gannon College.

- The professional Basketball Association of America was established for the 1946-47 season. After its third season in 1948-49, the BAA merged with the National Basketball League to form the National Basketball Association.

Hall-of-Famer Jim White ran the show for Prep's first City Champs. He later was the first Gannon College hoopster to start every game for four years.

Ed Hunter (Hyziewicz), Prep's "speedy blond forward."

1947 All-Opponent Team:

"Slim" Jim Dilling, St. Ignatius [Holy Cross]

Jim Lytle, Millcreek

Herm Hedderick, Millcreek [Canisius; NBA New York Knickerbockers]

Phil Zuravleff, Tech [Princeton]

Ed Palkovic, Tech [Gannon, football]

Albert Hasselo, Cathedral Latin [Ohio State, football]

Dick Kehl, Academy

Fran Gleason, Bradford St. Bernard's

Jackie Busch, Vincent (3rd team all-state)

Jim Panowicz, Dunkirk St. Mary's

Gene Rossi, Youngstown Ursuline

Gene Sundberg, Academy

Melvin "Sam" Nissel, St. Marys Central Catholic [Providence]

"Slim" Jim Schlimm, St. Marys Central Catholic [Providence]

Tom Bauer, St. Marys Central Catholic

Chuck Detzel, East

Gene Pecora, Bradford St. Bernard's

Jim Ruggiero, Tech

John "Jake" Williams, Vincent [Gannon]

John Weber, Sharpsville

John "Jabby" Ellison, Sharpsville [Indians Class B baseball]

Ramon Peet, Ashtabula [Cubs Class C baseball, Reds Class B]

Joe DeChurch, Ashtabula

Bobby Micklos, Johnstown Central Catholic

Eddie "Sam" Seman, Johnstown Central Catholic

LeRoy "Axle" Leslie, Johnstown Central Catholic [Notre Dame All-American]

Prep Smacked Down!

1947-48 (6-13)

Coach: Walter C. "Walt" Strosser
Captains: Chuck Genck, Don Laird
Manager: Ray Hooper

Rambler stars Jack Konkol and Don Fessler are tickled to find they are not on Sister Anna Marie's academic ineligibility list.

Date	PREP			Dec.	Loc.	High Scorer	Opponent
12/13	34	Cleveland (OH) St. Ignatius	42	L	H	Hilinski (13)	Dilling (17)
12/16	29	Technical	33	L	H	Luteran (8)	Ruggiero (19)
12/18	23	Corry	30	L	A	Hilinski (7)	Sturdevant (8)
12/20	33	Warren	31	W	H	Crotty (9)	Nelson (11)
12/30	37	Cleveland (OH) Cathedral Latin	45	L	H	Laird & Hilinski (7)	Theisen (12)
1/2	35	Cleveland (OH) St. Ignatius	52	L	A	Luteran (10)	Dilling (15)
1/6	30	Academy	31	L	H	Laird & Hilinski (10)	Kehl (15)
1/10	39	Bradford St. Bernard's	37	W	H	Konkol & Hilinski (9)	Camarco (11)
1/13	46	Strong Vincent	34	W	A	Hilinski (18)	Berg (11)
1/15	42	East	29	W	H	Hilinski (10)	Bernatowicz (13)
1/20	29	Technical	44	L	A	Konkol (8)	Zuravleff (18)
1/24		Ashtabula (OH) (POSTPONED—POOR CONDITION OF ROADS)		H			
1/28		Corry (POSTPONED—TRAVEL TO ROCHESTER)		H			
1/30	27	Rochester (NY) Aquinas	39	L	A	Crotty & Luteran (6)	Dimino (16)
2/5	31	Academy	53	L	A	Harabedian (9)	Kehl (19)
2/7	28	Bradford St. Bernard's	29	L	A	Hilinski (10)	Vinelli (11)
2/12	48	Strong Vincent	28	W	H	Laird (26)	Berg (8)
2/14	49	Corry	30	W	H	Hilinski (15)	Morgan (8)
2/17	30	Ashtabula (OH)	37	L	H	Hilinski (10)	Gephart (10)
2/19	36	East	38	L	A	Hilinski (9)	Demyanovich (12)
		P.C.I.A.A. STATE CATHOLIC H.S. TOURNAMENT					
3/6	37	Johnstown Central Catholic	59*	L	A	Crotty (13)	Leslie (28*)
	663 (34.9)		**721 (37.9)**				

Pos.	Player	Prior School	Class	G(GS)	FG	FT	Total	*PPG*	Career
C	Art Hilinski (#7)	St. Stan's	Jr.	19(18)	60	36	156	8.4	291
F	Don "Dummer" Laird (#5)	St. Andrew's	Sr.	18(13)	36	37	109	6.1	399
G	Jack Crotty (#4)	St. Andrew's	Soph.	19(18)	35	19	89	4.7	89
F	Johnny "Harpo" Harabedian (#3)	St. Peter's	Sr.	18(13)	23	35	81	4.5	102
G	Chuck Genck (#17)	St. Patrick's	Sr.	19(13)	20	13	53	2.8	372
F	Joe Luteran (#12)	St. Jos. Home	Sr.	14(10)	18	16	52	3.7	92
G	Jack Konkol (#16)	St. Stan's	Soph.	16(2)	19	8	46	2.9	46
F	Jim O'Brien (#6)	St. John's	Jr.	11(1)	12	7	31	2.8	31
G	Jack "Flannels" Flanagan (#13)	Sacred Heart	Sr.	13(5)	9	8	26	2.0	38
C	Art Middleton (#8)	St. Peter's	Jr.	7	4	1	9	1.3	9
G	Hank Glowacki (#18)	St. Stan's	Sr.	8(1)	2	1	5	0.6	8
F	Don Fessler (#14)	Holy Rosary	Jr.	6	1	0	2	0.3	2
F	Bob Young (#10)	St. Joseph's	Jr.	5	1	0	2	0.4	2
G	Jack Krahe (#15)	St. Joseph's	Jr.	9	1	0	2	0.2	2
C	Jerry Blackwood (#9)	Harborcreek	Jr.	4	0	0	0	0.0	0
F	Bill "Dippy" DiPlacido (#11)	Sacred Heart	Sr.	2	0	0	0	0.0	11

The 1948 Prep Ramblers. Kneeling, L to R: Konkol, Middleton; Second Row: Luteran, O'Brien, Crotty, Coach Strosser, Harabedian, Laird, Krahe; Back: Glowacki, Flanagan, Genck, Hilinski, Blackwood, Mgr. Hooper.

HIGHLIGHTS:

- **Walt Strosser's** second and final year as coach was a disappointment, despite the fact Prep had several returning veterans. The Ramblers suffered from lack of height and an inability to hold early leads. A football injury to star **Chuck Genck**, the city's leading scorer in 1946-47, also slowed him down considerably.

- The final standings in City Series basketball were as follows:

	W	L
Academy	7	1
Tech	6	2
Prep	3	5
Vincent	2	6
East	2	6

- The best moments of the season included **Don Laird's** 26-point performance (9 FGs and 8 FTs) against Strong Vincent (7-9), the most scored by a Rambler since **Herbert Perry** broke the record with 28 points against Wesleyville on December 17, 1929. Coach Strosser removed Laird from the lineup with four minutes remaining, and did not relent to the Rambler faithful chanting loudly for "Dummer's" return. Others were **Joe Luteran's** late shot before the buzzer to beat Bradford St. Bernard's (15-5); and the come-from-behind upset victory over Warren (27-4), the eventual District 10 champion.

- Warren went on a 22-game winning streak after its loss to Prep before losing to Pittsburgh Westinghouse, 42-41, in the PIAA Western Final. The Ramblers and the Dragons did not play again until they met thrice in 1973-74. Warren didn't win another D-10 title until 1983.

- After Prep suffered a pair of defeats to St. Ignatius (10-3), the Ramblers and Wildcats did not meet again for 47 years, until the 1994-95 season.

- Prep's victory over Corry (12-11) started a string of 22 straight against the Beavers through 2016. That game was reset from January 28 to February 14 to permit the Ramblers an evening off before embarking for Rochester Aquinas on January 30.

- Prep's loss to Cathedral Latin (9-5) was the only time all season the Lions played outside the city of Cleveland. The Ramblers outplayed the Lions for three quarters, but couldn't contend with 6'7" **Dick Theisen** in the final frame.

- Prep had a pair of close battles with Bradford St. Bernard's. Also dubbed the "Ramblers," St. Bernard's was coached by none other than **Richard "Dick" Detzel**, who became the Prep Ramblers coach the following season, 1948-49, through 1957.

- Ashtabula (16-4), which defeated Prep on the Rambler floor, won its third consecutive Lake Shore League title but was upset by Cleveland Heights, 44-32, in the first round of its sectional playoffs. The Ramblers and Panthers have never played again.

- The biggest disappointments were the City Series losses, particularly to kiddie corner rival Technical (10-8); to East (5-14) in the regular season finale; and the first round PCIAA ouster, after a 2 ½ week layoff, to Johnstown Central Catholic (21-3). The Crimson Crushers' and their star **LeRoy Leslie**, later of the Fighting Irish of Notre Dame, broke 23-year old opponents' records with 59 and 28 points respectively. The Johnstown squad eventually lost in the final to Allentown Central Catholic, 45-41, before 4,000 fans in Allentown. Leslie went on to coach the Crushers for five years, winning PCIAA state titles in 1960 and 1963.

- Though Prep did not play St. Marys Central Catholic (22-6) after four straight years of competition, the Crusaders made

HANS, OUR MASCOT

Hans, Prep's popular canine mascot.

it to the state PCIAA Class B final in 1948. There they lost to York Catholic, 44-42, on a controversial shot from beyond half court at the buzzer in a game played at Penn State University. The game ended with a 45-foot toss by York Catholic's **Bill Campbell** with the time remaining under dispute. The ball went into the basket, but the time keeper and referee both said the shot occurred after time had elapsed. They were overruled by the umpire who said that the goal did count. According to the *St. Marys Daily Press*: "Both teams were kept on the court as fans swarmed on the playing floor and fists began flying as partisans from both teams argued pro and con." Then, after more than an hour of confusion, the score was certified as being final. A protest never materialized as spring had arrived, high schools were beginning baseball, leaves were on the trees, soon graduation lists were being posted in newspapers in St. Marys and York, and no word ever arrived from the PCIAA. Even though the scoreboard on the wall at State College was never changed and read 42-42, the record books credit York Catholic (28-2) with a 44-42 win and the 1948 State Championship.

- Academy's (18-5) leap from last place in 1946-47 to the City Series title in 1947-48 was remarkable. It was the Lions' last city crown until 1974, a 26-year break.

- In a season-ending basketball extravaganza at the Prep gym, the Cathedral Prep Faculty defeated the Prep Dads' Club, 25-24. **Father Tom Geddes**, Rambler wrestling and boxing coach, was the hero for the faculty, sinking a field goal with 10 seconds remaining that brought the winners from behind. **Joe Filipkowski** and **Dave Ziegler** were the stars for the Dads.

- **Art Hilinski** emerged as a true star his junior season. Hilinski was the big noise as a grade school player at St. Stanislaus, once scoring a record 47 points in a game. His 7th and 8th grade teams won the first Erie Parochial League hoop titles ever for St. Stan's, beginning a string of seven straight for the Eagles (1944-1950) under

"Harpo" Harabedian, Prep's All-City fire wagon.

coach **Father Joseph Radziszewski**. "Father Joe" was also Prep's first JV basketball coach (1941).

- The *Erie Dispatch-Herald* and the *Erie Daily Times* sportwriters together selected the All-City All-Star squad, which included Prep's **Don Laird** and **Johnny Harabedian**. Laird and Harabedian (led all with 10 points) played in the 6th annual Coaches All-Star Game, while Prep's 1947 head football coach **Cyril "Cy" James** and Coach Strosser (7 points) also participated in the contest, won by the All-Stars over the Coaches, 47-29.

- **Walt Strosser** continued to coach basketball at Prep, guiding the junior varsity from 1948 through 1957. He further went on to guide the Rambler football squads through their "Golden Era", retiring with the highest winning percentage (58-15-6, .795) of any Erie coach at the time. Following his Prep career, Strosser became a successful football coach at Tech Memorial, and later that school's principal. One of Erie's iconic coaches, he was inducted into the Metropolitan Erie Sports Hall of Fame in 1988 and was a charter inductee into the Cathedral Prep Athletic Hall of Fame in 1992.

Chuck Genck led the city in scoring as a junior, but was hampered by a football injury as a senior.

- Three-year stars **Don Laird** and **Chuck Genck** finished as Prep's 4th and 5th all-time leading scorers, with 399 and 372 points respectively. Genck went on to star at Gannon College.

1948 All-Opponent Team:

Jim Dilling, St. Ignatius [Holy Cross]
Jim Ruggiero, Tech
Ray Barczak, Tech
Don Sturdivant, Corry
Chuck Geertson, Corry [Gannon, football]
Gail Nelson, Warren [Gannon]
Dick Theisen, Cathedral Latin [Duquesne]
Ed Harmon, St. Ignatius
Dick Kehl, Academy (3rd team all-state)
Carl "Dizzy" Bernatowicz, East
Fran Gleason, Bradford St. Bernard's
Phil Zuravleff, Tech [Princeton]
Andrew Dimino, Rochester Aquinas
Jim Rigney, Rochester Aquinas
Holland Morgan, Corry
Frank Frisina, Corry
Gene Gephart, Ashtabula [DePauw, football & basketball]
Nick Dellerba, Ashtabula
Delbert DeVaughn, Ashtabula
Billy Demyanovich, East
LeRoy "Axle" Leslie, Johnstown Central Cath. [Notre Dame All-American]

Dick Detzel and Prep's Golden Era!

1948-49 (19-6)

Coach: Richard "Dick" Detzel
Captain: Art Hilinski
Manager: Norb Gannon

Richard "Dick" Detzel came from Bradford St. Bernard's to take over the Prep helm.

Date	PREP			Dec.	Loc.	High Scorer	Opponen
12/3	40	Albion	25	W	H	Hilinski (16)	Patton (10)
12/7	46	Girard	21	W	H	Hilinski (12)	Frey (7)
12/13	42	Alumni	33	W	H	Hilinski (12)	Hyziewicz (10)
12/17	37	Cleveland (OH) Cathedral Latin	46	L	A	Krahe (13)	Manning (20)
12/21	39	Youngstown (OH) Ursuline	38	W	H	Hilinski (18)	Blaski (14)
12/27	45	Oil City St. Joseph's	15	W	H	Hilinski (11)	Stubler (6)
12/31	39	Conneaut (OH)	26	W	H	Crotty (15)	Hietikko (8)
1/4	48	Millcreek	31	W	H	Hilinski (21)	Komora & Brown (12)
1/6	39	East	25	W	A	Krahe (11)	Martin (7)
1/7	40	Bradford St. Bernard's	49	L	A	Hilinski (12)	Camarco (21)
1/11	43	Academy	34	W	H	Hilinski (12)	Whiteman (6)
1/12	46	Girard	47	L	A	Hilinski (14)	Frey (22)
1/14	38	Technical	32	W	H	Crotty (12)	Ruggiero (9)
1/18	51	Corry	38	W	A	Hilinski & Middleton (13)	Elston (16)
1/20	34	Strong Vincent	40	L	H	Hilinski (16)	Davis (12)
1/27	46	Millcreek	31	W	N	Hilinski (18)	Brown (12)
1/28	45	Bradford St. Bernard's	24	W	H	Middleton (17)	Camarco (10)
2/1	42	East	28	W	H	Middleton (14)	Demyanovich (11)
2/3	39	Academy	37	W	A	Hilinski (23)	Cacchione (16)
2/4	65	Oil City St. Joseph's	36	W	A	Middleton (22)	Tobin (12)
2/8	39	Technical	33	W	A	Middleton (14)	Borowicz (13)
2/10	49	Corry	33	W	H	Middleton (27)	Elston (13)
2/15	48	Strong Vincent	40	W	A	Crotty (13)	Davis (20)
2/19	30	Sharpsville	51	L	A	Hilinski (10)	Parker (17)

P.C.I.A.A. STATE CATHOLIC H.S. TOURNAMENT

Date	PREP			Dec.	Loc.	High Scorer	Opponen
2/24	39	Pittsburgh Central Catholic	43	L	A	Hilinski (15)	Pikunas (15)
	1069* (42.8*)		**869* (34.2)**				

Pos.	Player	Prior School	Class	G(GS)	FG	FT	Total	*PPG*	Career
F	Art Hilinski (#7)	St. Stan's	Sr.	25(24)	112*	69*-112	293*	11.7	584*
C	Art Middleton (#8)	St. Peter's	Sr.	25(25)	84	52-114*	220	8.8	229
G	Jack Crotty (#4)	St. Andrew's	Jr.	25(23)	67	30-65	164	6.6	253
G-F	Jack Krahe (#15)	St. Joseph's	Sr.	24(22)	61	30-74	152	6.3	154
F-G	Len Cyterski (#14)	Holy Trinity	Soph.	25(24)	39	20-50	98	3.9	98
G	Jack Konkol (#16)	St. Stan's	Jr.	24(1)	21	12-25	47	1.9	93
F	Jack Dalton (#3)	St. Andrew's	Jr.	20(1)	9	6-10	24	1.2	24
C	Jerry Blackwood(#9)	Harborcreek	Sr.	12(3)	5	8-22	18	1.5	18
F	Don Guerrein (#13)	St. Andrew	Jr.	13(1)	7	2-10	16	1.2	16
F	Jim O'Brien (#6)	St. John's	Sr.	15(1)	5	0-5	10	0.7	41
F	Mike Carey (#5)	St. Ann's	Jr.	4	2	1-4	5	1.3	5
G	Bob Fries (#17)	St. Peter's	Jr.	5	1	1-4	3	0.6	3
G	Bob Held (#12)	St. Ann's	Jr.	5	1	0-0	2	0.4	2

Prep's 1949 City Champs, L to R: Coach Detzel, Carey, Held, O'Brien, Fries, Dalton, Middleton, Blackwood, Hilinski, Krahe, Konkol, Cyterski, Crotty, Mgr. Gannon.

Coach Detzel accepts the 1949 City Series championship trophy from Jack Komora.

HIGHLIGHTS:

- Cathedral Prep overcame a pre-season "dark horse" tag and handily regained the City Series championship under first-year mentor **Richard "Dick" Detzel**, the former East High and St. Vincent's College star. Before coming to Prep, Detzel was a successful head coach in basketball and football at Bradford St. Bernard's. His 1947-48 hoop squad was good enough to hand the Ramblers a defeat in Bradford, 29-28.

- 1948-49 was the last season the City Series basketball games were played at the respective schools on a home-and-home basis. The exception was Tech, which had always played its home games at the Downtown YMCA. The second Millcreek game was played at Roosevelt Junior High.

- Several rules changes came into effect for the 1948-49 season, including: 1) Elimination of the rule making a substitute report to the referee before entering the game; 2) All jump balls were to be held in the nearest center circle or foul circle; 3) A player on whom a foul was called was expected to raise his hand, although there would be no penalty for failure to do so; and 4) Teams may go near the bench to talk to their coach during timeouts or intermissions between quarters.

- From 1945 through 1948, the top-ranked City Series public school played the better of Corry or Millcreek for the "Section One" championship in the first round of PIAA District 10 playoffs. In 1948-49 a new Section One league setup included Corry and Millcreek along with Academy, East, Vincent and Tech, therefore obviating the need for a Section One playoff within the District 10 tournament. A "Big Seven" was then formed, combining Cathedral Prep with the Section One teams.

- The final standings in City Series and "Combined City Series/Section I" (Big Seven) basketball were as follows:

	W	L		W	L
Prep	7	1	Prep	11	1
Tech	4	4	East	8	4
East	4	4	Tech	7	5
Vincent	3	5	Vincent	7	5
Academy	2	6	Academy	5	7
			Corry	3	9
			Millcreek	1	11

- The best moments of the season included the consistent scoring punch of **Art Hilinski**, the first Rambler to average in double figures since **Ted Morasky** in 1941; the exciting one-point verdict over Youngstown Ursuline (14-11) on Hilinski's midcourt shot with 35 seconds left; the big upset in the first Tech (16-7) game; the thrilling come-from-behind victory in the second Academy (8-13) contest; as well as 6'3" **Art Middleton's** 27-point performance (7 FGs, 13-23 FTs) against Corry (12-11), just one shy of the Prep record set by **Herbert Perry** in 1929.

Three-year star Art Hilinski retired as Prep's all-time leading scorer. The rugged competitor played football at Gannon College.

- Prep never played Albion (9-10) again after its season-opening win over the Redskins. Albion later merged with Cranesville and West Springfield, former Erie County League schools, to form Northwestern High School ("Wildcats") in 1958-59. Prep won the series over Albion, 5-0, and has never competed with Northwestern in athletics.

- Prep followed with a victory over Girard (14-10), but lost by one to the Yellow Jackets later in the season on the road. Girard has had success in basketball over the years, winning PIAA Class AA (formerly Class B) titles in 1988 and 1990. Girard did not play Prep in basketball again until the 2014-15 season, 6 ½ decades later!

- The disappointments were the lone city setback to underdog Vincent (11-6); the second straight loss to Cathedral Latin (12-5); the loss to **Dick Detzel's** former St. Bernard's (17-5) squad; the upset by Girard, its first win over the Ramblers since 1932; the pasting Prep took at District 10 champion Sharpsville (23-5), from Mercer County; and the PCIAA Western Semifinal ouster to eventual Class A state champion Pittsburgh Central Catholic (23-1).

- The St. Bernard's team tied for the Erie Diocesan League Eastern Division title, then defeated St. Mary's Central Catholic, 37-24, for the Eastern crown. The Ramblers then lost to Western Division winner Kanty Prep (15-6), 40-38, in the EDL championship tilt. Kanty then defeated Renovo St. Joseph's, 38-28, in inter-diocesan play, but was walloped by Pittsburgh St. Justin's in the Western Regional title clash, 40-29. St. Justin's then triumphed over Scranton St. Patrick's, 51-43, to win the PCIAA Class B state championship.

All-City center Art Middleton became a full star at Gannon College.

All-around athlete Jack Krahe went on to play football at Gannon.

- Pittsburgh Central Catholic's only loss was to Charleroi, 55-36, in a game that saw the Vikings playing with only four players on the court in the final minutes of the game, as the six other teammates had all fouled out!

- **Art Hilinski** and **Art Middleton** were honored as First Team All Scholastic choices by the *Erie Dispatch-Herald* and the *Lake Shore Visitor*. **Jack Krahe** was a Second Team choice in both papers, while **Jack Crotty** was named First Team by the *Visitor* and Second Team by the *Dispatch*. The *Erie Daily Times* listed Hilinski, Middleton and Crotty among its 11-man All-Star Team.

Jack Crotty gives maximum effort against Central Catholic at Duquesne Gardens.

Middleton (#8) plays solid defense as Hilinski (#7) and Cyterski (#14) help.

- The Prep-Central Catholic game was played before a crowd of 2,819 at the Duquesne Gardens and broadcast over WWSW radio in Pittsburgh. It is believed to be the first radio broadcast of any Prep sporting event, save the Prep-Wesleyville football game of 1929. The Ramblers lost the hotly contested battle by four, and were but 9-of-24 from the free throw line. The victorious Vikings then defeated Allenton Central Catholic in the finals, 54-42, at Pitt Pavilion, underneath Pitt Stadium. It was the Central Catholic's first and only state crown. Central made a PIAA Class AAAA finals appearance in 1988.

- Hilinski (7 points), Middleton (9) and Krahe (6) all played in the 7th annual Coaches All-Star Game. Prep's JV coach **Walt Strosser** (3 points) and Coach Detzel (6) also participated.

- Three-year star **Art Hilinski** retired as Prep's all-time leading scorer with 584 career points, and was the first Rambler to cross the 500-point plateau. A three-sport star at Prep, Hilinski also broke the single season records for FGs, FTs and points scored.

Rambler champions, L to R: Crotty, Krahe, Middleton, Hilinski, Cyterski and Coach Detzel.

- Hilinski received further recognition being named Second Team to the Northwestern Pennsylvania Second Annual All-Star basketball team by the named area's scribes. Notorious as a unanimous First Team selection was Franklin's **Ted Marchibroda**, later of St. Bonaventure, University of Detroit and NFL playing and coaching fame.

- Big **Art Middleton** went on to star at Gannon College, where he was named "Athlete of the Year" in 1953. **Art Hilinski** and **Jack Krahe**, both gridiron stars at Prep, played football at Gannon.

- The National Basketball League (NBL), formed in 1937, and the Basketball Association of America (BAA), formed in 1946, officially combined on August 3, 1949 to form the National Basketball Association (NBA), the foremost professional league in the history of basketball. The only two teams from the initial league that have remained in the same city and under the same name are the Boston Celtics and New York Knickerbockers.

1949 All-Opponent Team:

    John Patton, Albion
    Richard Manning, Cathedral Latin
    Dick Theisen, Cathedral Latin [Duquesne]
    Jack Blaski, Youngstown Ursuline [Youngstown State]
    Jim Hietikko, Conneaut [Ohio State, football]
    Jack Komora, Millcreek
    Cassius "Cash" Elston, Corry [Allegheny]
    Jim Davis, Vincent [Gannon]
    Ed Bordonaro, Vincent
    Gil Brown, Millcreek
    Patsy Camarco, Bradford St. Bernard's [Gannon, football]
    Larry Frey, Girard
    Jim Ruggiero, Tech
    Bill Demyanovich, East
    Tommy Cacchione, Academy
    Ed Borowicz, Tech
    Lee Parker, Sharpsville [Allegheny]
    Bill Dunder, Sharpsville [Thiel]
    William Powderly, Pittsburgh Central Catholic
    Tom Pikunas, Pittsburgh Central Catholic [Slippery Rock]
    Bernie Flowers, Tech [Purdue, football]

Coach Detzel's first starting five, L to R: Cyterski, Krahe, Middleton, Konkol, Hilinski.

The 1950's

The Cathedral Prep Ramblers hoist Coach Dick Detzel while celebrating their second consecutive state championship (1954).

City Series, Big 7 Logjam!

1949-50 (12-7)

Coach: Richard "Dick" Detzel
Captain: Jack Crotty
Manager: Norb Gannon

All-City guard Jack Crotty was in Prep's starting lineup three straight years.

Date	PREP			Dec.	Loc.	High Scorer	Opponent
11/30	37	North East	18	W	A	Hatkevich (9)	McAdoo (5)
12/9	43	Bradford St. Bernard's	35	W	A	Crotty (14)	Pecora (13)
12/17	42	Youngstown (OH) Ursuline	60*	L	A	Crotty (20)	Beck (19)
12/20	48	Conneaut (OH)	50	L	A	Cyterski(13)	Dombroski (23)
12/27	36	Cleveland (OH) Cathedral Latin	45	L	H	Cyterski(10)	Egan (22)
1/3	38	Technical	43	L	N	Hatkevich & Konkol (8)	Polagyi (13)
1/5	40	Millcreek	21	W	N	Hatkevich (18)	Jackson (6)
1/13	25	East	39	L	N	Hatkevich (10)	Bernatowicz (11)
1/17	46	Strong Vincent	41	W	N	Crotty (16)	Williams (16)
1/24	49	Corry	45	W	A	Hatkevich (13)	Spaulding (19)
1/26	53	Academy	40	W	N	Konkol (14)	Smoot (12)
2/2	34	Technical	47	L	N	Cyterski, Crotty, Hatkevich (7)	Morosky (14)
2/4	49	Bradford St. Bernard's	35	W	H	Cyterski (17)	Pecora (16)
2/7	48	Millcreek	27	W	N	Crotty & Konkol (11)	Komora (9)
2/14	48	East	45	W	N	Crotty & Konkol (12)	Latina (11)
2/16	55	Strong Vincent	43	W	N	Cyterski (20)	Shaw (10)
2/21	45	Corry	24	W	N	Hatkevich (12)	Pitts (9)
2/24	36	Academy	32	W	N	Cyterski (11)	Lindsey (9)
		P.C.I.A.A. STATE CATHOLIC H.S. TOURNAMENT					
3/14	37	Pittsburgh Central Catholic	42	L	H	Crotty (14)	Reamy (15)
	809 (42.6)		**732 (38.5)**				

Pos.	Player	Prior School	Class	G(GS)	FG	FT	Total	*PPG*	Career
G	Jack Crotty (#4)	St. Andrew's	Sr.	19(18)	66	40-66	172	9.1	425
F	Len Cyterski (#11)	Holy Trinity	Jr.	18(18)	52	39-66	143	7.9	241
C	Al Hatkevich (#16)	St. Patrick's	Soph.	19(19)	56	30-66	142	7.5	142
G-F	Jack Konkol (#9)	St. Stan's	Sr.	18(17)	40	44-71	124	6.9	217
F	Don Wolf (#15)	Sacred Heart	Soph.	19(2)	24	10-22	58	3.1	58
F	Jack "Mohawk" Dalton (#3)	St. Andrew's	Sr.	9(8)	24	4-12	52	5.8	76
F	Don Guerrein (#7)	St. Andrew's	Sr.	11(6)	16	6-21	38	3.5	54
G	Norm Zmyslinski(#10)	St. Peter's	Soph.	14(3)	10	4-15	24	1.7	24
G	Tom Eberlein (#6)	St. Patrick's	Jr.	12(2)	5	6-11	16	1.3	16
G	Dick Nolan (#8)	Toledo (OH) CC	Jr.	9	5	5-8	15	1.7	15
F	Bob Held (#12)	St. Ann's	Sr.	9(2)	6	0-3	12	1.3	14
F	Caesar Montevecchio (#5)	Roosevelt	Soph.	7	2	3-4	7	1.0	7
F	Nick Bruno (#14)	Sacred Heart	Soph.	5	1	1-2	3	0.6	3
C	Len "Stretch" Szczypinski (#17)	St. Stan's	Soph.	2	1	0-0	2	1.0	2
G	George Palmer (#13)	St. Joseph's	Jr.	3	0	0-0	0	0.0	0
G	Jim Dentel (#17)	St. Andrew's	Jr.	0	0	0-0	0	0.0	0
	Opponent goal				1	1	0-0	2	

Prep's 1950 squad tied with Tech and East for the city title. L to R: Coach Detzel, Held, Guerrein, Crotty, Dalton, Wolf, Dentel, Hatkevich, Nolan, Konkol, Palmer, Cyterski, Bruno, Eberlein, Montevecchio.

Hall-of-Famer Jack Konkol, about to bank one in.

Crotty lets go a perfect hook shot.

HIGHLIGHTS:

- Cathedral Prep went on a late-season tear to earn a City Series championship tie with Tech and East and a mythical "Big Seven" tie with East in **Dick Detzel's** second year at the helm. There was no provision for a playoff at the time. The Ramblers presented a nice blend of youth with experienced seniors **Don Guerrein, Bob Held** and the "three **Jacks**"—**Konkol, Dalton** and leading scorer **Crotty**.

- All City Series games, for the first time, were played at Gannon College's new Auditorium, colloquially called "the Audi". No longer were the league clashes played in the schools' respective gymnasiums. The only games played at the Prep gym were the Cathedral Latin and St. Bernard's contests. All other independent regular season contests were played on the road.

- Prep started the season with a convincing win over hard-luck North East (15-6), which had the best overall record in the Erie County League. The Grapepickers tied for the first half crown in the ECL, only to lose in a playoff to Girard, 39-38. North East also tied for the second half honors, then lost the playoff to Lawrence Park, 42-33.

- The St. Bernard's (6-14) lineup included sophomore **Don "Bud" Raabe**, the future head football coach at Cathedral Prep (1966-67).

- Youngstown Ursuline (16-7) became the first team to score 60 points against Prep. The Fighting Irish finished its season with three wins in the Northeast Ohio Tournament, before succumbing to Rayen, 51-38.

- Cathedral Latin (14-4) finished the season with its best record ever in the then-38 year history of its basketball program.

- Though unknown at the time, Prep's win over Millcreek (8-10) on February 7 was the 250th victory in Rambler history.

- The best moments of the season included winning 9 of the last 10 regular season games and the fine play of several underclassmen, including **Len Cyterski, Al Hatkevich** and **Don Wolf.** Cyterski finished 8th and Hatkevich 9th in the Big Seven regular season scoring race, while **Jack Crotty** came in place number 6.

- The biggest disappointments were the City Series losses to neighborhood rival Tech (14-9) and the first round loss at the Audi (after a 2 ½ week layoff) to Pittsburgh Central Catholic (19-6) in the PCIAA tourney. Central made it all the way to the PCIAA state final where it lost to Reading Central Catholic, 58-41.

- The final standings in City Series and "Big Seven" basketball leagues were as follows:

	W	L		W	L
Prep	5	3	Prep	9	3
Tech	5	3	East	9	3
East	5	3	Tech	8	4
Academy	4	4	Academy	8	4
Vincent	1	7	Vincent	3	9
			Millcreek	3	9
			Corry	2	10

- The Gannon College Faculty defeated the Cathedral Prep Faculty, 30-29, in a post-season matchup at the Gannon

Auditorium. Former Prep hoopsters **Lou Tullio** and **Father Fred Nies** led the Golden Knights' faculty with 9 and 8 points respectively, while **Father Ted Carter** and **Father Jim Sperry** each scored 9 markers to lead the Rambler faculty.

- **Jack Crotty** was honored as a First Team All Scholastic choice by both the *Erie Dispatch-Herald* and *Erie Daily Times*. **Len Cyterski** and **Jack Konkol** were Second Team choices, while **Al Hatkevich** made Honorable Mention. Crotty was also awarded the Jewish War Veterans Trophy as the best player in the city.

- **Jack Konkol**, an acknowledged football star, went on to star at Purdue in the gridiron sport. He was also the 1950 PCIAA discus champion, and was inducted into the Cathedral Prep Athletic Hall of Fame in 1993.

- **Jim Dentel** did not play basketball his senior year, but as a fastballing hurler later spent three years with the Brooklyn Dodgers organization. The Dentel family, from St. Andrew's parish, later moved to Pittsburgh where younger brother **Bob Dentel** became an all-sports star for Central Catholic. Bob played football at Miami (FL) where he started at center and was drafted by the AFL's Boston Patriots and NFL's Chicago Bears, though he did not play.

- **Tom Gola** of Philadelphia LaSalle (later of LaSalle College, Philadelphia/San Francisco Warriors and New York Knickerbockers fame) and **Mike DePaul** of Reading Central Catholic were the first private or Catholic school players ever to be named First Team Pennsylvania All-State by the Associated Press.

- The Basketball Association of America adopted the name National Basketball Association and merged with the National Basketball League to form the NBA for the 1949-50 season.

1950 All-Opponent Team:

Gordon Maas, North East
"Jumping Joe" Concilla, North East
Bill Pecora, Bradford St. Bernard's
Frank Beck, Youngstown Ursuline [Youngstown St.]
Jack Blaski, Youngstown Ursuline [Youngstown St.]
Bill Dombroski, Conneaut
Johnny Egan, Cathedral Latin (All-Catholic)
Don Polagyi, Tech (hm all-state) [Cincinnati]
Carl "Dizzy" Bernatowicz, East
Jimmy Smoot, Academy
Al Morosky, Tech
Dick "Skinny" Skonieczka, East [Gannon, football]
Sammy Williams, Vincent (hm all-state)
Doug Spaulding, Corry
Tom Reamy, Pittsburgh Central Catholic (hm all-state)

Tom Gola, LaSalle College H. S. '50.

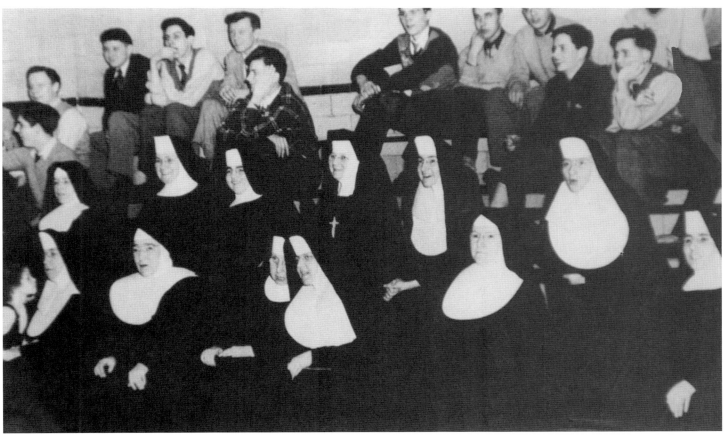

The faculty's good Sisters, thoroughly enjoying the destruction of another opponent.

Another 3-Way Tie for the City Crown!

All-around Hall-of-Fame athlete Lenny Cyterski later became a legendary Prep coach.

1950-51 (15-5)

Coach: Richard "Dick" Detzel
Captain: Len Cyterski
Manager: Jim Niederriter

Date	PREP			Dec.	Loc.	High Scorer	Opponent
12/12	75	North East	35	W	A	Hatkevich (15)	Karsh (15)
12/15	63	Bradford St. Bernard's	35	W	A	Hatkevich (13)	Yerdon (15)
12/19	40	Alumni	36	W	H	Cyterski (15)	Genck (15)
12/22	65	North East	18	W	H	Hatkevich (16)	Henderson (6)
12/27	37	Cleveland (OH) Cathedral Latin	51	L	A	Nolan (9)	Hollis (18)
12/29	58	East	37	W	N	Hatkevich (19)	Morris (11)
1/2	45	Millcreek	29	W	N	Zmyslinski (12)	Wigham (7)
1/12	36	Strong Vincent	38	L	N	Eberlein (8)	Williams (13)
1/16	52	Corry	33	W	N	Hatkevich (22)	Elchinski (9)
1/19	61	Technical	60*	W	N	Hatkevich (23)	Riazzi (27)
1/21	46	Academy	29	W	N	Hatkevich (12)	Infield (10)
1/30	31	East	50	L	N	Hatkevich (11)	Morris (17)
2/6	42	Strong Vincent	30	W	N	Wolf (14)	Williams (15)
2/9	51	Sharpsville	49	W	A	Cyterski(15)	Timmerman (13)
2/16	42	Technical	33	W	N	Hatkevich (14)	Riazzi (13)
2/20	56	Corry	38	W	N	Hatkevich (12)	Spaulding (12)
2/27	36	Academy	44	L	N	Cyterski & Hatkevich (12)	King (14)
3/1	48	Millcreek	38	W	N	Hatkevich (17)	Thompson (11)
3/2	48	Bradford St. Bernard's	30	W	H	Cyterski (14)	Raabe (14)
	P.C.I.A.A. STATE CATHOLIC H.S. TOURNAMENT						
3/5	50	Johnstown Central Catholic	53	L	H	Hatkevich (17)	Nathanic (15)
	934 (49.1)		**736 (38.7)**				

Pos.	Player	Prior School	Class	G(GS)	FG	FT	Total	*PPG*	Career
C	Al Hatkevich (#16)	St. Patrick's	Jr.	20(20)	97	67	261	13.1*	403
G	Len Cyterski (#13)	Holy Trinity	Sr.	20(20)	77	38	192	9.6	433
F	Len Tomczak (#3)	St. Stan's	Soph.	20(19)	49	27	125	6.3	125
F	Don Wolf (#15)	Sacred Heart	Jr.	20(19)	44	27	115	5.8	173
G	Norm Zmyslinski (#10)	St. Peter's	Jr.	19(16)	40	22	102	5.4	126
G	Ralph Malina (#14)	Wilson	Jr.	13(3)	17	12	46	3.5	46
G-F	Tom Eberlein (#6)	St. Patrick's	Sr.	15(2)	12	9	33	2.4	82
G	Caesar Montevecchio (#5)	Roosevelt	Jr.	9	13	3	29	3.2	36
C-G	Dick Nolan (#15)	Toledo (OH) CC	Sr.	8	7	11	25	3.2	40
G	Joe Peplinski (#11)	St. Ann's	Jr.	8(1)	10	1	21	2.6	21
F	Charles Maxwell (#7)	Sacred Heart	Jr.	9	6	4	16	1.8	16
F	Len "Stretch" Szczypinski (#17)	St. Stan's	Jr.	4	4	2	10	2.5	12
F	Nick Bruno (#8)	Sacred Heart	Jr.	4	0	1	1	0.3	4

The 1951 Prep Ramblers tied with Tech and Academy for the city diadem. L to R: Coach Detzel, Szczypinski, Maxwell, Peplinski, Hatkevich, Nolan, Malina, Cyterski, Zmyslinski, Eberlein, Bruno, Tomczak, Montevecchio.

HIGHLIGHTS:

- Cathedral Prep again earned a three-way tie for the well-balanced City Series championship in **Dick Detzel's** third year at the helm, this time with Technical and Academy. Again there was no provision for a playoff.

- All City Series contests, Big Seven games and the PCIAA elimination scrap were played at the Gannon Auditorium, with the exception of the second Millcreek contest, which was staged at East High. The Ramblers continued to play their independent home contests in the Prep gym.

- The final standings in City Series and "Big Seven" basketball were as follows:

	W	L		W	L
Prep	5	3	Prep	9	3
Tech	5	3	Tech	9	3
Academy	5	3	Academy	8	4
East	3	5	Vincent	6	6
Vincent	2	6	East	5	7
			Millcreek	4	8
			Corry	1	11

- The three-year try for Corry (5-18) in the Big Seven was not successful as the league records of the Beavers went from 3-9, to 2-10, to 1-11. Corry officials decided to rejoin the Class B Erie County League the following season.

- One big highlight of the season was Prep's two-point road win over District 10 champion Sharpsville (16-12). The Blue Devils upset a strong Meadville team in the D-10 final, 40-39.

- Other highlights of the season included the consistent scoring of **Al Hatkevich**, who broke the school record for points per game; the twin victories over Section One champ Tech (16-6), particularly in the controversial first battle when the Orange & Black overcame a 15-point third quarter deficit; and the fine showing against powerful Johnstown Central Catholic (27-0) in the PCIAA tourney.

- Prep walloped Bradford St. Bernard's (9-9) twice during the season. It was the last time the two schools which shared the nickname "Ramblers" ever competed. On the other hand, Prep began a series with Bradford High, beginning with the 1951-52 campaign. Prep finished on the long end of the series over the Bernies, 14 games to 3. St. Bernard's, a parish school that opened in 1885, closed following the 1961-62 school year. Bradford Central Christian opened in 1962 and served the Bradford area until its closure in 2000.

- The two pastings Prep handed its old Class B rival North East (6-16) were the last times the Ramblers and Grapepickers competed in basketball.

- Hatkevich finished third in the Big Seven regular season scoring race, while **Len Cyterski** finished 8th and **Len Tomczak** 9th.

- The biggest disappointments for the Ramblers were the City Series losses, particularly to the spoiler Academy Lions (10-10); a 4th straight loss to the Cathedral Latin Lions (14-3); and the 5th straight first round loss in the PCIAA tourney. Prep headmaster **Father Robert McDonald** was so peeved with the Johnstown PCIAA loss and exchanged words with Coach Detzel following the game. That argument resulted in Coach Detzel actually resigning his basketball and baseball coaching positions after the disagreements between the two. "Black Mac" flatly told Detzel he was not satisfied with his work and Detzel felt he had no choice but to quit. The sudden resignation stunned Erie's fans and was a choice subject of conversation not only about town, but across the state as well. It was the first time in Erie's long history of sports that a coach had abruptly resigned because of differences with the head of a school. Coaches simply did not resign in the middle of a

A pensive-looking Coach Detzel felt he had no choice but to resign after facing the wrath of Msgr. McDonald.

term, especially in the first year of a five-year contract. Days later harmony was restored and the pair reached a complete understanding while ironing out the difficulties which led to the resignation. Detzel resumed his duties at the school and did not report to the General Electric on the following Monday morning as he said he was going to do.

- Among Johnstown Central Catholic's regular season victims were District 6 champ Johnstown Public High and WPIAL titlist Farrell, which made it to the PIAA final before losing to Allentown, 66-55. After Prep, the Crimson Crushers defeated Pittsburgh Central Catholic in the PCIAA Western Final, 42-39. **Jack Twyman**, later an NBA star with the Rochester/Cincinnati Royals, and who appeared in 6 NBA All-Star games, led Pittsburgh Central Catholic with 10 points. Johnstown Central Catholic finished undefeated while winning its first of four state titles, ousting defending champ, Reading Central Catholic, 50-48, in the finals. Reading CC had beaten PIAA champ Allentown during the regular season, 56-54.

- The 1951 PCIAA state title was controversial. On the court, Johnstown Catholic won 50-48 at the new Johnstown War Memorial Auditorium, n/k/a War Memorial Arena, with over 5,000 fans in attendance. According to PCIAA rules, the state championship game each year rotated between the East and the West. The East had three Dioceses: Allentown, Scranton, and Harrisburg. The West also had three Dioceses: Erie, Pittsburgh, and Altoona/Johnstown. In 1950, the game was played in the East and Reading CC was the winner. Therefore, the 1951 game was to be played in the West. In 1948, the PCIAA passed a rule stating that "championship games were to be played on neutral floors." Johnstown CC announced that the game would be played at War Memorial, the problem being that even though it was not its home court, the Crushers had played 12 games there that season. Reading CC filed a written protest of that decision, which was taken up by the 18 member PCIAA Executive Board. The Board had 3 members from each Diocese: 9 from the East and 9 from the West. They split 9-9 on accepting or rejecting the protest. That put the decision into the hands of **Father Thomas J. Quigley** of Pittsburgh, the Chairman of the Executive Board. He ruled in favor of playing the game at the War Memorial Arena. Through the wrankling, the game was delayed from March 20 to April 2, which gave Crusher star **Ronnie Nathanic** a chance to get off his crutches and guard **Dick Osmar** time to mend a broken hand. The final result was a Johnstown victory, which Reading fans complained about for years.

- Johnstown Central Catholic had a remarkable senior cast. As freshmen they went 10-0 and as a JV squad went 24-0. As the varsity team in their junior year they had 17 consecutive wins before losing a game, and finished the season with a record of 26-3. This unit compiled 51 consecutive wins before losing in its junior year and compiled a four-year record of 87-3. Two of the three losses were by only one point. As a sidenote, Crimson Crusher coach **Joe Majer** was a classmate of Prep's **Dick Detzel** at St. Vincent's College.

- **Al Hatkevich** and **Len Cyterski** were honored as First Team All-Scholastic choices by the *Erie Daily Times* and the *Erie Dispatch-Herald*. **Norm Zmyslinski** was a Second Team choice for both papers, while **Dick Nolan** and **Tom Eberlein** both played in the Coaches All-Star game. Prep's coaches also participated.

- Hatkevich was also named Second Team on the 4th Annual All-Northwestern Pennsylvania basketball team selected by a poll of 13 area sportswriters. Cyterski was an Honorable Mention choice, as was a future Prep basketball mentor—**Dick Fox** of Linesville!

- Three-year star **Len Cyterski** retired as one of Prep's all-time leading scorers with 433 career points, and later went on to star at Gannon College after first attending Notre Dame as a football recruit. "Mr. Cy" returned to Prep in 1958 to teach English and coach JV football, JV basketball and varsity baseball. Highly successful in coaching as well, Cyterski was inducted into the Metropolitan Erie Sports Hall of Fame in 1991 and was a charter member of the Cathedral Prep Athletic Hall of Fame in 1992.

Five defenders attempt to stop Len Cyterski without success.

- 1951 was the first year the PIAA had a "Class C" championship. The new ruling dictated that "Class C" teams were those with school enrollments of 250 or less. District 10's Fredonia won the first state Class C title with a 49-43 verdict over Mount Joy. The Vocats also won the 1955 state Class C crown with a 50-44 verdict over Freeland.

1951 All-Opponent Team:

Chuck Yerdon, Bradford St. Bernard's
Johnny Hollis, Cathedral Latin [Case Tech]
Fred "Sina" Morris, East
Sammy Williams, Vincent
Carmen Riazzi, Tech [Dayton]
Don Polagyi, Tech [Cincinnati]
Fred Infield, Academy [Fenn]
Dick Timmerman, Sharpsville [Youngstown St.]
Doug Spaulding, Corry
Don Raabe, Bradford St. Bernard's [St. Bonaventure]
Ed Pavlick, Johnstown Central Catholic [Pitt]
Joe Resutek, Johnstown Central Catholic [Pitt]
Ronny Nathanic, Johnstown Central Catholic
    (2nd team all-state) [Seton Hall]

Zmyslinski looks on as Wolf goes up with a one-hander.

Headmaster Msgr. Robert McDonald, a/k/a "Black Mac," happily checks the scoreboard as his Ramblers pound another opponent.

Three Straight 3-Way City Series Title Ties!

1951-52 (12-6)

Coach: Richard "Dick" Detzel
Captain: Al Hatkevich
Manager: James Latimer

Al Hatkevich's 37 points against Tech stood as a Prep record for 16 years.

Date	PREP			Dec.	Loc.	High Scorer	Opponent
12/7	38	Bradford	36	W	H	Malina (17)	M. Goodman (15)
12/10	64	Greenville St. Michael's	51	W	H	Hatkevich (20)	Judge & B. Giardina (15)
12/21	47	East	49	L	N	Malina (18)	Cabeloff (14)
12/22	52	Cleveland (OH) Cathedral Latin	41	W	H	Zmyslinski (15)	Zielinski (13)
12/28	53	Youngstown (OH) Ursuline	46	W	A	Malina (18)	Ochman (12)
12/29	45	Greenville St. Michael's	51	L	A	Malina (19)	B. Giardina (15)
1/4	44	Strong Vincent	50	L	N	Hatkevich (16)	Wainwright (22)
1/11	50	Cleveland (OH) Benedictine	38	W	A	Hatkevich (18)	Weber (10)
1/18	41	Millcreek	34	W	N	Hatkevich (10)	Werner (14)
1/22	67	Technical	53	W	N	Hatkevich (37*)	Riazzi (15)
1/25	46	Academy	40	W	N	Fahey (10)	Price (14)
1/29	59	Millcreek	48	W	N	Hatkevich (25)	LeJeal (20)
2/1	56	East	30	W	N	Hatkevich (17)	Watral (8)
2/5	47	Bradford	54	L	A	Fahey (19)	Bizzaro (14)
2/15	50	Strong Vincent	40	W	N	Fahey (20)	Wainwright (11)
2/26	57	Technical	48	W	N	Hatkevich (21)	Riazzi (20)
2/29	44	Academy	47	L	N	Tomczak (13)	Becker (14)
	P.C.I.A.A. STATE CATHOLIC H.S. TOURNAMENT						
3/15	37	Pittsburgh Central Catholic	38	L	A	Tomczak (12)	Quinlan (9)
	897 (49.8*)		**794 (44.1*)**				

Pos.	Player	Prior School	Class	G(GS)	FG	FT	Total	PPG	Career
C-F	Al "Hacker" Hatkevich (#16)	St. Patrick's	Sr.	18(18)	90	61	241	13.4*	644*
F	Ralph Malina (#9/7)	Wilson	Sr.	18(14)	65	34	164	9.1	210
G	Norm Zmyslinski (#13)	St. Peter's	Sr.	16(16)	47	21	115	7.2	241
G	Len "Linda" Tomczak (#12/3)	St. Stan's	Jr.	18(17)	43	29	115	6.4	240
C	Jim "Red" Fahey (#17/9)	Sacred Heart	Jr.	16(12)	42	18	102	6.4	102
G-F	Richard "Dick" Salamon (#7)	St. Ann's	Jr.	12(4)	15	3	33	2.7	33
F	Chuck Maxwell (#11)	Sacred Heart	Sr.	10(1)	13	3	29	2.9	45
F	Jimmy Dailey (#3/17)	St. Ann's	Jr.	13	9	8	26	2.0	26
F	Don Wolf (#6)	Sacred Heart	Sr.	11(5)	10	5	25	2.3	198
G	Joe Peplinski (#10)	St. Ann's	Sr.	10(3)	6	11	23	2.3	44
G	Bob Hamm (#8)	St. Peter's	Jr.	3	1	3	5	1.7	5
G	Caesar "Chaz" Montevecchio (#4)	Roosevelt	Sr.	3	2	0	4	1.3	40
C	Len "Stretch" Szczypinski (#13)	St. Stan's	Sr.	3	2	0	4	1.3	16
G	Jim Lynch (#15)	St. Patrick's	Jr.	5	1	0	2	0.4	2
F	Johnny Donatucci (#14)	Roosevelt	Soph.	3	1	0	2	0.7	2
F	Rob "Zeke" Szoszorek (#9)	St. Joseph's	Jr.	0	0	0	0	0.0	0

The 1952 Ramblers tied for the city crown for the third straight year, this time with Tech and Academy. L to R: Coach Detzel, Zmyslinski, Fahey, Maxwell, Malina, Donatucci, Hatkevich, Peplinski, Wolf, Szoszorek, Hamm, Salamon, Tomczak, Lynch, Montevecchio, Dailey, Mgr. Latimer.

Monsignor Robert McDonald accepts the Trophy of Trophies from City Series director Lowell Drake. L to R: Dick Detzel, Mayor Tom Flatley, McDonald, Drake, Walt Strosser, Joe Robie, A.D. Msgr. Jim Gannon.

HIGHLIGHTS:

- Cathedral Prep earned its third straight three-way tie for the championship in the well-balanced City Series. The Ramblers were in the driver's seat until they blew a 9-point halftime lead in the regular season finale against Academy (8-10). Once again there was no provision for a playoff, despite the proposal of Prep headmaster **Monsignor Robert McDonald** to have the three teams that tied for city honors play it off. The main objection was that it should have been set before the season started, to which Monsignor McDonald replied, according to the *Erie Daily Times*: "Next year I'm going to make sure before the season opens that we have a playoff scheduled. This tie business is silly. It ruins the entire objective of the league".

- It was also the third straight city title tie for Technical (18-8) and Vincent's (13-6) first piece of the crown since 1936.

- All City Series games were played at the Gannon Auditorium, while the Ramblers continued to play their independent home contests in the Prep gym. The PCIAA game with Pittsburgh Central Catholic was contested at the Pitt Fieldhouse.

- The season started on a high note when **Jim "Red" Fahey**, according to the *Erie Dispatch*: "a massive 6-3, 230-pound junior playing in his first varsity game, batted in a follow-up shot with 25 seconds left to give Cathedral Prep a 38-36 squeaker over Bradford (18-3) in the opener for each school." According to the *Bradford Era*, the game-winning tap-in, his third immediate attempt, was made "in the final seconds" after

Fahey had missed a free throw and with less than 10 seconds left. The Owls defeated the Ramblers later in the season in Bradford. Bradford only lost one more regular season game, but lost to Punxsutawney in the District 9 final, 48-44.

- Prep and Bradford, situated in a valley in the Allegheny Mountains with a recent monopoly on PIAA District 9 championships, met for the first two times in 1951-52. The two engaged in a home-and-home series for the next two seasons also, as well as in 1955-56. The Ramblers and the Owls renewed the series in 1969-70 and played every year through the 1981-82 season.

- Scoring picked up overall, as both Prep (49.8 *PPG*) and its opponents (44.1 *PPG*) broke records for team points per game average.

- The final standings in City Series/Big Six basketball (Corry had rejoined the Erie County League) were as follows:

	W	L		W	L
Prep	5	3	Prep	7	3
Tech	5	3	Tech	7	3
Vincent	5	3	Vincent	6	4
Academy	4	4	Academy	5	5
East	1	7	Millcreek	4	6
			East	1	9

- More highlights of the season included the consistent play of **Al Hatkevich**, who broke a 22-year old school record for most points in a game with 37 against Tech, as well as the record for most points per game; the solid play of forward **Ralph Malina** and guards **Lenny Tomczak** and **Norm Zmyslinski**; the twin victories over rival Tech (Section

Norm Zmyslinski was inducted posthumously into the Prep Hall of Fame in 1993.

One champ); and the wins over out-of-state Catholic rivals Cathedral Latin, Ursuline and Benedictine.

- Hatkevich's 37-point performance broke the old city record for a single game set at 32 by Tech's **Joe Zuravleff**. His total also shattered the Gannon Audi record of 31 set by Vincent's **Sammy Williams** in 1951. More amazingly, "Hacker" scored his points after picking up three personal fouls in the first 5 minutes of the game. His school scoring record stood until broken by **Paul Pry** in 1968. Prep's total of 67 points also was a new Audi scoring mark for a high school quintet.

- In the victory over Cathedral Latin (4-10), the *Erie Dispatch* noted: "**Jim Dailey**, a 5-5 Rambler, surprised everyone when he pushed in 5 points [as soon as he entered near the end of the first half]…His slight stature befuddled the rangy visitors. They were unable to cover him in their zone defense."

- With Prep's victory over Youngstown Ursuline (9-12) on December 28, the Ramblers became the first team to defeat the Irish on its home court in five years, since Warren Harding did so in February, 1947. Though unknown at the time, Prep's win over Ursuline was the 500th basketball game played in Rambler history.

- A new opponent, Benedictine (3-11), is an all-male school founded in 1927 by the Benedictine monks of Cleveland. The original focus of the founders was to teach the sons of Slovakian immigrants. It is located on Martin Luther King Drive on Cleveland's east side and the Bengals have had success in basketball, winning Ohio state titles in 1997 and 1998.

- The biggest disappointments were the City Series losses, particularly the season finale to Academy which was again in the role of spoiler; the losses to Greenville St. Michael's (23-6) and Bradford after beating both combines to start the season; and the 6th straight first round loss in the PCIAA tourney, this time to Pittsburgh Central Catholic (17-5) on a tip-in by **Bob Szymanski** with 4 seconds remaining. The Vikings next defeated Altoona Catholic before bowing to Allentown Central Catholic (also the "Vikings") in the PCIAA Class A championship game. It was Allentown CC's third crown, also having won the titles in 1945 and 1948. It went on to win three more, in 1956, 1957 and 1964. Twice Allentown CC lost to Prep in PCIAA finals, in 1954 and 1971.

- Greenville St. Mike's, which upset Prep on December 29, had a total enrollment of only 90 boys and girls. The Irish won the Erie Diocesan Class B championship for the second straight season,

Hatkevich up for two against Benedictine.

defeating Ridgway St. Leo's, 65-42; St. Marys Central Catholic, 50-36; and Oil City St. Joseph's, 53-44, in the playoffs held at Gannon College. The Mikes then lost the PCIAA Western Regional to Pittsburgh power West End St. James, 55-40. St. James then defeated Williamsport St. Mary's, 69-55, for the state Class B crown. It was an all-time Pennsylvania scholastic basketball record 65th consecutive victory for the Spartans, who had not lost since February, 1950.

Norm Zmyslinski shows his form against Tech.

- **Al Hatkevich** was honored as a First Team All-Scholastic choice by the *Erie Daily Times*, the *Erie Dispatch* and the *Lake Shore Visitor*. **Jim Fahey** was named First Team by the *Visitor* and Second Team by the *Times* and *Dispatch*, while **Len Tomczak** was named First Team by the *Visitor*, Second Team by the *Times* and Honorable Mention by the *Dispatch*. **Norm Zmyslinski** and **Ralph Malina** were named Third Team choices by the *Visitor* and Honorable Mention by the *Times*. Zmyslinski was also a Second Team *Dispatch* pick.

Big Jim Fahey battles for a rebound with Academy's Becker.

- Three-year star **Al Hatkevich** retired as Prep's all-time leading scorer with 644 career points, and later went on to play football at Ohio State under coach **Woody Hayes**. "Hacker" was inducted into the Cathedral Prep Athletic Hall of Fame in 2005. **Don Wolf, Caesar Montevecchio** and **Jim Lynch** all went on to play football at the University of Detroit, while Tomczak continued at John Carroll and Zmyslinski at Xavier (OH) as

Tomczak grabs a rebound against Vincent, as Wolf and Dailey look on.

gridders. Zmyslinski was inducted posthumously into the Cathedral Prep Athletic Hall of Fame in 1993.

- **Lenny "Linda" Tomczak** ('53) and his four brothers who starred in many sports at Prep in the 1950's—**Dan "Dana"** ('54), **Bob "Clutch"** ('56), **Eugene "Jiggs"** ('57), and **Pat** ('60)—were all inducted into the Cathedral Prep Athletic Hall of Fame on the same evening in 2003. Lenny was also inducted into the Metro Erie Sports Hall of Fame in 1988.

Lenny Tomczak, first of the famous Tomczak brothers to star for Prep.

- **Leonard Szczypinski** (later "Sypinski") went on to study for the priesthood with the Oblates of St. Francis de Sales, who, at the time, taught at Cathedral Prep. Szczypinski was ordained an Oblate Father in 1964.

1952 All-Opponent Team:

Marvin Goodman, Bradford
Bob Giardina, Greenville St. Mike's [Detroit, football]
Frank Judge, Greenville St. Mike's
Joe Kulka, Greenville St. Mike's
Lee Cabeloff, East [Allegheny]
Walt Zielinski, Cathedral Latin
Edward "Ned" Ochman, Youngstown Ursuline
Willie "Five-Star" Wainwright, Vincent
Carmen Riazzi, Tech (1st team all-state) [Dayton]
Reno Strand, Vincent [Gannon]
Don Polagyi, Tech [Cincinnati]
John LeJeal, Millcreek
Pete Alex, Tech
Joe Bizzaro, Bradford
George Becker, Academy
Tom Smith, Pittsburgh Central Catholic
Bob Szymanski, Pittsburgh Central Catholic

First PCIAA State Championship! Eastern States Runner-up!

1952-53 (23-4)

Coach: Richard "Dick" Detzel
Captains: Jim Fahey, Jimmy Dailey
Manager: Mike Nolan

Coach Detzel draws a play for his state champs. Clockwise: Wittman, Hamm, Ruska, Lynch, Wedzik.

Date	PREP			Dec.	Loc.	High Scorer	Opponent
12/7	75	Titusville St. Joseph's Academy	35	W	A	Fahey (16)	English (13)
12/12	42	Sharon	48	L	H	Donatucci (13)	Shepard (13)
12/14	53	Pittsburgh St. Basil	31	W	H	Fahey (13)	Peszko (11)
12/19	82*	East	58	W	N	Sarvadi (22)	Laskoff (18)
12/22	95*	Titusville St. Joseph's Academy	30	W	H	Dillon (20)	McDonald (11)
12/27	78	Jamestown (NY)	65*	W	A	Fahey (23)	Johnson (22)
12/30	63	Strong Vincent	34	W	N	Fahey (17)	Wainwright (12)
1/1	70	Millcreek	54	W	N	Sarvadi (20)	Fiddler (18)
1/3	58	Rochester (NY) Aquinas	50	W	H	Fahey (18)	Mack (22)
1/9	55	Technical	65*	L	N	Fahey (16)	Riazzi (25)
1/10	48	Youngstown (OH) Ursuline	31	W	H	Fahey (13)	Kimmel (7)
1/13	70	Bradford	52	W	A	Dailey (22)	Girard (18)
1/16	67	Academy	38	W	N	Fahey & Sarvadi (19)	Shay (12)
1/23	52	Millcreek	39	W	N	Fahey (13)	Sampson (11)
1/30	55	Rochester (NY) Aquinas	62	L	A	Fahey (13)	Britz (17)
2/6	56	East	50	W	N	Donatucci (19)	Demyanovich (14)
2/7	53	Bradford	41	W	H	Dailey (13)	Girard (13)
2/10	61	Strong Vincent	37	W	N	Fahey & Sarvadi (13)	Vitale (9)
2/14	81	Cleveland (OH) Benedictine	51	W	H	Fahey (21)	Bartko (10)
2/20	82	Technical	50	W	N	Fahey (27)	Riazzi (13)
2/27	68	Academy	51	W	N	Fahey (20)	Schneider (19)
		P.C.I.A.A. STATE CATHOLIC H.S. TOURNAMENT					
3/6	70	Latrobe St. Vincent Prep	48	W	H	Fahey (13)	Sanzi (22)
3/18	54	Johnstown Central Catholic	49	W	H	Fahey (13)	Vilchinsky (14)
		P.C.I.A.A. STATE CATHOLIC CHAMPIONSHIP					
3/24	66	Harrisburg Catholic High	64	W	H	Fahey & Sarvadi (16)	Forjan (23)
		EASTERN STATES INVITATIONAL TOURNAMENT (GLENS FALLS, NY)					
3/26	54	Pawtucket (RI) St. Raphael's	51	W	N	Fahey (20)	Dragon & Marcil (18)
3/27	42	Buffalo (NY) Canisius	39	W	N	Fahey (21)	Cunningham (18)
3/28	57	Staunton (VA) Military Academy	63	L	N	Fahey (20)	Rosenbluth (32*)
	1704* (63.1*)		**1289* (47.7*)**				

Pos.	Player	Prior School	Class	G(GS)	FG	FT	Total	*PPG*	Career
C	Jim "Big Red" Fahey (#16)	Sacred Heart	Sr.	27*(27*)	165*	117*	447*	16.5*	549
G	Jim Dailey (#17)	St. Ann's	Sr.	27*(27*)	87	100	274	10.1	300
G	Joe Sarvadi (#7)	St. Andrew's	Jr.	26(22)	95	71	261	10.0	261
F	Johnny Donatucci (#10)	Roosevelt	Jr.	27*(27*)	70	21	161	6.0	163
C	Johnny "Sweetwater" Ruska (#3)	St. Patrick's	Jr.	27*(2)	55	38	148	5.5	148
F	Dana Tomczak (#11)	St. Stan's	Jr.	27*(25)	43	20	106	4.0	106
C	Chuck Dillon (#9)	Sacred Heart	Jr.	22	35	13	83	3.8	83
G	Jim Lynch (#13)	St. Patrick's	Sr.	22(3)	28	15	71	3.2	73
G	Jim Mraz (#4)	St. Mary's	Jr.	15	15	5	35	2.3	35
F	Robert "Bob" Hamm (#12)	St. Peter's	Sr.	18	13	4	30	1.6	35
F	Chuck Wittman (#14)	St. Andrew's	Jr.	15	11	6	28	1.9	28
F	Al Wedzik (#8)	St. Ann's	Sr.	17	9	7	25	1.5	25
G	Jim "Moe" Gross (#5)	St. Michael's	Jr.	18	7	5	19	1.0	19
G	Richard "Dick" Salamon (#15)	St. Ann's	Sr.	17(2)	5	8	18	1.1	51

HIGHLIGHTS:

- Cathedral Prep had its most successful season in history in 1952-53, winning its first state basketball championship in thrilling fashion. The Ramblers of coach **Dick Detzel** were fortunate to have a home court advantage with all 3 playoff games played at Gannon Auditorium. Prep also won the exciting City Series title and finished runner-up in the prestigious Eastern States Invitational Tournament. The 23-win season lasted as a Prep record until 1978. Included were a then-record 11 straight victories. The entire 1953 Prep basketball team was inducted into the Cathedral Prep Athletic Hall of Fame in 2005.

- Other highlights of the season included the consistent play of **Jimmy Dailey** and **Jim Fahey**, who both made the all-tourney

Fahey leaves Vincent's Colonels helpless.

team at Eastern States; Fahey breaking Prep records for field goals, free throws, points in a season and points per game; the huge win over powerful Section One champ Tech (18-5), after getting beat in the first battle with the Centaurs by blowing a fourth quarter 6-point lead; the pair of blowouts over a solid Academy (16-5) team; the pair of easy wins over District 9 champion Bradford (18-8); the city scholastic 95-point scoring record versus Titusville St. Joe's (7-21); the convincing win over St. Basil (28-5), a now-defunct (closed in 1978) parish school squad from the Carrick section of Pittsburgh, that went on to win the PCIAA state Class B title for 1953; the close PCIAA Western Final victory over Johnstown Central Catholic; and, of course, winning the City Series and PCIAA state togas. After the state championship battle with Harrisburg Catholic High, the headline of the *Erie Dispatch-Herald* proclaimed: "Ramblers Nail PCIAA Title in Wild Game."

Jimmy Dailey, a deceptive guard at only 5'6", was inducted into the Prep Hall of Fame in 1993.

All-American center Jim Fahey, later "Father Fahey," went on to star at Villanova.

Cathedral Prep's first State Champions (1953). L to R: Coach Detzel, Dailey, Sarvadi, Mraz, Wedzik, Gross, Lynch, Salamon, Hamm, Wittman, Donatucci, Tomczak, Dillon, Ruska, Fahey.

- A special rules change took place in 1952 whereby a fouled player received a second chance if he missed his first free throw. This rule was added for two reasons: to do away with intentional fouling to gain possession of the ball and to slow down the game and give athletes more time to rest. This rule was the target of the intense criticism that games were too long and students did not get home early enough at night.

Fahey reaches over Laskoff for another rebound.

- Sharon (26-4) defeated Prep on the Rambler floor early in the season, then went all the way to the PIAA state final before losing to Yeadon, 55-43, at the Palestra in Philadelphia. Sharon featured first team all-state junior **Bob Atterholt**. The Prep-Sharon battle was the first of an 11-year series between the two. Sharon High had a variety of different mascots and nicknames over the years, among them "Yellow Jackets," "Bronco-Busters," "Cow-Punchers," "Orange Tornado," "Kings," "Gypsies," and simply "Orange & Black." It finally settled on "Tigers," beginning with the 1934-35 school year.

- St. Basil was in Section 1 of the Pittsburgh Catholic B League. Other entrants in Section 1 were Allentown St. George, Ambridge St. Veronica, Carnegie St. Luke, Carrick St. Wendelin, Knoxville St. Canice, Mount Washington St. Justin and West End St. James. Section 2 consisted of Braddock St. Thomas, Mount Oliver St. Joseph, Mount Washington St. Mary of the Mount, Natrona St. Joseph, South Side St. Adalbert, South Side St. Casimir, Shadyside Sacred Heart, South Side St. Michael and Uniontown St. John. The Class A League consisted of Central Catholic, North Catholic and Latrobe St. Vincent Prep. All of these schools are now closed with the exception of Central Catholic, North Catholic and St. Joseph, which moved out to Natrona Heights and remains the only parish-operated high school in the Diocese of Pittsburgh.

- St. Basil, coached by **Jerry Unites**, defeated Kanty Prep in the PCIAA Class B Western Final at the Southside Market House, 65-43, before disposing Bethlehem Catholic in the title game, 57-51.

- Though Prep had a comfortable win in its first-ever game with Jamestown (7-13), the Red Raiders still broke an opponent record by scoring 65 points against the Ramblers. Later in the season Technical tied that mark in its 10-point triumph over Prep.

- Prep split a pair of wins with rival Rochester Aquinas (13-2), which won a mythical Rochester high school title.

- All City Series games were played at the Gannon Auditorium, while the Ramblers continued to play their independent home contests in the Prep gym. Gate sales for the first Prep-Tech contest were listed at a record 2,751, while the classic second contest, which decided the city title, crammed in over 3,000 fans.

- The final standings in City Series/Big Six basketball were as follows:

	W	L		W	L
Prep	7	1	Prep	9	1
Tech	6	2	Tech	8	2
Academy	4	4	Academy	6	4
East	3	5	East	5	5
Vincent	0	8	Millcreek	2	8
			Vincent	0	10

- Prep opened PCIAA play with an easy victory over undermanned St. Vincent's Prep (4-16), then scored a difficult, heated, Western Regional victory over Johnstown Central Catholic (20-8). Central Catholic's leading scorer, **Bob Vilchinsky**, went on to become one of Gannon College's early stars. He was a four-year starter for the Golden Knights and retired as Gannon's all-time leading scorer with 1,326 points.

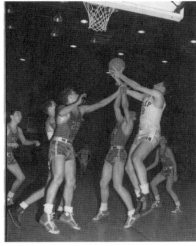

Chuck Dillon engages in tense action in the Millcreek game.

Vilchinsky was inducted into the Gannon Hall of Fame in 1984.

- Harrisburg Catholic's (24-5) path to the state championship game included a tense, 44-41 upset thriller over 23-1 Scranton Prep in an Eastern Semifinal. The very physical contest ended with famed referee **Mendy Rudolph**, of Wilkes-Barre, suffering a broken nose on the last play of the game. (Rudolph began his distinguished 22-year NBA officiating career the next season.) Harrisburg caught a break for the Eastern Regional Final, easily defeating Reading Central Catholic, 62-40. Reading had its worst team in 10 years, finishing 9-19, but it upset Allentown Central Catholic, 54-45, in the semifinals.

- Prep's first state title was not without controversy. Erie was the chosen site for the state championship game, as it was the Western Regional winner's turn to host the event. The Gannon Auditorium was the natural venue, but Harrisburg Catholic administrators protested, citing Gannon as "unacceptable" as Prep played 10 games there and it was therefore not a "neutral court," which the rules required. The PCIAA agreed and warned that Prep faced forfeiting if the game was not scheduled for another facility. The rhubarb was ostensibly settled when the Academy gym was booked, though the site was changed to East High, as its auditorium could accommodate 600 fans rather than 400 at Academy. Upon inspection when the Harrisburg squad arrived in Erie, coach **Lester Ginanni** found the East stage unacceptable because of poor lighting, warps on the playing surface and the fact that Headmaster **Monsignor Robert McDonald** sold every available seat to Prep students and fans. Monsignor McDonald had previously stated that Prep would agree to play in Harrisburg if the Ramblers weren't scheduled to depart for the Eastern States tourney the next day. An incensed Coach Ginanni finally agreed, under protest, to move the scrap to the Audi rather than to have his team and a half-dozen busloads of Crusader supporters turn around and go home.

- The state title contest ended in utter confusion for the 2,300 fans present. Led by double-digit scorers **Joe Sarvadi, Jim Lynch, Jimmy Dailey** and **Jim Fahey**, Prep led the entire way, despite the fact Fahey sat with four fouls with 5:42 left in the second quarter and did not re-enter the game until the 3:20 mark of the third period. Prep was ahead 66-62 when the final buzzer sounded and the fans stormed the court. But a frantic Harrisburg Catholic bench claimed three seconds actually remained as the timer had started the clock too soon on a final out-of-bounds play.

Sarvadi lays up a one-hander as Fahey and Donatucci approve.

The referees agreed and the floor was cleared. Harrisburg scored again to slice the final margin to two. Coach Ginanni protested violently after the game, citing "lousy officiating", and taking Prep officials to task for failing to allot tickets for the 300 Harrisburg supporters. What erupted was a full-scale free-for-all among fans swarming the court. Ginanni would not congratulate Prep coach **Dick**

Fahey up for two against Millcreek, with Tomczak close by.

Detzel as the brawl continued for at least five wild minutes after the game. Ginanni told both the *Harrisburg Evening News* and the *Harrisburg Patriot*: "I think on a neutral floor with neutral officials, we would have won the game!"

- **Les Ginanni** filed a formal protest with the PCIAA, stating: 1) The Gannon Audi was not a neutral court (as specified by PCIAA rules); and 2) The officials (**Naz Servidio** and **Walter "Deacon" Stanky**) should not have been from Erie. The PCIAA eventually ruled against Catholic and the Ramblers kept their first state championship trophy. Harrisburg Catholic is now known as Bishop McDevitt. The two schools never competed in basketball again, though they have had some very memorable PIAA football playoff battles in recent years.

- Harrisburg Catholic's 6'4" star **Jim Forjan** later became the legendary basketball coach at York Catholic (1959-70).

- The Ramblers left just hours after the PCIAA title game for Glens Falls (NY) to participate in the prestigious Eastern States Invitational. The squad and coaches traveled by overnight train to Albany, then by bus to Glens Falls. The Orange & Black became the "darlings" of the tourney after upsetting St. Raphael's (18-4) and Canisius (20-0 when Prep beat the three-consecutive Manhattan Cup champs), led by **Jim Cunningham**, later a Fordham star and third round draft choice of the Boston Celtics in 1958), but fell in the finals to the legendary 6'8" **Len Rosenbluth** (a Bronx, NY resident and later a two-time All-American at University of North Carolina; 1957 College Player of the Year; and Philadelphia Warriors star & first round draft choice in 1957) and Staunton Military Academy (20-1).

- Staunton Military Academy had a remarkable season in 1952-53. Its regular season schedule consisted only of other military schools and college freshmen combines. The Cadets scored over 100 points on nine occasions and averaged 95.2 *PPG* during the regular season. Staunton's only loss was in its opener to the University of Virginia Freshmen, 71-69. The Cadets avenged that defeat in their final regular season contest, defeating the U. Va. Frosh, 89-80. To Cathedral Prep's credit, the Ramblers held Staunton to its second lowest point total of the season. The lowest occurred in a semifinal the evening before, when the Cadets defeated Brooklyn (NY) Adelphi Academy, 54-53.

- Many notable American political and military leaders were graduates of Staunton Military Academy. With the 1960's came a new generation, geared to permissiveness and nonconformity, rather than regimentation and discretion.

Excitement at the post-season banquet. Indentifiable, L to R: "Ma" Kaiser, toastmaster Paul Allen, Msgr. McDonald, Bishop Gannon, guest speaker John Gallagher (head coach, Niagara Univ.), Fr. Gallagher, Mayor Flatley, Msgr. Gannon, Coach Detzel.

The fallout from Vietnam helped perpetuate an anti-military sentiment that further eroded enrollments at military schools throughout the country. Despite the best efforts of a dedicated and talented faculty and staff, inflation and unemployment weakened the schools finances and SMA closed in 1976.

- The Eastern States Scholastic Basketball Tournament (later, the "Eastern States Invitational Tournament") began in 1920 and was designed to serve public and private schools in the New England and Middle States sections of the country. Each year the tourney was held in Glens Falls (NY) for 8 representative schools. The tournament was cancelled from 1943-1946 due to wartime conditions. Schools from 10 different states were the principal participants during the history of the tournament, with private schools dominating the tourney until its finale in 1955, won by Lewisburg (WV) Greenbrier Military Academy. By that time the Eastern States Catholic Invitational Tournament at Newport (RI) was drawing many Catholic schools away from the Glens Falls tournament.

Jim Dailey breaks away for another score.

- For the second straight season both Prep (63.1 *PPG*) and its opponents (47.7 *PPG*) broke records for team points per game average. The Ramblers broke their school single game records with back to back wins over East (10-9) and Titusville St. Joe's. One bright spot in St. Joe's otherwise miserable season was its first victory over Oil City St. Joe's in 17 years!

- Prep finished as the #5 ranked Catholic team in the nation as reported by Chicago's archdiocesan newspaper, *The New World*. Los Angeles Loyola (34-2) finished #1; Boys Town (NE) (17-2) #7; New York City All Hallows (19-6) # 8; Philadelphia West Catholic (25-2) #10 and Buffalo Canisius (20-1) # 12.

- Big **Jim Fahey** (6'4") and little **Jimmy Dailey** (5'6") were honored as First Team All-Scholastic choices by

Mel Laskoff of East harrasses Johnny Donatucci.

the *Erie Daily Times*, *Erie Dispatch-Herald* and the *Lake Shore Visitor*. **Johnny Donatucci** was an Honorable Mention choice as selected by the *Times*. Fahey was also named a Fourth Team Catholic All-American by *The New World* and further selected by sportswriter **Gene Cuneo** as the "Sunbeam Bread Athlete of the Year".

- Other All-City choices of note included East great **Mel Laskoff** and the great **Carmen Riazzi** of Tech, who in one game against Lawrence Park scored 52 points, still an all-time Erie record! Riazzi also scored 39 against Meadville in 1951-52, breaking the city record of Prep's **Al Hatkevich**, who scored 37 against Riazzi and his Tech Centaurs in 1952. Riazzi finished the season with 568 points (City record 24.7 *PPG*) and his career with 1,294, both local records at the time. Laskoff had one more season at East, while Riazzi went on to star for the Flyers at the University of Dayton under legendary coach **Tom Blackburn**.

- Fahey (later **Father Jim Fahey**), the first Prepster to be accorded All-American status, went on to star at Villanova University. There he was a three-year starter under venerated coach **Alex Severance**. He later attended Christ the King Seminary and was ordained in 1963. Father Fahey, also a two-time state champion in the discus and shot put, was inducted posthumously into the Metro Erie Sports Hall of Fame in 1989 and the Cathedral Prep Athletic Hall of Fame in 1994.

- **Jim Dailey** continued his exploits at the University of Detroit under legendary coach **Bob Calihan** and was inducted into the Cathedral Prep Athletic Hall of Fame in 1993.

- **Jim Lynch** went on to star in football at the University of Detroit, and was a first round draft choice of the Detroit Lions. He was inducted posthumously into the Cathedral Prep Athletic Hall of Fame in 1995 and the Metro Erie Sports Hall of Fame in 2007.

1953 All-Opponent Team:

Charlie Shepard, Sharon
Charles Mitchell, Sharon (3rd team all-state)
Bob Atterholt, Sharon (1st team all-state) [Youngstown St.]
Tom Peszko, St. Basil's [Duquesne]
Robert "Duke" Schneider, St. Basil's [Duquesne]
Mel Laskoff, East (2nd team all-state) [Michigan State, Allegheny]
Denny Johnson, Jamestown
Harold "Hal" Fiddler, Millcreek
Ron Mack, Rochester Aquinas [LeMoyne, baseball & basketball]
Carmen Riazzi, Tech (1st team all-state) [Dayton]
Joey Girard, Bradford (hm all-state)
Greg Britz, Rochester Aquinas [Canisius]
Paul Demyanovich, East [Mount Union]
Jack Laraway, Academy [Purdue, football]
Pete Alex, Tech
Ron Sanzi, St. Vincent Prep [Waynesburg]
Bob Vilchinsky, Johnstown Central Catholic [Gannon]
Jim Forjan, Harrisburg Catholic [Millersville St.]
Ray Naccarato, Harrisburg Catholic
Mariano DeFilippo, Harrisburg Catholic
Jim Cunningham, Canisius [Fordham, NBA Boston Celtics, Baltimore Bullets]
Len Rosenbluth, Staunton [North Carolina, NBA Philadelphia Warriors]

Dan Tomczak grabs a rebound between a pair of Tech Centaurs.

Testimonial Banquet

HONORING

CATHEDRAL PREP BASKETBALL CHAMPIONS

City Series - Big Six - State

Eastern States Tournament Finalist

SUNDAY EVENING, APRIL 19, 1953
6:30 O'CLOCK

LAWRENCE HOTEL

Sponsors

CATHEDRAL PREP DADS' CLUB

KNIGHTS OF COLUMBUS

Ramblers Repeat as City, State Champs! Eastern States Catholic Runner-up!

1953-54 (22-3)

Coach: Richard "Dick" Detzel
Captains: Dan Tomczak, Johnny Donatucci
Manager: Mike Nolan

Nobody played better than "Moe" Gross by season's end. Sadly killed in a 1957 auto accident, Cathedral Prep continues to honor him with the James "Moe" Gross Trophy, given annually to Prep's MVP.

Date	PREP			Dec.	Loc.	High Scorer	Opponent
12/6	87	Titusville St. Joseph's Academy	32	W	A	Wittman (16)	McDonald (16)
12/11	51	Sharon	48	W	A	Ruska & Wittman (16)	Atterholt (28)
12/18	66	Academy	37	W	N	Ruska (18)	Russo (17)
12/23	47	Technical	33	W	N	Sarvadi (16)	DiFucci (16)
12/27	66	Buffalo (NY) Canisius	56	W	H	Sarvadi (17)	Cunningham (25)
12/29	63	Youngstown (OH) Ursuline	28	W	A	Sarvadi (22)	Kimmel (11)
1/2	47	Bradford	39	W	H	Gross & Wittman (13)	Coburn (16)
1/6	71	Titusville St. Joseph's Academy	16	W	H	Mraz (18)	McDonald (7)
1/8	73	Buffalo (NY) Canisius	64	W	A	Sarvadi (20)	Cunningham (30)
1/12	44	East	45	L	N	Sarvadi (11)	Laskoff (27)
1/17	54	Rochester (NY) Aquinas	58	L	H	Ruska (13)	Britz (28)
1/23	69	Strong Vincent	57	W	N	Sarvadi (17)	Simon (18)
1/28	69	Academy	40	W	N	Ruska & Gross (15)	Savelli (10)
2/2	55	Bradford	50	W	A	Dillon (15)	Coburn (14)
2/5	53	Technical	30	W	N	Ruska (9)	Jablonski (13)
2/16	61	Jamestown (NY)	34	W	H	Wittman (14)	Marshall (10)
2/19	45	East	33	W	N	Gross (13)	Demyanovich & Watral (9)
2/26	62	Strong Vincent	54	W	N	Wittman (30)	Simon (16)
		`CITY CHAMPIONSHIP PLAYOFF					
3/2	50	East	45	W	N	Wittman (18)	Laskoff (24)
		P.C.I.A.A. STATE CATHOLIC H.S. TOURNAMENT					
3/14	2	Latrobe St. Vincent' Prep (FFT)	0	W	n/a	no stats--forfeit	
3/18	75	Johnstown Central Catholic	46	W	A	Gross (26)	Kozora (23)
		P.C.I.A.A. STATE CATHOLIC CHAMPIONSHIP					
3/25	80	Allentown Central Catholic	58	W	A	Gross (25)	Egizio (16)
		EASTERN STATES CATHOLIC INVITATIONAL TOURNAMENT (NEWPORT, RI)					
3/26	65	Syracuse (NY) St. Lucy	64	W	N	Gross (22)	Daughton (24)
3/27	60	Newport (RI) De la Salle	51	W	N	Gross (20)	Harrington (23)
3/28	59	New York City (NY) All Hallows	73*	L	N	Gross (19)	Haynes (25)
	1472 (61.3)		**1095 (45.6)**				

Pos.	Player	Ht.	Prior School	Class	G(GS)	FG	FT	Total	PPG	Career
F	Chuck Wittman (#3)	6'3"	St. Andrew's	Sr.	23(22)	106	78	284	12.3	312
G	Jim "Moe" Gross (#5)	5'10"	St. Michael's	Sr.	23(9)	100	58	258	11.2	277
G	Joe Sarvadi (#7)	5'8"	St. Andrew's	Sr.	23(15)	80	69	229	10.0	490
C	Johnny "Sweetwater" Ruska (#15)	6'5"	St. Patrick's	Sr.	23(23)	75	68	218	9.5	366
G	Daniel "Dana" Tomczak (#11)	6'2"	St. Stan's	Sr.	23(23)	41	28	110	4.8	216
F	Johnny Donatucci (#10)	6'2"	Roosevelt	Sr.	23(21)	44	17	105	4.6	268
F	Chuck Dillon (#9)	6'3"	Sacred Heart	Sr.	23(1)	39	21	99	4.3	182
C	Bob "Clutch" Tomczak (#16)	6'2"	St. Stan's	Soph.	16(2)	16	12	44	2.8	44
F	Richard "Dick" Dill (#8)	6'0"	St. Patrick's	Jr.	15(1)	16	11	43	2.9	43
F	Al Montevecchio (#6)	6'1"	Roosevelt	Jr.	10(1)	13	9	35	3.5	35
G	Jim Mraz (#4)	5'11"	St. Mary's	Sr.	9(1)	13	2	28	3.1	63
G	Bernie Farabaugh (#12)	6'1"	St. Peter's	Jr.	7(1)	4	3	11	1.6	11

Prep's 1954 State Champions. Front, L to R: Gross, Donatucci, Dillon, Ruska, Wittman, D. Tomczak, Sarvadi; Back: Coach Detzel, Montevecchio, Farabaugh, B. Tomczak, Dill, Mgr. Nolan.

HIGHLIGHTS:

• Erie hoop fans saw one of the greatest seasons ever, as the Cathedral Prep Ramblers of coach **Dick Detzel** won their second PCIAA state basketball championship in thrilling fashion.

• The Ramblers were awarded a first round forfeit victory over St. Vincent's Prep (5-11) of Latrobe, when the St. Vincent College Fieldhouse was damaged by a storm and the insurance company said it would not be responsible for any injuries suffered by players or fans as a result of the damage. St. Vincent's Prep thus forfeited the game, stating it was not interested in scheduling the contest elsewhere. St. Vincent's Prep, opened in 1932, closed at the conclusion of the 1961-62 school year.

All-City Choice Chuck Wittman went on to star at Princeton.

• It was then **Jim "Moe" Gross** who stole the show with 26 points as Prep trounced Johnstown Central Catholic (12-11) in the Western Regional. Gross continued to amaze in the State Final with 27 points as the Orange & Black made shambles of Allentown Central Catholic (20-7). **Chuck Wittman** added 22, while **Dan Tomczak** put on a tenacious defensive performance, holding Allentown superstar **Alex DeLucia** to one measly field goal and 7 points. It must be noted that DeLucia, who averaged 20.5 *PPG* going into the state final, was a first team all-state AP & UPI selection, a squad that included Meadville's 6'9" center **Lloyd Sharrar** and Sharon's **Bob Atterholt**. Oh—and there was another on that all-state team—a 6'11" fellow from Philadelphia Overbrook by the name of **Wilt Chamberlain**! (Chamberlain was the first Mr. Basketball USA, 1955). Prep would play Allentown CC one more time—in the 1971 PCIAA state title game.

Defensive ace Dan Tomczak held Allentown superstar Alex DeLucia to 7 points.

First Team All-Stater Wilt Chamberlain scores two for Overbrook against Farrell.

• Prep had its best start ever to date with a hounding man-to-man defense and 9 straight wins, before losing nail-biters to East High (16-10) and to Rochester Aquinas' (18-0) greatest team. Later in the campaign the Ramblers broke the school record for most consecutive wins with 13.

- The Prep rout at Youngstown Ursuline (4-17) was the last the two competed in basketball, until the 2015-16 season. Prep and Ursuline have been common opponents in football a few times over the years.

- The senior-laden Ramblers won the City Series title in a playoff thriller with Section One champ East, staving off the Warriors and their great high-scoring star **Mel Laskoff**, before a sellout gallery of 3,000 fans. It was the first year ever with a tie-breaking provision after three consecutive three-way ties for the city crown in 1950, 1951 and 1952. Laskoff, who finished the season with 561 points (26.1 *PPG*) and his career with 1,196, started out at Michigan State before transferring and starring at Allegheny College.

- All City Series games were played at the Gannon Auditorium (where "turn-away" crowds were becoming the norm), while the Ramblers continued to play their independent home contests in the Prep gym, with the exception of the Aquinas and Jamestown games, which were played as preliminaries to Gannon College contests. The PCIAA Western Regional was played at Johnstown's War Memorial Auditorium, while the state championship game was played on the Muhlenberg College Memorial Field House floor.

- Big **Johnny Ruska** led the city in rebounding at 12.4 RPG, while **Chuck Wittman**, "the 6'3" stringbean," was fourth in scoring at 12.3 *PPG*. Mite-sized guard **Joe Sarvadi** completed his Prep career averaging exactly 10.0 *PPG* over two seasons. Sarvadi once scored a record 43 points in a 1950 parochial grade school game for St. Andrew's in a 69-19 win against St. John's. Just a week or so later, however, **Eddie Grucza** of St. Stanislaus broke Sarvadi's record, scoring 45 points in a 74-14 victory over that same St. John's team.

- The final standings in City Series basketball were as follows [only the four city public schools competed with Millcreek (which became the new school "McDowell" in 1954) in the "Section One" league]:

	W	L
*Prep	8	1
East	7	2
Vincent	3	5
Tech	2	6
Academy	1	7

won city championship playoff

- Coach **Dick Detzel** became the first Prep basketball coach to reach the 100-win plateau with the Ramblers March 18 verdict over Johnstown Central Catholic in the PCIAA's.

- Prep also participated in the prestigious 17th annual Eastern States Catholic Invitational Tournament in Newport (RI), playing three straight days immediately following the state championship win. The Ramblers were treated with a stay at the Hotel Viking, toured the historical sights of Newport, received free passes to movies, marched in a parade, played before standing room only crowds and attended parties following the games. Prep won the *Newport Daily News* Cup as tournament runner-up. It didn't help though, that after Prep's semifinal victory, De la Salle kids kept the Ramblers up until 3 a.m., throwing coke bottles through their windows, breaking into their rooms and spraying their beds with fire extinguishers!

- After holding off St. Lucy's (14-5) and hometown De la Salle Academy (19-8) in a pair of thrillers, the exhausted Ramblers,

the # 2 seed, finally bowed to the top-seeded Gaels of All Hallows Institute (19-7) and its great superstar, tourney MVP **Ernest Haynes**. The 6'4" Haynes, who averaged 22.5 *PPG* as a senior, was an all-ESCIT player three years running and was winner of the Mayor's Award for athletic ability and sportsmanship in New York City. All Hallows, which also won the tourney in 1953, is situated next to Yankee Stadium, maybe being one reason for its success!

- All Hallows (1909-) was one of the founding schools of the New York City Catholic High School Athletic Association (CHSAA) in 1927. Other founding members, from The Bronx: Fordham Prep (1841-); from Brooklyn: St. Francis Prep (1858-), Brooklyn Prep (1908-1972), Bishop Loughlin (1909-1969), St. John's Prep (1870-1972), Cathedral Prep (1914-1985) and Most Holy Trinity (1915-1972); and from Manhattan: St. Ann's Academy, n/k/a Archbishop Molloy (1892-), Xavier (1847-), Regis (1914-) and LaSalle Academy (1848-). Erie Cathedral Prep played a different Brooklyn Bishop Loughlin school in 1984 and 1991 and competed with LaSalle in 1993, 1996, 2000 and 2001.

Chuck Wittman skies high for another rebound.

- Elizabeth (NJ) St. Mary (24-2) won third place honors at the ESCIT with a 52-35 win over De la Salle, while Jersey City (NJ) St. Peter's Prep (18-6) won the consolation bracket with a 54-49 victory over St. Lucy's. Other participants included Manhattan (NY) Prep (22-3) and New Haven (CT) St. Mary (14-7).

- The Eastern States Catholic Invitational Tournament was inaugurated in 1938 and was sponsored by De la Salle Academy of Newport (RI). The tournament drew teams mainly from New York City, Philadelphia and New Jersey. With the demise of the National Catholic Interscholastic Basketball Tournament in 1941, the ESCIT emerged as the most significant event for Catholic schools in the country. Competition from several new big-name tourneys forced the Eastern States to abandon its project following the 1962 tournament, won by Washington (DC) DeMatha.

- The highlights of the season included the victory over 1953 PIAA finalist Sharon (11-8) and its two-time 1st team all-stater **Bob Atterholt**, the national high school player of the year; and the pair of big wins over a Canisius (12-9) team which featured future NBA star **Jim Cunningham**, voted the top Catholic player in the nation in 1954 by the Chicago archdiocesan

The Gaels of All Hallows swarm Donatucci.

newspaper, *The New World*. Also, the exceptional late-season heroics of **"Moe" Gross**, who made the all-tourney team at

Eastern States; the scoring and rebounding of **Chuck Wittman** and big **Johnny Ruska**; the stellar defensive play of **Dana Tomczak**; and, of course, again winning the City Series and PCIAA state togas.

Joe Sarvadi was just the second Rambler to average in double figures as both a junior and senior.

- Canisius' **Jim Cunningham** and All Hallows' **Ernie Haynes** both went on to Fordham University, where they led a spectacular freshmen team to a 20-0 record. There was great excitement in the Bronx when the Rams were ranked #8 pre-season for the 1955-56 season, but Haynes withdrew from school and Fordham finished the season with a record of 11-14.

- All Hallows' **Bobby Cunningham** (along with **Len Rosenbluth** from Staunton Military Academy's 1953 team that beat Prep) was a key member of North Carolina's 1957 NCAA championship team that came to be known as the "Subway Five." That UNC team finished 32-0, including a triple-overtime victory over **Wilt Chamberlain** and Kansas in the NCAA Final.

- **Chuck Wittman** and **Johnny Ruska** were honored as First Team All-Scholastic choices by the *Erie Dispatch-Herald*, while Ruska also made the *Erie Daily Times* First Team. **"Moe" Gross** was a Second Team choice for both papers, while Wittman and fast-breaking **Joe Sarvadi** were Second Team choices with the *Times*. Honorable Mention choices included **Johnny Donatucci** by the *Times*, Sarvadi by the *Dispatch*, and defensive ace **Dana Tomczak** by both newspapers. Tomczak was inducted into the Cathedral Prep Hall of Fame, with four of his brothers, in 2003.

- Several Ramblers went on to compete at the college level, including **Chuck Wittman** at Princeton, **Chuck Dillon** at Gannon and **Johnny Ruska** at Canisius. Ruska played in the 1957 NCAA Tournament for the Golden Griffins.

- **Johnny Donatucci**, a four-sport star at Prep, played baseball at Villanova. Donatucci also spent some time in the Detroit Tigers organization, playing with the Erie Sailors of the NYP, Valdosta Tigers of the Florida-Georgia League and the Durham Bulls of the Carolina League. Donatucci was inducted into the Metropolitan Erie Sports Hall of Fame in 1992 and was also a charter inductee into the Cathedral Prep Athletic Hall of Fame the same year.

All-City center Johnny Ruska took his wares to Canisius. He played in the 1957 NCAA Tournament for the Golden Griffins.

- **James "Moe" Gross** sadly died on September 18, 1957, as a result of an automobile accident in New Jersey. Considered a model student and athlete, Cathedral Prep continues to honor him to this day by awarding the James "Moe" Gross Trophy annually to the Ramblers' most valuable player.

1954 All-Opponent Team:

Bob Atterholt, Sharon (1st team all-state) [Youngstown St.]

Jim Cunningham, Canisius (*New World* Catholic All-American) [Fordham, NBA Boston Celtics, Baltimore Bullets]

Davey Kimmel, Youngstown Ursuline [Youngstown St., football]

Bob "Coon" Coburn, Bradford

Mel Laskoff, East (2nd team all-state) [Michigan State, Allegheny]

Paul Demyanovich, East [Mount Union]

Frank Simon, Vincent

Walt Askins, Vincent [Edinboro St.]

Walt Watral, East [Edinboro St.]

Len "Jabs" Jablonski, Tech

Joe Titus, Bradford [Georgetown]

Greg Britz, Rochester Aquinas [Canisius]

Jim Kozora, Johnstown Central Catholic

Jim Egizio, Allentown Central Catholic [Villanova, baseball]

Alex DeLucia, Allentown Central Catholic (1st team all-state, *New World* Catholic All-American) [Penn]

Ed Daughton, Syracuse St. Lucy's

Bobby Cunningham, NYC All Hallows [North Carolina]

Ernest Haynes, NYC All Hallows (*New World* Catholic All-American) [Fordham]

Milan High—the 1954 Indiana state champs and inspiration for the movie "Hoosiers."

Dethroned!

1954-55 (12-7)

Coach: Richard "Dick" Detzel
Captains: Dick Dill, Al Montevecchio
Manager: Victor Gallagher

Bishop Gannon marvels at the sight of the Trophy of Trophies. Others at the all-sports banquet, L to R: Fr. Skinner, Fr. Gallagher, Msgr. McDonald and Paul Allen, president of Prep's Dads' Club.

Date	PREP			Dec.	Loc.	High Scorer	Opponent
12/3	67	Conneaut (OH) Rowe	54	W	H	Kwiatkowski (19)	Hill (24)
12/7	50	Harborcreek	34	W	H	Dill & Montevecchio (12)	Akerly (8)
12/10	49	Sharon	77*	L	A	Montevecchio (12)	Tice (18)
12/23	67	Alumni	42	W	H	Kwiatkowski (21)	Gross (11)
12/27	63	Buffalo (NY) Canisius	45	W	H	Kwiatkowski (15)	Brady (14)
12/29	62	Technical	66	L	N	Kwiatkowski (26)	Loewel (16)
1/5	51	Harborcreek	47	W	A	Kwiatkowski (15)	Seifert & Lewis (13)
1/7	69	East	49	W	N	Tomczak (25)	Toran (15)
1/14	47	Strong Vincent	56	L	N	Dill (18)	Polagyi (22)
1/15	48	Conneaut (OH)	49	L	A	Feasler (18)	Ely (18)
1/21	61	Academy	50	W	N	Feasler (20)	Russo (23)
1/23	45	Buffalo (NY) Canisius	48	L	A	Keim (14)	Walsh (12)
1/28	61	Technical	51	W	N	Keim (13)	Loewel (13)
2/4	61	Rochester (NY) Aquinas	57	W	A	Feasler (20)	Burke (16)
2/10	50	East	26	W	N	Feasler (15)	Toran & Biletnikoff (9)
2/18	67	Strong Vincent	79*	L	N	Tomczak (19)	Simon (26)
2/25	74	Academy	42	W	N	Feasler (32)	Russo (19)
		P.C.I.A.A. STATE CATHOLIC H.S. TOURNAMENT					
3/9	62	Johnstown Central Catholic	55	W	H	Keim (18)	Horvath (14)
3/18	56	Pittsburgh North Catholic	70	L	A	Feasler (25)	Brown (27)
	1110 (58.4)		**997 (52.5*)**				

Pos.	Player	Prior School	Class	G(GS)	FG	FT	Total	*PPG*	Career
F-G	George Feasler (#13)	Holy Rosary	Jr.	18(13)	81	54	216	11.3	216
C-G	Vinny "Flowers" Kwiatkowski (#9)	St. Michael's	Jr.	19(15)	63	49	175	9.2	175
G-F	Al Montevecchio (#6)	Roosevelt	Sr.	19(14)	62	41	165	8.7	200
F-G	Jim Keim (#4)	St. Andrew's	Jr.	19(12)	61	35	157	8.3	157
F-C-G	Richard "Dick" Dill (#7)	St. Patrick's	Sr.	19(19)	56	38	150	7.9	193
G-F	Bob "Clutch" Tomczak (#3)	St. Stan's	Jr.	17(16)	55	31	141	8.3	185
F-G	Joe Regruth (#5)	Holy Family	Jr.	18(5)	22	17	61	3.4	61
F-G	Bob Timmons (#12)	St. Andrew's	Jr.	16(1)	5	2	12	0.8	12
G-F	Joe Schossler (#15)	Oil City Assumption	Jr.	11	2	3	7	0.6	7
F	Bernie Farabaugh (#8)	St. Peter's	Sr.	7	2	1	5	0.7	16
C	Victor Glembocki (#16)	St. Hedwig's	Jr.	5	1	0	2	0.4	2
F	Dominic "Pete" Donatucci(#10)	Roosevelt	Jr.	3	0	0	0	0.0	0
G	Charles Kaczmarek (#14)	Holy Trinity	Jr.	1	0	0	0	0.0	0
F	Ziggy Mazanowski (#17)	St. Stan's	Jr.	0	0	0	0	0.0	0
G	Ron Costello (#11)	Holy Rosary	Soph.	0	0	0	0	0.0	0

The 1955 Prep Ramblers. Front, L to R: Keim, Montevecchio, Dill, Tomczak, Feasler, Kwiatkowski, Regruth, Timmons; Back: Coach Detzel, Kaczmarek, Glembocki, Farabaugh, Donatucci, Schossler, Mgr. Gallagher.

HIGHLIGHTS:

- Cathedral Prep suffered from inexperience in **Dick Detzel's** seventh season at the helm, after losing all of its top stars from two consecutive PCIAA state championship teams. Considering the youth of the Ramblers, a second place finish to a great Strong Vincent squad was not too bad of a showing. **Al Montevecchio** and **Dick Dill** provided senior leadership, and the Ramblers further showed a strong junior class.

Al Montevecchio, team captain along with Dick Dill.

- All City Series games and the Johnstown playoff encounter were played at the Gannon Auditorium, while the Ramblers continued to play their independent home contests in the Prep gym.

- Prep opponents broke the record for most points per game average (52.5) for a season.

- Prep's victory over Conneaut Rowe (16-6) in the season lidlifter was the first the two competed in 15 years.

- Prep's early season loss to Sharon (15-4) was its worst in 15 years. The Tigers broke a Rambler opponent scoring record which was again broken later in the season by powerful Vincent.

- Academy's **Pete Russo**, who finished as the top scorer in the city, was held to two field goals in the regular season finale, but canned 15 free throws in 16 attempts for a Prep opponent record.

- With Erie County League school Harborcreek (8-10) joining Class A competition in the new Section One league (even though Prep was not a member), the Huskies and Ramblers

began a home-and-home series that ran through the 1960-61 season.

- The highlights of the season included the impressive wins over Rochester Aquinas (12-4), played as a preliminary to the LeMoyne-Boston College contest; and a strong Johnstown Central Catholic (20-4) team in the PCIAA tourney.

- Prep's one-point upset loss at Conneaut (9-10) was the first the two competed since the Trojans beat the Ramblers by two in Conneaut in 1950.

- Prep's close loss at Buffalo Canisius (13-9) broke a 5-game Rambler win streak over the Crusaders.

- The final standings in City Series basketball were as follows [only the four city public schools competed, with Millcreek (which became "McDowell" in 1954) and Harborcreek in the "Section One" league]:

	W	L
Vincent	8	0
Prep	5	3
Tech	3	5
Academy	3	5
East	1	7

- The biggest disappointments of the season were a pair of losses to Vincent's "Go-Go" Colonels (21-2), who won their first outright city title since 1936, and the PCIAA Western Final ouster to North Catholic (20-4) in a contest played at the Pitt Fieldhouse. After Prep's huge win over Johnstown CC, the Ramblers were unable to cope with a full court press, the rebounding of 6'8½" center **John Sparvero** and **George Brown** and the hot shooting of Brown. The Trojans then lost to St. Rose of Carbondale in the PCIAA Final, 63-56.

- Strong Vincent also won its first of seven District 10 titles for coach **Ralph "Baron" Calabrese**, but lost to Pittsburgh South in PIAA play, 67-64.

High-scoring George Feasler gets two more.

Vinny "Flowers" Kwiatkowski snares a carom.

- Big **George Feasler** was honored as a First Team All-City/All-Scholastic choice by both The *Erie Dispatch* and the *Erie Daily Times*. **Bob "Clutch" Tomczak** (both papers) and **Jim Keim** (*Times*) were Second Team choices, while **Dick Dill** was an Honorable Mention choice with both newspapers. Keim was also named HM by the *Dispatch*.

- **Dick Dill** went on to star in football and lacrosse at Penn State, and was inducted into the Cathedral Prep Hall of Fame in 1995, as a benefactor into the Behrend Athletic Hall of Fame in 1991 and the Metropolitan Erie Sports Hall of Fame in 2010.

- **"Clutch" Tomczak** was inducted into the Cathedral Prep Hall of Fame, with four of his brothers, in 2003. His son-in-law, **Mark Majewski**, is the current Rambler basketball coach.

1955 All-Opponent Team:

Dick Hill, Conneaut Rowe (hm all-state, OH) [Lockborn AFB]

Bob Williams, Conneaut Rowe

Delbert Tice, Sharon

Don Loewel, Tech

Len Jablonski, Tech

Mel Toran, East

Mike "Demon" Polagyi, Vincent

Paul "Zipper" Bruschi, Vincent

Walt Askins, Vincent [Edinboro St.]

Jim Ely, Conneaut

Bob Marcy, Conneaut

Pete Russo, Academy [Dayton, Gannon]

Jim Walsh, Canisius

Frank "Torch" Simon, Vincent

Jack Horvath, Johnstown Central Catholic

John Sparvero, North Catholic

Don DiPasquale, North Catholic

George Brown, North Catholic

Rough and Tumble City Series!

Jim Keim slices through for another bucket agains Tech.

1955-56 (16-7)

Coach: Richard "Dick" Detzel
Captains: George Feasler, Vinny Kwiatkowski
Manager: Victor Gallagher

Date	PREP			Dec.	Loc.	High Scorer	Opponent
11/26	75	Conneaut (OH) Rowe	43	W	H	Feasler (17)	Lynch (12)
12/2	77	Buffalo (NY) Canisius	52	W	H	Keim (25)	Broderick (11)
12/7	63	Bradford	51	W	A	Keim (16)	Barber (19)
12/9	68	Sharon	55	W	H	Kwiatkowski (20)	Fridley (11)
12/16	76	Conneaut (OH)	63	W	A	Kwiatkowski (17)	Strine (18)
12/22	80	Technical	75	W	N	Kwiatkowski (21)	Kovalesky (27)
12/27	71	Bradford	55	W	H	Feasler (30)	Devoe (15)
12/29	69	East	62	W	N	Feasler (22)	Sorenson (22)
1/4	67	Strong Vincent	68	L	N	Feasler (21)	Cahill (22)
1/11	65	McDowell	39	W	H	Feasler (14)	Darby (12)
1/13	54	Academy	57	L	N	Feasler (20)	Pierce (24)
1/17	76	Harborcreek	32	W	H	Keim (20)	Carlson (10)
1/20	77	McDowell	44	W	A	Keim (16)	Darby (14)
1/22	69	Buffalo (NY) Canisius	55	W	A	Kwiatkowski (21)	Broderick (27)
1/27	76	Technical	82*	L	N	Regruth (21)	Kovalesky (32*)
1/29	66	Rochester (NY) Aquinas	70	L	H	Feasler (27)	Burke (21)
2/3	65	East	49	W	N	Feasler (29)	Sorenson (11)
2/9	52	Strong Vincent	62	L	N	Feasler (18)	Cahill (29)
2/17	66	Academy	75	L	N	Feasler (18)	Pierce (36*)
2/21	80	Corry	42	W	H	Keim (15)	Mitchell (11)
2/24	86	Harborcreek	58	W	A	Kwiatkowski (18)	Carlson (23)
		P.C.I.A.A. STATE CATHOLIC H. S. TOURNAMENT					
2/29	79	Johnstown Central Catholic	77	W	A	Feasler (24)	Horvath (18)
3/9	65	Pittsburgh Central Catholic	68	L	H	Costello (16)	Twyman (25)
	1622 (70.5*)		**1334* (58.0*)**				

Pos.	Player	Ht.	Prior School	Class	G(GS)	FG	FT	Total	PPG	Career
C	George Feasler (#13)	6'4"	Holy Rosary	Sr.	23(23)	162	75-155	399	17.3*	615
F	Vinny "Flowers" Kwiatkowski (#9)	6'3"	St. Michael's	Sr.	23(23)	138	56-121	332	14.4	510
G	Jim Keim (#7)	5'11"	St. Andrew's	Sr.	23(18)	122	58-92	302	13.1	459
F	Joe Regruth (#8)	6'1"	Holy Family	Sr.	23(23)	70	63-96	203	8.9	264
G	Ron Costello (#12)	5'11"	Holy Rosary	Jr.	21(6)	38	19-34	95	4.2	95
C	Victor Glembocki (#3)	6'2"	St. Hedwig's	Sr.	21(6)	29	12-25	70	3.1	72
G	Bob Timmons (#11)	5'7"	St. Andrew's	Sr.	17(10)	25	19-34	69	4.1	81
F	Joe Schossler (#15)	5'8"	O.C. Assumption	Sr.	14(3)	17	12-17	46	3.7	53
F	Jim Ehrman (#6)	6'0"	St. Mary's	Jr.	15(3)	16	9-11	41	2.7	41
G	Ed Kopkowski (#5)	5'5"	St. Patrick's	Jr.	12	13	8-15	34	2.9	34
G	Dave Rouen (#17)	6'0"	St. Ann's	Jr.	8	5	2-4	12	1.5	12
G	Tom Quirk (#10)	6'0"	St. Patrick's	Jr.	6	4	0-1	8	1.3	8
F	Gene "Jiggs" Tomczak (#16)	6'0"	St. Stan's	Jr.	8	2	4-8	8	1.0	8
F	Dave Mitchell (#14)	6'3"	St. Andrew's	Jr.	6	3	0-0	6	1.0	6
F	Don "Vindi" Vollbrecht (#4)	6'2"	St. Patrick's	Jr.	1	1	0-0	2	2.0	2
F	Mike McCormick (#15)	6'1"	St. Peter's	Jr.	3	0	1-1	1	0.3	1
G	Bill Eberlein (#4)	5'9"	St. Patrick's	Soph.	1	0	0-0	0	0.0	0
G	Dominic "Pete" Donatucci (#10)	6'0"	Roosevelt	Sr.	1	0	0-0	0	0.0	0

The 1956 Prep Ramblers. Front, L to R: Feasler, Kwiatkowski, Regruth, Ehrman, Glembocki, Keim, Timmons, Coach Detzel; Back: Mitchell, Vollbrecht, McCormick, Tomczak, Rouen, Costello, Quirk, Kopkowski, Mgr. Gallagher.

HIGHLIGHTS:

- With a pre-season prediction to win the title in **Dick Detzel's** eighth season at the helm, Cathedral Prep's highest scoring team got off to an 8-0 start, but faded to a third place tie finish in the rough and tumble City Series. Poor free throw shooting at crucial times bogged the Ramblers down all season.

- All City Series games and the PCIAA Western Final were played at the Gannon Auditorium, while the Ramblers continued to play their independent home contests in the Prep gym.

- Prep opened the season with a victory over Conneaut Rowe (13-7), the last time the two competed. In 1963 Conneaut (OH) and East Lakeville (OH) merged and their respective high schools, the Conneaut Trojans and the Rowe Vikings, became one, the Conneaut High School Spartans.

- The final standings in City Series basketball were as follows (the four city public schools competed with McDowell and Harborcreek in the "Section One" league):

	W	L
Tech	7	1
Academy	6	2
Vincent	3	5
Prep	3	5
East	1	7

- The highlights of the season included the impressive wins over Canisius (9-12) and Sharon (13-8); the victory over city and section champion Tech (16-4); and the two-point thriller over a tough Johnstown Central Catholic (19-6) team at Johnstown's War Memorial Auditorium in the PCIAA tourney.

- Scoring picked up considerably in 1955-56, as both Prep (70.5) and its opponents (58.0) broke team records for most points per game. Prep and Technical combined for 158 points on January 27, breaking a Gannon Audi and City Series record to that point. An opponent team record was broken by Technical with 82 points in that contest, while the Centaurs' **Ray Kovalesky** tied the individual opponent scoring record with 32. Kovalesky's output remained as the highest point total a Tech Centaur ever scored against Prep. Though unknown at the time, that loss to the Centaurs was the 250th defeat in Rambler basketball history.

- 1955-56 was the first season Prep had three players score over 300 points for a season. Despite this fact, it was Prep's first losing season in the City Series since 1948. Both Tech, which lost to Hickory in the District 10 playoffs, 59-51, and Academy (20-4) dumped Prep twice.

- Academy's **Roger Pierce** then broke the single game Prep opponent record with 36 points, 3 shy of Tech star **Carmen Riazzi's** City Series record of 39 set in 1953. Pierce's 36 points lasted as a Prep opponent record until 1966-67, when **Bob Rhoads** of Mercer hit for 40 against the Ramblers. Pierce's effort remained the highest total ever for an Academy player against Prep, and was equaled by Lion **David Purdue's** 36-point display in 1972-73.

- East High's **Ken Biletnikoff** set a Warrior record with 44 points against Harborcreek.

- Strong Vincent's (11-6) fast-breaking Colonels became Erie's first team to score in triple digits, with a 100-60 victory over Geneva (OH).

- Prep and Bradford (10-10) discontinued their four-year "home and away" series until the 1969-70 season.

- The biggest disappointments of the season were the five City Series losses; the close loss at home to Rochester Aquinas (11-4); and the nail-biter to Pittsburgh Central Catholic (18-4) in the PCIAA Western Final, led by **Ned Twyman**, kid brother of **Jack Twyman**, former PCC, University of Cincinnati and Rochester/Cincinnati Royals star. **George Feasler** grabbed 22 rebounds in that contest, but Prep converted only 11 of 24 free throws. PCC, on the other hand, made 22 of 28 FTs and that told the story. The Vikings then lost in the final to Allentown Central Catholic. **Ned Twyman** went on to star at Duquesne University, and was a 6th round draft choice of the Boston Celtics in 1961.

- Big **George Feasler** finished as only the second Prepster ever to score more than 600 in a career. He also broke **Jim Fahey's** points per game average, a record which

Big George Feasler gets an "and one" against Tech.

Thrilling action in the Pittsburgh Central Catholic game?

stood until 1960 when broken by **Bobby Ward** (19.1).

- Feasler was again honored as a First Team All-City/All-Scholastic choice by the *Erie Dispatch* and the *Erie Daily Times*. **Vince Kwiatkowski** (both newspapers) and **Jim Keim** (*Dispatch*) were Second Team choices, while Keim was also an Honorable Mention choice with the *Times*.

- The *Erie Dispatch*'s All-City team was its final one, as the long-time Erie newspaper published its last edition on January 6, 1957. The *Erie Morning News* was inaugurated the next day, January 7, 1957.

- Kwiatkowski, Feasler and Keim all played in the First Annual City-County All-Star games, played on March 20, 1956. Kwiatkowski scored a game-high 18 for the victorious City "B" team (81-41), while Feasler led all scorers with 19 and Keim had 8 for the winning City "A" team (84-62). The idea for the games was started by **Father Francis Schlindwein**, St. Boniface pastor and former Prep assistant football coach, to benefit the less fortunate children of the Erie community.

Jim Keim later starred at John Carroll, then became one of Erie's greatest golfers.

- **Jim Keim**, also a fine golfer, went on to star at John Carroll and was inducted into both the Metro Erie Sports Hall of Fame in 1988 and the Cathedral Prep Hall of Fame in 1998. Keim is also an inductee into the Pennsylvania Golf Hall of Fame.

1956 All-Opponent Team:

Bill Lynch, Conneaut Rowe

Larry Beers, Conneaut Rowe

Stew Barber, Bradford [Penn St., football, NFL Buffalo Bills]

Ray Kovalesky, Tech [Detroit]

Tom Cahill, Vincent [Slippery Rock]

Dale Sorenson, East

Ken Biletnikoff, East

Roger Pierce, Academy

Don Chludzinski, Tech [Yankees rookie league baseball]

Jack McElroy, Tech

Mike Broderick, Canisius

Jim "Howdy" Burke, Rochester Aquinas

"Pistol" Pete Pavia, Rochester Aquinas

Tommy "Booty" Yacobozzi, Vincent [Edinboro St.]

Ed Plonsky, Academy

Jack Horvath, Johnstown Central Catholic

Ned Twyman, Pittsburgh Central Catholic [Duquesne]

Dick Detzel's Final Season!

1956-57 (14-10)

Coach: Richard "Dick" Detzel
Captain: Ron Costello
Manager: Leo Brugger

Hall-of-Famer Ron Costello, one of Prep's all-time, all-around greatest athletes.

Date	PREP			Dec.	Loc.	High Scorer	Opponent
12/9	48	Buffalo (NY) Canisius	50	L	H	Costello (14)	Wlodarczak (18)
12/11	44	Sharon	86*	L	A	Quirk & Costello (9)	DuMars (19)
12/15	50	Conneaut (OH)	67	L	H	Costello (19)	Lacey (21)
12/21	56	East	43	W	N	Carey (21)	Sorenson (14)
12/23	56	Buffalo (NY) Bishop Timon	53	W	H	Carey (14)	Gallo (15)
12/28	59	Strong Vincent	61(OT)	L	N	Costello (21)	Redinger (18)
1/4	79	Academy	26	W	N	Carey (19)	Feldman (6)
1/6	51	St. Marys Central Catholic	55	L	A	Carey (15)	Nicklas (16)
1/8	58	Harborcreek	45	W	A	Costello (24)	Carlson (16)
1/11	57	McDowell	48	W	A	Costello (26)	Trohoske & Darby (12)
1/18	70	Technical	66	W	N	Carey (20)	Felix (16)
1/20	34	Buffalo (NY) Bishop Timon	55	L	A	Eberlein (9)	Gallo (16)
1/25	52	East	44	W	N	Ehrman (16)	Sorenson (12)
2/1	61	Strong Vincent	76	L	N	Costello (23)	Redinger (23)
2/3	61	Buffalo (NY) Canisius	73	L	A	Costello (21)	Gabbey (18)
2/8	92	Academy	51	W	N	Ehrman & Costello (19)	Feldman (23)
2/12	68	McDowell	62	W	H	Tomczak (16)	Darby (20)
2/15	72	Harborcreek	55	W	H	Costello (28)	Hackenberg (16)
2/17	48	Rochester (NY) Aquinas	52	L	A	Ehrman (14)	Wagner & Pelcher (14)
2/18	74	Corry	58	W	A	Costello (32)	Turner (20)
2/22	54	Technical	38	W	N	Carey (15)	Seiersen (13)
3/3	80	St. Marys Central Catholic	45	W	H	Carey (19)	Hasselman (13)

P.C.I.A.A. STATE CATHOLIC H. S. TOURNAMENT

Date	PREP			Dec.	Loc.	High Scorer	Opponent
3/6	50	St. Marys Central Catholic	40	W	N	Carey (17)	Hasselman (14)
3/8	59	Pittsburgh Central Catholic	65	L	A	Costello (22)	Masa (28)
	1433 (59.7)		**1314 (54.7)**				

Pos.	Player	Prior School	Class	G(GS)	FG	FT	Total	*PPG*	Career
G	Ron Costello (#21)	Holy Rosary	Sr.	24(23)	150	71	371	15.4	466
F	Bill Carey (#42)	Hamburg (NY) HS	Sr.	21(21)	96	49	241	11.5	241
F	Jim Ehrman (#45)	St. Mary's	Sr.	23(22)	87	47	221	9.2	262
G	Ed Kopkowski (#14)	St. Patrick's	Sr.	21(14)	49	45	143	6.8	177
F	Gene "Jiggs" Tomczak (#43)	St. Stan's	Sr.	24(22)	49	39	137	5.7	145
G	Tom Quirk (#34)	St. Patrick's	Sr.	23(12)	41	29	111	4.8	119
G	Bill Eberlein (#41)	St. Patrick's	Jr.	14(1)	23	4	50	3.6	50
F	Al Stankiewicz (#15)	St. John's	Soph.	12	10	16	36	3.0	36
F	Bill Galla (#25)	Holy Family	Jr.	12(1)	9	16	34	2.8	34
F	Ralph Hellman (#24)	Sacred Heart	Sr.	13	11	8	30	2.3	30
C	Dave Mitchell (#54)	St. Andrew's	Sr.	10(2)	6	5	17	1.7	23
F	Tom Walkiewicz (#52)	Holy Trinity	Jr.	8(1)	6	4	16	2.0	16
G	Ed Wittman (#23)	St. Andrew's	Jr.	7(1)	5	5	15	2.1	15
G	Maury Marchant (#12)	St. Patrick's	Jr.	7	5	0	10	1.4	10
G	Jim Rudy (#32)	Sacred Heart	Soph.	5	3	0	6	1.2	6

Row one, left to right: L. Brugger, manager; J. Ehrman, T. Walkiewicz, W. Carey, D. Mitchell, J. Rudy, W. Galla, E. Tomczak, and Richard Detzel coach. *Row two*: E. Kopkowski, R. Costello, W. Eberlein, A. Stankiewicz, T. Quirk, R. Hellman, E. Wittmann, and M. Marchant.

HIGHLIGHTS:

- All City Series games were played at the frenzied Gannon Auditorium, while Cathedral Prep continued to play its independent home contests in the Prep gym.

- The free throw lane was widened from 6 feet to 12 feet, beginning with the 1956-57 season.

- Prep began with three straight losses, its worst start since the 1947-48 season. Canisius took down the Ramblers with a last-second jump shot by **Terry O'Connor** in the opener. This was followed by a complete drubbing from powerful Sharon (28-0) and an embarrassing loss to Conneaut (16-3) when Prep was outscored 25-2 in the fourth quarter—at home. The Ramblers had led by six at the end of three. Only Ashtabula, twice, and Ashtabula Harbor defeated the Trojans during the campaign. Two of Conneaut's victories were over McDowell.

- Sharon broke Tech's record for most points scored against Prep with 86. It was the largest defeat suffered by a Rambler team since 1926. The powerful Tigers featured 6'6" center **John Fridley** and **Mark DuMars**, a 5'10" sharpshooting guard. Sharon went on to win the PIAA state championship, defeating Chester in the final, 59-50, in Philadelphia's Palestra. The Tigers, in the WPIAL at the time, finished with a glossy, unbeaten season.

- The Ramblers started slow, but came on strong in City Series competition. Disappointing losses to Vincent's "Go-Go" Colonels (19-4) spelled the difference. The initial battle was Prep's first overtime game in nearly 15 years. In the second SV contest, lanky **"Mickey" Atkinson** had 33 rebounds for the Red & Black. That is believed to be a Prep opponent record. Vincent won its first of four consecutive District 10 titles in 1957.

- Prep's wins over McDowell (11-8) ran its string to 20 straight victories over the Trojans.

- Prep began a three-year home-and-home contract with a new opponent, Bishop Timon, an all-male Franciscan high school located in South Buffalo. Timon's coach was **Mel Palano**, who went on to coach the Tigers until 1989, for 37 years. Timon was previously an opponent of the Ramblers in football in 1950 and 1951. The school's name was changed to Bishop Timon-St. Jude in 1993, after a major benefactor's gift to the school.

- Canisius (17-3), which beat Prep twice, won Buffalo's Manhattan Cup after a three-year famine. The Crusaders dethroned Bishop Timon, who in 1956 had the Cup tourney MVP and future St. Bonaventure and NBA star **Ronald "Whitey" Martin.**

- Prep's loss to Rochester Aquinas (13-2) was the last time the two met until the 2014-15 season, a lapse of 58 years. In the meantime the Ramblers and Lil' Irish met 13 times in football.

- The final standings in City Series basketball were as follows:

	W	L
Vincent	8	0
Prep	6	2
Tech	4	4
East	1	7
Academy	1	7

- The highlights of the season were the two heated late season victories over St. Marys Central Catholic (18-6), the first to force a playoff to represent the Erie Diocese in the PCIAA tournament, and the second in the Diocesan final. The first of the two created quite a controversy, when it was reported that Prep Headmaster **Monsignor Robert McDonald** forced students to purchase tickets, selling every available seating space in the Prep gym to, in essence, "shut the door" and leave out St. Marys fans. Monsignor McDonald responded: "There was no intention to shut out St. Marys fans at Sunday's game. We knew this game would be a sell-out and we wanted to avoid any last-minute jams. We didn't want St. Marys fans coming here and then being turned away. We put tickets on sale in our homerooms, then had a Friday rally for all those who purchased tickets. We felt it was fair for only those interested to attend the rally. When we sold out all 800 tickets, I informed St. Marys so they wouldn't be disappointed on Sunday. This saved any last-minute mix-ups. We just didn't have room for everyone. It was a physical impossibility to get any more fans into our gym Sunday." St. Marys CC principal and athletic director **Father Donald, O.S.B.** was peeved at what he felt was rude treatment from "Black Mac".

- After the Ramblers crushed St. Marys, the best-of-three playoff was actually held in Jamestown (NY), with a sellout crowd and 750 tickets given to each school. It was possibly the only time a Pennsylvania state playoff game was actually contested in another state!

- The close loss in the PCIAA Western Semifinal, Prep's third straight to Pittsburgh Central Catholic (19-5), was played at Mt. Lebanon High School. The Ramblers could connect on only 9 of 17 free throws. The Vikings then lost in the Western Final to Johnstown Central Catholic, which then lost to Allentown Central Catholic for the state crown. It was Allentown's second straight PCIAA Class A diadem.

- Another highlight of the season was the impressive play of senior team leader **Ron Costello**, honored as a First Team All-Scholastic choice by the *Erie Daily Times*. Costello, a four-year class president, went on to star in football at Xavier (OH) and later returned to teach and coach at Prep (1960-65). After coaching football at Edinboro State for a year, Costello was appointed head football coach at Tech Memorial in 1968, where he retired as the Centaurs' all-time winningest coach after 20 years. He was inducted into the Cathedral Prep Athletic Hall of Fame in 1993 and the Metropolitan Erie Sports Hall of Fame in 1994. Prep posthumously honors Costello with the "Ronald G. Costello Courage Award", given each year to a Prep alumnus who has demonstrated the ability to "greet life's challenges with courage and dignity."

Transfer student Bill Carey had a fine senior season and went on to become one of Gannon's all-time greats, once scoring 54 points in a game.

"Jiggs" Tomczak drives against East's Conley.

- After a 10-year layoff because of what was reported as "bad blood" between the teams, Prep, in January, went to play St. Marys at what was supposed to be a public school location because of the Crusaders' "band-box" gym. When the Rambler squad and its coaches appeared, no one was there, so Prep was forced to play at St. Marys, where it suffered a close defeat. Following the game, St. Marys fans mauled the Prep team, knocking star **Bill Carey** down a flight of stairs! Prep and St. Marys CC never scheduled a regular season game again.

- **Bill Carey** came on strong as an outstanding point-maker and rebounder. An all-state transfer from Hamburg (NY) High School, Carey went on to become one of Gannon College's all-time greats. There, as a senior, he averaged 23.1 *PPG* and he still holds the single game scoring record with 54 points against Stewart Air Force Base in 1961. He earned a tryout with the NBA's St. Louis Hawks, and was chosen to compete on the U. S. cage team at the Pan-American games in 1963. He later coached the Armed Forces all-stars from 1979-89. Carey was inducted into the Cathedral Prep Athletic Hall of Fame in 1994.

Jimmy Ehrman was a dead-eye shooter.

1957 All-Opponent Team:

> Ed "Woody" Wlodarczak, Canisius [Canisius]
> Mark DuMars, Sharon (1st team all-state) [Penn State]
> John Fridley, Sharon (3rd team all-state) [Pitt]
> Bernie "Pete" Culp, Sharon (hm all-state) [Anderson (IN); ABA Cleveland Pipers]
> Jim Dombroski, Conneaut
> Bill Lacey, Conneaut [Baldwin Wallace, football]
> Dale Sorenson, East
> Don Gallo, Bishop Timon
> Hal "Buzz" Redinger, Vincent (2nd team all-state) [Slippery Rock]
> Renny Nicklas, St. Marys Central Catholic
> Emidio "Cat" Felix, Tech
> Tommy "Booty" Yacobozzi, Vincent (hm all-state) [Edinboro St.]
> Jim "Mickey" Atkinson, Vincent (hm all-state) [Flint (MI) JC]
> John Gabbey, Canisius [Canisius]
> Dick Darby, McDowell
> Roger Wagner, Rochester Aquinas
> Ken Pelcher, Rochester Aquinas
> Bill Turner, Corry
> LeRoy "Tubby" Hasselman, St. Marys Central Catholic
> Ray Masa, Pittsburgh Central Catholic

- Carey and **Jim Ehrman** were selected Second Team choices by the *Erie Daily Times*, while **Gene "Jiggs" Tomczak** was an Honorable Mention choice. Tomczak is also a Prep Hall of Fame inductee, given the honor with four of his brothers (of which Pat is the youngest) in 2003.

- The second annual City-County All-Star game was, this time, sponsored by the Belle Valley Lions Club. A new format to expect more evenly matched games divided the stars into East and West squads, with city and county players each simply facing their own. **"Jiggs" Tomczak** scored 6 for the victorious West squad (66-60), while Carey and Costello, toiling for the East side, scored 10 and 16 points respectively. East star **"Carney" Metzgar**, later head coach at East, led all scorers with 16.

- Coach **Richard "Dick" Detzel** retired from the hoops game after being named Prep's head football coach in 1957. In nine years as coach of the Rambler varsity basketball team, Detzel led his charges to three undisputed City Series championships and three more seasons in which the Ramblers shared the crown three ways. His 1952-53 and 1953-54 teams were Erie's first state championship teams. He finished as Prep's winningest coach with a "Golden Era" record of 145-55, for a .725 winning percentage. Detzel went on to coach a pair of city champ gridiron teams, finishing with a three year record of 16-9. He later became head football coach at Strong Vincent. Detzel was inducted into the Cathedral Prep Athletic Hall of Fame in 1993.

Slow Start for New Coach!

1957-58 (7-14)

Coach: Robert "Bob" Trombacco
Captains: Bill Galla, Bill Eberlein
Managers: Dave DeSante, Jim Karle

Coach Tombacco gives intructions to senior captains Bill Galla and Bill Eberlein.

Date	PREP			Dec.	Loc.	High Scorer	Opponent
12/7	48	Cleveland (OH) Cathedral Latin	59	L	H	Tomczak & Marchant (12)	Gacey & Baracz (18)
12/13	31	Sharon	66	L	A	Stankiewicz & Marchant (12)	Winters & Dadio (18)
12/17	38	Conneaut (OH)	62	L	H	Wittman (13)	Lacey (29)
12/19	58	Strong Vincent	54	W	N	Foster & Eberlein (16)	E. Smith (21)
12/27	57	Academy	52	W	N	Galla (16)	Feldman (19)
12/29	35	Buffalo (NY) Bishop Timon	49	L	H	Eberlein (14)	Guest (17)
1/3	57	Harborcreek	49	W	A	Galla (12)	Moorehead (21)
1/7	48	McDowell	50	L	H	Foster (15)	Trohoske (15)
1/10	49	Technical	65	L	N	Eberlein (19)	Litz (21)
1/17	61	East	64(OT)	L	N	Galla (15)	Conley (23)
1/19	49	Buffalo (NY) Canisius	56	L	A	Eberlein (13)	Agate (19)
1/24	50	Strong Vincent	55	L	N	Stankiewicz (14)	J. Smith (16)
1/31	37	Academy	48	L	N	Galla (11)	Feldman (18)
2/4	65	Harborcreek	45	W	H	Eberlein (21)	Moorehead (18)
2/7	55	McDowell	72	L	A	Foster (13)	Trohoske (22)
2/14	64	Technical	56	W	N	Wittman (19)	Parmeter (24)
2/21	46	East	51	L	N	Galla (21)	Fisher (16)
2/23	53	Buffalo (NY) Bishop Timon	62	L	A	Wittman (17)	McDonald (18)
2/28	82	Buffalo (NY) Canisius	68	W	H	Stankiewicz (27)	Agate (30)
		P.C.I.A.A. STATE CATHOLIC H. S. TOURNAMENT					
3/7	53	St. Marys Central Catholic	44	W	N	Wittman (18)	Meyer (21)
3/14	60	Pittsburgh North Catholic	78	L	H	Rudy (16)	Szykowny (28)
	1096 (52.0)		**1199 (57.0)**				

Pos.	Player	Ht.	Prior School	Class	G(GS)	FG	FT	Total	*PPG*	Career
G	Ed Wittman (#14)	5'10"	St. Andrew's	Sr.	21(21)	79	52-89	210	10.0	225
F	Bill Galla (#25)	6'1"	Holy Family	Sr.	20(19)	73	47-69	193	9.7	227
C	Herb Foster (#43)	6'3"	Wilson	Jr.	19(13)	60	14-31	134	7.1	134
G	Bill Eberlein (#41)	5'10"	St. Patrick's	Sr.	17(13)	57	15-32	129	7.6	179
F	Al Stankiewicz (#15)	6'0"	St. John's	Jr.	20(8)	46	34-49	126	6.3	162
F	Jim Rudy (#32)	6'2"	Sacred Heart	Jr.	13(9)	27	15-27	69	5.3	75
G	Chuck Bauder (#34)	5'10"	St. Andrew's	Jr.	15(6)	30	6-15	66	4.4	66
C	Pat Tomczak (#21)	6'2"	St. Stan's	Soph.	18(3)	22	19-44	63	3.5	63
G	Maury Marchant (#45)	5'7"	St. Patrick's	Sr.	10(7)	24	9-25	57	5.7	67
G	Joe Messina (#12)	6'0"	St. Patrick's	Jr.	14(4)	13	9-18	35	2.5	35
G	John Garbin (#54)	5'10"	St. Michael's	Jr.	11(2)	6	3-9	15	1.4	15
C	Rick Amendola (#32)	6'3"	St. Patrick's	Soph.	4	0	2-4	2	0.5	2
G	Steve Hanson (#42)	5'9"	St. John's	Jr.	1	3	0-0	6	6.0	6
F	Tom Walkiewicz (#24)	6'2"	Holy Trinity	Sr.	0	0	0-0	0	0.0	16
F	Tom Konkol (#52)	6'2"	St. Stan's	Jr.	0	0	0-0	0	0.0	0
F	Gary Gabutti (#23)	5'11"	St. Peter's	Jr	0	0	0-0	0	0.0	0

Coach Trombacco's first Prep team (1958). Front, L to R: Coach Trombacco, Hanson, Wittman, Bauder, Messina, Eberlein, Garbin, Mgr. DeSante, Mgr. Karle; Back: Stankiewicz, Walkiewicz, Galla, Rudy, Foster, Tomczak, Konkol, Gabutti.

SEASON HIGHLIGHTS:

- **Robert "Bob" Trombacco** was named Cathedral Prep's new basketball coach after the appointment of "**Dick**" **Detzel** as the new Rambler head football coach. Trombacco hailed from Farrell, where he was an assistant under legendary coach **Ed McCluskey** for six years (1951-57). The 32-year old played for Farrell High and was an all-state nominee his senior year. He co-captained the team his senior year and his squad lost in the 1943 PIAA Final to Lower Merion at the Palestra in Philadelphia, 29-28. He graduated from Gannon College in 1951, then moved back to Farrell as an assistant coach. A disciplinarian and a true protégé of the Coach McCluskey style, Trombacco made his players shoot free throws underhand but promised that the Ramblers would operate under a completely new system: "We'll run and gun!"

- Coach Trombacco's first Prep team suffered from inexperience and injuries, and the only returning letterman was **Bill Eberlein**. Another letterman, big **Tom Walkiewicz**, was unable to perform as he needed to recuperate from several football-related injuries. **Jim Rudy** missed a portion of the season when he broke a bone in his foot, while **Maury Marchant** was also out several games with a broken finger. Senior **Eddie Wittman** was the only Rambler to average in double figures for the season, right at 10.0.

- All City Series games and the North Catholic PCIAA game were played at the jam-packed Gannon Auditorium, while the Ramblers continued to play their independent home contests in the Prep gym.

- Prep was beaten in the home opener by Cathedral Latin (17-6), a team that was coming off a 23-1 season. Latin went on a late-season tear, winning its section title before losing to Columbus East in state playoffs, 61-59. One of the Lions' stars was **Don Gacey**, who later coached Cathedral Latin to its only Ohio state basketball championship in 1977 (24-2). Gacey also starred at John Carroll, finishing his career as the Blue Streaks' second all-time leading scorer.

- The opener was followed by a drubbing at Sharon (19-6), which made it to the WPIAL semifinal round before losing to Washington, 50-36. Prep then lost again on the home floor to Conneaut (15-3).

Leading scorer Eddie Wittman plows through for two more against McDowell.

- The final standings in City Series basketball were as follows:

	W	L
Vincent	6	2
East	5	3
Academy	4	4
Prep	3	5
Tech	2	6

Bill Eberlein shows perfect form sinking an outside jumper.

- The highlight of the season was the upset in the City Series opener versus the D-10 championship Vincent (17-5) squad, which featured stars **"Mickey" Atkinson** (3rd team all-state, AP), **Wally Knox, Esker Smith** and **Jim Smith**. **Herb Foster** and **Bill Eberlein** each scored 16 in Prep's first win over SV since 1954. The exciting "Go-Go" Colonels of coach **Ralph "Baron" Calabrese** made it all the way to the PIAA Western Final before bowing to Altoona, 58-53.

- The other big Prep win was over St. Marys Central Catholic (19-5) in PCIAA competition played at Northern Area High School in Sugar Grove, Warren County. **Ed Wittman**, the only Rambler to start every game for the season, broke loose for 18 points in that one. The Ramblers were then no match for eventual state champ North Catholic (24-3), which featured an outstanding performance from 6'2" all-stater **Matt Szykowny**. Fisticuffs marred the Prep-NC game with Szykowny and teammate **Dick Turici** both being ejected at 5:02 of the fourth quarter. Turici was exited after connecting on a couple of rights to the chin of Rambler

Jim Rudy, while Szykowny was sent to the showers after elbowing a Prepster on his way to the free throw line for his own fifth foul. Fast-breaking North followed with an easy 90-60 victory over Johnstown Bishop McCort in the Western Final, then triumphed over Harrisburg Bishop McDevitt (formerly Harrisburg Catholic) to win all the marbles.

- McDowell's (13-6) two wins over Prep were its first after twenty straight victories by the Ramblers.

- East High's (12-9) two wins over the Ramblers were its only against 22 victories for Prep during the years 1954 through 1965.

- Bishop Timon (17-4), which defeated Prep twice, made it to the Manhattan Cup final, where it lost to St. Francis, 67-52. At the time Timon and opponent Canisius operated in the Bishop Burke Division of Buffalo's Monsignor Martin Athletic Association, along with Buffalo Bishop Ryan, Buffalo Bishop Fallon, Buffalo St. Joseph's Collegiate Institute, Lackawanna Baker-Victory, and Niagara Falls Bishop Duffy. The Bishop Smith Division consisted of Buffalo Cardinal Dougherty, Athol Springs St. Francis, Williamsville Bishop Neumann, Batavia Notre Dame Academy, Lockport DeSales, Dunkirk Cardinal Midzenty and Lancaster St. Mary's.

- This was the first season since 1948 that Prep did not have a first or second team All Scholastic selection. Only **Bill Galla** was named an Honorable Mention choice by the *Erie Daily Times*.

- The third annual City-County All-Star game, sponsored by the Belle Valley Lions Club, reverted back to pitting the City squads against the County. **Maury Marchant** scored two for the City's victorious "B" squad, while **Ed Wittman** scored five and **Bill Galla** two in a losing effort in the "A" game. Prep coach **Bob Trombacco** was one of the coaches for the City. The games were played in the brand new Memorial Junior High gymnasium on Cherry Street.

1958 All-Opponent Team:

> Donald Gacey, Cathedral Latin [John Carroll]
> Joe Perrella, Cathedral Latin
> John Baracz, Cathedral Latin
> Ed Winters, Sharon [St. Francis (PA)]
> Bill Dadio, Sharon
> Bill Lacey, Conneaut [Baldwin Wallace, football]
> Tom Walter, Conneaut
> Jim "Mickey" Atkinson, Vincent (3rd team all-state)
>   [Flint (MI) JC]
> Esker Smith, Vincent
> Bob Feldman, Academy
> Brian Guest, Bishop Timon [Gannon,
>   basketball & baseball]
> Steve Moorehead, Harborcreek [Penn State,
>   cross country & track]
> Dick Feidler, McDowell [Syracuse, football]
> Walt Litz, Tech
> Tim Conley, East
> Charlie Fisher, East [Gannon]
> Bill McDonald, Bishop Timon (All-Catholic, NY)
> Tom Agate, Canisius
> Dave Parmeter, Tech
> LeRoy "Tubby" Hasselman, St. Marys Central Catholic
> Jake Meyer, St. Marys Central Catholic
> John Mauro, North Catholic [Gannon]
> Matt Szykowny, North Catholic (3rd team all-state)
>   [Iowa baseball, basketball & football;
>   Erie Sailors baseball]

Ramblers, Go-Go Colonels Present Thrilling Season!
1958-59 (16-6)

Coach: Robert "Bob" Trombacco
Captains: Herb Foster, Al Stankiewicz
Managers: Dave DeSante, Jim Karle

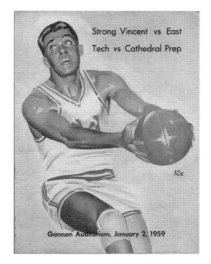

Strong Vincent vs East
Tech vs Cathedral Prep

Gannon Auditorium, January 2, 1959

Programs were only a dime, and they contained a wealth of information.

Date	PREP		Dec.	Loc.	High Scorer	Opponent
12/6	47	Cleveland (OH) Cathedral Latin	59	L	A	Tomczak & Ward (12)	Payne (17)
12/9	67	Linesville	43	W	A	Stankiewicz (19)	Carlson (10)
12/12	35	Sharon	38	L	H	Tomczak & Rudy (9)	Gibson (10)
12/14	68	Buffalo (NY) Canisius	66	W	H	Bauder (25)	Naples (19)
12/16	55	Conneaut (OH)	63	L	H	Foster (14)	Minor (17)
12/18	58	Academy	37	W	N	Bauder (26)	Blanchard (13)
12/22	69	Harborcreek	36	W	H	Bauder (19)	Henry (16)
12/28	64	Buffalo (NY) Bishop Timon	45	W	H	Stankiewicz (18)	Guest (17)
12/30	67	McDowell	61	W	A	Stankiewicz (21)	Sanders (21)
1/2	67	Technical	43	W	N	Stankiewicz (17)	Valahovic (16)
1/9	64	East	44	W	N	Stankiewicz (18)	Klopfer (13)
1/17	71	Strong Vincent	66	W	N	Tomczak (23)	Hickock (26)
1/23	46	Academy	45	W	N	Stankiewicz & Tomczak (16)	Deibler (16)
1/30	77	Harborcreek	53	W	A	Ward (16)	Henry (23)
2/3	85	McDowell	69	W	H	Stankiewicz (27)	Dingfelder (14)
2/6	64	Technical	41	W	N	Stankiewicz (15)	Biletnikoff (14)
2/13	62	East	51	W	N	Stankiewicz (22)	Gulick (19)
2/20	66	Strong Vincent	67	L	N	Bauder (21)	Smith (23)
2/22	48	Buffalo (NY) Bishop Timon	50	L	A	Foster (12)	Minkiewicz, Guest & Cipriani (14)
		CITY CHAMPIONSHIP PLAYOFF					
2/26	55	Strong Vincent	54	W	N	Nies (18)	Hickock (17)
		P.C.I.A.A. STATE CATHOLIC H. S. TOURNAMENT					
3/6	52	St. Marys Central Catholic	26	W	N	Foster (19)	Goetz (17)
3/13	54	Pittsburgh North Catholic	70	L	A	Foster (14)	Szykowny & Brown (18)
	1341 (61.0)		**1127 (52.1)**				

Pos.	Player	Ht.	Prior School	Class	G(GS)	FG	FT	Total	*PPG*	Career
F	Al Stankiewicz (#15)	6'1"	St. John's	Sr.	20(19)	100	80-132	280	14.0	442
C	Herb Foster (#43)	6'3"	Wilson	Sr.	22(22)	101	38-72	240	10.9	374
G	Chuck Bauder (#34)	5'10"	St. Andrew's	Sr.	22(19)	76	56-90	208	9.5	274
F	Pat Tomczak (#21)	6'2"	St. Stan's	Jr.	21(21)	81	32-63	194	9.2	257
G	Bernie Nies (#14)	5'10"	St. John's	Jr.	22(17)	59	44-61	162	7.4	162
F	Jim Rudy (#24)	6'2"	Sacred Heart	Sr.	21(7)	41	21-35	103	4.9	178
G	Bob Ward (#23)	5'11"	Holy Family	Jr.	17(3)	28	19-26	75	4.4	75
G	Joe Messina (#12)	6'0"	St. Patrick's	Sr.	19(1)	16	13-23	45	2.4	80
C	Rick Amendola (#32)	6'3"	St. Patrick's	Jr.	9(1)	3	2-6	8	0.9	10
F	Dave "Tex" Reuter (#45)	6'2"	St. Mary's	Jr.	8	3	1-5	7	0.9	7
F	Tom Yonko (#52)	5'11"	St. Casimir's	Jr.	3	0	5-5	5	1.7	5
F	Joe Lazorchak (#54)	6'0"	Holy Family	Jr.	4	2	0-0	4	1.0	4
G	Eddie Kuhar (#25)	5'9"	Holy Family	Jr.	3	0	2-2	2	0.7	2
G	Steve Moore (#41)	5'10"	St. Luke's	Jr.	1	1	0-0	2	2.0	2
G	Joe Blaszczyk (#42)	5'11"	Holy Rosary	Jr.	1	0	0-0	0	0.0	0

The 1959 Prep Ramblers, City Series playoff champs. Front, L to R: Messina, Lazorchak, Nies, Blaszczyk, Moore, Yonko, Kuhar, Mgr. DeSante; Back: Reuter, Stankiewicz, Tomzak, Amendola, Foster, Rudy, Ward, Mgr. Karle.

HIGHLIGHTS:

- An exciting season saw Cathedral Prep coach **Bob Trombacco** win his first City Series title in his second season at the Rambler helm. Turnaway crowds of over 3,000 were assured at the City Series doubleheaders, with games played at 7:30 and 9:00 p.m.

- All City Series games were played at the Gannon Auditorium, while the Ramblers continued to play their independent home contests in the Prep gym. The PCIAA playoff contest versus St. Marys Central Catholic (10-14) was played on a neutral court at Northern Area High School, in Sugar Grove, Warren County.

- Prep opened with another loss to Cleveland area sectional champ Cathedral Latin (15-5), which featured 6'7" **Alvin Payne**, who for the season averaged 20 *PPG* and 17.5 *RPG*. Two of the Lions losses were to powerful East Tech, 69-42 and 74-63.

- Prep's win over Linesville (16-6) came in the first year of a four-year home-and-away contract with the Lions, who won Crawford County League title in 1959.

- Prep's home loss to Sharon (17-5) was the Tigers' third straight victory over the Ramblers.

- Another thrilling win for Prep was the home court victory over Buffalo Canisius (5-9), when **Chuck Bauder** hit a 15-foot jump shot with two seconds left for a 68-66 final. Bauder poured in 25 points in the contest,

Chuck Bauder was the big hero of the Canisius game, sinking a 15-foot jumper with two seconds left for the win.

including 13-of-16 from the free throw line. Four days later, against Academy, Bauder would sink a school record 14 FT's.

- Prep suffered its third consecutive home court loss to Conneaut (16-4) after being outscored 20-7 in the fourth quarter. The Trojans fine record included a pair of wins over McDowell's Trojans. Conneaut's win over Prep was its fourth in the previous five seasons, with the Ramblers winning one. The series then laid dormant until the 1969-70 season.

All-City star Al Stankiewicz drives for two against Bishop Timon. He later became a successful professional boxer and his son played for the Yankees!

- Prep's home contest with Bishop Timon (19-5) on Sunday, December 28, was switched from an afternoon contest to an 8:00 p.m. start so that fans could witness the exciting televised NFL Championship game between the New York Giants and the Baltimore Colts. In what has been considered "the greatest

This amazing photo shows SV's Bill Senger scoring at the buzzer while lying flat on his back, giving the Colonels a one-point win and forcing a playoff for the City Series crown.

football game ever played" and the game which ushered in football's "television era," the **Johnny Unitas**-led Colts defeated the Giants in football's first overtime contest, 23-17.

- The final standings in City Series basketball were as follows (Harborcreek had joined with McDowell and the four city public schools to form a new "Section One"; along with Prep in football it formed the "Big Seven"):

	W	L
*Prep	8	1
Vincent	7	2
East	2	6
Tech	2	6
Academy	2	6

won city championship playoff

- The highlights of the season were a 12-game win streak and the heart-pounding wins over "Go-Go" Vincent's (19-4) defending champs during the regular season and in the City Series playoff for the title. In the first contest, **Pat Tomczak** scored 23 to defeat the foul-plagued Colonels by 5. **Esker Smith** scored 23 and **Bill "Dutch" Senger** scored the game-winner lying on his back as SV won the rematch in a one-point thriller. In the playoff battle, **Bernie Nies** hit the long bombs and **Jim Rudy**, on a feed from Tomczak, hit the game winner with 20 seconds left as the Orange & Black came from behind to win by one. That victory gave Prep its first city crown since 1954. Vincent won its third straight District 10 title, but lost in a PIAA Regional contest to DuBois, 50-48.

- Prep's three-year home-and-home series with Bishop Timon ended with a two-point Rambler loss in Buffalo. The Tigers showcased future Gannon College performer **Brian Guest**, who was only the second three-sport (also football and baseball) All-Catholic selection since the Monsignor Martin

Athletic Association was formed in 1948. Timon and Prep did not compete again until the 1985-86 season, when relations were renewed in football as well.

- The biggest disappointment was another loss to the great **Matt Szykowny** and his Pittsburgh North Catholic Trojans (25-2) in the PCIAA Western Final at the Pitt Fieldhouse. It was Prep's 10th straight loss to a Pittsburgh entry in the PCIAA's. Meanwhile, North Catholic went on to win its second consecutive PCIAA state title and its fifth overall, smothering Allentown Central Catholic, 83-67. Szykowny went on to star at quarterback for Iowa in the Big Ten. He still holds North Catholic's all-time career scoring record with 1,852 points.

North Catholic's Matt Szykowny shoots over Bauder in PCIAA action.

- **Al Stankiewicz** and **Herb Foster** were honored as First Team All Scholastic choices by the *Erie Daily Times*. **Bernie Nies, Chuck Bauder** and **Pat Tomczak** were all Second Team selections.

- Stankiewicz, also an excellent pole vaulter for the Ramblers, played hoops at Gannon College and later became a successful professional boxer under the name **Al Stankie**. He was inducted into the California Boxing Hall of Fame in 2012. Al's son, **Andy Stankiewicz**, caused a bit of a sensation in 1992 with the New York Yankees, breaking in at age 27 as a fine infielder. Andy played six more years in the majors, also with the Astros, Expos and Diamondbacks.

- **Herb Foster** went on to Syracuse University where he started two years at big forward. As senior team captain in 1962-63, Foster led the Orangemen in rebounding (5.5 *RPG*) and was second in scoring (10.6 *PPG*).

- All-around athlete **Joe Lazorchak** did not play basketball as a senior, but did go on to play baseball at Gannon College.

Herb Foster, Prep's First Team All-City center.

- The fourth annual City-County All-Star game, under the joint sponsorship of the Belle Valley Lions Club and the Erie County Retarded Children's Association, again saw the City All-Stars win both "A" & "B" games at the Memorial Junior High gym. In the "A" game, **Al Stankiewicz** starred with 15 points, while Bauder and Foster each scored two. SV's **Wally Knox** led all scorers with 25 for the City "A's".

Vincent's Wally Knox and Prep's Pat Tomczak engage in a steel cage death match for the ball.

1959 All-Opponent Team:

Alvin Payne, Cathedral Latin
Ronald Gibson, Sharon
Elvorne "Bucky" Ferguson, Sharon
Jim Naples, Canisius
Fred Minor, Conneaut
Gary McWilliams, Conneaut
Ron Hall, Conneaut
Brian Guest, Bishop Timon [Gannon, basketball & baseball]
Dick Valahovic, Tech
Ralph Sanders, Millcreek
Dave Hickock, Vincent [Muskingum, basketball & baseball]
Wally Knox, Vincent
Dave Henry, Harborcreek
Esker Smith, Vincent (hm, all-state)
Bill Senger, Vincent
Frank Cipriani, Bishop Timon [MLB Kansas City Athletics]
Tom Goetz, St. Marys Central Catholic [St. Vincent (PA)]
Tom Brown, North Catholic
Matt Szykowny, North Catholic (1st team all-state, Parade Magazine 2nd team All-American) [Iowa, baseball, basketball & football; Erie Sailors]

Herb Foster continued his career in the starting lineup at Syracuse University.

Pat Tomczak, determined to score again.

Joe Messina goes strong to the hoop.

The 1960's

Jubilant Ramblers celebrate their 8th outright and 11th overall city title (1964). In front: JV coach "Gus" Thomas, Pat Lupo, Tim Maloney, Dave Wenrick and coach "Red" Murray.

City Champs After a Four-Way Tie!

1959-60 (17-6)

Coach: Robert "Bob" Trombacco
Captain: Pat Tomczak

All-City star Bob Ward broke the points per game average with 19.1.

Date	PREP			Dec.	Loc.	High Scorer	Opponent
12/4	54	Linesville	48	W	H	Ward (19)	Headley (15)
12/8	93	Ashtabula (OH) St. John School	40	W	H	Tomczak (18)	Colin (13)
12/11	50	Buffalo (NY) Canisius	51	L	A	Tomczak (13)	Stasio (16)
12/15	38	Sharon	37	W	H	Ward (13)	Youkers (13)
12/18	72	Tech Memorial	70	W	N	Ward (22)	Golembeski (23)
12/26	64	Strong Vincent	48	W	N	Ward (18)	Lockwood (16)
12/29	72	McDowell	53	W	A	Ward (21)	Aitken (14)
1/3	56	Buffalo (NY) Canisius	51	W	H	Ward (26)	Smaldone & Stasio (14)
1/5	68	Ashtabula (OH) St. John School	46	W	H	Desser (19)	Morgan (13)
1/8	62	Academy	64	L	N	Tomczak (22)	Miller (26)
1/12	87	Harborcreek	64	W	H	Ward (23)	Gindelsperger (20)
1/15	70	East	41	W	N	Ward (24)	Gulick (22)
1/22	58	Tech Memorial	61	L	N	Tomczak (21)	Golembeski (17)
1/29	56	Strong Vincent	59	L	N	Ward (23)	Lockwood (17)
2/2	84	Harborcreek	49	W	A	Ward (23)	Kennedy (29)
2/5	40	Sharpsville	61	L	A	Ward (12)	Timmerman (16)
2/12	63	Academy	58	W	N	Ward (19)	Miller (18)
2/16	69	McDowell	46	W	H	Ward (23)	Conley (12)
2/19	75	East	50	W	N	Ward (34)	Gulick (26)
		CITY CHAMPIONSHIP PLAYOFFS					
2/26	74	Strong Vincent	60	W	N	Ward (27)	Lockwood (19)
3/1	59	Tech Memorial	58	W	N	Ward & Desser (16)	Golembeski (20)
		P.C.I.A.A. STATE CATHOLIC H. S. TOURNAMENT					
3/4	58	St. Marys Central Catholic	37	W	N	Ward (22)	Goetz (15)
3/8	57	Johnstown Central Catholic	58	L	H	Ward (18)	Foran (18)
	1479 (64.3)		**1210 (52.6)**				

Pos.	Player	Ht.	Prior School	Class	G(GS)	FG	FT	Total	PPG	Career
G	Bob Ward (#23)	6'1"	Holy Family	Sr.	23(23)	162	116	440	19.1*	515
F	Pat Tomczak (#21)	6'4"	St. Stan's	Sr.	23(23)	123	44	290	12.6	547
F	Tom Desser (#12)	6'2"	Holy Rosary	Sr.	22(11)	59	34	152	6.9	152
G	Joe Blaszczyk (#42)	5'11"	Holy Rosary	Sr.	22(15)	51	28	130	5.9	130
G	Bernie Nies (#14)	5'10"	St. John's	Sr.	3(18)	44	28	116	5.0	278
C	Rick Amendola (#32)	6'3"	St. Patrick's	Sr.	23(14)	40	14	94	4.1	106
G	Jim McCallion (#15)	5'11'	St. John's	Jr.	17(3)	34	10	78	4.6	78
G	Eddie Kuhar (#25)	5'9"	Holy Family	Sr.	18(3)	30	6	66	3.7	68
F	Dave "Tex" Reuter (#45)	6'2"	St. Mary's	Sr.	20(3)	28	6	62	3.1	69
F	Tom Yonko (#22)	5'11"	St. Casimir's	Sr.	12(2)	6	11	23	1.9	28
F	Paul Modzelewski (#41)	6'0"	St. Stan's	Sr.	4	6	1	13	3.3	13
G	John Fetzner (#31)	5'10"	Mt. Calvary	Jr.	3	1	4	6	2.0	6
G	Jim Murray (#34)	5'11"	Sacred Heart	Jr.	3	1	3	5	1.7	5
F	Dave Paris (#43)	6'0"	Wilson	Jr.	1	2	0	4	4.0	4
G	Bill Kleiner (#52)	5'10"	St. John's	Jr.	0	0	0	0	0.0	0
G	Rich Matlak (#53)	5'11"	Holy Rosary	Jr.	0	0	0	0	0.0	0
G	Armand Grassi (#35)	5'10"	Roosevelt	Jr.	0	0	0	0	0.0	0

Prep's 1960 City Champions. Front, L to R: Coach Trombacco, Grassi, Matlak, Murray, Kleiner, Fetzner; Back: McCallion, Nies, Reuter, Desser, Tomczak, Amendola, Ward, Blaszczyk, Kuhar, Yonko.

SEASON HIGHLIGHTS:

- **Bob Trombacco's** third campaign as Cathedral Prep coach is remembered as having one of the most surprising and hectic City Series races ever. Replete with unanticipated upsets and cliff-hanging, last-minute victories, 1959-60 surpassed all others with its unprecedented four-way tie for first place! Prep, Tech (18-4), Vincent (16-8) and Academy (12-9) all finished the regular season 5-3! Only East (9-13) couldn't win a city game. Though the senior-laden Ramblers were predicted to have little trouble repeating as city champs, three other schools were not to be counted out so easily. At one point the Ramblers were actually counted out with a 3-3 record, all three losses close. Prep did keep its city playoff record clean, first dumping

Vincent, and then beating Tech by one in a championship game spine-tingler.

- Earlier in the season, Vincent had broken an area record for most points in a game with a 112-point barrage against Harborcreek. The Colonels, with only an eventual third place tie in the city, went on to win their second straight Section One crown and their record-breaking fourth consecutive District 10 championship.

- Technical High School, located kiddie corner from Prep at 10th & Sassafras Streets, closed its doors following the 1958-59 school year. The entire faculty and student body then moved to the new facility on Cherry Street, near upper Peach Street. The name of the school was then changed to "Tech Memorial High School," though it did retain the unique nickname "Centaurs."

- In the first Tech contest, Prep staged a terrific 3rd quarter barrage of 32 points, nailing an unreal 15 straight field goals and 2 free throws without a miss, eventually winning by 2. Senior upstart **Bobby Ward** led the Ramblers with 22 markers. In the second battle, the Centaurs came from behind in the 4th quarter to win by 3. This was immediately followed by a loss to Vincent, which also came back in the 4th quarter to win by 3.

- Gannon Auditorium was the scene of a raucous, sold-out Friday night double-header, with the pairings of the four even squads drawn days before by the faculty managers at the home of **Lowell Drake**, the athletic director of Erie's public schools. Attending the session were **Father Jim Gannon** of Prep, **Al Humphrey** of Vincent, **Leonard Mattis** of Academy and **Henry Narducci** of Tech. In the opener, **Pat Tomczak** and **Bob Ward** combined for 50 points to lead the Ramblers to a convincing win over SV; in the thrilling 53-49 nightcap, Tech staved off a late Academy rally that cut the gap to one with 48 seconds remaining. Entering as sixth man for the Centaur cagers was **Bobby Biletnikoff**, a 9th-grade Memorial student who had recently broken junior high league single game scoring records with 38 and 46 points.

- In the City Series championship spine-tingler, **Tom Desser** came off the bench to lead the Orange & Black to a one-point victory with 16 points. For his efforts, Desser was awarded the 14" high Wolves Club Trophy as the outstanding player of the game. Ball-handler extraordinaire Ward also tallied 16 and Tomczak chipped in with 12 in the bruising battle. Tech's **Freddy Biletnikoff** failed to convert on an "and one" situation with just 13 seconds remaining which might have put the battle into overtime.

Team captain and All-City choice Pat Tomczak goes up for a block against Academy's Cleo Harris.

- The final standings in City Series basketball were as follows:

	W	L
*Prep	7	3
Tech	6	4
Vincent	5	4
Academy	5	4
East	0	8

won city championship playoffs

- All City Series games and the Johnstown PCIAA game were played at the Gannon Auditorium, while the Ramblers continued to play their independent home contests in the Prep gym. The St. Marys CC playoff tilt was played at Eisenhower High School (formerly Northern Area High) in Russell, just north of Warren.

- Season highlights included the impressive early season upset of Sharon (14-6) and the emergence of **Bobby Ward** as a full star. Ward, also senior class president, slashed his way to an all-time Prep points per game record (19.1) and fell only 7 points shy of **Jim Fahey's** single season record (447 in 27 games) set in 1954. Ward's 34 points against East were the second most ever by a Rambler at that point, only behind **Al Hatkevich's** 37 recorded against Tech in 1952.

- Ward finished second in the city in scoring, quite a bit behind East's **Johnny Gulick**, who finished with 518 points in 20 games (city record 25.9 *PPG*), third best ever total in the city to that point. **Carmen Riazzi** of Tech had 568 tallies in 1952-53 and **Mel Laskoff** of East had 561 points in 1953-54.

- Prep's two wins over Ashtabula St. John's (5-12) were the only times the Ramblers ever played the Fighting Heralds. St. John's most famous alumnus is current Ohio State football coach **Urban Meyer**.

Tom Desser won the Wolves Club Trophy as MVP in the city championship playoff game.

- Prep suffered a couple of tough road losses, first to Canisius (15-4), which scored 2 free throws in the last ten seconds to win by one; and to Sharpsville (20-4), the last time the Ramblers ever played the Blue Devils, who won three of the four contests between the two. Canisius, which Prep defeated in the rematch on the strength of **Bob Ward's** 26 points, finished as co-champions of Buffalo's Monsignor Martin Association and went on to win the Manhattan Cup. Canisius' **John Stasio** was the first Crusader to cross the 1,000 career point mark. Though common opponents since 1953, Prep and Canisius did not tangle again for 21 years, until 1981.

- Harborcreek (6-12) made a request to the local secondary schools governing board for permission to discontinue football and basketball relations with Prep at the end of the 1959-60 school year. Officials at Harborcreek pointed out that the "primary reason" was that Prep had too large a student body, with some 1,250 boys, compared to about 200 boys in the 10th, 11th and 12th grades at the suburban school. The move toward ending grid relations started in 1959 when the Ramblers laid a 46-0 pasting on the Huskies. Although nothing was said publicly, it was no secret that Harborcreek officials seethed over the way Prep poured it on in that game. Permission was not immediately granted because of contractual obligations, and an agreement was reached that the Huskies and Ramblers would compete in basketball through the 1960-61 season and in football through the 1961 season.

- The season's big disappointment was another loss in the PCIAA's, this time a real heartbreaker to Johnstown Central Catholic (20-4). What really hurt was that Prep, down by six at the half, rallied to a 56-50 lead with just 1:26 left on the scoreboard clock. The Ramblers' strategy from there was to "freeze" the ball. Prep was apparently ahead by one when time expired and the final buzzer sounded, but the official timekeeper informed the referees that one second remained in the game. The Crimson Crushers put the ball in play at mid-court to little **Mike Foran**, who took one step (some say three steps around players) and let fly with a hook shot that banked neatly through the net. The capacity crowd was stunned, even the 500 or so Johnstown fans who made their way to Erie. *Erie Daily Times* sportswriter **Gene Cuneo** wrote that he'd seen Johnny Podres beat the Yankees for the Dodgers' only pennant; he'd seen **Don Larsen** throw a perfect

Eddie Kuhar became a head coach at Iroquois and North East in the Erie County League.

game in the World Series; he'd seen **Johnny Unitas** lead his Colts to a championship when all had seemed lost; and he'd seen **Bob Cousy** single-handedly lead the Celtics to an NBA title. But he further added "we have never seen one specific quick clutch play as the one engineered by Foran."

- Johnstown went on the defeat defending champ Pittsburgh North Catholic in the Western Final and Norristown Bishop Kenrick in a 62-61 championship thriller. It was the third straight year Prep was ousted from the PCIAA's by the eventual state champ. The name Johnstown Central Catholic was changed to Bishop McCort High School in 1961, in honor of **Bishop John J. McCort**, who founded the diocesan Catholic high school in 1922.

Dave "Tex" Reuter with an old-fashioned, picture-perfect hook shot.

Rick Amendola with another bucket in the jam-packed Prep gym.

- **Pat Tomczak** and **Bobby Ward** were honored as First Team All-Big Seven Team choices by the *Erie Daily Times*, while **Tom Desser** was an Honorable Mention selection.

- The fifth annual City-County All-Star game, under the joint sponsorship of the Belle Valley Lions Club and the Erie County Retarded Children's Association, again saw the City All-Stars win both "A" & "B" games at the Memorial Junior High gym. **Bob Ward**, who went on to play for Gannon College, led all scorers with 16 as the City won the "A" game, 70-64. **Pat Tomczak** chipped in with 8 and **Bernie Nies** with 2 for the victorious Slickers.

- **Eddie Kuhar** became a high school basketball coach, first for the Iroquois girls (1977-80), then for the North East boys (1980-82).

- Team captain **Pat Tomczak** was the last of the five Tomczak brothers to rule Erie's high school sports scene and star for Prep. The others included **Lenny "Linda"** ('53), **Dan "Dana"** ('54), **Bob "Clutch"** ('56) and **Eugene "Jiggs"** ('57). All were inducted into the Cathedral Prep Athletic Hall of Fame on the same evening in 2003.

- On January 22, 1960, Pennsylvania's individual record for most points scored in one game was set by Bristol's **Pete Cimino,** who scored 114 against Palisades High. Cimino made 44 shots out of 79 attempts from the field and 26-of-29 free throw attempts. Bristol defeated Palisades, 132-86, and after the game Cimino stated, "All I wanted to do was break the league mark of 62. But the guys on the team kept getting the rebounds and I was able to score a lot on the fast break!" He later became a major league baseball pitcher with the Minnesota Twins (1965-66) and California Angels (1967-68).

- Not to be outdone, just four days later on January 26, 1960, **Danny Heater** of Burnsville (WV) scored an all-time high schoolboy record 135 points in a 173-43 victory over Widen High. Heater connected on 53-of-70 FG attempts and 29-of-41 free throws, grabbed 32 rebounds and had 7 assists!

1960 All-Opponent Team:

John Stasio, Canisius [Xavier (OH)]

Frank Youkers, Sharon

Jim "The Hands" Golembeski, Tech [Behrend]

Fred Biletnikoff, Tech [Florida St., football; NFL Oakland Raiders]

Jack Lockwood, Vincent [Westminster]

Jim Miller, Academy [Clarion St., football]

Johnny Gulick, East

Dan Kennedy, Harborcreek

Jim Timmerman, Sharpsville [Youngstown St.]

Tommy Goetz, St. Marys Central Catholic

Mike Foran, Johnstown Central Catholic

John Stofa, Johnstown Central Catholic [Buffalo, football; NFL Dolphins, Bengals]

Coach Trombacco forced his players to shoot foul shots underhand. Here, Pat Tomczak sinks another. He was the last of the famous Tomczaks to star at Prep. This photo gives a good idea of how the Gannon Auditorium appeared in the 1950's and 1960's.

Tech, SV, Best in Erie

Coach Trombacco has his team's attention while warning captain Jim McCallion not to miss a shot.

1960-61 (12-7)

Coach: Robert "Bob" Trombacco
Captain: Jim McCallion

Date	PREP			Dec.	Loc.	High Scorer	Opponent
12/2	51	Linesville	41	W	A	McCallion (17)	Nieman (13)
12/7	67	Oil City St. Joseph	45	W	H	McCallion (16)	Jarosz (16)
12/16	42	Sharon	68	L	A	McCallion (21)	Atterholt (15)
12/20	60	Alumni	51	W	H	McCallion & Whitby (15)	Rudy (13)
12/23	45	Tech Memorial	74	L	N	Whitby (11)	B. Biletnikoff (20)
12/30	51	Strong Vincent	70	L	N	Whitby (13)	Goodwin (25)
1/6	66	McDowell	52	W	A	McCallion (18)	Aitken (21)
1/13	60	Academy	55	W	N	McCallion (21)	Harris (16)
1/15	64	Oil City St. Joseph	44	W	A	McCallion (28)	Stubler (14)
1/17	60	Harborcreek	33	W	H	McCallion (19)	Dougan (10)
1/20	64	East	55	W	N	McCallion (20)	Battles (17)
1/27	61	Tech Memorial	64	L	N	Whitby (20)	F. Biletnikoff (21)
1/31	57	McDowell	48	W	H	Whitby (19)	Aitken (14)
2/3	54	Strong Vincent	67	L	N	McCallion (15)	Tansey, Haffa & Goodwin (16)
2/10	61	Harborcreek	45	W	A	McCallion (19)	Cook (13)
2/18	54	Academy	65	L	N	McCallion (26)	Thomas (22)
2/24	62	East	45	W	N	McCallion (18)	Montague (16)
		P.C.I.A.A. STATE CATHOLIC H. S. TOURNAMENT					
3/5	69	St. Marys Central Catholic	47	W	A	McCallion (20)	Hasselman (12)
3/9	53	Pittsburgh South Hills Catholic	61	L	A	McCallion (20)	Coll (20)
	1341 (61.0)		**1127 (52.1)**				

Pos.	Player	Ht.	Prior School	Class	G(GS)	FG	FT	Total	PPG	Career
G	Jim McCallion (#15)	5'11'	St. John's	Sr.	19(19)	109	105	323	17.0	401
C	Dave Whitby (#45)	6'2"	St. Mary's	Jr.	15(15)	60	31	151	10.1	151
F	Al Lubiejewski (#35)	6'1"	St. Stan's	Jr.	19(19)	53	38	144	7.6	144
G	John Fetzner (#41)	5'10"	Mt. Calvary	Sr.	17(12)	50	19	119	7.0	125
F	Rick Scheppner (#22)	5'11"	St. Andrew's	Jr.	15(7)	32	10	74	4.9	74
F	Jerry Kruszewski (#24)	6'2"	St. John's	Jr.	14(6)	26	15	67	4.8	67
C	Dan Bulishak (#42)	6'3"	St. Casimir's	Jr.	14(7)	25	10	60	4.3	60
G	Johnny Cardot (#34)	5'11"	St. John's	Sr.	6(5)	15	2	32	5.3	32
G	Dave Engel (#23)	5'8"	Bl. Sacrament	Jr.	8(3)	11	2	24	3.0	24
F	Charlie Fischer (#21)	6'0"	St. John's	Jr.	10	10	0	20	2.0	20
G	Mike Flaherty (#14)	5'9"	St. Joseph's	Soph.	12	5	5	15	1.3	15
G	Ron Chimenti (#25)	6'0"	St. John's	Jr.	8(2)	2	9	13	1.6	13
G	Jim Sitter (#32)	5'10"	St. Andrew's	Jr.	4	1	1	3	0.8	3
F	Jim Schwartz (#31)	5'10"	St. Luke's	Jr.	0	0	0	0	0.0	0
F	John Aquino (#43)	6'0"	St. Peter's	Jr.	0	0	0	0	0.0	0
G	Rich Matlak (#53)	5'11"	Holy Rosary	Sr.	0	0	0	0	0.0	0
G	Jerry Martin (#12)	5'10"	St. John's	Jr.	0	0	0	0	0.0	0

The 1961 Prep Ramblers. Front, L to R: Chimenti, Scheppner, Lubiejewski, Whitby, Bulishak, McCallion, Fetzner, Flaherty, Coach Trombacco. Back: Sitter, Matlak, Aquino, Fischer, Kruszewski, Schwartz, Martin, Engel.

Jim McCallion had an outstanding senior campaign for the Ramblers.

HIGHLIGHTS:

- Cathedral Prep suffered from inexperience and had but one letterman in the fold, that being high-scoring senior **Jim McCallion**. A somewhat weaker schedule and some solid performances by juniors **Dave Whitby** and **Al Lubiejewski** enabled the Ramblers to have a somewhat successful season, though not in City Series strife.

- The final standings in City Series basketball were as follows (this was the last year that Harborcreek was in Section One in basketball and the Big Seven in football):

	W	L
Tech	8	0
Vincent	6	2
Prep	3	5
East	2	6
Academy	1	7

- All City Series games were played at the Gannon Auditorium, while the Ramblers continued to play their independent home contests in the Prep gym.

- An obscure PIAA rule, one that had been on the books for many years but rarely enforced, had been revived locally for the 1960-61 season. The rule in question stated that any PIAA member school is not permitted to play any school that is coached by anyone who is not a member of that school's faculty. The issue was raised after a letter was received questioning a game between Tidioute and Oil City St. Joseph's, coached by highly-esteemed **Bill Eckert**, who was not a faculty member at St. Joe's. Obviously aimed at Catholic schools, this rule did not affect Cathedral Prep, but immediately affected Erie Diocesan Class B schools, which had to adjust staffs and schedules and deal with cancellations after the season had already started. **H. D. Leberman**, Academy High principal and PIAA District 10 chairman, was emphatic in his ruling that either the schools hire coaches who were faculty members or cancel games with public schools. Greenville St. Michael's was hardest hit, as 11 of its 24 games were scheduled against public schools.

Rick Scheppner (Allgeier) backs in as Dave Whitby sets a pick.

- Prep came to the aid of Oil City St. Joe's (15-6), which had to cancel five games, by hosting the Irish on December 7 to help them balance out their schedule. St. Joe's went on to win the Western Division of the Erie Diocesan League with a 12-0 loop record. Other teams in the West at that time included Clarion Immaculate Conception, Greenville St. Mike's, Kanty Prep, Meadville St. Agatha's, North East St. Gregory's and Titusville St. Joseph's. Eastern Division teams included Bradford St. Bernard's, DuBois St. Catherine's, Punxsutawney Sts. Cosmas and Damien, Ridgway St. Leo's and Clearfield St. Francis, which finished its regular season 18-0 then defeated Oil City St. Joe's, 56-48, in the Diocesan title game.

- Prep's wins over Harborcreek (5-10) ran its victory streak to 14 straight against the Huskies. The two did not compete again until the 1974 District 10 playoffs.

- The win over the Alumni was the Prep varsity's 18th consecutive and it was the last time the regular school team played a graduate combine in a regular season contest.

- City champion Tech Memorial (21-2) finished its regular season at 21-1, the finest record for an Erie combo to that point. The Centaurs were led by stars **Fred Biletnikoff** (later

of NFL fame), **Denny Cologrande, Bobby Biletnikoff, John Esser** and **Bobby Fragale**. The powerful Centaurs were then beaten soundly by Hickory (25-2) in District 10 competition, 61-40. The Hornets made it all the way to the state final where it lost to Nanticoke, 56-46. Vincent (17-3) also presented a strong unit, with 2 of its only 3 losses to Tech. In this regard, all of Prep's losses were to very tough teams, with the exception of the late-season Academy (9-10) upset.

- Though Vincent had its way with Prep in basketball, one great accomplishment for the Rambler school was its upset swimming meet triumph over the Colonels, 44-42, thus ending SV's unbelievable record of 116 consecutive dual meet victories! After both squads finished the City Series race with 7-1 records, Vincent left no question about its superiority in swimming by defeating Prep in a playoff, 58-27.

McCallion nails a jump shot over Tech's Denny Cologrande.

- Prep continued its mastery over St. Marys Central Catholic (17-8) in PCIAA playoff action, defeating the Crusaders for the fifth consecutive year before 775 foot-stomping Central partisans. The Ramblers were ahead, 40-23, at half-time, but couldn't score a second half field goal until **Jim McCallion** nailed one with 30 seconds left in the third quarter. In the meantime Central cut the Prep lead to two. In the fourth period the Ramblers went back to a full court press and rang up 16 unanswered points to breeze to victory.

- The biggest disappointment of the season was another loss to a Pittsburgh entry in the PCIAA tourney, the 11th straight suffered by the Ramblers. **John Fetzner** suffered a broken nose from a sucker punch in the contest, but played hard and finished the game. It was South Hills Catholic (24-7) of coach

Jerry Conboy this time, which then beat North Catholic and Scranton Prep to win its first state title. It was the first time Prep played South Hills Catholic, n/k/a Seton-LaSalle, but the fourth straight year Prep was ousted from the PCIAA's by the eventual state champ. The contest was played at Mt. Lebanon High School.

- South Hills Catholic, which opened in 1959, won the 1961 PCIAA Class A title, 41-40, in a cliff-hanger that was decided in the closing seconds when **Denny Coll** tossed in a field goal from the free throw circle. It was Scranton Prep's only defeat of the season against 20 wins. The SHC Rebels then entered the 8th annual Knights of Columbus Tournament at Georgetown University, but promptly lost both games it played.

- The season highlight was the fine outside shooting and the consistent scoring of **Jim McCallion**, who later went on to star at Gannon College. McCallion was named a First Team Big 7 All-Scholastic by the *Erie Daily Times*.

- **Rich Matlak**, a star hurler for the Ramblers, became a four-year letter winner in baseball at Gannon College. Matlak has been, for decades, the timekeeper at nearly every high school basketball game at Gannon's Hammermill Center.

- **John Cardot**, hampered throughout the season because of football-related injuries, was the star All-City halfback for the city champion Rambler gridders.

- The sixth annual City-County All-Star game was played at the Gannon Audi, under the sponsorship of the Belle Valley Lions Club, with proceeds going to the Erie County Retarded Children's Association. **John Fetzner** scored 15 as the City won the "B" game, 73-44. In the "A" game, **Jim McCallion** scored 6, but the County used the scoring strength of Lawrence Park's **Jim Cipalla** and **Earl Hall,** and Fort LeBoeuf's **Walley Mahle** to score a 79-77 overtime win.

- **Father John Poux** took over the position of Prep athletic director following the retirement of **Monsignor Jim Gannon** in the summer of 1961. "Monsignor Jim" guided Prep's athletic fortunes since 1946 in what has been referred to as Prep's "Golden Era." He began parish work at Our Lady of the Lake in Edinboro and later at St. Andrew's parish. Monsignor Gannon was a charter inductee into the Cathedral Prep Athletic Hall of Fame in 1992 and was inducted posthumously into the Metro Erie Sports Hall of Fame in 2001.

John Fetzner's senior photo was taken before he suffered a broken nose from a sucker punch in the South Hills Catholic game.

1961 All-Opponent Team:

Joe Atterholt, Sharon

Jerry Bodnar, Sharon [Gannon]

Bobby Biletnikoff, Tech [Miami (FL), football; Yankees Class AAA baseball]

John Esser, Tech

Norward Goodwin, Vincent [Buffalo]

Doug Aitken, McDowell

Cleo Harris, Academy

Don Dougan, Harborcreek [Edinboro St.]

Ike Battles, East

Fred Biletnikoff, Tech (hm all-state) [Florida St., football; NFL Oakland Raiders]

Denny Cologrande, Tech

Dick Schau, McDowell

Ken Faulkner, McDowell

Ed Tansey, Vincent [Edinboro St., St. Petersburg (FL) JC]

Bill Haffa, Vincent [Twins, Indians Class A baseball]

Chuck Thomas, Academy

Denny Montague, East

George Hasselman, St. Marys Central Catholic

Denny Coll, South Hills Catholic

City Champs!

1961-62 (17-9)

Coach: Robert "Bob" Trombacco
Captain: Game captains
Manager: John Anderson

First Team All-Big 7 star Dave Whitby was a scoring machine for the Ramblers.

Date	PREP			Dec.	Loc.	High Scorer	Opponent
12/1	75	Linesville	48	W	H	Whitby (26)	Jones (14)
12/5	56	Youngstown (OH) Card. Mooney	53	W	A	Whitby (18)	Porea & Lesi & Schneider (13)
12/12	92	Titusville St. Joseph's Academy	56	W	A	Whitby (18)	Snyder (17)
12/15	37	Sharon	54	L	H	Lubiejewski & Fisher (8)	Brewer (16)
12/16	70	Corry	42	W	A	Whitby (25)	McMahon (17)
12/19	58	Oil City St. Joseph's	33	W	A	Whitby (18)	Stubler (19)
12/22	65	East	52	W	N	Whitby (20)	Battles (24)
		MEADVILLE ELKS HOLIDAY INVITATIONAL					
12/26	44	Har-Brack	53	L	A	Whitby (16)	Paffrath (18)
12/27	46	Youngstown (OH) Chaney	59	L	A	Whitby (15)	Avery (19)
1/5	50	Strong Vincent	48	W	N	Whitby (15)	Carson (12)
1/13	75	Youngstown (OH) Card. Mooney	55	W	H	Whitby (26)	Velk (19)
1/16	52	McDowell	59	L	H	Kruszewski (11)	Zirkle (22)
1/19	49	Academy	48	W	N	Marnella & Whitby (12)	Crosby (16)
1/26	70	East	43	W	N	Marnella (15)	Battles (17)
1/28	53	Oil City St. Joseph's	46	W	H	Marnella & Whitby (17)	Stubler (26)
2/2	47	Tech Memorial	69	L	N	Kruszewski (13)	Kinnard (20)
2/4	65	Niagara Falls (NY) Bishop Duffy	67(OT)	L	H	Kruszewski (24)	Kontrabecki (17)
2/9	54	Strong Vincent	51	W	N	Whitby (16)	Massing (17)
2/13	75	Corry	50	W	H	Whitby (20)	McMahon (16)
2/16	44	McDowell	60	L	A	Scheppner (15)	Zirkle (20)
2/23	68	Academy	46	W	N	Whitby (20)	Thomas (22)
2/27	72	Tech Memorial	77(OT)	L	N	Whitby (15)	Kinnard (22)
		CITY CHAMPIONSHIP PLAYOFF					
3/6	60	Tech Memorial	58	W	N	Flaherty (18)	Biletnikoff (16)
		P.C.I.A.A. STATE CATHOLIC H.S. TOURNAMENT					
3/4	55	St. Marys Central Catholic	41	W	H	Whitby (20)	Mills (12)
3/9	50	Greensburg Central Catholic	38	W	H	Whitby (14)	Cornali (10)
3/14	47	Pittsburgh North Catholic	58	L	A	Whitby (16)	Lutz (16)
	1529 (58.8)		**1364* (52.4)**				

Pos.	Player	Ht.	Prior School	Class	G(GS)	FG	FT	Total	*PPG*	Career
F	Dave Whitby (#23)	6'2"	St. Mary's	Sr.	26(26)	142	118	402	15.5	553
F	Rick Scheppner (#35)	6'0"	St. Andrew's	Sr.	22(16)	76	34	186	8.5	260
G	Jim Marnella (#31)	6'1"	St. Peter's	Jr.	21(13)	68	21	157	7.5	157
C	Al Lubiejewski (#33)	6'1"	St. Stan's	Sr.	22(19)	53	50	156	7.1	300
G	Jerry Kruszewski (#13)	6'3"	St. John's	Sr.	19(16)	59	19	137	7.2	204
F	Charlie Fischer (#14)	6'0"	St. John's	Sr.	19(9)	54	12	120	6.3	140
G	Mike Flaherty (#24)	5'10"	St. Joseph's	Jr.	22(7)	40	25	105	4.8	120
C	Dan Bulishak (#32)	6'3"	St. Casimir's	Sr.	19(6)	45	11	101	5.3	161
G	Ron Chimenti (#15)	6'0"	St. John's	Sr.	20(18)	30	30	90	4.5	103
F	Jerry Fetzner (#3)	6'0"	St. Peter's	Jr.	8	9	4	22	2.8	22
G	Dave Engel (#4)	5'8"	Bl. Sacrament	Sr.	7	5	2	12	1.7	36
F	Tom Simmons (#30)	6'0"	St. Peter's	Jr.	5	2	3	7	1.4	7
F	Tom Schneider (#41)	6'1"	St. Joseph's	Jr.	1	2	0	4	4.0	4
G	Jim Reszkowski (Reske) (#5)	6'0"	St. Peter's	Jr.	5	1	1	3	0.6	3
G	Paul Simon (#34)	5'11"	St. Andrew's	Jr.	4	1	1	3	0.8	3
G	Jim Sitter (#41)	5'10"	St. Andrew's	Sr.	2	0	2	2	1.0	5
F	Ed Robasky (#41)	6'1"	St. Stan's	Jr.	2	1	0	2	1.0	2

ROW 1, J. Anderson, J. Sitter, J. Reszkowski, M. Flaherty, D. Engel, R. Chimenti, P. Simon, Coach, Mr. Robert Trombacco, K. Anderson, ROW 2, T. Simmons, J. Marnella, D. Whitby, D. Bulishak, J. Kruszewski, A. Lubiejewski, C. Fischer, and L. Robasky. G. Fetzner, missing.

Prep's surprising 1962 City Champions.

HIGHLIGHTS:

- One of Cathedral Prep's greatest and most thrilling wins of all time was the 60-58 City Series Championship playoff thriller over a good Tech Memorial (20-7) team before a jam-packed capacity crowd of 3,300 at the Gannon Auditorium. **Mike Flaherty** was the clutch hero for **Bob Trombacco's** Ramblers, impressing the crowd with several long-range two-handed set shots. Flaherty had a key bucket with a running one-hander with 21 seconds left. It was the fourth time in four tries that Prep won the title via the playoff route.

- Prep's opening game victories in 1960-61 and 1961-62 were the third and fourth straight wins over Linesville (21-5). **Dave Whitby** scored a season-high 26 points against Linesville to forecast a high-scoring season for the talented senior. The Ramblers and the Lions have never played again. In 2012, Linesville merged with fellow Crawford County schools Conneaut Lake and Conneaut Valley to form Conneaut Area High School.

- Linesville went on to defeat Youngsville in a District 10 Class B semifinal, 43-41, for its 17th straight victory, before losing to Mercer in the final, 56-37.

- The Meadville Elks Holiday Tournament was the first time Prep entered an in-season tourney, suffering poor losses to Har-Brack (9-12) and Youngstown Chaney (10-11). Meadville won the tourney on night two with a 67-60 verdict over Har-Brack.

- Prep's contests against Har-Brack, Greensburg Central Catholic and Youngstown Cardinal Mooney (7-11) were the only times these schools ever competed in basketball. The Ramblers played Chaney again in three consecutive seasons, from 1976-1979.

- Har-Brack was located in Natrona Heights, Allegheny County, and served Harrison Township and Brackenridge Borough.

It produced star athletes like **"Cookie" Gilchrist** and **Dick Modzelewski** of the NFL. Har-Brack is now closed and the area is served by Highlands High School.

- Cardinal Mooney, located on Youngstown's South Side, opened in 1956 and is well-known for football and for listing among its alumni San Francisco 49ers owner **Ed DeBartolo**; champion boxer **Ray "Boom-Boom" Mancini**; former controversial congressman **Jim Traficant**; and head football coaches **Bob Stoops** of Oklahoma, **Mark Stoops** of Kentucky, **Bo Pelini** of Nebraska and Youngstown State and **Carl Pelini** of Florida Atlantic.

- Chaney won more Youngstown city titles than any other school prior to the 2006–2007 school year when the Youngstown City Series was dissolved. Chaney lists among its many former star collegiate and NFL football players such notables as **Michael Zordich, Matt Cavanaugh** and Heisman Trophy winner and NFL MVP **Frank Sinkwich**. Sinkwich was also coach of the old Erie Vets semi-pro football squad in 1949.

- The Cardinal Mooney Cardinals and the Chaney Cowboys were members of the rugged Youngstown City Series, as were the Rayen School Tigers, East High Golden Bears, North High Bulldogs, South High Warriors, Ursuline Fighting Irish and Woodrow Wilson Presidents (later "Redmen").

- Oil City St. Joe's closed at the end of the 1961-62 school year, with the Hilltoppers on top in the all-time series, 15-12, despite the Ramblers winning 8 of the last 9. The Oil City area was then served by Venango Christian High School (1962-2016).

- Corry (9-13), routed twice by Prep, had not played the Ramblers in five years. The two Orange & Black squads did not meet again until the 1968-69 campaign.

- Other thrilling victories included the one-point win over Academy (13-10) and the 2 and 3-point wins over Strong Vincent (16-8), all part of capacity crowd doubleheaders at the Gannon Auditorium. In the victory over Academy, **Al Lubiejewski** grabbed a rebound from his own missed shot and scored at the buzzer, his only two points of the contest. Academy showcased a super sophomore in lefty gunner **Bob Thomas** (482 points, 21.0 PPG).

- In the first Vincent triumph, **Ron Chimenti** was intentionally fouled with 28 seconds remaining and Prep clinging to a 49-48 lead. Chimenti missed the first free throw, but nailed the second and the Colonels prepared for a final shot. SV's **Dennis Atkinson's** one-hander hit the rim and a wild scramble for the rebound ensued as the final gun sounded. In game

Lanky Jerry Kruszewski nails a jump shot.

two, the Ramblers overcame a 7-point, 4th quarter deficit with some hot shooting by **Rick Scheppner, Jerry Kruszewski**, and particularly **Charlie Fischer** to gain the victory.

Charlie Fischer extends in defending against SV's Sonny Carson.

- The final standings in City Series basketball were as follows:

	W	L
*Prep	7	2
Tech	6	3
Academy	4	4
Vincent	3	5
East	1	7

won city championship playoff

- All City Series games and the St. Marys and Greensburg PCIAA games were played at Gannon, while the Ramblers continued to play their independent home contests in the Prep gym. The St. Marys CC conquest was played on a Sunday afternoon and it marked the sixth consecutive year Prep eliminated St. Marys CC from title contention since the Crusaders vaulted into Class A competition. It was also the last time Prep and its heated rival St. Marys CC ever played, with the Ramblers winning the series over the Crusaders, 9 games to 6.

- Prep's two wins over St. Marys Central Catholic (19-4) and Greensburg Central Catholic (6-12) were its most in PCIAA tourney play since the state title season of 1953-54. While Greensburg CC was only in its third year of existence, St. Marys CC closed its doors following the 1961-62 school year. The St. Marys area is now served by Elk County Catholic.

- Biggest disappointments were regular season sweeps by Tech and McDowell (19-6) and the tense PCIAA Western Final playoff loss to heavily-favored North Catholic (25-5). The Ramblers held NC Trojan star **Larry Szykowny** to 8 points and battled back from a big early deficit, but couldn't overcome the eventual state champs. That made it *a dozen straight times* Prep lost to the Pittsburgh representative in the PCIAA tourney. A major donnybrook erupted with only 46 seconds remaining, resulting in a pair of ejections before nearly 2,000 fans at Mt. Lebanon High. Players and fans joined the action with Prep's **Mike Flaherty** and NC's **Paul Walter** both being sent off. A *Pittsburgh Post-Gazette* headline declared: "Fisticuffs Mar Game With Erie." Trojan coach **Don Graham** stated that Prep "was a scrappy team—in more ways than one!" The *PPG* further noted: "The contest was marred by an old-fashioned fistic brawl between the players of both teams…and to add a bit more spice to the game, Erie's [Rick] Scheppner was asked to leave the court by officials after he slammed North's Szykowny to the floor in no uncertain manner. Following the contest, an overly enthusiastic Erie rooter scored a direct hit on a North player's jaw as the teams were leaving the floor. Outside of these shenanigans, it was an otherwise clean-cut ball game!" The brawl spilled outside after the battle as well and Mt. Lebanon police were called to quell the fireworks. It was the fifth straight year the Ramblers were eliminated by the eventual state winners. It was the last of six PCIAA state titles for the Trojans.

- North Catholic went on to the K. of C. National Catholic Tournament in Washington (DC), but lost in the first round to Philadelphia St. Joseph's Prep and its star **Matt Goukas**, 63-50. The Trojans rebounded with a consolation win over New York City (NY) LaSalle, 70-56, but lost the consolation final to New Orleans (LA) St. Augustine, 62-60. Winner of the tourney was Hyattsville (MD) DeMatha Catholic.

- High-scoring Tech Memorial, led by juniors **Willie Kinnard, Bobby Biletnikoff, Carl Johnson** and **Joe Liedtke**, won the Section One title. Early in the season, Tech broke the all-time City Series record for points in a game with 94 against East. The Centaurs, however, blew a mid-third quarter 8-point lead in a D-10 semifinal against Meadville, then completely fell apart in the final three minutes to lose, 82-65. Kinnard led all scorers with 27 in that contest, played before 3,200 fans at Farrell High School.

- Another highlight included the consistent scoring punch of senior **Dave Whitby**, who was named First Team Big 7 All-Scholastic by the *Erie Times-News*. Whitby, the only Rambler to get post-season recognition, went on to play at the University of Detroit.

Dave Whitby hits another at the sold-out Gannon Audi.

- Cathedral Prep became engaged in a minor controversy when the Erie School District Athletic Governing Board, through secretary **Lowell Drake**, ordered that Prep must forfeit five junior varsity and one junior high game because of the use of ineligible players. Apparently a pair of 9th grade stars, **Tim Maloney** and **Dave Wenrick**, had been promoted and appeared in the JV games and later played in a junior high game against Memorial. Prep headmaster **Monsignor Robert McDonald** was incensed as both he and athletic director **Father**

Athletic Director Father John Poux was not shy about paddling misbehaving Prep boys.

John Poux already cleared eligibility for the two after the Wilson Junior High principal wouldn't permit them to compete against his team previously. Nevertheless, the Board reversed form and unfairly ruled that the two could not compete on the junior varsity nor the junior high levels, so the JV's went from 7-0 in the standings to 2-5, and the freshmen team dropped

from 6-2 to 5-3. And Maloney and Wenrick were done for the remainder of the season (but still had to practice!).

- The junior varsity ("Little Ramblers") and freshmen team ("Baby Ramblers") forfeits cost both squads their respective league titles. The JV's lost out on both the City Series and Big Seven, consisting of the city schools plus McDowell and Harborcreek. The Frosh (9-3 in the city) lost out to the squad that gained the forfeit, Memorial, which finished 10-2. The Baby Ramblers, however, did tie with Memorial for the Big 9 Junior High championship, both with 13-3 records. The City Series Junior High loop consisted of Prep, Memorial, Gridley, Roosevelt, Vincent, East and Wilson, while the Big 9 included the city schools plus Millcreek junior highs Westminster and Westlake.

- The seventh annual City-County All-Star game was played before 3,000 at the Gannon Audi, again under the sponsorship of the Belle Valley Lions Club, with proceeds going to the Erie County Retarded Children's Association. **Al Lubiejewski** scored 18, **Dan Bulishak** scored 15, and **Charlie Fischer** 3 as the City won the "B" game, 62-48. **Dave Whitby** poured in 17 in the "A" game as the City was again victorious, 65-

Al Lubiejewski was carried off the floor by teammates and fans after his buzzer-beater against Academy, his only two points in the game.

63, on two free throws after the final buzzer by East's **Denny Montague**.

- **Al Lubiejewski**, also a stellar end on the Rambler football team, was inducted into the Cathedral Prep Athletic Hall of Fame in 2008. Other All-City gridders who went on to play college football included the "Galloping Ghost," **Rick [Scheppner] Allgeier**, **Jim Sitter** and quarterback **Ron Chimenti**.

- On March 2, 1962, at Hersheypark Arena, **Wilt Chamberlain** of the Philadelphia Warriors scored 100 points against the New York Knicks, still an NBA record. Wilt's dominance eventually led to many rule changes: offensive basket interference, the widening of the foul lane and the rule that keeps the foul shooter behind the line

Wilt "The Stilt" Chamberlain scores 100 points at the Hersheypark Arena, where Prep won state titles in 1980 and 1993.

until the ball has reached the basket. Prep would win state championships in that same Hersheypark Arena in 1980 and 1993.

- Three Prep cagers received honors from WWYN radio station-sponsored dinner for the champion Ramblers. **Dave Whitby** received a $200 scholarship from WWYN, while a pair of the sponsors of Prep game radio broadcasts presented trophies: one by Meadowland Dairy to **Mike Flaherty** as the "Most

Improved Player," and the other by Marquette Building & Loan to **Rick Scheppner** as the "Outstanding Scholar-Athlete."

1962 All-Opponent Team:

Howard Sterling, Linesville

Bobby Porea, Cardinal Mooney [killed in
    Viet Nam, 1967]

Bill Brewer, Sharon

Dan Stubler, Oil City St. Joe's (hm all-state)

Ike Battles, East

Larry Paffrath, Har-Brack [William & Mary]

John Avery, Youngstown Chaney [Maryland]

Gene Velk, Cardinal Mooney

Joe Nigro, Cardinal Mooney [Youngstown St.]

Doug Zirkle, McDowell [Cornell, football & lacrosse]

Jim Titus, McDowell

Walt Crosby, Academy

Joe "Tippy" Pohl, East [Pitt, football]

Bobby Biletnikoff, Tech (hm all-state)[Miami (FL),
    football; Yankees Class AAA baseball]

Willie Kinnard, Tech (5th team all-state)

Carl Johnson, Tech [Edinboro]

Joe Liedtke, Tech [Louisville]

Phil Kontrabecki, Bishop Duffy [LaSalle]

Dale Massing, Vincent [Stetson, baseball]

Denny McMahon, Corry (hm all-state)

Chuck Faulkner, McDowell

Roosevelt "Sonny" Carson, Vincent

Bob Thomas, Academy (hm all-state) [Buffalo]

Dick Lutz, North Catholic [Gannon]

Bob Rojik, North Catholic [Gannon]

Larry Szykowny, North Catholic (3rd team
    all-state) [Pitt]

Jerry Fetzner drives for two more.

Tech Is the Big Story!

1962-63 (11-7)

Coach: Robert "Bob" Trombacco
Captains: Jim Marnella, Mike Flaherty
Managers: Ken Anderson, Ed Filipowicz

Three-sport star Jim Marnella led the Ramblers in scoring. For decades he's been color commentator for Prep football and basketball broadcasts.

Date	PREP			Dec.	Loc.	High Scorer	Opponent
11/30	92	Dunkirk (NY)	43	W	H	Lupo (18)	Valentine (14)
12/4	75	Southwestern (NY) Central	57	W	A	Marnella (30)	Coalier (20)
12/7		Beaver Falls (POSTPONED—SNOW)			H		
12/11		Dunkirk (NY) (CANCELLED—SNOW)			A		
12/18	38	Sharon	43	L	A	Druckemiller (11)	Tutt (16)
12/21	62	East	45	W	N	Lupo (21)	Watts (15)
12/28	45	Tech Memorial	78	L	N	Marnella & Lupo (13)	Kinnard (27)
1/4	46	Strong Vincent	68	L	N	Lupo (19)	Smith (25)
1/8	63	Meadville	55	W	A	Marnella (19)	Roberts (18)
1/15	67	McDowell	28	W	H	Marnella (22)	Amann (7)
1/18	53	Academy	56	L	N	Marnella (24)	Hitt (22)
1/20	61	Niagara Falls (NY) Bishop Duffy	51	W	A	Lupo (19)	Traverse (14)
1/25	61	East	43	W	N	Marnella (26)	Gallegos (17)
1/29		Beaver Falls (CANCELLED)			H		
2/1	71	Tech Memorial	74(OT)	L	N	Lupo (25)	Biletnikoff (22)
2/5	71	Jamestown (NY)	61	W	H	Marnella (16)	Morgan (21)
2/8	55	Strong Vincent	62	L	N	Marnella (17)	Smith (22)
2/12	80	Southwestern (NY) Central	46	W	H	Marnella (18)	Coalier (17)
2/15	62	McDowell	51	W	A	Marnella (17)	Moore (20)
2/22	62	Academy	56	W	N	Druckemiller (15)	Thomas (19)
		P.C.I.A.A. STATE CATHOLIC H.S. TOURNAMENT					
3/3	52	Johnstown Bishop McCort	59	L	A	Marnella (25)	Stofa (14)
	1116 (62.0)		**976 (54.2)**				

Pos.	Player	Ht.	Prior School	Class	G(GS)	FG	FT	Total	*PPG*	Career
G	Jim Marnella (#32)	6'1"	St. Peter's	Sr.	18(18)	128	36	292	16.2	449
F	Pat Lupo (#30)	6'0"	St. George's	Jr.	18(18)	102	37	241	13.4	241
C	Bill Druckemiller (#31)	6'7"	Memorial	Jr.	18(18)	62	28	152	8.4	152
F	Jerry Fetzner (#3)	6'0"	St. Peter's	Sr.	17(5)	46	8	100	5.9	122
G	Jim Reszkowski (Reske) (#5)	6'0"	St. Peter's	Sr.	18(13)	48	3	99	5.5	102
G	Mike Flaherty (#24)	5'10"	St. Joseph's	Sr.	11(11)	34	10	78	7.1	198
F	Tom Simmons (#33)	6'1"	St. Peter's	Sr.	13(4)	28	11	67	5.2	74
G	Paul Simon (#34)	5'11"	St. Andrew's	Sr.	14(3)	18	15	51	3.6	54
G	Fred Engel (#14)	5'10"	Bl. Sacrament	Jr.	8	7	0	14	1.8	14
G	Bob Alex (#4)	5'10"	St. Patrick's	Jr.	3	2	2	6	2.0	6
G	Dave Farrell (#23)	5'10"	St. Mary's	Soph.	4	1	3	5	1.3	5
C	Dave Lichtinger (#35)	6'2"	St. John's	Soph.	7	1	2	4	0.6	4
F	Tom Schneider (#41)	6'1"	St. Joseph's	Sr.	2	2	0	4	2.0	8
F	Dave Hambly (#15)	6'0"	St. Peter's	Sr.	2	1	0	2	1.0	2
F	Dick Scalise (#13)	6'0"	St. Peter's	Sr.	1	0	0	0	0.0	0
F	Dan Haley (#41)	6'2"	St. James	Soph.	1	0	0	0	0.0	0

The 1963 Prep Ramblers. Front, L to R: Farrell, Fetzner, Reske, Alex, Simon, Engel, Scalise, Flaherty; Back: Mgr. Anderson, Mgr. Filipowicz, Haley, Simmons, Marnella, Druckemiller, Lichtinger, Lupo, Coach Trombacco.

HIGHLIGHTS:

- 1962-63 was the last season in the six-year reign of **Bob Trombacco** as Cathedral Prep head coach. Trombacco, who resigned to take a position within the Erie City School District at Wilson Junior High, finished with an aggregate record of 80-49, with three City Series championships. The highlights of his Prep career were the thrilling playoff encounters to win those titles. His feat of winning the 1962 city championship was considered a minor miracle by fans and experts when his Ramblers knocked off Tech in the final playoff. On the downside, his Rambler quints were never able to get past the downstate representatives in the PCIAA tournaments. Trombacco was inducted into the Metro Erie Sports Hall of Fame in 1992.

- All City Series games were played at the Gannon Auditorium, while the Ramblers continued to play their independent home contests in the Prep gym. The PCIAA elimination contest was played at Windber High, outside Johnstown.

- Cathedral Prep suffered a bad break in the season opener, when star long-bomb artist **Mike Flaherty** went down with a severe ankle sprain. Though the role was capably filled by senior spot starters **Tom Simmons, Jim Reske, Jerry Fetzner,** and **Paul Simon**, Flaherty's absence was keenly felt as he missed the next seven contests and struggled through much of the season.

- A three-sport star, Flaherty went on to play quarterback for the University of Detroit and the University of Cincinnati, where

All-around athlete Mike Flaherty was inducted into the Prep Athletic Hall of Fame in 2013.

Sharp-shooting Tom Simmons, later an esteemed grade school coach.

he was named team captain his senior year. He was given the first "Ma" Kaiser Award, signifying him as Prep's best all-around athlete. (**"Ma" Kaiser** ran the Prep cafeteria for decades and was considered Prep's greatest fan.) Flaherty was inducted into the Cathedral Prep Athletic Hall of Fame in 2013.

- Prep suffered from a lack of height overall, with the exception of 6'7" rebounder **Bill Druckemiller**, a transfer who played for Memorial Junior High in 9th grade.

Who can stop big Bill Druckemiller?

- Prep had a one-point lead with a minute left at Sharon, but a late technical foul on Coach Trombacco spelled doom for the Ramblers. Trombacco was trying to break up a fight under the basket after some rough play in the game's final moments. Hard feelings by both schools made Prep's loss the last game of an 11-year series. The Tigers won 8 of the 11 and the teams did not compete again until 1981-82.

- Tech Memorial (25-2) ran away from the pack in City Series strife, led by 6'7" **Joe Liedtke, Bobby Biletnikoff** (1,144 career points), **Carl Johnson** and **Willie Kinnard** (499 points, 18.5 PPG, 1,094 for career). The Centaurs, District 10 champs and one of Erie's all-time greatest teams, lost to Norwin (24-4) and 6'9 ½", 280-pound **"Big John" Naponick** in the PIAA Western Final, 56-42. (In the WPIAL final, Norwin defeated Aliquippa, 69-64, behind Naponick's 33 points and 21 rebounds.) Norwin then lost in the state final to Plymouth-Whitemarsh (24-0), 74-54, despite Naponick's 28 points. One point of interest is that 6'7" Harborcreek superstar **Don Dougan** was to transfer to Tech before the season's start—a move that was protested by the Harborcreek School District. Dougan was forced to remain with the Huskies and had a stellar senior season, was named first team all-state and scored a Section One record 47 points against McDowell and 447 (26.3 PPG) for the season in just 17 games. Dougan's *PPG* average broke East High's **Johnny Gulick's** local record of 25.2 *PPG* set in 1960.

- The final standings in City Series basketball were as follows:

	W	L
Tech	8	0
Academy	5	3
Vincent	4	4
Prep	3	5
East	0	8

- Biggest disappointments were the 3-5 City Series record and the first round PCIAA playoff loss to Bishop McCort. McCort (25-4) went on to win its third state title under coach **Leroy Leslie,** the school's former luminary and later a star at Notre Dame. It was the *sixth* consecutive year the Ramblers were ousted from the tourney by the eventual state champion. Crimson Crusher stars **Ray Weaver** and **Dave Stofa** were both Big 33 choices at quarterback, in the 1963 and 1964 games respectively. Stofa was also a second team all-state QB for the 1963 season. He is also the younger brother of **John Stofa,** who played quarterback for the Miami Dolphins and Cincinnati Bengals. As a sidenote, Crusher football teams, from 1960-1963, had a combined record of 37-1-1.

- Prep's lopsided wins over Southwestern Central (located near Jamestown, NY) are the only two contests ever played between the schools. **Jim Marnella** burned the nets for 30 points in the first Southwestern encounter.

Pat Lupo lays one up for another bucket.

- The Ramblers did make a good accounting in the thrilling second Tech contest behind **Pat Lupo's** 25 points, a heartbreaking overtime Centaur victory.

- Tech's 87-84 win over Vincent (14-7), with its combined 171 points, broke the City Series and Gannon Audi records for most combined points, a mark previously held by Tech's 82-76 win over Prep in 1955-56.

- Prep's victory over Meadville (12-10) was the first game between the two since 1926. The Bulldogs entered the Ramblers schedule after winning the Section Two and District 10 titles in 1962 under new coach **Norm Sundstrom**. Meadville had

been coached by legendary **John Joy** from 1947 through 1961, winning several section and district championships and making it to the PIAA Western Final in both 1953 and 1954.

- Cathedral Prep held McDowell (8-12) to 3 FGs in their first contest on the Rambler floor. The 39-point Rambler edge was the widest margin ever between the two.

- Prep was able to get revenge against Bishop Duffy (7-11) after the previous season's overtime loss to the Monsignor Martin league's Manhattan Cup-winning Patriots. Bishop Duffy, only open from 1946 to 1974, never played the Ramblers again. Niagara Falls is now served by Niagara Catholic High School.

- Another highlight included the consistent scoring punch of senior **Jim Marnella,** who was named Second Team Big Seven by the *Erie Times-News.* Star junior **Pat Lupo** was also a Second Team choice.

Jerry Fetzner, forward.

- **Tom Schneider,** who was an All-City lineman on the Prep grid squad, played football at Boston College and later became a teacher and assistant football coach at Prep.

- **Jim Marnella** later became a three-sport star at Slippery Rock, and eventually was a top assistant coach for the Ramblers under **Marcel Arribi** (1987-99). Prior to coaching at Prep, Marnella was head basketball coach at Tech Memorial (1980-87). He has been a popular color commentator for Prep radio football and basketball broadcasts for many seasons.

Jim Reske, guard.

Marnella was inducted into the Metro Erie Sports Hall of Fame in 2001 and the Cathedral Prep Athletic Hall of Fame in 2006.

- The eighth annual Belle Valley Lions Club City-County All-Star game was played before 2,000 at the Gannon Audi, with Prep coach **Bob Trombacco** serving as co-coach of the City along with **Carney Metzgar** of East. **Jerry Fetzner** scored 7 as the City copped the "B" game, 66-46, while **Jim Marnella** (7 points), **Jim Reske** (5) and **Mike Flaherty** (2) helped the City to an easy win in the "A" game, 83-48.

- At the conclusion of the season, **Bob Springer,** President of McDowell High's Student Council, issued a direct challenge to **Tom Ridge,** Prep's Student Council President, for a basketball game that would benefit the March of Dimes. The contest pitted senior boys from McDowell against senior boys from Prep, the stipulation being that none could have had any varsity experience during the 1962-63 season. Though the Rambler seniors led 21-9 at the end of the first quarter, the Trojans dominated from there and won, 63-58, behind **Jim Jensen's** 19 points. Other Trojan participants included Springer, **Jim Meyer, Ken Meyer, Bill Wentling** and **Dick Conover. Mike Sullivan,** a star quarterback on the Prep gridiron squad, led all scorers with 24 points. Other Rambler stars included Ridge, **James Harris, Paul Wozniak, Len Robasky, Ed Robasky** and **Bob Liebel.** A large crowd attended and proceeds from admissions and the sale of candy went to the 1963 March of Dimes. Though the contest was an exciting match on its own merits, the fans enjoyed it even more knowing that handicapped children with birth defects, arthritis and polio would benefit.

1963 All-Opponent Team:

Marion Tutt, Sharon [Point Park JC, Arizona State]

Jeff Person, Sharon

Jim Coalier, Southwestern [Fredonia St.]

Willie Kinnard, Tech (3rd team all-state)

Bobby Biletnikoff, Tech (hm all-state) [Miami (FL),
        football; Yankees AAA baseball]

Joe Liedtke, Tech (2nd team all-state) [Louisville]

Jim Smith, Vincent [Gannon]

Larry Hitt, Academy

Bob Thomas, Academy (hm all-state) [Buffalo]

Walt Crosby, Academy

John Traverse, Bishop Duffy

Jack Watts, East

Carl Johnson, Tech [Edinboro]

Jim Anderson, Jamestown

Rocky Morgan, Jamestown

Tristy Moore, McDowell [Grove City]

Bill Amann, McDowell

Dave Stofa, Bishop McCort [Maryland, football]

Ray Weaver, Bishop McCort

Ted Kurowski, Bishop McCort

East High's Tippy Pohl has trouble working against Druckemiller.

Marnella and Druckemiller crash the boards.

The 1963 Tech Memorial Centaurs, one of Erie's all-time greatest teams. Front, L to R: Claude Harraway, Ed Crumbly, Ken Kruszewski, Joe Liedtke, Willie Kinnard, Bobby Biletnikoff, Carl Johnson; Back: Bill Franz, Donny Calabrese, Bob Williams, Alex Stasko, Paul Jenson.

City Series Champs with new Coach "Red" Murray!

1963-64 (18-3)

Coach: Richard "Red" Murray
Assistant: Rev. James Fahey
Captains: Bill Druckemiller, Pat Lupo
Managers: Dave Pross, Joe Kerner

Richard "Red" Murray's first year as Rambler mentor was a brilliant one.

Date	PREP			Dec.	Loc.	High Scorer	Opponent
11/30	49	Titusville St. Joseph's Academy	38	W	A	Druckemiller (18)	Romaniszyn (13)
12/10	68	Greenville St. Michael's	48	W	H	Druckemiller (26)	Ceremuga (11)
12/15	63	Elk County Christian	44	W	A	Maloney (25)	McGeehan (13)
12/17		Bradford Central Christian (CANCELLED—SNOW)			A		
12/21	72	Academy	54	W	N	Druckemiller (34)	Thomas (17)
12/26	46	Tech Memorial	45	W	N	Lupo (14)	Carson (21)
1/3	74	Strong Vincent	64	W	N	Maloney (22)	Atkinson (16)
1/5	61	Venango Christian	37	W	A	Maloney (19)	Schill (17)
1/7	75	Meadville	63	W	H	Lupo (24)	Vactor (17)
1/10	49	East	32	W	N	Wenrick (16)	Woodard (13)
1/12	79	Elk County Christian	49	W	H	Druckemiller (23)	Fritz (14)
1/17	60	McDowell	53	W	A	Druckemiller (17)	Moore (19)
1/24	65	Academy	68	L	N	Lupo (18)	Thomas (26)
1/31	56	Tech Memorial	66	L	N	Lupo (19)	Lofton (22)
2/2	81	Venango Christian	45	W	H	Druckemiller (16)	Schill (18)
2/4	67	McDowell	63	W	H	Druckemiller (21)	Moore (26)
2/7	77	Strong Vincent	69	W	N	Druckemiller (23)	Schauble (22)
2/11	77	Jamestown (NY)	65	W	A	Maloney (18)	Cole (28)
2/14	65	East	45	W	N	Maloney (16)	Gallegos (14)
2/21	77	Titusville St. Joseph's Academy	66	W	H	Lupo (28)	Snyder (25)
		CITY CHAMPIONSHIP PLAYOFF					
2/28	63	Academy	62	W	N	Druckemiller (20)	Hitt (26)
		P.C.I.A.A. STATE CATHOLIC H.S. TOURNAMENT					
3/8	42	Pittsburgh Central Catholic	48	L	H	Lupo (15)	Gage & Hart (11)
	1366 (65.1)		**1124 (53.5)**				

Pos.	Player	Ht.	Prior School	Class	G(GS)	FG	FT	Total	*PPG*	Career
C	Bill Druckemiller (#32)	6'8"	Memorial	Sr.	21(21)	133	60-97	326	15.5	478
F	Pat Lupo (#30)	6'0"	St. George's	Sr.	21(21)	134	54-103	322	15.3	563
F	Tim Maloney (#4)	6'0"	St. Patrick's	Jr.	20(20)	119	34-54	272	13.6	272
G	Dave Wenrick (#13)	5'10"	St. Patrick's	Jr.	21(19)	59	45-85	163	7.8	163
F	John Stano (#41)	6'4"	Holy Trinity	Jr.	21(18)	46	29-47	121	5.8	121
F-C	Dave Lichtinger (#35)	6'4"	St. John's	Jr.	21(4)	28	5-14	61	2.9	65
G	Dennis Cerami (#5)	5'10"	St. Patrick's	Jr.	17	11	3-8	25	1.5	25
F	Fred "Rick" Hanhauser (#24)	6'0"	St. Luke's	Jr.	15	9	3-7	21	1.4	21
G	Ron Hornyak (#3)	6'0"	St. James	Jr.	8	9	3-5	21	2.6	21
F	Jim Olszewski (#14)	6'1"	St. John's	Jr.	17	3	10-14	16	0.9	16
G	Fred Engel (#34)	5'10"	Bl. Sacrament	Sr.	15(2)	4	0-0	8	0.5	22
C	Chuck Shreve (#33)	6'4"	St. Joseph's	Jr.	6	2	0-2	4	0.7	4
G	Mike Heberle (#31)	5'11"	St. John's	Jr.	5	1	1-1	3	0.6	3
F	John Meister (#15)	6'0"	St. John's	Jr.	4	1	0-0	2	0.5	2
G	Dave Farrell (#23)	5'11"	St. Mary's	Jr.	11	0	1-1	1	0.1	6

Prep's 1964 City Champions. Front, L to R: Mgr. Pross, Heberle, Lupo, Lichtinger, Druckemiller, Stano, Maloney, Engel, Mgr. Kerner; Back: Asst. Coach Father Fahey, Cerami, Wenrick, Olszewski; Shreve, Meister, Hanhauser, Hornyak, Farrell, Coach Murray.

HIGHLIGHTS:

- **Richard "Red" Murray** moved up from the junior varsity ranks and his first year as head coach of Cathedral Prep was a brilliant one, as the Ramblers regained the City Series title. Despite returning only 3 seniors, the Orange & Black had great chemistry. Prep opened the season with a record 11 straight victories and had its best overall record since its 22-3 state championship season of 1953-54.

- Coach Murray was a 1943 graduate of Titusville High School and later of Slippery Rock State College. Following service in the Navy, he made his coaching debut at North Clarion High, going 17-3. Moving to Girard High in 1953, Murray clicked for five straight Erie County League titles, with respective season records of 18-7, 23-4, 14-10, 15-9 and 20-5. He then was hired at Prep and guided the JV teams to outstanding records from 1958 to 1963.

- Former Rambler and Villanova star **Father Jim Fahey**, then on the faculty at Prep, became the first varsity assistant coach (excluding JV and freshmen coaches) since **Father Joe Radziszewski** in 1942-43 and 1943-44.

- It was a strong year for City Series and Section One teams. Cathedral Prep, led by star seniors 6'8" **Bill Druckemiller** and **Pat Lupo**, at season's end, was crowned champion of the *Erie Daily Times* weekly basketball ratings and the *Erie Morning News* "Polly-Point" ratings system. Polly-Point rated 79 teams in the tri-state area. Tech (16-6) was slightly behind at #2, with Academy (14-6) close by at #3. Vincent (15-7), which won Section One but lost to Meadville (18-7) in the District 10 final, was rated 5th, with McDowell (14-6) close at #6 in Class A and 7th overall. The Trojans were just behind a great Mercer (26-2) squad, rated #1 in Class B and 6th overall. The Mustangs made it to the PIAA Class B state final, despite not having a starter above 6'0". Only East High (8-14) had a losing record in Erie, yet ranked #9 in Class A and 17th overall.

- After Prep's 11 straight wins came a pair of City Series losses. The Ramblers then finished the remainder of the regular season without a loss before beating Academy in a playoff for the City title

Druckemiller and Wenrick work hard against St. Mike's.

Dave Wenrick drives against Tech's Donny Calabrese, as Bill Druckemiller offers help.

in a last-second, 63-62 sizzler before a turn-away Audi crowd of 3,000. It was the fifth time in five tries that Prep won the title via the playoff route. **Dave Wenrick** hit the game winning free throw, while big **Bill Druckemiller** led the way with 20 points and 13 rebounds. This was the last time Prep had to contend with three-year Lion superstar **Bob Thomas,** who finished his career with 1,395 points, an all-time Erie area record. It was not broken until 1974 when Academy great **David Purdue** topped Thomas with 1,398 points. Thomas was also the first Wilson Junior High (9th grade) player to score over 300 points in a season.

- An impressive Prep victory was the one over Meadville (18-7), with **Pat Lupo** pouring in 24 points. The Bulldogs went on to win both the Section Two and District 10 titles, defeating Strong Vincent in the D-10 final, 76-67.

- Other big wins included the two over a very talented McDowell squad, the two against S-I champ Vincent, and the one at Jamestown (14-6), the Red Raiders eventually winning New York's Lake Shore League title. An early victory that turned out to be bigger than thought was that over Greenville St. Michael's (24-4), which went on to win its second consecutive PCIAA Class C title, with a 50-49 final's win over Williamsport St. Joseph's.

- All City Series games were played at the Gannon Auditorium (all in doubleheaders before screaming sellout crowds), while the Ramblers continued to play their independent home contests in the Prep gym. The PCIAA elimination contest was also played at Gannon.

- The final standings in the very talented and competitive City Series race were as follows:

	W	L
*Prep	7	2
Academy	6	3
Tech	4	4
Vincent	4	4
East	0	8

*won city championship playoff

- Prep began a five-year home-and-away series with Venango Christian (7-18), which opened its doors after the closing of Oil City St. Joe's in 1962. The Ramblers and the Vikings played twice a year through the 1968 season.

- Prep also began a four-year home-and-away series with Elk County Christian, which opened its doors after the closing of St. Marys Central Catholic in 1962. The Ramblers and the Crusaders played twice a year through the 1967 season.

- An early season trip to Bradford to play Bradford Central Christian, which opened after the closing of Bradford St. Bernard's in 1962, was cancelled because of snow. The game could not be rescheduled and there never was a contest between the two schools both nicknamed "Ramblers." And there never will be—Bradford Central Christian closed in 2000.

- Biggest disappointment was the first round PCIAA playoff loss to Pittsburgh Central Catholic (21-2). It was Prep's unlucky 13th straight loss to a Pittsburgh representative in the PCIAA state playoffs. Over 2,300 fans witnessed a vicious battle, with no less than 66 free throws being taken. A wild melee erupted with 36 seconds remaining, resulting in Erie police being called to the rescue and Rambler **Tim Maloney** being flattened by a kick to the head. Then came a major brawl in Perry Square with dozens of Central and Prep boys participating. It was Central's seventh straight win over Prep, every time in PCIAA tourney play. The Ramblers and Vikings did not play again for 19 years, until the 1982-83 season, the first time the two ever met in regular season play.

- Pittsburgh Central Catholic made it to the state title clash, but Allentown Central Catholic virtually stole the crown, rallying to wipe out a 10-point, fourth quarter deficit and winning, 59-57, in double overtime.

- Other highlights included the consistent scoring punch of seniors **Pat Lupo,** who was named First Team All-City by the *Erie Times-News,* and **Bill Druckemiller,** who was named to the Second Team All-City. High-scoring junior **Tim Maloney** was also named Second Team All-City, while junior playmaker **Dave Wenrick** was given Honorable Mention status.

- **Pat Lupo** and **Bill Druckemiller** also represented the Ramblers in the ninth annual Belle Valley Lions Club City-County All-Star "A" game, starring for the victorious City slickers who routed the County, 90-57. Lupo, a three-sport all-city star at Prep, later competed at John Carroll. He was given the 1964 "Ma" Kaiser Award and was inducted into the Cathedral Prep Athletic Hall of Fame in 2005. Druckemiller went on to star at Denison University, where he was All-Ohio Athletic Conference Most

Hall of Famer Pat Lupo was First Team All-City in football, baseball, and basketball.

Valuable Player in 1968. "Druck" also played in the collegiate SOS North-South All-Star Game in Erie in 1968, competing for the North which lost to the South, 124-104.

1964 All-Opponent Team:

Neil Romaniszyn , Titusville St. Joe's
Mike Ceremuga, Greenville St. Mike's
  [Youngstown St., baseball]
Bob Thomas, Academy (3rd team all-state) [Buffalo]
Roosevelt "Sonny" Carson, Tech
Denny "Hogman" Atkinson, Vincent
Frank Vendetti, Vincent [Edinboro St.]
Tony Schill, Venango Christian [Lycoming]
Tim Vactor, Meadville
"Chickie" Woodard, East
Tristy Moore, McDowell [Grove City]
Rob Wagner, McDowell [Nebraska]
Jim Mosher, McDowell [Princeton, baseball]
Ed Crumbly, Tech
Napoleon "Nate" Lofton, Tech
Dick Schauble, Vincent
Bob Childs, Vincent [Grove City]
Dick Cole, Jamestown [Jamestown
  Community College]
Dan Gallegos, East
Jim "Beaver" Snyder, Titusville St. Joe's
Larry Hitt, Academy
Kevin Hart, Pittsburgh Central Catholic
John Gage, Pittsburgh Central Catholic [Wheeling Jesuit;
  Orioles Class A baseball]

Denny Cerami lofts a bomb from outside the key, hopefully to the correct rim.

Maloney sinks another jump shot from the side.

Tim Maloney looks to drive against Meadville.

Big Dave Lichtinger tosses in a jump shot.

City Champs Again!

1964-65 (17-5)

Coach: Richard "Red" Murray
Assistant: Rev. James Fahey
Captains: Tim Maloney, Dave Wenrick
Managers: Joe Kerner, Nick Gervase

Team captain Dave Wenrick about to sink a one-handed jump shot. He later became head coach at Prep.

Date	PREP			Dec.	Loc.	High Scorer	Opponent
12/4	61	Titusville St. Joseph's Academy	37	W	A	Maloney (15)	Dahle (15)
12/8	48	Cleveland (OH) Gilmour Academy	75	L	A	Stano (19)	Walczuk (21)
12/10	70	Greenville St. Michael's	58	W	H	Maloney & Stano (17)	Zarecky (20)
12/12	49	Venango Christian	58	L	A	Stano (17)	Schill (21)
12/19	67	Academy	59	W	N	Stano (24)	Young (18)
12/30	62	Tech Memorial	56	W	N	Stano (18)	Gaines (20)
1/5	74	Meadville	60	W	A	Maloney (25)	Gray (17)
1/8	68	Strong Vincent	64	W	N	Maloney & Stano (19)	Schauble (26)
1/10	89	Elk County Christian	40	W	H	Maloney (16)	Fritz (11)
1/12	102*	Titusville St. Joseph's Academy	48	W	H	Hornyak (14)	Madden (14)
1/15	75	East	62	W	N	Stano (23)	Lavalais (17)
1/22	44	McDowell	40	W	A	Stano (15)	Peck & Heitzenrater (10)
1/24	58	Venango Christian	41	W	H	Maloney (17)	O'Malley (13)
1/29	74	Academy	63	W	N	Shreve (19)	Weakland (17)
2/6	52	Tech Memorial	54	L	N	Stano (21)	Gaines & Lofton (16)
2/9	70	McDowell	55	W	H	Maloney (21)	Wagner (20)
2/12	55	Strong Vincent	61	L	N	Stano (15)	Schauble (22)
2/14	70	Elk County Christian	31	W	A	Stano (17)	Fritz (14)
2/16	68	Jamestown (NY)	54	W	H	Stano (20)	Smrekar (19)
2/19	72	East	62	W	N	Stano (26)	Katchen (18)
	CITY CHAMPIONSHIP PLAYOFF						
3/1	61	Tech Memorial	34	W	N	Maloney (22)	Kinnard (9)
	P.C.I.A.A. STATE CATHOLIC H.S. TOURNAMENT						
3/16	56	Pittsburgh South Hills Catholic	58	L	H	Stano (19)	South (20)
	1445 (65.7)		**1169 (53.1)**				

Pos.	Player	Ht.	Prior School	Class	G(GS)	FG	FT	Total	*PPG*	Career
F	John Stano (#41)	6'5"	Holy Trinity	Sr.	22(22)	142	88-119	372	16.9	493
G	Tim Maloney (#30)	6'2"	St. Patrick's	Sr.	22(21)	129	55-79	313	14.2	585
C	Chuck Shreve (#32)	6'4"	St. Joseph's	Sr.	22(20)	81	26-50	188	8.5	192
G	Dave Wenrick (#13)	5'11"	St. Patrick's	Sr.	22(21)	49	57-92	155	7.0	318
F	Fred "Rick" Hanhauser (#31)	6'0"	St. Luke's	Sr.	21(11)	50	23-43	123	5.9	144
G	John Meister (#24)	6'0"	St. John's	Sr.	20(8)	27	17-26	71	3.6	73
F	Jim Olszewski (#14)	6'1"	St. John's	Sr.	14(2)	16	15-26	47	3.4	63
F	Ron Hornyak (#4)	5'11"	St. James	Sr.	16	20	6-7	46	2.9	67
G	Dave Lichtinger (#33)	6'5"	St. John's	Sr.	18(4)	18	5-7	41	2.3	102
G	Dennis Cerami (#5)	5'9"	St. Patrick's	Sr.	17(1)	13	8-13	34	2.0	59
C	Don Felix (#35)	6'3"	St. George's	Jr.	9	6	1-5	13	1.4	13
F	John Behan (#3)	5'11"	St. Andrew's	Jr.	3	5	2-2	12	4.0	12
F	Jim Flanigan (#15)	5'9"	St. Patrick's	Jr.	5	5	2-3	12	2.3	12
G	Dan Pakela (#23)	5'11"	St. Patrick's	Jr.	3	5	2-2	12	4.0	12
G	Jim Murray (#34)	5'8"	St. Luke's	Soph.	2	1	0-0	2	1.0	2

Prep's 1965 City Champs. Front, L to R: Behan, Hornyak, Cerami, Wenrick, Flanigan, Pakela, Murray; Back: Mgr. Gervase, Hanhauser, Meister, Felix, Lichtinger, Stano, Shreve, Olszewski, Maloney, Mgr. Kerner.

Maloney defends against Tech, as Shreve prepares to follow up.

HIGHLIGHTS:

- After opening the season at 2-2 with a stunning upset loss at Venango Christian, Cathedral Prep reeled off 10 straight wins before losing to Tech Memorial (13-9) in a 54-52 thriller. The Ramblers avenged that defeat, behind **Tim Maloney's** 22 points, with a surprising 61-34 rout of the Centaurs in a playoff for the City Series championship. It was the sixth time in six tries that Prep won the title via the playoff route.

- Prep had an excellent senior class, 10 men strong, led by high-scoring 6'5" forward **John Stano**; 6'4" center **Chuck Shreve**; and veteran guards **Tim Maloney** and **Dave Wenrick**. Other

star seniors included spot starters **Rick Hanhauser, John Meister, Jimmy Olszewski, Dave Lichtinger, Denny Cerami** and **Ron Hornyak**. Maloney, Wenrick, Cerami and juniors **Jim Flanigan** and **Dan Pakela** were all part of the St. Patrick's team that won Erie's Parochial League championship in 1961 and suffered its only defeat of the season in the grade school state championship game to Pittsburgh St. John's.

- All City Series games were played at the Gannon Auditorium, while the Ramblers continued to play their independent home contests in the Prep gym. The PCIAA elimination heartbreaker was also played at the Audi.

- The final standings in the talented and competitive City Series race were as follows:

	W	L
*Prep	7	2
Tech	6	3
Vincent	5	3
East	3	5
Academy	0	8

won city championship playoff

- Another highlight of the season was the record-breaking 102-point barrage against Titusville St. Joseph's Academy (5-15). **Ron Hornyak** led the way with 14 in that one. That total is a Prep record to this day, tied only when the Ramblers scored 102 against Academy in the 1982-83 season. It was the last time the Ramblers and the Blue Knights competed, with Prep finishing on the long end of the series ledger, 18-1. St. Joe's made it to the 1968 PCIAA Class C state final, but closed following the 1968-69 school year.

- It was also the last time Prep played Greenville St. Mike's (15-7), which closed following the 1964-65 school year. The Ramblers won the series over the Irish, 12-2. The Mikes lost their last game ever in the final of the Erie Diocesan Class C tourney to Clearfield St. Francis, 78-73. The Greenville area is now served by Kennedy Catholic, which opened its doors as Kennedy Christian in 1965.

- Gilmour Academy (17-3) star **Lee Walczuk**, a junior and son of former Cathedral Latin coach **Leo Walczuk**, left his squad late-season to finish the year playing for Lakewood (OH) St. Edward, an Ohio power that was 15-1 at the time. The reason Walczuk transferred, according to the *Cleveland Plain Dealer*, was for media exposure. Gilmour, a Catholic school with a boarding program located in Gates Mills (OH), was not a member of the Ohio High School Athletic Association then, which meant it was not part of the state tournament. St. Ed's, on the other hand, expected to go deep into the playoffs. St. Ed's won its last two games of the regular season with Walczuk taking his thirty shots and everybody else standing around watching. St. Ed's was out of sync and the chemistry was wrong. Coach **Jim Connors** fretted. In the first tournament game, St. Edward, which had a 17-1 record, was upset by Lakewood, a team that had gone 8-10. As a St. Ed's senior, Walczuk was named Third Team All-State by the *Associated Press*. Only 6', 175 pounds, Walczuk was later part of a UCLA national championship team (1969), playing with such Bruin stars as **Lew Alcindor** (n/k/a **Kareem Abdul-Jabbar**), **Kenny Heitz, Curtis Rowe, Lynn Shackelford, John Vallely, Sidney Wicks** and **Lucius Allen**. According to ESPN, the 1968–69 UCLA Bruins basketball team is the "Greatest Basketball Team" ever assembled, and Walczuk was part of that squad!

- In the early season loss to Venango Christian (12-9), Prep was caught off-guard with a full-court press that caused many bad passes and turnovers. A technical foul was also given to the Rambler bench when the coaches and reserves objected a little too strenuously to some bad calls by the officials. For VC it was called "the upset of the year" though just after the holiday it lost to lowly St. Mark's Seminary, 55-52. Prep was able to win the rematch handily on the Ramblers' floor, holding Viking star **Tony Schill** to two points. Schill entered the contest averaging 18.8 *PPG*. In the Erie Diocesan Class B championship game, Venango blew a 15-point halftime lead and lost to Bradford Central Christian, 65-62.

- Though Jamestown (11-8) fell to Prep on the Rambler floor, the Red Raiders did win New York's Lake Shore League championship.

- Biggest disappointment was the heartbreaking Western Final PCIAA playoff loss to eventual state champ South Hills Catholic (26-1). It was Prep's *14th straight loss* to a Pittsburgh representative in the PCIAA state playoffs. It was the outside shooting of **Tom Donahoe** and the all-around play of the first Dapper Dan Classic selectee and appropriately named **Hank South** that spelled doom for the fighting Orange & Black in the nip-and-tuck battle. The annual PCIAA melee between Prep kids and whomever "'m up from Pittsburgh" spilled into Perry Square, with no serious injuries reported. The Rebels went on to defeat powerful Allentown Central Catholic in the final, 64-60, behind South's 30 points. (As a side note, **Tom Donahoe**, grandson of former Pennsylvania governor **David Lawrence**, was head coach of Seton-LaSalle's WPIAL football champions in 1979 and 1980, and later became director of football operations with the Pittsburgh Steelers and GM and president of the Buffalo Bills. He played for the City-Catholic squad in the 1965 Dapper Dan preliminary against the Western PA stars.)

- Prior to South Hills Catholic beating Prep, the Rebels defeated Johnstown Bishop McCort in the Western Semifinal. Pittsburgh Canevin protested South Hills right to be in that game, contending that the Rebels should forfeit its games because of what should have been the ineligibility of 6'3" senior **Joe Laufer**. Laufer returned to the Rebels from North Carolina after his father, a marine, was assigned to overseas duty. The Pittsburgh Diocesan Board of Governors ruled in favor of South Hills Catholic and Canevin appealed to the PCIAA Western Regional Board, which also ruled in favor of the Rebels. South Hills' only loss of its championship campaign was inflicted by North Catholic during the regular season, 59-58.

- The Dapper Dan Roundball Classic was well known in the sports world as the first national high school all-star basketball game. Co-founded by **Sonny Vaccaro** and **Pat DiCesare** (of DiCesare-Engler concert promotions), it was sponsored by and used as a fundraising event for the Dapper Dan Charities in Pittsburgh. The games were played at the Civic Arena with the inaugural held in 1965. The format usually featured the U.S.A. All-Stars vs. the Pennsylvania All-Stars with a preliminary game that featured either the Western Pennsylvania stars against a Pittsburgh City-Catholic lineup or the Western PA All-Stars vs. Eastern PA All-Stars. The game came to be known as the premier high school basketball attraction in the entire nation, hosting crowds upwards of 17,000. Ultimately, the game was hurt by the emergence of other high school all-star games that followed, most notably the McDonald's High School All-Star Game that began in 1977. The 28th Annual Roundball Classic was the last to be played in Pittsburgh on April 11, 1992.

- Vincent (17-7), led by flashy **Dick Schauble's** 496 points (20.7 *PPG*) throughout the season, won Section One and then the District 10 title with victories over Hickory and Meadville. The Colonels then lost to Pittsburgh Schenley, 74-48, in the PIAA Western Semifinal.

- Other highlights included the consistent scoring punch of seniors **John Stano** and **Tim Maloney**, who both were named First Team All-City by the *Erie Times-News*. Both went on to star four years in college, Stano at Alliance College and Maloney at Edinboro State. **Dave Wenrick** was a Second Team All-City selection, while **Chuck Shreve** and **Rick Hanhauser** were Honorable Mention choices.

All-City star Tim Maloney, always determined.

- Stano and Maloney scored 11 and 15 respectively in the 10th annual Belle Valley Lions Club City-County All-Star "A" game, won by the City, 75-54; while Shreve (16 points), Wenrick (11) and Hanhauser (8) led the City to a 64-63 victory in the preliminary "B" contest.

- **Ron Hornyak** went on to a stellar career at Penn State-Behrend,

All-City choice John Stano scores against Tech at the sold-out Audi.

averaging 17.9 *PPG* (1965-67), third on the Cubs' all-time chart at the time (6th today). He was inducted into the Behrend Athletic Hall of Fame in 1991.

- **Dave Wenrick**, an acknowledged football star at quarterback, was given the 1965 "Ma" Kaiser Award, signifying him as Prep's best all-around athlete. He later became Prep's head football coach (1975-77) and the Ramblers' head basketball coach (1984-86) after many years as an assistant in both. Wenrick was also a 35-year teacher at Prep and was inducted into the Cathedral Prep Athletic Hall of Fame in 2015.

- **Chuck Shreve**, an outstanding pitcher on the Rambler baseball squad, went on to a professional career in the Los Angeles Dodgers' organization, playing for Class A teams Bakersfield (1969), Daytona Beach (1970) and Raleigh-Durham (1971). He compiled a lifetime mark of 23-33, with a 3.63 ERA.

Chuck Shreve expertly boxes out teammate Maloney.

1965 All-Opponent Team:
   Paul Dahle, Titusville St. Joe's
   Lee Walczuk, Gilmour Academy [UCLA]
   Tom Eby, Gilmour Academy
   Tom Selfridge, Gilmour Academy [Cincinnati, rugby]
   Phil Zarecky, Greenville St. Mike's
   Tony Schill, Venango Christian [Lycoming]
   Pat O'Malley, Venango Christian
   Jamie Young, Academy
   Napoleon "Nate" Lofton, Tech
   Larry Gaines, Tech
   Curtis Lofton, Tech
   Rollie Johnson, Tech
   Chris Buchanan, Meadville [Central St. (OH)]
   Ed Gray, Meadville
   Bob Lavalais, East
   Dave Heitzenrater, McDowell [Anderson (IN)]
   Rob Wagner, McDowell (4th team all-state) [Nebraska]
   George Weakland, Academy
   Norm Kuhn, Academy
   Dick Schauble, Vincent (hm, all-state)
   John Suesser, Vincent [Slippery Rock]
   Charley Knox, Vincent [Williams College]
   Dan Fritz, Elk County Christian
   Frank Smrekar, Jamestown [Brewton-Parker College]
   Dan Gallegos, East (hm all-state)
   Lee Katchen, East
   Hank South, South Hills Catholic (2nd team all-state) [Cornell]
   Joe Laufer, South Hills Catholic [St. Vincent (PA)]
   Tom Donahoe, South Hills Catholic

Leading scorer John Stano went on to a brilliant career at Alliance College.

Maloney cleanly blocks a Nate Lofton attempt.

Stano maintains he's open as Maloney takes a jump shot from the key.

Worst Prep Team Ever?

1965-66 (3-18)

Coach: Richard "Red" Murray
Assistant: Rev. Thomas Landgraf
Captains: Game captains
Manager: Nick Gervase

The hapless 1966 Prep Ramblers. Front, L to R: Mgr. Gervase, Flanigan, Hathaway, Gunter, Borgia, Davis, Asst. Coach Father Landgraf; Middle: Coach Murray, Barthelmes, Finegan, Pakela, Fessler, Nowak; Back: Belton, Lynch, Goehring, McCoy, Meuser, Felix.

Date	PREP			Dec.	Loc.	High Scorer	Opponent
12/3	51	Meadville	63	L	H	Davis (20)	Buchanan (12)
12/7	59	Cleveland (OH) Gilmour Academy	55	W	H	Pakela (12)	J. Strait (20)
12/11	39	Strong Vincent	54	L	N	Davis (16)	Carter (16)
12/15	53	Venango Christian	61	L	H	Belton (18)	Homan (30)
		GANNON INVITATIONAL CHRISTMAS TOURNAMENT					
12/28	64	Pittsburgh North Catholic	66	L	H	McCoy (13)	Miller (23)
12/29	62	Pittsburgh Bishop Canevin	71	L	H	Belton (14)	Prokell (28)
1/4	51	McDowell	53	L	H	Finegan (16)	Hampy (17)
1/7	70	Tech Memorial	89*	L	N	Finegan (22)	Gaines (23)
1/15	52	Academy	53	L	N	Finegan (17)	Twillie (18)
1/16	83	Elk County Christian	62	W	H	Finegan (20)	Geitner (18)
1/18	55	Jamestown (NY)	77	L	A	Finegan (15)	Smrekar (24)
1/21	47	East	65	L	N	Finegan (13)	Satyshur (15)
1/28	33	Strong Vincent	48	L	N	Davis (11)	Carter (20)
2/2	74	Venango Christian	56	W	A	Davis (24)	Homan (24)
2/4	45	McDowell	55	L	A	Belton (18)	Hampy (24)
2/11	47	Tech Memorial	62	L	N	Belton (16)	Gaines (19)
2/13	51	Elk County Christian	66	L	A	Belton (11)	Krieg (27)
2/19	64	Academy	71	L	N	Davis (25)	Harden (16)
2/22	63	Meadville	85	L	A	Fessler (15)	Lukasik (20)
2/25	57	East	69	L	N	Pakela (14)	Satyshur (20)
		P.C.I.A.A. STATE CATHOLIC H.S. TOURNAMENT					
3/7	58	Johnstown Bishop McCort	80	L	A	Finegan (17)	Munko (24)
	1178 (56.0)		**1371* (65.3*)**				

It might be best to get out of Mike McCoy's way.

Gunter, Fessler and Belton defend the hoop.

Pos.	Player	Ht.	Prior School	Class	G(GS)	FG	FT	Total	PPG	Career
G	Ray Davis (#4)	6'0"	St. Patrick's	Jr.	21(20)	90	39	219	10.4	219
F	Don Belton (#42)	6'3"	Sacred Heart	Jr.	19(16)	77	37	191	10.1	191
F	Tim Finegan (#12)	6"3"	St. James	Jr.	16(14)	72	34	178	11.1	178
F	Rick Fessler (#30)	6'0"	St. John's	Soph.	19(5)	57	20	134	7.1	134
C-F	Don Felix (#40)	6'3"	St. George's	Sr.	21(19)	51	21	123	5.9	136
F	Don Gunter (#50)	6'3"	St. Patrick's	Jr.	21(10)	47	17	111	5.3	111
C	Mike McCoy (#54)	6'5"	St. John's	Sr.	12(11)	27	23	77	6.4	77
G	Dan Pakela (#23)	6'0"	St. Patrick's	Sr.	12(2)	18	20	56	4.7	68
G	Otto Borgia (#10/#12)	5'6"	St. Patrick's	Soph.	7(6)	17	10	44	6.3	44
G	Jim Flanigan (#32)	5'11"	St. Patrick's	Sr.	10	8	7	23	2.3	35
G	John Behan (#10)	6'0"	St. Andrew's	Sr.	5	3	1	7	1.4	19
F	Jerry Nowak (#52)	6'2"	St. Luke's	Jr.	4(1)	3	0	6	1.5	6
F	Dan Lynch (#22)	6'1"	Mt. Calvary	Jr.	2(1)	2	0	4	2.0	4
F	Chuck Goehring (#24)	6'3"	St. John's	Jr.	1	1	0	2	2.0	2
G	Gerry Mifsud (#34)	5'7"	St. Paul's	Soph.	3	1	0	2	0.7	2
F	Norb Barthelmes (#44)	6'3"	St. George's	Sr.	1	0	0	0	0.0	0
G	Tommy Hathaway (#14)	5'11"	St. John's	Jr.	2	0	0	0	0.0	0
F	Chuck Meuser (#24)	6'2"	St. Andrew's	Jr.	0	0	0	0	0.0	0
	Unknown					0	1	1		

HIGHLIGHTS:

- Cathedral Prep's 3-18 mark, including 0-8 in the City Series and 0-10 in the Big Six, is the worst record suffered in the history of the school. After the graduation of 10 seniors in 1965, the Ramblers were beset by youth, a lack of veterans and mid-season injuries to **Dan Pakela** and **Tim Finegan**. Prep also suffered a pair of 7-game losing streaks.

- All City Series games were played at the Gannon Auditorium, while the Ramblers continued to play their independent home contests in the Prep gym. The PCIAA elimination contest was played at Johnstown's War Memorial Auditorium.

- Prep also lost two in the Gannon Invitational, played at the Audi. The first was a close one to North Catholic (16-10), the first time the Ramblers ever played the Trojans during the regular season. (North Catholic's **Bob Miller** played for the City-Catholic squad against the Western PA team in the 1966 Dapper Dan preliminary.) On night two was the Ramblers' first contest with Bishop Canevin High School (11-11), a co-educational Catholic school located in the Oakwood section of Pittsburgh that opened in 1959. McDowell won the tourney, defeating Canevin first, 72-69, and North Catholic, 74-68, next.

- Both North Catholic and Bishop Canevin were members of the Pittsburgh Catholic Class A League, which began in 1959-60. Other loop members, with their 1966 league records (with several weather cancellations) included South Hills Catholic (13-1, 1966 champ; 1959-1979, now Seton-

Big Mike McCoy blocks a Denny Satyshur drive.

LaSalle); Central Catholic (11-3, established 1927); North (9-5); Homestead Bishop Boyle (7-6, 1962-1987); McKeesport Serra Catholic (5-8, established 1961); Canevin (5-9); Mon Valley Catholic (4-9, 1959-1989); and Greensburg Central Catholic (0-13, established 1959).

- Of interest was the mid-season addition of big **Mike McCoy**, Prep's All-American football star, who had also competed in wrestling, water polo and track for the Ramblers. McCoy played well on the hardcourt before quitting in mid-February to concentrate on wrestling, from which he emerged as the PCIAA state heavyweight champion. He also won the 1966 "Ma" Kaiser Award as Prep's best all-around athlete. Defensive tackle McCoy, of course, went on to star at the University of Notre Dame and with the Packers, Giants, Raiders and Lions in an 11-year NFL career. He was a charter inductee of both Metro Erie Sports Hall of Fame in 1986 and the Cathedral Prep Athletic Hall of Fame in 1992.

- The final standings in City Series and Big Six basketball were as follows:

	W	L		W	L
Vincent	8	0	Vincent	9	1
Tech	5	3	McDowell	7	3
East	5	3	Tech	6	4
Academy	2	6	East	6	4
Prep	0	8	Academy	2	8
			Prep	0	10

- Tech (14-6) broke Sharon's record (86 in 1957) for most points scored against Prep with 89. This helped Rambler opponents break an all-time record for points in a season (1371) against the Orange & Black and points per game average (65.3) as well. The 1965-66 opponent *PPG* average lasts as a record to this day.

- Though McDowell (18-4) defeated Prep twice, the Ramblers held the Trojans well below their local record for most points per game at 75.2. That standard lasted until broken by Academy's high-scoring 1973-74 squad.

- Strong Vincent (19-3) won the "Triple Crown" of local basketball leagues—the City Series, Big Six and Section One. The Colonels of coach **Ralph Calabrese** were led by seniors **J.C. Carter, Charley Knox, Bill Lash, Richmond Flowers** and junior big man **Joe Tinko**. Meadville (21-4), however, which routed Prep twice, defeated SV in the playoffs, 54-51, and emerged as District 10 champion.

- The Ramblers never had a chance in their first round PCIAA playoff loss to Bishop McCort (28-2), formerly Johnstown Central Catholic. The Crimson Crushers, led by **Rudy Munko, Mike Patcher** and all-state footballer **Steve Smear**, went on to defeat South Hills Catholic in a 59-58 Western Final thriller and Harrisburg Bishop McDevitt in the state final, 88-83, to win their fourth PCIAA Class A state title. Of note in 1966 was the PCIAA Class C state champion Hazleton St. Gabriel's, coached by **Richard "Digger" Phelps**, later of Notre Dame coaching and television broadcasting fame.

Sophomore Otto Borgia gives maximum effort.

- Highlights included some fine individual scoring by juniors **Ray Davis, Don Belton,** and **Tim Finegan,** and some fine play by sophomores **Rick Fessler** and **Otto Borgia**. Finegan and senior **Donny Felix** were both accorded Honorable Mention Big 6 All-Scholastic by the *Erie Times-News*.

Donny Felix attempts to stop East's Jack Woods from behind.

- **Don Felix,** after college, became an assistant basketball coach and physics teacher at Prep before becoming head coach at DuBois Central Christian High School. He later moved on to a successful construction business career in Phoenix (AZ).

- Seniors **Dan Pakela** (5 points), **John Behan** (4), **Jim Flanigan** and **Norb Barthelmes** all played in the City-County All-Star "B" game, while no Prepsters were invited to the 11th annual "A" contest for the first time. The "Four Preps" helped the City slaughter the County, 64-39. The City "A's" also won, 55-52, giving the Slickers a combined 18-2 record over the course of the series. It was the 11th and last annual Belle Valley Lions Club game, which was started by former Prep assistant football coach **Father Francis Schlindwein** and benefited the Exceptional Children's Fund.

Felix slithers in for a field goal.

1966 All-Opponent Team:-

> Chris Buchanan, Meadville [Central State (OH)]
> Ed Lukasik, Meadville
> Pete Eby, Gilmour Academy
> Jay McKenna, Gilmour Academy
> Jim "J.C." Carter, Vincent [Clarion, Mercyhurst]
> Joe Tinko, Vincent [Duke, football]
> Joe Homan, Venango Christian
> Bob Miller, North Catholic [Point Park]
> Gary Gruseck, North Catholic [Point Park]
> Mike Graham, North Catholic [American University]
> Jim Prokell, Pittsburgh Canevin [Edinboro St.]
> Mickey Marracino, Pittsburgh Canevin
> Jack Burik, Pittsburgh Canevin [Fordham]
> Tony Hampy, McDowell [Brewton-Parker College]
> Steve Brandon, McDowell [Erie Business Center, Mercyhurst]
> Bobby Wheeler, McDowell
> Dave Heitzenrater, McDowell [Anderson (IN)]
> Larry Gaines, Tech
> Larry Troop, Tech
> Calvin Kinnard, Tech
> Tom Twillie, Academy
> Denny Geitner, Elk County Christian
> Frank Smrekar, Jamestown [Brewton-Parker College]
> Amos Goodwine, East [Fredonia St.]
> Lee Katchen, East
> Rollie Johnson, Tech
> Ambrose Krieg, Elk County Christian
> Mike Lecker, Elk County Christian
> Bob Barney, Academy
> Bob Glecos, Academy
> Denny Satyshur, East [Duke, football & golf]
> Rudy Munko, Bishop McCort
> Steve Smear, Bishop McCort [Penn State, football; CFL Montreal Alouettes, Toronto Argonauts & Saskatchewan Roughriders]
> Mike Patcher, Bishop McCort [Pitt]

Slow Start, Poor Finish: Murray Out!

1966-67 (13-9)

Coach: Richard "Red" Murray
Assistant: Rev. Thomas Landgraf
Captains: Tim Finegan, Ray Davis
Managers: Gary Miller, Tim Scully

Team captain Tim Finegan had a fine senior campaign and was named First Team All-Big Six.

Date	PREP			Dec.	Loc.	High Scorer	Opponent
12/2	61	Meadville	69	L	H	Finegan (15)	Buchanan (33)
12/6	66	Mercer	93*	L	A	Pry (20)	Rhoads (40*)
12/11	69	Elk County Christian	48	W	A	Davis (17)	Nedzinski (17)
12/16	51	Strong Vincent	64	L	N	Pry (14)	Tinko (14)
12/20	86	Venango Christian	50	W	H	Finegan (22)	Fonzo (15)
12/23	60	Kennedy Christian	52	W	A	Davis (24)	Morocco (19)
		GANNON INVITATIONAL CHRISTMAS TOURNAMENT					
12/28	69	Cleveland (OH) John F. Kennedy	74	L	H	Finegan & Pry (18)	Canty (21)
12/29	77	Ashtabula (OH) Edgewood	50	W	H	Pry (15)	Higgins & Waid (10)
1/3	71	McDowell	52	W	H	Finegan (26)	Wassell (18)
1/6	60	Tech Memorial	45	W	N	Davis (19)	Troop (17)
1/11	60	Venango Christian	45	W	A	Pry (17)	Fonzo (19)
1/13	54	Academy	56	L	N	Finegan (15)	Taylor & Matthews (11)
1/15	58	Elk County Christian	41	W	H	Fessler (18)	Werner (12)
1/20	56	East	54	W	N	Finegan (16)	Satyshur & Zenewicz (19)
1/27	49	Strong Vincent	53	L	N	Davis (17)	Tinko (14)
2/3	50	McDowell	51	L	A	Finegan (16)	Wassell (19)
2/7	77	Kennedy Christian	54	W	H	Finegan (15)	Westmeyer (22)
2/10	59	Tech Memorial	50	W	N	Finegan (15)	Troop (25)
2/14	69	Meadville	50	W	A	Finegan (19)	Hendricks (12)
2/17	85	Academy	68	W	N	Finegan (22)	L. Harden (18)
2/22	49	East	52(OT)	L	N	Fessler (14)	Satyshur (14)
		P.C.I.A.A. STATE CATHOLIC H.S. TOURNAMENT					
3/11	67	Pittsburgh Bishop Canevin	81	L	H	Belton (19)	Burik (27)
	1403 (63.8)		**1252 (56.9)**				

Pos.	Player	Ht.	Prior School	Class	G(GS)	FG	FT	Total	*PPG*	Career
F	Tim Finegan (#32)	6"3"	St. James	Sr.	22(21)	123	81-97	327	14.9	505
C	Paul Pry (#50)	6'4"	St. Patrick's	Jr.	22(22)	86	61-91	233	10.6	233
F	Rick Fessler (#14)	6'0"	St. John's	Jr.	22(19)	94	14-25	202	9.2	336
G	Ray Davis (#34)	6'0"	St. Patrick's	Sr.	21(17)	85	31-58	201	9.6	420
G	Jerry Mifsud (#30)	5'8"	St. Paul's	Jr.	21(14)	55	40-58	150	7.1	152
F	Don Belton (#42)	6'3"	Sacred Heart	Sr.	22(13)	61	20-42	142	6.5	333
F	Dave Van Volkenburg (#24)	6'1"	Sacred Heart	Jr.	20(1)	33	10-20	76	3.8	76
F	Pat Quinn (#20)	6'0"	St. Peter's	Jr.	12	11	11-21	33	2.8	33
F	Don Gunter (#52)	6'3"	St. Patrick's	Sr.	8(3)	9	4-5	22	2.8	133
G	Otto Borgia (#12)	5'7"	St. Patrick's	Jr.	11	7	3-6	17	1.5	61
G	Vern Gambill (#10)	5'6"	St. John's	Jr.	5	2	4-7	8	1.6	8
F	Jerry Nowak (#40)	6'2"	St. Luke's	Sr.	4	2	1-2	5	1.3	11
G	Keith Hardner (#4)	5'9"	St. John's	Jr.	4	1	0-0	2	0.5	2
G	Tom Hathaway (#22)	5'11"	St. John's	Sr.	3	1	0-0	2	0.7	2
F	Dan Lynch (#54)	6'1"	Mt. Calvary	Sr.	3	0	1-2	1	0.3	5
F	Jeff Trombacco (#44)	6'1"	St. George's	Jr.	3	0	0-0	0	0.0	0

Coach Murray's last Prep team (1967). Front, L to R: Mgr. Miller, Gambill, Borgia, Mifsud, Hardner, Mgr. Scully; Middle: Asst. Coach Father Landgraf, Gunter, Hathaway, Fessler, Davis, Van Volkenburg, Coach Murray; Back: Pry, Finnegan, Belton, Quinn, Trombacco, Nowak, Lynch.

HIGHLIGHTS:

- Though Cathedral Prep had ten more victories than the season before, it was **Richard "Red" Murray's** last of four years at the Rambler helm. He finished with an aggregate record of 51-35 for a winning percentage of .593, including two city championships, but had no victories in PCIAA playoff action.

- Coach Murray's surprise resignation came at the conclusion of the regular season, but before the PCIAA contest against Canevin. Though 35-8 with two city crowns via the playoff route in his first two years, it was rumored that Murray was on his way out after the disastrous 1965-66 campaign. It was no secret that Prep Headmaster **Monsignor Robert McDonald** was unhappy with the results, despite the fact the Prep ranks were depleted by

Headmaster Monsignor McDonald told the student body: "If we have another season like we had last year, we just won't have basketball here anymore."

graduation and injuries. When announcements for tryouts were given in Fall of 1966, "Black Mac" barked to the entire school over the P.A. system: "If we have another season around here like we had last year, we just won't have basketball here anymore!" The 1966-67 season was supposed to ride high with plenty of experienced hands around, but with the chugging start and then the dismal finish, Murray was done. Murray was known as a fine coach and gentleman, however, and was inducted into Titusville High School's Athletic Hall of Fame in 1994 and the Metro Erie Sports Hall of Fame in 2002.

- Seniors **Ray Davis** and **Don Gunter**, and juniors **Paul Pry**

and **Otto Borgia** were all part of St. Patrick's Grade School's 1963 state championship team, the first basketball state titlists from Erie at any level. Also on that squad was Vincent star **Cliff Root** and Tech star **Billy Callahan**.

- All City Series games were played at the Gannon Auditorium, while the Ramblers continued to play their independent home contests in the Prep gym. The PCIAA elimination contest was also played at the Audi.

Two-year starter Ray Davis was also a team captain.

- The season opened with **Chris Buchanan** of Meadville (17-6) scoring 33, the most against the Ramblers since **Roger Pierce** of Academy hit for 36 in 1956. The very next game **Bob "Posey" Rhoads** of Mercer (25-2) broke the all-time record for Prep opponents by tossing in 40 points. (Mercer records show he "only" scored 39.) It was the only time Prep and Mercer ever played, with the Mustangs breaking Tech's all-time team record for most points scored against Prep with 93. That mark lasted until 1991 when broken by Altoona, which scored 101 against Prep in an overtime playoff contest. Rhoads played for the Pennsylvania All-Stars against the U.S.A. in the 1967 Dapper Dan Roundball Classic, while Buchanan had 14 points and 13 rebounds for the victorious Western PA stars against the City-Catholic team in the preliminary match-up.

- Prep beat Meadville in the rematch, but Buchanan was not available for the Bulldogs in that one. The 6'7" pivot stalwart, averaging 28 points and 20 rebounds per game, was sidelined with a respiratory ailment and the Ramblers took advantage of his absence. Buchanan closed his career with 30 points against Hickory in a District 10 semifinal, but the Hornets won the battle, 63-57.

- Mercer won the 1967 PIAA Class B state championship for the second straight year (28-0 in 1965-66), with the Mustangs defeating Montrose in the final, 61-52, at the Harrisburg Farm Show Arena. It was Mercer's fifth trip to the finals in six years under coach **John Swogger,** amassing an overall record of 141-21 for that period. Rhoads next was in the starting lineup for three years at Wake Forest, then played professionally in Australia.

- When junior **Vern Gambill** entered the lineup on December 20 against Venango Christian (11-13), it marked the first time an African-American played in a varsity basketball game for Cathedral Prep.

- Prep began a four-year home-and away series with Kennedy Christian (18-8), which opened its doors after the closing of Greenville St. Mike's in 1965. The original name of the proposed school was changed from Shenango Catholic Prep to Kennedy Christian High School after the death of **President John F. Kennedy** in November, 1963. The school was renamed Kennedy Catholic in 2001. The Ramblers and the Eagles, who won the 1967 Erie Diocesan League Class B title, played twice a year through the 1970 season, then not again until 1992.

- Prep's loss to Cleveland Senate League member John F. Kennedy (13-5, opened in 1966) in the 2nd Gannon Invitational was the only time the Ramblers and Fighting Eagles competed and the only time Prep ever played a Cleveland city public school in basketball. JFK expected to do well at playoff time, but suffered its second upset of the season to Cathedral Latin in the second round, 72-59. Prep's consolation game against Ashtabula Edgewood (4-15) was also the only time the Ramblers and the Warriors ever met.

- Strong Vincent (14-5), which defeated Prep twice, repeated at city champion behind the strong play of **Roger Arrowsmith, Joe Tinko, Cecil Horton, Matt Darby, Ken Jewell** and **Cliff Root**. SV was the beneficiary of Prep's shocking two-point upset of East on a **Tim Finegan** tip-in with just seven seconds left on the clock. East won the regular season finale rematch over Prep in an overtime thriller, playing only five ironmen: **Denny Satyshur, Sid Booker, Alan Poole, Mark Karuba** and **Ed Zenewicz.**

- In an oddity, East High (21-3) won the Section One crown after a 50-42 playoff triumph over Vincent after each finished 7-1 in the regular season S-I standings. For the high-scoring Warriors (104 points against Warren earlier in the season), it was their first S-I crown since 1954. Hickory, however, emerged as District 10 champion.

- Prep's wins over Tech (6-15) and Academy (7-15) began strings of 11 wins in 12 tries against each from 1967 to 1972. The Ramblers lost to the Centaurs once in 1969; and to the Lions once in 1971.

- The final standings in City Series basketball (no Big Six standings this year) were as follows:

	W	L
Vincent	7	1
East	6	2
Prep	4	4
Academy	2	6
Tech	1	7

- 1966-67 was the last time Prep played Elk County Christian (12-9) until the 1994-95 Crusader Classic in St. Marys.

- Prep's first round PCIAA playoff loss to Pittsburgh Canevin (23-2), was its *16th straight loss* to a Pittsburgh representative in the PCIAA state playoffs. Canevin was then upset in the Western Regional by eventual Class A champion Altoona Bishop Guilfoyle, 67-66, at the Pitt Fieldhouse. Guilfoyle next defeated Shamokin Lourdes in the final, 61-57, finishing 20-6 for the season.

Rick Fessler surveys the situation.

- The consistent scoring punch of senior **Tim Finegan** earned him a First Team spot on the Big 6 All-Scholastic team of the *Erie Times-News.* Juniors **Rick Fessler** and **Paul Pry** were named Second Team and Honorable Mention, respectively. Finegan, who finished third in the City Series scoring race, went on to play at St. John Fisher College. Pry finished 8th in the city while Fessler checked in at number 14.

- **Don Belton** was also a stellar end on the Prep football team and a star on the track team. He was given the 1967 "Ma" Kaiser Award as Prep's best athlete, which was fitting as Belton was "Ma" Kaiser's grandson!

Tim Finegan battles against Vincent's Joe Tinko.

- **Don Gunter** was a Catholic All-American lineman on the Rambler football squad and played in the "Big 33" All-Star game in Hershey. He continued his gridiron career at Duke University.

- The Ramblers finished 4th of 31 Class A teams and 5th of 100 overall area teams (including western New York and eastern Ohio) on the *Erie Times-News* "Polly Point" scale, the *Times* exclusive ratings formula. East and Vincent finished as the top Class A teams, though Class B Mercer was #1 for all 100 tri-state area teams.

1967 All-Opponent Team:

    Chris Buchanan, Meadville (4th team all-state)
        [Central State (OH)]
    Bob "Posey" Rhoads, Mercer (1st team all-state)
        [Wake Forest]
    Dave Knowlton, Mercer [Edinboro St.]
    Denny Mathieson, Mercer
    Gary Nedzinski, Elk County Christian
    Joe Tinko, Vincent [Duke, football]
    Roger Arrowsmith, Vincent [Bucknell]
    Cecil Horton, Vincent
    Bill Eckert, Jr., Venango Christian
    Frank Westmeyer, Kennedy Christian
    Al Canty, Cleveland JFK
    John Wassell, McDowell [Gannon]
    Joe Fonzo, Venango Christian
    Larry Harden, Academy
    Larry Troop, Tech
    Tom Twillie, Academy
    Marlen "Chick" Matthews, Academy
    Ed Zenewicz, East [Waynesburg]
    Denny Satyshur, East (5th team all-state)
        [Duke, football & golf]
    Jack Burik, Pittsburgh Canevin [Fordham]
    Bob Cizmarik, Pittsburgh Canevin [Pitt]

Jerry Mifsud, Prep's feisty junior guard.

PCIAA State Champs!

1967-68 (19-5)

Coach: Richard "Dick" Fox
Assistant: Rev. Thomas Landgraf
Captains: Game captains
Manager: Manager: Randy Barko

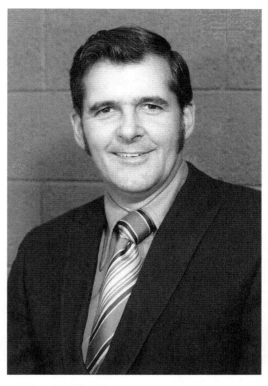

Coach Richard "Dick" Fox led Prep to state titles in 1968 and 1971.

Date	PREP			Dec.	Loc.	High Scorer	Opponent
12/1	45	Meadville	48	L	A	Fessler (20)	Griffin (13)
12/5	99	Kennedy Christian	51	W	H	Fessler (32)	Cattron (18)
12/12	89	Punxsutawney	61	W	A	Pry (25)	Pounds (29)
12/16	70	Venango Christian	61	W	A	Pry (15)	Lynch (28)
12/22	50	Strong Vincent	20	W	N	Pry (17)	Howard (7)
		McDOWELL INVITATIONAL CHRISTMAS TOURNAMENT					
12/28	59	Jamestown (NY)	46	W	N	Pry (18)	Johnston (17)
12/29	53	McDowell	50	W	A	Pry (18)	Hudson (22)
1/5	64	Tech Memorial	42	W	N	Pry (25)	Rastatter (11)
1/9	80	McDowell	58	W	H	Fessler (23)	Hudson (19)
1/12	55	East	61	L	N	Fessler (28)	Satyshur (26)
1/16	92	Venango Christian	41	W	H	Van Volkenburg (27)	Lynch (14)
1/19	68	Academy	40	W	N	Fessler (16)	Moffett (12)
1/26	83	McDowell	48	W	A	Pry (27)	Gunesch (9)
2/2	48	Strong Vincent	50	L	N	Pry (16)	Thompson (26)
2/3	65	Ashtabula (OH) Harbor	57	W	A	Pry (26)	Andrews (16)
2/6	63	Kennedy Christian	48	W	A	Van Volkenburg (17)	Morrocco (11)
2/9	73	Tech Memorial	50	W	N	Pry (23)	Rastatter & Troop (11)
2/11	62	Olean (NY) Bishop Walsh	70	L	H	Pry (23)	Metzler (20)
2/16	51	East	52(OT)	L	N	Fessler (17)	Poole (18)
2/17	89	Ashtabula (OH) Harbor	60	W	H	Pry (33)	Haight (21)
2/23	85	Academy	57	W	N	Pry (40*)	Smith (15)
		P.C.I.A.A. STATE CATHOLIC H.S. TOURNAMENT					
3/12	65	Pittsburgh Bishop Canevin	56	W	N	Fessler (24)	Wojdowski (15)
		P.C.I.A.A. STATE CATHOLIC CHAMPIONSHIP					
3/15	70	Shamokin Lourdes Regional	47	W	N	Pry (17)	Yagodzinski (11)
	1666 (69.4)		**1223 (50.9)**				

Pos.	Player	Ht.	Prior School	Class	G(GS)	FG	FT	Total	PPG	Career
C	Paul Pry (#50)	6'4"	St. Patrick's	Sr.	24(24)	186*	98-138	470*	19.6*	703
F	Rick Fessler (#14)	6'0"	St. John's	Sr.	24(24)	178	45-68	401	16.7	737*
G	Dave Van Volkenburg (#24)	6'1"	Sacred Heart	Sr.	24(24)	118	51-72	287	12.0	363
G	Jerry Mifsud (#30)	5'8"	St. Paul's	Sr.	24(22)	65	52-84	182	7.6	334
F	Gary Borowy (#32)	6'4"	St. Patrick's	Jr.	24(3)	50	25-51	125	5.2	125
F	Pat Quinn (#20)	6'0"	St. Peter's	Sr.	23(21)	29	35-62	93	4.0	126
G	Chuck Rosenthal (#44)	6'0"	St. John's	Jr.	20(2)	27	11-16	65	3.3	65
G	Gerry Mullen (#12)	5'10"	Sacred Heart	Jr.	10	6	2-5	14	1.4	14
G	Vern Gambill (#10)	5'6"	St. John's	Sr.	11	4	2-4	10	0.9	18
G	Pat Steenberge (#22)	6'1"	St. Luke's	Jr.	14	4	1-8	9	0.6	9
F	Rusty Felix (#34)	6'0"	St. George's	Jr.	10	3	0-0	6	0.6	6
F	Gary Bukowski (#42)	6'0"	St. John's	Jr.	7	1	2-3	4	0.6	4
C	Bill Giermak (#40)	6'5"	St. Luke's	Jr.	8	1	0-0	2	0.3	2
G	Tom Hansen (#34)	6'0"	Sacred Heart	Soph.	1	0	0-0	0	0.0	0

Cathedral Prep's 1968 State Champions. Front, L to R: Mgr. Barko, Gambill, Mullen, Bukowski, Steenberge, Rosenthal, Mifsud, Coach Fox; Back: Asst. Coach Father Landgraf, Felix, Fessler, Borowy, Pry, Giermak, Van Vokenburg, Quinn.

HIGHLIGHTS:

- The first campaign of new Cathedral Prep coach **Richard "Dick" Fox** resulted in the Ramblers' third PCIAA Class A state championship and first since 1954. Fox, an English teacher at Prep, was a product of Linesville, and was its high school's all-time leading scorer. He later starred for the Gannon Golden Knights (1955-57). He had coaching stints at Union City (1958-61), Gannon (assistant, 1961-63) and Corry (1963-67) before coming to Prep.

- All City Series games were played at the Gannon Auditorium, while the Ramblers continued to play their independent home contests in the Prep gym.

- The "dunk" shot was banned from 1967 through 1976. Said rule followed the NCAA's ruling banning the dunk in response to the dominant play of UCLA's **Lew Alcindor**, n/k/a **Kareem Abdul-Jabbar**.

- Senior **Paul Pry** and junior **Gary Borowy** were part of the St. Patrick's team that won the 1964 grade school CYO state championship, the second consecutive for the Shamrocks. Also on that squad were Tech Memorial stars **Mike Rastatter, Billy Callahan, Nick Vicentini** and **Dave Damore**.

- The Ramblers won a thrilling PCIAA Western Regional with a revenge victory over Pittsburgh Canevin (18-6), 65-56. Prep sold all of its 1,100 allotted tickets and sent 13 busloads of high-spirited supporters to sold-out Penn

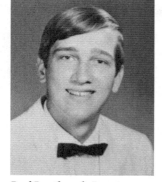

Paul Pry, the only Prepster to ever play in the NCAA Final Four.

Hills High School on that Tuesday night. The battle was nip-and-tuck all the way, until the final four minutes when some hot shooting by **Rick Fessler** and some clutch free throws by

Jerry Mifsud and Paul Pry helped the Orange & Black pull away. It was one of Prep's all-time greatest victories.

- A near riot nearly occurred at halftime, when several Canevin students stole the ram's head off Rambler mascot Joe Patora and began tossing it around the Viking student section. No less than 200 Prepsters came down from the stands to retrieve the article from the opposing side, until some quick-thinking Pittsburgh police officers stepped in to halt the posse. The ram's head was then quietly returned. Nevertheless, a major brawl still occurred at the game's conclusion near where the Prep bus convoy was located. Cooler heads prevailed after a full five-minute brawl, then the game, and the fights, were all officially declared over.

- Canevin was the squad that ousted Prep from the tourney the year before, in 1967. The Crusaders rebounded in 1969 to win their only PCIAA state title. All five Canevin starters that year went on to play in major college: one in football (Tom Clements, starting quarterback at Notre Dame) and four in basketball: Jack Wojdowski (Duquesne), Jim Bolla (Pitt), Tom Rosepink (George Washington) and Tom "Ralph" Pipich (Fordham). Clements was but a starting freshman guard for the Crusaders in the Western final against Prep.

- Canevin's Bob Cizmarik played in the 1968 Dapper Dan Roundball Classic preliminary with the City-Catholic team against the Western PA stars, while Wojdowski (12 points, 16 rebounds) and Pipich (11 points) played in the 1969 preliminary. Rosepink played in the 1970 prelim, while Clements played in 1971's main event with the Pennsylvania All-Stars against the United States.

Mifsud drives against unbeaten Bishop Walsh, as Fessler observes.

- The state final was almost anti-climactic with the easy rout of Shamokin Our Lady of Lourdes Regional (21-5), which had also been in the 1967 final when it lost to Bishop Guilfoyle, 61-57. Four Prep starters—Paul Pry (17), Rick Fessler (16), Dave Van Volkenburg (12) and Jerry Mifsud (10) scored in double figures and Gary Borowy and Pat Quinn were close with 9 and 6. Prep opened with a 12-point 1st quarter lead and simply ran through the Red Raiders press the rest of the way.

No less than twenty busloads of rowdy Prep students were in the crowd of over 4,000 at the Harrisburg Farm Show Arena, screaming: "Roll Ramblers!...Keep Rolling!" Coach Dick Fox told reporters: "I said last Tuesday that whoever won the Canevin game would win the state title."

Harrisburg Farm Show Arena, site of 20 busloads of Prep boys cheering the Ramblers on to the state title.

- The Prep-Lourdes title game was the second of a state championship doubleheader at the Farm Show Arena and didn't start until 9:30 pm. In the lidlifter, Scranton Cathedral defeated Pittsburgh St. Basil in a 77-76 thriller to win the PCIAA Class B crown. St. Basil's Ed Banaszak hit a bucket at the end which would have won the game, but the shot was ruled late by a half-second. The twenty busloads of Prepsters didn't arrive back in the Gem City until well after sunrise—very tired, but very happy to read Saturday's *Erie Morning News* sports headline that stated: "Holy Shamokin'! Prep State Kings!"

- Shamokin Lourdes, the Central Penn Catholic League titleholder and Harrisburg Diocese representative, earned a shot at the title by turning back a strong bid by Scranton Prep in the Eastern final, 68-63. Red Raiders coach Dave Maloney told the *Shamokin News-Dispatch* "The reason for our inability [to score against Prep was] a shakeup over a zone defense." The Ramblers, which the *News-Dispatch* referred to as "tall and classy," opened with a man-to-man but switched to a

Vern Gambill, Prep's first African-American varsity basketball player.

zone just three minutes into the contest. The switch befuddled Lourdes and strong rebounding by Pry and "Van" prevented the Raiders from getting even one second shot at the basket. When senior Vern Gambill scored the last point on a free throw, Prep had built an amazing 70-43 lead. It would have been worse had the Ramblers made more than 14-of-29 free throws. Tom Yagodzinskie was Lourdes leading scorer with 11, and he didn't even enter the contest until midway into the 4th period. Lourdes finally did win a state title, defeating Kennedy Christian, 55-54, to win the 1990 PIAA Class A crown at Hersheypark Arena.

- The 1967-68 Ramblers surrendered the fewest points per game (50.9) since the 1953-54 state championship season (45.6 *PPG*). The Orange & Black also averaged the most *PPG* (69.4) since the 1955-56 season. A highlight was the appearance of Notre Dame coach Johnny Dee as the main speaker at the season-ending championship banquet.

Vincen'ts Ed Davis about to make his second free throw, with time expired, for a 50-48 Colonel win.

- Though unknown at the time, Coach Fox's first victory as Prep mentor, over Kennedy Christian (12-9) on December 5, was the 500th win in school history. It was also the first year which the Eagles operated as a Class A team, which meant the Ramblers had to win their regular season contests with KC for the right to represent the Diocese in the PCIAA tourney.

- Bishop Walsh (18-0), an independent winner over the Orange & Black, finished with a perfect season, further winning Western New York's prestigious Manhattan Cup. The Ramblers and Eagles never played again.

- Prep had new opponents in the Punxsutawney (14-8) and Ashtabula Harbor (1-17). The Woodchucks tied DuBois and Bradford for the District 9 league title, but lost a playoff to DuBois. Harbor's only victory of the season was a 62-61 triumph over Jefferson in its second game. The Mariners proceeded to lose their next 16, including a lopsided pair to the Ramblers.

- The five-year series with Venango Christian (14-13) concluded with a pair of Prep victories and the Orange & Black on the long end of an 8-2 ledger. The Vikings, who won the 1968 Erie Diocesan League Class B title, and Ramblers never competed again, and VC was ordered closed at the conclusion of the 2015-16 school year as part of **Bishop Lawrence Persico's** plan to reorganize Catholic education in the Erie Diocese.

- Heavily-favored East High (22-3) won its first outright City Series championship in 24 years with stars like **Denny Satyshur, Alan Poole, Sid Booker, Leroy Goodwine** and **Doug Zimmerman**. The Warriors of coach **Clarence "Carney" Metzgar** won the District 10 title as well, their first since 1935. East ended the 1967-68 season in disappointing fashion, losing to Pittsburgh Allegheny in a PIAA Western Semifinal.

- The biggest disappointments of the season were the two tough losses to powerful East High. In the first contest, Prep held a commanding 49-31 lead at the end of three quarters in what looked to be a huge upset. The Warriors then went on a 30-6 tear in the final period to shock and humiliate the Ramblers, 61-55. **Denny Satyshur** and **Alan Poole** went wild for East in the fourth quarter, scoring 13 and 10 points respectively. It is considered one of Prep's greatest defeats and that game is talked about to this day. The close loss to Vincent also stung, especially when Prep held the Colonels to but 20 points earlier in the season. SV's **Ed Davis** nailed two free throws with one second remaining to give SV the 50-48 triumph.

- The second East battle looked to be a carbon copy of the first, only with the Sunrisers having an easy time of it after three periods, 45-31. Prep then went on its own furious 18-4 fourth quarter rally, finally sending the game in to overtime at 49-49. Fessler put Prep ahead, 51-50, with a jump shot at 2:15. A terrible 5th personal foul call against Pry on a cleanly blocked shot sent East's Zimmerman to the line, where he coolly sank two for a 52-51 Warrior lead at 0:29. With the Orange & Black running the clock down, East's Satyshur stole the ball, and was fouled with seven seconds left. He missed the front end of the one-and-one—with Rambler Borowy getting the rebound! He outed the ball to Fessler, and with the record-smashing Audi crowd of 3,600 in an utter frenzy, a patented Fessler jump shot fell just short before the final buzzer. The crowd at this game was so big that *fans were actually standing within the playing area* near the four corners of the court! Every space in all six aisles was also taken. Of the contest, Prep boss **Dick Fox** had but one comment: "This was the worst officiated game I've seen in my entire playing or coaching career."

- The final standings in City Series basketball were as follows:

	W	L
East	7	1
Prep	5	3
Tech	4	4
Vincent	3	5
Academy	1	7

- One of the season's many highlights included the consistent scoring punch of seniors **Rick Fessler** and **Paul Pry**. Pry finished the season as the leading scorer in the Big Six with

470 points, breaking [Father] **Jim Fahey's** Prep record of 447 set in 1953. Pry's 19.6 *PPG* broke **Bobby Ward's** mark of 19.1 set in 1960. Of particular note was Pry's 40-point output in his final Audi appearance versus Academy, breaking **Al Hatkevich's** record of 37 set against Tech in 1952. Pry finished his career with 703 tallies, second only to Fessler, who finished as Prep's career scoring leader with 737. "Fess" broke Hatkevich's career mark of 635.

Rick Fessler finished as Prep's all-time leading scorer. He later became the principal at Prep.

- Pry broke the all-time Prep and City Series single game scoring records with his incredible 40 points in the last city battle of the season, canning 13 FG's and 14 FT's. This helped Pry capture the regular season city scoring title, as he was running neck-and-neck with East High's classy **Denny Satyshur** for the crown. (Satyshur actually did finish ahead of Pry at season's end with 476 points, getting one extra game in the PIAA playoffs. "Saty" finished his career with 1,203 points, an East High record at the time.)

Dave Van Volkenburg is in the Prep Hall of Fame for his baseball and basketball exploits. He looks like he could have also been a tough wrestler.

- **Rick Fessler** and **Paul Pry** were named First Team Big 6 All-Scholastic by the *Erie Times-News*. **Jerry Mifsud** was a Second Team selection, while **Dave Van Volkenburg** was given Honorable Mention status. Pry was also given honorable mention status on the *Associated Press'* all-state team, while Fessler was HM on the *UPI* all-state team. Fessler and Pry were the first Prepsters to be accorded all-state honors.

- A proposed Metropolitan League, which would include the five city schools and McDowell, was nixed as the schools failed to reach an agreement on neutral sites for contests. McDowell was willing to compete on neutral sites for all sports, except football and basketball, while the city schools wanted the Trojans to play all football games at the Erie Stadium and all basketball games at the Gannon Audi. McDowell officials were reluctant to do this, thus an agreement could not be reached.

- **Pat Quinn**, also a star shot-putter on the Rambler track and field team, was given the first Guth Memorial Track Award, given in honor of **Jimmy Guth** '65, a Rambler track star who was sadly killed in an automobile accident on September 10, 1964.

Prep's three-sport all-star, Jerry Mifsud, operates against Kennedy Christian.

- **Jerry Mifsud** was a highly acclaimed three-sport star at Prep and was winner of the 1968 "Ma" Kaiser Award as Prep's best athlete. He played football at Edinboro State before joining the Kansas City Royals organization. He played with Billings in the Pioneer League in 1971 and with Waterloo in the Midwest league in 1972. Mifsud was inducted into the Cathedral Prep Athletic Hall of Fame in 1994 and the Metro Erie Sports Hall of Fame in 1995.

- **Dave Van Volkenburg** was an outstanding pitcher for the Ramblers. He was drafted in the 7th round by the Pittsburgh Pirates in 1968, but instead went on to Clemson University where he lettered 4 years (1969-72). "Van" is one of just two Tigers to hit a home run and pitch a shutout in the same game. He accomplished the feat in 1969 against Jacksonville University, a game in which he struck out 10. Van Volkenburg also pitched an 11-0 no-hitter against Florida State in 1971. He was inducted into the Cathedral Prep Athletic Hall of Fame in 1995 and the Metro Erie Sports Hall of Fame in 2012.

Paul Pry scored a record 40 points in the regular season finale against Academy.

- **Paul Pry** was the first recipient of the James "Moe" Gross Award, signifying him as Prep's best basketball

Both Prep-East games were tense, hard-fought, jam-packed affairs.

player. Pry went on to play at the University of Louisville, where he lettered three years and played in the 1972 NCAA Final Four for first-year coach **Denny Crum**. The Cardinals entered that Final Four with a 26-3 record, but lost to eventual national champ UCLA in the semifinals, 96-77, and to North Carolina in the consolation game, 105-91. Pry scored four points against the 30-0 Bruins, who boasted such stars as **Bill Walton, Keith Wilkes, Henry Bibby, Larry Hollyfield** and **Swen Nater**. Pry scored two against the Tar Heels, who also finished 26-5 under coach **Dean Smith** and rostered such stars as **Bob McAdoo, Dennis Wuycik** and **George Karl**. Pry is the only Prep Rambler ever to participate in an NCAA Final Four.

- **Rick Fessler** went on to compete at Saint Vincent College and Mercyhurst College. Fessler was the first recipient of Mercyhurst's esteemed Senior Student-Athlete of the Year Award in 1972. Fessler was head basketball coach at McDowell High School (1983-1990) and later became principal at Cathedral Prep.

- An upstart organization called the American Basketball Association emerged for the 1967-68 season. The ABA, with its red, white and blue basketballs and 3-point shots, briefly threatened the NBA's dominance until the rival leagues merged in 1976.

1968 All-Opponent Team:

  Sam Morocco, Kennedy Christian

  Larry Pounds, Punxsutawney

  Dave Lynch, Venango Christian

  Donn Johnston, Jamestown [North Carolina]

  Mike Rastatter, Tech [Clarion St.]

  Hank Hudson, McDowell

  Jimmy Trojan, McDowell

  Alan Poole, East (hm all-state)

  Denny Satyshur, East (2nd team all-state) [Duke, football & golf]

  Sid Booker, East [Edinboro St.]

  Mark Karuba, East [Hobart, football]

  Marlen "Chick" Matthews, Academy

  Greg Thompson, Vincent [Clarion St.]

  Mike Metzler, Bishop Walsh [Tufts, football]

  Doug Zimmerman, East [Slippery Rock]

  Ed Haight, Ashtabula Harbor

  Jack Wojdowski, Pittsburgh Canevin (2nd team all-state, 1969) [Duquesne]

  Bob Cizmarik, Pittsburgh Canevin [Pitt]

  Tom Clements, Pittsburgh Canevin [Notre Dame, football; CFL Rough Riders, Roughriders, Tiger-Cats, Blue Bombers; NFL Kansas City Chiefs]

Britton Injury Spoils Season!

1968-69 (14-7)

Coach: Richard "Dick" Fox
Captains: Gary Borowy, Pat Steenberge
Managers: Randy Barko, Dave Lastowski

Rosenthal and Hansen battle against Academy.

Date	PREP		Dec.	Loc.	High Scorer	Opponent
12/9	70	Corry	44	W	H	Britton (25)	Schwab (22)
12/13	55	Strong Vincent	65	L	N	Rosenthal (19)	Howard (21)
12/14	84	Punxsutawney	62	W	H	Rosenthal (25)	Williams (20)
12/16	70	Corry	57	W	A	Rosenthal (23)	Schwab (20)
12/22	57	Meadville	55	W	H	Rosenthal (20)	Seeley (15)
		McDOWELL INVITATIONAL CHRISTMAS TOURNAMENT					
12/27	71	Jamestown (NY)	45	W	N	Britton (23)	Johnston (17)
12/28	67	McDowell	49	W	A	Britton (19)	Peck (14)
1/3	53	Tech Memorial	70	L	N	Hansen (16)	Crotty (16)
1/5	58	Cleveland (OH) St. Joseph	74	L	H	Rosenthal (18)	Delaney (25)
1/7	68	McDowell	58	W	H	Rosenthal (27)	McKeag (24)
1/10	59	East	65	L	N	Borowy (19)	Allen (21)
1/14	55	Kennedy Christian	44	W	A	Borowy (21)	Glavin (13)
1/18	71	Academy	70(OT)	W	N	Borowy (26)	Harden (25)
1/24	53	Strong Vincent	49(OT)	W	N	Rosenthal (17)	Swartzman (14)
1/31	44	McDowell	47	L	A	Borowy (17)	McKeag & Peck (12)
2/4	66	Jamestown (NY)	65	W	A	Rosenthal (18)	Johnston (23)
2/7	50	Tech Memorial	48	W	N	Rosenthal (19)	Marucci (13)
2/11	50	Kennedy Christian	32	W	H	Borowy (15)	Gibbons (10)
2/14	61	East	79	L	N	Rosenthal (20)	Goodwine (22)
2/22	55	Academy	52	W	N	Borowy (24)	Barnes (15)
		P.C.I.A.A. STATE CATHOLIC H.S. TOURNAMENT					
3/7	56	Altoona Bishop Guilfoyle	62	L	N	Rosenthal (19)	Lambour (22)
	1277 (60.8)		**1192 (56.8)**				

Pos.	Player	Ht.	Prior School	Class	G(GS)	FG	FT	Total	*PPG*	Career
G	Chuck Rosenthal (#24/25)	6'0"	St. John's	Sr.	21(21)	146	69-107	361	17.2	426
F	Gary Borowy (#32/33)	6'4"	St. Patrick's	Sr.	21(21)	115	78-115	308	14.7	433
G	Tom Hansen (#34/35)	6'0"	Sacred Heart	Jr.	20(18)	72	33-50	177	8.9	177
F	Chuck Britton (#22/21)	5'10"	Gridley	Soph.	7(7)	46	38-56	130	18.6	130
G	Pat Steenberge (#10/11)	6'1"	St. Luke's	Sr.	21(18)	31	23-40	85	4.0	94
C	Bill Giermak (#40/41)	6'5"	St. Luke's	Sr.	9(6)	25	7-11	57	6.3	59
G	Willis Cardot (#20/23)	5'9"	St. John's	Soph.	15(5)	21	15-27	57	3.8	57
G	Dave Wieczorek (#14/15)	5'8"	St. John's	Jr.	17(5)	24	4-9	52	3.1	52
F	Jack Benson (#50/51)	6'2"	Bl. Sacrament	Sr.	17(4)	16	8-18	40	2.4	40
G	Gerry Mullen (#12/13)	5'10"	Sacred Heart	Sr.	8	2	1-3	5	0.6	19
C	Bob Kneib (#52/53)	6'4"	Mt. Calvary	Jr.	1	1	1-2	3	3.0	3
F	Rusty Felix (#44/45)	6'0"	St. George's	Sr.	1	1	0-0	2	2.0	8
F	Brian Flanagan (#30/31)	6'1"	St. Peter's	Jr.	2	0	0-0	0	0.0	0

The 1969 Prep Ramblers. L to R: Mgr. Barko, Cardot, Britton, Mullen, Rosenthal, Flanagan, Giermak, Borowy, Kneib, Benson, Steenberge, Felix, Hansen, Wieczorek, Coach Fox.

HIGHLIGHTS:

Vincent's Willie Giulianelli aims for two over Chuck Britton.

- The second campaign of Cathedral Prep coach **Richard "Dick" Fox** gave mixed results. The loss of star sophomore **Charley Britton** to injury in the seventh game of the season proved devastating. Highlights of the season included the thrilling back-to-back overtime victories over Academy and Strong Vincent before capacity crowds at the Gannon Auditorium, and the second consecutive championship of the four-team McDowell Invitational Christmas Tournament.

- Prep's two wins over Corry (3-19) were the last time the two played until the 1984-85 opener.

- Prep's victories over Jamestown (16-5) in the McDowell Invitational and later in the season at Jamestown were impressive. The Red Raiders won New York's Section 6 Class AAA title with a lopsided win over Niagara Falls at Buffalo's Memorial Auditorium.

Chuck Britton, one of Erie's greatest all-time athletes.

- Prep and Erie area fans were excited about the early season play of 5'10" sophomore **Chuck Britton**. A superb leaper with a soft touch, Britton led the Ramblers to a 6-1 record and a McDowell Christmas Tournament championship. Britton, unfortunately, was rammed into the wall in the second half of the championship game at McDowell (11-10), broke his leg, and was out for the season. The Ramblers proceeded to lose three of the next four games. This effectively ended Britton's Prep athletic career, as he transferred to Vincent and then to McDowell, where he became a full star in football, basketball and track. Considered one of Erie's all-time greatest athletes, Britton was awarded football and basketball scholarships to the University of Cincinnati.

- Though Britton's role was capably filled by seniors **Jack Benson, Bill Giermak** and **Gerry Mullen**, the Ramblers had to amend their style of play and Britton's absence was keenly felt as season wore on.

- Prep faced a new opponent in Cleveland St. Joseph (22-3), located on the shores of Lake Erie where Cleveland meets its important suburb of Euclid. St. Joe's was, at the time, the largest all-boys school in the state of Ohio, with over 2,000 students. St. Joe's was founded in by the Marianists in 1950 and quickly became a recognized athletic power. The Vikings

Borowy looks to get the tip verses Academy.

were the 1969 Crown Conference, OHSAA Sectional and OHSAA District champions. They also beat Tech, 81-70, and Vincent, 70-55, during the season. The Vikes faltered in a Regional final to Canton McKinley, 99-54. McKinley next defeated Dayton Chaminade but lost to unbeaten Columbus East in the AA state final, 71-56. In 1990 St. Joe's merged with Villa Angela Academy to form Villa Angela-St. Joseph High School (VASJ).

SV's Rein Pold watches as Borowy defends against Colonel center Bill Swartzman.

- The overtime victories over Academy (10-11) and Vincent (13-6) were, unbelievably, only the second and third times Prep ever won OT contests. The Ramblers were but 1-11 all-time in OT games to that point, the previous win being the famous victory over SV in 1942.

- City champion East High (18-7) won its third straight Section One championship and its second consecutive District 10 title and sixth overall. The Warriors didn't win another D-10 championship until taking the AA crown in 1984. The Warriors lost to Bradford in the first round of PIAA playoff action, 70-64.

- Prep's win at home over Kennedy Christian (6-15) may have been the *shortest* game ever played by the Ramblers. With 5:47 remaining in the third quarter, KC coach **Jack Burns** became visibly upset with an offensive foul call on Eagle **Jack Glavin**. Burns promptly called his club together then marched to the locker room. Officials **Ron Jones** and **Pete Lightner** waited three minutes before awarding Prep a forfeit victory at the said score. Kennedy Christian then scored a 56-53 season-ending upset over Bishop Guilfoyle, the team that ousted Prep in the PCIAA tourney.

- The final standings in the very talented and competitive City Series basketball were as follows:

	W	L
East	6	2
Vincent	5	3
Prep	4	4
Tech	3	5
Academy	2	6

- The biggest disappointments were the tough losses in City Series competition and the first round PCIAA loss to Bishop Guilfoyle (15-11). It was the first time the Ramblers and Marauders competed since 1929 when Guilfoyle was known as Altoona Catholic. Guilfoyle was then crushed, 74-52, by star-studded eventual state champ Pittsburgh Canevin (24-0),

Team captain Gary Borowy went on to a record career at Behrend.

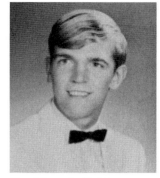

Chuck Rosenthal led the Ramblers in scoring and later played at Allegheny College.

but rebounded to win the 1970 title. Guilfoyle also won the Class A crown in 1967. The 1969 Canevin squad was the only PCIAA Class A team to finish undefeated since Johnstown Central Catholic (27-0) in 1951 and Pittsburgh North Catholic (28-0) in 1943.

- All City Series games were played at the Gannon Auditorium (all in doubleheaders before screaming sellout crowds), while the Ramblers continued to play their independent home contests in the Prep gym. The PCIAA elimination contest was played at Tech Memorial, the first time the Ramblers ever played in that venue.

- Seniors **Chuck Rosenthal** and **Gary Borowy** were named Second Team Big 6 All-Scholastic by the *Erie Times-News*. Rosenthal went on to play at Allegheny College (1969-71), while Borowy, winner of the James "Moe" Gross Award as Prep's best player, starred for Penn State-Behrend (1969-71) where he still holds the all-time scoring average at a record 22.0 *PPG* for the Cubs (now Lions). Borowy was inducted into Behrend's Athletic Hall of Fame in 1993.

Rosenthal from the corner for two!

- **Pat Steenberge**, an acknowledged football and baseball star, went on to start at quarterback at the University of Notre Dame and is famous for tossing the two-point conversion pass that beat Purdue, 8-7, in the rain in 1971. He was given the "Ma" Kaiser Award, signifying him as Prep's best all-around athlete and was inducted into the Cathedral Prep Athletic Hall of Fame in 2005.

All-around athlete Pat Steenberge went on to star as quarterback for Notre Dame.

- Part-time starter **Jack Benson** was also an outstanding receiver for the Prep gridders and a main target of **Pat Steenberge's** brilliant passing. "Bennie" could also toss the pigskin–he was 3-for-3 in the famous "Steenberge-to-Benson-to-Britton" trick plays for 90 yards and two touchdowns.

- Seniors **Jack Benson, Gerry Mullen** and **Rusty Felix** humorously referred to themselves as members of an infamous "30-30-30 Club." This simply meant that for Coach Fox to insert any of the three into the lineup, the Ramblers had to be either "up by thirty; down by thirty; or there has to be less than thirty seconds remaining to be played!"

Junior Tommy Hansen snares a rebound.

Mite-sized junior Dave Wieczorek leaps high for another bucket.

1969 All-Opponent Team:

Fred Schwab, Corry [Grove City]

Jack Howard, Vincent [Clarion St.]

Dave "Spinner" Crotty, Tech [Clarion St.]

Dan Williams, Punxsutawney

Gordon Seeley, Meadville

Donn Johnston, Jamestown (1st team all-state, NY) [North Carolina]

Billy "Bumpy" Callahan, Tech [Gannon]

Tim Delaney, Cleveland St. Joe's (3rd team all-state, OH) [Kenyon]

Pat Lyons, Cleveland St. Joe's [Dayton, John Carroll]

Roger Gunesch, McDowell [Colorado, football]

Bob McKeag, McDowell [Virginia, basketball & football]

Mike Ford, McDowell [Clarion St., baseball]

Eddie Woodard, East [Kent State, football]

Kenny Harden, Academy

Bobby Hoffman, Academy

Leroy Taylor, Academy

Rein Pold, Vincent [Clarion St.]

Bill Swartzman, Vincent [Pitt}

Mike Peck, McDowell [Duke, football]

John Marucci, Tech [Alliance]

Leroy Goodwine, East [Erie Business Center]

Claude Allen, East

Dan Porath, East [PSU-Behrend]

Tim Lambour, Bishop Guilfoyle [Georgetown]

The 1970's

Assistant Bill Flaherty and head coach Dick Fox celebrate with Prep fans following the dramatic victory for the 1971 state championship.

After 5-Year Drought: City Champs!

1969-70 (18-6)

Coach: Richard "Dick" Fox
Assistants: Bill Flaherty, Tom Schneider
Captains: Tom Hansen, Dave Wieczorek
Managers: Larry Piotrowicz, Dan Leifield

The Ramblers celebrate their first city series title in five years.
Identifiable: Wieczorek, Flaherty, Cardot, Massing, Mangold.

Date	PREP			Dec.	Loc.	High Scorer	Opponent
12/5	77	Bradford	80(OT)	L	A	Cardot (24)	Titus (23)
12/6	101	Ashtabula (OH) Harbor	63	W	H	Flanagan (23)	Milberg (28)
12/12	69	Tech Memorial	67	W	N	Bukowski (17)	Weber (24)
12/14	57	Pittsburgh South Hills Catholic	69	L	H	Cardot (20)	Pietro (24)
12/19	77	Strong Vincent	49	W	N	Flanagan (22)	Swartzman (14)
12/27	81	Lackawanna (NY) Baker-Victory	78	W	H	Wieczorek (18)	Weigel (34)
12/28	79	Pittsburgh North Catholic	78(OT)	W	H	Cardot (26)	DiPasquale (29)
1/2	55	McDowell	56	L	A	Bukowski (20)	Bartoszek (21)
1/9	77	Academy	59	W	N	Flanagan & Bukowski (18)	Bean (17)
1/13	100	Jamestown (NY)	42	W	H	Cardot (27)	Edstrom (15)
1/16	56	East	58	L	N	Cardot (16)	Baker (17)
1/17	79	Ashtabula (OH) Harbor	42	W	A	Cardot (28)	Milberg (12)
1/20	86	Kennedy Christian	51	W	A	Cardot (20)	Kranich (15)
1/23	65	Tech Memorial	52	W	N	Hansen (16)	Marucci (24)
1/25	73	Cleveland (OH) St. Joseph	78	L	A	Cardot (27)	Hill (33)
1/30	60	Strong Vincent	53	W	N	Cardot (22)	Swartzman (16)
2/6	73	Jamestown (NY)	68	W	A	Cardot (26)	Edstrom (21)
2/7	73	Conneaut (OH)	64	W	A	Bukowski (25)	Puffer (19)
2/10	69	Kennedy Christian	47	W	H	Cardot (20)	Welch (15)
2/14	78	Academy	58	W	N	Bukowski (26)	Twillie (18)
2/17	71	McDowell	70	W	H	Flanagan (26)	Britton (29)
2/20	64	East	57	W	N	Flanagan (18)	Woodard & Satyshur (16)
		P.C.I.A.A. STATE CATHOLIC H. S. TOURNAMENT					
3/1	63	Pittsburgh North Catholic	53	W	A	Cardot (17)	Pagani (19)
3/8	63	Altoona Bishop Guilfoyle	69	L	N	Bukowski (18)	Landolfi (25)
	1746* (72.8*)		**1461* (60.9)**				

Pos.	Player	Ht.	Prior School	Class	G(GS)	FG	FT	Total	*PPG*	Career
G	Willis Cardot (#12)	5'8"	St. John's	Jr.	24(24)	185	113-152	483*	20.1*	540
C	Brian Flanagan (#30)	6'3"	St. Peter's	Sr.	24(22)	120	97-158	337	14.0	337
F	Dan Bukowski (#32)	6'1"	St. John's	Jr.	24(24)	135	43-75	313	13.0	313
F	Tom Hansen (#34)	6'1"	Sacred Heart	Sr.	24(24)	99	46-70	244	10.2	421
G	Dave Wieczorek (#14)	5'8"	St. John's	Sr.	23(23)	98	47-77	243	10.6	295
F	John Reynders (#52)	6'3"	St. Luke's	Jr.	11	13	7-18	33	3.0	33
G	Ray Massing (#42)	5'9"	St. Luke's	Jr.	11(1)	9	9-17	27	2.5	27
F	Joe Cook (#44)	6'1"	Sacred Heart	Jr.	10	7	5-9	19	1.9	19
F	Tom Burke (#50)	6'1"	Pgh. St. Teresa	Jr.	7	5	4-8	14	2.0	14
G	Bobby Smith (#10)	5'9"	St. George's	Jr.	5	7	0-2	14	2.8	14
C	Bob Kneib (#54)	6'5"	Mt. Calvary	Sr.	16(2)	6	1-7	13	0.8	16
F	Dick Mangold (#24)	5'11"	Sacred Heart	Jr.	7	1	0-4	2	0.3	2
G	Jim Cox (#22)	5'8'	St. Peter's	Jr.	3	1	0-2	2	0.7	2
G	Kirk Hardner	5'8"	St. John's	Jr.	0	0	0-0	0	0.0	0

Prep's 1970 City, LSL Champions. Front, L to R: Massing, Wieczorek, Cardot, Cox, Smith, Mangold; Back: Coach Fox, Bukowski, Burke, Cook, Kneib, Reynders, Flanagan, Hansen, Mgr. Leifield, Mgr. Piotrowicz

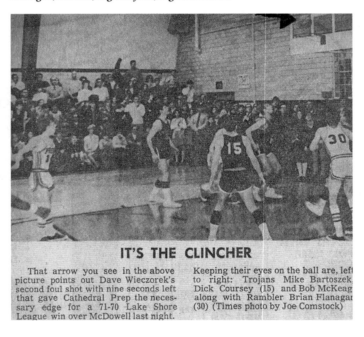

IT'S THE CLINCHER

That arrow you see in the above picture points out Dave Wieczorek's second foul shot with nine seconds left that gave Cathedral Prep the necessary edge for a 71-70 Lake Shore League win over McDowell last night. Keeping their eyes on the ball are, left to right: Trojans Mike Bartoszek, Dick Coursey (15) and Bob McKeag, along with Rambler Brian Flanagan (30) (Times photo by Joe Comstock)

HIGHLIGHTS:

- Cathedral Prep won its first City title in five years for third-year mentor **Dick Fox**, and tied for the Lake Shore League crown with McDowell. The Ramblers fell in the PCIAA Western Final for the second straight year to Altoona Bishop Guilfoyle (21-4) at Johnstown's War Memorial Auditorium. BG's **Bob Landolfi** was a one-man wrecking crew with 25 points and 19 rebounds. The Marauders then defeated Allentown Central Catholic, 76-74, on **Denny Tomassetti's** 15-foot jump shot with 3 seconds remaining, to win the Class A state championship. It was the last state championship ever for any Blair County high school.

- All City Series games were played at the Gannon Auditorium, while the Ramblers continued to play their independent home contests in the Prep gym. Strong Vincent and Pittsburgh North Catholic tussled as a preliminary to the Baker-Victory contest.

- The biggest highlight was the Rambler season scoring record of shooter-deluxe **Willis "Puck" Cardot**, who was unanimously

named First Team All Big Six by the *Erie Times-News* and the new *Erie Press*. The smooth junior southpaw with the soft touch led the Big Seven in scoring and broke **Paul Pry's** all-time single-season scoring record. He was also the first Prepster ever to average more than 20 points per game.

- In the season opener at eventual District 9 champion Bradford (21-2), **Jack Titus** of the Owls hit a hook shot from mid-court in the final second to send the game into overtime. Bradford fans listening on the radio had their own *Heidi* moment, unable to hear what happened in the final second of the game. According to the *Bradford Era*, as the announcer was calling the game someone tipped over the radio table, causing the remote control to disconnect and knock the WESB broadcast out for a few moments. Listeners were unaware of what happened until a voice came on stating the game was going into overtime, indicating that Titus' shot found the mark. Bradford, which played Prep without the services of leading scorer **Paul Stiles**, outscored the Ramblers, 7-4, in OT. The Owls' only two losses of the season were both to powerful Pittsburgh Schenley, once during the regular season and the second in a PIAA Western Semifinal. Schenley, with stars **Ricky Coleman, Clarence Hopson** and **Maurice Lucas,** was then upset by Beaver Falls in the Western Final, 87-83. Prep's OT loss to Bradford was the

The Prep seniors, L to R: Kneib, Flanagan, Wieczorek, Hansen.

first time the Ramblers engaged the Owls since 1956. The two schools then met annually through the 1981-82 season.

- The Baker-Victory contest was the first the Ramblers and the Braves competed in a quarter-century, when Baker-Victory was known as Our Lady of Victory and was the first team to play on Prep's new gymnasium floor on December 2, 1944.

- All six of Prep's losses were close encounters. In the first McDowell (16-6) battle the Ramblers simply went cold in the 4th quarter; and in the first East (11-11) contest Prep lost the services of classy guard **Dave "Wiz" Wieczorek**

Wieczorek was submarined by East's McIntosh and taken to Hamot Hospital.

when he was submarined by **Virg McIntosh** and taken to Hamot Hospital for treatment.

- One of the biggest wins of the season included the one-point thriller over rugged McDowell before a jam-packed throng in the Prep gym. Prep and McDowell fans even climbed through first floor restrooms windows to gain admittance to the long sold-out affair. **Brian Flanagan** led the Orange & Black with 26 points and 13 rebounds and **Dave Wieczorek** hit a pair of free throws on a pressure-packed "one-and-one" situation with 9 seconds left to offset **Chuck Britton's** drive at the buzzer for the Trojans. (High-scoring McDowell had scored 111 against Conneaut Valley earlier in the season).

Cardot drives against East, as Hewitt, Satyshur, and Baker attempt to defend. Others for Prep: Hansen, Massing, Flanagan.

Cardot still feels he might get the pass as "Wiz" takes a perfect jump shot.

- Also huge were a pair of slim victories over powerful North Catholic (21-4). **Tommy Hansen** was the hero in the first NC contest, sinking a pair of free throws after time had expired, and then scoring 4 more in the overtime. The Ramblers were down by 14 in the last period and scored 6 in the final minute to send the game into OT in one of Prep's finest comebacks! A nice little brawl between Prep students and the Trojan team occurred in the aftermath. The second NC upset came in the PCIAA Western Semifinal at the Pitt Fieldhouse. The Ramblers galloped to a 23-5 first quarter lead and were able to hold on the balance of the way.

- North Catholic star **Augie DiPasquale** (12 points) played in the 1970 Dapper Dan Roundball Classic preliminary for the City-Catholic team against the Western PA stars.

- Another big win for the Ramblers was the city title clincher against East, Prep's first win over the Warriors since 1967. Two easy wins over District 10 champion Vincent (14-10) also look good on the resume.

- The final standings in City Series and LSL basketball leagues were as follows:

	W	L		W	L
Prep	7	1	Prep	10	2
Vincent	6	2	McDowell	10	2
East	4	4	Vincent	9	3
Academy	2	6	East	6	6
Tech	1	7	Academy	4	8
			Tech	2	10
			Jamestown	1	11

- Prep clobbered Kennedy Christian (2-20) twice for the Erie Diocese Class A title. Kennedy had not been in the Class B/C Erie Diocesan League since the 1966-67 year, its second season of operation. By 1969-70, the EDL consisted only of: East—Elk County Christian, DuBois Central Christian, Bradford Central Christian and Clearfield St. Francis; and West—Venango Christian, St. Mark's Seminary and Kanty Prep. Elk CC, DuBois CC and Bradford CC had also joined the Allegheny Mountain League, along with Sheffield, Brockway and Johnsonburg. The Ramblers did not compete with Kennedy Christian again until 1991-92 in the Farrell Christmas Tourney.

- Prep also had two easy wins over Ashtabula Harbor (5-14). The Ramblers scored in triple digits at home and continued with hot shooting in Ashtabula, this despite having to sit in a cold bus after being held up by an accident on the way to the game. The Ramblers and Mariners never played again and Harbor merged with Ashtabula High in 2001 to form Lakeside

High School. Lakeside is now the only high school in the Ashtabula (OH) Area City School District.

- Prep won 10 of its last 11 regular season games, losing only to Crown Conference champion Cleveland St. Joseph (18-3) in that span. The Vikings also defeated Tech, 77-62, and East, 75-61, during the campaign.

- This was the last of 18 seasons at Vincent (1952-70) for former Prep coach (1937-38) **Ralph "Baron" Calabrese**. The Colonels came on strong at the end of the year with fine play from **Bill Swartzman, Billy Wagner, Mark Deane, Howie Horton** and **Danny Cantoni**. SV surprised McDowell in a Section One championship playoff, and then shocked Oil City to win the D-10 crown before losing to Pittsburgh Schenley in PIAA play. Included in Calabrese' record (254-120) for the Colonels are five City Series championships, nine Section One titles and seven D-10 crowns, including the 1970 trophy.

- As a team, the hard-working, well-balanced Ramblers broke their single season record with 1,746 points and 72.8 PPG. It was the only time in Prep basketball history that all five starters averaged in double figures. Never before or even since have four starters averaged in double figures! This edition of the Orange & Black was the first to score at least 100 points twice in one season. Opponents also broke a single season record with 1,461 points.

Flanagan defends against Vincent's 6'8" center Bill Swartzman.

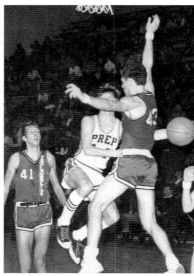

Wieczorek makes an amazing pass around the back of SV's Dan Cantoni, as Swartzman can only look on.

Shifty guard Dave Wieczorek clicks for another field goal.

Senior Class President Glenn Miller joins the well-dressed Ramblers on a road trip. Front, L to R: n/a, Cardot, Miller, Massing, Mangold, Smith, Cox, Burke; Middle: Reynders, Asst. Coach Flaherty, Wieczorek, Mgr. Piotrowicz; Back: Asst. Coach Schneider, Kneib, Borowy, Flanagan, Coach Fox, Bukowski, Cook.

- Seniors **Dave Wieczorek**, a smooth and shifty guard; **Brian Flanagan** (8th in Big 7 scoring), an undersized workhorse center who led the Ramblers with 318 rebounds (13.3 RPG); and defensive specialist **Tom Hansen** were named Second Team All Big Six by the *Erie Times-News* and the *Erie Press*; while junior **Danny Bukowski** (11th in Big 7 scoring) was awarded Honorable Mention by the *Erie Times-News*.

- **Dick Fox** was named "Coach of the Year" by the *Erie Press*, while **Brian Flanagan** won the prestigious James "Moe" Gross Award, signifying him as Prep's best player.

- Wieczorek went on to play at Clarion State and Mercyhurst College; Flanagan at Loyola (MD); and all-around athlete Hansen, a four-sport star at Prep and winner of the "Ma" Kaiser Award, played basketball and baseball at the University of Notre Dame. He was part of the 1973-74 Irish squad that, in a 71-70 victory, ended UCLA's all-time record 88-game winning streak that remains the longest in the history of college basketball. Hansen later played in the Detroit Tiger organization, first with Lakeland of the Florida State League, then with Clinton of the Midwest League.

- **Brian Flanagan** had a successful coaching career, first in the parochial grade schools; then at Fairview High School; then finally as JV, then head basketball coach at Prep (2004-08), where he compiled an outstanding overall record of 89-24 (.788), including four region championships, three District 10 titles and a PIAA Final Four appearance. "Bump's" winning percentage is the best, not only among Rambler coaches, but for all of Erie's coaches who mentored for more than two seasons.

- **Tom Hansen** also went on to become a teacher/coach at Prep and later the head basketball coach at McDowell (2001-07). He was inducted into the Metro Erie Sports Hall of Fame in 2000 and the Cathedral Prep Athletic Hall of Fame in 2008.

Hall-of-Famer Tom Hansen lettered in four sports as a senior, then went on to star at Notre Dame.

1970 All-Opponent Team:

Jack Titus, Bradford

Dick Glady, Bradford

Bob Millberg, Ashtabula Harbor

Rick Weber, Tech

John Marucci, Tech [Alliance]

Jim "Bimbo" Pietro, South Hills Catholic [Creighton]

Bill Swartzman, Vincent (hm all-state) [Pitt]

Gary Weigel, Baker-Victory [Gannon]

Augie DiPasquale, North Catholic [California (PA) St.]

Mike Bartoszek, McDowell [Ohio State, football]

Blaine Baker, East

Virgil McIntosh, East

Jim Hill, Cleveland St. Joe's

Pat Lyons, Cleveland St. Joe's (1st team all-state, OH)
    [Dayton, John Carroll]

Billy Wagner, Vincent

Chuck Britton, McDowell [Cincinnati,
    football & basketball]

Eddie Woodard, East [Kent State, football]

Bob Landolfi, Bishop Guilfoyle

Denny Tomasetti, Bishop Guilfoyle

Brian Flanagan leaps against East High's Blaine Baker while East's Jeff Satyshur and Danny Bukowski get ready.

Super-sub Ray Massing gets an important basket.

Cardot smoothly lays in another bucket.

PCIAA State Champs!

1970-71 (22-3)

Coach: Richard "Dick" Fox
Assistant: Bill Flaherty
Captains: Will Cardot, Dan Bukowski
Manager: Dan Leifield

Richard "Dick" Fox retired from Prep to take the new coaching job at Mercyhurst College. Fox mentored two state champion teams at Prep in just four years.

Date	PREP			Dec.	Loc.	High Scorer	Opponent
12/4	85	Bradford	50	W	H	Cardot (20)	Titus (17)
12/11	69	Tech Memorial	50	W	N	Cardot (20)	Chojnacki (14)
12/13	73	Pittsburgh South Hills Catholic	68	W	A	Cardot (26)	Albert (35)
12/18	54	Strong Vincent	51	W	N	Cardot (16)	Ekimoff (16)
12/19	57	Altoona Bishop Guilfoyle	52	W	A	Cardot (23)	McGeary (20)
		FREDONIA (PA) AMERICAN LEGION CHRISTMAS TOURNEY					
12/28	82	Hickory	51	W	N	Cardot (26)	Rust & Long (11)
12/29	73	Kinsman (OH) Joseph Badger	53	W	N	Cardot (25)	Bates (17)
1/8	72	McDowell	82	L	A	Cardot (25)	Britton (23)
1/12	93	Johnstown	79	W	A	Reynders (25)	Clayton (25)
1/15	71	Academy	79	L	N	Cardot (25)	Bean (22)
1/19	89	Jamestown (NY)	60	W	H	Reynders (27)	Briggs (27)
1/22	73	East	62	W	N	Cardot (24)	Satyshur (23)
1/29	71	Tech Memorial	47	W	N	Cardot (19)	Chojnacki (13)
2/5	76	Strong Vincent	74	W	N	Cardot (27)	Hollis (21)
2/6	72	Conneaut (OH)	43	W	H	Cardot (26)	Ferl (13)
2/12	99	Jamestown (NY)	88	W	A	Cardot (33)	Chili (27)
2/16	76	Ford City	61	W	A	Bukowski (28)	Heffner (17)
2/20	75	Academy	74	W	N	Cardot (29)	Twillie (21)
2/23	74	McDowell	62	W	H	Cook (20)	Britton (23)
2/24	85	Johnstown	72	W	H	Cardot (30)	Tomaselli (35)
2/26	63	East	69	L	N	Cardot (22)	Hewitt (25)
		CITY CHAMPIONSHIP PLAYOFF					
3/5	62	Academy	50	W	N	Cook (18)	Twillie (13)
		P.C.I.A.A. STATE CATHOLIC H. S. TOURNAMENT					
3/14	52	Pittsburgh South Hills Catholic	50(5OT*)	W	N	Cardot (20)	McBride (13)
		P.C.I.A.A. STATE CATHOLIC CHAMPIONSHIP					
3/19	65	Allentown Central Catholic	64	W	N	Cardot (22)	Kinek (21)
	1761*(73.4*)		**1491*(62.1)**				

Pos.	Player	Ht.	Prior School	Class	G (GS)	FG	FT	Total	PPG	Career
G	Willis "Puck" Cardot (#12)	5'9"	St. John's	Sr.	24(24)	212*	125*-181*	549*	22.9*	1089*
F	Dan Bukowski (#32)	6'1"	St. John's	Sr.	24(24)	162	39-52	363	15.1	676
C	John Reynders (#30)	6'4"	St. Luke's	Sr.	24(24)	128	81-127	337	14.0	370
F	Joe Cook (#14)	6'1"	Sacred Heart	Sr.	23(22)	68	61-86	197	8.6	216
G	Ray Massing (#10)	5'10"	St. Luke's	Sr.	21(13)	31	25-50	87	4.1	114
F	Tom Van Volkenburg (#24)	6'1"	Sacred Heart	Jr.	21(8)	19	30-65	68	3.2	68
F	Tom Burke (#50)	6'1"	Pgh. St. Teresa	Sr.	17(1)	24	3-6	51	3.0	65
G	Randy Bowers (#44)	6'0"	St. John's	Sr.	17(2)	17	6-14	40	2.4	40
F	Mark Borowy (#22)	6'2"	St. Patrick's	Jr.	17	14	5-8	33	1.9	33
C	Bob Repko (#40)	6'5"	St. James	Jr.	8	7	0-2	14	1.8	14
F	Don Wierbinski (#52)	6'2"	Sacred Heart	Jr.	7(1)	4	2-3	10	1.4	10
G	Joe Barabas (#34)	6'0"	Holy Family	Jr.	4	1	3-4	5	1.3	5
G	Dave Causgrove (#42)	5'11"	St. James	Jr.	3	0	3-4	3	1.0	3
G	Billy Bules (#4)	5'11"	OLP	Jr.	3	1	0-1	2	0.7	2
G	Tim Fox (#20)	5'9"	OLC	Jr.	5(1)	0	2-2	2	0.4	2
F	Larry Szoszorek (#54)	6'3"	St. George's	Jr.	2	0	0-0	0	0.0	0
F	John "Dezzie" Long (#45)	6'1"	St. Andrew's	Jr.	2	0	0-0	0	0.0	0

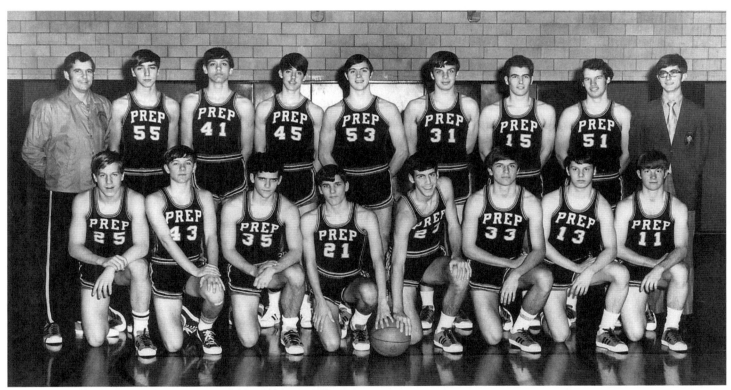

Prep's 1971 State Champions. Front, L to R: Van Volkenburg, Causgrove, Barabas, Fox, Borowy, Bukowski, Cardot, Massing; Back: Coach Fox, Szoszorek, Repko, Long, Wierbinski, Reynders, Cook, Burke, Mgr. Leifield.

Coach Fox and the Prep fans accept congratulations from a PCIAA director.

Coach Fox ponders the situation during a time out.

HIGHLIGHTS:

- Cathedral Prep won its fourth PCIAA state championship and second for fiery coach **Dick Fox** in four years. Fox was named "Coach of the Year" for the second straight season by the *Erie Press*.

- Coach Fox announced mid-season that he would become Mercyhurst College's first head basketball coach, beginning with the 1971-72 year. He finished with an aggregate Prep mark of 72-21 (.763) with two city titles as well as the two state championships. Fox coached at Mercyhurst six years (1971-75, 1976-78) with a total record of 101-43. He coached the Gannon College team for five years (1979-84), and for a half-season (1996), finishing with an overall mark of 100-58. Fox closed out his high school coaching career by guiding Corry to a 21-7 record in 1992-93. He was inducted to the Metro Erie Sports Hall of Fame in 1995.

The starting five, fired up for the state title game. Shown: Cook, "Van" and "Puck." Behind: "Bu" and Reynders.

- The state championship game was a nip-and-tuck thriller before 2,400 fans at St. Vincent's College in Latrobe. The Ramblers went ahead for the final 65-64 count with just 13 seconds left to play, when **John Reynders** outfought a trio of Allentown Central Catholic (14-13) players for a rebound and jammed the ball through. **Ray Massing** came off the bench to play excellent ball for Prep while high-scoring **Will Cardot** played his consistently great game. Starring for Central was **George Kinek, Jr.**, son of former Tulane and NFL star **George Kinek**, who was a football coach and athletic director at Central Catholic from 1956 to 1993. Prep also beat Central in the 1954 title clash, the only other time the two schools have met.

John Reynders scored the winning bucket in the state title game, then went on to play and coach at Allegheny College. He is now the president of Morningside College.

- The biggest wins of the regular season included early season upsets of South Hills Catholic (19-6) and defending state champ Bishop Guilfoyle (19-6); the one-point thriller over Academy (15-6); the two-point thriller over Vincent (4-13), where Prep missed 9 consecutive free throws in the 4th quarter; and the hotly-contested conquest of LSL champ McDowell (20-4), with **Joe Cook** leading the way (20 points, 14 rebounds).

- Bishop Guilfoyle's loss to Prep was the Marauders' only defeat in its first 17 games.

- Playoff features included the city championship playoff win over Academy and the incredible record five-overtime victory over South Hills Catholic before 4,000 fans at Edinboro's McComb Field House. **Will Cardot** hit the game-winner from 17 feet just five seconds before the end of overtime #5. The Rebels went on to win the PCIAA Class A title the next season (1972).

- Prep's championship verdict over Academy was the seventh time in seven tries that Prep won the City Series title via the playoff route.

- **Willis Cardot** and **Danny Bukowski** were selected to the All-Tournament team for victorious Prep at the Fredonia American Legion Christmas Tourney, hosted by Reynolds High School. The Ramblers faced new opponents in Joseph Badger (6-16), from Trumbull County, Ohio—named after **Reverend Joseph Badger**, a circuit riding minister of the late 18th century; and Hickory (3-19), located in Hermitage, Mercer County. The Hornets had long been a District 10 basketball power.

- Prep's win over Conneaut (12-7) was the last time the two competed, with the Ramblers on the short end of the series, 6 games to 5. The big win at Ford City (15-5), located about 40 miles northeast of Pittsburgh, was the only time the Ramblers and Sabers ever met. Ford City won the WPIAL Section 1 title, a division which also included Kiski, Highlands, Burrell, Valley and Kittaning. Winning that crown gave the Sabers a WPIAL record 30 sectional titles.

- Prep's wins over Greater Johnstown High School (11-12), located in the city most famous for its three major floods, were the first two games of 22 played between the Ramblers and Trojans through the 1986-87 season.

- Disappointing losses were those to Academy; at McDowell; and to East which cost the Ramblers a co-championship of the Lake Shore League.

"Tommy Van" looks to score over the outstretched arm of former Prepster Chuck Britton.

- The McDowell Trojans, featuring former Prepster **Chuck Britton** (scored 535 for the season, finished with 1,049 for his Prep/McDowell career), **Mike Bartoszek** (scored school record 43 against East), **Don Weiss** and **Jim Sperry**, finished with their first Section One title since 1946 and their first District 10 championship ever. McDowell was defeated in PIAA playoff action by one of Pennsylvania's all-time great teams: Pittsburgh Schenley, which featured **Maurice Lucas** (1971 Mr. Basketball USA), **Rickey Coleman**, and **Robert "Jeep" Kelly**. That Schenley team, representing District 8 and the Pittsburgh City League, defeated Norristown for the AAA Championship, 77-60. The Spartans were also considered national champions, along with East Chicago (IN) Washington.

- Schenley set a Pittsburgh City League single game scoring record when it defeated Allderdice during the regular season, 151-73. Other gaudy scores were over South High, 116-28 and 140-68. This was later topped by Albert Gallatin, which set a WPIAL record by beating hapless West Greene, 167-30!

- Schenley's Lucas (22 points, 16 rebounds) and Coleman (17 points) and Pittsburgh Canevin's **Tom Clements** all played for the Pennsylvania All-Stars in the 1971 Dapper Dan Classic, while South Hills Catholic's **Steve Albert** (4 points, 12 rebounds), who burned Prep for 35 and who later starred for Coach Fox at Mercyhurst College, played for the City-Catholic combine against Western PA in the preliminary.

- All City Series games were played at the Gannon Auditorium, while the Ramblers continued to play their independent home contests in the Prep gym. The LSL home game against McDowell was played in the Gannon Auditorium for the first time, before a screaming throng of 3,000.

- The final standings in City Series and LSL basketball leagues were as follows:

	W	L		W	L
*Prep	7	2	McDowell	10	2
Academy	6	3	Prep	9	3
East	5	3	Academy	8	4
Vincent	2	6	East	6	6
Tech	1	7	Jamestown	5	7
			Vincent	3	9
			Tech	1	11

won city championship playoff

- Another highlight was the all-time Rambler scoring record of senior lefty **Willis Cardot**, who finished his Prep career at 1,089 points. The first Rambler to score over 1,000 in a career, "Puck" was a pure shooter, named 6th team all-state and was awarded First Team All-Big Six unanimously for the second straight year by the *Erie Times-News*. Seniors **Dan Bukowski** and **John Reynders** were named to the Second Team, while senior **Joe Cook** made Honorable Mention.

- Cardot was also a unanimous First Team All-Scholastic choice of the *Erie Press*, which also named him "Most Valuable Player," "Outstanding Offensive Performer" and "Outstanding Collegiate Prospect." Bukowski was named to the Second Team, while Cook was accorded Honorable Mention. Reynders, who led the Ramblers in rebounds (329, 13.7 RPG), made the Erie Press' "Rebounding Dream Team," while junior **Tom Van Volkenburg** was runner-up to Academy's **Chuck Thomas** as the area's "Outstanding Defensive Performer." "Van" did a particularly good job on "D" in the playoff contests.

- For the second consecutive season, Prep broke team scoring

All-American Willis "Puck" Cardot retired as Prep's all-time leading scorer. Here, "Puck" scores again between a trio of Colonel defenders.

Danny Bukowski was named Second Team All-Big Six and graduated as Prep's fourth all-time leading scorer.

records (1761 points, 73.4 PPG), as did its opponents (1491 points).

- **Willis Cardot** rewrote the Prep season and career record books, becoming the leader in field goals, free throws made, free throws attempted, as well as total points and points per game. "Puck," who finished at the time third highest single season scorer in Erie schoolboy history, was also the first Prepster since Jim "Red" Fahey (in 1953) accorded All-American status. He was named Honorable Mention on the High School All-America team, as selected by the U. S. Basketball Writers Association, Coach & Athlete Magazine and Sunkist Growers. Cardot, winner of the "Moe" Gross Award, was inducted into the Cathedral Prep Athletic Hall of Fame in 2006. He led the freshmen team in scoring at Pitt, lettered as a sophomore, and went on to play for Coach Fox at Mercyhurst College.

- **Danny Bukowski's** 676 career tallies placed him fourth on Prep's all-time chart at the time. He next lettered four years for Coach Fox at Mercyhurst College.

- Also a star baseball player (City Series MVP and "Ma" Kaiser Award winner, 1971), **Joe Cook** went on to play in the Chicago White Sox organization, first with Sarasota in the Gulf Coast League, then with the Appleton Foxes of the Midwest League. He was inducted posthumously into the Metro Erie Sports Hall of Fame in 2006 and the Cathedral Prep Athletic Hall of Fame in 2008.

- **Ray Massing** won the Dave Tyzinski Memorial Trophy as Prep's best two-sport athlete, and went to the University of Maryland on a golf scholarship.

- **Randy Bowers**, retired Chief of Police of the City of Erie, went on to an esteemed coaching career in local girls' basketball. Bowers coached St. Luke's grade school to an amazing 170-18 record and five Diocesan titles in a six-year period (1988-94), and later coached at Mercyhurst Prep (1996-2005), compiling an overall 191-59 mark with four District 10 championships and PIAA state titles in his last two years.

- **John Reynders** went on to play at Allegheny College and later become head basketball coach at Woodridge (OH) High (1977-79) and at Allegheny (1979-1989), where he won the most games (181-78, .699) as coach in school history. He led the Gators to five NCAA Tournament appearances, two PAC championships and three NCAC titles. Reynders was twice named PAC Coach of the Year and once NCAC Coach of the Year. He was inducted into the Allegheny Hall of Fame in 1994.

1971 All-Opponent Team:

Steve Albert, South Hills Catholic [Mercyhurst]
Pat McGeary, Bishop Guilfoyle [St. Francis (PA)]
Chuck Britton, McDowell (5th team all-state) [Cincinnati, football & basketball]
Lou Clayton, Johnstown
Jim "Mack" Bean, Academy
Howard Briggs, Jamestown [Eastern Nazarene College]
Jeff Satyshur, East [Richmond, football]
John Chojnacki, Tech [Mercyhurst]
Essie Hollis, Vincent [St. Bonaventure; NBA Detroit Pistons]
David Twillie, Academy
Mike Bartoszek, McDowell [Ohio State, football]
Jim Sperry, McDowell [Slippery Rock]
Terry Chili, Jamestown [Duke]
Steve Heffner, Ford City
Dave Tomaselli, Johnstown
Vaughn Hewitt, East
George McBride, South Hills Catholic [Pitt]
George Kinek, Allentown Central Catholic [Ursinus]

Joe Cook closely guards Tech freshman Bruce Chrzanowski, as Sister Dorinda observes from the second row.

William "Bill" Flaherty, Prep's new coach at age 29.

Bill Flaherty era begins with city title!

1971-72 (18-5)

Coach: William "Bill" Flaherty
Captains: Game captains
Managers: Dave Benacci, Dan Skrzypczak

Date	PREP			Dec.	Loc.	High Scorer	Opponent
12/3	57	Bradford	38	W	A	Borowy (11)	Nazzo & Harris (10)
12/10	55	Johnstown	47	W	A	Repko (12)	Maser (20)
12/11	47	Altoona Bishop Guilfoyle	52	L	A	Fox (11)	Cordova (18)
12/17	63	East	58	W	N	Borowy (19)	Satyshur (22)
		FREDONIA (PA) AMERICAN LEGION CHRISTMAS TOURNEY					
12/27	74	Kinsman (OH) Joseph Badger	51	W	N	Orzechowski (19)	Bates (13)
12/28	63	Hickory	44	W	N	Repko, Orz, Borowy (12	Rust, Ream, Smith (8)
12/1	62	Tech Memorial	57	W	N	Borowy (17)	Chrzanowski & Keys (16)
1/7	61	Strong Vincent	55	W	N	Orzechowski (19)	Hollis (23)
1/14	44	Jamestown (NY)	66	L	A	VanVolkenburg (13)	Edstrom (19)
1/18	48	McDowell	39	W	H	Orzechowski (19)	Michaels (20)
1/21	56	Academy	55	W	N	Orzechowski (18)	Purdue (21)
1/28	64	East	57(OT)	W	N	Repko (20)	Gavin (18)
1/29	65	Johnstown	47	W	H	Orzechowski (22)	Maser (23)
2/1	76	Pittsburgh North Catholic	54	W	H	Orzechowski (26)	Jackson (21)
2/4	51	Tech Memorial	48	W	N	Orzechowski (14)	Keys (15)
2/11	46	Strong Vincent	51(OT)	L	N	Repko (14)	Hollis (23)
2/12	78	Cleveland (OH) St. Joseph	65	W	A	Borowy, Orz (20)	Guilfoyle (22)
2/15	68	New Castle	65	W	A	Van Volkenburg (18)	Scott, Beckwith, Wiley (13)
2/18	59	McDowell	56	W	A	Szoszorek, Orz (15)	Ricart (18)
2/22	57	Jamestown (NY)	63	L	H	Borowy (20)	Chili (27)
2/25	60	Academy	55	W	N	Orzechowski (17)	Purdue (20)
		P.C.I.A.A. STATE CATHOLIC H. S. TOURNAMENT					
3/8	51	Johnstown Bishop McCort	44	W	A	Orzechowski (16)	Fields (9)
3/12	42	Pittsburgh South Hills Catholic	46(2OT)	L	N	Orzechowski (22)	Yeckley (15)
	1347 (58.5)		**1213 (52.7)**				

Pos.	Player	Ht.	Prior School	Class	G (GS)	FG	FT	Total	PPG	Career
F	Marty Orzechowski (#30)	6'0"	Holy Trinity	Jr.	22(21)	136	49-68	321	14.6	321
F	Mark Borowy (#32)	6'3"	St. Patrick's	Sr.	23(22)	92	48-74	232	10.1	265
C	Bob Repko (#44)	6'6"	St. James	Sr.	22(22)	84	52-89	220	10.0	234
F	Tom Van Volkenburg (#22)	6'1"	Sacred Heart	Sr.	22(22)	58	80-133	196	8.9	264
G	Tim Fox(#10)	5'10"	OLC	Sr.	18(16)	50	21-33	121	6.7	123
F	Don Wierbinski (#50)	6'3"	Sacred Heart	Sr.	23(7)	38	28-50	104	4.5	114
F	Larry Szoszorek (#52)	6'3"	St. George's	Sr.	15(1)	17	14-24	48	3.2	48
G	Billy Bules (#14)	5'11"	OLP	Sr.	17(3)	17	12-17	46	2.7	48
G	Jack "Jason" Weber (#20)	5'10"	Bl. Sacrament	Jr.	10	15	10-13	40	4.0	40
G	Joe Mifsud (#34)	5'8"	St. Paul's	Jr.	7(1)	5	4-8	14	2.0	14
G	Tony Keim (#54)	5'9"	St. Peter's	Jr.	4	0	3-4	3	0.8	3
F	Fred Bartnicki (#42)	6'2"	St. Boniface	Jr.	3	1	0-1	2	0.7	2
G	Mike O'Brien (#12)	5'8"	Sacred Heart	Jr.	4	0	0-0	0	0.0	0
F	Tom Fessler (#40)	5'11"	St. Luke's	Jr.	4	0	0-1	0	0.0	0
F	Dan Nowak (#24)	6'3"	St. Luke's	Jr.	3	0	0-3	0	0.0	0

The 1972 Prep Ramblers. Front, L to R: Coach Flaherty, Orzechowski, Van Volkenburg, Wierbinski, Repko, Szoszorek, Bartnicki, Borowy, Weber; Back: Mgr. Skryzpczak, Mifsud, Bules, Fox, Keim, O'Brien, Fessler, Mgr. Benacci.

HIGHLIGHTS:

- Using the motto "the best offense is a good defense," Cathedral Prep won its third straight City Series crown for first-year coach **William "Bill" Flaherty**. The *Erie Press* named the rookie mentor "Coach of the Year" and the Ramblers "Team of the Year."

- Flaherty, just 29 years of age and a 1960 graduate of Prep, had been an assistant coach of the Ramblers since 1965, guiding the frosh to a 15-3 record in 1966-67 and an overall four-year mark of 64-12 (1967-1971) as JV mentor. Prior to his Prep job, he coached with success at St. Joseph's Grade School.

The Ramblers and coaches celebrate winning the City Series in Bill Flaherty's first year at the helm.

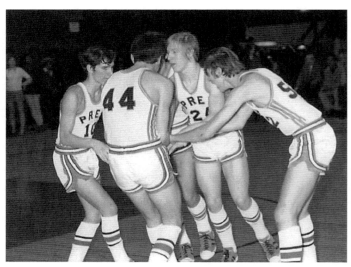

The Ramblers, ready to break. Shown, L to R: Fox, Repko, Van Volkenburg, Szoszorek.

- All City Series games and the McDowell home battle were played at the Gannon Auditorium, while the Ramblers continued to play their independent home contests, including the Jamestown LSL game, in the Prep gym. The PCIAA playoff contests were played at Windber (near Johnstown) and St. Vincent's College in Latrobe.

- Coach Flaherty broke with tradition and did not have a team captain named for his Rambler squads. With his strict philosophy that basketball is a "team game," Flaherty preferred that no individual gain honors over the team concept. Hence, captains were selected on a pre-game basis.

- Prep traveled to New Castle (10-12), located about 50 miles northwest of Pittsburgh, to face a new WPIAL opponent in the Red Hurricanes. It was part of Coach Flaherty's immediate upgrade of the Ramblers' schedule, which also included regular season contests with Bishop Guilfoyle, North Catholic, Cleveland St. Joe's and two with Johnstown.

- The biggest wins of the regular season included the close City Series thrillers, and the pairs of conquests over McDowell (9-12) and particularly Johnstown (19-8). The Johnnies, runners-up in District 6, lost a first round PIAA game to Keystone Oaks, 82-68.

"Marty O" buries one from the corner against Academy at the sold-out Gannon Audi.

- The rout of a fine North Catholic team was particularly notable, as Prep was without the services of starters **Bob Repko, Tim Fox** and **Tom Van Volkenburg**, all out with the flu. **Marty Orzechowski** led with his season-high 26 points and **Mark Borowy** followed with 19. It was seniors **Don Wierbinski, Bill Bules** and particularly **Larry Szoszorek**, with 17 points, that picked up the slack.

- Other highlights were the breakout of junior **Marty "Marty O" Orzechowski**, who led the scoring from midseason on; the stellar defensive work of **Tom Van Volkenburg**; and the rebounding of lanky senior **Bob Repko** (353 rebounds, 16.0 RPG).

- Orzechowski was named MVP and Repko was also All-Tourney as Prep copped its second straight Fredonia American Legion Christmas Tourney, hosted by Reynolds High School. Victories were over the same teams, Badger (5-18) and Hickory (9-12), as the year before.

- An oddity occurred as three different schools won the local league titles—Prep, City Series; Vincent (15-7), Section One; and Jamestown (19-2), featuring 6'10" **Terry Chili** and 6'3" **Mark Edstrom**, the Lake Shore League. Jamestown finished with New York's Section 6 championship and a final NY state ranking of #9, while Vincent won its second District 10 title in three years.

- The final standings in City Series and LSL basketball leagues were as follows:

	W	L		W	L
Prep	7	1	Jamestown	10	2
Vincent	6	2	Prep	9	3
Academy	3	5	Vincent	9	3
Tech	3	5	Academy	5	7
East	1	7	Tech	5	7
			East	2	10
			McDowell	2	10

- The disappointments were a pair of losses to the Jimtowners and the double-overtime heartbreaker to eventual PCIAA

The new Prep bench and the fans grimace at the action. On the bench, L to R: Repko, Sertz, Wenrick, Flaherty. Several past notable fans can be seen as well.

Defensive whiz Tommy Van Volkenburg gathers a loose ball between five Jamestown players. Standing, L to R: Jim Young, Mark Edstrom, Bill Johnson, Terry Chili, "Marty O," Tim Grissom.

state champ South Hills Catholic (19-5). That battle looked like it might be a repeat of 1971's five-overtime thriller. One of the Rebel stars was **Bobby Del Greco, Jr.** (5 steals, 11 assists), son of former Pittsburgh Pirates outfielder **Bobby Del Greco.** South Hills star **Rich Yeckley** unfortunately died of a heart attack at an Allegheny College practice, where he was a promising sophomore guard and teammate of Prep's **Marty Orzechowski.** Another Rebel star was **George McBride** (14 points, 8 rebounds), who competed for the City-Catholic unit against Western PA in the 1972 Dapper Dan preliminary. South Hills coach **Rick Keebler** made a curious post-game statement to the *Pittsburgh Press* following the encounter: "I might have oversold my team about their defense. We helped them. Their defense is not that good, but we made mistakes that might have been caused by fear of it." In reality, Prep's 6'5" **Bob Repko,** 6'3" **Mark Borowy,** and 6'1" **Tom Van Volkenburg** did a stellar job on Rebels' big men 6'7" McBride, 6'6" **Bob O'Connor** and 6'4" **Mark Albert,** holding the three combined to 24 points. The battle against South Hills Catholic was the last time Prep participated in the post-season tournament of the PCIAA, which sponsored its final brackets in 1973 for Class A, and in 1974 for Classes B and C.

- Prep's playoff victory over Johnstown Bishop McCort (12-13) was the last time the two competed. The Ramblers and the Crimson Crushers had met 15 times, each time in PCIAA playoff action. The Crushers won the series, 8 games to 7.

- In the championship final South Hills Catholic put injury-ridden Allentown Central Catholic out of its misery, 69-53. It was the third state championship for the Rebels (also won in 1961 and 1965) and the fourth consecutive state title game loss for Allentown's Vikings.

- This was also the last time Prep played South Hills Catholic. Seton-La Salle Catholic High School was formed in 1979 by the merger of the all-boys South Hills Catholic, served by the Christian Brothers, and the all-girls Elizabeth Seton High School, founded by the Sisters of Charity of Seton Hill. Seton-LaSalle, whom the Ramblers played once in the opening round of the Farrell Holiday Tournament in 2001-02, won the PIAA Class AAA state title in 1988.

- **Bob Repko,** winner of the James "Moe" Gross Award, was named First Team All-Big Six by the *Erie Times-News* and First Team All-City by the *Erie Press.* **Tom Van Volkenburg** and **Marty Orzechowski** were Second Team choices for the *Erie Times-News,* while **Mark Borowy** was an Honorable Mention selection by the *Times-News* and a Second Team choice by the *Press.* The *Press* made **Tim Fox** an Honorable Mention selection, while Repko was named "Top Rebounder" and Van Volkenburg the city's "Best Defensive Player."

Bob Repko was honored as team MVP and a First Team All-Big Six selection. Here, he outmaneuvers Dana Gibbs of East.

- Repko, Fox and super-sub **Larry Szoszorek** went on to star at Mercyhurst College, Thiel College and Behrend College respectively; **Donny Wierbinski,** winner of the 1972 "Ma"

Floor leader Tim Fox nails a perfect outside jumper before an overflow crowd at the Prep gym. The All-Big Six honoree went on to star at Thiel College.

Kaiser Award, played football at Cornell; and **Bill Bules** and **Tommy Van Volkenburg** both took to the pitching mound at Edinboro State.

- **Monsignor Robert B. McDonald,** the determined and demanding headmaster at Cathedral Prep, retired from his position at the close of the 1971-72 school year. During legendary "Black Mac's" tenure, Prep grew from 200 boys to a peak of 1,375 and became an academic and athletic powerhouse. Monsignor McDonald was a charter inductee to the Cathedral Prep Athletic Hall of Fame in 1992.

Repko establishes position against Academy's Bill Holter and Gerald Rankin.

1972 All-Opponent Team:

Donnie Maser, Johnstown [Duquesne]

Steve Cordova, Bishop Guilfoyle

Jeff Satyshur, East [Richmond, football]

Rick Bates, Kinsman Badger

Jerry Keys, Tech

Essie Hollis, Vincent [St. Bonaventure; NBA
Detroit Pistons]

David Purdue, Academy [Stetson]

Richie Gavin, East

Terry Chili, Jamestown [Duke]

Mark Edstrom, Jamestown [Alfred, football]

Tom Michaels, McDowell

Tom Jackson, North Catholic

Joe Guilfoyle, Cleveland St. Joe's

Rob Ricart, McDowell

Rich Yeckley, South Hills Catholic [Allegheny]

George McBride, South Hills Catholic [Pitt]

Bobby Del Greco, South Hills Catholic [Allegheny]

All-Big Six honoree Mark Borowy was second in scoring and rebounding for the Ramblers.

Just a friendly reminder to the new coach from Monsignor McDonald.

Prep Joins PIAA!

1972-73 (9-13)

Coach: William "Bill" Flaherty
Captains: Game captains
Managers: Dan Skrzypczak, Bob Blakeslee

Headmaster Father John Dollinger over-saw Prep's transition into the PIAA.

Date	PREP			Dec.	Loc.	High Scorer	Opponent
11/24	67	Bradford	60	W	A	R. Bengel (23)	Platko (14)
12/1	57	Bradford	48	W	H	Orzechowski (14)	Bond (15)
12/8	56	Johnstown	90	L	A	Weber (14)	Maser (42*)
12/9	52	Altoona Bishop Guilfoyle	53(OT)	L	A	O'Brien (20)	Stoehr (17)
12/15	52	East	58	L	N	O'Brien (14)	Gibbs (16)
12/22	47	Tech Memorial	63	L	N	Orzechowski (21)	Keys (21)
	WARREN HOLIDAY BASKETBALL TOURNAMENT						
12/28	38	Cleveland (OH) St. Joseph	85	L	N	Nowak, Weber & Orz (8)	Cannon (20)
12/29	60	Charleroi	43	W	N	Orzechowski (23)	Sharp (14)
1/5	52	Strong Vincent	54	L	N	Orzechowski (26)	Hollis (38)
1/12	79	Jamestown (NY)	43	W	A	Barron (13)	Waite (11)
1/16	70	Pittsburgh North Catholic	69	W	A	Orzechowski (25)	Carroll (26)
1/19	73	Academy	71	W	N	Barron (22)	Purdue (36)
1/23	80	McDowell	72(2OT)	W	H	Orzechowski (23)	Schmitt (20)
1/26	63	East	66	L	N	Nowak (12)	Gavin (26)
2/2	64	Tech Memorial	59	W	N	Barron (18)	Chrzanowski (14)
2/9	53	Strong Vincent	68	L	N	Barron (14)	Hollis (49*)
2/13	48	New Castle	54	L	A	Orzechowski (16)	Hailstock & DeJohn (13)
2/16	50	McDowell	54	L	A	Barron (16)	Michaels (18)
2/17	74	Jamestown (NY)	67	W	H	Orzechowski (26)	Waite (15)
2/23	59	Academy	69	L	N	Orzechowski (21)	Purdue (30)
2/24	62	Johnstown	73	L	H	Nowak (20)	Cummings (18)
	DISTRICT 10 PLAYOFF						
2/27	50	Strong Vincent	55	L	N	Barron (20)	Hollis (22)
	1310 (59.5)		**1391 (63.2)**				

Pos.	Player	Ht.	Prior School	Class	G (GS)	FG	FT	Total	PPG	Career
F	Marty Orzechowski (#30)	6'2"	Holy Trinity	Sr.	20(18)	145	35-52	325	16.3	646
G	Kevin Barron (#10)	5'10"	St. Andrew's	Jr.	19(14)	85	36-48	206	10.8	206
C	Dan Nowak (#54)	6'5"	St. Luke's	Sr.	22(22)	81	31-45	193	8.8	193
G	Joe Mifsud (#4)	5'9"	St. Paul's	Sr.	21(15)	53	16-28	122	5.8	136
F	Matt Scheppner (#40)	6'1"	St. Andrew's	Jr.	20(15)	54	12-20	120	6.0	120
G	Mike O'Brien (#12)	5'9"	Sacred Heart	Sr.	19(10)	40	24-34	104	5.5	104
F	Jack "Jason" Weber (#32)	5'11"	Bl. Sacrament	Sr.	17(11)	43	15-21	101	5.9	141
G	Rick Bengel (#22)	6'1"	Sacred Heart	Soph.	12(1)	18	11-14	47	3.9	47
G	Mark Van Volkenburg (#24)	5'11"	Sacred Heart	Jr.	13	11	11-21	33	2.5	33
F	Fred Bartnicki (#50)	6'3"	St. Boniface	Sr.	8(1)	11	3-8	25	3.1	27
F	Tom Fessler (#20)	6'0"	St. Luke's	Sr.	9(3)	5	1-3	11	1.2	11
G	Tony Keim (#44)	5'10"	St. Peter's	Sr.	4	2	2-4	6	1.5	9
F	Mark Cieslak (#52)	6'1"	OLC	Jr.	8	3	0-2	6	0.8	6
G	Mark DiPlacido (#14)	5'9"	St. Andrew's	Jr.	3	2	1-1	5	1.7	5
F	George Carrig (#42)	5'10"	St. Peter's	Jr.	5	1	2-6	4	0.8	4
G	Pat Cox (#34)	5'10"	St. Peter's	Jr.	3	0	2-5	2	0.7	2

The 1973 Prep Ramblers. Front, L to R: Mgr. Hansen, Weber, Cieslak, Fessler, O'Brien, Mifsud, Keim, Scheppner, DiPlacido, Mgr. Gatz; Back: Mgr. Blakeslee, Van Volkenberg, Cox, Bengel, Bartnicki, Nowak, Orzechowski, Barron, Mgr. Skrzypczak, Coach Flaherty.

HIGHLIGHTS:

- **Father John M. Dollinger** was appointed by **Bishop Alfred Watson** to succeed **Monsignor Robert B. McDonald** as the fourth headmaster of Cathedral Prep. Father Dollinger promised that the basic standards and traditions that had been with Prep through its history, both academically and athletically, would continue through his administration.

- Cathedral Prep suffered its first losing season since 1966 under second-year coach **Bill Flaherty**. Beset by inexperience, lack of height and injuries, the Ramblers nevertheless scored impressive victories over Pittsburgh foe and PCIAA Western champ North Catholic (14-13); Section I champion Tech (19-7); Academy (12-8); and arch-rival McDowell (11-11), a thrilling, double-overtime affair. Senior star **Marty "Marty O" Orzechowski** had some big, high-scoring games, despite being hobbled by a back injury for much of the campaign.

- All City Series games and the McDowell home battle were played at the Gannon Auditorium, while the Ramblers continued to play their independent home contests, including the Jamestown LSL game, in the Prep gymnasium.

- Disappointments included the overall poor City Series play, including two losses to East (12-10) and a trio to Strong Vincent (19-6), including Prep's first PIAA District 10 playoff game ever; and the 47-point pasting by Cleveland St. Joe's (20-2) in the Warren Tourney, the worst Rambler loss in history at the time. It

Nowak scores off the glass at McDowell.

broke the 46-point margin in a 55-9 loss to Alliance Academy on January 18, 1926 and lasted as a record until Lakewood St. Edward defeated the Ramblers by a 49-point margin, 84-35, in the 2016 Burger King Classic!

- Prep's win over Charleroi (9-11) in the Warren Tourney consolation game was the only time the Ramblers and Cougars ever met. Charleroi, located 21 miles south of Pittsburgh in Washington County, was in the WPIAL Section 4, along with Belle Vernon, Ringgold, Elizabeth-Forward, Thomas Jefferson, Monessen and Brownsville.

- Prep had difficulty containing the big scoring opponents like never before. Witness the 42-point record-breaking performance of **Don "The Laser" Maser** of Johnstown [Maser (16 points, 7 rebounds) played for the Western PA stars against the East in the 1973 Dapper Dan preliminary.]; the 36 and 30 point showings by Academy smoothie **David Purdue**; and the incredible 38 and 49 (of SV's 68) point extravaganzas by Vincent's **"Easy Essie" Hollis**! Hollis, of course, broke Maser's all-time opponent single game high, a record that remains to this day.

- A memorable line came from Coach Flaherty at a rollicking basketball rally the afternoon of the second Vincent game: "If we can hold Essie to 45 points, I think we'll win." Everyone roared, thinking 45 points was a joke, but Hollis got his 49 in a 15-point Colonel victory.

- Vincent won both the City Series and Lake Shore Leagues via a sold-out, exciting, 60-57 playoff victory over high-scoring Tech Memorial. It was noted that although 3,000 fans filled the Audi for that one, another 2,000 were turned away at the door. The Colonels had a genuine superstar in **Essie Hollis** and solid support from **Tim Turner** and **Ed Arrington**. SV then took down Prep, Warren and Tech again to win its second consecutive District 10 title and third in four years. The D-10 final over the Centaurs, the fourth time the two squads met, was a nip-and-tuck, 65-62 overtime thriller at sold-out McComb Fieldhouse. SV proceeded to dump Pittsburgh Oliver in PIAA action, as Hollis scored 46 of his team's 62 points in a 5-point triumph. The Colonels were then defeated by Aliquippa in a Western Quarterfinal heartbreaker, 56-55.

- In an oddity, Tech celebrated its first Section One championship in a decade, finishing 7-1 to SV's 6-2 in S-I play. This occurred by virtue of the Centaurs' two regular season wins over the Colonels. Tech was led by **"Jumpin' Joe" Blanks, Dave Kierzek, Bruce Chrzanowski, Jerry Keys, Leo Bennett** and **Mark Behringer**. Kierzek, Chrzanowski and Bennett were part of the **Dr. Bill Garvey**-coached St. John's grade school teams that won state championships in 1969 (30-1) and 1970 (32-1). Behringer later became head coach at Tech (1987-88) before becoming a 14-year assistant at Prep, mostly during the tenure of **Marcel Arribi**. Behringer was also Prep's head junior varsity coach for seven seasons (1992-1999).

- The final standings in unpredictable City Series and LSL basketball leagues were as follows:

	W	L		W	L
*Vincent	7	2	*Vincent	11	2
Tech	6	3	Tech	10	3
Academy	4	4	Academy	8	4
East	2	6	Prep	5	7
Prep	2	6	East	5	7
			McDowell	4	8
			Jamestown	0	12

won city & LSL playoff championship

A full capacity in the Prep gym sees "Marty O" sink two of his 26 points against Jamestown.

- The Lake Shore League folded after the 1972-73 season. Jamestown's (3-16) four-year experiment in the league with six Erie teams proved unsuccessful—Raider fans had little interest in the LSL, JHS was located a good 40 miles east of the Erie schools, and Jamestown officials felt it would be better for their program overall to compete with schools from their own state of New York.

- District 6 champion Johnstown (25-1), which toppled Prep twice, ran off 25 consecutive victories before a future Pitt and NFL star **Randy Holloway**-led Sharon team from District 7 destroyed the Trojans in front of 3,624 fans at Johnstown's War Memorial Auditorium in the PIAA quarterfinals, 77-41. Four Johnstown starters fouled out of the contest. Coach **Paul Litwalk** stated this was his greatest team over his 27-year career (1970-97) at JHS. Star Trojans included 6'9" **Pat Cummings**, who went on to score 1,762 points at the University of Cincinnati and play a dozen years in the NBA with five different teams, averaging 9.6 PPG and 5.6 RPG in 683 games.

- The final Pennsylvania Catholic Interscholastic Athletic Association (PCIAA) Class A tourney was held in 1973, but it was a shadow of itself because many Catholic schools had recently joined the Pennsylvania Interscholastic Athletic Association (PIAA), Cathedral Prep included. The final PCIAA Class B and C tourneys were held in 1974. In October, 1972, **Governor Milton Shapp** signed a bill into law that allowed private and parochial schools to join the 1,100 member PIAA organization. Under the old law, private and parochial schools could only compete with public schools during the regular season, but not in post-season playoffs. Prep had been a charter member of the offshoot PCIAA since 1943. Headmaster **Father John Dollinger** oversaw Prep's transition into the PIAA and within a short time he became a power within the District 10 committee.

- 1973 was also the first year the PIAA held a girls' state championship, with Allentown Central Catholic defeating Sharpsville in the title game, 65-38.

- Scranton Prep defeated Pittsburgh North Catholic in a 48-46 thriller in the final PCIAA Class A state title game ever played. North Catholic star **John Carroll** later became the son-in-law of venerated Trojan coach **Don Graham**, who amassed an 801-436 record while guiding the North Catholic program from 1948 through 1999. Graham's grandson, **Matt Carroll**, starred at Notre Dame and with the NBA's Dallas Mavericks; while his grandson, **Pat**, played at St. Joseph's (PA) University and in a Spanish professional league.

- Vincent's **Essie Hollis** finished the season with all-time area record 753 points (all-time local record 30.1 PPG) and was the first Erieite selected for the prestigious Dapper Dan Classic in Pittsburgh, scoring 8 points for the Pennsylvania All-Stars. Teammates included Schenley's **"Jeep" Kelly** and Donora's **Ulice Payne**, later the uncle of future Prep football great **Charles Rush**. But it was future Notre Dame and NBA star **Adrian Dantley** (25 points, 12 rebounds) who dominated that game in an 87-79 victory for the United States team. Hollis went on to star at St. Bonaventure and was captain of its 1977 NIT champs. He was inducted into the Bonnies' Hall of Fame in 1988.

- Top scorer **Marty Orzechowski** was named First Team All-Big Six by the *Erie Times-News*, while junior sharpshooter **Kevin Barron**, who didn't make Prep's starting five until mid-season, was a Second Team selection. "Marty O" won the James "Moe" Gross Award as Prep's finest player.

- **Jason Weber** continued his basketball career at Behrend College.

- **Marty Orzechowski** was selected to participate in the second annual Northwestern Senior All-Star game at St. Marys High School. He went on to star at Allegheny College and was inducted into its Athletic Hall of Fame in 1991. A two-time MVP and single season-scoring leader, "Marty O" concluded his collegiate career third on the all-time scoring list for the Gators, with 1,105 points, and was named to the first team All-Presidents Athletic Conference three times.

1973 All-Opponent Team:

Don "The Laser" Maser, Johnstown (2nd team all-state) [Duquesne]

Eric "Springer" Stoehr, Bishop Guilfoyle

Dana Gibbs, East

Jerry Keys, Tech

Joe Guilfoyle, Cleveland St. Joe's (2nd team all-state, OH)

Tim Cannon, Cleveland St. Joe's

David Purdue, Academy [Stetson]

John Carroll, North Catholic

Tom Michaels, McDowell

Jack Nill, McDowell

Joe Blanks, Tech [Gannon]

Bill Holter, Academy

Richie "Rabbit" Gavin, East

Tim Turner, Vincent

Lynn Hailstock, New Castle [Austin Peay, football]

Essie Hollis, Vincent (2nd team all-state) [St. Bonaventure; NBA Detroit Pistons]

Ken Horoho, Johnstown [St. Francis (PA)]

Pat Cummings, Johnstown [Cincinnati; NBA Milwaukee Bucks, NY Knicks, Dallas Mavericks, Miami Heat, Utah Jazz]

Starting forward Matt Scheppner makes a one-handed jumper.

Junior Mark Van Volkenburg breaks through for two.

Big center Dan Nowak, leading rebounder and the only Rambler to start every game of the season.

Prep's First D-10 Playoff Win!

1973-74 (14-11)

Coach: William "Bill" Flaherty
Captains: Game captains
Managers: Don Gatz, Bill Hansen

Scoring machine Kevin Barron poured in a near-record 39 points against Warren.

Date	PREP			Dec.	Loc.	High Scorer	Opponent
11/27	59	Bradford	62	W	A	Barron (17)	Lloyd (22)
11/29	64	Warren	60	W	H	Barron (39)	Bowen (16)
12/7	62	Altoona Bishop Guilfoyle	65	L	A	Barron (29)	Palazzi (24)
12/14	52	Academy	67	L	N	Webb (18)	Purdue (24)
12/21	46	Tech Memorial	54	L	N	Barron (15)	Chrzanowski (20)
12/22	75	Cleveland (OH) St. Joseph	57	W	H	Scheppner (27)	Gornik (14)
		WARREN HOLIDAY BASKETBALL TOURNAMENT					
12/27	63	Warren	59	W	N	Scheppner & Webb (16)	Young (18)
12/28	54	Cleveland (OH) St. Joseph	52	W	N	Webb (19)	Cyvas (20)
1/4	46	Strong Vincent	62	L	N	Scheppner (18)	Turner (23)
1/5	81	Cleveland (OH) Benedictine	66	W	H	Barron (29)	Robinson (28)
1/8	53	Johnstown	64	L	A	Barron (16)	Cummings (35)
1/12	67	East	48	W	N	Wierbinski (20)	Gibbs & Simpson (13)
1/15	86	Pittsburgh Bishop Canevin	50	W	H	Barron (21)	Pobicki (16)
1/17	66	McDowell	51	W	H	Barron (15)	Prentice (20)
1/25	45	Academy	68	L	N	Barron (11)	Purdue (23)
2/1	69	Tech Memorial	57	W	N	Scheppner (22)	Chrzanowski (22)
2/5	49	McDowell	47	W	A	Webb (11)	Schmitt (18)
2/8	70	Strong Vincent	56	W	N	R. Bengel (20)	Crockett (21)
2/15	63	East	50	W	N	R.Bengel, Webb & Wierbinski (14)	Gibbs (17)
2/19	67	Jamestown (NY)	70	L	A	Barron (25)	Rigoli (26)
2/23	49	Johnstown	85	L	H	Scheppner (12)	Buchan (41)
2/26	86	Jamestown (NY)	70	W	H	Scheppner (31)	Gill (16)
		DISTRICT 10 PLAYOFFS					
3/2	66	Harborcreek	61(OT)	W	H	R. Bengel (20)	Kennedy (22)
3/5	50	Warren	52	L	N	R. Bengel (17)	Bowen (18)
3/9	54	Hickory	59(OT)	L	N	Barron (19)	Bell (19)
	1561 (62.4)		**1503* (60.1)**				

Pos.	Player	Ht.	Prior School	Class	G (GS)	FG	FT	Total	PPG	Career
G	Kevin Barron (#10)	6'0"	St. Andrew's	Sr.	22(22)	167	60-85	394	17.9	600
F	Matt Scheppner (#40)	6'2"	St. Andrew's	Sr.	22(19)	133	34-49	300	13.6	420
F	John Webb (#50)	6'3"	St. Luke's	Jr.	21(18)	87	37-56	211	10.0	211
G	Mike Sisinni (#22)	6'0"	St. George's	Jr.	24(19)	63	36-46	162	6.8	162
G	Rick Bengel (#12)	6'1"	Sacred Heart	Jr.	22(19)	61	18-25	140	6.4	187
F	Steve Wierbinski (#54)	6'3"	Sacred Heart	Jr.	20(7)	54	32-48	140	7.0	140
G	Bob Bengel (#42)	6'1"	Sacred Heart	Jr.	20(4)	36	6-12	78	3.9	78
F	George Carrig (#52)	6'1"	St. Peter's	Sr.	14(6)	13	7-12	33	2.4	37
G	Mark Van Volkenburg (#24)	6'0"	Sacred Heart	Sr.	15(9)	7	13-19	27	1.8	60
G	Jim Feeney (#44)	6'0"	St. John's	Jr.	22(1)	8	8-26	24	1.1	24
C	Tim Niewierowski (#30)	6'3"	St. Patrick's	Jr.	16(1)	8	3-8	19	1.2	19
F	Pat Cox(#32)	6'1"	St. Peter's	Sr.	12	7	0-3	14	1.2	16
F	Mark Cieslak (#34)	6'1"	OLC	Sr.	10	2	7-15	11	1.1	17
G	Mark DiPlacido (#14)	5'9"	St. Andrew's	Sr.	6	2	2-3	6	1.0	11
G	Jay Simon (#20)	5'9"	St. Andrew's	Jr.	2	1	0-1	2	1.0	2
F	Jeff Maries (#43)	6'1"	OLC	Jr.	3	0	0-0	0	0.0	0
G	Maurice Myers (#4)	5'9"	St. Peter's	Jr.	1	0	0-0	0	0.0	0
F	Mark Leifield (#31)	6'0"	St. Luke's	Jr.	0	0	0-0	0	0.0	0

The 1974 Prep Ramblers. Front, L to R: Coach Flaherty, Barron, Van Vokenburg, Cox, Webb; Standing: Scheppner, Niewierowski, Feeney, B. Bengel, Maries, Leifield, R. Bengel, DiPlacido, Sisinni, Cieslak, Myers, Simon.

HIGHLIGHTS:

George Carrig has the pleasure of sitting next to Coach Flaherty on the bench.

- Cathedral Prep returned to a winning campaign under third-year coach **Bill Flaherty**, utilizing the shooting strength of seniors **Kevin Barron** and **Matt Scheppner** and the help of a strong junior class.

- 1973-74 was the first year the Ramblers were considered a part of the PIAA District 10 Section One league, the old "Big Six." Of note was Prep's first D-10 playoff victory, with the Ramblers erasing a 14-point deficit to top Harborcreek (16-7) in overtime. It was the first time the Ramblers and the Huskies had met since 1961. Unfortunately, Prep tried stalling but blew a 10-point fourth quarter lead, losing to Section Two champ Warren (21-5) in the D-10 semifinals. That one hurt,

Bob Bengel, determined to score again.

especially after Prep handed the Dragons two of their only three defeats in the regular season. Hickory (17-7) ended all Rambler hopes for advancement, overcoming a 9-point fourth quarter arrearage, then downing the Orange & Black in OT in the consolation match. At the time three D-10 Class A teams (large school) advanced to inter-district play.

- All City Series games, the McDowell home battle and the District 10 playoff against Harborcreek were played at the Gannon Auditorium, while the Ramblers continued to play their independent home contests in the Prep gym. The Warren and Hickory D-10 battles were played at Edinboro's McComb Fieldhouse.

Pat Cox goes underneath for a bucket.

- The final standings in City Series and Section One basketball leagues were as follows:

	W	L			W	L
Academy	8	0		Academy	10	0
Prep	4	4		Prep	6	4
Vincent	4	4		Vincent	4	6
Tech	3	5		Tech	4	6
East	2	6		McDowell	4	6
				East	2	8

- District 10 champion Academy (24-1), led by superstar **David Purdue**, ran away with the City Series and Section One titles. It was Academy's first D-10 crown since 1939 and first outright city title since 1948. The Lions won a record 24 straight contests before losing to Jeannette in the first round of the state playoffs, 83-71. Purdue, a three-time First Team All-City selection, scored 607 points for the season and completed his career as Erie's all-time leading scorer with 1,398 points. This Academy squad, to this day, holds the all-time record for most points per game, once defeating Conneaut Valley, 137-29. Purdue scored 50 in that one, just shy of Tech great **Carmen Riazzi's** local record 52 scored against Lawrence Park in 1953.

- Prep's three games against Warren were the first between the Ramblers and the Dragons since 1948. The first Prep-Warren battle was the middle contest of a tripleheader at the Audi. In the first game, Corry upset Vincent, 70-68; in the nightcap, Iroquois upset East, 66-60. Sharpshooter **Kevin Barron's** 39-point effort against Warren on that night was one point shy of **Paul Pry's** Prep record of 40, set against Academy in 1968.

Big Steve Wierbinski drives for two against Academy.

- Prep played well winning its second attempt in the Warren Holiday Basketball Tournament. Particularly gratifying was the close triumph over Cleveland St. Joe's, which completely pasted the Ramblers in the Warren tourney just the year before.

- Prep's second win over McDowell (13-9) was the first high school varsity basketball game ever played at the new Erie County Fieldhouse, located on Wattsburg Road (Route 8), just north of I-90. The Prep JV's defeated McDowell's JV's in the preliminary tilt, 40-31.

- Prep's two victories over East High (11-10) evened the all-time series between the two at exactly 40-40.

- Though unknown at the time, Prep's win over Tech (10-9) on February 1 was the 1,000th varsity basketball game played in the school's history.

John Webb boxes out McDowell's Dale Jennings and grabs the rebound.

- Prep's inability to hold down stars **Pat Cummings** and **Jack Buchan** made it four straight losses to District 6 AAA champion Johnstown (20-5). The Trojans lost to Pittsburgh Peabody in the PIAA first round, 51-48. District 6 AA champ Bishop Guilfoyle also defeated the Ramblers in a close one. It was the last time Prep and nemesis Bishop Guilfoyle played until the 1989 Great Chevy Shootout in Altoona.

- **Pat Cummings** played for the Pennsylvania All-Stars in the 1974 Dapper Dan Classic, while Academy's **David Purdue** scored 8 points in an 89-78 loss for Quaker State against Buckeye State in the preliminary.

- **Matt Scheppner's** 31 tallies against Jamestown (8-13) in the regular season finale ranked ninth on the single game Prep chart at the time.

- 1974 was the last year for PCIAA Class B and Class C tournaments. There was no Class A bracket because of a lack of Class A teams, most which had already joined the PIAA. The last Class B winner was Bradford Central Christian, which defeated Braddock St. Thomas, 66-61. In the final PCIAA game ever played, Delone Catholic upset Pittsburgh South Side Catholic, 60-59, for the Class C title.

Kevin Barron, a First Team All-Section One choice, operates against Vincent's Greg Grace.

- Prep opponents broke the record for most points (1,503) scored against the Ramblers in a season .

- **Mark Van Volkenburg** was the third of four Van Volkenburg brothers from Sacred Heart parish to toil for the Ramblers.

- High-scoring **Kevin Barron** was named First Team All-Section One by the *Erie Times-News*, while **Matt Scheppner**, the James "Moe" Gross Award winner, was a Second Team selection.

1974 All-Opponent Team:

> Dave Lloyd, Bradford
> Mike Palazzi, Bishop Guilfoyle [Fairfield]
> David Purdue, Academy (3rd team all-state) [Stetson]
> Bruce Chrzanowski, Tech
> Saulius "Saul" Cyvas, Cleveland St. Joe's [John Carroll]
> Tim Turner, Vincent
> Greg Grace, Vincent
> Mark Robinson Cleveland Benedictine
> John Matthews, Academy
> John Schmitt, McDowell
> Ross Rigoli, Jamestown
> Jack Buchan, Johnstown
> "Butch" Gill, Jamestown
> Jon Kennedy, Harborcreek
> Jim Bowen, Warren [California (PA) St.]
> Bill Bell, Hickory
> Pat Cummings, Johnstown (1st team all-state)
>   [Cincinnati; NBA Milwaukee Bucks, NY Knicks, Dallas Mavericks, Miami Heat, Utah Jazz]

Referee Vinnie Marchant closely watches Mike Sisinni on a steal and breakaway bucket.

Junior guard Mike Sisinni, fully in control.

Mark Cieslak scores from the outside.

First District 10 Crown!

1974-75 (22-6)

Coach: William "Bill" Flaherty
Captains: Game captains
Managers: Rick Carlotti, Mark O'Hara

The classic pose of Coach William "Bill" Flaherty.

Date	PREP			Dec.	Loc.	High Scorer	Opponent
11/29	61	Lackawanna (NY) Baker-Victory	35	W	H	Sisinni (20)	McDowell (12)
12/3	64	Bradford	43	W	H	R. Bengel & Sisinni (16)	Newberg & Schultz (16)
12/6	75	Lackawanna (NY) Baker-Victory	55	W	A	Webb (16)	McDowell (15)
12/14	73	Cuyahoga Falls (OH)	56	W	A	Webb (26)	Fraser (16)
12/17	80	McDowell	61	W	N	Sisinni (21)	Prentice (19)
12/20	68	Strong Vincent	50	W	N	R. Bengel (17)	Barnes (20)
		WARREN HOLIDAY BASKETBALL TOURNAMENT					
12/26	64	Greensburg Salem	66	L	N	R. Bengel (20)	Neurohr (26)
12/27	79	Jamestown (NY)	58	W	N	B. Bengel & Sisinni (18)	Reading (21)
12/30	65	Tech Memorial	46	W	N	B. Bengel (18)	Carson & Dougherty (14)
1/3	56	Penn Hills	69	L	A	R. Bengel & McCormick (14)	Genday (16)
1/7	66	Academy	65	W	N	R. Bengel (22)	Clark (22)
1/10	68	Johnstown	53	W	A	Sisinni (30)	Zupan (18)
1/14	68	Pittsburgh Bishop Canevin	45	W	A	R. Bengel & Webb (12)	Burik & Pollett (10)
1/17	57	East	53	W	N	Sisinni (15)	Brown & Hamilton (16)
1/21	52	Tech Memorial	54	L	N	R. Bengel (16)	Carson (23)
1/24	72	McDowell	63	W	N	R. Bengel (24)	Chojnacki (26)
1/28	65	Strong Vincent	66(OT)	L	N	Sisinni (22)	Barnes (23)
1/31	81	Pittsburgh Oliver	51	W	H	Sisinni (18)	Scott (15)
2/8	59	Academy	77	L	N	Sisinni (16)	Clark (24)
2/14	78	Altoona	74	W	H	Cousart (23)	Moore (25)
2/15	57	Johnstown	55	W	H	Webb (26)	Zupan (19)
2/21	62	East	36	W	N	R. Bengel (16)	House (10)
		SECTION ONE SECOND PLACE PLAYOFF					
2/25	71	Strong Vincent	67	W	N	Webb (28)	Barnes (29)
		DISTRICT 10 PLAYOFFS					
2/28	79	Harborcreek	37	W	N	Sisinni (17)	Helffrich (10)
3/4	52	Meadville	45	W	N	R. Bengel (23)	O'Laughlin (23)
3/8	66	Academy	62	W	N	Sisinni (21)	Clark (18)
		P.I.A.A. INTERDISTRICT PLAYOFFS					
3/12	83	Hempfield Area	66	W	N	R. Bengel (19)	Irwin (17)
3/15	48	Pittsburgh Schenley	76	L	N	R. Bengel & Webb (16)	Lewis & Smith (18)
	1869* (66.8)		**1584* (56.6)**				

Pos.	Player	Ht.	Prior School	Class	G (GS)	FG	FT	Total	PPG	Career
G	Rick Bengel (#12)	6'2"	Sacred Heart	Sr.	28*(28*)	186	63-83	435	15.5	622
G	Mike Sisinni (#22)	6'0"	St. George's	Sr.	28*(28*)	159	92-121	410	14.6	572
F	John Webb (#50)	6'3"	St. Luke's	Sr.	27(27)	110	56-86	276	10.2	487
F	Dave Cousart (#52)	6'2"	St. John's	Jr.	28*(13)	92	60-96	244	8.7	244
G	Bob Bengel (#42)	6'2"	Sacred Heart	Sr.	27(26)	104	35-45	243	9.0	321
F	Jim Feeney (#44)	6'0"	St. John's	Sr.	27(11)	38	23-50	99	3.7	123
C	Tim Niewierowski (#30)	6'3"	St. Patrick's	Sr.	16(7)	27	0-7	54	3.4	73
G	Jim McCormick (#4)	5'10"	St. Peter's	Jr.	10	16	0-3	32	3.2	32
G	Billy Fessler	5'11"	St. Luke's	Jr.	13	7	4-7	18	1.4	18
F	Bob Kraus	6'3"	St. Peter's	Jr.	15	5	2-3	12	0.8	12
F	John Hall	6'2"	Sacred Heart	Jr.	10	4	4-4	12	1.2	12
G	Rick Bordonaro (#10)	5'6"	J. S. Wilson	Jr.	7	4	2-2	10	1.4	10
F	Matt Hersch	6'1"	Millcreek Int.	Jr.	8	2	3-5	7	0.9	7
G	Dwight Pace	5'9"	St. Peter's	Jr.	9	0	6-8	6	0.7	6
G	John Greulich (#20)	5'11"	St. Peter's	Jr.	9	2	0-0	4	0.4	4
F	Steve Wierbinski (#54)	6'4"	Sacred Heart	Sr.	5	1	0-0	2	0.4	142
F	Mike Madonia	6'1"	Holy Rosary	Jr.	9	1	0-4	2	0.2	2
G	Brian Denard	5'10"	St. Peter's	Jr.	4	1	0-0	2	0.5	2
F	Jim MacKrell	6'0"	Sacred Heart	Sr.	6	0	1-4	1	0.2	2
G	Jim Heberle	5'10"	St. John's	Jr.	6	0	0-0	0	0.0	0

Prep's 1975 District 10 Champs. Front, L to R: Mgr. Carlotti, Heberle, Hersch, Hall, Madonia, Greulich, Fessler, Mgr. Orzechowski; Middle: Mgr. O'Hara, MacKrell, Denard, Bordonaro, McCormick, Pace, Cousart; Back: Coach Flaherty, R. Bengel, Sissini, Webb, Niewierowski, Feeney, B. Bengel, Asst. Coach Wenrick.

HIGHLIGHTS:

- Cathedral Prep's man-to-man and fast-breaking squad produced its first District 10 champions in a thrilling season. Coach **Bill Flaherty's** pattern of consistently upgrading the Prep schedule finally paid dividends, as it was also the first Rambler team to win in inter-district PIAA play. Stalwarts included veteran seniors **Mike Sisinni, John Webb** and the **Bengel** twins, **Rick** and **Bob**.

- Seniors **Rick Bengel, Bob Bengel, Steve Wierbinski** and **Jim MacKrell** and junior **John Hall** were all part of the Sacred Heart grade school team, coached by **Ron Sertz**, that finished 29-2 and won the 1971 Pennsylvania state CYO grade school basketball championship. Sertz was later to become a successful cross-country and basketball coach at Prep and later

the long-time Athletic Director and Director of Operations.

- Prep's 28 contests in 1974-75 broke Erie's all-time record for most games played in a season, previously held by Prep's 1952-53 state champions (23-4). Consequently, **Mike Sisinni** and **Rick Bengel** broke Prep records for most games played and started (both 28), while junior **Dave Cousart** also played in the record 28 games.

- For the second consecutive year, Prep opponents broke the record for most points (1,584) scored against the Ramblers in a season.

- New Rambler opponents included Cuyahoga Falls; Altoona; the WPIAL's Greensburg Salem, Penn Hills and Hempfield Area; and Pittsburgh City League entrants Oliver and Schenley. Both

Oliver and Schenley are now closed.

- Prep's victory over Cuyahoga Falls (10-10) was the only time the Ramblers and Black Tigers competed. The town of Cuyahoga Falls is well-known as the home of Blossom Music Center and the synthetic rock band Devo. The high school is notorious for being the place where legendary **Bobby Knight** got his first coaching stint (1962-63), before moving on to West Point and to Indiana University.

- Prep's contests against Oliver (6-12) and Schenley (24-4) were the first times the Ramblers ever competed in basketball against teams from the Pittsburgh City League. Schools in the Pittsburgh City League at the time included: Section 1— Fifth Avenue, Schenley, W e s t i n g h o u s e , Peabody, Taylor Allderdice, Carrick and South; Section 2: Perry, Allegheny, Oliver, Langley, South Hills and Gladstone. Only Westinghouse, Allderdice, Carrick and Perry (n/k/a Perry Traditional Academy) survive today. Schools which fielded teams in the City League which closed some years before 1975 include Ralston, Connelley Trade School, Allegheny Vocational and Washington Vocational.

- All City Series and Section One games, including both McDowell contests for the first time, were played at the Gannon Auditorium,

Junior Dave Cousart scores two more.

First Team All-Section One selection Mike Sisinni pulls down a rebound against McDowell.

- Prep's road contest with Baker-Victory (10-8) was played in Buffalo's Memorial Auditorium as a preliminary to the NBA's Buffalo Braves-Portland Trail Blazers battle, while Prep's home game against Johnstown (9-13) was a preliminary to the Gannon College-Siena clash. Baker-Victory, formerly known as Our Lady of Victory, was named after Buffalo's revered **Father Nelson Baker**. The Ramblers never played Baker-Victory again and the high school section of

Sisinni with a left-handed layup following a steal.

the school affiliated with Lackawanna's Our Lady of Victory parish and basilica is now closed.

- Prep's win against Jamestown (8-11) was its 16th in 20 games versus JHS since 1953. The Ramblers and the Red Raiders have only played one more time, that at the Jamestown Holiday Tournament in 1982-83.

- Another season highlight was Prep's stunning win over eventual District 6 titlist Altoona (21-4), as Rambler free throw shooters canned 30 of 33 attempts. The powerful Mountain Lions featured 6'1" **Johnny Moore**, later of University of Texas and NBA fame. He spent his entire career playing point guard for the San Antonio Spurs, save one game for the New Jersey Nets. In his 10-year NBA career, Moore averaged 9.4 points and 7.4 assists per game. The Spurs have honored Moore by retiring his number "00".

- It was an exciting year for nip-and-tuck City Series and Section One hoops. Overflow crowds at the Audi were the norm as Academy (19-5) showed its strength, winning both togas, but eventually losing to Prep in the D-10 final. The Lions pounded Punxsutawney, 75-60, but then lost to undefeated WPIAL champion Uniontown (27-1), 89-72, in state playoff action. Lion stalwarts included First Team All-City performers **James "PeeWee" Bolden, Walt Clark** and **Jeff Quinn**, as well as sophomore **Francis Spearman**.

as were the home games with Fr. Baker and Johnstown. The other independent home contests were held in the Prep gym. The Harborcreek D-10 opener was played in the Tech Memorial gym, while Prep's next four playoff battles were played at Edinboro's McComb Fieldhouse. Prep did not play Harborcreek again for the next 30 years.

Cousart and Sisinni apply pressure to Tech's Johnny Blanks.

- Prep's first three losses were of the disappointing sort. Greensburg Salem (14-8) finished third in WPIAL Section 2 and didn't qualify for the playoffs; Penn Hills (15-9) won WPIAL Section 7, but was crushed by **Sam Clancy** and Fifth Avenue, 68-49, in the PIAA first round; and the close Tech (10-9) defeat cost the Ramblers sole second place in the city and S-I.

- Prep's rout over Pittsburgh Canevin (3-13) was the last time the schools competed, Prep holding a 3-2 edge in the series. Canevin was among several Pittsburgh area Catholic schools, including Central Catholic, North Catholic, Vincentian Academy and all the traditional Class B parish schools, which had yet to join the WPIAL or PIAA. By the 1974-75 season, South Hills Catholic operated in WPIAL Section 10; Mon Valley Catholic, McKeesport Serra Catholic and Homestead Bishop Boyle were in Section 13; Baden Quigley Catholic was in Section 15; and Connellsville Father Geibel and Uniontown St. John's were in Section 19.

- Coach Flaherty was incensed at the officiating in Prep's overtime loss to Vincent (11-5), stating to the *Erie Daily Times*: "For the first time in my coaching career I want to publicly say I was disgusted with the way this game was called…my kids played well and did not deserve to lose this game!" The Ramblers won revenge against the young Colonels in a playoff for second place to determine a D-10 playoff spot, using a full-court press and incredibly rallying from a 17-point deficit in the second half to pull out the victory before over 3,000 fans. It was **John Webb** who lit up the scoreboard with an incredible 26 points in the second half alone. Webb was amazing and the comeback was considered Erie's greatest since East's 61-55 come-from-behind win over Prep in 1968 when the Warriors erased a 19-point fourth quarter deficit.

- The final standings in City Series and Section One basketball leagues were as follows:

	W	L		W	L
Academy	7	1	Academy	9	1
Prep	5	3	*Prep	7	3
Vincent	5	3	Vincent	7	3
Tech	2	6	Tech	4	6
East	1	7	East	3	7
			McDowell	0	10

won 2nd place playoff

- Prep's District 10 march began with a defensive gem over Harborcreek (12-11). Next was an exciting defensive struggle over a strong Meadville (19-6) squad, with **Jim Feeney** providing

Feeney appears to get whacked by SV's Mickey Hintz.

the spark with some fancy shooting; **Rick Bengel** tossing in the long bombs; and **Bob Bengel** playing super defense. Meadville defeated Warren in the consolation bout, but was torn apart by Valley (New Kensington area), 84-64, in first round PIAA play. The Bulldogs had to contend with the inside play of sophomore **Benjy Pryor** (12 points, 20 rebounds) and the awesome scoring display of **"B.B." Flenory** (49 points).

Jim Feeney goes up strong to pull down another rebound.

- The Prep-Academy D-10 sell-out final was considered the "Game of the Year" and it lived up to pre-game expectations. The Ramblers erased 12-point 1st quarter and 9-point halftime deficits to gain their first D-10 diadem behind the outside shooting of **Rick Bengel** and **Mike Sisinni** and the inside play of junior strongman **Dave Cousart**. Down 62-59 with but 52 seconds remaining, Sisinni nailed a baseline jumper; Cousart followed with a drive off a backcourt steal, and hit both ends of a one-and-one after a rebound; and Bengel cashed in a late technical foul shot to seal the 66-62 win. Prep then looked strong and balanced in eliminating Hempfield (19-6) in first round PIAA action.

- Prep's exciting 8-game win streak and exciting state playoff run was finally upended by the inside play of 6'11" **Kelvin Smith** and eventual state champion Pittsburgh Schenley. The Spartans defeated defending champion Abington in the PIAA Class A final, 65-64. It was Schenley's third state title in 10 years under legendary coach **Spencer Watkins**. Schenley was opened in 1916 and the building is located in the Oakland section of Pittsburgh on the edge of the Hill District.

- Schenley's Smith (14 points, 8 rebounds) and **Wayne Williams** both played for the Pennsylvania All-Stars against the U. S. in the 1975 Dapper Dan Classic, while Altoona's Moore played for the Keystone team against Garden State in the preliminary.

- 1975 was the last year the PIAA classifications were listed as "A", "B" and "C". They were changed to the politically correct "AAA", "AA" and "A" for the 1976 playoffs.

- **Rick Bengel** and **Mike Sisinni**, winner of the James "Moe" Gross Award, were both named First Team All-Section One by the *Erie Times-News*, while defensive ace **Bob Bengel** was a Second Team selection. **John Webb**, who had several huge games, was an Honorable Mention choice. All four represented Prep in a losing effort, 80-79, in the rejuvenated City-County All-Star tilt (considered the "first") played at McComb Fieldhouse. Sisinni starred with 15 points for the Slickers.

- The **Bengel** twins, **Rick** and **Bob**, were the first co-winners of Prep's "Ma" Kaiser Award, signifying both as the best Rambler athletes of the year.

- **Rick Bengel, Mike Sisinni** and **John Webb** all went on to star in college—Bengel at Harvard; Sisinni at Clarion State; and Webb at Allegheny. Bengel, who lettered two years for the Crimson, later became head women's basketball coach at Mercyhurst College (1985-1987). Sisinni was inducted into the Eagles' Athletic Hall of Fame in 1999.

1975 All-Opponent Team:

Steve McDowell, Baker-Victory

Scott Fraser, Cuyahoga Falls

Steve Prentice, McDowell [Pirates Class A baseball]

Dave Neurohr, Greensburg Salem [Bethany]

Jim McElrath, Jamestown

Ricky Genday, Penn Hills [Penn State, volleyball]

Walt Clark, Academy [Mercyhurst]

Mike Zupan, Johnstown

Jamie Carson, Tech

John "Red" Barnes, Vincent

Greg Grace, Vincent

Tim Watson, East

James "PeeWee" Bolden, Academy [
Pitt-Bradford, Gannon]

Jeff Quinn, Academy [Pitt-Bradford]

Dan Chojnacki, McDowell [Clarion St.]

Johnny Moore, Altoona [Texas; NBA San Antonio
Spurs & N. J. Nets]

Rick Federici, Vincent [Edinboro St.;
Pirates Class AA baseball]

Tom O'Laughlin, Meadville (S-II Player of the Year)

Nathan "Sonny" Lewis, Schenley [Pitt, Point Park]

Wayne Williams, Schenley (1st team all-state) [Pitt]

Kelvin Smith, Schenley [Pitt]

Bob Bengel, along with his twin, Rick, were co-winners of the "Ma" Kaiser Award, signifying them as Prep's best athletes.

Leading scorer Rick Bengel, First Team All-Section One. He went on to star at Harvard and later became head women's coach at Mercyhurst College.

Coach Flaherty pleads with the student body for maximum support.

No Post-season for Prep!

1975-76 (9-12)

Coach: William "Bill" Flaherty
Captains: Game captains
Managers: Rick Carlotti, Steve Orzechowski, Charles Jenkins, Lawrence Schaaf

Date	PREP			Dec.	Loc.	High Scorer	Opponent
11/25	82	DuBois Central Christian	36	W	H	Cousart (22)	Rossi & Mitchell (9)
12/2	74	Bradford	51	W	A	Cousart (18)	Scott (15)
12/3	77	Buffalo (NY) St. Joseph's Collegiate	51	W	H	Cousart (15)	Wilson (28)
12/12	62	East	60(OT)	W	N	Bensur (22)	Gausman (20)
12/16	41	Buffalo (NY) St. Joseph's Collegiate	65	L	A	Kraus (8)	Freeman & Downing (17)
12/19	62	Academy	50	W	N	Cousart (19)	Spearman (12)
		WARREN HOLIDAY BASKETBALL TOURNAMENT					
12/29	59	Pittsburgh North Catholic	81	L	N	Bensur (17)	Duerring (23)
12/30	80	Warren	70	W	N	Cousart (26)	Daley (20)
1/2	61	Strong Vincent	62	L	N	Bensur (15)	Barnes (19)
1/6		Pittsburgh Fifth Avenue (CANCELLED—TEACHERS' STRIKE)			H		
1/9	68	McDowell	65	W	N	Cousart (35)	Chojnacki (31)
1/13	51	Tech Memorial	56	L	N	Cousart (18)	Carson (19)
1/16	68	East	73	L	N	Cousart (22)	Brown & Gausman (20)
1/20	80	Dunkirk (NY)	71	W	H	Cousart & Elwell (15)	Jones (21)
1/27	65	Academy	71	L	N	Bensur (25)	Spearman (19)
1/30	61	Uniontown	82	L	A	Greulich (16)	Hozak (28)
2/3	61	Dunkirk (NY)	65(OT)	L	A	McCormick (21)	Carter (16)
2/6	38	Strong Vincent	42	L	N	Mifsud (11)	Carter (16)
2/13	61	McDowell	74	L	N	Cousart (19)	Chojnacki (17)
2/14	52	Johnstown	86	L	A	Hesch (12)	Pridgen (24)
2/17	54	Altoona	73	L	A	Bensur (12)	Futrell (21)
2/20	73	Tech Memorial	55	W	N	Cousart (21)	C. Blanks (16)
	1330 (63.3)		**1339 (63.8)**				

Pos.	Player	Ht.	Prior School	Class	G (GS)	FG	FT	Total	PPG	Career
G	Dave Cousart (#44)	6'2"	St. John's	Sr.	21(21)	121	77	319	15.2	563
C	Bill Bensur (#30)	6'5"	Bl. Sacrament	Jr.	19(16)	97	35	229	12.1	229
G	John Greulich (#20)	6'1"	St. Peter's	Sr.	21(21)	94	23	211	10.0	215
G	Rick Bordonaro (#10)	5'9"	J. S. Wilson	Sr.	18(17)	47	15	109	6.1	119
G	Jim McCormick (#4)	5'10"	St. Peter's	Sr.	16(2)	48	12	108	6.8	140
F	Bob Kraus (#42)	6'4"	St. Peter's	Sr.	18(14)	35	13	83	4.6	95
F	Kevin Elwell (#32)	6'1"	St. Andrew's	Jr.	17(1)	20	16	56	3.3	56
G	Fran Mifsud (#14)	5'7"	St. Paul's	Jr.	15(4)	22	11	55	3.7	55
F	Tom Smogorzewski (#50)	6'3"	St. John's	Jr.	17(7)	18	7	43	2.5	43
G	Tom Hesch (#24)	5'10"	Bl. Sacrament	Jr.	9(1)	16	9	41	4.6	41
G	Billy Fessler (#22)	6'0"	St. Luke's	Sr.	3(1)	6	2	14	4.7	32
F	Andy Paris (#54)	6'3"	Bl. Sacrament	Jr.	6	4	5	13	2.2	13
F	Dan DeDionisio (#40)	6'0"	St. Patrick's	Jr.	7	6	0	12	1.7	12
F	Dan Sculley (#52)	6'3"	OLP	Soph.	2	5	0	10	5.0	10
G	Ed Clark (#34)	5'10"	St. George's	Jr.	8	5	0	10	1.3	10
G	Jim Heberle (#12)	5'10"	St. John's	Sr.	8	3	1	7	0.9	7
G	Tim Brabender (#13)	5'10"	St. George's	Jr.	5	2	1	5	1.0	5
F	Jeff Joint (#35)	6'0"	OLC	Jr.	4	2	0	4	1.0	4

The 1976 Prep Ramblers. Front, L to R: Mgrs. Jenkins, Schaaf; Middle: Pace, Hesch, Brabender, Mifsud, DeDionisio, Joint, Clark, Heberle; Back: Mgrs. Orzechowski, Carlotti, Cousart, Bordonaro, Kraus, Greulich, Bensur, Madonia, Sculley, Elwell, Paris, Fessler, Smogorzewski, McCormick, Coach Flaherty.

HIGHLIGHTS:

- Coach **Bill Flaherty's** fifth season was a rebuilding one, with only senior **Dave Cousart** having significant experience. Though the season began with four straight victories, a second half tailspin gave Flaherty his second but last losing campaign as Cathedral Prep coach.

- All City Series and Section One games were played at the Gannon Auditorium, while independent home contests against Buffalo St. Joe's and Dunkirk were held in the Prep gym. The opener against DuBois Central Christian was the middle game of a high school tripleheader at Gannon, while the second St. Joe's battle was played in Buffalo's Memorial Auditorium.

- Juniors **Bill Bensur, Andy Paris** and **Tom Hesch** were all part of the Blessed Sacrament team that won the 1972 Pennsylvania

state grade school basketball crown. Also on that squad were Strong Vincent stars **Rick Federici** and **Mickey Hintz**.

- New opponents included DuBois Central Christian (now Central Catholic); Buffalo St. Joseph's Collegiate Institute; and the WPIAL's powerful Uniontown, located some 50 miles southeast of Pittsburgh. All three were never placed on a Prep schedule again, although the Ramblers did face Uniontown in 2001-02 PIAA playoff action.

- Prep had an extra-easy win in its opener against DuBois Central Christian (26-4). One reason was the absence of the Crusaders' 6'4" center and all-state candidate **Pat Felix**, whose foot was in a cast from a broken ankle. It was the only game Felix missed all season, and DuBois proceeded to the District 9 Class A (formerly "C") title and on to Hershey as a state final four participant. There the Crusaders lost the Western

Final to Uniontown St. John's, 76-68, but on the next night defeated Weatherly, 52-49, for consolation honors. Felix, who finished the season with 598 points and 1,396 for his career, was named MVP of the Dapper Dan preliminary game and later played at Duquesne University.

Bordonaro sinks a free throw in the victory against Buffalo St. Joe's.

- After defeating Prep in the opening round of the Warren Holiday Tourney, Pittsburgh North Catholic (15-5) lost to Harrisburg, 107-86, in the title clash. 1975-76 was the first year NC was in the WPIAL, where it finished second in Section 9 and therefore did not qualify for the playoffs. Prep defeated host Warren (15-8) in the consolation game, 80-70. The Dragons finished the season the third seed out of District 10, but lost in the PIAA first round to Valley, 78-54.

- Prep never played North Catholic again, the Trojans finishing on top in the series, 7-4. Five of the Trojan victories came in PCIAA playoff action out of six games. North Catholic was located in the deteriorating Troy Hill section of Pittsburgh and became co-educational in 1974. Despite enrollment problems it has had

Coming to Prep from J.S. Wilson, Ricky Bordonaro was Prep's gain, McDowell's loss.

success in athletics, particularly girls' basketball, although it now competes at the PIAA Class A level. In 2013 North Catholic moved to a new school in Cranberry Township and is now known as "Cardinal Wuerl North Catholic High School."

- The highlight of the season was rugged **Dave Cousart's** scoring punch and his 35-point performance in the victory over McDowell (17-7). Trojan **Dan Chojnacki's** 31-point effort in the same contest remains the highest total ever scored by a McDowell Trojan against the Ramblers.

- Most disappointing were the two close losses to City Series, Section One and District 10 champ Strong Vincent (19-5) and Prep losses in the second Buffalo St. Joe's (13-7), East (12-10), Academy (5-16), Dunkirk (16-5) and McDowell games, after the Ramblers defeated all those opponents in their first outings. What really made no sense was the 24-point loss at St.

Joe's. This occurred less than two weeks after Prep had completely routed the Marauders at home, a game which the Ramblers led 41-13 at halftime! These were the only two times Prep and St. Joe's competed in basketball, although they are regular opponents in football.

Rick Bordonaro controls the action against Jamestown.

- The Ramblers missed an opportunity to host powerful Pittsburgh Fifth Avenue (15-0) and its 6'6" junior superstar **Sam Clancy** because of the Pittsburgh School District's teachers' strike. The Archers won their only PIAA AAA state championship with a 53-42 victory over Norristown in the final. The state title clash was the last game ever for storied Fifth Avenue, which closed at the conclusion of the 1975-76 school year.

- Prep did not fare well at the other traditional downstate powers on its schedule. Uniontown (12-10), a squad that finished 27-1 in 1975 but did not make the playoffs in 1976, presented a 28-point, 22-rebound performance from **Mark Hozak** to crush the Ramblers. Johnstown (14-11) also took little time picking apart the Orange & Black. The Johnnies record was deceptive as some of their other losses were

Jim McCormick patiently awaits for another assist.

to good teams like DeMatha, Reading, Harrisburg, Farrell and Schenley, 59-52, in first round playoff action. The Ramblers were also blown out by District 6 champion Altoona (19-10). The Mountain Lions, a graduation-depleted squad, nevertheless made it to the PIAA Western Semifinals, but were completely outclassed in an 80-59 rout by eventual state champ Fifth Avenue. It was still admirable that the Prep brass scheduled such tough road contests, a strategy that was certain to pay future dividends. Gone from the schedule were the teams like Venango Christian, Kennedy Christian, Elk County Christian, etc.

- Prep broke a seven-game losing streak in the season finale against Tech (11-11), the only contest in which the Ramblers were able to avenge an earlier defeat.

- Prep did not play Dunkirk again until the 1982-83 Jamestown Holiday Tournament, the Ramblers and Marauders also meeting in 1947 and 1963. Dunkirk finished as the #19 ranked team in the state of New York.

- The final standings in City Series and Section One basketball leagues were as follows:

	W	L		W	L
Vincent	7	1	Vincent	9	1
Tech	5	3	McDowell	7	3
East	3	5	Tech	5	5
Prep	3	5	Prep	4	6
Academy	2	6	East	3	7
			Academy	2	8

- Prep gave Triple Crown winner Strong Vincent (City, S-I and D-10) a pair of close scares. In the first matchup, the Ramblers scored the final nine points in the last two minutes only to fall short by one, 62-61. **Rick Bordonaro** tossed in a couple of buckets; **John Greulich** flipped in a technical and followed with an arching 25-foot bomb; and **Dave Cousart** drove the baseline after an SV turnover. Prep had one last chance in the thriller after the front end of a one-and-one was missed with 10 seconds left, but a jump shot at the buzzer rolled harmlessly off the rim. In game two the "Never Say Die" Ramblers again had a nine-point 4th quarter deficit, but fought back and had a chance to tie it with a minute remaining. An outside shot missed and Vincent froze the ball until **John Barnes** hammered in a drive with 12 seconds left for the 42-38 SV verdict. An ugly disturbance erupted seconds after the final buzzer, order finally being restored with no reported injuries.

Johnny Greulich started every game, averaged in double figures.

- After winning District 10, Vincent was soundly beaten by Monessen, 81-64, in first round PIAA play. A brawl erupted on the court in the closing minutes and several Edinboro policemen had to control the highly vocal partisan crowd. Monessen then lost to Schenley; Schenley lost to Farrell; and Farrell lost to Fifth Avenue, which on the next evening in Hershey collected the state crown.

- 1975-76 was the first season Prep was not engaged in some type of post-season playoff since 1942!

- 1975-76 was the first year the PIAA used classifications listed as "AAA", "AA" and "A", rather than previously denoted "A", "B" and "C". Early signs of political correctness??

- **Dave Cousart**, the James "Moe" Gross Award winner, was named First Team All-Section One by the *Erie Times-News*, while **Bill Bensur** was an Honorable Mention choice. Cousart scored 16 while representing the Ramblers in a high-scoring second City-County All-Star tilt played at McComb Fieldhouse, with the City stars winning, 102-70.

Dave Cousart, a rugged performer and First Team All-Section One honoree.

1976 All-Opponent Team:

> Avery Wilson, Buffalo St. Joe's
> John Downing, Buffalo St. Joe's [New York Jets team doctor]
> Bill Duerring, North Catholic
> Jerry Koch, North Catholic [Slippery Rock, Duquesne, football]
> Tim Daley, Warren
> Ken McCune, Warren
> John "Red" Barnes, Vincent
> Rick Federici, Vincent (2nd team, all-state) [Edinboro St.; Pirates Class AA baseball]
> Mickey Hintz, Vincent
> Tim Antolik, Vincent [Gannon, baseball]
> Dan Chojnacki, McDowell [Clarion St.]
> Brian Merz, McDowell
> Jamie Carson, Tech
> Willie Blanks, Tech
> Danny Brown, East [Mercyhurst]
> Bill Gausman, East
> Ricky Pullium, East
> Francis Spearman, Academy [Tennessee St.]
> Mark Hozak, Uniontown [Waynesburg, basketball & baseball]
> Mike Pratt, Uniontown [Washington & Jefferson]
> Herman Jones, Dunkirk [Buffalo St.]
> Roy Carter, Vincent
> Tom Baronner, McDowell [Lock Haven]
> Tom Pridgen, Johnstown [Saint Vincent College]
> Al Futrell, Altoona

Flaherty Elevates Ramblers to Statewide Prominence!

1976-77 (20-5)

Coach: William "Bill" Flaherty
Captains: Game captains
Managers: Lawrence Schaaf, Gery Nietupski

Coach Flaherty's 1976-77 Ramblers were his first to make a serious PIAA run.

Date	PREP			Dec.	Loc.	High Scorer	Opponent
11/26	76	Tonawanda (NY) Cardinal O'Hara	47	W	H	Bensur (19)	Denzel (16)
11/30	65	Bradford	47	W	H	Bensur (14)	Hannon (19)
12/1	60	Pittsburgh Brashear	67	L	H	Szumigale (14)	Kennedy (22)
12/10	76	East	52	W	N	Sculley (16)	Barnett (15)
12/14	77	Warren	74	W	A	Achille (23)	Daley (26)
12/17	63	Academy	65	L	N	Elwell (16)	Spearman (31)
12/21	59	Strong Vincent	52	W	N	Sculley (24)	Antolik (17)
12/23	95	Clearfield	59	W	A	Bensur (16)	McNamee (14)
12/28	77	Cleveland (OH) St. Joseph	66	W	A	Bensur (19)	Kellogg (17)
12/30	86	Youngstown (OH) Chaney	78	W	H	Paris (16)	Mihalik (21)
1/7	55	McDowell	62	L	N	Bensur (22)	D. Birchard (16)
1/11	59	Tech Memorial	53	W	N	Szumigale (15)	Hammond (25)
1/14	83	East	51	W	N	Bensur (22)	Carson (14)
1/21		Johnstown (POSTPONED—SNOW & TEMPERATURES)			A		
1/25	67	Academy	63	W	N	Bensur (22)	Spearman (14)
1/28		Buffalo (NY) Nichols (CANCELLED—SNOW & TEMPERATURES)			A		
2/4		Strong Vincent (POSTPONED—SNOW & TEMPERATURES)			N		
2/11	62	McDowell	43	W	N	Bensur (23)	D. Birchard (16)
2/12	92	Johnstown	71	W	H	Bensur (34)	Varga & Cummings (13)
2/19	72	Tech Memorial	51	W	N	Bensur (20)	Hammond (17)
2/22	67	Johnstown	68	L	A	Elwell & Sculley (18)	Hipp & Boykin (18)
2/26	87	Strong Vincent	59	W	N	Sculley (17)	Krause (12)
		SECTION ONE CHAMPIONSHIP PLAYOFF					
3/1	63	Academy	43	W	N	Sculley (20)	Stone (11)
		DISTRICT 10 PLAYOFFS					
3/3	62	Hickory	42	W	N	Bensur (18)	Laskowitz (14)
3/10	57	Academy	54	W	N	Sculley (20)	Spearman (18)
		P.I.A.A. INTERDISTRICT PLAYOFFS					
3/16	61	Baldwin	59	W	N	Bensur (18)	O'Keefe & Kachulis (18)
3/19	74	State College	63	W	N	Bensur & Elwell (17)	Dodds (39)
3/23	52	Fox Chapel	68	L	N	Sculley & Bensur (16)	Lyon (24)
	1747 (69.9)		**1457 (58.3)**				

Pos.	Player	Ht.	Prior School	Class	G (GS)	FG	FT	Total	PPG	Career
C	Bill Bensur (#50)	6'6"	Bl. Sacrament	Sr.	25(24)	166	66	398	15.9	627
F	Dan Sculley (#52)	6'5"	OLP	Jr.	25(25)	115	94	324	13.0	334
F	Kevin Elwell (#44)	6'3"	St. Andrew's	Sr.	24(22)	106	52	264	11.0	320
G	Danny Achille (#20)	5'10"	Sacred Heart	Jr.	25(20)	73	69	215	8.6	215
F	Jeff Szumigale (#32)	6'4"	OLC	Jr.	23(12)	73	16	162	7.0	162
F	Hank Bujalski (#42)	6'2"	Mt. Calvary	Jr.	16(4)	29	15	73	4.6	73
F	Andy Paris (#34)	6'4"	Bl. Sacrament	Sr.	18	31	10	72	4.0	85
G	Chuck Longo (#24)	5'8"	St. George's	Jr.	12(5)	28	12	68	5.7	68
G	Fran Mifsud (#22)	5'7"	St. Paul's	Sr.	21(6)	28	9	65	3.1	120
F	Dan DeDionisio (#40)	6'3"	St. Patrick's	Sr.	12(1)	8	14	30	2.5	42
G	Tim Brabender (#30)	5'11"	St. George's	Sr.	9	7	8	22	2.4	27
G	Barry Roach (#14)	5'8"	St. John's	Jr.	10	8	3	19	1.9	19
G	Tom Hesch (#10)	5'11"	Bl. Sacrament	Sr.	8(1)	4	6	14	1.8	55
F	Vic Benoit (#54)	6'2"	OLC	Jr.	7	3	5	11	1.6	11
G	Dave Kosobucki (#34)	5'11"	St. John's	Jr.	2	2	2	6	3.0	6
G	Kevin Hughes (#12)	5'11"	OLC	Jr.	4	2	0	4	1.0	4

HIGHLIGHTS:

- Coach **Bill Flaherty's** sixth season was an exciting gem, as Cathedral Prep regained City, Section One and District 10 championships; and further advanced to the Western Semifinals of the state tournament.

- PIAA inter-district play gave Prep brand new opponents in Baldwin, State College and Fox Chapel. Baldwin and Fox Chapel are located in suburban Pittsburgh, while State College is the town dominated by Penn State University.

- All City Series and Section One games were played at the Gannon Auditorium, while independent home contests against Bradford, Youngstown Chaney and Johnstown were held in the Prep gym. The opener against Cardinal O'Hara was the middle game of a high school tripleheader at Gannon. The D-10 and Baldwin playoff games were played at Edinboro's McComb Fieldhouse; the State College battle was played at Beaver County Community College in Monaca; and the Fox Chapel matchup was contested at Westminster College in New Wilmington.

Prep's 1977 District 10 Champions. Kneeling, L to R: Achille, Bujalski, Sculley, Bunsur, Longo, Smogorzewski; Standing: Szumigale, Brabender, Paris, DeDionisio, Hesch, Coach Flaherty, Hughes, Benoit, Kosobucki.

- Another new opponent was Cardinal O'Hara (1-16), a Franciscan-affiliated school located in the suburb of Tonawanda, just north of Buffalo, founded in 1961. When Bishop Gibbons High School closed in 1971, the Felician Sisters took over and COHS became co-educational. Enrollment reached a peak of 1,200 in the 1960's, but hovers around 265 currently. Cardinal O'Hara competes in Buffalo's Monsignor Martin Athletic Association and its leading scorer against Prep was **Michael "Ding" Denzel**, a St. Francis Acolyte and Silicon Valley whiz kid.

- Brashear High's (22-3) first basketball victory ever was over the 1976-77 Ramblers. Brashear was created to help with segregation issues in the Pittsburgh public schools. The Board of Education closed 1976 state champ Fifth Avenue High, South Hills High (actually did not close until 1986) and Gladstone High in Hazelwood and merged the students into a huge building in Beechview with 5000 students attending. The school opened with protesters from the Brookline and Beechview communities, as well as the Hill and Hazelwood. The school had mass media coverage, and school security and local police were on hand the first week of school in 1976 to quell expected disturbances. The first Brashear team won the Pittsburgh City League title and made it to the PIAA second round before losing to Beaver Falls, 57-46.

- Prep's win at Clearfield (11-13) was the first of two occasions the Ramblers and Bisons have competed. Prep also defeated Clearfield easily in the 1994-95 season.

- Prep's contest with Youngstown Chaney (11-10) was the start of a three-year series between the two. The Ramblers previously

Longo works against McDowell.

Bensur stretches out to stop Academy.

Elwell on the fast break.

Franny Mifsud works against McDowell's Tom Baronner.

battled with the Cowboys in 1961-62.

- The wretched winter weather of 1976-77 wreaked havoc on all athletic schedules in the Erie area. For instance, the Ramblers had a 17-day break between the Academy and McDowell battles because of necessary cancellations. One of the games cancelled was at rugged Buffalo Nichols School. The Vikings had several cancellations because of miserable weather in Buffalo as well, but nevertheless finished 15-1 with a final #11 ranking in New York State.

- The final standings in City Series and Section One basketball leagues were as follows:

	W	L		W	L
Prep	7	1	*Prep	9	2
Academy	6	2	Academy	8	3
Vincent	4	4	McDowell	6	4
East	2	6	Vincent	4	6
Tech	1	7	East	3	7
			Tech	1	9

won championship playoff

- The highlights of the season were the thrilling victories at Warren (11-9); over a strong Academy (19-7) team; the revenge win over rival McDowell (16-7); and the exciting state playoffs run. The Prep brand of basketball, as well as the wildly original Rambler student cheering section, dubbed "The Sixth Man," had Prep being noticed statewide.

- Prep's S-1 championship verdict over Academy was the eighth time in eight tries that Prep won the City Series or Section One title via the playoff route.

- Prep's impressive win against Johnstown (11-9), with **Bill Bensur** scoring 34, was the last time the Ramblers played a home game in the Prep gym. The Gannon and Mercyhurst sites, with an ability to accommodate many hundreds more fans, became the preferred options for home games. DuBois High was actually scheduled to meet the Ramblers in the Prep gym during the 1987-88 season, but the contest was cancelled because DuBois was unable to bus to Erie because of wintery weather conditions.

- Other highlights included the stellar scoring and rebounding of **Bill Bensur** and **Kevin Elwell**; and the emergence of juniors **Dan Sculley**, **Danny Achille** and **Jeff Szumigale**.

Bujalski surveys the situation.

- The dramatic postseason playoff run was highlighted with a record five wins, including the D-10 semifinal over Hickory (11-9). The Academy triumphs, including the D-10 final, were marked by some chippy play, though full scale brawls were barely avoided. **Hank Bujalski** netted a pair of free throws to forge a tie with 10 seconds left, and **Kevin Elwell** took a **Dan Achille** pass and scored on a reverse layup right at the buzzer in an amazing comeback victory over Baldwin (17-6). Next the Ramblers got off to a huge first quarter lead and held off State College (23-5) and its superstar **Chris Dodds**. The run ended with a convincing loss to Fox Chapel, leaving the Ramblers one game shy

Achille drives through.

of a PIAA Western Final game. The Foxes (29-1) next downed Steelton Highspire, 81-71, to capture its first and only state championship.

Bensur looks for an opening against the Trojans.

Sculley blocks a Johnny Toran shot.

Mifsud nails one against McDowell.

- Fox Chapel's **Stu Lyon** and Brashear's **Sam Clancy** (14 points, 11 rebounds) and **D. J. Kennedy** played for the Pennsylvania All-Stars in the 1977 Dapper Dan Roundball Classic, while Baldwin's **Regis O'Keefe** (10 points) and Brashear's **Warner Macklin** (14 points) played in the preliminary with the Western PA stars.

- **Bill Bensur** was named First Team All-Section One by the *Erie Times-News*, while **Dan Sculley** was a Second Team choice. **Kevin Elwell** and **Danny Achille** were Honorable Mention selections. Bensur (10 points) and Elwell (8 points) represented the Ramblers in the third annual City-County All-Star tilt played at McComb Fieldhouse, with the City stars winning under Coach Flaherty, 96-86.

- Bensur, winner of the James "Moe" Gross Award, went on to star at Westminster College; Elwell toiled at Gannon College; and **Tim Brabender** played on the freshmen team at the University of Dayton. **Franny Mifsud** went on to play football at Allegheny College.

- The McDonald's High School All-American designation began in 1977 with the selection of the inaugural team. The teams are sponsored by McDonald's, the fast-food chain, with proceeds from annual games going to local Ronald McDonald House programs. The McDonald's All-American teams eventually surpassed the Dapper Dan all-stars as the best-known of the high school basketball All-American teams. Having the designation of McDonald's All-American instantly brands a player as one of the top high-school players in the United States or Canada. Every college team to win the NCAA men's championship since 1978 has had at least one McDonald's All-American on its roster, except for the 2002 Maryland Terrapins.

1977 All-Opponent Team:

    D.J. "Puffy" Kennedy, Brashear [Cincinnati]

    Sam Clancy, Brashear (1st team all-state) [Pitt; NFL Seahawks, Browns & Colts]

    Warner Macklin, Brashear [Allegheny CC, Point Park]

    Tim Daley, Warren

    Jay Duell, Warren

    Francis Spearman, Academy [Tennessee St.]

    Clark Kellogg, Cleveland St. Joe's (1st team all-state, OH, 1978 & 1979; OH Player of the year, 1979; 1979 McDonald's HS All-American; 1979 Mr. Basketball USA) [Ohio St.; NBA Indiana Pacers]

    Tim Mihalik, Youngstown Chaney

    Doug Birchard, McDowell [Mercyhurst]

    Al Hammond, Tech [Fort Valley St.]

    Joe Boykin, Johnstown

    Bill Hipp, Johnstown [Allegheny Community College]

    Regis O'Keefe, Baldwin [Yale]

    Chris Dodds, State College (2nd team all-state) [Davidson, Clemson]

    Dave Damico, Fox Chapel [Washington & Jefferson]

    Stu Lyon, Fox Chapel (2nd team all-state) [Oregon, Georgia Tech]

"Zoom" attempts to block a Walter Stone shot.

All the Way to the Western Final!
Thrilling year for Great Rambler Team!

1977-78 (26-3)

Coach: William "Bill" Flaherty
Assistant: Dave Wenrick
Captains: Game captains
Managers: Gery Nietupski, Tim Gallagher,
   Dave Kruszewski

Coach Flaherty offers encouragement to his Ramblers.

Date	PREP			Dec.	Loc.	High Scorer	Opponent
11/26	84	Meadville	55	W	H	Sculley & Gore (14)	Nickerson (14)
11/29	60	Bradford	43	W	A	Sculley (16)	Brocious (10)
12/9	46	New Castle	53	L	A	Szumigale (17)	Hall (18)
12/10		Cleveland (OH) St. Joseph (CANCELLED—SNOW & TEMPERATURES)			H		
12/13	75	Pittsburgh Brashear	56	W	H	Sculley (41*)	Townsend (16)
12/16	58	Strong Vincent	43	W	N	Szumigale (14)	Krause (20)
12/17	2 (53)	Pittsburgh Schenley (FFT)	0 (59)	W	H	Sculley (15)	Thornton (15)
12/20	56	McDowell	58	L	N	Gore (14)	D. Birchard (18)
12/23	88	Youngstown (OH) Chaney	53	W	A	Szumigale (19)	Bartell (28)
		WARREN HOLIDAY BASKETBALL TOURNAMENT					
12/28	74	Philadelphia Northeast Catholic	51	W	N	Sculley (21)	Sears (17)
12/29	67	Washington (DC) Eastern	48	W	N	Szumigale (16)	Chesley (12)
1/3	74	Tech Memorial	32	W	N	Achille (14)	Palimore (8)
1/7	55	Academy	53 (OT)	W	N	Sculley (19)	Carter (18)
		SILVER FOX TOURNAMENT (McMASTER UNIVERSITY, HAMILTON, ONT.)					
1/13	75	Hamilton (ONT) Southmont	45	W	A	Szumigale (21)	Fuller & Kerr (8)
1/14	65	Toronto (ONT) Runnymede	42	W	N	Szumigale (14)	Schiraldi (12)
1/14	63	Toronto (ONT) Oakwood	54	W	N	Szumigale (17)	Outschoern (14)
1/17	77	East	65	W	N	Sculley (26)	Dawson (18)
1/20		Strong Vincent (POSTPONED—SNOW & TEMPERATURES)			N		
1/24	56	McDowell	53	W	N	Gore (18)	D. Birchard (15)
1/27		Tech Memorial (POSTPONED—SNOW & TEMPERATURES)			N		
2/3	65	Academy	53	W	N	Szumigale (23)	Stone (15)
2/4	69	Tech Memorial	42	W	N	Szumigale (16)	Blanks (12)
2/7	62	Strong Vincent	46	W	N	Achille (20)	Barron (12)
2/10	75	East	46	W	N	Sculley (18)	R. Carson (11)
2/11	84	Johnstown	56	W	H	Sculley (18)	Petry (12)
2/22	91	Brookfield (OH)	83	W	A	Sculley (30)	Shelley (21)
		DISTRICT 10 PLAYOFFS					
3/1	75	Warren	50	W	N	Sculley & Achille (22)	Mong (18)
3/4	53	Academy	46	W	N	Gore (14)	Carter (10)
		P.I.A.A. INTERDISTRICT PLAYOFFS					
3/8	51	Baldwin	37	W	N	Sculley (15)	Kachulis (10)
3/11	65	Pittsburgh South Hills	54	W	N	Sculley (21)	Bibbens (16)
3/14	65	Belle Vernon	55	W	N	Achille (17)	Parks (23)
3/16	66	Pittsburgh Schenley	67 (OT)	L	N	Achille (15)	Thornton (29)
	1949* (67.2)		**1493 (51.7)**				

Pos.	Player	Ht.	Prior School	Class	G (GS)	FG	FT	Total	PPG	Career
C	Dan Sculley (#52)	6'6"	OLP	Sr.	28(28)	190	91	471	16.8	805
F	Jeff Szumigale (#32)	6'4"	OLC	Sr.	29*(29*)	174	35	383	13.2	545
G	Danny Achille (#20)	6'0"	Sacred Heart	Sr.	29*(27)	127	69	323	11.1	538
F	Tim Gore (#44)	6'3"	St. Andrew's	Soph.	29*(14)	102	66	270	9.3	270
F	Hank Bujalski (#42)	6'3"	Mt. Calvary	Sr.	29*(22)	54	22	130	4.5	203
G	Barry Roach (#10)	5'8"	St. John's	Sr.	28(25)	42	24	108	3.9	127
G	Dave Kosobucki (#34)	6'0"	St. John's	Sr.	24	25	15	65	2.7	71
G	Tim Emling (#24)	6'1"	St. George's	Jr.	15	22	4	48	3.2	48
F	Vic Benoit (#54)	6'3"	OLC	Sr.	14	12	20	44	3.1	55
F	Gary Metzgar (#40)	6'0"	St. Luke's	Jr.	11	6	12	24	2.2	24
F	Mike May (#50)	6'3"	St. George's	Jr.	12	9	4	22	1.8	22
G	Kevin Hughes (#12)	5'11"	OLC	Sr.	10	6	4	16	1.6	20
G	Tim Nies (#4)	5'11"	St. John's	Jr.	7	3	5	11	1.6	11
G	Joe Nolan (#22)	5'8"	OLC	Jr.	7	4	2	10	1.4	10
G	Mark Fuhrman (#30)	6'0"	St. Andrew's	Jr.	7	4	1	9	1.3	9

HIGHLIGHTS:

- Coach **Bill Flaherty's** seventh season was spectacular, as Cathedral Prep won Section One and District 10 championships; and further advanced to the Western Final of the state tournament. Prep broke City of Erie all-time records for most victories in a season (26) and most games played (29). The Ramblers easily broke the school record for consecutive victories (21) as well as points scored (1949).

- All Section One games, the season opener against Meadville (nightcap of a triple-header) and the first Schenley game (later forfeited by the Spartans) were played at the Gannon Auditorium, while the Brashear and Johnstown home games were contested at Mercyhurst's Campus Center. The D-10 and Baldwin playoff games were played at Edinboro's McComb Fieldhouse; the South Hills battle was played at Westminster College; the Belle Vernon Western Semifinal was

Prep's 1978 Western Finalists. Front, L to R: Mgr. Nietupski, Roach, Mgr. Gallagher, Fuhrman, Mgr. Kruszweski; 2nd Row: Achille, Nolan, Kosobucki; 3rd Row: Metzgar, Hughes, Emling, Nies; 4th Row: C. Wenrick, C. Flaherty, May, Bujalski; Back: Szumigale, Gore, Sculley, Benoit, C. Hansen.

contested at St. Vincent College in Latrobe; and the Western Final against Schenley was played at Memorial Fieldhouse at IUP.

- The horrendous winter weather of 1977-78 wreaked havoc on all athletic schedules in the Erie area, similar as it did the year before. The Ramblers had to cancel what could have been a showcase game against Cleveland St. Joe's and its superstar, **Clark Kellogg**, later of Ohio State, NBA and TV commentator fame.

- Senior **Dan Sculley** broke **Paul Pry's** single game record (40 vs. Academy, 1968) with a whopping 41 points against Brashear on December 13 at the Mercyhurst Campus Center. This record lasted until 1991 when broken by **Jim Hamilton** with 42 against Chattanooga (TN) Brainerd.

- **Marty Bartell** of Youngstown Chaney (3-16) broke the all-time Prep opponent record by sinking 16 of 18 free throws in a losing effort. The previous record was held by Academy's **Pete Russo**, who sank 15 foul shots against Prep in 1954-55.

- Prep's re-entry in the Warren Holiday Tourney was successful, the Ramblers posting a pair of impressive victories. It was the first time Prep had ever played teams from Philadelphia and Washington (DC). At one point Northeast Catholic High School (10-9) had the largest student body of any Catholic boys school in the world (close to 5,000 students), and today it is known for having the largest number of all-male alumni of any high school in the world. Northeast Catholic's Class of 1956 alone had 1,103 graduates, making it the largest all-boys Catholic high school graduating class ever in the world. From its founding in 1926 until its closing in 2010, "North" won more Philadelphia Catholic League Championships in soccer (22), bowling (16), wrestling (13) and baseball (11) than any other Philadelphia Catholic high school. It also had 8 titles each in football, basketball and swimming.

- Northeast Catholic operated in the Northern Division of the Philadelphia Catholic League, which also included Bishop Kenrick, Father Judge, LaSalle College, Archbishop Ryan, Bishop McDevitt, Cardinal Dougherty, Bishop Egan and Archbishop Wood. The Southern Division included Roman Catholic, Monsignor Bonner, St. John Neumann (formerly Southeastern Catholic), Cardinal O'Hara, West Philadelphia Catholic, Archbishop Carroll, St, James and St. Joseph's Prep.

- Eastern is a DC public school located near old RFK Stadium. Prep's win over Eastern—nicknamed the "Ramblers"— on December 29 was Coach Flaherty's 100th victory as Prep boss.

- Prep's pair of victories on January 14 in Canada was not the first time the Ramblers won two games in one day. Back in 1926 Prep defeated Ripley (NY) and Falconer (NY) on March 6 at the Brocton (NY) Invitational Tournament; on January 15, 1929 Prep defeated Corry St. Ed's and an Alumni aggregation on the same day. **Dan Sculley** was named MVP of the 1978 Silver Fox Tourney, then in its 7th year, with scoring leader **Jeff Szumigale** and **Danny Achille** joining him on the all-tournament team. It was the first time Prep ever played teams from outside the country and the Ramblers were the first U.S.

Dan Sculley, one of Prep's all-time greats. He later starred at Gannon University.

Danny Achille, outstanding Rambler guard. He went on to star at Gannon University.

Jeff Szumigale hides his identity before a big bucket against Schenley.

scholastic team ever in the Silver Fox Tourney. The Silver Fox, one of the best and longest running basketball tournaments in Canada, held its 45th annual showcase in Hamilton during the 2015-16 season.

- Other highlights included the trio of wins over a tough Academy (20-7) squad with **Rob Carter, Gary Page** and 6'9" **Walter Stone**; and the always enjoyable triumph over an excellent McDowell (18-5) team which featured the **Birchard** brothers, **Doug** and **Steve**, and **"Chip" Knight**. Doug had 538 points for the season and finished his career as McDowell's all-time leading scorer with 1,101 points. The Trojans won their first meeting with the Ramblers by 2 on the neutral Gannon court, with Coach Flaherty noting to *Erie Daily Times* reporter **Jim LeCorchick** post-game: "It's tough to win on the road. You can take that any way you want!"

- 1977-78 was the first season when standings for the 57-year old City Series were not kept. Prep was entrenched as a PIAA member by this time, and officials simply opted to have the former Big Six (the city schools and McDowell) as the only league and simply go by its official name of Section One.

- The final standings in the Section One basketball league were as follows:

	W	L
Prep	9	1
*Academy	8	3
McDowell	7	4
Vincent	3	7
Tech	2	8
East	2	8

won playoff for second seed in D-10 Tourney

- The highlight of the season was the thrilling state playoffs run to the PIAA Western Final. It was the first time any Erie team had reached that level since Tech's great 1962-63 squad. Prep's "Sixth Man" cheering section was legendary by then, witness dozens of busloads of students and hundreds of Erieites following the Orange & Black. Overflow crowds were present at every playoff encounter and Prep defeated very solid teams with some legitimate stars to get to the Western Final, including Baldwin (16-8), South Hills (19-6) and Belle Vernon (26-5). Before those battles Prep waltzed to the D-10 title with wins over Warren (12-10) and Academy.

- South Hills coach **Bruce Weston** complained that his entire starting five fouled out because two officials that refereed the game were from Erie. Weston sent a letter to PIAA Executive Director **Charlie McCullough** objecting to what he felt was an unusual choice of referees. McCullough has yet to write back.

- A particularly annoying situation occurred at the Western Semifinal in Latrobe. Prep and Belle Vernon were scheduled as the second game of a doubleheader, the first a girls' semi between Franklin Regional and North Catholic. Game officials sold 5,000 tickets for the 2,500 seat fieldhouse, hoping the first game's fans would exit at the buzzer. They didn't leave—and 14 busloads of Prep students and fans, traveling over 3 hours to see the game, waited outside, hoping to get in. Side note: all the Belle Vernon fans (30 minute drive) were admitted to the already jam-packed gym. Finally the Prep fans were admitted and told to find any nook or cranny they could to stand. It was a truly upsetting situation, and only the unusually good behavior of the Erieites prevented a disaster from happening.

- Prep's loss to Schenley (27-3) in the Western Final goes down as one of the most heartbreaking in Rambler history. The Orange & Black came from 10 down in the 3rd quarter to forge a 6-point lead with two minutes left in the game, only to have the Spartans send the battle into overtime at 60 on a **Larry Anderson** jumper with four seconds left to play. Schenley took a 67-66 lead at 0:33 in OT, and Prep had one last chance. **Dan Achille** missed a 15-footer, but **Dan Sculley** collected a loose ball under the hoop with three seconds left, went up for the shot and was crushed by Schenley's 6'7" **Dave Thornton**. Unbelievably, the officials made no call—possibly the worst non-call in Rambler history.

- The famous non-call sent Schenley to the championship game in Hershey, where it defeated 6'11'" superstar **Sam Bowie** and his Lebanon Cedars in a classic thriller, 51-50. Policemen rimmed the court to prevent violence in the tension-filled title game, which erupted briefly in a 3rd quarter dust-up between Schenley's Thornton and Lebanon's Bowie. Schenley's state title was its fourth between 1966 and 1978.

- Schenley's **Jamie Smith** and Baldwin's **George Kachulis** both played for the Pennsylvania All-Stars in the 1978 Dapper Dan Classic, while Schenley's Thornton and Belle Vernon's **Tom Parks** (17 points, 8 rebounds) played for Keystone against California in the preliminary.

- **Jeff Szumigale, Danny Achille, Hank Bujalski** and **Tim Gore** all set Prep records for most games played in a season, while Szumigale broke the record for most games starting in a season. "Zoom" was a great shooter and rebounder; Achille a very scrappy guard; Bujalski a steady performer; and Gore one of the best sophomores in the state. The unsung hero of the Ramblers was guard **Barry Roach**—all he did was handle the ball, dish out assists, play great defense, take charges and do the little things that made the 1977-78 Ramblers great.

Barry Roach, working hard for a rebound.

- The Rambler basketball Class of 1978 consisted of nine seniors: Sculley, Achille, Szumigale, Bujalski, Roach, **Dave Kosobucki, Vic Benoit, Chuck Longo** and **Kevin Hughes**. They capped a glossy four years of basketball with records of 21-2 as freshmen; 17-1 as JV's; and 20-5 and 26-3 on the varsity.

- **Dan Sculley** (unanimous), **Danny Achille** and **Jeff Szumigale** were named First Team All-Section One by the *Erie Morning News*, while **Barry Roach** was an Honorable Mention selection. Sculley, Achille and Szumigale represented the Ramblers in the fourth annual City-County All-Star tilt played at McComb Fieldhouse, with the City stars defeating the County, 93-71. Szumigale led all scorers with 20 points and was named MVP, while Sculley chipped in with 15 and Achille 8.

- Sculley finished his Rambler career as Prep's 2nd all-time leading career scorer, only behind **Willis "Puck" Cardot** (1089, 1968-71). He was also third on the single season chart (471), again only behind Cardot (549 & 483). Rebounds statistics were not reliable in this era, but it's a safe bet to say Sculley averaged about 15 per game. Sculley also won the James "Moe" Gross Award, signifying him as Prep's most valuable player.

- **Dan Sculley** then became only the third Prepster ever given all-state honors in basketball. The classy 6'6" center was named Second Team All-State by the *United Press International* (*UPI*) and Third Team All-State by the *Associated Press*. Both **Paul Pry** and **Rick Fessler** in 1968 were accorded honorable mention honors: Pry by the *AP* and Fessler by the *UPI*.

- **Dan Sculley** played first at Bucknell, then along with **Danny Achille** went on to star at Gannon College. **Jeff Szumigale** went on to star at Clarion State, where he was a teammate of now-famous University of Kentucky coach **John Calipari**.

- **Barry Roach** coached the Prep freshmen team to a 20-1 record and the Metro League championship in 1999-2000 and a 19-3 chart in 2005-06.

Barry Roach did all the little things that made the Ramblers click.

- Cathedral Prep's old war horse, **Anthony "Tony" Zambroski** '48, was named athletic director in 1977. "Zambo" was the former star athlete on Prep's football (all-city guard), wrestling (first Rambler to ever win an individual match) and track teams. A four-year varsity player at Notre Dame, he started at tackle under **Frank Leahy** and was a member of the Irish' 1949 national championship team. Zambroski returned to Prep in 1953 to teach and coach and did not retire from Prep until 1992, after 39 years of service. "Zambo" was the highly esteemed head football coach for five years (city titles in 1968 and 1970) and the head wrestling coach from 1956 to 1969 (state champs, 1964). "Mr. Z" served as AD with and until **Ron Sertz** took the title of Director of Athletic Operations in 1982. Zambroski was accorded the honorary title of AD Emeritus in 1988. Prep continues to honor him with the "Anthony J. Zambroski Legend Award," given to the alumnus of the year; and more recently with the "Coach Tony Zambroski Award," which will be given annually to the Rambler football player who best exemplifies the spirit, courage and honor of "Mr. Z." A campaign to have the award inaugurated was spearheaded by Prep grads **Ed Schneider** '71 and **Jim Gervase** '71, and first given to Rambler linebacker **Jake Galla** '15.

1978 All-Opponent Team:

> Glenn Hall, New Castle
> Billy Krause, Vincent
> David Thornton, Schenley (3rd team all-state)
>   [George Washington]
> Larry "Bread" Anderson, Schenley (1st team all-state)
>   [UNLV]

Doug Birchard, McDowell [Mercyhurst]

Steve Birchard, McDowell

Marty Bartell, Youngstown Chaney

Chris Sears, Philadelphia North Catholic

Rob Carter, Academy [Youngstown St.]

Andre Dawson, East

Walter Stone, Academy [Arizona St.]

Pat Barron, Vincent

Ray Shelley, Brookfield

Harold Mong, Warren [Alliance]

George Kachulis, Baldwin (2nd team all-state)
    [Bucknell, Westminster]

Cleveland "Shang" Bibbens, South Hills
    [Michigan State, Southern Illinois]

Tom Parks, Belle Vernon (1st team all-state)
    [Robert Morris]

Calvin Kane, Schenley [Lamar]

Jamie "Snuffy" Smith, Schenley [Wisconsin]

1978's seniors had a four-year record of 84-11. Front, L to R: Roach, Kosobucki, Longo, Achille; Back: Hughes, Benoit, Sculley, Szumigale, Bujalski.

D-10 Champs, Great State Run!

1978-79 (23-5)

Coach: William "Bill" Flaherty
Assistant: Dave Wenrick
Captains: Game captains
Managers: Richard Schodt, Guido Bucci, Dave Kruszewski

The Prep brain trust drawing plans for the next victory. L to R: coaches Flaherty, Hansen, Wenrick.

Date	PREP			Dec.	Loc.	High Scorer	Opponent
11/25	80	Youngstown (OH) Chaney	51	W	H	Gore (25)	Ford (14)
11/28	73	Bradford	45	W	H	Emling (14)	Naughton (15)
12/1	75	Punxsutawney	65	W	A	Emling (22)	Kopas (32)
12/2	55	Youngstown (OH) North	43	W	H	Gore (22)	Copeland & Haynes (13)
12/8	56	New Castle	64	L	A	Gore (15)	Hall (20)
12/12	66	Hickory	57	W	A	Gore (16)	Ogden (30)
12/15	46	Strong Vincent	65	L	N	Gore (14)	Barron (26)
12/16	61	Pittsburgh Brashear	57	W	H	May (15)	Townsend (20)
12/19	64	McDowell	63	W	N	Gore (18)	Shoskin (20)
12/22	51	Tech Memorial	48	W	N	Kaminsky (18)	Grafius (13)
		WARREN HOLIDAY BASKETBALL TOURNAMENT					
12/28	73	Churchill	58	W	N	Gore (18)	Brown (24)
12/29	71	Warren	48	W	A	Emling (17)	Mong (14)
1/2	46	Academy	41	W	N	Gore (21)	Stone (21)
1/9	49	Youngstown (OH) North	46	W	A	Emling (18)	Haynes (18)
1/12	61	East	47	W	N	Gore (17)	Young (15)
1/16	44	Strong Vincent	56	L	N	May (21)	Barron & McCallum (19)
1/19	46	McDowell	45	W	N	Gore (18)	Feick (14)
1/23	54	Tech Memorial	52	W	N	Gore (20)	Grafius (19)
1/30	55	Pittsburgh Peabody	45	W	A	Gore (16)	Upshaw (16)
2/2	54	Academy	58(OT)	L	N	Gore & May (15)	Stone (19)
2/9	72	East	49	W	N	Gore (16)	K. Johnson (15)
2/14	51	Johnstown	34	W	A	Gore (13)	Boykin (13)
		SECTION ONE PLAYOFF FOR SECOND PLACE					
2/20	55	Academy	48	W	N	Gore (20)	Stone (20)
		DISTRICT 10 PLAYOFFS					
2/28	49	Meadville	35	W	N	Gore (22)	McClure (13)
3/10	54	Strong Vincent	44	W	N	May (14)	Barron (14)
		P.I.A.A. INTERDISTRICT PLAYOFFS					
3/14	57	Indiana	49	W	N	Gore (19)	Milner (22)
3/17	56	Punxsutawney	42	W	N	Gore (22)	Kopas (18)
3/20	43	Beaver Falls	50	L	N	Gore (14)	Bryant (15)
	1617 (57.8)		**1405 (50.2)**				

Pos.	Player	Ht.	Prior School	Class	G (GS)	FG	FT	Total	PPG	Career
F	Tim Gore (#44)	6'5"	St. Andrew's	Jr.	28(28)	179	96	454	16.2	724
G	Tim Emling (#22)	6'2"	St. George's	Sr.	28(28)	111	45	267	9.5	315
C	Mike May (#42)	6'4"	St. George's	Sr.	28(28)	88	72	248	8.9	270
G	Andy Sisinni (#5)	6'1"	St. George's	Jr.	27(20)	65	56	186	6.9	186
C	Jim Roseto (#40)	6'4"	OLC	Jr.	15(3)	35	16	86	5.7	86
G	Tim Nies (#21)	6'0"	St. John's	Sr.	23(18)	33	19	85	3.7	96
F	Gary Metzgar (#52)	6'1"	St. Luke's	Sr.	19(9)	37	6	80	4.2	104
G	Jerry Kaminsky (#20)	6'0"	St. Peter's	Jr.	16(1)	31	15	77	4.8	77
G	Bob "Bo" Stevenson (#41)	6'1"	St. John's	Jr.	18(6)	23	15	61	3.4	61
G	Joe Bizjak (#12)	5'9"	OLC	Jr.	12	8	4	20	1.7	20
F	Bob Van Volkenburg (#24)	6'2"	Sacred Heart	Jr.	9	6	3	15	1.7	15
G	Jeff Metzgar (#23)	5'10"	St. Luke's	Jr.	6	3	4	10	1.7	10
F	Mark Maruca (#34)	6'2"	OLP	Jr.	6	4	0	8	1.3	8
F	Mark Fatica (#50)	6'3"	OLC	Sr.	8	2	2	6	0.8	6
G	Doug Geiger (#32)	6'0"	OLC	Jr.	6	3	0	6	1.0	6
G	Tim Steenberge (#11)	6'0"	St. Luke's	Sr.	2	2	0	4	2.0	4

Prep's 1979 Distrct 10 Champs. Front, L to R: Mgr. Bucci, Nies, Bizjak, Maruca, Kaminsky, J. Metzgar, Geiger, Stevenson, Mgr. Schodt; Back: Coach Flaherty, Mgr. Kruszewski, G. Metzgar, Emling, Fatica, Gore, Roseto, May, Van Volkenburg, Sisinni, Coach Wenrick.

HIGHLIGHTS:

- An over-achieving Cathedral Prep squad, finishing but in a second place tie for the Section One's regular season, stormed to its fourth District 10 championship in five seasons, then won a pair of PIAA inter-district clashes before bowing to powerful WPIAL champ Beaver Falls in a Western Semifinal.

Tim Emling was a deadeye outside shooter.

- This defensive-minded Prep squad surrendered the fewest points per game (50.2) in a quarter-century, since the 1953-54 state championship season (45.6 PPG). It was no secret that coach **Bill Flaherty** was a protégé of the defensive style of Indiana University coach **Bobby Knight**. The Ramblers were also a patient team on offense, controlling the tempo of games with fine ball handling guards **Andy Sisinni**, a junior, and seniors **Tim Emling** and **Tim Nies**. Coach Flaherty developed

a well-balanced squad with a true star in junior **Tim Gore** and rugged senior inside operators **Mike May** and **Gary Metzgar**.

- All Section One games, including the second place playoff battle against Academy, were played at the Gannon Auditorium, while the Bradford and Brashear home games were contested at Mercyhurst's Campus Center. The D-10, Indiana, Punxsutawney and Beaver Falls playoff games were all played at Edinboro's McComb

Timmy Nies, Prep's dependable starting guard.

Fieldhouse. The Prep-Beaver Falls clash was moved to Edinboro from Indiana because the PIAA felt that playing both that game and the Schenley-Valley battle the same night would have presented "attendance problems," similar to what happened the year before because of insufficient seating. Beaver Falls coach **Frank Chan** was fuming at the selection of Edinboro for the site, not even trying to disguise his anger to the *Beaver County Times*: "It is really unfair to make us go all the way up there when it's like a home court to Erie Prep." Chan was mad enough to drag out a map and ruler and note that Edinboro was 82 miles from Beaver Falls, but only 16 miles from Erie. "We have to travel two hours and that takes a lot out of the kids," Chan said.

- Prep's opening game win over Youngstown Chaney (2-16) was the last time the two competed, with the Ramblers taking three of the four games played. Chaney, which recently was one of only two traditional high schools left in the declining "Steel City," was changed to a vocal performing arts school in 2011. Chaney no longer sponsors athletics. The Chaney Cowboys produced many college and NFL standouts, including **Michael Zordich, Matt Cavanaugh, Jerry Olsavsky, Anthony Floyd, Brad Smith, Keilen Dykes** and particularly 1942 Heisman Trophy winner **Frank Sinkwich**, who also coached the old Erie Vets pro football team in the late 1940's.

- Chaney and a new Prep opponent, Youngstown North (13-8), which the Ramblers hung two losses on, were still part of the Youngstown City Series at the time, which also included East, Rayen, South and Wilson. Catholic schools Cardinal Mooney and Ursuline bolted for the Steel Valley Conference following the 1969-70 school year.

- **Terry Ogden**, who scored 30 in a loss to Prep, retired as Hickory's (8-16) all-time leading scorer with 1,361 points. The Hornets did not fare well in the D-10 playoffs, losing to Vincent, 77-56, and Meadville, 87-69.

- Prep looked impressive winning the Warren Holiday Tourney, with easy victories over Chuchill (5-17) and Warren (11-12). Churchill, which derived its name from the Beulah Church *on the hill*, was only open from 1963 through 1987 and Churchill students are now served by the Woodland Hills School District. The Chargers operated in WPIAL Section 5, along with champion Burrell, Wilkinsburg, Gateway, Penn Hills, Plum, Franklin Regional and Kiski Area.

- Prep's win against Pittsburgh Peabody (11-10) was the start of a six-year series against the Highlanders. Peabody, which opened in 1911, was located in the east Liberty section of Pittsburgh. The Pittsburgh school board voted to close the school and graduate its final class in 2011. Some of Peabody's honored graduates include actor/comedians **Frank Gorshin, Charles Grodin** and **Fritz Weaver**; actor/dancer **Gene Kelly**; former Cleveland Browns receiver **Dave Logan**; and *Pittsburgh Post-Gazette* sportswriter **Bob Smizik**.

- Last place Tech Memorial (6-16) nevertheless gave Prep a duo of tough ballgames. **Jerry Kaminsky** came off the bench to score 18 points in the three-point Rambler win, while **Tim Gore** and **Bob Stevenson** scored the big buckets in the two-point rematch Prep victory.

Tim Gore enjoys Andy Sisinni's future prediction.

- More thrills came with Prep's pair of nip-and-tuck one-point victories over rival McDowell (16-8). **Jim Roseto** hit the winning foul shot in the first battle, while two **Andy Sisinni** pressure free throws with 7 seconds remaining enabled the Ramblers to come from 7 points down in the final 5 minutes in the rematch. Prep was also the beneficiary of a late-season, overtime triumph by the Trojans over Academy, which allowed the Ramblers to tie for second place in S-I and keep their playoff hopes alive.

Sisinni drives for two against Academy before a jam-packed Gannon Audi crowd.

- Prep had to defeat the tough Academy (16-8) squad, with its all-section players **Scott Palimore** and 6'10" **Walter Stone**, in a playoff for second place in Section One just to earn a spot in the D-10 format. Prep's verdict over Academy was the tenth time in ten tries that Prep had won a post-season playoff in City Series or Section One competition. In the first Prep-Academy game earlier in the season, a thrilling but crucial 5-point win for the Ramblers, a fight broke out on the floor with 34 seconds remaining that nearly escalated into a full-scale brawl. **Tim Gore** and Stone battled on even terms in that one, while **Andy Sisinni** made some clutch free throws down the stretch. Game two was a pulsating overtime win for the Lions before a roaring packed house at the Audi.

- The final standings in the close Section One basketball league were as follows:

	W	L
Vincent	8	2
*Prep	8	3
Academy	7	4
McDowell	5	5
East	2	8
Tech	1	9

won playoff for second seed in D-10 Tourney

- Prep opened District 10 play with a methodical handling of Section Two titlist Meadville (13-10). **Tim Gore** was the big noise, scoring 22 points and grabbing 19 rebounds, while **Jim Roseto**, hampered most of the season with a knee injury, tallied 9 points off the bench.

- The D-10 upset final over Strong Vincent (20-5) was particularly gratifying for Prep, as the Section One champion Colonels had twice handily bounced the Ramblers during the regular season. Prep employed a 1-2-2 zone defense to stymie SV stars **Pat Barron, John Corkan** and **Henry McCullum** before 4,200 fans in that one. Vincent upset the WPIAL's number two seed Burrell,

All-Section One junior Tim Gore banks one in from middle at Pittsburgh Peabody. Gore was the first underclassman to win the coveted "Moe" Gross Award.

68-58, in first round PIAA play before running into the Schenley (26-2) freight train, losing a 66-63 Western Quarterfinal to the defending state champs.

- Prep opened PIAA inter-district play with a pair of impressive wins over Indiana (24-6) and District 9 champ Punxsutawney (23-7). The Indians had a 26 *PPG* scorer in **Stanford Webb**, but Gore denied him the ball, holding Webb to just 8 points and only two in the first three quarters. In the St. Patrick's Day battle against Punxy, Gore scored 22 points, while smooth-shooting **Tim Emling** cashed in with 14. On a sidenote, Punxy's **John "Sarge" Mizerock** still holds the Pennsylvania high school record for most assists in a season (344, 11.86 APG, 1978-79) and career (754, 10.19 APG, 1976-79).

- Beaver Falls' (29-2) stars **Dwight Collins** and **Damon Bryant** were then a bit too much for the young Prepsters to handle. But the playoff experience before 5,000 fans, including the incredibly noisy Rambler "Sixth Man," was certain to bode well for the very near future.

- The **Billy Varner** and **Gosby "Goose" Pryor** (inducted posthumously into Gannon's Hall of Fame in 1984) combo led Valley High School to stunning victories in its final three over defending state champ Schenley by 30, WPIAL titlist Beaver Falls and Allentown Allen, 72-66, to claim the 1979 PIAA Class AAA state crown.

- After a successful run of 14 years as a one-night gala, the 1979 Dapper Dan Roundball Classic gambled by changing its format to a two-night extravaganza with four teams vying for the championship: U. S. Mideast, U. S. Midwest, U. S. Southwest and Pennsylvania. Academy's **Walter Stone** was selected and scored a total of 16 points and gathered 8 rebounds for both games, a 97-92 loss to U. S. Southwest and a 109-95 loss to U. S. Midwest. Stone's teammates included Beaver Falls' **Damon Bryant**, Valley's **Billy Varner** and Schenley's **Larry Anderson** (46 points in 2 games), as well as luminary **Sam Bowie** from Lebanon. Stone was only the second Erieite to be so honored.

- **Tim Gore** became the first Rambler junior to win the James "Moe" Gross Award, given annually to Prep's best player. **Mike May** was given the 1979 "Ma" Kaiser Award as best all-around athlete, the first hoopster so honored since the Bengel twins in 1975.

- Junior star **Andy Sisinni** finally got around to having his arm checked post-season, only to find it had been broken since the Prep-Vincent D-10 final!

- **Tim Gore** was unanimously named First Team All-Section One by the *Erie Morning News*, while **Tim Emling** and **Mike May** were Honorable Mention selections. Emling and May represented Prep in the fifth annual City-County All-Star classic played at McComb Fieldhouse, with the City stars defeating the County, 78-66.

Mike May, tough customer, nice tux.

1979 All-Opponent Team:

Mike Kopas, Punxsutawney [Gannon]
Anthony Haynes, Youngstown North
Glen Hall, New Castle
Terry Ogden, Hickory
Pat Barron, Vincent
John Corkan, Vincent
Ricky Townsend, Brashear
Stu Shoskin, McDowell [Edinboro, track]
John Feick, McDowell
Tony Brown, Churchill
Harold Mong, Warren [Alliance]
Walter Stone, Academy [Arizona St.]
Darrell Grafius, Tech [Mercyhurst]
Greg Wells, Tech
Gary Page, Academy
Mark Milner, Indiana [Allegany (MD) CC]
Stanford Webb, Indiana [Kentucky Wesleyan]
John "Sarge" Mizerock, Punxsutawney
    [MLB Houston Astros, Atlanta Braves]
Damon Bryant, Beaver Falls (1st team all-state)
    [South Alabama]
Dwight Collins, Beaver Falls (2nd team all-state)
    [Pitt, football; NFL Minnesota Vikings]

Tim Gore with some tight defense on Vincent's John Corkan.

The 1980's

The jubilant Cathedral Prep Ramblers celebrate their first PIAA state championship (1980).

Erie's First PIAA State champs!

1979-**80** (33-1)

Coach: Bill Flaherty
Assistant: Dave Wenrick
Captains: Game captains
Managers: John Detisch, Richard Schodt,
Guido Bucci, Ken Bauer, Jeff O'Brien

Coach Flaherty proudly displays Erie's first PIAA championship trophy.

Date	PREP			Dec.	Loc.	High Scorer	Opponent
11/23	76	Plum	49	W	H	Gore (20)	Knapp (32)
11/27	61	Bradford	32	W	A	Roseto (16)	Woods & R. Smith (10)
12/1	72	Punxsutawney	39	W	H	Stevenson (14)	Levy (11)
12/4	59	Cleveland (OH) St. Joseph	47	W	H	Sisinni (14)	Dudley (14)
12/7	58	Academy	34	W	N	Gore (15)	Harden (11)
12/11	86	Hickory	46	W	H	Gore (24)	Weigle (20)
12/14	67	Strong Vincent	39	W	N	Roseto (20)	Hollis (8)
12/18	47	McDowell	45	W	N	Gore (16)	Feick (14)
		CHARTIERS VALLEY BASKETBALL CLASSIC					
12/22	80	Pittsburgh Oliver	30	W	N	Roseto (12)	Gist (10)
12/26	75	Clairton	52	W	N	Gore (23)	Moore (13)
		MEADVILLE ELKS HOLIDAY TOURNAMENT					
12/27	89	Meadville	44	W	A	Gore (17)	Allen (9)
12/28	75	Pittsburgh Schenley	55	W	N	Gore (24)	Halsel (19)
		CHARTIERS VALLEY BASKETBALL CLASSIC FINAL					
12/29	52	Ambridge	56	L	N	Gore (21)	Edwards (23)
1/2	67	Tech Memorial	29	W	N	Gore & Roseto (12)	Du.Jackson & Brown (8)
1/4	73	East	46	W	N	Gore & Roseto (17)	E. Jones (12)
1/8	76	Academy	42	W	N	Gore (24)	Harden (19)
1/12	90	Youngstown (OH) North	56	W	H	Gore (23)	Campbell (18)
1/15	86	Strong Vincent	31	W	N	Sisinni (17)	Blanks & Atkinson (7)
1/25	59	McDowell	48	W	N	Gore (28)	Shoskin & Feick (11)
1/26	67	Pittsburgh Peabody	49	W	H	Roseto (30)	Upshaw & Jackson (12)
2/1	41	State College	32	W	A	Gore (14)	Miller (10)
2/2	75	Williamsport	51	W	A	Gore (24)	Hance (18)
2/8	78	East	37	W	N	Gore (16)	E. Jones (9)
2/9	50	Susquehanna Township	47	W	N	Gore (16)	Dean (19)
2/14	70	Johnstown	47	W	H	Roseto (21)	Myers (22)
2/15	51	Tech Memorial	35	W	N	Sisinni (15)	Dv. Jackson (13)
		DISTRICT 10 PLAYOFFS					
2/25	67	Oil City	35	W	N	Roseto (19)	McGinnis & McCauley (6)
2/28	58	Hickory	37	W	N	Roseto (18)	Hampton (11)
3/8	66	McDowell	58	W	N	Gore (20)	Feick (17)
		P.I.A.A. INTERDISTRICT PLAYOFFS					
3/12	50	Indiana	42	W	N	Sisinni (18)	May (12)
3/15	85	West Mifflin North	58	W	N	Gore (25)	Kecman (23)
3/18	64	Beaver Falls	40	W	N	Gore (24)	Collins (16)
3/20	53	McDowell	43	W	N	Roseto (18)	Nesdore (12)
		P.I.A.A. CLASS AAA STATE CHAMPIONSHIP					
3/22	50	Allentown William Allen	40	W	N	Gore (23)	Lucien (10)
	2273* (66.9)		**1471 (43.3)**				

Pos.	Player	Ht.	Prior School	Class	G (GS)	FG	FT	Total	PPG	Career
F	Tim Gore (#44)	'5"	St. Andrew's	Sr.	33(32)	233*	115	581*	17.6	1305*
C	Jim Roseto (#40)	6'4"	OLC	Sr.	33(33)	190	76	456	13.8	542
G	Andy Sisinni (#5)	6'1"	St. George's	Sr.	34*(34*)	134	115	383	11.3	569
G	Bob "Bo" Stevenson (#41)	6'1"	St. John's	Sr.	33(3)	80	39	199	6.0	260
G	Jerry Kaminsky (#20)	6'0"	St. Peter's	Sr.	34*(34*)	67	32	166	4.9	243
G	Jeff Metzgar (#23)	5'10"	St. Luke's	Sr.	34*(34*)	45	28	118	3.5	128
C	Chuck Brower (#52)	6'9"	Spirit of Christ	Jr.	21	28	21	77	3.7	77
F	Bob Van Volkenburg (#24)	6'2"	Sacred Heart	Sr.	23	18	22	58	2.5	73
G	John Achille (#21)	6'0"	Sacred Heart	Jr.	19	15	12	42	2.2	42
G	Doug Geiger (#32)	6'0"	OLC	Sr.	21	15	7	37	1.8	43
F	Chris Fatica (#45)	6'2"	OLC	Jr.	20	12	12	36	1.8	36
G	Joe Bizjak (#22)	5'9"	OLC	Sr.	20	14	5	33	1.7	53
F	Joe Tarasovitch (#34)	6'0"	St. John's	Jr.	20	14	9	26	1.9	26
G	Pete Russo (#42)	6'0"	St. George's	Jr.	15	9	4	22	1.5	22
F	Jim Kaiser (#50)	6'0"	Spirit of Christ	Jr.	14	8	3	19	1.4	19
G	Mike Smith (#12)	6'0"	OLP	Jr.	15	4	1	9	0.6	9

Cathedral Prep's 1980 State Champions. Kneeling, L to R: managers Detisch, O'Brien, Schodt, Bauer, Bucci; Middle: coaches Flaherty, Hansen, Wenrick & custodian Norm Lizotte; Players: Kaiser, Smith, Tarasovitch, Kaminsky, Metzgar, Stevenson, Sisinni, Gore, Brower, Roseto, Van Volkenburg, Fatica, Geiger, Russo, Achille, Bizjack.

HIGHLIGHTS:

- **Bill Flaherty's** ninth year as Cathedral Prep mentor produced what is regarded as not only Prep's, but the City of Erie's greatest high school basketball team ever. The final record speaks for itself, and to this day the 1979-80 Ramblers still hold the record for most victories (33) and most games played in a season (34). Crowd support from the then state-famous "Sixth Man," Rambler alumni and other well-wishing Erieites was phenomenal in the Orange & Black run to the state crown. The Prep faithful's pre-game routine during the playoffs was deafening. First came the warmup with the "Two-Minute Spaz," when everybody cheered, waved their hands and went crazy for two minutes. Next came player introductions, when the entire student group turned its back to the court when opponents were announced and shouted "Who's he?!! Who cares?!!"

- Prep's starting lineup of **Tim Gore, Jim Roseto, Andy Sisinni, Jeff Metzgar** and **Jerry Kaminsky**, as well as super-sub sixth man **Bob "Bo" Stevenson**, had great chemistry and were the near-perfect lineup for Coach Flaherty's deliberate, defense oriented style of play. Others part of a fine senior cast included seventh man **Bob Van Volkensburg**, **Doug Geiger** and **Joe Bizjak**. The squad's only loss was to Ambridge by four, and that occurred on a *fourth consecutive night* of ballgames, a scheduling quandary that may have prevented this team from having a completely undefeated season.

- The Prep Ramblers won their first PIAA state basketball championship and fifth state crown overall with a thrilling 50-40 victory over Allentown William Allen (31-6, Allentown High School until 1960), a team that had also been in the 1979 title game. Senior **Tim Gore**, sensational throughout his entire Prep career, led the Ramblers over Allen in the AAA (large school) final with 23 points, 12 rebounds, 4 blocked shots, 3 steals and 3 assists before a crowd of 7,206 at Hersheypark Arena. Gore won the Most Valuable Player award for the tourney.

All-American Andy Sisinni about to sink a free throw in the state title game.

Hersheypark Arena, March 22, 1980. The largest crowd ever to attend a Prep basketball game.

Prep students rejoice as Tim Gore hits another jump shot in Hershey.

- Gore started the title bout against Allentown like a house afire, scoring 6 points as Prep went on a 10-0 burst at the outset. The Canaries closed to within 21-17 at the half, but the Ramblers pulled away behind guard Sisinni (11 points) and center Roseto (12 points, 10 rebounds) who combined for 21 points in the second half.

- Prep brought no less than 16 busloads of orange-clad supporters to Hershey. Hundreds more went by car. Before the game, Prep students sang the National Anthem with full-throated vigor, sounding like a massive chorus. During the game, four tuxedo-clad students led the Rambler cheers.

Prep boys showing their "Never Say Die" spirit in Hershey.

- Cathedral Prep was the first school from Erie ever to win a PIAA state basketball crown. East High made it to the final in 1926 and Strong Vincent did so in 1932. The Warriors bowed to Nanticoke, 44-25, while the Colonels lost to Old Forge, 24-19.

- This defensive-minded Prep squad, with its rugged man-to-man, surrendered the fewest points per game (43.3) for a Rambler team in 29 years, since the 1950-51 season (38.7 PPG).

- All Section One games and home games were played at the Gannon Auditorium, with the exception of the Hickory and Youngstown North home games that were contested at Mercyhurst's Campus Center. The D-10, Indiana, West Mifflin North and McDowell Western Final playoff games were all held at Edinboro's McComb Fieldhouse, while the Beaver Falls PIAA Western Semifinal was played before 3,500 fans at Chartiers Valley High School, the same venue where the Ramblers suffered their only defeat of the season.

Sisinni drives for two against Indiana.

A mob of well-wishers greet the victorious Ramblers on their return from Hershey.

- Prep had difficulty stopping high-scoring **Sean Knapp** in its otherwise easy opening game victory over the WPIAL's Plum (12-12). The Pennsylvania Turnpike runs through Plum Borough and golfers might recognize that Oakmont Country Club is wholly located within Plum's borders. The Ramblers and the Mustangs have played just one more time, that a 58-49 Prep victory in the 1998 opener.

- Prep crushed a solid Punxsutawney (18-7) team, the last time the Ramblers and Woodchucks ever competed. Prep holds a 4-0 ledger in the series.

- Prep opened the Chartiers Valley Basketball Classic with a 50-point breeze over Pittsburgh Oliver (0-23), the worst team, record-wise, the Ramblers ever played. Oliver, located in the Northside area of Pittsburgh, was closed as an active city high school for the 2012-13 school year as part of an approved facility reform plan adopted in 2011 by the Pittsburgh Board of Education. The staff and students were then relocated to Pittsburgh Perry Traditional High School.

Sisinni leaves behind a Meadville opponent at the Elks' Club Tourney, as Gore and Roseto position for a rebound.

- Prep followed in Chartiers with a route over eventual WPIAL Section 10 champion Clairton (23-7), which featured 6'8" sophomore center **Lloyd Moore**. It was the only time the Ramblers played the Bears, who made it to the 1980 PIAA Class AA Western Final. Clairton is a Monongahela River mill town with a thoroughly Pittsburgh attitude. Clairton was the setting for the 1979 movie *The Deer Hunter*, though the stateside scenes were actually filmed in Cleveland and Mingo Junction (OH). In recent years Clairton has been a Class A football power, winning a state record 66 consecutive games between 2009 and 2013.

- The Chartiers Valley Tourney was interrupted by the Meadville Elks Tourney, which Prep won with resounding victories over the host team and Pittsburgh Schenley (14-9). **Andy Sisinni** was named MVP of the Elks' Tourney. Then it was back to Chartiers four a fourth straight night of battles, including the Ramblers' only loss of the season. It was Ambridge (23-8) who stunned Prep to win the Chartiers Tourney, 56-52. The Bridgers held a 10-point halftime margin, but the Ramblers came back to take a 52-51 lead with two minutes left to play. Ambridge came on strong down the stretch, however, scoring the game's last five points for its triumph. **Tim Gore** and Sisinni both made the All-Tourney team. The Ramblers never had a chance to avenge that defeat until its exciting PIAA second round win over the Bridgers in 2015.

- Ambridge is an Ohio River town where steel and blast furnaces were a symbol of its strength. Its named was derived from the American Bridge Company, which bought the town called Harmony Society in 1901. Hollywood took cue in 1983 in a high school football movie called *All the Right Moves*, where the setting was a western Pennsylvania steel town called "Ampipe," for the "American Pipe Company."

- Rambler victim Youngstown North (11-12) lost its final seven games of the regular season, but rallied to win three Ohio state Class A (small school) playoff games before losing to Windham, 79-66, in the Bulldogs' final game ever. North, called Scienceville High School until 1945, was shuttered at the end of the 1979–1980 school year due to declining enrollment in a declining city. The Bulldogs, however, still hold the Ohio state record for consecutive losses in football—64, from 1957 to 1964!

- Prep's back-to-back games at State College (12-13) and Williamsport (11-16) were the first of five annual February weekend trips to mid-Pennsylvania where the Ramblers would

The 1980 Western Finalists McDowell Trojans. Front, L to R: DiBacco, G. Sweeting, Schauble, Hawley, Kuligowski, Tushak, Fiddler; Back: Bresslin, Birchard, Shoskin, Holland, Feick, Stroup, Merryman, Nesdore, S. Sweeting.

play the Little Lions on a Friday evening, then the Millionaires the next night. For four years following the State College-Williamsport series, Prep alternated at Johnstown and Altoona on the Saturday evenings after playing State College on the Friday night.

- One of Prep's great wins for the season was the verdict over Susquehanna Township (35-3), played at Waldo Tippin Gymnasium at Clarion University. The Indians won the 1980 PIAA Class AA State Championship, defeating Greensburg Central Catholic in the title game, 71-62. Susquehanna still holds the record for most games ever played in a season in Pennsylvania boys' high school basketball with its 38 games.

- One of Prep's all-time great wins was the Western Semifinal verdict over favored WPIAL champ Beaver Falls (26-4), which,

like Prep, was operating on an 18-game winning streak. The Tigers, expected to be a shoo-in for the Western crown, could not handle the Ramblers' full-court press or the boisterous Prep fans, and several times their frustration showed. Over two-thirds of Prep's 900 students (17 busloads) and another thousand Erieites were there. **Tim Gore** set the tone for the evening, blocking superstar **Dwight Collins** first shot of the game. Though down 24-20 at the half, three straight baskets by **Andy Sisinni** put the Ramblers ahead, 26-24, to stay. Prep's pressure defense completely befuddled the Tigers from there on as the Ramblers' rolled to a 44-16 advantage over the final 16 minutes. It was mostly unsung guards **Jeff Metzgar** and **Jerry Kaminsky** that did the defensive damage as Prep forced an amazing 30 turnovers, while Gore (24 points, 10 rebounds), **Jim Roseto** (20) and Sisinni (10) all scored in double figures. Downstate sportwriters, including those from the *Pittsburgh Press*, *Pittsburgh Post-Gazette*, and *Beaver County Times*, all opined the reason Prep blew BF away was because of an ankle injury to star Tiger guard **Forest "Bay" Grant** in the first half! BF coach **Frank Chan** felt the same way: "the difference between us winning and losing was Forest...we thought this was our year...that's the way life goes." Grant played briefly in the second half but had a bad limp and scored only six points with four assists and the Ramblers won handily, 64-40.

- **Dwight Collins** (16 points, 11 rebounds) took the loss the hardest of all the Beaver Falls players. After the game he collapsed on the floor in tears and had to be helped off the court by Coach Chan. Collins went to the Prep dressing area with his coach and again broke down in tears as he wished the

Father Dollinger beams as the state championship trophy is hoisted high at school upon the team's return.

Art teacher Jim Sabol greeted the student body with another of his great paintings.

Ramblers well. As Collins left the room the Prepsters gave him a sincere round of applause.

- To get to the matchup with Beaver Falls, Prep breezed to the District 10 title with victories over Oil City (8-15), Section Two titlist Hickory (19-9) and McDowell (27-5). This was followed by a pair of inter-district wins over Indiana (23-6) and West Mifflin North (24-4), both excellent fives.

- An amazing part of the season was that Prep was able to hang four losses on arch-rival McDowell—twice during the regular season, in the D-10 final and in the first time ever all-Erie Western Final. The 1979-80 Trojans were considered their finest team ever—27-1 if they did not have to play Prep! Star Trojans included **John Feick, Stu Shoskin, Bruce Nesdore, Bobby DiBacco** and **Greg Sweeting**.

- Prep's 10-point win over McDowell in the high-spirited Western Final before a throng of 4,200 in Edinboro was considered the biggest high school game ever on the local scene at the time. The Trojans were just coming off an impressive Western Semifinal win over Uniontown (28-4), 65-60, and hoping "the fourth time would be a charm." The classy Ramblers, led by Roseto's 18 points and Sisinni's 15, controlled the tempo, played great defense and frustrated the Trojans as they had done in the previous three meetings.

- The final standings in the Section One basketball league were as follows:

	W	L
Prep	10	0
McDowell	8	2
East	5	5
Academy	4	6
Tech	3	7
Vincent	0	10

- Gore led the Ramblers in rebounding with 315 (9.5 RPG), while Roseto was next with 256 (7.8 RPG) and Sisinni third with 177 (5.2 RPG). **Bob Stevenson** also chipped in with 102 rebounds (3.1 RPG).

- Prep received state, regional and national recognition for its outstanding season. Aside from being the first Catholic school to win Pennsylvania's large school state title, the Ramblers were ranked 2nd in the Mid-Atlantic Region by the *Philadelphia Enquirer* and 12th in the nation by *Basketball Weekly*.

- Consistently sensational **Tim Gore** broke Prep's single season (581) and career (1305) scoring records and was unanimously

Coach Flaherty instructs his boys before the opening tip in the state title game.

selected First Team Section One Dream Team by the *Erie Morning News*. He was then named First Team All-State by the *Associated Press* and the *United Press International*, the first Prepster to be so honored. Tim was further honored as a First Team Catholic Prep All-American. His single season scoring record remained until broken by **Jim Hamilton** in 1991 and his career record stood until four-year star **Jed Ryan** broke it in 1995.

- **Andy Sisinni** and **Jim Roseto** were also unanimously named First Team Section One Dream Team, while **Jeff Metzgar, Bob Stevenson** and **Jerry Kaminsky** were Honorable Mention selections. Sisinni was also given Honorable Mention status on the *Associated Press* All-State team and was named Second Team Catholic Prep All-American. Roseto was a Third Team Catholic Prep All-American choice.

- The **Jean** and **Bob Stevenson, Sr.** family certainly had an enjoyable 1979-80 basketball season watching their boys compete. Prep senior "**Bo" Stevenson** was, of course, the high-leaping, capable sixth man for the Ramblers' state champs; sophomore **Jack Stevenson** was a star on the Rambler junior varsity that finished 22-3 with a Metro League championship; and young 8th-grader **Jimmy Stevenson** was a top player for St. John's Grade School that finished 29-1 and won the Pennsylvania State Parochial Grade School title. The aggregate record for the year in this family of champions was 84-5.

8—LAKE SHORE VISITOR

Jim Stevenson   Bo Stevenson   Jack Stevenson

Stevenson family had enjoyable cage season

Bob and Jean Stevenson of St. John's Parish, Erie, were kept hopping this basketball season but they couldn't have been happier.

They had three sons — Bo, Jack and Jim — playing on teams and all they witnessed was two state championships and a junior varsity title. In all, the three Stevenson were involved in just five losses all season.

Bo, a senior at Prep, played on the Rambler edition that finished with a 33-1 record and became the first Erie team to ever win the PIAA AAA state crown.

Jack, a sophomore at Prep, was on the Rambler junior varsity that finished with a 22-3 record and a Metro League championship.

Jim, an eighth-grader at St. John's, was one of the top players on a state champion five that ended the season with a glossy 29-1 chart.

While Jack wasn't a member of a state championship team this season, he was part of all the fun at Prep, he enjoyed watching his younger brother win and he was a member of a the St. John's team that won state three years ago.

Said Jim, with a smile, "I guess we're just the family of champions.

"When Prep won the state championship two weeks before us, I just knew we had to win. I didn't want to be second to him."

The nifty shooter added, "I went down state with Jack's team when they won it and I've dreamed of winning it ever since."

Bo, a great leaper at 6-1, commented, "It was great being part of the state championship team at Prep because it meant so much to Erie. The people have been great and it also lets everyone in the state know there are some pleyers in Erie."

He also said, "Going to St. John's really helped. They have a great program and it helped me get ready to play basketball in high school."

Bo will be going to the University of Pittsburgh where he will probably play baseball. He has been a two-year starter for the Ramblers diamond squad.

While Bo will be moving on to college, Jack will be moving up to the Rambler varsity and Jim will be playing for the one of the Rambler underclass teams. He will also be joined there by most of his teammates from the St. John's powerhouse as Rambler rooters are already talking about another state championship team in a couple of years.

Jack and Jim also excell in baseball and continue to play that sport in the Erie Boys Baseball program.

While it was an exciting winter for the Stevensons - one they'll never forget - and a busy one, next year will be just as much fun. Win or lose.

- With the Orange & Black having so many individual stars, the annual James "Moe" Gross Award, which is traditionally given to Prep's best player, was awarded to the entire 1979-80 basketball team.

- Roseto represented Prep and was named MVP with 13 points at the sixth annual City-County All-Star classic, played at the Gannon Auditorium. The City stars defeated the County in a thriller, 67-66, under the guidance of Prep assistants **Dave Wenrick** and **Tom Hansen**. Gore and Sisinni were unavailable to play and Flaherty was unavailable to coach because all were participating in the Dapper Dan Classic in Pittsburgh the same evening.

- Sisinni scored 4 points and grabbed 2 rebounds in the Dapper Dan preliminary matchup for the victorious (93-91) Western PA all-stars, while Gore scored 6 points and had 4 rebounds for the Pennsylvania squad in the feature game, won by the United States, 89-87. Sisinni and Gore were the first Prepsters to be so honored at the prestigious Classic.

- Gore's teammates at the Dapper Dan Classic included Susquehanna's **Brian Dean** and Beaver Falls' **Dwight Collins** (13 points), while Sisinni teamed with Brashear's **Cleveland Bibbens** (23 points), who as a sophomore starred for South Hills against Prep in the 1978 PIAA playoffs. West Mifflin North's **Doug Kecman** played for the Western PA stars in the 1981 Classic preliminary and Clairton's **Lloyd Moore** (15 points) played in the 1982 feature game.

- A post-season exhibition matchup between the Russian Junior National Team and an Erie AAU squad made up of the Prep seniors and **John Feick** and **Bruce Nesdore** of McDowell was played before 2,800 enthusiastic fans at the old Erie County Field House on Route 97 on May 3, 1980. The Erie team, coached by **Bill Flaherty**, suffered from several weeks layoff and shot only 28% from the field in a losing effort, 83-61. The game was close with 5 minutes left to play, but the tall Russians dominated the tired Erie team for the remainder.

- **Jeff Metzgar** went on to star at John Carroll University, where he led the Blue Streaks in assists as a senior in 1984 at 3.4 APG.

- **Tim Gore** went on to letter four years at Michigan State under legendary coach **Jud Heathcote**, where he played with such stars as **Sam Vincent** and **Scott Skiles**. Gore was inducted into the Metro Erie Sports Hall of Fame in 2002 and the Cathedral Prep Athletic Hall of Fame in 2003.

Jeff Metzgar surveys the Allentown defense before making a key assist.

- **Andy Sisinni** was a four-year starter at Duquesne University under coaches **Mike Rice** and **Jim Satalin**. Sisinni was the winner of Duquesne's 1984 Sihugo Green Award, named in honor of the only two-time consensus All-American in Duquesne history (1955 and 1956) and presented annually to the top upperclassman on the Dukes' roster. Andy later became head basketball coach at Strong Vincent and at Prep (2001-2004), compiling a three-year Rambler record of 54-26 (.675).

Headmaster Father Dollinger proudly hands manager Jeff O'Brien a $10 check and thanks him for all his hard work during the past season.

- The entire 1980 Cathedral Prep basketball team was inducted into Cathedral Prep Athletic Hall of Fame at a banquet in 2008.
- Colorful manager **John Detisch** (now **Father John Detisch**) was inducted into the Cathedral Prep President's Hall of Fame in 2015. Father Detisch easily ranks as one of Prep's all-time notorious and greatest fans.

1980 All-Opponent Team:

Sean Knapp, Plum [IUP]

Lloyd Moore, Clairton (3rd team all-state, 1st team 1982) [Marquette, Rutgers]

Tom Edwards, Ambridge

Tim Campbell, Youngstown North

John Feick, McDowell (hm all-state)

Bruce Nesdore, McDowell (hm all-state) [Allegheny]

Stu Shoskin, McDowell [Edinboro, track]

Bobby DiBacco, McDowell

Mark Halsel, Schenley [Northeastern]

Brian Dean, Susquehanna (1st team all-state) [Penn State]

Doug Kecman, West Mifflin North [Cincinnati]

Forest "Bay" Grant, Beaver Falls (hm, all-state) [Robert Morris]

Ron Rowan, Beaver Falls [Notre Dame, St. John's, NBA Portland Trail Blazers]

Dwight Collins, Beaver Falls (2nd team all-state) [Pitt, football; NFL Minnesota Vikings]

Congratulations **Cathedral PREP** **PIAA STATE CHAMPS** *Roll on Ramblers!*

Tim Gore

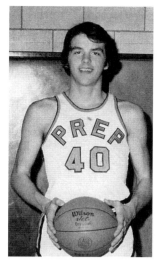

Jim Roseto

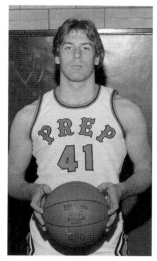

Bob Stevenson

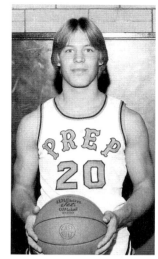

Jerry Kaminsky

Jeff Metzgar

Bob Van Volkenburg

Andy Sisinni

Section One Champs!

1980-81 (20-8)

Coach: Bill Flaherty
Assistant: Dave Wenrick
Captains: Game captains
Managers: Dave Lurty, Ken Bauer, Chris Spadacene

Father Dollinger pores over the demerit reports before deciding who is and who is not eligible.

Date	PREP			Dec.	Loc.	High Scorer	Opponent
11/21	72	Warren	35	W	A	Brower (20)	Bowen (14)
11/25	74	Bradford	49	W	A	Tarasovitch (17)	Woods (14)
11/28	43	Beaver Falls	53	L	H	Alberstadt (13)	Rowan (20)
12/2	69	Hickory	46	W	A	Brower (17)	Flowers (14)
12/5	74	Academy	56	W	N	Tarasovitch (21)	Blatt (18)
12/9	49	Pittsburgh Peabody	47	W	A	Alberstadt & Miller (10)	Benton (12)
12/12	56	Strong Vincent	51	W	N	Tarasovitch (12)	C. Hollis (17)
12/16	60	McDowell	46	W	N	Alberstadt (16)	Taylor (26)
12/20	49	Aliquippa	67	L	N	Tarasovitch (23)	Klenovich (24)
		MEADVILLE ELKS HOLIDAY INVITATIONAL					
12/29	60	Phoenixville	53	W	N	Alberstadt (14)	Gianpetro (15)
12/30	55	Gahanna (OH) Columbus Academy	59	L	N	Tarasovitch (13)	Richardson (29)
1/2	50	Tech Memorial	47	W	N	Alberstadt (16)	Graml (13)
1/6	65	East	43	W	N	Brower (24)	Lewis (9)
1/9	43	Academy	41(OT)	W	N	Brower (12)	Henderson (14)
1/13	73	Warren	44	W	H	Tarasovitch (21)	Bowen (23)
1/16	62	Strong Vincent	42	W	N	Fatica (12)	Billups (16)
1/17	59	Buffalo (NY) Canisius	54	W	A	Alberstadt (22)	Hokaj (22)
1/22	47	Altoona	48	L	A	Tarasovitch (17)	McGinnis (13)
1/30	50	McDowell	54	L	N	Alberstadt (12)	Taylor (25)
2/6	73	Tech Memorial	60	W	N	Tarasovitch (19)	UNREPORTED
2/13	65	State College	53	W	A	Achille (18)	Miller (20)
2/14	64	Williamsport	62	W	A	Achille & Alberstadt (15)	Lee (17)
2/20	67	East	62	W	N	Alberstadt (16)	Norton & Thompson (17)
2/21	46	Johnstown	44	W	A	Achille (13)	Pisarcik & C. Hall (15)
2/27	62	Buffalo (NY) Canisius	65	L	H	Hitt (20)	Merriweather (24)
		DISTRICT 10 PLAYOFFS					
3/10	38	Warren	68	L	N	Achille (12)	Bowen & Buerkle (23)
3/12	48	Meadville	39	W	N	Achille (16)	Sheridan (16)
		P.I.A.A. INTERDISTRICT PLAYOFF					
3/18	41	Uniontown	50	L	N	Alberstadt (12)	Gabriel (12)
	1541 (55.0)		**1374 (49.1)**				

Pos.	Player	Ht.	Prior School	Class	G (GS)	FG	FT	Total	PPG	Career
F	Joe Tarasovitch (#32)	6'0"	St. John's	Sr.	28(28)	126	55	311	11.1	337
F	John Alberstadt (#50)	6'4"	Bl. Sacrament	Jr.	28(26)	101	75	277	9.9	277
C	Chuck Brower (#52)	6'9"	Spirit of Christ	Sr.	23(19)	85	58	228	9.9	305
G	John Achille (#5)	6'0"	Sacred Heart	Sr.	26(24)	86	48	224	8.6	266
G	Pete Russo (#20)	6'0"	St. George's	Sr.	28(25)	67	32	166	5.9	188
G	Stacy Hitt (#21)	5'11"	Kanty Prep	Jr.	18(2)	50	20	120	6.7	120
F	Chris Fatica (#45)	6'3"	OLC	Sr.	24(12)	37	18	92	3.8	128
F	Doug Carter (#40)	6'3"	Wilson	Jr.	17(3)	26	5	57	3.4	57
F	Mark Zappia (#41)	6'3"	OLC	Jr.	15	20	13	53	3.5	53
F	Gary Miller (#42)	6'2"	St. Luke's	Jr.	14	13	6	32	2.3	32
G	Mike Smith (#22)	6'0"	OLP	Sr.	10(1)	6	1	13	1.3	22
G	Jack Stevenson (#23)	5'10"	St. John's	Jr.	6	4	1	9	1.5	6
G	Felix Orzechowski (#44)	6'0"	Holy Trinity	Jr.	6	4	1	9	1.5	6
G	John Schwab (#12)	5'10"	Girard St. John's	Jr.	5	3	2	8	1.6	8
F	Joe Corella (#34)	5'11"	St. Paul's	Jr.	5	2	2	6	1.2	6

Prep's 1981 Section One Champions. Kneeling, L to R: managers Lurty, Bauer, Spadacene; Middle: coaches Lesniewski, Hansen, Flaherty, Wenrick, custodian Norm Lizotte; Players: Hitt, Tarasovitch, Orzechowski, Corella, Smith, Fatica, Zappia, Brower, Carter, Alberstadt, Miller, Achille, Russo, Stevenson, Schwab.

HIGHLIGHTS:

- Cathedral Prep's defending PIAA state champions won the Section One title and looked poised to make a serious run in the state playoffs again, until a late-season slump derailed the Orange & Black. The Ramblers appeared to be on the right track with five straight wins after mid-season losses to Altoona and McDowell. Losses in 3 of the last 4, including the devastating blunder to Warren in the District 10 semifinal, gave what essentially was a great season, with another Section One championship, a very disappointing finish for a very good team.

- The 1980-81 school year brought many new faces to Prep, including star junior transfer **Stacey Hitt**. Hitt was a student at St. John Kanty Prep, which closed its doors forever in 1980. This alone brought about 100 new boys to Prep and this, combined with a larger freshmen class, skyrocketed Prep's enrollment from 885 to 1,013 in one short year.

- Senior **Joe Tarasovitch** and junior **Jack Stevenson** were both part of the 1977 St. John's grade school team that won the Pennsylvania CYO state championship.

- Defense was this Rambler edition's calling card, surrendering only 49.1 points per game.

- The season opener against Warren was part of a triple-header at Gannon Auditorium, while the Aliquippa contest was part of a unique triple-header played at Slippery Rock. All Section One games and Prep independent home games were played at the Gannon Auditorium, except the second Warren contest which was played at the Mercyhurst College Campus Center. The D-10 battles were played at Edinboro's McComb Fieldhouse, while the Uniontown game was played at Chartiers Valley.

- Remarkable for this squad was winning 8 of the 9 games not played at home or on neutral courts. This includes victories over fine teams like Bradford (22-7), Hickory (14-11), Peabody (Pittsburgh City League champion, 22-8), Canisius (Monsignor

Tarasovitch nails a picture-perfect jump shot. He was Prep's MVP.

Martin League champion, 20-3), State College (19-9), Williamsport (District 4 champion, 19-11) and Johnstown (15-11) fives, with the only loss by one point at District 6 champion and PIAA Western Finalist Altoona (23-9).

- Though unknown at the time, Prep's 49-47 win over Peabody on December 9 was the 750th victory in Rambler history. Prep's 62-42 victory over Strong Vincent (13-11) on January 16 was the 100th game between the two, with the Colonels winning 54 of the contests.

- Prep was 7-2 going into the Meadville Elks' Holiday Invitational, with its only losses to tough Beaver Falls (19-10) and WPIAL runner-up Aliquippa (28-4). The Tigers season ended when upset by Center in the WPIAL playoffs. The Quips were poised for a PIAA Western Final showdown with eventual state champ Uniontown, until they were derailed by Altoona in a Western Semifinal, 61-60, on a 45-foot half-court toss at the buzzer by Mountain Lion **Cory Gehret**, a shot considered the greatest in Altoona history.

- Though Prep lost in the final of the Meadville Elks' Tourney to Columbus Academy (27-1), **Chuck Brower**, **John Alberstadt**

and **Joe Tarasovitch** all made the All-Tourney team. Columbus Academy lost only to Kalida (also 27-1) in the Class A (small school) state final, 58-44, before 14,000 fans at St. John Arena at Ohio State University. **Kevin Richardson**, the Vikings' 6'5" first team all-stater, was MVP of the Meadville tourney.

- Prep's two battles with Canisius were the first time the two competed in 21 years. Canisius star **Larry Hokaj** was no less the son of **Ed Hokaj** '54, a former Prep gridiron star who was a First Team All-City center for the Ramblers in 1953! **Larry Hokaj** had a fine career at the University of Rochester and was later inducted into the Yellowjackets' Hall of Fame.

- McDowell's (21-7) win over Prep ended an 8-game Rambler win streak against the Trojans and also ended Prep's 19-game win skein in Section One competition. McDowell won the D-10 playoffs, beating Warren, 81-64, and made it to the Western Semifinal before getting bounced by state champ Uniontown.

- The final standings in the Section One basketball league were as follows:

	W	L
Prep	9	1
McDowell	7	3
East	6	4
Vincent	5	5
Tech	3	7
Academy	0	10

- The lowlight of the campaign was the shocking upset and embarrassing 30-point loss in the D-10 semifinal to Warren (16-11), particularly after Prep had crushed the Dragons by 37

Brower goes up strong against Beaver Falls.

and 29 points during the regular season. Though the Ramblers rebounded with a fine win over Meadville (15-11) in the consolation game, the loss to Warren caused Prep to be D-10's #3 seed, which meant a first round loss to the WPIAL's top seed and eventual state champion, Uniontown (32-2).

Leading scorer Joe Tarasovitch later became a highly-esteemed high school football coach.

- Prep actually played well against Uniontown and led 22-21 at the half on a **Joe Tarasovitch** jump shot at the buzzer. The Orange & Black were up by three entering the 4th quarter, but the Red Raiders reeled off five straight points to take a 36-34 lead. Another Tarasovitch jumper tied it at 36-all, but Prep never got the lead again. Four straight **Chuck Brower** free throws brought it to 42-40 with two minutes remaining, but Uniontown nailed eight straight freebies to seal the win. The Red Raiders went on to Hershey, where they defeated Springfield Delco in the PIAA State Final, 73-61.

Leading rebounder Chuck Brower went on to perform at Siena and Mercyhurst College.

- Beaver Falls' **Ron Rowan**, Peabody's **Darryl Shepard**, Aliquippa's **Dave Klenovich** and Uniontown's **Earl Minor** all played with the Pennsylvania All-Stars against the United States in the 1981 Dapper Dan Roundball Classic. Aliquippa's **Mark Banks** and Uniontown's **Greg Gabriel** played for the Western PA Stars in the Dapper Dan preliminary.

- While no Prepsters were named First Team S-1 Dream Team by the *Erie Times-News* (3rd place East had three 1st team choices!), junior **John Alberstadt** and seniors **Joe Tarasovitch, Chuck Brower** and **Pete Russo** were all Second Team selections. Senior **John Achille** was an Honorable Mention choice.

John Achille is now the highly successful head coach at Lampeter-Strasburg High School.

Tarasovitch, the "Moe" Gross Award winner, led all scorers with 15 in the 7th annual City-County Cage Classic as the City defeated the County, 72-52. Achille and Brower were other Rambler All-Stars in the contest.

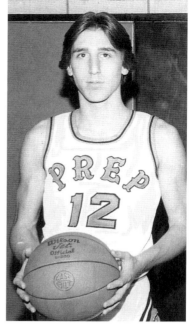

Starting gaurd Pete Russo was named second team All-Section One.

- **Chuck Brower** went on to perform at Siena and at Mercyhurst College, while **Joe Tarasovitch** later became the esteemed head football coach at Central, Ft. Le Boeuf and McDowell high schools.

- **John Achille** is the highly successful head coach at Lampeter-Strasburg High in southeastern Pennsylvania. In 12 seasons guiding the Pioneers, Achille has an overall record of 183-118. His fine 2015-16 squad finished 24-5 with a spot in the second round of the PIAA Class AAA state tournament.

- Spot starter and sixth man **Chris Fatica** was a consistent performer all season. A star first baseman on Prep's baseball team, Fatica was one of only three unanimous choices on the First Team All-Metro nine.

1981 All-Opponent Team:

Dave Woods, Bradford

James Benton, Peabody

Darryl Shepard, Peabody [Pitt]

Charles Hollis, Vincent

Tom Taylor, McDowell [Cheyney St., Edinboro]

Ron Rowan, Beaver Falls [Notre Dame, St. John's, NBA Portland Trail Blazers]

Carliss Jeter, Beaver Falls [UT-Chattanooga]

Dave Klenovich, Aliquippa [Youngstown St.]

Mark Lay, Aliquippa [Columbia]

Kevin Richardson, Columbus Academy (1st team all-state, OH) [William & Mary]

Chip Lewis, East [Mercyhurst]

Lawrence Hokaj, Canisius [Rochester]

Cory Gehret, Altoona

Lonnie Lee, Williamsport [Catawba]

Dave Pisarchik, Johnstown

Tony Merriweather, Canisius [Erie Community College]

Don Buerkle, Warren

John Bowen, Warren (1st team all-state) [Notre Dame, William & Mary, Gannon; Washington Generals]

Earl Minor, Uniontown

Greg Gabriel, Uniontown [Carnegie-Mellon]

Trojans Oust Ramblers from Top Spot!

1981-82 (19-10)

Coach: Bill Flaherty
Assistant: Dave Wenrick
Captains: Game captains
Managers: Mike Jefferys, Ron Cieslikowski, Steve Flaherty, Dave Beveridge

John Alberstadt scores two of his 25 in the big win over Johnstown.

Date	PREP			Dec.	Loc.	High Scorer	Opponent
11/20	63	Warren	56	W	H	Alberstadt (20)	Bowen (29)
11/24	60	Bradford	40	W	A	Stevenson (16)	Sexton (14)
11/27	53	Beaver Falls	57	L	A	Hitt (14)	Jeter (25)
12/1	76	Hickory	48	W	H	Miller (15)	Hampton & Kovach (10)
12/4		Tech Memorial (POSTPONED—TEACHER'S STRIKE)		N			
12/5	37	Hyattsville (MD) DeMatha Catholic	50	L	H	Hitt (12)	Alexander (17)
12/9	65	Pittsburgh Peabody	45	L	H	Alberstadt (16)	Hefflin (16)
12/11	51	Penn Hills	55	L	A	Alberstadt (14)	Knight (14)
12/12		Strong Vincent (POSTPONED—TEACHER'S STRIKE)		N			
12/15		McDowell (POSTPONED—ONE WEEK)		N			
12/18	37	Farrell	48	L	H	Alberstadt (20)	Phillips (14)
12/22		Academy (POSTPONED—TEACHER'S STRIKE)		N			
12/22	54	McDowell	51	W	N	Alberstadt (21)	Dowling & Taylor (17)
12/30	52	Altoona	53(OT)	L	A	Hitt (14)	O'Donald (15)
1/5	73	Sharon	59	W	A	Alberstadt (22)	Mansell (33)
1/8	63	Warren	56	W	A	Alberstadt (13)	Bowen (28)
1/9	76	Tech Memorial	46	W	N	Carter (24)	Rush (18)
1/12	65	East	38	W	N	Hitt (16)	Shirley (9)
1/15	86	Tech Memorial	47	W	N	Miller (18)	Menc (12)
1/19	72	Strong Vincent	45	W	N	Zappia (15)	Billups & Jones (12)
1/22	43	McDowell	49	W	N	Schwab & Hitt (13)	Lewis (13)
1/29	57	Strong Vincent	54	W	N	Hitt (16)	Horn & Jones (12)
2/5	68	State College	37	W	A	Alberstadt (11)	Yoder & Nelson (10)
2/6	56	Williamsport	65	L	A	Hitt (18)	Lee (18)
2/9	49	McDowell	62	L	N	Stevenson (12)	Dowling (25)
2/12	66	Academy	46	W	N	Alberstadt (18)	M. Williams (11)
2/16	61	Youngstown (OH) Rayen	54	W	H	Miller (21)	McClendon (20)
2/20	77	Johnstown	65	W	H	Alberstadt (25)	Walker (16)
2/23	70	East	48	W	N	Miller (26)	Salter (13)
2/26	71	Academy	44	W	N	Alberstadt (21)	Drayer (19)
	DISTRICT 10 PLAYOFFS						
3/9	58	Warren	64	L	N	Stevenson (16)	Bowen (33)
3/11	76	Meadville	68	W	N	Hitt (20)	Parry (25)
	P.I.A.A. INTERDISTRICT PLAYOFF						
3/17	51	New Castle	55	L	N	Miller (16)	Bruce (20)
	1735 (59.8)		**1505 (51.9)**				

Pos.	Player	Ht.	Prior School	Class	G (GS)	FG	FT	Total	PPG	Career
F	John Alberstadt (#50)	6'4"	Bl. Sacrament	Sr.	28(28)	139	85	363	13.0	640
G	Stacy Hitt (#21)	5'11"	Kanty Prep	Sr.	29(29)	130	61	321	11.1	441
F	Gary Miller (#42)	6'3"	St. Luke's	Sr.	29(29)	120	64	304	10.5	336
G	Jack Stevenson (#20)	5'11"	St. John's	Sr.	29(11)	74	23	171	5.9	177
F	Doug Carter (#40)	6'3"	Wilson	Sr.	24(5)	51	36	138	5.8	195
C	Mark Zappia (#41)	6'4"	OLC	Sr.	22(14)	54	23	131	5.7	184
G	John Schwab (#5)	5'11"	Girard St. John's	Sr.	24(16)	44	29	117	4.9	125
G	Felix Orzechowski (#24)	6'0"	Holy Trinity	Sr.	25(13)	38	13	89	3.6	95
F	Shawn Dombrowski (#52)	5'11"	Bl. Sacrament	Jr.	23	22	40	84	3.7	84
F	Jim Schaaf (#45)	6'3"	St. Joseph's	Jr.	9	9	11	29	3.2	29
F	Joe Corella (#32)	6'0"	St. Paul's	Sr.	14	8	1	17	1.2	23
C	Jody Jefferson (#34)	6'5"	OLC	Sr.	7	5	2	12	1.7	12
F	Kevin Gallagher (#22)	6'1"	OLC	Jr.	7	2	3	7	1.0	7
G	Jon Russo (#12)	6'1"	St. George's	Jr.	6	0	0	0	0.0	0
F	Dana Stewart (#23)	5'10"	St. Peter's	Jr.	6	0	0	0	0.0	0

The 1982 Prep Ramblers. Front, L to R: Mgr. Jefferys, Stewart, Orzechowski, Stevenson, Schwab, Russo, Hitt, Corella, Mgr. Cieslikowski, Custodian Lizotte; Back: Coach Flaherty, Mgr. Flaherty, Gallagher, Dombrowski, Schaaf, Alberstadt, Jefferson, Zappia, Miller, Carter, Mgr. Beveridge, Asst. Coach Wenrick.

HIGHLIGHTS:

- **Bill Flaherty's** 11th season at the helm of Cathedral Prep basketball showed another successful campaign, though a disappointing one in certain respects. The senior-laden Ramblers had impressive early season victories over eventual PIAA Western Semifinalist McDowell and over Section Two champion Warren twice and further had a 9-game mid-season winning streak. A first round District 10 upset by that same Warren squad led to a disappointing finish in PIAA play.

- Prep presented a well-balanced offense with top scorers **John Alberstadt, Stacy Hitt** and **Gary Miller**; and fine contributions from role players **Jack Stevenson, John Schwab, Mark Zappia, Doug Carter** and **Felix Orzechowski** (all seniors); and junior **Shawn Dombrowski.**

- Several Prep "home" games were played at Mercyhurst College's Campus Center, including the Hickory, Peabody,

Farrell, Rayen and Johnstown contests. The season opener against Warren was part of a triple-header at the Gannon Auditorium, where all the Section One games were played as well. For years the Gannon Auditorium had been colloquially referred to as "the Audi," but from the year 1981 on was known as the "Hammermill Center."

- The season began with an Erie School District teachers' strike (which included coaches) in progress which caused scheduling difficulties. Athletic Director **Ron Sertz** and Coach Flaherty had to scramble to schedule independent games in the spaces that were created by postponements. One such contest was the first of the three McDowell games. Eventually the strike was settled and the full complement of Metro League games was played out with new dates.

- There was great excitement in Erie when the Ramblers hosted famed high school power Hyattsville DeMatha Catholic (28-3). DeMatha's athletic teams, the Stags, received national recognition for achievement in a variety of sports, particularly basketball. The Stags first gained national recognition in 1962 with their initial national championship under coach **Morgan Wootten**. In 1965, the DeMatha basketball team won its second national championship, defeating Manhattan (NY) Power Memorial, with then **Lew Alcindor**, in a game called "The Greatest High School Basketball Game Ever." By the time Wooten brought the Stags to Erie, they had won 19 of their 21 previous Washington Catholic Athletic Conference titles and Wootten had an overall coaching record of 679-93. Tickets went on sale weeks in advance, and the Gannon Auditorium sellout crowd was treated to a gallant, if losing effort by the high-spirited Prep team.

Leading scorer John Alberstadt was Prep's MVP.

- Hard-working but tentative Prep did not play well against DeMatha, until scoring the final five points of the 3rd quarter to reduce the Stags' lead to 36-25. A hustling 4th quarter surge by **Doug Carter**, a bucket by **John Schwab** and a steal by **Stacy Hitt** had the crowd roaring and brought Prep to within four, 41-37, with just three minutes left in the game. DeMatha settled down from that point, scoring the final 9 points for its margin of victory in a game that was closer than the final score indicated. Hitt finished in double figures while Carter, in only 10 minutes of action, scored 8 points, grabbed 6 rebounds and blocked three shots.

- For more than 20 years, every senior who played for DeMatha's **Morgan Wootten** received a scholarship. The 1983-84 squad finished 29-2 and was the last of five national championship squads coached by Wootten, a member of the Basketball Hall of Fame. He won 1,274 games before retiring in November, 2002.

- Disappointments were early season road losses at Beaver Falls (12-12), Penn Hills (25-8) and at District 6 champ Altoona (19-9) in overtime; the home loss to Farrell (15-8); the tough loss at District 4 champion Williamsport (24-5) and the two regular season losses to Section One and District 10 champion McDowell (23-9).

Doug Carter could leap out of the gym. This amazing rebounder and shot blocker had a strong performance against national power DeMatha.

- Prep made a fine accounting in the four-point loss at powerful Penn Hills. The Indians were led by **Mark Knight**, younger

brother of Pitt and NBA star **Billy Knight**, and a pair of slick ball handlers in **Dow Misenhelter** and **Chris Seneca**. Penn Hills won its first state playoff games in 1982, making it to the PIAA Western Final, where it lost a memorable 101-95 shootout to New Castle.

- The Prep-Farrell game was the first time the two competed in basketball. Under legendary coach **Eddie McCluskey**, the Steelers won PIAA state championships in 1952, 1954, 1956, 1959, 1960, 1969 and 1972. In 29 years at Farrell, McCluskey finished with 574 wins and 153 losses. He was once named the National High School Coach of the Year and in January, 2000 was named one of Western Pennsylvania's Top 100 Sports Figures of the 20th Century by the *Pittsburgh Post-Gazette*.

- Prep's victory over Sharon (11-12) was the first time the two competed in 19 years. Before that the Ramblers and Tigers played eleven straight years from 1953 to 1963.

- Sharon's 6'7" **Jack Mansell** was Mercer County scoring leader with 433 points. He was the only Tiger player ever selected to play for the Pennsylvania team in Pittsburgh's Dapper Dan Roundball Classic, starting for the team that upset the heavily favored United States squad. McDowell's **Tom Taylor** and New Castle's **Barry Whetzel** played in the preliminary for the Keystone team, which lost to the Ohio All-Stars, 99-88.

- The final standings in the Section One basketball league were as follows:

	W	L
McDowell	10	0
Prep	8	2
Vincent	5	5
Academy	3	7
East	2	8
Tech	2	8

- The Erie teachers' strike and corresponding lack of pre-season practice was devastating for the Erie public school teams, witness the final records of Academy (5-8), East (4-11) and Tech (4-11). Only Vincent (11-8) finished respectably, making it into the second round of the PIAA Class AA tourney.

- Prep's victory over Warren (22-8) on January 8 was the 200th in coach **Bill Flaherty's** career as head Prep mentor. The huge disappointment, however, was the first round District 10 loss to the **John Bowen**-led Dragons for the second year in a row. The contest was played at Allegheny College's David Mead Fieldhouse in Meadville. The set-up was similar to the previous season when the Ramblers defeated Warren twice during the regular season, only to have to beat rugged Meadville (19-8) at McComb for a third place finish to gain a PIAA bid. This lower seed paired Prep with powerful WPIAL champion New Castle (27-5), which beat the Ramblers in a nail-biter by 4 at Farrell. The Hurricanes made it to Hershey, only to lose to Whitehall, 42-38, in the AAA state final.

Gary Miller started every contest and was a second team All-City choice.

- **Stacy Hitt** and **John Alberstadt** were named to the First Team Section One All-Star Basketball Team by the

Erie Times-News, while **Gary Miller** was a Second Team selection. **John Schwab** was an Honorable Mention choice, while Hitt, Alberstadt and Miller represented the City in the Northwest Jaycees 8th Annual City-County Basketball Classic at Hammermill Center. The City topped the County, 98-91, with Miller contributing 14 points.

Classy All-City guard Stacy Hitt started every game and later starred at Gannon University.

- **Doug Carter,** the leaping rebounder and shot blocker, was also a star on the Rambler track team, breaking high jump records in the city (6'8 5/8") and District 10 (6'7 7/8"). Carter won the Guth Memorial Track Award in 1982, signifying him as Prep's track and field MVP. He went on to star in the high jump at Ashland College.

- **John Alberstadt** was also winner of the James "Moe" Gross Award, given annually to Prep's best player.

- **Stacy Hitt** went on to star at guard for Gannon University, performing for the only Golden Knights' team to play in the NCAA Division II national championship game.

1982 All-Opponent Team:

John Bowen, Warren (1st team all-state) [Notre Dame, William & Mary, Gannon; Washington Generals]

Carliss Jeter, Beaver Falls [UT-Chattanooga]

Mike Alexander, DeMatha [Boston University]

Tony Graves, DeMatha [Georgia Southern]

Mark Knight, Penn Hills

Dow Misenhelter, Penn Hills [Alliance]

Rob Phillips, Farrell

Tom Taylor, McDowell [Cheyney St., Edinboro]

Mike Dowling, McDowell (2nd team, all-state) [Akron]

Bob O'Donald, Altoona [Waynesburg]

Jack Mansell, Sharon [Georgia Tech]

Lonnie Lee, Williamsport [Catawba]

Mark McClendon, Youngstown Rayen

Ralph Drayer, Academy

Ray Parry, Meadville

Barry Whetzel, New Castle (2nd team all-state)

Russell Bruce, New Castle [Westminster]

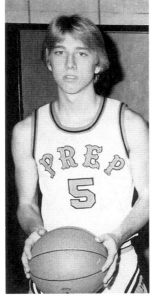

John Schwab

Mark Zappia

Felix Orzechowski

Jack Stevenson

The role players all made strong contributions.

Prep Regains Metro Title!

1982-83 (20-10)

Coach: Bill Flaherty
Assistant: Dave Wenrick
Captains: Game captains
Managers: Rick Scarpino, David Soule

Bill Flaherty elevated Prep to statewide prominence.

Date	PREP			Dec.	Loc.	High Scorer	Opponent
11/23	46	Warren	48	L	H	Schaaf (18)	Buerkle (16)
11/26	55	Beaver Falls	52	W	H	Schaaf (18)	Lee (17)
11/27	67	Pittsburgh Central Catholic	52	W	N	P. Bowen (18)	Bauer (30)
12/3	53	Strong Vincent	65	L	N	P. Bowen (16)	Hollis (24)
12/7	66	Pittsburgh Peabody	69	L	H	Schaaf (21)	Poston (21)
12/11	102	Academy	54	W	N	Schaaf (16)	Brunson (10)
12/14	77	Tech Memorial	57	W	N	Schaaf (24)	Lofton (14)
12/17	61	McDowell	55	W	N	Atkinson & Stevenson (14)	Lewis (16)
12/18	56	Philadelphia Roman Catholic	65	L	H	Schaaf (17)	Lawton (21)
12/22	66	Altoona	61	W	H	Atkinson (19)	West (26)
		JAMESTOWN (NY) HOLIDAY BASKETBALL TOURNAMENT					
12/28	90	Dunkirk (NY)	53	W	N	Atkinson (18)	Lockett (14)
12/30	72	Jamestown (NY)	43	W	A	Schaaf (16)	O'Boyle (14)
1/7	76	East	68	W	N	Dombrowski (17)	Pullium (17)
1/8	60	Warren	61	L	H	Schaaf (17)	Bowen (26)
1/12	77	Tech Memorial	54	W	N	Schaaf & Atkinson (16)	Horn (26)
1/14	66	Strong Vincent	46	W	N	Schaaf (19)	Atkinson (12)
1/15	81	Sharon	59	W	H	Dombrowski & Atkinson (16)	Dawson (20)
1/21	61	Farrell	60	W	A	Atkinson (20)	Shannonhouse (24)
1/28	76	Academy	58	W	N	Schaaf (18)	Brunson (24)
2/4	67	McDowell	69(2OT)	L	N	Atkinson (20)	Nesdore & Kovalesky (18)
2/11	74	State College	54	W	A	P. Bowen (18)	Washington (16)
2/12	70	Williamsport	76	L	A	Schaaf (20)	Churba (22)
2/17	65	Norwin	54	W	N	Schaaf (20)	Lewandowski (14)
2/18	91	East	56	W	N	Atkinson (25)	Pullium (27)
2/25	53	Hyattsville (MD) DeMatha Catholic	72	L	H	Stadtmiller (14)	Valentine (17)
2/26	73	Johnstown	60	W	A	Stadtmiller (18)	T. Callahan (17)
		DISTRICT 10 PLAYOFFS					
3/9	63	Meadville	47	W	N	Schaaf (16)	Parmeter (12)
3/12	49	Warren	51(OT)	L	N	P. Bowen & Dombrowski (10)	Parry (17)
		P.I.A.A. INTERDISTRICT PLAYOFFS					
3/16	61	Butler	47	W	N	Schaaf (14)	Beichner (16)
3/19	62	McKeesport	63	L	N	Atkinson (22)	Leonard (25)
	2036 (67.9)		**1729* (57.6)**				

Pos.	Player	Ht.	Prior School	Class	G (GS)	FG	FT	Total	PPG	Career
F	Jim Schaaf (#42)	6'3"	St. Joseph's	Sr.	30(30)	188	60	436	14.5	465
F	Mark Atkinson (#41)	6'3"	OLP	Jr.	30(30)	134	87	355	11.8	355
F	Shawn Dombrowski (#40)	6'0"	Bl. Sacrament	Sr.	29(26)	118	55	291	10.0	375
F	Preston Bowen (#52)	6'4"	Girard	Jr.	30(5)	79	75	233	7.8	233
G	Jim Stevenson (#5)	6'1"	St. John's	Jr.	27(17)	66	69	201	7.4	201
F	Mike Stadtmiller (#12)	6'2"	Bl. Sacrament	Jr.	30(24)	85	21	191	6.4	191
G	Joe Fessler (#21)	6'0"	St. John's	Jr.	30(15)	57	55	169	5.6	169
C	John Bowen (#50)	6'3"	Girard St. John's	Jr.	10	11	21	43	4.3	43
G	Jon Russo (#20)	6'1"	St. George	Sr.	14	15	4	34	2.4	34
G	Jim Webb (#34)	6'0"	St. Luke's	Jr.	14	10	6	26	1.9	26
F	Kevin Gallagher (#32)	6'3"	OLC	Sr.	12(3)	8	8	24	2.0	31
C	Sonny Watson (#51)	6'4"	St. John's	Jr.	10	2	5	17	1.7	17
F	David Repko (#24)	6'1"	St. James	Sr.	8	3	2	8	1.0	8
G	John Perrotti (#22)	6'0"	St. Peter's	Jr.	10	0	5	5	0.5	5

HIGHLIGHTS:

- A major study of the operations of the Cathedral Prep athletic program was commissioned by headmaster **Father John Dollinger** and the result was restructuring and the promotion of **Ron Sertz** as Director of Athletic Operations. Sertz, from the Prep Class of 1965, had been at the school since 1971 and was well-known as a successful coach in cross-country, basketball and track. His ten-year record as head coach of the harriers was 111-4 and his record as freshmen basketball coach was 95-5! Prior to his Prep job, Sertz coached Sacred Heart to a 27-1 record and the Pennsylvania grade school state championship in 1971. Within a few years Sertz brought the Rambler program into not only state, but national prominence.

Prep's 1983 Metro League Champions. Front, L to R: coaches Wenrick, Flaherty; Middle: Stadtmiller, Webb, Stevenson, Fessler, Russo, Perrotti, Repko; Back: Mgr. Soule, Dombrowski, J. Bowen, Watson, Atkinson, P. Bowen, Schaaf, Gallagher, Mgr. Scarpino.

- Juniors **Jim Stevenson, Joe Fessler** and **Sonny Watson** were all stars on the St. John's grade school team that won the 1980 Pennsylvania CYO state championship.

- Cathedral Prep again won the Section One League title in 1983, though most local followers felt the young Ramblers would not even be a contender. Behind the high scoring of **Jim Schaaf** and the all-around play of **Shawn Dombrowski,** plus the emergence of several top juniors, particularly **Mark Atkinson,** Prep made it to the Western Quarterfinals round of PIAA inter-district play after defeating Butler (17-9), only to

All-Metro selection Mark Atkinson leaves a befuddled McDowell Trojan in his wake.

suffer a heart-breaking loss to state finalist McKeesport (29-4) on a tip-in at the buzzer by **Sam Commodore.** The Tigers went on to the state final where it lost to Chester, 82-66.

- Prep's points per game average (67.9) was the highest since the 1976-77 season.

- All Section One (a/k/a Metro League) games and most home contests were played at Gannon's Hammermill Center, while home games against Pittsburgh Peabody (20-8) and Sharon (12-11) were played at Mercyhurst College's Campus Center. The season opener against Warren was part of a double-header at Gannon, with Girard outlasting McDowell, 56-53, in the lid-lifter.

- Prep's inter-district games against Butler and McKeesport were the first time the Ramblers played these schools, although they had been opponents on occasion in football. These games were played at super-loud Westminster College and New Castle High School, respectively. The District 10 playoff against Meadville was played at Allegheny College's David Mead Fieldhouse, while the D-10 final against Warren was played at Edinboro's McComb Fieldhouse.

- Prep's great independent wins were over Beaver Falls (17-8), Pittsburgh Central Catholic (14-11), Altoona (19-13), Johnstown (14-17) and particularly at Farrell (23-7), as the Steelers made it to the PIAA AAA Western Final, only to lose to McKeesport, 62-57.

- Prep's unusual game against Pittsburgh Central Catholic was played in Slippery Rock as a preliminary to the Slippery Rock-Carnegie-Mellon collegiate contest. It was the first time the Ramblers ever defeated the Vikings, having lost on seven previous occasions, each time in PCIAA tournament play.

- Prep's 77-57 victory over a good Tech Memorial (19-8) team was the 100th game between the two, with the Ramblers winning 58 of the contests.

- Erie had a major attraction when Philadelphia Roman Catholic (24-5) and its 6'9" superstar **Dallas Comegys** came to town. The powerful Cahillites (named after the school's founder, businessman **Thomas Cahill**) were 8-0 and ranked as high as fourth in the nation by some publications at the time and Comegys was considered the top player out of the Philly area. Roman is located in Philadelphia's center city and has been prominent in athletics, particularly basketball, since the Philadelphia Catholic League's founding in 1920. Tuition was free at Roman from its inception in 1890 until well into the 1960's.

- Roman Catholic won the 1983 Philadelphia Catholic League's regular season Southern Division. The Cahillites lost a semifinal playoff game, however, to eventual Catholic League champ Monsignor Bonner, 43-42, despite Comegys' 21 points, 21 rebounds and 5 blocks.

- **Jim Schaaf**, who really came into his own as a senior, was named Most Valuable Player at the Jamestown Holiday Tournament, while **Mark Atkinson** and **Shawn Dombrowski** earned berths on the All-Tournament Team. Prep's win over Dunkirk (11-8) was the last time the two competed, with the Ramblers holding a 4-1 advantage over the Marauders. Dunkirk competed in the Chautauqua-Cattaraugus Interscholastic Athletic Conference with the likes of Falconer, Silver Creek, Olean, Salamanca, Fredonia, Gowanda and Southwestern. Prep's triumph against Jamestown (9-11) was the first game the two played since they competed 20 times between 1953 and 1975. It was also the last contest ever between the Ramblers and the Red Raiders, with Prep holding a 17-4 edge.

- Prep had a tough loss at Williamsport (25-6). The Millionaires went on to win their third straight District 4 title and make it to the PIAA Eastern semifinals. Another tough loss was the rematch with DeMatha Catholic (27-4), which again finished as the number one-ranked team in the DC area.

- The Rambler squad had a big thrill defeating Norwin (11-12) at the Pittsburgh Civic Arena, in a game that was played as a preliminary to the Duquesne University-St. Francis (PA) collegiate battle. Prep fans who stayed enjoyed seeing former Rambler star **Andy Sisinni** '80 lead the Dukes to a 78-70 victory over St. Francis.

- When Prep smashed Academy (10-12), 102-54, the Ramblers established new records for most points scored in local high school league competition. The mark eclipsed was held by the 1961-62 Tech Centaurs who rung up 92 points against East. Prep also knotted the school record of 102 engineered against Titusville St. Joe's in the 1964-65 campaign. The Ramblers remarkably hit 30 of 36 free throws against Academy.

- Prep opponents broke the record for most points (1,729) scored against the Ramblers in a season.

- The two Prep-McDowell (14-13) rivalry games were interesting matchups, if for no other reason than junior guard **Joe Fessler's** older brother, former Prep star **Rick Fessler** '68, was in his first year as head coach of the Trojans. **Rick Fessler**, of course, graduated as Prep's all-time leading scorer and was an integral part of the Ramblers' 1968 state championship team.

- The final standings in the Section One basketball league, a/k/a Metro League were as follows:

	W	L
Prep	8	2
Tech	7	3
McDowell	6	4
Vincent	5	5
Academy	3	7
East	1	9

- Prep routed Meadville (13-9) with solid team play in the District 10 semifinal. However, most disappointing was Prep's three losses to Warren (29-3), including in the pulsating D-10 overtime final, by a total of five points. The Dragons met disaster in their first round PIAA playoff game against Uniontown, blowing an 18-point lead before succumbing in double-overtime, 82-76.

- Warren had been led for four years by 6'8" **John Bowen**, who finished his high school career with an amazing 2,884 points (25.5 PPG), 4th all-time in Pennsylvania at the time, 8th today, and 2,162 rebounds (19.1 RPG). Warren's record against Prep with Bowen on the squad was 5-4—and the Dragons won the big ones—D-10 playoff games three years in a row. Bowen later played at Notre Dame, William & Mary and Gannon; professionally in Germany and Israel; and with the famous Washington Generals of Harlem Globetrotters fame. He later became the successful head coach at Strong Vincent and Central high schools, and currently is an assistant at Cathedral Prep.

- 1982-83 was the first time Prep had as opponents three future NBA players—Roman's **Dallas Comegys**, Altoona's **Doug West** and DeMatha's 6'10" **Danny Ferry**.

- Comegys (10 points, 11 rebounds), Warren's Bowen (7 points, 8 rebounds) and **Billy Leonard** (10 points) of McKeesport all played for the Pennsylvania All-Stars against the U. S. in the 1983 Dapper Dan Roundball Classic, while McKeesport's **Todd Preston** and Farrell's **Roland Shannonhouse** (12 points) played with the Western PA team against the East in the preliminary. The Pennsylvania All-Stars were coached by Prep's **Bill Flaherty**, the first Erie mentor to be so honored. The United States team won the game, 123-121, behind such stars as **Steve Alford, Tyrone Bogues, Antoine Joubert, Reggie Williams** and **Dwayne "Pearl" Washington**.

- **Mark Atkinson** (unanimous) and **Jim Schaaf** were named to the First Team Section One All-Star Basketball Team by the *Erie Times-News*, while Shawn Dombrowski was a Second Team selection. **Jim Stevenson** and **Mike Stadtmiller** were Honorable Mention choices, while Schaaf and Dombrowski

Hall-of-Famer Shawn Dombrowski starred in football at Boston College, where he was Doug Flutie's favorite receiver.

represented the City in the Northwest Jaycees 9th Annual City-County Basketball Classic at Hammermill Center. The City won the high-scoring affair, 115-103, with Schaaf contributing 16 points and Dombrowski 6.

• **Shawn Dombrowski** was an acknowledged football star, having led the Ramblers to a 10-0 season as a senior in 1982. He was given the 1983 "Ma" Kaiser Award, signifying him as Prep's best all-around athlete. He went on to star at Boston College, where he was a top receiver for famous quarterback **Doug Flutie**. Dombrowski was inducted into the Cathedral Prep Athletic Hall of Fame in 2008.

• **Jim Schaaf** was also winner of the James "Moe" Gross Award, signifying him as Prep's best player.

• Senior **Dave Repko** later became a Prep varsity assistant under head coach **Mark Majewski**.

Dave Repko later became an assistant to current Prep mentor Mark Majewski.

Leading scorer Jim Schaaf had an outstanding senior season and was named First Team All-Metro.

1983 All-Opponent Team:

Don Buerkle, Warren

Ken Estelle, Beaver Falls

Bob Bauer, Pittsburgh Central Catholic

Willie Hollis, Vincent

LeRoy Poston, Pittsburgh Peabody

Tim Lewis, McDowell

Dallas Comegys, Roman Catholic (1st team all-state, McDonald's HS All-American) [DePaul; NBA Nets,Spurs]

Tim Lawton, Roman Catholic [Millersville]

Doug West, Altoona [Villanova; NBA Timberwolves, Grizzlies]

Ernie Lockett, Dunkirk

David Pullium, East

Billy Nesdore, McDowell

Ray Kovalesky, McDowell

John Bowen, Warren (1st team all-state) [Notre Dame, William & Mary, Gannon; Washington Generals]

Brian Horn, Tech

Roland Shannonhouse, Farrell [Gannon]

Michael Brunson, Academy [Robert Morris]

Jim Mextorf, Williamsport [Siena]

Jeff Churba, Williamsport [Shippensburg]

Danny Ferry, DeMatha (McDonald's HS All-American in 1985, 1985 USA Today Player of the Year & Mr. Basketball USA) [Duke, All-American, National Player of the Year; NBA Cavaliers, Spurs]

Carlton Valentine, DeMatha [Michigan State]

Bennie Bolton, DeMatha [North Carolina State]

Quenton Jackson, DeMatha [North Carolina State]

Ray Parry, Warren

Billy Leonard, McKeesport [Towson St.]

Todd Preston, McKeesport [Duquesne]

Senior Jon Russo played well when called upon.

The pre-game Ramblers enjoy spacious locker room accomodations at a welcoming opposing school.

Ramblers in First Quad-A State Title Game!
Bill Flaherty Retires After Sensational Campaign!

1983-84 (27-6)

Coach: Bill Flaherty
Assistant: Dave Wenrick
Captains: Game captains
Managers: Rick Scarpino, David Soule,
Tom Chylinski, Dan Scully

Bill Flaherty announces his retirement after 13 years as head coach at a news conference while displaying the state runner up trophy.

Date	PREP			Dec.	Loc.	High Scorer	Opponent
11/25	78	Warren	38	W	H	Stevenson (19)	Erickson (12)
11/26	56	Farrell	54	W	H	P. Bowen (17)	Booth (16)
11/28	78	McKeesport	48	W	H	Atkinson (22)	McTurner (15)
		McDONALD'S CLASSIC					
12/2	54	Philadelphia Roman Catholic	52(OT)	W	H	Stevenson (19)	Stevenson (23)
12/3	63	Brooklyn (NY) Bishop Loughlin	70	L	H	Atkinson (24)	Kibbler (20)
12/7	63	Pittsburgh Peabody	59	W	H	Atkinson (18)	Robinson (24)
12/10	93	East	54	W	N	Atkinson (21)	Pullium (18)
12/13	71	Strong Vincent	60	W	N	Atkinson & Stevenson (22)	Jones (23)
12/16	57	Meadville	54	W	A	Atkinson (23)	Zelasko (21)
12/21	64	Tech Memorial	56	W	N	Atkinson (20)	Amos (16)
12/23	62	Academy	56	W	N	Stevenson (17)	Brunson (20)
		LAS VEGAS (NV) HOLIDAY PREP CLASSIC					
12/27	79	Louisville (KY) Harry Doss	56	W	N	Atkinson (27)	McMichael (16)
12/28	59	Paradise (NV) Chaparral	74	L	N	Atkinson (22)	E. Williams (18)
12/29	82	Gardena (CA) Junipero Serra	70	W	N	Stevenson (24)	Cannady (23)
12/30	55	Compton (CA) Manuel Dominguez	49	W	N	Atkinson (21)	UNREPORTED
1/3	74	McDowell	36	W	N	Atkinson (15)	Moss (10)
1/11	76	Warren	49	W	A	P. Bowen (19)	Erickson (18)
1/14	62	Strong Vincent	48	W	N	Stevenson & Stadtmiller (17)	ones (16)
1/17	81	East	56	W	N	P. Bowen (24)	Goudy (23)
1/20	68	Tech Memorial	57	W	N	P. Bowen (19)	Lofton (21)
1/27	71	Farrell	56	W	A	Atkinson (24)	Smith (17)
1/31	52	Altoona	59	L	A	P. Bowen (21)	West (20)
2/4	87	Academy	63	W	N	Stadtmiller (18)	Brunson (20)
2/10	87	State College	65	W	A	P. Bowen (31)	Washington (28)
2/11	50	Williamsport	70	L	A	Atkinson (15)	Graves (17)
2/17	69	McDowell	38	W	N	Atkinson (16)	Legenzoff (9)
2/24	82	Johnstown	50	W	H	P. Bowen (14)	Horner (14)
		DISTRICT 10 PLAYOFFS					
3/10	51	Meadville	59	L	N	Atkinson (14)	Seidel (15)
		P.I.A.A. INTERDISTRICT PLAYOFFS					
3/17	66	Bethel Park	62	W	N	Atkinson (15)	Cwalina (19)
3/21	59	Pittsburgh Taylor Allderdice	47	W	N	Atkinson & Stadtmiller (14)	Dobbs (18)
3/24	59	Pittsburgh Central Catholic	49	W	N	Stevenson (16)	Sullivan (10)
3/28	58	Meadville	48	W	N	Stevenson (20)	Mudger (13)
		P.I.A.A. CLASS AAAA STATE CHAMPIONSHIP					
3/31	61	Williamsport	68	L	N	Stevenson (16)	White (26)
	2227 (67.5)		**1830* (55.5)**				

Pos.	Player	Ht.	Prior School	Class	G (GS)	FG	FT	Total	PPG	Career
F	Mark Atkinson (#41)	6'5"	OLP	Sr.	33(33)	216	105	537	16.3	892
G	Jim Stevenson (#20)	6'1"	St. John's	Sr.	33(33)	153	139*	445	13.5	646
F	Preston Bowen (#52)	6'6"	Girard	Sr.	33(33)	146	88	380	11.5	613
G	Joe Fessler (#21)	6'0"	St. John's	Sr.	32(32)	130	48	308	9.6	477
F	Mike Stadtmiller (#12)	6'3"	Bl. Sacrament	Sr.	32(32)	114	41	269	8.4	460
C	John Bowen (#42)	6'5"	Girard St. John's	Sr.	32(2)	26	29	81	2.5	124
G	Jim Webb (#34)	6'0"	St. Luke's	Sr.	23	21	15	57	2.5	83
F	John Donikowski (#50)	6'3"	Holy Rosary	Jr.	8	7	8	22	2.8	22
G	John Perrotti (#22)	6'1"	St. Peter's	Sr.	21	5	8	18	0.9	23
G	Jeff Kapsar (#30)	6'2"	Mt. Carmel	Jr.	10	5	3	13	1.3	13
F	Jeff Quirk (#31)	5'10"	OLC	Jr.	9	5	2	12	1.3	12
F	Vinnie DiNicola (#10)	6'1"	OLC	Jr.	6	5	2	12	2.0	12
F	Chris Keim (#51)	6'3"	OLP	Jr.	10	5	0	10	1.0	10
G	Jerry Cooley (#32)	5'10"	Bl. Sacrament	Jr.	8	3	3	9	1.1	9
G	Bill Snider (#11)	5'9"	Holy Rosary	Jr.	9	2	4	8	0.9	8

Prep's 1984 State Finalists. Front, L to R: Cooley, Mgr. Soule, Mgr. Scarpino, Quirk, Fessler, Snider, Mgr. Chylinski; Middle: Asst. Coach Wenrick, Mgr. Scully, Kapsar, Stevenson, Stadtmiller, DiNicola, Perrotti, Coach Flaherty. Back: Donikowski, Keim, J. Bowen, P. Bowen, Atkinson, Webb.

HIGHLIGHTS:

- 1983-84, the year the PIAA expanded to four divisions, was a thrilling season for the Cathedral Prep Ramblers, going undefeated in the Metro League and storming all the way to the first PIAA AAAA (large school) State Final. Prep had a daunting schedule, but an outstanding cast of seniors which presented a near-perfect blend of strong inside play—6'5" **Mark Atkinson**, 6'6" **Preston Bowen** and 6'5" **John Bowen**; and outstanding guard play—**Jim Stevenson, Joe Fessler, Jim**

Webb and **John Perrotti**. All could shoot well, handle the ball, play defense and rebound. It was a culmination of years of how coach **Bill Flaherty's** players and his successful brand of Prep basketball was molded—conservative, deliberate, disciplined, relentless and smart.

- The title game at Hersheypark Arena matched Prep against the Williamsport Millionaires (30-0). In a hectic, see-saw, down-to-the-last minute affair, the Millionaires prevailed, 68-61, behind the hot shooting of its head coach's son, **Pete White, Jr.,**

Stevenson scores a big bucket in the state title game in Hershey.

The dejected Ramblers receive their runner-up medals, not immediately realizing the magnitude of their accomplishments. L to R: Atkinson, Stadtmiller, P. Bowen, Fessler, Stevenson, J. Bowen, Webb.

The proud starting five with the PIAA Runner-Up Trophy, L to R: Stadtmiller, Atkinson, Bowen, Fessler, Stevenson.

to become the first AAAA champion in PIAA history. White was 9 of 15 from the floor and 8 of 9 from the foul line for 26 points.

- State champion Williamsport finished its season undefeated, including two wins over the Orange & Black. Prep also lost by 20 during the regular season at Williamsport. It was the fifth straight year the Ramblers met the Millionaires in their Magic Dome. The Millionaires averaged more than a whopping 87 points per game on their way to the District 4 and the first PIAA Class AAAA state title.

- Williamsport coach **Pete White,** a native of Farrell, was a graduate of Gannon College and had successful head coaching stints at North East St. Gregory's and Redbank Valley before taking the reins at Williamsport in 1980-81. Dubbed the "Wizard of West Fourth Street" in Williamsport, White's four-year record with the Millionaires to that point was 96-22.

- The day after Prep lost in the state final to Williamsport, the Rambler ice hockey team defeated Philadelphia Archbishop Ryan, 4-1, to win the PIAA Class AAA state championship at the Pittsburgh Civic Arena. Prep ice stars included **Chris Chane, Matt Gavula, Tim Presta, Johnny Sala, Sean Carroll, Sean Haley, Eric Anderson** and goalkeeper **Tim Swail**. The Ramblers were guided by long-time coach **Nels White**.

Preston Bowen battles for a rebound against Warren, as Jim Webb looks to help.

- All Metro League games and home games against Warren, Peabody and Johnstown were played at Gannon's Hammermill Center, while the home game against Farrell was played at Mercyhurst College's Campus Center as the preliminary to the Mercyhurst-St. Francis (PA) collegiate contest. (Division I St. Francis was coached at the time by former Red Flash and NBA star **Kevin Porter**.)

- For the second consecutive year, Prep opponents broke the mark for most points (1,830) scored against the Ramblers in a season. It is a record that lasts to this day.

Stevenson for two against Warren.

- Prep's decisive early season revenge wins over Warren (5-18) and McKeesport (19-8) helped take some sting out of the previous season's devastating losses. The Prep-McKeesport game was the first high school basketball contest ever played at Erie's brand new Erie Civic Center, located between East 8th and 9th Streets, between French and Holland Streets.

- The inaugural McDonald's High School Basketball Classic provided a weekend of high school basketball excitement

Floor leader Jim Stevenson takes charge in the McDonald's Classic final.

unequaled in Erie's history. The four-team tourney, the brainchild of coach **Bill Flaherty** and Prep athletic director **Ron Sertz** in conjunction with **Sam Covelli**, the owner at the time of the 11 local McDonald's restaurants, was a complete success and continues to this day, described as "the best four-team tournament in the country." The initial McDonald's competitors included Prep, East Coast power Philadelphia Roman Catholic, Beaver Falls and Bishop Loughlin Memorial, the defending New York state champ from the Fort Greene section of Brooklyn. Loughlin (26-3 in 1983), with 38 points by **Mark Jackson**, later of St. John's University, NBA and ESPN fame, won the 1983 New York State large-school division title with a 102-89 victory over North Babylon in the championship game. The initial McDonald's tourney was played at the new Erie Civic Center and featured the "All-Erie County High School Band," a collection of the most talented musicians from all the local high schools. It drew 2,712 fans the first night and 3,382 the next.

- Tournament director **Ron Sertz** pointed to a variety of factors that made such a tourney a reality: a great new place to play—the Erie Civic Center; a strong local host—Cathedral Prep; Erie's (really Sertz's) ability to attract powerhouse competition; and a community-minded advertising backer—Covelli and McDonald's Restaurants.

Stadtmiller drives for two between three Bishop Loughlin defenders.

- On the Friday night opening of the McDonald's Classic, powerful Bishop Loughlin (19-5), behind **Andre Kibbler**, a transfer from Brooklyn's Alexander Hamilton High, easily defeated Beaver Falls, 93-66. The nightcap was a thriller and was one of Prep's all-time great wins, a 54-52 overtime verdict over highly regarded Roman Catholic (19-8) and its 6'6" superstar, **Mark Stevenson** (a 1985 McDonald's All-American). Another Stevenson—Prep's **Jim Stevenson**—proved to be the best player on the floor with 19 points. Roman defeated Beaver

Atkinson and Stevenson wait as Stadtmiller fires one up against Roman Catholic.

Falls in the consolation game on Saturday night, 57-46, and then Loughlin beat the Ramblers, 70-63, for the Classic's first title.

- Roman Catholic was barred from the Philadelphia Catholic League for the 1983-84 season for the alleged recruitment of 6'3" freshman **Scott Odom** by coach **Barry Brodzinski.** Northeastern Catholic filed a complaint against Roman when Odom enrolled after attending St. Boniface, a Kensington area traditional feeder parish for North. Odom was ruled ineligible as a freshman and transferred to Camden (NJ) Catholic after being unhappily relegated to the Roman JV team as a sophomore.

- Prep's win over Pittsburgh city champion Peabody (23-5) was

the last time the Ramblers and Highlanders competed after a six-year run. After 100 years in operation, the Pittsburgh school board voted to close the school and graduate its final class in 2011. The Barack Obama Academy of International Studies now occupies the building and the Peabody name is no longer used.

- Prep recorded two huge wins over WPIAL champion Farrell (23-9), a school with a Class A enrollment that was competing at a Quad-A level. A third Prep-Farrell battle in the playoffs was averted when Taylor Allderdice, the Pittsburgh City League's #3 team, upset the Steelers in the first round. Prep's second win over Farrell was immediately followed by a loss at District 6 champion Altoona (24-7).

- Prep's trip to the 7th annual Las Vegas Holiday Prep Basketball Classic was the first time ever the program traveled such a great distance for a holiday tourney. The Holiday Prep Classic began in 1977 and has been the biggest, most respected and most well-known tournament in the country as well as a Christmastime fixture in the Las Vegas Valley. It later became known as the Reebok Las Vegas Holiday Prep Classic then after several years the Powerade Las Vegas Holiday Prep Classic. The tourney always features dozens of top-flite teams from around the country and by 2002 engaged 96 teams from 22 different states. Prep fared well in winning three of four, losing only to nationally-ranked tournament winner Chaparral. Consistently strong **Mark Atkinson**, with 92 points in the four games, was named to the Classic's all-tournament team.

- Of Prep's Holiday Classic opponents: Doss, which Prep played again in 1995-96, was opened in the late 1960's to help with overcrowding of Jefferson County (KY) schools; Chaparral, with over 3,000 students, is located on Annie Oakley Drive in Las Vegas and has "Kevin the Cowboy" as its mascot; Junipero

Prep's famous "Sixth Man."

Serra, named after the founder of the California Missions, is a Diocese of Los Angeles school originally run by the Marianists from the University of Dayton (1950-1994), but turned over to the Diocese because of lack of staffing; and Manuel Dominguez is an athletic power which boasts many MLB, NFL and NBA players, and is named after a California rancher. Manuel Dominguez was crowned national champion in 2000 by *USA Today* with a record of 35-2.

- Prep's 38-point win over McDowell on January 3 was the widest margin between the two since the 67-28 Rambler victory in 1963.

- Prep's victory on January 17 over East High was the 100th meeting between the two, with the Ramblers holding a won-lost edge of 59-41. It was also Coach Flaherty's record 250th win at the Rambler helm.

- The final standings in the Section One basketball league, a/k/a Metro League were as follows:

	W	L
Prep	10	0
Tech	7	3
Academy	5	5
Vincent	4	6
East	2	8
McDowell	2	8

- 1983-84 turned out to be one of the finest years for Erie's local teams. Tech Memorial (18-7) qualified for the AAAA playoffs and had its best season since its great 1962-63 campaign;

Academy (20-10) won its first District 10 title (in AAA) since 1974 and made it to the PIAA Western Quarterfinals behind star **Michael Brunson**; East High (22-12) won its first District 10 title (in AA) since 1969 and went all the way to the PIAA Western Final behind stars **Shannon Pulliam** (later the esteemed Vincent head coach) and **Tony Goudy**; and Strong Vincent (14-13) finished as D-10 runner-up (in AAA) and entered PIAA inter-district play. Only McDowell (7-21) finished disappointingly.

- The 1983-84 Tech Memorial Centaurs were coached by Prep Hall of Famer **Jim Marnella** '63 and had an interesting starting lineup that consisted of four former Prepsters: **Dave Dombkowski**, **Sonny Watson**, **Marcus Amos** and **Brent**

Prep's infamous "P-Flop."

The Prep fans show intensity before the start of the Western Final.

The Prep fans and bench implore for a converted free throw in the Western Final.

Preston Bowen drives against Meadville in the D-10 final.

The Prep coaches and bench are entranced by the sight of the good-looking Bethel Park cheerleaders.

Taylor. Marnella later became **Marcel Arribi's** top assistant at Prep (1987-99).

- Prep's regular season-ending victory over Johnstown (8-13) was its seventh straight over the Trojans.

- Prep's biggest win of the season was the 58-48 thriller over powerful Meadville (30-3, two losses to Prep) in the Western Final before a capacity crowd of over 4,200 at McComb Fieldhouse in Edinboro. This was a payback to the Bulldogs who beat the Ramblers at McComb in the exciting District 10 Final. Prep had beaten Meadville the 9 previous times the two competed. The Bulldogs presented one of their greatest teams ever and were led by such stars as **Paul Burnett, Dave Zelasko, Bob Mudger, Mike Burnett, Terry Gray** and **Rich Seidel**.

- To get to a rematch with Meadville in the Western Final, the Ramblers' pressure defense made for impressive inter-district victories over strong Pittsburgh area representatives Bethel Park (21-10), Taylor Allderdice (23-6) and Central Catholic (25-5). Bethel Park is a suburban school; Allderdice is located in the Squirrel Hill section of Pittsburgh; and Central Catholic is located in Oakland area. These games were played at McComb, at New Castle High School and at the Westminster Fieldhouse, respectively.

- The trip to Hershey was on the line with the Prep-Meadville Western Final. Tickets came at a premium for the McComb Fieldhouse affair, where as many as 3,000 were shut out attempting to get into the Rambler-Bulldog D-10 title game just 18 days before. Meadville coach **Norm Price** rejected a request that the battle be moved to roomier Civic Center in Erie. "There's really no reason to put the game into the city of the home team," Price said. "Maybe we should have looked at the Pitt Fieldhouse if we wanted a larger arena."

- Meadville took a 10-point 2nd quarter lead in the Western Final, but Prep battled back behind the play of **Jim Stevenson**, who was spectacular in the Rambler playoff run to Hershey. Second half adjustments by Coach Flaherty and clutch shooting by **Mike Stadtmiller** helped Prep take a 3rd period lead and pull away in the fourth. **Joe Fessler** struck three times from long range, but more importantly nailed 5 of 6 free throws in the waning moments to break the hearts and 22-game winning streak of the Bulldogs.

- **Jim Stevenson**, the third and last of the great Stevenson brothers, broke school records for most free throws made in a game (sinking 16 of 17 against Junipero Serra), breaking **Jim McCallion's** record of 15 made against Academy in 1960-61; and also most free throws made in a season (137), breaking **Will Cardot's** record of 125 set in 1970-71. The Stevenson name was on the Prep varsity roster for six consecutive seasons!

- **Mark Atkinson** (unanimous) and **Jimmy Stevenson** were named First Team Section One All-Stars by the *Erie Times-News*. **Preston Bowen** and **Joe Fessler** were Second Team selections, while **Mike Stadtmiller** was an Honorable Mention choice. The five seniors all participated in balanced scoring as the City defeated the County, 111-89, in the 10th post-season City-County All-Star game held at Gannon. Atkinson and Stevenson had a dozen

Jim Webb went on to become a three-year starter at PSU-Behrend and later women's coach at Mercyhurst College.

Named First Team All-Metro, Mark Atkinson later became MVP at Bucknell University.

Classy guard Joe Fessler went on to play at Mercyhurst College.

Mike Stadtmiller, Prep's best athlete, was the star quarterback for the Ramblers' gridiron team.

points each, while Fessler and Stadtmiller each scored 10 and Bowen had 9.

- For the first time ever, the James "Moe" Gross Award was given to two great players: Atkinson and Stevenson. Stadtmiller, also a star quarterback on the Rambler eleven, was given the prestigious "Ma" Kaiser Award as Prep's best all-around athlete.

- **Mark Atkinson** was selected to play in the 1984 Dapper Dan Roundball Classic preliminary, scoring 5 points and collecting 9 rebounds for the City-Catholic team in a 93-87 loss to the Western PA stars. One Division I coach remarked of Atkinson: "For his size, there's not a better power player in America!" Rambler opponents toiling for the West included Academy's **Mike Brunson** (12 points), McKeesport's **Tony McTurner** and Beaver Falls' **Ken Estelle**. Prep opponents in the main go against the United States stars included Peabody's **Johnny Robinson**, Roman Catholic's **Tarone Thornton** and **Collins Dobbs** of Taylor Allderdice.

John Bowen was the reliable sixth man for the Ramblers.

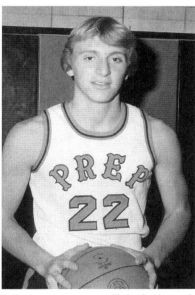
John Perrotti was a capable back-up guard.

- Many of the Prep luminaries went on to star in college, including **Mark Atkinson** at Division I Bucknell, where he won the Kribbs Award (team MVP) and is one of only 17 Bisons to record over 1,000 points (1,029) and 500 rebounds (520) in a career; **Preston Bowen** at Baldwin-Wallace where he was All-Ohio Athletic Conference in 1987; **Mike Stadtmiller** at John Carroll; **Joe Fessler** at Mercyhurst; and **Jim Webb**, a three-year starter at Penn State-Behrend. Webb became head women's basketball coach at Mercyhurst College from 1994 through 2001.

- The fledging *USA Today*, which began publication in the fall of 1982, revealed its preseason Super 25 high school basketball rankings in the first week of December, 1983. Mater Dei of Santa Ana (CA) was tabbed # 1 followed by DeMatha.

- 1983-84 was **Bill Flaherty's** final season coaching the Prep Ramblers. It was strictly a financial situation, as Flaherty had four children approaching college age. He finished with a colorful 13-year mark of 260-95, for a winning percentage of .732, including six Metro League championships, five District 10 championships, one state championship (1980) and 1984's runner-up. Flaherty and AD **Ron Sertz** built the program from one that played local and Diocesan schools; to one that took on regional competition; then became a statewide power; to one that competed against programs on a national level. Prep basketball had become the #1 high school show in town. Flaherty retired as Prep's all-time winningest coach and was inducted into both the Cathedral Prep Athletic Hall of Fame and the Metropolitan Erie Sports Hall of Fame in 1994. Flaherty, who was only 42 years of age at the time, spent 20 years coaching at Prep and 19 teaching. He was the first Rambler mentor to win a District 10 title; to win a PIAA state championship; to coach at the Dapper Dan Classic; to coach at the McDonald's Classic; and the first to coach in a PIAA Quad-A Final. Flaherty left the school to become the full-time director of Youth Activities for the Erie Diocese, having previously served on a part-time basis for 15 years. He later assisted his son, **Pat Flaherty**, head coach at Mercyhurst Prep (2000-10); and followed with a coaching stint at Our Lady's Christian grade school. **Pat Flaherty** became head coach at Fairview in 2015, succeeding the 14-year reign of former Prepster **Keith Nies**.

1984 All-Opponent Team:

James Booth, Farrell

Shawn Roberts, Farrell [Akron]

Tony McTurner, McKeesport [Kent State, LaRoche]

Tarone Thornton, Roman Catholic [South Carolina, Northeastern]

Mark Stevenson, Roman Catholic [Notre Dame, Duquesne]

Andre Kibbler, Bishop Loughlin [St. Francis (NY)]

James Major, Bishop Loughlin [Seton Hall]

John Robinson, Pittsburgh Peabody (2nd team all-state) [Youngstown St.]

Shannon Pullium, East [Slippery Rock]

Todd Jones, Vincent

Dave Zelasko, Meadville

Terry Gray, Meadville [Allegheny]

Doug West, Altoona [Villanova; NBA Minnesota Timberwolves, Vancouver Grizzlies]

Michael Brunson, Academy [Robert Morris]

Jeff Penix, Chaparral (NV Player of the Yr.) [Colorado]

Jerrol Williams, Chaparral [Purdue, football; NFL Steelers, Chargers, Chiefs & Ravens]

Zarak Cannady, Gardena Serra

Tony Goudy, East

Darryl Lofton, Tech

Darryl Washington, State College [Penn State, football]

Marc Graves, Williamsport [Wilkes]

Rich Seidel, Meadville [Allegheny]

Collins Dobbs, Allderdice (2nd team all-state) [Duquesne]

Bob Mudger, Meadville

Pete White, Williamsport (1st team all-state) [Yale]

The Ramblers enjoy some foolishness before the coaches return.

Joey Fessler drains a 20-footer in the state championship game.

Dave Wenrick Deals with Injuries, Inexperience and Shooting Woes; SV Colonels Win PIAA State Crown!

1984-85 (7-14)

Coach: Dave Wenrick
Assistant: Tom Hansen
Captains: Bill Snider, Chris Keim
Managers: Tom Chylinski, Peter Kern, Phil Alberstadt, John Kleiner

Head coach Dave Wenrick, a true Prep thoroughbred.

Date	PREP		Dec.	Loc.	High Scorer	Opponent
12/7	81	Corry	37	W	H	Jefferson (19)	Coleman (16)
12/11	46	East	47	L	N	Jefferson & Donikowski (9)	Winters (15)
		McDONALD'S CLASSIC					
12/14	50	Williamsport	51	L	H	Manczka (19)	Niklaus (21)
12/15	63	Richmond (VA) Benedictine	48	W	H	Jefferson (14)	Carpin (18)
12/19	54	Meadville	56	L	H	Manczka (17)	P. Burnett (21)
12/21	59	Academy	68	L	N	Jefferson (22)	T. Brewington (21)
12/27	34	Cleveland (OH) St. Joseph	71	L	A	Dalton & Donikowski (6)	Batts (23)
1/2	45	McDowell	51	L	N	Jefferson (12	Boetger (12)
1/4	64	Mercyhurst	31	W	N	Dalton (14)	Goring (9)
1/5	48	Farrell	63	L	A	Ianello (14)	Roberts (25)
1/11	53	Strong Vincent	60	L	N	Ianello (15)	Harris (19)
1/17	38	Altoona	4	L	H	Kaczenski (10)	West (16)
1/19		Pittsburgh Schenley (CANCELLED—SNOW)			H		
1/22		Tech Memorial (POSTPONED—SNOW)			N		
1/29	59	East	74	L	N	Ianello (12)	Winters (25)
2/1	53	Academy	50	W	N	Kaczenski (19)	T. Brewington (12)
2/5	68	Mercyhurst	50	W	N	Snider (16)	Beck (12)
2/8	45	McDowell	62	L	N	Kaczenski (10)	Legenzoff (21)
2/13	41	Strong Vincent	49	L	N	Kaczenski & Dalton (9)	Blanks & Dickens (13)
2/15	51	State College	42	W	A	Kaczenski (13)	Williams (18)
2/16	38	Johnstown	58	L	A	Ianello (9)	McNair (23)
2/22	60	Tech Memorial	59	W	N	Keim (16)	Amos (14)
2/26	66	Tech Memorial	69	L	N	Keim (15)	Keys (17)
	1116 (53.1)		**1150 (54.8)**				

Pos.	Player	Ht.	Prior School	Class	G (GS)	FG	FT	Total	PPG	Career
G	Bob Kaczenski (#30)	6'1"	St. John's	Jr.	20(17)	86	25	197	9.9	197
F	Mike Manczka (#40)	6'3"	Sacred Heart	Jr.	17(13)	64	16	144	8.5	144
G	Mark Dalton (#42)	6'0"	Sacred Heart	Jr.	20(9)	45	28	118	5.9	118
C	Jon Jefferson (#41)	6'5"	OLC	Jr.	11(9)	52	8	112	10.2	112
G	Bill Snider (#11)	5'10"	Holy Rosary	Sr.	21(18)	38	19	95	4.5	103
F	Chris Keim (#51)	6'3"	OLP	Sr.	19(9)	35	20	90	4.7	100
F	Joe Ianello (#52)	6'2"	OLP	Jr.	14(6)	40	7	87	6.2	87
F	John Donikowski (#50)	6'3"	Holy Rosary	Sr.	18(3)	36	13	85	4.7	107
G/F	Tom Filipkowski (#21)	6'3"	St. John's	Jr.	20(14)	32	11	75	3.8	75
G	Jerry Cooley (#32)	5'10"	Bl. Sacrament	Sr.	13	16	2	34	2.6	43
G	Jeff Torrelli (#10)	6'0"	St. John's	Jr.	9(2)	9	0	18	2.0	18
G	Vinnie DiNicola (#12)	6'2"	OLC	Sr.	5(3)	7	2	16	3.2	28
F	Chris Geisler (#22)	6'1"	St. Peter's	Jr.	7	7	2	16	2.3	16
F	Jeff Quirk (#31)	5'10"	OLC	Sr.	12(2)	5	4	14	1.2	26
G	Mark Hansen (#20)	5'11"	Sacred Heart	Jr.	8	3	2	8	1.0	8

The 1985 Prep Ramblers. Front, L to R: Mgr. Kleiner, Mgr. Kern, Mgr. Chylinski, Cooley, Snider, Hansen, Torrelli, Mgr. Alberstadt. Back: Coach Wenrick, Quirk, Dalton, Ianello, Manczka, Keim, Donikowski, Jefferson, Filipkowski, DiNicola, Kaczenski, Asst. Coach Hansen.

HIGHLIGHTS:

- **Bishop Michael Murphy** named **Monsignor John B. Hagerty** as the fifth Cathedral Prep headmaster following the retirement of esteemed leader **Monsignor John Dollinger**. Monsignor Hagerty, a true sports lover, was Prep's first alumnus headmaster and brought a wealth of experience in school administration. He was determined to maintain Prep's "lofty tradition of excellence in academics, activities and athletics."

New headmaster Msgr. John Hagerty, a true sports lover.

- First-year coach **David C. "Dave" Wenrick** was the former Cathedral Prep basketball and football star from the Class of 1965. He was the fiercely loyal assistant to **Bill Flaherty** and was also a former head football coach of the Ramblers (1975-77). Wenrick was a knowledgeable coach and a true Prep thoroughbred.

- It could be stated that "the cupboard was left bare" for Coach Wenrick's initial campaign at the helm, witness the returning players contributed a total of just 73 points combined the previous season. Concerning the loss of so many Rambler stars from the previous state finalist team, Coach Wenrick stated pre-season: "This will be a stern test, but this will be a team that improves as the season wears on."

- Juniors **Tom Filipkowski, Jeff Torrelli** and **Bob Kaczenski** were all part of the St. John's team that won the 1982 Pennsylvania CYO grade school state championship. Academy's **Tyrone Brewington** was also a member of that squad.

- All Metro League games and home games were played at Gannon's Hammermill Center. It was the first time in 8 years that no Prep games were played at Mercyhurst College's Campus Center. The McDonald's Classic was again held at the Erie Civic Center.

- The 1984-85 Prep squad was the first not to have post season action since 1975-76 and only the second since 1941-42. Though Coach Wenrick's system was basically the same as prior coach **Bill Flaherty's**, the Ramblers suffered from a serious lack of experience, injuries and poor shooting. A knee injury to senior starter **Vinnie DiNicola** during the McDonald's Classic and the mid-season departures of promising juniors **Jon Jefferson** and **Jeff Torrelli** didn't help either. Jefferson left Prep to star for McDowell, while Torrelli quit the hoops game to concentrate on baseball and football, for which he excelled.

- This was most likely the worst free throw shooting team in the history of Prep, with a final mark hovering around 44%. This fact cost the Ramblers dearly, particularly in close, early season losses to East by one (6 for 22 from the free throw line); to Williamsport by one in the McDonald's Classic (6 for 15); and to Meadville by two (6 for 19). Other miserable performances at the charity stripe were in the loss to Academy (11 for 24); the loss to Altoona (4 for 12); and the two losses to McDowell (3 for 12 and 11 for 29).

Vinnie DiNicola suffered a season-ending knee injury in the fifth game of the season. His loss was keenly felt.

Junior Mike Manczka about to bank one in against Williamsport, as Mark Dalton and Chris Keim look to help.

- Prep's points per game average was the lowest since the 1957-58 season, when the Ramblers also went 7-14. It was also the first time since the 1949-50 season that Prep did not have a player, who finished the season with the team, average in double figures.

- On the other hand, Tech (17-7), under coach **Jim Marnella** (Prep '63), and Strong Vincent (29-1), under coach **Pete Flinn**, presented fine units, the Centaurs winning their first District 10 title (AAAA) since their great 1962-63 season. Tech beat Meadville (19-6) to win the D-10 crown, but lost to Kiski Area, 81-66, in the first round of the PIAA's. Vincent won the AAA district crown, then breezed its way to the PIAA Class

AAA state championship behind stars **Matt Harris, Mike Smith, John Blanks** and **Anthony Dickens**. Along the way the Colonels easily defeated Franklin (79-51), Sharon (71-47), Academy (82-71), Southmoreland (47-30), Ellwood City (58-41), Aliquippa (68-50), Beaver Falls (57-44) and Nanticoke (70-53) to become only the second team in history from Erie to win a PIAA state basketball title.

Strong Vincent's Matt Harris looks for an opening against the Rambler defense. Harris is currently a varsity assistant with Prep.

- Prep's opening game blowout over Corry (8-14), despite a 5 for 20 chart at the FT line, was part of a triple-header at Gannon. It was the first time the two competed since the 1968-69 season opener.

- East's (12-13) pair of wins over Prep broke a string of 16 straight Rambler victories over the Warriors and 21 out of 22.

- The second McDonald's High School Basketball Classic presented a nip-and-tuck rematch of Pennsylvania's 1984 state championship clash between Prep and eventual D-4 champ Williamsport (15-8) along with national power Queens (NY) Christ the King Regional, and perennial Virginia state champ Richmond Benedictine College Preparatory.

- Adding to the excitement of the McDonald's Classic '84 was an appearance by the Greenup County (KY) High School cheerleaders, the defending four-time national cheerleading champions, and the second edition of McDonald's "All-Erie County High School Band," under the direction of **Ronald Stitt**.

- Christ the King (23-4) won the McDonald's Classic after victories over Benedictine and Williamsport. And the big star for the Royals: 6'7" center **Brian Royal**! A large co-ed school located in the Middle Village section of Queens, Christ the King is noted for having among its alumni several NBA players, but more particularly for graduating well-known female basketball stars **Sue Bird** and **Chamique Holdsclaw**. The Royals, at the time, were defending New York State Class A Catholic state champions and listed their chief rival as Brooklyn Bishop

Loughlin Memorial, the first McDonald's Classic winner in 1983.

- Benedictine College Preparatory is a private Catholic military high school that established a national record for public or private schools by winning 14 straight Virginia state Catholic basketball titles. Before coming to Erie, the Cadets of esteemed coach **Warren Rutledge**, one of the winningest high school coaches in the nation, had won 20 state titles in the 27 previous seasons. Rutledge coached Benedictine until he passed away in 2000, finishing 43 seasons with 26 state crowns and a record of 949-334, the highest victory total in Virginia and seventh in the nation according to the *National High School Record Book*. Needless to say, Prep's victory over Benedictine was its best win of the season.

- Academy's (12-12) win over Prep broke an 11-game Rambler win streak over the Lions. The Orange & Black had won 18 of the previous 19 between the two. That game also marked the 100th meeting between the two, with the Ramblers holding the series lead, 67-33.

- Prep's 37-point defeat to Cleveland St. Joseph (18-5) was the worst Rambler beating in a dozen years, since the same Vikings defeated Prep, 85-38, in the 1972-73 season. St. Joe's was the 25th-ranked team in the nation at the time, according to *USA Today*. On the Viking roster was sophomore **Treg Lee** (named after his father's best friends: Tony, Ronnie, Eddie and Greg), who two years later would be a 6'8" McDonald's All-American.

- Prep's first loss to McDowell (15-9) was the 100th meeting between the two, with the Ramblers holding the series lead, 68-32.

- Prep's loss at Johnstown (12-12) was the Trojans' first victory over the Ramblers in eight games.

- Tech's win over Prep in the season finale ended a Rambler string of 18 consecutive victories over the Centaurs.

- The Erie high school basketball league was no longer referred to as "Section One", but only as the "Metro League." The final standings in the Metro League, which by then included Mercyhurst Prep, were as follows:

	W	L
Vincent	12	0
*Tech	9	4
McDowell	8	5
Academy	5	7
East	4	8
Prep	4	8
Mercyhurst	1	11

won playoff for second place

- 1984-85 marked the entry of Mercyhurst Preparatory School (5-16) into the Metro League basketball wars. Founded as all-girls Mercyhurst Seminary in 1926 by the Sisters of Mercy, Mercyhurst Prep became co-educational in 1974. Mercyhurst is located on East Grandview Boulevard in Erie, directly behind Mercyhurst College, now known as Mercyhurst University. The Ramblers easily defeated the Lakers in the initial contest between the two, despite being 8 for 18 at the free throw line, and were ahead, 48-12, after the first three quarters. The very next evening Prep took a beating at Farrell (24-2).

- Altoona (27-1), led by stars **Mike Iuzzolino** and 6'6" **Doug West,** the Mountain Lions' all-time scoring leader, rattled off 27 straight victories before being upset in the PIAA Western Final by Brashear, a team it had dominated by 26 points earlier in the season. No less than seven Altoona players went on to play basketball at the collegiate level. Brashear was then beaten by Carlisle and its First Team *USA Today* All-American, **Jeff Lebo**, for Pennsylvania's second AAAA state title.

Manczka drives over Mercyhurst's Jim Lydic, as Kaczenski and Filipkowski are about to crash the boards.

Rambler MVP Bill Snider.

Rambler all-star Chris Keim.

- **Bill Snider**, winner of the James "Moe" Gross Award, was named Second Team Metro League All-Star by the *Erie Times-News*, while junior **Bob Kaczenski** was an Honorable Mention choice. Snider (2 points) and **Chris Keim** (4 points) participated in the 11th post-season City-County All-Star game, won by the City, 112-94, at Gannon.

- Prep opponents selected to the Pennsylvania team in the 1985 Dapper Dan Roundball Classic included MVP **Doug West** of Altoona (16 points), Strong Vincent's **Anthony Dickens** (4 points, 5 rebounds), Farrell's **Shawn Roberts** and **Mark Stevenson** (18 points) of Philadelphia Roman Catholic. Meadville's **Paul Burnett** was selected to play for the Quad-A squad against the City-Western

PA team in the preliminary. Johnstown's **Tim McNair** made the Pennsylvania All-Star team for the 1986 Classic.

1985 All-Opponent Team:

Kenny Winters, East

Rik Niklaus, Williamsport [Lycoming]

John Carpin, Benedictine

Paul Burnett, Meadville [IUP]

Tyrone Brewington, Academy

Billy Batts, Cleveland St. Joe's (2nd team all-state, Ohio) [Virginia]

Treg Lee, Cleveland St. Joe's [Ohio State]

Shawn Roberts, Farrell [Akron]

Matt Harris, Vincent [Millersville]

Doug West, Altoona [Villanova; NBA Timberwolves, Grizzlies]

Mike Iuzzolino, Altoona [Penn State, St. Francis (PA); NBA Dallas Mavericks]

Bob Bradfield, Altoona [Millersville]

Craig Curry, Altoona [Midland (TX) JC, Westmoreland Community College]

Tom Legenzoff, McDowell

John Blanks, Vincent

Anthony Dickens, Vincent [Robert Morris]

Tim McNair, Johnstown [Youngstown St.]

Marcus Amos, Tech [Allegheny]

Senior Ramblers, Front, L to R: Quirk, Snider, Cooley; Back: DiNicola, Donikowski, Keim.

Strong Vincent's 1985 State Champs. Team members: Dickens, Blanks, M. Harris. M. Smith, Giannelli, McDaniel, Wiley, Pelton, Beard, Duncan, C. Harris, T. Smith, McLaurin, Sala. Coaches: Pete Flinn, Jim Delsandro.

Spot-starter John Donikowski.

RAMBLERS SHOW IMPROVEMENT! But Trojans take D-10 Crown!

1985-86 (15-9)

Coach: Dave Wenrick
Assistant: Tom Hansen
Captain: Game captains
Managers: Peter Kern, John Kleiner

Filipkowski drives for two against East.

Date	PREP		Dec.	Loc.	High Scorer	Opponent
	McDONALD'S CLASSIC					
12/6	50	Hopkinsville (KY)	61	L	H	DiRienzo (12)	Quarles & Ware (21)
12/7	46	Canton (OH) McKinley	41	W	H	May (11)	Jackson & Sistrunk (12)
12/11	75	Academy	71	W	N	Manczka (23)	K. Williams (30)
12/13	61	State College	42	W	H	Kaczenski (12)	Williams (17)
12/17	56	East	38	W	N	Manczka & M. Dalton (15)	Kuna (14)
12/20	67	Buffalo (NY) Bishop Timon	43	W	A	Kaczenski (14)	Murphy & Jakubczak (10)
	JAMESTOWN (NY) HOLIDAY TOURNAMENT (postponed two days, snow)						
12/28	56	Buffalo (NY) Mt. St. Joseph	52	W	N	Manczka (17)	Ferguson (25)
12/30	60	Buffalo (NY) Grover Cleveland	61	L	N	Manczka (20)	Robinson (25)
1/3	43	McDowell	49	L	N	Manczka (16)	Morrow (19)
1/4	93	Mercyhurst	55	W	N	Manczka (19)	Keith Mundy (22)
1/7	58	DuBois	51	W	A	Manczka & Kaczenski (16)	Strouse (18)
1/10	60	Strong Vincent	58	W	N	Manczka (17)	Harris (20)
1/17	60	Tech Memorial	46	W	N	Manczka (15)	Jones (11)
1/18	65	Buffalo (NY) Canisius	57	W	H	Kaczenski (17)	Flannery (20)
1/24	60	East	38	W	N	Manczka (16)	Baughman (15)
1/28	47	Academy	66	L	N	Manczka (15)	M. Williams (20)
1/31	77	Mercyhurst	55	W	N	Manczka (19)	Keith Mundy (17)
2/1	47	Meadville	45	W	A	Manczka & Kaczenski (14)	M. Burnett (14)
2/5	50	McDowell	51	L	N	Manczka (14)	Morrow (29)
2/7	60	Strong Vincent	61	L	N	Manczka & M. Dalton (17)	Harris (22)
2/8		Pittsburgh Schenley (CANCELLED)			H		
2/14	43	State College	53	L	A	Kaczenski (16)	three with (11)
2/15	62	Altoona	69	L	A	M. Dalton (22)	Iuzzolino (33)
2/18	66	Tech Memorial	49	W	N	Manczka (16)	Keys (19)
	DISTRICT 10 PLAYOFF						
2/27	43	Meadville	48	L	N	May (17)	Pero (13)
	1405 (58.5)		**1262 (52.8)**				

Pos.	Player	Ht.	Prior School	Class	G (GS)	FG	FT	Total	PPG	Career
F	Mike Manczka (#41)	6'3"	Sacred Heart	Sr.	24(22)	144	59	347	14.5	491
G	Bob Kaczenski (#30)	6'1"	St. John's	Sr.	24(22)	104	33	241	10.0	438
G	Mark Dalton (#42)	6'0"	Sacred Heart	Sr.	24(22)	74	52	200	8.3	318
C	Brian May (#51)	6'5"	Wilson	Jr.	24(2)	71	44	186	7.8	186
G	Ricky DiRienzo (#10)	5'11"	OLC	Jr.	23(15)	43	25	111	4.8	111
G/F	Tom Filipkowski (#21)	6'3"	St. John's	Sr.	23(11)	34	24	92	4.0	167
F	Joe Ianello (#52)	6'2"	OLP	Sr.	24(21)	40	12	92	3.8	179
F	Bill Parry (#40)	6'1"	OLC	Jr.	21(1)	19	18	56	2.7	56
G	Pat Mastrian (#31)	6'0"	OLC	Jr.	11(1)	9	6	24	2.2	24
F	Claye Greene (#32)	6'4"	Girard St. John's	Jr.	6	2	3	7	1.2	7
G	Andy Mraz (#22)	6'0"	OLC	Jr.	8	3	1	7	0.9	7
F	Rick Demski (#50)	6'5"	Holy Rosary	Jr.	7	2	2	6	0.9	6
G	Kevin Dalton (#20)	6'0"	Sacred Heart	Jr.	10(1)	1	4	6	0.6	6
F	Mike Szewczykowski (#11)	6'3"	St. James	Jr.	6(2)	0	4	4	0.7	4

The 1986 Prep Ramblers. Front, L to R: DiRienzo, Mraz, Mastrian, K. Dalton; Back: Coach Wenrick, Parry, Ianello, Szewczykowski, Kaczenski, Manczka, Demski, May, Filipkowski, Greene, M. Dalton, Asst. Coach Hansen.

A cameraman surprises Meadville coach Norm Price and Prep coach Dave Wenrick as they exchange notes at halftime.

HIGHLIGHTS:

- Cathedral Prep improved immensely under second-year coach **Dave Wenrick**, but a late season slide, losing 6 of the final 9 games, was the Ramblers' undoing. The 1985-86 Ramblers had great, close wins over Canton McKinley, defending District 10 champions Academy and Vincent, Canisius (12-1 at the time) and Meadville, but one-point losses to Grover Cleveland, Vincent and McDowell, and other close losses to District 6 champion Altoona and Meadville spelled doom for the Orange & Black.

- All Metro League games and the home game against Canisius were played at Gannon's Hammermill Center, while the home game against State College was played at Mercyhurst College's Campus Center. The McDonald's Classic was again held at the Erie Civic Center, with the two-night crowd of 3,377 considered disappointing. The D-10 playoff game against Meadville was played at Edinboro's McComb Fieldhouse.

- In the third McDonald's High School Basketball Classic,

Kentucky's defending state champion, Hopkinsville, defeated Prep, then shocked the nation's # 1 ranked team, DeMatha Catholic, 74-69, to win the tourney. The Tigers' victory over the Stags is considered their all-time greatest win.

Clay Greene did not get much rest on the eve of team photo day.

- Adding to the excitement of the McDonald's Classic '85 was an encore appearance by the Greenup County (KY) High School cheerleaders and the third edition of McDonald's "All-Erie County High School Band," this time under the direction of Prep's **Roy Fronzaglia**.

- Prep played well in the season-opening McDonald's Classic and even led Hopkinsville by 8 with 7 minutes remaining, before succumbing to the Tigers' hawking defense. The Ramblers then bounced back with fine defense of their own to defeat an excellent Canton McKinley (20-6) squad for consolation honors. Then just four nights later the Orange & Black upset a strong Academy (22-5) five. The Lions went on to win their second D-10 AAA crown in three years, and made it to

Junior guard Ricky DiRienzo started 15 contests. He missed his entire senior season due to injury.

the second round of PIAA action before bowing to Ellwood City, 80-78.

- Canton McKinley, well-known for having one of the nation's all-time greatest high school football programs, is just as famous for its basketball program. McKinley is #5 all-time in the nation in wins, #1 all-time in the nation in winning seasons, and #1 all-time in the nation in winning percentage among teams with 1500+ victories. McKinley is also #1 all-time in Ohio in victories, having won state championships in 1984, then later in 2005 and 2006. The Bulldogs have been state runners-up 8 times and hold Ohio records for most appearances in the championship game (11), Final Four appearances (23) and Sweet Sixteen appearances (48). McKinley has had several players move on to the NBA, including **Nick Weatherspoon, Phil Hubbard, Gary Grant, Eric Snow, Michael Hawkins** and **Keith McCleod**. McKinley has had a graduate in the NBA

continuously since 1974, which is believed to be a record.

- Prep's win over Buffalo Bishop Timon-St. Jude (14-11) was the first time the two competed since 1959. Still coaching the Tigers was venerated **Mel Polano**, who finally retired in 1989 as the Monsignor Martin Athletic Association's and Western New York's winningest coach, compiling a 544-202 record over 37 years. At the time the MMAA consisted of: AA—Canisius, Mount St. Joseph, St. Francis, Turner/Carroll, St. Joseph's and Timon; A—DeSales, Niagara Catholic, Bishop O'Hara, Lancaster St. Mary's and St. Mary's School for the Deaf.

- Prep split a pair of games against Buffalo teams in the Jamestown Holiday Tournament. Oddly enough, both schools are now closed. Mount St. Joseph Academy (16-8) was founded by the Sisters of St. Joseph in 1891 as a K–12 boarding school for girls. In the 1970's MSJA began admitting boys, but in 1987 the high school portion of MSJA was closed due to declining enrollment. Grover Cleveland High School (21-3) was formed in 1931 as a school serving the Lower West Side of Buffalo. During the 1970's, Grover Cleveland was designated as the school to serve foreign language-speaking students within the City of Buffalo.

- Prep had a nice win at District 9 league champion DuBois (14-7), the first time the Ramblers and Beavers ever competed in basketball.

- **Bob Kaczenski** hit a 22-foot bomb at the buzzer in Prep's thrilling 2-point win over Vincent (14-13) on January 10.

Two-year starter Bob Kaczenski was also a star on the gridiron for the Ramblers.

Rambler all-star Mark Dalton.

- Prep lost a pair of super-heated thrillers to arch-rival McDowell before overflow crowds at the Hammermill Center. A full-scale brawl erupted with just 12 seconds remaining in the second battle when **Brian May** intentionally fouled Trojan star **Jeff Morrow**, who was trying to extend McDowell's 50-48 lead with a fast-break layup. It took a full ten minutes to restore order after both benches cleared, punches were exchanged and fans poured onto the floor. Morrow converted one of two, then **Mark Dalton** connected from the corner to narrow the gap to one. The Trojans bungled the inbounds pass, but a short Prep jumper at the last second rimmed out. Prep had blown a 10-point lead it had with just 7:20 left to play.

- Prep's loss at State College (11-14) on Valentine's Day was its first to the Little Lions in 9 games. It was not a good weekend as the Ramblers were beaten the next evening at D-6 titlist Altoona (22-5), a squad that featured future NBA player **Mike Iuzzolino**. 1985-86 was also the first season Prep did not compete against traditional rival Johnstown (22-5) since 1969-70.

Big junior Brian May shows fine form as he buries an outside jump shot against Tech.

- The final standings in the Metro League were as follows:

	W	L
McDowell	11	1
Academy	9	3
Prep	8	4
Vincent	6	6
Tech	5	7
East	3	9
Mercyhurst	0	12

First Team All-Metro choice Mark Manczka played in the Dapper Dan Classic.

- Prep's loss to Meadville (18-11) in the District 10 semifinal was heartbreaking, especially since the Ramblers defeated the Bulldogs during the regular season in a two-point thriller. With there being four state classifications rather than three, D-10 was allotted only two slots for inter-district play rather than the customary three. McDowell (24-4) won its fourth D-10 championship, defeating Meadville in the final, 55-51.

- Meadville pulled a stunning upset over 26-0 Norwin in a PIAA first round playoff, 46-45. Norwin had just defeated Kiski Area to become the second team since 1967 to win the WPIAL's highest classification with an undefeated record (Ambridge did it in 1967 and Uniontown in 1975). McDowell in PIAA play easily defeated Penn Hills, 58-31, before bowing to Kiski Area in the Western Quarterfinal, 65-60. Kiski lost to Carlisle, led by later Syracuse and NBA star **Billy Owens**, in the state final, 61-59. It was Carlisle's second straight PIAA AAAA championship.

- Consistent scorer **Mike Manczka** was named First Team Metro League All-Star by the *Erie Times-News*, while **Mark Dalton** and **Bob Kaczenski** were Honorable Mention choices. Dalton scored 14 as the City defeated the County, 103-91, in the post-season City-County All-Star game held at Gannon. Manczka was selected but did not play, as he was further selected to participate with the City/West Penn Stars against the WPIAL Stars in the preliminary of the 1986 Dapper Dan Roundball Classic in Pittsburgh the same weekend. Manczka played 17 minutes in a 78-77 loss, finishing with 4 points, 2 assists, 3 steals and 4 rebounds.

- Prep opponent **Mike Iuzzolino** of Altoona was selected to the Pennsylvania All-Stars for the Dapper Dan Classic, while Academy's **Mike Williams** joined Manczka on the City/West Penn Stars in the loss to the WPIAL Stars in the preliminary.

- **Mike Manczka** was also given the James "Moe" Gross Award as Prep's best player for the season. Manczka went on to star in baseball at Allegheny College.

- **Tom Filipkowki** went on to play basketball at Mercyhurst College.

Tom Filipkowski went on to play at Mercyhurst College.

1986 All-Opponent Team:

Jeff Quarles, Hopkinsville

LaMont Ware, Hopkinsville

Tim Jackson, Canton McKinley (HM all-state, OH)

Kevin Williams, Academy

Mike Williams, Academy

Keith Robinson, Buffalo Grover Cleveland (NY's 1st Mr. Basketball, McDonald's HS All-American) [Notre Dame]

Fergie Ferguson, Buffalo Mt. St. Joseph

Jeff Morrow, McDowell [Westminster]

Dave Fragale, McDowell

Jon Jefferson, McDowell [Iowa Wesleyan]

Paul Bamberger, McDowell [Clarion]

Danny Merryman, McDowell

Matt Harris, Vincent [Millersville]

Keith Mundy, Mercyhurst

Ray Flannery, Canisius

Mike Burnett, Meadville [St. Bonaventure]

Mike Pero, Meadville

Mike Williams, State College

Chris Spielvogel, State College

Mike Iuzzolino, Altoona (1st team all-state) [Penn State, St. Francis (PA); NBA Mavericks]

Frank Dicken, Altoona [Mt. Aloysius, IUP]

Senior forward Joe Ianello goes up strong against Tech.

Former Prepster Jon Jefferson tries to bank one in as Manczka, DiRienzo and Kaczenski defend.

Wenrick Retires as Prep Coach!

Dave Wenrick retired from coaching after three years at the Rambler helm.

1986-87 (14-12)

Coach: Dave Wenrick
Assistant: Tom Lesniewski
Captain: Game captains
Managers: Jeff Jones, Darren Dusza

Date	PREP			Dec.	Loc.	High Scorer	Opponent
	McDONALD'S CLASSIC						
12/5	44	Meadville		60	L	H	Parry (8)	M. Burnett (22)
12/6	59	Philadelphia Roman Catholic		58	W	H	Dalton (14)	Smith (20)
12/10	67	East		53	W	N	May (22)	Flemings (16)
12/12	56	State College		47	W	H	May (17)	Washington (19)
12/16	74	Tech Memorial		48	W	N	Demski (18)	Keys (17)
12/19	66	Meadville		71	L	A	Dalton & Demski (17)	three with (17)
12/23	62	Mercyhurst		41	W	N	Demski (16)	Bakka (10)
	McDONALD'S CELRIVER HOLIDAY CLASSIC (ROCK HILL, SC)						
12/27	71	Brookville (NY) Long Island Lutheran	65	W	N	Demski (21)	Birindelli (16)
12/29	65	Huntersville (NC) North Mecklenburg	73	L	N	Dalton (12)	Moore (20)
12/30	60	York (SC) Comprehensive		66	L	N	Szewczykowski (14)	Dickson (19)
1/6	61	Academy		64(OT)	L	N	May (18)	Williams (24)
1/10	59	McDowell		47	W	N	May (20)	Flowers (18)
1/13	52	Strong Vincent		55	L	N	Demski (16)	Smith & Oatis (15)
1/16	51	East		46	W	N	May (16)	Baughman (23)
1/23	53	Canton (OH) McKinley		66	L	A	May (11)	Robinson (15)
1/27	49	Tech Memorial		51	L	N	Demski (13)	Eddy (17)
1/30	69	Mercyhurst		60	W	N	May (18)	Bakka (19)
2/6	67	State College		41	W	A	Szewczykowski (16)	Washington (13)
2/7	46	Johnstown		50	L	A	Szewczykowski (10)	Harris (20)
2/10	53	Academy		49	W	N	Demski (14)	Barney (20)
2/14	65	McDowell		47	W	N	Demski (16)	Watts (18)
2/20	46	Strong Vincent		43	W	N	May (13)	Smith & Oatis (13)
2/21	48	Altoona		52	L	A	Szewczykowski (12)	Brumbaugh (32)
	DISTRICT 10 PLAYOFFS						
2/26	85	Warren		42	W	N	Demski (24)	Molinaro (10)
3/5	55	Meadville		61	L	N	May (16)	Pero (19)
	P.I.A.A. INTERDISTRICT PLAYOFF						
3/14	64	Penn Hills		65	L	N	Szewczykowski (18)	Tate (21)
	1494 (57.5)			**1421 (54.7)**				

Pos.	Player	Ht.	Prior School	Class	G (GS)	FG	FT	Total	PPG	Career
C	Brian May (#51)	6'5"	Wilson	Sr.	26(24)	102	63	267	10.3	453
F	Rick Demski (#50)	6'5"	Holy Rosary	Sr.	25(24)	93	55	241	9.6	247
F	Mike Szewczykowski (#11)	6'3"	St. James	Sr.	26(26)	67	53	187	7.2	191
G	Kevin Dalton (#20)	6'0"	Sacred Heart	Sr.	24(20)	72	28	172	7.2	178
G	Olivier Allinei (#30)	6'2"	France	Jr.	23(18)	53	22	128	5.6	128
F	Eric Lewandowski (#52)	6'3"	Holy Rosary	Jr.	19(2)	26	17	69	3.6	69
G	Andy Mraz (#22)	6'0"	OLC	Sr.	20(5)	26	7	59	3.0	66
F	Bill Parry (#40)	6'1"	OLC	Sr.	15(6)	18	22	58	3.9	114
G	Pat Mastrian (#31)	6'0"	OLC	Sr.	19(2)	18	9	45	2.4	69
F	Jim Camp (#41)	6'4"	Holy Rosary	Jr.	20(1)	16	13	45	2.3	45
G	John Mundy (#12)	5'10"	St. Joseph's	Sr.	16(2)	8	16	32	2.0	32
F	Dean Heidt (#42)	6'2"	St. George's	Jr.	13	8	6	22	1.7	22
G	Kevin Misko (#32)	6'0"	OLP	Jr.	9	3	3	9	1.0	9
F	Steve Ziegler (#12)	6'2"	St. John's	Soph.	1	2	1	5	5.0	5
G	Mike Heberle	6'1"	St. John's	Soph.	1	2	0	4	4.0	4
F	Jason Steiner (#21)	6'0"	Bl. Sacrament	Jr.	7	1	1	3	0.4	3
G	Ricky DiRienzo (#10)	5'11"	OLC	Sr.	0	0	0	0	0.0	111

HIGHLIGHTS:

- Third-year coach **Dave Wenrick** resigned following a winning, but disappointing season, wherein 9 of the 12 losses were by 6 or fewer points. The 1986-87 Ramblers were beset by a tough schedule, relative inexperience, some bad luck and various injuries, particularly to star senior guard **Ricky DiRienzo** who missed the entire season. Coach Wenrick's final three-year record was 36-35, for a .507 winning percentage. He remained at Prep teaching for many more years and was often the beloved featured speaker at athletic rallies. Also a great athlete in his days at Prep, Wenrick was inducted into the Cathedral Prep Athletic Hall of Fame in 2015.

- In the fourth McDonald's High School Basketball Classic, Cleveland (OH) St. Joseph's, behind superstars **Treg Lee**, the 1987 *Associated Press* Player of the Year in Ohio, 6'11" **Eric Riley** and 6'10" **John Beauford**, defeated defending Philadelphia Catholic League champion Roman Catholic, then won a thriller over Meadville, 68-65, to win the tourney.

- Prep played poorly in the season-opening McDonald's game against Meadville (28-3), but came back strong to upset Roman Catholic (23-5) by one the following evening in one of the Ramblers' best wins of the season. Roman made it to the final of the Philadelphia Catholic League post-season tourney, but there it was upset by Northeast Catholic, 63-59. It was North's first Catholic League title since 1967.

- Other fine wins for Prep were the upsets over Metro champ Academy (20-9) and District 10 AAA titlist Strong Vincent (21-7), as well as the pair over arch-rival McDowell (9-17) after four straight losses to the Trojans over two seasons. Academy made it to the second round of PIAA inter-district action before losing a buzzer beater to Beaver, 49-47.

Brian May establishes position in the season opener against Meadville.

French transfer student Oliver Allinei scores against McDowell.

- Vincent won the D-10 AAA crown over Academy in one of the most incredible finishes in local history. With no time remaining on the clock in regulation, Academy's **Kevin Williams** made his first of two free throws to give the Lions an apparent 48-47 victory and the district championship. Academy coach **Paul Demyanovich** and his squad ran onto the floor for the victory celebration and a two-shot technical foul was immediately whistled. In shock, Williams nevertheless made the second shot for a 49-47 lead. Then SV's **Tony Harper** cooly sank both technicals to send the game into overtime, 49-49. From there the Colonels went on to win in double OT, 57-56, and claim the title. Vincent then lost a heartbreaker to Thomas Jefferson, 66-64, in the first round of the PIAA tourney.

- Disappointing losses were the three to state finalist Meadville; the two-point upset by Tech (9-15), particularly when the Ramblers defeated the Centaurs by 26 earlier in the season; four-point losses on the road to Johnstown (20-7) and reigning D-6 champion Altoona (17-10); and the one-point heartbreaker to WPIAL champion Penn Hills (22-9) in first round PIAA tournament action at Chartiers Valley.

- Prep's loss at Johnstown was the last time the two competed, with the Ramblers winning the overall series, 14-8. Prep and Johnstown had played at least once every season since 1970-71, sans 1985-86.

- **E. J. Sandusky** scored 10 points for State College (10-15) in its first game against Prep. He is the son of disgraced former Penn State football assistant **Jerry Sandusky**, currently serving a 30 to 60 year prison sentence for various morals charges.

- The Ramblers went on a distant Christmas trip for three games to the old Civil War town of Rock Hill (SC), winning one and losing two, including to nearby York Comprehensive. The win was over Long Island Lutheran and the other loss to North Mecklenburg. Prep has never played any of these schools a second time.

- Long Island Lutheran High School is a Lutheran college preparatory school, founded and built in 1960 on a 32-acre estate. Long Island Lutheran, commonly known as LuHi, has students coming from more than 50 school districts throughout Long Island and New York City. LuHi is known for its storied basketball program, which included former NBA players **Reggie Carter** and **Bill Chamberlain**. The Crusaders have won 7 New York State Federation Championships, including the 1981 and 1982 titles.

- North Mecklenburg High School, founded in 1951, has the largest student body in North Carolina. The school mascot is the Viking, and school colors are royal blue, red, and white. The original mascot was a Rebel who was often seen flying a confederate flag during the period when the school was segregated. Along with the Rebel, the original red and black school colors were also changed when the school was integrated in the 1960's.

- Canton McKinley (25-3) made it to the Ohio state AAA (large school) championship game, only to lose to Dayton Dunbar, 70-65. Both **Tim Jackson** and **Terry Jackson** made the All-State Tournament team. The "Pups" followed with a 24-2 record the next season, when 7-footer **Bill Robinson** was named first team all-state and the Player of the Year in Ohio.

- All Metro League games were played at Gannon's Hammermill Center, while the home game against State College was played at Mercyhurst College's Campus Center. The McDonald's Classic was held at the Erie Civic Center for the fourth consecutive year.

- The final standings in the Metro League were as follows:

	W	L
Academy	10	2
Prep	9	3
Vincent	9	3
Tech	4	8
McDowell	4	8
East	4	8
Mercyhurst	2	10

- In Prep's regular season ending loss, **Joey Brumbaugh** scored 32 of Altoona's 52 points. Brumbaugh's sister, **Jill Brumbaugh**, was at the time the starting point guard at the University of Connecticut under now-legendary coach **Geno Auriemma**. Jill was a four-year starter and remains one of UConn's all-time greats.

- The Warren (8-17) D-10 game was played at McComb Fieldhouse, while the hard-fought D-10 title game loss to Meadville was played before an overflow crowd of 5,678 as the nightcap of a doubleheader at the Erie Civic Center. The first game featured the girls' D-10 championship, with Villa Maria Academy upsetting favored McDowell in a 57-53 overtime thriller. These were the first high school playoff games ever played at ECC and at the time the crowd was the largest ever to witness a PIAA doubleheader.

- In the first round loss to Penn Hills, Prep erased a 16-point second half deficit and actually took a 56-55 lead with 3 minutes remaining after a jump shot by **Andy Mraz** and a layup by **Eric Lewandowski**. The Indians countered quickly with five unanswered points and held on to win by one, despite two inside FG's each by **Rick Demski** and **Brian May**. Penn Hills was then knocked of the tournament with a one-point loss to Taylor Allderdice, 40-39.

Brian May, a Second Team All-Metro selection, was also a Rambler football star.

- The 1986-87 Meadville Bulldogs presented the finest team in the school's history. Under Coach **Norm Price**, the 'Dogs finally made it to the state championship game after being eliminated in the Western Final two of the previous three seasons. In a thrilling, hard-fought title bout, the Carlisle Thundering Herd, led by future Syracuse and NBA star **Billy Owens**, handed Meadville a 48-47 loss. Bulldog stars included **Tom Wofford**, **Joey Gray**, **Mike Pero** and brothers **Don** and **Mike Burnett**.

- In an oddity, the Metro League's last place team, Mercyhurst Prep (15-13), was actually the last local team to be eliminated from post-season play. The Lakers defeated Ridgway, 79-68, in PIAA Class A first round action before losing to Wilmington in a heartbreaker, 66-65.

- Seniors **Brian May** and **Ricky Demski** were named Second Team Metro All-Stars by the *Erie Times-News*, while **Mike Szewczykowski** and French transfer exchange student **Olivier**

A pensive Coach Wenrick ponders his resignation.

Allinei were Honorable Mention choices. May was also winner of the "Moe" Gross Award, signifying him as Prep's best player.

- **Dave Wenrick** coached the City All-Stars to an NBA-sized 116-102 victory over the County in the 13th post-season City-County All-Star game held at the Hammermill Center. Prepster Rick Demski led all scorers with 24 points, while **Mike Szewczykowski** poured in 11. Of more note is the fact that this was the first high school game in Erie to use the 3-point field for completed shots from outside the 19'9" arc. Szewczykowski nailed a 3-pointer, and in this regard he is the first Prepster ever to score a 3-point field goal.

6'3" stringbean Mike Szewczykowski, in a post-season all-star game, was the first Rambler to bury a 3-point shot. He went on to a stellar career at Rockford University.

Named Second Team All-Metro, Rick Demski went on to become PSU-Behrend's all-time leading scorer.

- The 1987 Dapper Dan Roundball Classic featured an East vs. West format for the first time. Until this game a Pennsylvania all-star team always met a U.S. team. Meadville's **Mike Burnett** and St. Joe's **Treg Lee** both participated on the East squad.

- **Mike Szewczykowski** went on to star as a 6'5" forward at Rockford University, where he was twice named All-Northern Illinois Intercollegiate Conference, averaging close to 20 points per game his junior and senior seasons.

- **Rick Demski** became a full star at Penn St.-Behrend, where he graduated as the school's all-time leading scorer with 1,466 points and finished third all-time in rebounds with 806. Demski was a four-year starter under coach **Doug Zimmerman** and he captained the Lions for two seasons. He led the Lions to their first ECAC post-season bid in 1989 and was inducted into Behrend's Athletic Hall of Fame in 2001.

- The three-point field goal was introduced to college basketball for the first time in 1986-87.

1987 All-Opponent Team:

> Mike Burnett, Meadville [St. Bonaventure]
> Mike Pero, Meadville
> Eugene Smith, Roman Catholic
> Mike Washington, State College
> Don Burnett, Meadville [St. Bonaventure]
> Pierre Birindelli, L.I. Lutheran
> Bobby Moore, N. Mecklenburg [North Carolina A & T]
> Bernard Dickson, York Comprehensive
> Kevin Williams, Academy
> Tim Smith, Vincent [Lock Haven]
> Dean Oatis, Vincent
> Randy Baughman, East [PSU-Behrend]
> Bill Robinson, Canton McKinley [Ohio State]
> Terry Jackson, Canton McKinley (1st team all-state, OH) [NE Oklahoma JC]
> Tim Jackson, Canton McKinley (3rd team all-state, OH) [Youngstown St.]
> Steve Harris, Johnstown
> Curtis Barney, Academy
> Joey Brumbaugh, Altoona
> John Tate, Penn Hills [Massachusetts]
> Tim Timko, Penn Hills [Mercyhurst]
> Doug Bakka, Mercyhurst

Starting guard Kevin Dalton.

Andy Mraz

Jason Steiner

John Mundy

Pat Mastrian

Bill Parry

These spot starters played well when called upon.

Marcel Arribi Brings a New Style! Ramblers Surprise McDonald's, Metro, D-10 Winners!

1987-88 (24-5)

Coach: Marcel Arribi
Assistants: Jim Marnella, Tom DelFratte
Captains: Jim Camp, Olivier Allinei
Manager: Rick Gudowski

Marcel Arribi brought a wealth of basketball knowledge to Cathedral Prep.

Date	PREP		Dec.	Loc.	High Scorer	Opponent
	McDONALD'S CLASSIC					
12/11	56	McDowell	54	W	H	Ziegler (20)	Maus (14)
12/12	58	Mouth of Wilson (VA) Oak Hill Academy	48	W	H	Allinei (16)	Vega (18)
12/19	40	Toledo (OH) Scott	38	W	H	Allinei (10)	Scrutchins (11)
12/22	77	East	48	W	N	Ziegler (19)	Patterson (12)
1/2	69	Tech Memorial	60	W	N	Allinei & Ziegler (16)	Keys (21)
1/5	71	Academy	51	W	N	Allinei (15)	Williams (16)
1/8	64	Meadville	57	W	H	Heberle (19)	Hamilton (19)
1/12	55	Mercyhurst	46	W	N	Heberle (22)	Beck (19)
	BASS PRO TOURNAMENT OF CHAMPIONS (SPRINGFIELD, MO)					
1/14	50	Springfield (MO) Central	49	W	A	Allinei (14)	Adams (18)
1/15	57	Kansas City (MO) Paseo	59(OT)	L	N	Allinei (16)	Peeler (36)
1/16	50	Ballwin (MO) Parkway West	46	W	N	Toohey (16)	Pederson (21)
1/19	52	McDowell	46	W	N	Heberle (17)	Maus (15)
1/22	54	South Bend (IN) St. Joseph's	62	L	A	Allinei (25)	Holmes (23)
1/26	71	Strong Vincent	64	W	N	Toohey (23)	Smith (21)
1/27	74	East	50	W	N	Allinei (26)	Johnson (11)
1/29	78	Mercyhurst	66	W	N	Heberle (26)	Beck (20)
2/2	58	Tech Memorial	54	W	N	Allinei (18)	Keys (20)
2/12	49	Academy	35	W	N	Toohey (14)	Cooper (13)
2/13		DuBois (CANCELLED—SNOW)			H		
2/16	45	Strong Vincent	57	L	N	Allinei (16)	Smith (20)
2/19	67	McDowell	66	W	N	Allinei (24)	Wilhelm (24)
	METRO LEAGUE CHAMPIONSHIP PLAYOFF					
2/23	48	Strong Vincent	38	W	N	Camp (13)	Smith (18)
2/26	58	State College	43	W	A	Toohey (13)	Carlin (13)
2/27	52	Altoona	55	L	A	Toohey (15)	Brumbaugh (18)
	DISTRICT 10 PLAYOFFS					
3/9	81	Warren	46	W	N	Ziegler (17)	Berdine (16)
3/12	57	Meadville	49	W	N	Toohey (19)	Burnett (22)
	P.I.A.A. INTERDISTRICT PLAYOFFS					
3/15	62	Latrobe	52	W	N	Allinei (21)	Pellathy (12)
3/17	65	Fox Chapel	53	W	N	Allinei & Ziegler (16)	Ostrowski (19)
3/19	51	Farrell	49	W	N	Toohey (15)	Craig (21)
3/23	59	Pittsburgh Central Catholic	61	L	N	Allinei (18)	McCoy (26)
	1728 (59.6)		**1502 (51.7)**			

Pos.	Player	Ht.	Prior School	Class	G (GS)	FG (3)	FT	Total	PPG	Career
F	Olivier Allinei (#30)	6'3"	France	Sr.	29(29)	145(27*)	94	411	14.2	539
G	Jim Toohey (#20)	6'0"	St. George's	Sr.	28(28)	111(24)	75	321	11.5	321
F	Steve Ziegler (#22)	6'3"	St. John's	Jr.	25(16)	101(14)	46	262	10.5	267
G	Mike Heberle (#21)	6'1"	St. John's	Jr.	22(20)	100(13)	38	251	11.4	255
C	Jim Camp (#50)	6'5"	Holy Rosary	Sr.	29(19)	53	58	164	5.7	209
F	Phil Kraus (#42)	6'4"	St. George's	Jr.	29(26)	60	26	146	5.0	146
F	Tony Yonko (#40)	6'0"	Holy Rosary	Sr.	21	19(5)	15	58	2.8	58
G	Jeff Cardot (#11)	5'10"	St. Luke's	Soph.	24(7)	16(1)	10	43	1.8	43
G	John Steiner (#31)	6'0"	Bl. Sacrament	Jr.	7	7(1)	8	23	3.3	23
G	Bill Speros (#10)	5'11"	Villa Maria	Jr.	7	4(1)	8	17	2.4	17
F	John Smith (#41)	6'1"	St. James	Jr.	4	6	2	14	3.5	14
F	Joe Hellman (#32)	6'1"	St. James	Jr.	8	3	7	13	1.9	13
F	Todd Stablein (#51)	6'2"	OLP/McDowell	Soph.	1	1	0	2	2.0	2
F	Tom Huff (#52)	6'2"	St. Andrew's	Soph.	1	0	0	0	0.0	0

The 1988 District 10 Champions. Front, L to R: Mgr.   , Smith, Cardot, Steiner, Yonko, Toohey, Speros, Mgr.   , Mgr. Gudowski; Back: Asst. Coach Del Fratte, Asst. Coach Marnella, Heberle, Kraus, Camp, Ziegler, Allinei, Hellman, Coach Arribi, Headmaster Msgr. Hagerty.

HIGHLIGHTS:

- **Marcel Arribi**, a Cliffside (NJ) native and former star at Gannon University, was hired at Cathedral Prep to take over coaching responsibilities after the three-year reign of **Dave Wenrick**. The 35-year old Arribi was a fierce starting point guard for the Golden Knights and brought a wealth of experience as head coach at St. Luke's Grade School; as JV coach at Kanty Prep; as a Gannon assistant; as an assistant at Division I La Salle; and as East Coast Scouting Director for the NBA's Golden State Warriors.

Coach Arribi came from New Jersey to be a feisty star at Gannon College.

- Coach Arribi promised to transform the Prep Ramblers into a new-look team, and despite the fact there were only two players who returned from the previous season, the results

were astounding. Prep got off to a 9-0 start and showcased a more free-wheeling, transitional team, rather than the methodical offense and swarming defense teams of coaches Flaherty and Wenrick. The Orange & Black regained Metro and District 10 titles, created great excitement in a PIAA playoff run and finished but one contest away from Hershey, losing to Pittsburgh Central Catholic in the Western Final. This was accomplished despite mid-season injuries to star juniors **Steve Ziegler**, **Mike Heberle** and **John Smith**.

Jim Toohey did not play as a junior, but as a senior was named First Team All-Metro.

- Ziegler and Heberle were the stars on the St. John's grade school team that won the 1985 Pennsylvania CYO state grade school title. Tech Memorial's **Ed Gieza** was also a star on that championship squad.

- **Jim Toohey**, along with fellow 12th-grader **Tony Yonko**, were cut from the team as juniors, but got their chance when football stars **Eric Lewandowski** and **Dean Heidt** decided not to participate, leaving the Ramblers short-handed. Toohey and Yonko had stellar senior seasons, while Heidt went on to play football at Temple and Lewandowski at Penn State. Toohey, also a football star for the 1987 Ramblers that went 11-1, won the "Ma" Kaiser Award and went on to play basketball at Gannon University.

- Prep did not look impressive against McDowell (8-16) in Coach Arribi's debut as Rambler mentor in the season-opening McDonald's High School Basketball Classic, sneaking by with a two-point verdict. The next evening, however, Prep pulled off a stunning 10-point upset over the nation's # 4 team, Oak Hill Academy (21-7), to win the tournament for the first time. Oak Hill had crushed a strong St. Anthony's team from Long Island just the night before, 86-52, with **Orlando Vega**, from Brooklyn (NY), pouring in 38 points. Prep baffled Oak Hill with a spread offense and held the 6'4" Vega, who was averaging 40, to 18 points. Vega did, however, nail the first 3-pointer ever in a Rambler regular season game. Oak Hill Academy is a Baptist-affiliated boarding school with only 150 students, yet with over 25 alumni listed as former NBA basketball players, including **Carmelo Anthony, Kevin Durant** and **Rajon Rondo**.

- The McDonald's Classic was held at the Erie Civic Center for the fifth consecutive year, with repeat performances by the McDonald's All-County Band and the nationally famous Greenup County (KY) Cheerleaders. All Metro League games were played at Gannon's Hammermill Center, while the home game against Toledo Scott, the District 10 playoff games and the Latrobe playoff contest were held at the Erie Civic Center as well. The Meadville home game was played at Mercyhurst College's Campus Center.

The Ramblers celebrate their first McDonald's Classic Championship.

- An all new era was launched in 1987-88 with use of the three-point field goal. Nine states had tried it with much success on an optional basis for the previous two years. The National Federation of High School Athletic Associations then decreed use of the same 19-foot, 9-inch distance, used nationally in college basketball in 1986-87, for high schools across the United States, beginning with the 1987-88 season. **Dr. Russell T. Werner,** executive director of the PIAA, saw the three-point goal as adding to the excitement of high school basketball in Pennsylvania. "If what we've been seeing in college basketball

Dr. Brian Stark, Notre Dame's leprechaun mascot, from the Prep Class of 1984, speaks to the players during their trip to South Bend.

on television is any indication of how it has changed the game, we're in for some real excitement," said the PIAA chief who considered himself a fundamentalist favoring whatever will give "the little guys in the game, who are often your best outside shooters, a chance to play more."

Mike Heberle breaks free for a layup.

- The first 3-pointers ever scored by Prepsters in a regular season game occurred when senior star **Olivier Allinei, Steve Ziegler** and **Mike Heberle** each nailed one in the win over Oak Hill Academy in the second game of the season. Allinei established the initial 3-point FG records with 5 against South Bend St. Joe's and 27 for the season.

- Other fine wins for Prep were the two over Metro League pre-season favorite Vincent, including a playoff battle for the league title; two more close ones over arch-rival McDowell; the win over Toledo Scott (20-9) on **Mike Heberle's** shot at the buzzer; and the pair over Meadville, including the victory in the D-10 title matchup. The Prep-Meadville rivalry had become white-hot by this time.

- Toledo Scott's basketball program has been historically known as a powerhouse in the Toledo City League with its biggest rivals being the Toledo Macomber and Toledo Libbey. Macomber was the big rival until that school's closure in 1991, and Libbey was the main rival until it was closed in 2010. Scott's oldest rival is Toledo Waite, as its school was built a year after Scott and prompted an annual Thanksgiving Day football matchup that ran from 1914-1963 and generated the interest of many Midwestern newspapers. The nucleus of the 1987-88 Scott team, that Prep beat, won Scott's only Ohio Division I state title in 1990, with a 59-57 overtime win over Canton McKinley and a final record of 27-1.

- Prep took two of three and an impressive 3rd place finish in the 4th annual Bass Pro Tournament of Champions, a prestigious 8-team event in Springfield (MO). New Rambler opponents in the tourney included three Missouri teams—Springfield Central (14-11), tournament champion Kansas City Paseo (27-3) and Ballwin Parkway West (23-7). Though unknown at the time, Prep's loss to Paseo, Coach Arribi's first setback, was the 500th defeat in Rambler basketball history. Paseo's **Anthony Peeler** ran all over Prep in that one, earning tournament MVP honors. **Olivier Allinei** and **Jim Toohey** were both selected to the All-Tourney team. Bass Pro hosted its 30th annual tourney in Springfield in 2014.

- Central was the first high school built in Springfield. The old school building is well known for having many stories of "ghosts," "spooks," and other haunting-related tales surrounding it.

- Paseo High School, which served Kansas City's Blue Hills neighborhood, is now known as Paseo Academy of Fine and Performing Arts. During the 1960's, Paseo High School experienced rapid white flight and had a predominantly African-American student body by the 1970's. Students are now required to pass an audition to be enrolled into the school.

The Prep squad visits The Grotto at Notre Dame.

- Parkway West opened in 1968 and has won more state championships than any other high school in Missouri, though most are in the water sports of swimming, diving and water polo.

- Saint Joseph High School (23-2) began classes in 1953 as the first consolidated, co-institutional Catholic high school in the

Phil Kraus grabs a rebound against South Bend St. Joe's as Jeff Cardot looks on.

South Bend area. The school is very well known for its location, directly across the street from the University of Notre Dame. Many visitors who go to Notre Dame football games in the Fall know of St. Joe's solely on its location. The school was made up of students from Central Catholic High School, Saint Hedwig School, Saint Joseph's Academy, and South Bend Catholic High School. Suffice to say the Prep staff was not impressed with some of the officiating there, resulting in one of the few season's losses.

- The Prep-DuBois game was scheduled to be the first varsity game in the Prep gym since the 1976-77 season, but the Beavers were unable to bus into Erie because of wintery weather conditions and the game had to be cancelled. There has not been a varsity game in the Prep gym since that time.

- Prep's championship verdict over Vincent (22-8) was the ninth time in nine tries that Prep won the City Series, Section One or Metro League title via the playoff route. The Ramblers were eleven for eleven including playoffs for second place. SV showcased its all-time leading scorer, **Tim Smith** (1,418 points, 6th all-time in Erie area), winning the AAA District 10 title. Tech Memorial (11-14) also presented its all-time leading scorer in **Bruce Keys** (1,420 points, 5th all-time in Erie area).

- The final standings in the Metro League were as follows:

	W	L
*Prep	12	1
Vincent	11	2
Tech	6	6
Academy	5	7
Mercyhurst	4	8
McDowell	4	8
East	1	11

*won Metro championship playoff

- Prep crushed a weak Warren (8-18) team in the District 10 semifinal, then faced defending champion Meadville (18-9) in the D-10 final. The Bulldogs led most of the first half until a pair of **Olivier Allinei** 3-point bombs gave Prep a 27-21 lead at the half. **Jim Toohey** and **Mike Heberle**, who had come off the bench after missing 7 games with an ankle injury, proved too much for Meadville with their scoring in half two.

- Prep's PIAA inter-district playoff run was thrilling for Prep's famed "sixth man" students, alumni and fans. Toohey and particularly Allinei continued their strong play during the stretch. The Ramblers defeated Latrobe (18-6) handily at the Erie Civic Center, where they had already played five games earlier in the season. Hordes of fans followed the Ramblers to Westminster for the impressive win over Fox Chapel (23-6), in revenge for the 1977 playoff loss to the Foxes; to Edinboro for the thrilling triumph over Farrell (23-6) before a capacity crowd of 4,000; and finally to Sharon for the heartbreaking loss to Central Catholic (29-3) in the Western Final.

Jim Camp had a big senior season for the Ramblers.

- All of Prep's five losses were close, with the one to Pittsburgh Central Catholic in the PIAA Western Final the biggest heartbreaker of all. Central Catholic, which defeated heavily-favored Allderdice, 38-28, before meeting Prep, did not fare well in the state title game in Hershey, however, losing to undefeated Carlisle by a whopping 80-54 margin. Carlisle won its fourth straight crown and was led by future Syracuse and NBA star **Billy Owens**, who was 19 for 22 (one 3-pointer) from the floor and 14 of 16 at the free throw line for an incredible 53 points! It was the finest display ever in a Pennsylvania state championship game.

- **Olivier Allinei** and first-year player **Jim Toohey** were named First Team Metro League All-Stars by the *Erie Times-News*. **Mike Heberle** was a Second Team selection, while senior

Olivier Allinei was the first Rambler to receive All-State recognition since Tim Gore in 1980. He played at Allegheny and then became a full star in his native France.

surprise **Jim Camp** was an Honorable Mention choice. Allinei was also recipient of the annual James "Moe" Gross Award, naming him Prep's most valuable player.

- **Joe Hellman** did not play the next season, preferring to concentrate on track and field. He was the 1989 winner of the Guth Memorial Track Award

- **Olivier Allinei**, a consistently excellent scorer and defender, was further honored with an Honorable Mention selection on the *Associated Press* All-State team, the first Prepster to be given all-state recognition since **Tim Gore's** first team selection in 1980. Allinei went on to star at Allegheny College, then returned to his native France where he started at point guard on the 1992 French Olympic Team and the 1993 French National Team. He also played in the French Pro League, commanding a $150,000 salary.

- **Marcel Arribi** coached the City All-Stars to an 88-83 victory over the County, coached by General McLane's **Andy Schulz**, in the Northwest Jaycees 14th annual post-season City-County All-Star game held at the Hammermill Center. Those representing Prep included Toohey (10 points), Allinei (4 points) and Camp (6 points).

- Prep opponents selected to the 1988 Dapper Dan Roundball Classic included Oak Hill Academy's **Orlando Vega**, MVP of the East team; and **Anthony Peeler** of Kansas City Paseo, MVP of the West team. After the 1987-88 season, Vega was recruited by Arizona State and later transferred to Providence but never played, returning to Puerto Rico where he played professional ball for 18 seasons.

Hellman and Kraus vie for a loose ball at Altoona.

1988 All-Opponent Team:

Orlando Vega, Oak Hill Academy [Arizona State, Providence]

Alex Blackwell, Oak Hill Academy [Monmouth College; NBA Lakers]

Sean Scrutchins, Toledo Scott [Dayton]

Bruce Keys, Tech (hm all-state) [Akron, football]

Don Burnett, Meadville (2nd team all-state) [St. Bonaventure]

Anthony Peeler, KC Paseo (McDonald's All-American) [Missouri; NBA Lakers, Grizzlies, Timberwolves, Kings & Wizards]

Evan Pederson, St. Louis Parkway West [Northwestern, St. Louis]

Rodney Holmes, South Bend St. Joseph's [Michigan State, Ball State]

Tim Smith, Vincent (4th team all-state) [Lock Haven]

Cliff Beck, Mercyhurst [Mercyhurst]

Joe Brumbaugh, Altoona (hm all-state)

Dave Ostrowski, Fox Chapel (hm all-state)

Gravelle Craig, Farrell (2nd team all-state) [Cleveland State; head coach Bethune-Cookman]

Jim McCoy, Pittsburgh Central Catholic (1st team all-state) [Massachusetts]

Junior Billy Speros.

Prep Runs Away With Metro Title!

1988-89 (19-8)

Coach: Marcel Arribi
Assistants: Jim Marnella, Tom DelFratte
Captains: Steve Ziegler, Mike Heberle
Manager: Rick Gudowski

Coach Marcel Arribi shows intensity on the sideline.

Date	PREP			Dec.	Loc.	High Scorer	Opponent
12/9	48	Philadelphia Roman Catholic	68	L	H	Heberle (27)	Watkins (23)
12/16	76	East	53	W	N	Ziegler (21)	Jones (13)
12/17	72	Warren	47	W	A	Ziegler (21)	Farr (12)
12/20	73	Mercyhurst	43	W	N	Heberle (21)	Thomes (15)
		CITY OF PALMS CLASSIC (FT. MYERS, FL)					
12/26	62	Stuart (FL) Martin County High	64	L	N	Heberle (18)	McWilliams (16)
12/2	70	Naples (FL) Baron G. Collier	49	W	N	Ziegler (24)	Dinesen (22)
12/29	59	Pensacola (FL) B. T. Washington	56	W	N	Ziegler (16)	Donald (21)
12/30	55	Gainesville (FL) F. W. Buchholz	69	L	N	Ziegler (23)	Fox (18)
1/3	81	Academy	55	W	N	Pecarski (25)	Page (13)
1/5	59	Strong Vincent	48	W	N	Ziegler (20)	Blanks (16)
1/7	61	State College	40	W	H	Pecarski (16)	Cronemiller (17)
1/10	57	McDowell	46	W	N	Pecarski (13)	Hersperger (17)
1/17	85	Tech Memorial	46	W	N	Kraus (17)	Buerger (13)
		McDONALD'S CLASSIC					
1/20	38	Cleveland (OH) St. Joseph's	61	L	H	Cardot (12)	Redding (16)
1/21	50	Lorain (OH) Admiral King	51	L	H	Heberle (15)	Gladden (20)
1/27	58	Mercyhurst	4	W	N	Ziegler (13)	Thomes (10)
1/28	43	Meadville	61	L	A	Ziegler (14)	Dumancic (16)
2/4	84	DuBois	50	W	H	Heberle (23)	Volansky (21)
2/7	71	East	46	W	N	Pecarski (21)	Johnson (13)
2/10	68	Tech Memorial	50	W	N	Ziegler (21)	Gieza (22)
2/17	58	Academy	57	W	N	Kraus (18)	Williams (17)
2/23	63	McDowell	57	W	N	Ziegler (18)	Wilhelm (20)
2/26	59	Strong Vincent	51	W	N	Heberle (14)	Blanks (17)
		DISTRICT 10 PLAYOFFS					
3/4	82	Franklin	43	W	N	Ziegler (21)	Koziara (13)
3/9	55	Meadville	60	L	N	Ziegler & Stablein (18)	Newsome (17)
		P.I.A.A. INTERDISTRICT PLAYOFFS					
3/15	57	Butler	43	W	N	Heberle (21)	Cooper (16)
3/18	50	Pittsburgh Brashear	56	L	N	Ziegler (11)	Booth (15)
	1694 (62.7)		**1414 (52.4)**				

Pos.	Player	Ht.	Prior School	Class	G(GS)	FG(3)	FT	Total	PPG	Career
F	Steve Ziegler (#22)	6'3"	St. John's	Sr.	25(21)	147(8)	64	366	14.6	633
G	Mike Heberle (#21)	6'2"	St. John's	Sr.	26(26)	138(16)	44	336	12.9	591
F	Sasha Pecarski (#30)	6'1"	Yugoslavia	Sr.	27(22)	73(27*)	41	214	7.9	214
G	Jeff Cardot (#11)	5'9"	St. Luke's	Jr.	24(23)	59(27*)	59	204	8.5	247
F	Phil Kraus (#42)	6'4"	St. George's	Sr.	27(26)	87(2)	26	202	7.5	348
F	Todd Stablein (#32)	6'2"	OLP/McDowell	Jr.	26(12)	66(2)	31	165	6.3	167
G	John Donnelly (#20)	5'8"	Fairview	Soph.	23(2)	12(1)	18	43	1.9	43
F	Jim Hamilton (#51)	6'0"	OLC	Soph.	18	17(4)	4	42	2.4	42
F	John Smith (#41)	6'1"	St. James	Sr.	10	14(2)	8	38	3.8	52
F	Rich Toohey (#40)	6'0"	St. George's	Jr.	13	12	7	31	2.4	31
G	Kevin Trapp (#10)	5'2"	St. Boniface	Jr.	15(1)	6(4)	12	28	1.9	28
G	John Steiner (#31)	6'1"	Bl. Sacrament	Sr.	18(1)	8	10	26	1.6	49
F	Mike Kujawinski (#50)	6'0"	St. Peter's	Jr.	10	2	0	4	0.4	4
G	Todd Filipkowski (#12)	5'8"	St. John's	Soph.	1	0	0	0	0.0	0

HIGHLIGHTS:

- **Marcel Arribi's** second season at the Cathedral Prep helm produced another exciting, successful season. The favored Ramblers breezed to the Metro League title at 12-0, their best league record ever, and had easy wins in playoff encounters against Franklin and Butler. Prep showcased an experienced senior cast with top scorer **Steve Ziegler**, all-around star **Mike Heberle** and a solid big man in **Phil Kraus**; a welcomed transfer in **Sasha Pecarski**; and a pair of excellent juniors in **Jeff Cardot** and **Todd Stablein**. And, of course, there was the intense coaching of Arribi.

Prep's 1989 Metro League champions. Front, L to R: Manager, Cardot, Donnelly, Toohey, Trapp, Steiner, Smith, Filipkowski; Back: Huff, Heberle, Kujawinski, Stablein, Kraus, Ziegler, Pecarski, Hamilton, Coach Arribi.

- All Metro League games and Prep home games were played at Gannon's Hammermill Center. The District 10 semifinal was held at McComb Fieldhouse, while the final was played at the Erie Civic Center before 4,381 fans. The Butler inter-district contest was played at the Pitt Fieldhouse and the second round loss to Brashear was nevertheless decided with a home court advantage at the Hammermill Center.

Yugoslavian Sasha Pecarski with an "and one" versus DuBois.

- Prep finished 8th in the 16-team field at the City of Palms Basketball Classic with a 2-2 record. The tournament began in 1973 with a format of seven local teams. By 1985 the tourney had skyrocketed into a major national event. Currently, the tournament consists of a 16-team national bracket, with selected "Sunshine Series" games (featuring additional high school teams from Florida and Georgia) dotting the schedule throughout the typically five- or six-day event. Fort Myers High School hosted the event from 1985 through 1989. The 1988 champion was Miami (FL) Carol City High, with orange and black colors no less.

- Of the Florida opponents: Stuart County won three state basketball championships in the 1970's; contrary to popular belief Collier was never in fact a prison, but was and continues to be a school; Booker T. Washington first opened in 1916 as a segregated black school and remained that way until 1969, when it was integrated as a result of a federal court order, and its school song is Cream's "I'm So Glad"; and Buchholz, which lost to state champion Miami Senior in the Florida 4A (large school) semifinals, 73-56, is the largest public high school in Gainesville, with an enrollment over 3,000.

- The sixth annual McDonald's Classic moved from a tip-off tournament to mid-January and from the Erie Civic Center to the jam-packed Gannon University Hammermill Center for the first time. Jersey City (NJ) St. Anthony, led by stars **Bobby Hurley, Terry Dehere** and **Jerry Wallace**, made easy pickings of Admiral King, 69-50, and Cleveland St. Joseph, 65-47, and went on to finish the season as national champion with a final record of 32-0. St. Anthony's four-year record with Hurley as point guard was 115–5. Hurley became a first team All-American at Duke, winning a pair of NCAA titles, and further played with the NBA's Sacramento Kings and Vancouver Grizzlies. Hurley is now head coach at the University of Buffalo. Dehere starred at Seton Hall and had an NBA career with the Kings, Grizzlies and Los Angeles Clippers.

Heberle scores a bucket against Cleveland St. Joe's in the McDonald's Classic.

• Prep failed to win a McDonald's Classic game for the first time since the tournament's inception in 1983, losing to both Cleveland St. Joe's (20-7) and Admiral King (20-3). The Ramblers shot horribly against the Vikings the first night and against the Admirals in the consolation match a valiant rally fell just short. St. Joe's finished the season strong, winning its district, regional and state semifinal games, before losing to Toledo Macomber-Whitney in the Ohio Division I state championship game, 75-72, in overtime.

• Admiral King's **Jamie Gladden** in 1988-89 scored 554 points while averaging 23.1 PPG. The Admirals were Erie Shore Conference co-champions, Sectional champs and District runners-up, losing to St. Edward, 65-60, in the final. Gladden's outstanding play carried the team to a third place ranking in Ohio's final AP poll. As a side note, the Admirals were the winningest Division I team in Ohio in the 1980's (281-34). Since that time Admiral King merged with Lorain High to form Lorain Admiral King. In 2010 the school merged with Lorain Southview and that city's only public high school is now simply known as Lorain High.

• Prep completely dismantled a good Franklin (18-6) team in the District 10 opener with a full team effort. Disheartening, however, were the pair of losses to white-hot rival Meadville (23-4), including in the D-10 final. It was the sixth straight year the Bulldogs played in the D-10 championship game and their second crown in three years. The Rambler-Bulldog matchups were interesting if for no other reasons both teams presented Yugoslavian foreign exchange students—Meadville's 6'10" center **Dominik Dumancic** and Prep's long-range shooting artist, senior **Sasha Pecarski**.

• Prep dedicated its first round PIAA playoff game against Butler (25-3) to **Todd Stablein**, who was home with a fever. **Mike Heberle** scored 21 points and **Steve Ziegler** added 14 as the Ramblers upset the WPIAL's Section 3 champs by simply outhustling the Golden Tornadoes down the floor.

• Prep's loss in a PIAA Western Quarterfinal to Brashear (20-7) was particularly disappointing, in that even with the home court advantage the Ramblers could shoot only 28% from the floor, including only 4 of 23 in 3-point shots. Prep outrebounded the Bullets, 49-30, but was sunk when the Ramblers missed their first 13 shots of the second half. Brashear advanced all the way to the state final, where it lost to Chester, 72-57.

• The final standings in the Metro League were as follows:

	W	L
Prep	12	0
Vincent	8	4
Academy	8	4
McDowell	7	5
Tech	3	9
Mercyhurst	3	9
East	1	11

Long-range bomber Sasha Pecarski, along with Cardot, set the first Rambler 3-point shot records.

• Leading scorer **Steve Ziegler** was named First Team Metro League All-Star by the *Erie Times-News.* Versatile **Mike Heberle** and dependable **Phil Kraus** were Second Team selections, while **Jeff Cardot** was an Honorable Mention choice.

• Ziegler led the City All-Stars with 14 points, Heberle added 10 and Kraus 6 in the Northwest Jaycees 15th annual post-season City-County All-Star game held at the Hammermill Center. The City won its 14th straight, 98-91.

Phil Kraus was a versatile inside star.

• Prep opponents selected to the 1989 Dapper Dan Roundball Classic included Roman Catholic's **Alan Watkins**, who scored 19 points in a 96-84 win for the East over the West; and Meadville's Dumancic, who scored 14, including three 3-pointers, for the West Penn stars in a 133-121 lost to the City/Quad A team in the preliminary.

- Three-sport star **John Smith** proved to be one of Prep's all-time running backs, gaining 1,049 yards for coach **Mina George's** 1988 District 10 champion Ramblers.

- **Steve Ziegler** was winner of the annual James "Moe" Gross Award, signifying him as Prep's Most Valuable Player, while **Mike Heberle**, a star quarterback who played at Pitt, won the "Ma" Kaiser Award, signifying him as Prep's best athlete.

- In a mysterious situation, **Steve Ziegler** simply vanished and has been reported as a missing person since May 3, 2005. He was last seen late-night in an Erie tavern eating a hamburger and drinking pop. Erie police have been baffled by the disappearance and they have had difficulty finding a trace of the low-profile Ziegler, as he had no credit cards, mortgage, phone bills or records, rental contracts, etc.

Leading scorer Steve Ziegler was a First Team All-Metro selection and the Ramblers' MVP. Nobody knows where he is right now.

1989 All-Opponent team:

Alan Watkins, Roman Catholic (3rd team all-state) [Duquesne]

Michael Blanks, Vincent (hm all-state)

Nick Kupetz, Cleveland St. Joe's [Clarion]

Dave Wojciechowski, Cleveland St. Joe's [Clarion]

Tony Redding, Cleveland St. Joe's [Mercyhurst]

Jamie Gladden, Admiral King (1st team all-state, OH) [Xavier (OH)]

Joel Volansky, DuBois

Ed Gieza, Tech (hm all-state) [Mercyhurst]

Mark Wilhelm, McDowell (hm all-state)

Pat Swick, Meadville

Dominik Dumancic, Meadville (sm all-state) [Pitt]

Bill "Bucky" Newsome, Meadville

Steve Cooper, Butler

Mike Booth, Brashear [West Virginia, football]

Brian Brown, Brashear

John Smith was a three-sport star at Prep. Stats show he and Steiner led the team in scoring during warm-ups.

John Steiner was reliable off the bench. Stats show he and Smith led the team in scoring during warm-ups.

Heberle gets two of his 27 against Roman Catholic.

Team captain Mike Heberle, also a star QB, won the "Ma" Kaiser Award as Prep's best all-round athlete. He played football at Pitt.

Ziegler for two more versus Dubois.

Kraus is unstoppable against Roman Catholic.

The 1990's

A tense situation in the closing moments of the Western Final. On the bench, L to R: Coleman, Dennett, Reid, Summerville, Bielak. (1993)

Prep players and fans celebrate as the final buzzer signifies the huge upset over New Castle in the Western Final at Edinboro. (1993)

Metro League, District 10 Champs!

1989-90 (21-5)

Coach: Marcel Arribi
Assistant: Jim Marnella
Captains: Todd Stablein, Jeff Cardot
Managers: Dave Mucha, Jon Trapp, Steve Demyanovich

Coach Marcel Arribi molded a team with great chemistry.

Date	PREP		Dec.	Loc.	High Scorer	Opponent
	LATROBE ROTARY CLUB TIP-OFF CLASSIC					
12/8	61	Philadelphia Benjamin Franklin	72	L	N	Stablein (22)	West (16)
12/9	71	Latrobe	49	W	A	Hamilton (19)	Saunders (18)
12/15	73	Mercyhurst Prep	32	W	N	Stablein (17)	Horton & Cameron (7)
12/19	95	East	57	W	N	Hamilton (17)	A. Johnson (19)
	GREAT CHEVY SHOOTOUT (ALTOONA)					
12/22	78	Altoona Bishop Guilfoyle	55	W	A	Cardot (25)	Ronan (13)
12/23	81	Baltimore (MD) Cardinal Gibbons	64	W	N	Stablein (26)	Musick (19)
	BURGER KING PREPSTAR SHOOTOUT (FAYETTEVILLE, NC)					
12/28	53	Bladenboro (NC)	60	L	N	Stablein (19)	Owens (22)
12/29	88	Fayetteville (NC) Academy	53	W	A	Stablein (17)	Inman (15)
12/30	65	Raleigh (NC) Athens Drive	47	W	N	Hamilton (17)	Rice & Brown (9)
1/3	64	Academy	60	W	N	Stablein (18)	Jordan & Knight (13)
1/9	62	McDowell	51	W	N	Cardot (17)	Morrow (17)
1/11	68	Strong Vincent	48	W	N	Cardot (20)	Sansom (15)
1/16	97	Tech Memorial	69	W	N	Cardot (21)	Jells (19)
	McDONALD'S CLASSIC					
1/19	68	Baltimore (MD) Dunbar	62	W	H	Hamilton (20)	Bright (20)
1/20	63	Mouth of Wilson (VA) Oak Hill Academy	76	L	H	Hamilton (26)	Cade (27)
1/26	64	Mercyhurst Prep	57	W	N	Stablein & Cardot (17)	Horton (18)
2/2	77	East	55	W	N	Cardot (18)	A. Johnson (16)
2/6	83	Tech Memorial	46	W	N	Stablein (16)	Lanager (10)
2/9	81	State College	65	W	A	Cardot (21)	Ermol (16)
2/10	69	Williamsport	85	L	A	Stablein (22)	Bullock (21)
2/17	54	Academy	42	W	N	Stablein (16)	McDonald (15)
2/22	64	McDowell	48	W	N	Stablein (14)	Morrow & Roward (11)
2/24	59	Strong Vincent	35	W	N	Toohey (12)	Orlando (11)
	DISTRICT 10 PLAYOFFS					
3/2	62	Meadville	43	W	N	Stablein (12)	Newsome (18)
3/8	79	Franklin	51	W	N	Hamilton (27)	Koziara (15)
	P.I.A.A. INTERDISTRICT PLAYOFF					
3/17	72	Shaler Area	77	L	N	Hamilton (22)	Jones (24)
	1851 (71.2)		**1459 (56.1)**			

Pos.	Player	Ht.	Prior School	Class	G(GS)	FG(3)	FT	Total	PPG	Career
F	Jim Hamilton (#32)	6'3"	OLC	Jr.	26(25)	140(46*)	63	389	15.0	430
C	Todd Stablein (#41)	6'3"	OLP/McDowell	Sr.	25(25)	154(3)	70	381	15.2	548
G	Jeff Cardot (#31)	5'9"	St. Luke's	Sr.	26(26)	110(32)	107	359	13.8	606
G	Todd Filipkowski (#21)	5'10"	St. John's	Jr.	26(24)	80(13)	47	220	8.5	220
F	Rich Toohey (#22)	6'0"	St. George's	Sr.	26(24)	56(2)	8	122	4.7	153
F	Mark Tate (#20)	5'10"	Luther Memorial	Soph.	23	39	34	112	4.9	112
F	Mike Kujawinski (#50)	6'0"	St. Peter's	Sr.	24(3)	30	29	89	3.7	93
G	John Donnelly (#30)	5'8"	Fairview	Jr.	21(2)	18(2)	20	58	2.8	101
F	Drew Hoffman (#12)	5'10"	St. George's	Sr.	15(1)	17(1)	4	39	2.6	39
G	Kevin Trapp (#10)	5'2"	St. Boniface	Sr.	18	9(4)	15	37	2.1	65
G	Joe Gaeta (#40)	5'7"	Sacred Heart	Jr.	15	8(1)	7	24	1.6	24
F	Paul Samlock (#42)	6'0"	St. Luke's	Jr.	16	6	9	21	1.3	21

HIGHLIGHTS:

- **Art Bergamasco** became Cathedral Prep's first lay headmaster and sixth overall following the retirement of **Monsignor John Hagerty**. Bergamasco, a native of Meadville, had been a principal within the Millcreek School District for eight years and brought to Prep what was termed "strong business experience."

- **Marcel Arribi's** third year as Cathedral Prep mentor produced an excellent season, as the Ramblers again won the Metro League, going 12-0; returned as District 10 champions after a one-year absence; won consolation honors at the Latrobe Tip-Off Tourney; won the 1st annual Great Chevy Shootout; finished third at the Fayetteville Prepstar Shootout; and were runners-up in the 7th annual McDonald's Classic. The Ramblers had great chemistry, despite battling through several injuries throughout the season. Not a big team by any stretch, Prep showcased uncanny shooting (51% FG, including 45% from 3-point range) and ball control, as well as a relentless full court man-to-man defense.

Prep's 1990 Metro League and District 10 Champions. Front, L to R: Gaeta, Trapp, Donnelly; Middle: Tate, Hoffman, Filipkowski, Cardot; Back: Samlock, Kujawinski, Stablein, Hamilton, Toohey.

- All Metro League games were played at Gannon's Hammermill Center; the Great Chevy Shootout was played at the Jaffa Mosque in Altoona, the first games at the storied Mosque in 17 years; the 8-team Fayetteville tourney was played at the Cumberland County Memorial Arena; and the McDonald's Classic was played at the Hammermill Center. The Meadville D-10 game was oddly played at McDowell, while the Erie Civic Center hosted the title clash versus Franklin.

- Benjamin Franklin High (9-9), a new opponent that defeated Prep in the season opener at the Latrobe Tip-Off, is located just north of Philadelphia's Center City. The Electrons have produced several NBA players over the years, including **"Pooh" Richardson, "Snoop" Graham, Randy Woods** and **Fred Carter**, as well as Philly playground legend **Bryant "Sad Eye" Watson**. Also listed among Franklin alumni is esteemed former Cheyney State and Temple coach **John Chaney**. Prep's victory over host Latrobe (20-7) turned out to be a good one, as the Wildcats made it to the PIAA second round before losing to Peabody, 48-47.

- Benjamin Franklin High operated in Division C of the Philadelphia Public League, which also included Franklin Learning Center, Dobbins, Mastbaum, Edison, University City and William Penn.

Stablein increases the lead against Tech.

- Prep's win over Bishop Guilfoyle in the Great Chevy Shootout was the first time the two competed since 1974. **Todd Stablein** was named MVP of the tourney, while **Jeff Cardot** also made the all-tournament team. Stablein also made the all-tourney team in Fayetteville.

Cardot accepts congratulations for making the All-Tourney team at the Prepstar Shootout.

- Prep's third place finish in its only entry in the Burger King Prepstar Shootout was impressive. Of the Ramblers' Prepstar opponents: Bladenboro High no longer exists, as in 2002 students from Bladenboro, Tar Heel High and Clarkton High combined to form West Bladen High School; Fayetteville Academy is an independent, non-sectarian, college preparatory school that opened in 1970; Athens Drive is a large public school that opened in 1978 and lists as its most famous athlete **Josh Hamilton** of major league baseball fame.

- The McDonald's Classic featured another outstanding lineup, headed by renowned nationally ranked Baltimore Dunbar (22-4) and #2 Oak Hill Academy (29-0). Dunbar was defending Baltimore city champ and ranked pre-season by *USA Today* at #18. The Poets could lay claim as the best high school team of the 1980's, winning national championships in 1982, 1983 and 1985. Oak Hill was on a 56-game winning streak and *Sports Illustrated* noted at the time "In a catalog of hoop powers, Oak Hill belongs on its own page."

- In one of their all-time wins, the Prep Ramblers upset Dunbar, 68-62, on opening night after Oak Hill disposed of Meadville, 86-49. Dunbar then overwhelmed Meadville for consolation

honors, 72-48, while the Ramblers lost a hard-fought battle to Oak Hill in the final, 76-63. Led by 6'9" center **Anthony Cade**, from Bronx (NY), Oak Hill moved to 21-0 on the season and went on to finish undefeated and ranked #2 in the nation. Prep junior **Jim Hamilton** caught fire against Oak Hill, nailing six 3-pointers, giving him a record 8 for the tourney.

- Prep jumped out to a 22-0 lead in the first game against Tech (4-19); and in the second Vincent (10-13) game scored a stretch of 30 unanswered points and led 34-6 early in the second half! In the second Tech contest, **Todd Stablein** was 7 of 7 from the field and 2 for 2 from the line, while sophomore **Mark Tate** was 5 for 5 from the floor and 4 for 4 from the stripe. The 1989-90 Centaurs were their worst team ever, record-wise.

- Prep's easy pair of victories over rival McDowell (16-9) made for nine straight for the Ramblers over the Trojans.

- The final standings in the Metro League were as follows:

	W	L
Prep	12	0
McDowell	9	3
Academy	8	4
East	4	8
Mercyhurst	4	8
Vincent	3	9
Tech	2	10

- Prep returned as king of D-10 hoops after a one-year absence, using its pressure defense to breeze to victory over Meadville (15-8) and **Jim Hamilton's** season-high 27 points to rout Franklin (19-5) in the final. This put the Ramblers in a favorable part of the PIAA state bracket, having to face the WPIAL's 7th seeded team.

- The season's biggest disappointment was Prep's shocking first round upset loss in PIAA inter-district play to Shaler (19-9). Played at the McComb Fieldhouse, the Ramblers ran into foul trouble, committed 6 fourth quarter turnovers and blew a 13-point third quarter lead. Regardless, the 1989-90 Ramblers were considered overachievers and the season was deemed very successful.

Senior spot-starter Mike Kujawinski.

Senior reserve Drew Hoffman.

Jumping junior Jim Hamilton led the Ramblers in scoring and was named Second Team All-Metro. Here, Kujawinski watches as "The Hammer" tallies again.

- Leading scorer **Todd Stablein** shot an amazing 60.8 % from the floor and in only 3 games all season did he shoot less than 50 %. Stablein also led the Ramblers in rebounding (7.8 RPG), while guards **Todd Filipkowski** (4.4 APG) and **Jeff Cardot** (4.3 APG) led the squad in the assist department. Cardot led the Orange & Black in free throw shooting at 80.5 % and hit 10 of 11 against Cardinal Gibbons and 10 of 10 against Academy. Sharpshooter **Jim Hamilton** set a record with 46 three-pointers for the year.

- Senior **Kevin Trapp**, at only 5'2", is considered to be the smallest player ever to wear a Prep varsity uniform. One could not measure the size of his heart.

- Erie County League entrant Girard won the PIAA Class AA state title with a 59-49 verdict over Wilkes Barre GAR Memorial in the final. The Yellowjackets finished with a 32-0 record and were led by **Marc Blucas**, later of Wake Forest and currently a star Hollywood actor.

Kevin Trapp, believed to be the smallest Prep hoopster ever. One could not measure the size of his heart.

- Prep opponents **Joe Saunders** of Greater Latrobe and **"Bucky" Newsome** of Meadville competed for the City/AAAA team against West Penn in the preliminary game of the 1990 Dapper Dan Classic. Newsome starred with 13 points and 8 rebounds in a 115-110 loss.

- Seniors **Jeff Cardot** and **Todd Stablein** were both named First Team on the 1989-90 All-Metro Basketball Team as announced by the *Erie Times-News*, while junior **Jim Hamilton** was a Second Team selection.

- Girard's Blucas helped the County All-Stars snap a 14-game losing streak by scoring a team-high 19 points in a 107-85 thumping of the City. Prep's Stablein led the City in scoring with 19, while Cardot chipped in 8.

Starting senior forward Rich Toohey, now known as "Father Rich Toohey."

- **Rich Toohey**, later **"Father Rich Toohey,"** was named winner of the Dave Tyzinski Memorial Trophy, signifying him as Prep's best two-sport athlete. As a priest Father Toohey organized the "Running Revs," a squad of clergymen that ministered to and competed against various parish basketball teams.

- **Jeff Cardot** and **Todd Stablein** were co-winners of the prestigious James "Moe" Gross Award as Prep's most valuable players. Stablein went on to star at Gannon University, scoring 649 career points.

1990 All-Opponent Team

    Tyrone West, Philadelphia Ben Franklin
    Dajuan Williams, Philadelphia Ben Franklin
    Joe Saunders, Latrobe [St. Vincent's]
    A.J. Johnson, East
    Trelonnie Owens, Bladenboro (NC Player of the Year) [Wake Forest]
    Wilbert Hunter, Athens Drive [East Carolina]
    Chris Morrow, McDowell [Penn St.-Behrend]
    Dietrich Jells, Tech [Pitt, football; NFL Patriots, Eagles]
    Donta Bright, Baltimore Dunbar [Massachusetts]
    Anthony Cade, Oak Hill Academy (McDonald's All-American) [Connors St. JC, Seminole St. JC]
    Carlos Cofield, Oak Hill Academy [Rhode Island]
    Gandhi Jordan, Oak Hill Academy [Hartford]
    Jason Bullock, Williamsport [IUP]
    Bill "Bucky" Newsome, Meadville [Gannon]
    Kevin Hannan, Shaler
    Tim Jones, Shaler

Co-MVP and three-year star Jeff Cardot was a First Team All-Metro pick.

Co-MVP Todd Stablein, a First Team All-Metro selection. He went on to star at Gannon University.

Ramblers Reach Amazing 38 Straight Metro Wins! McDonald's Classic, Metro and D-10 Winners!

1990-91 (22-5)

Coach: Marcel Arribi
Assistants: Jim Marnella, Wes Alexander
Captains: Jim Hamilton, Todd Filipkowski
Managers: Dave Mucha, Jon Trapp,
    Steve Demyanovich

The Ramblers rejoice at capturing the McDonald's Classic in thrilling fashion.

Date	PREP		Dec.	Loc.	High Scorer	Opponent
	STEELTON ROLLER INVITATIONAL					
12/7	55	York Catholic	66	L	N	Hamilton (33)	Calhoun (23)
12/8	83	Ringgold	64	W	N	Hamilton (20)	Miller (23)
12/14	61	Academy	52	W	N	Hamilton (25)	McDonald (28)
	KING OF BLUEGRASS TOURNAMENT (FAIRDALE, KY)					
12/19	81	Chattanooga (TN) Brainerd	76 (OT)	W	N	Hamilton (42)	Alexander (22)
12/20	77	Huntsville (AL) S.R. Butler	66	W	N	Hamilton (26)	McGinnis (32)
12/21	65	Fairdale (KY)	70	L	A	Hamilton (23)	Morris (19)
12/22	73	Louisville (KY) Male Traditional	75 (2OT)	L	N	Hamilton (24)	Osborne (22)
	FARRELL HOLIDAY TOURNAMENT					
12/27	82	Butler	68	W	N	Hamilton (29)	Heiman (22)
12/28	63	Farrell	66	L	N	Hamilton (30)	B. Brodie (20)
1/2	61	McDowell	54	W	N	Hamilton (20)	Metzger (26)
1/5	69	State College	61	W	H	Hamilton & Dennett (18)	Farbaugh (23)
1/8	76	Strong Vincent	39	W	N	Hamilton & Tate (13)	Montie (19)
1/12	69	Tech Memorial	68	W	N	Hamilton (28)	J. Roberts (16)
1/15	86	East	37	W	N	Filipkowski (16)	Crosby (8)
	McDONALD'S CLASSIC					
1/18	82	Trumbull (CT) St. Joseph	65	W	H	Hamilton (26)	Gras (21)
1/19	70	Brooklyn (NY) Bishop Loughlin	69	W	H	Hamilton (28)	Anderson (16)
1/25	74	Mercyhurst Prep	56	W	N	Hamilton (25)	Horton (23)
2/2	47	Academy	31	W	N	Hamilton (14)	McDonald (10)
2/8	62	McDowell	48	W	N	Filipkowski (18)	Roward (10)
2/12	76	Strong Vincent	58	W	N	Hamilton (21)	Bennett (17)
2/15	75	Tech Memorial	44	W	N	Hamilton (21)	J. Roberts (20)
2/19	93	East	50	W	N	Filipkowski (17)	Mitchell (14)
2/21	76	Mercyhurst Prep	58	W	N	Hamilton (21)	Horton (32)
	DISTRICT 10 PLAYOFFS					
2/28	81	Franklin	63	W	N	Hamilton (33)	Davis (23)
3/7	56	McDowell	35	W	N	Hamilton (21)	Hubert (10)
	P.I.A.A. INTERDISTRICT PLAYOFFS					
3/12	83	Fox Chapel	42	W	N	Hamilton (22)	Hudak & Ostrosky (14)
3/14	98	Altoona	101*(2OT)	L	N	Hamilton (37)	Taneyhill (34)
	1974 (73.1)		**1582 (58.6)**				

Pos.	Player	Ht.	Prior School	Class	G(GS)	FG(3)	FT	Total	PPG	Career
F	Jim Hamilton (#32)	6'3"	OLC	Sr.	27(27)	238*(86*)	83-113	645*	23.9*	1076
G	Todd Filipkowski (#21)	5'10"	St. John's	Sr.	25(25)	130(23)	74-98	357	14.3	577
G	John Donnelly (#30)	6'0"	Fairview	Sr.	27(27)	64(7)	82-118	217	8.0	318
F	Mark Tate (#20)	5'10"	Luther Memorial	Jr.	27(27)	72	56-88	200	7.4	312
F	Cliff Dennett (#41)	6'3"	Fairview	Soph.	27(7)	63(20)	19-28	165	6.1	165
G	Josh Schneidmiller (#10)	5'9"	Holy Rosary	Sr.	27(2)	49(12)	37-48	147	5.4	147
F	Paul Samlock (#42)	6'0"	St. Luke's	Sr.	27(20)	52(1)	16-35	121	4.5	142
C	Rick Kaczenski (#52)	6'2"	St. John's	Soph.	13	13	4-7	30	2.3	30
G	Mike King (#31)	5'10"	St. Patrick's	Jr.	10	8(1)	8-11	25	2.5	25
F	Mike Guelcher (#51)	6'0"	OLC	Jr.	10	11	2-4	24	2.4	24
F	Eugene Tomczak (#40)	5'11"	St. Stan's	Soph.	10	6	2-3	14	1.4	14
G	Derrick Reid (#11)	5'6"	St. John's	Soph.	8	5	0-0	10	1.3	10
F	Matt Bennett (#50)	6'0"	OLC	Soph.	7	1	6-8	8	1.1	8
G	Jim Sitter (#12)	5'8"	St. George's	Jr.	6	2	3-6	7	1.2	7
F	Mike Wernicki (#22)	5'9"	OLMC/St. James	Sr.	6	1	1-2	3	0.5	3
	Unknown					0	1-1	1		

Prep's 1991 Metro League and District 10 Champions. Front, L to R: King, Donnelly, Filipkowski, Wernicki, Reid; Middle: Schneidmiller, Sitter, Bennett, Tomczak, Guelcher; Back: Samlock, Kaczenski, Dennett, Hamilton, Coleman. Missing: Tate.

Senior Josh Schneidmiller was also a star quarterback for the Orange & Black.

HIGHLIGHTS:

• **Marcel Arribi's** fourth year as Cathedral Prep coach was spectacular, as the Ramblers were barely challenged in the Metro League, going 12-0 for the third straight season; again won the District 10 championship; won consolation honors at the Roller Classic; took 4th place at the King of Bluegrass Tourney; and became the first team to win the McDonald's Classic for a second time. Record-setting senior **Jim Hamilton** had an outstanding season, shattering several Prep scoring records. Other stars included experienced senior guards **Todd Filipkowski** and **John Donnelly**, as well as dependable senior **Paul Samlock**, junior football star **Mark Tate**, senior **Josh Schneidmiller** and sophomore transfer **Cliff Dennett**. The Ramblers once again displayed great chemistry and superb coaching by Arribi, only to lose in second round PIAA inter-district action in an extra memorable performance with Altoona after a 17-game winning streak.

• All Metro League games were played at Gannon's Hammermill Center, while the State College home game was the first played at the Mercyhurst College Campus Center in three years. The Roller Classic was contested at Steelton-Highspire High School; the December tournaments were at Fairdale (KY) High School and Farrell High School; and the McDonald's Classic was played at the Hammermill Center. The Franklin and Fox Chapel playoff games were played at Edinboro's McComb Fieldhouse, while the Erie Civic Center hosted the D-10 title clash versus McDowell. Clarion University's Waldo

Athletic Director Ron Sertz and Coach Arribi embrace after beating McDowell for the District 10 crown, as assistant Wes Alexander is all smiles.

Tippin Gym was the scene of the Altoona loss.

- Prep faced new opponents in the season-opening Steelton Roller Invitational, the 2nd annual. (31-1) had just won the 1990 PIAA AAA state title and had also won four previous state championships: in 1978 (AA), 1979 (AA) and 1987 (AAA); as well as a PCIAA Class B crown in 1948. Fighting Irish 6' floor general **Brian Pearl** later in the season became the first York/Adams Counties player to cross 2,000 career points. YC's win over Prep was its 27th consecutive victory. It went on to win District 3 and remain undefeated (57 straight) until upset by Pottstown in the PIAA Eastern Final.

Dependable senior forward Paul Samlock.

Mark Tate slices through the Altoona defense.

- Prep's consolation game win in Steelton over Ringgold (17-7) was impressive, as the Rams were coming off a 29-3 season and a berth in the 1990 PIAA Quad-A state title game, where they lost to Glen Mills, 76-74. Ringgold is known as the alma mater of NFL great **Joe Montana** and was formed in 1964 by the merger in of three high schools: Donora, Monongahela and Finleyville. Donora and Monongahela actually kept two separate campuses until the new school was built in 1979 and had separate athletic programs until 1969-70 when they merged and formed the "Ringgold Rams." Ringgold was named in honor of the "Ringgold Cavalry" and **Samuel Ringgold** of Mexican War fame, also known as the "Father of Modern Artillery."

Hamilton draws a foul at York Catholic.

- Prep won an impressive fourth place finish in the 16-team field at the 10th annual King of Bluegrass Tournament, the only time the Ramblers have participated in the high class event which lasts to this day. **Jim Hamilton** and **Todd Filipkowski** were both named to the All-Tourney team. Hamilton's incredible 42 points, including seven 3-pointers, in the great win over Brainerd is considered one of the all-time performances at the Bluegrass. That broke **Dan Sculley's** Prep record of 41 set in 1977-78 against Pittsburgh Brashear and lasts as a Rambler record to this day. Both Brainerd and S. R. Butler were 9-0 when beaten by Prep; Kentucky's defending state champ Fairdale was ranked #5 in the nation by *USA Today*; and Male Traditional was #7 in Kentucky.

- King of Bluegrass opponent Brainerd won state basketball championships in 1984, 1988 and the next year in 1992. By

Hall-of-Famer Jim Hamilton pads the lead against Butler in the Farrell Tourney.

the time 69-year old **Robert High** was let go in 2013, he had coached the Panthers 37 seasons, compiling an overall record of 1,001-307. He is one of only 13 high school coaches nationally to earn over 1,000 victories. His teams won at least 20 games a season 31 times.

- Of Prep's other Bluegrass opponents: S. R. Butler (30-4) has won six state titles, one in 1966 and the others since its meeting with the Ramblers; host Fairdale (37-5) won state championships in 1990, 1991 and 1994 and are thus the last team in Kentucky to win back-to-back titles; Louisville Male opened in 1856 and is famous for listing as alumni many professional athletes. Male has won four state basketball crowns, though none since 1975.

- Eventual WPIAL champion Butler's (27-4) sharpshooter **Dan Heiman** nailed a Prep opponent record six 3-pointers against the Ramblers at the Farrell Holiday Tournament, won by the Farrell Steelers (18-7), who beat Prep in the final. The 5'7", 130-pound Heiman played for the WPIAL All-Stars in the preliminary at the 27th annual Dapper Dan Roundball Classic at the Pittsburgh Civic Arena.

- Prep's win over Vincent (13-15) on January 8 evened the all-time series between the Ramblers and Colonels at 60-60.

- Detroit Country Day School, which featured All-American and future Michigan and NBA star **Chris Webber** (1991 *USA Today* Player of the Year), came to the 8th annual McDonald's Classic as the heavy favorite, but was upset by Brooklyn Bishop Loughlin (23-3), 71-69. Loughlin then fell victim to several "back door" plays and a dramatic and memorable 3-point shot with four seconds left by Prep's **Jim Hamilton** in the most exciting Classic game to date. That shot was one of the greatest in Rambler history and it won the tourney over a team that finished ranked #3 in the state

High scoring First Team All-Metro forward Jim Hamilton is one of Prep's all-time greats.

of New York by season's end. Prep outscored Loughlin with 3-pointers, 11-0, with Hamilton nailing a McDonald's Classic record seven.

- Opening night Rambler victim Trumbull St. Joseph opened in 1962 and had but one coach in its entire history. By the time 80-year-old **Vito Montelli** retired in 2013, he completed 50 years at St. Joseph with a brilliant 878-329 record and 11 state championships. Montelli is the winningest coach in New England history and the only one to win Connecticut state basketball titles in all four classes.

- Among Prep's great victories were the three over rival and Metro League pre-season favorite McDowell (21-7), which boasted an imposing front line of 6'10" **Bryan Eisert**, 6'8" **Jeremy Metzger** and 6'6" **Steve Roward**. That made for a dozen consecutive wins for the Ramblers over the Trojans. Hamilton broke Prep's all-time single season scoring record in

the fourth quarter of the D-10 final against McDowell, when he scored his 17th point following a rebound on a fast break. The previous record was held by **Tim Gore**, who scored 581 in the Ramblers' 1979-80 state championship season. Hamilton had two more games to pad his record and finished with 645 for the campaign. His single-season points record lasted for four years, until broken by **Jed Ryan** in 1994-95, though Hamilton still owns the PPG record at 23.9. Hamilton retired as Prep's third all-time leading scorer, behind only **Tim Gore** and **Willis Cardot**.

- Hamilton also broke Prep's single season records for field goals (238) and 3-pointers (86).

- Prep's third straight perfect Metro League season (36-0, three seasons) ran its amazing consecutive Metro victory skein to 38 games. The final standings in the Metro League were as follows:

	W	L
Prep	12	0
Mercyhurst	8	4
McDowell	8	4
Vincent	6	6
Academy	5	7
Tech	3	9
East	0	12

- After Prep coasted to the District 10 title, the Ramblers walloped Fox Chapel (13-15) by 41 in PIAA first round action. The Foxes snuck into the tournament after upsetting the *Pittsburgh Post-Gazette*'s #3-ranked team, Mount Pleasant, 56-49.

- The classic double-overtime nip-and-tuck Western Semifinal battle with Altoona (23-8) at the jam-packed Clarion gym goes down as one of Prep's all-time memorable and heartbreaking losses. The Ramblers nailed an incredible 15 three-pointers, including six by **Jim Hamilton**, but the Mountain Lions, behind 6'7" freshman **Danny Fortson** (27 points), 6'7" **Brian**

Donnelly looks for an opening at York Catholic.

Filipkowski scores again versus Academy.

Rehm (30 points) and star gridiron quarterback 6'4" **Steve Taneyhill** (34 points), played inspired basketball and hung on in the superbly played contest. It was the only time in the history of Prep basketball that an opponent scored in triple figures. Altoona went on to win the Western title by defeating Butler, 60-57, before falling in the PIAA Quad-A title game to Glen Mills, 81-75.

- The high-scoring Prepsters came close to breaking the points per game average at 73.1, just shy of the 73.4 PPG mark set by the Ramblers twenty years before, in 1970-71.

- Metro League entrant Mercyhurst Prep (27-5), 0-14 all-time versus Prep to this point, brought glory to Erie—its Lakers boys' team won the AA state championship with a 58-55 verdict over Wilkes-Barre GAR Memorial—and the MPS girls' squad won the AAA crown with a 67-55 decision over Allentown Central Catholic! Junior **Khyl Horton** was the big star of the Lakers and

Classy guard John Donnelly started every game and was named Second Team All-Metro.

after the 1991-92 season was the Erie area's all-time leading scorer with 1,884 points. This stayed as a local record until broken by Prep's **Jed Ryan** with 1,926 just three years later. **Angie Potthoff**, later of Penn State, WNBA and Notre Dame coaching fame was the Lady Lakers big star.

- Seniors **Jim "Hammer" Hamilton** and **Todd "Flip" Filipkowski** were both named First Team on the 1990-91 All-Metro Basketball Team as announced by the *Erie Times-News*, while **John Donnelly** was a Second Team selection. Of note were the Honorable Mention honors accorded to **Cliff Dennett**, making him the first Prep sophomore ever to be given post-season recognition.

First Team All-Metro gaurd Todd Filipkowski was a fierce competitor. He went on to star at Mercyhurst College.

- Hamilton was game-high with 25 points, including four 3-pointers, though the County defeated the City for the second straight year, 117-109, in the 17th annual City-County All-Star Classic, sponsored by the Northwest Jaycees. Filipkowski added 17 points and 7 rebounds, while Donnelly also participated for the Slickers.

- Hamilton also played for the City-West Penn team in a 124-99 triumph over the WPIAL All-Stars in the preliminary game at the 1991 Dapper Dan Roundball Classic. Rambler opponents **Steve Roward** of McDowell and Academy's **James McDonald** also played for City-West Penn.

- "The Hammer" was named to the all-tourney teams of all four in-season tournaments Prep played in and further was named as one of the top 15 players in Pennsylvania by *USA Today*.

- **Jim Hamilton** was named Third Team All-State by the *Associated Press* and was also winner of the prestigious James "Moe" Gross Award as Prep's best player. Hamilton went on to star at the Naval Academy, where he broke the all-time Midshipmen career record for 3-point field goals with 138 (still second on the list). Just in 1994, Jim hit a buzzer-beater as Navy beat Colgate, 68-67; nailed seven 3-pointers against Holy Cross; and scored 14 against Missouri in NCAA tourney action. He was inducted into the Cathedral Prep Athletic Hall of Fame in 2013.

- **Todd Filipkowski** went on to star at Mercyhurst College, while **John Donnelly** became the successful head basketball coach at Villa Maria Academy.

- **Rick Kaczenski** did not play after his promising sophomore season, preferring to concentrate on the gridiron sport. Kaczenski went on to start for three years at center for the Fighting Irish of Notre Dame. He was inducted into the Metro Erie Sports Hall of Fame in 2007. He spent seven years on the staff at the University of Iowa and currently is the defensive line coach at the University of Nebraska.

• **Mike Wernicki** went on to play at the University of Pittsburgh. During his career, the Panthers made appearances in the 1992 NIT and the 1993 NCAA Tournament. Wernicki has since had assistant coaching positions at Franklin Regional High School, Mercyhurst College and Canisius College; and since 2006 has been an assistant coach and the recruiting coordinator at Division I Youngstown State.

Mike Wernicki went on to play at Pitt, and is currently an assistant at Youngstown State.

1991 All-Opponent Team:

Brian Pearl, York Catholic (2nd team all-state) [Delaware]Shawn Calhoun, York Catholic

Brian Miller, Ringgold (4th team all-state) [Penn State, football

James "Khibi" McDonald, Academy [Duquesne, Oregon State]

Demetrius Alexander, Brainerd [Hutchinson (KS) CC, Alabama]

Delvin Sullivan, S.R. Butler [North Alabama, Alabama A & M, football]

Tony "T-Mack" McGinnis, S.R. Butler (1st team all-state, AL) [Texas A & M]

Jermaine Brown, Fairdale (KY Mr. Basketball) [Tennessee, Georgetown (KY)]

Maurice Morris, Fairdale [Southern Mississippi]

Carlos "Rollo" Turner, Fairdale [signed w/South Carolina, DNP]

Jason Osborne, Louisville Male (KY Mr. Basketball, 1993) [Louisville]

Dan Heiman, Butler (5th team all-state) [Slippery Rock]

Jeremy Metzger, McDowell [Richmond, Penn State]

Bryan Eisert, McDowell [Bucknell]

Jerry Roberts, Tech

Matt Gras, Trumbull St. Joseph's (1st team all-state, CT) [Siena]

Andre "The Rejector" Riddick, Bishop Loughlin [Kentucky]

Dietrich Jells, Tech [Pitt, football; NFL Patriots, Eagles]

Khyl Horton, Mercyhurst (1st team all-state) [George Mason, Gannon]

Steve Taneyhill, Altoona [South Carolina, football]

Brian Rehm, Altoona (1st team all-state)

Danny Fortson, Altoona (3rd team all-state; McDonald's All-American, 1994) [Cincinnati; NBA Nuggets, Celtics, Warriors, Mavericks, SuperSonics]

Future Bright with Young Talent!

D-10 Crown in Trojan Hands!

Senior co-captain Mike King beats Meadville's Brook Bright to the ball in a District 10 playoff.

1991-92 (16-11)

Coach: Marcel Arribi
Assistants: Jim Marnella, Wes Alexander
Captains: Mark Tate, Mike King, Jim Sitter
Manager: Matt Kujawinski

Date	PREP			Dec.	Loc.	High Scorer	Opponent
	CARLISLE HS TIP-OFF TOURNAMENT						
12/6	55	Waynesboro	57	L	N	Dennett (21)	Balistrere (23)
12/7	55	Hollidaysburg	48	W	N	Dennett (20)	Salerne (17)
12/15	60	Strong Vincent	48	W	N	Dennett (29)	Selby (15)
	OCEANIC-IOLANI (HI) PREP CLASSIC						
12/18	54	Kailua (HI) Kalaheo	50	W	A	Dennett (18)	Shane (14)
12/19	37	Potomac (MD) Harker Prep	65	L	N	Ryan (15)	Hipp (16)
12/20	48	Los Angeles (CA) Fairfax	37	W	N	Dennett (23)	Harris (12)
12/21	55	Philadelphia Roman Catholic	66	L	N	Dennett (17)	Locke (19)
	FARRELL DRESCH-McCLUSKEY MEMORIAL CHRISTMAS TOURNAMENT						
12/27	49	Valley	46	W	N	Dennett (16)	Pipkins & Banks (11)
12/28	49	Kennedy Christian	37	W	N	Tate (17)	Patrick (16)
1/4	54	McDowell	64	L	N	Dennett (16)	Hubert (15)
1/7	62	East	42	W	N	King (11)	Jordan & Thompson (10)
	McDONALD'S CLASSIC						
1/10	66	Dayton (OH) Dunbar	71	L	H	King (17)	Brown (30)
1/11	28	Mouth of Wilson (VA) Oak Hill Academy	70	L	H	Dennett & Ryan (7)	Davis (21)
1/14	76	Tech Memorial	32	W	N	Dennett (16)	T. Roberts (10)
1/21	64	Academy	49	W	N	Dennett (17)	Ellis (20)
1/24	64	Mercyhurst Prep	45	W	N	King (19)	Horton (18)
1/25	63	Strong Vincent	45	W	N	Dennett (17)	UNREPORTED
2/1	44	McDowell	54	L	N	Ryan (15)	Hubert (15)
2/4	67	East	51	W	N	Dennett (25)	C. Crosby (18)
2/8	53	Niagara Falls (ONT) A.N. Myer	59	L	A	Dennett (16)	Guarasci & Newton (20)
2/13	52	Butler	53	L	A	Dennett (17)	Sease (18)
2/15	58	Tech Memorial	46	W	N	Dennett (13)	UNREPORTED
2/18	71	Academy	62	W	N	Dennett (26)	Ellis (23)
2/21	73	Mercyhurst Prep	58	W	N	Dennett (25)	Horton (20)
	DISTRICT 10 PLAYOFFS						
2/29	51	Meadville	44	W	N	King (13)	Raga (18)
3/9	42	McDowell	49	L	N	Dennett & King (10)	Metzger (18)
	P.I.A.A. INTERDISTRICT PLAYOFF						
3/14	56	North Allegheny	58	L	N	Tate (17)	Billeter (37)
	1506 (55.8)		**1406 (52.1)**				

Pos.	Player	Ht.	Prior School	Class	G(GS)	FG(3)	FT	Total	PPG	Career
F	Cliff Dennett (#44)	6'4"	Fairview	Jr.	27(26)	128(31)	76-106	425	15.7	590
F	Jed Ryan (#32)	6'5"	Girard St. John's	Fr.	27(27)	105(9)	40-65	277	10.3	277
G	Mike King (#10)	5'10"	St. Patrick's	Sr.	27(27)	63(7)	50-86	197	7.3	222
F	Mark Tate (#23)	6'0"	Luther Memorial	Sr.	24(8)	70(3)	47-84	196	8.2	396
G	Jim Sitter (#12)	5'9"	St. George's	Sr.	18(1)	27(10)	26-37	110	6.1	117
C	Booker Coleman (#41)	6'6"	Jamestown (NY)	Soph.	27(25)	40	19-36	99	3.7	99
F	Matt Bennett (#50)	6'2"	OLC	Jr.	27(2)	18(7)	20-31	77	2.9	85
G	Kenny Duck (#22)	5'9"	Holy Trinity	Soph.	26(13)	26(1)	15-25	70	2.7	70
F	Eugene Tomczak (#40)	6'0"	St. Stan's	Jr.	13(6)	6	7-10	19	1.5	33
F	Mike Guelcher (#51)	6'1"	OLC	Sr.	12	5(1)	4-5	17	1.4	41
G	Pat Marnella (#20)	5'8"	Bl. Sacrament	Jr.	5	3	1-2	7	1.4	7
G	Harry Izbicki (#30)	5'10"	Mount Calvary	Jr.	5	3	0-0	6	1.2	6
G	Derrick Reid (#11)	5'6"	St. John's	Jr.	9	2	0-0	4	0.4	14
G	Courtney Mooney (#21)	5'8"	St. John's	Jr.	3	1	0-0	2	0.7	2
F	Keith Anthony (#31)	6'3"	St. George's	Soph.	2	0	0-0	0	0.0	0

HIGHLIGHTS:

- 1991-92 was a rebuilding year in Marcel Arribi's fifth season as Cathedral Prep coach. After the departure of stars like **Jim Hamilton, Todd Filipkowski, Paul Samlock** and **John Donnelly**, the Ramblers were considered young and inexperienced. Prep won the Farrell Christmas tourney, but surrendered Metro League and District 10 crowns to pre-season favorite and arch-rival McDowell. The Ramblers counted heavily on 6'4" junior **Cliff Dennett**, who became a scoring machine; seniors **Mark Tate, Mike King** and **Jim Sitter**; and a trio of highly-touted underclassmen: **Jed Ryan**, a 6'5" freshman; **Booker Coleman**, a 6'6" sophomore; and **Kenny Duck**, a 5'9" sophomore. Ryan had just led Girard St. John's to the 1991 state Catholic grade school title and was the first freshman to play in a varsity contest for Prep since **Art Hilinski** played in one game in 1945-46. Ryan was also the first freshman in the starting lineup for the Ramblers in 50 years, since **"Syl" Mannarino** in 1941-42. Coleman was a transfer from Jamestown (NY) and was considered to have outstanding potential.

- Juniors **Derrick Reid** and **Courtney Mooney** were part of the St. John's grade school team that won the 1989 Pennsylvania CYO state championship. **Josh DeBello** of Mercyhurst Prep was also part of that squad, as were Prep gridders **Rick Kaczenski** and **Shawn Kendrick**.

- All Metro League games and the 9th annual McDonald's Classic were played at the Gannon's Hammermill Center. The

The 1992 Prep Ramblers, thoroughly enjoying a Hawaiin lifestyle. L to R: King, Tomczak, Anthony, Marnella, Izbicki, Coleman, Ryan, Dennett, Sitter, Guelcher, Tate, Reid, Bennett, Mooney, Duck.

Highly-touted Jed Ryan was the first freshman to dot the Prep starting lineup in 50 years.

McDonald's contests were the only two games which were considered "home" games all season.

- Of new Rambler opponents in the season-opening tournament at Carlisle High School, Waynesboro (23-4) derived its name from Erie's own **General "Mad Anthony" Wayne**; and Hollidaysburg might say its town's most famous resident was old-time Hollywood gossip columnist **Hedda Hopper**. Both Waynesboro and Hollidaysburg were Quad-A schools that joined the Mid-Penn Conference after the 1991-92 season, the MPC being the largest conference in the state. Waynesboro had previously been a member of the Blue Mountain League and was its champion for the instant season, while Hollidaysburg dropped out of the MPC and is now independent.

- Prep's first battle against Strong Vincent (10-15) was moved from a Friday night, December 13, to two nights later on Sunday to accommodate both schools' athletes and fans who were immersed in the PIAA state football finals that Saturday, Prep in AAAA versus Central Bucks West, and SV in AAA against Conestoga Valley. Though the Ramblers lost and the Colonels won, both squads were honored at halftime of the basketball game, with about 1,200 fans present to applaud their gridiron heroes. Prep battled back to beat SV behind **Cliff Dennett's** season-high 29 points, but Rambler fans were really

Jed Ryan tosses one from the paint against Kalaheo in Hawaii.

Kenny Duck and Mike King leap high for a rebound against Kalaheo in Hawaii.

impressed with the play of the freshman phenom **Jed Ryan**, who scored 16 and showed plenty of poise on the court.

- Prep took an impressive sixth place after losing to Philadelphia Roman Catholic (25-5) at the 16-team Oceanic-Iolani Prep Classic, all the way in Honolulu (HI), some 5,000 miles away and definitely a Prep record! Roman went on to win its fourth straight Philadelphia Catholic League title. Of Prep's other opponents in Hawaii: Kalaheo is located on the island of Oahu; and financially troubled Harker Prep, which closed following the instant season, was coached by notable **Stu Vetter**, who coached two teams to # 1 national rankings by *USA Today*—Oakton (VA) Flint Hill Prep in 1985-86 and Frederick (MD) St. John's Prospect Hall in 1997-98—and further led Rockville (MD) Montrose Christian to the 2011 National High School Invitational championship. By the time Vetter retired in 2013 after a 37-year career, he was twice named *USA Today's* Coach of the Year and had 878 career wins at four schools, where he was uncanny at bringing national-caliber transfers in. Vetter was 44-3 in two seasons at Harker Prep. A ghost seen by many is said to roam the building where Harker Prep used to be.

- Also in Hawaii: Los Angeles Fairfax (15-10) had an incredible roster of alumni, of which the following is just a partial list: athletes **Chris Mills, Jack Kemp, Barry Latman, Larry Sherry** and **Norm Sherry**; actors **David Janssen, David Arquette, Timothy Hutton, Mila Kunis, Carole Lombard, Demi Moore, Ricardo Montalban** and **Mickey Rooney**; and musicians **Herb Alpert, Jermaine Jackson, Jerry Leiber** (Leiber & Stoller), **Allan Sherman, Warren Zevon, Slash, Phil Spector** and the Red Hot Chili Peppers!

- As a sidelight, it has been noted that the quality of Los Angeles city basketball has plummeted since the **Rodney King** riots in April, 1992. Many African-Americans fled South L.A. for safer school districts after the riots. The city schools now have higher student populations of Latino students who appear more interested in baseball and soccer, and hence, the hoops game has suffered dramatically.

- Of Prep's opponents at the Farrell Christmas Tournament: Valley High School was formed by the merger in 1967 of New Kensington and Arnold high schools; and Prep's win over Kennedy Christian in the final was the first time the two squared off since 1970. Kennedy Christian was renamed Kennedy Catholic in 2001. Prior to the change, the Eagles won PIAA Class A titles in 1986, 1987, 1998, 1999, 2000 and 2001. The Ramblers and Golden Eagles did not meet again until the 2003-04 season.

- Prep's win over Valley (17-9) was particularly impressive in that the Ramblers held superstar **Tom Pipkins**, averaging 30 per game, to just 11 points. **Pipkins**, the WPIAL's all-time leading scorer with 2,838 points from 1989-93, scored 878 one season and still ranks as # 10 in the state for career points scored. Valley, with Pipkins and emotional leader **Monte Banks**, made it to the PIAA AAA title game the next season, in 1993, where it lost to Pottstown, 85-66, and finished 30-3. Kennedy Christian (21-7) finished third in D-10 Class A play, then lost its first round PIAA tourney game to Sto-Rox, 54-46.

- **Cliff Dennett** made the all-tourney teams at both the Carlisle and Farrell events.

- Prep did not fare well in the 9th annual McDonald's Classic, losing opening night to a new opponent in Dayton Dunbar and suffering one of its most lopsided defeats in history to Oak Hill Academy (34-2) on night two. The Ramblers' 28 points against the Warriors was their lowest point total since scoring 25 against the Warriors of East High in 1950—42 years! Dunbar is the only historically African-American high school in Dayton, created in the early 1930's to educate African-American youth and to employ teachers of color. A power in basketball, the Wolverines have won OHSAA state championships in 1987, 2006, 2007, 2010 and 2012.

- The nation's top-ranked team, the Baltimore (MD) Dunbar Poets, led by stars **Michael Lloyd, Keith Booth** and first team All-American **Donta Bright**, thrashed # 2 ranked Oak Hill on

Coach Arribi does a little sideline hokey-pokey in the waning moments of the Dunbar game.

opening night, then easily disposed of Dayton Dunbar, 82-66, for the McDonald's crown. The Poets stayed undefeated at 29-0 and wound up as national champs.

- Though unknown at the time, the 1991-92 season would be the last time Prep ever played ancient rivals Tech and Academy in basketball. With the controversial and political closing of Academy, and the transferring of its students to the Tech building which would then be called "Central High School," the Metro League as it was known and the great rivalries with the Centaurs and the Lions were over for good, in one fell swoop. The Ramblers finished on top in the all-time series with both schools: 75-44 versus Tech and 80-35 against Academy.

- Prep's loss at Canadian power A.N. Myer Secondary School was the first time Prep played an opponent outside the USA since 1978.

- Causing ire was the poorly officiated defeat at Butler (23-4). In a chance for a major upset, **Kenny Duck** picked up a rebound and was clobbered underneath the hoop before the buzzer. Unfortunately, no foul was called and Prep lost by one. The Golden Tornadoes had been ranked the WPIAL's number one team for much of the year.

- The Ramblers' final two wins over the Academy Lions (23-6) were two of their best for the season. Coach Arribi gained his 100th career victory for Prep in the second contest.

- Academy finished its 73-year basketball history with its first-ever trip to the PIAA Final Four. The Lions, under coach **Tom Whalen,** only in his third year at the helm, won the D-10 AAA toga then disposed Pittsburgh North Catholic, 62-53, Pittsburgh Perry, 58-55, and Aliquippa, 77-75, in inter-district play. Academy's last game ever was a loss in the Western Final to state champ Blackhawk (32-1) and its superstar **Dante Calabria**, 73-50. Aside from the 1973-74 Lions that went 24-1, this Academy squad was the finest on the hilltop, a fine last hurrah and a real tribute to Coach Whalen.

- Tech Memorial (5-16), on the other hand, finished its 61-year history with one of its worst records ever, including two losses to Prep.

- The final standings in the Metro League, the final year that the league included Academy and Tech, were as follows:

	W	L
McDowell	12	0
Prep	10	2
Academy	8	4
Mercyhurst	6	6
Vincent	3	9
East	2	10
Tech	1	11

Leading scorer and First Team All-Metro selection Cliff Dennett is hacked by Meadville's Manuel Raga in a D-10 semifinal.

- Prep had a big victory over Meadville (20-5) in the District 10 semifinal in Edinboro, the 1,500[th] game in Rambler basketball history. The Bulldogs presented an interesting character in Swiss national **Manuel Raga, Jr**. Raga is the son of **Manuel Raga**, nicknamed the "Flying Mexican", one of the first great athletic guards in European basketball and arguably the best Mexican basketball player ever. A great defensive player with outstanding jumping and rebounding skills, Raga helped Varese to three Italian League crowns, three Italian Cups and three Euroleague titles from 1968 to 1975 as one of the most fun-to-watch players in basketball. The "Flying Mexican" was simply unstoppable and way ahead of his own era. In 1970 he became the first player from an international league to be selected in the NBA draft when the Atlanta Hawks took him with the 167th overall pick. Raga, however, never played in the NBA.

- The biggest disappointments for the season were the three losses to arch-rival McDowell (25-3). The first defeat broke Prep's record 39-game Metro League winning streak since

Tate looks to drive against McDowell in the D-10 final.

1988. The D-10 final was played before 6,018 fans, the biggest basketball crowd ever at the Erie Convention Center to that point. The Trojans then defeated a strong Butler team by 10 in inter-district play before getting bounced by Altoona, 57-55.

- Finally, there was the season-ending, two-point loss in Butler to North Allegheny (23-6) and its little point guard **Devin Billeter**, who personally pummeled Prep with 12 field goals (two 3's) and 11 free throws for 37 points, 23 coming in the second half. It was one of the greatest performances against Prep, ever. Prep could have won, but sunk only 5 of 15 foul shots.

- **Cliff Dennett** was named First Team on the 1991-92 All-Metro Basketball Team as announced by the *Erie Times-News*, while **Mike King** and

Hall-of-Famer Mark Tate was an All-State running back. He starred at Penn State and later played with the NFL's Patriots and Eagles.

Jed Ryan were Second Team selections. Ryan was the first Rambler freshman ever to receive post-season honors. **Mark Tate** was accorded Honorable mention status.

- **Mark Tate**, aside from being a fine basketball player, was also one of the greatest Rambler football stars ever. He led the Rambler gridders to a 14-1 record in 1991 and a berth in the PIAA state championship game. Named First Team All-State RB by the *Associated Press*, Tate also won the 1992 "Ma" Kaiser Award as Prep's best all-around athlete. He starred four years on the gridiron at Penn State and later played with the NFL's New England Patriots and Philadelphia Eagles, as well as with the Saskatchewan Rough Riders of the CFL. Tate was inducted into the Cathedral Prep Athletic Hall of Fame in 2008.

Versatile Jim Sitter went on to star in football at W & J.

- Other roundballers that were Prep football stars included quarterback **Harry Izbicki** and wide receiver **Jim Sitter**, who

Senior Mike King won the "Moe" Gross Award for outstanding basketball ability.

went on to star in football at Washington & Jefferson, the same place where his father, **Jim Sitter, Sr.** '62, was also a star.

- **Mike King** was winner of the prestigious James "Moe" Gross Award for outstanding basketball ability.

- Tate scored 9 points and King 16 as the City All-Stars obliterated the County's two-year winning streak, 127-89, in the 18th annual City-County All-Star Classic, sponsored by the Northwest Jaycees.

- The 28th Annual Dapper Dan Roundball Classic was the last to be played in Pittsburgh, on April 11, 1992. Prep opponents **Devin Billeter** (9 points) of North Allegheny, **Jeremy Metzger** (7) of McDowell and **Khyl Horton** (15, team MVP) of Mercyhurst all played in the final preliminary matchup for the Quad-A/West Penn team, which lost to the City/WPIAL squad, 113-95.

- Rumors were spreading for weeks that youngsters **Booker Coleman** and **Jed Ryan** were unhappy at Prep and decided to transfer. The wild, untrue stories got so out of hand that Prep A.D. **Ron Sertz** invited *Erie Daily Times* sportswriter **Pat Cuneo** to Prep to interview the boys. Coleman and Ryan, who both ranked near the top of their respective classes, assured Cuneo, who then wrote an expose, that they loved Prep; loved playing for Coach Arribi; and harbored no thoughts about ever attending school anywhere else.

1992 All-Opponent Team:

Jeff Balistrere, Waynesboro (5th team all-state) [Mount St. Mary's]

Serge Zwikker, Harker Prep (McDonald's All-American) [North Carolina; NBA Houston Rockets]

Exree Hipp, Harker Prep [Maryland; Harlem Globetrotters]

Jeremy Dean, Harker Prep [William & Mary]

Burt Harris, L.A. Fairfax [Southern Cal]

Kyle Locke, Roman Catholic [Coppin State]

James "Flame" Lewis, Roman Catholic

Tom Pipkins, Valley [Ducuesne]

Mark Patrick, Kennedy Christian

Richard "TuTu" Brown, Dayton Dunbar [Miami (OH)]

Chris Davis, Oak Hill Academy (McDonald's All-American) [Auburn]

Martice Moore, Oak Hill Academy (McDonald's All-American) [Colorado]

Peter Guarasci, A.N. Myer [Fairfield, Simon Fraser; Canadian National Team]

Greg Newton, A. N. Myer [Duke; Canadian National Team]

Aaron Sease, Butler

Jaron Hilovsky, Butler

Brian Ellis, Academy [Canisius]

Khyl Horton, Mercyhurst (1st team all-state) [George Mason, Gannon]

Jeremy Metzger, McDowell (5th team all-state) [Richmond, Penn State]

Jimmy Delsandro, McDowell [Westminster]

Manuel Raga, Meadville [Clarendon JC, Cal Poly-San Luis Obispo; Switzerland National Team]

Devin Billeter, North Allegheny

PIAA State Champs! Rugged Schedule Is Formula for State Run!

1992-93 (21-7)

Coach: Marcel Arribi
Assistants: Jim Marnella, Wes Alexander
Captains: Gene Tomczak, Cliff Dennett
Managers: Matt Kujawinski, Rick Herbstritt

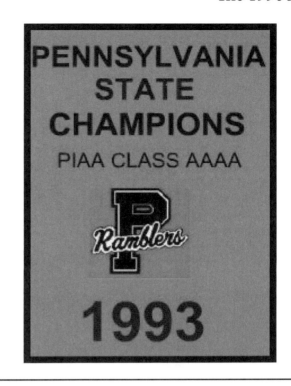

PENNSYLVANIA STATE CHAMPIONS
PIAA CLASS AAAA
P Ramblers
1993

Date	PREP		Dec.	Loc.	High Scorer	Opponent
	GREAT CHEVY SHOOTOUT (ALTOONA)					
12/11	CANCELLED—SNOW		N			
12/12	CANCELLED—SNOW		N			
12/18	58	Butler	41	W	H	Dennett (21)	three w/ (7)
12/22	77	Central	67	W	N	Dennett (29)	Benjamin (23)
	ARBY'S HIGH SCHOOL BASKETBALL CLASSIC (BRISTOL, TN)					
12/28	49	Kingsport (TN) Dobyns-Bennett	92	L	N	Dennett (15)	Mills (21)
12/29	78	Sullivan (TN) North	55	W	N	Dennett (21)	Painter (11)
12/30	46	Marrero (LA) John Ehret	53	L	N	Dennett (15)	Allen (18)
1/5	63	Mercyhurst Prep	40	W	N	Ryan (19)	Tate (9)
	McDONALD'S CLASSIC					
1/8	53	Middletown (OH)	44	W	H	Dennett (16)	Lucas (14)
1/9	38	NYC (NY) LaSalle Academy	32	W	H	Ryan (17)	Wells & Austin (7)
	BASS PRO TOURNAMENT OF CHAMPIONS (SPRINGFIELD, MO)					
1/14	52	Lee's Summit (MO)	54	L	N	Dennett (16)	Zoller (18)
1/15	51	Springfield (MO) Hillcrest	35	W	N	Ryan & Tomczak (14)	Montgomery (15)
1/16	50	Memphis (TN) East	51	L	N	Dennett (16)	Henderson (17)
1/19	52	McDowell	55	L	N	Dennett (18)	Delsandro (19)
1/22	46	Strong Vincent	40 (OT)	W	N	Coleman (15)	Selby (19)
1/27	73	East	47	W	N	Dennett (22)	C. Crosby (18)
1/29	70	Central	68 (OT)	W	N	Ryan (20)	Benjamin (29)
2/5	61	Altoona	70	L	A	Dennett (19)	Churchill (18)
2/9	87	East	50	W	N	Dennett (21)	T. Crosby (18)
2/12	73	Mercyhurst Prep	52	W	N	Ryan (25)	Vallimont (15)
2/16	61	Strong Vincent	48	W	N	Dennett (16)	Selby (16)
2/24	75	McDowell	57	W	N	Ryan (20)	Martineau (17)
	METRO LEAGUE PLAYOFF					
3/1	55	McDowell	65	L	N	Ryan (20)	Cronk (24)
	DISTRICT 10 PLAYOFFS					
3/4	57	Meadville	52	W	N	Coleman (15)	Raga (21)
3/11	54	McDowell	49	W	N	Ryan (20)	Delsandro (21)
	P.I.A.A. INTERDISTRICT PLAYOFFS					
3/20	62	Shaler	42	W	N	Dennett (20)	Hunter (14)
3/24	72	Altoona	52	W	N	Ryan (15)	Churchill (17)
3/27	67	Butler	53	W	N	Duck (16)	Bellis (22)
3/31	64	New Castle	61	W	N	Ryan (21)	Zarilla (23)
	P.I.A.A. CLASS AAAA STATE CHAMPIONSHIP					
4/3	41	Hazleton Area	30	W	N	Coleman (11)	Long (19)
	1685 (60.2)		**1455 (52.0)**			

Pos.	Player	Ht.	Prior School	Class	G(GS)	FG(3)	FT	Total	PPG	Career
F	Jed Ryan (#32)	6'6"	Girard St. John's	Soph.	28(28)	141(25)	109-146	416	14.9	693
F	Cliff Dennett (#43)	6'5"	Fairview	Sr.	28(28)	156(20)	80-118	412	14.7	1002
C	Booker Coleman (#41)	6'7"	Jamestown (NY)	Jr.	28(28)	99	88-140	286	10.2	385
G	Kenny Duck (#21)	5'9"	Holy Trinity	Jr.	28(24)	74(2)	57-87	207	7.4	277
G	Eugene Tomczak(#40)	5'10"	St. Stan's	Sr.	28(27)	62(17)	18-33	159	5.7	192
G	Pat Marnella (#20)	5'8"	Bl. Sacrament	Sr.	28(1)	29(12)	13-20	83	3.0	90
F	Matt Bennett (#50)	6'1"	OLC	Sr.	27(4)	10(5)	22-41	47	1.7	132
F	Keith Anthony (#31)	6'3"	St. George's	Jr.	22	12	3-7	27	1.2	27
G	Derrick Reid (#11)	5'6"	St. John's	Sr.	23	7	3-9	17	0.7	31
F	Nick Bielak (#30)	6'3"	Bl. Sacrament	Jr.	3	4(1)	0-2	9	3.0	9
G	Keith Nies (#22)	5'6"	St. John's	Fr.	6	3(1)	0-1	7	1.2	7
F	Shawn Summerville (#23)	6'0"	St. Patrick's	Jr.	8	2	2-3	6	0.8	6
G	Ryan Infield (#12)	5'10"	St. George's	Jr.	9	2	1-2	5	0.6	5
G	Craig Fomich (#10)	5'8"	St. John's	Soph.	7	1	0-0	2	0.3	2
C	Kevin Anthony (#42)	6'4"	St. George's	Jr.	9	1	0-2	2	0.2	2

Cathedral Prep's 1993 State Champions. Front, L to R: Summerville, Infield, Fomich, Reid, Marnella, Duck, Nies. Back: Tomczak, Bielak, Ryan, Coleman, Dennett, Kevin Anthony, Keith Anthony, Bennett.

Booker Coleman had an army of fans.

HIGHLIGHTS:

- 1992-93 was an incredible season as Cathedral Prep won its sixth state championship overall and second in the PIAA. The Ramblers were ranked # 20 in the nation in the preseason *USA Today* Super 25 Rankings even though they were but 16-11 in 1991-92 and didn't even win the Metro League. It was the first time Prep was ever included in the *USA Today* rankings in basketball and it brought the school national attention. There were some tough losses along the way, but by the winning streak at season's end the Ramblers jelled into the best team in Pennsylvania. Blessed with talent, size, experience, intelligence, poise, a good bench and outstanding coaching by **Marcel Arribi**, this Prep squad had a lofty goal in mind—and succeeded!

- The big man at center was **Booker Coleman**, who developed into a fierce presence inside; forwards **Cliff Dennett** and **Jed Ryan** could rebound and score underneath and were also dangerous

The student body keep the Ramblers fired up at the Western Final.

from 3-point range; and guards **Kenny Duck** and **Gene Tomczak** ran the backcourt with aplomb. Seniors **Pat Marnella**, **Matt Bennett** and **Derrick Reid** gave the Ramblers bench strength all season long.

Senior gaurd Derrick Reid gave the Ramblers strength off the bench.

- Also on the Prep roster were juniors **Kevin Anthony** and **Keith Anthony**, the second set of twins to play varsity basketball for the Ramblers, the first being **Rick Bengel** and **Bob Bengal** in the 1970's.

- All Metro League games, the opener against Butler and the 10th annual McDonald's Classic were played at Gannon University's Hammermill Center. Edinboro's McComb Fieldhouse hosted the District 10 semifinal against Meadville, the PIAA first round against Shaler and the Western semifinal and final against Butler and New Castle. The D-10 final was held before the largest crowd ever (6,193) at the Erie Civic Center. The Western quarterfinal against Altoona was played at Clarion while the state championship game was played at the famous Hersheypark Arena in Hershey, before a sold-out crowd

Coleman with a power slam at the crowded Hammermill Center.

of 8,392, the largest ever to witness a Prep basketball game.

- Erie Central High School, inaugurated with the 1992-93 school year, was formed after the highly controversial and political closing of Erie's Academy High School. The argument was that the grand old school high on the hill in South Erie was so decrepit that it had to be torn down. Never mind that it was reopened just a couple of years later as what some considered the showcase public school in Erie, Collegiate Academy.

Academy's students were moved to the Tech Memorial building on Cherry Street and without much thought Tech was simply renamed Central. At least Academy alumni and supporters had the chance to argue and complain about the school's closing—nobody was even told there would be the demise of Tech. Those alumni have been lost forever. In any regard, new Central High's (13-9) first game ever in the Metro League was a loss to Cathedral Prep.

- Prep suffered its most lopsided loss in 20 years (an oddity for a state championship team) at the Arby's Basketball Classic, despite being ranked at #17 in the U. S. at the time, at Viking Hall in Bristol (TN), to renowned Dobyns-Bennett (35-2) of Kingsport (TN), winners of the tourney. Originally called the Mountain Empire Classic, the Arby's Classic has been sponsored by Arby's since it began in 1983.

- Dobyns-Bennett, through 2016, has the winningest basketball program in the country with over 2,100 wins. Longtime basketball coach **Buck van Huss** ranks in the top ten in wins in the country in basketball. Thanks in part to the school's long history, in January, 2007, a victory made the Indians the first basketball program in the country—high school, college or professional—to win 2,000 games. Dobyns-Bennett finished the 1992-93 season with a loss in the Tennessee state quarterfinals.

- Prep's other loss at the Arby's tourney was to the John Ehret Patriots, who went on to win the 1993 Class 5A (large school) Louisiana state basketball championship with a 79-48 victory over district rival Higgins. Ehret boasts as alumni former NFL stars **Kordell "Slash" Stewart** and **Reggie Wayne**, and it won the 5A title again in a magical 2005-06 season. This followed Hurricane Katrina on August 31, 2005, a time when many fled the New Orleans area and did not return. Others returned and found their schools decimated and unable to open. Coach **Al Collins** meshed a group from different backgrounds and schools and the Patriots became a story-book, championship team. The story proved so compelling that Hollywood noticed and made a film titled *Hurricane Season*, with Academy Award winner **Forest Whitaker** starring as Coach Collins.

- The annual McDonald's High School Basketball Classic was in its 10th year and had earned an excellent reputation for bringing in top caliber competition. Newcomers for the 1993 lineup included the Middletown (OH) Middies, which in the 1940's and 1950's boasted one of the most respected high school basketball programs in the country with seven state titles; and LaSalle Academy, a small school run by the Christian Brothers and located in Manhattan's East Village, right across from McSorley's, New York's oldest tavern. Middletown brought along 6'10" **J. J. Lucas**, son of former Middletown, University

Rambler cheerleaders created quite a ruckus at Hersheypark Arena.

of Cincinnati, U. S. Olympian and NBA star **Jerry Lucas**, considered Middletown's most famous citizen. LaSalle's most famous alumni were former N3A star **John Roche** and MLB star **John Candelaria**. Two cardinals of the Catholic Church graduated from La Salle: **Patrick Cardinal Hayes** and **George Cardinal Mundelein**, archbishops of New York and Chicago, respectively. For this reason, La Salle athletes are known as the Cardinals.

- LaSalle Academy (17-10) upset a terrific Brooklyn Bishop Loughlin (17-7) team on Friday night in a 48-47 thriller, before Prep easily disposed of the very good Middletown five. The Ramblers then won a 38-32 chess match against LaSalle to win their third McDonald's title and second in three years before a sold out Hammermill crowd of 3,082.

Dennett with his patented one-hand jumper.

- Prep lost two close games to finish sixth in the 8-team field at the 9th annual Bass Pro Tournament of Champions, its second foray in the tourney that Coach Arribi felt was the best in the country. Defense oriented Lee's Summit (20-7) overcame a 12-point halftime deficit to beat the Ramblers on opening night, followed by Prep playing two inspired halves to down Hillcrest (16-9). Finally it was Memphis East (27-7) that downed the Orange & Black in a nailbiter, as a Prep shot at the buzzer didn't fall. **Cliff Dennett** made the all-tourney team.

- The final standings in the Metro League, the first year that the league included the new Central High School Falcons, were as follows:

	W	L
*McDowell	10	1
Prep	9	2
Central	6	4
Vincent	3	7
East	2	8
Mercyhurst	1	9

won championship playoff

- Prep's rivalry with the McDowell Trojans (21-5) of coach **Pete Flinn** was nothing less than fierce. After splitting two games during the regular season, the Trojans won the playoff for the Metro League title. It was the first time the Ramblers ever lost a league title via the playoff route after being successful nine times in nine previous tries over the years. In D-10 play, Prep made 19 of 20 free throws to deflate Meadville (23-2), which had been ranked the #3 team in the state by the Harrisburg Patriot-News. Then a record-setting crowd at the Civic Center saw the Ramblers dictate the action and dethrone McDowell for its third district title in four years and eighth crown overall.

- Prep's run to the PIAA title was thrilling for the school, its alumni and Erie fans in general. There was excitement at the Shaler (17-9) game when frustrated Titan star **Tino Hunter** took a swing at **Cliff Dennett** with 2:52 left in the game and was ejected. Prep's bench emptied, resulting in an automatic technical foul. Moments later the Rambler

Super-sub Pat Marnella was great during the Ramblers' playoff run.

bench was issued another technical, which resulted in Coach Arribi's ejection for the only time in his career. That win was followed by a revenge victory over Altoona (16-11) and a bruising victory over WPIAL runner-up Butler (23-8), a contest in which 44 fouls were called. Super-sub **Pat Marnella** was hot off the bench with 20 points in the wins over Butler and Altoona.

The Prep boys could care less about who's in the New Castle starting lineup.

- Prep's thrilling triumph over WPIAL champion New Castle (27-5) in the Western Final at sold-out McComb Fieldhouse, and before a WICU-Channel 12 viewing audience, was particularly satisfying. The Red Hurricanes, ranked #2 in the state by the *Harrisburg Patriot-News*, were heavily favored and presented a pair of transfer students from Texas, **Marcus Thomas** and **Rick Steele**, as well as NC's all-time leading scorer, **Jason Zarilla**, in their lineup. The Ramblers fell behind 10-0 as red-bedecked fans went wild when NC made its first five shots in the game's opening minute. Prep, down by six midway in the 3rd quarter, lost **Cliff Dennett** on a technical foul after he questioned the referee about a poor call on a 4th personal foul. To make matters worse, the Ramblers then lost **Booker Coleman**, who had 14 points and 12 rebounds, on fouls midway through the final chapter. But **Pat Marnella's** 3-pointer started an 11-0 run that gave Prep a lead it never relinquished. In an attempt to tie the score the frantic final 30 seconds, NC attempted four 3-point shots until **Gene Tomczak** came down with a clutch rebound, then sank both ends of a one-and-one to seal the Rambler victory. **Jed Ryan** was Prep's main star with 21 points, 8 rebounds and 4 assists.

Cliff Dennett about to sink a free throw in the state title game.

WJET-Channel 24's Mike Gallagher interviews a very happy Coach Arribi after the state final.

The Prep boys get a little nutty at McComb Fieldhouse.

- Prep's victim in the state title bout was Hazleton Area (29-2), in its first year of existence after the consolidation of Freeland, Hazleton and West Hazleton high schools. The Cougars lost their season opener to Carlisle, 62-58, then reeled off an amazing 29 consecutive victories. Hazleton disposed of West Scranton and Tunkhannock in the district playoffs, and methodically put Upper Darby, Lancaster McCaskey, Upper Merion and Chester away in the state tournament. Not only did the Cougars take their fans on a magic carpet ride to the state final, but their success helped to unite a student body still coming to grips with no longer being called "Mountaineers," "Wildcats" or "Whippets." The title game was broadcast live on WJET-Channel 24 in Erie.

- Prep became the first Western Pennsylvania team to win the AAAA crown since the classification began in 1984. The 41-30 verdict over Hazleton was also the lowest-scoring game in the top boys' division since Norristown defeated Ford City, 30-23, in 1948. Neither of the two deliberate offenses could find any touch in the face of the respective tightly-packed zone defenses. Down but 14-13 at the half, the Ramblers wore down the Cougars and took control in the second half. Though Prep made only 9 FG's in the contest, it was 22 of 33 from the free throw line. Scoring was balanced, with Coleman getting 11 markers, Ryan and Dennett 10 and Duck 9. The Ramblers also received gutsy play from Tomczak and super subs Marnella and Bennett.

- **Jed Ryan** and **Booker Coleman** were both named First Team on the 1992-93 All-Metro Basketball Team as announced by the *Erie Times-News*, while **Cliff Dennett** was a Second Team selection. **Kenny Duck** was an Honorable Mention choice. Ryan, who at one point in the season made a Prep-record 25 consecutive free throws, was the first Prep sophomore to receive such lofty honors. He then became the first Prep underclassman to receive all-state honors as he was named 5th

Team All-State by the *Associated Press.*

- **Cliff Dennett** (14 points) and **Gene Tomczak** helped the City defeat the County, 87-78, in the 19th annual City-County All-Star Classic, sponsored by the Northwest Jaycees. Tomczak and his Dad, **Gene "Jiggs" Tomczak** '57, thus became Prep's first Father-Son combo to play in the City-County all-star games.

All-star guard Gene Tomczak. He and his Dad, "Jigs," were the first father-son combo to play in the city-county all-star games.

- Prep opponents **Manuel Raga** of Meadville and **Jimmy Delsandro** of McDowell both played in the Asics Roundball Classic in Pittsburgh, resulting in a 114-73 victory for Pennsylvania over the USA team. Billed "the 29th annual," it was an attempt to keep the spirit of the Dapper Dan games alive, but it did not draw the top players in the country or even in Pennsylvania for that matter.

- Seniors **Cliff Dennett, Matt Bennett, Gene Tomczak, Pat Marnella** and **Derrick Reid** were all winners of Prep's prestigious James "Moe" Cross Award for basketball excellence. Dennett, a three-year star at Prep after transferring from Fairview, went on to a fine career at Gannon University, scoring 795 career points.

Team Captain and three-year star Cliff Dennett went on to a fine career at Gannon.

Senior forward Matt Bennett, a valuable seventh man.

A portrait of Prep pride. Exhausted teammates Marnella and Dennett embrace after the big win over New Castle.

1993 All-Opponent Team:

Matt Clement, Butler [MLB Padres, Marlins, Cubs, Red Sox]

Roosevelt Benjamin, Central [Kings River (CA) CC, Clarion, football]

JaMichael Mills, Dobyns-Bennett [Pensacola (FL) JC, Sullivan (KY) JC]

Rayshard Allen, John Ehret [Tulane]

J. J. Lucas, Middletown (2nd team all-state, OH) [Vanderbilt, Hawaii Pacific]

Shammgod Wells, NYC LaSalle [Providence; NBA Washington Wizards]

Ed Elisma, NYC LaSalle [Georgia Tech]

Robby Montgomery, Hillcrest (2nd team all-state, MO)

Cedric Henderson, Memphis East [Memphis; NBA Cavaliers, Warriors]

Desmond "Dez" Merriweather, Memphis East [Lane College]

Jimmy Delsandro, McDowell [Westminster]

Lamont Selby, Vincent

Tony Crosby, East

Clifton Crosby, East [Maryland, football; NFL Bengals, Rams, Colts, Chiefs]

Jeff Churchill, Altoona [St. Francis (PA)]

Brad Martineau, McDowell

Scott Cronk, McDowell

Lucas Marsh, McDowell [Geneva]

Manuel Raga, Meadville (Clarendon JC, Cal Poly-San Luis Obispo; Switzerland National Team]

Brook Bright, Meadville (5th team all-state) [Kent State]

Tino Hunter, Shaler (2nd team all-state) [North Carolina State]

Shawn Bellis, Butler [Clarion]

Jason Zarilla, New Castle (5th team all-state)

Chris Long, Hazleton (3rd team all-state)

The traditional awarding of gold medals to the new state champions!

A very impressive scene as the Ramblers warm up for their championship tussle against Hazleton.

PIAA State Finalist!

1993-94 (24-7)

Coach: Marcel Arribi
Assistants: Jim Marnella, Wes Alexander
Captains: Kenny Duck, Booker Coleman, Jed Ryan-
Managers: Matt Kujawinski, Rick Herbstritt

The Ramblers win a prestigious Kreul Classic in Florida.

Date	PREP			Dec.	Loc.	High Scorer	Opponent
		GREAT CHEVY SHOOTOUT (ALTOONA)					
12/10	79	Altoona Bishop Guilfoyle	38	W	A	Coleman (20)	Hooper (13)
12/11	46	Hamilton (ONT) Cathedral	47	L	N	Ryan (22)	UNREPORTED
		LATROBE ROTARY INVITATIONAL					
12/17	65	Latrobe	29	W	A	Coleman (22)	Dias (10)
12/18	35	Philadelphia Simon Gratz	42	L	N	Ryan (11)	Stokes & Stewart (13)
		KREUL HOLIDAY CLASSIC (CORAL SPRINGS, FL)					
12/20	73	Lauderdale Lakes (FL) Boyd H. Anderson	61	W	A	Ryan (22)	Bonner (21)
12/21	62	Ft. Lauderdale (FL) St. Thomas Aquinas	46	W	A	Ryan (27)	Brown & Crep (11)
12/22	60	South Miami (FL)	58	W	A	Coleman (19)	Miller (17)
		SLAM DUNK TO THE BEACH HOLIDAY TOURNAMENT (LEWES, DE)					
12/28	63	Redmond (WA)	53	W	N	Ryan (31)	Fulsom (18)
12/29	51	Queens (NY) Christ the King Regional	47	W	N	Coleman (24)	Seronik (13)
12/30	52	New Castle (DE) William Penn	65	L	A	Coleman (13)	Brown (18)
1/4		East (POSTPONED—SNOW)			N		
1/5	73	East	49	W	N	Coleman (26)	C. Crosby (15)
1/7	67	Mercyhurst Prep	59	W	N	Ryan (20)	Carpenter (15)
1/11	65	Strong Vincent	66	L	N	Ryan (25)	Britton (26)
		McDONALD'S CLASSIC					
1/14	61	Cleveland (OH) VASJ	71	L	H	Coleman (18)	Levett (32)
1/15	62	Elizabeth (NJ) St. Patrick's	47	W	H	Ryan (21)	Holloway (16)
1/18	74	Central	49	W	N	Ryan (20)	Jackson (12)
1/28	73	McDowell	56	W	N	Ryan (24)	Ehrensberger (18)
2/2	97	East	52	W	N	Ryan (17)	Moye (18)
2/4	78	Mercyhurst Prep	41	W	N	Ryan (19)	Kaiser (9)
2/9	65	Strong Vincent	37	W	N	Coleman (21)	Munson (14)
		TORONTO CHALLENGE (TORONTO, ONT.)					
2/11	53	Toronto (ONT) Lester B. Pearson	63(OT)	L	A	Ryan (25)	Lyte (22)
2/12	62	Toronto (ONT) Eastern Commerce	41	W	A	Ryan (20)	UNREPORTED
2/15	79	Central	51	W	N	Coleman (23)	Hamilton (12)
2/23	51	McDowell	49	W	N	Coleman (21)	Delsandro & Marsh (16)
		DISTRICT 10 PLAYOFFS					
3/1	72	Meadville	41	W	N	Coleman & Ryan (16)	Goodrum (14)
3/7	53	McDowell	50(OT)	W	N	Coleman (17)	Marsh (15)
		P.I.A.A. INTERDISTRICT PLAYOFFS					
3/12	70	McKeesport	63	W	N	Ryan (27)	Weiss (21)
3/16	76	North Allegheny	45	W	N	Coleman (15)	Barnes (10)
3/19	49	Upper St. Clair	41	W	N	Coleman (17)	Kaylor & O'Neill (11)
3/23	62	Penn Hills	43	W	N	Coleman (21)	Horne (18)
		P.I.A.A. CLASS AAAA STATE CHAMPIONSHIP					
3/26	65	Chester	69	L	N	Coleman (25)	Carroll (22)
	1993 (64.3)		**1569 (50.6)**				

Pos.	Player	Ht.	Prior School	Class	G(GS)	FG(3)	FT	Total	PPG	Career
F	Jed Ryan (#32)	6'7"	Girard St. John's	Jr.	31(31)	202(33)	114-149	551	17.8	1244
C	Booker Coleman (#43)	6'8"	Jamestown (NY)	Sr.	29(29)	174	154*-243	502	17.3	887
G	Kenny Duck (#23)	5'10"	Holy Trinity	Sr.	30(30)	86(2)	61-107	235	7.8	512
G	Keith Nies (#22)	5'8"	St. John's	Soph.	31(22)	73(42)	31-45	219	7.1	226
G	Craig Fomich (#21)	5'9"	St. John's	Jr.	31(24)	58(14)	29-48	159	5.1	161
F	Keith Anthony (#31)	6'4"	St. George's	Sr.	31(10)	55	28-40	138	4.5	165
F	Nick Bielak (#30)	6'5"	Bl. Sacrament	Sr.	27(9)	36(10)	1-3	83	3.1	92
C	Graham Witherspoon (#41)	6'3"	St. Luke's	Fr.	15	10	1-9	21	1.4	21
C	Kevin Anthony (#42)	6'5"	St. George's	Sr.	11	4	8-12	16	1.5	18
G	Gregor Martin (#11)	5'8"	St. Luke's	Jr.	11	4	7-9	15	1.4	15
G	Justin Izbicki (#10)	5'10"	Mount Calvary	Jr.	16	4(1)	6-9	15	0.9	15
F	Matt Marnella (#20)	6'3"	Bl. Sacrament	Jr.	18	7	1-3	15	0.8	15
G	Ryan Infield (#12)	5'10"	St. George's	Sr.	15	4	5-7	13	0.9	18
F	John Trocki (#40)	6'2"	St. John's	Soph.	9	4(1)	2-3	11	1.2	11

Cathedral Prep's 1994 State Finalists. Front L to R: Mgr. Kujawinski, Martin, Nies, Izbicki, Mgr. Herbstritt; Middle: Coach Arribi, Duck, Trocki, Fomich, Infield, Marnella, Headmaster Bergamasco; Back: A. D. Sertz, Asst. Coach Marnella, Kth. Anthony, Kv. Anthony, Coleman, Ryan, Bielak, Witherspoon, Asst. Coach Behringer.

HIGHLIGHTS:

- 1993-94 was another incredible season for coach **Marcel Arribi** and his Cathedral Prep Ramblers, as they showcased size, talent, superior coaching and state championship experience to win the Metro League and District 10 titles, then blow through four WPIAL powers on their way to a second straight appearance PIAA state championship game at Hersheypark Arena in Hershey. And, of course, there was the matter of the formidable and rugged schedule that once again prepared the Ramblers well for post-season activity.

- Senior big man **Booker Coleman** added 20 pounds of muscle and became only the sixth Prepster to score over 500 points in one season; he averaged 13 rebounds per game; he broke the single-season record for free throws made; and he had a whopping 92 blocked shots and plenty of slam-dunks for the season. **Jed Ryan** became the only Prepster to twice score over 500 in a season—and he was only a junior! Three-year starter **Kenny Duck** blended smoothly at guard with sophomore sensation **Keith Nies**, a 3-point specialist; spot starters **Craig Fomich, Keith Anthony** and **Nick Bielak** were dependable and when not starting Fomich was a super 6th man off the bench.

- All Metro League games and the McDonald's Classic were played at the Gannon University's Hammermill Center, while the Erie Civic Center was the site of the District 10 playoff games. Edinboro's McComb Fieldhouse hosted the PIAA first round against McKeesport, while the Western quarterfinal and final games against North Allegheny and Penn Hills were played at Sharon High School. The Western semifinal against Upper St. Clair was played at Grove City College.

- Prep participated in a record six regular season tournaments, taking second place finishes in the Great Chevy, Latrobe and Slam Dunk events and winning the prestigious 5th annual Kreul

Ryan with his patented jump shot.

Holiday Classic of which **Booker Coleman** was voted the Most Valuable Player.

Jed Ryan accepts Prep's runner-up trophy at the Slam Dunk Tourney.

- Canada's Hamilton Cathedral, whom Prep lost to by one in the final of the Great Chevy Shootout, moved to 10-0 with its victory. The Gaels went on to finish the season undefeated with the All-Ontario championship and a #1 ranking in the entire country of Canada. Cathedral was coached by Canadian legend **Mark Walton**, who had a remarkable career record of 723-86 with the Gaels.

- Although holding superstar **Shawn "Reds" Smith** to a mere four points, Prep lost in the Latrobe final to Simon Gratz, an inner-city Philadelphia school coming off a 31-0 national championship season in 1992-93. The Bulldogs were also 1991 national champions, led by **Rasheed Wallace**, later of North Carolina and NBA fame. Three future Division I players dotted the Bulldog lineup that held the Ramblers to a season low of 35 points. Other prominent alumni of Simon Gratz include the Brooklyn Dodgers' **Roy Campanella, Leroy Kelly** of the Cleveland Browns and entertainer **Eddie Fisher**.

- Prep won one of the premier high school basketball tournaments in the country, the Kreul Classic, with stunning upsets over eventual Florida state champion Boyd Anderson (30-5) and a 12-0 South Miami team which was ranked #2 in Florida at the time. The Kreul Classic features top-caliber boys' teams from across the nation. Held annually the week before Christmas in Coral Springs, Florida, the 16-team event is considered a model of excellence by which other tourneys gauge their performance.

- Of Prep's Kreul opponents: Boyd Anderson High School is a public school known more for its track and field and cross-country programs, and whose only previous claim to fame in

As always, Coach Arribi is determined to get it right.

basketball, before winning the 1994 Class 5A (large school) Florida state title, was the high school career of NBA guard **Mitch Richmond**. St. Thomas Aquinas has won seven Florida state football titles, a couple of baseball crowns and the 2001 state basketball championship; and in 2011 was named the nation's top athletic program by *MaxPreps*. South Miami lists among its alumni several former NFL players as well as **Senator Marco Rubio**. The Cobras were upset by Miami Senior in the first round of the Florida state tourney.

- The Slam Dunk to the Beach Tournament annually drew many of the nation's top players and teams to Delaware beginning in 1990. The tournament came to an end in 2003 after then-director **Bobby Jacobs** pleaded guilty to theft and forgery charges for stealing tens of thousands of dollars from the program and received two years in prison. After a decade of dormancy, the Slam Dunk was rejuvenated in the year 2014.

- Of Prep's Slam Dunk opponents: Redmond High, which has produced a few MLB players, has its fight song set to the *Blazing Saddles* theme; Christ the King (17-7), though never having played Prep before, did win the second McDonald's Classic in Erie in 1984; and William Penn, the largest high school in Delaware, won its first state basketball title in 1994, and three more since that time. The team Prep lost to in the Slam Dunk has been called Delaware's "Team of the Decade."

- Though unknown at the time, Prep's victory over Mercyhurst on January 7 was its 1,000th in school history.

- Manhattan's Rice High School (25-4) arrived at the 11th annual McDonald's High School Basketball Classic in Erie as the nation's #1 team, led by **Felipe Lopez**, "Mr. NY Basketball" and considered the best player in the country. The Raiders did not disappoint, demolishing St. Pat's, 78-49, then Ohio's eventual Division II state champ Villa Angela-St. Joseph (22-5), 80-58, to win the title. The Raiders finished the season as the State of New York's number one team as well. Rice was a private, Catholic, college preparatory school in the Central Harlem neighborhood, established in 1938 by the Christian Brothers. It produced great basketball players such as **Dean Meminger, Charlie Yelverton, Kenny Satterfield** and **Kemba Walker**, among others. Rice held its final graduation ceremony in 2011.

- In 1990, Cleveland St. Joseph, once the largest all-male school in Ohio with over 2,000 students, merged with all-girls Villa Angela Academy to form co-ed "Villa Angela-St. Joseph High School," commonly referred to as simply "VASJ." VASJ won Ohio state Division II basketball crowns in 1991 and 1992, and won again in the instant season, 1994. St. Patrick's athletic program is also noted for its storied basketball program, one that has produced numerous college and professional level players. Often a national powerhouse, St. Pat's has been a staple in many national rankings, including the ESPN Fab 50, *USA Today* Super 25, and the *MaxPreps* Top 25.

- Prep played well in the McDonald's Classic, taking consolation honors with an impressive win over St. Patrick's. On night one, however, the Ramblers suffered a 10-point loss to Ohio's eventual state champ, VASJ. In one memorable play, Viking great **Melvin Levett** drove in for a layup and soared directly over the head of **Keith Nies** who was settled in and poised to take the charge. Levett, known as "The Helicopter," never touched Nies and slam-dunked the ball to the amazement and roaring approval of the capacity crowd. Years later, Nies remarked: "It was a 2-on-1 break and I moved to take the charge. Levett got a bounce pass, took off and jumped right over me and all I remember is seeing the bottom of his shoes. The crowd went nuts on both sides. I get razzed about it to this day!"

- Of Prep's opponents in Toronto: **Lester B. Pearson** was himself prime minister of Canada in the mid-1960's; and Eastern Commerce, despite its small size, is well known for its elite basketball program.

- The final standings in Metro League basketball were as follows:

	W	L
Prep	9	1
McDowell	7	3
East	6	4
Vincent	3	7
Central	3	7
Mercyhurst	2	8

- Prep's one-point loss to Vincent (11-12) was its first after 11 straight wins against the Colonels. SV's **Ryan Munson** was the star, nailing a 22-footer at 0:02 to win the one-point thriller for the Colonels.

Kenny Duck and Booker Coleman congratulate each other in the waning moments of the Western Final victory over Penn Hills.

- Of exceptional note were Prep's three big wins over a strong McDowell (19-8) team. Each game was sold out and jam-packed before the warm-up drills. The Rambler two-point win in the regular season finale and the overtime victory in the D-10 final were particularly exciting. Every Prep-McDowell battle, for several years running, had become well-attended, intense, physical, bruising spectacles involving fans, students, players and even a white-hot rivalry between coaches **Marcel Arribi** of the Ramblers and **Pete Flinn** of the Trojans.

- Prep, ranked Pennsylvania's #1 team at the time, began its road back to Hershey by manhandling Meadville (12-11), then surviving the intense overtime thriller against McDowell in the D-10 final before 3,708 fans. The Ramblers then rattled off four straight inter-district wins, the final three over the WPIAL's top three teams. First they held off McKeesport (15-7), which had whittled a 15-point Prep lead to three, before **Jed Ryan** took over to ensure victory. The Ramblers played perhaps their finest game next, routing North Allegheny (18-9). Prep then defeated the state's #5 team, Upper St. Clair (25-5), in a very tense contest. Finally, the Ramblers whipped the #2 team, Penn Hills (27-5), ripping its renowned full-court press to shreds. Ryan and particularly **Booker Coleman** had

A couple of Chester Clippers are in awe of the power dunk by Booker Coleman.

monstrous games down the stretch.

- The nip-and-tuck state final was an instant classic, with 24 lead changes and 12 ties. Neither team led by more than four until Chester (28-4) forged a brief 69-63 edge in the closing seconds. The Clippers used 11 players to operate its full-court, harassing defense which led to a choppy, twisted game of peaks and valleys on both sides. Coleman, who had four different players covering him in that swarming man-to-man defense, led all scorers with 25. But it was **Randy Maultsby's** short baseline jumper at 1:32 that put the Clippers up for good, 63-61. Chester's **Raymond Carroll** hit two FT's with 33 seconds left to seal the Clippers' third state title.

- **Booker Coleman** was named First Team All-State by the *Associated Press*, only the second Prepster ever to be so

The Ramblers employ a rugged defense in the state final against Chester.

honored and the first since **Tim Gore** in 1980. **Jed Ryan** was named Fourth Team All-State, the first Rambler accorded all-state honors two years in a row.

A small portion of the Nies family prepares for the road trip to Hershey to cheer on Keith and the Ramblers.

Coach Arribi consoles Coleman with a silver medal after Prep's 3-point loss in the state final.

- Coleman and Ryan, of whom one or the other led Prep in scoring every game of the season, were both named First Team on the 1993-94 All-Metro Basketball Team as announced by the *Erie Times-News*, while **Kenny Duck** was a Second Team selection. Young **Keith Nies** was accorded Honorable Mention recognition.

- Duck and dependable **Keith Anthony** each scored 6 points for the City All-Stars in an 82-68 win over the County in the 20th annual City-County All-Star Classic, sponsored by the Northwest Jaycees. Coleman was selected but did not play, as he was on an official recruiting visit to the University of Wisconsin, where he eventually lettered for four years under coaches **Stan Van Gundy** and **Dick Bennett**. Coleman played in the 1996 NIT and 1997 NCAA's for the Badgers.

First Team All-State center Booker Coleman, only the second Rambler ever to be so highly honored. Coleman continued his career at Wisconsin.

- **Nick Bielak** went on to play for Division II Lock Haven, where he lettered three years (1994-97).

- **Booker Coleman**, now an attorney, and **Jed Ryan** were co-winners of the prestigious James "Moe" Gross Award as Prep's most valuable players. Coleman was also the "Ma" Kaiser Award recipient as Prep's best athlete. Coleman, perhaps more than any other Prepster had ever done, altered opponents plans on both offense and defense—witness the intentional fouls when he was underneath the hoop and his season records for free throws made and attempted (154 of 243). Coleman was inducted inot the Prep Athletic Hall of Fame in 2017.

Three-year star Kenny Duck about to convert a free throw in the state final.

Coleman with a left-handed hook as Duck, Fomich and Ryan prepare to crash.

1994 All-Opponent Team:

Joe Martin, Hamilton Cathedral [Virginia Commonwealth]

Steve Maga, Hamilton Cathedral [Simon Fraser, McMaster Univ., Canadian Player of the Year, 2001]

Lynard Stewart, Simon Gratz (1st team all-state) [Temple]

Shawn "Reds" Smith, Simon Gratz [LaSalle]

Terrell Stokes, Simon Gratz [Maryland]

Pat Bonner, Boyd Anderson [Temple, Florida A & M, football]

Charlie Miller, South Miami (McDonald's All-American, FL Player of the Year) [Indiana]

Gary Lumpkin, William Penn (2nd team all-state, DE) [Xavier (OH)]

Lenny Brown, William Penn (1st team all-state, DE) [Xavier (OH)]

William "Tail" Davis, William Penn (2nd team all-state, DE) [Virginia Union]

Clifton Crosby, East [Maryland, football; NFL Bengals, Rams, Colts, Chiefs]

Matt Britton, Vincent

Ryan Munson, Vincent

Melvin "The Helicopter" Levett, VASJ (2nd team all-state, OH) [Cincinnati]

Babe Kwasniak, VASJ [Army]

Shaheen Holloway, St. Pat's (2nd team *Parade Magazine* All-American, 1996; McDonald's All-American, 1997) [Seton Hall]

Richie Lyte, Lester B. Pearson [SE Missouri St.]

Jerry Ambooken, Meadville (4th team all-state) [Allegheny]

Lucas Marsh, McDowell [Geneva]

Jarrod O'Neill, Upper St. Clair [Susquehanna]

Justin Kaylor, Upper St. Clair [Washington & Jefferson]

Chris Horne, Penn Hills (3rd team all-state) [William & Mary]

Eric Roberson, Penn Hills [Bradley]

Raymond Carroll, Chester (2nd team all-state) [Fordham]

Randy Maultsby, Chester [Neumann College]

Four defenders can't stop Jed Ryan, Prep's leading scorer and 4th Team All-State pick.

Dependable all-star Keith Anthony.

Spot starter Nick Bielak went on to a fine career at Lock Haven.

Loss to Ringgold Overshadows Great Accomplishments

1994-95 (25-4)

Coach: Marcel Arribi
Assistants: Jim Marnella, Wes Alexander
Captains: Keith Nies, Jed Ryan, Craig Fomich
Managers: Matt Kujawinski, Rick Herbstritt

Jed Ryan, Erie's all-time leading scorer, is introduced at the Hammermill Center for the last time.

Date	PREP		Dec.	Loc.	High Scorer	Opponent
	CHOCOLATE WORLD BASKETBALL CLASSIC (HERSHEY)					
12/2	58	Hempfield	51	W	N	Ryan (32)	Hanse (21)
12/3	55	Whitehall	46	W	N	Ryan (20)	Lisicky (19)
12/9	101	Clearfield	46	W	H	Ryan (28)	Corkle (20)
12/10	70	Cleveland (OH) St. Ignatius	66	W	A	Nies (23)	Fox (25)
	ELK COUNTY CHRISTIAN CRUSADER CLASSIC (ST. MARYS)					
12/16	70	Tonawanda (NY) Cardinal O'Hara	54	W	N	Ryan (25)	Price (22)
12/17	42	Elk County Christian	25	W	A	Nies (13)	Straub (12)
	SCENIC CITY SHOOTOUT (CHATTANOOGA, TN)					
12/21	72	Chattanooga (TN) Lookout Valley	60	W	A	Ryan (33)	Fears (33)
12/22	59	Chattanooga (TN) Brainerd	73	L	A	Ryan (35)	Walker (18)
12/23	61	Chattanooga (TN) Baylor School	51	W	A	Ryan (26)	Womack (21)
	SUN USA CUP (TORONTO, CANADA)					
12/28	69	Ottawa (ONT) St. Matthew Catholic	56	W	N	Ryan (34)	Martin (16)
12/29	57	Queens (NY) Msgr. McClancy	54	W	N	Nies (21)	Cook (16)
12/30	46	Toronto (ONT) Runnymede	35	W	A	Szewczykowski (16)	Cain (9)
1/6	94	East	47	W	N	Ryan (24)	Moye (18)
1/10	70	Mercyhurst Prep	57	W	N	Ryan (28)	Emick (18)
	McDONALD'S CLASSIC					
1/13	59	Chester	52	W	H	Ryan (31)	Carroll (14)
1/14	55	Paterson (NJ) Catholic	62	L	H	Ryan (24)	Thomas (23)
1/17	75	Strong Vincent	36	W	N	Ryan (23)	Barron (12)
1/20	69	Central	55	W	N	Ryan & Trocki (23)	Benjamin (18)
1/25	52	McDowell	40	W	N	Ryan (23)	Delsandro (16)
1/31	78	East	42	W	N	Ryan (15)	Mrv. Goodwine (19)
2/3	81	Mercyhurst Prep	48	W	N	Ryan (32)	Emick (18)
2/7	87	Strong Vincent	47	W	N	Ryan (25)	Orlando (13)
2/10	69	Central	65	W	N	Ryan (21)	Dixon (22)
2/17	47	McDowell	50	L	N	Ryan (17)	Witgen (13)
	P.I.A.A. DISTRICT 10 PLAYOFFS					
2/23	66	Meadville	35	W	N	Ryan (21)	Acker & Engelbert (6)
3/6	58	McDowell	55	W	N	Ryan (17)	Finazzo (13)
	P.I.A.A. INTERDISTRICT PLAYOFFS					
3/11	73	New Castle	53	W	H	Ryan (27)	Lucas (19)
3/15	73	North Allegheny	55	W	N	Ryan (24)	MacMurdo (24)
3/18	67	Ringgold	77(2OT) L		N	Szewczykowski (19)	Horan (29)
	1933 (66.7)		**1493 (51.5)**			

Pos.	Player	Ht.	Prior School	Class	G(GS)	FG(3)	FT	Total	PPG	Career
F	Jed Ryan (#32)	6'7"	Girard St. John's	Sr.	29(29)	243*(43)	153-194	682*	23.5	1926*
G	Keith Nies (#22)	5'9"	St. John's	Jr.	29(29)	102(48)	58-70	310	10.7	536
F	Brian Szewczykowski (#42)	6'3"	St. James	Jr.	29(28)	101(31)	57-71	290	10.0	290
F	John Trocki (#31)	6'4"	St. John's	Jr.	27(26)	84(20)	40-57	228	8.4	239
G	Craig Fomich (#43)	5'11"	St. John's	Sr.	29(5)	42(13)	50-60	147	5.1	308
G	Justin Izbicki (#10)	5'10"	Mount Calvary	Sr.	29(27)	52(9)	20-44	133	4.6	148
F	Matt Marnella (#20)	6'3"	Bl. Sacrament	Sr.	21	15	6-17	36	1.7	51
G	Gregor Martin (#11)	5'8"	St. Luke's	Sr.	13	10(2)	10-14	32	2.5	47
C	Graham Witherspoon (#50)	6'4"	St. Luke's	Soph.	19(1)	9	9-15	27	1.4	48
F	Doug Lecker (#40)	6'4"	St. Boniface	Jr.	14	12	2-6	26	1.9	26
F	Bob Vahey (#21)	6'2"	St. John's	Jr.	11	4(3)	0-1	10	1.0	10
G	Mike McMahon (#12)	5'8"	St. Peter's	Jr.	7	2(2)	0-0	6	0.9	6
G	Brandon Ralph (#23)	5'11"	Corry	Soph.	4	1	3-5	5	1.2	5

Cathedral Prep's 1995 Western Finalists. Front, L to R: Fomich, McMahon; Middle: Vahey, Martin, Nies, Izbicki, Marnella; Back: Trocki, Lecker, Ryan, Witherspoon, Szewczykowski.

HIGHLIGHTS:

- 1994-95 was another spectacular season for coach **Marcel Arribi** and his Cathedral Prep Ramblers. Favored again to win the Metro League despite returning only two starters, it was an indication of where Coach Arribi and his top assistant, **Jim Marnella**, had brought the program—elite statewide, and even a national reputation with its tournament-heavy schedule from year to year. The returning starters were good ones: **Jed Ryan**, only the second four-year starter in Prep basketball history (**Ted Morasky** was the first, 1938-42), and junior **Keith Nies**. Juniors **John Trocki** and particularly **Brian**

Starting gaurd Justin Izbicki was a defensive specialist.

Ryan scored 55 points in the two McDonald's Classic games.

Szewczykowski emerged as strong scorers and rebounders, while **Justin Izbicki**, star Rambler quarterback on the gridiron, was a steady defensive specialist. As important as the starters was **Craig Fomich**, nothing less than a "super sixth man." They all had designs on returning the Ramblers to Hershey in a quest for another state crown.

- All Metro League games, the Clearfield home game (Prep's only home game in the month of December), the McDonald's Classic and the PIAA first round matchup against New Castle were played at the Gannon University's Hammermill Center, while Edinboro's McComb Fieldhouse hosted the District 10 semifinal and the PIAA Western Quarterfinal against North Allegheny. The Western Semifinal against Ringgold was played at New Castle High School.

- Prep opened the season with a return to Hershey and a championship in the Chocolate World Basketball Classic against a pair of solid Quad-A teams it had never played before. Hempfield (22-4) was picked apart by the Ramblers, who then took down the Whitehall Zephyrs (16-13). The Black Knights,

The Ramblers huddle-up at the Hammermill before tearing apart another opponent.

from the Lancaster-Lebanon League, have not enjoyed much athletic success. Whitehall, from the Lehigh Valley Conference, won a PIAA AAA crown in 1982, defeating New Castle in the final, 42-38, in Hershey.

- **Keith Nies** took MVP honors at the Elk County Christian Classic, leading the Ramblers to its second tourney title of the season with a victory over New York's 1994 Catholic Class C state champion, Cardinal O'Hara, and a slowdown win over the hometown ECC Crusaders (19-10) in the final.

- Prep's wins over Clearfield and Cardinal O'Hara (15-8) were the first time the Ramblers played these schools since 1977; the Orange & Black triumph over Elk County Christian, which made it to the second round of the PIAA Class A tourney, was the first the two competed since 1967; and Prep's impressive victory over St. Ignatius (9-12) was the first Ramblers-Wildcats battle since 1948. Despite St. Ignatius' mediocre record, the Wildcats did make it to their sectional final, where they lost to Parma, 60-55. Prep and St. Ignatius did not play again for another decade.

- **Jed Ryan** set a three-game Scenic City Shootout record with 94 points as Prep took third place consolation honors with a win over perennial powerhouse Chattanooga Baylor. The Baylor School is a private college prep and boarding school that was honored twice by *Sports Illustrated* with having the top high school sports program in Tennessee with over 150 state championships in various sports.

- The Ramblers followed with its third tourney championship at the 8-team *Toronto Sun* USA Cup in Canada. Impressive were victories over 10-0 St. Matthew's, Ottawa's top program, and 9-0 Msgr. McClancy (20-5), from the East Elmhurst neighborhood in Queens. Again winning an MVP award, **Keith Nies** converted a fadeaway 3-pointer from the top of the key at the buzzer in the thrilling win over McClancy. Prep bounced Toronto Runnymede in the title clash. Owing to its red school jackets, Runnymede came to be known as the Redmen in the 1930's. Over time an Indian logo was adopted, but the nickname and logo were both retired in 1994 by political correctness and the Redmen became known as the Ravens.

- The 12th annual McDonald's High School Basketball Classic featured a recent opponent and a new foe for the Ramblers. The defending state champs Chester Clippers have a long-standing tradition of excellence in basketball, winning eight state championships, including 1994; also in 1983 and 1989, and later in 2000, 2005, 2008, 2011 and 2012. Chester was state runner-up on 10 occasions. Since the 1981-82 season, the Clippers have qualified for the state tournament every year except for 1991-92. The Paterson Catholic Cougars had a strong athletic history, but due to dwindling enrollment and monetary problems, the Paterson Diocese closed the school at the end of the 2009-10 school year.

- Opening night of the 12th annual McDonald's High School

Basketball Classic saw a Classic record 41-point performance by the nation's number one player, **Tim Thomas**, as Paterson Catholic edged Simon Gratz, 69-66. Prep then took down Chester High, but fell to Paterson in the final, despite holding Thomas to 23 markers.

- Prep ran its all-time series record against cross-town rival Mercyhurst Prep (14-13) to 22-0. After the Ramblers forced 10 consecutive Laker turnovers with a wicked 3rd quarter press in the February 3 contest, MPS coach **Bill Gausman** engaged in a heat-of-the-moment shouting exchange with Coach Arribi. The verbiage was smoothed over with post-game handshakes.

- The final standings in Metro League basketball were as follows:

	W	L
Prep	9	1
McDowell	8	2
Central	7	3
Mercyhurst	4	6
*East	2	9
Vincent	1	10

won playoff for AAA title

- The Prep-McDowell (22-5) series continued to be a heated affair—both teams were excellent and *loved* to beat the other; and both teams *hated* to lose to the other. All three games were televised by WSEE-Channel 35 as the rivalry had drawn so much interest. The Ramblers won the first contest handily, but the rugged Trojan defense disrupted Prep and knocked the Ramblers out of a number one state ranking in game two, this despite the fact the Ramblers had already been crowned Metro League champs. The fiercely bitter opponents both had outstanding 22-3 records by the time they met in the District 10 final, of which Prep gained a hard-fought win before 4,675 fans at the Erie Civic Center. Trojan star **Jake Delsandro** tried to tie the game with a 3-pointer, but after a miss and scramble for the ball, **Keith Nies** came up with the rebound with 0:02 left. The Ramblers inbounded and won their third straight D-10 crown and fifth in six years.

- Prep established dominance over Meadville (8-17) with its fifth straight D-10 semifinal win over the Bulldogs in the 1990's. Meadville had given Prep quite a dose of trouble in the mid-to late-1980's.

- Prep looked to be on its way back to Hershey with easy inter-district wins over New Castle (20-7) and North Allegheny (21-8). About the only thing Prep couldn't contain against NA was **Matt MacMurdo's** shooting—and his temper. MacMurdo hit five 3-pointers, but it was his flagrant foul on Nies in the middle of a 10-0 Prep run with less than three minutes to play that got him ejected and ultimately did in the Tigers. "That incident fired us up a little bit," stated coach **Marcel Arribi**. And from the crowd's reaction, it fired up the Rambler faithful *a lot* of bit.

Marcel Arribi, with his animated coaching instructions.

- The most devastating defeat in the history of Prep basketball occurred in the next outing, the Western Semifinal contest against Ringgold (25-6) at New Castle High School. After a pulsating 11 ties and 14 lead changes, the Ramblers comfortably led, 57-54, with only five ticks left on the clock after **Keith Nies** iced a pair of free throws. He got to the line courtesy of **Jed Ryan**, who drew a

Reliable 7th man, Matt Marnella.

charge when the Rams attempted a go-ahead shot. Then Ringgold's **Jeremy "Czar" Walsh**, a name that will forever live in infamy in Prep basketball annals, was able to get a running, one-handed prayer off at the buzzer as he fell into the bench from 35 feet away. The high-arching desperation shot swished right through. Though it only sent the game into overtime, the bomb at the end of regulation seemed to deflate the Ramblers. Prep regrouped behind **Brian Szewczykowski** in the first OT after falling behind, but by the second OT the Ramblers had been sapped of their strength. The Rams went on a 13-0 run while Prep missed its first six shots in OT 2 and only scored at the final buzzer on a 3-pointer by **Justin Izbicki**. It was a stinging defeat to a team that many called Prep's best ever.

- Ryan was seen as heartbroken when he fouled out of his last game in the closing moments of the second overtime. "This isn't the way we envisioned it," said Jed, who started every game in his amazing four-year career. "But everything comes to an end. It's sad that it's over and hard to take off the Prep jersey for the last time." Added master psychologist **Marcel Arribi**: "It's hard for these 16 and 17-year old boys to accept right now that it's over. They're feeling a lot of pain and a lot of hurt, and that's understandable. But they've accomplished a great deal going 25-4 and I couldn't be prouder of them. This is character building. They are going to learn a great deal from this."

- Ringgold went on to become the first WPIAL team to win a PIAA Class AAAA title with a 71-66 victory over Williamsport.

- **Jed Ryan** became only the third player in Rambler history to be named First Team All-State by the *Associated Press*. He is the only Erieite to be given all-state honors three years running. Ryan was named to no less than ten all-tournament teams over his career and is the all-time Prep single season record holder in field goals made (243) and points scored (682); and the all-time Prep career record holder in games played and started

Named First Team All-State, Jed Ryan is the only Erieite to be given all-state recognition three straight years.

(115), field goals made (700), free throws made (416), points scored (1,926, also the Metro League record). Jed also added 700 career rebounds and 243 career assists to his resume.

Super-sub and all-star Craig Fomich has recently joined the Prep staff.

- Unanimous choice **Jed Ryan** and **Keith Nies** were both named First Team on the 1994-95 All-Metro Basketball Team as announced by the *Erie Times-News*, while **John Trocki** was a Second Team selection. **Brian Szewczykowski** was an Honorable Mention choice, giving the Ramblers three juniors with post-season honors. Ryan is the only Prepster in history named First Team three consecutive years.

- **Jed Ryan** led the City All-Stars with 18 points in a high-scoring 114-113 victory over the County in the 21st annual City-County All-Star Classic, sponsored by the Northwest Jaycees. Rambler dependables **Craig Fomich** and **Justin Izbicki** were also selected to the All-Star squad. Fomich is now an assistant coach at Prep and Izbicki, also a star quarterback for the Rambler gridders, has become an assistant at Prep and now at McDowell.

Four-year star Jed Ryan, Prep's all-time greatest basketball player. His number 32 is retired.

- Ryan and Central's **Roosevelt Benjamin** were both selected to play for Pennsylvania in the "Shootout against Maryland" in Mechanicsburg. This was considered the premier high school all-star game in the state after the demise of the Dapper Dan Roundball Classic.

- Promising sophomore **Brandon Ralph** transferred to Corry High School, where he became an All-County star, averaging 16.5 PPG as a senior.

- **Jed Ryan**, Prep's Student Government president, was also winner of the prestigious James "Moe" Gross Award as Prep's most valuable player, the first Rambler hoopster to win the honor two consecutive years. He led the Orange & Black to three District 10 AAAA crowns, the PIAA title as a sophomore, and a return trip to Hershey the following year. Jed, Prep's first four-year letter winner in a half-century, went on to star at the University of Pennsylvania, scoring in double figures with the Quakers for three straight years. Ryan once nailed seven 3-pointers against Yale and in NCAA tournament action hit six 3-pointers in a near upset of Florida, a performance that has been called one of Penn's Top 10 of all time. Cathedral Prep's greatest basketball player ever, Ryan was inducted into the Cathedral Prep Athletic Hall of Fame in 2008 and the Metro Erie Sports Hall of Fame in 2009. His #32 is now retired.

1995 All-Opponent Team:

Justin Stewart, Hempfield (5th team all-state) [UNC-Greensboro]

Terry Hanse, Hempfield

Gabe Lisicky, Whitehall [East Tennessee St.]

Tom Fox, St. Ignatius (3rd team all-state, OH)

Calvin Price, Cardinal O'Hara

Robert Fears, Lookout Valley [Walters St. CC, UT-Chattanooga]

Harris Walker, Brainerd (Mr. Tennessee Basketball, 1998) [Tennessee, Mountain St.]

C.J. Black, Brainerd [Tennessee]

Shamek Cook, Msgr. McClancy [Maryland-Eastern Shore]

Tim Thomas, Paterson Catholic (1996 McDonald's All-American; 1996 1st team *Parade Magazine* All-American) [Villanova; NBA 7 teams]

Alexander "Vincent" Mitchell, Paterson Catholic

Rodney Rodgers, Paterson Catholic [St. Peter's]

Raymond Carroll, Chester (2nd team all-state) [Fordham]

Jake Delsandro, McDowell [Allegheny]

Willie Dixon, Central

Roosevelt Benjamin, Central [Kings River (CA) CC, Clarion, football]

Brad Orlando, Vincent

Brent Witgen, McDowell

Damon Finazzo, McDowell [Grove City]

Matt MacMurdo, North Allegheny

Mike Horan, Ringgold (2nd team all-state) [Fairfield]

Jeremy "Czar" Walsh, Ringgold

PIAA Western Champions!
Loss to Kobe Bryant Team Can't Erase Great Win Over McDowell!

1995-96 (24-8)

Coach: Marcel Arribi
Assistants: Jim Marnella, Wes Alexander
Captains: Keith Nies, John Trocki,
          Brian Szewczykowski
Managers: Rick Herbstritt

The Ramblers held Lower Merion superstar Kobe Bryant to a season-low 17 points. Here, Fiorelli checks Bryant closely.

Date	PREP			Dec.	Loc.	High Scorer	Opponent
	FARRELL TIP-OFF TOURNAMENT						
12/1	70	Canfield (OH)	57	W	N	Nies (25)	Kish (17)
12/2	67	Farrell	48	W	A	Trocki (16)	Page (21)
	COCA-COLA BASKETBALL CHALLENGE (GANNON UNIVERSITY)						
12/8	67	Lakewood (OH) St. Edward	68(OT)	L	H	Trocki (17)	Clancy (16)
12/9	75	Ringgold	35	W	H	Fiorelli (13)	Thomas (15)
12/15	80	Whitehall	53	W	H	Trocki (26)	Lloyd (13)
	REEBOK HOLIDAY BASKETBALL TOURNAMENT (LAS VEGAS, NV)						
12/18	60	Franklin-Simpson (KY)	65	L	N	Sz'ki, Nies & Fiorelli (11)	Chatman (18)
12/19	61	Orem (UT)	58(OT)	W	N	Szewczykowski (23)	Webb (16)
12/20	45	Oakland (CA) Fremont	35	W	N	Nies (12)	Milstead (14)
12/21	62	Louisville (KY) Harry Doss	56	W	N	Szewczykowski (20)	Williams (14)
12/21	55	Huntsville (AL) S. R. Butler	56	L	N	Szewczykowski (22)	Strong (15)
	OIL CITY VILLAGE AUTO HOLIDAY BASKETBALL TOURNAMENT						
12/28	69	Knox Keystone	43	W	N	Nies (20)	Corcetti (11)
12/29	72	Oil City	40	W	A	Trocki (15)	Schill (13)
1/6	68	East	50	W	N	Fiorelli (19)	Woodard (18)
1/9	74	Mercyhurst Prep	43	W	N	Nies (13)	Kaiser (15)
1/12	72	Central	52	W	N	Nies (22)	Bush (16)
1/16	94	Strong Vincent	54	W	N	Fiorelli (14)	Barron (20)
	McDONALD'S CLASSIC						
1/19	60	Baltimore (MD) St. Frances Academy	86	L	H	Vahey (15)	Jones & Hampton (16)
1/20	40	NYC (NY) LaSalle Academy	44(2OT)	L	H	Szewczykowski (17)	Artest (24)
1/24	47	McDowell	62	L	N	Nies & Trocki (11)	Witgen & Delsandro (15)
1/30	68	East	42	W	N	Trocki (19)	Woodard (13)
2/2	67	Mercyhurst Prep	38	W	N	Trocki (17)	Slomski (9)
2/6	91	Strong Vincent	35	W	N	Szewczykowski (15)	Whitted (14)
2/9	72	Central	46	W	N	Nies (24)	Bush (24)
2/16	52	McDowell	48	W	N	Blanks (15)	Garrity (16)
	METRO LEAGUE PLAYOFF						
2/20	55	McDowell	49	W	N	Szewczykowski (23)	Garrity (17)
	P.I.A.A. DISTRICT 10 PLAYOFFS						
2/24	83	Warren	31	W	N	Fiorelli (17)	Rondinelli (11)
3/4	56	McDowell	69	L	N	Fiorelli (16)	Delsandro (25)
	P.I.A.A. INTERDISTRICT PLAYOFFS						
3/9	66	Upper St. Clair	49	W	N	Szewczykowski (19)	Keeley (17)
3/13	65	Bradford	38	W	N	Szewczykowski (20)	Grice (14)
3/16	60	Pittsburgh Schenley	44	W	N	Fiorelli (16)	Jackson (20)
3/20	47	McDowell	44	W	N	Nies (14)	Witgen (15)
	P.I.A.A. CLASS AAAA STATE CHAMPIONSHIP						
3/23	43	Lower Merion	48	L	N	Nies (12)	Bryant (17)
	2063 (64.5)		**1586 (49.6)**				

Pos.	Player	Ht.	Prior School	Class	G(GS)	FG(3)	FT	Total	PPG	Career
F	Brian Szewczykowski (#42)	6'3"	St. James	Sr.	32(32)	142(61)	58-66	403	12.6	693
G	Keith Nies (#22)	5'9"	St. John's	Sr.	32(32)	123(46)	60-76	352	11.0	888
F	John Trocki (#31)	6'4"	St. John's	Sr.	30(30)	116(16)	68-93	316	10.5	555
G	R. J. Fiorelli (#23)	6'1"	St. Luke's	Jr.	32(6)	106(24)	54-74	290	9.1	290
G	Julian Blanks (#21)	5'11"	St. John's	Soph.	32(29)	93(21)	34-55	241	7.5	241
C	Graham Witherspoon (#50)	6'4"	St. Luke's	Jr.	30(22)	61	26-48	148	4.9	196
F	Doug Lecker (#40)	6'4"	St. Boniface	Sr.	32(9)	59	12-26	130	4.1	156
F	Bob Vahey (#43)	6'2"	St. John's	Sr.	27	25(14)	7-14	71	2.6	81
G	Mike McMahon (#14)	5'8"	St. Peter's	Sr.	25	17(5)	10-13	49	2.0	55
G	Jim Gemler (#33)	5'11"	Bl. Sacrament	Soph.	21	15(6)	2-4	38	1.8	38
F	Brad Kons (#20)	6'3"	OLP	Jr.	20	6	4-7	16	0.8	16
G	Chris Dunham (#41)	5'11"	California	Jr.	16	3	3-4	9	0.6	9

HIGHLIGHTS:

- 1995-96 was another sensational season for the Cathedral Prep program and coach **Marcel Arribi**. This well-balanced, veteran crew won a pair of in-season tournaments, faced strong opposition independently and gave fans one of the most exciting post-season runs in Rambler history—and an extra memorable victory over McDowell in the PIAA Western Final.

- Prep was well-stocked with experienced seniors, including leading scorer **Brian Szewczykowski**; tough inside man **John Trocki**; and four-year guard and team leader, **Keith Nies**. Other senior stars included journeymen **Doug Lecker, Bob Vahey** and **Mike McMahon**. The Ramblers also received excellent play from super-sixth man **R. J. Fiorelli**, a junior, and big junior center

Cathedral Prep's 1996 State Finalists, the third time in four years. Front, L to R: Dunham, Nies, McMahon, Blanks; Middle: Fiorelli, Gemler, Vahey, Kons; Back: Trocki, Lecker, Szewczykowski, Witherspoon.

Graham Witherspoon, who had already spent two years with the varsity. Witherspoon is the son of former Gannon College great **Mel Witherspoon** and was named after another Gannon great, **Cal "Cracker" Graham**, who was big "Spoon's" best pal when they both starred for the Golden Knights.

- **Father Bruce R. Allison**, from Prep's Class of 1954, was appointed Prep's seventh headmaster in 1995 by **Bishop Donald Trautman**.

- **Mrs. Joann Mullen**, Prep's esteemed mathematics teacher and a big Rambler sports fan since 1967, was appointed the school's first principal in 1995 by Bishop Trautman. Mrs. Mullen had been an assistant headmaster since 1989 and Director of Academics since 1987.

- All Metro League games, the Whitehall home game, the Coca-Cola Challenge and the McDonald's Classic were played at Gannon University's

Prep's rugged inside man, John Trocki.

Hammermill Center. Edinboro's McComb Fieldhouse hosted the District 10 semifinal, while the D-10 title game and the PIAA Western Final, both against McDowell, were played at the Erie Civic Center. The PIAA first round clash against Upper St. Clair was played at Robert Morris University, while the Western Quarterfinal against Bradford was held at Clarion. The Western Semifinal against Schenley was played at Grove City College, while the Ramblers played in their third state final in four years at Hersheypark Arena.

- Prep opened the season with a championship in the Farrell Tip-Off Tourney and hosting the Coca-Cola Basketball Challenge at the Hammermill Center. The victory over host Farrell (24-7) was impressive, as by season's end Farrell was the top-ranked AA team in the WPIAL and the Steelers made it to the Western Final before being run over by

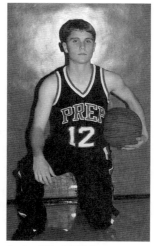

Senior Mike McMahon was reliable off the bench.

eventual state champ George Jr. Republic, 84-52. The Coca-Cola Challenge featured nine games with teams at all levels of play from grade school through high school, boys and girls. The concept developed by Prep A.D. **Ron Sertz** was new and it gave area fans a chance to see basketball at every level—grade school JV's and varsity, 9th grade, junior varsity and varsity teams. On Friday night Prep lost a close one to a new opponent in Lakewood St. Ed's, but on Saturday the Ramblers paid back defending state champ Ringgold (9-15) by a 40-point revenge margin. Preliminaries to the Prep contests included Cleveland VASJ versus Franklin and on Saturday Elk County Christian against Kennedy Christian.

- St. Edward (21-5), which beat Prep in overtime in the Coca-Cola Challenge, played three eventual Division I stars and another who eventually starred on the Division II national championship team. The Eagles made it to the Ohio Division I state semifinals, where it lost to Cincinnati LaSalle, 60-54. St. Ed's, founded by the Brothers of Holy Cross, Notre Dame (IN) in 1949, is located in Cleveland's important western suburb of

Trocki guards LaSalle's "Masked Marvel."

Lakewood and is one of only three remaining all-male Catholic high schools in the Greater Cleveland area (Benedictine and St. Ignatius being the others). The Eagles' main historic rivalry was with St. Joseph High School (which became VASJ). The rivalry pitted a large east suburban school, St. Joe's, against a large west suburban school, St. Ed's. After merging with Villa Angela Academy, the enrollment of VASJ dropped and the rivalry has pretty much faded. With the rise to football and overall sports prominence of St. Ignatius, along with the proximity of the two schools, St. Ignatius replaced VASJ as the main rival of "Ed's" with St. Edward replacing the closed (and now reopened/merged) Cathedral Latin for St. Ignatius.

- Prep had an impressive rout over Whitehall (21-7), which was ranked the #2 team in Pennsylvania at the time. **John Trocki** meshed a season-high 26 points in that one. The Zephyrs finished disappointingly, losing to Plymouth-Whitemarsh in the first round of the state playoffs.

- In the first Prep-East (12-14) game, the Warriors bolted out to an 11-0 lead and led by 12 early in the 2nd quarter. On came the Rambler press and down went the Warriors, who let Prep have a 17-0 run in period three.

- Prep faced stiff competition at the 19th annual Reebok Holiday Prep Classic in Las Vegas, playing well in winning three of five. **Brian Szewczykowski** proved remarkable with his smooth-shooting ability throughout the tourney. The Ramblers faced three brand new opponents at the Reebok, including Franklin –Simpson, a rural school close to the Kentucky-Tennessee border; Oakland Fremont, an urban public school;

First Team All-Metro choice Brian Szewczykowski was the leading Prep scorer in a well-balanced offense.

and Orem, which has been dubbed "Family City USA." In fact, *Time* and *Forbes* magazines rated the Provo-Orem area as one of the best places to live for spiritual well-being, due to a high population of members of The Church of Jesus Christ of the Latter-day Saints. Opponents Doss and S. R. Butler were defeated by Prep in 1984 and 1991 respectively. At the time the Reebok Classic was considered one of the most prestigious tournaments in the nation. It was Prep's second trip to Las Vegas, the first time being a dozen years before.

- The 13th annual McDonald's High School Basketball Classic returned to the Hammermill Center welcoming three top teams, including defending champion Paterson Catholic, featuring 6'10" All-American **Tim Thomas**; Baltimore St. Frances Academy with 6'5" **Mark Karcher**; and New York City's LaSalle Academy, presenting 6'6" **Ron Artest**. Paterson was the first team in the history of the Classic to be invited to defend its championship. With credit given to A.D. **Ron Sertz**, coach **Jim Salmon** was happy to accept: "We've been all over the country, from Florida to Las Vegas, in the top high school tournaments and the Classic ranks with the best! In terms of hospitality, it can't be beat!"

- Opening night of the McDonald's Classic saw Prep get swamped by St. Frances (30-4), despite a phenomenal

The 1996 Ramblers, enjoying their stay at the Excalibur in Las Vegas.

shooting performance by Rambler senior **Bob Vahey**, who at one point scored 11 in a 54 second span. Though the Ramblers held Panther superstar Karcher, a 1997 McDonald's All-American, to just 13 points, he dished out 10 assists and had a game-high 9 rebounds. St. Frances finished the season the #14 team in the *USA Today* Top 25 Poll. In the opener Paterson Catholic easily defeated LaSalle. The consolation match was a double-overtime thriller, with LaSalle (17-6) beating Prep, 44-40, behind Artest's 24 points. The next year LaSalle finished 27-1 and was the #2 rated team in the nation for most of the

Senior Bob Vahey had a great shooting touch. At one point, in the McDonald's Classic, he scored 11 points in a 54-second span, which must be some kind of record somewhere.

season. The title clash saw Paterson storm past St. Frances, 70-50, with Thomas scoring 29, despite a box-and-one defense employed by St. Frances. St. Frances was founded in 1828 as the Baltimore School for Colored Girls. It changed its name in the 1850's and became coeducational in the 1970's.

- The 56-point rout of hapless Strong Vincent (2-22) was Prep's largest winning margin since the Ramblers pounded Jamestown, 100-42, in 1970.

- The final standings in Metro League basketball were as follows:

	W	L
*Prep	10	1
McDowell	9	2
Central	5	5
Mercyhurst	3	7
East	4	6
Vincent	0	10

won championship playoff

- The intense Prep-McDowell (23-8) series reached its zenith in 1996. The Trojans of coach **Pete Flinn** and his top assistant **Jim Delsandro**, ranked #1 in the state pre-season by the *Harrisburg Patriot-News*, presented an outstanding lineup with spunky veterans **Jake Delsandro** and **Damon Finazzo** at the guards; 3-point artist **Aaron Garrity** at wing; **John Park** and **Shawn Blakeslee** underneath; and the big man, **Brent Witgen**, at center. They fired the first salvo against Prep with a convincing 15-point win. In the second engagement in the ongoing war, the Ramblers, behind sophomore smoothie **Julian Blanks** 15 points, broke McDowell's 12-game win streak to forge a Metro League regular season tie. In the battle for the Metro crown just four days later, before a capacity crowd at Gannon, Prep overcame a 7-point 4th quarter deficit to win its third straight title and seventh in 9 years. It was the tenth time in 11 tries that Prep won the City Series or Metro title via the playoff route. After Prep overwhelmed Warren (7-18) and McDowell beat Meadville in the District 10 semifinals, the stage was set for

meeting number four before a capacity crowd of 5,500 at the Erie Civic Center. There the Trojans halted Prep's seven-game win streak and three-year run as D-10 champ with a sensational second half performance, particularly by Delsandro.

Sophomore smoothie Julian Blanks rolls one in.

- Prep took care of business in PIAA inter-district play, impressively crushing WPIAL champ Upper St. Clair (23-6); District 9 titlist Bradford's greatest team in years (24-3); and Pittsburgh city champion Schenley (25-5). In the meantime, McDowell handily defeated New Castle, Franklin Regional and State College. All these victories set the stage for a record fifth meeting between the long-time rivals, both evenly matched with records of 23-7, for the AAAA Western Final. There had not been a game of this magnitude in Erie for 16 years, evoking thoughts of Prep's 1980 championship run when the Ramblers completed a four-game sweep over the Trojans

Hot-shooting junior R.J. Fiorelli was a super-sixth man.

in the Western Final. On game day the front page headline of the *Erie Morning News* read: "Super Ball V: The Western Finals." Right below the sub-headline stated: "Tonight's historic 5th game between McDowell and Prep will send both squads packing: One will head for Hershey, while the other will head home."

Mike McMahon, relentless on defense against Bradford.

Keith Nies operates against McDowell's Jake Delsandro in Western Final. Moments later Nies stole the ball in the game's closing moments–the greatest defensive play in Rambler basketball history.

Julian Blanks works against McDowell's Damon Finazzo in the 5th battle against McDowell.

- There was more on the line than just a trip to the state final for Prep and McDowell. It was more than just a basketball game— it seemed to be the one event that would settle the argument for all time as to which team was better in sports and simply a better school overall. It was decades of intense hatred between Prep and McDowell, boiling down to one basketball game. Prep students responded with unbounded enthusiasm and spirit. A rally on the morning of game day included dozens of alumni who were there to fire up the student body. The rally proceeded to the cafeteria, where several Prep alums stood on tables giving impassioned speeches. The old-timers were there to impress upon the student body that *this was more* than just a basketball game—it just might mean bragging rights for all time. Those who could not secure ducats were able to hang in all the crowded bars in Erie to watch the game on WJET-Channel 24 and *two* Erie radio stations (1330 AM and 1400 AM) carried the contest. One could walk on the level of enthusiasm shown by both schools.

- The fifth battle between Prep and McDowell, this time for the PIAA Western Championship, goes down as the single greatest high school sporting event in the history of Erie. A sellout crowd of over 6,000 face-painted, pumped-up fans crammed every nook and cranny of the Erie Civic Center for the climactic game which wasn't decided until the final seconds. Prep was up by a point, but McDowell had the ball for a last shot. The crowd was in a complete frenzy as Trojan star **Jake Delsandro**, ball in hand, tried to drive the lane. There **Keith Nies** stripped the ball, gained possession and was fouled in one of the greatest defensive plays in Rambler history. The Civic Center exploded with a barrage of Hershey kisses and the sonic noise of high-spirited students and the rest of the Prep faithful. Nies hit both gut-wrenching foul shots with 4 seconds left and Prep, after watching Delsandro miss a last-second 3-pointer, scored a 47-44 verdict for a third state title berth in four years! A riotous celebration by Rambler fans ensued. The classy McDowell coaches and players gave it their all, deserved to win as much and were gracious in defeat despite the heartache. The tight defensive struggle was immediately determined "a classic." The next day the front page of the *Erie Morning News* simply proclaimed "Ramblers Rule!" A headline on the front sports page read: "Nies Hands Trojans the Kiss of Death!"

- Prep dictated the pace and held the upper hand for much of the PIAA championship game before a sellout crowd of 9,000 against the #1 team in the state, Lower Merion (32-3). The

Three-point artist Keith Nies drains another.

The Ramblers meet alumnus Governor Tom Ridge '63 in Hershey on the day of the big game.

Aces featured the best high school player in America, future Los Angeles Laker **Kobe Bryant**. The Ramblers shot out to a 7-0 lead; led by six at the half; and still led by two with 3 minutes left. Prep fell behind after some brilliant play by Bryant, but had the ball with a little over one minute remaining and only down by two. The Ramblers couldn't find the range, however, and lost, 48-43, in a game they led throughout and could have won in the closing moments. A greatly designed defense frustrated NBA-bound Bryant and kept him to a season-low 17 points. Kobe had several smart assists and some powerful dunks, however, and plenty of help from his teammates as Lower Merion won its first state crown since 1943.

- In an interview some twenty years later, **Keith Nies** stated: "That championship game brings back a lot of great memories, but the one thing that wears at me to this day is that we lost a game that we had a chance to win. The cards just didn't fall into place. But it was amazing to compete against a Hall of Fame player like **Kobe Bryant,** and that's what I'll always remember most about my basketball career." Nies met up with Bryant in Cleveland during Bryant's farewell tour of 2016. When Kobe noticed Keith at a press conference, he stated: "I remember you! You guys trapped the hell out of me and forced me to pass the ball! Luckily my teammates made some great shots! We had to rally to win!" The two exchanged pleasantries later and embraced when Nies presented Bryant with a brand-new Prep t-shirt "for his trophy case!"

- Lower Merion High School is located on Philadelphia's Main Line. It has won seven PIAA basketball titles: in 1933, 1941, 1942, 1943, 1996, 2006 and 2013. Though Lower Merion's athletic teams are called the "Aces", its football team is known as the "Bulldogs." As for **Kobe Bryant**, he has won five NBA championships, is an 18-time NBA All-Star and was named NBA MVP in 2008.

- The 1995-96 Prep team was the first since the state champs of 1979-80 to score more than 2,000 points as a team and also the first since 1980-81 to give up less than 50 PPG.

First Team All-Metro star Brian Szewczykowski led the Ramblers in scoring.

- **Brian Szewczykowski** and **Keith Nies** were both named First Team on the 1995-96 All-Metro Basketball Team as announced by the *Erie Times-News*, while **John Trocki** and sophomore smoothie **Julian Blanks** were Second Team selections.

- The County upset the City, 99-94, in the 22nd annual City-County All-Star Classic, sponsored by the Northwest Jaycees. **Keith Nies** wowed the crowd at McDowell's Paul Goll Gymnasium with a game-high 24 points, including five 3-pointers. Also playing well were Prep all-stars **John Trocki** (6 points), **Doug Lecker** (8) and **Brian Szewczykowski** (6).

- Both **Brian Szewczykowski** and **John Trocki** went on to star in college, Szewczykowski at Clarion, and Trocki at Pitt-Titusville, then at Gannon. John met an untimely death in 2009, and since that time former teammates, including **Bob Vahey**, **Keith Nies** and **Justin Izbicki**, have organized the annual John Trocki Memorial Golf Scramble to benefit the Trocki children.

- **Keith Nies**, just the fifth four-year letterman in Rambler history, was also winner of the prestigious James "Moe" Gross Award as Prep's most valuable player. Nies went on to star at Mercyhurst University where he also lettered four years. He later became the successful 14-year head coach at Fairview High School (2001-15), where he compiled an overall record of 238-109, with 11 playoff appearances and a District 10 title in 2009.

1996 All-Opponent Team:

Jason Page, Farrell

Sam Clancy, Lakewood St. Ed's [Southern Cal]

Gino Bartolone, Lakewood St. Ed's [Kentucky Wesleyan]

Steve Logan, Lakewood St. Ed's [Cincinnati]

Steve LePore, Lakewood St. Ed's [Northwestern, Wake Forest]

Gabe Lisicky, Whitehall [East Tennessee St.]

Jerry Lloyd, Whitehall [Mount St. Mary's]

Mark Karcher, Baltimore St. Frances (*Baltimore Sun* Player of the Year) [Temple]

Ron Artest, NYC LaSalle [St. John's; NBA 6 teams]

Richard Bush, Central [Gannon]

Jake Delsandro, McDowell (4th team all-state) [Allegheny]

Brent Witgen, McDowell [Westminster]

Damon Finazzo, McDowell [Grove City]

Aaron Garrity, McDowell [Gannon]

Naron Jackson, Schenley (3rd team all-state) [Robert Morris]

Kobe Bryant, Lower Merion (1st team all-state; McDonald's All-American; 1st team *Parade Magazine* All-American & Player of the Year) [NBA Los Angeles Lakers]

Keith Nies, just the 5th four-year letter winner in the history of Prep basketball, was named team MVP.

Coach Arribi Proclaims '97 "Team" His Best!

Metro, D-10 Champs Suffer Devastating PIAA Loss to Schenley

Coach Marcel Arribi called his 1996-97 Ramblers his best "team" ever.

1996-97 (24-3)

Coach: Marcel Arribi
Assistants: Jim Marnella, Wes Alexander
Captains: R. J. Fiorelli, Graham Witherspoon

Date	PREP			Dec.	Loc.	High Scorer	Opponent
	COCA-COLA BASKETBALL CHALLENGE (GANNON UNIVERSITY)						
12/7	68	Penn Hills	54	W	H	Blanks (19)	UNREPORTED
	TORONTO MARTINGROVE INVITATIONAL (ETOBICOKE, ONT)						
12/12	74	Etobicoke (ONT) Martingrove	54	W	A	Blanks (20)	Faulkner (24)
12/13	58	Scarborough (ONT) Bethune	55	W	N	Blanks (23)	Reid (20)
12/13	62	Welland (ONT) Centennial	18	W	A	Fiorelli (15)	Bowen (8)
12/17	73	Strong Vincent	47	W	N	Fiorelli (22)	Barron (14)
	STATE FARM INSURANCE INVITATIONAL (PARKERSBURG, WV)						
12/20	57	Cincinnati (OH) Taft	42	W	N	Fiorelli (19)	Martin (12)
12/21	60	Parkersburg (WV)	43	W	A	Fiorelli (20)	UNREPORTED
	STEAKBALL CLASSIC (SANDUSKY, OH)						
12/27	58	Olmsted Falls (OH)	53	W	N	Fiorelli (18)	Schaefer (29)
12/28	57	Sandusky (OH)	53	W	A	Fiorelli (18)	UNREPORTED
1/3	62	Mercyhurst Prep	47	W	N	Fiorelli (19)	Coleman (16)
1/4	79	Central	70	W	N	Blanks (25)	Bush (17)
	McDONALD'S CLASSIC						
1/10	53	Lorain (OH) Admiral King	44	W	H	Fiorelli (14)	Taylor (19)
1/11	41	Lakewood (OH) St. Edward	52	L	H	Witherspoon (15)	Bartolone (14)
1/14	75	East	49	W	N	Fiorelli (17)	Wiley (20)
	BASS PRO TOURNAMENT OF CHAMPIONS (SPRINGFIELD, MO)						
1/16	60	St. Louis (MO) Riverview Gardens	54	W	N	Fiorelli & Blanks (14)	Robinson (23)
1/17	56	Bronx (NY) St. Raymond	50	W	N	Fiorelli & Blanks (13)	Brown (14)
1/18	47	St. Louis (MO) Christian Brothers	55	L	N	Fiorelli (14)	Hughes (34)
1/21	42	McDowell	35	W	N	Witherspoon (18)	Schodt (20)
1/23	80	Strong Vincent	49	W	N	Fiorelli (18)	Barron (19)
1/28	61	Mercyhurst Prep	42	W	N	Witherspoon (20)	Coleman (14)
1/31	85	Central	60	W	N	Fiorelli (21)	McLaurin (20)
2/7	62	East	48	W	N	Blanks (19)	Wiley (15)
2/14	54	McDowell	51	W	N	Fiorelli (21)	Caldwell (15)
	P.I.A.A. DISTRICT 10 PLAYOFFS						
2/22	83	Central	76(2OT)	W	N	Fiorelli & Blanks (22)	Bush (23)
2/28	74	Meadville	63	W	N	Blanks (29)	Smith (30)
	P.I.A.A. INTERDISTRICT PLAYOFFS						
3/8	76	Kiski Area	59	W	N	Fiorelli (21)	Long (15)
3/12	33	Pittsburgh Schenley	36	L	N	Fiorelli (16)	Jackson (21)
	1690 (62.6)		**1359 (50.3)**				

Pos.	Player	Ht.	Prior School	Class	G(GS)	FG(3)	FT	Total	PPG	Career
F-G	R. J. Fiorelli (#23)	6'3"	St. Luke's	Sr.	27(27)	160(55)	65-96	440	16.3	730
G	Julian Blanks (#21)	6'2"	St. John's	Jr.	26(26)	139(19)	73-97	370	14.2	611
C	Graham Witherspoon (#50)	6'4"	St. Luke's	Sr.	27(27)	130	86-138	346	12.8	542
G	Jim Gemler (#33)	5'11"	Bl. Sacrament	Jr.	27(20)	66(39)	29-39	200	7.4	238
F	Ben Straub (#42)	6'3"	Girard St. John's	Jr.	25(21)	44(7)	27-36	122	4.9	122
F	Adam Montie (#41)	6'2"	Millcreek	Soph.	27(7)	33(12)	20-24	98	3.6	98
F-G	Adam Straub (#22)	6'0"	Girard St. John's	Soph.	27(7)	19(8)	11-17	57	2.1	57
F	Brad Kons (#20)	6'5"	OLP	Sr.	17	9(1)	3-6	22	1.3	38
C	Brian Root (#40)	6'5"	Millcreek	Fr.	14	4	7-8	15	1.1	15
G	Steve Noonan (#14)	5'10"	Bl. Sacrament	Soph.	9	2(1)	2-6	7	0.8	7
G	Chris Dunham (#43)	5'11"	California	Sr.	16	4	4-6	12	0.8	21
C	Greg Dufala (#31)	6'3"	St. Peter's	Jr.	4	0	1-2	1	0.3	1

Prep's 1997 Metro League and District 10 Champs, L to R: Root, Kons, Fiorelli, Dufala, Witherspoon, B. Straub, Blanks, Montie, A. Straub, Dunham, Gemler.

HIGHLIGHTS:

- The 1996-97 season started with Cathedral Prep ranked the #2 AAAA team in Pennsylvania by the *Harrisburg Patriot-News*. By this time **Marcel Arribi's** Ramblers cemented their reputation as one of the state's elite programs, with state finals appearances in three of the previous four seasons, including the 1993 state championship. The 1994-95 team, which lost to Ringgold in the final eight, may have been Prep's and Arribi's best team of all. Arribi felt, though, this team was special, and with its chemistry—his best "team."

- Captains **R. J. Fiorelli** and **Graham Witherspoon** really blossomed as seniors, Fiorelli with uncanny outside shooting ability and Witherspoon doing the yeoman's work inside. Guard **Julian Blanks** became a star with his smooth all-around play and **Jim**

Three-sport star Jim Gemler was the first underclassman to win the "Ma" Kaiser Award as Prep's best athlete.

Gemler proved he could also be deadly from 3-point range. Both were only juniors, as was the fifth starter, workhorse **Ben Straub**.

- The 1996-97 Prep squad did not disappoint. Rather, the Ramblers finished with the second best winning percentage (.889) in 73 years of Prep basketball history, only behind 1980's state champs (33-1, .971). That lofty status lasts to this day, well over 90 years of Rambler basketball history. These Prepsters won three in-season tournaments, their fourth straight Metro League title, won back the District 10 crown and went on to the PIAA Western Quarterfinals.

- All Metro League games, the Coca-Cola Challenge, the McDonald's Classic and the District 10 semifinal were played at the Gannon University's Hammermill Center. Edinboro's McComb Fieldhouse hosted the D-10 title game and Prep's two PIAA inter-district games.

Fiorelli scores easily against Penn Hills in the Coca-Cola Challenge.

- Prep opened the season with championships in the Coca-Cola Challenge, the Martingrove and State Farm Invitationals, the Steakball Classic and opening night of the McDonald's Classic, springing out to a 12-0 won-lost record, tying the 1979-80 squad for the best start in Rambler history.

- Prep's Coca-Cola victim, Penn Hills (13-12), qualified for the WPIAL playoffs for the 18th straight year, but lost to Central Catholic in the first round, 64-60.

- Of Prep's new Canadian opponents: Martingrove Collegiate has a fine basketball reputation; Dr. Norman Bethune Collegiate Institute has over 1300 students, most of Chinese descent; and the 18 points scored by Welland Centennial was the lowest output by a Prep opponent since the Ramblers defeated Titusville St. Joe's, 71-16, in the 1953-54 season. The victory over Bethune was Coach Arribi's 200th as Rambler mentor.

- Of Prep's new Ohio opponents: Cincinnati Taft won state titles in 1962 and 2011; Olmsted Falls and Sandusky are west of Cleveland and were Division II schools at the time. Although Sandusky is known for its football tradition, they have had great basketball teams and players throughout the school's history as well. **Scott May**, the Blue Streaks' all-time leading scorer, went on to become the NCAA Player of the Year on **Bobby Knight's** undefeated 1976 Indiana Hoosier basketball team, an Olympic Games gold medalist, and the Chicago Bulls' first round pick in 1976.

- One of Prep's great wins was over Olmstead Falls (23-2) at the Steakball Classic. It was the only loss of the regular season for the Bulldogs, who won the Southwest Conference and district playoff titles. The 1996-97 squad is considered Olmstead Falls greatest team ever.

- Parkersburg High is the second-largest school in the state of West Virginia and has the largest campus in the state. Erstwhile MLB outfielder **Nick Swisher** (class of 1999) is one of its esteemed graduates. Parkersburg is known as "The School of Champions" and holds twice as many state titles in athletics as any other high school in West Virginia. PHS was rated by *Sports Illustrated* as the #9 sports high school of all time due to its long winning traditions. It has won WV state basketball titles in 1916, 1917, 1923, 1932, 1958, 1960 and 1970.

- Lakewood St. Ed's (24-2) won the 14th annual McDonald's High School Basketball Classic, with a win over Prep in the final, after the Ramblers defeated a good Lorain Admiral King team in the first round. Prep neutralized St. Ed's star **Sam Clancy** who scored only 9 points, but **Steve Logan** and **Gino Bartolone** combined for 27 to stymie the Orange & Black. The Eagles were *USA Today's* #9 team in the nation until upset by Zanesville, 58-54, in the Ohio Division I state semifinals. Admiral King, with **Javin Hunter's** 30 points, won the consolation match beating Detroit Country Day School, whose First Team *Parade Magazine* All-American **Shane Battier** was injured and did not play.

- Prep finished as runner-up in its third trip to the Bass Pro tourney in Missouri, after impressive, close wins over Riverview Gardens (20-8) and Bronx St. Raymond (12-14). Christian Brothers College High (28-4) handed the Ramblers its second of only two regular season losses in the final. The Cadets' 6'5" **Larry Hughes** dominated the tourney with 95 points, earning MVP honors and later a lengthy NBA career. Ramblers **R. J. Fiorelli** and **Julian Blanks** both made the prestigious all-tournament team, while **Jim Gemler** won the tourney's first Father John Savage Award for sportsmanship. Christian Brothers steamrolled to the Missouri Class 4A (large school) state title with a 51-35 victory over Truman. CBC is a large, all-boys school, founded in 1850, which operates in

Bass Pro Tournament of Champions runner-up, L to R: Dunham, Blanks, Gemler, Fiorelli, Witherspoon, Montie.

the competitive St. Louis Metro Catholic Conference with Chaminade College Prep, DeSmet Jesuit, St. John Vianney and St. Louis University High.

- The final standings in Metro League basketball were as follows:

	W	L
Prep	10	0
McDowell	7	3
East	6	4
Central	4	6
Vincent	3	7
Mercyhurst	0	10

- Prep dominated the local scene with another undefeated Metro season and by waltzing to another District 10 title. The Ramblers were nearly eliminated early from post-season competition by a stout Central High (13-12) team. Prep then overwhelmed Meadville (20-7) for the sixth straight time, despite Maplewood transfer **Nate Smith's** 30 points, this one in the D-10 final. **Julian Blanks** was right there with 29 points, a season-high for the Ramblers, including a perfect 10-for-10 from the free throw line in the last two minutes. Meadville beat Pittsburgh Central Catholic in PIAA first round action, then got beat by Uniontown in the Western Quarterfinals.

R.J. Fiorelli, a First Team All-Metro pick, was deadly from 3-point range.

- Prep easily defeated the Kiski Cavaliers (17-10) in PIAA first round action, but Pittsburgh Schenley (24-5) ruined the Ramblers' quest for a fourth trip to the PIAA Final in five years, rallying from an 8-point deficit in the final quarter to hand Prep the unexpected loss. **R. J. Fiorelli** lit up the score board with a trio of 3-pointers as Prep shot out to a 17-4 lead at the end of the first period. From there the Spartans chipped away at the lead and allowed the Orange & Black but five buckets the rest of the way. It was one of Prep's most heartbreaking defeats, ever, and a major disappointment for both the coach and the team as they had played in Hershey three of the previous four seasons. At the time, Prep was ranked #1 in the state according to the *Harrisburg Patriot-News*. "We only look at one thing, and that's the final goal in Hershey," said the highly successful coach **Marcel Arribi** to *Erie Morning News* reporter **Joe Mattis**, "it's hard to take as these kids worked so hard for six months and they won't get there." Arribi then stated, "This was my best 'team.'"

A big and tough center, Graham Witherspoon was First Team All-Metro and a four-year letter winner.

- **R. J. Fiorelli, Graham Witherspoon** and **Julian Blanks** were all named First Team on the 1996-97 All-Metro All-Star Team as announced by the *Erie Times-News*. It was the first time three Ramblers were named first team all-league since 1978, when **Dan Sculley, Jeff Szumigale** and **Danny Achille** were all named first team by the *Times*.

- Fiorelli was game-high with 18 points as the City defeated the County, 82-79, in the 23rd annual City-County All-Star Classic, sponsored by the Northwest Jaycees. Witherspoon also helped the City Slickers with 8 points.

Witherspoon collars a rebound, with Ben Straub close by.

- **Julian Blanks** was further honored by being named Fifth Team Pennsylvania Big School (AAAA and AAA) All-State Team by the *Associated Press*.

- **Graham Witherspoon** and **R. J. Fiorelli** were co-winners of the prestigious James "Moe" Gross Award as Prep's most valuable players, while junior **Jim Gemler**, also a star in football and baseball, became the first underclassman to win the "Ma" Kaiser Award as Prep's best athlete.

- Witherspoon played college basketball at Roberts Wesleyan, while Fiorelli went on to star for St. John Fisher College, where he still holds the all-time record for most points in a game with 40. He also ranks #16 on the Cardinals' all-time career points total chart with 1,050.

- **R. Ron Sertz** retired as Cathedral Prep athletic director at the end of the 1996-97 school year, to become an owner and general manager of the Erie Otters hockey team of the Ontario Hockey League. Sertz had many years and volumes of achievement at Prep, serving on the staff from 1971 to 1997 and being the major athletic official from 1982 to 1997. Sertz was the primary force behind Prep's movement into national caliber competition and his high-profile leadership brought state and national prominence through success in all the Ramblers' sports programs. He would continue his role as director of the McDonald's Classic through 25 years. Sertz was also the founder and original director of the Cathedral Prep Athletic Hall of Fame, to which he was inducted in 2003. Since 2010 Sertz has been the executive director of the Erie Sports Commission, an organization that hosts and supports major sporting events in the Erie area. He is also Chairman of Pennsylvania Sports, heading sports tourism initiatives for the state. In 2016 Sertz was honored as the "National Sports Tourism Executive of the Year," a prestigious award sponsored by the National Association of Sports Commissions.

1997 All-Opponent Team:

    Vernon "Jake" Schifino, Penn Hills [Akron, football; NFL Titans, Texans]

    Damian Reid, Bethune Collegiate [St. Joseph's]

    Tim Schaefer, Olmsted Falls (1st team all-state, OH)

    John Storey, Olmstead Falls (hm all-state, OH)

    Richard Bush, Central [Gannon]

    Doug Taylor, Admiral King (HM all-state, OH) [Tiffin]

    Sam Clancy, Lakewood St. Ed's [Southern Cal]

    Gino Bartolone, Lakewood St. Ed's [Kentucky Wesleyan]

    Steve Logan, Lakewood St. Ed's (1st team all-state, OH) [Cincinnati]

    Shannon Wiley, East

    Bryant Robinson, Riverview Gardens

    Ernest Brown, Bronx St. Raymond [Mesa CC, Indian Hills CC; NBA Miami Heat]

    Justin Tatum, Christian Brothers [St. Louis]

    Larry Hughes, Christian Brothers (1st team all-state, MO) [St. Louis; NBA six teams]

    Ryan Johnson, Christian Brothers [Memphis]

    Rob Schodt, McDowell [Edinboro]

    John Barron, Vincent

    Nate Smith, Meadville

    Scott Long, Kiski Area [Pitt, football]

    Naron Jackson, Schenley [Robert Morris]

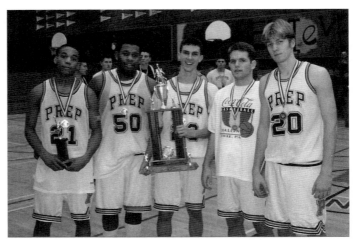

Toronto Challenge Champions, L to R: Blanks, Witherspoon, Fiorelli, Dunham, Kons.

Ramblers Regroup!

1997-98 (17-10)

Coach: Marcel Arribi
Assistants: Jim Marnella, Wes Alexander,
 Mark Behringer
Captains: Julian Blanks, Jim Gemler

*Hall-of-Fame and All-State honoree
Julian Blanks starred at LaSalle
and later played professionally in
Portugal and France.*

Date	PREP		Dec.	Loc.	High Scorer	Opponent
	INDIANA (PA) PIZZA HUT TIP-OFF TOURNAMENT					
11/28	58	Plum	49	W	N	Blanks (23)	Vargo (16)
11/29	46	Indiana	57	L	A	Blanks (21)	Woodall (15)
	COCA-COLA BASKETBALL CHALLENGE (GANNON UNIVERSITY)					
12/6	46	Hamilton (ONT) Cathedral	52	L	H	Gemler (18)	Julius (15)
	GONZAGA HS BASKETBALL TOURNAMENT (WASHINGTON, DC)					
12/12	31	Washington (DC) Gonzaga College	51	L	A	Gemler (21)	McCloskey (15)
12/13	42	Washington (DC) Woodrow Wilson	46	L	N	Montie (12)	Browner (11)
12/14	47	Ft. Wash. Germantown Academy	62	L	N	Gemler (15)	Burke (24)
12/19	82	Niagara Falls (ONT) A. N. Myer	38	W	A	Montie (17)	Medic & Jankovic (12)
12/20	75	St.Catharine's (ONT) Denis Morris	59	W	A	Blanks (26)	McKenna (19)
	BEACH BALL CLASSIC (MYRTLE BEACH, SC)					
12/28	58	San Diego (CA), University of, HS	61(OT)	L	N	Gemler (23)	UNREPORTED
12/29	40	West Charlotte (NC)	56	L	N	Blanks (10)	Parker (20)
12/30	42	Myrtle Beach (SC) Socastee	50	L	A	Blanks (16)	Hilton (17)
1/4	52	Mercyhurst Prep	38	W	N	Blanks (17)	Schlaufman (12)
1/6	43	Central	38	W	N	Blanks (22)	Coleman (12)
	McDONALD'S CLASSIC					
1/9	46	Hatboro-Horsham	69	L	H	Blanks (15)	M. Carroll (25)
1/10	51	Philadelphia Simon Gratz	42	W	H	Gemler (23)	Sims (16)
1/14	57	East	39	W	N	Blanks (24)	Jones (13)
1/16	50	Strong Vincent	41	W	N	Blanks (26)	Rivera (20)
1/21	37	McDowell	35	W	N	Blanks (19)	Slocum (16)
1/24	60	Lockport (NY)	57	W	H	Blanks (29)	Croff (22)
1/30	69	Mercyhurst Prep	39	W	N	Blanks (21)	Schlaufman (14)
1/31	63	Central	49	W	N	Blanks (20)	McLaurin (12)
2/6	51	East	42	W	N	Blanks (14)	Jones (11)
2/10	73	Strong Vincent	42	W	N	Blanks (16)	Whitted (16)
2/13	64	McDowell	54	W	N	Blanks (24)	Cocolin (15)
	P.I.A.A. DISTRICT 10 PLAYOFFS					
2/21	66	Central	47	W	N	Blanks (24)	Coleman (29)
2/26	65	Meadville	55	W	N	Blanks (29)	Power (17)
	P.I.A.A. INTERDISTRICT PLAYOFF					
3/7	49	Pittsburgh Central Catholic	64	L	N	Blanks (21)	Horan (19)
	1690 (62.6)		**1359 (50.3)**				

Pos.	Player	Ht.	Prior School	Class	G(GS)	FG(3)	FT	Total	PPG	Career
G	Julian Blanks (#21)	6'2"	St. John's	Sr.	27(27)	186(35)	84-116	491	18.2	1102
G	Jim Gemler (#33)	5'11"	Bl. Sacrament	Sr.	27(27)	110(65)	15-26	300	11.1	538
F-G	Adam Straub (#22)	6'1"	Girard St. John's	Jr.	27(27)	81(21)	32-48	215	8.0	272
G	Steve Noonan (#20)	5'10"	Bl. Sacrament	Jr.	21(18)	40(7)	46-64	133	6.3	140
F	Adam Montie (#51)	6'2"	Millcreek	Jr.	13(6)	27(13)	11-15	78	6.0	176
C	Chris Bates (#40)	6'4"	St. Peter's	Sr.	27(3)	32	13-22	77	2.9	77
F	Jim Fetzner (#30)	6'0"	Walnut Creek	Soph.	16	17(5)	6-7	45	2.8	45
G	Mike Malloy (#23)	6'0"	St. Luke's	Soph.	24	12(3)	10-13	37	1.5	37
F	Ben Straub (#42)	6'3"	Girard St. John's	Sr.	11(8)	13(2)	7-13	35	3.2	157
C	Brian Root (#50)	6'5"	Millcreek	Soph.	27(19)	14	4-11	32	1.2	47
G	John Weber (#41)	5'10"	St. Luke's	Jr.	12	8	0-0	16	1.3	16
G	Chris Kowalski (#12)	6'0"	Sacred Heart	Jr.	16	2	0-2	4	0.3	4

HIGHLIGHTS:

- The 1997-98 Cathedral Prep Ramblers began the season with a #9 state ranking, but had a sub-par 3-8 start through December. Head coach **Marcel Arribi**, however, stated "this may be the best 3-8 team in the country!" Then an upset victory by Prep over powerful Simon Gratz in the McDonald's Classic consolation game jump-started the Ramblers to a 12-game win streak; a fifth straight Metro League title with a second consecutive 10-0 record; and a second consecutive District 10 title, Coach Arribi's eighth overall and fifth in six years. It was another admirable coaching job, as the Prep squad was whittled to 10 players when star senior **Ben Straub** was unfortunately injured and ruled out for the season after the Beach Ball Classic; and junior **Adam Montie** quit the squad for personal and injury-related reasons after 13 games. The Ramblers mostly rode the back of veteran superstar **Julian Blanks**, who had a spectacular senior season.

- Erie attorney **Anthony "Tony" Himes** succeeded **Ron Sertz** as the new athletic director at Prep.

- The Coca-Cola Challenge, the McDonald's Classic, all Metro League games and the home game versus Lockport were held at Gannon University's Hammermill Center.

- Prep had not played its opening opponents in the Indiana Holiday tourney, Plum (6-18) and Indiana (20-8), since the state championship season of 1979-80. Blanks and **Adam Straub** were selected to the All-Tourney team at

The 1998 Prep Ramblers. Front, L to R: Gemler, Noonan, A. Straub, Fetzner, Weber; Back: Montie, B. Straub, Bates, Root, Blanks, Malloy.

Senior star Ben Straub missed over half the season after an injury at the Beach Ball Classic.

Indiana. The Lil' Indians made it to the second round of the PIAA tourney, where they lost in a shootout to Penn Hills, 90-83.

- Prep faced several new opponents in Washington, including all three which handed the Ramblers defeats at the Gonzaga tourney. Gonzaga College High (21-10) was founded by the Jesuits in 1821 and is the oldest boys' high school in the District of Columbia. A recent *Wall Street Journal* editorial referred to the institution as "the premier Catholic high school of Washington." Its roster of alumni includes politician **Pat Buchanan**; "drug czar" **William Bennett**; and the boy who was the victim of the alleged possession chronicled in the book and movie *The Exorcist*. Woodrow Wilson (15-13) is a large DC public school and Germantown Academy is the oldest nonsectarian day school in the United States and was founded in 1759. Germantown Academy is now in the Philadelphia suburb of Fort Washington, having moved from its original Germantown campus in 1965.

- Germantown Academy (23-9), under esteemed coach Jim Fenerty, won its fourth consecutive Philadelphia Inter-

Academic League championship and its sixth in seven years. Other schools in the Inter-Ac include Episcopal Academy, The Haverford School, Malvern Prep (formerly Villanova Prep), Chestnut Hill Academy and William Penn Charter. The Germantown Academy Patriots compete annually in the finest of basketball showcases, and in 1998 GA was crowned champion of the Laker Classic hosted by the Boys Latin School of Towson (MD).

- Prep's five straight early-season losses made for the longest Rambler losing streak since 1972-73.

- Other new Rambler opponents included Canada's Denis Morris Catholic High School, the Lockport Lions and all three the Ramblers faced at the Beach Ball Classic in Myrtle Beach (SC). The University of San Diego High School (26-4) was a Catholic, co-educational, college preparatory school located in San Diego (CA). In 2005, the school was closed and reopened in Del Mar (CA) as Cathedral Catholic High School. West Charlotte is well known for its athletic programs but nearly faced closing because of poor test scores; and its star player, 6'8" **Jason Parker**, wore a size 19 shoe! Socastee (23-10), a large public school, was the hometown favorite of the tourney. An interesting stat at the Beach Ball Classic: Prep shot only six free throws the entire tourney, all three games combined. West coast power San Diego outshot the Ramblers in FT's 41-4; West Charlotte 22-1; and Socastee 21-1! Socastee made it to the South Carolina AAAA state final, where it lost to South Aiken, 45-44, on a last second shot.

- All-American **Matt Carroll** scored 25 on the opening night of the 15th annual McDonald's Classic, leading Hatboro-Horsham (27-5) over Prep, but the Ramblers came back strong in the consolation game to upset Simon Gratz (21-7). The "Hatters," who made it to the PIAA Eastern Semifinals before losing to eventual state champ Harrisburg, are from the strong Suburban One League outside Philadelphia and its district covers Horsham Township and Hatboro Borough. New York City Rice (24-4), eventual New York Federation state champ however, became only the third team in Classic history to win more than one title by thoroughly dominating H-H, 80-61. Senior **Jim Gemler** scored 23 in the great win over Simon Gratz, including five 3-pointers. Gratz lost to Franklin Learning Center, 43-38, in the semifinals of the Philadelphia Public League post-season tourney.

- Prep ran off 21 unanswered points against Mercyhurst (12-16), after spotting the Lakers a 2-0 lead.

- Prep's biggest win was the 3-point margin over Lockport (22-4), champions of the Niagara-Frontier League, which at the time included Kenmore West, Niagara Falls, North Tonawanda, LaSalle and Lockport in the Niagara Division; and Niagara-Wheatfield, Lew-Port, Kenmore East, Grand Island and Nichols in the Frontier Division. Lockport made it all the way to New York State's Class A (large school) semifinals, where it lost to Hempstead, 69-65.

- Other big Prep wins included the pair over rival McDowell (13-12). In the first McDowell contest, the Ramblers held a 37-35 lead, but the Trojans rebounded a missed free throw with just 15 seconds remaining. With the crowd in a complete frenzy, the Trojans moved the ball up court hoping for one last shot to either tie or win the game. **Steve Noonan** then made the game's big play, stepping into the breach and swiping the ball with just four seconds remaining to preserve the Rambler victory.

- The final standings in the Metro League, were as follows:

	W	L
Prep	10	0
McDowell	7	3
East	6	4
Central	3	7
Mercyhurst	3	7
Vincent	1	9

- Prep played a strong second half to defeat Central (10-14) in the D-10 semifinals, then in the final doused Meadville (21-6) for the seventh consecutive time in D-10 competition behind the brilliant play of **Julian Blanks**, who scored 29 points, collected 6 rebounds, dished out 5 assists and had 3 steals. Playing against the Bulldogs seemed to bring out the best in Blanks, who also had 29 points against them in the 1997 D-10 title clash.

- Prep's 12-game win streak and season came to a screeching halt against Pittsburgh Central Catholic (24-5) in PIAA first round action. The Ramblers shot poorly and displayed a lackluster performance, despite having home-court advantage with the contest being held at Gannon.

- **Julian Blanks** and **Jim Gemler** were both named First Team on the 1997-98 Metro All-Star Basketball Team as announced by the *Erie Times-News*, while junior **Adam Straub** was a Second Team choice. Blanks was the only unanimous selection to the team.

- Blanks, who finished as Prep's third all-time leading scorer with 1,102 points (now fourth), behind only **Jed Ryan** and **Tim Gore**, was further honored by being named Second Team Pennsylvania Big School (AAAA and AAA) All-State Team by the *Associated Press*.

- **Julian Blanks** was also winner of the prestigious James "Moe" Gross Award as Prep's most valuable player. He received a full scholarship and went on to star at LaSalle University where he was in the starting lineup all four years. Blanks was team captain his senior year and is among the Explorers' all-time leaders in assists and steals. He later played professional ball with teams in Portugal and France. Blanks, a cancer survivor, was inducted into the Metro Erie Sports Hall of Fame in 2011 and the Cathedral Prep Athletic Hall of Fame in 2015.

- **Jim Gemler**, also a star quarterback and baseball player for Prep, became the first double-winner of the "Ma" Kaiser Award, signifying him as Prep's finest athlete. The long-range bomber's 65 3-pointers rank him second on the all-time single season chart, behind only **Jim Hamilton**, who nailed 86 in 1990-91. Gemler went on to play four years of

Three-point bomber Jim Gemler was First Team All-Metro and the first double-winner of the "Ma" Kaiser Award as Prep's best athlete. This star quarterback went on to a fine collegiate baseball career.

Division I baseball, first at UNC-Asheville, then three years at Akron where he was named Academic All-MAC in 2000. A long ball hitter, Gemler finished with a .288 collegiate career batting average with 19 home runs.

• Gemler and Blanks represented Prep as the City All-Stars crushed the County, 107-86, in the 24th annual City-County All-Star Classic, sponsored by the Northwest Jaycees. Blanks scored 16 for the City.

1998 All-Opponent Team:

Jerry Vargo, Plum

Dave "Gator" Woodall, Indiana

Kevin Rado, Indiana

Kyle Julius, Hamilton Cathedral [Guelph; Team Canada]

Mihai Raducano, Hamilton Cathedral [Coastal Carolina]

Tom McCloskey, Gonzaga (hm all-DC)

Rahsaan Johnson, Gonzaga [Monmouth]

Gary Wade, Wilson

Brian Burke, Germantown Academy (2nd team all-state) [Lafayette]

Chris Krug, Germantown Academy (1st team all-state) [Princeton]

Kevin McKenna, Denis Morris

Jason Parker, West Charlotte (NC Mr. Basketball) [Kentucky]

Derrick Hilton, Socastee

Matt Carroll, Hatboro-Horsham (1st team all-state, AP Player of the Year) [Notre Dame; NBA Trail Blazers, Spurs, Bobcats, Mavericks]

Pat Carroll, Hatboro-Horsham [St. Joseph's]

Bryan Martin, Hatboro-Horsham [St. Francis (PA)]

Rasheem Sims, Simon Gratz [Coppin St.]

Sharod Carroll, Simon Gratz [Cheyney St.]

Aaron Slocum, McDowell [Geneva, football]

Charles Croff, Lockport (all-Western NY)

Cory Coleman, Central [Gannon]

Phil Power, Meadville

Casey Miller, Meadville [Allegheny]

Jim Horan, Pittsburgh Central Catholic [Bucknell, football]

Adam Montie surveys the action against East.

Arribi Era Ends Abruptly!
Rival Trojans Advance to State Final!

1998-99 (13-14)

Coach: Marcel Arribi
Assistants: Jim Marnella, Wes Alexander,
          Mark Behringer
Captain: Adam Straub

*First Team All-Metro selectee Adam Straub was the
lone senior on the young and troubled Prep Team.*

Date	PREP			Dec.	Loc.	High Scorer	Opponent
	FARRELL TIP-OFF TOURNAMENT						
12/4	47	Farrell	66	L	A	Straub (17)	Flint (17)
12/5	67	Beaver Falls	29	W	N	Straub (19)	Little (9)
	COCA-COLA CHALLENGE (GANNON UNIVERSITY)						
12/12	34	Cleveland (OH) Benedictine	61	L	H	Hairston (16)	Matthews (12)
	SCENIC CITY SHOOTOUT (CHATTANOOGA, TN)						
12/18	54	Chattanooga (TN) Tyner Academy	41	W	N	Fetzner (15)	Long (14)
12/19	50	Cleveland (TN) Bradley Central	66	L	N	Fetzner (16)	Carpenter (23)
12/21	25	Chattanooga (TN) Brainerd	37	L	A	Fetzner (9)	Davis (11)
	KENTUCKY HOLIDAY CLASSIC (LEXINGTON, KY)						
12/27	33	Baton Rouge (LA) Southern Univ. Lab	66	L	N	Fetzner (9)	Tarver (23)
12/28	37	Flemingsburg (KY) Fleming County High	43	L	N	Chase (12)	Graham (14)
12/29	73	Decatur (GA) Cathedral Academy	52	W	N	Malloy (19)	Carruth (18)
1/8	73	Strong Vincent	46	W	N	Fetzner (16)	Testrake (11)
1/12	41	Mercyhurst Prep	35	W	N	Dolak (13)	Wilcox (13)
	McDONALD'S CLASSIC						
1/15	47	Washington (DC) Archbishop Carroll	54	L	H	Straub (16)	Hawkins (20)
1/16	45	Los Angeles (CA) Westchester	65	L	H	Hairston (11)	Wright (17)
1/19	54	Central	46	W	N	Straub (25)	Mitchell (15)
1/22	54	East	47	W	N	Fetzner (20)	Jamison (15)
1/26	52	McDowell	53(OT)	L	N	Straub (16)	Shouse (17)
	TORONTO (ONT) CHALLENGE						
1/29	70	Scarborough (ONT) Mother Teresa	50	W	N	Hairston (18)	Breto (12)
1/30	29	North York (ONT) Westview Centennial	30	L	N	Dolak (14)	Johnson (13)
1/31	59	Toronto (ONT) St. Michael's College	53	W	N	Fetzner (22)	Yonker (10)
2/2	60	Strong Vincent	35	W	N	Straub (21)	Rivera (17)
2/5	49	Mercyhurst Prep	47	W	N	Straub (15)	Sammons (15)
2/9	54	Central	42	W	N	Straub (24)	Mitchell (15)
2/16	48	McDowell	68	L	N	Fetzner (11)	Komorek (23)
2/19	51	East	54	L	N	Fetzner (18)	Cooley (20)
	P.I.A.A. DISTRICT 10 PLAYOFFS						
2/27	67	Warren	37	W	N	Chase (17)	Hoden (18)
3/4	37	McDowell	55	L	N	Hairston (12)	Delsandro (16)
	P.I.A.A. INTERDISTRICT PLAYOFF						
3/13	41	Penn Hills	52	L	N	Walker (13)	Schifino (23)
1	351 (52.0)		1330 (51.2)				

Pos.	Player	Ht.	Prior School	Class	G(GS)	FG(3)	FT	Total	PPG	Career
F	Jim Fetzner (#30)	6'0"	Walnut Creek	Jr.	27(27)	92(40)	67-83	291	10.8	336
F-G	Adam Straub (#22)	6'0"	Girard St. John's	Sr.	27(27)	105(6)	70-116	286	10.5	558
F	David Hairston (#31)	6'3"	Erie Day School	Jr.	25(20)	79(5)	33-56	196	7.8	196
C	Jason Dolak (#41)	6'3"	St. Luke's	Jr.	25(20)	58(1)	31-46	148	5.9	148
G	Mike Malloy (#23)	6'0"	St. Luke's	Jr.	27(23)	44(13)	32-44	133	4.9	170
G	Mark Chase (#10)	6'1"	Luther Memorial	Fr.	26(12)	47(15)	23-32	132	5.1	132
C	Dale Williams (#50)	6'7"	OLP	Soph.	18	21	10-18	52	2.9	52
G	Zach Meeder (#14)	6'0"	Garwood	Soph.	22(2)	10(2)	13-20	35	1.6	35
G	Jawan Walker (#20)	5'10"	Sacred Heart	Fr.	7	5(1)	15-16	27	3.9	27
F-C	Aaron DeCoursey (#33)	6'3"	Holy Rosary	Soph.	16(4)	9(2)	7-10	27	1.7	27
G	Ed Hinkel (#21)	6'0"	OLC	Soph.	5	6(1)	8-13	21	4.2	21
F-C	Noah Pelkowski (#40)	6'3"	Villa Maria	Soph.	7	2	0-0	4	0.6	4
C	Jeff Daisley (#42)	6'10"	Girard	Soph.	5	0	0-0	0	0.0	0

McDowell's 1999 State Finalists. Front, L to R: Delsandro, Spronatti, Finazzo, Vacanti, Shouse, Komorek, Curtis, Bohrer; Back: St. George, Coach Flinn, Panighetti, Juhlin, Miller, Grieshober, Caldwell, Schodt, Werntz, Amann, Coach Delsandro, Funaro.

HIGHLIGHTS:

- Cathedral Prep coach **Marcel Arribi's** 12th and final season at the helm was his only losing campaign. The 1998-99 Ramblers were considered extremely young with but one senior, **Adam Straub**, on the 13-man roster which included six sophomores and two freshmen.

- Several Prep gridiron stars, including **Jason Dolak, Dale Williams, Ed Hinkel** and **Jawan Walker**, were late in joining the Rambler cage team because of Prep's exciting post-season football playoff run which lasted into December. Further complicating matters were the absences of 1997-98 starters **Brian Root** and **Steve Noonan**. Root decided to concentrate on baseball and Noonan, also a star running back for the Ramblers, was nursing football-related bruises then began training for baseball as well. Noonan was given the 1999 "Ma" Kaiser Award, signifying him as Prep's best all-around athlete.

- **Mark Chase**, star of the 1998 St. Luke's grade school team that finished 32-2 and made it to the state final, was the first freshman to dot the starting lineup for Prep since **Jed Ryan** in 1991-92. Chase and fellow classmate **Jawan Walker** were just the second and third freshmen to play varsity ball at Prep since 1946!

- At the season-opening Tip-Off Tourney at Farrell (26-5), the Steelers presented another good team that made it to the PIAA AA Quarterfinals before losing to Quaker Valley. Prep's win over Beaver Falls (4-17) was the first time the two competed since their memorable battles in the early 1980's. That game

was played the same night of Prep's thrilling Western Final football contest against New Castle before some 10,000 fans at the Erie Stadium.

- Prep's loss to two-time Ohio defending state champ Benedictine (20-7) in the Coca-Cola Challenge was the first time the two competed since 1974. The Bengals missed an opportunity for a third straight title when they lost to Philo in a semifinal, 48-46.

- Prep lost two of three in its second entry in the Scenic City Shootout, the victory an impressive one over Tyner High (26-6), which made it to the quarterfinal round of the Tennessee state tourney. **Jimmy Fetzner** proved to be Prep's most effective weapon at the Shootout. Of Prep's new Chattanooga opponents: Tyner is now known as Tyner Academy of Math, Science and Technology; Bradley Central is known mostly for its wrestling program, with 22 Tennessee state championships; and the Ramblers' 25 points against Brainerd was their lowest point total since scoring 25 against the Warriors of East High in 1950—nearly half-century before!

- Prep did not fare well in the Kentucky Holiday Classic, defeating only Decatur Cathedral Academy, a very small, Christian-affiliated school. Of Prep's other Lexington opponents: Fleming County High (24-9) is a large, suburban school that made it to Kentucky's Sweet Sixteen in 1998 and 1999; and Southern University Laboratory High School (35-3), or "Southern Lab," provides a training ground for teacher preparation programs and further has the most Louisiana state championships (15), winning 11 of 13 titles between

1993 and 2005. Southern won the 1999 crown with a 45-39 overtime win in the final over Dunham. The Jaguars won the 1998 title with a final's win over Dunham, though Dunham was declared the champion after Southern Lab was ruled to have an ineligible player.

- Elizabeth (NJ) St. Patrick's overcame its disappointing 1994 performance and won the 16th annual McDonald's Classic crown with an opening night 55-47 win over Los Angeles Westchester and a 57-45 victory over Washington Archbishop Carroll in the final. **Jerome Holman** and **Sam Dalembert** were the Celtic standouts, while Prep lost to both Carroll and Westchester (19-10). Both were new opponents for the Orange & Black.

- In 1989, the Archdiocese of Washington merged several high schools—Archbishop Carroll, All Saints, Mackin, the Academy of Notre Dame, and Holy Spirit—into one school on the Archbishop Carroll site, and, at that point, the school became co-educational. Today, Carroll enrolls only about 400 students, and it remains as the only high school owned and operated by the Archdiocese of Washington. Once the standard-bearer for DC athletics, Carroll now struggles amid declining enrollment, dwindling funds and facilities that are inferior to its DC Catholic counterparts. L. A. Westchester, with nearly 3,000 students, has since been reconfigured as Westchester Enriched Sciences Magnets (WESM).

- Prep won two of three in its second attempt in the Toronto Challenge. Of the Ramblers' new Canadian opponents: Mother Teresa is now known as "Blessed Mother Teresa Catholic Secondary School," and its nickname is the "Teresa Titans"; Centennial is added to the Westview school name is for the reason that the school was built 100 years after Canada had claimed its independence from England; and St. Michael's College School is a private, all-boys Roman Catholic school, administered by the Basilian Fathers. St. Mike's is the largest school of its kind in Canada, with an enrollment of nearly 1,000 students. It is more renowned for its football and hockey programs (the NHL **Mahovlich brothers**, **Gerry Cheevers** and several others are grads), rather than basketball. St. Michael's nickname is the "Kerry Blues" and its mascot is "Babbalou," which, in urban dictionary lingo, is considered "a really cool dude with the chicks."

- East High's (16-11) stunning victory over Prep on February 19 was its first since 1985. The Ramblers defeated the Warriors 27 consecutive times before that loss. Coach Arribi's all-time record versus East: 23-1.

- Prep's two wins over Strong Vincent (6-16) ran the Ramblers' winning streak over the Colonels to 11, without any of the contests even being competitive. Coach Arribi's all-time record versus Vincent: 23-2.

- With Prep's two wins over Mercyhurst (16-12), the Ramblers ran their all-time record over the Lakers to an amazing 30-0, including 24-0 under Coach Arribi!

- Against Central High (9-15), Coach Arribi was 16-0, including the triumph on February 9, which was Arribi's 250th victory at the Rambler helm. **Adam Straub** scored a Rambler season-high 25 in that one.

- The Coca-Cola Challenge, the McDonald's Classic, and the Metro League games were held at Gannon University's Hammermill Center. The District 10 semifinal against Central was held at the Mercyhurst Athletic Center, while Edinboro's McComb Fieldhouse hosted the D-10 final.

- The final standings of the Erie Metro League:

	Won	Lost
McDowell	10	0
Prep	7	3
East	6	4
Mercyhurst	4	6
Central	3	7
Vincent	0	10

- McDowell's (26-5) three wins over Prep, all before sellout crowds, was the first time the Trojans swept a season's series between the two since 1991-92. In the process the Ramblers' 29-game Metro League winning skein was snapped. Trojan stars included **Justin Shouse**, **J.J. Delsandro**, **Dave Komorek** and **Mike Caldwell**. After winning the District 10 title, the Trojans mowed down Greensburg Salem, Pittsburgh Brashear and Hollidaysburg in PIAA action. McDowell, after a stunning 52-48 victory over nationally ranked New Castle in the Western Final, met its match in the PIAA championship game in Hershey. Williamsport and its star **Chevon "Chevy" Troutman** ended the Trojans' dream of a state championship with a 64-40 triumph. Coach Arribi's all-time record versus arch-rival McDowell: 24-11.

- Prep could not contain Penn Hills' (21-7) **Drew Schifino**, the WPIAL's leading scorer, and was ousted in the first round of the inter-district playoffs at Robert Morris University. This defeat sealed the Ramblers' first losing season since 1984-85. Penn Hills then lost to New Castle by 15 in the next round.

- **Adam Straub** was named First Team 1998-99 Metro All-Star as announced by the *Erie Times-News*, while junior **Jim Fetzner** was a Second Team selection. Straub then scored 13 points in a losing cause in the silver anniversary of the City-County All-Star Classic, won by the County, 85-66.

- **Adam Straub**, the only senior on the squad, was also winner of the prestigious James "Moe" Gross Award as Prep's most valuable player. He then went on to star at Allegheny College where he lettered four years.

- **Marcel Arribi** resigned after the 1998-99 campaign following complaints by some disgruntled parents of four players over playing time and what they considered harsh treatment to their sons by the coach. Under Coach Arribi, Cathedral Prep compiled a 251-87 (.743) record in twelve seasons, ranking him second in all-time wins, only behind **Bill Flaherty** (1971-84; 260-95, .732). That remarkable success was charted against one of the nation's toughest schedules. Included in Arribi's list of sterling accomplishments were 9 Metro League championships with an amazing league record of 122-11; eight District 10 titles with an overall 20-4 chart in D-10 play; three McDonald's Classic crowns from six appearances in the final game; a PIAA state championship in 1993 and appearances in the state title game in 1994 and 1996. A 24-3 record in 1996-97 led to another ranking as Pennsylvania's #1 team entering the state playoffs, where only a close upset loss to Pittsburgh Schenley prevented yet another assault on the state crown. Arribi's best team may have been his 1994-95 crew (25-4), which suffered what the coach called his "most difficult loss," to eventual state champ Ringgold after a kid named **"Czar" Walsh** lofted through a 40-foot prayer to send the Western Semifinal into overtime.

- An impressive roster of Prep players trained by Coach Arribi received Division I scholarships, including **Jim Hamilton** (Navy), **Booker Coleman** (Wisconsin), **Jed Ryan** (Penn) and **Julian Blanks** (LaSalle). Locally, **Jim Toohey**, **Todd Stablein**,

Cliff Dennett and **John Trocki** all made their mark at Division II Gannon; **Todd Filipkowski** and **Keith Nies** did so at Division II Mercyhurst; and **Brian Szewczykowski** played at Division II Clarion. Division III stars who played under Coach Arribi include **R. J. Fiorelli** (St. John Fisher), **Graham Witherspoon** (Roberts Wesleyan), **Adam Straub** (Allegheny) and **Jim Fetzner** (Grove City), while **Olivier Allinei** returned to France and became a top guard in European pro basketball.

• Several Arribi protégés have become successful high school basketball coaches, including **John Donnelly** (Villa Maria girls); **Craig Fomich** (assistant at Central); **Justin Izbicki** (assistant at Prep and McDowell); **Jason Dolak** (Harborcreek) and **Keith Nies** (Fairview); while **Mike Wernicki**, who played at Pitt, has coached in the college ranks at Mercyhurst, Canisius and currently at Youngstown State.

1999 All-Opponent Team:

Urbie Flint, Farrell (3rd team all-state)

Chris Leanza, Benedictine (1st team all-state, OH; OH Player of the Year) [Yale]

Michael Woods, Benedictine (3rd team all-state, OH)

Gary Long, Tyner

Jack Carpenter, Bradley Central

Josh Hare, Bradley Central (TN Mr. Basketball, 2000) [Virginia]

Marty Davis, Brainerd

Victor Tarver, Southern Lab [Southern University]

Josh Graham, Fleming County (3rd team all-state, KY) [VCU, Morehead State]

Rashaad Carruth, Cathedral Academy (McDonald's All-American, 2001) [Kentucky, Southern Mississippi]

David Hawkins, Archbishop Carroll (2nd team All-DC Catholic) [Temple]

Lou Wright, Westchester [SW Tennessee JC, Tennessee]

Chris Osborne, Westchester [Arizona State]

Justin Shouse, McDowell (3rd team all-state) [Mercyhurst]

Brendan Johnson, Westview Centennial

Joe Rivera, Vincent [Gannon]

Dave Komorek, McDowell [Mercyhurst, golf]

Pierre Cooley, East

J. J. Delsandro, McDowell [Mercyhurst]

Drew Schifino, Penn Hills (3rd team all-state) [West Virginia, California (PA)]

Marcel Arribi retired after a dozen years as the most highly accomplished coach in the history of Cathedral Prep and Erie Area basketball.

Jim Marnella retired after a long and distinguished athletic career. He can now be heard as the color commentator on Prep football and basketball radio broadcasts.

The 2000's

The victorious Cathedral Prep Ramblers hoist the 2009 District 10 championship trophy after the huge upset win over arch-rival McDowell.

Bob Ronai Brings College Experience!
Rival McDowell Is the Local Power!

1999-2000 (12-12)

Coach: Robert "Bob" Ronai
Assistant Coach: Bob Achille
Captains: Jim Fetzner, Jason Dolak, David Hairston,
      Mike Malloy
Manager: Nate Cox

Bob Ronai brought a wealth of collegiate coaching experience to Cathedral Prep.

Date	PREP		Dec.	Loc.	High Scorer	Opponent
	GREAT CHEVY SHOOTOUT (ALTOONA)					
12/3	73	Altoona Bishop Guilfoyle	53	W	N	Hairston (15)	Henneman (13)
12/4	58	Butler	50	W	N	Hairston (13)	Gallagher (21)
	COCA-COLA CHALLENGE					
12/12	75	Buffalo (NY) Canisius	59	W	H	Ronai & Malloy (15)	Vera (25)
	REEBOK HOLIDAY PREP SHOOTOUT (LAS VEGAS, NV)					
12/18	58	Spring Valley (NV) Durango	76	L	N	Chase (15)	Johnson (15)
12/20	67	Los Angeles (CA) Westchester	81	L	N	Chase (17)	Cook (21)
12/21	55	Mesa (AZ) Dobson	67	L	N	DeCoursey (13)	Legge (18)
	FESTIVAL OF LIGHTS HOLIDAY CLASSIC (WHEELING, WV)					
12/27	65	Toledo (OH) Scott	72	L	N	Fetzner (20)	Springs (23)
12/28	52	Detroit (MI) Country Day School	67	L	N	Fetzner (15)	Aikens & Brown (12)
12/29	80	Farmington (WV) North Marion	71	W	N	Ronai (24)	Exilus (30)
1/4	83	Strong Vincent	69	W	N	Chase (18)	Rivera (24)
1/7	59	Central	45	W	N	Malloy (14)	Carson (12)
1/11	51	Mercyhurst Prep	47	W	N	Chase (14)	Wilcox (15)
	McDONALD'S CLASSIC					
1/14	44	New York City (NY) La Salle Academy	59	L	H	Dolak (12)	Cooke (23)
1/15	30	Simon Gratz	59	L	H	Chase (9)	McKie (15)
1/21	54	East	65	L	N	DeCoursey (16)	Matt Jones (29)
1/25	34	McDowell	42	L	N	Hairston (12)	Shouse (17)
1/28	78	Strong Vincent	48	W	N	Fetzner (17)	Dragoone (11)
1/29	74	North Hills	62	W	H	Fetzner (19)	Branvold (13)
2/1	60	Central	71	L	N	Chase (21)	Mitchell (29)
2/4	54	Mercyhurst Prep	48	W	N	Malloy (11)	Dill (25)
2/9	85	Warren	57	W	H	Hairston (17)	Curran (15)
2/15	44	McDowell	54	L	N	Hairston (14)	Shouse (16)
2/18	75	East	67	W	N	Fetzner (20)	Mark Jones (16)
	METRO LEAGUE SECOND PLACE PLAYOFF					
2/22	56	Central	58	L	N	Fetzner (25)	Mitchell (26)
	1464 (61.0)		**1447 (60.3)**				

Pos.	Player	Ht.	Prior School	Class	G(GS)	FG(3)	FT	Total	PPG	Career
F	David Hairston (#31)	6'3"	Erie Day School	Sr.	23(23)	97(15)	31	240	10.4	436
G	Jim Fetzner (#30)	6'3"	Walnut Creek	Sr.	24(24)	76(42)	45	239	10.0	575
F-C	Aaron DeCoursey (#33)	6'3"	Holy Rosary	Jr.	24(9)	75(6)	63	219	9.1	246
G-F	Mark Chase (#5)	6'3"	Luther Memorial	Soph.	24(24)	60(20)	55	195	8.1	327
G	Jared Ronai (#10)	5'10"	Bishop Walsh	Soph.	24(24)	43(17)	85	188	7.9	188
G	Mike Malloy (#23)	6'3"	St. Luke's	Sr.	24(16)	52(21)	21	146	6.1	316
C	Jason Dolak (#24)	6'3"	St. Luke's	Sr.	17	28	17	73	4.3	221
G	Joe Mifsud (#12)	5'7"	Bl. Sacrament	Sr.	24	14(10)	7	45	1.9	45
G	Andy Kubinski (#52)	6'1"	OLC	Soph.	15	15(4)	2	36	2.4	36
G	Ed Hinkel (#11)	6'1"	OLC	Jr.	14	13(5)	3	34	2.4	55
C	Steve Kubinski (#20)	6'5"	OLC	Sr.	14	4	19	27	1.9	27
G	John Yaple (#15)	6'0"	St. Boniface	Soph.	8	4(1)	0	9	1.1	9
C	Dale Williams (#50)	6'7"	OLP	Jr.	4	3(1)	1	8	2.0	60
G	Kevin Bogacki (#4)	6'2"	OLC	Sr.	12	1	0	2	0.2	2
F-C	Noah Pelkowski (#40)	6'5"	Villa Maria	Jr.	4	1	0	2	0.5	6
C	Jeff Daisley (#42)	6'10"	Girard	Jr.	3	0	0	0	0.0	0
G	Julio Achille	6'0"	Bl. Sacrament	Soph.	1	0	0	0	0.0	0

HIGHLIGHTS:

- Rebuilding after Cathedral Prep's first losing season in 15 years was the focus for the Ramblers' new head basketball coach, **Robert "Bob" Ronai**. Ronai joined the Prep staff in July, 1999, returning to high school teaching and coaching after 18 years of heading up college programs. A native of Ramsey (NJ), Ronai was a multi-sport athlete at Don Bosco Prep and St. Francis University in Fort Wayne (IN). He received a master's degree from Ball State while coaching high school basketball in the Fort Wayne area. He had coaching stints at Woodstock (VA) Massanutten Academy and five years at Mars Hill College (60-87 record) before becoming head coach at Urbana University, compiling an overall record of 210-140 from 1986 through 1997. Included were three 26-win seasons, two NAIA District 22 titles and "Coach of the Year" honors. The next two years he compiled an aggregate 23-28 mark at Frostburg State, before coming to Prep. Coach Ronai was expected to do well with the Ramblers, especially with senior veterans **Jimmy Fetzner, David Hairston, Mike Malloy** and **Jason Dolak**; and returning sophomore starter **Mark Chase**. Furthermore, Ronai brought with him a bonus—his son, sophomore point guard **Jared Ronai**. On his hiring, Ronai stated: "The biggest reason I wanted to come back to high school is I'm tired of being on the road recruiting. My second concern is I wanted to get into a good situation—a school with good academics and athletics—and Cathedral Prep fits the bill!"

The 2000 Prep Ramblers opened the season with titles at the Great Chevy Shootout and the Coca-Cola Challenge. Kneeling, L to R: Frank Mezler, A. Kubinski, Ronai, DeCoursey; Standing: Coach Ronai, S. Kubinski, Malloy, Pelkowski, Hairston, Bogacki, Mifsud, Fetzner, Yaple, Daisley, Hairston, Asst. Coach Achille.

- Coach Ronai's tenure began on a grand note with Prep titles in the Great Chevy Shootout and the Coca-Cola Challenge. The win over eventual WPIAL runner-up Butler (20-9) was one of the best of the season, with **David Hairston** leading the way. Prep's win over Canisius (10-14) in the Coke was the first time the two competed since 1986. The game was moved from Saturday, December 11, to Sunday, December 12, to accommodate Rambler football fans who had witnessed in Hershey a heartbreaking 14-13 loss to Central Bucks West in one of the most exciting championship football games ever played in the state. The entire Prep gridiron team, which included cagers **Jason Dolak, Ed Hinkel** and **Dale Williams**, arrived to a thunderous, 5-minute standing ovation before 1,000 spectators at the Erie Civic Center. They were honored before and at halftime of the Prep-Canisius contest.

Three-year star Mike Malloy.

Coach Ronai had his players training hard with runs to the beach.

- Things went south on Prep's third Las Vegas holiday trip when the Ramblers got dumped in all three outings. Of the Ramblers' new Las Vegas opponents: Durango had about 3,600 students at the time and won state basketball titles in 1995 and 1996; and Mesa Dobson (21-8), with about 2,800 students, is one of the largest schools in Arizona.

- Prep then lost a pair to Toledo Scott (17-7) and Detroit Country Day School in the Festival of Lights tourney before rebounding against the defending West Virginia state champ, North Marion.

- Detroit Country Day School is a private, expensive, secular school actually located in Beverly Hills, just north of Detroit. The Yellowjackets compete in the Class B Michigan HSAA. Country Day's **Chris Webber** (1991) and **Shane Battier** (1997) each won Naismith Player of the Year awards as the top prep players in the nation. In 2004 the MHSAA recommended that Country Day voluntarily forfeit three state basketball championships won between 1989 and 1991, claiming that Webber had violated his amateur status via his relationship with a University of Michigan athletic booster. Country Day declined to follow the MHSAA's suggestion.

- NYC LaSalle Academy finally took home a McDonald's Classic crown in the 17th annual. Led by **Rodney Epperson** and **Famous Brown**, the Cardinals ousted defending Pennsylvania state champ Williamsport and All-American **Chevy Troutman**, 63-55. LaSalle routed Prep on opening night, while Williamsport dismantled Simon Gratz, 70-52. Gratz came through with consolation honors over Prep on night two as the Ramblers shot just 17.5%. The Bulldogs made it to the Philadelphia Public School final where it lost to Strawberry Mansion, 60-49.

- It was an interesting scenario when a hotdog from LaSalle named **Lenny Cooke** shattered the backboard at the south end of Hammermill Center during warm-ups for the McDonald's Classic's second game on Friday night. Workers replaced the backboard, but the LaSalle-Prep matchup was delayed by one hour, 23 minutes. After transferring from LaSalle the next season, Cooke was rated the #4 high school player in the United States in

LaSalle's Lenny Cooke shattered the backboard during warm-ups for the McDonald's Classic. The Prep-LaSalle contest was delayed for one hour, 23 minutes.

the Prep Stars Recruiter's Handbook. Unable to compete as a senior because his high school eligibility had run out, Cooke had other options for basketball: North Carolina, Seton Hall, St. John's, Miami and Ohio State. Cooke, however, chose to declare himself eligible for the 2002 NBA Draft, though he went undrafted. When all 29 NBA teams passed on Cooke in both rounds, he turned to the Rucker Park Summer League in New York and later foundered around with different minor league teams. In 2013 he became the subject of a documentary on a "star-to-be that never was," a look at athletes who declared NBA eligibility early but never fulfilled their once presumed destinies to become NBA stars.

- Prep's win over North Hills (9-15) was the first time the two competed in basketball. The Indians have a storied history in football, but have never won as much as a WPIAL title in basketball.

All-star Jim Fetzner started every game as a junior and senior.

- Biggest disappointments of the season were the pair of losses to arch-rival McDowell (27-1) and the two losses to Central (17-11), particularly in the play-in game for a District 10 berth. **Jim Fetzner** closed out his fine career with a season-high 25 points, but the two-point loss was devastating. It was the first time since 1985 that Prep had no post-season and the first time since 1986 that Prep did not advance to the PIAA inter-district playoffs (a final round of 32 teams). Central's two victories over Prep were its first ever after 17 straight Rambler wins since 1992-93.

Jim Fetzner moves the ball quickly up court. "Fetz" was a Second Team All-Metro selection.

- McDowell had a spectacular campaign under coaches **Pete Flinn** and **Jim Delsandro**, winning the Metro League and D-10 titles and finishing the regular season undefeated. Ranked the #1 team in Pennsylvania at the time, the Trojans were upset by Uniontown, 49-40, in the PIAA Western Semifinal. Senior **Justin Shouse** was the big star for McDowell, finishing his Trojan career with 1,337 points, a McDowell record at the time. Other Trojan luminaries included **J.J. Delsandro, Matt Miller, Mike Schodt, Dusty Ras** and **Matt Amann**.

- East High (19-9) won the District 10 AAA title, its first district crown since 1984. Leading the way was **Matt Jones**, currently the East head coach, who finished the 1999-2000 season as the Warriors' all-time leading scorer with 1,400 points, 7th on the Erie area's all-time chart. East defeated Valley in the PIAA's, but was soundly beaten by Montour in the second round, 72-43.

- The final standings of the Erie Metro League:

	Won	Lost
McDowell	10	0
*Central	7	4
Prep	6	5
East	5	5
Mercyhurst	3	7
Vincent	0	10

*won playoff for second place

Steve Kubinski barrells in for two more against Warren, with Fetzner close by.

- The McDonald's Classic, all Metro League games and Prep's home games against North Hills and Warren were held at Gannon's Hammermill Center.

- Seniors **Jim Fetzner** and **David Hairston** were both named Second Team Metro All-Stars by the *Erie Times-News*, while junior **Aaron DeCoursey** was an Honorable Mention choice. Fetzner and Hairston both played in the 26th annual City-County all-star classic at McComb Fieldhouse, won by the County for the second straight year, 89-80. Both Ramblers played well, Hairston scoring 12 and Fetzner 11.

"One, Two, Three, Team!"

- **Dave Hairston**, Prep's leading scorer, was winner of the James "Moe" Gross Award for outstanding basketball ability. He went on to star at Penn State-Behrend, while **Jim Fetzner** went on to play at Grove City College.

- **Jason Dolak**, who set several Prep place-kicking records on the gridiron, went on to star in basketball at LaRoche College. He ranks #18 on the Redhawks' all-time scoring chart. As a senior (2003-04) he made the Allegheny Mountain Collegiate Conference All-Academic team, and further was awarded the conference's Faculty Representative Award. Dolak was head coach at Harborcreek High School from 2009 through 2014.

2000 All-Opponent Team:

Jake Henneman, Bishop Guilfoyle

Ben Gallagher, Butler [Juniata]

Joe Vera, Canisius

Martrel Johnson, Durango [Montana St.]

Jordan Legge, Mesa Dobson [Santa Clara]

Ashanti Cook, Westchester [Georgetown]

Dennis Springs, Toledo Scott [Ferris State]

Ashton Aikens, Detroit Country Day [Northwestern, football]

Chris Exilus, North Marion (1ˢᵗ team all-state, WV) [Virginia Tech, DePaul]

Joe Rivera, Vincent [Gannon]

Leonard Cooke, NYC LaSalle

Rodney Epperson, NYC LaSalle [Midland (TX) JC, St. John's, Mountain St.]

Percell Coles, Simon Gratz (4ᵗʰ team all-state) [Cleveland State]

Shaun McKie, Simon Gratz [Salem International]

Matt Jones, East (4ᵗʰ team all-state) [Gannon]

Justin Shouse, McDowell (2ⁿᵈ team all-state) [Mercyhurst]

Mike Biletnikoff, McDowell

Matt Miller, McDowell

Torry Mitchell, Central [Mercyhurst, Edinboro]

Dan Dill, Mercyhurst

James Curren, Warren (5ᵗʰ team all-state) [Behrend]

J. J. Delsandro, McDowell [Mercyhurst]

Kubinski banks one in against Vincent.

Better Record, but Ronai Gone!

2000-01 (16-9)

Coach: Robert "Bob" Ronai
Assistants: Coach: Bob Achille, Joe Spinelli
Captains: Aaron DeCoursey, Jared Ronai
Managers: Mark Marasco, Dave Parker,
Gary Sienicki

The boyz, enjoying their time at the KSA Tourney. Front, L to R: Chase, Braham; Middle: McCloskey, Ronai, Tarasovitch, Sertz, White, Yaple; Back: Daisley, Fetzner.

Date	PREP		Dec.	Loc.	High Scorer	Opponent
		BISHOP TIMON TOURNAMENT (BUFFALO, NY)				
12/1	65	Hamburg (NY)	39	W	N	Chase (16)	Babicz (11)
12/2	48	Buffalo (NY) Bishop Timon-St. Jude	83	L	A	Samailovic (12)	Herring (21)
		HAMOT SPORTS MEDICINE CHALLENGE				
12/10	76	Butler	52	W	H	DeCoursey (16)	Saeler (20)
		KSA TOURNAMENT (KISSIMMEE, FL)				
12/14	63	Woodlake (CA) Union	21	W	N	McCloskey (10)	Valencia (7)
12/15	61	Sebring (FL)	57	W	N	DeCoursey (19)	Zwayer (16)
12/16	41	Orlando (FL) Maynard Evans	55	L	N	Chase (19)	Baker (21)
		CELRIVER CLASSIC (ROCK HILL, SC)				
12/27	67	Dreher (SC)	66	W	N	Samailovic (16)	Epps (20)
12/28	49	NYC (NY) Frederick Douglass	72	L	N	Samailovic (13)	Edwards (16)
12/29	65	Rock Hill (SC)	49	W	A	DeCoursey (23)	Simpson (13)
1/3	70	Mercyhurst Prep	62	W	N	Chase (17)	Merski (26)
1/6	70	Warren	51	W	A	Chase (16)	UNREPORTED
1/9	79	Strong Vincent	66	W	N	Samailovic (18)	Williams (23)
		McDONALD'S CLASSIC				
1/12	66	Lexington (KY) Catholic	74	L	H	Chase (19)	Heissenbuttel (25)
1/13	47	NYC (NY) LaSalle Academy	49	L	H	Chase (19)	Sterling (22)
1/16	51	East	35	W	N	Samailovic (12)	McInnis (10)
1/19	54	Central	46	W	N	Chase (17)	Mitchell & Heidelberg (12)
1/20	94	St.Catharine's (ONT) Dennis Morris	49	W	H	Chase (20)	UNREPORTED
1/26	36	McDowell	33	W	N	Daisley (14)	Ras (12)
1/27	46	Mercyhurst Prep	48	L	N	DeCoursey (13)	Merski (15)
2/2	61	Strong Vincent	50	W	N	Samailovic (22)	Madigan (14)
2/6	53	East	55(2OT)	L	N	Samailovic (19)	Matt Jones (15)
2/9	58	Central	68	L	N	DeCoursey (20)	Mitchell (18)
2/10	58	Meadville	54	W	H	Samailovic (15)	UNREPORTED
2/16	54	McDowell	40	W	N	DeCoursey (17)	Delsandro (14)
		DISTRICT 10 PLAYOFF				
2/22	63	George Junior Republic	70(OT)	L	H	DeCoursey (14)	Warner (24)
	1495 (59.8)		**1344 (53.8)**				

Pos.	Player	Ht.	Prior School	Class	G(GS)	FG(3)	FT	Total	PPG	Career
F	Srboljub Samailovic (#4)	6'5"	North East HS	Sr.	24(24)	113(8)	62-89	296	12.3	296
F	Aaron DeCoursey (#33)	6'3"	Holy Rosary	Sr.	25(25)	110(8)	58-82	286	11.4	532
G-F	Mark Chase (#5)	6'4"	Luther Memorial	Jr.	23(23)	100(24)	56-83	280	12.2	607
G	Jared Ronai (#10)	5'11"	Bishop Walsh	Jr.	25(25)	65(20)	40-63	190	7.6	378
F	Andy Kubinski (#52)	6'2"	OLC	Jr.	25(25)	53	33-53	139	5.6	175
G	John Yaple (#15)	6'2"	St. Boniface	Jr.	25(3)	34(21)	5-9	94	3.8	103
C	Jeff Daisley (#42)	7'0"	Girard	Sr.	24	22	24-29	68	2.8	68
G	Casey McCloskey (#30)	6'1"	St. Luke's	Soph.	24	14(5)	4-6	37	1.5	37
G	Mike Sertz (#12)	5'10"	OLP	Jr.	12	7(3)	2-3	19	1.6	19
G-F	Nick Tarasovitch (#24)	6'1"	J. S. Wilson	Jr.	11	7	4-6	18	1.6	18
F	Steve White (#20)	6'2"	St. Luke's	Jr.	12	5(4)	3-4	17	1.4	17
G	Adam Braham (#31)	5'1"	OLC	Jr.	11	4	7-11	15	1.4	15
G	Julio Achille (#40)	6'1"	Bl. Sacrament	Jr.	12	2	2-2	12	1.0	12
F	Dan Fetzner (#23)	6'3"	St. Peter's	Jr.	12	1	5-8	7	0.6	7

HIGHLIGHTS:

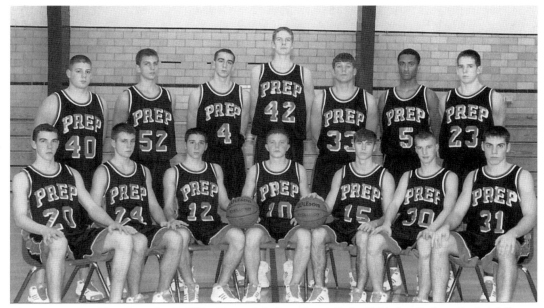

- **Father Scott Jabo** was appointed Cathedral Prep's eighth headmaster following the retirement of **Monsignor Bruce Allison** in 2000. The personable Father Jabo, a native of Warren, continues to promote the spiritual, moral and academic development of Prep's young men. He serves as team chaplain and can always be seen on Prep's sideline or bench supporting his Ramblers.

- **Bill Flanagan** took the reigns as Cathedral Prep athletic director in 2000. A Prep graduate from the Class of 1987, Flanagan was a successful radio and television sports announcer and spent some time with ESPN as well. Flanagan has since kept the Prep sports program at the forefront of state and national prominence.

The 2001 Prep Ramblers. Front, L to R: White, Tarasovitch, Sertz, Ronai, Yaple, McCloskey, Braham; Back: Achille, Kubinski, Samailovic, Daisley, DeCoursey, Chase, Fetzner.

- The Prep team was bolstered with the addition of 6'5" First Team All-County transfer **Srboljub "Srba" Samailovic** from North East. Samailovic, a Serbian foreign exchange student, averaged 17.0 PPG for the Grapepickers as a junior in 1999-2000.

- Prep opened the season with a win in an only-ever game against Hamburg (12-9), but lost badly to the tip-off tourney's powerful host Bishop Timon-St. Jude (27-2). It was the first time the Ramblers and Tigers squared off since 1986 and it was the largest losing margin for the Orange & Black since 1984-85. At the time Hamburg was a member of the Erie County (NY) Interscholastic Conference I (ECIC I), along with Williamsville North, Jamestown, Orchard Park, Frontier, Clarence and Lancaster.

- The new Hamot Sports Medicine Challenge was delayed one day to accommodate Prep players, students, alumni and fans who again trekked to Hershey, only this time to see the Ramblers win their first state football championship with a thrilling 41-35 overtime victory over Central Bucks West, breaking CBW's three-year stranglehold on the state title and its 59-game winning streak. "We Are the Champions!" blared from the loudspeakers as the Rambler gridders marched into a raucous Hammermill Center after arriving via police escort. After a victory medals presentation and congratulatory speeches from the mayor, city council, **Bishop Donald Troutman,** Headmaster **Father Scott Jabo** and football coach **Mike Mischler,** the Rambler basketball squad methodically picked apart Butler (6-18) to win the Challenge.

- Several Rambler star football players, including first team all-state gridders **Ed Hinkel, Dale Williams** and **Jawan Walker**, were unable to rejoin the basketball squad because of the lateness of the pigskin season and the fact they were all being heavily recruited by football powers. Hinkel, winner of the "Ma" Kaiser Award as Prep's finest athlete, had a spectacular career in the Big Ten at the University of Iowa, where he was team MVP and "Permanent Team Captain" for the Hawkeyes. Williams and Walker both played at the University of Pittsburgh. Williams was named to the 2004 Big East All-Academic team, while Walker, to this day, is the only Pitt Panther to run for a touchdown, catch a pass for a touchdown and throw a TD pass all in one game!

- Prep made its first of several trips to the KSA Holiday tourney near Orlando (FL). KSA Events is considered one of the premier hosts of high school sporting events and participating teams come from Florida to Alaska and from Massachusetts to California, providing a national competition format that brings together teams that otherwise would not meet.

- Of Prep's new KSA opponents: Woodlake Union's 21 points were the fewest scored by a Rambler opponent since Wellington

Centennial scored 18 in 1996-97; Sebring High is located near Sebring International Raceway; and Maynard Evans High was named after a man who once owned a downtown Orlando soda shop!

- Prep made its first trip to the Celriver Classic since 1985-86 and as it did in the KSA tourney, won two of three. Of Prep's new Celriver opponents: Dreher has won five South Carolina state titles and lists NBA Hall of Famer **Alex English** as an alumnus; Frederick Douglass Academy, founded in 1991, is a co-ed public school of about 1,700 students that competes in high school basketball's highest levels and is located in West Harlem.

- New York City Rice won its third McDonald's Classic title in the tournament's 18th year, with an easy 79-61win over Lexington Catholic. **Shagari Alleyne**, Rice's 7'3" sophomore sensation, teamed with **Ken Eusey** for 43 points. LaSalle nudged Prep on an **Eric Sterling** shot with 5.6 seconds left in the consolation thriller after **Jack Heissenbuttel** led Lexington Catholic (25-8) over Prep on opening night. Another star for the LC Knights was **Brian Smith**, son of former Kentucky coach **Tubby Smith**. Lexington Catholic was formed in 1951 through the merger of St. Catherine's Academy and Lexington Latin. The Knights won the Kentucky state championship in 2002, finishing #10 in

Ron and his girls at the 2001 Classic.

Pennsylvania Governor Tom Ridge '63 congratulates the Rice coach on winning the McDonald's Classic.

the nation in the final *USA Today* Super 25 poll with a 33-2 record.

- Long-time LaSalle coach **Bill Aberer** complimented Erie, Prep and McDonald's Classic director **Ron Sertz**: "We've been to tournaments in Alaska, Hawaii, Florida, Arkansas, and of all of them, the McDonald's treats you the nicest...The accomodations are nice and the competition is excellent. It's a

Daisley, Prep's only legitimate 7-footer, slams one down for Mercyhurst College.

nice little trip. The kids like it. I always let the kids vote on where they want to go, and the McDonald's Classic is always a unanimous selection!"

- One notable loss for Prep was its first ever to Mercyhurst (18-10), after 33 consecutive Rambler victories! This came the night after Prep's emotional win over McDowell (18-7) before a capacity crowd at the Hammermill Center. **Jeff Daisley** sparked the Ramblers from a 10-point second half deficit to a 36-33 upset over the Trojans, coming off the bench to score 14 points, collect 10 rebounds, block 3 shots and nail 10 of 11 from the free throw line. Following the game was the well-publicized "basket-brawl" that involved, according to the *Erie Times-News*, "at least 30 and as many as 90 students" outside the Hammermill. Needless to say, the Prep-McDowell rivalry was still quite heated.

- Biggest disappointments of the season were losing the rematches with three out of the five Metro League opponents: Mercyhurst, East and Central. The first meetings with these same teams were all comfortable Rambler victories. When Prep beat Mercyhurst on January 3, the Lakers were 11-0 at the time.

- Prep's win over Meadville (9-15) was the first regular season scheduled game between the two since 1989, though the Ramblers and Bulldogs met in playoff situations eight times in between.

- Central (20-8) won its first and only championship of the very competitive Erie Metro League. The Falcons made it to the PIAA Western Quarterfinals where they were crushed by state finalist Pittsburgh Schenley, 71-42.

- The final standings of the Metro League:

	Won	Lost
Central	8	2
Prep	7	3
McDowell	6	4
East	5	5
Mercyhurst	4	6
Vincent	0	10

- The McDonald's Classic, all Metro League games, Prep home games against Denis Morris and Meadville and the D-10 playoff were held at Gannon's Hammermill Center.

- The season's final disappointment came with the overtime loss to powerful George Junior Republic (25-4) in the District 10 semifinal. George Junior Republic is an all-boys juvenile institution near Grove City that houses, schools and disciplines about 400 high school-aged kids from troubled backgrounds. The Junior Republic is characterized by its successful athletics, most notably its basketball team. The Tigers won PIAA AA state titles in 1996 and 1998, have a plethora of District 10 championships and have graduated several who went on to play at the collegiate level. In February, 2000, fourteen principals representing the Mercer County Athletic Conference decided to vacate GJR's conference titles for 1998 and 1999 and the Junior Republic volunteered to give up the 1999-2000 title that it earned with a 20-0 record. These actions resulted when it came to light that GJR had used the wrong enrollment figures for their participation in Class AA. GJR participated as a Class AAAA team for the first time in 2000-01, resulting in the first meeting between Prep and the Junior Republic.

- The Ramblers made a fine comeback to put the George Junior Republic playoff game into OT, but ran out of steam from there. GJR then made it all the way to the PIAA Western Final, where it lost to Schenley (29-3) in an overtime thriller, 83-77. The Spartans then lost to Coatesville (30-1) in the state final, 70-57.

- **Aaron DeCoursey** and juniors **Mark Chase** and **Jared "J-Ro" Ronai** were all named Second Team All-Metro by the *Erie Times-News*. **Srba Samailovic** was an Honorable Mention choice.

MVP Aaron DeCoursey was also a star hurler for the Ramblers. He went on to pitch for St. Bonaventure in the A-10.

- Samailovic scored 8 points for the City All-Stars against his former County mates in the 27th annual City-County all-star clash, a 67-64 City victory. DeCoursey was unavailable for the contest as he was with the Prep baseball squad on its annual Florida competition trip.

- **Aaron DeCoursey**, a consistent two-year star for the Ramblers, was winner of the James "Moe" Gross Award for outstanding basketball ability. Also a star pitcher, DeCoursey received a scholarship and played Division I baseball for St. Bonaventure in the Atlantic 10 Conference.

- **Jeff Daisley**, to this day Prep's only legitimate 7-footer, played one year at Naval Academy Prep School before starring at Mercyhurst College. Daisley went on to play professional basketball in China and Yugoslavia, as well as with the Buffalo Silverbacks of the ABA and the Rio Grande Valley Silverados of the CBA.

Jeff Daisley went on to a pro career in China and Yugoslavia; and with the ABA and CBA.

- After graduation from Prep in 2001, **Srba Samailovic** returned to Europe and has played professional basketball in both Serbia and Romania.

- **Bob Ronai** resigned as head coach at season's end after rumors were rampant that he would be stepping down. Ronai's record of 28-21 after two seasons was considered substandard after the outstanding 12-year record of **Marcel Arribi**. The Ramblers improved in Ronai's season 2, but were eliminated in the first round of the District 10 playoffs by GJR in an overtime semifinal game. Several years later (2011), in a situation eerily similar to Ronai's situation at Prep, the Middletown (OH)

athletic department announced that Coach Ronai resigned after eight seasons with the Middies. Ronai guided Middletown to an 18-5 mark his final season, but was only 97-79 overall with the Middies. It was reported that Ronai was "caught off guard" when he was told that the Middletown administration wanted to go in a different direction. Ronai has more than 550 wins in his 34-year coaching career at the college and high school levels. Prior to Middletown, Ronai served as basketball coach at London High

Jared Ronai left with his Dad after his junior year to London (OH), where he was named First Team All-State as a senior.

School in Ohio. After Middletown, Ronai became the Director of Athletics at Toledo (OH) St. John's Jesuit, whom Cathedral Prep played for the first time in the 2013-14 season.

- Coach Ronai's departure also meant the loss of two-year point guard **Jared Ronai**. Jared played his senior season for London (OH), where he averaged 18.4 PPG and was named to Ohio's First Team Division II All-State Team along with another notable: **LeBron James** of Akron St. Vincent-St. Mary and later of the NBA's Miami Heat and Cleveland Cavaliers! Jared redshirted at UNC-Asheville before transferring and completing his playing career at Georgia Southwestern State. There he was a two-year starter at the point guard position and served as a team captain in 2005-06. Ronai was a recipient of the Champions of Character award, which is presented annually to only 32 players across the United States. He is now an assistant coach at UNC-Asheville.

2001 All-Opponent Team:

Corey Herring, Bishop Timon-St. Jude (1st team all-state, NY) [Baylor]

Fran Snyder, Bishop Timon-St. Jude [RIT]

Charlie Comerford, Bishop Timon-St. Jude [Holy Cross, football & basketball]

Clint Zwayer, Sebring [VMI, Longwood]

Aaron Baker, Maynard Evans

Maurice Epps, Dreher

LaMarcus Nero, Dreher [Benedict (SC) College, football]

Sam Edwards, Frederick Douglass Academy [S. New Hampshire]

Alonzo Brown, Frederick Douglass Academy [American International]

Tahan Engram, Frederick Douglass Academy [Niagara]

Doug Merski, Mercyhurst [Behrend]

Jovan Williams, Vincent

Brian Smith, Lexington Catholic [Mississippi]

Jack Heissenbuttel, Lexington Catholic

Eric Sterling, NYC LaSalle

Dusty Ras, McDowell

Matt Jones, East [Gannon]

Torry Mitchell, Central (4th team all-state) [Mercyhurst, Edinboro]

Mark Wilcox, Central

J.J. Delsandro, McDowell (3rd team all-state) [Mercyhurst]

Brad Warner, GJR

Andy Sisinni Returns to Prep!

Trojans win D-10 in OT Thriller!

2001-02 (19-10)

Coach: Andy Sisinni
Assistants: Jim Stevenson, Brian Flanagan
Captains: Mark Chase, Andy Kubinski
Managers: Matt Detisch, Mark Marasco,
Dave Parker

Andy Kubinski was honored as the Metro League "Player of the Year."

Roger Randolph, GJR (5ᵗʰ team all-state)

Date	PREP		Dec.	Loc.	High Scorer	Opponent
	MIDLAND TIP-OFF TOURNAMENT					
11/30	47	Uniontown	70	L	N	Chase (24)	Jenkins (23)
12/1	59	East Liverpool (OH)	61	L	A	Chase (20)	Kirby (21)
12/5	59	Franklin	62	L	A	Kubinski (18)	Grill (19)
12/9	67	Buffalo (NY) Bishop Timon/St. Jude	45	W	H	Kubinski (20)	Snyder (14)
12/14	78	Warren	52	W	H	Chase (33)	Maljovec (13)
	IOLANI PREP CLASSIC (HONOLULU, HI)					
12/18	36	Honolulu (HI) 'Iolani School	65	L	A	Chase (12)	Nash (20)
12/20	76	Honolulu (HI) Roosevelt	48	W	N	Kubinski (20)	Borges (16)
12/21	41	Honolulu (HI) Punahou School	43	L	N	Kubinski (9)	Fergus (14)
12/22	57	Mililani (HI)	43	W	N	Kubinski (20)	Broadus (15)
	FARRELL HOLIDAY TOURNAMENT					
12/27	59	Pittsburgh Seton-LaSalle	36	W	N	Chase (18)	Buffington (10)
12/28	54	Farrell	51	W	A	Kubinski (15)	Lowe (13)
1/2	30	Mercyhurst Prep	46	L	N	McCloskey & Kubinski (10)	Johnson (21)
1/8	55	Strong Vincent	51	W	N	Chase (18)	Selby (18)
1/10	51	Meadville	42	W	A	Kubinski (21)	Dixon (19)
1/12	56	East	43	W	N	Kubinski (21)	Johnson (15)
1/15	65	Central	52	W	N	Chase (20)	McCreary (17)
	McDONALD'S CLASSIC					
1/18	48	Chester	54	L	H	Kubinski (16)	Swiggett (11)
1/19	69	Washington (DC) Dunbar	62	W	H	Kubinski (29)	Kelly (20)
1/23	46	McDowell	42	W	N	Chase (14)	Schodt (9)
1/25	50	Mercyhurst Prep	37	W	N	Kubinski (16)	Nies & Merski (11)
1/30	60	Strong Vincent	48	W	N	McCloskey (18)	Williams (20)
2/5	50	East	44	W	N	Chase (19)	Johnson (14)
2/8	69	Central	63	W	N	Kubinski (22)	McCreary (23)
2/15	54	McDowell	63(OT)	L	N	Kubinski (20)	Schodt (18)
	DISTRICT 10 PLAYOFFS					
2/21	68	George Junior Republic	51	W	H	Stewart (22)	White (17)
2/28	59	McDowell	64(OT)	L	N	Chase (19)	G. Hoffman (23)
	P.I.A.A. INTERDISTRICT PLAYOFFS					
3/9	52	Kiski Area	46	W	N	Kubinski (17)	Tuchstone (17)
3/13	57	Pittsburgh Schenley	49	W	N	Chase (18)	Bryant (14)
3/16	45	Uniontown	48	L	N	Kubinski (19)	Jacobs (18)

Pos.	Player	Ht.	Grade School	Class	G(GS)	FG(3)	FT	Total	PPG	Career
F	Andy Kubinski (#4)	6'4"	OLC	Sr.	29(29)	174(19)	91-122	458	15.8	633
G-F	Mark Chase (#5)	6'4"	St. Luke's	Sr.	28(27)	146(19)	99-133	410	14.6	1017
G	Casey McCloskey (#52)	6'1"	St. Luke's	Jr.	27(24)	99(12)	33-52	243	9.0	280
F	Phil Stewart (#31)	6'3"	Fairview	Jr.	26(6)	45(24)	13-16	127	4.9	127
G	John Yaple (#15)	6'2"	St. Boniface	Sr.	26(13)	31(18)	16-22	96	3.7	199
G	Joe Jones (#30)	6'1"	Luther Memorial	Soph.	26(19)	26(5)	14-21	71	2.7	71
G	Mike Sertz (#12)	6'0"	OLP	Sr.	23(11)	21(12)	10-17	64	2.8	83
G	Kyle Brabender (#11)	6"2"	St. Luke's	Jr.	21(6)	13(2)	7-12	35	1.7	35
G-F	Nick Tarasovitch (#24)	6'1"	J. S. Wilson	Sr.	16(2)	11(4)	3-5	29	1.8	47
F	Bob Barber (#33)	6'3"	St. Peter's	Jr.	19	12	5-6	29	1.5	29
F	Steve White (#20)	6'3"	St. Luke's	Sr.	21(3)	6(2)	4-6	18	1.1	35
F	Jim MacKrell (#40)	6'3"	Erie Day School	Jr.	7(3)	6	6-9	18	2.6	18
F	Dan Fetzner (#42)	6'3"	St. Peter's	Sr.	22(2)	4	4-8	12	0.5	19
C	Mike Daisley (#50)	6'6"	Girard	Jr.	13	2	1-4	5	0.4	5
G	Greg Durr (#23)	6'1"	St. John's	Jr.	2	1	0-2	2	1.0	2

1617 (55.8)
1481 (51.1)
HIGHLIGHTS:

- First-year coach **Andrew "Andy" Sisinni**, a prominent Erie lawyer, was a 1980 graduate of Cathedral Prep and was a star guard on the Ramblers' 1980 state championship team that finished 33-1. Sisinni later started four years at point guard at Duquesne University. The Prep head coach job was Sisinni's dream job after coaching stints at Duquesne, Adelphi University, Prep (freshman coach, 1989-90) and Strong Vincent (head coach, 1990-95).

- Coach Sisinni brought on as assistants a pair of former Prep stars with vast coaching experience and basketball knowledge—**Brian Flanagan** '70, who led Prep to the 1970 city title and later played at Division I Loyola (MD); and **Jim Stevenson** '84, a two-year starting point guard who led the Ramblers to the state final in 1984.

Prep's 2002 Metro League Champions. Front, clockwise: Mgr. Detisch, Brabender, Durr, McCloskey, Sertz, Yaple, Tarasovitch, Jones, Asst. Coach Stevenson; Back: Asst. Coach Flanagan, MacKrell, Stewart, Kubinski, Daisley, Barber, Chase, Fetzner, White, Coach Sisinni.

- Cathedral Prep won its first Metro League championship since 1998 under the new coach. Veterans **Andy Kubinski** and **Mark Chase** provided excellent senior leadership while some underclassmen stepped forward with some good work. Other highlights were winning the Farrell Holiday tourney, a good showing in the McDonald's Classic and an impressive and exciting PIAA run before losing to state finalist Uniontown (30-2) in the PIAA Western Semifinals. **Andy Sisinni** was named the *Erie Times-News* "Coach of the Year," as selected by his peers.

- Junior **Greg Durr** was a star on the 1999 St. John's team that won the Pennsylvania CYO state grade school title. McDowell's **Sean Hoffman** was also a star on that squad.

- All Metro League games, the McDonald's Classic, home dates with Bishop Timon-St. Jude and Warren and the District 10 semifinal versus George Junior Republic were played at Gannon's Hammermill Center. The D-10 final was contested in Edinboro; the PIAA first round in Butler; and the Western Quarterfinal and Semifinal at Slippery Rock's Morrow Fieldhouse.

- Prep opened the season the way it would finish—with a loss to the powerful Uniontown Red Raiders, first in the Midland Tip-off tourney. Prep then lost the Midland consolation prize to a new opponent in East Liverpool, despite an amazing six 3-pointers by senior long-bomb artist **John Yaple**. **Mark Chase** won a spot on the all-tourney team. The EL Potters most famous alumnus is former college and pro football coach and erstwhile TV football analyst **Lou Holtz**.

- Prep made its second holiday trip to the 'Iolani Classic in 'Iolani, Hawaii, the first being ten years before. The 'Iolani was in its 19th year and 16 teams participated, with Los Angeles (CA) Fairfax winning the title. Eight different Ramblers received in-season suspensions totaling 21 games, anywhere from one to three individually, for certain disciplinary violations during the 'Iolani trip. The suspensions were served on a rotating basis which caused lineup disruptions until the final three games of the regular season.

- Of Prep's Hawaii opponents: 'Iolani in the Hawaiian language means "heavenly hawk," though the Episcopalian school's nickname is the "Raiders"; President Theodore Roosevelt High School, one of the oldest public schools in Hawaii, is used as a backdrop in several movie and television productions; Mililani is one of Hawaii's largest public schools; and The Punahou School's sports program was ranked best in the country by *Sports Illustrated*, having won more state championships than any other high school in the nation. Notre Dame's 2012 Heisman Trophy finalist, **Manti Te'o**, went to Punahou. **U.S. President Barack Obama** is said to have graduated from Punahou in 1979, though this could not be independently verified and no transcripts have been produced.

Father Jabo enjoying a Christmas vacation in Hawaii with the players and coaches.

- Prep easily bounced Seton-LaSalle (14-13), then got by the hometown Farrell Steelers (17-7, forced to forfeit 13 games, 4-20) to win its second Farrell Holiday Tournament in three years and fourth overall. **Mark Chase** and **Andy Kubinski** were selected to the all-tourney team, with Chase capturing MVP honors. Seton-La Salle, the largest co-educational high school in the Diocese of Pittsburgh, was formed in 1979 by the merger of all-boys South Hills Catholic, one of Prep's former nemeses, and all-girls Elizabeth Seton High School. It was the first time the Ramblers and Rebels clashed in three decades, since some very memorable PCIAA overtime playoff encounters.

- Los Angeles Westchester entered the 19th McDonald's Classic as the nation's #1 team and easily crushed Washington Dunbar, 93-51, and Chester, 100-50, to steal the show. Chester (24-5) edged Prep on opening night, but the Ramblers bounced back to take consolation honors over Dunbar (13-12), behind a spectacular 20-point shooting performance by **Mike Sertz**, son of **Ron Sertz**, the McDonald's Classic founder and director.

- The Dunbar Crimson Tide competes in the D.C. Interscholastic Athletic Association, and its football team historically has been strong. Originally named "Preparatory High School for Colored Youth", Dunbar

Spot starter Mike Sertz lit up the Hammermill Center during the McDonald's Classic.

Classic director Ron Sertz congratulates his son, Mike, for his outstanding play against Dunbar.

was America's first public high school for black students. Dunbar rebounded in 2002-03, finishing 23-6 with the DCIAA championship.

- Good Prep wins in the strong Metro League included the pairs over city rivals Strong Vincent (17-8) and East (15-9), as well as the victory over Mercyhurst Prep (26-5). The Lakers' made it all the way to the PIAA Class AA Western Final under coach **Pat Flaherty**, son of Prep's legendary Hall of Fame coach **Bill Flaherty**.

- Prep's biggest victory was the District 10 semifinal win over #6 rated George Junior Republic (22-3). The heavily favored Tigers had just come off an overtime victory over nationally-ranked Akron (OH) St. Vincent-St. Mary and superstar **LeBron James**, later of Cleveland Cavaliers, Miami Heat and NBA fame. **Phil Stewart**, Prep's transfer from Fairview where he started as a sophomore, displayed some uncanny shooting

Red-hot Mike Sertz buries another perimeter shot against Dunbar.

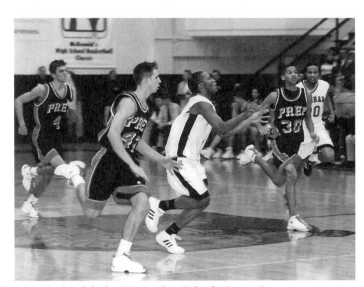

Racing back to defend against Dunbar: Kubinski, Fetzner, Jones.

Fetzner battles a trio of Crimson Tide for a loose ball.

- The final standings of the Erie Metro League:

	Won	Lost
Prep	8	2
Mercyhurst	7	3
McDowell	6	4
East	4	6
Vincent	3	7
Central	2	8

- Prep went deep into the PIAA playoffs, with impressive victories over Kiski Area (22-6) and Schenley (18-10), and the hard-fought, near upset of powerful Uniontown in the Western Semifinals. The Red Raiders made it all the way to Hershey, where it lost to Harrisburg (30-3) in the state championship game, 69-62.

- Villa Maria Academy's girls team (27-6) defeated Mercyhurst Prep (25-7) in a PIAA Western Final thriller at Edinboro, 44-39. The Victors of coach **Scott Dibble** used the leadership of **Sarah Grab** and four free throws by **Colleen Behringer** and **Maria DiVecchio** in the final 32 seconds to beat the Lakers for the third time in the season. VMA then lost to powerful Allentown Central Catholic (30-1) at the state final in Hershey.

Nobody messed with Danny Fetzner when he entered the Prep lineup.

with no less than six 3-pointers and 22 points to lead the Orange & Black.

- Biggest disappointments of the season were a pair of overtime losses to rival McDowell (20-7), including the District 10 finale. In that battle, Trojan **Greg Hoffman** made three pressure-packed free throws after time expired to send the game into OT. It was the 50th time McDowell had beaten Prep through the years.

- Consistent outstanding play from **Andy Kubinski** earned him a spot on the *Erie Times-News* Metro Stars First Team. More importantly, Andy was named "Player of the Year" in the Metro League by the *Times*, having scored in double figures in 26 of 29 games and averaging 8.9 RPG. He was also selected to play in the 28th annual City-County All-Star game, won by the Slickers, 84-60. Finally, Kubinski was named to the *Associated Press* Big School All-State Fourth Team.

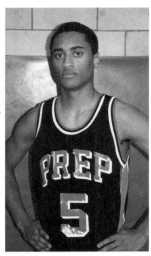

First Team Metro Star Mark Chase, one of only three 4-year starters in the history of Prep basketball.

- **Mark Chase** was also an *Erie Times-News* First Team Metro star, while **Casey McCloskey** was a Second Team choice. One of only three four-year starters in the history of Prep basketball (the others were **Ted Morasky**, 1938-42; and **Jed Ryan**, 1991-95), Chase finished his fine Prep career with 1,017 points, only the seventh player in Rambler history at the time to cross the 1,000 mark. Though selected for the City-County All-Star clash, he opted on the same evening to play in the Sportsmanship I All-Star Game at Clarion for the Western Pennsylvania All-Stars. Chase scored 15 to help lead his squad to a 123-54 victory over the Keystone Shortway Athletic Conference All-Stars, featuring players from District 9.

MVP Andy Kubinski led the Ramblers all season and went on to a fine career at Mercyhurst College.

- **Andy Kubinski** was winner of the James "Moe" Gross Award for outstanding basketball ability. He went on to star four years at Mercyhurst College, where he made the GLIAC All-Academic Team and as a senior made the conference's All-Defensive squad.

- **Kyle Brabender**, who did not play as a senior, started three years on Prep's District 10 champion soccer teams (2000-01-02), which included the Ramblers PIAA state championship team in 2001. Brabender was named First Team All-State in 2002 and played four years at Indiana University, where he was twice part of the Hoosiers' NCAA national championship soccer teams (2003 & 2004).

2002 All-Opponent Team:

Terrance Vaughn, Uniontown [Clarion]

Dierre Jenkins, Uniontown [Penn State-Fayette]

Nick Hager, Franklin [Juniata]

Fran Snyder, Bishop Timon-St. Jude (6th team all-state, NY) [RIT]

Bobby Nash, 'Iolani (1st team all-state, HI) [Hawaii]

Derrick Low, 'Iolani (1st team all-state, Player of the Year, HI) [Washington St.]

Dane Uperesa, Punahou (3rd team all-state, HI) [Hawaii, football]

Alex Fergus, Punahou

Rashaun Broadus, Mililani (1st team all-state, HI) [Western Nebraska CC, Brigham Young]

Myron Lowe, Farrell [Casper (WY) CC]

Jovon Johnson, Mercyhurst [Iowa, football; CFL Roughriders, Blue Bombers]

Jermaine Selby, Vincent

Charles Dixon, Meadville

Jamal Swiggett, Chester

Alfrie "Tre" Kelly, Washington Dunbar [South Carolina]

Jovan Williams, Vincent

T. J. McCreary, Central

Pat Schodt, McDowell [Behrend]

Greg Hoffman, McDowell

Joey Tuchstone, Kiski Area

Larry Bryant, Schenley [Edinboro UP]

Chris Jacobs, Uniontown [Fairmont St.]

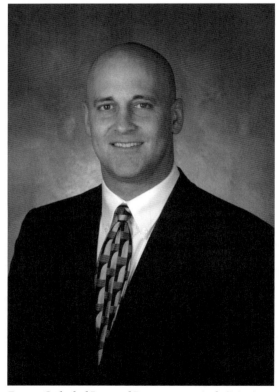

Former Cathedral Prep and Duquesne star Andy Sisinni considered the Rambler coaching position his "dream job."

Kyle Brabender moves past a Chester defender in the McDonald's Classic. Brabender later played for two Indiana University NCAA champion soccer teams.

Andy Kubinski shoots over a Timon defender for 2 of his 20 points.

Though just a sophomore, Joe Jones started 19 games for the Ramblers.

Three-point artist John Yaple made the all-tourney team at the Midland Tip-Off.

Scoring in double figures in 26 of 29 games, Andy Kubinski was named Fourth Team All-State.

Late Season Slump!

2002-03 (17-9)

Coach: Andy Sisinni
Assistants: Jim Stevenson, Brian Flanagan
Captain: Casey McCloskey
Managers: Matt Detisch

The 2002-03 coaching staff, L to R: Brian Flanagan, Andy Sisinni, Jim Stevenson.

Date	PREP		Dec.	Loc.	High Scorer	Opponent
	HAMOT SPORTS CHALLENGE @ BEHREND COLLEGE					
11/29	52	Buffalo (NY) Bishop Timon/St. Jude	45	W	H	McCloskey (25)	Dunford (22)
12/4	70	Warren	65(OT)	W	A	McCloskey (21)	Maljovec (16)
12/7	43	Franklin	42	W	H	McCloskey (16)	O'Brien (13)
12/10	67	Strong Vincent	40	W	N	Dolak (14)	Thomas (17)
12/13	59	Central	53	W	N	Jones (16)	McNeil (16)
12/16	52	New Castle	50	W	A	Scholz (13)	Ward (17)
	KSA CLASSIC (LAKE BUENA VISTA, FL)					
12/19	76	Cumming (GA) Covenant Christian	46	W	N	McCloskey (14)	Williams (20)
12/20	83	Tampa Bay (FL) Technical	61	W	N	McCloskey (18)	Edwards & Girod (12)
12/21	46	Brea (CA) Brea-Olinda	48	L	N	McCloskey (14)	Smith (15)
	MEADVILLE SERTOMA CHRISTMAS TOURNAMENT					
12/27	75	Avella	30	W	N	Jones & Knight (10)	Kettler (19)
12/28	61	Meadville	67	L	A	Jones (17)	Hughes (16)
1/2	54	East	55(OT)	L	N	Jones (24)	Presley (17)
1/4	50	Mercyhurst Prep	32	W	N	Jones & McCloskey (13)	Wiley (10)
1/7	53	Villa Maria Academy	43	W	N	Jones (18)	Buczynski (18)
1/14		McDowell	POSTPONED		N		
	McDONALD'S CLASSIC					
1/17	50	Rochester (NY) McQuaid Jesuit	78	L	H	McCloskey (21)	O'Sullivan (20)
1/18	43	N. Bethesda (MD) Georgetown Prep	49	L	H	McCloskey (16)	Hibbert (25)
1/21	58	Strong Vincent	48	W	N	McCloskey (25)	Richmond (12)
1/23	59	McDowell	36	W	N	Jones (13)	Smiley (12)
1/28	51	George Junior Republic	52	L	H	McCloskey (12)	Bates (26)
2/1	78	Central	52	W	N	McCloskey (14)	Williams (23)
2/4	67	East	50	W	N	McCloskey (18)	Bean (14)
2/6	56	Mercyhurst Prep	27	W	N	McCloskey (15)	Wiley (12)
2/8	63	Villa Maria Academy	44	W	N	Jones (16)	Buczynski (20)
2/14	55	McDowell	62	L	N	McCloskey (26)	Smiley (19)
	METRO LEAGUE CHAMPIONSHIP PLAYOFF					
2/18	43	Strong Vincent	50	L	N	Jones & McCloskey (10)	Williams & Thomas (14)
DISTRICT 10 PLAYOFF						
2/22	40	McDowell	48(OT)	L	N	Jones (16)	Stoczynski (15)
	1504 (57.8)		**1273 (49.0)**			

Pos.	Player	Ht.	Prior School	Class	G(GS)	FG(3)	FT	Total	PPG	Career
G	Casey McCloskey (#52)	6'1"	St. Luke's	Sr.	24(24)	131(44)	62-85	368	15.3	648
G	Joe Jones (#25)	6'3"	Luther Memorial	Jr.	26(26)	112(15)	39-65	278	10.7	349
F	Billy Scholz (#34)	6'4"	St. George's	Jr.	26(26)	77(37)	17-29	208	8.0	208
G	Adam Dolak (#23)	6'1"	St. Luke's	Jr.	26(22)	62(11)	28-41	163	6.3	163
G	Cory Knight (#3)	5'9"	OLP	Soph.	24(3)	27(16)	12-16	82	3.4	82
F	Bob Barber (#33)	6'3"	St. Peter's	Sr.	24(8)	33(6)	9-16	81	3.4	110
F	Anthony Easterling (#30)	6'3"	Stephenson (GA) HS	Jr.	23(6)	26(2)	12-22	66	2.9	66
G	Tony DeMichele (#11)	5'10"	Sacred Heart	Jr.	24(2)	18(7)	17-21	60	2.5	60
G-F	Dejan Milasinovic (#15)	6'2"	Yugoslavia	Sr.	17	16(10)	5-9	47	2.8	47
C	Jon Vincent (#45)	6'3"	Wilson	Sr.	21(11)	20	5-8	45	2.1	45
F	Robbie Fugate (#10)	6'1"	St. George's	Jr.	11(1)	13(2)	5-11	33	3.0	33
C	Mike Daisley (#55)	6'6"	Girard	Sr.	15(1)	16	1-4	33	2.2	38
G-F	Greg Durr (#5)	6'0"	St. John's	Sr.	14	7(1)	3-12	18	1.3	20
G	Derek Candela (#13)	5'10"	OLC	Jr.	10	4	5-6	13	1.3	13
G	Dave Weber (#22)	5'10"	North East	Sr.	6	3	0-0	6	1.0	6
F	Phil Stewart (#31)	6'3"	Fairview	Sr.	9	1(1)	0-2	3	0.3	130

HIGHLIGHTS:

- Prep got off to a great start under second-year coach **Andy Sisinni**, before losing by two in the KSA final in Florida. The Ramblers were 8-0 and ranked as high as #6 in the state, but could only win half of its remaining games, with several losses close. Prep closed out disappointingly, with three season-ending losses—to Strong Vincent for the Metro League title and two to McDowell, the latter a District 10 semifinal.

- All Metro League games, the home battle against Franklin and the McDonald's Classic games were played at Gannon's Hammermill Center, while the home game versus George Junior Republic was contested at Behrend College's Junker Center.

- Senior **Dejan Milasinovic** was the second Prep basketball player to hail from the former Yugoslavia, the first being Rambler star **Sasha Pecarski** (1988-89).

- **Casey McCloskey's** turn-around three-pointer at the buzzer from 25 feet away gave Prep its thrilling 43-42 victory over Franklin (24-6). The Knights of esteemed coach **Bill Hager** would go on to the PIAA Class AAA Semifinals, where it lost to state runner-up Perry Traditional Academy.

- Prep came from 7 points down in the second half to win before a sold-out throng at perennial power New Castle (16-9). The Red Hurricanes had just been beaten the day before by **LeBron James**-led Akron (OH) St. Vincent-St. Mary, 82-48.

- Prep's second trip to the KSA tourney saw the Ramblers defeat a very small Christian school, Covenant Christian, and a very large technical school, Tampa Bay Tech, before falling to undefeated Brea-Olinda in their bracket final. Brea-Olinda won 20 straight before taking a defeat.

Junior Joe Jones averaged in double figures and was Second Team All-Metro.

- Prep blew a 10-point fourth quarter lead to Meadville (11-13) in the final of the Meadville Sertoma tourney, after defeating little Avella (3-20), a Class A squad from Washington County, the night before. It was the Bulldogs' first win against the Ramblers since 1989, with nine Orange & Black victories in between. Coach Sisinni was given a two-game suspension by the Prep administration for his vocal locker room outburst following that contest. Top assistant **Jim Stevenson** ran the team in Sisinni's absence. Next, against East (12-12), a 3-point shot at the end of regulation and a baseline jumper with four seconds left in overtime, both by **Andre Dawson**, helped the Warriors to a one-point victory.

- **Casey McCloskey** and **Joe Jones** both made the All-Tournament team at the Meadville Sertoma Christmas Tourney.

- Prep's tenacious defense held Mercyhurst (15-13) to just one FG in the second half of the 50-32 win.

- Villa Maria Academy (9-16) presented its boys' basketball squad into the Metro League and competed against Prep for the first time, easy victories for the Ramblers. The Victors, only a Class A team, were admitted to the Metro after performing well for several years (20-4 in 1999-2000) under future Prep coach **Mark Majewski**. Villa Maria was established in 1892 as an all-girls school by the Sisters of St. Joseph. Since the closing of St. Benedict Academy, VMA is the oldest Catholic high school in Erie. It was originally located at 8th and Liberty Streets before being moved to the westside in 1954. The school became co-educational in 1989 and first sponsored varsity basketball in 1992-93. On January 8, 2009, Villa announced a merger with Prep and no longer accepted male students.

- The Villa Victors had a genuine star in left-handed junior **Kevin Buczynski**, who, after the following season (2003-04), finished 3rd on the Erie area's all-time scoring chart with 1,616 points.

- Rochester McQuaid (27-1), rated #2 in the nation at season's end, showcased a spectacular shooting team, winning the 20th annual McDonald's Classic and later the New York state title. Pummeling the Ramblers with 15 three-pointers, the Knights continued their hot shooting in the McDonald's final, defeating NYC Rice, 69-63, to claim the crown. Prep couldn't contend with 7'2" **Roy Hibbert** of Georgetown Prep (20-6) in the consolation match. Hibbert had 25 points, 11 rebounds and 4 blocked shots, not to mention forcing the Ramblers to alter many shots with his long arms. He's believed to be Prep's tallest individual opponent ever.

- Of Prep's McDonald's opponents: Georgetown Preparatory

School, founded by the Jesuits in 1789, is a highly selective, prestigious, college preparatory boarding and day school and the oldest all-male school in the U.S. McQuaid Jesuit is also an all-male college prep school, founded 165 years after Georgetown Prep, in 1954.

- Prep got off to a horrible start against eventual D-10 champ George Junior Republic (16-11), trailing by 19 in the second quarter. The Ramblers fought back to tie the game in the final period, but were never able to take the lead. The Junior Republic went on to defeat McDowell in the district final.

- The first Prep-McDowell (20-7) contest on January 13 was postponed to January 23 because of the untimely death of esteemed McDowell athletic director **Dave Hanlon**. The Ramblers outscored the Trojans 34-9 in the fourth quarter on their way to a one-sided win in the rivals' first contest, as "Na Na, Hey, Hey" was the prevalent game-ending cheer. But Prep's biggest disappointments were the late season loss to McDowell to force a tie with Vincent for the Metro title, then the first round D-10 loss to the Trojans in overtime at Edinboro's McComb Fieldhouse. Though unknown at the time, it was the 150th meeting between Prep and McDowell.

- The Ramblers dumped Metro champ Vincent (22-7) twice during the regular season, but blew a 13-point first half lead to the Colonels in a playoff for the Metro crown at Mercyhurst's Campus Center. It was the second consecutive time the Ramblers lost a league title via the playoff route after being successful nine times in nine previous tries over the years. It was also the first SV win over Prep after the Ramblers had won 19 straight and 30 of the previous 31 contests between the two.

- Senior **Jon Vincent**, though just a part-time starter, led Prep in rebounding (4.6 RPG and blocked shots (1.0 PG).

- The final standings of the Erie Metro League, which for the first time included Villa Maria Academy:

	Won	Lost
*Vincent	11	2
Prep	10	3
McDowell	8	4
Central	2	10
East	6	6
Mercyhurst	5	7
Villa Maria	1	11

won championship playoff

- **Casey McCloskey** was named first team Metro All-Star and was honored for his stellar season as the *Erie Times-News* Metro League "Player of the Year." McCloskey led Prep in scoring, steals and assists. **Joe Jones**, who led the Ramblers in FG percentage (48.3%) was named Second team All-Metro.

- McCloskey led all scorers in the 29th City-County All-Star game, draining 22 points in a 76-55 City victory.

- **Casey McCloskey** was also winner of the James "Moe" Gross Award as Prep's most outstanding basketball player. He went on to star for four years at Allegheny College where he is tied for 19th place on the Gators' all-time scoring list with 1,056 points, and is 10th in three-point field goals with 326. McCloskey was appointed head basketball coach at Franklin High School beginning with the 2013-14 season. His cagers faced Prep in the 2015 District 10 playoffs.

- It was announced by the PIAA that Philadelphia's public schools would join and compete for state titles in all sports. It was expected that high school playoffs will have an entirely different look. Talks were also under way with Philadelphia's Catholic League schools, to which Prep AD **Bill Flanagan** stated: "I hope they join the party!"

2003 All-Opponent Team:

Ryan Dunford, Bishop Timon-St. Jude [Pitt, baseball]

Ben Maljovec, Warren [Syracuse, football]

James McNeil, Central [Buffalo St.]

Leon Ward, New Castle

Marcel Smith, Brea Olinda

Evan Moore, Brea Olinda [Stanford, football & basketball; NFL Packers, Browns, Seahawks, Eagles]

Mikel Kettler, Avella

Darius Hughes, Meadville

Matt Werle, Meadville [Juniata, volleyball]

Mathie Presley, East

Andre Dawson, East [Colgate, football]

Tyler Relph, McQuaid (NY Player of the Year) [West Virginia, St. Bonaventure]

Ryan Pettinella, McQuaid [Penn, Virginia]

Jack Leasure, McQuaid [Coastal Carolina]

Marty O'Sullivan, McQuaid [Fairfield]

Roy Hibbert, Georgetown Prep (hm, DC) [Georgetown; NBA Indiana Pacers]

James Bates, GJR

Tyrae Denmark, GJR [New Mexico JC]

Kevin Buczynski, Villa Maria Academy [Behrend]

Jovan Williams, Vincent

Sean Smiley, McDowell [Buffalo]

Sean Bach, McDowell

Tyler Stoczynski, McDowell [UMass-Lowell, Gannon]

Casey McCloskey, the Metro League "Player of the Year."

Sisinni Reign Over

Prep's 2003-04 staff, L to R: coaches Trigilio, Sisinni, Irwin.

2003-04 (18-7)

Coach: Andy Sisinni
Assistants: Mark Trigilio, Dave Irwin
Captains: Adam Dolak, Billy Scholz, Tony DeMichele, Joe Jonesi
Manager: Adam Grode

Date	PREP			Dec.	Loc.	High Scorer	Opponent
		FARRELL THANKSGIVING TOURNAMENT					
11/29	61	Kennedy Catholic	59	W	N	Jones (18)	Fuller (15)
11/30	59	Farrell	49	W	A	Knight (16)	Clay (19)
12/5	54	Strong Vincent	35	W	N	Jones (20)	Thomas (12)
12/10	84	Central	66	W	N	Scholz (25)	Roddy (22)
12/12	81	Villa Maria Academy	48	W	N	Dolak, Demski & Arrigo (10)	Buczynski (23)
		KSA CLASSIC (ORLANDO, FL)					
12/18	52	Las Vegas (NV)	54	L	N	Dolak & Scholz (15)	Howard (22)
12/19	76	Mars Area	35	W	N	Jones (15)	three w/ (7)
12/20	79	Erwin (TN) Unicoi County High	39	W	N	Knight (17)	Grindstaff (14)
12/23	76	East	56	W	N	Scholz (23)	Jones (21)
12/30	61	Athol Springs (NY) St. Francis	48	W	A	Jones & Dolak (16)	Dziduch (17)
1/3	53	Mercyhurst Prep	31	W	N	Dolak (18)	McFadden (10)
1/9	72	Warren	43	W	H	Dolak (13)	R. Johnson (11)
1/13	70	McDowell	71(OT)	L	N	Jones (23)	Stoczynski (30)
		McDONALD'S CLASSIC					
1/16	43	Mount Vernon (NY)	72	L	H	Haller (11)	Benjamin (23)
1/17	60	Philadelphia Cardinal Dougherty	78	L	H	Dolak (22)	Lowry (18)
1/20	67	Strong Vincent	59	W	N	Knight (29)	Thomas (26)
1/22	81	Central	64	W	N	Scholz (24)	Horton (19)
1/24	58	Villa Maria Academy	50	W	N	Jones (20)	Buczynski (23)
		HAMOT SPORTS MEDICINE CHALLEGE					
1/31	84	Buffalo (NY) Bishop Timon/St. Jude	45	W	H	Dolak (30)	Dunford (14)
2/3	51	East	64	L	N	Jones (13)	Jordan (17)
2/5	57	Mercyhurst Prep	52	W	N	Jones (20)	Moore (12)
2/7	55	George Junior Republic	52	W	A	Jones (21)	Roberts & Daniels (17)
2/13	50	McDowell	57	L	N	Haller (14)	Morrison (15)
2/17	64	Franklin	57	W	A	Mahoney (14)	Edmondson (15)
		DISTRICT 10 PLAYOFF					
2/23	52	George Junior Republic	59	L	N	Knight (12)	Roberts (20)
	1600 (64.0)		**1343 (53.7)**				

Pos.	Player	Ht.	Prior School	Class	G(GS)	FG(3)	FT	Total	PPG	Career
G	Joe Jones (#5)	6'1"	Luther Memorial	Sr.	25(25)	129(32)	46	336	13.4	685
G	Adam Dolak (#23)	6'1"	St. Luke's	Sr.	25(24)	116(24)	34	290	11.6	453
G	Cory Knight (#4)	5'10"	OLP	Jr.	24(23)	99(42)	41	281	11.7	363
F	Billy Scholz (#24)	6'3"	St. George's	Sr.	25(24)	80(32)	32	224	9.0	432
G	Nick Haller (#15)	5'10"	St. Luke's	Jr.	25(3)	40(23)	5	108	4.3	108
G	Brian Mahoney (#20)	5'11"	OLC	Jr.	23(4)	27(9)	42	105	4.6	105
F	Mark Demski (#12)	6'4"	Bl. Sacrament	Soph.	25(3)	33	14	80	3.2	80
G	Tony DeMichele (#31)	5'10"	Sacred Heart	Sr.	25(19)	28(6)	16	78	3.1	138
F	Mike Arrigo (#33)	6'2"	Sacred Heart	Jr.	11	13	12	38	3.5	38
F	Derek Brower (#30)	6'4"	Mount Carmel	Soph.	13	15	7	37	2.8	37
G	Alex Fatica (#11)	5'10"	OLC	Jr.	11	7	0	14	1.3	14
F	Dana Revel (#42)	6'2"	Meadville	Jr.	4	4	1	9	2.3	9

The 2004 Prep Ramblers. Front, L to R: Arrigo, Fatica, Mahoney, DeMichele, Knight, Haller; Back: Coach Sisinni, Asst. Coach Irwin, Revel, Brower, Demski, Scholz, Jones, Dolak, Asst. Coach Trigilio, Mgr. Grode.

HIGHLIGHTS:

Tony DeMichele, energetic starting guard.

- The Cathedral Prep Ramblers again got off to a great start, winning 11 of their first 12 under third-year mentor **Andy Sisinni**. Included was first place trophy in the Farrell Thanksgiving tourney and taking two of the three at the prestigious KSA Classic in Florida. The Ramblers had a well-stocked senior class with shooters **Joe Jones** and **Billy Scholz** and workhorses **Adam Dolak** and **Tony DeMichele**; and several promising juniors, most prominently **Cory Knight**.

- All Metro League games, the McDonald's Classic and the Warren home game were played at Gannon's Hammermill Center, while the Hamot Sports Medicine Challenge clash versus Bishop Timon-St. Jude was played at Behrend's Junker Center. The George Junior Republic games were played at Slippery Rock's Morrow Fieldhouse and Edinboro's McComb Fieldhouse, respectively.

- The PIAA took its cue from football and initiated its version of the basketball "mercy rule", beginning with the 2003-04 campaign. The new rule stated if a team leads by 40 or more points in the third quarter, or 30 or more points in the fourth quarter, a running clock goes into effect, with exceptions for timeouts, flagrant or technical fouls, injuries or to make correctable errors.

- Junior **Brian Mahoney**, in his first Prep varsity game, nailed a 3-point game-winner in the closing moments of the season opener against Kennedy Catholic (24-5) at the Farrell tourney. It was the first time in a dozen years and the last time ever the Ramblers and Eagles competed, with Prep holding a lopsided 10-0 edge over KC. Kennedy was ranked the number one Class A team in Pennsylvania the entire season, until being upset by Vincentian, 38-36, in the second round of PIAA tourney action. The Ramblers won the Farrell event the following night, defeating the hometown Farrell Steelers (12-12) behind seven 3-pointers.

- Though Prep had competed several times in football with St. Francis (8-15), its basketball victory over the Red Raiders was a first. St. Francis is an all-boys school about the size of Prep, located just south of Buffalo near Lake Erie and is operated under the jurisdiction of the Black Franciscans.

- Of Prep's KSA opponents: Las Vegas High School, founded in 1931, is the oldest school in its area and the Wildcats athletics programs are some of the best in Nevada; Mars (8-13) appears to put more emphasis in soccer than other sports; and Unicoi, which in the Cherokee language means "hazy" or "fog-like," is located in the subrange of the Blue Ridge Mountains, near the Nolichucky River and the Appalachian Trail.

- The 21st annual McDonald's Classic featured three of the nation's best teams, according to the National Prep poll. Included were Philadelphia Cardinal Dougherty (ranked #10, #1 in Pennsylvania), Mt. Vernon (#5), and Orlando (FL) Edgewater (#3). Prep was a huge underdog in the format, but fought hard and earned respect despite losing twice. *Parade Magazine* All-American **Darius Washington** (later starred at Memphis) scored the final points as Edgewater defeated Mt. Vernon (finished 27-3, # 7 in the nation according to *USA Today*) in the final, 69-67.

- Mount Vernon (27-3) lies on the border of the New York City borough of the Bronx. Mount Vernon is a perennial powerhouse in the State of New York as well as the nation. Northside Mount Vernon has a suburban look while Southside Mount Vernon has a very urban feel, nearly mirroring its border with the Bronx. The Knights went on to win the 2004 New York AA state and Federation titles. They were named the "Team of the Decade" in the Lower Hudson Valley.

- Cardinal Dougherty High School (24-5) was established in 1955 in the Olney section of Philadelphia's north side. By 1965 CDHS became the largest Catholic high school in the world with a student enrollment surpassing 6,000. There were 1,435 graduates each in the classes of 1969 and 1970 alone, and the school has over 40,000 alumni world-wide. Cardinal Dougherty's enrollment began to shrink because of one key factor—the demographics of the surrounding neighborhood changed and there were not enough eligible youth available to meet the required enrollment levels. Cardinal Dougherty sadly closed at the end of the 2009-10 academic year.

- Prep's lopsided win over Bishop Timon-St. Jude was highlighted by **Adam Dolak's** 30-point performance. It was the Ramblers' second straight Hamot Sports win over the Tigers and the third consecutive triumph over BTSJ since the beating the Tigers put on the Ramblers in 2001. It was also the last time Prep and BTSJ competed in basketball, with the Ramblers holding a 6-5 series edge.

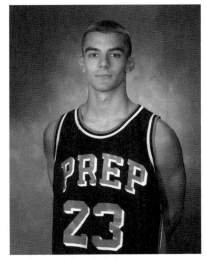

Workhorse Adam Dolak was a two-year starter for the Ramblers.

- Both Prep-McDowell (26-2) clashes were classics before a sellout crowds at Hammermill Center. The Trojans, 12-0 and ranked third in the state, led by as many as 16 in the first contest, but the 11-1 Ramblers battled back and forced overtime. Though ahead in OT, 68-64, Prep could not hold on and lost by one.

- McDowell was 22-1 and ranked second in PA at the time of the second game. Though Prep held McDowell star **Tyler Stoczynski**, the *Erie Times-News* "Player of the Year" who had 30 the first game, to only 8 points, the Ramblers blew a 6-point fourth quarter lead before succumbing by 7. The Trojans finished the regular season as the top-ranked team in Pennsylvania, only to lose to Pittsburgh Central Catholic, 65-61, in overtime in the second round of the PIAA playoffs. It was their only loss of the season to a Pennsylvania school. The Trojans had defeated Upper St. Clair in the first round, 62-45. (Note: **Tyler Stoczynski** is now the successful head coach at Highlands, a WPIAL AAA entrant. His four-year chart with the Rams has shown steady improvement: 1-21, 9-13, 13-13 and 23-6, with a spot in the PIAA state tourney's second round.)

- Though unknown at the time, East High's (11-12) triumph over Prep was the 150th meeting between the Warriors and Ramblers, with Prep on the long end of the series, 92-48.

- Prep's biggest wins of the season were the pair over Strong Vincent (18-10); the come-from-behind verdict against George Junior Republic (20-7); and the trouncing of Franklin (22-4), when the Ramblers hit 27 of 31 FT's. Both the GJR and Franklin battles were road contests.

- George Junior Republic abruptly ended Prep's season in the rematch in District 10 play, even though the Ramblers held star **Tyrae Denmark** to only 13 points. It was the second consecutive season the Ramblers failed to make the D-10 final. GJR clobbered New Castle in PIAA first round action, but lost to WPIAL champ Chartiers Valley in the second round.

- 2003-04 was the last year of Prep's affiliation in the "Metro League," in existence since the mid-70's. Prep enjoyed an affiliation in basketball with the Metro and its predecessor, the "City Series," since the 1942-43 season. The PIAA District 10 committee would realign all leagues in the area following the season, hoping to make better competition by grouping schools with others of similar size.

- The final standings of the Erie Metro League:

	Won	Lost
McDowell	12	0
Prep	9	3
Vincent	7	5
East	6	6
Central	3	9
Mercyhurst	3	9
Villa Maria	2	10

- Senior guard **Joe Jones** was named First Team Metro All-Star by the *Erie Times-News*. **Adam Dolak** won Second Team honors, while **Billy Scholz** and **Cory Knight** were Honorable Mention selections.

- Jones (8 points) and Dolak (6 points) helped lead the City to a close 67-64 victory over the County in the 30th annual All-Star game.

- **Joe Jones** was also recipient of the James "Moe" Gross Award as Prep's most valuable player. He went on to star at Edinboro

Joe Jones, MVP and First Team All-Metro. He went on to a spectacular career at EUP.

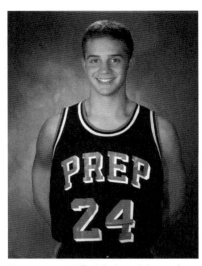

Two-year star Billy Scholz could score from inside or outside.

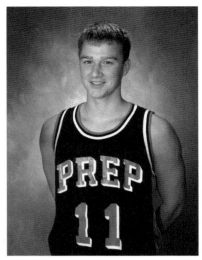

Junior guard Alex Fatica.

University (2006-09), where he ranks 6th on the Scots' all-time scoring chart with 1,465 points.

- Only 10 days after the conclusion of Prep's season, **Andy Sisinni** was fired by Prep AD **Bill Flanagan**, who cited "administrative differences" and the need to "move in a different direction with the program." Sisinni finished with a fine three-year record at Prep of 54-26, but was only 2-6 against arch-rival McDowell, with four of those losses in OT, and the Ramblers failed to win a playoff game in 2003 or 2004. The Ramblers won the Metro League title and advanced deep in the PIAA playoffs Sisinni's first season, 2001-02.

2004 All-Opponent Team:

Kevin Buczynski, Villa Maria [PSU-Behrend]

Kenny Howard, Las Vegas

J. T. Jones, East

Tyler Stoczynski, McDowell [UMass-Lowell, Gannon]

Cory Dziduch, St. Francis

Keith Benjamin, Mount Vernon [Pitt]

Dexter Gray, Mount Vernon [St. John's, Iona]

Jonathan Mitchell, Mount Vernon [Florida, Rutgers]

Kyle Lowry, Cardinal Dougherty (1st team all-state, Player of the Year) [Villanova; NBA Grizzlies, Raptors]

Shane Clark, Cardinal Dougherty [Villanova]

DeSean White, Cardinal Dougherty [Providence]

Tywaun Thomas, Vincent

Delvon Jordan, East

Terrence Roberts, George Junior Republic

Adam Morrison, McDowell

Tyrae Denmark, George Junior Republic [New Mexico JC]

Ramblers Advance to Final Four!

The new Prep coach, Brian Flanagan, former Ramblers and Loyola star.

2004-05 (26-5)

Coach: Brian Flanagan
Assistants: Mark Behringer, Jack Tufts
Captains: Nick Haller, Cory Knight, Brian Mahoney
Manager: Adam Grode

Date	PREP			Dec.	Loc.	High Scorer	Opponent
12/3	66	Cleveland (OH) St. Ignatius	73	L	H	Demski (12)	Parris (22)
12/4	54	Mercyhurst Prep	36	W	A	Knight (16)	UNREPORTED
12/7	64	Strong Vincent	51	W	N	Knight (20)	Henderson (11)
12/10	55	East	46	W	N	Kaiser (15)	Jones (14)
12/14	61	Fort LeBoeuf	45	W	H	Haller (10)	Whittelsey (13)
12/15	52	Franklin	48	W	H	Haller & Knight (16)	Urda (21)
	KREUL HOLIDAY CLASSIC (CORAL SPRINGS, FL)						
12/19	58	Queens (NY) Holy Cross	62(OT)	L	N	Knight (17)	Ogletree (20)
12/20	53	St. Petersburg (FL)	48	W	N	Haller & Demski (14)	Bowens & Boyle (10)
12/21	49	Marion (MS) Tabor Academy	42	W	N	Knight (15)	Rhines (12)
12/22	71	Hollywood (FL) South Broward	33	W	N	Kaiser (16)	Ferguson (10)
12/30	71	Warren	53	W	N	Knight (16)	C. Johnson (13)
1/4	60	Central	50	W	N	Haller (16)	Harrison (23)
1/7	84	George Junior Republic	44	W	H	Blazek (12)	Mack (14)
1/11	76	Corry	47	W	A	Demski (18)	Cirigliano (11)
	McDONALD'S CLASSIC						
1/14	58	Arlington (VA) Bishop O'Connell	79	L	H	Haller (12)	Ginyard (34)
1/15	46	Houston (TX) Westbury Christian	51	L	H	Knight (11)	Coleman (19)
1/19	74	McDowell	52	W	N	Knight (19)	Smiley (19)
1/21	56	Central	25	W	N	Brower & Knight (8)	Murphy (11)
1/27	67	Strong Vincent	62(OT)	W	N	Knight (22)	M. Williams (17)
1/29	60	Harborcreek	51	W	H	Matson (13)	Brine & McQueeney (15)
1/31	83	General McLane	77(OT)	W	A	Haller (29)	Stauffer (25)
2/2	68	East	48	W	N	Haller (15)	Thomas (15)
2/4	70	George Junior Republic	35	W	A	Demski & Pluta (12)	Gyton (11)
2/8	59	McDowell	39	W	N	Mahoney (14)	Smiley (15)
	DISTRICT 10 PLAYOFFS						
2/19	64	Central	49	W	N	Mahoney (18)	Hairston (15)
2/22	75	McDowell	66	W	N	Knight & Haller (21)	Harris (18)
	P.I.A.A. INTERDISTRICT PLAYOFFS						
2/26	83	Hollidaysburg	49	W	N	Knight (19)	Vite (12)
3/5	94	North Hills	64	W	N	Haller (22)	Wink (16)
3/9	78	Mt. Lebanon	74	W	N	Knight (25)	Kestler (31)
3/12	53	Pittsburgh Schenley	49	W	N	Kaiser (15)	Kennedy (20)
3/16	54	Lower Merion	65	L	N	Demski (14)	Williamson (22)
	2016 (65.0)		**1613 (52.0)**				

Pos.	Player	Ht.	Prior School	Class	G(GS)	FG(3)	FT	Total	PPG	Career
G	Cory Knight (#5)	5'10"	OLP	Sr.	31(31)	133(47)	94-125	407	13.1	770
G	Nick Haller (#15)	5'10"	St. Luke's	Sr.	30(30)	125(56)	39-50	345	11.5	447
G	Adam Kaiser (#30)	5'10"	St. Peter's	Jr.	31(20)	99(34)	30-43	262	8.5	262
F	Mark Demski (#12)	6'5"	Bl. Sacrament	Jr.	30(30)	106(3)	41-52	256	8.5	336
G	Brian Mahoney (#10)	5'11"	OLC	Sr.	31(24)	67(3)	70-99	207	6.7	308
F	Matt Pluta (#23)	6'3"	St. George's	Jr.	30(8)	68(7)	11-12	154	5.1	154
F	Earl Matson (#11)	6'3"	Sacred Heart	Jr.	31(11)	54(5)	21-27	134	4.3	134
G	Mark Blazek (#4)	6'0"	Harborcreek	Fr.	19	21(11)	24-27	77	4.1	77
C	Derek Brower (#31)	6'5"	Mount Carmel	Jr.	26(1)	32(2)	8-14	74	2.8	111
F	Marty Lindenberger (#50)	6'5"	Walnut Creek	Jr.	17	15	9-14	39	2.3	39
G	Mike Hubert (#24)	6'1"	OLC	Jr.	15	11(3)	7-10	32	2.1	32
F	Eric Schumacher (#52)	6'3"	Bl. Sacrament	Jr.	13	5	5-9	15	1.2	15
G	Alex Eaton (#33)	5'10"	Harding	Jr.	11	3	2-8	8	0.7	8

HIGHLIGHTS:

- **Brian Flanagan**, a 1970 graduate of Cathedral Prep, was named the new Rambler cage mentor after posting a spectacular four-year record of 88-7 as coach of the Prep JVs. Flanagan was also head coach at Fairview in 2000-01, where he led the Tigers to a 20-7 mark and the District 10 AA championship. He was also a star on Prep's 1970 city championship squad, and later played Division I ball at Loyola (MD) University.

- When his appointment was announced to the press, Coach Flanagan stated "the future is now...I've worked with all these players and I know their strengths and weaknesses...we're not in a situation pointing to two or three years away...we're going to win this year." Flanagan was speaking of his veteran guards **Cory Knight**, **Nick Haller** and **Brian Mahoney**, along with a host of juniors from his championship JV squad.

- Coach Flanagan's inaugural season was great, as Prep employed a new, aggressive, push-it-up-the-court style and a four-guard offense to garner its first 20-win season since 1997; won the first Region 6 crown; won three of four at the Kreul Classic to win the silver medal; won its first District 10 crown since 1998; and put together a thrilling playoff run to advance to the PIAA AAAA Final Four.

- Prep opened the season with a loss to renowned athletic power Cleveland St. Ignatius (18-5). It was the first battle between the Ramblers and the Wildcats since 1994-95 and only the second since 1947-48. St. Ignatius made it to the district final in Ohio state playoffs, only to lose to Solon, 53-50.

- Prep's schedule began to look radically different from years gone as the District 10 committee of the PIAA realigned school classifications, putting Prep into a little four-team AAAA league with the ridiculous name "Region 6," which included McDowell, Central and George Junior Republic. Gone was the Metro League and meaningful games with East and Vincent. Also meeting its demise was the Erie County League, which had been in existence since the 1920's. Former ECL and Metro League Class AAA schools were forced to schedule games within an AAA-AAAA setup in an effort to provide more fair competition between area teams, a strategy that has not proved successful over the years. On the Rambler schedule for the first time ever were contests against former ECL representatives Fort LeBoeuf and General McLane, as well as a renewal of the rivalries with Corry and Harborcreek. Prep hadn't played Corry in two decades and Harborcreek in three decades.

- All Prep home games, Region 6 games with Central and McDowell and the McDonald's Classic were played at Gannon's Hammermill Center. The Ramblers played at Mercyhurst Prep High School for the first time, while the Warren contest was played at Behrend College's Junker Center. Prep's game in Corry was the first time the Ramblers traveled to Erie County's second city since 1969. The play-in and first round PIAA games were contested at Edinboro's McComb Fieldhouse; the second round against Mount Lebanon was contested at Westminster College, Prep's first trip there since the 1987-88 playoffs.

- One of Prep's best wins was over powerful Franklin (26-2), the eventual D-10 AAA champion. The Knights only other loss was to Strong Vincent, 41-36, in the quarterfinals of the PIAA AAA tourney. Another great Prep win was the overtime victory over Vincent (23-8), which made it all the way to the AAA Western Final where it lost to Johnstown, 47-46. Unknown at the time, it was the 150th meeting between the Ramblers and the Colonels, with the Orange & Black holding an 88-62 edge.

- Also noteworthy was Prep's trio of convincing wins over McDowell (17-10). Unknown at the time, Prep's victory over McDowell on February 8th was the 100th time the Ramblers defeated the Trojans in basketball. An interesting sidelight of the Rambler-Trojan games was that head coaches **Brian Flanagan** of Prep and **Tom Hansen** of McDowell were both all-city classmates on Prep's 1970 city championship hoop squad.

- McDowell also showcased its all-time leading scorer, **Sean Smiley**, who finished his Trojan career with 1,426 points, 4th on the Erie area's all-time chart. Smiley caused a bit of a sensation when a **Mike Gallagher** photo of one of his dunks was featured in *Sports Illustrated*.

- Of Prep's new opponents at the Kreul Classic: Holy Cross is an all-male school of about 1,000 located in Flushing, Queens, and lists among its star basketball players from years gone by such notables as **Mike Riordan** and **Derrick Chievous**; St. Pete High was billed as "the nation's first million dollar high school" in 1898; Tabor Academy is a select private boarding school known mostly in athletics for its fine rowing teams; and South Broward is a marine science magnet school that has an excellent football program.

- The 22nd annual McDonald's Classic, called "the best 4-team tournament in the country" by **Eddie Oliver** of *HoopsUSA* magazine, featured three of the nation's best teams, including winner Memphis (TN) Fairley, with St. John's recruit **Anthony Mason, Jr.**, son of former NBA all-star **Anthony Mason**; Houston Westbury Christian, with 12 of the previous 14 private school state championships in Texas and superstars **Jeremy Barr** and **Sean Coleman**; and Arlington Bishop O'Connell (31-3), ranked #21 in the nation in 2004 and undefeated going into the tourney with North Carolina recruit **Marcus Ginyard**, who was spectacular in O'Connell's opening night win over Prep.

- The first Prep-General McLane (22-5) matchup ever was

a classic before a capacity crowd of 1,700 in Edinboro. The Lancers opened with a 16-3 lead, but the Ramblers battled back, taking the lead in the fourth quarter. McLane's **Ben Swank** then took an in-bounds lob pass from mid-court for a layup before the buzzer that sent the game into overtime at 64-all. Prep roared ahead in OT with **Nick Haller** scoring 9 of his 29 points, the most by a Rambler in a single game all season. McLane thus suffered only its fourth loss ever on its home court since its new gym opened in 1991! The Lancers finished 2005 losing to Vincent in the AAA Western Semifinals.

- 2004-5 was the first year Prep was not in the "City Series," "Big Seven," "Big Six," "Lake Shore League," "Section One" or "Metro League" (all variations of the local league) since the 1942-43 season. The Ramblers won every region game by a rout, winning the first-ever Region 6 title with a perfect record. The final standings:

	Won	Lost
Cathedral Prep	6	0
McDowell	4	2
Central	2	4
George Junior Republic	0	6

- The Ramblers won their first District 10 title in seven years, and followed with four impressive PIAA tournament wins to reach the PIAA AAAA Final Four. Opponents were unable to handle Prep's transition game and **Nick Haller, Cory Knight** and **Adam Kaiser** displayed spectacular 3-point shooting ability. The Hollidaysburg (18-8) and North Hills (17-11) routs were followed by thirteen 3-pointers and a great fourth quarter

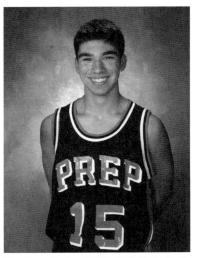

First Team Region All-Star Nick Haller had a remarkable 3-point shot.

Rambler rally to defeat Mt. Lebanon (22-8). Mt. Lebo led by 9 to start the final period, but the Rambler defense keyed a 20-3 run for an 8-point lead and perfect free throw shooting at the end preserved the Orange & Black victory.

- The win over Schenley (25-5) was particularly great, despite the fact it may have been the worst officiated game in Prep history. Prep staged a furious defensive comeback before a sold-out, packed throng at Slippery Rock, forcing three turnovers in the final minute to key an 8-0 run to shock the heavily-favored Pittsburgh city champions. The Spartans had overcome a 29-11 second quarter deficit and the loss of

Schenley's tough trio, L to R: DeJaun Blair, Jamal Bryant, D.J. Kennedy.

superstar **DeJuan Blair** to injury and had a 49-45 lead with a little more than a minute remaining in the game. With the score knotted at 49-49, an official called **Brian Mahoney** for palming the ball with 29.9 seconds remaining, possibly the worst call the Ramblers received in PIAA play since **Dan Sculley** was hacked in 1978.

- Lower Merion (25-9) finally derailed Prep's 14-game win streak, fourth longest in Prep history, before a packed throng in the state semifinal at State College High School. The Ramblers had a 6-point third quarter lead, but went on a dry spell the remainder of the contest, sinking but one-of-14 shots in the third period and only 6 of 32 for the second half. Lower Merion lost to Chester in the championship game at the Giant Center in Hershey, 74-61, but defeated Schenley, 60-58, in the state final the next year, 2006.

- Mercyhurst Prep's girls' team became the first Erie school to win back-to-back state championships with a 57-33 verdict over Jenkintown St. Basil Academy. The Lakers of two-time state "Coach of the Year" and former Prep hoopster **Randy Bowers** '71 were led by three Division I recruits: **Mashea Williams** (Penn State), **Chelsea Gordon** (Illinois) and **Erin Kerner** (Quinnipiac).

- Many changes occurred in the PIAA playoff system with the addition of a new District 12 for Philadelphia public schools. District 10 was no longer guaranteed two spots in the bracket, as both Districts 6 and 9 were added to a four-team sub-region bracket. Furthermore, there was no more "Western Bracket," as the state was now top-heavy with Quad-A teams from the East. Prep's "Final Four" entry was no longer considered a "Western Final."

Cory Knight, the District 10 "Player of the Year."

- Sharpshooting freshman **Mark Blazek** gave signs of big things to come by nailing his first 15 free throws of his career and not missing until the month of February. He finished remarkably, making 24 of 27 for the year for an 88.8%. As a team the Ramblers shot FTs at an excellent 73.7%, with some of the better shooters being **Matt Pluta** (91.7%), **Mark Demski** (78.8%), **Nick Haller** (78%), **Earl Matson** (77.7%) and **Cory Knight** (75.2%).

- Knight was lauded by Coach Flanagan: "Cory's transition game, from foul line to foul line, I have not seen anybody get it up the court better in all my years." Aside from his 13.1 PPG, Knight had 4.1 APG, 2.5 steals per game and a

Senior Brian Mahoney was Second Team Region All-Star.

3-point shooting percentage of 47.1%.

- For his efforts **Cory Knight** was named "Player of the Year" by the *Erie Times-News*, as well as first team All-District 10, the first year the *Times* had an All D-10 team. Knight and **Nick Haller** were named first team Region 6 All-Stars, while **Brian Mahoney, Mark Demski** and **Earl Matson** garnered second team honors.

- Knight was named Third Team All-State by the *Associated Press*, while Haller, Mahoney and Knight all played in the 31st annual City-County All-Star Classic.

- **Cory Knight** was also winner of the prestigious James "Moe" Gross Award for outstanding basketball ability, while **Adam Kaiser** won the "Ma" Kaiser Award as Prep's best athlete. Kaiser was only the second underclassman to ever win that honor. **"Ma" Kaiser**, who ran Prep's cafeteria for years and is considered by many to be the Prep's all-time biggest fan, was Adam's great-grandmother!

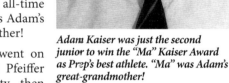

Adam Kaiser was just the second junior to win the "Ma" Kaiser Award as Prep's best athlete. "Ma" was Adam's great-grandmother!

- **Cory Knight** went on to star first at Pfeiffer (NC) University, then at Gannon University, where in 2008-09 he helped the Golden Knights set a team record of wins with a 30-4 slate. **Nick Haller** took his 3-point shooting wares first to John Carroll University, then to Penn State-Behrend.

2005 All-Opponent Team:

Robby Parris, St. Ignatius [Notre Dame, football]

Jude Urda, Franklin [IUP]

Nate Byham, Franklin (2nd team all-state) [Pitt, football; NFL 49ers, Buccaneers]

Kevin Ogletree, Holy Cross [Virginia, football; NFL Cowboys, Buccaneers, Lions]

Eric Harrison, Central

Marcus Ginyard, Bishop O'Connell [North Carolina]

Dave Neal, Bishop O'Connell [Maryland]

Rockwell Moody, Bishop O'Connell [St. Joseph's]

Sean Coleman, Westbury Christian [Tulsa, Blinn JC, Houston]

Jeremy Barr, Westbury Christian [Southern Cal]

Sean Smiley, McDowell [Buffalo]

Maurice "Moe" Williams, Vincent [Pitt, football]

Bobby Stauffer, General McLane (3rd team all-state) [Edinboro]

Drew Astorino, General McLane [Penn State, football]

Ben Swank, General McLane [Edinboro, football & basketball]

Preston Harris, McDowell [Gannon]

Geoff Kestler, Mt. Lebanon (3rd team all-state) [Princeton]

DeJuan Blair, Schenley (2nd team all-state) [Pitt; NBA Spurs, Mavericks]

D. J. Kennedy, Jr., Schenley [St. John's]

Jamaal "Onion" Bryant, Schenley [Broward (FL) CC]

Ryan Brooks, Lower Merion (2nd team all-state) [Temple]

Dan Capkin, Lower Merion [Gettysburg]

Garrett Williamson, Lower Merion (1st team all-state) [St. Joseph's]

Region, District 10 Champs!

2005-06 (22-6)

Coach: Brian Flanagan
Assistants: Mark Behringer, Jack Tufts
Captains: Mark Demski, Adam Kaiser
Manager: Adam Grode

Demski gets the tip at the start of the McDonald's Classic final versus Rufus King.

Date	PREP			Dec.	Loc.	High Scorer	Opponent
12/2	54	Mercyhurst Prep	48	W	H	Harris (25)	McFadden (14)
12/7	65	Franklin	62	W	A	Blazek (18)	Urda (17)
12/8	69	East	51	W	N	Harris (18)	W. Baker (12)
12/12	77	Athol Springs (NY) St. Francis	53	W	H	Harris (17)	Ross & Halbina (13)
12/16	61	Fort LeBoeuf	45	W	A	Harris (10)	Lathrop (22)
12/19	65	Chicago (IL) Quigley Prep	39	W	A	Demski (12)	Santella (12)
12/20	59	Oak Park (IL) Fenwick	61	L	A	Harris (21)	Humphrey (20)
12/22	54	Chicago (IL) St. Rita of Cascia	49	W	A	Harris (14)	Russell (19)
12/30	62	Warren	59	W	A	Harris (20)	C. Johnson (16)
1/3	80	Central	32	W	N	Pluta & Harris (10)	Caccavo (8)
1/6	53	McDowell	39	W	N	Harris (23)	Kimball (9)
1/10	44	Strong Vincent	46	L	N	Demski (14)	Evans (14)
		McDONALD'S CLASSIC					
1/13	88	Chester	84(OT)	W	H	Harris (33)	Govens (40)
1/14	48	Milwaukee (WI) Rufus King	65	L	H	Blazek (10)	Cotton & Harris (16)
1/17	72	George Junior Republic	57	W	H	Harris (16)	Adams (21)
1/20	79	Corry	22	W	H	Demski (12)	Flick (5)
1/27	67	Central	35	W	N	Harris (13)	Henderson (10)
1/28	81	Cleveland (OH) St. Ignatius	84(OT)	L	A	Harris (28)	Kirbus (28)
1/31	70	George Junior Republic	55	W	A	Harris (23)	Masten (19)
2/4	70	McDowell	54	W	N	Harris (22)	Keim (18)
2/7	63	Harborcreek	46	W	A	Kaiser (15)	Brine & Bowen (11)
2/10	55	Strong Vincent	39	W	N	Harris (26)	Evans (14)
2/13	63	General McLane	65	L	H	Kaiser (20)	Stauffer (22)
2/17	55	East	52	W	N	Blazek (12)	Baker (18)
		DISTRICT 10 PLAYOFFS					
3/1	61	McDowell	54	W	N	Harris (18)	Spronatti (17)
		P.I.A.A. INTERDISTRICT PLAYOFFS					
3/4	69	State College	68	W	H	Harris (24)	Meister (22)
3/11	77	Pittsburgh Central Catholic	66	W	N	Harris (30)	Berenato (33)
3/15	47	McKeesport	54	L	N	Harris (19)	Alexander (11)
	1808 (64.6)		**1484 (53.0)**				

Pos.	Player	Ht.	Prior School	Class	G(GS)	FG(3)	FT	Total	PPG	Career
G	Preston Harris (#42)	6'3"	McDowell HS	Sr.	28(28)	177(36)	109-155	499	17.8	499
F	Adam Kaiser (#30)	5'10"	St. Peter's	Sr.	28(28)	104(41)	43-53	292	10.4	554
F	Mark Demski (#20)	6'5"	Bl. Sacrament	Sr.	28(27)	108(12)	60-89	288	10.3	624
G	Mark Blazek (#4)	6'0"	Harborcreek	Soph.	26(26)	77(25)	59-78	238	9.2	315
F	Matt Pluta (#23)	6'3"	St. George's	Sr.	26(26)	63(3)	20-31	149	5.7	303
F	Derek Brower (#31)	6'5"	Mount Carmel	Sr.	22(4)	35(4)	23-30	97	4.4	134
G	Josh Licata (#12)	5'10"	Mount Carmel	Jr.	18	20(6)	12-17	58	3.2	58
C	Jeff Wisinski #52)	6'5"	Mount Carmel	Jr.	21	24	8-12	56	2.7	56
G	Mike Hubert (#24)	6'1"	OLC	Sr.	14	17(9)	10-11	53	3.8	85
F	G. T. Miller (#10)	6'2"	Villa Maria	Jr.	11	13(1)	3-4	30	2.7	30
G	Ryan Heidt (#11)	5'9"	Villa Maria	Jr.	26(1)	9(6)	5-11	29	1.1	29
C	Deon Harvard (#50)	6'6"	Holy Family	Fr.	7	4	3-9	11	1.6	11
G	Brendan Barber (#40)	6'1"	St. Peter's	Soph.	9	4	1-2	9	1.0	9
G	T. J. Fessler (#33)	6'2"	St. Luke's	Jr.	9	1	1-2	3	0.3	3

Prep's 2006 District 10 Champions. Front, L to R: Heidt, Blazek, Barber, Fessler, Mgr. Grode, Miller, Hubert, Kaiser, Licata; Back: Asst. Coach Tufts, Pluta, Demski, Wisinski, Harvard, Brower, Harris, Asst. Coach. Behringer, Coach Flanagan.

HIGHLIGHTS:

- **Brian Flanagan's** second year at the helm produced tremendous results. Led by transfer student **Preston Harris**, along with veterans **Mark Demski** and **Adam Kaiser**, Cathedral Prep won its second straight Region 6 and District 10 titles.

- Harris played two years on arch-rival McDowell's varsity, averaging 16 PPG and 6 RPG as a junior, before transferring to

Demski draws a foul.

Prep at the conclusion of the 2004-05 season. He was a First Team Region 6 All-Star in 2004-05. He immediately showed Orange & Black fans what he could do, scoring 25 points in the season-opening win over eventual District 10 AA champion Mercyhurst (21-8). It was the last time Prep and MPS played, the Ramblers having a 40-2 edge in the 22-year series.

- The opening win was followed by one of Prep's best triumphs of the season at powerful Franklin (27-5), which finished the season as PIAA Class AAA state champs. With the Knights looking for a last shot, **Mark Blazek** stole the ball with four seconds remaining, drove down the court, then hit a 22-footer at the buzzer to seal the win in the much anticipated battle before an overflow crowd in Franklin.

- The Prep team made an interesting trip to Chicago in December, playing three away games in four days. Of the Ramblers' new Chicago opponents: Archbishop Quigley Prep (10-12) was a private high school seminary for those aspiring to the priesthood, located in downtown Chicago, that was closed by its Diocese in 2007; Fenwick (18-9), a suburban co-ed school, is the only high school in the United States run by the Dominican Friars. It lists among its alumni **Johnny Lattner**, the 1953 Heisman Trophy winner from Notre Dame; and St. Rita of Cascia (9-16), an all-male school of about 750 students, located on the southwest side of

Senior guard Mike Hubert was an outside marksman and a 91% free throw shooter.

Chicago and was one of the eight original founders of the Chicago Catholic League in 1912.

- The final standings in Region 6:

	Won	Lost
Cathedral Prep	6	0
McDowell	3	3
George Junior Republic	3	3
Central	0	6

- All Prep home games, the Region 6 contests against Central and McDowell, the McDonald's Classic, the D-10 final and the PIAA play-in game against State College were all played at Gannon's Hammermill Center. The PIAA first round encounter was played at McComb Fieldhouse, while the second round game versus McKeesport was staged at Sharon High School.

First Team Region All-Star Mark Demski brought the crowd to its feet with a resounding dunk against McDowell.

- Prep handily defeated arch-rival McDowell (10-17) three times, with **Preston Harris** leading the way, despite constant taunting from his former McDowell schoolmates. "I heard the chants," stated Harris to the *Erie Times-News*. "It's only fuel to play a lot harder. We got the wins and that's all that matters!" A great play occurred in the series when **Mark Demski** took a pass, dribbled around his back through three Trojan defenders down the left baseline, then put through a resounding slam dunk that brought the crowd to its feet.

- The 23rd annual McDonald's Classic featured some of the nation's best teams, including champion Rufus King International (21-4), five-time Wisconsin state champions and

a *USA Today* Super 25 pre-season pick; Mount Vernon, eight-time New York state champions, ranked #25 in the nation; and defending PIAA state champion Chester (26-8, five times PIAA state champs), whom the Ramblers shocked in an overtime thriller after squandering a 17-point second half lead. This despite the Clippers' **Darrin Govens** incredible 40-point effort, the most scored by a Prep opponent in 32 years. Harris had a career high of 33 on remarkable 13-for-17 shooting, while Demski and Kaiser combined for 33 and **Matt Pluta** added 13 to lead the assault. Rufus King, which beat Prep in the final, is considered the top-rated public school academically in the state of Wisconsin.

- Prep's 57-point margin over Corry (6-18), 5th largest all-time, was the Ramblers' biggest point spread since the 1969-70 season when Coach Flanagan led the Ramblers to a 100-42 rout of Jamestown (NY).

Starting forward Matt Pluta was also a star in water polo for the Ramblers.

- One disappointment included the 2-point loss to Vincent (21-7), the Colonels' second win over Prep in a dozen years. The Ramblers nearly erased an 18-point deficit, but fell short on a last-second **Matt Pluta** shot that just missed the mark. The Ramblers crushed SV in the rematch behind Harris' 26 as he crossed the 1,000 point plateau for his career at McDowell and Prep.

- Other downsides were the 40-foot 3-pointer by **Robbie Parris** at the buzzer when the Ramblers lost in OT at St. Ignatius (13-9); and the home loss to General McLane (26-5) when **Bobby Stauffer** drove the floor and scored with 0.7 seconds left on the clock. Lancer players directly taunted Prep fans at the game's conclusion. GM made it to the PIAA Final Four, only to lose to state titlist Franklin.

- Probably the best Rambler victory of the season was the PIAA playoff thriller over State College (19-8). The Little Lions got out to a 19-3 lead and led by 6, with the ball, with only 1:30 remaining. **Preston Harris** nailed a 24-footer at 0:14 for Prep's only lead of the game, then **Adam Kaiser** drew a charge with just 4 seconds left for the clutch play of the afternoon.

- Prep then made quick work of Pittsburgh Central Catholic (13-15) behind Harris' 30 points and a spectacular effort by **Mark Demski**, who cashed in with 14 points, 13 rebounds and 2 blocked shots.

- Prep could not match athleticism of

Pluta slices through against Schenley.

McKeesport (22-8) in the second round and lost a heartbreaker. Losing 46-41 with less than three minutes remaining, **Adam Kaiser** and **Mark Blazek** both nailed 3-pointers to give the Ramblers a 47-46 lead at 1:57. There **Devon Alexander** of the Tigers was fouled on a put-back bucket at 1:33. He sank the free throw and the Ramblers could not recover. McKeesport then lost in the quarterfinals to Schenley, which made it to the state championship game where it lost to Lower Merion, 60-58.

Senior Derek Brower, spot starter and reliable 6th man.

- **Preston Harris** finished one point shy of 500, making it the 8th best single season point total in Prep history and the best since **Jed Ryan's** record-breaking season in 1994-95. Demski led the Ramblers in rebounding at 8 RPG, while Kaiser led the squad in 3-point shooting and free throw percentage at 81.1%. Other top free throw shooters included reliable senior 6th man **Derek Brower** (76.7%) and Blazek (75.6%).

- **Preston Harris** was named first team All-District 10 and Region 6 Player of the Year by the *Erie Times-News*. Harris and **Mark Demski** were both named First Team Region 6 All-Stars, while **Adam Kaiser**, **Mark Blazek** and **Matt Pluta** all garnered Second Team honors.

Preston Harris transferred from McDowell to Prep for his senior season and was named D-10 "Player of the Year."

- Harris was further named third team all-state by the *Associated Press*, while Harris, Kaiser and Demski all played in the annual City-County all-star classic. Coach Flanagan was mentor of the city squad, which won handily, 87-60.

- **Preston Harris** was also winner of the James "Moe" Gross Award as Prep's most valuable player. Both he and **Mark Demski** went on to play for the Gannon University Golden Knights. **Matt Pluta** received a scholarship to Queens College—for water polo! He did come back, however to be the offensive star in the pool for Penn State-Behrend.

- **Adam Kaiser** became only the second Prepster to win the prestigious "Ma" Kaiser Award twice as the Ramblers' finest all-around athlete. **"Ma" Kaiser**, known as Prep's greatest fan, was Adam's great-grandmother! Kaiser went on to star at Penn State-Behrend, where he started three years and was team captain his senior year. He holds the Lions' career record for 3-pointers and crossed the 1,000 point plateau his senior year. Kaiser is now Prep's junior varsity coach after serving for a year on Behrend's coaching staff.

2006 All-Opponent Team:

Jude Urda, Franklin (1st team all-state) [IUP]

Xavier Humphrey, Fenwick [Winona St.]

Roshawn Russell, St. Rita [North Park]

Kyle Smith, St. Rita [Danville (IL) Area CC, Alaska-Fairbanks]

Craig Johnson, Warren

Brandon Evans, Vincent

Darrin Govens, Chester (1st team all-state) [St. Joseph's]

Shakiyl Reid, Chester [Harcum (PA) JC]

Troy Cotton, Rufus King (2nd team all-state, WI) [UW-Green Bay]

Leneal Harris, Rufus King [Frank Phillips (TX) JC, Wisconsin-Parkside]

Devon Adams, GJR

Rudy Kirbus, St. Ignatius [John Carroll]

Robbie Parris, St. Ignatius [Notre Dame, football]

Sean Masten, GJR

Garrett Keim, McDowell

Bobby Stauffer, General McLane (2nd team all-state) [Edinboro]

Drew Astorino, General McLane [Penn State, football]

Willie Baker, East

Zach Spronatti, McDowell [Behrend]

Eric Meister, State College [Holy Cross]

Kevin Scholly, State College [Shippensburg, baseball]

Nate Stupar, State College [Penn State, football; NFL 49ers, Jaguars]

Joe Berenato, Pittsburgh Central Catholic [California (PA)]

Devon Alexander, McKeesport [Point Park]

Prep's finest all-around athlete, Adam Kaiser. He starred at PSU-Behrend and is now the Rambler JV coach.

Region, D-10 Champs—Again!

2006-07 (23-5)

Coach: Brian Flanagan
Assistants: Mark Behringer, Jack Tufts
Captains: Josh Licata, Ryan Heidt, Jeff Wisinski
Manager: Mark Wagner

Brian Flanagan cemented his reputation as a great coach with Prep's third straight impressive playoff run.

Date	PREP			Dec.	Loc.	High Scorer	Opponent
		MIDLAND TIP-OFF TOURNAMENT					
12/1	63	Blackhawk	50	W	N	Licata (19)	Childs (31)
12/2	62	Mt. Lebanon	53	W	N	Licata (21)	Phillips (24)
12/12	70	East	61	W	N	Licata (22)	Rogers (22)
12/16	47	Meadville	43	W	H	Blazek (10)	Barton (16)
12/22	52	Hickory	61	L	A	Licata (13)	Szabo and Durisko (11)
		GULFSHORE SHOOTOUT (NAPLES, FL)					
12/27	47	Mount Dora (FL)	58	L	N	Licata (18)	Labelle (27)
12/28	70	Davie (FL) Western	45	W	N	Licata (19)	Todd (14)
12/29	61	Coral Gables (FL) Gulliver Prep	49	W	N	Blazek (17)	Sealy (15)
12/30	74	Englewood (FL) Lemon Bay	56	W	N	Wisinski (21)	Reed (17)
1/3	53	Strong Vincent	45	W	N	Blazek (25)	Lofton (19)
1/5	60	Corry	42	W	A	Licata (18)	Anderson (12)
1/9	72	Central	33	W	N	Blazek (12)	A. Lockett & Dunn (6)
		McDONALD'S CLASSIC					
1/12	53	Solon (OH)	63	L	H	Blazek (17)	Lauderdale (18)
1/13	64	Los Angeles (CA) Westchester	60	W	H	Blazek (15)	Suttle (18)
1/17	70	George Junior Republic	51	W	H	three with (10)	Cantino (28)
1/20	49	McDowell	41	W	N	Blazek (13)	Loomis (14)
1/23	70	East	59	W	N	Blazek (16)	Thomas (27)
1/27	75	Harborcreek	55	W	H	Blazek (24)	Bowen (14)
1/30		Oil City (CANCELLED—SNOW)			A		
2/2	83	General McLane	81(OT)	W	A	Blazek (32)	Wreh-Wilson (23)
2/7	60	Central	49	W	N	Wisinski (29)	Marley-Ellis (15)
2/10	56	Strong Vincent	49	W	N	Wisinski (23)	Williams & Barney (13)
2/15	60	George Junior Republic	49	W	A	Licata (15)	Cantino (20)
2/16	53	McDowell	57(OT)	L	N	Blazek (22)	Spronatti (20)
		DISTRICT 10 PLAYOFFS					
2/24	63	East	36	W	N	Blazek (15)	Crockett (13)
2/28	43	Strong Vincent	41	W	N	Blazek (11)	Williams (9)
		P.I.A.A. INTERDISTRICT PLAYOFFS					
3/3	73	State College	52	W	N	Blazek (24)	Kerr (18)
3/10	46	Pine-Richland	36	W	N	Blazek (20)	Duerr (17)
3/14	53	Moon Area	62	L	N	Blazek (16)	Dowdell (19)
	1702 (60.8)		**1437 (51.3)**				

Pos.	Player	Ht.	Prior School	Class	G(GS)	FG(3)	FT	Total	PPG	Career
G	Mark Blazek (#4)	6'0"	Harborcreek	Jr.	25(24)	130(28)	86-113	374	15.0	679
G	Josh Licata (#30)	6'0"	Mount Carmel	Sr.	28(28)	115(25)	86-122	341	12.2	399
C	Jeff Wisinski #42)	6'5"	Mount Carmel	Sr.	26(26)	118	47-70	283	10.9	339
G	Steve Piotrowicz (#3)	5'8"	OLC	Jr.	25(20)	59(21)	56-76	195	7.8	195
G	Ryan Heidt (#11)	5'9"	Villa Maria	Sr.	28(28)	54(25)	46-63	179	6.4	208
G	Mike Bukowski (#25)	6'1"	St. Peter's	Jr.	26(1)	41(8)	17-23	107	4.1	107
F	G. T. Miller (#21)	6'3"	Villa Maria	Sr.	28(11)	23(9)	13-18	68	2.4	98
F	Dan Marz (#34)	6'4"	Villa Maria	Jr.	21	25	6-13	56	2.7	56
F	Brendan Barber (#40)	6'2"	St. Peter's	Jr.	18(2)	12	11-23	35	1.9	44
G	Tim Mikotowicz (#22)	6'0"	St. Luke's	Jr.	12	7(4)	6-10	24	2.0	24
F	T. J. Fessler (#33)	6'3"	St. Luke's	Sr.	18	5(2)	0-2	12	0.7	15
G	Dave Galleher (#35)	5'11"	OLP	Jr.	12	7	0-3	14	1.2	14
G	Merle Page (#14)	6'0"	St. John's	Soph.	9	6	2-6	14	1.6	14

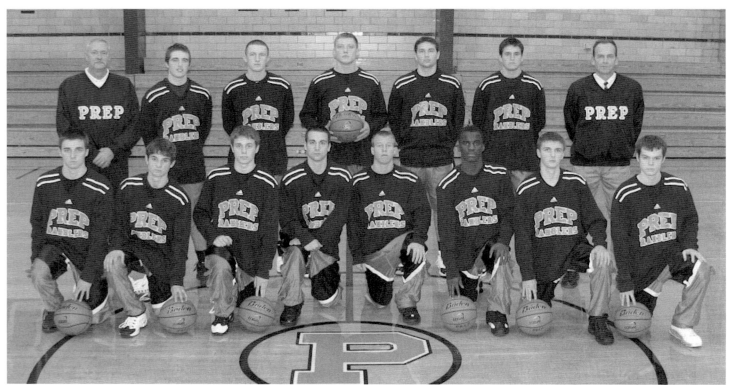

Prep's 2007 District 10 Champions. Front, L to R: Bukowski, Piotrowicz, Mikotowicz, Licata, Heidt, Page, Blazek, Gallaher; Back: Asst. Coach Behringer, Barber, Miller, Wisinski, Marz, Fessler, Coach Flanagan.

HIGHLIGHTS:

- **Brian Flanagan's** third year at the Cathedral Prep helm again produced excellent results with what was usually a four-guard offense. Led by junior veteran **Mark Blazek**, the Ramblers won their third straight region title (this time re-aligned as Region 7), third straight District 10 title and further won a pair of PIAA playoffs games before getting doused by Moon Area in the second round. Prep's cast of seniors, including center **Jeff Wisinski**; guards **Josh Licata** and **Ryan Heidt**; and forwards **G.T. Miller** and **T.J. Fessler**, were all relatively untested but finished over-achieving in a big way.

- The season started off with a bang as Prep won the Midland tip-off tourney with impressive wins over Blackhawk (16-11) and Mt. Lebanon (18-10). Blackhawk, actually located in Chippewa, PA, is noted for producing all-state basketball stars **Dante Calabria, Sean Miller** (current head coach at Arizona) and **Ryan "Archie" Miller** (current head coach at Dayton).

- Late in the season the Mt. Lebo team became embroiled in controversy when star junior guard **Shane Phillips** sent a profanity-laced e-mail to his coach, **Joey David**, informing him that several teammates were at a drinking party where several were cited by the police. David then suspended Phillips for the first game of the WPIAL playoffs for sending the e-mail, but took no action against the others involved with alcohol! David's father then sent the e-mail and explained his son's position to the two Pittsburgh newspapers, the *Post-Gazette* and the *Tribune-Review*, and the matter became a full-blown storm in the tony suburb. As a postscript, Phillips transferred to and starred at Wheeling (WV) Central Catholic for his senior season, where he was named first team all-state and further led the Maroon Knights to the West Virginia state championship.

- Prep's first loss of the season was at Hickory (18-8), where the Hornets finished 14-0 on their home court. It was the first contest between the Ramblers and Hornets in a quarter-century, since 1982.

- Prep gained the consolation prize at the 11th annual Gulfshore Shootout, by winning a trio of contests after losing the opener. It has been Prep's only trip to the Gulfshore, which started in 1997 and has a 16-team format. Of the Ramblers' Gulfshore opponents: Mount Dora (19-8) won the Shootout; Western's (10-15) mascot is the Wildcat and the official colors are Black

An irate General McLane fan doesn't like the call...

and is miffed as the Ramblers celebrate a dramatic overtime victory...

he decides he's had enough...

and realizes it is futile.

Mike Bukowski goes up high for a bucket against the Fightin' Planets.

and "Vegas Gold;" Gulliver Prep (15-10) originally started in 1926 and was for students from New England that were wintering in South Florida; and Lemon Bay (19-9), mascot "Manta Rays," was featured in the second season of *The Principal's Office*, a reality television show on TruTv.

• The 24th annual McDonald's Classic featured some of the nation's best teams, including undefeated champion Lakewood St. Edward (25-1), featuring 6'8" superstar **Delvon Roe**. St. Ed's was ranked as high as #8 in the nation until upset by Cincinnati Moeller in the Ohio Division I state semifinal playoffs; Ohio power Solon (19-5), a southeastern suburb of Cleveland, which Prep hung tough against on night one; and perennial Los Angeles powerhouse Westchester (26-7), ranked #10 in the nation by *USA Today*. The Ramblers pulled a huge

Senior all-star Josh Licata scores over Solon's Dallas Lauderdale.

Blazek leaves a trio of Moon defenders in his wake.

G.T. Milller, with some intense defense against Solon in the McDonald's Classic.

upset over the Comets for consolation honors, canning 19 of 20 free throws in the process.

- One of Prep's best triumphs was at #1 AAA state-ranked rival General McLane (28-4), which eventually won the PIAA Class AAA state championship. In that one **Mark Blazek** hit a last-second buzzer beater after a great pass from workhorse **Ryan Heidt** to dump the powerful Lancers in overtime on their sold-out home court. Hundreds of fans watched the fierce battle on closed-circuit TV that was set up in the GM cafeteria. McLane thus suffered only its 6th loss ever on its home court since its new gym opened over a quarter-century before, in 1991. And Prep was then 2-0 in that gym!

- Other great Prep wins were the hard-fought triumph over arch-rival McDowell (16-9); a trio of comeback victories over Strong Vincent (18-8), particularly the defensive struggle for the D-10 crown; and a pair of PIAA tourney wins. The season's biggest disappointments included the overtime loss to McDowell after erasing a 17-point second half deficit and the loss to Moon Area in the state tourney.

- The final standings of Region 7:

	Won	Lost
Cathedral Prep	9	1
Strong Vincent	8	2
McDowell	7	3
George Junior Republic	3	7
East	3	7
Central	0	10

- The big play in the PIAA play-in game against State College (12-12) was **Josh Licata's** tip-in at the very end of the third period, which ignited a 31-7 fourth quarter run for the Orange & Black. Prep then stole Pine-Richland's (18-9) reputation as the state's best defensive team in first round action, holding the Rams' leading scorer to just two points. And this was without the services of star center **Jeff Wisinski**, who had aggravated a stress fracture in his foot the week before in gym class. It must be noted that Pine-Richland's baseball, girls' soccer, hockey, gymnastics, and volleyball teams were all state champions in the 2005-2006 school year.

Prep grads Jim LeCorchick '65 and Carl Lombardo '79 protect rowdy Rambler students from interfering General McLane officials.

Wisinski with a huge block on McDowell's Glen Conner, as Licata offers help.

- Prep went stone cold from the floor in the loss to well-balanced Moon (25-5), the 6th-seeded team from District 7. The Ramblers went over nine minutes in the 2nd and 3rd periods without scoring and netted but 21 points until the fourth quarter. Though down by 17 early in the final frame, Prep never gave up and never let the Tigers relax, nailing eight

3-pointers in the final 6:41. Moon next lost in the quarterfinals to eventual state champ Pittsburgh Schenley, 73-59.

- All Prep home games, the McDonald's Classic and the D-10 final against Vincent were at Gannon's Hammermill Center. The D-10 semifinal against East and the PIAA first round games were played at Edinboro's McComb Fieldhouse; the PIAA play-in game versus State College was played at General McLane High School; and the second round loss to Moon Area was played at Slippery Rock's Morrow Fieldhouse.

- **Josh Licata** was the leading rebounder for the Ramblers with 179 (6.4 RPG), while Blazek lead the team with 37 steals.

- **Mark Blazek** was named first team All-District 10 by the *Erie Times-News*. Blazek and **Jeff Wisinski** were named First Team Region 7 All-Stars, while **Josh Licata**, who really came on strong for his senior year, and **Steve Piotrowicz** garnered Second Team honors. Blazek was also honored as Region 7's "Co-Player of the Year" with George Junior Republic's **Chris Cantino**.

- **Jeff Wisinski**, who missed the last two games of the season, made a return for the 33rd annual City-County All-Star Classic, joining teammates **Ryan Heidt** and **Josh Licata**. The County prevailed, however, 84-70, as Licata scored eight, Wisinski two and Heidt one.

- **Jeff Wisinski** went on to perform at Penn State on the track & field team as a discus thrower.

- **Mark Blazek** was also winner of the James "Moe" Gross Award as Prep's best player, only the second underclassman ever to win the honor.

2007 All-Opponent Team:

Antoine Childs, Blackhawk (1st team all-state, 2008) [Western Carolina]

Shane Phillips, Mt. Lebanon [South Carolina]

Gil Rogers, East

Jeremy Thomas, East

Aaron Barton, Meadville [Pitt-Titusville]

Brian Szabo, Hickory [Washington & Jefferson, baseball]

Matt Durisko, Hickory [Mercyhurst]

Scott Labelle, Mount Dora [Thiel]

Jordan Reed, Lemon Bay

Darryl Lofton, Vincent

Dallas Lauderdale, Solon [Ohio State]

Anthony Burns, Solon

Jarred DuBois, Westchester [Loyola Marymount, Utah]

Chris Cantino, George Junior Republic [Palm Beach State, Xavier (OH)]

Blidi Wreh-Wilson, General McLane [Connecticut, football; NFL Titans]

Shawn Walker, General McLane (1st team all-state) [Edinboro, football]

Bobby Stauffer, General McLane (3rd team all-state) [Edinboro]

Drew Astorino, General McLane [Penn State, football]

Rakim Marley-Ellis, Central [Gannon, football]

Maurice "Moe" Williams, Vincent [Pitt, football]

Zach Spronatti, McDowell [Behrend]

Jordan Bukowski, McDowell [Mercyhurst, football]

Andrew Kerr, State College [Princeton, football]

Eric Duerr, Pine-Richland [Case-Western Reserve]

Andy Dowdell, Moon Area [Villanova, rowing]

Brian Walsh, Moon Area [Xavier (OH)]

Chris Jeannot, Moon Area [New Hampshire, football]

Keir Jeter, Moon Area [Edinboro, football]

Shooter par excellence Mark Blazek sinks a free throw against Pine-Richland.

Miller hits a jump shot from the corner, as Ofcr. D.J. Fuhrman observes from his usual perch.

Ryan Heidt takes an open "three" from the corner as G.T. Miller implores him not to shoot.

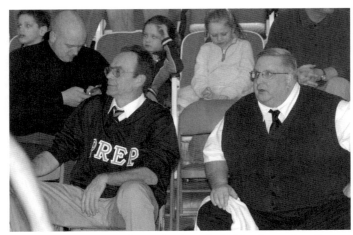

Coach Brian Flanagan and trusted assistant Jack Tufts observe the action, while a front row fan plays Candy Crush.

Piotrowicz takes a "three" as Coach Flanagan lines it up.

Hammermill Center regulars Ernie DiSantis, Ron DiSantis, Bob Achille, Tim Boetger and Bruce Stone watch as "Pio" works against McDowell.

Licata gets past the Trojans for two as Miller follows.

Ryan Heidt gets good advice from veteran coach Mark Behringer.

Brendan Barber sinks a free throw in the Pine-Richland state playoff win.

Senior T.J. Fessler, definitely serious about defense.

Heidt suffocates GM's Drew Astorino.

MVP Mark Blazek nails a perfect 3-pointer against his old pals from Harborcreek.

All-star Ryan Heidt adds to the lead over McDowell.

Wisinski for two in the rout of the Junior Republic.

Coach Flanagan with some worthy instructions to the starting five.

First Team Region all-star Jeff Wisinski scores in the big win at McLane.

Flanagan Retires with Best Winning Percentage Among Prep Coaches!
Rival McDowell Spoils D-10 Hopes!

2007-08 (18-8)

Coach: Brian Flanagan
Assistants: Mark Behringer, Jack Tufts
Captains: Mark Blazek, Steve Piotrowicz

The coach awards Blazek a plaque for crossing 1,000 points.

Date	PREP		Dec.	Loc.	High Scorer	Opponent
	MIDLAND TIP-OFF TOURNAMENT					
11/30	47	Blackhawk	57	L	A	Piotrowicz (14)	Childs (27)
12/1	66	Beaver Falls	60	W	A	Thrower (19)	Phillips (20)
12/4	65	Harborcreek	41	W	A	Thrower (17)	Pawlak (10)
12/6	62	East	59	W	N	M. Blazek (22)	Rogers (24)
12/11	59	Meadville	44	W	A	Piotrowicz (14)	Cowan & Hamilton (9)
	TOM KEENAN MEMORIAL CLASSIC (BUFFALO, NY)					
12/14	66	Buffalo (NY) Grover Cleveland	70	L	A	Thrower (20)	T. Edwards (21)
12/15	64	Cleveland (OH) St. Ignatius	62(OT)	W	A	Spoden (16)	Becker (18)
12/16		Niagara (NY) Catholic (CANCELLED)			N		
12/18	80	Hickory	57	W	H	M. Blazek & Thrower (17)	Shepard (16)
12/29	52	Massillon (OH) Washington	57	L	A	M. Blazek (22)	J. Turner (16)
1/2	67	Corry	42	W	H	Thrower (13)	Mike Anderson (18)
1/4	73	Central Tech	51	W	N	M. Blazek (18)	Altland (18)
1/8	68	Strong Vincent	62	W	N	Thrower (20)	Crosby (21)
1/10	67	George Junior Republic	51	W	A	Bukowski (13)	Lennon (15)
1/12	65	McDowell	61	W	N	M. Blazek (21)	Spronatti (15)
1/15	83	East	56	W	N	M. Blazek (19)	Ratliff (26)
	McDONALD'S CLASSIC					
1/18	63	New York City (NY) Rice	87	L	H	Thrower (14)	Fouch (26)
1/19	52	Lakewood (OH) St. Edward	60	L	H	Thrower & Spoden (14)	Pritchard (15)
1/22	70	Oil City	47	W	H	M. Blazek (19)	Carson (24)
1/26	72	General McLane	62	W	H	M. Blazek (32)	Walker (21)
1/29	70	Central Tech	40	W	N	Thrower (15)	Marley-Ellis (14)
2/2	69	Strong Vincent	57	W	N	Thrower (18)	Pennamon (20)
2/4	81	George Junior Republic	46	W	H	M. Blazek (16)	Floyd (17)
2/8	39	McDowell	62	L	N	Thrower (17)	Loomis (20)
	DISTRICT 10 PLAYOFFS					
2/16	65	East	56	W	N	Spoden (18)	Rogers (15)
2/20	50	McDowell	64	L	N	Piotrowicz (17)	Spronatti (28)
	P.I.A.A. INTERDISTRICT PLAYOFF					
2/23	58	State College	60	L	N	M. Blazek (21)	St. Andrews (21)
	1673 (64.3)		**1471 (56.6)**				

Pos.	Player	Ht.	Prior School	Class	G(GS)	FG(3)	FT	Total	PPG	Career
G	Mark Blazek (#4)	6'0"	Harborcreek	Sr.	26(26)	152(38)	32-50	374	14.4	1053
G	RaSean Thrower (#10)	6'1"	Wilson	Soph.	26(26)	150(34)	23-38	357	13.7	357
G	Steve Piotrowicz (#3)	5'9"	OLC	Sr.	24(24)	68(32)	50-64	218	9.1	413
F	Bob Spoden (#11)	6'3"	St. George's	Jr.	26(22)	81(23)	11-15	196	7.5	196
F	Brendan Barber (#40)	6'2"	St. Peter's	Sr.	24(13)	65(1)	37-54	168	7.0	212
G	Mike Bukowski (#25)	6'1"	St. Peter's	Sr.	26(5)	45(8)	14-21	112	4.3	219
F	Dan Marz (#34)	6'3"	Villa Maria	Sr.	25(7)	39(1)	18-31	97	3.9	153
G	Dave Galleher (#35)	5'10"	OLP	Sr.	24	13(5)	10-10	41	1.7	55
G	Tim Mikotowicz (#22)	6'0"	St. Luke's	Sr.	14	10(6)	7-15	33	2.4	57
G	Andy Sweny (#33)	6'1"	OLC	Jr.	11	11	8-12	30	2.7	30
F	Ryan Dougan (#30)	6'3"	OLC	Jr.	11	5	10-15	20	1.8	20
G	Keith Blazek (#14)	5'10"	Harborcreek	Jr.	21(7)	5(1)	3-5	14	0.7	14
F	Zach Hess (#21)	6'3"	St. Peter's	Jr.	9	4	3-6	11	1.2	11
G	Pat Barber (#42)	6'2"	St. Peter's	Jr.	9	1	0-2	2	0.2	2

Prep's 2008 Region Champions. Front, L to R: P. Barber, Sweeny, Piotrowicz, M. Blazek, K. Blazek, Bukowski, Mikotowicz, Gallaher; Back: Coach Flanagan, Thrower, Spoden, B. Barber, Marz, Hess, Dougan, Asst. Coach Tufts, Asst. Coach Behringer.

The Ramblers rejoice after another hard-fought victory.

HIGHLIGHTS:

- **Brian Flanagan's** fourth and final year at the Cathedral Prep helm produced good, but mixed results. Led by senior veterans **Mark Blazek** and **Mark Piotrowicz**, the Ramblers won their fourth straight region title, but bowed to McDowell for the District 10 title and lost the PIAA play-in game to State College.

- The final standings of a strong Region 7:

	Won	Lost
Cathedral Prep	9	1
McDowell	8	2
Strong Vincent	6	4
East	3	7
George Junior Republic	2	8
Central	2	8

- All Prep home games were at Gannon's Hammermill Center, while the East D-10 semifinal was at Mercyhurst College; the McDowell D-10 final at McComb Fieldhouse; and the State College play-in game at Tyrone Middle school.

- Prep opened the season with a loss in the Midland Tip-Off opener to Blackhawk (25-6), which went on to win the 2008

WPIAL AAA championship.

- Prep's first win against East (9-14) was the 100th time in history that the Ramblers defeated the Warriors.

- Prep lost in the first round to a very good Grover Cleveland (21-2) team in the first round of the Keenan Classic in Buffalo, but followed with an impressive overtime win over St. Ignatius (13-9). In 2010, Grover Cleveland was closed to new students by the New York State Department of Education due to low test scores and the remaining seniors graduated in 2011.

- Prep recorded a nice revenge victory over Hickory (14-11), as **Brendan Barber, Dave Galleher, Mike Bukowski, Dan Marz, Bobby Spoden, Ryan Dougan** and **Rasean Thrower** combined to nail 20 straight free throws to offset the Hornets' hot 3-point shooting.

Senior gaurd Mike Bukowski, read to go after a little lecture from the coach.

- Prep had an interesting matchup against Massillon Washington, a school and town completely known for football and historically one of the winningest teams in the nation, second only to Valdosta (GA) High School. A total of 23 professional players, 3 NFL coaches and 14 collegiate all-Americans have graduated from Massillon High School. The Tigers have also been recognized as the *Associated Press* National Champions nine times – in 1935, 1936, 1939, 1940, 1950, 1952, 1953, 1959, and 1961—the most in the nation. Not known for basketball, Massillon

Spot starter Dan Marz lets go a free throw, just under the 5-second limit.

(8-15) was nevertheless able to hang an upset on the Ramblers, the first time the two schools ever competed.

- Central High School (8-14), beginning with the 2007-08 school year, became known as "Central Career and Technical School", or simply, "Central Tech." The name change didn't seem to help—Prep's wins over the Falcons made for 15 straight.

- The Silver Anniversary edition (25th annual) of the McDonald's Classic featured a first: three preseason national top 10 teams, including the winner, New York City power Rice High (19-5), which clobbered Prep after a tight first half on Friday night

Mark Blazek is congratulated by family and friends as he crosses the career 1000 point mark.

then defeated perennial Elizabeth (NJ) powerhouse St. Patrick in a 60-57 final. Lakewood (OH) St. Ed's (25-5), without injured superstar **Delvon Roe**, was the consolation winner over Prep. Rice, led by *Parade Magazine* All-American **Kemba Walker**, finished as the #12 team in the nation according to *USA Today*, while St. Pat's (24-4), led by *Parade Magazine* All-American **Dexter Strickland**, was listed at #16. St. Ed's made it to the Ohio state final where it lost to Newark, 65-52. The McDonald's Classic was named the top 4-team tournament in the nation for the seventh straight year by *HoopsUSA*.

- Rice's **Chris Fouch** put on a spectacular shooting performance against Prep, nailing eight 3-pointers in just 11 tries to lead the Raiders. Fouch's eight treys was a McDonald's Classic record until broken by Mount Vernon's **Jabarie Hinds** two years later with nine. Though it was Rice's fifth appearance in the Classic, it was only the first time it was matched against the Ramblers.

Senior gaurd Dave Gallaher surveys the situation.

- **Ron Sertz**, the McDonald's Classic director for the entire glorious 25 years, announced before the championship game that it was his "100th and final" game as director. "I've made a decision that 25 years is a pretty good run," Sertz said. "I'm really proud of the event."

Captain Mark Blazek for three!

- Prep's best triumphs were the wins over arch-rivals McDowell (26-3), ranked #5 in AAAA in the state at season's end but lost to Pittsburgh Central Catholic in the PIAA second round, 49-47; Strong Vincent (18-8), twice; and General McLane (26-4), ranked #1 in AAA in the state at season's end but lost to Steelton-Highspire in a state semifinal, 58-43; and the early-season victory in the Midland tourney over AA Beaver Falls (22-5), ranked #4 in PA at season's end but lost to Farrell in the first round, 82-71.

- The biggest individual highlight of the season was **Mark Blazek's** 32-point effort against General McLane, one of the greatest performances ever displayed in Erie area hoops. He was 11 of 12 from the floor, including six 3-pointers, and 4-for-4 from the line.

- The season's biggest disappointments included the batterings from McDowell, one on Senior Night, and the other in the D-10 title game; and the PIAA play-in game loss to State College (18-9), when the Ramblers blew a 15-point second half lead. The Ramblers suffered from poor shot selection and shoddy defense and shot only 7 free throws compared to 27 for the Lions. State College then lost in the first round to Mechanicsburg, 46-45.

Junior forward Bobby Spoden dribbles down the side.

- Prep's 62-39 loss to McDowell was the worst margin suffered by the Ramblers against the Trojans, matched only by Millcreek's 41-18 victory over Prep in 1937.

- Sophomore starter **Rasean Thrower** led the Ramblers in rebounding (144/5.5 RPG) and steals (42), but also turnovers (64). Junior forward **Bob Spoden** led the squad with 21 blocked shots, while **Steve Piotrowicz** had the most assists (130/5.4 APG).

- **Mark Blazek**, the *Erie Times-News* "Pre-season Player of the Year", was later named First Team Region 7 All-Star as well as the Region 7 "Player of the Year." **Steve Piotrowicz** was also honored as a First team Region 7 All-Star, along with sophomore **RaSean Thrower**.

- Blazek scored eight and Piotrowicz two for the losing city squad in the 34th annual City-County All-Star Game held at Behrend's Junker Center. The final: County 73, City 53.

- **Mark Blazek** completed his fantastic four-year career at Prep and won the James "Moe" Gross Award, for the second time, for outstanding basketball ability. Only Blazek, **Jed Ryan** '95 and

Sophomore Rasean Thrower was a First Team All-Region choice.

Sheldon Zablotny '13 have won the award twice. The senior class salutatorian, Mark was also winner of Cathedral Prep's Headmaster's award for exemplary character and school leadership. He went on to star for four years at Hartwick College, where he is fourth on the all-time career list in 3-point field goals (185) and eighth on the all-time scoring list (1,366). He completed his Hartwick career honored as winner of Frederick Binder Scholar Athlete Award.

Blazek, with the soft touch.

- Aside from being a tough, hard-nosed player, **Steve Piotrowicz** was also a student-athlete. He went on to play at Behrend for one year then starred at point guard for Gannon the next three. Steve received the Division II Athletics Directors Academic Achievement award and was further named to the National Association of Basketball Coaches (NABC) Honors Court for strong academic work. He became an assistant coach for the IUP Red Hawks and is presently an assistant coach at Cathedral Prep.

- **Brendan Barber** won Prep's Dave Tyzinski Memorial Award for athletic talent, leadership and sportsmanship, as voted by student council, class advisors and all the Rambler coaches. He went on to play football four years for the Wildcats at Northwestern University, where he was a three-time Academic All-Big Ten honoree.

- Unfortunately for Cathedral Prep, coach **Brian Flanagan** resigned at season's end, stating: "My desire and commitment to coach 12 months a year are not there anymore." He finished at Prep with an outstanding four-year mark of 89-24, the top winning percentage (.788) of any Rambler basketball coach in history. A seven-week search for a new coach ended with the promotion of freshmen coach **Mark Majewski** to the head mentor's position.

First Team Region all-star Steve Piotrowicz had superb collegiate career at Gannon.

Brendan Barber banks it in. He went on to a football career at Northwestern.

2008 All-Opponent Team:

Antoine Childs, Blackhawk (1st team all-state) [Western Carolina]

David Phillips, Beaver Falls [Geneva]

Todd Thomas, Beaver Falls (2nd team all-state) [Pitt, football]

Gil Rogers, East

Tyshawn Edwards, Grover Cleveland [Erie (NY) CC, West Texas A & M]

Kirby Becker, St. Ignatius [Marietta, baseball]

Jaymee Shepard, Hickory [Slippery Rock, baseball]

Justin Turner, Massillon [Michigan, Scottsdale (AZ) CC, football]

Gio Caracillo, Massillon

Michael Anderson, Corry

Vadim Altland, Central Tech

Mike Crosby, Vincent

Zach Spronatti, McDowell (3rd team all-state) [Behrend]

Corey Ratliff, East

Chris Fouch, NYC Rice [Drexel]

Kemba Walker, NYC Rice [Connecticut; NBA Charlotte Bobcats]

Durand Scott, NYC Rice [Miami (FL)]

Tom Pritchard, Lakewood St. Ed's (1st team all-state, OH) [Indiana]

Justin Staples, Lakewood St. Ed's [Illinois, football]

Nic Carson, Oil City

Shawn Walker, General McLane (1st team all-state) [Edinboro, football]

Kellen O'Neill, General McLane [Slippery Rock, Edinboro, football]

Rakim Marley-Ellis, Central [Gannon, football]

Paris Pennamon, Vincent

Dillon Loomis, McDowell

Pat St. Andrews, State College [Behrend]

Junior gaurd Andy Sweny defends.

Floor leader Steve Piotrowicz.

Senior Mike Bukowski looks for an opening against GM.

Co-captain Piotrowicz goes way up for a basket.

Senior guard Tim Mikotowicz with another bucket.

Mark Majewski and a New Era!
Strong Finish after Mid-Season Slump!

Coach Majewski instructing his charges.

2008-09 (17-10)

Coach: Mark Majewski
Assistants: Bob Maxson, Dave Repko
Captain: Keith Blazek, Bob Spoden
Managers: Zack Comi, Tim Corder

Date	PREP		Dec.	Loc.	High Scorer	Opponent
	MOON TIP-OFF TOURNAMENT					
12/5	61	Hopewell	57	W	N	Dougan (17)	Faletta (17)
12/6	47	Peters Township	48	L	N	Dougan (23)	Wilcox (24)
12/11	68	General McLane	60	W	H	Thrower (19)	DiVito (18)
12/13	61	Penn Hills	63	L	H	Sweny (16)	Anthony (17)
12/16	73	East	59	W	N	Sweny (21)	Rogers (19)
	DISNEY-KSA PRE-HOLIDAY TOURNAMENT (KISSIMMEE, FL)						
12/18	44	San Diego (CA) Horizon Christian	38	W	A	Sweny (11)	Iglehart (17)
12/19	49	San Francisco (CA) Lowell	39	W	A	Spoden (10)	Ng (12)
12/20	69	Chartiers Valley	84	L	A	Spoden (16)	McConnell (36)
12/27	62	Massillon (OH) Washington	52	W	H	Thrower (21)	Malinowski (10)
1/3	61	Warren	49	W	A	Dougan (16)	Mangini (14)
1/6	63	George Junior Republic	44	W	A	Thrower (15)	Hanton (14)
1/10	62	Central Tech	46	W	N	Thrower (15)	Wallace (13)
1/13	57	Strong Vincent	62	L	N	Thrower (19)	Jones & Marlow (15)
	McDONALD'S CLASSIC						
1/16	62	Chester	69	L	H	Spoden (19)	Jefferson (26)
1/17	42	Houston (TX) Westbury Christian	58	L	H	Spoden (18)	Perry (18)
1/19	79	George Junior Republic	64	W	H	Sweny (24)	Lemon (21)
1/24	35	McDowell	43	L	A	Spoden (14)	Keim (15)
1/30	36	Cleveland (OH) St. Ignatius	53	L	A	Blazek (11)	Parker (16)
2/2	61	Strong Vincent	63	L	N	Thrower (24)	Harden-Pullium (22)
2/7	84	DuBois	48	W	A	Spoden (18)	Peterson (15)
2/12	64	Harborcreek	47	W	H	Sweny (20)	Rzepecki (15)
2/14	47	McDowell	43	W	H	Sweny (14)	Keim (16)
	DISTRICT 10 PLAYOFFS						
2/19	74	Strong Vincent	68	W	N	Thrower (21)	Harden-Pullium (21)
2/27	55	McDowell	51	W	H	Thrower (23)	Keim & Stano (11)
	P.I.A.A. INTERDISTRICT PLAYOFFS						
3/7	54	North Hills	43	W	N	Spoden (12)	Patton (17)
3/11	60	Pittsburgh Central Catholic	58	W	N	Sweny & Thrower (16)	Tsudis (20)
3/14	41	Mt. Lebanon	51	L	N	Sweny (10)	Pierce (15)
	1571 (58.2)		**1460 (54.1)**				

Pos.	Player	Ht.	Prior School	Class	G(GS)	FG(3)	FT	Total	PPG	Career
G	Andy Sweny (#4)	6'1"	OLC	Sr.	27(27)	124(11)	71-95	330	12.2	360
G	RaSean Thrower (#3)	6'1"	Wilson	Jr.	24(24)	115(43)	38-59	311	13.0	668
F	Bob Spoden (#11)	6'3"	St. George's	Sr.	27(25)	118(29)	39-52	304	11.3	500
F	Ryan Dougan (#30)	6'3"	OLC	Sr.	24(20)	61(3)	86-132	211	8.8	231
G	Keith Blazek (#14)	5'10"	Harborcreek	Sr.	24(21)	39(7)	31-43	116	4.8	130
G	Adam Blazek (#45)	5'10"	Harborcreek	Soph.	27(6)	36(5)	22-26	99	3.7	99
C	Mike Knoll (#40)	6'3"	Mount Carmel	Soph.	24(3)	25	13-27	63	2.6	63
G	A.J. Schumacher (#22)	6'0"	Bl. Sacrament	Sr.	26(6)	15(7)	6-9	43	1.7	43
C	Noel Oduho (#35)	6'5"	St. John/HR	Jr.	14(1)	13	5-10	31	2.2	31
G	Pat Barber (#10)	6'2"	St. Peter's	Sr.	21(2)	8(1)	4-5	21	1.0	23
G	Eric Hess (#42)	5'11"	St. James	Soph.	14	7(4)	1-2	19	1.4	19
F	Phil Hampy (#33)	6'2"	Walnut Creek	Jr.	8	4(1)	4-8	13	1.6	13
G	Joel Nunez (#34)	5'9"	Wilson	Sr.	7	2	1-2	5	0.7	5
G	Jordan Rydzewski (#25)	5'9"	St. Luke's	Jr.	6	1	1-4	3	0.5	3
F	Zach Hess (#21)	6'3"	St. Peter's	Sr.	7	1	0-2	2	0.3	13

Prep's 2009 District 10 Champions. Front, L to R: Hampy, Nunez, E. Hess, K. Blazek, Thrower, Rydzewski, A. Blazek; Back: Coach Majewski, Asst. Coach Repko, Z. Hess, Knoll, Sweny, Dougan, Oduho, P. Barber, Schumacher, Asst. Coach Flanagan, Asst. Coach Maxson.

HIGHLIGHTS:

- **Mark Majewski**, age 42, a 1983 graduate of Cathedral Prep, was named the new Rambler cage mentor after posting a two-year record of 40-6 as coach of the Prep Freshmen team, including 22-1 in 2007-08. Majewski cut his coaching eyeteeth at St. Stanislaus Grade School and St. Benedict Academy, and was also head coach at Villa Maria for 10 years, where he led the Class A Victors to a 135-119 aggregate mark and a #5 state ranking with a 21-9 record in 2005-06. Also rumored in the application mix were former Prep stars **Keith Nies, Tom Hansen** and **Adam Dolak**; Mercyhurst Prep coach **Pat Flaherty**; and Strong Vincent coach **Shannon Pullium**.

- On Friday, November 7 at 9:30am, **Bishop Donald Trautman, Headmaster Father Scott Jabo, Mayor Joe Sinnott**, and officials from Cathedral Prep participated in a ground breaking ceremony for the new Cathedral Prep Events Center at 12th and Cherry Streets in Erie. The initial phase provided for a football field and regulation 8-lane track, as well as ample locker rooms and concession areas. A natatorium and gymnasium would be added in the future, bringing Prep into a new, modern era of athletics.

Senior Pat Barber was also a star quarterback for the Ramblers.

- The **Mark Majewski** era began with a victory over a new opponent, Hopewell (11-14), in the Moon Tip-Off Tourney. Hopewell, located just outside Aliquippa, was coached by former Beaver Falls and college standout **Ron Rowan** and is further known as the high school of Pitt Panther and NFL great **Tony Dorsett**. Prep lost the following evening in the final to another new opponent, Peters Township (23-3), a Washington County school that went on to win the WPIAL title in 2009.

- Prep then followed with an exciting, come-from-behind win over General McLane (18-7). Junior **RaSean Thrower** ignited the comeback with three consecutive 3-pointers to open the second half. The Prep-GM rivalry by this time had become fierce, topped only by the intensity of the Prep-McDowell series.

Senior Zack Hess rattles a GJR ballhandler.

- Prep then lost a close one to Penn Hills (14-7), its third WPIAL opponent in its first four games. The Ramblers played a record seven WPIAL teams during the season. It was the last time Prep and Penn Hills played, the Indians holding a 5-2 series edge.

- East High (19-8) and Central Tech (7-15), and Tech Memorial before, for the first time since Prep joined the City Series in 1942-43, only scheduled one regular season game, rather than two, against the Ramblers.

- All Prep home games were at Gannon's Hammermill Center. The KSA Tourney was played at Disneyworld, while the first PIAA interdistrict game was at Edinboro's McComb Fieldhouse. The last two interdistrict games were played at Sharon High School.

- Prep made its fourth trip to the KSA Tourney near Orlando (FL). KSA Events, the nation's premier host of high school sporting events, hosts many classics and holiday tournaments in several different sports. Participating teams come nationwide from Alaska to Florida and from California to Massachusetts, providing a true national competition format that brings teams together that would otherwise never meet on the court.

- Prep did well at KSA, defeating a pair of West Coast teams, but ran into a backyard buzzsaw with Chartiers Valley (25-2) and its shooting star, **T. J. McConnell**. The Colts beat the Ramblers in the Thomas Jefferson Bracket final, then proceeded to stay undefeated through the regular season. Chartiers Valley lost in

the WPIAL semifinal to Highlands, 66-59, then to Greensburg Salem in the PIAA second round, 68-66.

- The McDonald's High School Basketball Classic continued with its 26th edition under the direction of Prep Athletic Director **Bill Flanagan**. The event did not lose a beat with Flanagan taking over. Chester High (24-5), coming in with a 1-5 all-time tournament record, nudged the host Ramblers before pounding Washington (DC) Archbishop Carroll in an anti-climactic final, 64-39. Prep took a beating from eventual Texas state champion Westbury Christian (27-6) for consolation honors.

- Prep's easy victory at DuBois (4-18) was the first the Ramblers and Beavers competed in 20 years.

- This was the first year since 1974 that the Ramblers played at McDowell's Paul Goll Gymnasium. Trojan officials controversially decided to discontinue playing designated "home" games at the Gannon site, preferring to use their own facilities for all such "home" contests. "Without the Metro League, things have changed," said **Brian Fuller**, McDowell's associate A.D. "We decided it was time to do it. We're getting that high school flavor back in the home gym." The game at McDowell, which held less than half the seating available at Gannon's Hammermill Center, needed a lottery for ticket allocation and closed-circuit TV in another school gym to satisfy public demand. The battle was also shown on Time-Warner Cable-TV station 8.

The final standings of Region7:

	Won	Lost
McDowell	5	1
Strong Vincent	4	2
Cathedral Prep	3	3
George Junior Republic	0	6

- The highlight of the season was Prep's exciting late-season surge, avenging losses to Vincent (14-9) and McDowell (16-7) to win its 17th District 10 title. **Bobby Spoden** was the big noise in the emotional SV win, scoring 10 fourth quarter points and capping it off with a steal and resounding slam dunk with just 20 seconds remaining. Prep's all-around best performance was in the D-10 final against the Trojans, with junior **Rasean Thrower** scoring 23 in the upset, including three 3-pointers, and also collecting 6 rebounds, 4 steals and 3 blocks.

A picture-perfect 3-pointer by Spoden as the Trojan bench marvels.

- A pair of state tourney wins then put the Ramblers into the PIAA Elite Eight for the 13th time. The Ramblers took care of North Hills (18-10) early, and made several clutch plays down the stretch to down Pittsburgh Central Catholic (17-10) in a thriller.

- After Prep's playoff win against North Hills, the *Pittsburgh Post-Gazette* noted: "Erie Prep has to have the best student section in the state. They're creative with chants, they're loud and they're funny. They sang 'Sweet Caroline' and 'Living on a Prayer' at halftime, as well as some other songs. They did it without any music. But the most unbelievable thing Erie Prep's student section did was this: All of a sudden in the middle of the game, one of the students was in nothing but a Speedo swim suit as he was dancing in the middle of the section. Police and game officials eventually got him out of the crowd and made him leave the gym."

The Rambler student section was called the "Best in the State" by the Pittsburgh Post-Gazette. Here, all fired up for McDowell.

- Prep had difficulty with three Mt. Lebanon (24-6) skyscrapers and some hot 3-point shooting by **Evan Pierce** and **Mike Martin** in a 10-point loss in the state quarterfinals. The Ramblers had a 40-37 lead with 3 minutes left in the heartbreaker, before 6'8" **Deion Turman** made a monster dunk that sent Mt. Lebo on a 14-1 run to close out the contest. Turman also had 15 rebounds for the Blue Devils, who lost to eventual state champ Penn Wood in the semifinal, 79-58.

MVP Mark Blazek was honored as Region 7 "Player of the Year." He went on to a stellar career at Hartwick.

- On January 8, 2009 Cathedral Prep announced a merger with Villa Maria Academy, which at the conclusion of the school year would no longer accept male students. The official name of the merged schools is Erie Catholic Preparatory School, though Prep and Villa maintain their original names and separate all-male and all-female campuses.

- Villa Maria Academy's girls' team (27-3) held off a furious second half comeback to defeat three-time defending champion York Catholic (27-6) to win its first PIAA state championship, 56-51. The Victors, coached by **Scott Dibble**, were led by Pennsylvania "Player of the Year" **Kayla McBride's** 20 points and by feisty point guard **Kaylyn Maruca's** 15 points.

- Senior workhorses **Andrew Sweny** (216/8.0 RPG) and **Ryan Dougan** (151/6.3 RPG) led the Ramblers in rebounding.

- **Bobby Spoden, Andrew Sweny** and **RaSean Thrower** were all named First Team Region 7 All-Stars by the *Erie Times-News*, while **Ryan Dougan** was a Second Team choice.

Villa Maria Academy won the state title in the initial year of its merger with Cathedral Prep. Some champion Victors, front, L to R: Kayla McBride, Kaylyn Maruca, Chelsea Laskey, Ashley Prischak; Back: Alexandra Brickell.

Bobby Spoden with a ferocious block of a Mychal Molnar shot.

- Spoden, Sweny and **Keith Blazek** were all chosen to play for the City All-Stars in the 35th annual City-County All-Star game. The City, coached by Prep's **Mark Majewski** and Villa Maria's **Joe Lunger**, defeated the County, 80-72. Spoden was the big star with 17 points and a couple of slam dunks, including a power dunk at the game's end. Sweny contributed seven points and Blazek two for the Slickers.

- **RaSean Thrower** became only the third Rambler junior, and the first since **Adam Kaiser** in 2005, to win the "Ma" Kaiser Award as Prep's best all-around athlete.

- Hard-working **Andrew Sweny**, who came on strong for his senior campaign, was honored with the James "Moe" Gross Award, signifying him as Prep's most valuable player. He went on to play at Gannon University.

- **Keith Blazek**, the second of four Blazek brothers to star back-to-back for Prep, was the winner of the Dave Tyzinski Memorial award for being the Ramblers' best two-sport athlete. He went on to a solid baseball career at Baldwin-Wallace where he also won several academic honors.

MVP Andy Sweny was a Region 7 First Team all-star.

First Team Region all-star Bob Spoden, ready to deal on McDowell's Zach Stano.

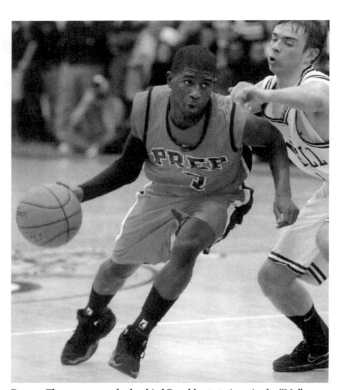

Rasean Thrower was only the third Rambler to twice win the "Ma" Kaiser Award as Prep's best athlete.

Senior forward Andy Sweny goes up strong against Chester in the McDonald's Classic.

2009 All-Opponent Team:

Nick Wilcox, Peters Twp. (3rd team all-state) [Bethany]

Craig Wolcott, Peters Twp. [Duquesne]

Dom DiVito, General McLane [Penn St.-Behrend]

Gil Rogers, East

Wendell Torres, East (3rd team all-state) [Nyack]

T. J. McConnell, Chartiers Valley (2nd team all-State) [Duquesne, Arizona]

Ashton Pullium-Jones, Vincent [Lakeland (OH) CC]

Rahlir Jefferson, Chester (1st team all-state) [Temple]

Kevin Perry, Westbury Christian [UTEP, football]

Mike Lemon, GJR

Deon Hanton, GJR

Tom Parker, St. Ignatius [Lake Erie College]

Courtney Harden-Pullium, Vincent [Edinboro]

Garret Peterson, DuBois [Slippery Rock, baseball]

Jason Keim, McDowell

Brandon Marlow, Vincent [Edinboro UP, football]

Cody Patton, North Hills

Evan Tsudis, Pittsburgh Central Catholic [Case Western Reserve]

Evan Pierce, Mt. Lebanon (2nd team all-state) [Wagner]

Deion Turman, Mt. Lebanon [Robert Morris, Wingate (NC)]

The 2010's

Father Scott Jabo, announcing the $10 million gift which eventually helped build the Joann Mullen Gymnasium. With Father Jabo are Board of Trustees chairman Dave Slomski '72 and Director of Operations Chris Hagerty '75.

The beautiful Cathedral Prep Events Center, prior to the building of the gymnasium and natatorium.

Rollercoaster Season!

Adam Blazek drives against Mount Vernon in the McDonald's Classic.

2009-10 (15-11)

Coach: Mark Majewski
Assistants: Bob Maxson, Dave Repko,
    Mike Flanagan
Captain: Rasean Thrower, Phil Hampy,
    Noel Oduho
Manager: Zack Comi

Date	PREP			Dec.	Loc.	High Scorer	Opponent
		HARRY JENKINS CLASSIC (FOX CHAPEL)					
12/11	71	Pittsburgh Schenley	54	W	N	Thrower (18)	B. Johnson (21)
12/12	66	Pittsburgh Peabody	44	W	N	Thrower (17)	Baskins (11)
12/15	50	General McLane	43	W	A	Thrower (18)	Jahn (10)
		BISHOP GORMAN HOLIDAY CLASSIC (LAS VEGAS, NV)					
12/17	51	Las Vegas (NV) Bishop Gorman	87	L	A	Thrower (14)	Winder (24)
12/18	69	Melbourne (Australia) Collegiate	59	W	N	Thrower (22)	Campos (14)
12/18	43	Ulm (Germany) Urspring Academy	64	L	N	Blazek (13)	Wolf (16)
12/19	47	Provo (UT) Timpview	59	L	N	Thrower (15)	Warner & Robison (12)
12/23	63	East	55(OT)	W	N	Thrower (21)	Torres (26)
12/29	67	Warren	58	W	N	Thrower (15)	M. Schoenborn (16)
1/6	82	DuBois	25	W	H	Thrower (19)	Avery (7)
1/9	63	Buffalo (NY) Canisius	66	L	A	Blazek (22)	Nevins (19)
1/11	74	Central Tech	38	W	N	Blazek (19)	Wallace (18)
		McDONALD'S CLASSIC					
1/15	57	Buffalo (NY) Nichols School	68	L	H	Thrower (17)	Wier (25)
1/16	67	Mount Vernon (NY)	79	L	H	Knoll (19)	Hinds (39)
1/19	56	Strong Vincent	73	L	N	Thrower (16)	Harden-Pullium (28)
1/22	60	Cleveland (OH) St. Ignatius	54	W	H	Thrower (17)	Hammond (13)
1/26	80	George Junior Republic	51	W	H	Thrower (21)	Johnson (18)
2/2	63	McDowell	47	W	H	Thrower (17)	Molnar (21)
2/9	57	Strong Vincent	65	L	N	Thrower (20)	Harden-Pullium (21)
2/15	75	George Junior Republic	52	W	A	Thrower (20)	Lawrence (13)
2/18	71	Harborcreek	52	W	A	Thrower (16)	Rzepecki (19)
2/20	54	McDowell	55(OT)	L	A	Thrower (17)	Roach & Kimball (14)
		DISTRICT 10 PLAYOFFS					
2/25	57	McDowell	49	W	N	Thrower (22)	Conner (12)
3/4	60	Strong Vincent	68	L	N	Thrower (15)	Harden-Pullium (22)
		P.I.A.A. INTERDISTRICT PLAYOFFS					
3/9	48	Upper St. Clair	42	W	A	Thrower (11)	Albert (12)
3/13	41	Hollidaysburg	50	L	N	Thrower (15)	Swauger (16)
	1592 (61.2)		**1457 (56.0)**				

Pos.	Player	Ht.	Prior School	Class	G(GS)	FG(3)	FT	Total	PPG	Career
G	Rasean Thrower (#3)	6'1"	Wilson	Sr.	26(26)	159(42)	66-98	426	16.4	1094
G	Adam Blazek (#4)	6'0"	Harborcreek	Jr.	26(26)	95(34)	53-76	277	10.7	376
C	Mike Knoll (#22)	6'4"	Mount Carmel	Jr.	26(19)	94(1)	43-64	232	8.9	232
G	Sheldon Zablotny (#34)	5'9"	Perry	Fr.	26(3)	62(9)	28-39	161	6.2	161
F	Phil Hampy (#11)	6'2"	Walnut Creek	Sr.	26(22)	54(3)	36-69	147	5.7	160
F	Joe Gnacinski (#35)	6'5"	St. George's	Jr.	26(5)	46	8-13	100	3.8	100
F	Dominic Sansone (#33)	6'5"	St. Andrew/OLP	Jr.	23(4)	24(5)	12-15	65	2.8	65
C	Noel Oduho (#10)	6'5"	St. John/HR	Sr.	23(7)	22	9-15	53	2.3	84
G	Jordan Rydzewski (#21)	5'10"	St. Luke's	Sr.	23(9)	20(8)	2-2	50	2.2	53
F	Dominic DiRaimo (#42)	6'1"	Harborcreek	Jr.	22(7)	17(3)	6-11	43	2.0	43
G	Joe Mikotowicz (#14)	5'10"	St. Luke's	Jr.	18(2)	9(3)	4-8	25	1.4	25
G	Ben Tate (#30)	5'11"	St. John/HR	Jr.	15	3(2)	0-3	8	0.5	8
G	Joe Sweny (#25)	5'8"	OLC	Jr.	14	2(1)	0-0	5	0.4	5
G	Nico Sisinni (#40)	6'0"	OLP	Soph.	2	0	0-3	0	0.0	0
F	Delton Williams (#45)	6'2"	Joanna Connell	Fr.	1	0	0-0	0	0.0	0
G	Shyquawn Pullium (#45)	6'1"	St. George's	Sr.	0	0	0-0	0	0.0	0

HIGHLIGHTS:

- It was a rollercoaster season in **Mark Majewski's** second year at the helm. Cathedral Prep had some impressive victories, but suffered three bad losses to Region 7 champion Vincent (19-6). The D-10 final was particularly disappointing, as Prep blew a 10-point second half lead. This edition of the Orange & Black was plagued by an abundance of turnovers and poor shot selection throughout the season.

The 2010 Prep Ramblers. Front, L to R: Mgr. Comi, Pulliam, Mikotowicz, Zablotny, Tate, Sweny, Blazek, Rydzewski; Back: Coach Majewski, Asst. Coach Repko, Oduho, Knoll, Sansone, Gnacinski, DiRaimo, Hampy, Thrower, Asst. Coach Flanagan, Asst. Coach Maxson.

- Prep opened the season winning the Fox Chapel Tourney with easy victories over Pittsburgh City League foes Schenley (6-16) and Peabody (9-13). **Rasean Thrower** started his senior season in fine order, leading the Ramblers in scoring both nights.

- The highlights of the season were Prep's come-from-behind win at rival General McLane (10-8), moving the Ramblers to 3-0 on the Lancers' home court (McLane thus suffered only its 7th loss ever on its home court since its gym opened 28 years before, in 1991); the victory over state-ranked East (21-3); the win over Ohio power St. Ignatius (19-5), which won the Solon

District title but lost to St. Ed's in the Region final, 53-49; and the D-10 Semifinal when the Ramblers overcame a 10-point fourth quarter deficit to beat McDowell (12-9) by 8.

- Prep's pounding from Bishop Gorman (30-2) in the Las Vegas tourney was no disgrace—the Gaels finished with the Nevada 4A state championship. Their only losses were to Henderson (NV) Findlay College Prep, the #3 ranked team in

Father Scott Jabo and Father John Detisch discuss the finer points of the roundball sport.

Rambler students made a good showing at McDowell, a one-point overtime loss.

the *USA Today* Super 25 national rankings, and Santa Ana (CA) Mater Dei, the #9 team in the nation. Bishop Gorman, the only Catholic School in southern Nevada, finished as the #11 team in the nation. The Gaels have become the most prominent high school athletics program in the state of Nevada, winning numerous state championships each year. Additionally,

Sheldon Zablotny had an impressive freshman season on the Rambler varsity.

Bishop Gorman has been recognized by *Sports Illustrated* as one of the top athletic programs in the nation.

- This was Prep's fourth journey to a holiday tournament in Las Vegas—the other trips occurring in 1983, 1995 and 1999.

- The Gorman tourney also saw Prep play, for the first time, teams from outside the North America continent. A team from Melbourne, Australia (5-12) was beaten by the Ramblers, although a huge squad from Germany had a fairly easy time with the Orange & Black. That team, Urspring Academy (2-6), is a basketball training center where talented student players have the opportunity to play on the best of the German school teams or to receive

Dominic DiRaimo is carried from the floor after an injury in the Vincent game.

scholarships from outstanding American colleges. Prep also lost to eventual Utah 4A state titlist Provo Timpview (12-7), a large Utah school mostly known for football championships.

- Prep's ridiculously easy win over DuBois (7-15) was the last time the two played, with the Ramblers holding a 4-0 series edge.

- Prep's close loss to a good Canisius (21-6) squad in Buffalo was the start of a yearly home-and-home series with the Crusaders which continues to this day.

- In the 27th edition of the McDonald's High School Basketball Classic, defending PIAA state champion Lansdowne Penn Wood defeated Buffalo Nichols, 64-53. In its consolation match over Prep, Mount Vernon's (18-7) **Jabarie Hinds** set a McDonald's Classic record for 3-pointers in one game with an unbelievable nine and narrowly missed the scoring record with 39 points. Hinds' nine 3-pointers were not only a McDonald's Classic record, but the most 3-pointers ever made in a Prep game. Hinds led Mount Vernon to the New York State Public High School Athletic Association Class AA title. This was the last "McDonald's Classic," giving way to the "Burger King Classic" the following season.

- In Nichols School's (24-7) victory over Prep, the Vikings' **Stan**

Wier set a Classic record with a perfect 9-for-9 at the free throw line. Only a sophomore, Weir led Nichols to the New York Federation Class A championship, then transferred out of state for the 2010-11 season. Weir then came back to play for East Aurora his senior season (2011-12), where he also played as a freshman. Nichols, an expensive, private non-denominational school located on 30 acres in North Buffalo, nevertheless competes in the Buffalo's Catholic Monsignor Martin Athletic Association.

- The final standings of Region 7:

	Won	Lost
Strong Vincent	6	0
Cathedral Prep	3	3
McDowell	3	3
George Junior Republic	0	6

- Prep overcame a 7-point halftime deficit with a 12-0 third quarter start in the PIAA play-in win over Upper St. Clair (15-10). Consecutive buckets by **Noel Oduho, RaSean Thrower, Mike Knoll, Adam Blazek** and **Phil Hampy** gave the Ramblers a lead for good. The Ramblers next blew a 12-point first quarter lead and lost handily to Hollidaysburg (16-9), which then lost to Gateway, 46-37, in the second round.

Defensive demon Phil Hampy blocks a shot by SV's Deuel Pacley.

- All Prep home games were at Gannon's Hammermill Center, with the exception of the Warren contest, which was played at Erie Civic Center. The PIAA play-in game was on Upper St. Clair's home court, while the first round loss to Hollidaysburg was played at the Altoona Fieldhouse.

- Villa Maria Academy's girls' team (28-2) won its second consecutive PIAA AA state championship with a 52-44 win, again over perennial powerhouse York Catholic. McDonald's All-American and two-time Pennsylvania "Player of the Year" **Kayla McBride** led the Victors with 29 points and 11 rebounds. McBride, who went on to become an *Associated Press* First Team All-American at Notre Dame, scored 17 straight second half points and 19 of the last 22 in VMA's conquest of York.

- **Rasean Thrower** closed out a high-scoring three-year career for the Ramblers with 1094 points, fourth on Prep's all-time chart. He was

MVP Rasean Thrower retired as Prep's fourth all-time leading scorer.

Named First Team All-Region as a junior, the determined Adam Blazek averaged 3 steals per game.

Named Second Team All-Region, Phil Hampy was the main reason DuBois was held to 25 points.

only the second Rambler ever to score more than 300 points in a season for three consecutive years. Thrower also led Prep in rebounding (197/7.6 RPG), while rugged **Phil Hampy** (134/5.2 RPG) and **Mike Knoll** (133/5.1 RPG) were second and third. **Adam Blazek** led the Orange & Black with 78 steals, or three per game.

- **Rasean Thrower** and **Adam Blazek** were both named First Team Region 7 All-Stars by the *Erie Times-News*, while **Phil Hampy**, also a Rambler gridiron star, garnered Second Team honors.

- Thrower and Hampy represented the Ramblers in the 36th annual City-County All-Star Game, played at Behrend's Junker Center. The City, coached by Prep's **Mark Majewski**, beat the County, 89-86, with Thrower scoring 9 and Hampy 4.

- **Rasean Thrower** was the first double winner since **Booker Coleman** in 1994 to win both the James "Moe" Gross Award and the "Ma" Kaiser Award, signifying him not only Prep's best basketball player, but also the best all-around athlete. It was Thrower's second "Ma" Kaiser Award, making him only the third double winner of that honor in Prep history, the first being **Jim Gemler** in 1997-98 and the second being **Adam Kaiser** in 2005-06. Thrower also played for a professional basketball team called the Erie Hurricane in 2013-14.

- **Noel Oduho** went on to star four years at wide receiver for Division I Duquesne University.

2010 All-Opponent Team:

Brandon Johnson, Schenley [Mercyhurst-North East]
Anson Winder, Bishop Gorman [BYU]
Ryan Parks, Bishop Gorman [Warner Pacific (OR)]
Eli Robison, Timpview [Utah Valley]
Wendell Torres, East (2nd team all-state) [Nyack]
Aaron Nevins, Canisius [Utica]
Mark Schoenborn, Warren
Jabarie Hinds, Mount Vernon [West Virginia]
Stan Wier, Buffalo Nichols [Buffalo]
Ashton Pullium-Jones, Vincent [Lakeland (OH) CC]
Courtney Harden-Pullium, Vincent (2nd team all-state) [Edinboro]
Omar Johnson, GJR
Mychal Molnar, McDowell [Thomas More]
DeAndrye Henderson, Vincent [Mercyhurst-North East]
Colin Kimball, McDowell [Mercyhurst, football]
Jordan Albert, Upper St. Clair [Mount Union]
Jordan Swauger, Hollidaysburg [Penn Highlands CC]

Prep Regains Region, D-10 Crowns!

2010-11 (14-10)

Coach: Mark Majewski
Assistants: Bob Maxson, Dave Repko,
Matt Harris, Sr
Captain: Adam Blazek, Mike Knoll,
Dominic DiRaimo
Manager: Nick Sorenson

Adam Blazek, Region 8 "Player of the Year."

Date	PREP			Dec.	Loc.	High Scorer	Opponent
	HOLLIDAYSBURG TOURNAMENT						
12/10	38	Butler	66	L	N	Zablotny (12)	Herald & Swartwout (13)
12/11	62	Franklin Regional	46	W	N	Zablotny (18)	Ayasso (11)
12/14	44	General McLane	59	L	H	Zablotny (14)	Mountain (15)
12/16	80	Corry	45	W	A	A. Blazek & Zablotny (20)	Mosher (16)
12/18	45	Morgantown (WV)	63	L	A	A. Blazek (17)	Price (23)
	SHOOTOUT BY THE SEA TOURNAMENT (N. MYRTLE BEACH, SC)						
12/20	51	Lexington (SC) White Knoll	43	W	N	DiRaimo (15)	Creed (13)
12/21	48	Clover (SC)	57	L	N	Williams & Harris (11)	Thomason (15)
12/22	64	Easley (SC)	72	L	N	A. Blazek (19)	McGowens & Pickel (24)
12/30	56	North Allegheny	58	L	A	Zablotny (19)	Howard (14)
1/5	69	Buffalo (NY) Canisius	58	W	H	A. Blazek (19)	Lyons (20)
1/7	67	George Junior Republic	25	W	H	Zablotny (17)	Swinton (7)
1/11	74	Strong Vincent	62	W	H	A. Blazek (24)	Henderson (12)
	BURGER KING CLASSIC						
1/15	57	Charlotte (NC) Christian	68(OT)	L	H	A. Blazek (16)	Rooks (22)
1/16	57	Lakewood (OH) St. Edward	70	L	H	Sansone (15)	Brown (14)
1/18	41	McDowell	35	W	A	A. Blazek (18)	Roach (11)
1/21	55	Cleveland (OH) St. Ignatius	58	L	A	A. Blazek (19)	Farris (13)
1/24	71	Harborcreek	18	W	H	A. Blazek & DiRaimo (10)	King (5)
2/8	61	Ft. LeBoeuf	30	W	A	Sansone (16)	D. Kress (11)
2/11	66	Central Tech	40	W	H	A. Blazek (23)	Edwards (13)
2/14	60	Strong Vincent	57	W	H	A. Blazek (19)	Pullium (12)
2/16	77	George Junior Republic	51	W	A	Sansone (22)	White (11)
2/18	52	McDowell	41	W	H	A. Blazek (19)	Kimball (16)
	DISTRICT 10 PLAYOFF						
3/2	51	McDowell	40	W	H	A. Blazek (16)	Kimball (16)
	P.I.A.A. INTERDISTRICT PLAYOFF						
3/12	52	Butler	60	L	H	A. Blazek (18)	Swartout (25)
	1399(58.3)		1222 (50.9)				

Pos.	Player	Ht.	Prior School	Class	G(GS)	FG(3)	FT	Total	PPG	Career
G	Adam Blazek (#5)	5'11"	Harborcreek	Sr.	24(24)	130(29)	64-82	353	14.7	729
G	Sheldon Zablotny (#2)	5'10"	Perry	Soph.	24(24)	109(20)	40-55	278	11.6	439
F	Dominic Sansone (#11)	6'5"	St. Andrew/OLP	Sr.	23(21)	100(1)	25-43	226	9.8	291
F	Joe Gnacinski (#21)	6'5"	St. George's	Sr.	24(13)	71	22-26	164	6.8	264
F-G	Dominic DiRaimo (#3)	6'2"	Harborcreek	Sr.	24(22)	60(24)	13-18	157	6.5	200
G	Nico Sisinni (#4)	5'10"	OLP	Jr.	24(11)	24(2)	10-25	60	2.5	60
F	Matt Harris (#34)	5'11"	St. Peter's	Fr.	19	17(8)	6-6	48	2.5	48
F	Delton Williams (#40)	6'2"	Joanna Connell	Soph.	18(4)	17	9-23	43	2.4	43
G	Dan Blazek (#15)	5'10"	Harborcreek	Soph.	17(1)	7(1)	6-6	21	1.2	21
G	Ben Tate (#10)	6'1"	St. John/HR	Sr.	11	8(1)	1-1	18	1.6	26
C	Mike Knoll (#22)	6'5"	Mount Carmel	Sr.	7	7	0-0	14	2.0	246
G	Conor Colpoys (#35)	6'0"	St. George's	Soph.	8	1	4-4	6	0.8	6
G	Chris Francis (#25)	5'10"	Bl. Sacrament	Soph.	8	2(1)	0-0	5	0.6	5
F	Kimani Smith (#45)	6'3"	Wilson	Jr.	5	1(1)	0-0	3	0.6	3
G	Matt Hess (#33)	5'10"	St. George's	Soph.	4	1(1)	0-0	3	0.8	3
G	Jeremy Lynch (#14)	5'6"	OLP	Soph.	7	0	0-0	0	0.0	0
F	Damion Terry (#42)	6'4"	Bl. Sacrament	Soph.	0	0	0-0	0	0.0	0

Prep's 2011 District 10 Champions. Front, L to R: Sisinni, Harris, Francis, Zablotny, Lynch, D. Blazek, Hess, A. Blazek; Back: Assistants Maxson, Bowen, and Harris, Smith, DiRaimo, Gnacinski, Knoll, Sansone, Terry, Williams, Colpoys, Tate, Asst. Repko, Coach Majewski.

Zablotny exalts with a huge bucket as McDowell's Colin Kimball is helpless and ref signals "three."

HIGHLIGHTS:

• Cathedral Prep, sparked by the fine play of senior **Adam Blazek**, came on strong after a pair of losses in the First Annual Burger King Classic, winning 8 of its next 9, before bowing to Butler in PIAA competition.

• The highlights of the season were Region 8 and District 10 titles and Prep's trio of victories over arch-rival McDowell, as well as the superb late-season play of Blazek.

• Though unknown at the time, Prep's win over Franklin Regional (10-13) on December 11 was game number 2,000 in Rambler basketball history!

• Prep got off to a slow start, losing 3 of its first 5, including at Morgantown (WV) (23-4), in which actor **Don Knotts** is probably its most famous alumnus; and 6 of its first 9, including a pair at the Shootout by the Sea tourney. Morgantown made it to the West Virginia AAA semifinals before losing to eventual state champ George Washington, 52-37.

All-star senior Joe Gnacinski goes high for a bucket in the Burger King Classic.

- The Shootout by the Sea Holiday Tournament was the 7th annual and featured host North Myrtle Beach and five other South Carolina schools, as well as one from North Carolina. The three tough Prep opponents never played before or again: White Knoll (19-8), Clover (18-11) and Easley (20-6).

- One of Prep's toughest losses of the campaign was the nip-and-tuck battle at North Allegheny (21-6), the only regular season battle ever scheduled

Mike Knoll scores over Central's Francis Nosant.

between the two. The Tigers' junior star, **Anthony Dallier** (24.7 PPG), once scoring 47 in a game for NA, transferred after the season to Northfield Mount Hermon (MA), where he led the Hoggers to the national prep championship as a senior.

- In the first edition of the Burger King High School Basketball Classic, Prep played well, taking North Carolina power Charlotte Christian (27-6) to OT before succumbing to a 10-point effort by **Patrick Rooks** in the extra four minutes. CC, which lost in the North Carolina state final, lost to underdog Lansdowne Penn Wood in the Burger King final, 58-51.

- On night two sophomore **Elijah Brown** led St. Edward (18-6) to the consolation victory over Prep. Brown is the son of **Mike Brown**, the NBA's Cleveland Cavaliers' all-time winningest head coach. **Elijah Brown** transferred after the season to Santa Ana (CA) Mater Dei, where he led the Monarchs to a two-year record of 68-4 and back-to-back state titles. He was second team all-state in California as a senior.

- The final standings of Region 8 (formerly Region 7):

	Won	Lost
Cathedral Prep	6	0
Strong Vincent	3	3
McDowell	3	3
George Junior Republic	0	6

- The 18 points surrendered to Harborcreek (8-14) was the lowest point total given up by Prep in 57 years, since Titusville St. Joseph's scored but 16 against the Ramblers in 1953-54. The defense-minded Ramblers gave up the fewest PPG (50.9) since the 2002-03 campaign.

- The Ramblers were beset by an off-season injury to star center **Mike Knoll**, who was expected to have a big senior season. Knoll was able to help sparingly by season's end. Inside operator **Dominic Sansone** (53% FG, 5.5 RPG) came on strong as the season progressed, but he unfortunately suffered a knee injury driving to the hoop in the last regular season game, and was not able to be used effectively from that point on.

- Prep's season unfortunately finished the way it began, with a loss to Butler (17-11). Golden Tornado coach **Matt Clement**, a former star MLB pitcher, stated post-game to **Tom Reisenweber** of the *Erie Times-News*: "All week all we heard was we had to come up to Erie and play on their home court. I think it was a blessing in disguise because it got us motivated and gave us an edge." Clement also noted that **Mark Majewski** "is an unbelievable coach with a great team" and "#21 [**Joe Gnacinski**] might be the most improved player I've seen all season!" Butler thus earned its first playoff win since 1998 and next defeated Taylor Allderdice before losing to Mount Lebanon in the state quarterfinals.

- All Prep's home games, the Burger King Classic and the two playoff encounters were held at Gannon's Hammermill Center.

Dominic Sansone, a First Team All-Region all-star, suffered a late-season knee injury.

- 2010-11 was the first campaign in 70 years that Cathedral Prep did not play the East High Warriors.

- Villa Maria Academy's girls' team (28-2), under the direction of interim coach **Doug Chuzie**, won its third consecutive PIAA AA state title with a resounding 62-39 verdict over Dunmore. **Lisa Mifsud's** floor leadership and **Abbey Steudler's** 17 points sparked the Victors, who also had fine play from **Adrienne Kloecker and Karlee McBride**. VMA is the only Erie school to have won three consecutive state crowns.

- **Adam Blazek** and **Dominic Sansone** were named First Team Region 8 All-Stars by the *Erie Times-News*, while **Sheldon Zablotny** and **Dominic DiRaimo** garnered Second Team honors.

- **Adam Blazek** was further named Region 8 "Player of the Year"; First Team All-District 10; and District 10 "Player of the Year" by the *Erie Times-News*. Blazek, a slick ball-handling guard, finished the season as Prep's leading scorer (14.7 ppg), top rebounder (5.9 RPG), leading assists man (4.7 apg) and best defender (2.7 steals pg). A complete player with a host of "intangibles," his floor leadership and clutch performances were the main reason the Ramblers easily won the Region and District crowns.

- Blazek, Sansone, DiRaimo and **Joe Gnacinski** represented the Ramblers in the 37th annual City-County All-Star Game, played at Behrend's Junker Center. Sansone, however, was unable to play because of his late-season knee injury. The City, led by Blazek's 16 points, pulled out a thrilling 69-68 verdict.

Gnacinski drives for two against the Trojans at the packed Hammermill Center.

- **Mike Knoll** went on to star at Penn State-Behrend, where he won Scholar-Athlete and Athletic Service Awards.

- **Adam Blazek**, the third of four brothers to perform for the Ramblers, was winner of the James "Moe" Gross Award for outstanding basketball ability. Blazek went on to become one of Gannon University's all-time greats. A three-time National Association of Basketball Coaches All-American and the PSAC Western Division's "Athlete of the Year," he finished his Golden Knights career as Gannon's all-time leader in steals (243); and among the top ten in 3-pointers (4th, 190); assists (7th, 373); and points scored (7th, 1,650).

MVP Adam Blazek became one of Gannon University's all-time greats.

2011 All-Opponent Team:

   J. R. Mountain, General McLane
   Taylor Price, Morgantown [West Virginia Wesleyan]
   Nathan Adrian, Morgantown (1st team all-state, WV) [West Virginia]
   Ashleyn Thomason, Clover [Caldwell (NC) CC & TI]
   Troy McGowens, Easley [Charleston Southern, football]
   Tim Pickel, Easley
   J. C. Howard, North Allegheny [Saint Vincent College]
   Anthony Dallier, North Allegheny (2nd team all-state) [Yale]
   Gordon Lyons, Canisius [SUNY-Geneseo]
   Patrick Rooks, Charlotte Christian [Clemson]
   Anthony Gill, Charlotte Christian [Virginia]
   Trent Walker, Charlotte Christian [Randolph-Macon]
   Elijah Brown, St. Ed's [Butler]
   Jake Lorbach, St. Ed's [Ohio State]
   Kyle Pisco, St. Ed's [John Carroll]
   Charles Farris, St. Ignatius
   Jack Tupa, St. Ignatius
   Colin Kimball, McDowell [Mercyhurst, football]
   Cody Herald, Butler [Seton Hill, baseball]
   Bobby Swartout, Butler [West Virginia Wesleyan, baseball]

Coach Majewski leads his Ramblers to a nice win at McDowell. On the bench, having no difficulty hearing the coach, are, L to R: Knoll, Hess, Lynch, Colpoys, Tate, Harris, Sisinni.

Ramblers Return to Final Four!

Zablotny drives for two more at McDowell.

2011-12 (21-6)

Coach: Mark Majewski
Assistants: Bob Maxson, Dave Repko,
Matt Harris, Sr.
Captain: Sheldon Zablotny, Conor Colpoys
Manager: Nick Sorenson

Date	PREP			Dec.	Loc.	High Scorer	Opponent
12/13	46	General McLane	51	L	A	Zablotny (15)	Mason (17)
12/16	71	Athol Springs (NY) St. Francis	44	W	H	Zablotny (14)	Wagner (13)
		KSA TOURNAMENT (KISSIMMEE, FL)					
12/19	56	Letcher County (KY) Central	54	W	N	Zablotny (19)	Gregory (13)
12/20	57	Landrum (SC)	40	W	N	Williams (12)	McDowell & Wilson (12)
12/21	67	Miami (FL) Gulliver Prep	34	W	N	Zablotny (22)	Thomas (7)
12/28	47	Cleveland (OH) St. Ignatius	50	L	A	Francis & Zablotny (12)	Sloan (12)
12/30	71	East	52	W	A	Zablotny (23)	Qualls (17)
1/5	91	George Junior Republic	64	W	A	Zablotny (24)	Richardson (19)
1/8	63	Shanghai (China) Nanyang	26	W	H	Zablotny (19)	Yang (8)
1/9	59	Strong Vincent	60	L	N	Zablotny (23)	Pullium (31)
		BURGER KING CLASSIC					
1/13	61	Jamesville-DeWitt (NY)	74	L	H	Zablotny (20)	Cavanaugh (27)
1/14	65	Niagara Falls (NY)	60	W	H	Zablotny (25)	Burton (18)
1/18	65	McDowell	56	W	H	Zablotny (19)	Lewis (18)
1/21	59	Buffalo (NY) Canisius	72	L	A	Zablotny (16)	MacDonald (23)
1/23	73	Corry	21	W	H	Zablotny & Harris (10)	Taydus (8)
1/25	50	Harborcreek	38	W	A	Zablotny (19)	Zoltowski (17)
1/27	62	North Allegheny	54	W	H	Zablotny (19)	Howard (22)
2/2	70	George Junior Republic	58	W	H	Colpoys (22)	Richardson (21)
2/6	59	Fort LeBoeuf	36	W	H	Colpoys (16)	Hering (13)
2/10	64	Central Tech	59(OT)	W	A	Harris & Colpoys (16)	Nosant (15)
2/13	60	Strong Vincent	59	W	N	Harris (19)	Jones (16)
2/17	47	McDowell	45	W	A	Zablotny (16)	Beck (23)
		DISTRICT 10 PLAYOFF					
3/1	85	Strong Vincent	43	W	N	Zablotny (26)	Jones (12)
		P.I.A.A. INTERDISTRICT PLAYOFFS					
3/10	79	Pittsburgh Obama Academy	57	W	H	Harris (18)	Byrd (21)
3/14	50	Pittsburgh Central Catholic	49(OT)	W	N	Zablotny (25)	Vrbanic (13)
3/17	52	Shaler	49	W	N	Zablotny (17)	Taylor (19)
3/21	48	Lower Merion	79	L	N	Colpoys (13)	Reynolds (20)
	1677 (62.1)		**1384 (51.3)**				

Pos.	Player	Ht.	Prior School	Class	G(GS)	FG(3)	FT	Total	PPG	Career
G	Sheldon Zablotny (#2)	5'11"	Perry	Jr.	25(24)	165(41)	64-85	435	17.4	874
F	Conor Colpoys (#35)	6'3"	St. George's	Jr.	27(25)	105(1)	62-82	273	10.1	279
F	Matt Harris (#25)	6'0"	St. Peter's	Soph.	26(20)	81(32)	20-25	214	8.2	262
G	Chris Francis (#4)	6'0"	Bl. Sacrament	Jr.	27(27)	84(12)	17-32	197	7.3	202
F	Delton Williams (#5)	6'2"	Joanna Connell	Jr.	25(20)	59(2)	30-50	150	6.0	193
G	Matt Hess (#21)	6'1"	St. George's	Jr.	27(3)	41(16)	20-26	118	4.4	121
G	Jeremy Lynch (#10)	5'8"	OLP	Jr.	26(5)	24(7)	30-38	85	3.3	85
G	Dan Blazek (#11)	6'0"	Harborcreek	Jr.	27(11)	26(4)	10-18	66	2.4	87
F	Alex Geanous (#14)	6'2"	St. George's	Jr.	27	13	15-29	41	1.5	41
F	Kimani Smith (#45)	6'3"	Wilson	Sr.	15	17	3-8	37	2.5	40
F	Malik Moffett (#22)	6'2"	Luther Memorial	Jr.	18	11(2)	6-7	30	1.7	30
G	Kyle Carmosino (#3)	5'10"	St. Luke's	Jr.	11	8(1)	2-5	19	1.7	19
G	Joe Causgrove (#34)	5'9"	St. George's	Soph.	8	3(3)	0-0	8	1.0	8
F	Alex Greenawalt (#40)	6'4"	Westlake	Soph.	9	2	0-0	4	0.4	4

Cathedral Prep's 2012 District 10 champs and Final Four entrants. Front, L to R: Geanous, Zablotny, Harris, Francis, Blazek, Lynch, Causgrove, Mgr. Sorenson; Back: Asst's Maxson, Bowen, and Harris, Hess, Smith, Greenawalt, Colpoys, Williams, Moffett, Carmosino, Asst. Coach Repko, Coach Majewski.

HIGHLIGHTS:

- **Mark Majewski's** fourth year at the helm was a thrilling one for Cathedral Prep with many big moments. Sparked by the fine play of an outstanding junior class, the Ramblers won three in the Orlando KSA Tournament; got their first Burger King (McDonald's) win since 2007, over a good Niagara Falls (17-5) team; beat a team from China; defeated rival McDowell twice; won the Region title; and easily pounded Vincent in the District 10 final after two regular season nail-biters. Prep then won the first three rounds of PIAA inter-district play, including a victory over Shaler in a quarterfinal, before bowing to powerful nemesis Lower Merion in the PIAA semifinals (Final Four).

- All of Prep's six losses were to good teams, including General McLane (26-1), St. Ignatius (16-6), Vincent (15-10), Jamesville-DeWitt (22-3), Canisius (21-7) and Lower Merion (29-4).

The Ramblers revel at winning the D-10 title. Front, L to R: Harris, Zablotny, Williams, Greenawalt; Middle: Hess, Lynch, Francis; Back: Maxson, Harris, Geanous, Carmosino, Colpoys, Moffett, Causgrove, Repko, Majewski, Sr. and Jr.

Though the Ramblers were crushed by 31 by Lower Merion in the AAAA semifinals, the Aces were crushed by undefeated perennial powerhouse Chester in the title game, 59-33.

- Cathedral Prep's opener at General McLane was disappointing as the Ramblers blew an early 17-3 lead. It was the only time the Ramblers lost at GM in five contests. The post-mortems were noteworthy if for no other reason than the firestorm controversy surrounding respected long-time Prep teacher/coach **Chet Moffett**, who in an e-mail chided the entire Prep student body for not showing stronger school spirit at the McLane game. As first reported by the *Erie Times-News*, Moffett stated "Never should a bunch of mayonnaise sandwich eating, sister loving, trailer park dwelling clowns at general mclane ever chant 'we can't hear you' to Cathedral Prep!" He also referred to rivals "general mcLame" and "mercyworst." Prep suspended Moffett without pay for two weeks, and split what it would have paid him with General McLame and Mercyworst, er General McLane and Mercyhurst, for their student programs. **Father Scott Jabo**, Prep's president, told the *Erie Times-News* that Moffett, at the school since 1998, twice offered to resign, but Prep insisted on keeping him because of the good work he had done in the past, his lack of prior problems, and Moffett's contrition for his words.

- **Sheldon Zablotny** scored 52 points in the three KSA games and was awarded the Blue Bracket MVP Award. It was Prep's fifth trip to the KSA tourney since 2000 and the first time it took home a first place finish. There were three other second place finishes. Particularly noteworthy was the win over Letcher (19-14), when **Jeremy Lynch** drained a 3-pointer with just 1.2 seconds left; and the triumph over Landrum (24-4), which lost to eventual state champ Great Falls in the South Carolina semifinals, 49-44.

Jeremy Lynch and Alex Geanous get specific instructions from Coach Majewski.

- KSA final victim Gulliver Prep (14-12) was founded in 1926 and initially enrolled students from New England that were wintering in South Florida. The *Miami Herald* recently awarded Gulliver the All-Sports Award for having the top program for small schools in Miami-Dade County.

- Prep hosted the first team from the Orient ever to play in Erie. Shanghai Nanyang Model High School, five-time Chinese national champion, was playing its first of five games in the United States. The Tiger players spent the night with Prep families and the teams met at half-court prior to the start of the contest to exchange gifts. The Chinese national anthem was sung before the U.S. National Anthem and goodwill was shown by all.

- Prep converted only 10 of 22 free throws in its one-point loss to Strong Vincent and lost the game when SV's **Peris Husband** nailed a 3-pointer with but 3.8 seconds left in the contest.

- Alpharetta (GA) Milton won the second edition of the Burger King High School Basketball Classic (29th time Prep has hosted, including the McDonald's Classic). The Eagles brought four Division I recruits, including **Shaquille Johnson**, considered "the best dunker in high school basketball." Johnson, now at Auburn University, wowed the crowd with 7 dunks as Milton defeated the Jamesville-Dewitt Red Rams (22-3) in the final, a team ranked first in New York State and 17th nationally at the time. Milton (28-4, 3 forfeit losses) went on to win the 2012 Georgia 5-A state championship. The Red Rams, who defeated Prep on the first evening, lost in the semifinals of the New York Class A state tourney to Tappan Zee. Prep's victim on night two, Niagara Falls (17-5), was national champion in 2005. It was the only time the Ramblers and the Cataract City boys competed.

- Prep's victory over Corry (3-19) made for 20 straight wins over the Beavers. The last time Corry beat the Ramblers was in 1948. Prep's wins over George Junior Republic (8-13) made for 16 straight against the Tigers.

- One of Prep's more impressive victories of the season was over North Allegheny (16-7). That win put the Ramblers ahead in the series versus the Tigers, 3-2.

A Rambler jersey was placed over the seat from where principal Joann Mullen watched every game. Three years later the new gym at the PVEC was named after her.

Tense action as Colpoys grabs a rebound against Niagara Falls in the Burger King Classic.

- The Ramblers got their 14th win of the season with an emotional 59-36 victory over Fort LeBoeuf (8-11) at the Hammermill Center just hours after long time Prep teacher and principal **Joann Mullen** died after a battle with cancer. Players wore black ribbons on their jerseys and a Prep basketball jersey was laid over beloved Mrs. Mullen's empty seat where she would watch every game from. Cathedral Prep and Villa Maria will continue to honor the memory of Mrs. Mullen as the new gymnasium, opened in the Fall of 2015, was christened the "Joann Mullen Gymnasium."

- Prep's win at Central Tech (11-12) was the first time in 40 contests with the Falcons that the game was not held at Hammermill Center. It was only the second time the Ramblers ever played in the old Tech Memorial gym, the first being in the 1969 PCIAA elimination contest against Altoona Bishop Guilfoyle.

- The final standings of Region 8:

	Won	Lost
Cathedral Prep	5	1
Strong Vincent	5	1
McDowell	2	4
George Junior Republic	0	6

- All Prep's home games and the Burger King Classic were held at Gannon's Hammermill Center. The victory over East High (5-16), with **Sheldon Zablotny** scoring 16 fourth quarter points, was the first time since 1949 the two competed on the Warriors' home court. From 1950 through 2010 all the Prep-East matchups were held at the Gannon Auditorium/Hammermill Center.

- Prep students held a wild post-game rally in Perry Square and throughout the streets of downtown Erie after the Ramblers' first drubbing of McDowell at Gannon. Prep's thrilling 2-point win in the regular season finale at the jam-packed, sold-out McDowell (9-12) gym was accomplished when Rambler strongman **Delton Williams** collected a rebound and drove the length of the floor with just 8 seconds remaining to give Prep its winning margin.

- Prep opened PIAA play easily disposing Pittsburgh Barack Obama Academy of International Studies (17-7), a public school established in 2009 and housed in the former Peabody High School building. **Matt Hess** was superb, with 17 points, 6 rebounds and 2 blocked shots. The Prep cheering section appeared in patriotic garb, hoisting American flags and chanting "USA! USA! USA!" One character even paraded around Hammermill Center wearing a **George W. Bush** mask to the many cheers of those in attendance. It was safe to assume there were not present many fans of our 44th president, aside from those from the Smoky City.

- Obama Academy sponsored its first basketball team for the instant season and did well enough to finish second to Taylor Allderdice in the Pittsburgh City League and make the PIAA playoffs. Obama Academy's entrance into the City League made for a nine-team loop, though it turned out to be the final campaigns for Oliver, Langley and Peabody. All three were closed at the conclusion of the 2011-12 school year. Other schools remaining in the City League include Brashear, Perry Traditional Academy, Westinghouse, Allderdice and Carrick.

- Round two of the PIAA's was thrilling overtime battle royale at Sharon, as **Sheldon Zablotny** used a screen by **Delton Williams** to drive down the left side of the lane and hit a short jumper as time expired against old rival Pittsburgh Central Catholic (16-12). The Ramblers were down by one and forced

District 10 "Player of the Year" Sheldon Zablotny, acknowledging victory over Shaler in a PIAA Quarterfinal.

to foul with 20 seconds remaining. The front end of a 1-and-1 missed the mark and Prep set up for a final chance—and "Z" made good.

- Prep proved to be best in the west, with its PIAA Quarterfinal win over a strong Shaler (25-4) outfit. The Ramblers neutralized 22 PPG all-stater **Geno Thorpe** (only 3 points) with solid defense from Zablotny, **Matt Harris** and particularly **Chris Francis**. In the olden days this would have been the Western Final, with the victory a ticket from Sharon to Hershey.

- Old nemesis Lower Merion used its superior size, speed and leaping ability to upend Prep in the PIAA Semifinal at Bald Eagle High School, of all places. It was the third time the Aces defeated the Ramblers, including the 2005 semifinal and the 1996 state championship game when they had a fellow by the name of **Kobe Bryant**.

- **Sheldon Zablotny**, only a junior but a complete player, led the Ramblers in scoring, blocks and steals, and further shot 51% from the floor and 75% from the foul line. He was also a high-leaping rebounder, despite his short appearance. Blue collar worker **Conor Colpoys**, another tough rebounder, also led Prep in FG percentage (57%), while **Matt Harris** (80%) and **Jeremy Lynch** (79%) were the best free throw shooters. **Kevin Francis**, who started every contest at point guard, led in the assist department (2.7 APG).

- **Sheldon Zablotny** and **Conor Colpoys** were named First Team Region 8 All-Stars by the *Erie Times-News*, while **Chris Francis** and **Delton Williams** garnered Second Team honors.

First Team Region All-Star Conor Colpoys.

- Zablotny was further named First Team All-District 10 and District 10 "Player of the Year" by the *Erie Times-News*. He also was named Third Team All-State by the *Associated Press*, the first Rambler underclassman since **Julian Blanks** to be given all-state recognition. Zablotny further became just the third junior to win the James "Moe" Gross Award, signifying him as Prep's most valuable player.

Kimani Smith was the only senior on the Prep roster. He went on to star in football at Robert Morris.

- No Ramblers were selected to play in the City-County All-Star Game for the first time ever. The 38th annual was won by the City, 71-62. The only senior on the Rambler squad was part-timer **Kimani Smith**, who went on to star at outside linebacker at Division I Robert Morris University, where he won several Northeast Conference "Player of the Week" awards.

- **Dan Blazek** was the fourth of four brothers to star for the Ramblers, the others being **Mark '08, Keith '09 and Adam '11**. The Blazeks were topped in number of Prep ballplayers only by the famous **Tomczaks: Len '53, Dan '54, "Clutch" '56, "Jiggs" '57 and Pat '60**.

- **Delton Williams**, also an all-state gridiron star for the Ramblers, won the "Ma" Kaiser Award as Prep's best all-around athlete, only the fourth junior in Rambler history to be so honored.

- **Malik Moffett** has become a record-breaking sprinter (100 and 200 meters) at Penn State-Behrend and later at the PSU main campus.

Three fired-up Ramblers, L to R: Hess, Williams, Zablotny.

2012 All-Opponent Team:

Jaymon Mason, General McLane (2nd team all-state) [Edinboro]

Chad Kulka, General McLane [Slippery Rock, football]

Cody Gregory, Letcher County Central [Pikeville]

Logan Johnson, Letcher County Central [Morehead St., football]

Derek Sloan, St. Ignatius (hm all-state, OH) [Cleveland St.]

Darion Qualls, East

Malquan Pullium, Vincent [Penn State-Behrend]

Denzel Jones, Vincent

Tyler Cavanaugh, Jamesville-DeWitt (1st team all-state, NY) [Wake Forest]

DaJuan Coleman, Jamesville-DeWitt (Mr. NY Basketball, McDonald's All-American) [Syracuse]

Pete Drescher, Jamesville-DeWitt [Hobart]

Jafar Kinsey, Jamesville-DeWitt [Robert Morris]

Jermaine Crumpton, Niagara Falls [Canisius]

Jamir Burton, Niagara Falls [St. Edward's (TX)]

Matt MacDonald, Canisius [Fairleigh Dickinson]

Adam Weir, Canisius [Canisius]

J. C. Howard, North Allegheny [Saint Vincent College]

Marlon Richardson, GJR

Francis Nosant, Central Tech [Mercyhurst-North East]

DeAndrye Henderson, Vincent [Mercyhurst-North East]

Mike Beck, McDowell [Edinboro]

Deandre Byrd, Obama Academy

Lincoln Davis, Pittsburgh Central Catholic [Fairfield]

Claude Scott, Pittsburgh Central Catholic [Allegheny CC]

Sam Calhoun, Pittsburgh Central Catholic [Allegheny]

Garrett Vrbanic, Pittsburgh Central Catholic [Seton Hill, baseball]

Zack Taylor, Shaler [Carlow]

Geno Thorpe, Shaler (1st team all-state) [Penn State]

Darryl Reynolds, Lower Merion (2nd team all-state) [Villanova]

B. J. Johnson, Lower Merion (1st team all-state) [Syracuse]

JaQuan Johnson, Lower Merion [Central Arizona JC]

Elite Eight Squad One of Prep's Best Ever!

2012-13 (23-3)

Coach: Mark Majewski
Assistants: Bob Maxson, Dave Repko,
Matt Harris, Sr.
Captains: Sheldon Zablotny, Conor Colpoys,
Dan Blazek
Manager: Anthony Mezler

The Ramblers rejoice in victory over Hampton in the state tourney.

Date	PREP			Dec.	Loc.	High Scorer	Opponent
12/8	70	Toronto (ONT) Pope John Paul II	60	W	A	C. Colpoys (17)	Alleyne (24)
12/10	68	Strong Vincent	41	W	N	Harris (20)	Coleman (11)
12/12	65	East	42	W	H	Zablotny (17)	Henderson & Kirkland (9)
12/15	75	Fort LeBoeuf	32	W	A	Zablotny & Colpoys (12)	Kress (16)
12/17	76	Harborcreek	36	W	H	Zablotny (15)	Zoltowski (11)
		KSA PRE-HOLIDAY TOURNAMENT (KISSIMMEE, FL)					
12/20	82	Carriere (MS) Pearl River Central	53	W	N	Harris (19)	Woodson (31)
12/21	54	Homewood (AL)	60(OT)	L	N	C. Colpoys (21)	Cook (20)
12/22	68	Midlothian (VA) James River	57	W	N	Zablotny (21)	Regimbal (17)
12/28	84	East	57	W	A	Zablotny (23)	Kirkland (13)
1/4	76	Central Tech	66	W	A	Zablotny (33)	Husband (32)
1/8	84	Athol Springs (NY) St. Francis	37	W	A	Zablotny (21)	Cullen (12)
1/12	63	General McLane	53	W	H	Zablotny (22)	Mason (22)
1/16	72	Franklin	27	W	H	Zablotny (18)	Jones (6)
		BURGER KING CLASSIC					
1/18	47	Philadelphia Imhotep Charter	74	L	H	Zablotny (12)	Austin (16)
1/19	80	Arlington (VA) Bishop O'Connell	75	W	H	Zablotny (19)	Trimble (33)
1/24	69	McDowell	46	W	A	Zablotny (30)	C. Lewis (13)
1/26	68	Warren	59	W	A	Zablotny (18)	Sandberg (21)
1/28	74	Central Tech	60	W	H	C. Colpoys (23)	Husband (19)
1/31	74	Strong Vincent	44	W	N	Zablotny (27)	Pullium (25)
2/2	78	Pittsburgh Perry Traditional	34	W	H	Zablotny (16)	Cox (14)
2/7	72	Buffalo (NY) Canisius	53	W	H	Harris (20)	Weir (20)
2/14	73	McDowell	50	W	H	Zablotny (27)	C. Lewis (19)
		DISTRICT 10 PLAYOFF					
3/2	64	McDowell	46	W	N	Zablotny (16)	C. Lewis (12)
		P.I.A.A. INTERDISTRICT PLAYOFFS					
3/9	79	Seneca Valley	54	W	N	Harris (17)	Bazzoli (17)
3/13	58	Hampton	50	W	N	Zablotny (21)	C. Luther (22)
3/16	70	New Castle	80	L	N	Zablotny (24)	Anderson (20)
	1843(70.9)		**1346 (51.8)**				

Pos.	Player	Ht.	Prior School	Class	G(GS)	FG(3)	FT	Total	PPG	Career
G	Sheldon Zablotny (#2)	6'0"	Perry	Sr.	26(26)	176(39)	106-129	497	19.1	1371
F	Matt Harris (#22)	6'0"	St. Peter's	Jr.	26(26)	135(38)	46-56	354	13.6	616
G	Conor Colpoys (#33)	6'3"	St. George's	Sr.	26(26)	121(16)	46-60	304	11.7	583
G	Chris Francis (#4)	6'0"	Bl. Sacrament	Sr.	26(26)	77(9)	18-30	181	7.0	383
G	Matt Hess (#21)	6'1"	St. George's	Sr.	25(26)	63(17)	13-16	156	6.2	277
F	Jarret Pound (#15)	6'2"	Seneca	Soph.	22	31(5)	21-28	88	4.0	88
G	Dan Blazek (#11)	6'0"	Harborcreek	Sr.	26(1)	30(6)	9-12	75	2.9	162
G	Jeremy Lynch (#3)	5'8"	OLP	Sr.	16(9)	23(6)	7-12	59	3.7	144
F	Marlon Tyree (#5)	6'3"	Wilson	Jr.	18	13	4-5	30	1.7	30
F	Matt Viera (#40)	6'2"	St. George's	Jr.	17	12	5-9	29	1.7	29
G	Joe Causgrove (#10)	5'9"	St. George's	Jr.	17	7(1)	9-11	24	1.4	32
G	Anthony Pearson (#25)	5'11"	Wayne	Jr.	16	9(3)	2-3	23	1.4	23
F	Delton Williams (#5)	6'2"	Joanna Connell	Sr.	4	7	2-2	16	4.0	209
G	Antonio Frisina (#34)	5'10"	Seton Catholic	Soph.	10	2	3-4	7	0.7	7
G	Jack Lindenberger (#51)	6'1"	Walnut Creek	Soph.	1	0	0-0	0	0.0	0
G	Carter Cross (#14)	6'0"	Walnut Creek	Fr.	1	0	0-0	0	0.0	0
F	Matt Colpoys (#33)	6'0"	St. George's	Soph.	1	0	0-0	0	0.0	0

Cathedral Prep's 2013 District 10 Champions. Front, L to R: Mgr. Mezler, Pearson, Frisina, Cross, Blazek, Lynch, Causgrove, Majewski Jr.; Back: Asst's Maxson, Harris, and Bowen, Francis, Harris and Bowen, Francis, Harris, Viera, Hess, Pound, Colpoys, Tyree, Williams, Zablotny, Coach Majewski, Asst. Repko.

HIGHLIGHTS:

- **Mark Majewski's** fifh year at the helm produced one of Cathedral Prep's greatest teams in its history, storming to Region 7 and District 10 titles and outscoring opponents by nearly 20 points per game. The Ramblers .885 winning percentage ranks third on Prep's all-time chart, behind only the 1979-80 state champions (33-1, .971) and the 1977-78 semifinalists (26-3, .897). Prep's misfortune was running into exceptionally powerful roadblock, undefeated New Castle, in the PIAA state quarterfinals.

Coach Mark Majewski molded the 2013 Ramblers into one of Prep's best squads ever.

- The 2012-13 Ramblers presented no real big men, but did have an outstanding senior class, including savvy veterans **Sheldon Zablotny**, the *Erie Times-News* Pre-season District 10 Player of the Year; inside man **Conor Colpoys**; playmakers **Chris Francis** and **Jeremy Lynch**; reliable **Matt Hess**; and defenseman **Dan Blazek**, the fourth of four brothers to perform for the Ramblers. Zablotny, Colpoys, Francis and junior **Matt Harris** started all 26 games.

"Z! No!" Coach Majewski implores Zablotny not to shoot.

- The 2012-13 Prepsters were an outstanding shooting team, hitting 50% from the floor, including 38% from 3-point range. The Ramblers also shot 77% from the free throw line, with Zablotny, Harris and junior **Joe Causgrove** at 82% and Hess clipping in at 81%.

Matt Harris with his patented one-hand jumper.

- Unknown at the time, Prep's early season victory over Strong Vincent was the 100th time the Ramblers defeated the Colonels.

- The 30th Burger King Classic and all Prep home games were at Gannon's Hammermill Center, including both Vincent contests. The D-10 title game and the PIAA Final Four contest against New Castle were held at Edinboro's McComb Fieldhouse. The PIAA inter-district clashes against Seneca Valley and Hampton were held at General McLane and Farrell high schools, respectively.

- **Sheldon Zablotny** became the 10th Rambler all-time to cross the 1,000 career point mark on December 28 at East High's Bill Brabender Gymnasium. Zablotny, a four-year letterman for the Ramblers, finished the campaign as Prep's second all-time leading scorer (1,371 points), ahead of **Tim Gore** (1,305; 1977-80) and behind only **Jed Ryan** (1,926; 1991-95). One of Prep's all-time greatest players ever, Zablotny also finished #11 on the all-time Erie area scoring chart.

- Senior **Delton Williams**, an all-state star RB and DB for the 2013 Cathedral Prep football state champions, was honored before the Harborcreek game. Williams, who did not finish the hoop season because of football commitments, has gone on to star for the Michigan State Spartans on the gridiron with another Rambler football great, all-state quarterback **Damion Terry**.

- Prep took impressive consolation honors at the KSA tournament, losing but once in overtime to a solid Homewood (AL) (23-6) team. It was Prep's sixth trip to the KSA since the year 2000.

- Impressive independent wins for the Ramblers included the pounding of Canisius (23-5), which made it to New York's Class A state championship game at Fordham University, only to lose to Brooklyn Nazareth, 46-40; and the verdict over General McLane (21-6), which made it to the AAA quarterfinals, only to lose to Montour, 42-40. Great defense by **Matt Harris** and **Kevin**

Point gaurd Kevin Francis, a terror on defense.

Francis held GM's all-state star **Jaymon Mason** scoreless in the first half. Mason scored his 22 when the game was out of reach for the Lancers.

- Prep's slaughter of St. Francis was the last the two competed in basketball, with the Ramblers on the long end of a 4-0 series ledger. The two remain common opponents in football.

- The annual Burger King Classic presented three eventual state champions along with the exciting Prep Ramblers team. Imhotep Charter (28-5), the 2013 PIAA AAA champion, crushed Prep on opening night, then got by 2013 PIAA AAAA state titlist Lower Merion, 64-61. The Ramblers took consolation honors with a stunning upset over #15 nationally ranked Bishop O'Connell (29-7), which won the 2013 the Virginia state crown with an 85-75 verdict over Richmond Benedictine in the final.

Starting guard Matt Hess works against Imhotep in the Burger King Classic.

- Bishop O'Connell fell out of the *USA Today* Super 25 Rankings after suffering consecutive losses to Lower Merion and Prep, but the Knights were having bigger problems to worry about. There were grumblings by coaches and a *Deadspin* report that 6'7" forward star **"Junior" Etou**, a transfer from the Republic of Congo, was actually 20 years of age, rather than 18 as claimed by Etou and his coach, **Joe Wootten**. Etou and Wootten vehemently denied the reports and publicly stated they had documentation of proof of age. Etou continued to play and O'Connell won the DC area and Virginia titles. FIBA, basketball's international governing body, completed an investigation and found that Etou competed during the entire 2012-13 season while being 20 years old, two years too old for league regulations. Needless to say, the coaches who were topped by Etou's dominant show of force were less than pleased to learn that they were duped by the prep star who went on to play at Rutgers as a 21-year old freshman.

- Prep faced a new opponent in Pittsburgh Perry Traditional Academy (12-14), formerly simply Perry High School, a partial magnet school which emphasizes academics, attendance and positive behavior. The Commodores won the Pittsburgh City League title, but lost in the PIAA first round to Hampton, which the Ramblers next beat.

- Central Tech (17-6) gave Prep a battle on its home court behind **Eugene Husband's** 32 points and kept it close until the fourth quarter. The Falcons, however, could not overcome an amazing 33-point performance by Zablotny. In the second Central Tech contest, the Ramblers made 19 of 20 foul shots and easily beat the Falcons.

- Satisfying to the Prep fans were the three beatdowns handed to archrival McDowell (12-12) in regular season play and in the D-10 final. **Sheldon Zablotny** was spectacular throughout the series, and scored 30 on the Trojans' home floor in game one. The Ramblers drained eleven 3-pointers in the rematch at Gannon and in the D-10 final overcame a 6-point halftime deficit with a tremendous second half show.

Zablotny always played his best against rival McDowell.

- The final standings of the new Region 7, a ridiculous three-team farce forced upon AAAA schools by the PIAA District 10:

	Won	Lost
Cathedral Prep	4	0
Central Tech	2	2
McDowell	0	4

- Prep was 21-2 and ranked #5 in the state heading into the PIAA playoffs. In the first round, the Ramblers rode **Matt Harris'** 17 first half points (5 for 5 from the floor, including four 3-pointers) to an easy win over Seneca Valley (17-9). The second round battle against Hampton (21-6) was more contentious, as the Talbots presented the 6'8" **Luther twins, Ryan and Collin**, and a "triangle-and-two" defense to try and thwart Prep in the dark Farrell gym. Prep hung on in the exciting, tense battle. The next season Hampton, with the Luther twins still in the lineup, made it to the state semifinals and finished with a 24-5 record and #2 ranking in the state.

Conor Colpoys slices through a pair of Hurricane defenders.

- In the much-hyped PIAA Quarterfinal matchup against WPIAL champ New Castle (30-1), before a raucous sellout crowd, Prep held an early lead. The Red Hurricanes, however, went 6 for 6 from 3-point range in the 2nd period and the Ramblers, though clawing and scratching admirably the rest of the way, could not catch up. New Castle then lost in the state final to Chester, but

came back in 2014 to win the PIAA crown with a state final victory over Philadelphia LaSalle College to finish 31-0.

- Zablotny led the Ramblers in scoring, blocks and steals, and further shot 50% from the floor. He was also a high-leaping rebounder at 5.2 RPG, despite his short appearance. Blue collar worker **Conor Colpoys**, who typically was assigned to guarding opponents always several inches taller, again led Prep in FG percentage (56%) and rebounds (6.2 RPG), including a 20-rebound performance against Central Tech. Point guard **Kevin Francis** again led in the assist department (3.2 APG) and was a hounding defensive point guard.

- Three-year letterman **Jeremy Lynch**, who unfortunately suffered a pre-season knee injury and was slowed down much of the season, came on strong for the Ramblers at playoff time. He went on to play for Edinboro University for two seasons.

Jeremy Lynch battled injuries his senior year, but came on strong as the season progressed.

Colpoys for two from the charity stripe.

- **Sheldon Zablotny** was named to the *Erie Times-News* All-District 10 team and was also a First Team Region 7 All-Star, along with **Conor Colpoys**.

- Zablotny was further honored by being named Second Team Class AAAA All-State by the Pennsylvania Sports Writers. Only Zablotny, **Jed Ryan** and **Julian Blanks** are the Prepsters to be named all-state on more than one occasion.

- Zablotny wowed the crowd, draining four 3-pointers amid his game-high 16 points, as the City defeated the County, 73-55, in the 39th annual City-County All-Star Game, played at Behrend's Junker Center. Colpoys and Francis also represented the Ramblers, scoring two and five, respectively.

- **Sheldon Zablotny** became just the third double-winner, along with Prep greats **Jed Ryan** and **Mark Blazek**, to win the James "Moe" Gross Award for outstanding basketball ability. Zablotny went on to star at Niagara County CC, averaging 12.7 PPG as a freshman and 20.3 PPG as a sophomore. He now starts for Florida Southern College, the 2015 NCAA Division II national champion.

2013 All-Opponent Team:

Joey Zoltowski, Harborcreek [Hiram]

Ashton Woodson, Pearl River Central [Jones County (MS) JC]

Malik Cook, Homewood [Alabama-Huntsville]

Kevin Regimbal, James River [Christopher Newport]

Jaymon Mason, General McLane (2nd team all-state) [Edinboro]

Romelo "Melo" Trimble, Bishop O'Connell [Maryland]

Luc Tselan "Junior" Etou, Bishop O'Connell [Rutgers]

Brandon Austin, Imhotep Charter (1st team all-state) [Providence]

Carson Lewis, McDowell

Matt Sandberg, Warren

Eugene Husband, Central Tech

Malquan Pullium, Vincent [Penn St.-Behrend]

Adam Weir, Canisius (*Buffalo News* Player of the Year) [Canisius]

Easton Bazzoli, Seneca Valley [Cedarville]

Ryan Luther, Hampton (3rd team all-state) (Player of the Year, 2014) [Pitt]

Collin Luther, Hampton [Elon]

Shawn Anderson, New Castle (1st team all-state) [Navy]

Anthony Richards, New Castle [West Virginia Wesleyan]

Brandon Domenick, New Castle [Gannon, Westminster]

The Prep Faculty lineup, which squared off against the CYO All-Stars, L to R: Father Bill Barron, Corey Ferraro, Mark Brooks, Will Pituch, Dustin Burger, Dave Swanson, Chet Moffett, Matt Hubert.

Region Champions!
Season Ends Abruptly with Loss to McDowell!

2013-14 (15-8)

Coach: Mark Majewski
Assistants: Bob Maxson, Dave Repko,
John Bowen, Sr
Captains: Matt Harris, Felix Manus-Schell,
Matt Colpoys
Manager: Anthony Mezler, Dillon Wolbert

All-state star Matt Harris with his patented one-hand 3-pointer from the corner.

Date	PREP		Dec.	Loc.	High Scorer	Opponent
12/7		Toronto (ONT) Pope John Paul II (POSTPONED—SNOW)		A		
12/11	65	East	61	W	H	Colpoys (18)	Burzic (13)
12/16	57	Harborcreek	27	W	A	Cross (11)	I. Mattson (8)
		TARKANIAN CLASSIC (LAS VEGAS, NV)				
12/19	48	Lynwood (CA)	33	W	N	Fustine (10)	Hill (8)
12/20	66	El Cajon (CA) Foothills Christian	55	W	N	Harris (28)	Leaf (28)
12/20	44	Orem (UT)	78	L	N	Harris (15)	Holt (23)
12/21	52	Provo (UT) Timpview	66	L	N	Harris (29)	Wright (17)
12/23	76	Fort LeBoeuf	30	W	H	Harris (16)	Miller (11)
12/27	60	Toledo (OH) St. John's Jesuit	67	L	N	Harris (29)	Glover (21)
1/3	58	Central Tech	44	W	A	Harris (22)	Wells (13)
1/6		Strong Vincent (POSTPONED—WEATHER)			N		
1/11	49	General McLane	38	W	A	Harris (23)	Kulka (16)
		BURGER KING CLASSIC				
1/17	35	Philadelphia Archbishop Carroll	47	L	H	Colpoys & Harris (15)	Taylor & Tilghman (13)
1/18	46	Cleveland (OH) VASJ	64	L	H	Harris (11)	Bragg (24)
1/23	52	McDowell	47	W	H	Harris (24)	Beck (16)
1/25		Warren (POSTPONED—WEATHER)			H		
1/27	74	Central Tech	69(OT)	W	H	Harris (38)	Tracy (23)
1/29		Strong Vincent (POSTPONED—WEATHER)			N		
2/1	91	Toronto (ONT) Pope John Paul II	86(OT)	W	A	Harris (40)	Ramirez (24)
2/5		Pittsburgh Perry Traditional (POSTPONED—WEATHER)			A		
2/6	53	Pittsburgh Perry Traditional	64	L	A	Harris (14)	N. Taylor (18)
2/8	54	Buffalo (NY) Canisius	56	L	A	Colpoys (17)	Huffman (18)
2/10	87	Warren	63	W	H	Fustine & Harris (14)	Fantaskey (15)
2/11	63	Franklin	56	W	A	Harris (14)	Ritchey (17)
2/14	59	McDowell	47	W	A	Harris (29)	Beck (16)
2/15	70	Strong Vincent	58	W	N	Harris (22)	Pointer & Morris (14)
2/17	61	Strong Vincent	60	W	N	Harris (15)	Morris (23)
		DISTRICT 10 PLAYOFF				
2/25	52	McDowell	66	L	H	Harris (25)	Beck (17)
	1372 (59.7)		**1282 (55.7)**			

Pos.	Player	Ht.	Prior School	Class	G(GS)	FG(3)	FT	Total	PPG	Career
G	Matt Harris (#22)	6'2"	St. Peter's	Sr.	23(23)	148(51)	123-147	470	20.4	1086
F	Matt Colpoys (#33)	6'0"	St. George's	Jr.	23(22)	80(11)	72-95	243	10.6	243
G	Carter Cross (#14)	6'0"	Walnut Creek	Soph.	23(18)	38(17)	24-39	117	5.1	117
F	Felix Manus-Schell (#11)	6'0"	St. Luke's	Sr.	21(14)	39(4)	16-30	98	4.7	98
F	Joe Fustine (#4)	6'2"	OLP	Jr.	23	34(11)	14-19	93	4.0	93
G	Taylor Mackowski (#15)	6'1"	Bl. Sacrament	Jr.	20(11)	31(3)	14-25	79	4.0	79
G	Jack Lindenberger (#21)	6'1"	Walnut Creek	Jr.	23(5)	27(7)	6-8	67	2.9	67
F	Marlon Tyree (#5)	6'3"	Wilson	Sr.	18(7)	20(1)	11-15	52	2.9	82
G	Antonio Frisina (#2)	5'10"	Seton Catholic	Jr.	22(4)	18(5)	9-18	50	2.3	57
G	Joe Causgrove (#10)	6'0"	St. George's	Sr.	23(9)	18	9-22	45	2.0	77
F	Michael Douds (#34)	6'3"	OLP	Jr.	15	6	7-12	19	1.3	19
G	Matt Falconer (#35)	5'9"	Walnut Creek	Jr.	12	6(4)	0-1	16	1.3	16
F	Matt Viera (#3)	6'2"	St. George's	Sr.	20(1)	5	2-3	12	0.6	41
F	Billy Fessler (#40)	6'1"	OLC	Sr.	15(1)	3	5-10	11	0.7	11

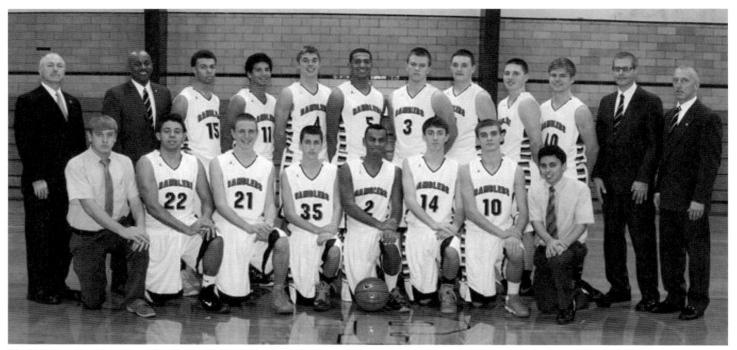

The 2014 Prep Ramblers. Front, L to R: Mgr. Wolbert, Harris, Lindenberger, Falconer, Frisina, Cross, Causgrove, Mgr. Mezler; Back: Coach Majewski, Asst. Harris, Mackowski, Manus, Fustine, Tyree, Viera, Douds, Colpoys, Fessler, Asst's Repko, Maxson.

Harris ready to drive against McDowell's Michael Beck, the Region "Player of the Year."

HIGHLIGHTS:

- **Mark Majewski's** sixth year at the Cathedral Prep helm was considered one for rebuilding as the Ramblers were decimated by graduation. The lineup was brand-new with the exception of veteran **Matty Harris**, who was named the District 10 Preseason Player of the Year by the *Erie Times-News*. Harris had already signed on to a full scholarship to Division I Massachusetts-Lowell. He went on to have a spectacular season as the Prep repeated as Region 7 champion over McDowell and Central.

- Prep's win over a very good East High (20-6) team made for 16 straight over the Warriors; the Rambler triumphs over Central Tech (12-11) made for 23 consecutive against the Falcons.

- Early in the season the Ramblers flew to Las Vegas for the 2nd annual Tarkanian Classic, honoring the godfather of Las Vegas basketball, former UNLV coach **Jerry Tarkanian**. It was the fifth time since 1983 that Prep engaged in a Las Vegas holiday tourney. The 44-team event was highlighted by four of the nation's top five teams as ranked by *MaxPreps.com*, and four defending state champions. Prep won an impressive 4th place finish in the 16-team Gold Division after opening with two victories. Wasatch Academy from Mt. Pleasant (UT) won the

Gold Division, while host Bishop Gorman High School won the Platinum Division.

- Prep was to play at Columbus DeSales on December 27, but that game was cancelled and replaced by a contest with Toledo St. John's (18-6), which agreed to meet half-way and play in New Philadelphia (OH), some 110 miles northwest of Columbus. All-male St. John's was founded in 1898 by the Jesuits as St. John's College and in 2004 began featuring grades 6 through 12. The Titans have never won an Ohio state basketball title, but have been to the Final Four six times and in the final thrice. Former Prep coach **Bob Ronai** is the A.D. at St. John's.

Carter Cross gets an earful from Coach Majewski.

- Always good was an easy win at rival General McLane (15-8), as a spectacular 17-point second quarter outburst by **Matt Harris** led the way. McLane was a paltry 3 for 18 from the free throw line. The Lancers thus suffered only their 16th loss ever on their home court since their gym opened over two decades before, in 1991. The Ramblers are 4-1 at McLane!

- The Prep-Central Tech game of January 3 was originally scheduled to be played at Hammermill Center, but a fire at the facility several days before necessitated the move to Central's gym.

Marlon Tyree gets a monster block against Carroll in the BK Classic, as team-mate Jack Lindenberger watches in amazement.

- The 4th annual Burger King High School Basketball Classic (referred to as the 31st to include the McDonald's Classic games) featured several big-time Division I recruits from all four participating teams. Archbishop Carroll (23-5) stars **Derrick Jones** (1st team all-state) and **Ernest Aflakpui** (2nd team all-state) were held in check point-wise, but the Patriots' tenacious zone defense forced Prep into an 0-for-17 stretch in the 2nd and 3rd quarters and a lousy 29.3% overall shooting night. The consolation match found Prep playing Cleveland Villa Angela-St. Joseph (21-9) for the first time in two decades. The Ramblers had a difficult time handling impressive 6'10" junior **Carlton Bragg** and were never really in the contest.

- Archbishop Carroll is a co-ed school of about 900 students that competes in the Philadelphia Catholic League. The Patriots won state championships in 2009 and 2013 and beat St. Rita of Cascia (21-8), 64-38, in the Burger King final. Most considered that score a surprise since St. Rita looked so powerful opening night versus VASJ. St. Rita is located on the southwest side of Chicago and was one of the eight original founders of the Chicago Catholic League in 1912. St. Rita, founded in 1906, is an all-male school of about 750 boys.

- Prep put together a great defensive effort to upset arch-rival McDowell (23-4), 14-1 at the time, in a 52-47 thriller before a packed house at the Hammermill Center. The Ramblers erased an early 18-6 deficit, clawing and scratching their way to victory, despite missing 11 free throws in the 4th quarter.

Felix Manus-Schell drives past Central Tech's Josh Wells.

- The second Prep-Central battle was moved to the Hammermill Center, a thrilling overtime win for the Ramblers. **Matty Harris** burned the nets for 38 points, fifth highest single game effort in Prep history. Harris scored Prep's final 18 points, including all 12 in OT. Prep had a three-point lead in regulation until the Falcons' **Josh Wells**, son of esteemed General McLane football coach **Jim Wells**, buried a turnaround 3-pointer from the top of the key to send the game into overtime. The Prep victory made for 23 straight over the Falcons.

- Harris followed with a remarkable 40-point game, third highest in Prep history, in another overtime battle in Toronto. His spectacular two-game 78-point output is a Rambler record for most points scored in back-to-back games. It was also Coach Majewski's 100th win at the Rambler helm.

- Two of Prep's toughest losses were the back-to-back upset loss at Perry (11-12) and the two-point setback at powerful Buffalo Canisius (23-3).

- Prep handed McDowell its second of only 3 regular season losses at sold-out Paul Goll Gymnasium to capture its fourth consecutive Region title and eighth overall since District 10 dissolved the 7-team Metro League following the 2003-04 season. **Matt Harris** put together one of the greatest performances in a Rambler uniform, scoring 29 points,

Matt Harris, up and over McDowell's Quinn Lewis.

Diving Matty Harris giving maximum effort against the Trojans.

including 18 in the 4th period, despite being double and sometimes triple-teamed. The game's key play was a 3-pointer by **Felix Manus-Schell** that tied the game at 40-40, after McDowell erased an early 14-point deficit and had taken a 4th quarter lead. Harris then scored the battle's next 12 points as the Ramblers buried the Trojans for the 11th straight time.

• The final standings of Region 7:

	Won	Lost
Cathedral Prep	4	0
McDowell	2	2
Central Tech	0	4

• Prep concluded the regular season with a pair of emotional make-up games against Strong Vincent (17-9). The Colonels hung tough in both outings behind freshman phenom **David Morris** and 6'4", 360-pound center **Kyle Pointer**. SV nearly won the second battle, but couldn't convert a short put-back at the buzzer after an errant **Simeal Wofford** shot. Wofford had given the Colonels a 60-59 lead with 15 seconds remaining, but **Matt Colpoys** made the clutch play of the evening with a key rebound and short put-back with 5.1 seconds remaining.

• Prep's season ended abruptly with a 66-52 loss to favored McDowell (23-4) in the District 10 championship game. The Ramblers unfortunately gave their poorest showing of the season, this despite a 25-point performance by **Matt Harris**, which included five 3-pointers and 10 of 10 at the FT line.

Harris' last shot of his Prep career was a picture perfect 25-foot trey in the game's final minute, giving him 1,086 points for his four-year stay on the Rambler varsity. He was taken out of the game to a standing ovation by Prep fans moments later.

Lindenberger for three!

• Prior to the start of the season finale there was a moment of silence for highly respected teacher **Antonio "Tony" Del Rio**, who passed away earlier that day. Mr. Del Rio, only 61, was a 34-year veteran of the Prep faculty, a tireless moderator for many student activities and a pillar of the Erie community.

• All Prep's home games, the Burger King Classic and the D-10 final were at Gannon's Hammermill Center.

• **Mike Douds** did not play basketball his senior year. However, as a fine third-baseman on the Rambler baseball team, Douds was named First Team Region 8 All-Star in 2015 by the *Erie Times-News*. He has gone on to star on the diamond at Westminster College (PA).

• **Matt Harris**, son of Prep assistant **Matt Harris, Sr.**, was named First Team All-District 10 and First Team Region 7 All-Star by the *Erie Times-News*. Harris' 20.4 PPG average places him 4th on the Rambler single season chart and his 1,086 career point total ranks him 7th for most points scored in a Prep uniform.

• Four-year star **Matt Harris,** who started every game his junior and senior seasons, was further honored with a spot on the *Associated Press* AAAA All-State Third Team and was finally given the James "Moe" Gross Award as Prep's finest player. He now stars

Prep's record-setting quarterback, Billy Fessler, joined the Rambler hoop squad after leading the Orange & Black to the state football crown.

at Division I Massachusetts-Lowell, averaging over 20 minutes per game and scoring in double figures consistently for the River Hawks.

- **Billy Fessler**, a first team All-State quarterback for the Ramblers, now performs on the gridiron for Penn State University.

- Harris and **Felix Manus-Schell** represented Prep in the 40th annual City-County All-Star Game, played at Behrend's Junker Center. Harris led all scorers with 24 points, including an amazing six 3-pointers, as the City routed the County, 101-74. Manus-Schell also played well and chipped in with 7 points.

Matt Colpoys gets past Girard's Williams.

2014 All-Opponent Team:

T. J. Leaf, Foothills Christian [UCLA]
Cooper Holt, Orem [Salt Lake CC]
Dalton Nixon, Orem (1st team all-state, UT) [Brigham Young]
David Wright, Timpview
Anthony Glover, Toledo St. John's (3rd team all-state, OH) [Chicago St.]
Samir Taylor, Archbishop Carroll
Austin Tilghman, Archbishop Carroll (3rd team all-state) [Monmouth]
Derrick Jones, Archbishop Carroll (1st team all-state) [UNLV]
Ernest Aflakpui, Archbishop Carroll (2nd team all-state) [Temple]
Carlton Bragg, VASJ (2nd team all-state, OH) [Kansas]
Brian Parker, VASJ (1st team all-state, Player of the Year, OH) [Marist]
Mike Beck, McDowell [Edinboro]
Malik Brinson, Central Tech [Penn St.-Behrend]
Anthony Tracy, Central Tech [Mercyhurst-North East]
Brandon Ramirez, Pope John Paul II
Norman Taylor, Pittsburgh Perry
Josh Huffman, Canisius [Maine, football]
Collin Fantaskey, Warren [Mercyhurst, baseball]
Kyle Ritchey, Franklin [Westminster]
David Morris, Vincent [Tennessee St.]
Kyle Pointer, Vincent
Simeal Wofford, Vincent
Andrew Stromenger, McDowell

The top student section in the state. Enough said.

Overachieving Ramblers Place in Final Four

2014-15 (22-7)

Coach: Mark Majewski
Assistants: Bob Maxson, Matt Harris, Sr.,
John Bowen, Sr
Captain: Matt Colpoys
Managers: George Dufala, Brendan Flanagan

Fustine scores 2 of his 20 in the two-point triumph on McDowell's home floor.

Date	PREP			Dec.	Loc.	High Scorer	Opponent
12/8	60	Sharon	55	W	A	Colpoys (27)	Austin (14)
	KSA ATLANTIS BEACH BASH & SAND JAM (PARADISE ISLAND, BAHAMAS)						
12/11	61	St. Augustine in the Carribean	47	W	N	Colpoys (25)	Adderley (19)
12/12	81	Sault St. Marie (ONT) Korah Collegiate	49	W	N	Fustine (24)	Niccoletta (13)
12/13	66	Upper St. Clair	47	W	N	Colpoys (19)	Pateras (12)
12/19	73	Fort LeBoeuf	32	W	A	Fustine (18)	Tserger (10)
12/23	64	Corry	39	W	H	Fustine (17)	Haenel (14)
1/2	55	Central Tech	51	W	H	Fustine (16)	Davis (19)
1/5	72	Warren	47	W	A	Colpoys (17)	Suppa (14)
1/8	68	Harborcreek	24	W	H	Colpoys (13)	Kaschalk (6)
1/10	39	Girard	30	W	A	Fustine (17)	Harbaugh (7)
1/13	71	East	56	W	H	Fustine (20)	Davis (26)
	BURGER KING CLASSIC						
1/16	56	Philadelphia Constitution	61	L	H	Colpoys (22)	Gilbert (20)
1/17	43	Sparta (NJ) Pope John XXIII	68	L	H	Fustine (10)	Diagne (18)
1/22	53	McDowell	51	W	A	Fustine (20)	Q. Lewis (16)
1/24	54	General McLane	60(OT)	L	H	Cross (13)	Jay (25)
1/27	58	Strong Vincent	53	W	N	Colpoys (14)	Morris (21)
1/30	71	East	55	W	A	Colpoys (22)	Davis (16)
2/3	45	Central Tech	50	L	A	Cross (12)	Brinson (19)
2/5	57	Buffalo (NY) Canisius	47	W	H	Fessler (16)	Huffman (19)
2/7	35	Rochester (NY) Aquinas	48	L	A	Cross (8)	Roberts (18)
2/10	38	McDowell	46	L	H	Fustine (12)	Kerr (18)
2/14	58	Strong Vincent	53(OT)	W	N	Cross (17)	Morris (21)
	DISTRICT 10 PLAYOFFS						
2/19		Franklin (POSTPONED—WEATHER)			N		
2/21	50	Franklin	39	W	N	Colpoys (18)	Drain (22)
2/24	47	Girard	40	W	N	three with (12)	Williams (13)
2/27	41	Strong Vincent	40	W	N	Fessler (12)	Morris (19)
	P.I.A.A. INTERDISTRICT PLAYOFFS						
3/6	86	Hampton	70	W	N	Fustine (26)	Lafko (19)
3/10	53	Ambridge	39	W	N	Colpoys (16)	Carter (22)
3/13	62	Mars	56	W	N	Colpoys (18)	Castello (16)
3/17	32	Philadelphia Archbishop Carroll	59	L	N	Colpoys (12)	Jones (27)
	669 (57.6)		**1412 (48.7)**				

Pos.	Player	Ht.	Prior School	Class	G(GS)	FG(3)	FT	Total	PPG	Career
F	Matt Colpoys (#5)	6'1"	St. George's	Sr.	29(29)	121(22)	120-168	384	13.2	627
F	Joe Fustine (#25)	6'2"	OLP	Sr.	24(23)	115(38)	35-49	303	12.6	396
G	Carter Cross (#14)	6'0"	Walnut Creek	Jr.	29(29)	78(27)	33-48	216	7.4	333
F	Charlie Fessler (#4)	6'4"	OLC	Sr.	27(14)	89	31-61	209	7.7	209
G	Dajon Heidelberg (#21)	6'1"	Wilson	Jr.	28(3)	53(4)	31-50	141	5.0	141
G	Antonio Frisina (#3)	5'11"	Seton Catholic	Sr.	26(11)	28(5)	38-49	99	3.8	153
G	Jack Lindenberger (#10)	6'1"	Walnut Creek	Sr.	29(17)	33(10)	9-12	85	2.9	152
G	Jaryn Simpson (#15)	5'9"	St. George's	Soph.	28(15)	24(17)	20-28	85	3.0	85
C	Jose Casiano (#45)	6'4"	Wilson	Jr.	22(1)	14	5-15	33	1.5	33
F	John "J.T." Bowen (#35)	6'4"	St. Peter's	Jr.	20(2)	12	5-6	29	1.5	29
G	Taylor Mackowski (#2)	6'1"	Bl. Sacrament	Sr.	8(1)	9(4)	5-6	27	3.4	106
G	Peter Jefferys (#33)	5'10"	OLC	Jr.	13	4(3)	0-0	11	0.8	11
G	Mark Majewski (#40)	5'11"	OLP	Soph.	9	4	1-2	9	1.0	9
F	Jake Narring (#42)	6'4"	Jefferson	Jr.	12	3	2-5	8	0.7	8
G	Matt Falconer (#11)	5'9"	Walnut Creek	Sr.	6	2(2)	0-0	6	1.0	22
C	Bruce Fagan	6'8"	Walnut Creek	Soph.	1	0	0-0	0	0.0	0

Cathedral Prep 2015 District 10 Champs and PIAA Final Four participants. Front, L to R: Simpson, Jefferys, Majewski, Frisina, Falconer, Cross, Mackowski; Back: Coach Majewski, Bowen, Lindenberger, Fessler, Cross, Casiano, Fustine, Heidelberg, Colpoys, Asst's Harris, Maxson, Mgr. Flanagan, Asst. Bowen.

HIGHLIGHTS:

- Cathedral Prep administrators made a two-year decision to drop from Quad-A to AAA in its PIAA classification for the 2014-15 and 2015-16 school years. This decision marked the first time that Prep, in basketball, did not compete in the highest, or largest, school classification since its entry into the PCIAA in 1943 and the PIAA in 1973. This move, though criticized in some quarters, was understandable as the Quad-A bar for student enrollments had been elevated significantly with the entry of all the large Philadelphia public and private schools. The Philadelphia area is top-heavy with Quad-A schools, with 75 such in Districts 1 and 12 alone. The AAA set-up is further preferable in District 10, where there are 18 AAA schools (including Prep) and but two Quad-A schools— Central Tech and McDowell, which has over twice as many students as Central Tech. D-10 Quad-A playoffs had become a farce, while AAA playoffs, with many more eligible teams, was certainly more meaningful. The enrollment figures for the current AAA classification are 235-411—and Prep was listed as having exactly 411 boys in grades 10-12. The questions, then, were: should Cathedral Prep be the smallest Quad-A school in the state? Or should Prep be the largest AAA school in the state?

- Coach **Mark Majewski** and his capable staff, including assistants **Bob Maxson**, **Matt Harris** and **John Bowen**, put together another remarkable season in his seventh year at the Rambler helm. While the Ramblers were rated, pre-season, no better than third in the five-team Region 7, by the end of the campaign the Orange & Black showed great chemistry and gained their 21st District 10 title, 10th entry into the PIAA's post-season Final Four and a final ranking of #8 in the state, according to the *Harrisburg Patriot-News*.

Carter Cross, always giving 100%.

- Despite the loss of superstar **Matty Harris** to Division I Massachusetts-Lowell, the Ramblers looked to be strong with two-year starters **Matt Colpoys** and **Carter Cross**, along with several returning spot starters, including **Taylor Mackowski**, **Jack Lindenberger** and **Antonio Frisina**. The big improvement came from smooth-shooting forward **Joe Fustine**, who didn't start one game as a junior, but developed into Prep's most reliable performer of the season.

- Of key importance for Prep was the emergence at mid-season of 6'4" senior **Charlie Fessler**, a First Team All-State wide receiver who did not play basketball the previous season, despite a pair of fine years on the JV's. His defense, rebounding and slam-dunk ability was a big factor in the late-season success of the Ramblers.

- In 2013 the National Federation of High School Associations (NFHSA) put rules in place that dictated what basketball table announcers could and could not say. The NFSHA restated those rules for the 2014-15 campaign with points of emphasis and the PIAA adopted the same. Though not considered a serious problem anywhere in the state, announcers were encouraged not to be "cheerleaders," which is fine. But the rules went ridiculously further and announcers are now ordered not to state the number of points a player scores; the number of fouls on a player; the number of team fouls; the number of timeouts a team has remaining; the time remaining in any period; the type of foul or violation; and giving emphasis to any 2- or 3-point shot. It will be comical to see what penalties or sanctions will be meted out to announcers, almost always volunteers, by the overreaching of the NFHSA and PIAA.

Matt Colpoys dribbles around Girard's Dontae Williams, who dons possibly the worst-looking uniform ever seen locally.

- Prep opened the season with a victory at Sharon (13-10), an opponent it had not faced in over three decades, since 1983. Later in the season were a pair of victories over Girard (14-10), an old foe the Ramblers had not played in 6 ½ decades, since 1949.

- Early in the season the Prep team flew to the Bahamas for the second annual KSA Atlantis Beach Bash and Sand Jam, held at Paradise Island. There the Ramblers won three straight in a clean sweep, including a rout of Upper St. Clair (16-8).

- Prep was off to its best start since the 1996-97 season, and was 11-0 before losing a thriller to Philadelphia Constitution High School (24-8) in the 5th annual Burger King High School Basketball Classic (referred to as the 32nd annual to include the McDonald's Classic games). The Ramblers got an exceptional 22-point performance from **Matt Colpoys**, but couldn't contain 6'9" stringbean left-handed guard **Ahmad Gilbert**. Constitution was defending state Class AA champion and

Ducats for the last Burger King Classic held at the Hammermill Center.

easily won the 2015 Class A division state title with an easy 85-53 finals triumph over perennial power Farrell. Founded in 2006, Constitution is a small public college preparatory school located in Center City Philadelphia and is the only history based high school in the state. Constitution draws upon the historical resources of Philadelphia and hopes to deliver future leaders in government, public policy and law.

- Sparta Pope John XXIII (29-4), a co-ed school of about 1,000 students near Paterson (NJ), undefeated at the time of the Classic, ranked #2 in New Jersey and #14 in the nation according to *MaxPreps*, had an easy way with Prep in the consolation game. The Ramblers had difficulty with the Lions' size, particularly 6'9" monster **Moustafa Diagne**. Lakewood (OH) St. Ed's (22-7), ranked #8 in Ohio and led by 6'9" junior **Derek Funderburk**, defrocked Pope John on Friday night, 57-43, and won the tourney with a thrilling 70-63 overtime victory over Constitution. Pope John finished second in New Jersey's season-ending Tournament of Champions, losing to nationally-ranked Roselle Catholic in the final, 57-45.

- Prep's mid-season two-point triumph over McDowell (18-7) marked the fifth consecutive year the Ramblers defeated the Trojans at McDowell's Paul Goll Gymnasium. **Joe Fustine** was the hero, grabbing a rebound and scoring with only 3.5 seconds remaining. Fustine led all scorers with 20 points on an 8-for-9 FG performance.

- The big McDowell win was followed by an injury-filled overtime upset loss to General McLane (11-11). **Carter Cross** led a fourth quarter comeback, but the Ramblers could not overcome 15 missed free throws (9-of-24) and poor shooting from the field. Star **Joe Fustine** left the contest early after twisting an ankle and was forced to miss Prep's next five games.

- Prep's victories over East High (9-13) made for 18 straight over the Warriors. The Ramblers are on the long end of the series with the Sunrisers, 110-48.

- Central Tech's (14-9) victory over Prep on February 3 halted a 24-game Rambler win streak against the Falcons. Prep was outscored 19-7 in the fourth frame and converted but 10-of-20 free throws. The loss most likely cost the Ramblers the outright Region 7 title.

- Prep won an impressive triumph over Canisius (25-5), as the Crusaders finished winning its fourth Manhattan Cup in five years and the NYSCHSAA (Catholic) state championship at Fordham University.

- Prep's loss at undefeated Rochester Aquinas (22-1) was the first the two met in 58 years, since 1956-57. In the meantime the Ramblers and Little Irish met 13 times on the gridiron. Aquinas was 15-0 after beating Prep but met its match in the NYSPHSAA (public, opted into by Aquinas) Class AA state tournament semifinal, losing to Brentwood, the Long Island champion, 63-56.

- McDowell won a share of the Region 7 crown by virtue of its big win over Prep at Gannon. The Trojans then only had to defeat Central Tech to win the D-10 Quad-A title. Powerful Pittsburgh Allderdice ended McDowell's season in a PIAA playoff held at Brashear High School.

- Prep overcame a 9-point second half deficit when it defeated pre-season favorite Strong Vincent on January 27 behind the strong play of **Antonio Frisina**. The rematch on February 14 was a classic, as the Ramblers battled back the entire game and finally forced overtime with a 3-pointer by **Carter Cross,** with just seconds remaining, after **Charlie Fessler** found him open in the right corner . **Matt Colpoys**, who had only two points in regulation, drained six straight pressure free throws to seal the OT win and gain Prep the co-championship of Region 7.

- East High and Strong Vincent were added to Region 7 for the 2014-15 campaign. This formation was the closest setup to the old City Series, Big Six or Metro leagues since District 10 forced the Erie schools to abolish their traditional alignment and be placed in the ridiculous "Region" divisions beginning in 2004. More interest came with the addition of the Warriors

and Colonels, and a five-team region, with all decent teams, was certainly preferable to the pathetic three-team region of the previous two seasons. What were still missing were plenty of the good old-fashioned doubleheaders at Gannon, since only Prep and SV were using Gannon for home games. It was also unfortunate not to have a provision for a championship playoff, as a third meeting between Prep and McDowell would have been a huge draw. The final standings of Region 7:

	Won	Lost
Cathedral Prep	6	2
McDowell	6	2
Strong Vincent	5	3
Central Tech	2	6
East	1	7

Triumphant Ramblers greet schoolmates after the big win over Mars in the state playoffs.

Ramblers whoop and holler after the victory over Mars down in Sharon.

Fessler with another rousing dunk against Hampton in PIAA action.

Senior big man Charlie Fessler scores in the thriller over Ambridge.

- 2014-15 was Prep's first foray into the AAA playoffs since the PIAA went to four classifications in 1983-84. The Ramblers won their District 10 quarterfinal matchup with a Franklin (13-11) squad that gave it trouble and kept the battle close until there were about four minutes remaining. An interesting sidenote is that the Knights are coached by former Prep and Allegheny College great **Casey McCloskey** '03. It was the

Ramblers' 9th victory in 10 games over Franklin. The Ramblers then downed a scrappy Girard combine for the second time in the semifinal matchup.

- The campaign's biggest thrill came in the D-10 final, the third intense contest of the season against Strong Vincent (17-9). The Colonels, led by sophomore star **David Morris**, had beaten a fine Meadville team in the semifinals and outplayed the Ramblers in the title game. Prep never had a lead and was down by 5 with only 1:03 remaining. **Joe Fustine** drove for two and the teams traded free throws make it 40-37, Vincent, with 27.2 seconds left. **Charlie Fessler** scored inside and Prep fouled immediately, to make it 40-39 with 10 seconds remaining. SV's **Bryon Williams** missed the front end of a one-and-one and **Dajon Heidelberg**, who grabbed the rebound, passed out to **Carter Cross** who fed back to Heidelberg who missed on a driving layup. A Rambler putback was swatted out-of-bounds by Vincent's **Kyle Pointer**, and with exactly 1.0 second to go, it was Ramblers' ball underneath. Heidelberg made a pass to the left corner to his last option—Fessler, the only man open. Charlie arched a contested fadeaway 17-footer, the buzzer sounded and the ball fell through for Prep's 21st D-10 crown. And the huge Prep crowd made the welkin ring and began an unbridled victory celebration!

Joe Fustine with the put-back in the Elite Eight win over Mars.

- Prep opened PIAA interdistrict play with a high-scoring victory over Hampton (20-7), the second time in three years the Ramblers ousted the Talbots from state contention. Five Prepsters scored in double figures, with **Joe Fustine** leading the way with 26 points and 10 rebounds. The second round opponent was Ambridge (17-9), a team which Prep had met only once before. That was in 1980, when the Bridgers handed the Ramblers their only defeat in a 33-1 season. The Orange & Black exploded in the second half behind a pair of crowd-pleasing slam dunks by **Charlie Fessler** and strong defense throughout. More excitement came late in the contest when 6'4" Ambridge star **Daylon Carter** was whistled for a foul and a technical and nearly started a brawl on-court and with fans behind his bench.

- Prep next won a tense 62-56 PIAA Quarterfinal thriller over Mars (26-3), which had just gained a 3-point upset over Beaver Falls in the second round. **Dajon Heidelberg** came off the bench and erupted for three big buckets and a steal in the closing moments to gain the Ramblers the impressive victory. **Matt Colpoys** led all scorers with 18, while **Joe Fustine** had 17 markers and 11 rebounds.

- Prep's exciting run finally ended in the PIAA Semifinal against powerful Archbishop Carroll (23-7) at Bald Eagle High School. The Patriots' inside game with Pennsylvania Player of the Year **Derrick Jones** was just too much for the Ramblers to handle. Carroll then lost in the state final to Philadelphia Neumann-Goretti (formerly Southeastern Catholic), 69-67.

Colpoys with an inside tally in the PIAA triumph over Hampton.

- All Prep's home games and the Burger King Classic were held at Gannon's Hammermill Center. This was the last year the Ramblers used Gannon as its home court as the new gymnasium at the Cathedral Prep Events Center was scheduled to open for the 2015-16 season. All three D-10 games and the Hampton PIAA battle were played at Edinboro's McComb Fieldhouse, while the Ambridge and Mars PIAA games were hosted in Sharon.

Antonio Frisina softly lays in a bucket.

- **Matt Colpoys**, snubbed for post-season recognition as a junior, was named First Team All-District 10 and First Team Region 7 All-Star by the *Erie Times-News*. **Joe Fustine** was also named a First Team Region 7 All-Star by the *Times*.

Construction moved quickly for the PVEC's new gymnasium.

- Colpoys, winner of the James "Moe" Gross Award as Prep's best player, went on to play his college ball at Penn St.-Behrend. Fustine plays at Gannon University, while **Antonio Frisina** competes at Allegheny College in his hometown of Meadville.

- **Charlie Fessler**, a First Team *Associated Press* All-State football player and winner of the "Ma" Kaiser Award as Prep's all-around best athlete, is on a football scholarship at Northwestern University in the Big Ten.

- Colpoys (10 points), Fustine (10) and Fessler (9) all represented the Ramblers in the 41st annual City-County All-Star Game, played at Behrend's Junker Center. The "Slickers" came out on top, 80-55.

- At the annual Cathedral Prep/Villa Maria Academy Legacy Gala on April 27, 2015, it was announced that the Cathedral Prep Events Center was renamed the "Prep & Villa Events Center," or "PVEC." It was further announced that the gym will now be referred to as the "Joanne Mullen Gymnasium" and the pool will be called the "David M. Hallman III Aquatics Center."

2015 All-Opponent Team:

Justice Davis, Central Tech [Mercyhurst-North East]

Malik Brinson, Central Tech [Penn St.-Behrend]

Justus Davis, East

Ahmad Gilbert, Constitution [George Mason]

Kimar Williams, Constitution [Florida International]

Moustapha Diagne, Pope John XXIII [Syracuse]

Jeromy Rodriguez, Pope John XXIII [Northwest Florida St.]

Quinn Lewis, McDowell [Dayton, rugby]

Ryan Reagan, General McLane [Navy]

Alex Jay, General McLane

David Morris, Vincent (3rd team all-state)

Kyle Pointer, Vincent

Josh Huffman, Canisius [Maine, football]

D. J. Roberts, Rochester Aquinas

Max Kerr, McDowell [Gannon]

Isaac Drain, Franklin [Mercyhurst-North East]

Daylon Carter, Ambridge (2nd team all-state) [Shippensburg]

John Castello, Mars (2nd team all-state) [Shippensburg]

Josh Sharkey, Archbishop Carroll (3rd team all-state) [Samford]

Derrick Jones, Archbishop Carroll (1st team all-state, Player of the Year) [UNLV]

Prep Embarks on New Era!

Prep's first game in the impressive, brand new Joann Mullen Gymnasium.

2015-16 (16-10)

Coach: Mark Majewski
Assistants: Bob Maxson, Matt Harris, Sr.,
    John Bowen, Sr
Captain: Carter Cross, J.T. Bowen,
    Dajon Heidelberg
Managers: George Dufala, Brendan Flanagan

Date	PREP	Dec.	Loc.	High	Scorer	Opponent	
12/4	40	Youngstown (OH) Ursuline	43	L	H	Simpson (10)	Parella (25)
12/9	63	Fort Le Boeuf	41	W	H	Bowen (14)	Greggs (15)
12/11	63	General McLane	53	W	A	Simpson (21)	Reagan (23)
		TARKANIAN CLASSIC (LAS VEGAS, NV)					
12/16	57	Las Vegas (NV) Adelson School	48	W	N	Cross (17)	Pitts & Elharrar (14)
12/17	51	N. Las Vegas (NV) Cheyenne	52	L	N	Cross (15)	Moore (20)
12/18	63	San Bernardino (CA)	48	W	N	Cross (25)	Kayonda (17)
12/19	69	Campbell County (WY)	61	W	N	Cross (22)	Holst (29)
12/22	72	Corry	35	W	A	Cross (20)	Xander (20)
1/2	58	Central Tech	55	W	A	Cross (14)	Clark (16)
1/5	79	Warren	43	W	H	Heidelberg (18)	Suppa (17)
1/7	66	Harborcreek	50	W	A	Simpson (15)	Boyd (22)
1/9	51	Girard	44	W	H	Cross (14)	Williams (18)
1/12	67	East	46	W	A	Cross (30)	Manus (18)
		BURGER KING CLASSIC					
1/15	58	Toronto (ONT) St. Michael's College	61	L	H	Cross & Jefferys (11)	Djurcic (22)
1/16	35	Lakewood (OH) St. Edward	84	L	H	Upperman (9)	Schmock (16)
1/22	68	McDowell	38	W	H	Cross & Simpson (14)	Dirkmaat (9)
1/26	57	Strong Vincent	70	L	A	Heidelberg (14)	Morris (31)
1/29	64	East	51	W	H	Heidelberg (20)	Manus (33)
2/2	61	Central Tech	52	W	H	Cross (21)	Clark (22)
2/6	45	Buffalo (NY) Canisius	51	L	A	Cross (10)	Ayiy (19)
2/9	48	McDowell	57	L	A	Simpson (16)	Kuna (16)
2/12	60	Strong Vincent	63	L	H	Cross (26)	Morris (19)
		DISTRICT 10 PLAYOFFS					
2/19	68	Hickory	31	W	H	Cross (17)	Three w/(8)
2/21	65	General McLane	52	W	N	Four w/ (11)	Reagan (32)
2/24	52	Meadville	56	L	N	Cross (19)	Foster (33)
2/27	51	Girard	55(OT)	L	N	Simpson (22)	Harbaugh (20)
	1531 (58.9)		1340 (51.5)				

Pos.	Player	Ht.	Prior School	Class	G(GS)	FG(3)	FT	Total	PPG	Career
G	Carter Cross (#5)	6'0"	Walnut Creek	Sr.	26	133(36)	75-99	377	14.5	710
G	Jaryn Simpson (#2)	5'9"	St. George's	Jr.	26	88(29)	60-76	265	10.2	350
C	John "J.T." Bowen (#35)	6'4"	St. Peter's	Sr.	26	62	29-49	153	5.9	182
F	Dajon Heidelberg (#21)	6'1"	Wilson	Sr.	16	58(2)	30-60	148	9.3	289
G	Mark Majewski (#33)	5'11"	OLP	Jr.	26	53(25)	14-20	145	5.8	154
G	Adam Upperman (#40)	6'0"	J.S. Wilson	Soph.	24	39(7)	17-25	102	4.3	102
G	Franco Agnello (#10)	5'10"	McDowell	Jr.	25	27(9)	16-27	79	3.2	79
G	Peter Jefferys (#3)	5'10"	OLC	Sr.	22	23(16)	4-4	66	3.0	77
F	Jake Narring (#25)	6'4"	Jefferson	Sr.	9	18	10-15	46	5.1	54
G	Tommy Russo (#34)	6'0"	St. George's	Soph.	26	16(7)	12-19	51	2.0	51
F	Eddie Thompson (#4)	6'0"	Wilson	Jr.	13	11	9-13	31	2.4	31
C	Bruce Fagan (#14)	6'8"	Walnut Creek	Jr.	22	13	4-7	30	1.4	30
C	Jose Casiano (#45)	6'4"	Wilson	Sr.	14	9	5-16	23	1.6	56
G	Jeremy Hill (#42)	6'0"	OLP	Sr.	8	1(1)	3-5	6	0.8	8
F	Nate Serafin (#15)	6'2"	OLP	Jr.	7	2	1-2	5	0.7	5
G	Trousie Thrower (#11)	5'8"	Bl. Sacrament	Jr.	5	1	0-0	2	0.4	2
G	Joe Mischler (#11)	6'0"	OLP	Soph.	1	1	0-0	2	2.0	2
G	Adam Malesiewski (#35)	5'11"	North East	Soph.	1	0	0-0	0	0.0	0
G	Kenny Harden (#22)	6'1"	St. Peter's	Jr.	0	0	0-0	0	0.0	0

HIGHLIGHTS:

- Cathedral Prep opened coach **Mark Majewski's** eighth season as Rambler mentor with the inauguration of a new era and the spectacular Joann Mullen Gymnasium at the $12.5 million Prep & Villa Events Center (PVEC). Many Prep alumni, students, fans and well-wishers have been in awe of the modern, gorgeous facility, built entirely with private donations. With a seating capacity of 1,800 and plenty of space for SRO, the "Mullen" is certain to be a source of pride for the Prep community and the site of many thrilling athletic events for both Prep and Villa Maria Academy. All of Prep's home games, the Burger King Classic and the first round District 10 playoff were held at the PVEC, while only the second Strong Vincent contest was held at Gannon's Hammermill Center. Prep's last three D-10 playoff encounters were staged at Edinboro's McComb Fieldhouse.

The 2016 Prep Ramblers. Front, L to R: Hill, Jefferys, Agnello, Majewski, Upperman; Middle: Dufala, Heidelberg, Russo, Simpson, Thompson, Serafin, Narring; Back: Casiano, Bowen, Fagan, Cross.

- Villa Maria's girls actually played the first varsity contest in the new gym, a 49-22 victory over Youngstown Ursuline in a preliminary to the Prep opener. What followed for the Ramblers was a three-point loss to Ursuline (19-7) after being ahead for 3 ½ quarters. It was senior **Carter Cross** who made Prep's first free throw in the new facility; Cross who made the first 2-point bucket; and senior **Peter Jefferys** who buried the first 3-point shot. It was the first time the Ramblers and the Fighting Irish squared off in hoops in 62 years!

- Another great early season victory was the 10-point, upset win at General McLane (18-6). **Jaryn Simpson** poured in 23 points as the Ramblers, with a later playoff win over GM, moved their all-time record against the Lancers to 9-4. The first GM contest was played at the same moment the Prep football squad was engaged in its incredible come-from-behind,

The Burger King final shows how gorgeous the new Joann Mullen Gymnasium is.

38-34, PIAA Semifinal victory over Harrisburg Bishop McDevitt (formerly Harrisburg Central Catholic.) Star gridders that had to postpone their individual hoop seasons included **Dajon Heidelberg**, **Jose Casiano**, Jeremy Hill and Joe Mischler. GM officials would not agree to postpone the game to accommodate Rambler fans, and when they announced the halftime score with the Rambler gridders behind, 34-21, the Lancer fans applauded.

Jose Casiano was also a rugged gridiron star for the Ramblers.

- Early in the season the Prep team flew to Las Vegas for the 4th annual Tarkanian Classic, where the Ramblers played well, winning three of four. It was the sixth time since 1983 that Prep engaged in a Las Vegas holiday tourney. The 77-team event was broken into five categories, with Prep taking 5th place in the 12-team Premier Division, won by the squad that defeated the Ramblers on a jump shot at the buzzer, the Cheyenne Desert Shields. **Carter Cross**, who averaged almost 20 PPG at the event, was honored with a berth on the Premier Division All-Tourney team.

- Of Prep's new opponents in Las Vegas: state-of-the-art Adelson (12-10), the first Jewish high school in the Las Vegas area, opened in 2007 after a $25 million donation from casino magnates and multi-billionaires **Dr. Miriam and Sheldon Adelson**; Cheyenne (16-7), opened in 1991, has 2,500 students in a growing, middle class suburban community; San Bernardino is the city that just weeks before suffered a horrific Islamic terrorist attack. SBHS (10-17), founded in 1885, lists as prominent alumni *Miami Vice* actor **Philip Michael Thomas** and the guy who composed the theme songs for *Huckleberry Hound, The Jetsons, The Flintstones and The Smurfs*; and Campbell County (19-8), located on the plains between the Black Hills of South Dakota and the Big Horn Mountains of Wyoming, owns no less than 15 Wyoming state basketball championships. The Camels finished third in 2016.

- One of Prep's best victories of the season was the 51-44 verdict over Girard (22-5), which invaded the PVEC with an 11-0 record. Unfortunately, the Yellow Jackets later ended the Ramblers' season with an overtime victory in the D-10 consolation matchup. Girard leads the overall series, 7-6.

The ducat to see Prep's largest point spread defeat ever.

- The 33rd annual Burger King Classic was held for the first time in the Joann Mullen Gymnasium at the PVEC after 27 years at Gannon's Hammermill Center. The clear winner was Philadelphia power Neumann-Goretti (29-4), formerly known as Southeastern Catholic, eventual Class AAA state titleist. Neumann-Goretti is located smack-dab in the middle of South Philly's Little Italy section and the Saints have now won six PIAA state championships in the past seven seasons. They coasted to 80-60 and 80-53 victories over defending champion Lakewood St. Edward (13-7) and Toronto St. Michael's College to win their first BK title.

- Prep lost a nail-biter on opening night at the classic, when **Danilo Djurcic** buried a 3-pointer with two seconds remaining as St. Mike's defeated the Ramblers, 61-58. The consolation match was a complete disaster for Prep, as St. Ed's 49-point triumph was the largest margin of

Coach Majewski instructs the Ramblers at the first Burger King Classic at the PVEC.

defeat in the entire 92-year history of Rambler basketball.

Junior gaurds Jaryn Simpson and Mark Majewski, Jr. defend against St. Michael's.

Prep fans make their presence known in a 53-51 victory at McDowell.

The previous record was a 47-point margin foisted upon the Ramblers by Cleveland St. Joe's during the 1972-73 season.

- After the Burger King Classic disaster, Prep bounced back with a surprisingly easy, 30-point massacre over McDowell (9-14). The Rambler victory came before the first capacity crowd ever at the "Mullen." The Trojans upset Prep in the rematch at sold-out Paul Goll Gymnasium, eliminating the Orange & Black from Region 7 title contention. It was McDowell's first home court win against Prep in six years.

- In the East second contest, held at the PVEC, East's **Brevin Manus** tallied 33 points, the most ever scored by a Warrior against the Ramblers. Manus was 16-of-23 from the foul line, thus equalizing the all-time record for free throws made in a Prep game, first set by Youngstown Chaney's **Marty Bartell** in 1977-78, then tied by Prep's **Jim Stevenson** in 1983-84.

- After defeating McDowell for its first D-10 title in school history, the Falcons trounced DuBois in a PIAA sub-regional contest, before getting beat by the state's number one team at the time, Pittsburgh Taylor Allderdice, in a second sub-regional.

- The Canisius Crusaders still operate in Class AA of Buffalo's Monsignor Martin Athletic Association, along with Bishop Timon/St. Jude, St. Joseph's and Athol Springs St. Francis. Current Class A schools in the MMAA include Nichols School, Olean Archbishop Walsh, Tonawanda Cardinal O'Hara, Niagara Catholic, Lancaster St. Mary's and the Park School of Buffalo. Nichols and Park are private, non-denominational schools. Canisius won its second straight New York State Catholic Class A title with a 44-41 victory over Staten Island Monsignor Farrell.

- After nine consecutive Prep victories over Strong Vincent (19-8), including the three thrillers from the previous season, the D-10 champion Colonels finally gained revenge over the Ramblers, 70-57, before another big crowd at the "Mullen." Junior superstar **David Morris** was outstanding with 31 points, including five 3-pointers and a jaw-dropping windmill tomahawk slam dunk that garnered an ovation even from the home crowd. Within hours the video of Morris' dunk received national attention and was a highlight on ESPN's SportsCenter that evening. In the rematch, Morris nailed a 3-pointer in the opening seconds to make him not only Vincent's, but the Erie School District's all-time leading scorer, with yet another season to go. The Orange & Black kept game two close behind the hot-shooting of **Carter Cross**, but fell short as a 3-point attempt by **Jaryn Simpson** at the buzzer just missed. The Red & Black made 30-of-39 free throws in the contest, including 11-of-12 by **Simeal Wofford**.

- Vincent won its first District 10 title in 27 years, since 1989. The Colonels mowed down Grove City, Girard and Meadville to capture the crown, then defeated Hampton, 71-51, in PIAA

first round action. SV's season closed in the second round with a heartbreaking loss to Mars, 58-56. Coach **Shannon Pullium** retired from the Vincent job post-season to become the new head coach at Mercyhurst-North East.

- The final standings of Region 7:

	Won	Lost
Strong Vincent	8	0
Cathedral Prep	5	3
Central Tech	3	5
McDowell	3	5
East	1	7

Dajon Heidelberg drives in a playoff victory over General McLane.

- The Prep cagers, seeded #3 in the 14-team District 10 AAA playoffs, opened with 15 players seeing action in an easy 68-31 win over Hickory (9-14). Next was another convincing victory over General McLane, despite a 32-point effort by Lancer star **Ryan Reagan**, the most ever scored by a GM player against Prep. The downside was a season-ending elbow injury to

The nationally-ranked 2016 Villa Maria Victors. Members: Anna Sweny, Amanda Heidt, Emily Bauer, Addisyn Cross, Julia Casella, Sarah Agnello, Natalie Bird, Molly Mraz, Andrea McCormick, Jaclyn Kitts, Madison Demski, Victoria Sanders, Autumn Byes, Megan Howe, Jennifer Oduho, Sydney Palermo.

Rambler star **Dajon Heidelberg**, who had already been offered a football scholarship to Edinboro University of Pennsylvania.

- Next came a disappointing semifinal loss to Meadville (21-5), the first time the two competed since 2008. The Orange & Black could not stop a 33-point onslaught by **Armoni Foster**. It was also the first playoff matchup between the Ramblers and Bulldogs since the fierce playoff rivalry of the 1980's and 1990's. Prep's season-ending tailspin continued with the overtime loss to Girard, making it just the second time since 2004 that the Ramblers were unable to compete in the PIAA's state-wide playoffs.

- 2015-16 was Prep's last foray into the AAA playoffs, since the PIAA was moving to a ridiculous six classifications, beginning with the 2016-17 season. The Ramblers will be operating in Class 5-A.

- Villa Maria Academy (29-1) ranked as high as number 9 in the nation according to *USA Today*. The Victors, led by senior all-state Division I recruits **Anna Sweny, Sarah Agnello** and **Jennifer Oduho**, finished as the number two team in Pennsylvania after a championship final loss to Philadelphia Archbishop Wood (25-6), 46-29.

- **"J. T." Bowen** led Prep in rebounding (151), while **Jaryn Simpson** led in assists (83). Always causing havoc on defense, the ever-hustling **Carter Cross** led the squad in steals (58) and blocked shots (15).

Defensive workhorse Carter Cross hauls in another rebound.

- **Carter Cross** was twice named the *Erie Times-News* District 10 Player of the Year—in baseball! A standout pitcher the leading hitter on the Rambler nine, Cross will play his collegiate baseball at the University of Nebraska.

- **"J. T." Bowen** and **Mark Majewski** were also star hurlers and First Team Region All-Stars for the D-10 champion Ramblers.

- Workhorse **Carter Cross** was named First Team Region 7 All-Star by the *Erie Times-News*, while **Dajon Heidelberg** and **Jaryn Simpson** were Second Team choices.

- Cross, Heidelberg and **"J. T." Bowen** were all selected to participate in the 42nd annual City-County All-Star Game. Cross did not participate because of his commitment to the Rambler baseball squad, while Bowen scored 5 points in a 75-72 losing effort. Late in the first half the County took a bench technical foul to let the injured Heidelberg sub into the game, giving him one last chance to step onto the floor and shoot free throws. The classy move "meant a lot to me," stated Heidelberg.

- **Mr. James Smith** was appointed principal of Cathedral Prep beginning with the 2016-17 school year. A former principal in the Erie School District at East High and Harding Elementary, Smith was an outstanding athlete in his own right. He spent three years in baseball's minor leagues, first in the Kansas City Royals organization, then the Milwaukee Brewers organization. "Smitty" was a pitcher with Eugene of the Northwest League; Appleton and Beloit of the Midwest League; and Memphis of the Southern League.

2016 All-Opponent Team:

Greg Parella, Youngstown Ursuline (2nd team all-state, OH) [John Carroll]

Alex Jay, General McLane [Edinboro]

William Moore, Cheyenne [Tacoma (WA) CC]

Dewayne Alexander, Cheyenne

Dalton Holst, Campbell County [Chadron St., football]

Derrick Clark, Central Tech

Riley Boyd, Harborcreek

Dontae Williams, Girard [Mercyhurst]

Danilo Djurcic, Toronto St. Michael's [Harvard]

Thomas Schmock, St. Ed's

Jack Sullivan, St. Ed's

David Morris, Vincent (2nd team all-state) [Tennessee St.]

Brevin Manus, East

Madut Ayiy, Canisius (5th team, all-WNY)

Mike Stone, Vincent

Bryon Williams, Vincent

Simeal Wofford, Vincent

Ryan Reagan, General McLane [Navy]

Armoni Foster, Meadville [IUP]

Keith Harbaugh, Girard [Thiel]

Prep Makes PIAA Class 5-A Run!

2016-17 (14-13)

Coach: Mark Majewski
Assistants: Bob Maxson, Craig Fomich, Matt Harris
Captain: Jaryn Simpson, Bruce Fagan, Mark Majewski
Managers: Jack Halli, Bob Ek

Senior leader Jaryn Simpson drives over Meadville's 6'8" Lashon Lindsey.

Date	PREP			Dec.	Loc.	High Scorer	Opponent
12/13	76	Fort Le Boeuf		49	W	A	Simpson (16)	Dahn (19)
		KSA TOURNAMENT (ORLANDO, FL)						
12/15	64	Homewood (AL)		72	L	N	McBride (13)	Jemison (24)
12/16	59	Ralston Valley (CO)		42	W	N	Fagan (12)	Asquith (10)
12/17	71	Tottenville (NY)		31	W	N	Upperman (15)	Jean Pierre (11)
12/21	65	General McLane		61	W	A	Simpson (20)	Jay (29)
12/23	79	Buffalo (NY) Canisius		59	W	H	Upperman (19)	Johnson (15)
		I-90 HOLIDAY CLASSIC (BUFFALO, NY)						
12/29	48	Athol Springs (NY) St. Francis		53	L	N	Simpson (18)	Cunningham (14)
1/4	69	Meadville		72	L	A	Simpson (17)	Foster (46)
1/6	58	Strong Vincent		60	L	H	McBride, Fagan & Simpson (12)	Morris (24)
1/10	67	East		65	W	H	Simpson (14)	Thompson (22)
		BURGER KING CLASSIC						
1/13	54	Westerville (OH) South		82	L	H	Majewski (10)	Wesson (43)
1/14	37	Cleveland (OH) VASJ		60	L	H	Russo (11)	Higgins (13)
1/17	56	Central Tech		58	L	H	Simpson (17)	L. Johnson (25)
1/21	52	Harborcreek		44	W	H	Upperman (19)	Boyd (13)
1/26	55	McDowell		49	W	H	Upperman (19)	B. Lewis (15)
1/28	52	Toronto (ONT) St. Michael's		61	L	A	Upperman & Simpson (14)	
1/31	54	Meadville		67	L	H	Upperman (15)	Foster (23)
2/3	57	East		49	W	A	Simpson (21)	Jones (18)
2/7	64	Central Tech		43	W	A	Upperman & McBride (18)	Williams (14)
2/10	50	Youngstown (OH) Ursuline		58	L	A	McBride (17)	
2/11	51	Rochester (NY) Aquinas		56	L	H	Upperman (13)	Puckett (22)
2/14	63	McDowell		53	W	A	Simpson (21)	Kuna & Becker (17)
		DISTRICT 10 PLAYOFFS						
2/23	55	Central Tech		43	W	N	Simpson (17)	Johnson (20)
2/28	48	Meadville		68	L	N	Simpson (17)	Foster (30)
		PIAA SUB-REGIONAL						
3/3	42	Pittsburgh Obama Academy		41	W	N	Simpson (15)	Strothers (13)
		PIAA INTERDISTRICT PLAYOFFS						
3/10	55	Central Mountain		46	W	N	Simpson (13)	Baker (14)
3/16	61	Mars		72	L	N	Simpson (23)	Carmody (45)
	1531 (58.9)			**1340 (51.5)**				

Pos.	Player	Ht.	Prior School	Class	G(GS)	FG(3)	FT	Total	PPG	Career
G	Jaryn Simpson (#2)	6'2"	St. George's	Sr.	27(27)	113(27)	128	381	14.1	731
G	Mark Majewski (#33)	5'11"	OLP	Sr.	27	43(19)	14	119	4.4	273
G	Adam Upperman (#11)	6'1"	J.S. Wilson	Jr..	27	120(39)	40	319	11.8	421
G	Franco Agnello (#10)	5'10"	McDowell	Sr.	7	11(3)	5	30	4.3	109
G	Aaron McBride (#10)	5'10"	Bl. Sacrament	Jr.	27	74(19)	63	230	8.5	230
G	Tommy Russo (#5)	6'1"	St. George's	Jr.	27	51(6)	45	153	5.7	204
G	Marcus Lewkowicz (#15)	5'10"	Walnut Creek	Jr.	10	0	1	1	0.1	1
C	Bruce Fagan (#14)	6'9"	Walnut Creek	Sr.	24	57	12	126	5.3	156
G	Ethan Rys (#21)	5'10"	Walnut Creek	Jr.	10	0	0	0	0.0	0
F	Alex Douds (#22)	6'1"	OLP	Jr.	20	22(2)	19	65	3.3	65
G	Joe Mischler (#45)	6'0"	OLP	Jr.	16	27(11)	10	75	4.7	77
G	Adam Malesiewski (#4)	6'1"	North East	Jr.	12	10(4)	4	28	2.3	28
C	Collin Irwin (#34)	6'4"	Harborcreek	Jr.	18	7(1)	1	16	0.9	16
G	Anthony Lupo (#40)	5'6"	St. George's	Jr.	4	0	0	0	0.0	0
G	Tyler Oedekoven (#42)	6'1"	Oregon	Jr.	16	4	4	12	0.8	12
F	Henry Fessler	6'0"	OLC	Jr.	19	2(1)	4	9	0.5	9

The 2016-17 Prep Ramblers.

HIGHLIGHTS:

- Cathedral Prep coach **Mark Majewski**'s ninth season as Rambler mentor was somewhat disappointing. Though appearing to have some marked talent, particularly with three-year starter **Jaryn Simpson**, the Ramblers suffered from poor shooting in big games. Unable to defend effectively as well, three of the top four all-time individual single game scoring highs were accomplished by opponents in the instant season.

- Prep's early season victory over Fort LeBoeuf (9-14) put the Ramblers on the long end of a 9-0 series over the Bison. The triumph over Harborcreek (18-8) put the Ramblers on the very long end of a 29-0 series over the Huskies.

- Prep's win at Canisius (18-10) was the 32nd meeting between the two, with the Ramblers holding a 19-13 edge in the series. A visiting team has not won a game in that series since it was renewed in 2010. The Crusaders won Buffalo's 2017 Manhattan Cup title.

- Meadville's (26-2) **Armoni Foster** put on an incredible 46-point barrage, including a 3-point buzzer beater, in the Bulldogs' 72-69 victory over Prep. Foster's 46 is second on Prep's all-time single game opponents' chart, behind only Strong Vincent's **Essie Hollis**, who had 49 points in 1972-73. Foster's 17 converted free throws are the most ever made in a Prep game. Game two with Meadville, played at the PVEC, the Ramblers had an early 14-point lead, but completely fell apart in the 2nd and 3rd quarters and lost by 13. Foster, Meadville's all-time leading scorer, destroyed Prep in the District 10 playoff with 30 points. Meadville went on to defeat Chartiers

Simpson up for two in his final game, a playoff loss to Mars.

Valley, Franklin Regional, Mars and Northeastern to reach the PIAA Class 5-A state final, where it was crushed by powerful

Warminster Archbishop Wood, 73-40. Prep still leads the all-time series between the Ramblers and Bulldogs, 28-18.

- **Joe Mischler, Adam Malesiewski, Anthony Lupo, Collin Irwin, Henry Fessler** and **Tyler Oedekoven** were among the some 80 players and coaches honored at halftime of the Meadville game at the Mullen, all receiving gold medals as part of Prep's incredible 2016 PIAA State Football Championship. The undefeated Ramblers (14-0) scored an incredible upset over powerful Philadelphia Imhotep Charter, 27-20, in the title game at Hersheypark Stadium. Prep was behind, 20-9, in the fourth quarter but exploded for a field goal by Lupo; an interception return TD by **Terry Roberts**; a 2-point conversion by Mischler; a Mischler to Oedekoven TD pass; and a PAT by Lupo, all in a six-minute final period span to seal the improbable victory.

- Prep's victories over East High (6-15) made for 22 straight over the Warriors. The Ramblers are on the long end of the series with the Sunrisers, 114-48.

- Strong Vincent (27-4) won its second consecutive District 10 title, this time in Class 4-A, defeating Sharon and Grove City in the playoffs. The Colonels squared off with Prep just once this season, a close, two-point victory for SV. Vincent had an exciting PIAA playoff run, knocking off South Fayette (67-48); highly-rated Beaver Falls (71-48) and New Castle (68-43); and Quaker Valley (73-64) to win the trip to Hershey. There the Colonels ran into a buzzsaw in the form of Philadelphia powerhouse Imhotep Charter, which defeated Vincent, 80-52. SV standout **David Morris** completed his career with 2,270 points, easily outdistancing Prep's **Jed Ryan** to become the Erie area's all-time leading scorer. Though Prep will own the all-time series over Vincent, 106-72, no team has beaten the Ramblers more than the Colonels.

- Arlington (VA) Paul VI won the 34th annual Burger King Classic, held for the second time in the Joann Mullen Gymnasium at the PVEC. Paul VI won in the final against Westerville (OH) South, which had crushed Prep the evening before with a spectacular 43-point performance from 6'10" Division I recruit **Kaleb Wesson**. It was the third highest individual point total ever against the Ramblers. Prep then lost the consolation match against VASJ, which holds an 8-4 advantage in the all-time series.

- Prep won two of three games with Central Tech (10-13), including the D-10 semifinal, giving the Ramblers a whopping 46-5 edge in the all-time series between the two.

- Despite Prep's loss at Youngstown Ursuline, the Ramblers still hold an overall edge in the series, 4-3. The very next night Prep blew a 12-point halftime lead at the PVEC to Rochester Aquinas. The Li'l Irish hold a commanding 7-3 lead in the series.

Adam Upperman dives for a loose ball against Vincent.

- Prep scored wins over arch-rival McDowell (13-10) before a pair of sell-out crowds, first on the home court, then on the Trojan floor. Both games were nip-and-tuck until the Ramblers pulled away with clutch free throw shooting. In game one

Adam Upperman nailed five 3-pointers, while **Aaron McBride** and **Jaryn Simpson** nailed the free throws down the stretch. In game two **Bruce Fagan** had a big night with 14 points, 7 rebounds and 3 blocked shots, while Simpson buried 6 straight free throws in the final minute. It was also the 186th meeting between the Ramblers and Trojans, with Prep holding a big 124-62 margin.

- The PIAA, with its infinitely politically correct wisdom, expanded school classifications from four to a ridiculously watered down six divisions. In this regard, Prep, Class AAA previously, began operating in Class 5-A. The final standings of ever-changing Region 7:

	Won	Lost
Meadville	8	0
Cathedral Prep	5	3
McDowell	4	4
Central Tech	3	5
East	0	8

- Prep, as the second seed out of D-10, defeated Obama Academy (13-10) in a PIAA sub-regional contest at Carrick High School in Pittsburgh. Obama finished second to Allderdice in the Pittsburgh City League. Next was a first round victory over first time opponent Central Mountain (17-9) at Bald Eagle High School. In the second round game played against Mars (17-10), the Fightin' Planets displayed 6'4" junior Robby Carmody, who pulverized Prep with 45 points en route to an easy win over the Ramblers.

- Senior **Mark Majewski**, also a fine baseball player for the Orange & Black, will continue his athletic career on scholarship as a member of Gannon University's golf team.

- **Jaryn Simpson**, who led the Ramblers in scoring, rebounding (5.0 RPG) and assists (3.4 APG) was named First Team All-Region 7. He was also winner of the "Moe" Gross Award, signaling him as Prep's best player. Simpson finished 20th on Prep's all-time career scoring chart.

- Simpson and **Bruce Fagan** were selected to play in the 43rd City-County All-Star game, a 75-72 County victory.

- In the spring of 2017, the Erie School Board voted to convert East and Strong Vincent high schools to middle schools and to eliminate Central Tech as its own entity. Thus, as similar to what happened with Academy and Tech Memorial in 1993, Prep will have no further competition with the Warriors, Colonels, or Falcons. In its place will be a new school combining East, Vincent and Central, located in the Central Tech facility, originally the Tech Memorial building. The name of the new school is Erie High School; its mascot nickname is the "Royals;" and its colors are Purple & Gold. Cathedral Prep will compete with the Erie Royals in all sports.

2017 All-Opponent Team:

    Trey Jemison, Homewood

    Alex Jay, General McLane [Edinboro]

    David Morris, Vincent (1st team all-state, D-10 POY) [Tennessee St.]

    Armoni Foster, Meadville (1st team all-state, D-10 POY) [IUP]

    Kaleb Wesson, Westerville South [Ohio State]

    Leonard Johnson, Central Tech

    Bailey Lewis, McDowell

    Jalen Puckett, Rochester Aquinas

    Lashon Lindsey, Meadville

    Robby Carmody, Mars [Notre Dame]

CATHEDRAL PREP'S 100 GREATEST BASKETBALL VICTORIES

Dejected Vincent star David Morris exits the court, as Prep boys mob Charlie Fessler after his dramatic shot to win the 2015 D-10 crown.

The Top Dozen

1) **3/20/1996—Prep 47, McDowell 44.** An historic fifth battle between the Ramblers and Trojans, this time for the PIAA Western Championship, goes down as the single greatest high school sporting event in the history of Erie. A sellout crowd of over 6,000 pumped-up fans cram every nook and cranny of the Erie Civic Center for the climactic game in the history of both programs which isn't decided until the final seconds when Keith Nies, who led the Ramblers with 14 points, steals the ball from the Trojans. It is Prep's greatest victory.

2) **3/24/1953—Prep 66, Harrisburg Central Catholic 64.** The Ramblers win their first state crown in a thrilling contest which ends in utter confusion for the 2,300 fans present at the Gannon Auditorium. Prep is ahead 66-62 when the final buzzer sounds and the fans storm the court. But a frantic HCC bench claims three seconds actually remain as the timer had started the clock too soon on a final out-of-bounds play. The referees agree and the floor is cleared. Harrisburg scores again to slice the final margin to two—and later files a protest of the final result.

3) **3/14/1971—Prep 52, Pittsburgh South Hills Catholic 50 (5 OT's).** It takes a record 5 overtimes for the Ramblers to upset the Rebels in a PCIAA Western Final thriller before 4,000 fans at Edinboro's McComb Field House. Will Cardot hits the game-winner from 17 feet just five seconds before the end of overtime #5. Ramblers go on to defeat Allentown Central Catholic in state final thriller, 65-64.

4) **12/12/1987—Prep 58, Mouth of Wilson (VA) Oak Hill Academy 48.** The Marcel Arribi era begins at the Erie Civic Center with Olivier Allinei tallying 16 markers in an amazing upset over the nation's top program to win the McDonald's Classic for the first time.

5) **3/18/1980—Prep 64, Beaver Falls 40.** Prep marches toward its first PIAA state crown in huge upset over the Tigers at Chartiers Valley. Unsung guards Jeff Metzgar and Jerry Kaminsky do the defensive damage, while Tim Gore, Jim Roseto and Andy Sisinni all score in double figures.

6) **3/31/1993—Prep 64, New Castle 61.** The jam-packed McComb Field House is the site, as Jed Ryan scores 21 points in a thrilling comeback in the PIAA Western Final versus the WPIAL's best. The Ramblers then outmaneuver Hazleton, 41-30, to win their second PIAA state championship and sixth state title overall.

7) **2/27/2015 & 2/14/2015 & 1/27/2015—Prep 41, Strong Vincent 40 & Prep 58, Strong Vincent 53 (OT) & Prep 58, Strong Vincent 53.** The Ramblers defeat the Colonels for the third time in the season, this time for the District 10 championship. Prep never has a lead and is down by 5 with only 1:03 remaining. The deficit is whittled to 40-39 with exactly 1.0 second to go, Ramblers ball underneath. Dajon Heidelberg makes a pass to the far left corner to his last option—Charlie Fessler, the only man open. Fessler arches a contested fadeaway 17-footer, the buzzer sounds and the ball falls through for Prep's 21st D-10 crown. Less than two weeks before against SV, the Ramblers battle back and force overtime with a 3-pointer by Carter Cross with just seconds remaining. Matt Colpoys drains six straight pressure free throws to seal the OT win and gain Prep the co-championship of Region 7. In the first battle between the two, the Ramblers erase a 9-point second half deficit to gain the victory.

8) **3/6/1962—Prep 60, Tech 58.** Big upset in City Series championship playoff for Prep, which was beaten twice by the Centaurs during the regular season. Mike

Flaherty's running one-hander with 21 seconds remaining puts the Ramblers ahead in the jam-packed thriller at the Gannon Audi.

9) **3/28/1984—Prep 58, Meadville 48.** The Section II and District 10 champion Bulldogs enter a PIAA Western Final with a 30-2 record. Jim Stevenson tallies 20 points in a thrilling victory before a capacity crowd of over 4,200 at McComb Fieldhouse in Edinboro and the Ramblers earn their second trip to Hershey.

10) **2/28/1964—Prep 63, Academy 62.** The Ramblers win a sizzling, last-second city championship playoff encounter over the Bob Thomas-led Lions, before a turn-away crowd of over 3,000 fans at the Audi. Dave Wenrick hits the game winning free throw, while big Bill Druckemiller leads the way with 20 points and 13 rebounds.

11) **3/12/1968—Prep 65, Pittsburgh Canevin 56.** A nip-and-tuck PCIAA Western Final thriller at Penn Hills, until the final four minutes when some hot shooting by Rick Fessler and some clutch free throws by Jerry Mifsud and Paul Pry help

Sensing an upset victory over Meadville in the 1984 Western Final, Jim Stevenson displays his Prep Power fist.

the Orange & Black pull away. Ramblers next crush Shamokin Lourdes at the Harrisburg Farm Show Arena, 70-47, for their first state crown in 14 years.

12) **2/26/1959—Prep 55, Strong Vincent 54.** In a nail-biting playoff battle for the city championship, Bernie Nies hits the long bombs and Jim Rudy, on a feed from Pat Tomczak, hits the game winner with 20 seconds left as Ramblers erase a 5-point last minute deficit to defeat SV's "Go-Go" Colonels to win their first city crown since 1954.

Jim Rudy scored the game-winner in Prep's exciting playoff victory over Vincent for the 1959 city title.

Jerry Mifsud made the clutch free throws in the great victory over Pittsburgh Canevin in the 1968 Western Final.

The Rest in Chronological Order

13) **2/13/1925—Prep 36, Greenville St. Mike's 11.** Prep's first win ever and first victory on the home court.

14) **2/19/1926—Prep 20, Titusville St. Titus 19.** Prep gains upset on Kenny Sechrist's free throw in closing moments.

15) **3/2/1927—Prep 23, West Millcreek 21.** Prep's first game against arch-rival now known as the McDowell Trojans—a victory! Ken Sechrist leads the Orange & Black with 11 points.

16) **2/16/1929—Prep 33, North East 32.** Herb Perry, "leaving a sick bed to take his place in the Cathedral lineup," enters early in the 2nd quarter and scores in the final seconds to beat the Grapepickers in an exciting battle. Perry finishes with a then-Prep record 23 points.

17) **12/15/1930—Prep 18, Wesleyville 3.** Fewest points ever surrendered by a Prep team.

18) **1/29/1932—Prep 12, Oil City St. Joe's 11.** The Ramblers hand 23-3 Hilltoppers their first loss ever on their home court in a defensive gem.

19) **2/15/1932—Prep 21, West Millcreek 20.** The Ramblers, down 20-13 early in the 4th quarter, rally to score 8 unanswered points, including 4 in the last 20 seconds (FGs by Len Kuziora and Eugene Coleman).

20) **2/17/1933—Prep 30, Cleveland (OH) St. Ignatius 27.** The Ramblers, after trailing for three quarters and being down 24-20 entering the 4th period, outscore the Golden Tornado 10-3 in the final session for the conquest. Len Kuziora scores 15 points to lead Prep.

21) **2/17/1934—Prep 19, North East 10.** The Ramblers avenge an early season 20-point loss to defeat the 9-0 Grapepickers. Eugene "Dog" Coleman scores 9 for the Orange & Black.

22) **1/29/1935—Prep 24, Wesleyville 23.** With the Ramblers on the short end of a 23-19 score with only 1:30 left to play, Bob Culhane breaks through for a couple of baskets and star senior "Mickey" McLaughlin scores the winning free throw with just seconds remaining. At the rematch in Wesleyville, another Prep victory, a fistfight between Culhane and a feisty Bulldog guard named McMahon leads to a five-year severance of relations between the bitter rivals.

23) **2/24/1936—Prep 24, Oil City St. Joe's 17.** The Ramblers upset the Hilltoppers, who enter the contest with a record of 20-0.

24) **2/17/1941—Prep 2, Buffalo (NY) Canisius 0.** The Ramblers gain a forfeit win over the Crusaders when coach Johnny Barnes pulls his team from the floor after referee Chuck Bauder refuses to reverse his ejection of Canisius player Jack Connelly, who "kneed" Rambler Rodger Lamb after a jump ball call. Some reports have Canisius ahead at the time, 22-18 in the 2nd quarter, while other accounts state the game was tied at that moment, 20-20.

25) **2/10/1942—Prep 36, Strong Vincent 34 (2OT's).** Prep's first win over the west-side rival Colonels and first win in an overtime contest. Johnny Flanigan is the hero, nailing a free throw to put the game into OT, then sinking the game-winner from the side of the foul circle 1:32 into the second OT, which was played under "sudden death" rules.

26) **12/13/1943—Prep 29, Oil City St. Joe's 27.** With Prep down, 27-25, Johnny DeLuca is fouled underneath the hoop with four seconds remaining. Irish coach Father Charles Hurley vehemently disputes the call and draws a technical foul. DeLuca makes two of three free throws to knot the score, with Prep retaining possession underneath. Regaining the leather on a pass from a teammate, DeLuca lets go from the sidecourt and the final buzzer sounds as the ball is in the air. The sphere swishes through, referee Jack Komora calls it "good" and the Ramblers win, 29-27.

27) **12/2/1944—Prep 20, Lackawanna (NY) Our Lady of Victory 7.** First game played in the new Prep gymnasium resembles a football score.

Prep's 1968 State Champions. Front, L to R: Asst. Coach Father Landgraf, Steenberge, Van Volkenburg, Borowy, Pry, Giermak, Quinn, Fessler, Rosenthal, Coach Fox; Back: Mgr. Barko, Mifsud, Hansen, Mullen, Felix, Bukowski, Gambill.

28) **3/12/1945—Prep 37, Johnstown Central Catholic 22.** Johnny DeLuca scores 18 points as Prep upsets Johnstown Central Catholic, 37-22, for its first win in PCIAA state tournament play.

29) **1/5/1946—Prep 21, St. Marys Central Catholic 19.** Don Laird leads the Ramblers to impressive win over 19-3 Crusaders.

30) **3/7/1946—Prep 33, Johnstown Central Catholic 32.** Jim White's set shot with only four seconds remaining beats Johnstown Central Catholic in a PCIAA tourney thriller, 33-32.

31) **2/20/1947—Prep 39, Strong Vincent 35.** The Ramblers rally behind Art Hilinski's 15 points, gain revenge to clinch first City Series title.

32) **12/20/1947—Prep 33, Warren 31.** Come-from-behind verdict over eventual District 10 champs and only win in 1947-48 season's first seven games. Sophomore Jack Crotty leads the Ramblers with 9 points.

33) **1/14/1949 & 2/8/1949—Prep 38, Tech 32 & Prep 39, Tech 33.** The Ramblers upset Tech twice on way to City Series, Big Seven titles. Jack Crotty scores 12 in the first contest and Art Middleton tallies 14 in game two.

34) **1/19/1951—Prep 61, Tech 60.** Thrilling win over Carmen Riazzi-led Centaurs. Al Hatkevich scores 23 to lead the Ramblers, while Riazzi leads Tech with 27.

35) **2/9/1951—Prep 51, Sharpsville 49.** Close win on the road over eventual D-10 champs. Len Cyterski leads the Ramblers with 15.

36) **3/18/1953—Prep 54, Johnstown Central Catholic 49.** The Ramblers defeat the Crimson Crushers in a thriller for Prep's first PCIAA Western title. Jim Fahey scores 13.

37) **3/26 & 27/1953—Prep 54, Pawtucket (RI) St. Raphael's 51 and Prep 42, Buffalo (NY) Canisius 39.** The state champ Ramblers are the darlings of the prestigious Eastern States Invitational Tourney (ESIT), opening with an impressive victory over St. Raphael's, then scoring a great win over 20-0 Canisius. Big Jim Fahey leads the way with 20 and 21 points.

38) **3/2/1954—Prep 50, East 45.** The Ramblers use Chuck Wittman's 18 points to win a thriller over the Mel Laskoff-led Warriors in the first playoff ever for a City Series title. Laskoff scores 24.

39) **3/25-26/1954—Prep 80, Allentown Central Catholic 58 & Prep 65, Syracuse (NY) St. Lucy's 64.** The Ramblers dominate the Vikings for their second consecutive PCIAA state title as James "Moe" Gross thrills the crowd with 25 points. On the very next evening the Ramblers open the prestigious Eastern States Catholic Invitational Tournament (ESCIT) impressively, as Gross scores 22.

40) **3/9/1955—Prep 62, Johnstown Central Catholic 55.** The Ramblers upset the 20-3 Crimson Crushers at the Gannon Auditorium behind Jim Keim's 18 points in PCIAA tourney play.

41) **12/22/1955—Prep 80, Tech 75.** Nice win over Ray Kovalesky-led Tech, eventual City and Section I champ. Vinny "Flowers" scores 21 to lead the Ramblers. Kovalesky pours in 27.

42) **2/29/1956—Prep 79, Johnstown Central Catholic 77.** Big George Feasler scores 24 at the Audi in this PCIAA tourney thriller.

43) **3/6/1957—Prep 50, St. Marys Central Catholic 40.** PCIAA tourney win over a tough Crusader squad, and the only time a Pennsylvania state playoff game is held in another state—New York, in the city of Jamestown! Bill Carey leads Ramblers with 17 points.

44) **12/19/1957—Prep 58, Strong Vincent 44.** Herb Foster and Bill Eberlein each score 16 as Ramblers upset SV's "Go-Go Colonels," eventual District 10 champions.

45) **3/1/1960—Prep 59, Tech 58.** Tom Desser comes off the bench to lead the Ramblers in a City Series playoff thriller, while Centaur great Fred Biletnikoff misses a free throw that would have sent the game into overtime.

46) **1/19/1962—Prep 49, Academy 48.** Al Lubiejewski grabs a rebound from his own missed shot and scores at the buzzer, his only two points of the contest, and is carried off the floor by his teammates after this City Series thriller.

47) **1/7/1964—Prep 75, Meadville 63.** The Ramblers defeat the eventual Section II and D-10 champion Bulldogs behind Pat Lupo's 24 points.

48) **1/12/1965—Prep 102, Titusville St. Joe's 48.** First time Ramblers score

Ron Hornyak led the 1965 Ramblers in the record setting 102-point outburst against Titusville St. Joe's. Hornyak went on to star at PSU-Behrend.

in triple digits. The points are spread around, with Ron Hornyak leading Prep with 14.

49) **3/1/1965—Prep 61, Tech 34.** Tim Maloney with 22 points leads the Ramblers to a surprisingly easy City Series title playoff win.

50) **1/20/1967—Prep 56, East 54.** The Ramblers shock the Warriors on Tim Finegan's tip-in with only seven seconds remaining.

51) **12/5/1967—Prep 99, Kennedy Christian 51.** Rick Fessler scores 32 points as the Ramblers gain their 500th win in history.

52) **3/17/1968—Prep 70, Shamokin Lourdes 47.** Easy win in state final, the Ramblers' third PCIAA title. Paul Pry leads Prep with 17 markers.

Will Cardot fires over the outstretched arms of McDowell's Mike Bartoszek, while Jim Sperry helps defend. The thrilling Rambler victory was the first time Prep and McDowell squared off in the Gannon Audi.

Dave Wieczorek, with perfect form, shoots over Jim Sperry in the last Prep-McDowell game held in the Prep gym (1970).

53) **12/28/1969—Prep 79, Pittsburgh North Catholic 78 (OT).** "Puck" Cardot scores 26, but Tommy Hansen is the hero, sinking a pair of free throws after time expires, then scoring 4 more in the overtime. The Ramblers were down by 14 in the last period and scored 6 in the final minute to send the game into OT. A couple of months later Prep hands North Catholic its second of only four losses for the season, 63-53, in the PCIAA playoffs.

54) **2/17/1970—Prep 71, McDowell 70.** Brian Flanagan leads the Orange & Black with 26 points and 13 rebounds and Dave Wieczorek hits a pair of free throws on a pressure-packed "one-and-one" situation with 9 seconds left to offset Chuck Britton's drive at the buzzer for the Trojans. An overflow crowd witnesses the last Prep-McDowell game played in the Prep gym.

55) **2/23/1971—Prep 74, McDowell 62.** This hotly-contested triumph over the Trojans is the first time the two teams ever played at Gannon Auditorium. Joe Cook plays his finest game with 20 points and 14 rebounds, while Danny Bukowski, John Reynders and all score in double figures to offset the high-scoring Trojan trio of Chuckie Britton, Jim Sperry and Mike Bartoszek.

John Reynders scored the slam dunk that won the 1971 state title for Prep. He is now the president of Morningside College.

56) **3/19/1971—Prep 65, Allentown Central Catholic 64.** The Ramblers go ahead with just 13 seconds left to play, when John Reynders outfights a trio of Viking players for a rebound and jams the ball through as Prep wins its fourth PCIAA state championship. Willie Cardot leads the Orange & Black with 22 points.

57) **2/25/1972—Prep 60, Academy 55.** Marty "O", with 17 points, leads Prep over the David Purdue-led Lions as the Ramblers wrap up another city title. Purdue scores 20.

Bill Bensur and Jeff Szumigale defend against Francis Spearman in the 1977 thriller over Academy.

58) **3/2/1974—Prep 66, Harborcreek 61.** It's the Ramblers' first victory ever in District 10 PIAA playoff competition. Rick Bengel scores 20 to lead the way.

59) **2/25/1975—Prep 71, Vincent 67.** John Webb goes wild with 26 second half points as the Ramblers erase a 17-point deficit to keep PIAA playoff hopes alive.

60) **3/8/1975—Prep 66, Academy 62.** The Ramblers erase a 9-point halftime deficit and upset the Lions behind Mike Sisinni's 21 points to claim their first District 10 title.

61) **3/1/1977 & 3/10/1977—Prep 63, Academy 43 & Prep 57, Academy 54.** With Dan Sculley scoring 20 points in each contest, the Ramblers first down Lions for the Section One crown then do it again in a hotly-contested District 10 championship thriller.

62) **3/4/1978—Prep 53, Academy 46.** Sophomore Tim Gore leads Ramblers to a D-10 title.

63) **3/14/1978—Prep 65, Belle Vernon 55.** The Ramblers gain an impressive PIAA Western Semifinal win in the only battle ever against the Leopards. Danny Achille scores 17 to lead the Orange & Black.

64) **3/10/1979—Prep 54, Strong Vincent 44.** After the Colonels twice trounce the Ramblers during regular season, Prep bounces back to upset SV in the District 10 final. Mike May leads Prep with 14 points.

65) **3/20/1980—Prep 53, McDowell 43.** Prep's 4th straight victory of the season over the 27-5 Trojans, this time in the PIAA Western Final. Jim Roseto leads the Ramblers with 18 points, while Andy Sisinni chips in with 15.

66) **3/22/1980—Prep 50, Allentown Allen 40.** The Ramblers win Erie's first PIAA state crown. Tim Gore, sensational throughout his entire Prep career, leads Prep with 23 points, 12 rebounds, 4 blocked shots, 3 steals and 3 assists before a crowd of 7,206 at Hersheypark Arena.

67) **12/9/1981—Prep 49, Pittsburgh Peabody 47.** Jon Alberstadt and Gary Miller each tally 10 points to lead Prep's 750th win in history.

68) **12/2/1983—Prep 54, Philadelphia Roman Catholic 52 (OT).** Jimmy Stevenson scores 19 points in an impressive McDonald's Classic win over a big-time program.

69) **12/6/1986—Prep 59, Philadelphia Roman Catholic 58.** Kevin Dalton scores 14 in a thrilling win over the Philly powerhouse at the McDonald's Classic.

70) **2/23/1988—Prep 48, Strong Vincent 38.** The Ramblers defeat the Colonels in a Metro League championship playoff behind Jim Camp's 13 points.

71) **3/19/1988—Prep 51, Farrell 49.** Jim Toohey scores 15 points and steals the ball in the final second in this PIAA Western Semifinal thriller.

72) **1/19/1990—Prep 68, Baltimore (MD) Dunbar 62.** Jim Hamilton drops in 20 in this huge McDonald's Classic win over the #18-ranked team in the nation.

73) **12/19/1990—Prep 81, Chattanooga (TN) Brainerd 76.** Jim Hamilton scores a Prep record 42 points, including seven 3-pointers in an impressive victory over Tennessee's top program.

74) **1/19/1991—Prep 70, Brooklyn (NY) Bishop Loughlin 69.** Jim Hamilton's 3-point buzzer beater wins the McDonald's Classic in the most thrilling Classic game ever.

75) **1/9/1993—Prep 38, NYC (NY) LaSalle Academy 32.** The Ramblers stun LaSalle to win their third McDonald's Classic championship behind sophomore Jed Ryan's 17 points.

76) **3/4/1993—Prep 57, Meadville 52.** Booker Coleman's 15 points leads the Ramblers to a great D-10 playoff win over the third-ranked 23-2 Bulldogs.

77) **3/11/1993—Prep 54, McDowell 49.** Jed Ryan tallies 20 in the fourth Ramblers-Trojans meeting of the season. The D-10 final was held before 6,193 fans, the largest crowd ever at the Erie Civic Center.

78) **4/3/1993—Prep 41, Hazleton Area 30.** The verdict over the 29-2 Cougars is the lowest-scoring title game in the top boys' division since Norristown defeated Ford City, 30-23, in 1948. It's Prep's second PIAA state crown and sixth state toga overall. The Hersheypark Arena crowd of 8,392 is the largest to ever witness a Prep basketball game.

79) **1/7/1994—Prep 67, Mercyhurst Prep 59.** Though unknown at the time, it's the 1,000th victory in Rambler basketball history. Jed Ryan scores 20 to lead the way.

80) **3/7/1994—Prep 53, McDowell 50 (OT).** Booker Coleman powers in 17 points in this very intense overtime thriller in a District 10 final. An Erie Civic Center crowd of 3,708 are witnesses.

81) **1/13/1995—Prep 59, Chester 52.** Jed Ryan bangs in 31 points in a McDonald's Classic revenge triumph over the defending state champs. The Clippers had defeated the Orange & Black in 1994's PIAA final.

82) **3/6/1995—Prep 58, McDowell 55.** The Ramblers win the rubber match, before 4,675 fans at the Erie Civic Center, as both teams enter this intense D-10 final with identical 22-3 records.

83) **2/28/1997—Prep 74, Meadville 63.** Julian Blanks garners 29 points as the Ramblers outplay the Bulldogs in a District 10 final at the McComb Fieldhouse.

84) **1/10/1998—Prep 51, Philadelphia Simon Gratz 42.** Jim Gemler pours in 23 points, including five 3-pointers, in an impressive win over the strong Philly power.

85) **1/26/2001—Prep 36, McDowell 33.** Jeff Daisley sparks the Ramblers from a 10-point second half deficit to a three-point upset, coming off the bench to score 14 points, collect 10 rebounds, block 3 shots and nail 10 of 11 from the free throw line. Following the game was the well-publicized "basket-brawl" that involved "at least 30 and as many as 90 students" outside the Hammermill Center.

86) **2/21/2002—Prep 68. George Junior Republic 51.** Phil Stewart goes wild with six 3-pointers and 22 points to lead the Orange & Black to an upset over the state's #6 team in a D-10 semifinal.

87) **1/31/2005—Prep 83, General McLane 77 (OT).** The Lancers open with 16-3 lead, but the Ramblers battle back and take a fourth quarter lead. GM's Ben Swank then takes an in-bounds lob pass from mid-court for a layup that sends game into overtime at 64-all. Prep roars ahead in OT with Nick Haller scoring 9 of his 29 points. GM thus suffers only its 4th loss ever on its home court since its new gym opened in 1991!

88) **3/12/2005—Prep 53, Pittsburgh Schenley 49.** The Ramblers stage a furious defensive comeback before a sold-out, packed throng at Slippery Rock, forcing three turnovers in the final minute to key an 8-0 run to shock the heavily favored Pittsburgh City champions and the referees in a tense PIAA Elite Eight playoff.

89) **12/7/2005—Prep 65, Franklin 62.** Mark Blazek buries a 22-footer at the buzzer to defeat the eventual state champions before a packed throng in Franklin.

90) **1/13/2006—Prep 88, Chester 84 (OT).** Preston Harris tallies 33 points in an exciting McDonald's Classic victory over the defending state champs.

91) **1/13/2007—Prep 64, Los Angeles (CA) Westchester 60.** The Ramblers shock the nationally-ranked Comets for the McDonald's Classic consolation honors.

92) **2/2/2007—Prep 83, General McLane 81 (OT).** The Ramblers defeat the eventual state champs on their home floor behind Mark Blazek's amazing 32 points on 11-of-12 shooting and his game-winning bucket at the buzzer.

93) **1/12/2008—Prep 65, McDowell 61.** The Ramblers hand the Trojans one of only three losses in their entire campaign behind Mark Blazek's 21 points.

94) **2/19/2009—Prep 74, Strong Vincent 68.** The Ramblers avenge earlier defeats to the Colonels in a District 10 semifinal. Bobby Spoden caps off the emotional win, scoring 10 fourth quarter points and finishing with a steal and resounding slam dunk with just 20 seconds remaining.

95) **2/17/2012—Prep 47, McDowell 45.** Rambler strongman Delton Williams collects a rebound and drives the length of the floor with just 8 seconds remaining to give Prep its winning margin at the jam-packed, sold-out McDowell Paul Goll gym.

96) **3/1/2012—Prep 85, Strong Vincent 43.** The Ramblers crush the Colonels for a District 10 crown after a pair of regular season nail-biters versus SV. Sheldon Zablotny leads the way with 26 points.

97) **3/14/2012—Prep 50, Pittsburgh Central Catholic 49 (OT).** Sheldon Zablotny hits a short jumper at the buzzer as the Ramblers down the nemesis Vikings in thrilling PIAA playoff action.

98) **1/19/2013—Prep 80, Arlington (VA) Bishop O'Connell 75.** The Ramblers score a stunning upset over the nation's #15 ranked team to take Burger King Classic consolation honors.

99) **3/13/2013—Prep 58, Hampton 50.** The Ramblers overcome the Talbots' skyscrapers and "triangle-and-two" defense in a thrilling PIAA Sweet 16 encounter. Sheldon Zablotny scores 21.

100) **1/23/2014 & 2/14/2014—Prep 52, McDowell 47 & Prep 59, McDowell 47.** The Ramblers erase an early 18-6 deficit in the first game, clawing and scratching their way over the 14-1 Trojans behind Matt Harris' 24 points. Harris tallies 18 fourth quarter points in game two and totals 29 as the Ramblers upset the Trojans at jam-packed, sold-out Paul Goll gym. The Blue & White finish the regular season with just three defeats—two to the Orange & Black!

Jim Hamilton '91 led Prep to several of its greatest wins.

PREP'S 100 GREATEST PLAYS AND PERFORMANCES

Moments before Keith Nies stole the ball from Jake Delsandro to clinch the 1996 Western Final, the greatest single play in Prep basketball history.

Jim Hamilton's buzzer-beating 3-pointer won the 1991 McDonald's Classic. Hamilton also holds Prep single game record with 42 points.

The Top Dozen

1) **3/20/1996**—With Prep leading McDowell by one with just two seconds left in a thrilling PIAA Western Final, **Keith Nies** strips the ball from Trojan star **Jake Delsandro**, gains possession and is fouled in the greatest defensive play in Rambler history. Nies sinks both free throws and Prep defeats McDowell, 47-44, in Prep's greatest victory.

2) **1/19/1991**—**Jim Hamilton** nails his last of seven 3-pointers with four seconds remaining to upset powerful Brooklyn Bishop Loughlin, 70-69, in the most exciting McDonald's Classic title game ever played.

3) **1/26/2008**— **Mark Blazek** gives one of the greatest performances ever displayed in Erie area hoops, draining 11-of-12 from the floor, including six 3-pointers, and going 4-for-4 from the line for 32 points in a 72-62 win over top-ranked General McLane.

4) **3/22/1980**—Sensational **Tim Gore** leads the Ramblers over Allentown Allen, 50-40, in the PIAA AAA (large school) state championship game with 23 points, 12 rebounds, 4 blocked shots, 3 steals and 3 assists before an impressed crowd of 7,206 at the Hersheypark Arena.

5) **12/19/1990**—**Jim Hamilton** scores a Prep record 42 points, including seven 3-pointers, in an 81-76 OT victory over Chattanooga Brainerd in one of the greatest performances ever at the prestigious King of Bluegrass Tournament in Fairdale (KY). That broke **Dan Sculley's** Prep record of 41 set in 1977-78 against Pittsburgh Brashear and lasts as a Rambler record to this day.

6) **2/23/1968**—**Paul Pry** breaks the all-time Prep and City Series single game scoring records with 40 points in the last city battle of the season, canning 13 FGs and 14 FTs. This helps Pry capture the regular season city scoring title, as he was running neck-and-neck with East High's **Denny Satyshur** for the crown.

7) **3/14/1991**—**Jim Hamilton** scores 37 points in his final game, including six 3-pointers, in a classic, double-overtime, nip-and-tuck, 101-98 PIAA Western Semifinal battle with Altoona at the jam-packed Clarion gym in one of Prep's all-time memorable and heartbreaking losses.

8) **3/14/1971**—**Will Cardot** hits the game-winner from 17 feet just five seconds before the end of the record fifth overtime to beat Pittsburgh South Hills Catholic in a PCIAA Western Final, 52-50.

9) **2/27/2015**—Prep never has a lead and is down by 5 with only 1:03 remaining. The deficit is whittled to 40-39 with exactly 1.0 second to go, Ramblers ball underneath. **Dajon Heidelberg** makes a pass to the far left corner to his fourth option—**Charlie Fessler**, the only man open. Fessler arches a fadeaway 17-footer, the buzzer sounds and the ball falls through for a thrilling 41-40 victory over Strong Vincent and Prep's 21st D-10 crown.

10) **2/14/2014**—In a thrilling 59-47 victory at McDowell, **Matt Harris** completely takes over in one of the greatest performances in a Rambler uniform, scoring 29 points, including 18 in the fourth period, despite being double and sometimes triple-teamed.

11) **1/22/1952**—**Al Hatkevich's** 37-point performance in a 67-53 victory over Tech breaks the old city record for a single game of 32 by Tech's **Joe Zuravleff**. His total also shatters

Will Cardot hit the game winner in the 5th overtime to win the Western Final on the way to the PCIAA state crown.

Matt Harris gave one of the best performances ever in a Rambler uniform in the 2014 victory at McDowell.

Al Hatkevich scored 37 points in this game against Tech, a Prep record that lasted 16 years. Defending for the Centaurs: Spiro Woolis (21), Dan Yurkovic (41) and Pete Alex (14).

the Gannon Audi record of 31 set by Vincent's **Sammy Williams** in 1951. More amazingly, "Hacker" scores his points after picking up three personal fouls in the first 5 minutes of the game. His school scoring record stands until broken by **Paul Pry** in 1968.

12) 2/25/1975—**John Webb** goes wild, scoring 26 second half points, as the Ramblers erase a 17-point second half deficit to keep their PIAA playoff hopes alive in a revenge victory over Vincent, 71-66.

The Rest in Chronological Order

13) 1/16/1925—**George Murphy** scores Prep's first field goal ever and **Ralph Cochrane** makes Prep's first free throw ever in a loss to the Central Seconds, 30-19.

14) 2/19/1925—**Kenny "Ribs" Sechrist** sinks the winning field goal "on a pretty heave from the side" in the closing moments to upset Titusville St. Titus, 20-19.

John Webb's wild 26-point second half performance put Prep into the 1975 playoffs.

15) 1/13/1928—**Don Hayes** becomes the first Prepster to score 20 points in a game, defeating Corry St. Ed's, 55-13. Hayes was also the first to average in double digits for PPG.

16) 2/16/1929—**Herb Perry**, "leaving a sick bed to take his place in the Cathedral lineup," enters early in the second quarter, and later scores in the final seconds as Prep wins an exciting battle at North East, 33-32. "The Galloping Ghost of the Hardwood" finishes with a then-Prep record 23 points.

17) 12/17/1929—**Herb Perry** scores 28 points in a 52-5 victory over Wesleyville, a record that lasts 22 years.

18) 2/15/1932—The Ramblers, down 20-13 to West Millcreek early in the fourth quarter, rally to score 8 unanswered points, including four in the last 20 seconds on FGs by **Len Kuziora** and **Eugene Coleman**, to win 21-20.

19) **1/29/1935**—With the Ramblers on the short end of a 23-19 score with only 1:30 left to play, **Bob Culhane** breaks through for a couple of baskets and **"Mickey" McLaughlin** nails a free throw with only seconds remaining to beat Wesleyville, 24-23.

20) **2/10/1942**-- **Johnny Flanigan** is the hero in Prep's first-ever win over Strong Vincent, nailing a free throw to put the game into OT, then sinking the game-winner from the side of the foul circle 1:32 into the second OT, which was played under "sudden death" rules. Final score: 36-34.

21) **12/13/1943**—With Prep down, 27-25, **Johnny DeLuca** is fouled underneath the hoop with four seconds remaining. Oil City St. Joe's coach **Father Charles Hurley** vehemently disputes the call and draws a technical foul. DeLuca makes two of three free throws to knot the score, with Prep retaining possession underneath. Regaining the leather on a pass from a teammate, DeLuca lets go from the sidecourt and the final buzzer sounds as the ball is in the air. The sphere swishes through, referee **Jack Komora** calls it "good" and the Ramblers win, 29-27.

22) **3/10/1945**—Prep coach **Sam Yezerski** nails a 3-point field goal in the Coaches All-Star Game, thus making him the first person affiliated with Prep to score a "trey." It's the first game ever played in Erie using Tech coach **Eddie Abramoski's** 3-point play rule.

23) **3/12/1945**—Johnny DeLuca scores 18 points as Prep upsets Johnstown Central Catholic, 37-22, for its first ever win in PCIAA state tournament play.

24) **3/7/1946**—Jim White's long bomb set shot with only four seconds remaining beats Johnstown Central Catholic in a PCIAA tourney thriller, 33-32.

25) **2/12/1948**—Don Laird scores 26 points, second highest in Prep history at the time, as the Ramblers crush Vincent, 48-28. Coach **Walt Strosser** removes Laird from the lineup with four minutes remaining, and did not relent to the Rambler faithful chanting loudly for Laird's return.

26) **1/10/1948**— Joe Luteran's late shot before the buzzer beats Bradford St. Bernard's, 39-37.

27) **2/20/1953 through 3/28/1953**—The consistently strong play of big **Jim Fahey** and little **Jimmy Dailey** leads Prep to City Series and PCIAA state crowns and a second place finish in the prestigious Eastern States Invitational Tournament in Glens Falls (NY).

28) **2/26/1954 & 3/2/1954**—Chuck **Wittman** scores 30 against Strong Vincent and then follows with 18 to lead Prep to a thrilling 50-45 verdict over East in a City Series championship playoff.

29) **3/18/1954 & 3/25/1954**—Prep is led by the outstanding play and floor leadership of **James "Moe" Gross**, who scores 26 in the 75-46 win over Johnstown Central Catholic in the PCIAA Western Final and 25 in the state championship game against Allentown Central Catholic, an 80-58 rout. Gross continues his outstanding play as Prep makes it to the final of the prestigious Eastern States Catholic Invitational Tournament in Newport (RI).

Jim White's set shot with four seconds left beat Johnstown CC in the 1946 PCIAA tourney.

Don Laird might have broken the Prep record for most points in a game had Coach Strosser not removed him from the lineup with four minutes remaining.

30) **2/25/1955**—Big **George Feasler** scores 32 points in a 74-42 rout of Academy.

31) **2/18/1957**—Ron Costello scores 32 points in a 74-58 victory over Corry.

32) **12/14/1958**—Chuck Bauder hits a 15-foot jump shot with two seconds left for a 68-66 triumph over Buffalo (NY) Canisius.

33) **2/26/1959**—In a nail-biting playoff battle for the city championship, **Jim Rudy**, on a feed from **Pat Tomczak**, hits the game winner with 20 seconds left as the Ramblers erase a 5-point last minute deficit to defeat SV's "Go-Go" Colonels, 55-54, and win their first city crown since 1954.

34) **2/19/1960 & 3/1/1960**—High-scoring **Bobby Ward** pours in 34 in a 75-60 win over East High. Just 11 days later **Tom Desser** comes off the bench to score 16 and lead Prep to a 59-58 City Series championship playoff sizzler over Tech.

35) **1/19/1962**—Al Lubiejewski grabs a rebound from his own missed shot and scores at the buzzer, his only two points of the contest, and is carried off the floor by his teammates after this thrilling 49-48 conquest of Academy.

36) **3/6/1962**— Mike Flaherty gets a key bucket on a running one-hander with 21 seconds left in the thrilling 60-58 City Series championship playoff thriller over Tech Memorial. Flaherty is the clutch hero for the Ramblers, impressing the crowd with several long-range two-handed set shots.

37) **12/4/1962**—Jim Marnella scores 30 points in a 75-57 win against Southwestern (NY) Central.

38) **12/21/1963**—6' 8" **Bill Druckemiller** scores 34 points in a 72-54 victory over Academy.

39) **2/28/1964**—Dave Wenrick hits the game winning free throw, while big **Bill Druckemiller** leads the way with 20 points and 13 rebounds in a last-second, 63-62 sizzler over Academy in a playoff for the City Series title.

40) **1/20/1967**—Prep shocks East, 56-54, on a **Tim Finegan** tip-in with just seven seconds remaining.

41) **12/5/1967 & 2/17/1968**—Rick Fessler pours in 32 points in a 99-51 win over Kennedy Christian and **Paul Pry** scores 33 in an 89-60 victory over Ashtabula (OH) Harbor.

42) **3/12/1968**—Hot shooting by **Rick Fessler** and clutch free throws by **Jerry Mifsud** and **Paul Pry** help the Ramblers pull away from rugged Pittsburgh Canevin in a thrilling 65-56 win in a PCIAA Western Final at Penn Hills High School.

43) **12/28/1969**—Tom Hansen is the hero in a 79-78 win over Pittsburgh North Catholic, sinking a pair of free throws after time expires, and then scoring 4 more in the overtime. The Ramblers were down by 14 in the last period and scored 6 in the final minute to send the game into OT!

44) **2/17/1970**—Brian Flanagan leads the Orange & Black with 26 points and 13 rebounds in a thrilling 71-70 victory over McDowell. **Dave Wieczorek** hits a pair of free throws on a pressure-packed "one-and-one" situation with 9 seconds left to offset **Chuck Britton's** drive at the buzzer for the Trojans.

45) **2/12/1971**—Willis "Puck" Cardot scores 33 points in a 99-88 win over Jamestown (NY).

46) **2/23/1971**—Joe Cook leads the way with 20 points and 14 rebounds in a hotly-contested 74-62 triumph over McDowell, the first time the two teams ever played at Gannon Auditorium.

47) **3/19/1971**—John Reynders outfights a trio of Allentown Central Catholic players for a rebound and jams the ball through with just 13 seconds remaining in a 65-64 state championship thriller over Allentown Central Catholic.

48) **3/12/1972**—Bob Repko and Tom Van Volkenburg are heroes in defeat, holding big men 6'7" **George McBride**, 6'6" **Bob O'Connor** and 6'4" **Mark Albert** combined to 24 points in the 46-42 double-overtime PCIAA Western Final loss to Pittsburgh South Hills Catholic.

49) **11/29/1973**—Kevin Barron scores 39 points, just one shy of the Prep record 40 set by **Paul Pry** in 1968, in a 64-60 win over Warren. Barron tallies a Rambler record 17 field goals in the process.

50) **2/26/1974**—Matt Scheppner scores 31 points in an 86-70 victory over Jamestown (NY).

51) **1/17/1975**—Mike Sisinni pours in 30 points in a 68-53 triumph over Johnstown.

52) **1/9/1976**—Dave Cousart scores 35 points as Prep wins a 68-65 heart pounder against McDowell. Cousart outlasts the Trojans' **Dan Chojnacki**, who scores 31.

53) **2/22/1977**—Bill Bensur tallies 34 points in a 92-71 win over Johnstown.

54) **3/1/1977 & 3/10/1977**—Dan Sculley scores 20 points each in back-to-back wins over Academy for the Section I and District 10 titles.

55) **3/16/1977**— Hank Bujalski nets a pair of free throws to forge a tie with 10 seconds left, then **Kevin Elwell** takes a **Dan Achille** pass and scores on a reverse layup right at the buzzer in an amazing comeback victory over Baldwin in state playoff action, 61-59.

Kevin Elwell scored on a reverse layup at the buzzer to defeat Baldwin in a 1977 PIAA playoff thriller.

56) **12/13/1977—Dan Sculley** scores a Prep record 41 points in a 75-56 victory over Pittsburgh Brashear.

57) **12/19/1978—Jim Roseto** hits the winning free throw in a thrilling 64-63 triumph over McDowell.

58) **1/19/1979**—Clutch free throw shooting by **Andy Sisinni** down the stretch, including two pressure free throws with 7 seconds remaining, enables the Ramblers to come from 7 points down in the final five minutes to beat McDowell, 46-45.

59) **3/18/1980—Tim Gore** sets the tone and blocks superstar **Dwight Collins** first shot of the game in a shocking 64-40 PIAA Western Semifinal upset over Beaver Falls. Though down 24-20 at the half, Prep's pressure defense, led by **Jeff Metzgar** and **Jerry Kaminsky**, completely befuddles the Tigers as the Ramblers' roll to a 44-16 advantage over the final 16 minutes.

60) **3/20/1980**—The Ramblers, led by **Jim Roseto's** 18 points and **Andy Sisinni's** 15, control the tempo, play great defense and frustrate the McDowell Trojans for the fourth time in the 1979-80 season, this time in a PIAA Western Final, 53-43.

61) **2/10/1984— Preston Bowen** scores 31 points in an 87-65 win at State College.

62) **3/10/1984—Jim Stevenson's** 20-point performance lifts Prep over powerful Meadville in the first PIAA AAAA Western Final, 58-48.

63) **1/10/1986— Bob Kaczenski** hits a 22-foot bomb at the buzzer in Prep's thrilling 60-58 victory over defending state champion Strong Vincent.

64) **4/1/1987—Mike Szewczykowski** nails a 3-pointer in the City-County All-Star Game, and thus is the first Prepster ever to score a 3-point field goal.

65) **12/12/1987**— The first 3-pointers ever scored by Prepsters in a regular season game occur when **Olivier Allinei, Steve Ziegler** and **Mike Heberle** each nail one in an amazing 58-48 win over nationally ranked Mouth of Wilson (VA) Oak Hill Academy.

66) **12/19/1987—Mike Heberle** hits a clutch shot at the buzzer to defeat Toledo (OH) Scott, 40-38.

67) **3/19/1988—Jim Toohey** steals the basketball in the final second as Prep defeats Farrell, 51-49, in a PIAA Western Semifinal.

68) **12/9/1988—Mike Heberle** scores 27 of Prep's 48 points in a season-opening, 20-point loss to powerful Philadelphia Roman Catholic.

69) **12/22-23/1989**—All-tourney players **Jeff Cardot** (25 points vs. Bishop Guilfoyle, 78-55 win) and MVP **Todd Stablein** (26 vs. Cardinal Gibbons, 81-64 win) lead Prep to the championship of the Great Chevy Shootout in Altoona.

70) **1/20/1990—Jim Hamilton** catches fire in a McDonald's Classic final, nailing six 3-pointers, giving him a record 8 for the tourney and finishes with 26 points in a 76-63 loss to Oak Hill Academy.

71) **3/24/1993 & 3/27/1993 & 3/31/1993**—The outstanding play of sixth man **Pat Marnella** sparks Prep to PIAA state tourney wins over Altoona, Butler and New Castle on the way to a state title.

72) **3/31/1993**—Sophomore **Jed Ryan** leads Prep to a 64-61 upset over New Castle in a PIAA Western Final, with 21 points, 8 rebounds and 4 assists.

73) **3/12/1994 through 3/23/1994**—Monstrous games by **Jed Ryan** and **Booker Coleman** lead the Ramblers to four playoff victories and a berth in a PIAA state final in Hershey.

74) **3/26/1994**—**Booker Coleman** is a hero in defeat, scoring 25 points in a 69-65 loss to Chester in a PIAA AAAA state championship final.

75) **12/21-22-23/1994**—**Jed Ryan** sets a three-game scoring record at the Scenic City Shootout in Chattanooga (TN), with 33, 35 and 26 points against Lookout Valley, Brainerd and Baylor.

76) **12/29/1994**—**Keith Nies** converts a fadeaway 3-pointer from the top of the key

Andy Sisinni made the pressure free throws in the comeback victory over McDowell (1979).

Preston Bowen scored 31 in the road triumph at State College (1984).

at the buzzer in a thrilling 57-54 win over Queens (NY) Msgr. McClancy at the *Toronto Sun* USA Cup.

77) **1/19/1996—Bobby Vahey** comes off the bench and scores 11 points in a 54-second span on opening night of the McDonald's Classic, though Prep loses to powerful Baltimore (MD) St. Frances Academy, 86-60.

78) **3/23/1996**—A **Marcel Arribi**-designed defense holds superstar **Kobe Bryant** to a season-low 17 points, though Lower Merion beats Prep for the PIAA state title, 48-43.

79) **2/28/1997—Julian Blanks** pours in 29 points as Prep downs Meadville for a District 10 title, 74-63.

80) **1/21/1998—Julian Blanks** dominates with 19 points and **Steve Noonan** swipes the ball with just four seconds remaining to preserve a 37-35 Rambler thriller over rival McDowell.

81) **2/26/1998**—Prep dumps Meadville for the seventh consecutive time in D-10 competition behind the brilliant play of **Julian Blanks**, who scores 29 points, collects 6 rebounds, dishes out 5 assists and has 3 steals.

82) **1/26/2001—Jeff Daisley** comes off the bench to score 14 points, collect 10 rebounds, block 3 shots and nail 10 of 11 from the free throw line and rally the Ramblers from a 10-point second half deficit to a 36-33 upset of rival McDowell before the infamous "basket-brawl."

83) **1/19/2002—Mike Sertz** puts on a spectacular shooting performance in the McDonald's Classic, scoring 20 as Prep upsets powerful Washington (DC) Dunbar, 69-62.

84) **2/21/2002—Phil Stewart** lights up the Hammermill Center with six 3-pointers and 22 points as Prep upsets George Junior Republic, 68-51, in District 10 playoff action.

85) **12/7/2002—Casey McCloskey's** turn-around three-pointer at the buzzer from 25 feet away gives Prep a thrilling 43-42 victory over a strong Franklin team.

86) **11/29/2003**—Junior **Brian Mahoney**, in his first Prep varsity game, nails a 3-point game-winner in the closing moments of a season opening 61-59 win against Kennedy Catholic at the Farrell Thanksgiving tourney.

Mike Heberle's clutch shot at the buzzer beat Toledo scott by two (1987).

87) **1/31/2005—Nick Haller** scores 29 points, including 9 in overtime, as Prep defeats General McLane in OT, 83-77, in the first Rambler -Lancer battle ever.

88) **3/9/2005—Cory Knight** scores 25 points in an exciting 78-74 PIAA playoff victory over Mount Lebanon.

89) **12/7/2005**—Franklin looks for a last shot, but **Mark Blazek** steals the ball with four seconds remaining, drives down the court, then hits a 22-footer at the buzzer to seal the 65-62 win over the Knights.

90) **1/13/2006—Preston Harris** scores 33 points, burying 13 of 17 shots in an 88-84 overtime McDonald's Classic thriller over Chester, the defending state champs.

91) **2/4/2006—Mark Demski** embarrasses McDowell, taking a pass, dribbling around his back through three Trojan defenders down the left baseline, and slamming through a resounding dunk in a 70-54 Rambler victory.

92) **2/2/2007—Mark Blazek** (32 points) hits a last-second buzzer beater after a great pass from **Ryan Heidt** to dump eventual state champ General McLane in overtime on the Lancers' sold-out home court, 83-81.

93) **2/19/2009—Bobby Spoden** caps off an emotional win over Vincent in D-10 playoff, scoring 10 fourth quarter points and finishing with a steal and resounding slam dunk with just 20 seconds remaining in a 74-68 victory.

94) **2/27/2009—Rasean Thrower** scores 23, including three 3-pointers, and also collects 6 rebounds, 4 steals and 3 blocks in 55-51 District 10 final win over McDowell.

95) **1/18/2011 & 2/18/2011 & 3/2/2011—Adam Blazek** gives outstanding performances in a trio of victories over arch-rival McDowell, scoring 18, 19 and 16 points as Prep wins 41-35, 52-41 and 51-40 for the District 10 title.

96) **12/19/2011—Jeremy Lynch** drains a 3-pointer with just 1.2 seconds left as Prep defeats Letcher County (KY) Central, 56-54, at the KSA Tourney in Florida.

97) **2/17/2012**—Rambler strongman **Delton Williams** collects a rebound and drives the length of the floor with just 8 seconds remaining to give Prep a thrilling 47-45 win at the jam-packed, sold-out, Paul Goll Gymnasium at McDowell.

98) **3/14/2012**— **Sheldon Zablotny** uses a screen by **Delton Williams** to drive down the left side of the lane and nail a short jumper as time expires in a thrilling, 50-49 overtime win against Pittsburgh Central Catholic in the PIAA playoffs.

99) **1/3/2013 & 1/24/2013—Sheldon Zablotny** scores 33 points in a 76-66 triumph over Central Tech, and three weeks later completely takes over and amazes the crowd with 30 points as Prep hands McDowell a 69-46 beatdown on the Trojans' home court.

100) **1/27/2014 & 2/1/2014—Matty Harris** burns the nets for 38 points in a 74-69 overtime victory over Central Tech. Harris scores Prep's final 18 points, including all 12 in OT. Harris follows his 38-point performance with a remarkable 40-point game, third highest in Prep history, in another overtime battle in Toronto (ONT) against Pope John Paul II. His spectacular two-game 78-point output is a Rambler record for most points scored in back-to-back games.

Sheldon Zablotny '13 at the top of his game at McDowell.

Zablotny hit the bucket that beat Central Catholic in overtime in the 2013 state tourney.

CATHEDRAL PREP's 100 GREATEST BASKETBALL DEFEATS

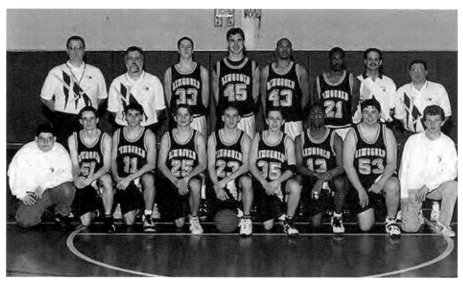

The state champion Ringgold Rams broke Rambler hearts in the 1995 Western Final. "Czar" Walsh, front row fifth from left.

The Top Dozen

1. **3/18/1995—Ringgold 77, Prep 67 (2 OT).** Ringgold's "Czar" Walsh, a name that forever lives in infamy in Prep basketball annals, gets a running, one-handed prayer off at the buzzer as he falls into the bench from 35 feet away. The high-arching, desperation shot swishes right through to send the game into overtime. The deflated Ramblers lose in double OT, 77-67, ending Prep's season and ruining chances for a third straight trip to Hershey.

2. **3/16/1978--Pittsburgh Schenley 67, Prep 66 (OT).** The Ramblers outplay the Spartans, but the famous non-call on an obvious foul on Dan Sculley's drive to the bucket at the buzzer gives the Spartans a huge PIAA Western Final playoff gift at IUP's Memorial Fieldhouse.

Sid Booker, East High's great star in football, basketball and track (1968).

3. **1/12/1968 & 2/16/1968—East 61, Prep 55 & East 52, Prep 51 (OT).** In the first battle, the Ramblers blow a 19-point lead and are outscored by the powerful Warriors, 30-6, in the fourth quarter before an overflow sell-out crowd at the Gannon Auditorium. In game two, a great Rambler comeback falls short before the largest Audi crowd ever, with Prep coach Dick Fox telling reporters post-game: "This was the worst officiated game I've seen in my entire playing or coaching career."

Alan Poole's 10 fourth-quarter points helped East engineer the greatest comeback in City Series history (1968).

4. **3/8/1960—Johnstown Central Catholic 58, Prep 57.** With the Crimson Crushers given a second chance after time expired, little Mike Foran takes one step and lets fly a half-court hook shot that banks neatly through the net. Ramblers lose the PCIAA thriller at Gannon, while the Crushers go on to win their third state title.

5. **3/14/1991—Altoona 101, Prep 98 (2 OT).** A hard-fought, emotional battle and the highest combined scoring game ever results in a Rambler defeat, ending a 17-game win streak in a classic PIAA Western Quarterfinal clash at Clarion.

6. **3/23/1996—Lower Merion 48, Prep 43.** The Ramblers are in the game until the final moments, but Kobe Bryant and the Aces prevail in this state championship battle in Hershey.

7. **3/14/1946—Pittsburgh North Catholic 34, Prep 33.** The Ramblers are edged by one in the PCIAA Western Final before 1,400 fans at East High on a hook shot from the foul line by Trojan Dick Rauluk with less than a minute remaining. That shot spoils a great comeback by the Orange & Black, who were down by 12 midway in the third quarter. NC goes on to win its second of six PCIAA Class A state titles.

8. **2/28/2002—McDowell 64, Prep 59 (OT).** The Trojans win after Greg Hoffman makes three pressure-packed free throws with time expired to send a District 10 final into overtime.

9. **2/13/2006—General McLane 65, Prep 63.** The Lancers gain their first win over the Ramblers when Bobby Stauffer drives the floor and scores a bucket with but 0.7 left on the clock at the Hammermill Center.

10. **3/12/1997—Pittsburgh Schenley 36, Prep 33.** The Spartans ruin the Ramblers' quest for a fourth trip to the PIAA Final in five years, rallying from an 8-point deficit in the final quarter to hand

Lower Merion defeated Prep in the 1996 state final, Kobe Bryant's last game before turning pro.

Greg Hoffman's three pressure-packed free throws with no time left sent the 2002 D-10 final into OT for victorious McDowell.

The great Len Rosenbluth, of Staunton Military Academy, North Carolina and the NBA, MVP of the 1953 ESIT.

Bobby Stauffer drove the length of the floor and scored with less than one second remaining to give GM its first win over Prep (2006).

Prep the unexpected loss. Prep shoots out to a 17-4 lead at the end of the first period, but the Spartans chip away at the lead and allow the Orange & Black but five buckets the rest of the way.

11. **3/26/1994—Chester 69, Prep 65.** The nip-and-tuck PIAA state final is an instant classic, with 24 lead changes and 12 ties. Neither team leads by more than four until the Clippers forge a brief 69-63 edge in the closing seconds. Chester keeps the Ramblers from repeating as state champs.

12. **3/28/1953—Staunton Military Academy (VA) 63, Prep 57.** The Ramblers show class, but lose in the Eastern States Invitational Tournament championship game. Len Rosenbluth, later of North Carolina and NBA fame, scores 32 points for the winners.

The Rest in Chronological Order

13. **1/16/1925—Central High Seconds 30, Prep 19.** Prep's first basketball game in history results in a loss.

14. **1/18/1926—Alliance Academy 55, Prep 9.** Stayed as record for the largest losing margin for a Prep team for 47 years.

15. **1/21/1927 & 2/11/1927—Titusville St. Titus 16, Prep 15 & Titusville St. Titus 24, Prep 19.** Two losses to St. Titus cost Prep a chance to be invited to the National Catholic Tournament in Chicago.

16. **3/23/1927—West Millcreek 28, Prep 26.** First loss ever to the Trojans (later became McDowell High).

17. **1/20/1928 & 2/17/1928—both games Erie St. Stanislaus 20, Prep 19.** Two close losses to local rival in first year of organized league play.

18. **3/7/1929—Altoona Catholic 26, Prep 15.** Prep's first post-season bid, to the Pennsylvania State Catholic Tournament at Duquesne University, ends in first round defeat.

19. **1/6/1931—Vincent 25, Prep 15.** It's the Ramblers' first game against the rival Colonels.

Strong Vincent's first team, 1931. Top players; Ralph Calabrese, Al Farkas, Chuck Bauder, Kenny Bossart, Lou Sickafus, Jerry Rosenthal, John Amendola, Art McDonald.

20. **1/19/1931—Corry 11, Prep 10.** Two technical fouls are called on the Ramblers in the game's final moments. The first is for "delaying the game," while the second is called while time is out, presumably for Father Conway giving Referee Burns "a piece of his mind." Though the first free throw is missed, the second one is made to provide for the Beavers' margin of victory.

The 1931 Academy Lions. Top players: Lugo, Snell, Tell, Mumford, T. Schreckengost, M. Schreckengost, French, Keiper, Beck, Spath, McCart.

21. **1/29/1931—Academy 36, Prep 14.** It's the Ramblers' first game against the rival Lions.

22. **2/10/1931—East 26, Prep 16.** It's the Ramblers' first game against the rival Warriors.

The 1931 East Warriors. Front, L to R: George Blossey, Stan Andrezejczak, Paul Prizinsky, Jack Laraway, Bob Arrowsmith; Back: Coach Hyde, Zig Andrusking, Ed Hiller, Don Eppler, Bob Weber, Paul DeTuerk.

23. **2/22/1932—Tech 34, Prep 11.** It's the Ramblers' first game against the rival Centaurs.

24. **2/3/1933—Cleveland (OH) St. Ignatius 28, Prep 16.** The game in Cleveland held up for an hour at the end of the third quarter, when coach Father Conway, dissatisfied with the officiating of Referee Murphy, refuses to continue until a new official is substituted! It didn't help, the Ramblers lose!

25. **1/19/1934—Oil City St. Joe's 27, Prep 26.** Prep loses 22-6 halftime and 25-14 third quarter leads.

26. **1/30/1934— Edinboro 15, Prep 14.** Wayne "Windy" Crawford sinks a half-court shot with one second remaining to beat the Ramblers.

27. **2/7/1936—Oil City St. Joseph's 31, Prep 15.** The Ramblers have a stretch of 19 minutes, 37 seconds without scoring and lose handily.

28. **1/4/1937—Millcreek 32, Prep 18.** It's the 100th loss in Rambler basketball history.

The 1937 Millcreek Trojans. Front, L to R: Jim Flanagan, Wes Freeburg, Bob Tracy, Sam Willis, Frank Bolte; Back: Bob Green, John Fails, Harry Love, Mike Salvatore, Coach Anderson.

29. **1/21/1937—Corry St. Edward's 32, Prep 28.** The Ramblers own a 22-1 ledger against St. Ed's. This is the one they lost.

30. **2/5/1937—Titusville St. Joseph's 39, Prep 31.** The Ramblers own an 18-1 ledger against the Robots. This is the one they lost.

31. **1/12/1940—Wesleyville 21, Prep 20.** An odd technical foul at the game's conclusion dooms the Ramblers. This is the first time the Ramblers and Bulldogs compete since the famous 1935 brawl and the last time there is any athletic relations between the two through Wesleyville's closing in 1966.

32. **1/22/1940—Tech 41, Prep 38.** It's a bitter loss to the kiddie-corner rival Centaurs.

33. **2/6/1940—Vincent 30, Prep 11.** A capacity crowd sees the Colonels crush the Ramblers. The proceedings are enlivened at the opening of the 4th quarter when Prep center Rodger Lamb tosses a punch at SV's Dick DiTullio. Referee Paul Fitting banishes Lamb from the game.

34. **3/7/1941—Oil City St. Joseph's 37, Prep 35 (OT).** A close loss in the season finale to the Irish, who go on to win their second state Catholic crown in three years.

35. **12/8/1942—East 38, Prep 22.** The Ramblers lose their first-ever City Series encounter.

36. **3/19/1943—Johnstown Central Catholic 35, Prep 25.** The Ramblers lose their first-ever PCIAA playoff game, played at the Strong Vincent gym.

37. **3/9/1944—Johnstown Central Catholic 20, Prep 19.** It's a heartbreaking PCIAA tournament loss to the state finalist Crimson Crushers.

38. **1/11/1947 & 2/8/1947—St. Marys Central Catholic 27, Prep 25 & St. Marys Central Catholic 44, Prep 38.** It's the last of regular season relations between the Crusaders and the Ramblers because of what is considered "bad blood" between them. Fistfights between players and fans of the two rivals are commonplace. The Ramblers and the Crusaders do not meet again for another decade, until the 1956-57 season.

39. **3/6/1948—Johnstown Central Catholic 59, Prep 37.** The Ramblers can't handle a two and one-half week layoff before a PCIAA playoff, as Leroy Leslie and the Crimson Crushers score an easy victory.

40. **2/24/1949—Pittsburgh Central Catholic 43, Prep 39.** Ramblers lose a close Western Semifinal as the Vikings eventually go on to win their first and only PCIAA state crown.

41. **1/30/1950—Tech 43, Prep 38.** It's the first game at the new Gannon Auditorium.

42. **3/14/1950—Pittsburgh Central Catholic 42, Prep 37.** Another two and one-half week layoff doesn't help the Ramblers against the PCIAA state finalist Vikings.

43. **2/27/1951—Academy 44, Prep 36.** A loss to the spoiler Lions lowers the Ramblers into a three-way tie for the city crown with Tech and Academy.

44. **3/5/1951—Johnstown Central Catholic 53, Prep 50.** Headmaster Monsignor Robert McDonald, incensed with another PCIAA playoff loss, exchanges barbs with coach Dick Detzel, who then resigns. Days later harmony is restored and the pair reaches a complete understanding while ironing out the difficulties which led to the resignation.

45. **2/29/1952—Academy 47, Prep 44.** A loss again to the spoiler Lions lowers Ramblers into a three-way tie for the city crown, this time with Tech and Vincent.

46. **3/6/1952—Pittsburgh Central Catholic 38, Prep 37.** A sixth straight PCIAA opening round loss is a heartbreaker and occurs when Viking Bob Szymanski tips one in with just four seconds remaining.

47. **1/9/1953—Tech 65, Prep 55.** Carmen Riazzi pours in 25 points as the Centaurs hand the Ramblers one of their only two regular season defeats.

The 1952 Tech Centaurs. Front, L to R: Bob Schwellinger, Bernie Kieklak, Frank Minichelli, Eddie Grucza, Rich Zielinski, Tom Maries, Jim Vicary; Back: Octavio Chiappazzi, Spiro Woolis, Pete Alex, Hank Baltine, Don Polagyi, Carmen Riazzi, Dan Yurkovic, Denny Polatas.

48. **1/12/1954—East 45, Prep 44.** Mel Laskoff with 25 points leads the Warriors in one of only two regular season losses for the Orange & Black.

49. **3/28/1954—New York City (NY) All Hallows 73, Prep 59.** The boys from the Bronx overpower the Ramblers in the Eastern States Catholic Invitational Tournament final.

50. **2/18/1955—Vincent 79, Prep 67.** The "Go-Go" Colonels dethrone the Ramblers and break the opponent team scoring record in the process.

51. **1/27/1956—Tech 82, Prep 76.** Ray Kovalesky scores 32 for the Centaurs as the Ramblers suffer their 250th loss in history.

52. **3/9/1956—Pittsburgh Central Catholic 68, Prep 65.** The Ned Twyman-led Vikings nip the Ramblers in a PCIAA Western Final.

53. **12/11/1956—Sharon 86, Prep 44.** The Tigers hand the Ramblers their worst defeat since 1926 and break an opponent team scoring record in the process. This followed a 50-48 loss to Buffalo Canisius just two days before, when a Terry O'Connor shot at the buzzer sank the Ramblers.

54. **3/14/1958—Pittsburgh North Catholic 78, Prep 60.** The Ramblers are no match for Matt Szykowny and the eventual PCIAA state champ Trojans, even though Szykowny and teammate Dick Turici are ejected for fighting with five minutes remaining,

55. **2/20/1959—Vincent 67, Prep 66.** Esker Smith scores 23 and Bill Senger scores the game-winner lying on his back as SV wins a thriller to force a City Series tie.

56. **12/23/1960—Tech 74, Prep 45.** The powerful Centaurs rout the Ramblers with Bobby Biletnikoff scoring 20 points.

57. **2/22/1962—Tech 77, Prep 72 (OT).** Willie Kinnard nets 22 as the Centaurs forge a City Series tie.

58. **12/18/1962—Sharon 43, Prep 38.** A brawl under the hoop in the closing moments ends with a technical foul against Coach Trombacco. The two schools don't compete again for two decades.

59. **1/24/1964—Academy 68, Prep 65.** Bob Thomas scores 26 points as the Lions ruin an 11-game Rambler win streak.

Academy star Larry Hitt (1964).

60. **3/8/1964—Pittsburgh Central Catholic 48, Prep 42.** It's Prep's unlucky 13th straight loss to the Pittsburgh representative in the PCIAA state playoffs. Over 2,300 fans witness this vicious battle, with no less than 66 free throws taken. A wild melee erupts with 36 seconds remaining, Rambler Tim Maloney is flattened by a kick to the head and Erie police are called to the rescue. Then comes a major brawl in Perry Square with dozens of Central and Prep boys participating.

61. **3/16/1965—Pittsburgh South Hills Catholic 58, Prep 56.** It's another Western Final PCIAA playoff loss to the eventual state champ Rebels. The outside shooting of Tom Donahoe and the all-around play of appropriately named Hank South spell doom for the fighting Orange & Black. The annual PCIAA melee between Prep kids and whomever 'mup from Pittsburgh spills into Perry Square, with no serious injuries reported.

62. **3/11/1967—Pittsburgh Canevin 81, Prep 67.** The Ramblers' 16th straight loss to the Pittsburgh area representative in PCIAA tourneys spells doom for coach "Red" Murray.

63. **3/12/1972—Pittsburgh South Hills Catholic 46, Prep 42 (2 OT).** The Rebels prevent the Ramblers from a state title repeat and win a thriller in the last PCIAA tournament game ever played by the Orange & Black.

Appropriately-named Hank South of South Hills Catholic (1965).

64. **2/9/1973—Vincent 68, Prep 53.** SV's Essie Hollis bangs in a Prep opponent record 49 points before a packed house at the Audi.

65. **3/5/1974—Warren 52, Prep 50.** After being beaten by the Orange & Black twice during the regular season, the Dragons upset the Ramblers in a District 10 playoff.

New York City All Hallows, 1954 ESCIT champions. Ernest Haynes, back-row, 4th from left.

66. **3/23/1977—Fox Chapel 68, Prep 52.** The Foxes end the Ramblers' first real exciting PIAA playoffs run.

67. **3/20/1979—Beaver Falls 50, Prep 43.** A powerful Tiger quint ends the Ramblers' thrilling PIAA playoff run in a Western Semifinal.

68. **12/29/1979—Ambridge 56, Prep 52.** A fourth game in four nights is the only time the Ramblers lose in a great 33-1 state championship season.

69. **3/10/1981—Warren 68, Prep 38.** The Ramblers suffer an embarrassing loss in a District 10 playoff game after routing the Dragons twice during the regular season.

70. **12/5/1981—DeMatha Catholic (MD) 50, Prep 37.** The Ramblers give their all in a loss to the first "big time" national power to traipse to Erie.

71. **3/9/1982—Warren 64, Prep 58.** The John Bowen-led Dragons again jinx Prep in a D-10 playoff after falling twice to the Ramblers in regular season.

72. **3/19/1983—McKeesport 63, Prep 62.** Sam Commodore's tip-in at the buzzer wins a Western Quarterfinal for the Tigers.

73. **3/31/1984—Williamsport 68, Prep 61.** The unbeaten Millionaires prevail in the first PIAA Quad-A state championship game.

74. **12/11/1984—East 47, Prep 46.** The Warriors break a 16-game losing skein to the Ramblers, as Prep goes 6 of 22 from the free throw line.

75. **3/5/1987—Meadville 61, Prep 55.** A bumper crowd of 5,678 watches the first District 10 final held at the Erie Civic Center.

76. **1/15/1988—Kansas City (MO) Paseo 59, Prep 57 (OT).** Coach Arribi's first loss as Rambler mentor at the Bass Pro tourney is Prep's 500th defeat in history.

77. **3/23/1988—Pittsburgh Central Catholic 61, Prep 59.** The playoff nemeses Vikings end the Orange & Black season in a PIAA Western Final.

78. **3/18/1989—Pittsburgh Brashear 56, Prep 50.** Even with the home court advantage in a PIAA Western Quarterfinal, Ramblers shoot only 28% from the floor, including only 4-of-23 from 3-point range.

79. **3/17/1990—Shaler 77, Prep 72.** The Ramblers blow 13-point second half lead and are upset in PIAA first round action in Edinboro.

80. **1/11/1992—Oak Hill Academy (VA) 70, Prep 28.** An old-fashioned beatdown by the famed national power in the McDonald's Classic.

81. **3/14/1992—North Allegheny 58, Prep 56.** The Ramblers miss 10 of 15 free throws while NA's Devin Billeter sinks 37 points in a PIAA first round battle.

82. **3/1/1993—McDowell 65, Prep 55.** The Trojans win a Metro League playoff over the eventual state champion Ramblers. Scott Cronk leads the way for the Blue & White with 24 markers.

83. **12/18/1993—Philadelphia Simon Gratz 42, Prep 35.** The Ramblers lose in a Latrobe Rotary Invitational final to the defending national champions.

84. **3/4/1996—McDowell 69, Prep 56.** Jake Delsandro wreaks havoc with 26 points as the Trojans win a District 10 crown in the fourth battle of season between the two. A fifth battle will take place 16 days later in the PIAA Western Final.

85. **3/7/1998—Pittsburgh Central Catholic 64, Prep 49.** The Vikings end a 12-game Rambler win streak and turn-around season in a first round PIAA playoff. Poor shooting and an overall lackluster performance contribute to defeat.

86. **2/22/2000—Central 58, Prep 56.** A second place playoff loss results in the first time since 1985 that Prep has no post-season and the first time since 1986 that Prep does not advance to the PIAA inter-district playoffs (final round of 32 teams).

DeMatha's Danny Ferry, later a star at Duke and in the NBA (1993).

John Bowen, one of Pennsylania's all-time greats, twice destroyed Prep for Warren in D-10 finals. Bowen is now a Rambler assistant.

87. **1/27/2001—Mercyhurst 48, Prep 46.** It's Prep's first loss to the Lakers after 33 consecutive victories.

88. **3/16/2002—Uniontown 48, Prep 45.** The Ramblers lose a hard-fought, near-upset in a PIAA Western Semifinal.

89. **12/28/2002—Meadville 67, Prep 61.** The Ramblers blow a 10-point fourth quarter lead in the final of the Meadville Sertoma tourney, which leads to a post-game outburst and a two-game suspension for Coach Sisinni.

90. **2/18/2003—Strong Vincent 50, Prep 43.** The Ramblers blow a 13-point first half lead to the Colonels in a playoff for the Metro crown at Mercyhurst's Campus Center.

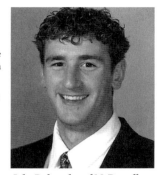

Jake Delsandro of McDowell destroyed Prep with 25 points in the 1996 D-10 final.

91. **3/16/2005—Lower Merion 65, Prep 54.** The Aces derail Prep's 14-game win streak before a packed throng in a PIAA Semifinal at State College High School.

92. **2/8/2008 & 2/20/2008—McDowell 62, Prep 39 and McDowell 64, Prep 50.** The Ramblers suffer two embarrassing defeats to the Trojans with poor play. The first is the worst margin suffered by the Ramblers against the Trojans and the second is in a District 10 final.

93. **2/23/2008—State College 60, Prep 58.** The Ramblers suffer from poor shot selection and shoddy defense and blow 15-point second half lead in a PIAA play-in game.

94. **3/14/2009—Mount Lebanon 51, Prep 41.** The Ramblers have a 40-37 lead with three minutes left in the heartbreaker, before Mt. Lebo goes on a 14-1 run to close out this PIAA Quarterfinal.

95. **3/4/2010—Vincent 68, Prep 60.** The Ramblers suffer their third of three bad losses to the Colonels, losing a 10-point second half lead in this D-10 final.

Lower Merion star B.J. Johnson (2012).

96. **3/21/2012—Lower Merion 79, Prep 48.** The Ramblers and their 12-game win streak are crushed in a PIAA Final Four loss at Bald Eagle High School.

97. **3/16/2013—New Castle 80, Prep 70.** The WPIAL champs display uncanny shooting in a PIAA Quarterfinal to end an 11-game Orange & Black win streak.

98. **2/25/2014—McDowell 66, Prep 52.** The Trojans advance with a District 10 final victory, after the Ramblers had twice crushed them during regular season.

99. **3/17/2015—Philadelphia Archbishop Carroll 59, Prep 32.** The Ramblers are no match for Derrick Jones and the rest of his Philly power teammates in this PIAA Semifinal.

100. **1/16/2016—Lakewood (OH) St. Edward 84, Prep 35.** The Ramblers suffer their all-time losing margin.

New Castle star Shawn Anderson (2013).

Archbishop Carroll star Derrick Jones (2014).

Three Tech Memorial legends, L to R: Willie Kinnard, Coach Al Calabrese, Bobby Biletnikoff (1963).

The 49 points Essie Hollis of Strong Vincent scored is still the all-time record in a Prep game (1973).

Mt. Vernon's Jabarie Hinds destroyed Prep with 39 points in the 2010 McDonald's Classic. Here, with AD Bill Flanagan.

"Czar" Walsh, a name that lives in infamy in Prep basketball annals (1995).

PREP OPPONENTS' 100 GREATEST PLAYS AND PERFORMANCES

Kobe Bryant was held to a season-low 17 points, but he did the other things necessary to ensure the 1996 state title for Lower Merion.

The Top Dozen

1. 3/18/1995—**"Czar" Walsh** is a name that will forever live in infamy in Prep basketball annals. Walsh gets a running, one-handed prayer off at the buzzer as he falls into the bench from 35 feet away. The high-arching, desperation shot swishes right through and sends the game into overtime. The deflated Ramblers then lose the playoff to Ringgold in double OT, 77-67, ending Prep's dream season and ruining chances for a third straight trip to Hershey.

2. 2/9/1973—Strong Vincent's **"Easy Essie" Hollis,** later of St. Bonaventure and NBA fame, tallies what is easily an all-time Prep opponent record 49 points as the Colonels down the Ramblers, 68-53.

3. 1/16/2010—**Jabarie Hinds'** spectacular performance for Mount Vernon in the McDonald's Classic: 14 FGs, including Prep opponent record nine 3-pointers, and 2 FTs for 39 points, beats the Ramblers, 79-67.

4. 3/8/1960—Johnstown Central Catholic's **Mike Foran's** half-court hook shot with no time remaining beats Prep in the PCIAA tourney, 58-57.

5. 3/16/1978—The famous non-call on an obvious foul on Rambler **Dan Sculley's** drive to the bucket at the buzzer gives Pittsburgh Schenley a huge PIAA Western Final playoff victory in overtime, 67-66.

6. 1/12/1968—**Denny Satyshur** scores 13 of his total 26 points and **Alan Poole** adds 10 more in an incredible 30-6 fourth quarter edge, as East High's comeback shocks Prep, 61-55.

7. 2/28/2002—McDowell's **Greg Hoffman** makes three pressure-packed free throws after time expires to send the game into OT. The Trojans then win a thrilling District 10 final, 64-59.

8. 1/26/2016—Vincent's **David Morris** registers 31 points, including five 3-pointers and an electrifying windmill tomahawk slam dunk as the Colonels gain awaited revenge, 70-57. Morris' slam receives national attention and is highlighted on ESPN's SportCenter that evening.

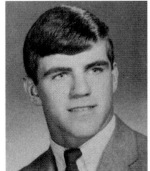

All-State in football, basketball and golf, East High's Denny "Do-it-all" Satyshur is one of Erie's all-time greats (1968).

9. 3/14/1991—**Steve Taneyhill** of Altoona gives an inspired 34-point performance in the Mountain Lions' 101-98 double OT win over a great Prep team in the state playoffs.

10. 2/20/1959—Strong Vincent's **Bill Senger** tosses in the winning bucket while lying on his back under the hoop to beat Prep, 67-66, forcing a playoff for a City Series title.

11. 2/13/2006—**Bobby Stauffer** drives the floor and scores a bucket with but 0.7 left on the clock as General McLane defeats Prep for the first time, 65-63.

12. 3/28/1953—Legendary **Len Rosenbluth,** later of North Carolina and NBA fame, destroys Prep with 32 points as Staunton Military Academy wins an Eastern States Invitational Tourney's championship game.

The Rest in Chronological Order

13. 2/21/1925—**Chester LaPrice** sets the early record with 27 points as Schaller Morticians wallop "the Preps," 58-27.

14. 1/21/1927—**Walter McDonald's** (Monsignor McDonald's brother) long heave with 20 seconds remaining enables Titusville St. Titus to defeat Prep, 16-15.

15. 1/29/1929—**Art Jacobsen,** with a minute to go, "pegged one from the side that swished through the hoop" as Girard halts a 7-game Prep winning streak, 18-16.

16. 1/30/1934— Edinboro's **Wayne "Windy" Crawford** sinks a half-court shot with one second remaining to beat Prep, 15-14.

17. 3/7/1941—Oil City St. Joe's 25-5 team beats Prep in overtime, 37-35, with a spectacular 17-point performance by **Forrest Hall.**

18. 2/18/1944—After Prep takes its first lead of the game, Tech's

Strong Vincent luminary David Morris is now Erie's all-time leading scorer (2017).

GM's Bobby Stauffer buries a "trey" against Prep (2007).

Ed Maras cooly sinks two free throws with 5 seconds remaining to win it for the Centaurs, 39-38.

19. 3/14/1946-- The Ramblers are edged, 34-33, in a PCIAA Western Final before 1,400 fans at East High on a hook shot from the foul line by North Catholic's **Dick Rauluk** with less than a minute remaining.

20. 2/19/1948—**Egilio Alo's** bucket with 6 seconds remaining caps a late East rally and beats the Ramblers, 38-36.

21. 3/6/1948—**Leroy Leslie's** record-breaking 28-point performance for Johnstown Central Catholic in the PCIAA tourney beats Prep, 59-37.

22. 3/6/1952—The Ramblers suffer a first round, 38-37 loss in the PCIAA tourney to Pittsburgh Central Catholic on a tip-in by **Bob Szymanski** with 4 seconds remaining.

23. 1/9/1953—Tech's **Carmen Riazzi** gives spectacular 25-point performance in a 65-55 victory over the eventual state champ Ramblers.

24. 12/11/1953—First team all-stater **Bob Atterholt** tallies 28 points, but Sharon loses to the eventual state champ Ramblers, 51-48.

25. 12/27/1953 & 1/8/1954—Future NBA star **Jim Cunningham** scores 25 and 30 points, but Prep beats Canisius twice, 66-56 and 73-64.

26. 1/12/1954—East High star **Mel Laskoff** pours in 27 points as Warriors down Prep, 45-44.

27. 3/28/1954—Eastern States Catholic Invitational Tourney MVP **Ernest Haynes** leads NYC All Hallows over Prep with 25 points in the title clash, 73-59.

28. 3/18/1955—**George Brown's** 27 points for North Catholic crushes Rambler hopes for a third straight PCIAA state crown, 70-56.

29. 1/27/1956—**Ray Kovalesky** (32 points) and his high-scoring Tech Centaurs defeat Prep, 82-76.

30. 2/17/1956—**Roger Pierce** is on fire with a record-breaking 36 points as Academy downs the Ramblers, 75-66.

31. 3/9/1956—Pittsburgh Central Catholic gains a PCIAA win over Prep, 68-65, behind **Ned Twyman's** 25 markers.

32. 12/9/1956—Buffalo Canisius flattens Prep in season opener, 50-48, on **Terry O'Connor's** jump shot at the buzzer.

33. 3/8/1957—**Ray Masa's** 28 points helps Pittsburgh Central Catholic beat the Ramblers in PCIAA action, 65-59.

34. 12/17/1957—29 points by rugged **Bill Lacey** helps Conneaut (OH) rout Prep, 62-38.

Tech's all-time great Carmen Riazzi (1953). He later starred for the Dayton Flyers.

All Hallows' Ernest Haynes, MVP of the 1954 ESCIT.

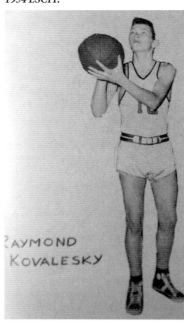

Ray Kovalesky scored 32 points as Tech beat Prep in 1956.

35. 3/14/1958—All-American **Matt Szykowny** with 28 points ensures Pittsburgh Central Catholic ends Prep's season, 78-60.

36. 12/28/1962—**Willie Kinnard** registers 27 points as talented Tech Memorial routs the Ramblers, 78-45.

37. 1/24/1964—**Bob Thomas** of Academy dials in 26 points as the Lions nip Prep, 68-65.

38. 3/16/1965—Appropriately-named **Hank South** (20 points) and eventual state titlist South Hills Catholic edge Prep in the PCIAA's, 58-56.

39. 12/2/1966—Meadville's **Chris Buchanan** records 33 points in 69-61 season opener over Prep.

40. 12/6/1966—**Bob "Posey" Rhoads,** later of Wake Forest, pours in 40 points as eventual state champ Mercer pounds the Ramblers, 93-66.

41. 2/2/1968—Vincent's **Greg Thompson** is unstoppable with 26 markers and **Ed Davis** sinks a pair of free throws with one second remaining as the Colonels upset the Ramblers, 50-48.

42. 12/5/1969—**Jack Titus** of Bradford nails a half-court hook shot at the buzzer to tie the game, giving the Owls the chance to beat Prep in overtime, 80-77.

North Catholic's great Matt Szykowny became a three-sport star at Iowa.

Mercer's Bob Rhoades pummeled Prep with 40 points (1967).

43. 3/8/1970—The Ramblers again fall in the PCIAA Western Final to Bishop Guilfoyle, as BG's **Bob Landolfi** is a one-man wrecking crew with 25 points and 19 rebounds.

44. 12/13/1970 & 2/24/1971—35-point performances by **Steve Albert** and **Dave Tomaselli** can't stop Rambler victories over South Hills Catholic, 73-68, and Johnstown, 85-72.

45. 1/8/1971—Former Prepster **Chuck Britton** scores 23 as McDowell bops the Ramblers, 82-72.

46. 2/22/1972—Future Duke star **Terry Chili** drops in 27 points as Lake Shore League champ Jamestown whips Prep, 63-57.

47. 12/8/1972—Don **"The Laser" Maser** pours in 42 points as Johnstown crushes Prep, 90-56.

Academy great David Purdue works against Tom Van Volkenburg. (1972).

48. **1/19/1973 & 2/23/1973**—Academy sharpshooter **David Purdue** scores 36 and 30 points as Prep wins, 73-71, and loses, 69-59.

49. **1/8/1974 & 2/23/1974**—Future NBA star **Pat Cummings** slams in 35 points and quarterback **Jack Buchan** scores 41 as Johnstown twice defeats the Ramblers, 64-53 and 85-49.

50. **2/14/1975**—Future San Antonio Spurs star **Johnny Moore** of Altoona scores 25 points in a losing effort, 78-74.

51. **1/9/1976**—**Dan Chojnacki** scores 31 for McDowell, but the Ramblers upend the Trojans, 68-65.

52. **12/17/1976**—**Francis Spearman** runs wild with 31 points as Academy nips Prep, 65-63.

53. **3/19/1977**—**Chris Dodds** pours in 39 points, but a State College comeback falls short in PIAA action, 74-63.

54. **3/23/1977**—**Stu Lyon's** 24 points leads eventual state champ Fox Chapel to 68-52 Western Semifinal win over the Ramblers.

55. **12/1/1978**—Punxsutawney's **Mike Kopas** tallies 32 points, but Prep downs the Woodchucks, 75-65.

56. **2/2/1979**—6'10" **Walter Stone** of Academy scores 19 points in a tense Lion win over Prep, 58-54.

57. **11/23/1979**—Plum's **Sean Knapp** scores 32 of his team's 49 points, but Prep romps, 76-49.

58. **3/10/1981**—**John Bowen** and **Don Buerkle** each score 23 as Warren embarrasses the Ramblers in a D-10 semifinal, 68-38.

59. **1/5/1982**—**Jack Mansell** tallies 33 points, though Prep beats Sharon, 73-59.

60. **3/9/1982**—Warren defeats Prep in D-10 play, 64-58, behind big **John Bowen's** 33 points.

61. **3/19/1983**—McKeesport's **Billy Leonard** dumps in 25 points and **Sam Commodore** tips one in at the buzzer as the Tigers nip the Ramblers in a PIAA Western Quarterfinal, 63-62.

62. **3/31/1984**—**Pete White, Jr.** goes 9 of 15 from the floor and 8 of 9 from the foul line for 26 points in Williamsport's 68-61 PIAA state title victory over the Orange & Black.

63. **2/5/1986**—McDowell's **Jeff Morrow** racks up 29 points in a Trojan nail-biter over Prep, 51-50.

64. **2/15/1986**—Future NBA star **Mike Iuzzolino** records 33 points in Altoona's 69-62 victory over Prep.

65. **2/21/1987**—**Joe Brumbaugh** scores 32 in Altoona's 52-48 win over the Ramblers.

66. **1/15/1988**—Future NBA star **Anthony Peeler** leads Kansas City Paseo to a 59-57 overtime victory over Prep with 36 points.

67. **3/23/1988**—**Jim McCoy** leads Pittsburgh Central Catholic with 26 points in a tense 61-59 PIAA Western Final win over Prep.

68. **1/20/1990**—McDonald's All-American **Anthony Cade** of Oak Hill Academy impresses a McDonald's Classic crowd with 27 points in 76-63 tourney final win over Prep.

Pat Cummings, Johnstown (1974). Prep had no way to stop this future Cincinnati and NBA star.

"Kopas from the corner!" Mike Kopas, Punxsutawney (1979).

McDowell Hall-of-Famer Jeff Morrow scored 29 points in the 51-50 victory over Prep (1986).

Anthony Cade of Oak Hill Academy (1990).

69. **12/27/1990**—Sharpshooter **Dan Heiman** nails six 3-pointers against the Ramblers at the Farrell Holiday Tournament, but Prep beats Butler, 82-68.

70. **2/21/1991**—Mercyhurst Prep's **Khyl Horton** scores 32 points, but Prep wins, 76-58.

71. **1/10/1992**—**Richard "TuTu" Brown** burns Prep for 30 points as Dayton Dunbar downs the Ramblers in the McDonald's Classic, 71-66.

72. **3/14/1992**—Little point guard **Devin Billeter** personally pummels Prep with 12 field goals (two 3's) and 11 free throws for 37 points, 23 coming in the second half. North Allegheny wins a close one in the PIAA first round, 58-56.

73. **1/11/1994**—**Ryan Munson's** 3-pointer at 0:02 gives Vincent a 66-65 upset win over Prep.

74. **1/14/1994**—**Melvin Levett** of Villa Angela-St. Joseph wows the crowd and leap-frogs directly over the head of **Keith Nies** for an easy layup, two of his 32 points as the Vikings beat Prep in the McDonald's Classic, 71-61.

75. **1/20/1996**—Future NBA star **Ron Artest** tallies 24 points in a 44-40 double overtime victory for NYC LaSalle Academy over the Ramblers in the McDonald's Classic.

76. **3/4/1996**—McDowell's **Jake Delsandro** destroys Prep with 25 points in the D-10 final, 69-56.

77. **3/23/1996**—Though held to a season-low 17 points, future NBA superstar **Kobe Bryant's** all-around performance wins a PIAA state title game for Lower Merion over Prep, 48-43.

78. **3/12/1997**—Schenley's **Naron Jackson** (23 points) does most of the scoring as the Spartans overcome an early 17-4 deficit to derail Rambler title hopes, 36-33.

79. **1/9/1998**—**Matt Carroll** does it all as Hatboro-Horsham crushes the Ramblers in the McDonald's Classic, 69-46. The future Notre Dame and NBA star scores 25 points.

80. **1/21/2000**—**Matt Jones** lights up 29 points as East upsets Prep, 65-54.

81. **2/22/2000**—**Torry Mitchell** scores 26 points as Central nips the Ramblers in D-10 play, 58-56.

82. **1/3/2001**—Seven 3-pointers by **Doug Merski** isn't enough as Prep downs Mercyhurst, 70-62.

83. **1/12/2001**—**Jack Heissenbuttel's** 25 points, including seven 3-pointers, takes care of the Ramblers for Lexington Catholic in the McDonald's Classic, 74-66. On the next evening, NYC LaSalle's **Eric Sterling's** running, off-balance shot off the left baseline beats Prep in the consolation match, 49-47.

Prepster Keith Nies will never forget Melvin "The Helicopter" Levett (1994).

Future Notre Dame star Matt Carroll was the highlight of the 1998 McDonald's Classic for Hatboro-Horsham.

Eric Sterling's off-balance shot gave LaSalle the consolation victory over Prep in the 2001 McDonald's Classic.

84. **1/2/2003—Andre Dawson's** 3-point shot at the end of regulation, then a baseline jumper by Dawson with four seconds left in overtime gives East a 55-54 victory.

85. **1/18/2003—**Prep can't contend with 7'2" **Roy Hibbert** of Georgetown Prep in McDonald's Classic consolation match, 49-43. The future Georgetown and NBA star gets 25 points, 11 rebounds and 4 blocked shots, not to mention forcing the Ramblers to alter many shots with his long arms.

It's not hard to understand that Prep had difficulty with 7'2" Roy Hibbert of Georgetown Prep (2003).

86. **1/13/2004—Tyler Stoczynski** pours in 30 points as McDowell beats Prep in overtime, 71-70.

McDowell great Tyler Stoczynski is now the successful head coach at Highlands in the WPIAL.

87. **1/14/2005—**Future North Carolina star **Marcus Ginyard** pours in 34 points as Arlington Bishop O'Connell routs Prep in the McDonald's Classic, 79-58.

88. **3/9/2005—Geoff Kestler** scores 31, but Prep edges Mount Lebanon in the PIAA second round, 78-74.

89. **1/13/2006—Darrin Govens** sinks 40 points, including six 3-pointers, the most by a Prep opponent in 32 years, but the Ramblers defeat defending state champ Chester in overtime, 88-84.

90. **1/28/2006—Robbie Parris** buries a 40-foot 3-pointer at the buzzer as St. Ignatius beats Prep in overtime, 84-81.

91. **3/11/2006—Joe Berenato** tallies 33 points for Pittsburgh Central Catholic, but the Ramblers win the state playoff game, 77-66.

92. **1/18/2008—Chris Fouch** puts on a spectacular shooting performance against Prep, nailing eight 3-pointers in just 11 tries to lead NYC Rice over the Ramblers in the McDonald's Classic, 87-63.

93. **2/20/2008—**McDowell embarrasses Prep in a District 10 final, 64-50, as **Zach Spronatti** dominates with 28 points.

94. **12/20/2008—**Chartiers Valley's **T. J. McConnell** destroys Prep with outside shooting for 36 points in 84-69 Rambler defeat at the KSA tourney in Florida.

95. **1/15/2010—**In Buffalo Nichols 68-57 McDonald's victory over Prep, the Vikings' **Stan Wier** sets a Classic record with a perfect 9-for-9 at the free throw line. He scores 25.

96. **1/19/2010 & 2/9/2010 & 3/4/2010—**Strong Vincent's **Courtney Harden-Pulliam** gives three great performances, scoring 28, 21 and 22 points in three wins over Prep, 73-56, 65-57 and 68-60.

97. **2/20/2010—**McDowell's **Myke Molnar's** free throw with three seconds remaining in OT beats Prep, 55-54.

98. **1/15/2011—**Prep takes North Carolina power Charlotte Christian to OT before succumbing to a 10-point effort by **Patrick Rooks** in the extra four minutes, 68-57. Rooks finishes with 22.

99. **3/12/2011—Bobby Swartout** scores 25 as Butler ends the Rambler season in a first round PIAA playoff, 60-52.

100. **1/9/2012—Malquan Pullium** tallies 31 markers as Vincent nips Prep, 60-59.

Courtney Harden-Pulliam was the main cog in three Strong Vincent victories over Prep (2010).

6'10" Walter Stone of Academy went on to star at Arizona State. Here, in 1979.

Canisius star Jim Cunningham (1954).

Altoona star Mike Iuzzolino (1986).

Chester's Darren Govens burned Prep for 40 points in the 2006 McDonald's Classic.

Bob Atterholt, Sharon's 1954 First Team All-State selection.

Chuck Britton, one of Erie's all-time greatest athletes. (1971).

Academy's feisty star Francis Spearman (1977).

"Puck" Cardot '71 was the first Rambler to average over 20 PPG and the only player to do it twice.

Paul Pry '68 is the only Erieite to ever perform in the NCAA Final Four. Pry's 40 points against Academy stood as a Rambler record for 10 years.

Hall-of-Famer Jim Hamilton is in the starting lineup of Prep's all-time greats, as is attested by his name being all over the scoring charts. Here, along with his family and Coach Arribi, Jim signs with the Naval Academy.

Matty Harris '14 is one of just four Prepsters to average more than 20 PPG in a season.

Two great men always seen at the Prep games: statisticians Sam Mancini '73 and Larry Piotrowicz '70.

Dan Sculley '78 held Prep single game scoring record with 41 points for 13 years.

All-Time Statistical Records

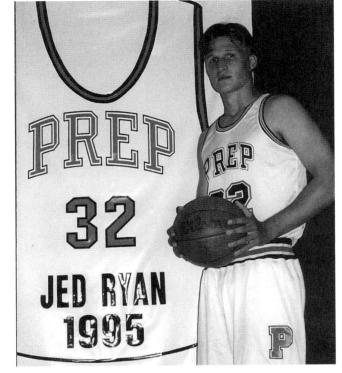

Erie's all-time career scoring leader, Jed Ryan '95, #32. His number is just the second of two to be retired at Prep.

Most Points in Game (Prep, Individual Record Holders):

16—Lester Hahn, vs. Schaller Morticians, 1924-25
20—Don Hayes, vs. Corry St. Edward's, 1927-28
23—Herb Perry, vs. North East, 1928-29
28—Herb Perry, vs. Wesleyville, 1929-30
37—Al Hatkevich, vs. Tech, 1951-52
40—Paul Pry, vs. Academy, 1967-68
41—Dan Sculley, vs. Pittsburgh Brashear, 1977-78
42—Jim Hamilton, vs. Brainard (TN), 1990-91

Most Points in Game (Prep, Individual):

42—Jim Hamilton, vs. Chattanooga (TN) Brainerd, 1990-91
41—Dan Sculley, vs. Pittsburgh Brashear, 1977-78
40—Paul Pry, vs. Academy, 1967-68
40—Matt Harris, vs. Toronto (ONT) Pope John Paul II, 2013-14
39—Kevin Barron, vs. Warren, 1973-74
38—Matt Harris, vs. Central Tech, 2013-14
37—Al Hatkevich, vs. Tech, 1951-52
37—Jim Hamilton, vs. Altoona, 1990-91
35—Dave Cousart, vs. McDowell, 1975-76
35—Jed Ryan, vs. Chattanooga (TN) Brainerd, 1994-95
34—Bobby Ward, vs. East, 1959-60
34—Bill Druckemiller, vs. Academy, 1963-64
34—Bill Bensur, vs. Johnstown, 1976-77
34—Jed Ryan, vs. Ottawa (ONT) St. Matthew's, 1994-95
33—Paul Pry, vs. Ashtabula (OH) Harbor, 1967-68
33—Willis Cardot, vs. Jamestown (NY), 1970-71
33—Jim Hamilton, vs. York Catholic, 1990-91
33—Jim Hamilton, vs. Franklin, 1990-91
33—Jed Ryan, vs. Lookout Valley (TN), 1994-95
33—Mark Chase, vs. Warren, 2001-02
33—Preston Harris, vs. Chester, 2005-06
33—Sheldon Zablotny, vs. Central Tech, 2012-13
32—Ron Costello, vs. Corry, 1956-57
32—Rick Fessler, vs. Kennedy Christian, 1967-68
32—Jed Ryan, vs. Hempfield, 1994-95
32—Jed Ryan, vs. Mercyhurst Prep, 1994-95
32—Mark Blazek, vs. General McLane, 2006-07
32—Mark Blazek, vs. General McLane, 2007-08
31—Matt Scheppner, vs. Jamestown (NY), 1973-74
31—Jed Ryan, vs. Redmond (WA), 1993-94
31—Jed Ryan, vs. Chester, 1994-95
30—Chuck Wittman, vs. Vincent, 1953-54
30—George Feasler, vs. Bradford, 1955-56
30—Jim Marnella, vs. Southwestern Central (NY), 1962-63
30—Willis Cardot, vs. Johnstown, 1970-71
30—Mike Sisinni, vs. Johnstown, 1974-75
30—Dan Sculley, vs. Brookfield (OH), 1977-78
30—Jim Roseto, vs. Pittsburgh Peabody, 1979-80
30—Jim Hamilton, vs. Farrell, 1990-91
30—Adam Dolak, vs. Buffalo (NY) BT/SJ, 2003-04
30—Preston Harris, vs. Pittsburgh Central Catholic, 2005-06
30—Sheldon Zablotny, vs. McDowell, 2012-13
30—Carter Cross, vs. East, 2015-16

Most Points in Season (Prep, Individual Record Holders):

64—Frank Kaltenbach, 1924-25
84—Joe Gorny, 1925-26
157—Joe Gorny, 1926-27
184—Herbert Perry, 1928-29
260—Herbert Perry, 1929-30
293—Art Hilinski, 1948-49
447—Jim Fahey, 1952-53
470—Paul Pry, 1967-68
483—Willis Cardot, 1969-70
549—Willis Cardot, 1970-71
645—Jim Hamilton, 1990-91
682—Jed Ryan, 1994-95

300 CLUB—Most Points in Season (Prep, Individual):

682—Jed Ryan, 1994-95
645—Jim Hamilton, 1990-91
581—Tim Gore, 1979-80
551—Jed Ryan, 1993-94
549—Willis Cardot, 1970-71
537—Mark Atkinson, 1983-84
502—Booker Coleman, 1993-94
499—Preston Harris, 2005-06
497—Sheldon Zablotny, 2012-13
491—Julian Blanks, 1997-98
483—Willis Cardot, 1969-70
471—Dan Sculley, 1977-78
470—Paul Pry, 1967-68
470—Matt Harris, 2013-14
458—Andy Kubinski, 2001-02
456—Jim Roseto, 1979-80
454—Tim Gore, 1978-79
447—Jim Fahey, 1952-53
445—Jim Stevenson, 1983-84
440—Bob Ward, 1959-60
440—R. J. Fiorelli, 1996-97
436—Jim Schaaf, 1982-83
435—Rick Bengel, 1974-75
435—Sheldon Zablotny, 2011-12
426—RaSean Thrower, 2009-10
425—Cliff Dennett, 1991-92
416—Jed Ryan, 1992-93
412—Cliff Dennett, 1992-93

Hall of Fame great Tim Gore '80 still ranks third on Prep's all-time career scoring chart. His #44 was the first to be retired at Prep.

411—Olivier Allinei, 1987-88
410—Mike Sisinni, 1974-75
410—Mark Chase, 2001-02
407—Cory Knight, 2004-05
403—Brian Szewczykowski, 1995-96
402—Dave Whitby, 1961-62
401—Rick Fessler, 1967-68
399—George Feasler, 1955-56
398—Bill Bensur, 1976-77
394—Kevin Barron, 1973-74
389—Jim Hamilton, 1989-90
384—Matt Colpoys, 2014-15
383—Jeff Szumigale, 1977-78
383—Andy Sisinni, 1979-80
381—Todd Stablein, 1989-90
381—Jaryn Simpson, 2016-17
380—Preston Bowen, 1983-84
374—Mark Blazek, 2006-07
374—Mark Blazek, 2007-08
372—John Stano, 1964-65
371—Ron Costello, 1956-57
370—Julian Blanks, 1996-97
366—Steve Ziegler, 1988-89
368—Casey McCloskey, 2002-03
363—Dan Bukowski, 1970-71
363—John Alberstadt, 1981-82
361—Chuck Rosenthal, 1968-69
359—Jeff Cardot, 1989-90
357—Todd Filipkowski, 1990-91
357—Rasean Thrower, 2007-08
355—Mark Atkinson, 1982-83
354—Matt Harris, 2012-13
353—Adam Blazek, 2010-11
352—Keith Nies, 1995-96
347—Mike Manczka, 1985-86
346—Graham Witherspoon, 1996-97
345—Nick Haller, 2004-05
341—Josh Licata, 2006-07
337—Brian Flanagan, 1969-70
337—John Reynders, 1970-71
336—Mike Heberle, 1988-89
336—Joe Jones, 2003-04
332—Vinnie "Flowers" Kwiatkowski, 1955-56
330—Andy Sweny, 2008-09
327—Tim Finegan, 1966-67
326—Bill Druckemiller, 1963-64
325—Marty Orzechowski, 1972-73
324—Dan Sculley, 1976-77
323—Dan Achille, 1977-78
322—Pat Lupo, 1963-64
321—Marty Orzechowski, 1971-72
321—Stacy Hitt, 1981-82
323—Jim McCallion, 1960-61

321—Jim Toohey, 1987-88
319—Dave Cousart, 1975-76
319—Adam Upperman, 2016-17
316—John Trocki, 1995-96
313—Tim Maloney, 1964-65
313—Dan Bukowski, 1969-70
311—Joe Tarasovitch, 1980-81
311—Rasean Thrower, 2008-09
310—Keith Nies, 1994-95
308—Gary Borowy, 1968-69
308—Joe Fessler, 1983-84
304—Gary Miller, 1981-82
304—Conor Colpoys, 2012-13
304—Bob Spoden, 2008-09
303—Joe Fustine, 2014-15
302—Jim Keim, 1955-56
300—Matt Scheppner, 1973-74
300—Jim Gemler, 1997-98

Highest PPG Average
(Prep, Individual Record Holders):

6.9—Harrison Clemens, 1924-25
8.3—Joe Gorny, 1926-27
10.4—Don Hayes, 1927-28
11.8—Herbert Perry, 1929-30
13.1—Al Hatkevich, 1950-51
13.4—Al Hatkevich, 1951-52
16.5—Jim Fahey, 1952-53
17.3—George Feasler, 1955-56
19.1—Bob Ward, 1959-60
19.6—Paul Pry, 1967-68
20.1—Willis Cardot, 1969-70
22.9—Willis Cardot, 1970-71
23.9—Jim Hamilton, 1990-91

Highest PPG Average
(Prep, Individual):

23.9—Jim Hamilton, 1990-91
23.5—Jed Ryan, 1994-95
22.9—Willis Cardot, 1970-71
20.4—Matt Harris, 2013-14
20.1—Willis Cardot, 1969-70
19.6—Paul Pry, 1967-68
19.1—Bob Ward, 1959-60
19.1—Sheldon Zablotny, 2012-13
18.6—Chuck Britton, 1967-68
18.2—Julian Blanks, 1997-98
17.8—Jed Ryan, 1993-94
17.8—Preston Harris, 2005-06
17.6—Tim Gore, 1979-80
17.4—Sheldon Zablotny, 2011-12
17.3—George Feasler, 1955-56
17.3—Booker Coleman, 1993-94
17.2—Chuck Rosenthal, 1968-69
17.0—Jim McCallion, 1960-61
17.0—Kevin Barron, 1973-74
16.9—John Stano, 1964-65
16.8—Dan Sculley, 1977-78
16.7—Rick Fessler, 1967-68
16.5—Jim Fahey, 1952-53
16.4—RaSean Thrower, 2009-10
16.3—Marty Orzechowski, 1972-73
16.3—Mark Atkinson, 1983-84
16.3—R. J. Fiorelli, 1996-97
16.2—Jim Marnella, 1962-63
16.2—Tim Gore, 1978-79
15.9—Bill Bensur, 1976-77
15.8—Andy Kubinski, 2001-02

15.7—Cliff Dennett, 1991-92
15.5—Dave Whitby, 1961-62
15.5—Bill Druckemiller, 1963-64
15.5—Rick Bengel, 1974-75
15.4—Ron Costello, 1956-57
15.3—Pat Lupo, 1963-64
15.3—Casey McCloskey, 2002-03
15.2—Dave Cousart, 1975-76
15.2—Todd Stablein, 1989-90
15.1—Dan Bukowski, 1970-71
15.0—Jim Hamilton, 1989-90
15.0—Mark Blazek, 2006-07

Most Points in Career
(Prep, Individual Record Holders):

112—Lester Hahn, 1924-26
255—Joe Gorny, 1924-27
444—Herbert Perry, 1928-30
447—Ted Morasky, 1938-42
498—Johnny DeLuca, 1942-45
584—Art Hilinski, 1946-49
644—Al Hatkevich, 1949-52
737—Rick Fessler, 1965-68
1089—Willis Cardot, Prep, 1968-71
1305—Tim Gore, Prep 1977-80
1926—Jed Ryan, Prep, 1991-95

500 CLUB—Most Points in Career
(Prep, Individual):

1926—Jed Ryan, 1991-95
1371—Sheldon Zablotny, 2009-13
1305—Tim Gore, 1977-80
1114—Preston Harris, McDowell/
      Prep, 2003-06
1102—Julian Blanks, 1994-98
1094—RaSean Thrower, 2007-10
1089—Willis Cardot, 1968-71
1086—Matt Harris, 2010-14
1076—Jim Hamilton, 1988-91
1053—Mark Blazek, 2004-08
1049—Charlie Britton,
      Prep/McDowell, 1968-71
1017—Mark Chase, 1998-2002
1002—Cliff Dennett, 1990-93
892—Mark Atkinson, 1982-84
888—Keith Nies, 1992-96
887—Booker Coleman, 1991-94
805—Dan Sculley, 1975-78
770—Cory Knight, 2002-05
737—Rick Fessler, 1965-68
731—Jaryn Simpson, 2014-17
730—R. J. Fiorelli, 1995-97
729—Adam Blazek, 2008-11
703—Paul Pry, 1966-68
693—Brian Szewczykowski, 1994-96
685—Joe Jones, 2001-04
676—Dan Bukowski, 1969-71
648—Casey McCloskey, 2000-03
646—Marty Orzechowski, 1971-73
646—Jim Stevenson, 1982-84
644—Al Hatkevich, 1950-52
633—Steve Ziegler, 1986-89
633—Andy Kubinski, 1999-2002
627—Bill Bensur, 1975-77
627—Matt Colpoys, 2012-15
624—Mark Demski, 2003-06
622—Rick Bengel, 1972-75
615—George Feasler, 1954-56

Rasean Thrower '10 stands 6th on Prep's career scoring chart.

613—Preston Bowen, 1982-84
606—Jeff Cardot, 1987-90
600—Kevin Barron, 1972-74
591—Mike Heberle, 1986-89
585—Tim Maloney, 1963-65
584—Art Hilinski, 1946-49
583—Conor Colpoys, 2010-13
577—Todd Filipkowski, 1988-91
575—Jim Fetzner, 1997-2000
572—Mike Sisinni, 1973-75
563—Pat Lupo, 1962-64
563—Dave Cousart, 1974-76
555—John Trocki, 1993-96
554—Adam Kaiser, 2004-06
553—Dave Whitby, 1960-62
549—Jim Fahey, 1951-53
548—Todd Stablein, 1987-90
547—Pat Tomczak, 1957-60
545—Jeff Szumigale, 1976-78
542—Graham Witherspoon, 1993-97
539—Olivier Allinei, 1986-88
538—Dan Achille, 1976-78
538—Jim Gemler, 1995-98
532—Aaron DeCoursey, 1998-2001
515—Bob Ward, 1958-60
512—Kenny Duck, 1991-94
510—Vinnie "Flowers" Kwiatkowski, 1954-56
505—Tim Finegan, 1965-67
500—Bob Spoden, 2007-09
499—Preston Harris, 2005-06
498—Johnny DeLuca, 1942-45

Most Field Goals in Game
(Prep, Individual Record Holders):

8—Lester Hahn, vs. Schaller Morticians, 1924-25
10—Don Hayes, vs. Corry St. Edward's, 1927-28
13—Herb Perry, vs. Wesleyville, 1929-30
15—Al Hatkevich, vs. Tech, 1951-52
16—Bill Druckemiller, vs. Academy, 1963-64
17—Kevin Barron, vs. Warren, 1973-74

Most Field Goals in Game
(Prep, Individual):

17—Kevin Barron, vs. Warren, 1973-74
16—Bill Druckemiller, vs. Academy, 1963-64
16—Dan Sculley, vs. Pittsburgh Brashear, 1977-78
15—Al Hatkevich, vs. Tech, 1951-52
15—Rick Fessler, vs. Kennedy Christian, 1967-68
15—Matt Scheppner, vs. Jamestown, 1973-74
14—Ron Costello, vs. Corry, 1956-57
14—Bobby Ward, vs. East, 1959-60
14—Paul Pry, vs. Ashtabula (OH) Harbor, 1967-68
14—Kevin Barron, vs. Bishop Guilfoyle, 1973-74
14—Jim Hamilton, vs. Chattanooga (TN) Brainerd, 1990-91
14—Jed Ryan, vs. Chattanooga (TN) Brainerd, 1994-95
13—Herb Perry, vs. Wesleyville, 1929-30
13—Paul Pry, vs. Academy, 1967-68
13—Willis Cardot, vs. Jamestown (NY), 1969-70
13—Willis Cardot, vs. Ashtabula (OH) Harbor, 1969-70
13—Willis Cardot, vs. Jamestown (NY), 1970-71
13—Jim Hamilton, vs. York Catholic, 1990-91
13—Jim Hamilton, vs. Altoona, 1990-91
13—Jed Ryan, vs. Lookout Valley (TN), 1994-95
13—Preston Harris, vs. Chester, 2005-06
13—Sheldon Zablotny, vs. Central Tech, 2012-13
13—Matt Harris, vs. Toronto (ONT) Pope John Paul II, 2013-14

Four-year star Sheldon Zablotny '13 ranks second on Prep's all-time career scoring chart.

Hall-of-Famer Julian Blanks '98 ranks 5th on Prep's career chart with 1102.

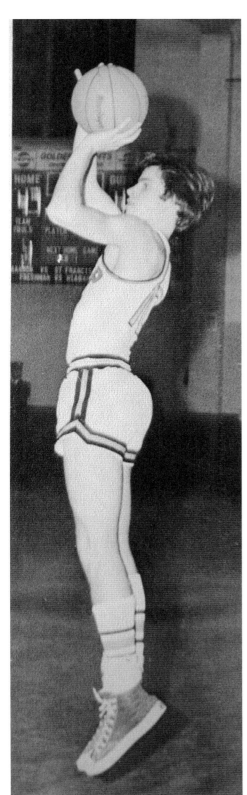

Kevin Barron '74 holds the Prep record for most field goals in a game with 17.

Most Field Goals in Season
(Prep, Individual Record Holders):

31—Lester Hahn, 1924-25
33—Joe Gorny, 1925-26
63—Joe Gorny, 1926-27
65—Herb Perry, 1928-29
109—Herb Perry, 1929-30
112—Art Hilinski, 1948-49
165—Jim Fahey, 1952-53
186—Paul Pry, 1967-68
212—Willis Cardot, 1970-71
233—Tim Gore, 1979-80
238—Jim Hamilton, 1990-91
243—Jed Ryan, 1994-95

Most Field Goals in Season
(Prep, Individual):

243—Jed Ryan, 1994-95
238—Jim Hamilton, 1990-91
233—Tim Gore, 1979-80
212—Willis Cardot, 1970-71
212—Mark Atkinson, 1983-84
202—Jed Ryan, 1993-94
190—Dan Sculley, 1977-78
190—Jim Roseto, 1979-80
186—Paul Pry, 1967-68
186—Rick Bengel, 1974-75
186—Julian Blanks, 1997-98
185—Willis Cardot, 1969-70
180—Jim Schaaf, 1982-83
179—Tim Gore, 1978-79
178—Rick Fessler, 1967-68
177—Preston Harris, 2005-06
176—Sheldon Zablotny, 2012-13
174—Jeff Szumigale, 1977-78
174—Booker Coleman, 1993-94

Most 3-Point Field Goals in Game
(Prep, Individual Record Holders):

5—Olivier Allinei, vs. South Bend (IN)St. Joseph's, 1987-88
6—Jim Hamilton, vs. Oak Hill Academy (VA), 1989-90
7—Jim Hamilton, vs. Chattanooga (TN) Brainerd, 1990-91

Most 3-Point Field Goals in Game (Prep, Individual):

7—Jim Hamilton, vs. Chattanooga (TN) Brainerd, 1990-91
7—Jim Hamilton, vs. Brooklyn (NY) Bishop Loughlin, 1990-91
6—Jim Hamilton, vs. Oak Hill Academy (VA), 1989-90
6—Jim Hamilton, vs. Huntsville (AL) S.R. Butler, 1990-91
6—Jim Hamilton, vs. Altoona, 1990-91
6—Keith Nies, vs. Brooklyn (NY) Msgr. McClancy, 1994-95
6—John Yaple, vs. East Liverpool (OH), 2001-02
6—Phil Stewart, vs. George Junior Republic, 2001-02
6—Nick Haller, vs. North Hills, 2004-05
6—Adam Kaiser, vs, Cleveland (OH) St. Ignatius, 2005-06
6—Mark Blazek, vs. General McLane, 2007-08
5—Olivier Allinei, vs. South Bend (IN) St. Joseph's, 1987-88
5—Jim Hamilton, vs. Academy, 1990-91
5—Jim Hamilton, vs. Fairdale (KY), 1990-91
5—Jim Hamilton, vs. Franklin, 1990-91
5—Jed Ryan, vs. Ottawa (ONT) St. Matthew's, 1994-95
5—Brian Szewczykowski, vs. Upper St. Clair, 1995-96
5—R. J. Fiorelli, vs. Bethune Collegiate (ONT), 1996-97
5—Jared Ronai, vs. Farmington (WV) N. Marion, 1999-2000
5—Jim Fetzner, vs. Vincent, 1999-2000
5—Cory Knight, vs. Vincent, 2003-04
5—Nick Haller, vs. McDowell, 2004-05
5—Nick Haller, vs. Mt. Lebanon, 2004-05
5—Mark Blazek, vs. State College, 2007-08
5—RaSean Thrower, vs. Vincent, 2008-09
5—Sheldon Zablotny, vs. Vincent, 2011-12
5—Sheldon Zablotny, vs. Harborcreek, 2011-12
5—Sheldon Zablotny, vs. McDowell, 2012-13
5—Matt Harris, vs. Toronto (ONT) Pope John Paul II, 2013-14
5—Matt Harris, vs. McDowell, 2013-14

Most 3-Point Field Goals in Season
(Prep, Individual Record Holders):

27—Olivier Allinei, 1987-88
27—Sasha Pecarski, 1988-89
27—Jeff Cardot, 1988-89
46—Jim Hamilton, 1989-90
86—Jim Hamilton, 1990-91

Most 3-Point Field Goals in Season
(Prep, Individual):

86—Jim Hamilton, 1990-91
65—Jim Gemler, 1997-98
61—Brian Szewczykowski, 1995-96
56—Nick Haller, 2004-05
55—R. J. Fiorelli, 1996-97
51—Matt Harris, 2013-14
48—Keith Nies, 1994-95
47—Cory Knight, 2004-05
46—Jim Hamilton, 1989-90
46—Keith Nies, 1995-96
44—Casey McCloskey, 2002-03
43—Jed Ryan, 1994-95
43—Rasean Thrower, 2008-09
42—Keith Nies, 1993-94
42—Jim Fetzner, 1999-2000

42—Cory Knight, 2003-04
42—RaSean Thrower, 2009-10
41—Adam Kaiser, 2005-06
41—Sheldon Zablotny, 2011-12
39—Jim Gemler, 1996-97
39—Sheldon Zablotny, 2012-13
38—Mark Blazek, 2007-08
38—Matt Harris, 2012-13
38—Joe Fustine, 2014-15

Most Free Throws Made in Game
(Prep, Individual Record Holders):

4—Frank Kaltenbach, The "L" Club, 1924-25
4—Joe Gorny, vs. St. Titus, 1925-26
4—Maurice "Casey" Jones, vs. Edinboro 1926-27
4—Richard Schumacher, vs. St. Titus, 1926-27
9—Herb Perry, vs. North East, 1928-29
13—Art Middleton, vs. Corry, 1948-49
13—Chuck Bauder, vs. Buffalo (NY) Canisius, 1958-59
14—Chuck Bauder, vs. Academy, 1958-59
14—Bobby Ward, vs. Buffalo (NY) Canisius, 1959-60
15—Jim McCallion, vs. Academy, 1960-61
16—Jim Stevenson, vs. Gardena (CA) Serra, 1983-84

Most Free Throws Made in Game
(Prep, Individual):

16—Jim Stevenson, vs. Gardena (CA) Serra, 1983-84
15—Jim McCallion, vs. Academy, 1960-61
14—Chuck Bauder, vs. Academy, 1958-59
14—Bobby Ward, vs. Buffalo (NY) Canisius, 1959-60
14—Paul Pry, vs. Academy, 1967-68
14—Julian Blanks, vs. Meadville, 1996-97
14—Brian Mahoney, vs. Franklin, 2003-04
13—Art Middleton, vs. Corry, 1948-49
13—Chuck Bauder, vs. Buffalo (NY) Canisius, 1958-59
13—Willis Cardot, vs. Academy, 1970-71
13—Willis Cardot, vs. Vincent, 1970-71
13—Nick Haller, vs. General McLane, 2004-05
13—Casey McCloskey, vs. Vincent, 2002-03
13—Jaryn Simpson vs. Mars, 2016-17
12—George Feasler, vs. Bradford, 1955-56
12—Willis Cardot, vs. East, 1970-71
12—Gary Miller, vs. East, 1981-82
12—Olivier Allinei, vs. Fox Chapel, 1987-88
12—Jed Ryan, vs. Redmond (WA), 1993-94
12—Mark Blazek, vs. State College, 2006-07
12—Matt Harris, vs. Central Tech, 2013-14

Jim McCallion '61 made 15 foul shots against Academy, a Prep record that stood for 23 years. His 17 PPG average as a senior was third highest at the time.

Most Free Throws Made in Season (Prep, Individual Record Holders):

10—Frank Kaltenbach, 1924-25
18—Joe Gorny, 1925-26
31—Joe Gorny, 1926-27
54—Herb Perry, 1928-29
59—Johnny DeLuca, 1944-45
69—Art Hilinski, 1948-49
117—Jim Fahey, 1952-53
125—Willis Cardot, 1970-71
137—Jimmy Stevenson, 1983-84
154—Booker Coleman, 1993-94

Booker Coleman '94 holds the Prep record for most free throws made in a season. The 6'8" center was also an amazing rebounder and shot-blocker.

Most Free Throws Made in Season (Prep, Individual):

154—Booker Coleman, 1993-94
153—Jed Ryan, 1994-95
137—Jimmy Stevenson, 1983-84
128—Jaryn Simpson, 2016-17
125—Willis Cardot, 1970-71
123—Matt Harris, 2013-14
120—Matt Colpoys, 2014-15
118—Dave Whitby, 1961-62
117—Jim Fahey, 1952-53
116—Bobby Ward, 1959-60
115—Andy Sisinni, 1979-80
115—Tim Gore, 1979-80
114—Jed Ryan, 1993-94
113—Willis Cardot, 1969-70
110—Mark Atkinson, 1983-84
109—Jed Ryan, 1992-93
109—Preston Harris, 2005-06
107—Jeff Cardot, 1989-90
106—Sheldon Zablotny, 2012-13
105—Jim McCallion, 1960-61
100—Jimmy Dailey, 1952-53
98—Paul Pry, 1967-68
97—Brian Flanagan, 1969-70
96—Tim Gore, 1978-79

Most Points in Game (Opponents, Individual Record Holders):

27—Chester LaPrice, Schaller Morticians, 1924-25
28—LeRoy Leslie, Johnstown Central Catholic, 1947-48
32—Len Rosenbluth, Staunton Military Academy, 1952-53
32—Ray Kovalesky, Tech, 1955-56
36—Roger Pierce, Academy, 1955-56
40—Bob Rhoads, Mercer, 1966-67
42—Donnie Maser, Johnstown, 1972-73
49—Essie Hollis, Vincent, 1972-73

Most Points in Game (Opponents, Individual):

49—Essie Hollis, Vincent, 1972-73
46—Armoni Foster, Meadville, 2016-17
45—Robby Carmody, Mars, 2016-17
43—Kaleb Wesson, Westerville (OH) South, 2016-17
42—Donnie Maser, Johnstown, 1972-73
41—Jack Buchan, Johnstown, 1973-74
40—Bob Rhoads, Mercer, 1966-67
40—Darrin Govens, Chester, 2005-06
39—Chris Dodds, State College, 1976-77
39—Jabarie Hinds, Mt. Vernon (NY), 2009-10
38—Essie Hollis, Vincent, 1972-73
37—Devin Billeter, North Allegheny, 1991-92
36—Roger Pierce, Academy, 1955-56
36—David Purdue, Academy, 1972-73
36—Anthony Peeler, Kansas City (MO) Paseo, 1987-88
36—T. J. McConnell, Chartiers Valley, 2008-09
35—Steve Albert, Pittsburgh South Hills Catholic, 1970-71
35—Dave Tomaselli, Johnstown, 1970-71
35—Pat Cummings, Johnstown, 1973-74
34—Gary Weigel, Lackawanna Fr. Baker, 1969-70
34—Steve Taneyhill, Altoona, 1990-91
34—Marcus Ginyard, Bishop O'Connell (VA), 2004-05
33—Chris Buchanan, Meadville, 1966-67
33—Jim Hill, Cleveland (OH) St. Joe's, 1969-70
33—Jack Mansell, Sharon, 1981-82
33—John Bowen, Warren, 1981-82
33—Mike Iuzzolino, Altoona, 1985-86
33—Robert Fears, Chattanooga (TN) Lookout Valley, 1994-95
33—Joe Berenato, Pittsburgh Central Catholic, 2005-06
33—Melo Trimble, Bishop O'Connell (VA), 2012-13
33—Brevin Manus, East, 2015-16
33—Armoni Foster, Meadville, 2015-16
32—Len Rosenbluth, Staunton Military Academy, 1952-53
32—Ray Kovalesky, Tech, 1955-56
32—Mike Kopas, Punxsutawney, 1978-79
32—Sean Knapp, Plum, 1979-80
32—Joe Brumbaugh, Altoona, 1986-87
32—Tony McGinnis, Huntsville (AL) S.R. Butler, 1990-91
32—Khyl Horton, Mercyhurst, 1990-91
32—Melvin Levett, Cleveland (OH) VASJ, 1993-94
32—Eugene Husband, Central Tech, 2012-13
32—Ryan Reagan, General McLane, 2015-16
31—Dan Chojnacki, McDowell, 1975-76
31—Francis Spearman, Academy, 1976-77
31—Geoff Kestler, Mount Lebanon, 2004-05
31—Antoine Childs, Blackhawk, 2006-07
31—Malquan Pulliam, Vincent, 2011-12
31-- Ashton Woodson, Pearl River (MS) Central, 2012-13
31—David Morris, Vincent, 2015-16
30—Jim Cunningham, Buffalo (NY) Canisius, 1953-54
30—Tom Agate, Buffalo (NY) Canisius, 1957-58
30—Joe Homan, Venango Christian, 1965-66
30—David Purdue, Academy, 1972-73
30—Terry Ogden, Hickory, 1978-79
30—Bob Bauer, Pittsburgh Central Catholic, 1982-83
30—Kevin Williams, Academy, 1985-86
30—Brian Rehm, Altoona, 1990-91
30—Richard "TuTu" Brown, Dayton (OH) Dunbar, 1991-92
30—Nate Smith, Meadville, 1996-97
30—Chris Exilus, Farmington (WV) North Marion, 1999-2000
30—Tyler Stoczynski, McDowell, 2003-04
30—Armoni Foster, Meadville, 2016-17

Most Field Goals in Game (Opponents, Individual Record Holders):

12—Chester LaPrice, Schaller Morticians, 1924-25
15—Len Rosenbluth, Staunton Military Academy, 1952-53
15—Roger Pierce, Academy, 1955-56
15—Donnie Maser, Johnstown, 1972-73
22—Essie Hollis, Vincent, 1972-73

Most Field Goals in Game (Opponents, Individual):

22—Essie Hollis, Vincent, 1972-73
18—Jack Buchan, Johnstown, 1973-74
17—Pat Cummings, Johnstown, 1973-74
16—John Bowen, Warren, 1981-82
15—Len Rosenbluth, Staunton Military Academy, 1952-53
15—Roger Pierce, Academy, 1955-56
15—Donnie Maser, Johnstown, 1972-73
15—Khyl Horton, Mercyhurst, 1990-91
15—Marcus Ginyard, Bishop O'Connell (VA), 2004-05
15—Kaleb Wesson, Westerville (OH) South, 2016-17
14—Chris Buchanan, Meadville, 1966-67
14—Bob Rhodes, Mercer, 1966-67
14—Dave Tomaselli, Johnstown, 1970-71
14—David Purdue, Academy, 1972-73
14—Sean Knapp, Plum, 1979-80
14—Jabarie Hinds, Mt. Vernon (NY), 2009-10
14—Robby Carmody, Mars, 2016-17

Most 3-Point Field Goals in Game (Opponents, Individual Record Holders):

5—Cliff Beck, Mercyhurst, 1987-88
6—Dan Heiman, Butler, 1990-91
6—Terry Hanse, Hempfield, 1994-95
7—Jack Heissenbuttel, Lexington (KY) Catholic, 2000-01
7—Doug Merski, Mercyhurst, 2000-01
8—Chris Fouch, NYC Rice (NY), 2007-08
9—Jabarie Hinds, Mt. Vernon (NY), 2009-10

Most 3-Point Field Goals in Game (Opponents, Individual):

9—Jabarie Hinds, Mt. Vernon (NY), 2009-10
8—Chris Fouch, NYC Rice (NY), 2007-08
7—Jack Heissenbuttel, Lexington (KY) Catholic, 2000-01
7—Doug Merski, Mercyhurst, 2000-01
7—T. J. McConnell, Chartiers Valley, 2008-09
7—Armoni Foster, Meadville, 2016-17
6—Dan Heiman, Butler, 1990-91
6—Terry Hanse, Hempfield, 1994-95
6—Nate Smith, Meadville, 1996-97
6—Torry Mitchell, Central, 1999-2000
6—Darrin Govens, Chester, 2005-06
6—Joe Berenato, Pittsburgh Central Catholic, 2005-06
6—Michael Anderson, Corry, 2007-08
6—Ryan Reagan, General McLane, 2015-16
5—Cliff Beck, Mercyhurst, 1987-88
5—Matt MacMurdo, North Allegheny, 1994-95
5—Aaron Garrity, McDowell, 1995-96
5—Charles Dixon, Meadville, 2002-03
5—Ryan Dunford, Buffalo (NY) BT/SJ, 2002-03
5—J. T. Jones, East, 2003-04
5—Tyler Stoczynski, McDowell, 2003-04
5—Keith Benjamin, Mount Vernon (NY), 2003-04
5—Marcus Daniels, George Junior Republic, 2003-04
5—Bobby Stauffer, General McLane, 2004-05
5—Geoff Kestler, Mt. Lebanon, 2004-05
5—Kirby Becker, Cleveland (OH) St. Ignatius, 2007-08
5—Dillon Loomis, McDowell, 2007-08
5—Mark Schoenborn, Warren, 2009-10
5—Courtney Harden-Pullium, Vincent, 2009-10
5—David Morris, Vincent, 2015-16

Most Free Throws Made in Game (Opponents, Individual Record Holders):

6—Jim Lawler, Ridgway St. Leo's, 1926-27
7—Robert Gilmore, North East, 1928-29
8—Leroy Leslie, Johnstown Central Catholic, 1947-48
10—Denny Johnson, Jamestown (NY), 1952-53
10—Ron Sanzi, Latrobe St. Vincent Prep, 1952-53
10—Jim Cunningham, Buffalo (NY) Canisius, 1952-53
10—Bob Atterholt, Sharon, 1953-54
15—Pete Russo, Academy, 1954-55
15—Al Hammond, Tech, 1976-77
16—Marty Bartell, Youngstown (OH) Chaney, 1977-78
17—Armoni Foster, Meadville, 2016-17

Academy's Pete Russo '55 once buried 15 free throws against Prep, an opponent record that lasted 23 years.

Most Free Throws Made in Game (Opponents, Individual):

16—Armoni Foster, Meadville, 2016-17
16—Marty Bartell, Youngstown (OH) Chaney, 1977-78
16—Brevin Manus, East, 2015-16
15—Pete Russo, Academy, 1954-55
15—Al Hammond, Tech, 1976-77
15—Jeff Morrow. McDowell, 1985-86
15—Matt Jones, East, 1999-2000
14—Ray Kovalesky, Tech, 1955-56
14—Floyd Rush, Tech, 1981-82
14—Robby Parris, Cleveland (OH) St. Ignatius, 2004-05
13—Steve Moorhead, Harborcreek, 1957-58
13—Jim Golembeski, Tech, 1959-60
13—Dan Kennedy, Harborcreek, 1959-60
13—Essie Hollis, Vincent, 1971-72
13—Chris Dodds, State College, 1976-77
13—Larry Hokaj, Buffalo (NY) Canisius, 1980-81
13—Mike Horan, Ringgold, 1994-95
13—Bobby Swartout, Butler, 2010-11
13—Robby Carmody, Mars, 2016-17

Tech Memorial's Floyd Rush '82 once nailed 14 free throws in a game against Prep.

Best Prep Season Starts:

12-0—1979-80
12-0—1996-97
11-0—1963-64
11-0—2014-15
9-0—1946-47
9-0—1953-54
9-0—1987-88
8-0—1955-56
8-0—2002-03
7-0—1928-29
7-0—1941-42
7-0—1970-71
7-0—1994-95
6-0—1938-39
6-0—1945-46
6-0—1974-75
6-0—2005-06
6-0—2012-13

Worst Prep Season Starts:

0-5—1942-43
0-4—1924-25
0-3—1947-48
0-3—1956-57
0-3—1957-58
0-3—2001-02
0-2—1966-67

Longest Prep Winning Streaks:

23—1979-80 through 1980-81
21—1977-78 (record for most in a single season)
17—1990-91
14—2004-05
13—1953-54
12—1958-59
12—1979-80
12—1996-97
12—1997-98
12—2011-12
11—1952-53
11—1963-64
11—1983-84
11—2012-13

11—2014-15
10—1964-65
10—1970-71
9—1946-47
9—1953-54
9—1981-82
9—1987-88
9—1993-94
9—1996-97

Longest Prep Losing Streaks:

9—1943-44
8—1942-43
7—1966-67
7—1966-67 (not a typo, happened twice!)
7—1975-76
6—1957-58
5—1924-25
5—1930-31
5—1934-35
5—1935-36
5—1942-43
5—1972-73
5—1997-98
5—1999-2000

Most Points, Prep, Game:

102—vs. Titusville St. Joseph's, 1964-65
102—vs. Academy, 1982-83
101—vs. Ashtabula (OH) Harbor, 1969-70
101—vs. Clearfield, 1994-95
100—vs. Jamestown (NY), 1969-70
99—vs. Kennedy Christian, 1967-68
99—vs. Jamestown (NY), 1970-71
98—vs. Altoona, 1990-91
97—vs. Tech, 1989-90
97—vs. East, 1993-94
95—vs. Titusville St. Joseph's, 1952-53
95—vs. Clearfield, 1976-77
95—vs. East, 1989-90
94—vs. East, 1994-95
94—vs. Vincent, 1995-96
94—vs. St. Catharine's (ONT) Dennis Morris, 2000-01
94—vs. North Hills, 2004-05
93—vs. Ashtabula (OH) St. John, 1959-60
93—vs. East, 1983-84
93—vs. Mercyhurst, 1985-86
93—vs. East, 1990-91

Least Points, Prep, Game:

9—vs. Alliance Academy, 1925-26
9—vs. Silver Creek (NY), 1925-26
9—vs. Kanty Prep, 1927-28
10—vs. Titusville St. Titus, 1930-31
10—vs. Corry, 1930-31
11—vs. St. Mary's Gems, 1925-26
11—vs. Alliance Academy, 1925-26
11—vs. Girard, 1928-29
11—vs. Bradford St. Bernard's, 1928-29
11—vs. Erie DeMolay, 1930-31
11—vs. Technical, 1931-32
11—vs. Erie DeMolay, 1931-32
11—vs. East, 1935-36
11—vs. Dunkirk (NY) St. Mary's, 1935-36
11—vs. Vincent, 1939-40

Most Points, Opponent, Game:

101—Altoona, 1990-91
93—Mercer, 1966-67
92—Kingsport (TN) Dobyns-Bennett, 1992-93
90—Johnstown, 1972-73
89—Tech, 1965-66
88—Jamestown (NY), 1970-71
87—New York City (NY) Rice, 2007-08
87—Las Vegas (NV) Bishop Gorman, 2009-10
86—Sharon, 1956-57
86—Johnstown, 1975-76
86—Baltimore (MD) St. Frances, 1995-96
86—Toronto (ONT) Pope John Paul II, 2013-14
85—Meadville, 1965-66
85—Cleveland (OH) St. Joseph, 1972-73
85—Johnstown, 1973-74
85—Williamsport, 1989-90
84—Chester, 2005-06
84—Cleveland (OH) St. Ignatius, 2005-06
84—Chartiers Valley, 2008-09
84—Lakewood (OH) St. Edward, 2015-16
83—Brookfield (OH), 1977-78
83—Buffalo (NY) Bishop Timon-St. Jude, 2000-01
82—Tech, 1955-56
82—McDowell, 1970-71
82—General McLane, 2006-07

Least Points, Opponent, Game:

3—Wesleyville, 1930-31
4—Ripley (NY) Central, 1925-26
5—Fairview, 1928-29
5—Wesleyville, 1929-30
6—Wesleyville, 1930-31
7—Kanty Prep, 1934-35
7—Meadville St. Agatha's, 1936-37
7—Meadville St. Agatha's, 1938-39
7—Lackawanna (NY) Our Lady of Victory, 1944-45
7—North East, 1945-46
8—Titusville St. Titus, 1928-29
9—Bradford St. Bernard's, 1929-30
9—Corry St. Edward's, 1934-35
10—Corry St. Edward's, 1928-29
10—Corry St. Edward's, 1931-32
10—North East, 1933-34
10—Oil City St. Joseph's, 1936-37

Largest Winning Margin, Prep, Game:

66—vs. Meadville St. Agatha's, 1940-41 (78-12)
65—vs. Titusville St. Joseph's, 1952-53 (95-30)
59—vs. Meadville St. Agatha's, 1940-41 (75-16)
58—vs. Jamestown (NY), 1969-70 (100-42)
57—vs. Corry, 2005-06 (79-22)
57—vs. DuBois, 2009-10 (82-25)
56—vs. Vincent, 1995-96 (91-35)
55—vs. Titusville St. Joseph's, 1953-54 (87-32)
55—vs. Titusville St. Joseph's, 1953-54 (71-16)
55—vs. Clearfield, 1994-95 (101-46)
54—vs. Corry St. Edward's, 1940-41 (71-17)
54—vs. Titusville St. Joseph's, 1940-41 (68-14)
54—vs. Titusville St. Joseph's, 1964-65 (102-48)
53—vs. Academy, 1956-57 (79-26)
53—vs. Harborcreek, 2010-11 (71-18)
52—vs. Warren, 1995-96 (83-31)
52—vs. Corry, 2011-12 (73-21)
51—vs. Venango Christian, 1967-68 (92-41)
50—vs. Pittsburgh Oliver, 1979-80 (80-30)

Largest Losing Margin, Prep, Game:

49—vs. Lakewood (OH) St. Edward, 2015-16 (84-35)
47—vs. Cleveland (OH) St. Joe's, 1972-73 (85-38)
46—vs. Alliance Academy, 1925-26 (55-9)
43—vs. Kingsport (TN) Dobyns-Bennett, 1992-93 (92-49)
42—vs. Sharon, 1956-57 (86-44)
42—vs. Oak Hill (VA) Academy, 1991-92 (70-28)
40—vs. Strong Vincent, 1935-36 (59-19)
37—vs. Cleveland (OH) St. Joe's, 1984-85 (71-34)
36—vs. Johnstown, 1973-74 (85-49)
35—vs. Sharon, 1957-58 (66-31)
35—vs. Buffalo (NY) Bishop Timon-St. Jude, 2000-01(83-48)
34—vs. East, 1935-36 (45-11)
34—vs. Johnstown, 1972-73 (90-56)
34—vs. Johnstown, 1975-76 (86-52)
34—vs. Orem (UT), 2013-14 (78-44)
33—vs. Strong Vincent, 1937-38 (45-12)
33—vs. Tech Memorial, 1962-63 (78-45)
33—vs. Baton Rouge (LA) Southern U. Lab, 1998-99 (66-33)
31—vs. Schaller Morticians, 1924-25 (58-27)

Most Points in Game (Erie, Individual):

Bold indicates individual school record.

52—**Carmen Riazzi, Tech,** vs. Lawrence Park, 1952-53
51—**Essie Hollis, Vincent,** vs. Pittsburgh Oliver, 1972-73
50—Pete Alex, Tech, vs. Alumni, 1952-53
50—**David Purdue, Academy,** vs. Conneaut Valley, 1973-74
49—Essie Hollis, Vincent, vs. Prep, 1972-73
49—**Richard Bush, Central,** vs. Warren (OH) Harding, 1995-96
48—**David Morris, Vincent** vs. Mt. St. Michael (NY), 2016-17
47—**Don Dougan, Harborcreek,** vs. McDowell, 1962-63

Tech's great Carmen Riazzi '53 still holds the all-time Erie record with 52 points in a game. Carmen went on to star with the Dayton Flyers.

46—Essie Hollis, Vincent, v. Pittsburgh Oliver, 1972-73
45—Sammy Williams, Vincent, vs. Girard, 1951-52
45—Don Dougan, Harborcreek, vs. Tech, 1960-61
44—**Ken Biletnikoff, East,** vs. Harborcreek, 1955-56
43—**Mike Bartoszek, McDowell,** vs. East, 1970-71
43—Jeremy Thomas, East, vs. St. Catharine (ONT) Simcoe, 2006-07
42—**Jim Hamilton, Prep,** vs. Chattanooga (TN) Brainerd, 1990-91

Villa Maria's Kevin Buczynski is fourth on Erie's all-time scoring chart.

Tim Smith '88 was Vincent's all-time leading scorer until David Morris '17 came around.

Bruce Keys '88, Tech Memorial's forever all-time scoring leader.

Sean Smiley '05, McDowell's all-time leading scorer.

Josh Chojnacki '10 ranks second on Mercyhurst Prep's career scoring chart behind Khyl Horton '92.

41—Sammy Williams, Vincent, vs. Millcreek, 1951-52
41—Dan Sculley, Prep, vs. Pittsburgh Brashear, 1977-78
40—Paul Pry, Prep, vs. Academy, 1967-68
40—Lucas Marsh, McDowell vs. Franklin, 1993-94
40—Matt Harris, vs. Toronto (ONT) Pope John Paul II, 2013-14
39—Barry Thompson, East vs. McDowell, 2016-17
39—Carmen Riazzi, Tech, vs. Meadville, 1951-52
39—Kevin Barron, Prep vs. Warren, 1973-74
39—David Morris, Vincent vs. Farrell, 2015-16
38—Essie Hollis, Vincent, vs. Tech, 1972-73
38—Matt Harris, Prep, vs. Central Tech, 2013-14
37—Al Hatkevich, Prep, vs. Tech, 1951-52
37—Mike Polaygi, Vincent, vs. Mercer, 1954-55
37—Jim Hamilton, Prep vs. Altoona, 1990-91
36—Roger Pierce, Academy, vs. Prep, 1955-56
36—Kenny Harden, Academy vs. McDowell, 1968-69

McDowell's all-around great Mike Bartoszek '71 holds the Trojan single-game record with 43 points against East.

Most Points in Season (Erie, Individual):

Bold indicates individual school record.
753—**Essie Hollis, Vincent,** 1972-73
682—Jed Ryan, Prep, 1994-95
661—**Mike Dowling, McDowell,** 1981-82
649—**Matt Jones, East,** 1999-2000
645—Jim Hamilton, Prep, 1990-91
628—**Khyl Horton, Mercyhurst,** 1990-91
607—**David Purdue, Academy,** 1973-74
597—Tim Smith, Vincent, 1987-88
586—Lucas Marsh, McDowell, 1993-94
581—Tim Gore, Prep, 1979-80
575—Khyl Horton, Mercyhurst, 1991-92
574—Tyler Stoczynski, McDowell, 2003-04
569—**Richard Bush, Central,** 1995-96
568—**Carmen Riazzi, Tech,** 1952-53
561—Mel Laskoff, East, 1953-54
551—Jed Ryan, Prep, 1993-94
549—Willis Cardot, Prep, 1970-71
547—John Jones, East, 1980-81
543—David Morris, Vincent, 2015-16
540—John Feick, McDowell, 1979-80
538—Doug Birchard, McDowell, 1977-78
537—Mark Atkinson, Prep, 1983-84
535—Chuck Britton, McDowell, 1970-71
532—**Kevin Buczynski, Villa Maria,** 2003-04
531—Kevin Williams, Academy, 1986-87
527—Brian Ellis, Academy, 1991-92

522—Davis Morris, Vincent, 2014-15
518—John Gulick, East, 1959-60
510—Kevin Buczynski, Villa Maria, 2001-02
502—Booker Coleman, Prep, 1993-94
501—Khyl Horton, Mercyhurst, 1989-90
499—Willie Kinnard, Tech, 1962-63
499—Kevin Buczynski, Villa Maria, 2002-03
499—Preston Harris, Prep, 2005-06
498—Pat Wiley, Mercyhurst, 2002-03
497—Sheldon Zablotny, Prep, 2012-13
496—Dick Schauble, Vincent, 1964-65
496—Bruce Keys, Tech, 1987-88
495—Bruce Nesdore, McDowell, 1979-80
491—Julian Blanks, Prep, 1997-98
490—Jeff Morrow, McDowell, 1985-86
490—Justin Shouse, McDowell, 1998-99
489—Carmen Riazzi, Tech, 1951-52
489—Jovan Williams, Vincent, 2001-02
483—Willis Cardot, Prep, 1969-70
482—Bob Thomas, Academy, 1961-62
479—Matt Harris, Vincent, 1985-86
479—Tywaun Thomas, Vincent, 2003-04
478—Tony Hampy, McDowell, 1965-66
477—Tim Smith, Vincent, 1986-87
477—James McNeil, Central, 2002-03
477—Josh Chojnacki, Mercyhurst, 2008-09
477—David Morris, Vincent, 2013-14
476—Denny Satyshur, East, 1967-68
471—Dan Sculley, Prep, 1977-78
470—Paul Pry, Prep, 1967-68
470—Wil Pituch, Villa Maria, 1999-2000
470—Matt Harris, Prep, 2013-14
467—Tom Taylor, McDowell, 1980-81
462—Bob Thomas, Academy, 1962-63
458—Essie Hollis, Vincent, 1971-72
458—David Purdue, Academy, 1971-72
458—Torry Mitchell, Central, 1999-2000
458—Andy Kubinski, Prep, 2001-02
457—Sean Smiley, McDowell, 2004-05
456—Jim Roseto, Prep, 1979-80
454—Tim Gore, Prep, 1978-79
452—Joe Blanks, Tech, 1972-73
451—Bob Thomas, Academy, 1963-64
449—Rob Wagner, McDowell, 1964-65
449—Al Hammond, Tech, 1976-77
447—Jim Fahey, Prep, 1952-53
447—**Don Dougan, Harborcreek,** 1962-63
446—Justus Davis, East, 2014-15
445—Jamie Carson, Tech, 1975-76
445—Jim Stevenson, Prep, 1983-84
444—Denny Satyshur, East, 1966-67
444—John Wassell, McDowell, 1966-67
443—Justin Shouse, McDowell 1999-2000
442—Sean Smiley, McDowell, 2003-04
441—Kevin Williams, Academy, 1985-86
440—Bob Ward, Prep, 1959-60
440—R. J. Fiorelli, Prep, 1996-97
440—Tywaun Thomas, Vincent, 2002-03
439—Malquan Pulliam, Vincent, 2012-13
436—Jim Schaaf, Prep, 1982-83
435—Larry Gaines, Tech, 1965-66
435—Rick Bengel, Prep, 1974-75
435—Sheldon Zablotny, 2011-12
434—Walt Clark, Academy, 1974-75
434—Steve Prentice, McDowell, 1974-75
434—Chris Morrow, McDowell, 1989-90
432—Joe Rivera, Vincent, 1999-2000
430—Michael Beck, McDowell, 2013-14

Most Points in Career (Erie, Individual):

Bold indicates individual school record.
2270—**David Morris, Vincent,** 2013-17
1926—**Jed Ryan, Prep,** 1991-95
1884—**Khyl Horton, Mercyhurst,** 1988-92
1616—**Kevin Buczynski, Villa Maria,** 2000-04
1426—Sean Smiley, McDowell, 2001-05
1420—**Bruce Keys, Tech,** 1984-88
1418—Tim Smith, Vincent, 1984-88
1400—**Matt Jones, East,** 1996-2000
1398—**David Purdue, Academy,** 1971-74
1395—Bob Thomas, Academy, 1961-64
1385—Wil Pituch, Villa Maria, 1997-2001
1381—Essie Hollis, Vincent, 1970-73
1371—Sheldon Zablotny, 2009-13
1337—Justin Shouse, McDowell, 1996-2000
1321—Josh Chojnacki, Mercyhurst, 2007-10
1305—Tim Gore, Prep 1977-80
1300—Kevin Williams, Academy, 1984-87
1298—Cliff Crosby, East, 1991-94
1294—Carmen Riazzi, Tech, 1950-53
1273—Tony McLaurin, Villa Maria, 1991-95
1259—**Eugene Husband, Central Tech,** 2010-13
1235—Richard Bush, Central, 1994-97
1235—Torry Mitchell, Central, 1998-2001
1233—Larry Gaines, Tech, 1963-66
1221—Jovan Williams, Vincent, 2000-03
1211—Tony Crosby, East, 1991-94
1203—Denny Satyshur, East, 1964-68
1196—Mel Laskoff, East, 1950-54
1193—Mike Henderson, Villa Maria, 1993-97
1189—Michael Brunson, Academy, 1981-84
1186—Michael Beck, McDowell, 2011-14
1182—Lucas Marsh, Corry/McDowell, 1991-94
1171—Joe Rivera, Vincent, 1997-2000
1157—Tywaun Thomas, Vincent, 2001-04
1150—Joe Blanks, Tech, 1970-73
1149—Doug Merski, Mercyhurst, 1999-2002
1144—Bobby Biletnikoff, Tech, 1959-63
1141—Wendell Torres, East 2007-10
1128—Lamont Selby, Vincent, 1990-93
1120—Brian Ellis, Academy, 1993-96
1119—Jim Delsandro, McDowell, 1990-93
1114—Preston Harris, McDowell/Prep, 2003-06
1102—Julian Blanks, Prep, 1994-98
1101—Doug Birchard, McDowell, 1975-78
1094—Willie Kinnard, Tech, 1960-63
1094—RaSean Thrower, Prep, 2007-10
1091—Bruce Chrzanowski, Tech, 1970-74
1089—Willis Cardot, Prep, 1968-71
1086—Walter Stone, Academy, 1976-79
1086—Zach Spronatti, McDowell, 2004-08
1086—Matt Harris, 2013-14
1078—Pat Wiley, Mercyhurst, 2000-03
1076—Jim Hamilton, Prep, 1988-91
1070—Mike Dowling, McDowell, 1979-82
1063—Mark Blazek, Prep, 2004-08
1061—Anthony Dickens, Vincent, 1982-85
1059—Maurice Williams, Vincent, 2004-07
1057—Jeff Morrow, McDowell, 1983-86
1054—J. J. Delsandro, McDowell, 1998-2001
1049—Charlie Britton, Prep/McDowell, 1968-71
1047—Mark Edstrom, Jamestown (NY), 1969-72

Essie Hollis of Strong Vincent '73 holds the records for most FGs (22) and points (49) in a Prep game. No one is close to his Erie single-season record 753 points.

McDowell's Mike Dowling '82 is third on Erie's single-season chart with 661 points.

1019—Pete Alex, Jr., Iroquois/Mercyhurst, 1980-83
1017—Mark Chase, Prep, 1998-2002
1016—Tom McCloskey, Mercyhurst, 1978-81
1005—Curtis Barney, Academy, 1984-87
1002—Cliff Dennett, Prep, 1990-93

J.J. Delsandro, McDowell '01.

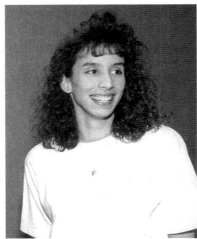

Mercyhurst Prep's great Teresa Szumigala '91, Erie's all-time career leading scorer, boys included, until David Morris showed up.

GIRLS

1961—**Teresa Szumigala, Mercyhurst**, 1987-91
1773—**Lisa Fessler,** Villa Maria/**McDowell,** 1985-89
1728—Chelsea Gordon, Mercyhurst, 2001-05
1727—**Kayla McBride, Villa Maria,** 2006-10
1669—Mashea Williams, Mercyhurst, 2001-05
1654—**Helen Marz, St. Benedict's,** 1974-78
1519—Kirsten Olowinski, Mercyhurst, 2005-09
1493—**Kelly Reedy, Academy,** 1977-81
1467—Sue Heidt, Mercyhurst, 1982-86
1404—Maria DiVecchio, Villa Maria, 1998-2002
1393—Nicole DiRaimo, Harborcreek/Villa Maria, 2002-06
1360—Erin Popovich, Villa Maria, 1987-91
1338—Erin Kerner, Mercyhurst, 2001-05
1319—Cheryl Tomczak, St. Benedict's, 1984-88
1299—Shelly Respecki, McDowell, 1984-88
1279—Karlee McBride, Villa Maria, 2009-13
1271—Kristen Baginski, St. Benedict's, 1984-88
1267—Angie Potthoff, Mercyhurst, 1988-92
1239—Lisa Maxson, Mercyhurst, 1982-86
1206—Amy Galla, Mercyhurst, 1993-97
1166—Amy Barickman, Villa Maria, 1986-90
1148—**Maniqua Williams, Central**, 2003-07
1124—Jane Marshall, St. Benedict's, 1973-76
1122—Lisa Donikowski, Villa Maria, 1985-88
1122—Jessie Montie, McDowell, 1999-2002
1121—Lisa Mifsud, Fairview/Villa Maria, 2008-12
1113—Elisha Pancoast, McDowell, 1997-2000
1103—**Sharese Hamer, Vincent**
1090—Julie Popovich, Villa Maria, 1993-96
1072—Erica Potter, Villa Maria, 1995-98
1043—Cindy Maus, Villa Maria, 1971-74
1035—Amanda Berchtold, Mercyhurst, 2009-12
1021—Allison Braun, McDowell, 2006-09

Kayla McBride, VMA '10 led the Victors to a pair of state titles; was the Pennsylvania "Player of the Year"; a First Team All-American at Notre Dame; and now stars in the WNBA.

Most Points in Game (Erie, Team):

Bold indicates individual school record.

137—**Academy**, vs. Conneaut Valley, 1973-74
117—Academy, vs. Conneaut Valley, 1971-72
117—Academy, vs. Titusville, 1985-86
114—Jamestown, vs. Academy, 1971-72
112—**Vincent**, vs. Harborcreek, 1959-60
111—**McDowell**, vs. Conneaut Valley, 1969-70
110—Academy, vs. Linesville, 1969-70
107—Academy, vs. Kennedy Christian, 1973-74
106—**Central**, vs. Warren (OH) Harding, 1995-96
104—**East**, vs. Warren, 1966-67
104—McDowell, vs. Warren, 1979-80 (twice)
104—Vincent, vs. East, 2006-07
103—East, vs, Venango Christian, 1970-71
103—Academy, vs. North East, 1978-79
102—**Prep**, vs. Titusville St. Joseph, 1964-65
102—East, vs. Warren, 1968-69
101—Prep, vs. Ashtabula Harbor (OH), 1969-70
101—Prep, vs. Clearfield, 1994-95
100—Vincent v. Geneva (OH), 1955-56
100—Vincent, vs. Corry, 1965-66
100—Prep, vs. Jamestown (NY), 1969-70
99—Prep, vs. Kennedy Christian, 1967-68
99—Prep, vs. Jamestown (NY), 1970-71
99—Academy, vs. Jamestown (NY), 1973-74
99—McDowell, vs. Franklin, 1973-74
98—East, vs. Hickory, 1967-68
98—**Tech** vs. Conneaut Valley, 1971-72
98—Prep, vs. Altoona, 1990-91
97—Vincent, vs. Millcreek, 1954-55
97—Tech v. Franklin, 1960-61
97—Vincent, vs. Dunkirk (NY), 1963-64
97—Prep, vs. Tech, 1989-90
97—Prep, vs. East, 1993-94
96—Academy, vs. Cambridge Springs, 1967-68
96—Tech, vs. Conneaut Valley, 1971-72
95—Prep, vs. Titusville St. Joseph's, 1952-53
95—Tech, vs. Warren, 1965-66
95—East, vs. Wattsburg, 1968-69
95—Academy, vs. North East, 1970-71
95—Academy, vs. Union City, 1970-71
95—Academy, vs. McDowell, 1971-72
95—Prep, vs. Clearfield, 1976-77
95—Prep, vs. East, 1989-90
94—Tech, vs. East, 1961-62
94—Tech, vs. Ellwood City, 1962-63

94—East, vs. Wattsburg, 1965-66
94—Prep, vs. East, 1994-95
94—Prep, vs. Vincent, 1995-96
94—Vincent, vs. George Junior Republic, 2009-10

McDonald's/Burger King Classic Records

Champions

1983—Brooklyn (NY) Bishop Loughlin
1984—Queens (NY) Christ the King
1985—Hopkinsville (KY)
1986—Cleveland (OH) St. Joseph
1987—CATHEDRAL PREP
1989—Jersey City (NJ) St. Anthony's
1990—Mouth of Wilson (VA) Oak Hill Academy
1991—CATHEDRAL PREP
1992—Baltimore (MD) Dunbar
1993—CATHEDRAL PREP
1994—Manhattan (NY) Rice
1995—Paterson (NJ) Catholic
1996—Paterson (NJ) Catholic
1997—Lakewood (OH) St. Edward
1998—Manhattan (NY) Rice
1999—Elizabeth (NJ) St. Patrick's
2000—New York City (NY) LaSalle
2001—Manhattan (NY) Rice
2002—Los Angeles (CA) Westchester
2003—Rochester (NY) McQuaid Jesuit
2004—Orlando, (FL) Edgewater
2005—Memphis (TN) Fairley
2006—Milwaukee (WI) Rufus King
2007—Lakewood (OH) St. Edward
2008—Manhattan (NY) Rice
2009—Chester
2010—Lansdowne Penn Wood
2011—Lansdowne Penn Wood
2012—Alpharetta (GA) Milton
2013—Philadelphia Imhotep Charter
2014—Philadelphia Archbishop Carroll
2015—Lakewood (OH) St. Edward
2016—Philadelphia Neumann-Goretti
2017—Arlington (VA) Paul VI

Most Points (Individual, Game)

43—Kaleb Wesson, Westerville South vs. Prep, 2017
41—Tim Thomas, Paterson (NJ) Cath. vs. Phl. Simon Gratz, 1995
40—Darrin Govens, Chester vs. Prep, 2006
40—Felipe Lopez, NYC (NY) Rice vs. Cle. (OH) VASJ, 1994
40—Chris Webber, Detroit (MI) Country Day vs. Bklyn. (NY) Loughlin, 1991
39—Jabarie Hinds, Mount Vernon (NY) vs. Prep, 2010
39—Orlando Vega, Oak Hill Academy (VA) vs. S. Htgn. (NY) St. A, 1987

Most Points (Individual, Tournament)

67—Darrin Govens, Chester, 2006
66—Darius Washington, Orlando, (FL) Edgewater, 2004
64—Tim Thomas, Paterson (NJ) Catholic, 1995
61—Chris Webber, Detroit (MI) Country Day School, 1991
60—Felipe Lopez, Manhattan (NY) Rice, 1994
59—Anthony Cade, Oak Hill Academy (VA), 1990

Most Points (Team, Game)

100—Los Angeles (CA) Westchester, vs. Chester, 2002
93—Brooklyn (NY) Bishop Loughlin, vs. Beaver Falls, 1983
93—L.A. (CA) Westchester, vs. Wash. (DC) Dunbar, 2002
93—Alpharetta (GA) Milton, vs. Jamesville-DeWitt (NY), 2012

Mercyhurst Prep's great Angie Potthoff '92 went on to star at Penn State and in the WNBA.

The 1974 Academy Lions averaged more PPG than any team in Erie, once scoring 137 against Cambridge Springs.

Fewest Points (Team, Game)

28—Prep, vs. Oak Hill Academy, 1992
30—Prep, vs. Simon Gratz, 2000
32—NYC LaSalle, vs. Prep, 1993
35—Prep, vs. Archbishop Carroll, 2014
35—Prep, vs. Neumann-Goretti, 2016

Most Rebounds (Individual, Game)

23—Treg Lee, Cle. St. Joe's vs. Phl. Roman Catholic, 1986
21—Tim Thomas, Paterson (NJ) Cath. vs. Phl. Simon Gratz, 1995
19—Jeromy Rodriguez, Sparta (NJ) Pope John XXIII vs. Prep, 2015

19—Kaleb Wesson, Westerville South vs. Arlington (VA) Paul VI, 2017
18—Andre Kibbler, Bklyn. (NY) Loughlin, vs. Beaver Falls, 1983
18—Andre Kibbler, Bklyn. (NY) Loughlin, vs. Prep, 1983

Most Assists (Individual, Game)

15—Charles Mann, Alpharetta (GA) Milton, vs. Jamesville-DeWitt (NY), 2012
13—Bobby Hurley, Jersey City (NJ) St. Anthony's vs. Cleveland (OH) St. Joseph, 1989
12—J. C. Ajemian, Richmond (VA) Benedictine vs. Queens (NY) Christ the King, 1984
12—Terrell Stokes, Philadelphia Simon Gratz, vs. Paterson (NJ) Catholic, 1995
12—Terrell Stokes, Philadelphia Simon Gratz, vs. Chester, 1995

7'4" Shagari Alleyne, NYC Rice '03.

Athletic Director Ron Sertz '65 elevated Prep to national prominence with the McDonald's Classic.

Superstar Tim Thomas, Paterson Catholic '96, scored 41 points and grabbed 21 rebounds against Simon Gratz in the McDonald's Classic.

Dallas Lauderdale, with a slam dunk for Solon in the 2007 McDonald's Classic.

Fr. Scott Jabo with the 2014 Burger King Classic champs, Archbishop Carroll.

Cathedral Prep's Awards and Honors Winners

All-State and All-D10 choice Matt Harris '14, Prep's last four-year letter winner.

Cathedral Prep's All-State Honorees

1968—Paul Pry, Honorable Mention, *AP*
1968—Rick Fessler, Honorable Mention, *UPI*
1971—Willis "Puck" Cardot, 6th team, *AP*
1978—Dan Sculley, 2nd team, *UPI*; 3rd team *AP*
1980—Tim Gore, 1st Team, *AP & UPI*
1980—Andy Sisinni, Honorable Mention, *AP*
1988—Olivier Allinei, Honorable Mention, *AP*
1991—Jim Hamilton, 3rd team, *AP*
1993—Jed Ryan, 5th team, *AP*
1994—Booker Coleman, 1st team, *AP*
1994—Jed Ryan, 4th team, *AP*
1995—Jed Ryan, 1st team, *AP*
1997—Julian Blanks, 5th team, *AP*
1998—Julian Blanks, 2nd team, *AP*
2002—Andy Kubinski, 4th team, *AP*
2005—Cory Knight, 3rd team, *AP*
2006—Preston Harris, 3rd team, *AP*
2012—Sheldon Zablotny, 3rd team, *AP*
2013—Sheldon Zablotny, 2nd team, *AP*
2014—Matt Harris, 3rd team, *AP*

Cathedral Prep's All-Americans

1953—Jim Fahey, *The New World* 4th team Catholic All-American
1971—Willis "Puck" Cardot, Honorable Mention, U. S. Basketball Writers Association; Honorable Mention, *Coach & Athlete Magazine*; and Honorable Mention, Sunkist Growers
1980—Tim Gore, *The New World* 1st team Catholic All-American
1980—Andy Sisinni, *The New World* 2nd team Catholic All-American
1980—Jim Roseto, *The New World* 3rd team Catholic All-American

Cathedral Prep's James "Moe" Gross Award

*Awarded to Prep's Most Valuable Player in the spirit of James "Moe" Gross, a model student and sparkplug of the Ramblers' 1953 and 1954 state champions. "Moe" was sadly killed in an automobile accident on September 18, 1957.

1968—Paul Pry
1969—Gary Borowy
1970—Brian Flanagan
1971—Willis "Puck" Cardot
1972—Bob Repko
1973—Marty Orzechowski
1974—Matt Scheppner
1975—Mike Sisinni
1976—Dave Cousart
1977—Bill Bensur
1978—Dan Sculley

1979—Tim Gore
1980—Team
1981—Joe Tarasovitch
1982—John Alberstadt
1983—Jim Schaaf
1984—Mark Atkinson, Jim Stevenson
1985—Bill Snider
1986—Mike Manczka
1987—Brian May
1988—Olivier Allinei
1989—Steve Ziegler
1990—Jeff Cardot, Todd Stablein
1991—Jim Hamilton
1992—Mike King
1993—Cliff Dennett, Matt Bennett, Gene Tomczak, Pat Marnella, Derrick Reid

James "Moe" Gross '54.

1994—Booker Coleman, Jed Ryan
1995—Jed Ryan
1996—Keith Nies
1997—Graham Witherspoon, R. J. Fiorelli
1998—Julian Blanks
1999—Adam Straub
2000—David Hairston
2001—Aaron DeCoursey
2002—Andy Kubinski
2003—Casey McCloskey
2004—Joe Jones
2005—Cory Knight
2006—Preston Harris
2007—Mark Blazek
2008—Mark Blazek
2009—Andrew Sweny
2010—RaSean Thrower
2011—Adam Blazek
2012—Sheldon Zablotny
2013—Sheldon Zablotny
2014—Matt Harris
2015—Matt Colpoys
2016—Carter Cross

Cathedral Prep's Four-year Letter Winners

1938-42—Ted Morasky
1940-44—Richard "Red" Doyle
1941-45—Ray Oldakowski (Oldach)
1991-95—Jed Ryan
1992-96—Keith Nies
1998-2002—Mark Chase
2004-08—Mark Blazek
2009-13—Sheldon Zablotny
2010-14—Matt Harris

Cathedral Prep's First Team All-City, All-Big 6, All-Big 7, All-Metro, All-Section I, All-Region and All-District 10 All-Stars

*As selected by the *Erie Times-News*, the *Erie Dispatch-Herald*, the *Erie Press* and/or the *Lake Shore Visitor* as noted.

1943—Johnny DeLuca *(D-H)*
1947—Jim White *(D-H)*
1948—Don Laird *(D-H & T-N)*
　　　Johnny Harabedian *(D-H & T-N)*
1949—Art Hilinski *(D-H, T-N & LSV)*
　　　Art Middleton *(D-H, T-N & LSV)*
　　　Jack Crotty *(TN & LSV)*

1950—Jack Crotty (D-H & T-N)
1951—Al Hatkevich (D-H & T-N)
 Len Cyterski (D-H & T-N)
1952—Al Hatkevich (D-H, T-N & LSV)
 Jim "Red" Fahey (LSV)
 Lenny Tomczak (LSV)
1953—Jim "Red" Fahey (D-H, T-N & LSV)
 Jimmy Dailey (D-H, T-N & LSV)
1954—Johnny Ruska (D-H & T-N)
 Chuck Wittman (D-H)
1955—George Feasler (D-H & T-N)
1956—George Feasler (D-H & T-N)
1959—Al Stankiewicz (T-N)
 Herb Foster (T-N)
1960—Pat Tomczak (T-N)
 Bobby Ward (T-N)
1961—Jim McCallion (T-N)
1962—Dave Whitby (T-N)
1964—Pat Lupo (T-N)
1965—John Stano (T-N)
 Tim Maloney (T-N)
1967—Tim Finegan (T-N)
1968—Rick Fessler (T-N)
 Paul Pry (T-N)
1970—Willis "Puck" Cardot (T-N & EP)
1971—Willis "Puck" Cardot (T-N & EP)
1972—Bob Repko (T-N & EP)
1973—Marty Orzechowski (T-N)
1974—Kevin Barron (T-N)
1975—Rick Bengel (T-N)
 Mike Sisinni (T-N)
1976—Dave Cousart (T-N)
1977—Bill Bensur (T-N)
1978—Dan Sculley (T-N)
 Danny Achille (T-N)
 Jeff Szumigale (T-N)
1979—Tim Gore (T-N)
1980—Tim Gore (T-N)
 Andy Sisinni (T-N)
 Jim Roseto (T-N)
1982—Stacy Hitt (T-N)
 John Alberstadt (T-N)
1983—Mark Atkinson (T-N)
 Jim Schaaf (T-N)
1984—Mark Atkinson (T-N)
 Jimmy Stevenson (T-N)
1986—Mike Manczka (T-N)
1988—Jim Toohey (T-N)
 Olivier Allinei (T-N)
1989—Steve Ziegler (T-N)
1990—Jeff Cardot (T-N)
 Todd Stablein (T-N)
1991—Jim Hamilton (T-N)
 Todd Filipkowski (T-N)
1992—Cliff Dennett (T-N)
1993—Jed Ryan (T-N)
 Booker Coleman (T-N)
1994—Jed Ryan (T-N)
 Booker Coleman (T-N)
1995—Jed Ryan (T-N)
 Keith Nies (T-N)
1996—Brian Szewczykowski (T-N)
 Keith Nies (T-N)
1997—R. J. Fiorelli (T-N)
 Graham Witherspoon (T-N)
 Julian Blanks (T-N)
1998—Jim Gemler (T-N)
 Julian Blanks (T-N)
1999—Adam Straub (T-N)
2002—Mark Chase (T-N)
2003—Casey McCloskey (T-N)
2004—Joe Jones (T-N)
2005—Cory Knight (T-N)
 Nick Haller (T-N)
2006—Preston Harris (T-N)
 Mark Demski (T-N)
2007—Mark Blazek (T-N)
 Jeff Wisinski (T-N)
2008—Mark Blazek (T-N)
 Steve Piotrowicz (T-N)
 RaSean Thrower (T-N)
2009—Bobby Spoden (T-N)
 Andrew Sweny (T-N)
 RaSean Thrower (T-N)
2010—Adam Blazek (T-N)
 RaSean Thrower (T-N)
2011—Adam Blazek (T-N)
 Dominic Sansone (T-N)
2012—Sheldon Zablotny (T-N)
 Conor Colpoys (T-N)
2013—Sheldon Zablotny (T-N)
 Conor Colpoys (T-N)
2014—Matt Harris (T-N)
2015—Matt Colpoys (T-N)
 Joe Fustine (T-N)
2016—Carter Cross (T-N)

Cathedral Prep's All-Star Game Participants

1942—Ted Morasky (1st East-West)
 Ray Laughlin
 Joe McCafferty
1943—Johnny DeLuca (1st Coaches')
 Richard "Red" Doyle
1944—Sil Mannarino (2nd Coaches')
 Richard "Red" Doyle
1945—Johnny DeLuca (3rd Coaches')
 Ray Oldach
 Coach Sam Yezerski
 Sil Mannarino (Coaches' Red Cross)
 Coach Sam Yezerski
 Father Jim Sperry
 Father Len Kuziora
1946—No Prepsters selected (4th Coaches')
1947—Jim White (5th Coaches')
 Dick Trombetta
 Ed Hyziewicz
1948—Don Laird (6th Coaches')
 Johnny Harabedian
 Coach Cyril "Cy" James
 Coach Walt Strosser
1949—Art Hilinski (7th Coaches')
 Art Middleton
 Jack Krahe
 Coach Walt Strosser
 Coach Dick Detzel
1950-55—No All-Star games
1956—George Feasler (1st City-County)
 Jim Keim
 Vinny Kwiatkowski
1957—Eugene "Jiggs" Tomczak (2nd City-County)
1958—Ed Wittman (3rd City-County "A")
 Bill Galla ("A")
 Maury Marchant ("B")
 *City coached by Bob Trombacco
1959—Al Stankiewicz (4th City-County "A")
 Chuck Bauder ("A")
 Herb Foster ("A")
1960—Bob Ward (5th City-County "A")
 Pat Tomczak ("A")
 Bernie Nies ("A")
1961—Jim McCallion (6th City-County "A")
 John Fetzner ("B")
1962—Dave Whitby (7th City-County "A")
 Al Lubiejewski ("B")
 Dan Bulishak ("B")
 Charlie Fischer ("B")
1963—Jim Marnella (8th City-County "A")
 Jim Reske ("A")
 Mike Flaherty ("A")
 Jerry Fetzner ("B")
 *City coached by Bob Trombacco
1964—Pat Lupo (9th City-County "A")
 Bill Druckemiller ("A")
1965—John Stano (10th City-County "A")
 Tim Maloney ("A")
 Chuck Shreve ("B")
 Dave Wenrick ("B")
 Rick Hanhauser ("B")
1966—Dan Pakela (11th City-County "B")
 John Behan ("B")
 Jim Flanigan ("B")
 Norb Barthelmes ("B")
1967-1974—No All-Star games

*NOTE—The eleven City-County All-Star games from 1956-1966 were sponsored by the Belle Valley Lions' Club for the benefit of the Exceptional Children's Fund. It was Father Francis Schlindwein who was the original promoter of these games. Beginning in 1975 the City-County All-Star Games have been sponsored by the Northwest Jaycees.

1975—Mike Sisinni (1st City-County)
 Rick Bengel
 Bob Bengel
 John Webb
1976—Dave Cousart (2nd City-County)
1977—Bill Bensur (3rd City-County)
 Kevin Elwell
 *City coached by Bill Flaherty
1978—Dan Sculley (4th City-County)
 Jeff Szumigale, MVP
 Dan Achille
1979—Tim Emling (5th City-County)
 Mike May
1980—Tim Gore, selected but DNP (6th City-County)
 Andy Sisinni, selected but DNP
 *City coached by Dave Wenrick and Tom Hansen
 Tim Gore (16th Dapper Dan Classic)
 Andy Sisinni (Dapper Dan preliminary)
1981—Joe Tarasovitch (7th City-County)
 John Achille
 Chuck Brower

1982—Stacy Hitt (8th City-County)
 John Alberstadt
 Gary Miller
1983—Jim Schaaf (9th City-County)
 Shawn Dombrowski
1984—Mark Atkinson (10th City-County)
 Jim Stevenson
 Preston Bowen
 Joe Fessler
 Mike Stadtmiller
 Mark Atkinson (20th Dapper Dan preliminary)
1985—Bill Snider (11th City-County)
 Chris Keim
1986—Mark Dalton (12th City-County)
 Mike Manczka (22nd Dapper Dan preliminary)
1987—Rick Demski (13th City-County)
 Mike Szewczykowski
 *City coached by Dave Wenrick
1988—Jim Toohey (14th City-County)
 Olivier Allinei
 Jim Camp
 *City coached by Marcel Arribi
1989—Steve Ziegler (15th City-County)
 Mike Heberle
 Phil Kraus
1990—Jeff Cardot (16th City-County)
 Todd Stablein
1991—Jim Hamilton (17th City-County)
 Todd Filipkowski
 John Donnelly
 Jim Hamilton (27th Dapper Dan preliminary)
1992—Mark Tate (18th City-County)
 Mike King
1993—Cliff Dennett (19th City-County)
 Gene Tomczak
1994—Kenny Duck (20th City-County)
 Keith Anthony
 Booker Coleman, selected but DNP
1995—Jed Ryan (21st City-County)
 Craig Fomich
 Justin Izbicki
1996—Keith Nies (22nd City-County)
 John Trocki
 Doug Lecker
 Brian Szewczykowski
1997—R. J. Fiorelli (23rd City-County)
 Graham Witherspoon
1998—Jim Gemler (24th City-County)
 Julian Blanks
1999—Adam Straub (25th City-County)
2000—Jim Fetzner (26th City-County)
 David Hairston
2001—Srba Samailovic (27th City-County)
 Aaron DeCoursey, selected but DNP
2002—Andy Kubinski (28th City-County)
2003—Casey McCloskey (29th City-County)
2004—Joe Jones (30th City-County)
 Adam Dolak
2005—Cory Knight (31st City-County)
 Brian Mahoney
 Nick Haller
2006—Preston Harris (32nd City-County)
 Adam Kaiser
 Mark Demski
 *City coached by Brian Flanagan
2007—Jeff Wisinski (33rd City-County)
 Ryan Heidt
 Josh Licata
2008—Mark Blazek (34th City-County)
 Steve Piotrowicz
2009—Bobby Spoden (35th City-County)
 Andrew Sweny
 Keith Blazek
 *City -----coached by Mark Majewski
2010—RaSean Thrower (36th City-County)
 Phil Hampy
 *The City was coached by Mark Majewski
2011—Adam Blazek (37th City-County)
 Dominic DiRaimo
 Dominic Sansone, selected but DNP
 Joe Gnacinski
2012—No Prepsters selected (38th City-County)
2013—Sheldon Zablotny (39th City-County)
 Conor Colpoys
 Kevin Francis
2014—Matt Harris (40th City-County)
 Felix Manus-Schell
2015—Matt Colpoys (41st City-County)
 Joe Fustine
 Charlie Fessler
2016—John Bowen (42nd City-County)
 Carter Cross, selected but DNP
 Dajon Heidelberg

Rick Fessler '68 was Prep's first to receive All-State recognition. Retiring as the Ramblers' all-time leading scorer, "Fess" later became prinicipal at Prep.

Julian Blanks '98, twice named All-State, started four years at LaSalle. Pictured here at his Prep Hall of Fame induction.

All-American Willis "Puck" Cardot '71.

Sheldon Zablotny '13, twice made the All-State team and was the 2012 District 10 "Player of the Year."

Jim "Red" Fahey '53 (#17) was Prep's first All-American. With him is Johnny Ruska '54, another All-City performer.

Andy Sisinni '80 received All-State and All-American recognition. He started four years at Duquesne and later became Prep's head coach.

Receiving All-State recognition and winning the "Moe" Gross Award, Olivier Allinei '88 later starred on the French National Team and in the French pro leagues.

All-City star and "Moe" Gross winner Marty Orzechowski '73 buries another outside jumper.

All-City center Bob Repko '72 also won the James "Moe" Gross Award.

Booker Coleman in for the slam dunk in the 1994 state championship game.

Booker Coleman '94, just the second Rambler ever to be named First Team All-State.

"Moe" Gross Award winner Steve Zeigler '89 mysteriously vanished in 2005.

All-Section performer Stacy Hitt '82 starred on Gannon's only team to make it to the national championship game.

Cory Knight '05, District 10 "Player of the Year" and Third Team All-State.

"Here comes Cardot!" Five Vincent Colonels surround the Rambler superstar, but can't stop him (1971).

All-Section star Danny Achille '78 went on to a fine career at Gannon College.

All-time Erie High School Basketball Records (1905-2017)

	WON	LOST	TIED	.PCT
Erie High School (1905-1920)	159	71	1*	.6904
Erie Central Fighting Colonels (1920-1929)	136	61	0	.6903
Erie Cathedral Prep Ramblers (1924-2017)	1446	735	0	.663
Millcreek McDowell Trojans (1921-2017)	1406	754	0	.651
Erie Strong Vincent Colonels (1930-2017)	1166	824	2*	.586
Erie Academy Lions (1919-1992)	887	687	4*	.563
Erie East High Warriors (1921-2017)	1207	945	2*	.561
Erie Mercyhurst Prep Lakers (1983-2017)	604	485	0	.555
Erie Tech Memorial Centaurs (1931-1991)	685	601	0	.533
Erie Central Tech Falcons (1992-2017)	275	314	0	.467
Total	**7971**	**5477**	**9***	**.593**

*Ties are considered .50 win and .50 loss when computing winning percentages.

Cathedral Prep "Ramblers" Basketball History (1924-2017)

Year	Won	Lost	Coach	Team Honors
1924-25	5	12	Wilmot Quillman	1st Team
1925-26	7	7	James "Gyp" Sullivan	
1926-27	12	7	Sullivan	
1927-28	4	7	Nelson "Fat" Schumacher	
1928-29	14	6	Rev. Walter Conway	State Catholic Tourney Bid
1929-30	15	7	Rev. Conway	
1930-31	8	11	Rev. Conway	
1931-32	7	12	Rev. Conway	
1932-33	10	7	Rev. Conway	
1933-34	10	6	Rev. Conway	
1934-35	8	10	Rev. Conway	
1935-36	9	9	Rev. Conway	
1936-37	6	8	Rev. Conway	
1937-38	8	9	Ralph "Baron" Calabrese	
1938-39	9	6	George Williams	
1939-40	5	10	Williams	
1940-41	11	5	Salvatore "Jimmy" Foti	
1941-42	12	2	Albert "Al" Calabrese	
1942-43	4	15	Rev. Leonard Kuziora	1st Year PCIAA Tourney
1943-44	7	17	Rev. Kuziora	
1944-45	13	8	Florian "Sam" Yezerski	PCIAA Final Four
1945-46	14	9	Yezerski	PCIAA Final Four
1946-47	19	6	Walter "Walt" Strosser	City Series Champs
1947-48	6	13	Strosser	
1948-49	19	6	Richard "Dick" Detzel	City Series Champs
1949-50	12	7	Detzel	City Series Champs (tie)
1950-51	15	5	Detzel	City Series Champs (tie)
1951-52	12	6	Detzel	City Series Champs (tie)
1952-53	23	4	Detzel	City Series/PCIAA State Champs/Eastern States
1953-54	22	3	Detzel	City Series/PCIAA State Champs/ESCIT
1954-55	12	7	Detzel	PCIAA Final Four
1955-56	16	7	Detzel	PCIAA Final Four
1956-57	14	10	Detzel	
1957-58	7	14	Robert "Bob" Trombacco	
1958-59	16	6	Trombacco	City Series Champs/PCIAA Final Four
1959-60	17	6	Trombacco	City Series Champs/PCIAA Final Four
1960-61	12	7	Trombacco	
1961-62	17	9	Trombacco	City Series Champs/PCIAA Final Four
1962-63	11	7	Trombacco	
1963-64	18	3	Richard "Red" Murray	City Series Champs
1964-65	17	5	Murray	City Series Champs/PCIAA Final Four
1965-66	3**	18*	Murray	
1966-67	13	9	Murray	
1967-68	19	5	Richard "Dick" Fox	McDowell Xmas Champs/PCIAA State Champs
1968-69	14	7	Fox	McDowell Xmas Champs
1969-70	18	6	Fox	City Series/LSL (tie) Champs/PCIAA Final Four
1970-71	21	3	Fox	Fredonia Tourney/City/PCIAA State Champs
1971-72	18	5	William "Bill" Flaherty	Fredonia Tourney/City Champs/PCIAA Final Four
1972-73	9	13	Flaherty	1st year in PIAA
1973-74	14	11	Flaherty	Warren Xmas Champs
1974-75	22	6	Flaherty	Section I/District 10 Champs
1975-76	9	12	Flaherty	
1976-77	20	5	Flaherty	City Series/Section I/District 10 Champs
1977-78	26	3	Flaherty	Silver Fox/Warren Xmas/Metro/D-10 Champs/ PIAA Final Four
1978-79	23	5	Flaherty	Warren Xmas/District 10 Champs
1979-80	33*	1**	Flaherty	Meadville Elks/City/Metro/D-10/PIAA State Champs
1980-81	20	8	Flaherty	Metro Champs
1981-82	19	10	Flaherty	
1982-83	20	10	Flaherty	Jamestown Xmas/Metro Champs
1983-84	27	6	Flaherty	Metro/PIAA Western Champs
1984-85	7	14	David "Dave" Wenrick	
1985-86	15	9	Wenrick	
1986-87	14	12	Wenrick	
1987-88	24	5	Marcel Arribi	McDonald's Classic/Metro/D-10 Champs/ PIAA Final Four
1988-89	19	8	Arribi	Metro Champs
1989-90	21	5	Arribi	Great Chevy Shootout/ Metro/District 10 Champs
1990-91	23	5	Arribi	McDonald's Classic/Metro/District 10 Champs
1991-92	16	11	Arribi	Farrell Xmas Champs
1992-93	21	7	Arribi	McDonald's Classic/District 10/PIAA State Champs
1993-94	24	7	Arribi	Kreul/ Metro/District 10/PIAA Western Champs
1994-95	25	4	Arribi	Chocolate World/ Elk Co. Xian Classic/Sun USA Cup/ Metro/District 10/PIAA Final Four
1995-96	24	8	Arribi	Farrell/Oil City/Metro/PIAA Western Champs
1996-97	24	3	Arribi	Toronto/State Farm/Steakball/Metro/ District 10 Champs
1997-98	17	10	Arribi	Metro/District 10 Champs
1998-99	13	14	Arribi	
1999-2000	12	12	Robert "Bob" Ronai	Great Chevy Shootout Champs
2000-01	16	9	Ronai	
2001-02	19	10	Andrew "Andy" Sisinni	Farrell Tourney/Metro Champs
2002-03	17	9	Sisinni	
2003-04	18	7	Sisinni	Farrell Tourney Champs
2004-05	26	5	Brian Flanagan	Region 6/District 10 Champs/PIAA Final Four
2005-06	22	6	Flanagan	Region 6/District 10 Champs
2006-07	23	5	Flanagan	Midland Tourney/Region 7/District 10 Champs
2007-08	18	8	Flanagan	Region 7 Champs
2008-09	17	10	Mark Majewski	District 10 Champs
2009-10	15	11	Majewski	Fox Chapel Tourney Champs
2010-11	14	10	Majewski	Region 8/District 10 Champs
2011-12	21	6	Majewski	KSA/Region 8 (tie)/D-10 Champs/PIAA Final Four
2012-13	23	3	Majewski	Region 7/District 10 Champs
2013-14	15	8	Majewski	Region 7 Champs
2014-15	22	7	Majewski	Region 7 (tie)/D-10 AAA Champs/PIAA Final Four
2015-16	16	10	Majewski	
2016-17	14	13	Majewski	

ALL-TIME RECORD: 1446-735 (.663)
FOURTEEN (14) CITY SERIES CHAMPIONSHIP (11 OUTRIGHT, 3 TIES)
THREE (3) BIG SEVEN CHAMPIONSHIPS (1 OUTRIGHT, 2 TIE)
TWO (2) BIG SIX CHAMPIONSHIPS (1 OUTRIGHT, 1 TIE)
ONE (1) LAKE SHORE LEAGUE CHAMPIONSHIP (TIE)
TWO (2) SECTION ONE CHAMPIONSHIPS
FOURTEEN (14) METRO LEAGUE CHAMPIONSHIPS
NINE (9) REGION CHAMPIONSHIPS (7 OUTRIGHT, 2 TIES)
TWENTY-ONE (21) DISTRICT 10 CHAMPIONSHIPS (20 AAAA, 1 AAA)
TWENTY-THREE (24) FINAL FOUR APPEARANCES (14 PCIAA, 10 PIAA)
NINE (9) STATE FINALS APPEARANCES (4 PCIAA, 5 PIAA)
SIX (6) STATE CHAMPIONSHIPS (4 PCIAA, 2 PIAA)

Cathedral Prep Varsity Coaching Records

Name	Years	Seasons	Won	Lost	Pct.
Wilmot Quillman	1**	1924-1925	5	12	.294
James "Gyp" Sullivan	2	1925-1927	19	14	.576
Nelson "Fat" Schumacher	1	1927-1928	4**	7	.364
Rev. Walter Conway	9	1928-1937	87	76	.534
Ralph "Baron" Calabrese	1**	1937-1938	8	9	.471
George Williams	2	1938-1940	14	16	.467
Salvatore "Jimmy" Foti	1**	1940-1941	11	5	.688
Albert "Al" Calabrese	1**	1941-1942	12	2**	.857*
Rev. Leonard "Len" Kuziora	2	1942-1944	11	32	.256**
Florian "Sam" Yezerski	2	1944-1946	27	17	.614
Walter "Walt" Strosser	2	1946-1948	25	19	.568
Richard "Dick" Detzel	9	1948-1957	145	55	.725
Robert "Bob" Trombacco	6	1957-1963	80	49	.620
Richard "Red" Murray	4	1963-1967	51	35	.593
Richard "Dick" Fox	4	1967-1971	72	21	.774
William "Bill" Flaherty	13*	1971-1984	260*	95*	.732
David "Dave" Wenrick	3	1984-1987	36	35	.507
Marcel Arribi	12	1987-1999	251	87	.743
Robert "Bob" Ronai	2	1999-2001	28	21	.571
Andrew "Andy" Sisinni	3	2001-2004	54	26	.675
Brian Flanagan	4	2004-2008	89	24	.788
Mark Majewski	9	2008-present	157	78	.668
			1446	**735**	**.663**

Cathedral Prep Junior Varsity Records

Year	Won	Lost	Coach	Team Honors
1925-26	12	7		
1930-31	1	0		
1932-33	0	1		
1934-35	0	2		
1935-36	0	1		
1937-38	0	5		
1939-40	1	1		
1940-41	0	1	Rev. Joseph Radzisiewski	
1941-42	1	0	Rev. Radzisiewski	
1942-43	1**	17	Rev. Radzisiewski	
1943-44	1**	18*	Rev. Radzisiewski	
1944-45	3	12	B. Regis "Sox" Harrison	
1945-46	7	5	Harrison	
1946-47	16	4	Theodore "Ted" Sowle	City Champs
1947-48	9	3	Cyril "Cy" James	City Champs
1948-49	14	5	Walter "Walt" Strosser	City Champs
1949-50	14	0	Strosser	City Champs (tie)
1950-51	7	4	Strosser	
1951-52	12	2	Strosser	City Champs
1952-53	13	1	Strosser	City Champs
1953-54	7	5	Strosser	City Champs
1954-55	5	5	Strosser	
1955-56	9	4	Strosser	
1956-57	7	5	Strosser	
1957-58	14	1	Richard "Red" Murray	City Champs
1958-59	11	2	Murray	City Champs (tie)
1959-60	8	3	Murray	
1960-61	10	3	Murray	
1961-62	12	8	Murray	17-3 before 5 forfeits
1962-63	16	2	Murray	
1963-64	12	7	David "Gus" Thomas	
1964-65	16	4	Thomas	City/ Big 6 Champs
1965-66	17	3	Thomas	City/ Big 6 Champs
1966-67	19	2	Thomas	City/ Big 6 Champs
1967-68	16	3	William "Bill" Flaherty	City/ Big 6 Champs
1968-69	15	3	Flaherty	City/ Big 6 Champs
1969-70	18	2	Flaherty	City/ LSL Champs
1970-71	15	4	Flaherty	
1971-72	15	4	David "Dave" Wenrick	City/ LSL Champs
1972-73	16	2	Wenrick	City/ LSL Champs
1973-74	14	6	Wenrick	
1974-75	14	4	Wenrick	City/ Section I Champs
1975-76	17	1	Wenrick	City/ Section I Champs
1976-77	14	4	Wenrick	Metro Champs
1977-78	17	0**	Tom Hansen	Metro Champs
1978-79	16	2	Hansen	Metro Champs
1979-80	22	3	Hansen	Metro Champs
1980-81	17	2	Hansen	Metro Champs
1981-82	23*		Hansen	Metro Champs
1982-83	13	6	Hansen	
1983-84	14	5	Hansen	Metro Champs
1984-85	15	2	Tom Lesniewski	Metro Champs
1985-86	17	2	Lesniewski	Metro Champs
1986-87	18	2	Bob Achille	Metro Champs
1987-88	16	1	Tom Del Fratte	Metro Champs
1988-89	14	2	Del Fratte	
1989-90			Rick Sertz	
1990-91	13	4	Sertz	
1991-92	15	2	Sertz	Metro Champs
1992-93	6	6	Mark Behringer	
1993-94	11	4	Behringer	
1994-95	15	4	Behringer	
1995-96	15	7	Behringer	Metro Champs (tie)
1996-97	22	1	Behringer	Metro Champs
1997-98	18	2	Behringer	Metro Champs (tie)
1998-99	6	3	Behringer	
1999-2000	21	3	Brian Flanagan	
2000-01	15	8	Mike Kujawinski	
2001-02	23*	1	Brian Flanagan	Metro Champs
2002-03	23*	1	B. Flanagan	Metro Champs
2003-04	23*	1	B. Flanagan	Metro Champs
2004-05	21	3	Mike Flanagan	
2005-06	19	6	M. Flanagan	
2006-07	21	1	M. Flanagan	
2007-08	18	5	Jason Dolak	
2008-09	15	7	Justin Izbicki	
2009-10	13	9	Izbicki	
2010-11	19	2	Mike Colpoys	
2011-12	17	4	Colpoys	
2012-13	18	2	Colpoys	
2013-14	19	3	Colpoys	
2014-15	18	4	Colpoys	
2015-16	17	4	Adam Kaiser	
2016-17	13	9	Kaiser	
	1085	311	.777	

Year	Won	Lost	Coach	Team Honors
1950-51	11	3	Rev. Reilly	
1951-52	7	5	Rev. Reilly	
1952-53	9	3	Rev. Reilly	City Champs
1953-54	11	4	Rev. Reilly	
1954-55	8	4	Rev. Reilly	
1955-56	7	5	Rev. Reilly	
1956-57	12	0	James "Jim" DeCarlo	City Champs
1957-58	7	5	Chris Filipkowski	
1958-59	12	0	Len Cyterski	City Champs
1959-60	9	4	Cyterski	
1960-61	3**	9	Cyterski	
1961-62	13	3	David "Gus" Thomas	Big 9 Champs (tie)
1962-63	4	10*	Thomas	
1963-64	No Team			
1964-65	No Team			
1965-66	7	7	William "Bill" Flaherty	
1966-67	15	3	Flaherty	
1967-68	19	0	William "Bill" Garvey	City Champs
1968-69	15	3	Garvey	
1969-70	9	8	Thomas "Tom" Schneider	
1970-71	16	2	David "Dave" Wenrick	
1971-72	17	1	R. Ronald "Ron" Sertz	Metro Champs
1972-73	19	0	Sertz	Metro Champs
1973-74	17	1	Sertz	Metro Champs
1974-75	21	2	Sertz	Metro Champs
1975-76	14	2	Dave Kordich	
1976-77	21	1	Ron Sertz	
1977-78	11	2	Tom Del Fratte	
1978-79	11	1	Del Fratte	
1979-80	13	4	Tom Lesniewski	
1980-81	17	1	Lesniewski	
1981-82	22	1	Lesniewski	
1982-83	19	0	Lesniewski	
1983-84	17	3	Lesniewski	
1984-85	16	0	Tom DelFratte	
1985-86	9	4	DelFratte	
1986-87	n/a		Del Fratte	
1987-88	15	5	Dave Kosobucki	
1988-89	13	4	Kosobucki	
1989-90	19	1	Andy Sisinni	
1990-91	19	1	Wes Alexander	
1991-92	14	1	Alexander	
1992-93	16	2	Joe Sarvadi, Jr.	
1993-94	14	6	Sarvadi	
1994-95	14	4	Sarvadi	
1995-96	14	4	Jim Stevenson	
1996-97	19	2	Stevenson	
1997-98	17	2	Stevenson	
1998-99	15	3	Stevenson	
1999-2000	20	1	Barry Roach	Metro Champs
2000-01	21	3	Ryan Ball	
2001-02	23*	0**	Mark Trigilio	Metro Champs
2002-03	22	2	Trigilio	Metro Champs
2003-04	20	3	Mike Flanagan	
2004-05	21	2	Jason Dolak	
2005-06	19	3	Barry Roach	
2006-07	18	5	Mark Majewski	
2007-08	22	1	Majewski	
2008-09	12	10*	Chris Caldwell	
2009-10	22	2	Mike Colpoys	
2010-11	18	4	Mike Flanagan	
2011-12	17	5	M. Flanagan	
2012-13	19	3	Bill Carideo	
2013-14	18	2	Adam Kaiser	
2014-15	20	2	Kaiser	
2015-16	21	0	Anthony Easterling	
2016-17	17	5	Easterling	
	985	201	.831	

Erie High School "Red & Black" History (1905-1920)

Year	Record	Coach	Team Honors
1905-06	5**-3	George Wilson (mgr.)	
1906-07	9-9*	Harold Thompson (mgr.)	
1907-08	14-8	D. G. "Doc" Evans	
1908-09	13-6	Evans	City Champs
1909-10	14-4	Evans	
1910-11	7-3-1	Mr. Stewart	
1911-12	6-4	Theodore Miller (mgr.)	
1912-13	12-5	"Oc" Anderson (capt.)	City Champs
1913-14	17*-2**	Warner Brockway (mgr.)	
1914-15	12-3	D. G. "Doc" Evans	
1915-16	7-9*	Evans	
1916-17	10-5	Evans	
1917-18	7-7	Evans	
1918-19	15-1	Evans	
1919-20	11-4	Evans	City Series Champs

FINAL ALL-TIME RECORD: 159-71-1 (.690)
TWO (2) CITY CHAMPIONSHIPS (WHICH INCLUDED CITY CLUB TEAMS)
ONE (1) CITY SERIES CHAMPIONSHIP (INAUGURAL CHAMPS)

Cathedral Prep Freshmen Records

Year	Won	Lost	Coach	Team Honors
1938-39	0	2		
1947-48	no games			Rev. Henry Heminghaus
1948-49	3**	3	Rev. George Groucutt	
1949-50	5	7	Rev. Robert J. Reilly	

Prep's 1944 JV's. Coaches Fr. Radziszewski, Fr. Kuziora.

Prep's 1946 senior team, which lost out to the juniors! Front, L to R: Dick Roberts, Bob Ferretti, Dick Rettger; Back: Carl Carlotti, Jim Minton, Coach Father Watson (later "Bishop Watson"), Charlie Colvin, Jim Carideo.

The famous Stevenson brothers get together for a few cold ones before heading down to the Prep game. L to R: Jim, Bob, Jack.

Joey Fessler '84 in his Mercyhurst College uniform.

Len Cyterski '51, Prep's legendary athlete, teacher, coach and rally speaker.

A familiar sight at the Prep games – Walter Helminski '50.

Tim Maloney up for two in a 1963 JV game.

Mike Sisinni '75 is in the Clarion Eagles Hall of Fame.

Chuck Brower '81 about to put another bucket in for Mercyhurst College.

Prep's 1946 JV's. Front, L to R: Harabedian, DiPlacido, Hilinski, Luteran, Nardo; Middle: Fessler, O'Brien, Flanagan, Filipkowski, Brendle, Lynch; Back: Coach "Sox" Harrison, Mauro, Manucci, D'Renz, Abbate, Mgr. Hafey.

Prep's 1948 City Champion JV's. Front: Gannon; Middle, L to R: Carey, Fries, Anthony, Guerrein, Held; Back: Wilwohl, DeLuca, Aquino, Coach James, Kreidinger, Cyterski, Kierzek.

Academy coach "Oc" Anderson.

Erie Academy "Lions" Basketball History (1919-1992)

Year	Record	Coach	Team Honors
1919-20	5-6	Orson Graham	
1920-21	8-10	Oscar "Oc" Anderson	
1921-22	12-7	Anderson	
1922-23	10-8	Anderson	
1923-24	14-6	Lowell Drake	Tri-State Tourney Champs
1924-25	9-13	Drake	Allegheny College Tourney Champs
1925-26	6-9	Drake	
1926-27	6-8	Vic Wright	
1927-28	10-7	Wright	
1928-29	20-2	James "Darby" Mannix	City Series Champs
1929-30	15-4	Mannix	
1930-31	21-4	Howard Kelly	City Series Champs
1931-32	17-2	Kelly	
1932-33	6-13	Kelly	
1933-34	12-8	Kelly	
1934-35	10-12	Kelly	
1935-36	9-12	Kelly	
1936-37	11-12	Kelly	
1937-38	16-10-1	Kelly	
1938-39	15-8-1	Ed "Pee Wee" Thomas	City Series/District 10 Champs
1939-40	14-2-2	Thomas	City Series Champs
1940-41	9-11	Thomas	
1941-42	8-12	Thomas	
1942-43	12-8	Thomas	
1943-44	19-7	Thomas	
1944-45	7-12	Thomas	
1945-46	8-14	John "Jack" Komora	
1946-47	4**-16	Komora	
1947-48	18-6	Komora	City Series Champs
1948-49	8-13	Komora	
1949-50	12-10	Komora	
1950-51	10-10	Komora	City Series Champs (tie)
1951-52	8-10	Komora	
1952-53	16-5	Mike Ferrare	
1953-54	6-14	Ferrare	
1954-55	16-8	Ferrare	
1955-56	20-4	Ferrare	
1956-57	8-12	John "Jack" Komora	
1957-58	10-10	Komora	
1958-59	9-9	Komora	

Year	Record	Coach	Team Honors
1959-60	12-9	Komora	
1960-61	9-10	Komora	
1961-62	13-10	Don Zonno	Scholastic Invitational Champs
1962-63	14-8	Zonno	
1963-64	14-6	Zonno	
1964-65	6-15	Zonno	
1965-66	5-17	Christ Lambros	
1966-67	7-15	Ron Severo	
1967-68	12-8	Lou DiBacco	
1968-69	10-11	DiBacco	
1969-70	12-10	DiBacco	
1970-71	15-6	DiBacco	
1971-72	12-9	DiBacco	
1972-73	12-8	DiBacco	
1973-74	24*-1**	DiBacco	City Series/Section I/District 10 Champs
1974-75	19-5	DiBacco	City Series/Section I Champs
1975-76	5-16	DiBacco	
1976-77	19-7	DiBacco	
1977-78	20-7	DiBacco	
1978-79	16-8	DiBacco	
1979-80	11-12	Paul Demyanovich	
1980-81	4**-18*	Demyanovich	
1981-82	5-8	Demyanovich	
1982-83	10-12	Demyanovich	
1983-84	20-10	Demyanovich	District 10 AAA Champs
1984-85	12-12	Demyanovich	
1985-86	22-5	Demyanovich	District 10 AAA Champs
1986-87	20-9	Demyanovich	Metro League Champs
1987-88	10-15	Demyanovich	
1988-89	16-11	Demyanovich	
1989-90	15-13	Tom Whalen	
1990-91	12-14	Whalen	
1991-92	23-6	Whalen	District 10 AAA Champs/PIAA Final Four

FINAL ALL-TIME RECORD: 890-685-4 (.565)
EIGHT (8) CITY SERIES CHAMPIONSHIPS (7 OUTRIGHT, 1 TIE)
ONE (1) METRO LEAGUE CHAMPIONSHIP
FIVE (5) DISTRICT 10 CHAMPIONSHIPS
ONE (1) PIAA FINAL FOUR APPEARANCE

Erie Central "Fighting Colonels" History (1920-1930)

Year	Record	Coach	Team Honors
1920-21	13-3**	Marcelle La Framboise	City Series Champs
1921-22	14-4	Gus Anderson	City Series Champs
1922-23	16-7	Andy Fletcher	City Series Champs
1923-24	11-10*	Fletcher	
1924-25	13-6	Fletcher	
1925-26	15-4	James "Jim" Hyde	
1926-27	15-5	Hyde	City Series Champs
1927-28	17*-7	Hyde	City Series Champs
1928-29	14-6	Hyde	
1929-30	8**-9	Harold "Sam" Kramer	

FINAL ALL-TIME RECORD: 136-61 (.690)
FIVE (5) CITY SERIES CHAMPIONSHIPS

Erie Central Tech High "Falcons" History (1992-2017)

Year	Record	Coach	Team Honors
1992-93	13-9	Greg Majchrzak	
1993-94	8-13	Majchrzak	
1994-95	14-6	Majchrzak	
1995-96	10-13	Don Dougan	
1996-97	13-12	Dougan	
1997-98	10-14	Rick Emerick	
1998-99	9-15	John Bowen	
1999-2000	17-11	Bowen	
2000-01	20*-8	Bowen	Metro Champs

Prep's first Freshmen Team (1948). Far right, Coach Fr. Heminghaus hands the ball to Dalton. Front, L to R: Wolf, Rougeux; Middle: Adsit, Bova, Palmer, Fromnecht; Back: Peitrzak, Dahlkemper, Grode, Torrelli, Eberlein, Kaczenski, Dawley, Dentel, Borkowski, Herzog, Hoenes.

Calvin Kinnard, Tech '65

2001-02	9-14	Bowen
2002-03	9-15	Tom Koval
2003-04	8-16	Koval
2004-05	9-14	John Bowen
2005-06	2**-22*	Bowen
2006-07	2**-20	Bob Rieger
2007-08	8-14	Rieger
2008-09	7-15	Tom Koval
2009-10	15-12	Koval
2010-11	14-9	Koval
2011-12	11-12	Koval
2012-13	17-6**	Koval
2013-14	12-11	Koval
2014-15	14-9	Koval
2015-16	14-11	Koval	District 10 AAAA Champs
2016-17		

ALL-TIME RECORD: 265-301 (.468)
ONE (1) METRO LEAGUE CHAMPIONSHIP
ONE (1) DISTRICT 10 CHAMPIONSHIP

Erie East High "Warriors" Basketball History (1921-2017)

Year	Recor	Coach	Team Honors
1921-22	8-11	Chet Louden	
1922-23	11-5	Gus Anderson	District 8 Champs
1923-24	15-6	Anderson	City Series Champs
1924-25	21-2**	Anderson	City Series/District 8 Champs/PIAA Final Four
1925-26	25*-2**	Anderson	City Series/District 8 Champs/State Final
1926-27	15-3	Anderson	
1927-28	13-4	Anderson	
1928-29	7-10	Anderson	
1929-30	19-5	James "Jim" Hyde	City Series Champs
1930-31	18-3	Hyde	
1931-32	11-5-1	Hyde	
1932-33	13-6	Hyde	City Series/District 10 Champs
1933-34	15-6	Hyde	City Series/District 10 Champs
1934-35	21-6	John "Jack" Komora	City Series/District 10 Champs
1935-36	20-5	Komora	
1936-37	15-9	Komora	City Series Champs
1937-38	16-7	Komora	City Series Champs
1938-39	14-5	Komora	
1939-40	11-10	Komora	
1940-41	18-6-1	Komora	City Series/Section I Champs
1941-42	14-5	Komora	City Series/Section I Champs
1942-43	16-6	Komora	City Series/Section I Champs
1943-44	20-9	Komora	City Series/Section I Champs
1944-45	10-6	Komora	
1945-46	14-7	Wilford Pomeroy	
1946-47	13-8	Robert "Bob" Arrowsmith	Section I Champs
1947-48	5-12	Arrowsmith	
1948-49	14-8	Arrowsmith	Section I Champs
1949-50	14-11	Arrowsmith	City Series (tie)/Section I Champs
1950-51	9-12	Arrowsmith	
1951-52	8-14	Arrowsmith	
1952-53	10-9	Arrowsmith	
1953-54	16-10	Arrowsmith	Section I Champs
1954-55	7-13	Arrowsmith	
1955-56	7-11	Arrowsmith	
1956-57	8-11	Arrowsmith	
1957-58	12-9	Arrowsmith	
1958-59	11-9	Arrowsmith	
1959-60	9-13	Arrowsmith	
1960-61	12-10	Arrowsmith	

1961-62	9-14	Arrowsmith	
1962-63	6-11	Clarence "Carney" Metzgar	
1963-64	8-14	Metzgar	
1964-65	15-7	Metzgar	
1965-66	16-6	Metzgar	
1966-67	21-3	Metzgar	Section I Champs
1967-68	22-3	Metzgar	City Series/Section I Champs
1968-69	18-7	Metzgar	City Series/Section I/District 10 Champs
1969-70	11-11	Metzgar	
1970-71	12-10	Metzgar	
1971-72	9-13	Metzgar	
1972-73	12-10	Metzgar	
1973-74	11-10	Metzgar	
1974-75	6-12	Donald "Don" Kolakowski	
1975-76	12-10	Kolakowski	
1976-77	11-10	Kolakowski	
1977-78	9-13	Kolakowski	
1978-79	10-12	Kolakowski	
1979-80	16-9	Kolakowski	
1980-81	18-11	Kolakowski	
1981-82	4-11	Kolakowski	
1982-83	6-13	Kolakowski	
1983-84	22-12	Kolakowski	District 10 AA Champs/PIAA Final Four
1984-85	12-13	Kolakowski	
1985-86	8-15	Kolakowski	
1986-87	8-14	Kolakowski	
1987-88	9-14	Kolakowski	
1988-89	4-20*	Kolakowski	
1989-90	11-13	Kolakowski	
1990-91	4-18	Chip Lewis	
1991-92	7-16	Lewis	
1992-93	12-11	Lewis	
1993-94	17-7	Lewis	
1994-95	10-15	Rick Binder	
1995-96	12-14	Binder	
1996-97	15-9	Binder	
1997-98	20-8	Bill Gausman	
1998-99	16-11	Gausman	
1999-2000	19-9	Gausman	District 10 AAA Champs
2000-01	15-9	Gausman	
2001-02	15-9	Gausman	
2002-03	12-12	George Ogeka	
2003-04	11-12	Ogeka	
2004-05	10-14	Steve Huefner	
2005-06	11-14	Huefner	
2006-07	12-12	Matt Jones	
2007-08	9-14	Jones	
2008-09	19-8	Jones	
2009-10	21-3	Jones	
2010-11	14-8	Jones	
2011-12	5-16	Jones	
2012-13	12-13	Jones	
2013-14	20-6	Jones	
2014-15	9-13	Jones	
2015-16	3-19	Jones	
2016-17	6-15	Jones	

ALL-TIME RECORD: 1207-945-2 (.561)
SIXTEEN (16) CITY SERIES CHAMPIONSHIPS (15 OURIGHT, 1 TIE)
ELEVEN (11) SECTION ONE CHAMPIONSHIPS
EIGHT (8) DISTRICT 10 CHAMPIONSHIPS (INCLUDES 3 AS D-8)
TWO (2) PIAA FINAL FOUR APPEARANCES
ONE (1) PIAA STATE FINAL APPEARANCE

Academy High School, now Collegiate Academy.

Academy's Dave Wiley, in 1939, became the first Erieite named First Team All-State by the Associated Press.

Larry Hitt, Academy '64.

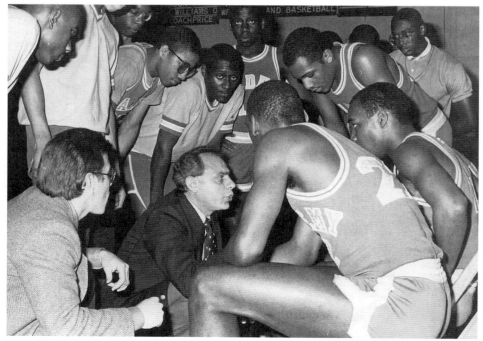

John DiTullio, Academy.

Coach Paul Demyanovich gives a pep talk to his Academy Lions.

Academy coach Don Zonno, Bob Thomas, Freddy Williams (1963).

Academy's Forney Mumford, in 1929, became the Erie School District's First African-American varsity basketball player. By 2015 every varsity player in the ESD was African-American, except one.

Ralph Drayer, Academy '82.

Academy's Walt Clark with a left-handed hook shot over Prep's Tim Niewierowski (1975).

Ty Brewington, Academy.

Steve Spearman, Academy.

Academy's great Michael Brunson '84.

Academy coach Lowell Drake.

"PeeWee" Bolden, Academy '75.

Academy's Bobby Hoffman moves the ball upcourt against the Ramblers (1970).

Curtis Barney, Academy '87.

The Academy High coaching staff, 1936.

Basketball practice on the third floor of the old Central High.

Erie Central High, later Technical High, kiddie corner from Prep.

The original Erie East High School.

East High's 1925 City Series and District 8 Champions. Front, L to R: Tommy Dowler, Augie Newcamp, Ted Meier, Syl Gromacki, Charlie "Bus" Downing; Back: n/a, Cyril "Blubber" Sullivan, Eddie Clouser, n/a, Coach Gus Anderson.

Charlie Downing, East High '26.

East High's great Eddie Woodard (1970).

Viola Andrews, East principal through the 1960s glory years.

Randy Baughman, East '87.

East High's 1930 City Champions. Front, L to R: Oscar Palmquist, Don Eppler, Earnest Forest, Howard Trostmiller, Paul Prizinski, Carl Forsberg; Back: Coach Hyde, Ken Fargo, Ed "Muckles" Hiller, George "Juda" Blossey, Abe Heller.

Tommy Dowler, East '26. He later played with the NFL's Brooklyn Dodgers.

East High's 1944 City Champions. Front, L to R: Bill Biletnikoff, Bob Swanson, Tom Andrews, Dick Praetzel, Joe Jablonski; Middle: Mgr. MacDonald, Pete Bechtos, Lee Kontis, Don George, Tom Zygai, Coach Komora; Back: Joe Novello, Pete Karuba, Art Amendola, Wally Biletnikoff.

Sid Booker, East High '68.

Chris Lucas, East High '83.

Mike Jones, East High '89.

East High's 1969 City Series, District 10 Champions. Kneeling, L to R: Goodwine, Beard; Middle: Mgr. Causgrove, McIntosh, Brown, Crotty, Woodard, Coach Metzgar; Back: Porath, Gallegos, Allen, Baker, Wilkinson, Wilcox.

Shannon Pulliam, East '84. He later became the highly successful coach at Strong Vincent.

Sil Gromacki, East High '26.

Dan Gallegos, East High '65.

McDowell High School.

Old Millcreek High School, later Westminster Jr. High.

McDowell Hall-of-Famer Mike Bartoszek '71. He later starred for Woody Hayes in football at OSU.

Dave Fragale, McDowell '86.

Tim Merryman, McDowell '81.

Jack Nill, McDowell '73.

Brent Sperry, McDowell '85.

Tim Lewis, McDowell '83.

McDowell Hall-of-Famer Tom Taylor '82.

Tony Agnello, McDowell '74.

Jim Feronti, McDowell '88.

McDowell Hall-of-Famer Rob Wagner '65.

Jeremy Metzger '92.

McDowell Hall-of-Famer Stu Shoskin '80.

McDowell great Mike Dowling drives against Prep's Tarasovitch and Alberstadt (1981).

Jim Delsandro, McDowell '92.

Millcreek's Herm Heddrick '47 had a fine career with Canisius and the New York Knicks.

Mike Bauer, McDowell '88.

McDowell Hall-of-Famer Steve "Buzz" Brandon '66.

Tony Hampy, McDowell '66.

Bobby DiBacco, McDowell '80.

Jim Sperry, McDowell '71.

Doug Zirkle, McDowell '62.

McDowell's Dillon Loomis sinks a "three" against Prep at the sold-out Hammermill Center (2007).

Bill Amann, McDowell '63.

A tense battle in the Millcreek High gym (1948).

Art Patterson, Millcreek High '47.

Erie McDowell "Trojans" Basketball History (1921-2017)

Year	Record	Coach	Team Honors
1921-22	2**-2	Bruce Goodrich	
1922-23	8-5	Mr. Schaffer	
1923-24	5-7	William Ives	ECIL Champs
1924-25	17-3	Paul Martin	ECIL Champs
1925-26	27*-3	Martin	ECIL Champs
1926-27	16-10	Martin	
1927-28	10-9	Martin	
1928-29	17-4	Martin	ECL Champs
1929-30	16-7	Martin	
1930-31	4-3	Gus Anderson	
1931-32	12-5	Anderson	
1932-33	13-5	Anderson	
1933-34	10-9	Anderson	
1934-35	5-10	Anderson	
1935-36	12-4	Anderson	
1936-37	18-5	Anderson	
1937-38	12-7	Anderson	
1938-39	21-4	Anderson	
1939-40	18-4	Anderson	
1940-41	11-7	Anderson	
1941-42	20-3	Anderson	ECL Champs
1942-43	9-3	Anderson	ECL Champs
1943-44	19-1**	Anderson	ECL Champs
1944-45	17-4	Anderson	ECL Champs
1945-46	15-7	Anderson	ECL/Section I Champs
1946-47	17-4	John Kola	ECL Champs
1947-48	16-4	Gus Anderson	
1948-49	6-11	John Kola	
1949-50	8-10	Kola	
1950-51	10-10	Kola	
1951-52	11-11	Kola	
1952-53	6-13	Naz Servidio	
1953-54	11-5	Ronald "Bud" McCoy	
1954-55	2-18	McCoy	
1955-56	6-15	McCoy	
1956-57	11-8	Al Kline	
1957-58	13-6	Kline	
1958-59	9-10	Kline	
1959-60	9-11	Kline	
1960-61	9-11	Kline	
1961-62	19-6	Kline	
1962-63	8-12	Kline	
1963-64	14-6	Kline	
1964-65	15-7	Kline	
1965-66	18-4	Kline	
1966-67	12-10	Jack Henning	
1967-68	9-12	Henning	
1968-69	11-10	Henning	
1969-70	16-6	Paul Siegel	LSL Champs (tie)
1970-71	20-4	Siegel	Section I/LSL/District 10 Champs
1971-72	9-12	Siegel	
1972-73	11-11	Siegel	
1973-74	13-9	Siegel	
1974-75	9-13	Richard "Dick" Fuller	
1975-76	17-7	Fuller	
1976-77	16-7	Fuller	
1977-78	18-5	Fuller	
1978-79	16-8	Fuller	
1979-80	27-5	James "Jim" Romaniszyn	PIAA Final Four
1980-81	21-7	Romaniszyn	District 10 Champs
1981-82	23-9	Romaniszyn	Section I/District 10 Champs

Michael Beck the 2014 Region "Player of the Year."

Year	Record	Coach	Team Honors
1982-83	14-13	Richard "Rick" Fessler	
1983-84	7-21*	Fessler	
1984-85	15-9	Fessler	
1985-86	24-4	Fessler	District 10 Champs
1986-87	9-17	Fessler	
1987-88	8-16	Fessler	
1988-89	13-11	Fessler	
1989-90	16-9	Fessler	
1990-91	21-7	Pete Flinn	
1991-92	25-3	Flinn	Metro/District 10 Champs
1992-93	21-5	Flinn	
1993-94	19-8	Flinn	
1994-95	22-5	Flinn	
1995-96	23-8	Flinn	District 10 Champs/PIAA Final Four
1996-97	16-9	Flinn	
1997-98	13-12	Flinn	
1998-99	26-5	Flinn	Metro/District 10 Champs/PIAA Western Champs
1999-2000	27*-1**	Flinn	Metro/District 10 Champs
2000-01	18-7	Flinn	
2001-02	20-7	Thomas "Tom" Hansen	District 10 Champs
2002-03	20-7	Hansen	
2003-04	26-2	Hansen	Metro/District 10 Champs
2004-05	17-10	Hansen	
2005-06	10-16	Hansen	
2006-07	17-9	Hansen	
2007-08	26-3	Kraig Hetz	District 10 Champions
2008-09	16-7	Hetz	
2009-10	14-9	Hetz	
2010-11	17-9	Hetz	
2011-12	9-12	Hetz	
2012-13	14-10	Kevin O'Connor	
2013-14	23-4	O'Connor	District 10 Champions
2014-15	18-7	O'Connor	Region 7 Champs (tie)/District 10 Champs
2015-16	9-14	O'Connor	
2016-17	13-10	O'Connor	

ALL-TIME RECORD: 1406-754 (.651)
TEN (10) ERIE COUNTY LEAGUE CHAMPIONSHIPS (INCLUDES ERIE COUNTY INTERSCHOLASTIC LEAGUE)
THREE (3) SECTION ONE CHAMPIONSHIPS
TWO (2) LAKE SHORE LEAGUE CHAMPIONSHIPS (1 OUTRIGHT, 1 TIE)
FOUR (4) METRO LEAGUE CHAMPIONSHIPS
ONE (1) REGION CHAMPIONSHIP (TIE)
THIRTEEN (13) DISTRICT 10 CHAMPIONSHIPS
THREE (3) PIAA FINAL FOUR APPEARANCES
ONE (1) PIAA STATE FINAL APPEARANCE

Erie Mercyhurst Prep "Lakers" History (1974-2017)

Year	Record	Coach	Team Honors
1974-75	9-4	Joe Cook	
1975-76	12-9	Cook	PONY Conf. of Private Schools
1976-77	14-7	Ed Zenewicz	Upper Allegheny Valley League Champs
1977-78	19-8	Zenewicz	UAVL Champs
1978-79	15-11	Zenewicz	UAVL Champs
1979-80	20-9	Zenewicz	UAVL Champs
1980-81	25-5	Zenewicz	District 10 AA Champs
1981-82	11-11	Zenewicz	
1982-83	6-19	Zenewicz	
1983-84	3**-16	Zenewicz	
1984-85	5-16	Zenewicz	1st year Metro League
1985-86	5-19	Zenewicz	
1986-87	15-13	Zenewicz	
1987-88	14-10	Zenewicz	

Mercyhurst Prep.

Pat Flaherty, highly successful coach at Mercyhurst Prep, now at Fairview.

Mercyhurst's Jovan Johnson '01 had a tremendous football career at Iowa and the CFL.

1988-89	7-15	Zenewicz	
1989-90	9-18	Zenewicz	
1990-91	27*-5	Greg Majchrzak	District 10/PIAA AA State Champs
1991-92	15-11	Al Rush	
1992-93	7-15	Bill Gausman	
1993-94	9-14	Gausman	
1994-95	14-13	Gausman	
1995-96	7-17	Gausman	
1996-97	3**-21*	Gausman	
1997-98	12-16	Bob Amendola	
1998-99	16-12	Amendola	
1999-2000	10-15	Art Laird	
2000-01	18-10	Pat Flaherty	
2001-02	26-5	Flaherty	N. Broward Holiday/D-10 Champs/ PIAA AA Final Four
2002-03	15-13	Flaherty	
2003-04	9-16	Flaherty	
2004-05	17-8	Flaherty	
2005-06	21-8	Flaherty	District 10 AA Champs
2006-07	16-9	Flaherty	
2007-08	15-10	Flaherty	
2008-09	22-4	Flaherty	Region 4 Champs (tie)
2009-10	25-4	Flaherty	Region 4 Champs
2010-11	14-12	Sean Baer	
2011-12	24-3**	Baer	Region 5/District 10 AA Champs
2012-13	18-10	Baer	Region 4 Champs
2013-14	19-8	Baer	
2014-15	14-12	Baer	
2015-16	10-13	Baer	
2016-17	12-11	Baer	

ALL-TIME RECORD: 604-485 (.555)
FOUR (4) UAVL CHAMPIONSHIPS
FOUR (4) REGION CHAMPIONSHIPS (3 OUTRIGHT, 1 TIE)
FIVE (5) DISTRICT 10 CHAMPIONSHIPS
TWO (2) PIAA FINAL FOUR APPEARANCES
ONE (1) STATE CHAMPIONSHIP

Erie Strong Vincent "Colonels" History (1930-2017)

Year	Record	Coach	Team Honors
1930-31	12-12	Harold "Sam" Kramer	
1931-32	24-3-1	Kramer	City Series/District 10 Champs/State Final
1932-33	16-5	Kramer	
1933-34	9-9	Kramer	
1934-35	10-9	Kramer	
1935-36	21-5	Kramer	City Series Champs
1936-37	16-9	Kramer	
1937-38	12-14	Kramer	
1938-39	9-12-1	Kramer	
1939-40	9-12	Kramer	
1940-41	5-14	Kramer	
1941-42	11-11	Kramer	
1942-43	8-11	Reno Strand	
1943-44	8-15	Strand	
1944-45	5-14	Vince Bell	
1945-46	13-8	Bell	
1946-47	11-8	Art "Duke" Detzel	
1947-48	7-9	Mike Ferrare	
1948-49	11-6	Vince Bell	
1949-50	5-14	Bell	
1950-51	6-12	Bell	
1951-52	13-6	Bell	City Series Champs (tie)
1952-53	2**-18	Ralph "Baron" Calabrese	
1953-54	12-8	Calabrese	
1954-55	21-2	Calabrese	City Series/Section I/District 10 Champs
1955-56	11-6	Calabrese	
1956-57	19-4	Calabrese	City Series/Section I/District 10 Champs
1957-58	17-5	Calabrese	City Series/Section I/District 10 Champs
1958-59	19-4	Calabrese	Section I/District 10 Champs
1959-60	16-8	Calabrese	Section I/District 10 Champs
1960-61	17-3	Calabrese	
1961-62	16-8	Calabrese	
1962-63	14-7	Calabrese	
1963-64	15-7	Calabrese	Section I Champs
1964-65	17-7	Calabrese	Section I/District 10 Champs

Year	Record	Coach	Team Honors
1965-66	19-3	Calabrese	City Series/Big 6/Section I Champs
1966-67	14-5	Calabrese	City Series/Section I (tie) Champs
1967-68	8-9	Calabrese	
1968-69	13-6	Calabrese	
1969-70	14-10	Calabrese	Section I/District 10 Champs
1970-71	4-13	Robert "Bob" Trombacco	
1971-72	15-7	Trombacco	Section I/District 10 Champs
1972-73	19-6	Trombacco	City Series/LSL/District 10 Champs
1973-74	9-11	Trombacco	
1974-75	11-5	Trombacco	
1975-76	19-5	Trombacco	City Series/Section I/District 10 Champs
1976-77	9-9	Walt Watral	
1977-78	9-10	Pete Flinn	
1978-79	20-5	Flinn	Section I Champs
1979-80	7-14	Flinn	
1980-81	13-11	Flinn	
1981-82	11-8	Flinn	
1982-83	10-13	Flinn	
1983-84	14-13	Flinn	
1984-85	29*-1**	Flinn	Metro/District 10/PIAA AAA State Champs
1985-86	14-13	Flinn	
1986-87	21-7	Flinn	District 10 AAA Champs
1987-88	22-8	Flinn	District 10 AAA Champs
1988-89	19-9	Flinn	District 10 AAA Champs
1989-90	10-13	Flinn	
1990-91	13-15	Andrew "Andy" Sisinni	
1991-92	10-15	Sisinni	
1992-93	9-15	Sisinni	
1993-94	11-12	Sisinni	
1994-95	5-20	Sisinni	
1995-96	2-22*	John Bowen	
1996-97	13-12	Bowen	
1997-98	9-16	Bowen	
1998-99	6-16	Cass Wright	
1999-2000	10-13	Shannon Pullium	
2000-01	9-15	Pullium	
2001-02	17-8	Pullium	
2002-03	22-7	Pullium	Metro Champs
2003-04	18-10	Pullium	
2004-05	23-8	Pullium	PIAA AAA Final Four
2005-06	21-7	Pullium	
2006-07	18-8	Pullium	
2007-08	16-8	Pullium	
2008-09	14-9	Pullium	
2009-10	19-6	Pullium	
2010-11	12-11	Pullium	
2011-12	15-10	Pullium	Region 8 Champs (tie)
2012-13	14-12	Pullium	
2013-14	17-9	Pullium	
2014-15	17-9	Pullium	
2015-16	19-8	Pullium	Region 7/District 10 AAA Champs
2016-17	27-4	Pullium	Region 6/District 10/PIAA State Final

ALL-TIME RECORD: 1166-824-2 (.586)
TEN (10) CITY SERIES CHAMPIONSHIPS (9 OUTRIGHT, 1 TIE)
THIRTEEN (13) SECTION ONE CHAMPIONSHIPS (12 OUTRIGHT, 1 TIE)
ONE (1) BIG SIX CHAMPIONSHIP
TWO (2) METRO LEAGUE CHAMPIONSHIPS
THREE (3) REGION CHAMPIONSHIPS (2 OUTRIGHT, 1 TIE)
SEVENTEEN (17) DISTRICT 10 CHAMPIONSHIPS
THREE (3) PIAA FINAL FOUR APPEARANCES
THREE (3) PIAA STATE FINALS APPEARANCES
ONE (1) PIAA STATE CHAMPIONSHIP

Erie Tech Memorial "Centaurs" History (1931-1992)

Year	Record	Coach	Team Honors
1931-32	7-8	Eddie Abramoski	
1932-33	12-3	Abramoski	
1933-34	6-10	Abramoski	
1934-35	13-7	Abramoski	
1935-36	17-5	Abramoski	
1936-37	13-9	Abramoski	
1937-38	12-6	Abramoski	
1938-39	7-8	Abramoski	
1939-40	8-9	Abramoski	
1940-41	12-7	Albert "Al" Calabrese	
1941-42	4**-15	William "String" Nash	
1942-43	9-9	Nash	
1943-44	6-11	Nash	
1944-45	17-3	Robert "Ted" Robb	City Series/Section I Champs
1945-46	17-7	Robb	City Series Champs
1946-47	10-9	Robb	
1947-48	10-8	Robb	
1948-49	16-7	Albert "Al" Calabrese	
1949-50	14-9	Calabrese	City Series Champs (tie)
1950-51	16-6	Calabrese	City Series (tie)/Section I Champs
1951-52	18-8	Calabrese	City Series (tie)/Section I Champs
1952-53	18-5	Calabrese	Section I Champs
1953-54	10-12	Calabrese	
1954-55	11-9	Robert "Ted" Robb	
1955-56	16-4	Robb	City Series/Section I Champs
1956-57	8-10	Robb	
1957-58	9-12	Albert "Al" Calabrese	
1958-59	8-12	Walter "Walt" Strosser	

Year	Record	Coach	Team Honors
1959-60	18-4	Albert "Al" Calabrese	
1960-61	21-2	Calabrese	City Series/Section I Champs
1961-62	20-7	Calabrese	Section I Champs
1962-63	25*-2**	Calabrese	City Series/Section I/District 10 Champs/Western Final
1963-64	16-6	Calabrese	
1964-65	13-9	Calabrese	
1965-66	14-6	Calabrese	
1966-67	6-15	Calabrese	
1967-68	5-13	Calabrese	
1968-69	8-14	Calabrese	
1969-70	5-16	Calabrese	
1970-71	6-15	Calabrese	
1971-72	11-11	Calabrese	
1972-73	19-7	Calabrese	Section I Champs
1973-74	10-9	Calabrese	
1974-75	4**-12	Calabrese	
1975-76	11-11	Calabrese	
1976-77	5-18	Johnny Johnson	
1977-78	8-13	Johnson	
1978-79	6-16	Johnson	
1979-80	7-14	Johnson	
1980-81	10-12	James "Jim" Marnella	
1981-82	4**-11	Marnella	
1982-83	19-8	Marnella	
1983-84	18-7	Marnella	
1984-85	17-7	Marnella	District 10 Champs
1985-86	11-13	Marnella	
1986-87	9-15	Marnella	
1987-88	11-14	Mark Behringer	
1988-89	5-18	Johnny Johnson	
1989-90	4**-19*	Johnson	
1990-91	10-13	Dan Chojnacki	
1991-92	5-16	Chojnacki	

FINAL ALL-TIME RECORD: 685-601 (.533)
EIGHT (8) CITY SERIES CHAMPIONSHIPS (5 OUTRIGHT, 3 TIES)
NINE (9) SECTION ONE CHAMPIONSHIPS
TWO (2) DISTRICT 10 CHAMPIONSHIPS
ONE (1) PIAA FINAL FOUR APPEARANCE

Erie Villa Maria "Victors" Basketball History (1992-2010)

Year	Record	Coach	Team Honors
1992-93	2**-16	Don Myers	
1993-94	2**-21*	Myers	
1994-95	6-18	Myers	
1995-96	5-19	Myers	
1996-97	10-14	Mark Majewski	
1997-98	12-12	Majewski	
1998-99	15-12	Majewski	
1999-2000	20-4**	Majewski	
2000-01	15-8	Majewski	
2001-02	9-15	Majewski	
2002-03	9-16	Majewski	1st year in Metro League
2003-04	11-14	Majewski	Last year of Metro League
2004-05	13-13	Majewski	
2005-06	21*-9	Majewski	Ranked 5th in state
2006-07	4-20	Joe Lunger	
2007-08	10-14	Lunger	
2008-09	19-5	Lunger	
2009-10	16-7	Lunger	

ALL-TIME RECORD: 199-237 (.456)

Corry High "Beavers" Basketball History (1944-1951)
(While in Section One Only)

Year	Record	Coach	Team Honors
1944-45	16*-11	John Tinson	
1945-46	8-15	John Milanovich	
1946-47	11-10**	Lou Hanna	
1947-48	12-11	Hanna	
1948-49	12-11	Hanna	
1949-50	7-15	Hanna	
1950-51	5**-18*	Hanna	

OVERALL RECORD WHILE IN SECTION ONE: 71-91 (.438)

George Junior Republic "Tigers" History (2004-2012)
(While in Regions 6, 7 & 8 Only)

Year	Record	Coach	Team Honors
2004-05	3**-17*	Pat Devine	
2005-06	12*-9**	Gary Revale	
2006-07	6-12	Revale	
2007-08	5-16	Revale	
2008-09	8-14	Brad Landfair	
2009-10	8-14	Landfair	
2010-11	6-13	Pat Devine	
2011-12	8-13	Devine	

OVERALL RECORD WHILE IN REGIONS 6, 7, & 8: 56-108 (.341)

The 1972 Jamestown Red Raiders, LSL Champions.

Michelle Sertz, with a wonderful rendition of the National Anthem at the 1996 McDonald's Classic.

Harborcreek "Huskies" Basketball History (1954-1965)
(While in Section One Only)

Year	Record		Coach	Team Honors
1954-55	8-10	Lloyd Leary		
1955-56	3**-14	Leary		
1956-57	4-13	Robert Black		
1957-58	6-11	Black		
1958-59	4-14	Black		
1959-60	6-12	Leroy Pallotto		
1960-61	5-10	Pallotto		
1961-62	8-10	Pallotto		
1962-63	10*-7**	Pallotto		
1963-64	4-16*	Pallotto		
1964-65	5-14	Pallotto		

OVERALL RECORD WHILE IN SECTION ONE: 63-131 (.325)

Jamestown (NY) High "Red Raiders" History (1969-1973)
(While in Lake Shore League Only)

Year	Record		Coach	Team Honors
1969-70	2**-16*	John "Dutch" Leonard		
1970-71	10-10	Leonard		
1971-72	19*-2**	Leonard		LSL Champs
1972-73	3-16*	Leonard		
OVERALL RECORD WHILE IN LSL:			34-44 (.436)	

ONE (1) LAKE SHORE LEAGUE CHAMPIONSHIP

The tuxedoed McDonald's Girls at the 1998 Classic! L to R: Michelle Sertz, Andrea Antolik, Tracy Seib, Antera Sertz.

Erie City Series Champions
(Overall Record, Coach)
* Academy, Erie High
1920—Erie High School (11-4, D. G. "Doc" Evans)
*Academy, Central (1920-21 to 1921-22)
1921—Central (13-3, Marcelle LaFramboise)
*Academy, Central, East
1922—Central (14-4, Gus Anderson)
1923—Central (16-8, Andy Fletcher)
1924—East (15-6, Gus Anderson)
1925—East (21-2, Gus Anderson)
1926—East (25-2, Gus Anderson)
1927—Central (15-5, Jim Hyde)
1928—Central (17-7, Jim Hyde)
1929—Academy (20-2, Darby Mannix)
1930—East (19-5, Jim Hyde)
*Academy, East, Vincent
1931—Academy (21-4, Howard Kelly)
*Academy, East, Tech, Vincent
1932—Vincent (25-2-1, Sam Kramer)
1933—East (13-6, Jim Hyde)
1934—East (15-6, Jim Hyde)
1935—East (21-6, Jack Komora)
1936—Vincent (21-5, Sam Kramer)
1937—East (16-9, Jack Komora)
1938—East (16-7, Jack Komora)
1939—Academy (14-8, "Pee Wee" Thomas)
1940—Academy (14-2-2, "Pee Wee" Thomas)
1941—East (18-6-1, Jack Komora)
1942—East (14-5, Jack Komora)
*Academy, East, Prep, Tech, Vincent
1943—East (16-6, Jack Komora)
1944—East (20-9, Jack Komora)
1945—Tech (17-3, Ted Robb)
1946—Tech (17-7, Ted Robb)
1947—Prep (19-6, Walt Strosser)
1948—Academy (18-5, Jack Komora)
1949—Prep (19-6, Dick Detzel)
1950—Prep (12-7, Dick Detzel), East (14-11, Bob Arrowsmith) & Tech (14-7, Al Calabrese) [tie]
1951—Prep (15-5, Dick Detzel), Academy (10-10, Jack Komora) & Tech (16-6, Al Calabrese) [tie]
1952—Prep (12-6, Dick Detzel), Vincent (13-6, Vince Bell) & Tech (18-8, Al Calabrese) [tie]
1953—Prep (23-4, Dick Detzel)
1954—Prep (22-3, Dick Detzel)
1955—Vincent (21-2, Ralph Calabrese)
1956—Tech (16-4, Ted Robb)
1957—Vincent (19-4, Ralph Calabrese)
1958—Vincent (17-5, Ralph Calabrese)
1959—Prep (16-6, Bob Trombacco)
1960—Prep (17-6, Bob Trombacco)
1961—Tech (21-2, Al Calabrese)
1962—Prep (17-9, Bob Trombacco)
1963—Tech (25-2, Al Calabrese)
1964—Prep (18-3, "Red" Murray)
1965—Prep (17-5, "Red" Murray)
1966—Vincent (19-3, Ralph Calabrese)
1967—Vincent (14-5, Ralph Calabrese)
1968—East (22-3, Carney Metzgar)
1969—East (18-7, Carney Metzgar)
1970—Prep (18-6, Dick Fox)
1971—Prep (21-3, Dick Fox)
1972—Prep (18-5, Bill Flaherty)
1973—Vincent (19-7, Bob Trombacco)
1974—Academy (24-1, Lou DiBacco)
1975—Academy (19-5, Lou DiBacco)
1976—Vincent (19-5, Bob Trombacco)
1977—Prep (20-5, Bill Flaherty)

Big Seven Champions
(Overall Record, Coach)
* Academy, Corry, East, Millcreek, Prep, Tech, Vincent
1949—Prep (19-6, Dick Detzel)
1950—Prep (12-7, Dick Detzel), East (14-11, Bob Arrowsmith) [tie]
1951—Prep (15-5, Dick Detzel) & Tech (16-6, Al Calabrese) [tie]

Big Six Champions
(Overall Record, Coach)
* Academy, East, Millcreek, Prep, Tech, Vincent
1952—Prep (12-6, Dick Detzel) & Tech (18-8, Al Calabrese) [tie]
1953—Prep (23-4, Dick Detzel)
* Academy, East, McDowell, Prep, Tech, Vincent
1966—Vincent (19-3, Ralph Calabrese)

Lake Shore League Champions
(Overall Record, Coach)
* Academy, East, Jamestown (NY), McDowell, Prep, Tech, Vincent
1970—Prep (18-6, Dick Fox) & McDowell (16-6, Paul Siegel)
1971—McDowell (20-4, Paul Siegel)
1972—Jamestown (19-2, "Dutch" Leonard)
1973—Vincent (19-7, Bob Trombacco)

Section One Champions
(Overall Record, Coach)
*Playoff between City Series and Erie County League A champs
1941—East (18-6-1, Jack Komora)
1942—East (14-5, Jack Komora)
1943—East (16-6, Jack Komora)
1944—East (20-9, Jack Komora)
1945—Tech (17-3, Ted Robb)
1946—Millcreek (15-7, Gus Anderson)
1947—East (13-6, Bob Arrowsmith)
* Academy, Corry, East, Tech, Vincent
1948—Academy (18-5, Jack Komora)
* Academy, Corry, East, Millcreek, Tech, Vincent
1949—East (14-8, Bob Arrowsmith)
1950—East (14-11, Bob Arrowsmith)
1951—Tech (16-6, Al Calabrese)
* Academy, East, Millcreek, Tech, Vincent
1952—Tech (18-8, Al Calabrese)
1953—Tech (18-5, Al Calabrese)
1954—Tech (16-10, Bob Arrowsmith)
*Academy, East, Harborcreek, McDowell, Tech, Vincent
1955—Vincent (21-2, Ralph Calabrese)
1956—Tech (16-4, Ted Robb)
1957—Vincent (19-4, Ralph Calabrese)
1958—Vincent (17-5, Ralph Calabrese)
1959—Vincent (19-4, Ralph Calabrese)
1960—Vincent (16-8, Ralph Calabrese)
1961—Tech (21-2, Al Calabrese)
1962—Tech (20-6, Al Calabrese)
1963—Tech (25-2, Al Calabrese)
1964—Vincent (15-7, Ralph Calabrese)
1965—Vincent (17-7, Ralph Calabrese)
*Academy, East, McDowell, Tech, Vincent
1966—Vincent (19-3, Ralph Calabrese)
1967—East (21-3, Carney Metzgar) & Vincent (14-5, Ralph Calabrese) [tie]
1968—East (22-3, Carney Metzgar)
1969—East (18-7, Carney Metzgar)
1970—Vincent (14-10, Ralph Calabrese)
1971—McDowell (20-4, Paul Siegel)
1972—Vincent (15-7, Bob Trombacco)
1973—Tech (19-6, Al Calabrese)
* Academy, East, McDowell, Prep, Tech, Vincent (Metro League)
1974—Academy (24-1, Lou DiBacco)
1975—Academy (19-5, Lou DiBacco)
1976—Vincent (19-5, Bob Trombacco)
1977—Prep (20-5, Bill Flaherty)
1978—Prep (26-3, Bill Flaherty)
1979—Vincent (20-5, Pete Flinn)
1980—Prep (33-1, Bill Flaherty)
1981—Prep (20-8, Bill Flaherty)
1982—McDowell (23-9, Jim Romaniszyn)
1983—Prep (20-10, Bill Flaherty)
1984—Prep (27-6, Bill Flaherty)

Metro League Champions
(Overall Record, Coach)
* Academy, East, McDowell, Mercyhurst, Prep, Tech, Vincent
1985—Vincent (29-1, Pete Flinn)
1986—McDowell (24-4, Rick Fessler)
1987—Academy (20-8, Paul Demyanovich)
1988—Prep (24-5, Marcel Arribi)
1989—Prep (19-8, Marcel Arribi)
1990—Prep (21-5, Marcel Arribi)
1991—Prep (23-5, Marcel Arribi)
1992—McDowell (25-3, Pete Flinn)
* Central, East, McDowell, Mercyhurst, Prep, Vincent
1993—McDowell (21-5, Pete Flinn)
1994—Prep (24-7, Marcel Arribi)
1995—Prep (25-4, Marcel Arribi)
1996—Prep (24-8, Marcel Arribi)
1997—Prep (24-3, Marcel Arribi)
1998—Prep (17-10, Marcel Arribi)
1999—McDowell (26-5, Pete Flinn)
2000—McDowell (27-1, Pete Flinn)
2001—Central (20-8, John Bowen)
2002—Prep (19-10, Andy Sisinni)
* Central, East, McDowell, Mercyhurst, Prep, Villa Maria, Vincent
2003—Vincent (22-7, Shannon Pullium)
2004—McDowell (26-2, Tom Hansen)

Region 6 Champions
(Overall Record, Coach)
* Central, George Junior Republic, McDowell, Prep,
2005—Prep (26-5, Brian Flanagan)
2006—Prep (22-6, Brian Flanagan)

Region 7 Champions
(Overall Record, Coach)
* Central, East, George Junior Republic, McDowell, Prep, Vincent
2007—Prep (23-5, Brian Flanagan)
2008—Prep (18-8, Brian Flanagan)
* George Junior Republic, McDowell, Prep, Vincent

2009—McDowell (14-9, Kevin Hetz)
2010—Vincent (19-6, Shannon Pullium)
* Central Tech, McDowell, Prep
2013—Prep (23-3, Mark Majewski)
2014—Prep (15-8, Mark Majewski)
*Central Tech, East, McDowell, Prep, Vincent
2015—Prep (22-7, Mark Majewski) & McDowell (18-7, Kevin O'Connor)
2016—Vincent (19-8, Shannon Pullium)
*Central Tech, East, McDowell, Prep, Vincent
2017—Meadville (26-2, Mark McElhinney)

Region 8 Champions
(Overall Record, Coach)
* George Junior Republic, McDowell, Prep, Vincent
2011— Prep (14-10, Mark Majewski)
2012— Prep (21-6, Mark Majewski) & Vincent (15-10, Shannon Pullium) [tie]

PIAA District 10
Large School Champions
(Erie teams in BOLD) (Overall Record, Coach)
*Erie teams which won smaller division titles are also listed.
When known as N.W.P.I.A.L.
1920—Sharon (20-5, A. Warner "Pop" Dickerson)
1921—Oil City (17-5, Bill Fountain)
1922—Franklin (10-12, R.M. Atticks)
1923—East High (11-5, Gus Anderson)
When known as District 8
1924—Greenville Penn (14-9, Harry Pierson)
1925—East High (21-2, Gus Anderson)
1926—East High (25-2, Gus Anderson) *STATE FINALIST*
1927—Sharon (25-2, A. Warner "Pop" Dickerson) *STATE FINALIST*
1928—Sharon (15-8, A. Warner "Pop" Dickerson)
1929—Sharon (18-4, A. Warner "Pop" Dickerson) *WESTERN CHAMPS*
1930—Sharon (23-1, A. Warner "Pop" Dickerson) * STATE CHAMPS*
1931—Farrell (22-3, William Ganaposki)
District 8 designation changed to District 10
1932—Strong Vincent (25-2-1, Sam Kramer) *WESTERN CHAMPS*
1933—East High (13-6, Jim Hyde)
1934—East High (15-6, Jim Hyde)
1935—East High (21-6, Jack Komora)
1936—Sharon (18-5, A. Warner "Pop" Dickerson)
1937—Sharon (18-4, Pete Collodi)
1938—Farrell (23-4, Tudor Lewis)
1939—Academy (14-8, Edmund L. Thomas)
1940—Farrell (25-6, Tudor Lewis)
1941—Sharpsville (22-5, Harry Sigel)
1942—Sharon (20-5, Pete Collodi) *WESTERN CHAMPS*
1943—Farrell (23-2, Tudor Lewis) *WESTERN CHAMPS*
1944—Sharon (22-3, Donald "Dudey" Moore)
1945 A—Sharpsville (23-5, Bob "Red" Johnston)
1946 A—Warren (22-4, Joe Massa)
1947 A—Titusville (18-4, J. Gordon Smock)
1948 A—Warren (27-4, Joe Massa)
1949 A—Sharpsville (23-5, Bob "Red" Johnston)
1950 A—Hickory (23-6, Keith Stoner)
1951 A—Sharpsville (16-12, Bob "Red" Johnston)
1952 A—Meadville (17-8, John Joy)
1953 A—Meadville (21-5, John Joy)
1954 A—Meadville (28-2, John Joy)
1955 A—Strong Vincent (21-2, Ralph Calabrese)
1956 A—Meadville (19-6, John Joy)
1957 A—Strong Vincent (19-4, Ralph Calabrese)
1958 A—Strong Vincent (17-5, Ralph Calabrese)
1959 A—Strong Vincent (19-4, Ralph Calabrese)
1960 A—Strong Vincent (16-8, Ralph Calabrese)
1961 A—Hickory (25-2, Fran Webster) *WESTERN CHAMPS*
1962 A—Meadville (23-2, Norm Sundstrom)
1963 A—Tech Memorial (25-2, Al Calabrese)
1964 A—Meadville (18-7, Norm Sundstrom)
1965 A—Strong Vincent (17-7, Ralph Calabrese)
1966 A—Meadville (21-4, Norm Sundstrom)
1967 A—Hickory (19-5, Ed McGlumphy)
1968 A—East High (22-3, Carney Metzgar)
1969 A—East High (18-7, Carney Metzgar)
1970 A—Strong Vincent (14-10, Ralph Calabrese)
1971 A—McDowell (20-4, Paul Siegel)
1972 A—Strong Vincent (15-7, Bob Trombacco)
1973 A—Strong Vincent (19-7, Bob Trombacco)
1974 A—Academy (24-1, Lou DiBacco)
1975 A—Cathedral Prep (22-6, Bill Flaherty)
1976 AAA—Strong Vincent (19-5, Bob Trombacco)
1977 AAA—Cathedral Prep (20-5, Bill Flaherty)
1978 AAA—Cathedral Prep (26-3, Bill Flaherty)
1979 AAA—Cathedral Prep (23-5, Bill Flaherty)
1980 AAA—Cathedral Prep (33-1, Bill Flaherty) *STATE CHAMPS*
1981 AAA—McDowell (21-7, Jim Romaniszyn)
*1981 AA—Mercyhurst Prep (25-5, Ed Zenewicz)

1982 AAA—**McDowell** (23-8, Jim Romaniszyn)
1983 AAA—Warren (26-2, Andy Randas)
1984 AAAA—Meadville (30-3, Norm Price)
1984 AAAA (2nd)—**Cathedral Prep** (27-6, Bill Flaherty) *WESTERN CHAMPS*
*1984 AAA—**Academy** (20-10, Paul Demyanovich)
*1984 AA—**East High** (22-12, Don Kolakowski)
1985 AAAA—**Tech Memorial** (17-7, Jim Marnella)
1985 AAA—Strong Vincent (29-1, Pete Flinn) *STATE CHAMPS
1986 AAAA—**McDowell** (24-4, Rick Fessler)
*1986 AAA—**Academy** (22-5, Paul Demyanovich
1987 AAAA—Meadville (28-3, Norm Price) *WESTERN CHAMPS*
*1987 AAA—**Strong Vincent** (21-7, Pete Flinn)
1988 AAAA—**Cathedral Prep** (24-5, Marcel Arribi)
*1988 AAA—**Strong Vincent** (22-8, Pete Flinn)
1989 AAAA—Meadville (24-4, Norm Price)
*1989 AAA—**Strong Vincent** (19-9, Pete Flinn)
1990 AAAA—**Cathedral Prep** (21-5, Marcel Arribi)
1991 AAAA—**Cathedral Prep** (23-5, Marcel Arribi)
1991 AA—Mercyhurst Prep (27-5, Greg Majchrzak) *STATE CHAMPS
1992 AAAA—**McDowell** (25-3, Pete Flinn)
*1993 AAA—**Academy** (23-6, Tom Whalen)
1993 AAAA—Cathedral Prep (21-7, Marcel Arribi) *STATE CHAMPS*
1994 AAAA—**Cathedral Prep** (24-7, Marcel Arribi) *WESTERN CHAMPS*
1995 AAAA—**Cathedral Prep** (25-4, Marcel Arribi)
1996 AAAA—**McDowell** (23-8, Pete Flinn)
1996 AAAA (2nd)—**Cathedral Prep** (24-8, Marcel Arribi) *WESTERN CHAMPS*
1997 AAAA—**Cathedral Prep** (24-3, Marcel Arribi)
1998 AAAA—**Cathedral Prep** (17-10, Marcel Arribi)
1999 AAAA—**McDowell** (26-5, Pete Flinn) *WESTERN CHAMPS*
2000 AAAA—**McDowell** (27-1, Pete Flinn)
2001 AAAA—George Junior Republic (25-4, Bob McConnell)
2002 AAAA—**McDowell** (20-7, Tom Hansen)
*2002 AA—**Mercyhurst Prep** (26-5, Pat Flaherty)
2003 AAAA—George Junior Republic (16-11, Bob McConnell)
2004 AAAA—**McDowell** (26-2, Tom Hansen)
2005 AAAA—**Cathedral Prep** (26-5, Brian Flanagan)
2006 AAAA—**Cathedral Prep** (22-6, Brian Flanagan)
*2006 AA—**Mercyhurst Prep** (21-8, Pat Flaherty)
2007 AAAA—**Cathedral Prep** (23-5, Brian Flanagan)
2008 AAAA—**McDowell** (27-3, Kraig Hetz)
2009 AAAA—**Cathedral Prep** (17-10, Mark Majewski)
2010 AAAA—**Strong Vincent** (19-6, Shannon Pullium)
*2010 AA—**Mercyhurst Prep** (25-4, Pat Flaherty)
2011 AAAA—**Cathedral Prep** (14-10, Mark Majewski)
2012 AAAA—**Cathedral Prep** (21-6, Mark Majewski)
2013 AAAA—**Cathedral Prep** (23-3, Mark Majewski)
2014 AAAA—**McDowell** (23-4, Kevin O'Connor)
2015 AAAA—**McDowell** (18-7, Kevin O'Connor)
*2015 AAA—**Cathedral Prep** (22-7, Mark Majewski)
2016 AAAA—**Central Tech** (14-11, Tom Koval)
2016 AAA—**Strong Vincent** (19-8, Shannon Pullium)
2017 4-A—**Strong Vincent** (27-4, Shannon Pullium) *STATE FINALIST*
2017 5-A—Meadville (26-2, Mark McElhinny) *STATE FINALIST*

Pennsylvania (PIAA) Large School State Champions

(Erie teams games in BOLD) (Overall Record, Coach)
*Erie teams which won smaller division titles are also listed.

1920—Harrisburg Tech (21-2, Clarence Miller)	38-34	Bellevue
1921—McKeesport (24-0, A. H. Clyde)	24-21	Williamsport (Earl Bartholomew)
1922—Mahanoy City (23-3, Johnny Goepfert)	22-17	Harrisburg Tech (19-7, Ike McCord)
1923—Nanticoke (Frank McDermott)	23-21	Monessen
1924—Homestead (George Gould)	32-21	Nanticoke (Frank McDermott)
1925—Uniontown (31-2, Abe "Pop" Everhart, Sr.)	21-14	Williamsport (Earl Bartholomew)
1926—Nanticoke (28-1, Dick Leary)	**44-25**	**Erie East High (25-2, Gus Anderson)**
1927—Steelton (23-1, J. Nelson Hoffman)	34-26	Sharon (25-2, A. Warner "Pop" Dickerson)
1928—Hazleton (19-1, Hugh McGeehan)	35-31	Lewistown
1929—Hazleton (21-0, Hugh McGeehan)	34-22	Sharon (18-4, A. Warner "Pop" Dickerson)
1930—Sharon (23-1, A. Warner "Pop" Dickerson)	18-14	Lower Merion (25-1, Bill Anderson)
1931—North Braddock Scott (26-5, Johnny Reed)	28-15	Lower Merion (22-2, Bill Anderson)
1932—Old Forge (21-0, Danny Semenza)	**24-19**	**Erie Strong Vincent (25-2-1, Sam Kramer)**
1933—Lower Merion (24-2, Bill Anderson)	21-16	Altoona (19-1, "Snaps" Emanuel)
1934—Pittsburgh South High (32-0, Grover "Pappy" Washabaugh)	42-17	Reading (15-4, Johnny Dietrich)
1935—Allentown (28-2, J. Birney Crum)	32-19	Rankin (27-4, "Jock" Rosenberg)
1936—Newport Township (16-2, Chet Rogowicz)	36-34	New Castle (20-4, Phil Bridenbaugh)
1937—Pittsburgh South High (25-1, Grover "Pappy" Washabaugh)	38-28	Newport Township (28-2, Chet Rogowicz)
1938—Hazleton (23-1, Hugh McGeehan)	29-27	Altoona (19-2, "Snaps" Emanuel)
1939—Homestead (22-6, Paul Birch)	29-24	Lower Merion (22-2, Bill Anderson)
1940—Lebanon (18-5, Bernie Thrush)	37-32	Conemaugh (23-3, Othmar Wuenschel)
1941—Lower Merion (22-2, Bill Anderson)	32-24	Duquesne (24-3, Bill Lemmer)
1942—Lower Merion (25-1, Bill Anderson)	32-27	Sharon (20-5, Pete Collodi)
1943—Lower Merion (23-1, Bill Anderson)	29-28	Farrell (23-2, Tudor Lewis)
1944—Duquesne (25-3, Bill Lemmer)	43-35	Hazleton (21-6, Hugh McGeehan)
1945 A—Allentown (28-1, J. Birney Crum)	40-38	Donora (27-4, Jerry Wunderlich)
1946 A—Allentown (28-0, J. Birney Crum)	45-27	Homestead (27-1, Charles "Chick" Davies)
1947 A—Allentown (30-2, J. Birney Crum)	46-42	Duquesne (26-4, Bill Lemmer)
1948 A— Norristown (24-3, Lawson Earl)	30-23	Ford City (23-5, Hubert Rupert)
1949 A—Aliquippa (29-0, Sam Milanovich)	63-51	York (25-2, Don Cockley)
1950 A—Homestead (27-3, Charles "Chick Davies)	48-42	Swoyerville (29-1, Eddie Chiampi)
1951 A—Allentown (21-5, Joseph Milo Sewards)	66-55	Farrell (28-3, Ed McCluskey)
1952 A—Farrell (29-1, Ed McCluskey)	63-55	Coatesville (23-4, Walter Funk)
1953 A—Yeadon (22-2, John Naegeli)	55-43	Sharon (26-4, Blaine "Bud" Laycock)
1954 A—Farrell (28-2, Ed McCluskey)	63-52	Chester (Bob Forwood)
1955 A—McKeesport (25-3, C.P. "Neenie" Campbell)	54-48	Chester (26-2, Bob Forwood)
1956 A—Farrell (27-4, Ed McCluskey)	57-45	Palmerton (24-5, Win Evans)
1957 A—Sharon (28-0, Blaine "Bud" Laycock)	59-50	Chester (28-2, Bob Forwood)
1958 A—Haverford (25-3, Steve Juenger)	67-45	Altoona (22-5, Jim O'Donnell)
1959 A—Farrell (27-3, Ed McCluskey)	76-66	Chester (27-2, Bob Forwood)
1960 A—Farrell (30-1, Ed McCluskey)	61-40	Radnor (25-2, Ellis Dwyer)
1961 A—Nanticoke (22-1, Syl "Stretch" Bozinski)	56-46	Hickory (25-2, Fran Webster)
1962 A—Uniontown (29-2, Abe Everhart, Jr.)	90-57	Norristown (22-5, Gene Kauler)
1963 A—Plymouth-Whitemarsh (24-0, Hank Stofko)	74-54	Norwin (24-4, Lyman Stough)
1964 A—Uniontown (28-0, Abe Everhart, Jr.)	62-51	Plymouth-Whitemarsh (24-2, Hank Stofko)
1965 A—Midland (28-0, Hank Kuzma)	90-61	Steelton-Highspire (26-3, Marty Benkovic)
1966 A—Pittsburgh Schenley (19-2, Willard Fisher)	74-64	Chester (25-2, Ray McLaughlin)
1967 A—Ambridge (27-0, Chuck DiVenzio)	93-61	Chester (27-1, Ray McLaughlin)
1968 A—Laurel Highlands (26-2, Harold "Horse" Taylor)	63-56	Cheltenham (26-1, Paul Westhead)
1969 A—Farrell (27-1, Ed McCluskey)	61-50	Steelton-Highspire (21-7, Marty Benkovic)
1970 A—Beaver Falls (25-4, Frank Chan)	82-58	Haverford (25-2, Steve Juenger)
1971 A—Pittsburgh Schenley (23-3, Spencer Watkins)	77-60	Norristown (27-2, Bill Werkiser)
1972 A—Farrell (27-3, Ed McCluskey)	56-55	Chester (24-6, Juan Baughn)
1973 A—General Braddock (22-5, Paul Burch)	63-62	Reading (26-2, Jim Gano)
1974 A—Abington (28-3, Jim Wilkinson)	53-48	Pittsburgh Peabody (22-5, Norm Frey)
1975 A—Pittsburgh Schenley (24-4, Spencer Watkins)	65-64	Abington (23-8, Jim Wilkinson)
1976 AAA—Pittsburgh Fifth Avenue (15-0, Elmer Guckert)	53-42	Norristown (26-5, Bill Werkeiser)
1977 AAA—Fox Chapel (29-1, Rick Keebler)	81-71	Steelton-Highspire (29-3, Marty Benkovic)
1978 AAA—Pittsburgh Schenley (27-3, Fred Yee)	51-50	Lebanon (30-3, Chic Hess)
1979 AAA—Valley (29-5, Jim Patterson)	72-66	Allentown Allen (30-6, John Danmoyer)
1980 AAA—Cathedral Prep (33-1, Bill Flaherty)	**50-40**	**Allentown Allen (31-6, John Danmoyer)**
1981 AAA—Uniontown (32-2, James "Lash" Nesser)	73-61	Springfield Delco (28-5, Gerry Quedenfeld)
1982 AAA—Whitehall (35-2, Dick Tracy)	42-38	New Castle (27-5, Don Ross)
1983 AAA—Chester (32-5, Clifford Wilson)	82-66	McKeesport (29-4, Dan Pacella)
1984 AAAA—Williamsport (30-0, Pete White)	**68-61**	**Cathedral Prep (27-6, Bill Flaherty)**
1985 AAAA—Carlisle (28-2, Dave Lebo)	74-64	Pittsburgh Brashear (21-5, Elmer Guckert)
***1985 AAA—Strong Vincent (29-1, Pete Flinn)**	**70-53**	**Nanticoke (23-4, Syl "Stretch" Bozinski)**
1986 AAAA—Carlisle (29-4, Dave Lebo)	51-49	Kiski Area (27-5, Sam Intrieri)
1987 AAAA—Carlisle (28-5, Dave Lebo)	48-47	Meadville (28-3, Norm Price)
1988 AAAA—Carlisle (33-0, Dave Lebo)	80-54	Pittsburgh Central Catholic (28-3, Chuck Crummie)
1989 AAAA—Chester (30-2, Alonzo Lewis)	82-57	Pittsburgh Brashear (20-7, Elmer Guckert)
1990 AAAA—Glen Mills (28-3, Tom Mann)	76-74	Ringgold (29-3, Phil Pergola)
1991 AAAA—Glen Mills (31-1, Tom Mann)	81-75	Altoona (23-8, Larry Betar)
***1991 AA—Mercyhurst Prep (27-5, Greg Majchrzak)**	**58-55**	**Wilkes-Barre GAR (30-1, John Hopkins)**
1992 AAAA—Steelton-Highspire (31-2, Ken Richter)	58-49	Punxsutawney (27-3, Bill Vassallo)
1993 AAAA—Cathedral Prep (21-7, Marcel Arribi)	**41-30**	**Hazleton (29-2, Bruce Leib)**
1994 AAAA—Chester (28-5, Alonzo Lewis)	**69-65**	**Cathedral Prep (24-7, Marcel Arribi)**
1995 AAAA—Ringgold (25-6, Phil Pergola)	71-66	Williamsport (23-5, Pete White)
1996 AAAA—Lower Merion (32-3, Gregg Downer)	**48-43**	**Cathedral Prep (24-8, Marcel Arribi)**
1997 AAAA—Plymouth-Whitemarsh (30-3, Al Angelos)	50-45	Franklin Regional (29-4, Rob Greenleaf)
1998 AAAA—Harrisburg (32-1, Kirk Smallwood)	69-53	New Castle (30-2, John Sarandrea)
1999 AAAA—Williamsport (29-2, Michael Bailey)	**64-40**	**McDowell (26-5, Pete Flinn)**
2000 AAAA—Chester (28-4, Fred Pickett)	73-48	Uniontown (25-4, Dave Shuck)
2001 AAAA—Coatesville (30-1, Jim Smith)	70-57	Pittsburgh Schenley (29-3, Fred Skrocki)
2002 AAAA—Harrisburg (30-3, Kirk Smallwood)	69-62	Uniontown (30-2, Dave Schuck)
2003 AAAA—State College (25-6, Drew Frank)	76-71	Chester (27-7, Fred Pickett)
2004 AAAA—Penn Hills (24-6, Jim Rocco)	57-48	Parkland (24-10, Rich Fatzinger)
2005 AAAA—Chester (26-6, Fred Pickett)	74-61	Lower Merion (24-9, Gregg Downer)
2006 AAAA—Lower Merion (28-6, Gregg Downer)	60-58	Pittsburgh Schenley (30-2, Fred Skrocki)
2007 AAAA—Pittsburgh Schenley (29-3, Fred Skrocki)	78-71	Chester (28-6, Fred Pickett)
2008 AAAA—Chester (33-1, Fred Pickett)	81-77	Norristown (32-2, Mike Evans)
2009 AAAA—Penn Wood (28-4, Clyde Jones)	72-53	William Penn (31-2, Troy Sowers)
2010 AAAA—Plymouth-Whitemarsh (30-2, Jim Donofrio)	58-51	Penn Wood (27-4, Clyde Jones)
2011 AAAA—Chester (31-1, Larry Yarbray)	72-60 (OT)	Mount Lebanon (27-4, Joey David)
2012 AAAA—Chester (32-0, Larry Yarbray)	59-33	Lower Merion (29-4, Gregg Downer)
2013 AAAA—Lower Merion (30-3, Gregg Downer)	63-47	Chester (28-4, Larry Yarbray)
2014 AAAA—New Castle (31-0, Ralph Blundo)	52-39	Philadelphia LaSalle (23-7, Joe Dempsey)
2015 AAAA—Philadelphia Roman Catholic (29-2, Chris McNesby)	62-45	Philadelphia MLK (23-9, Sean Colson)
2015 AAA—Philadelphia Neumann-Goretti (29-2, Carl Arrigale)	69-67	Phila. Archbishop Carroll (23-7, Paul Romanmczuk)
2016 AAAA—Philadelphia Roman Catholic (27-4, Chris McNesby)	73-62	Pittsburgh Allderdice (28-2, Buddy Valinsky)
2016 AAA—Philadelphia Neumann-Goretti (29-4, Carl Arrigale)	99-66	Mars (23-7, Rob Carmody)
2017 6-A—Reading (30-3, Rick Perez)	64-60	Pine-Richland (32-3, Jeff Ackerman)
2017 5-A—Archbishop Wood (29-3, John Mosco)	73-40	Meadville (26-2, Marl McElhinny)
2017 4-A—Imhotep Charter (31-2, Andre Noble)	80-52	Strong Vincent (27-4, Shannon Pullium)

National Interscholastic Basketball Tournament In Chicago (IL)

NIBT Champions (Coach)		Runners-up
1917—Evanston (IL) Township (James Bixby)	27-22(OT)	Freeport (IL)
1918—*No tournament (World War I)*		
1919—*No tournament (World War I)*		
1920—Wingate (IN) (Merrill Eaton)	22-16	Crawfordville (IN)
1921—Cedar Rapids (IA) Washington (Leo Novak)	43-19	West Lafayette (IN)
1922—Lexington (KY) (John Barclay)	46-28	Mount Vernon (IL)
1923—Kansas City (KS) (C. W. Corsant)	43-21	Rockford (IL)
1924—Windsor (CO) (Joseph Ryan)	25-6	Yankton (SD)
1925—Wichita (KS) (A. R. Young)	27-6	El Reno (OK)
1926—Fitchburg (MA) (Clarence Arniott)	25-14	Fargo (ND)
1927—Cicero (IL) Morton (H. K. Long)	18-16	Batesville (AR)
1928—Ashland (KY) (James Anderson)	15-10	Canton (IL)
1929—Athens (TX) (Jimmy Kitts)	25-21	Oklahoma City (OK) Classen
1930—Athens (TX) (Jimmy Kitts)	22-16	Jena (LA)

National Champions*

*as chosen by the National Sports News Service, National Prep Poll, USA Today, MaxPreps or by popular acclaim.

Champions (Overall Record, Coach)	Star Players
1952—Compton (CA) (32-0, Ken Fagans)	Woody Sauldsberry, George Selleck
1953—Pampa (TX) (26-0, Clifton McNeely)	Jimmy Bond
1954—Pampa (TX) (28-0, Clifton McNeely)	Jimmy Bond
1955—Indianapolis (IN) Crispus Attucks (31-1, Ray Crowe)	Oscar Robertson
1956—Middletown (OH) (25-0, Paul Walker);	Jerry Lucas
Indianapolis (IN) Crispus Attucks (31-0, Ray Crowe) [tie]	Oscar Robertson
1957—Middletown (OH) (27-0, Paul Walker)	Jerry Lucas
1958—Oakland (CA) McClymonds (21-0, Paul Harless)	Paul Silas
1959—Oakland (CA) McClymonds (22-0, Paul Harless)	Paul Silas
1960—Oakland (CA) McClymonds (22-0, Paul Harless)	Paul Silas
1961—Collinsville (IL) (32-0, Vergil Fletcher)	Bogie Redmon
1962—Hyattsville (MD) DeMatha Catholic (29-3, Morgan Wootten)	John Austin
1963—New York City (NY) Power Memorial (27-0, Jack Donahue)	Lew Alcindor (n/k/a Kareem Jabbar)
1964—New York City (NY) Power Memorial (30-0, Jack Donahue)	Lew Alcindor (n/k/a Kareem Jabbar)
1965—Hyattsville (MD) DeMatha Catholic (28-1, Morgan Wootten)	Sid Catlett, Bernie Williams, Bob Whitmore
1966—Bronx (NY) DeWitt Clinton (21-0, Robert Buckner)	Nate "Tiny" Archibald
1967—Ambridge (PA) (27-0, Charles DeVenzio)	Dennis Wuycik
Newark (NJ) Weequahic (26-0, Lester Fein) [tie]	Mo Layton
1968—Compton (CA) (32-0, Bill Armstrong)	Larry Hollyfield
1969—Compton (CA) (30-0, Bill Armstrong)	Larry Hollyfield
1970—Houston (TX) Wheatley (39-0, Jackie Carr)	Dwight Jones
1971—East Chicago (IN) Washington (29-0, John Molodet)	Pete Trgovich, "Junior" Bridgeman
Pittsburgh (PA) Schenley (24-3, Spencer Watkins)	Maurice Lucas, Rickey Coleman, "Jeep" Kelly
1972—Dolton (IL) Thornridge (33-0, Ron Ferguson)	Quinn Buckner
1973—Houston (TX) Wheatley (43-1, Jackie Carr)	Eddie Owens
Los Angeles (CA) Verbum Dei (29-2, George McQuarn) [tie]	Lewis Brown
1974—Los Angeles (CA) Verbum Dei (30-2, John Sneed)	David Greenwood
1975—Houston (TX) Kashmere (46-0, Weldon Drew)	Karl Godine, Jarvis Williams
Los Angeles (CA) Verbum Dei (28-1, John Sneed)	David Greenwood, Roy Hamilton
1976—Washington (DC) Dunbar (29-0, Joe Dean Davidson)	Craig "Big Sky" Shelton
Brooklyn (NY) Canarsie (24-0, Mark Reiner)	Curtis Redding
1977—Philadelphia (PA) West Philadelphia (30-0, Joey Goldenberg)	Gene Banks, Clarence Tillman
1978—Hyattsville (MD) DeMatha Catholic (28-0, Morgan Wootten)	Sidney Lowe, Dereck Whittenburg
1979—Macon (GA) Southwest (28-0, Don Richardson)	Jeff Malone, Terry Fair
1980—Inglewood (CA) (29-0, Vince Combs)	Ralph Jackson, Jay Humphries
1981—Quincy (IL) (33-0, Jerry Leggett)	Mike Payne, Bruce Douglas
1982—Towson (MD) Calvert Hall (34-0, Mark Amatucci)	Duane Ferrell
1983—Baltimore (MD) Dunbar (31-0, Bob Wade)	Reggie Williams, Reggie Lewis, Tyrone Bogues
1984—Hyattsville (MD) DeMatha Catholic (29-2, Morgan Wootten)	Danny Ferry
Long Beach (CA) Poly (31-2, Ron Palmer) [tie]	Terry Stallworth
1985—Washington (DC) Springarn (31-0, John Wood)	Sherman Douglas
Baltimore (MD) Dunbar (28-1, Bob Wade)	Daryl Wade, Terry Dozier
1986—Camden (NJ) (30-0, Clarence Turner)	Louis Banks
1987—Oakton (VA) Flint Hill (23-0, Stu Vetter)	Dennis Scott
1988—Bronx (NY) Tolentine (30-1, John Sarandrea)	Malik Sealy, Adrian Autry, Brian Reese
1989—Jersey City (NJ) St. Anthony (32-0, Bob Hurley, Sr.)	Bobby Hurley, Terry Dehere
1990—Chicago (IL) King (32-0, Landon Cox)	Jamie Brandon
1991—Philadelphia (PA) Simon Gratz (27-1, Bill Ellerbee)	Rasheed Wallace
Detroit (MI) Southwestern (26-1, Perry Watson) [tie]	Jalen Rose
1992—Baltimore (MD) Dunbar (29-0, Pete Pompey)	Donta Bright
1993—Mouth of Wilson (VA) Oak Hill Academy (30-0, Steve Smith)	Jerry Stackhouse, Jeff McInnis
Philadelphia (PA) Simon Gratz (31-0, Bill Ellerbee) [tie]	Rasheed Wallace
1994—Mouth of Wilson (VA) Oak Hill Academy (30-1, Steve Smith)	Curtis Staples, Alex Sanders
1995—New Orleans (LA) St. Augustine (37-1, Bernard Griffith)	Maurice Robertson
1996—Jersey City (NJ) St. Anthony (31-0, Bob Hurley, Sr.)	Anthony Perry, Ajmal Basit
1997—Peoria (IL) Manual (31-1, Wayne McClain)	Sergio McClain, Marcus Griffin
1998—Frederick (MD) St. John's (25-0, Stu Vetter)	Jason Capel, Damien Wilkins
1999—Mouth of Wilson (VA) Oak Hill Academy (31-0, Steve Smith)	Steve Blake, Ron Slay
2000—Compton (CA) Dominguez (35-2, Russell Otis)	Tyson Chandler
2001—Mouth of Wilson (VA) Oak Hill Academy (33-0, Steve Smith)	DeSagana Diop
2002—Dallas (TX) Lincoln (40-0, Leonard Bishop)	Chris Bosh
2003—Akron (OH) St. Vincent-St. Mary (26-0, Dru Joyce)	LeBron James
2004—Mouth of Wilson (VA) Oak Hill Academy (33-0, Steve Smith)	Rajon Rondo, Josh Smith
2005—Niagara Falls (NY) (28-1, Dan Bazzani)	Paul Harris, Jonny Flynn
2006—Indianapolis (IN) Lawrence North (29-0, Jack Keefer)	Greg Oden
2007—Mouth of Wilson (VA) Oak Hill Academy (40-1, Steve Smith)	Nolan Smith, Brandon Jennings
2008—Jersey City (NJ) St. Anthony (32-0, Bob Hurley, Sr.)	Mike Rosario
2009—Henderson (NV) Findlay Prep (33-0, Michael Peck)	Avery Bradley
2010—Houston (TX) Yates (32-0, Greg Wise)	Joseph Young, Brandon Peters
2011—Jersey City (NJ) St. Anthony (33-0, Bob Hurley, Sr.)	Myles Mack, Kyle Anderson
2012—Mouth of Wilson (VA) Oak Hill Academy (44-0, Steve Smith)	Tyler Lewis, Jordan Adams
2013—Highland (UT) Lone Peak (26-1, Quincy Lewis)	Eric Mika, Nick Emery, T.J. Haws
Montverde (FL) Academy (26-2, Kevin Boyle) [tie]	Jalynn Patterson
2014—Montverde (FL) Academy (28-0, Kevin Boyle)	Ben Simmons, DeAngelo Russell
2015—Montverde (FL) Academy (31-1, Kevin Boyle)	Ben Simmons
2016—Chino Hills (CA) (34-0, Steve Baik)	Lonzo Ball, LiAngelo Ball, LaMelo Ball
2017—LaPorte (IN) LaLumiere (27-1, Shane Heirman)	Jaren Jackson, Brian Bowen

Current Prep coach Mark Majewski instructs his 2009 Ramblers.

50 Selected Erie All-time Coaching Records

		WON	LOST	TIED	.PCT	YEARS
1.	Brian Flanagan, Prep (2004-08)	89	24		.788	4
2.	Richard "Dick" Fox, Prep (1967-71)	72	21		.774	4
3.	Gus Anderson, C (1921-22), E (1922-29), Millcreek (1930-46, 47-48)	353	116		.753	25
4.	Marcel Arribi, Prep (1987-99)	251	87		.743	12
5.	Jim Hyde, Central (1925-29), East (1929-34)	137	47	1	.743	9
6.	Paul Martin, Millcreek (1924-30)	103	36		.741	6
7.	William "Bill" Flaherty, Prep (1971-84)	260	95		.732	13
8.	Richard "Dick" Detzel, Prep (1948-57)	145	55		.725	9
9.	D. G. "Doc" Evans, Erie (1907-10, 1915-20)	103	44		.701	8
10.	Pete Flinn, Vincent (1977-90), McDowell (1990-2001)	430	195		.688	24
11.	Tom Hansen, McDowell (2001-07)	110	51		.683	6
12.	Pat Flaherty, Mercyhurst (2000-10)	184	87		.679	10
13.	Kraig Hetz, McDowell (2007-12)	82	40		.672	5
14.	Ralph "Baron" Calabrese, Prep (1937-38), Vincent (1952-70)	262	129		.670	19
15.	Shannon Pullium, Vincent (1999-2016)	308	162		.655	18
16.	Richard "Dick" Fuller, McDowell (1974-79)	76	40		.655	5
17.	Robert "Ted" Robb, Tech (1944-48, 54-57)	89	50		.640	7
18.	Lou DiBacco, Academy (1967-79)	164	96		.631	12
19.	Kevin O'Connor, McDowell (2012-17)	77	45		.631	5
20.	Paul Siegel, McDowell (1969-74)	69	42		.622	5
21.	Robert "Bob" Trombacco, Prep (1957-63), Vincent (1970-76)	157	96		.621	12
22.	Mike Ferrare, Vincent (1947-48), Academy (1952-56)	65	40		.619	5
23.	Sean Baer, Mercyhurst (2010-17)	111	69		.617	7
24.	Al Kline, McDowell (1956-66)	125	81		.607	10
25.	Clarence "Carney" Metzgar, East (1962-74)	161	105		.605	12
26.	Al Calabrese, Prep (1941-42), Tech (1940-41, 48-54, 57-58, 59-76)	337	227		.598	26
27.	Mark Majewski, Villa Maria (1996-2006), Prep (2008-16)	292	197		.597	19
28.	Ed Abramoski, Tech (1931-40)	95	65		.594	9
29.	Richard "Red" Murray, Prep (1963-67)	51	35		.593	4
30.	John "Jack" Komora, East (1934-45), Academy (1946-52, 56-61)	291	203	1	.589	22
31.	Howard Kelly, Academy (1930-38)	102	73	1	.582	8
32.	Edmund L. "PeeWee" Thomas, East (1938-45)	84	60	3	.582	7
33.	John "Dutch" Leonard, Jamestown (1963-77)	158	120		.568	14
34.	Harold "Sam" Kramer, Central (1928-29), Vincent (1930-42)	162	124	2	.566	13
35.	Jim Marnella, Tech (1980-87)	89	73		.549	7
36.	Paul Demyanovich, Academy (1979-89)	130	112		.537	10
37.	Father Walter Conway, Prep (1928-37)	87	36		.534	9
38.	John Kola, Millcreek (1946-47, 48-52)	52	46		.531	5
39.	Rick Fessler, McDowell (1982-90)	106	100		.515	8
40.	Matt Jones, East (2006-17)	130	127		.506	11
41.	Tom Koval, Central Tech (2002-04, 08-17)	131	129		.504	11
42.	Andy Sisinni, Vincent (1990-95), Prep (2001-04)	102	103		.498	8
43.	Bill Gausman, Mercyhurst (1992-97), East (1997-2002)	125	126		.498	10
44.	Bob Arrowsmith, East (1946-62)	164	174		.485	16
45.	Ed Zenewicz, Mercyhurst (1976-90)	168	177		.487	14
46.	Vince Bell, Vincent (1944-46, 48-52)	53	60		.469	6
47.	Don Kolakowski, East (1974-90)	156	202		.436	16
48.	John Bowen, Vincent (1995-98), Central (1998-2002, 04-06)	90	134		.402	9
49.	Leroy Pallotto, Harborcreek (1959-65)	38	69		.355	6
50.	Johnny Johnson, Tech (1976-80, 88-90)	35	98		.263	6

Al Kline, McDowell.

Jim Marnella, Tech, Prep.

Most Years Coaching

1. Al Calabrese (Tech, Prep) — 26
2. Gus Anderson (Central, East, Millcreek) — 25
3. Pete Flinn (Vincent, McDowell) — 24
4. John "Jack" Komora (East, Academy) — 22
5. Ralph "Baron" Calabrese (Prep, Vincent) — 19
6. Mark Majewski (Villa Maria, Prep) — 19
7. Shannon Pullium (Vincent) — 18
8. Bob Arrowsmith (East) — 16
9. Don Kolakowski (East) — 16
10. Ed Zenewicz (Mercyhurst) — 14

Most Coaching Victories

1. Pete Flinn (Vincent, McDowell) — 430
2. Gus Anderson (Central, East, Millcreek) — 353
3. Al Calabrese (Tech, Prep) — 337
4. Shannon Pullium (Vincent) — 308
5. John "Jack" Komora (East, Academy) — 291
6. Mark Majewski (Villa Maria, Prep) — 282
7. Ralph "Baron" Calabrese (Prep, Vincent) — 262
8. Bill Flaherty (Prep) — 260
9. Marcel Arribi (Prep) — 251
10. Pat Flaherty (Mercyhurst) — 184

Most Coaching Losses

1. Al Calabrese (Tech, Prep) — 227
2. John "Jack" Komora (East, Academy) — 203
3. Don Kolakowski (East) — 202
4. Mark Majewski (Villa Maria, Prep) — 197
5. Pete Flinn (Vincent, McDowell) — 195
6. Ed Zenewicz (Mercyhurst) — 177
7. Bob Arrowsmith (East) — 174
8. Shannon Pullium (Vincent) — 162
9. John Bowen (Vincent, Central) — 134
10. Ralph "Baron" Calabrese (Prep, Vincent) — 129

Highest Winning Percentage (At Least 10 Years)

1. Gus Anderson (Central, East, Millcreek) — .753
2. Marcel Arribi (Prep) — .743
3. Bill Flaherty (Prep) — .732
4. Pete Flinn (Vincent, McDowell) — .688
5. Pat Flaherty (Mercyhurst) — .679
6. Ralph "Baron" Calabrese (Prep, Vincent) — .670
7. Shannon Pullium (Vincent) — .655
8. Lou DiBacco (Academy) — .631
9. Bob Trombacco (Prep, Vincent) — .621
10. Al Kline (McDowell) — .607

Shannon Pulliam, Vincent.

John Bowen, Vincent, Central, Prep.

Johnny Johnson, Tech.

Gus Anderson, later years.

Kevin O'Connor, McDowell.

John Kola, Millcreek.

Sam Kramer, Central, Vincent.

Rick Fessler, McDowell.

Tom Koval, Central Tech.

Dave Wenrick, Prep.

Al Calabrese, Prep, Tech.

Andy Sisinni, Vincent, Prep.

Don Zonno, Academy.

Jim Hyde, Central, East.

Paul Demyanovich, Academy.

Sean Baer, Mercyhurst.

Don Kolakowski, East.

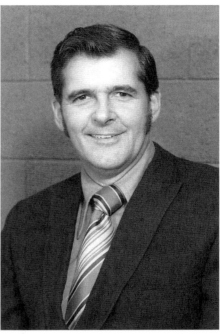

Dick Fox, Prep.

Lou DiBacco, Academy.

Bill Flaherty, Prep.

Ralph Calabrese, Prep, Vincent.

Pat Flaherty, Mercyhurst.

Dick Fuller, McDowell.

Dick Detzel, Prep.

Matt Jones, East.

Pete Flinn, Vincent, McDowell.

Brian Flanagan, Prep.

Carney Metzgar, East.

Ed Zenewicz, Mercyhurst.

Marcel Arribi, Prep.

Father Walter Conway, Prep.

"Dutch" Leonard, Jamestown.

Gus Anderson, Central, East, Millcreek.

Jack Komora, East, Academy.

Kraig Hetz, McDowell.

Eddie Abramoski, Technical.

"Puck" Cardot gets a teammate's bear hug after scoring the winning basket in the 5th overtime against South Hills Catholic (1971).

PREP'S OVERTIME GAMES (Won 30, Lost 48)

DATE	DEC.	SCORE
3/15/1928	L	Oil City St. Joe's 28, Prep 22.
1/14/1930	L	St. Ignatius 27, Prep 26.
2/13/1932	L	Canisius 30, Prep 24.
3/7/1941	L	Oil City St. Joe's 37, Prep 35.
2/10/1942	W (2 OT's)	Prep 36, Vincent 34.
12/28/1956	L	Vincent 61, Prep 59.
1/17/1958	L	East 64, Prep 61.
2/4/1962	L	Bishop Duffy 67, Prep 65.
2/27/1962	L	Tech 77, Prep 72.
2/1/1963	L	Tech 74, Prep 71.
2/22/1967	L	East 52, Prep 49.
2/16/1968	L	East 52, Prep 51.
1/18/1969	W	Prep 71, Academy 70.
1/24/1969	W	Prep 53, Vincent 49.
12/5/1969	L	Bradford 80, Prep 77.
12/28/1969	W	Prep 79, North Catholic 78.
3/14/1971	W (5 OT's)	Prep 52, South Hills Catholic 50.
1/28/1972	W	Prep 64, East 57.
2/11/1972	L	Vincent 51, Prep 46.
3/12/1972	L (2 OT's)	South Hills Catholic 46, Prep 42.
12/9/1972	L	Bishop Guilfoyle 53, Prep 52.
1/23/1973	W (2 OT's)	Prep 80, McDowell 72.
3/2/1974	W	Prep 66, Harborcreek 61.
3/9/1974	L	Hickory 59, Prep 54.
11/28/1975	L	Vincent 66, Prep 61.
12/12/1975	W	Prep 62, East 60.
2/3/1976	L	Dunkirk 65, Prep 61.
1/7/1978	W	Prep 55, Academy 53.
3/16/1978	L	Pittsburgh Schenley 67, Prep 66.
2/2/1979	L	Academy 58, Prep 54.
1/9/1981	W	Prep 43, Academy 41.
12/30/1981	L	Altoona 53, Prep 52.
2/4/1983	L (2 OT's)	McDowell 69, Prep 67.
3/12/1983	L	Warren 51, Prep 49.
12/2/1983	W	Prep 54, Phila. Roman Catholic 52.
1/6/1987	L	Academy 64, Prep 61
1/15/1988	L	Kansas City Paseo 59, Prep 57
12/19/1990	W	Prep 81, Chattanooga Brainerd 76.
12/22/1990	L (2 OT's)	Louisville Male 75, Prep 73.
3/14/1991	L (2 OT's)	Altoona 101, Prep 98.
1/22/1993	W	Prep 46, Vincent 40.
1/29/1993	W	Prep 70, Central 68.
2/11/1994	L	Toronto Pearson 63, Prep 53.
3/7/1994	W	Prep 53, McDowell 50.

DATE	DEC.	SCORE
3/18/1995	L (2 OT's)	Ringgold 77, Prep 67.
12/8/1995	L	Lakewood St. Ed's 68, Prep 67.
12/19/1995	W	Prep 61, Orem (UT) 58.
1/20/1996	L (2 OT's)	NYC LaSalle 44, Prep 40.
2/22/1997	W (2 OT's)	Prep 83, Central 76.
12/26/1997	L	Univ. of San Diego 61, Prep 58.
2/26/1999	L	McDowell 53, Prep 52.
2/6/2001	L (2 OT's)	East 55, Prep 53.
2/22/2001	L	George Junior Republic 70, Prep 63.
2/15/2002	L	McDowell 63, Prep 54.
2/28/2002	L	McDowell 64, Prep 59.
12/4/2002	W	Prep 70, Warren 65.
1/2/2003	L	East 55, Prep 54.
2/22/2003	L	McDowell 48, Prep 40.
1/13/2004	L	McDowell 71, Prep 70.
12/19/2004	L	Queens Holy Cross 62, Prep 58.
1/27/2005	W	Prep 67, Vincent 62.
1/31/2005	W	Prep 83, General McLane 77.
1/13/2006	W	Prep 88, Chester 84.
1/28/2006	L	St. Ignatius 84, Prep 81.
2/2/2007	W	Prep 83, General McLane 82.
2/16/2007	L	McDowell 57, Prep 53.
12/15/2007	W	Prep 64, St. Ignatius 62.
12/23/2009	W	Prep 63, East 55.
2/20/2010	L	McDowell 55, Prep 54.
1/15/2011	L	Charlotte (NC) Christian 68, Prep 57.
2/10/2012	W	Prep 64, Central Tech 59.
3/14/2012	W	Prep 50, Pgh. Central Catholic 49.
12/21/2012	L	Homewood (AL) 60, Prep 54.
1/27/2014	W	Prep 74, Central 69.
2/1/2014	W	Prep 91, Toronto Pope John Paul II 86.
1/24/2015	L	General McLane 60, Prep 54.
2/14/2015	W	Prep 58, Vincent 53.
2/27/2016	L	Girard 55, Prep 51.

Vs. Academy:	**3-2**
Vs. Central/Central Tech:	**4-0**
Vs. East:	**3-5**
Vs. General McLane:	**2-1**
Vs. McDowell:	**2-8**
Vs. Tech Memorial:	**0-1**
Vs. Strong Vincent:	**4-4**

The Ramblers rejoice after the thrilling OT playoff victory over Central Catholic (2012).

Mark Blazek scored 32, including the buzzer-beater, in the OT victory at General McLane (2007).

Justin Shouse scored 17 in McDowell's 1999 overtime triumph over Prep.

Steve Taneyhill scored 34 in Altoona's dramatic double-overtime playoff win over Prep (1991).

Future NBA star Ron Artest scored 24 in LaSalle's 44-40 double OT win over Prep in the McDonald's Classic (1996).

Anthony Peeler of K.C. Paseo poured in 36 points as Prep lost, 59-57 in OT at the 1988 Pro Bass tourney.

Robbie Paris of St. Ignatius buried a 40-foot 3-pointer at the buzzer in overtime to beat Prep (2006).

Kevin Williams scored 24 in Academy's 1987 overtime win over Prep.

The Three-Point Play was Invented in Erie, PA!
Tech's Eddie Abramoski is the "Father of the Three-Point Play"

Technical coach Ed Abramoski.

Erie Technical High coach **Eddie Abramoski** (1931-40) was a true visionary and innovator in the world of basketball. In the April, 1943 edition of *The Athletic Journal,* Abramoski wrote of a thought-provoking experiment carried out in his intramural sports program at Tech, prompted by severe criticism heaped upon the game by: 1) the elimination of the center jump, which was intended to restrain the giants of the game, but boomeranged, putting the game in the hands of "behemoths". Rather than having one "beanpole", teams would have five, leaving no place for the small, clever players; and 2) the establishment of the 10-second rule, which was intended to keep teams from "stalling" in the backcourt but enhanced the use of zone defenses, challenging the offensive team to penetrate its bulwarks. The offense then usually had two choices—to shoot over the heads of the zone defenses or beat a team down the court to the area around the basket. This led to the most severe criticism of the game—that the game had become nothing but "race horse tactics" or "fire engine style".

The new scoring plan improvised for Abramoski's 25 intramural teams required a 20-foot arc from the center of the basket inscribed on the floor. Within the arc a field goal would still be valued at two points, while a field goal from a shot outside the arc would carry a value of three points. Abramoski felt such a scoring plan, from the observation of his intramural teams, would have the following effects: 1) the "fast break" would give way to the presence of set-shot artists who could sink "triple-deckers"; 2) it would spread out zone defenses, allowing clever ball-handlers to regain their place in the game; 3) it would de-emphasize the advantage of height; 4) it would allow a team trailing by a few points an opportunity to get back in the game, keeping spectators glued to their seats; 5) "freezing" the ball in the closing minutes would be less attractive; 6) it would create a

trend away from the rough tactics of the game since the defense would have to spread; and 7) it would once again make the entire court the playing area.

The first local contest ever played using Abramoski's three-point play was the 1945 Coaches All-Star Game, pitting Erie's Scholastic All-Stars against a team of coaches from the city schools. A 21-foot arc was plied to the Strong Vincent floor and a capacity crowd was on hand to witness the demonstration of new scoring rules. The All-Stars scored a 53-50 victory, but the coaches proved more proficient at long-range shooting, caging six 3-pointers while the high school kids were content with a trio of "triple-deckers." Cathedral Prep coach **Sam Yezerski** led all scorers with 19 points, including one 3-pointer, thus making him the first person affiliated with Prep to score a "trey." Other coaches scoring 3-pointers included Academy's **Edmund "Pee-Wee" Thomas** and **Marion "Bimp" Lewis**; and **Vincent's "Red" Cochrane** and **Johnny Grasberger**, who nailed two. All-Stars tossing in 3-pointers included Academy's **Bill Roach** and East High's **Billy Biletnikoff** and **Pete Bechtos**.

Abramoski admitted at the time his innovation had little chance of widespread adoption, but he hoped that coaches would just think about the matter. Fordham and Columbia universities employed Abramoski's new rule about a week before the Erie game and it was reported that "fans liked the new scoring plan because it opened up play by giving the additional point award for a longer shot."

It took a little over four decades to be adopted nationally, but the three-point play did become integral and did forever change the nature of the game. It was Erie's **Eddie Abramoski's** brainchild, and he can truly be called the "Father of the Three-Point Play."

Records against Individual Opponents

(November or December games are credited to the next calendar year.)

The GM crowd, all worked up for a visit from Prep (2007).

Versus Erie Area

Old AllianceAcademy.

Alliance Academy (PNA College, Cambridge Springs) "Eagles" (2-3)

1926	9-55	L	A
1926	11-25	L	H
1934	22-20	W	H
1934	17-35	L	A
1936	31-30	W	A

Albion "Redskins" (5-0)

1927	25-13	W	H
1927	23-21	W	A
1941	26-17	W	A
1942	31-17	W	H
1949	40-25	W	H

Alumni "Ramblers" (18-0)

1926	19-17	W	H
1927	26-19	W	H
1928	31-25	W	H
1929	22-19	W	H
1930	54-34	W	H
1932	34-21	W	H
1933	28-15	W	H
1936	16-11	W	H
1938	21-18	W	H
1939	55-27	W	H

1942	36-20	W	H
1945	30-28	W	H
1946	33-11	W	H
1947	43-33	W	H
1949	42-33	W	H
1951	40-36	W	H
1955	67-42	W	H
1961	60-51	W	H

Bradford "Owls" (19-3)

1952	38-36	W	H
1952	47-54	L	A
1953	70-52	W	A
1953	53-41	W	H
1954	47-39	W	H
1954	55-50	W	A
1956	63-51	W	A
1956	71-55	W	H
1970	77-80 (OT)	L	A
1971	85-50	W	H (8-2)
1972	57-38	W	A
1973	67-60	W	A
1973	57-48	W	H
1974	59-62	L	A
1975	64-43	W	H
1976	74-51	W	A
1977	65-47	W	H
1978	60-43	W	A
1979	73-45	W	H
1980	61-32	W	A
1981	74-49	W	A (17-3)
1982	60-40	W	A
1996	65-38	W	N

Bradford St. Bernard's "Bernies" or "Ramblers" (14-3)

1927	17-12	W	A
1929	25-14	W	H
1929	11-18	L	A
1930	34-9	W	H
1930	32-22	W	A
1946	38-11	W	H
1946	48-21	W	A
1947	48-30	W	A
1947	51-26	W	H
1948	39-37	W	H
1948	28-29	L	A (8-2)
1949	40-49	L	A
1949	45-24	W	H
1950	43-35	W	A
1950	47-35	W	H
1951	63-35	W	A
1951	48-30	W	H

Carlton Druggists (Erie) (0-2)

1925	18-27	L	H
1925	17-19	L	A

Corry "Beavers" (26-6)

1928	27-30	L	A
1931	13-29	L	A
1931	10-11	L	H
1933	21-16	W	A
1933	45-23	W	H
1938	15-32	L	H
1938	16-37	L	A
1945	34-16	W	A
1945	37-23	W	H
1948	23-30	L	A (4-6)
1948	49-30	W	H
1949	51-38	W	A
1949	49-33	W	H
1950	49-45	W	A
1950	45-24	W	N
1951	62-33	W	N
1951	56-38	W	N
1956	80-42	W	H
1957	74-58	W	A
1962	70-42	W	A (14-6)
1962	75-50	W	H
1969	70-44	W	H
1969	70-57	W	A
1985	81-37	W	H
2005	76-47	W	A
2006	79-22	W	H
2007	60-42	W	A
2008	67-42	W	H
2011	80-45	W	A
2012	73-21	W	H (24-6)
2015	64-39	W	H
2016	72-35	W	A

Old Corry St. Edwards.

Corry St. Edward's "Shamrocks" (23-1)

1928	55-13	W	H
1928	52-12	W	A
1929	27-10	W	H
1929	35-21	W	A
1930	48-21	W	A
1930	40-22	W	H
1931	25-11	W	A
1931	41-14	W	H
1932	34-10	W	H

Mike Williams, Academy '86.

The 1926 Academy Lions. Front, L to R: Pasqual, Weschler, Thomas, Grasberger; Back: Coach Drake, Keintzel, Blazewski, Geisler, Hostetler, Fuller, Lancaster.

The 1932 Academy Lions. Front, L to R: French, T. Schreck, McCart, M. Schreck, Lugo, Keiper, Tell, Ross, Baker; Back: Mattimore, Wuenschel, Dwarokowski, Karznia, Kopec, Warner, McKees, Sarrity, Coach Kelly.

John Mathews, Academy '74.

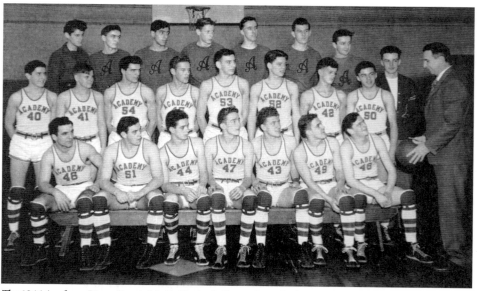

The 1946 Academy Lions. Front, L to R: Cipriani, Coyne, Breault, Carr, Farnbaugh, Barthelson, Morgan, Coach Komora; Middle: Schultz, Denniston, Krape, Burgess, Rosequist, Hammond, Sonnenberg, Wolfe, Penske; Back: Hill, Bean, Yomtob, Bartnicki, Sundberg, Coasta, Folga.

Academy's Gerald Rankin leaps over Prep's "Marty O" (30) to score as Tim Fox (10) can only observe (1972).

The Academy Lion mascot knows where to sit.

Academy's 1975 City Champs. Front, L to R: Johnson, Spearman, Quinn, Hobson, Jordan; Back: Coach DiBacco, Andrews, Walters, Bolden, Clark, Gustafson, Asst. Severo.

Justice Davis, Central Tech '16.

Central Tech's Eugene Husband and Vincent's D'Andre Henderson battle for a loose ball (2012).

Malik Brinson, Central Tech '15.

1932	36-22	W	A (10-0)
1933	28-19	W	A
1933	28-16	W	H
1934	19-13	W	A
1934	58-18	W	H
1935	26-9	W	A
1935	43-17	W	H
1937	31-19	W	H
1937	28-32	L	A
1938	34-12	W	H
1938	34-32	W	A (19-1)
1939	49-23	W	H
1939	51-22	W	A
1940	29-21	W	H
1941	68-17	W	H

Edinboro "Turtles" (3-4)

1927	31-36	L	H
1933	24-17	W	A
1933	26-29	L	H
1934	14-15	L	H
1934	31-22	W	A
1938	21-17	W	H
1938	15-32	L	A

Elk County Christian "Crusaders" (8-1)

1964	63-44	W	A
1964	79-49	W	H
1965	89-40	W	H
1965	70-31	W	A
1966	83-62	W	H
1966	51-66	L	A
1967	69-48	W	A
1967	58-41	W	H
1995	42-25	W	A

Erie Academy "Lions" (80-35)

1931	14-36	L	H
1931	17-38	L	A
1943	18-36	L	H
1943	23-40	L	A
1943	45-47	L	N
1943	40-31	W	N
1944	13-27	L	A
1944	25-39	L	H
1944	23-49	L	A
1944	26-38	L	H (1-9)
1945	20-27	L	H
1945	36-24	W	A
1945	29-28	W	N
1946	19-11	W	H
1946	26-22	W	A
1946	47-31	W	N
1947	38-25	W	H
1947	48-36	W	A
1948	30-31	L	H
1948	31-53	L	A (8-12)
1949	43-34	W	H
1949	39-37	W	A
1950	53-40	W	N
1950	48-27	W	N
1951	46-29	W	N
1951	36-44	L	N
1952	46-40	W	N
1952	44-47	L	N
1953	67-38	W	N
1953	68-51	W	N (16-14)
1954	66-37	W	N
1954	69-40	W	N
1955	61-50	W	N
1955	74-42	W	N
1956	54-57	L	N
1956	66-75	L	N
1957	79-26	W	N
1957	92-51	W	N
1958	57-52	W	N
1958	37-48	L	N (23-17)
1959	58-37	W	N
1959	46-45	W	N
1960	62-64	L	N
1960	63-58	W	N
1961	60-55	W	N
1961	54-65	L	N
1962	49-48	W	N
1962	68-46	W	N
1963	53-56	L	N

1963	62-56	W	N (30-20)
1964	72-54	W	N
1964	65-68	L	N
1964	63-62	W	N
1965	67-59	W	N
1965	74-63	W	N
1966	52-53	L	N
1966	64-71	L	N
1967	54-56	L	N
1967	85-68	W	N
1968	68-40	W	N (36-24)
1968	85-57	W	N
1969	71-70 (OT)	W	N
1969	55-52	W	N
1970	77-59	W	N
1970	78-58	W	N
1971	71-79	L	N
1971	75-74	W	N
1971	62-50	W	N
1972	56-55	W	N
1972	60-55	W	N (45-25)
1973	73-71	W	N
1973	59-69	L	N
1974	52-67	L	N
1974	45-68	L	N
1975	66-65	W	N
1975	59-77	L	N
1975	66-62	W	N
1976	62-50	W	N
1976	65-71	L	N
1977	63-65	L	N (49-31)
1977	67-63	W	N
1977	63-43	W	N
1977	57-54	W	N
1978	55-53 (OT)	W	N
1978	65-53	W	N
1978	53-46	W	N
1979	46-41	W	N
1979	54-58	L	N
1979	55-48	W	N
1980	58-34	W	N (58-32)
1980	76-42	W	N
1981	74-56	W	N
1981	43-41 (OT)	W	N
1982	66-46	W	N
1982	71-44	W	N
1983	102-54	W	N
1983	76-58	W	N
1984	62-56	W	N
1984	87-63	W	N
1985	59-68	L	N (67-33)
1985	53-50	W	N
1986	75-71	W	N
1986	47-66	L	N
1987	61-64 (OT)	L	N
1987	53-49	W	N
1988	71-51	W	N
1988	49-35	W	N
1989	81-55	W	N
1989	58-57	W	N
1990	64-60	W	N (75-35)
1990	54-42	W	N
1991	61-52	W	N
1991	47-31	W	N
1992	64-49	W	N
1992	71-62	W	N

Erie Business College (1-1)

1927	22-16	W	A
1927	31-32	L	H

Erie Central High Seconds "Fighting Colonels" (1-1)

1925	19-30	L	H
1925	15-12	W	A

Erie Central Tech, f/k/a Central "Falcons" (46-5)

1993	77-67	W	N
1993	70-68 (OT)	W	N
1994	74-49	W	N
1994	79-51	W	N
1995	69-55	W	N
1995	69-65	W	N
1996	72-52	W	N

1996	72-46	W	N
1997	79-70	W	N
1997	85-60	W	N (10-0)
1997	83-76 (2OT)	W	N
1998	43-38	W	N
1998	63-49	W	N
1998	66-47	W	N
1999	54-46	W	N
1999	54-42	W	N
2000	59-45	W	N
2000	60-71	L	N
2000	56-58	L	N
2001	54-46	W	N (18-2)
2001	58-68	L	N
2002	65-52	W	N
2002	69-63	W	N
2003	59-53	W	N
2003	78-52	W	N
2004	84-66	W	N
2004	81-64	W	N
2005	60-50	W	N
2005	56-25	W	N
2005	64-49	W	N (27-3)
2006	80-32	W	N
2006	67-35	W	N
2007	72-33	W	N
2007	60-49	W	N
2008	73-51	W	N
2008	70-40	W	N
2009	62-46	W	N
2010	74-38	W	N
2011	66-40	W	H
2012	64-59 (OT)	W	A (37-3)
2013	76-66	W	A
2013	74-60	W	H
2014	58-44	W	A
2014	74-69 (OT)	W	H
2015	55-51	W	H
2015	45-50	L	A
2016	58-55	W	A
2016	61-52	W	H
2017	56-58	L	H
2017	64-43	W	A
2017	55-43	W	N

Erie DeMolay (0-4)

1931	19-24	L	H
1931	11-13	L	A
1932	16-26	L	H
1932	11-22	L	A

Erie East "Warriors" (114-48)

1931	16-26	L	H
1931	20-26	L	A
1935	17-29	L	H
1935	20-39	L	A
1936	11-45	L	A
1937	13-34	L	H
1938	24-48	L	A
1939	20-49	L	A
1942	12-31	L	H
1943	22-38	L	H (0-10)
1943	37-48	L	A
1943	32-52	L	N
1943	38-48	L	N
1944	30-34	L	H
1944	14-31	L	A
1944	24-46	L	H
1944	25-51	L	A
1945	17-31	L	H
1945	31-41	L	A
1945	33-23	W	N (1-19)
1946	19-27	L	A
1946	31-25	W	H
1946	24-30	L	N
1947	31-28	W	H
1947	35-52	L	A
1948	42-29	W	H
1948	36-38	L	A
1949	39-25	W	A
1949	42-28	W	H
1950	25-39	L	N (6-24)
1950	48-45	W	N
1951	58-37	W	N
1951	31-50	L	N

East's 1941 City Champs. Front, L to R: Hatkevich, Oldach, Lundstrom, Kuhl, Skovron, Lininger; Middle: Witkowski, Venor, Varchola, Mahon, Hill, Coach Komora; Back: Dowd, Karuba, Marchant, Shannon, Wodarski.

East's Jim Davis goes up as Prep's Dan Nowak defends (1973).

East's 1943 City Champs. Front, L to R: Bilecki, Andrews, Karuba, Praetzel, Becker; Middle: McDonald, Baranowski, George, Pontoriero, Droast, Coach Komora; Novello, Razanauskus, Jablonski, Borgia.

Wayne Patterson, East '84.

The 1970 East Warriors. Front L to R: Turos, Satyshur, Woodard, L. McIntosh, Norton, B. McIntosh, Coach Metzgar; Back: O'Rourke, Hewitt, Miller, Zimmerman, Wilcox, Gallegos, Baker, Crotty.

East High's Eddie Woodard beats Prep's Tom Hansen to the hoop (1969).

Wenrick and Lupo defend against East's Dan Gallegos (1964).

Jack Watts gets past Pat Lupo to score for East (1963).

1952	47-49	L	N		1978	75-46	W	N		2005	68-48	W	N
1952	56-30	W	N		1979	61-47	W	N		2006	69-51	W	N
1953	82-58	W	N		1979	72-49	W	N (49-41)		2006	55-52	W	N
1953	56-50	W	N		1980	73-46	W	N		2007	70-61	W	N
1954	44-45	L	N		1980	78-37	W	N		2007	70-59	W	N
1954	45-33	W	N		1981	65-43	W	N		2007	63-36	W	N
1954	50-45	W	N (13-27)		1981	67-62	W	N		2008	62-59	W	N
1955	69-49	W	N		1982	65-38	W	N		2008	83-56	W	N
1955	50-26	W	N		1982	70-48	W	N		2008	65-56	W	N (102-48)
1956	69-62	W	N		1983	76-68	W	N		2009	73-59	W	N
1956	65-49	W	N		1983	91-56	W	N		2010	63-55 (OT)	W	N
1957	56-43	W	N		1984	93-54	W	N		2012	71-52	W	A
1957	52-44	W	N		1984	81-56	W	N (59-41)		2013	65-42	W	H
1958	61-64 (OT)	L	N		1985	46-47	L	N		2013	84-57	W	A
1958	46-51	L	N		1985	59-74	L	N		2014	65-61	W	H
1959	64-44	W	N		1986	56-38	W	N		2015	71-56	W	H
1959	62-51	W	N (21-29)		1986	60-38	W	N		2015	71-55	W	A
1960	70-41	W	N		1987	67-53	W	N		2016	67-46	W	A
1960	75-50	W	N		1987	51-46	W	N		2016	64-51	W	H (112-48)
1961	64-55	W	N		1988	77-48	W	N		2017	67-65	W	H
1961	62-45	W	N		1988	74-50	W	N		2017	57-49	W	A
1962	65-52	W	N		1989	76-53	W	N					
1962	70-43	W	N		1989	71-46	W	N (67-43)		**Erie McDowell f/k/a West Millcreek &**			
1963	62-45	W	N		1990	95-57	W	N		**Millcreek "Trojans" (124-62)**			
1963	61-43	W	N		1990	77-55	W	N		1927	23-21	W	A
1964	49-32	W	N		1991	86-37	W	N		1927	26-28	L	H
1964	65-45	W	N (31-29)		1991	93-50	W	N		1930	16-17	L	A
1965	75-61	W	N		1992	62-42	W	N		1931	23-12	W	A
1965	72-62	W	N		1992	67-51	W	N		1931	18-21	L	H
1966	47-65	L	N		1993	73-47	W	N		1932	26-28	L	A
1966	57-69	L	N		1993	87-50	W	N		1932	21-20	W	H
1967	56-54	W	N		1994	73-49	W	N		1933	22-31	L	H
1967	49-52 (OT)	L	N		1994	97-52	W	N (77-43)		1933	22-24	L	H
1968	55-61	L	N		1995	94-47	W	N		1934	24-18	W	A (4-6)
1968	51-52 (OT)	L	N		1995	78-42	W	N		1934	35-13	W	A
1969	59-65	L	N		1996	68-50	W	N		1935	15-29	L	A
1969	61-79	L	N (34-36)		1996	68-42	W	N		1935	43-26	W	H
1970	56-58	L	N		1997	75-49	W	N		1936	29-41	L	A
1970	64-57	W	N		1997	62-48	W	N		1937	18-32	L	H
1971	73-62	W	N		1998	57-39	W	N		1937	18-41	L	A
1971	63-69	L	N		1998	51-42	W	N		1938	16-36	L	H
1972	63-58	W	N		1999	54-47	W	N		1938	19-38	L	A
1972	64-57 (OT)	W	N		1999	51-54	L	N (86-44)		1940	25-28	L	A
1973	52-58	L	N		2000	54-65	L	N		1940	33-15	W	H (7-13)
1973	63-66	L	N		2000	75-67	W	N		1941	32-37	L	A
1974	67-48	W	N		2001	51-35	W	N		1942	31-22	W	H
1974	63-50	W	N (40-40)		2001	53-55 (2OT)	L	N		1942	19-14	W	A
1975	57-53	W	N		2002	56-43	W	N		1946	31-20	W	A
1975	62-36	W	N		2002	50-44	W	N		1946	32-27	W	H
1976	62-60 (OT)	W	N		2003	54-55 (OT)	L	N		1947	42-26	W	H
1976	68-73	L	N		2003	67-50	W	N		1947	47-33	W	A
1977	76-52	W	N		2004	76-56	W	N		1949	48-31	W	H
1977	83-51	W	N		2004	51-64	L	N (92-48)		1949	46-31	W	H
1978	77-65	W	N		2005	55-46	W	N		1950	40-21	W	N (16-14)

The 1939 Millcreek Trojans. Front, L to R: Ripley, Gay, McIntosh, Findley, Willis, Ford, Foye; Middle: Taylor, Redmond, Richard, Christensen, Richard, Coursey, Redmond, Luther, Bricker; Back: Coughlin, Santos, Coach Anderson, Love, Kline.

Millcreek's 1947 County League Champs. Front: Mgrs. Harrington, Mitchell; Seated: Patterson, Lytle, Hanable, Hedderick, Quinn; Standing: Zimmer, Doi, Trask, Komora, Dahlquist, Coach Kola.

Ray Hedderick, Millcreek '46.

Chet Moffett, McDowell '88, now a Prep coach.

Gary Maus, McDowell '88.

Jim Sperry, McDowell '71.

Dillon Loomis, McDowell '08.

Dusty Ras, McDowell '01.

Billy Heintz, McDowell '73, nails a free throw.

Zach Spronatti nails an outside jumper against Prep (2007).

Bruce Nesdore, McDowell '80.

Ken Faulkner, McDowell '62.

Tom Taylor, McDowell '82, scores against the Ramblers before a capacity crowd.

Rob Dowling, McDowell '77.

Colin Kimball, McDowell '11.

Chris Morrow, McDowell '90.

McDowell fans do get fired up for Prep.

Steve Prentice, McDowell '75.

Danny Merryman, McDowell '87.

Don Weiss, McDowell '72.

Sean Hoffman, McDowell '03.

Rob Ricart, McDowell '73.

Mark Wilhelm, McDowell '89.

Todd DeBello, McDowell 86.

Billy Nesdore, McDowell '83.

Year	Score	W/L	Site
1950	48-27	W	N
1951	45-29	W	N
1951	48-38	W	N
1952	41-34	W	N
1952	59-48	W	N
1953	70-54	W	N
1953	52-39	W	N
1956	65-39	W	H
1956	77-44	W	A
1957	57-48	W	A (26-14)
1957	68-62	W	H
1958	48-50	L	H
1958	55-72	L	A
1959	67-61	W	A
1959	85-69	W	H
1960	72-53	W	A
1960	69-46	W	H
1961	66-52	W	A
1961	57-48	W	H
1962	52-59	L	H (33-17)
1962	44-60	L	A
1963	67-28	W	H
1963	62-51	W	A
1964	60-53	W	A
1964	67-63	W	H
1965	44-40	W	A
1965	70-55	W	H
1966	51-53	L	H
1966	45-55	L	A
1967	71-52	W	H (40-20)
1967	50-51	L	A
1968	53-50	W	A
1968	80-58	W	H
1968	83-48	W	A
1969	67-49	W	A
1969	68-58	W	H
1969	44-47	L	A
1970	55-56	L	A
1970	71-70	W	H
1971	72-82	L	A (46-24)
1971	74-62	W	H
1972	48-39	W	H
1972	59-56	W	A
1973	80-72 (2OT)	W	H
1973	50-54	L	A
1974	66-51	W	H
1974	49-47	W	A
1975	80-61	W	N
1975	72-63	W	N
1976	68-65	W	N (55-25)
1976	61-74	L	N
1977	55-62	L	N
1977	62-43	W	N
1978	56-58	L	N
1978	56-53	W	N
1979	64-63	W	N
1979	46-45	W	N
1980	47-45	W	N
1980	59-48	W	N
1980	66-58	W	N (62-28)
1980	53-43	W	N
1981	60-46	W	N
1981	50-54	L	N
1982	54-51	W	N
1982	49-62	L	N
1983	61-55	W	N
1983	67-69 (OT)	L	N
1984	74-36	W	N
1984	69-38	W	N
1985	45-51	L	N (68-32)
1985	45-62	L	N
1986	43-49	L	N
1986	50-51	L	N
1987	59-47	W	N
1987	65-47	W	N
1988	56-54	W	N
1988	52-46	W	N
1988	67-66	W	N
1989	57-46	W	N
1989	63-57	W	N (75-35)
1990	62-51	W	N
1990	64-48	W	N
1991	61-54	W	N
1991	62-48	W	N
1991	56-35	W	N
1992	54-64	L	N
1992	44-54	L	N
1992	42-49	L	N
1993	52-55	L	N
1993	75-57	W	N (81-39)
1993	55-65	L	N
1993	54-49	W	N
1994	73-56	W	N
1994	51-49	W	N
1994	53-50 (OT)	W	N
1995	52-40	W	N
1995	47-50	L	N
1995	58-55	W	N
1996	47-62	L	N
1996	52-48	W	N (88-42)
1996	55-49	W	N
1996	56-69	L	N
1996	47-44	W	N
1997	42-35	W	N
1997	54-51	W	N
1998	37-35	W	N
1998	64-54	W	N
1999	52-53 (OT)	L	N
1999	48-68	L	N
1999	37-55	L	N (94-46)
2000	34-42	L	N
2000	44-54	L	N
2001	36-33	W	N
2001	54-40	W	N
2002	46-42	W	N
2002	54-63 (OT)	L	N
2002	59-64 (OT)	L	N
2003	59-36	W	N
2003	55-62	L	N
2003	40-48 (OT)	L	N (98-52)
2004	70-71 (OT)	L	N
2004	50-57	L	N
2005	74-52	W	N
2005	59-39	W	N
2005	75-66	W	N
2006	53-39	W	N
2006	70-54	W	N
2006	61-54	W	N
2007	49-41	W	N
2007	53-57 (OT)	L	N (105-55)
2008	65-61	W	N
2008	39-62	L	N
2008	50-64	L	N
2009	35-43	L	A
2009	47-43	W	H
2009	55-51	W	N
2010	63-47	W	H
2010	54-55 (OT)	L	A
2010	57-49	W	N
2011	41-35	W	A (111-59)
2011	52-41	W	H
2011	51-40	W	H
2012	65-56	W	H
2012	47-45	W	A
2013	69-46	W	A
2013	73-50	W	H
2013	64-46	W	N
2014	52-47	W	H
2014	59-47	W	A
2014	52-66	L	H (120-60)
2015	53-51	W	A
2015	38-46	L	H
2016	68-38	W	H
2016	48-57	L	A
2017	55-49	W	H
2017	63-53	W	A

Erie Mercyhurst Prep "Lakers" (40-2)

Year	Score	W/L	Site
1985	64-31	W	N
1985	68-50	W	N
1986	93-55	W	N
1986	77-55	W	N
1987	62-41	W	N
1987	69-60	W	N
1988	55-46	W	N
1988	78-66	W	N
1989	73-43	W	N
1989	58-44	W	N (10-0)
1990	73-32	W	N
1990	64-57	W	N
1991	74-56	W	N
1991	76-58	W	N
1992	64-45	W	N
1992	73-58	W	N
1993	63-40	W	N
1993	73-52	W	N
1994	67-59	W	N
1994	78-41	W	N (20-0)
1995	70-57	W	N
1995	81-48	W	N
1996	74-43	W	N
1996	67-38	W	N
1997	62-47	W	N
1997	61-42	W	N
1998	52-38	W	N
1998	69-39	W	N
1999	41-35	W	N
1999	49-47	W	N (30-0)
2000	51-47	W	N
2000	54-48	W	N
2001	70-62	W	N
2001	46-48	L	N
2002	30-46	L	N
2002	50-37	W	N
2003	50-32	W	N
2003	56-27	W	N
2004	53-31	W	N
2004	57-52	W	N (38-2)
2005	54-36	W	A
2006	54-48	W	H

Erie St. Stanislaus "Eagles" (2-2)

Year	Score	W/L	Site
1927	25-17	W	H
1927	28-26	W	A
1928	19-20	L	A
1928	19-20	L	A

Erie Strong Vincent "Colonels" (106-72)

Year	Score	W/L	Site
1931	12-25	L	A
1932	12-35	L	A
1932	15-36	L	A
1935	15-19	L	A
1936	19-59	L	A
1937	14-40	L	A
1938	12-45	L	A
1939	24-50	L	A
1940	11-30	L	A
1941	27-33	L	A (0-10)
1942	36-34 (2 OT)	W	A
1943	31-51	L	A
1943	32-50	L	A
1943	35-45	L	N
1943	48-40	W	N
1944	42-24	W	A
1944	27-30	L	A
1944	24-34	L	A
1944	31-44	L	A
1945	24-32	L	H (3-17)
1945	39-36	W	A
1945	39-29	W	N
1946	29-36	L	H
1946	22-24	L	A
1946	39-43	L	N
1947	26-35	L	N
1947	39-35	W	N
1948	46-34	W	A
1948	48-28	W	H
1949	34-40	L	H (8-22)
1949	48-40	W	A
1950	46-41	W	N
1950	55-43	W	N
1951	36-38	L	N
1951	42-30	W	N
1952	44-50	L	N
1952	50-40	W	N
1953	63-34	W	N
1953	61-37	W	N
1954	69-57	W	N (16-24)
1954	62-54	W	N
1955	47-56	L	N
1955	67-79	L	N
1956	67-68	L	N
1956	52-62	L	N
1957	59-61 (OT)	L	N
1957	61-76	L	N

Tom Martin, Vincent '40.

Mike Polaygi, Vincent '55.

Gridley Junior High, 1964. Can you name these guys?

The 1944 Strong Vincent Colonels. Front, L to R: Modica, Phillips, Herbstritt, McIntyre, Cerami, Herbstritt, Horn; Back: Oblom, Gallagher, Talerico, Rufini, Arkelian, Wroth, Tompkins, Coach Strand.

Strong Vincent and McDowell battle it out in the Colonels' gym, 1963.

Strong Vincent's 1979 Metro League Champs. Kneeling: Coaches Flinn, Delsandro; L to R: Flatley, McCullum, Dahlstrand, McNeal, Easterling, Corkan, Lillis, Martin, Barron, Hollis, Anuszkiewicz, Knoll, Amendola.

Wally Knox, Vincent '59.

Chris Knoll, Vincent '79.

Willie Hollis, Vincent '83.

Year	Score	W/L	Site		Year	Score	W/L	Site		Year	Score	W/L	Site
1958	58-54	W	N		1983	66-46	W	N		2009	74-68	W	N (95-65)
1958	50-55	L	N		1984	71-60	W	N		2010	56-73	L	N
1959	71-66	W	N (19-31)		1984	62-48	W	N		2010	57-65	L	N
1959	66-67	L	N		1985	53-60	L	N		2010	60-68	L	N
1959	55-54	W	N		1985	41-49	L	N		2011	74-62	W	N
1960	64-48	W	N		1986	60-58	W	N		2011	60-57	W	N
1960	56-59	L	N		1986	60-61	L	N (52-58)		2012	59-60	L	N
1960	74-60	W	N		1987	52-55	L	N		2012	60-59	W	N
1961	51-70	L	N		1987	46-43	W	N		2012	85-43	W	N
1961	54-67	L	N		1988	71-64	W	N		2013	68-41	W	N
1962	50-48	W	N		1988	45-57	L	N		2013	74-44	W	N (101-69)
1962	54-51	W	N		1988	48-38	W	N		2014	70-58	W	N
1963	46-68	L	N (24-36)		1989	59-48	W	N		2014	61-60	W	N
1963	55-62	L	N		1989	59-51	W	N		2015	58-53	W	N
1964	74-64	W	N		1990	68-48	W	N		2015	58-53 (OT)	W	N
1964	77-69	W	N		1990	59-35	W	N		2015	41-40	W	N
1965	68-64	W	N		1991	76-39	W	N (60-60)		2016	57-70	L	H
1965	55-61	L	N		1991	76-58	W	N		2016	60-63	L	A
1966	39-54	L	N		1992	60-48	W	N		2017	58-60	L	H
1966	33-48	L	N		1992	63-45	W	N					
1967	51-64	L	N		1993	46-40 (OT)	W	N					
1967	49-53	L	N		1993	61-48	W	N					

Erie Tech Memorial f/k/a Technical "Centaurs" (75-44)

Year	Score	W/L	Site		Year	Score	W/L	Site
1968	50-20	W	N (28-42)		1932	11-34	L	H
1968	48-50	L	N		1935	24-22	W	H
1969	55-65	L	N		1935	22-29	L	A
1969	53-49 (OT)	W	N		1936	20-25	L	H
1970	77-49	W	N		1937	19-24	L	H
1970	60-53	W	N		1938	14-39	L	H
1971	54-51	W	N		1939	14-29	L	H
1971	76-74	W	N		1940	38-41	L	H
1972	61-55	W	N		1941	20-24	L	H
1972	46-51 (OT)	L	N		1942	30-26	W	H (2-8)
1973	52-54	L	N (34-46)		1943	29-46	L	A
1973	53-68	L	N		1943	36-47	L	H
1973	50-55	L	N		1943	25-33	L	N
1974	46-52	L	N		1943	37-50	L	N
1974	70-56	W	N		1944	31-29	W	A
1975	68-50	W	N		1944	22-20	W	H
1975	65-66 (OT)	L	N		1944	37-40	L	H
1975	71-67	W	N		1944	38-39	L	A
1976	61-62	L	N		1945	17-31	L	A
1976	38-42	L	N		1945	32-29	W	H (5-15)
1977	59-52	W	N (38-52)		1945	22-31	L	N
1977	87-59	W	N		1946	38-44	L	H
1978	58-43	W	N		1946	35-38	L	A
1978	62-46	W	N		1946	41-33	W	N
1979	46-65	L	N		1947	32-24	W	H
1979	44-56	L	N		1947	39-34	W	A
1979	54-44	W	N		1948	29-33	L	H
1980	67-39	W	N		1948	29-44	L	A
1980	86-31	W	N		1949	38-32	W	H
1981	56-51	W	N		1949	39-33	W	A (10-20)
1981	62-42	W	N (46-54)		1950	38-43	L	N
1982	72-45	W	N		1950	34-47	L	N
1982	57-54	W	N		1951	61-60	W	N
1983	53-65	L	N		1951	42-33	W	N

The following additional entries belong to the middle column:

Year	Score	W/L	Site
1994	65-66	L	N
1994	65-37	W	N
1995	75-36	W	N
1995	87-47	W	N
1996	94-54	W	N (69-61)
1996	91-35	W	N
1997	73-47	W	N
1997	80-49	W	N
1998	50-41	W	N
1998	73-42	W	N
1999	73-46	W	N
1999	60-35	W	N
2000	83-69	W	N
2000	78-48	W	N
2001	79-66	W	N (79-61)
2001	61-50	W	N
2002	55-51	W	N
2002	60-48	W	N
2003	67-40	W	N
2003	58-48	W	N
2003	48-50	L	N
2004	54-35	W	N
2004	67-59	W	N
2005	64-51	W	N
2005	67-62 (OT)	W	N (88-62)
2006	44-46	L	N
2006	55-39	W	N
2007	53-45	W	N
2007	56-49	W	N
2007	43-41	W	N
2008	68-62	W	N
2008	69-57	W	N
2009	57-62	L	N
2009	61-63	L	N

A 1937 practice session at old Technical High.

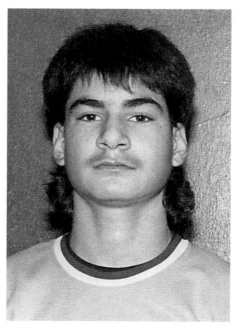

Joey Karpinski, Tech '88.

Joe Blanks, Tech '73.

Ed Crumbly, Tech '64.

Larry Gaines, Tech '66.

The 1964 Tech Centaurs. Front, L to R: Gaines, Kinnard, Calabrese, Lofton, Carson, Crumbly; Middle: Lorigo, Atkinson, Brewton, Monti, Smith, Semzcuk, Boback; Back: Coach Calabrese, Husband, Roberts, Baker, Soderberg, Merski.

1952	67-53	W	N	
1952	57-48	W	N	
1953	55-65	L	N	
1953	82-50	W	N	
1954	47-33	W	N	
1954	53-30	W	N (17-23)	
1955	62-66	L	N	
1955	61-51	W	L	
1956	80-75	W	N	
1956	76-82	L	N	
1957	70-66	W	N	
1957	54-38	W	N	
1958	49-65	L	N	
1958	64-56	W	N	
1959	67-43	W	N	
1959	64-41	W	N (24-26)	
1960	72-70	W	N	
1960	58-61	L	N	
1960	59-58	W	N	
1961	45-74	L	N	
1961	61-64	L	N	
1962	47-69	L	N	
1962	72-77	L	N	
1962	50-48	W	N	
1963	45-78	L	N	
1963	71-74 (OT)	L	N (27-33)	
1964	46-45	W	N	
1964	56-66	L	N	
1965	62-56	W	N	
1965	52-54	L	N	
1965	61-34	W	N	
1966	70-89	L	N	
1966	47-62	L	N	
1967	60-45	W	N	
1967	59-50	W	N	
1968	64-42	W	N (33-37)	
1968	73-50	W	N	
1969	53-70	L	N	
1969	50-48	W	N	
1970	69-67	W	N	
1970	65-52	W	N	
1971	69-50	W	N	
1971	71-47	W	N	
1972	62-57	W	N	
1972	51-48	W	N	
1973	47-63	L	N (41-39)	
1973	64-59	W	N	
1974	46-54	L	N	
1974	69-57	W	N	
1975	65-46	W	N	
1975	52-54	L	N	
1976	51-56	L	N	
1976	73-55	W	N	
1977	59-53	W	N	
1977	72-51	W	N	
1978	74-32	W	N (48-42)	
1978	69-42	W	N	
1979	51-48	W	N	
1979	54-52	W	N	
1980	67-29	W	N	
1980	51-35	W	N	
1981	50-47	W	N	
1981	73-60	W	N	
1982	76-46	W	N	
1982	86-47	W	N	
1983	77-57	W	N (58-42)	
1983	77-54	W	N	
1984	64-56	W	N	
1984	68-57	W	N	
1985	60-59	W	N	
1985	66-69	L	N	
1986	60-46	W	N	
1986	66-49	W	N	
1987	74-48	W	N	
1987	49-51	L	N	
1988	69-60	W	N (66-44)	
1988	58-54	W	N	
1989	85-46	W	N	
1989	68-50	W	N	
1990	97-69	W	N	
1990	83-46	W	N	
1991	69-68	W	N	
1991	75-44	W	N	
1992	76-32	W	N	
1992	58-46	W	N	

Erie Villa Maria Academy "Victors" (4-0)

2003	53-43	W	N
2003	63-44	W	N
2004	81-48	W	N
2004	58-50	W	N

Fairview "Tigers" (2-0)

| 1929 | 39-21 | W | A |
| 1929 | 29-5 | W | H |

Legendary Farrell coach Ed McCluskey.

Farrell "Steelers" (7-4)

1982	37-48	L	H
1983	61-60	W	A
1984	56-54	W	H
1984	76-49	W	A
1985	48-63	L	A
1988	51-49	W	N
1991	63-66	L	A
1996	67-48	W	A
1999	47-66	L	A
2002	54-51	W	A
2004	59-49	W	A

Fort LeBoeuf (Waterford) "Bison" f/k/a "Bisons" (9-0)

2005	61-45	W	H
2006	61-45	W	A
2011	61-30	W	A
2012	59-36	W	H
2013	75-32	W	A
2014	76-30	W	H
2015	73-32	W	A
2016	63-41	W	H
2017	76-49	W	A

Franklin "Knights" (9-1)

1989	82-43	W	N
1990	79-51	W	N
1991	81-63	W	N
2002	59-62	L	A
2003	43-42	W	H
2004	64-57	W	A
2005	52-48	W	H
2006	65-62	W	A
2012	63-56	W	A
2015	50-39	W	N

General McLane (Edinboro) "Lancers" (10-4)

| 2005 | 83-77 (OT) | W | A |
| 2006 | 63-65 | L | H |

2007	83-82 (OT)	W	A
2008	72-62	W	H
2009	68-60	W	H
2010	50-43	W	A
2011	44-59	L	H
2012	46-51	L	A
2013	63-53	W	H
2014	49-38	W	A (7-3)
2015	54-60 (OT)	L	H
2016	63-53	W	A
2016	65-52	W	N
2017	65-61	W	A

Chris Cantino, George Junior Republic '07.

George Junior Republic (Grove City) "Tigers" (18-3)

2001	63-70 (OT)	L	N
2002	68-51	W	H
2003	51-52	L	H
2004	55-52	W	A
2004	52-59	L	N
2005	84-44	W	H
2005	70-35	W	A
2006	72-57	W	H
2006	70-55	W	A
2007	70-51	W	H (7-3)
2007	60-49	W	A
2008	67-51	W	A
2008	81-46	W	H
2009	63-44	W	A
2009	79-64	W	H
2010	80-51	W	H
2010	75-52	W	A
2011	67-25	W	H
2011	77-51	W	A
2012	91-64	W	A (17-3)
2012	70-58	W	H

Girard "Yellow Jackets" (6-7)

1929	16-18	L	H
1929	11-25	L	A
1930	18-30	L	A
1930	14-16	L	H
1932	15-31	L	H
1940	18-14	W	H
1940	45-28	W	A
1949	46-21	W	H
1949	46-47	L	A
2015	39-30	W	A (4-6)
2015	47-40	W	N
2016	51-44	W	H
2016	51-55 (OT)	L	N

Jude Urda, Franklin '06.

Nick Hager, Franklin '02.

Blidi Wreh-Wilson, General McLane '07.

GM coach Andy Schulz, in his younger days.

Bobby Stauffer, General McLane '07.

McLane's great Drew Astorino of '07 was a thorn in Prep's side in football and basketball.

Old Kanty Prep.

Greenville St. Michael's "Irish" or "Mikes" (12-2)

1925	36-11	W	H
1925	31-24	W	A
1926	14-12	W	H
1926	23-16	W	A
1927	30-31	L	A
1927	20-16	W	H
1941	39-18	W	H
1941	41-30	W	A
1942	26-17	W	A
1942	35-23	W	H (9-1)
1952	65-50	W	H
1952	45-51	L	A
1964	68-48	W	H
1965	70-58	W	H

Harborcreek "Huskies" (29-0)

1955	50-34	W	H
1955	51-47	W	A
1956	76-32	W	H
1956	86-58	W	A
1957	58-45	W	A
1957	72-55	W	H
1958	57-49	W	A
1958	65-45	W	H
1959	69-36	W	H
1959	77-53	W	A (10-0)
1960	87-64	W	H
1960	84-49	W	A
1961	60-33	W	H
1961	61-45	W	A
1974	66-61 (OT)	W	H
1975	79-37	W	N
2005	60-51	W	H
2006	63-46	W	A
2007	75-55	W	H
2008	65-41	W	A (20-0)
2009	64-47	W	H
2010	71-52	W	A
2011	71-18	W	H
2012	50-38	W	A
2013	76-36	W	H
2014	57-27	W	A
2015	68-24	W	H
2016	66-50	W	A
2017	52-44	W	H

Harlock Pentagons (Erie) (1-0)

1925	28-25	W	H

Hickory (Hermitage) "Hornets" (10-2)

1971	82-51	W	N
1972	63-44	W	N
1974	54-59 (OT)	L	N
1977	62-42	W	N
1979	66-57	W	A
1980	86-46	W	H
1980	58-37	W	N
1981	69-46	W	A
1982	76-48	W	H
2007	52-61	L	A (8-2)
2008	80-57	W	H
2016	68-31	W	H

Kanty Prep/ Kanty College (Wesleyville) "Eagles" (14-8)

1927	21-23	L	H
1928	9-35	L	H
1928	15-33	L	A
1935	44-7	W	H
1936	35-15	W	A
1936	38-22	W	H
1937	23-33	L	A
1937	30-17	W	H
1938	39-36	W	H
1938	28-42	L	A (5-5)
1939	28-19	W	H
1939	29-31	L	A
1940	20-22	L	H
1940	23-25	L	A
1941	44-30	W	A
1941	35-24	W	H
1942	35-27	W	H
1942	42-20	W	A (10-8)
1943	38-35	W	H
1943	51-31	W	A
1944	46-19	W	A
1944	44-21	W	H

Kennedy Christian n/k/a Kennedy Catholic (Hermitage) "Golden Eagles" (10-0)

1967	60-52	W	A
1967	77-54	W	H
1968	99-51	W	H
1968	63-48	W	A
1969	55-44	W	A
1969	50-32	W	H
1970	86-51	W	A
1970	69-47	W	H
1992	49-37	W	H
2004	61-59	W	N (10-0)

Lawrence Park "Tigers" or "Parkers" (3-0)

1932	21-19	W	H
1933	36-20	W	H
1933	25-17	W	H

"L" Club (Erie) (1-0)

1925	27-25	W	H

Linesville "Lions" (4-0)

1959	67-43	W	A
1960	54-48	W	H
1961	51-41	W	A
1962	75-48	W	H

Bucky Newsome, Meadville '87,

Meadville "Bulldogs" (28-18)

1926	13-27	L	A
1963	63-55	W	A
1964	75-63	W	H
1965	74-60	W	A
1966	51-63	L	H
1966	63-85	L	A
1967	61-69	L	H
1967	69-50	W	A
1968	45-48	L	A
1969	57-55	W	H (5-5)
1975	52-45	W	N
1978	84-55	W	H
1979	49-35	W	N
1980	89-44	W	A
1981	48-39	W	N
1982	76-68	W	N
1983	63-47	W	N
1984	57-54	W	A
1984	51-59	L	N
1984	58-48	W	N (14-6)
1985	54-56	L	H
1986	47-45	W	A
1986	43-48	L	N
1987	44-60	L	H
1987	66-71	L	A
1987	55-61	L	N
1988	64-57	W	H
1988	57-49	W	N
1989	43-61	L	A
1989	55-60	L	N (17-13)
1990	62-43	W	N
1992	51-44	W	N
1993	57-52	W	N
1994	72-41	W	N
1995	66-35	W	N
1997	74-63	W	N
1998	65-55	W	N
2001	58-54	W	H
2002	51-42	W	A
2003	61-67	W	A (26-14)
2007	47-43	W	H
2008	59-44	W	A
2016	52-56	L	N
2017	69-72	L	A
2017	54-67	L	H
2017	48-68	L	N

Meadville St. Agatha's "Aggies" (9-0)

1928	41-11	W	A
1936	50-18	W	A
1936	37-14	W	A
1937	41-7	W	H
1938	33-12	W	H
1938	30-15	W	A
1939	30-7	W	A
1941	78-12	W	H
1941	75-16	W	A

Mercer "Mustangs" (0-1)

1967	66-93	L	A

North East "Grapepickers" (9-4)

1929	33-18	W	H
1929	33-32	W	A
1930	15-20	L	H
1930	17-27	L	A
1934	10-30	L	A
1934	19-10	W	H
1935	16-22	L	A
1935	21-16	W	H
1946	32-7	W	H
1946	40-22	W	A (6-4)
1950	37-18	W	A
1951	75-35	W	A
1951	65-18	W	H

Oil City "Oilers" (3-0)

1980	67-35	W	N
1996	72-40	W	A
2008	70-47	W	H

Oil City St. Joseph's "Irish" or "Hilltoppers" (12-15)

1928	22-28 (OT)	L	A
1932	12-11	W	A
1932	23-26	L	H
1933	18-22	L	A
1933	25-34	L	A
1934	26-27	L	H
1934	10-17	L	A
1936	15-31	L	A
1936	24-17	W	H
1937	25-21	W	H (3-7)
1937	12-10	W	A
1939	18-36	L	A
1939	30-31	L	H
1940	21-27	L	H
1940	26-52	L	A
1941	13-39	L	H
1941	35-37 (OT)	L	A
1942	21-22	L	H
1942	29-26	W	A
1944	29-27	W	H (6-14)
1944	18-25	L	A

Old Oil City St. Joseph's.

1949	45-15	W	H
1949	65-36	W	A
1961	67-45	W	H
1961	64-44	W	A
1962	58-33	W	A
1962	53-46	W	H

Phillips Fruits (Erie) (0-1)
1925	13-21	L	H

Ridgway St. Leo's "Lions" (5-1)
1927	26-13	W	A
1927	17-8	W	H
1929	21-14	W	H
1929	12-21	L	A
1930	41-26	W	A
1930	45-20	W	H

St. Mary's Gems (Erie) (0-1)
1926	11-18	L	H

St. Marys Central Catholic "Crusaders" (9-6)
1944	37-40	L	A
1945	33-21	W	H
1945	29-35	L	A
1946	21-19	W	H
1946	24-44	L	A
1947	25-27	L	A
1947	38-44	L	H
1957	51-55	L	A
1957	80-45	W	H
1957	50-40	W	N (4-6)
1958	53-44	W	N
1959	52-26	W	N
1960	58-37	W	N
1961	69-47	W	N
1962	55-41	W	H

Schaller Morticians (Erie) (0-1)
1925	27-58	L	H

Sharon "Tigers" (6-8)
1953	42-48	L	H
1954	51-48	W	A
1955	49-77	L	A
1956	68-55	W	H
1957	44-86	L	A
1958	31-66	L	A
1959	35-38	L	H
1960	38-37	W	H
1961	42-68	L	A
1962	37-54	L	H (3-7)
1963	38-43	L	A
1982	73-59	W	A
1983	81-59	W	H
2014	60-55	W	A

Sharon Sacred Heart (0-2)
1925	29-47	L	A
1925	22-25	L	H

Sharpsville "Blue Devils" (1-3)
1947	29-45	L	A
1949	30-51	L	A
1951	51-49	W	A
1960	40-61	L	A

Sharrer's Elites " Green & White" (Erie) (0-1)
1925	15-31	L	H

Titusville St. Joseph's "Robots"/ "Blue Knights" (18-1)
1934	25-16	W	A
1934	31-16	W	H
1936	32-11	W	H
1936	35-15	W	A
1937	30-22	W	H
1937	31-39	L	A
1939	22-21	W	A
1939	32-22	W	H
1940	36-14	W	A
1941	68-14	W	A (9-1)
1953	75-35	W	A
1953	95-30	W	H
1954	87-32	W	A
1954	71-16	W	H
1962	92-56	W	A
1964	49-38	W	A
1964	77-66	W	H
1965	61-37	W	A
1965	102-48	W	H

Elvorne Ferguson, Sharon '59.

Titusville St. Titus "Shamrocks" (4-5)
1926	20-23	L	A
1926	20-19	W	H
1927	15-16	L	H
1927	24-19	W	A
1928	13-37	L	A
1929	16-26	L	A
1929	28-8	W	H
1931	10-28	L	H
1932	27-17	W	A

Union City "Bears" (1-1)
1925	27-44	L	H
1938	34-28	W	A

Venango Christian (Oil City) "Vikings" (8-2)
1964	61-37	W	A
1964	81-45	W	H
1965	49-58	L	A
1965	58-41	W	H
1966	53-61	L	H
1966	74-56	W	A
1967	86-50	W	H
1967	60-45	W	A
1968	70-61	W	A
1968	92-41	W	H (8-2)

Warren's great John Bowen '83.

Warren "Dragons" (31-6)
1948	33-31	W	H
1974	64-60	W	H
1974	63-59	W	A
1974	50-52	L	N
1976	80-70	W	N
1977	77-74	W	A
1978	75-50	W	N
1979	71-48	W	N
1981	72-35	W	A
1981	73-44	W	H (9-1)
1981	38-68	L	N
1982	63-56	W	H
1982	63-56	W	A
1982	58-64	L	N
1983	46-48	L	H
1983	60-61	L	H
1983	49-51 (OT)	L	N
1984	78-38	W	H
1984	76-49	W	A
1987	85-42	W	N (14-6)
1988	81-46	W	N

Old Wesleyville High.

1989	72-47	W	A
1996	83-31	W	N
1999	67-37	W	N
2000	85-57	W	H
2001	70-51	W	A
2002	78-52	W	H
2003	70-65 (OT)	W	A
2004	72-43	W	H
2005	71-53	W	N (24-6)
2006	62-59	W	A
2009	61-49	W	A
2010	67-58	W	N
2013	68-59	W	A
2014	87-63	W	H
2015	72-47	W	A
2016	79-43	W	H

Wayne Methodist Episcopal (Erie) (0-2)
1925	27-30	L	A
1925	21-26	L	H

Wesleyville "Bulldogs" (10-5)
1929	20-19	W	H
1929	26-14	W	H
1930	52-5	W	H
1930	35-12	W	A
1931	18-3	W	H
1931	27-6	W	A
1932	14-18	L	A
1932	21-23	L	H
1933	25-32	L	A
1933	39-12	W	H (7-3)
1934	22-11	W	H
1934	12-17	L	A
1935	24-23	W	H
1935	36-21	W	A
1940	20-21	L	A

Youngsville "Eagles" (4-0)
1929	40-24	W	H
1929	47-34	W	A
1930	34-17	W	H
1930	37-18	W	A

Versus Pittsburgh Area

Aliquippa "Indians" (0-1)
1981	49-67	L	N

Daylon Carter, Ambridge '16.

Ron Rowan, Beaver Falls, '81.

Ambridge "Bridgers" (1-1)
1980	52-56	L	N
2015	53-39	W	N

Avella "Eagles" (1-0)
2003	75-30	W	N

Baldwin "Fighting Highlanders" (2-0)
1977	61-59	W	N
1978	51-37	W	N

Beaver Falls "Tigers" (4-3)
1979	43-50	L	N
1980	64-40	W	N
1981	43-53	L	H
1982	53-57	L	A
1983	55-52	W	H
1999	67-29	W	N
2008	66-60	W	N

Belle Vernon "Leopards" (1-0)
1978	65-55	W	N

Bethel Park "Black Hawks" (1-0)
1984	66-62	W	N

Blackhawk "Cougars" (1-1)
2007	63-50	W	N
2008	47-57	L	N

Butler "Golden Tornado" (7-3)
1983	61-47	W	N
1989	57-43	W	N
1991	82-68	W	N
1992	52-53	L	A
1993	58-41	W	H
1993	67-53	W	N
2000	58-50	W	N
2001	76-52	W	H
2011	38-66	L	N
2011	52-60	L	H (7-3)

Charleroi "Cougars" (1-0)
1973	60-43	W	N

Chartiers Valley "Colts" (0-1)
2009	69-84	L	N

Churchill "Chargers" (1-0)
1979	73-58	W	N

Clairton "Bears" (1-0)
1980	75-52	W	N

Antoine Childs, Blackhawk '08.

Major leauger Matt Clement, later head coach at Butler.

Ford City "Sabers" (1-0)
1971   76-61   W   A

Fox Chapel "Foxes" (2-1)
1977   52-68   L   N
1988   65-53   W   N
1991   83-42   W   N

Franklin Regional "Panthers" (1-0)
2011   62-46   W   N

Greensburg "Golden Lions" (0-1)
1975   64-66   L   N

Greensburg Central Catholic '["Centurions" (1-0)
1962   50-38   W   H

Ryan Luther, Hampton '14.

Hampton "Talbots" (2-0)
2013   58-50   W   N
2015   86-70   W   N

Har-Brack "Tigers" (0-1)
1962   44-53   L   N

Hempfield Area "Spartans" (1-0)
1975   83-66   W   N

Hopewell "Vikings" (1-0)
2009   61-57   W   N

Kiski Area "Cavaliers" (2-0)
1997   76-59   W   N
2002   52-46   W   N

Latrobe Area "Wildcats" (3-0)
1988   62-52   W   N
1990   71-49   W   A
1994   65-29   W   A

Latrobe St. Vincent's Prep "Bearcats" (2-0)
1953   70-48   W   H
1954   2-0 (FFT)   W   n/a

Mars Area "Fightin' Planets" (2-1)
2004   76-35   W   N
2015   62-56   W   N
2017   61-72   L   N

McKeesport "Tigers" (2-2)
1983   62-63   L   N
1984   78-48   W   H
1994   70-63   W   N
2006   47-54   L   N

Moon "Tigers" (0-1)
2007   53-62   L   N

Shane Phillips, Mt. Lebanon.

Mt. Lebanon "Blue Devils" (2-1)
2005   78-74   W   N
2007   62-53   W   N
2009   41-51   L   N

New Castle "Red Hurricanes" (4-5)
1972   68-65   W   A
1973   48-54   L   A
1978   46-53   L   A
1979   56-64   L   A
1982   51-55   L   N
1993   64-61   W   N
1995   73-53   W   H
2003   52-50   W   A
2013   70-80   L   N

North Allegheny "Tigers" (3-2)
1992   56-58   L   N
1994   76-45   W   N
1995   73-55   W   N
2011   56-58   L   A
2012   62-54   W   H

North Hills "Indians" (3-0)
2000   74-62   W   H
2005   94-64   W   N
2009   54-43   W   N

Norwin "Knights" (1-0)
1983   65-54   W   N

Anthony Dallier, North Allegheny '11.

Sam Clancy, Pittsburgh Brashear '77.

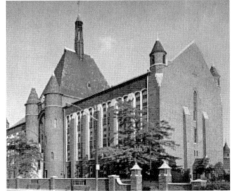

Pittsburgh Central Catholic.

Penn Hills "Indians" (2-5)

1975	56-69	L	A
1982	51-55	L	A
1987	64-65	L	N
1994	62-43	W	A
1997	68-54	W	H
1999	41-52	L	N
2009	61-63	L	H

Peters Township "Indians" (0-1)

2009	47-48	L	N

Pine-Richland "Rams" (1-0)

2007	46-36	W	N

Pittsburgh Bishop Canevin Catholic "Crusaders" (3-2)

1966	62-71	L	H
1967	67-81	L	H
1968	65-56	W	N
1974	86-50	W	H
1975	68-45	W	A

Pittsburgh Brashear "Bullets" (2-1)

1977	60-67	L	H
1978	75-56	W	H
1979	61-57	W	H

Jim McCoy, Pittsburgh Central Catholic '88.

Pittsburgh Central Catholic "Vikings" (5-9)

1945	22-30	L	A
1949	39-43	L	A
1950	37-42	L	H
1952	37-38	L	A
1956	65-68	L	H
1957	59-65	L	N
1964	42-48	L	N
1983	67-52	W	N
1984	59-49	W	N
1988	59-61	L	N (2-8)
1998	49-64	L	H
2006	77-66	W	N
2009	60-58	W	N
2012	50-49 (OT)	W	N

Pittsburgh North Catholic "Trojans" (4-7)

1946	33-34	L	N
1955	56-70	L	A
1958	60-78	L	H
1959	54-70	L	A
1962	47-58	L	A
1966	64-66	L	H
1970	79-78 (OT)	W	H
1970	63-53	W	N
1972	76-54	W	H
1973	70-69	W	A (4-6)
1976	59-81	L	N

Pittsburgh Obama Academy "Soaring Eagles" (2-0)

2012	79-57	W	H
2017	42-41	W	N

Pittsburgh Oliver "Bears" (2-0)

1975	55-45	W	A
1980	80-30	W	N

Pittsburgh Peabody "Highlanders" (6-1)

1979	81-51	W	H
1980	67-49	W	H
1981	49-47	W	A
1982	65-45	W	H
1983	66-69	L	H
1984	63-59	W	H
2010	66-44	W	N

Pittsburgh Perry Traditional "Commodores" (1-1)

2013	78-34	W	H
2014	53-64	L	A

Pittsburgh St. Basil's "Sabers" (1-0)

1953	53-31	W	H

Pittsburgh Schenley "Spartans" (6-3)

1975	48-76	L	N
1978	2(53)-0(59) FFT	W	H
1978	66-67 (OT)	L	N
1980	75-55	W	N
1996	60-44	W	N
1997	33-36	L	N
2002	57-49	W	N
2005	53-49	W	N
2010	71-54	W	N

Pittsburgh South Hills "Tigers" (1-0)

1978	65-54	W	N

Pittsburgh South Hills Catholic n/k/a Seton-LaSalle "Rebels" (3-4)

1961	53-61	L	A
1965	56-58	L	H
1970	57-69	L	H
1971	73-68	W	A
1971	52-50 (5OT)	W	N
1972	42-46 (2OT)	L	N
2002	59-36	W	N

Pittsburgh Taylor Allderdice "Dragons" (1-0)

1984	59-47	W	N

Plum "Mustangs" (2-0)

1980	76-49	W	H
1998	58-49	W	N

Ringgold "Rams" (2-1)

1991	83-64	W	N
1995	67-77 (2OT)	L	N
1996	75-35	W	H

Seneca Valley "Raiders" (1-0)

2013	79-54	W	N

Shaler Area "Titans" (2-1)

1990	72-77	L	N
1993	62-42	W	N
2012	52-49	W	N

Uniontown "Red Raiders" (0-4)

1976	61-82	L	A
1981	41-50	L	N
2002	47-70	L	N
2002	45-48	L	N

Upper St. Clair "Panthers" (4-0)

1994	49-41	W	N
1996	66-49	W	N
2010	48-42	W	N
2015	66-47	W	N

Valley "Vikings" (New Kensington) (1-0)

1992	49-46	W	N

Tom Pipkins, Valley '93.

West Mifflin North "Vikings" (1-0)

1980	85-58	W	N

DeJaun Blair, Schenley '05.

Old Pittsburgh Schenley.

Versus Other Pennsylvania

Allentown Central Catholic "Vikings" (1-1)
1954	80-58	W	A
1971	65-64	W	N

Allentown William Allen "Canaries" (1-0)
| 1980 | 50-40 | W | N |

Altoona "Mountain Lions" (4-9)
1975	78-74	W	H
1976	54-73	L	A
1981	47-48	L	A
1982	52-53 (OT)	L	A
1983	66-61	W	H
1984	52-59	W	A
1985	38-54	L	H
1986	62-69	L	A
1987	48-52	L	A
1988	52-55	L	A (3-7)
1991	98-101 (2OT)	L	N
1993	61-70	L	A
1993	72-52	W	N

Altoona Bishop Guilfoyle "Marauders" f/k/a Altoona Catholic "Yellow Jackets" (4-6)
1929	15-26	L	N
1969	56-62	L	N
1970	63-69	L	N
1971	57-52	W	A
1972	47-52	L	A
1973	52-53 (OT)	L	A
1974	62-65	L	A

Doug West, Altoona '86.

Danny Fortson, Altoona, Shaler '94.

1990	78-55	W	A
1994	79-38	W	A
2000	73-53	W	N (4-6)

Central Mountain "Wildcats" (1-0)
| 2017 | 55-46 | W | N |

Chester "Clippers" (2-3)
1994	65-69	L	N
1995	59-52	W	H
2002	48-54	L	H
2006	88-84 (OT)	W	H
2009	62-69	L	H

Clearfield "Bisons" (2-0)
1977	95-59	W	A
1995	101-46	W	H

DuBois "Beavers" (4-0)
1986	58-51	W	A
1989	81-50	W	H
2009	84-48	W	A
2010	82-25	W	H

DuBois Central Christian "Cardinals" (1-0)
| 1976 | 82-36 | W | H |

Germantown Academy (Fort Washington) "Patriots" (0-1)
| 1998 | 47-62 | L | N |

Harrisburg Catholic High n/k/a Bishop McDevitt "Crusaders" (1-0)
| 1953 | 66-54 | W | H |

Hatboro-Horsham "Hatters" (0-1)
| 1998 | 46-69 | L | H |

Hazleton "Cougars" (1-0)
| 1993 | 41-30 | W | N |

Hempfield "Black Knights" (1-0)
| 1995 | 58-51 | W | N |

Hollidaysburg "Golden Tigers" (2-1)
1992	55-48	W	N
2005	83-49	W	N
2010	41-50	L	N

Indiana "Lil' Indians" (2-1)
1979	57-49	W	N
1980	50-42	W	N
1998	46-57	L	A

Johnstown "Trojans" (14-8)
1971	93-79	W	A
1971	85-72	W	H
1972	55-47	W	A
1972	65-47	W	H
1973	56-90	L	A
1973	62-73	L	H
1974	53-64	L	A
1974	49-85	L	H
1975	68-53	W	A
1975	57-55	W	H (6-4)
1976	52-86	L	A
1977	92-71	W	H
1977	67-68	L	A
1978	84-56	W	H
1979	51-34	W	A
1980	70-47	W	H
1981	46-44	W	A
1982	77-65	W	H
1983	73-60	W	A
1984	82-50	W	H (14-6)
1985	38-58	L	A
1987	46-50	L	A

Johnstown Bishop McCort f/n/a Johnstown Central Catholic "Crimson Crushers" (7-8)
1943	25-35	L	H
1944	19-20	L	A
1945	37-22	W	H
1946	33-32	W	A
1947	38-47	L	N

1948	37-59	L	A
1951	50-53	L	H
1953	54-49	W	H
1954	75-46	W	A
1955	62-55	W	H (5-5)
1956	79-77	W	A
1960	57-58	L	H
1963	52-59	L	A
1966	58-80	L	A
1972	51-44	W	N

Knox Keystone "Panthers" (1-0)
| 1996 | 69-43 | W | N |

Lower Merion "Aces" (0-3)
1996	43-48	L	N
2005	54-65	L	N
2012	48-79	L	N

Philadelphia Archbishop Carroll "Patriots" (0-2)
2014	35-47	L	H
2015	32-59	L	N

Philadelphia Benjamin Franklin "Electrons" (0-1)
| 1990 | 61-72 | L | N |

Kyle Lowry, Cardinal Dougherty '04.

Philadelphia Cardinal Dougherty "Cardinals" (0-1)
| 2004 | 60-78 | L | H |

Philadelphia Constitution "Generals" (0-1)
| 2015 | 56-61 | L | H |

Philadelphia Imhotep Charter "Panthers" (0-1)
| 2013 | 47-74 | L | H |

Philadelphia Roman Catholic.

Imhotep Charter.

John Mizerock, Punxsutawney '79. He had a fine MLB career.

Philadelphia Overbrook.

Nate Stupar, State College '07.

Dallas Comegys, Roman Catholic '83.

Terrell Stokes, Simon Gratz '94.

Philadelphia Northeast Catholic "Falcons" (1-0)

1978	74-51	W	N

Philadelphia Roman Catholic (2-3) "Cahillites"

1983	56-65	L	H
1984	54-52	W	H
1987	59-58	W	H
1989	48-68	L	H
1992	55-66	L	N

Philadelphia Simon Gratz "Bulldogs" (1-2)

1994	35-42	L	N
1998	51-42	W	H
2000	30-59	L	H

Phoenixville "Phantoms" (1-0)

1981	60-53	W	N

Punxsutawney "Woodchucks" (5-0)

1968	89-61	W	A
1969	84-62	W	H
1979	75-65	W	A
1979	56-42	W	N
1980	72-39	W	H

Shamokin Our Lady of Lourdes "Red Raiders" (1-0)

1968	70-47	W	N

State College "Little Lions" (16-2)

1977	74-63	W	N
1980	41-32	W	A
1981	65-53	W	A
1982	68-37	W	A
1983	74-54	W	A
1984	87-65	W	A
1985	51-42	W	A
1986	61-42	W	H
1986	43-53	L	A
1987	56-47	W	H (9-1)
1987	67-41	W	A
1988	58-43	W	A
1989	61-40	W	H
1990	81-65	W	A
1991	69-61	W	H
2006	69-68	W	N
2007	73-52	W	N
2008	58-60	L	N

Susquehanna Township "Indians" (1-0)

1980	50-47	W	N

Waynesboro "Indians" (0-1)

1992	55-57	L	N

Whitehall "Zephyrs" (2-0)

1995	55-46	W	N
1996	80-53	W	H

Williamsport "Millionaires" (2-6)

1980	75-51	W	A
1981	64-62	W	A
1982	56-65	L	A
1983	70-76	L	A
1984	50-70	L	A
1984	61-68	L	N
1985	50-51	L	H
1990	69-85	L	A

York Catholic "Fighting Irish" (0-1)

1991	55-66	L	N

Versus Ohio

Ashtabula (OH) "Panthers" (1-1)

1947	38-35	W	A
1948	30-37	L	H

Ashtabula (OH) Edgewood "Warriors" (1-0)

1967	77-50	W	H

Ashtabula (OH) Harbor "Mariners" (4-0)

1968	65-57	W	A
1968	89-60	W	H
1970	101-63	W	H
1970	79-42	W	A

Ashtabula (OH) St. John "Heralds" (2-0)

1960	93-40	W	H
1960	68-46	W	H

Brookfield (OH) "Warriors" (1-0)

1978	91-83	W	A

Canfield (OH) "Cardinals" (1-0)

1996	70-57	W	N

Canton (OH) McKinley "Bulldogs" (1-1)

1986	46-41	W	H
1987	53-66	L	A

Cincinnati (OH) Taft "Senators" (1-0)

1997	57-42	W	N

Cleveland (OH) Benedictine "Bengals" (3-1)

1952	50-38	W	A
1953	81-51	W	H
1974	81-66	W	H
1999	34-61	L	H

Cleveland (OH) Cathedral Latin "Lions" (3-8)

1925	13-41	L	A
1935	24-27	L	A
1935	17-19	L	H
1947	44-31	W	H
1948	37-45	L	H
1949	37-46	L	A
1950	35-45	L	H
1951	37-51	W	A
1952	52-41	W	H
1958	48-59	L	H (3-7)
1959	47-59	L	A

Cleveland (OH) Gilmour Academy "Lancers" (1-1)

1965	48-75	L	A
1966	59-55	W	H

Cleveland (OH) JFK (0-1) "Fighting Eagles" (0-1)

1967	69-74	L	H

Cleveland (OH) St. Ignatius "Wildcats" f/k/a "Golden Tornado" (5-10)

1930	26-27(OT)	L	H
1930	27-28	L	A
1933	16-28	L	A
1933	30-27	W	H
1947	40-23	W	H
1948	34-42	L	H
1948	35-52	L	A
1995	70-66	W	A
2005	66-73	L	H
2006	81-84 (OT)	L	A (3-7)
2008	64-62 (OT)	W	N
2009	36-53	L	A
2010	60-54	W	H
2011	55-58	L	A
2012	47-50	L	A

Ray Peet, Ashtabula '47.

Gene Gephart, Ashtabula '48.

Cleveland St. Ignatius.

Cleveland St. Joseph, now VASJ.

Clark Kellogg, Cleveland St. Joe's '79.

Carlton Bragg, VASJ '14.

Brian Parker, VASJ '14.

Tom Pritchard, St. Ed's '08.

Cleveland (OH) St. Joseph, n/k/a Villa Angela-St. Joseph "Vikings" (4-8)

1969	58-74	L	H
1970	73-78	L	A
1973	38-85	L	N
1974	75-57	W	H
1974	54-52	W	N
1977	77-66	W	A
1980	59-47	W	H
1985	34-71	L	A
1989	38-61	L	H
1994	61-71	L	H (4-6)
2014	46-64	L	H
2017	37-60	L	H

Conneaut (OH) "Trojans"/ "Spartans" (5-6)

1944	32-30	W	H
1944	23-25	L	A
1949	39-26	W	H
1950	48-50	L	A
1955	48-49	L	A
1956	76-63	W	H
1957	50-67	L	H
1958	38-62	L	H
1959	55-63	L	H
1970	73-64	W	A (4-6)
1971	72-43	W	H

Conneaut (OH) Rowe "Vikings" (4-1)

1939	27-25	W	A
1939	33-27	W	H
1940	28-30	L	A
1955	67-54	W	H
1956	75-43	W	H

Cuyahoga Falls (OH) "Black Tigers" (1-0)

1975	73-56	W	A

Dayton (OH) Dunbar "Wolverines" (0-1)

1992	66-71	L	H

East Liverpool (OH) "Potters" (0-1)

2002	59-61	L	A

Gahanna (OH) Columbus Academy "Vikings" (0-1)

1981	55-59	L	N

Kinsman (OH) Joseph Badger "Braves" (2-0)

1971	73-53	W	N
1972	74-51	W	N

Lakewood (OH) St. Edward "Eagles" (0-5)

1996	67-68 (OT)	L	H
1997	41-52	L	H
2008	52-60	L	H

Jamie Gladden, Lorain Admiral King '89.

2011	57-70	L	H
2016	35-84	L	H

Lorain (OH) Admiral King "Admirals" (1-1)

1989	50-51	L	H
1997	53-44	W	H

Massillon (OH) Washington "Tigers" (1-1)

2008	52-57	L	A
2009	62-52	W	H

Middletown (OH) "Middies" (1-0)

1993	53-44	W	N

Olmstead Falls (OH) "Bulldogs" (1-0)

1997	58-53	W	N

Sandusky (OH) "Blue Streaks" (1-0)

1997	57-53	W	A

Solon (OH) "Comets" (0-1)

2007	53-62	L	A

Toledo (OH) St. John's Jesuit "Titans" (0-1)

2014	60-67	L	N

Toledo (OH) Scott "Bulldogs" (1-1)

1988	40-38	W	H
2000	65-72	L	N

Westerville (OH) Scott "Wildcats" (0-1)

2017	54-82	L	H

Old Youngstown South High.

Prep's Grant Miller closely gaurding Solon's big Dallas Lauderdale (2007).

Youngstown (OH) Cardinal Mooney "Cardinals" (2-0)

1962	56-53	W	A
1962	75-55	W	H

Youngstown (OH) Chaney "Cowboys" (3-1)

1962	46-59	L	N
1977	86-78	W	H
1978	88-53	W	A
1979	80-51	W	H

Youngstown (OH) North "Bulldogs" (3-0)

1979	55-43	W	H
1979	49-46	W	A
1980	90-56	W	H

Youngstown (OH) The Rayen School "Tigers" (1-0)

1982	61-54	W	H

Youngstown (OH) Ursuline "Fighting Irish" (4-3)

1947	52-38	W	H
1949	39-38	W	H
1950	42-60	L	A
1952	53-46	W	H
1954	63-28	W	A
2016	40-43	L	H
2017	50-58	L	A

Versus New York and New Jersey

Athol Springs (NY) St. Francis "Red Raiders" (4-1)

2004	61-48	W	A
2006	77-53	W	H
2012	71-44	W	H
2013	84-37	W	A
2017	48-53	L	N

Brocton (NY) Central "Bulldogs" (1-1)

1926	28-30	L	A
1926	42-17	W	H

Bronx (NY) St. Raymond's "Ravens" (1-0)

1997	56-50	W	N

Brookville (NY) Long Island Lutheran "Crusaders" (1-0)

1987	71-65	W	N

Brooklyn (NY) Bishop Loughlin Memorial "Lions" (1-1)

1984	63-70	L	H
1991	70-69	W	H

Buffalo (NY) Bishop Timon "Tigers" (6-5)

1957	56-53	W	H
1957	34-55	L	A
1958	35-49	L	H
1958	53-62	L	A
1959	64-45	W	H
1959	48-50	L	A
1986	67-43	W	A
2001	48-83	L	A
2002	67-45	W	H
2003	52-45	W	H (5-5)
2004	84-45	W	H

Buffalo (NY) Canisius "Crusaders" (19-13)

1930	22-20	W	H
1930	18-16	W	A
1932	18-31	L	A
1932	24-30 (OT)	L	H
1939	13-31	L	H
1941	2-0 (FFT)	W	H
1953	42-39	W	N
1954	66-56	W	H
1954	73-64	W	A
1955	63-45	W	H (7-3)
1955	45-48	L	A
1956	77-52	W	H
1956	69-55	W	A
1957	48-50	L	H
1957	61-73	L	A
1958	49-56	L	A
1958	82-68	W	H
1959	68-66	W	H
1960	50-51	L	A
1960	56-51	W	H (12-8)
1981	59-54	W	A
1981	62-65	L	H
1986	65-57	W	H
2000	75-59	W	H
2010	63-66	L	A
2011	69-58	W	H
2012	59-72	L	A
2013	72-53	W	H
2014	54-56	L	A
2015	57-47	W	H (18-12)
2016	45-51	L	A
2017	79-59	W	H

Buffalo (NY) Grover Cleveland "Presidents" (0-2)

1986	60-61	L	N
2008	66-70	L	N

Buffalo (NY) Mount St. Joseph (1-0)

1986	56-52	W	N

Buffalo (NY) Nichols "Vikings" (1-0)

2010	57-68	L	H

Brooklyn Bishop Loughlin.

Buffalo Canisius.

The great 1954 Canisius Crusaders.

Front row: T. Mueller, D. Morris, J. Cunningham, *Capt.*; T. McGuire, D. McDonald, J. Rodgers. Second row: Fr. R. Balduf, S.J., *Director of Athletics*; Mr. D. Lento, *Coach*; R. O'Connor, J. Wlodarczak, G. Jacobs, D. Breen, R. Webb. *Absent*: R. Raczynski, R. McKinnon.

Buffalo (NY) St. Joseph's Collegiate Institute "Marauders" (1-1)

1976	77-51	W	H
1976	41-65	L	A

Dunkirk (NY) "Marauders" (4-1)

1947	35-18	W	H
1963	92-43	W	H
1976	80-71	W	H
1976	61-65	L	A
1983	90-53	W	N

Dunkirk (NY) St. Mary's "Lions" (3-4)

1935	16-19	L	A
1935	14-24	L	H
1936	19-39	L	A
1936	11-28	L	H
1941	30-23	W	A
1947	42-16	W	A
1947	54-19	W	H

Elizabeth (NJ) St. Patrick's "Celtics" (1-0)

1994	62-47	W	H

Falconer (NY) Central "Golden Falcons" (1-0)

1926	30-16	W	N

Hamburg (NY) "Bulldogs" (1-0)

2001	65-39	W	N

Jamestown (NY) "Red Raiders" (17-4)

1953	78-65	W	A
1954	61-34	W	H
1963	71-61	W	H
1964	77-65	W	A
1965	68-54	W	H
1966	55-77	L	A
1968	59-46	W	N
1969	71-45	W	N
1969	66-65	W	A
1970	100-42	W	H (9-1)
1970	73-68	W	A
1971	89-60	W	H
1971	99-88	W	A
1972	44-66	L	A
1972	57-63	L	H
1973	79-43	W	A
1973	74-67	W	H
1974	67-70	L	A
1974	86-70	W	H
1975	79-58	W	N (16-4)
1983	72-43	W	A

DaJuan Coleman, Jamesville-DeWitt '12.

Jamesville-DeWitt (NY) "Red Rams" (0-1)

2012	61-74	L	H

Ernest Haynes, All Hallows '54.

Bob Cunningham, All Hallows '53.

NYC LaSalle.

NYC All Hallows.

Shammgod Wells, LaSalle Academy '93.

Kemba Walker, NYC Rice '08.

NYC Rice.

7'3" Serge Zwikker, Msgr. McClancy '95.

Three-point artist Tyler Relph, Rochester McQuaid '03.

Moustafa Diagne, Pope John XXIII '15.

Lackawanna (NY) Baker-Victory f/k/a Our Lady of Victory (5-0) "Braves"

1945	20-7	W	H
1945	33-31	W	A
1970	81-78	W	H
1975	61-35	W	H
1975	75-55	W	A

Lockport (NY) "Lions" (1-0)

1998	60-57	W	H

Mount Vernon (NY) "Knights" (0-2)

2004	43-72	L	H
2010	67-79	L	H

New York City (NY) All Hallows "Gaels" (0-1)

1954	59-73	L	N

New York City (NY) Frederick Douglass Academy "Lions" (0-1)

2001	49-72	L	N

New York City (NY) LaSalle Academy "Cardinals" (1-3)

1993	38-32	W	H
1996	40-44 (2OT)	L	H
2000	44-59	L	H
2001	47-49	L	H

NYC Power Memorial.

Rochester Aquinas.

New York City (NY) Rice "Raiders" (0-1)

2008	63-87	L	H

Niagara Falls (NY) "Wolverines" (1-0)

2012	65-60	W	H

Niagara Falls (NY) Bishop Duffy "Patriots" (1-1)

1962	65-67 (OT)	L	H
1963	61-51	W	A

Niagara Falls (NY) St. Mary's "Cataracts" (3-0)

1931	25-17	W	A
1931	22-15	W	H
1942	34-27	W	A

Olean (NY) Bishop Walsh "Eagles" (0-1)

1968	62-70	L	H

Paterson (NJ) St. Patrick's "Cougars" (0-1)

1995	55-62	L	H

Queens (NY) Christ the King Regional "Royals" (1-0)

1994	51-47	W	N

Queens (NY) Holy Cross "Knights" (0-1)

2005	58-62 (OT)	L	N

Queens (NY) Msgr. McClancy Memorial "Crusaders" (1-0)

1995	57-54	W	N

Ripley (NY) Central "Eagles" (1-0)

1926	17-4	W	N

Rochester (NY) Aquinas Institute "Li'l Irish" (3-7)

1947	46-36	W	H
1948	27-39	L	A
1953	58-50	W	H
1953	55-62	L	A
1954	54-58	L	H
1955	61-57	W	A
1956	66-70	L	H
1957	48-52	L	A
2015	35-48	L	A
2017	51-56	L	H (3-7)

Rochester (NY) McQuaid Jesuit "Knights" (0-1)

2003	50-78	L	H

Silver Creek (NY) Central "Knights" (0-1)

1926	9-14	L	N

Silver Creek (NY) St. Columban's Seminary (2-0)

1930	40-16	W	A
1931	28-19	W	H

Southwestern (NY) Central "Trojans" (2-0)

1963	75-57	W	A
1963	80-46	W	H

Sparta (NJ) Pope John XXIII "Lions" (0-1)

2015	43-68	L	H

Syracuse (NY) St. Lucy (1-0)

1954	65-64	W	N

Tonawanda (NY) Cardinal O'Hara "Hawks" (2-0)

1977	76-47	W	H
1995	70-54	W	N

Tottenville (NY) "Pirates" (1-0)

2017	71-31	W	N

Versus New England

Newport (RI) De la Salle (1-0)

1954	60-51	W	N

Pawtucket (RI) St. Raphael's "Saints" (1-0)

1953	54-51	W	N

Trumbull (CT) St. Joseph "Cadets" (1-0)

1991	82-65	W	H

Versus the South

Junior Etou, Bishop O'Connell '13.

Arlington (VA) Bishop Denis J. O'Connell "Knights" (1-1)

2005	58-79	L	H
2013	80-75	W	H

Baltimore (MD) Cardinal Gibbons "Crusaders" (1-0)

1990	81-64	W	N

Baltimore (MD) Dunbar "Poets" (1-0)

1990	68-62	W	H

Baltimore (MD) St. Frances Academy "Panthers" (0-1)

1996	60-86	L	H

Baton Rouge (LA) Southern Univ. Lab "Jaguars" (0-1)

1999	33-66	L	N

Bladenboro (NC) (0-1)

1990	53-60	L	N

Chattanooga (TN) Brainerd "Panthers" (1-2)

1991	81-76 (OT)	W	N
1995	59-73	L	N
1999	25-37	L	A

Chattanooga (TN) Lookout Valley "Yellowjackets" (1-0)

1995	72-60	W	N

Chattanooga (TN) Tyner Academy "Rams" (1-0)

1999	54-41	W	N

Cleveland (TN) Bradley Central "Bears" (0-1)

1999	50-66	L	N

Clover (SC) "Blue Eagles" (0-1)

2011	48-57	L	N

Coral Gables (FL) Gulliver Prep "Raiders" (1-0)

2007	61-49	W	N

Cumming (GA) Covenant Christian Academy "Rams" (1-0)

2003	76-46	W	N

Davie (FL) Western "Wildcats" (1-0)

2007	70-45	W	N

Decatur (GA) Cathedral Academy (1-0)

1999	73-52	W	N

Dreher (SC) Cathedral Academy (1-0)

2001	67-66	W	N

Easley (SC) "Green Wave" (0-1)

2011	64-72	L	N

Englewood (FL) "Manta Rays" (1-0)

2007	74-56	W	N

Erwin (TN) Unicoi County "Blue Devils" (1-0)

2004	79-39	W	N

Fairdale (KY) "Bulldogs" (0-1)

1991	65-70	L	A

Farmington (WV) North Marion "Huskies" (1-0)

2000	80-71	W	N

Fayetteville (NC) Academy "Eagles" (1-0)

1990	88-53	W	N

Flemingsburg (KY) Fleming County "Panthers" (0-1)

1999	37-43	L	N

Ft. Lauderdale (FL) St. Thomas Aquinas "Raiders" (1-0)

1994	62-46	W	N

Franklin-Simpson (KY) "Wildcats" (0-1)

1996	60-65	L	N

Gainesville (FL) F. W. Buchholz "Bobcats" (0-1)

1989	62-64	L	N

Hollywood (FL) South Broward "Bulldogs" (1-0)

2005	71-33	W	N

Homewood (AL) "Patriots" (0-2)

2013	54-60 (OT)	L	N
2017	64-72	L	N

Hopkinsville (KY) "Tigers" (0-1)

1986	50-61	L	H

Huntsville (AL) S.R. Butler "Rebels" (1-1)

1991	77-66	W	N
1996	55-56	L	N

Hyattsville (MD) DeMatha Catholic "Stags" (0-2)

1982	37-50	L	H
1983	53-72	L	H

Kingsport (TN) Dobyns-Bennett "Indians" (0-1)

1993	49-92	L	N

Kingsport (TN) Sullivan North "Raiders" (1-0)

1993	78-55	W	N

Landrum (SC) "Cardinals" (1-0)

2012	57-40	W	N

Lauderdale Lakes (FL) Boyd H. Anderson "Cobras" (1-0)

1994	73-61	W	N

Letcher Co. (KY) Central "Cougars" (1-0)

2012	56-54	W	N

Lexington (KY) Catholic "Knights" (0-1)

2001	62-74	L	H

Lexington (SC) White Knoll "Timberwolves" (1-0)

2011	51-43	W	N

Louisville (KY) Harry Doss "Dragons" (2-0)

1984	79-56	W	N
1996	62-56	W	N

Louisville (KY) Male Traditional "Bulldogs" (0-1)

1991	73-75 (2OT)	L	N

Marion (MS) "Seawolves" (1-0)

2005	49-42	W	N

Marrero (LA) John Ehret "Patriots" (0-1)

1993	46-53	L	N

Cedric Henderson, Memphis East '93.

Memphis (TN) East "Mustangs" (0-1)

1993	50-51	L	N

Miami (FL) Gulliver Prep "Raiders" (1-0)

2012	67-34	W	N

Midlothian (VA) James River "Rapids" (1-0)

2013	68-57	W	N

Morgantown (WV) "Mohigans" (0-1)

2011	45-63	L	A

Mount Dora (FL) "Hurricanes" (0-1)

2007	47-58	L	N

Mouth of Wilson (VA) Oak Hill Academy "Warriors" (1-2)

1988	58-48	W	H
1990	63-76	L	H
1992	28-70	L	H

Myrtle Beach (SC) Socastee "Braves" (0-1)

1998	42-50	L	A

Naples (FL) Baron G. Collier "Cougars" (1-0)

1989	70-49	W	N

New Castle (DE) William Penn "Colonials" (0-1)

1994	52-65	L	N

N. Bethesda (MD) Georgetown Prep "Li'l Hoyas" (0-1)

2003	43-49	L	H

Parkersburg (WV) "Big Reds" (1-0)

1997	60-43	W	N

Pensacola (FL) Booker T. Washington "Wildcats" (1-0)

1989	59-56	W	N

Potomac (MD) Harker Prep "Navigators" (0-1)

1992	37-65	L	N

Raleigh (NC) Athens Drive "Panthers" (1-0)

1990	65-47	W	N

Richmond (VA) Benedictine College Preparatory "Cadets" (1-0)

1985	63-48	W	H

Rock Hill (SC) "Bearcats" (1-0)

2001	65-49	W	A

St. Petersburg (FL) "Green Devils" (1-0)

2005	53-48	W	N

Sebring (FL) "Blue Streaks" (1-0)

2001	61-57	W	N

South Miami (FL) "Cobras" or "Serpents" (1-0)

1994	60-58	W	N

Staunton (VA) Military Academy "Cadets" (0-1)

1953	57-63	L	N

Stuart (FL) Martin County High "Tigers" (0-1)

1989	62-64	L	N

Tampa Bay (FL) Technical "Titans" (1-0)

2003	83-61	W	N

Washington (DC) Archbishop Carroll "Lions" (0-1)

1999	47-54	L	H

Washington (DC) Dunbar "Crimson Tide" (1-0)

2002	69-62	W	H

Washington (DC) Eastern "Ramblers" (1-0)

1978	67-48	W	N

Washington (DC) Gonzaga College High "Eagles" (0-1)

1998	31-51	L	A

Washington (DC) Woodrow Wilson "Tigers" (0-1)

1998	42-46	L	N

West Charlotte (NC) "Lions" (0-1)

1998	40-56	L	N

York (SC) Comprehensive "Cougars" (0-1)

1987	60-66	L	N

Versus the Midwest

Chicago (IL) Quigley Prep "Phoenix" (1-0)

2006	73-58	W	A

Chicago (IL) St. Rita of Cascia "Mustangs" (1-0)

2006	54-49	W	A

Detroit (MI) Country Day School "Yellwjackets" (0-1)

2000	52-67	L	N

Milwaukee (WI) Rufus King International "Generals" (0-1)

2006	48-65	L	H

Oak Park (IL) Fenwick "Friars" (0-1)

2006	59-61	L	A

South Bend (IN) St. Joseph's "Indians" (0-1)

1988	54-63	L	H

Versus the West

Ballwin (MO) Parkway West "Longhorns" (1-0)

1988	50-46	W	N

Campbell County (WY) "Camels" (1-0)

2016	69-61	W	N

Houston (TX) Westbury Christian "Wildcats (0-2)

2005	46-51	L	H
2009	42-58	L	N

Kansas City (MO) Paseo "Pirates" (0-1)

1988	57-59 (OT)	L	N

Las Vegas (NV) "Wildcats" (0-1)

2004	52-54	L	N

Las Vegas (NV) Adelson School "Lions" (1-0)

2016	57-48	W	N

Las Vegas (NV) Bishop Gorman "Gaels" (0-1)

2010	51-87	L	N

Lee's Summit (MO) "Tigers" (0-1)

1993	52-54	L	N

Mesa (MO) Dobson "Mustangs" (0-1)

2000	55-67	L	N

N. Las Vegas (NV) Cheyenne "Desert Shields" (0-1)

2016	51-52	L	N

Orem (UT) "Golden Tigers" (1-1)

1996	61-58 (OT)	W	N
2014	44-78	L	N

Paradise (NV) Chaparral "Cowboys" (0-1)

1984	59-74	L	N

Provo (UT) Timpview "Thunderbirds" (0-2)

2010	47-59	L	N
2014	52-66	L	N

Ralston Valley (CO) "Mustangs" (1-0)

2017	59-42	W	N

St. Louis (MO) Christian Brothers "Cadets" (0-1)

1997	47-55	L	N

St. Louis (MO) Riverview Gardens "Rams" (1-0)

1997	60-54	W	N

The Bishop Gorman complex.

Spring Valley (NV) Durango
"Trailblazers" (0-1)
2000   58-76   L   N

Springfield (MO) Central
"Bulldogs" (1-0)
1988   50-49   W   A

Springfield (MO) Hillcrest
"Hornets" (1-0)
1993   51-35   W   N

Versus the Far West

Brea (CA) Brea-Olinda "Wildcats" (0-1)
2003   46-48   L   N

Compton (CA) Manuel Dominguez
"Dons" (1-0)
1984   55-49   W   N

El Cajon (CA) Foothills Christian
"Knights" (1-0)
2014   66-55   W   N

Gardena (CA) Junipero Serra
"Cavaliers" (1-0)
1984   82-70   W   N

Honolulu (HI) 'Iolani School
"Raiders" (0-1)
2002   36-65   L   A

Honolulu (HI) Roosevelt
"Rough Riders" (1-0)
2002   76-48   W   N

Honolulu (HI) Punahou School
"Buff n' Blue" (0-1)
2002   41-43   L   N

Kailua (HI) Kalaheo "Mustangs" (1-0)
1992   54-50   W   N

Los Angeles (CA) Fairfax "Lions" (1-0)
1992   48-37   W   N

Los Angeles (CA) Westchester
"Comets" (1-2)
1999   45-65   L   H
2000   67-81   L   N
2007   64-60   W   H

Lynwood (CA) "Knights" (1-0)
2014   48-33   W   N

Mililani (HI) "Trojans" (1-0)
2002   57-43   W   N

Oakland (CA) Fremont "Tigers" (1-0)
1996   45-35   W   N

Redmond (WA) "Mustangs" (0-1)
1994   63-53   W   N

San Bernardino (CA) "Cardinals" (1-0)
2016   63-48   W   N

San Diego (CA) Horizon Christian
"Panthers" (1-0)
2009   44-38   W   N

San Diego (CA), University of;
"Dons" (0-1)
1998   58-61 (OT)   L   N

San Francisco (CA) Lowell
"Cardinals" (1-0)
2009   49-39   W   N

Woodlake (CA) Union "Tigers" (1-0)
2001   63-21   W   N

Versus Ontario, Canada

Etobicoke (ONT) Martingrove Collegiate
"Bears" (1-0)
1997   74-54   W   A

Hamilton (ONT) Cathedral "Gaels" (0-2)
1994   46-47   L   N
1998   46-52   L   H

Hamilton (ONT) Southmont (1-0)
1978   75-45   W   N

Niagara Falls (ONT) A. N. Myer
"Marauders" (1-1)
1992   53-59   L   A
1998   82-38   W   A

Ottawa (ONT) St. Matthew Catholic
"Tigers" (1-0)
1995   69-56   W   N

St. Catharine's (ONT) Denis Morris
Catholic "Redmen" (2-0)
1998   75-59   W   A
2002   94-49   W   H

Sault St. Marie (ONT) Korah Collegiate
"Colts" (1-0)
2015   81-49   W   N

Scarborough (ONT) Bethune
"Bears" (1-0)
1997   58-55   W   N

Scarborough (ONT) Mother Teresa
"Teresa Titans" (1-0)
1999   70-50   W   N

Toronto (ONT) Eastern Commerce
Collegiate "Panthers" (1-0)
1994   62-41   W   A

Toronto (ONT) Lester B. Pearson
"Bengals" (0-1)
1994   53-63 (OT)   L   A

Toronto (ONT) Oakwood Collegiate
Institute "Barons" (1-0)
1978   63-54   W   N

Toronto (ONT) Pope John Paul II
"Saints" (2-0)
2013   70-60   W   A
2014   91-86 (OT)   W   A

Toronto (ONT) Runnymede Collegiate
Institute "Ravens" f/k/a "Redmen" (2-0)
1978   65-42   W   N
1995   46-35   W   A

Toronto (ONT) St. Michael's College
School "Kerry Blues" (1-2)
1999   59-53   W   N
2016   58-61   L   H
2017   52-61   L   A

Toronto (ONT) Westview Centennial
"Wildcats" (0-1)
1999   29-30   L   N

Welland (ONT) Centennial "Bears" (1-0)
1997   62-18   W   N

Versus Other International

Melbourne (AUSTRALIA) College (1-0)
2010   69-59   W   N

St. Augustine in the Carribean
"Falcons" (1-0)
2015   61-47   W   N

Shanghai (CHINA) Nanyang Model
"Tigers" (1-0)
2012   63-26   W   H

Ulm (GERMANY) Urspring Academy (0-1)
2010   43-64   L   N

Tyler McCready, Honolulu Iolani '02.

The 1992 Ramblers, enjoying some down time in Hawaii.

CHAPTER 22

Pennsylvania State Catholic Champions

Cathedral Prep's 1971 State Champs celebrate with a very pleased Monsignor Mc-Donald.

The premier national high school tournament in the country in the 1920's was the National Interscholastic Basketball Tournament (NIBT) conducted by Amos Alonzo Stagg and sponsored by the University of Chicago. The tourney existed as an avenue whereby Stagg could recruit basketball talent to the University of Chicago, which is why he invited public school state champions only. In 1923, Chicago (IL) Loyola Academy specifically asked Stagg to include Catholic and private schools into the tournament, but was rebuffed, as Stagg did not see the Catholic schools as potential feeders into the university's athletic program. Loyola Academy AD Father Joseph Thorning then proposed to Loyola University that it establish a national Catholic tournament

patterned after that of Stagg's. Tremendous support was immediately received and the tournament began in 1924. This invitational meet featured competition between 32 outstanding teams representing various sections or states of the United States. The most popular entrant making regular appearances was the St. Francis (SD) Mission School for Sioux Indians. Some of the Mission's stars over the years carried names like Redfish, Red Elk, Quick Bear, Iron Wing and Crazy Thunder. The National Catholic Interscholastic Basketball Tournament thrived, while Stagg's tournament came under fire until it foundered and was cancelled in 1930. The NCIBT, also known as the "Cardinal's Cup Classic", became a catalyst for state tournaments across the nation and featured

as participants such luminaries as Ed "Moose" Krause, Ray Meyer and George Ireland, all of later collegiate fame. The tournament lasted until 1941, cancelled because of "national emergency" once the United States entered World War II after the bombing of Pearl Harbor.

The first known Pennsylvania State Catholic Tournament was held at St. Francis College in Loretto, March 23-25, 1927. It was announced that the tourney would be staged under PIAA regulations "with competent officials in charge." Any Catholic school in the state was invited to participate, though only four decided to enter: Altoona Catholic, Renovo St. Joseph's, Clearfield St. Francis and DuBois St. Catherine's. The Loretto tournament lasted but one more year, as three of the eight teams entered in 1928 failed to show and Loretto St. Francis Prep won its consolation game over Johnstown Central Catholic via forfeit.

Cathedral Prep received a bid in 1929 to the first annual Pennsylvania State Catholic High School Tournament at Duquesne University in Pittsburgh, featuring Diocesan champions from across the state. In charge of the event was none other than Elmer Layden, the Duquesne football coach and a former member of the famed "Four Horsemen" of Notre Dame. The teams that went to Pittsburgh from other parts of the state had their expenses paid by the university and the champion had the right to represent Pennsylvania in Chicago for the National Catholic Interscholastic Tournament, with all expenses paid. "On to Chicago!" was the slogan of the tournament.

The Duquesne state tournament was a classy event which usually hosted around a dozen teams. The tourney winner

Old Pittsburgh St. Justin's.

was awarded the Bishop Hugh C. Boyle Cup for one year's possession and the Duquesne Alumni Cup for permanent possession. The runner-up was awarded the Reverend M. A. Hehir (president of Duquesne University) Trophy for one year's possession and the Emil Fryer Cup for permanent possession. The consolation winner received the James Philip O'Connor Cup. The Pittsburgh Catholic Cup was awarded to the best Pittsburgh team, while the Notre Dame Club Cup was awarded to the best sportsmanship team. There were also all-tournament teams, most valuable player cups and even a Catholic Observer Cup, which was awarded to the best dressed team! The Duquesne tournament was a victim of the Great Depression, lasting only through 1932.

In 1937 the Williamsport Knights of Columbus chapter started a State Catholic Invitational Tournament (SCIT). The tournament committee members searched annually for whom they considered the best Catholic teams in the state of Pennsylvania. It was an honor for a school to be selected and sometimes teams with excellent records felt snubbed if they were not invited to Williamsport to what was usually an 8-team, single elimination bracket. The winner was considered the Catholic state champion and usually went on to the national tournament in Chicago.

In 1943 the Pennsylvania Catholic Interscholastic Athletic Association (PCIAA) was organized. It was modeled somewhat after the Pennsylvania Interscholastic Athletic Association (PIAA), a voluntary membership organization that consisted at the time of almost all of the public high schools in the Commonwealth of Pennsylvania. The PIAA was formed in Pittsburgh in 1913 by a group of high school principals who wanted to eliminate abuses, establish uniform rules, and place interscholastic athletics in the overall context of secondary education. The PIAA had a long history of bigotry against Catholic schools and always on many occasions over the years denied admittance to the Catholics. Generally stated, the function of PCIAA was to develop and enforce similar rules regulating Catholic interscholastic athletic competition.

Under PCIAA rules, championship basketball teams were determined from each of six dioceses in the state, with the winners meeting in inter-diocesan play along the same lines as the PIAA district competition. The state championship game each year rotated between the East and

Old Pittsburgh St. Basil's.

the West. The East had three Dioceses: Allentown, Scranton, and Harrisburg. The West also had three Dioceses: Erie, Pittsburgh, and Altoona/Johnstown. Each year on a rotating basis one of the diocesan winners in both the East and West received a bye and went directly to the East and West Regional Finals. The Regional winners then met in the state title games. The Philadelphia Diocese was also represented in the early years of PCIAA competition but opted out in 1948.

From 1943 to 1948 there was competition between the SCIT and the PCIAA, similar to what colleges across the nation experienced between the NIT and NCAA. Two state champs were crowned, although in 1943 Pittsburgh North Catholic won both tournaments (similar to CCNY winning both the NIT and NCAA tourney in 1950). Finally the growth and popularity of the PCIAA tourney forced the demise of the Williamsport K. of C. event. The 12th and last Knights of Columbus State Catholic Invitational Tournament was held in 1948.

Pittsburgh North Catholic won the most PCIAA Class A state championships with six, followed by Cathedral Prep, Allentown Central Catholic and Johnstown Central Catholic/Bishop McCort with four each. Johnstown also won a pair of K. of C. titles while ACC finished runner-up nine times, including a duo of losses to Prep in the state finals in 1954 and 1971. A trio of Pittsburgh parish schools won the most PCIAA Class B crowns with three, including St. Casimir's, St. George's and St. James. Hazleton St. Gabriel's garnered the most PCIAA Class C titles with three, including 1966 when future

Notre Dame coach Richard "Digger" Phelps guided the G-Men to the diadem.

The PCIAA thrived until October, 1972, when Governor Milton Shapp signed a bill into law that allowed private and parochial schools to join the 1,100 member PIAA organization. Under the old law, private and parochial schools could only compete with public schools during the regular season, but not in post-season playoffs. The bill was shepherded through by State Representative Frank Stanley, D-Lehigh, who believed it wasn't fair that the Catholic schools couldn't compete in the "coveted" PIAA tournament. It was thought the PIAA was more competitive than the PCIAA and that Catholic schools should be able to compete against the best. Sportswriters in the state predicted Stanley's legislation would lead to a merger of the PCIAA and PIAA. They were being kind as there was no merger. So many Catholic schools opted into the PIAA that just two years later, after an abbreviated state championship tournament in 1974, the PCIAA just sadly disappeared. Now all the high schools in the state could compete for one state title. At the time, no one could have conceived that Catholic or private schools would one day dominate the PIAA tournaments as they do now.

The final PCIAA Class A tourney was held in 1973, but it was a shadow of itself because many Catholic schools had already joined the PIAA, Cathedral Prep included. The final PCIAA Class B (only four Western teams) and Class C (8 teams, four from each side of the state) tourneys were held in 1974. Headmaster Father John Dollinger oversaw the transition into the PIAA for Cathedral Prep, which had been a charter member of the PCIAA since 1943.

Another National Catholic Invitational Basketball Tournament from 1954 to 1978 was sponsored by the national Knights of Columbus organization and played at a series of venues around the Washington (DC) area, including Catholic University, Georgetown and George Mason. The tournament was usually a three-day affair held in late March and teams would often get tours of the White House, Capitol Building and the Supreme Court building. In the latter years of the tournament some local public high schools were invited, as in 1975, when the public high school, Washington Dunbar, won the tournament. Tournament officials terminated the event in 1978 because of competing local tournaments and increasing charges for tournament sites, such as for paid union security guards that had to be used at some locations.

The following lists the Catholic champions (final record, coach) and the scores by which they defeated the runners-up:

Old Pittsburgh St. George's.

Old Johnstown Central Catholic

State Catholic Tournament at St. Francis College, Loretto

State Champions		Runners-up
1927—Altoona Catholic (13-4, Pete Schlegel)	29-19	Renovo St. Joseph's (Lou Bruno)
1928—Duquesne Prep (9-3)	21-18	Greenville St. Michael's (9-2)

State Catholic Invitational Tournament at Duquesne University

State Champions (Bishop Hugh C. Boyle Cup)		Runners-up
1929—Philadelphia Northeast Catholic (21-1, Bill "Butch" Dougherty)	10-8	Altoona Catholic (23-10, Pete Schlegel)
1930—Altoona Catholic (19-8, Pete Schlegel)	16-15	Duquesne Prep (15-5, Pete Collodi)
1931—Duquesne Prep (9-3, Pete Collodi)	39-11	Pittsburgh St. Mary of the Mount (6-6)
1932—Philadelphia Northeast Catholic (16-5, John "Jocko" Collins)	33-28	Scranton St. Thomas (18-4, Tommy Foley)

Knights of Columbus State Catholic Invitational Tournament at Williamsport

State Champions (Bishop William Hafey Cup)		Runners-up
1937—Altoona Catholic (15-4, Norb Rascher)	25-23	Johnstown Central Catholic (17-9, Al DeLuca)
1938—Johnstown Central Catholic (20-1, Al DeLuca)	47-35	Pittsburgh St. Basil's (16-4)
1939—Oil City St. Joseph's (23-4, Joe Connors)	26-22	Pittsburgh Central Catholic (10-7)
1940—Johnstown Central Catholic (21-2, Nick Szabados)	32-26	Oil City St. Joseph's (19-11, Joe Connors)
1941—Oil City St. Joseph's (26-6, Joe Connors)	36-33	Hazleton St. Gabriel's
1942—Philadelphia LaSalle College (24-3, Joe Meehan)	59-37	Pittsburgh North Catholic (19-4, Joe Thomas)
1943—Pittsburgh North Catholic (28-0, Joe Zerilla)	36-32	West Phila. Catholic (16-3, Bob Dougherty)
1944—Easton Catholic (Joseph "Sho" Parino)	43-26	Pittsburgh St. Basil's (22-9, Bill Rahl)
1945—Reading Central Catholic (28-2, Joe Schaaf)	41-26	Pittsburgh St. Joseph's (18-8, Nick Jacobs)
1946—Reading Central Catholic (22-4, Joe Schaaf)	29-22	Chester St. James (19-7, Jimmy Murphy)
1947—Pittsburgh Central Catholic (18-4, Al Stanish)	43-34	St. Marys Central Catholic (27-1, Jimmy Goetz)
1948—Philadelphia Southeastern Catholic (Jack Kraft)	61-46	Oil City St. Joseph's (19-7, Rev. C. M. Hurley)

Pennsylvania Catholic Interscholastic Athletic Association (PCIAA) State Catholic Tournament

PCIAA State Champions		Runners-up
1943 A—Pittsburgh North Catholic (28-0, Joe Zerilla)	30-29	Philadelphia Roman Catholic (12-9, Jordan Olivar)
1943 B—Pittsburgh St. Joseph's (24-7, Nick Jacobs)	37-26	Tamaqua St. Jerome's (14-4, Joe Farber)
1944 A—Philadelphia Southeastern Catholic (16-10, John McGarry)	38-20	Johnstown Central Catholic (21-11, Nat Hickey)
1944 B—Pittsburgh St. Joseph's (23-5, Nick Jacobs)	44-24	York Catholic (12-10, William Wogan)
1945 A—Allentown Central Catholic (23-4, Leo Crowe)	41-38	Pittsburgh Central Catholic (25-4, Al Standish)
1945 B—Pittsburgh St. Casimir's (21-6, Gus Krop)	39-33	Wilkes-Barre St. Mary's (Bill Morgan)
1946 A—Pittsburgh North Catholic (25-6, Joe Thomas)	45-42	Allentown Central Catholic (22-5, Clem Crowe)
1946 B—Pittsburgh St. Casimir's (25-4, Gus Krop)	38-34	Easton Catholic (22-1, Joseph "Sho" Parino)
1947 A—Pittsburgh North Catholic (17-5, Joe Thomas)	43-37	Philadelphia St. Joseph's Prep (16-4, Joe Oakes)
1947 B—Pittsburgh St. George's (21-9, Eddie Artman)	43-41	Mauch Chunk Catholic (31-5, Joe O'Donnell)
1948 A—Allentown Central Catholic (26-5, Joseph Krajsa)	45-41	Johnstown Central Catholic (21-3, Joe Majer)
1948 B—York Catholic (28-2, John Clark)	44-42	St. Marys Central Catholic (22-6, Jimmy Goetz)
1949 A—Pittsburgh Central Catholic (23-1, Joe Penzelik)	54-42	Allentown Central Catholic (23-7, Joe Krajsa)
1949 B—Pittsburgh St. Justin's (22-6, John McDermott)	51-43	Scranton St. Patrick (Fiore Cesare)
1950 A—Reading Central Catholic (29-5, Joe Schaaf)	58-41	Pittsburgh Central Catholic (19-6, Joe Penzelik)
1950 B—Pittsburgh St. James (27-3, Dick Diethorn)	61-55	Bethlehem Catholic (23-7, John Howard)
1951 A—Johnstown Central Catholic (27-0, Joe Majer)	50-48	Reading Central Catholic (23-6, Joe Schaaf)
1951 B—Pittsburgh St. James (29-0, Dick Diethorn)	66-53	Bethlehem Catholic (John Howard)
1952 A—Allentown Central Catholic (19-7, Joe Petro)	49-37	Pittsburgh Central Catholic (17-5, Joe Penzelik)
1952 B—Pittsburgh St. James (29-0, Dick Diethorn)	69-55	Williamsport St. Mary's (21-4, Rupert Morgan)
1953 A—Erie Cathedral Prep (23-4, Dick Detzel)	**66-64**	**Harrisburg Central Catholic (24-5, Les Ginanni)**
1953 B—Pittsburgh St. Basil's (28-5, Jerry Unites)	57-51	Bethlehem Catholic (27-2, John Howard)
1954 A—Erie Cathedral Prep (22-3, Dick Detzel)	**80-58**	**Allentown Central Catholic (20-7, John Wargo)**
1954 B—Pittsburgh St. Michael's (27-1, Howard Ruppen)	66-62	York Catholic (23-6, John Sinkovitz)
1955 A—Carbondale St. Rose (33-2, Ed Kassler)	63-56	Pittsburgh North Catholic (22-4, Don Graham)
1955 B—Pittsburgh St. Canice (32-1, Art Martin)	79-65	Shamokin St. Edwards's (21-6, Joe Shumock)
1956 A—Allentown Central Catholic (24-5, Emil Carazo)	68-60	Pittsburgh Central Catholic (18-4, Joe Penzelik)
1956 B—Pittsburgh St. Casimir's (25-2, Gus Krop)	67-58	Bethlehem Catholic (19-9, Paul Calvo)
1957 A—Allentown Central Catholic (18-10, John Compardo)	60-46	Johnstown Central Catholic (21-4, Don Johnson)
1957 B—Plymouth St. Vincent's (27-0, Joe Evan)	76-65	Pittsburgh St. Casimir's (25-1, Gus Krop)
1958 A—Pittsburgh North Catholic (24-3, Don Graham)	88-65	Harrisburg Bishop McDevitt (23-4, Les Ginanni)
1958 B—Ashley St. Leo's (28-2, Jack Collins)	64-46	Pittsburgh St. Casimir's (23-4, Gus Krop)
1959 A—Pittsburgh North Catholic (25-2, Don Graham)	83-67	Allentown Central Catholic (20-7, John Compardo)
1959 B—Pittsburgh St. George's (24-6, Abiathar "Abby" Bishop)	65-49	Pottstown Pius X (25-4, Dan Dougherty)
1960 A—Johnstown Central Catholic (20-4, Leroy Leslie)	62-61	Norristown Bishop Kenrick (24-3, J. Brown)
1960 B—Bethlehem Catholic (25-7, Paul Calvo)	54-50	Pittsburgh St. Adalbert's (30-4, Ted Kaczorowski)
1961 A—Pittsburgh South Hills Catholic (24-7, Jerry Conboy)	41-40	Scranton Prep (20-1, John Gallagher)
1961 B—Scranton South Catholic (19-6, Bob Dipipi)	61-52	Pittsburgh St. Canice (26-3, Dick Diethorn)
1962 A—Pittsburgh North Catholic (25-5, Don Graham)	75-67	Levittown Bishop Egan (17-6, Johnny Clark)
1962 B—Bethlehem Catholic (28-4, Paul Calvo)	40-29	Greenville St. Michael's (21-7, Denny Driscoll)
1963 A—Johnstown Bishop McCort (25-4, Leroy Leslie)	57-40	Scranton Prep (13-8, John Gallagher)
1963 B—Carbondale St. Rose (28-3, Jerry Finan)	56-54	Natrona St. Joseph's (24-5, Joe Nee)
1963 C—Greenville St. Michael's (22-3, Denny Driscoll)	69-64	Williamsport St. Joseph's (24-1, Charley Blackburn)
1964 A—Allentown Central Catholic (21-5, John Compardo)	59-57 (2OT)	Pgh. Central Catholic (21-2, John Killian)
1964 B—Pittsburgh St. Canice (31-1, Dick Diethorn)	86-80	Scranton Cathedral (21-8, Dan Donovan)
1964 C—Greenville St. Michael's (24-4, Denny Driscoll)	50-49	Williamsport St. Joseph's (23-4, Charley Blackburn)
1965 A—Pittsburgh South Hills Catholic (26-1, Jerry Conboy)	64-60	Allentown Central Catholic (24-2, John Compardo)
1965 B—McKees Rocks St. Francis DeSales (32-1, Ted Kazcorowski)	78-77	Shamokin Lourdes (Dave Maloney)
1965 C—Uniontown St. John's (19-9, James "Lash" Nesser)	64-60	Williamsport St. Joseph's (22-4, Frank Sullivan)
1966 A—Johnstown Bishop McCort (28-2, Bill Merkovsky)	88-83	Harrisburg Bishop McDevitt (23-4)
1966 B—Pittsburgh St. George's (26-1, Abiathar "Abby" Bishop)	85-61	Scranton Cathedral (25-2, Dan Donovan)
1966 C—Hazleton St. Gabriel's (21-6, Richard "Digger" Phelps)	91-59	Masontown Kolb Memorial (15-7, Frank Wydo)
1967 A—Altoona Bishop Guilfoyle (20-6, Bill Gaffey)	61-57	Shamokin Lourdes (22-3, Dave Maloney)
1967 B—Scranton Cathedral (28-1, Dan Donovan)	79-70	Connellsville Father Geibel (22-4, Ken Misiak)
1967 C—Hazleton St. Gabriel's (23-3, Jack Cryan)	68-60	North East Gregory's (18-9, Pete White)
1968 A—Erie Cathedral Prep (19-5, Dick Fox)	**70-47**	**Shamokin Lourdes (21-5, Dave Maloney)**
1968 B—Scranton Cathedral (21-5, Bob Meckwood)	77-76	Pittsburgh St. Basil's (24-2, Ed Miller)
1968 C—Spring Grove St. Francis Prep (15-10, Lou Sabler)	77-55	Titusville St. Joseph's (12-9, Jim Snyder)
1969 A—Pittsburgh Canevin (24-0, Ronald "Cy" Cygrymus)	80-57	Allentown Central Catholic (19-7, Mike Koury)
1969 B—Pittsburgh St. Basil's (26-1, Ed Miller)	44-42	West Chester Bishop Shanahan (24-2, Pete Bruni)
1969 C—Spring Grove St. Francis Prep (23-4, Lou Sabler)	84-52	Uniontown St. John's (13-10, "Lash" Nesser)
1970 A—Altoona Bishop Guilfoyle (21-4, Tom Lane)	76-74	Allentown Central Catholic (20-7, Mike Koury)
1970 B—Reading Holy Name (27-2, Lloyd Wolf)	59-58	Connellsville Father Geibel (10-13, Ken Misiak)

1970 C—Hazleton St. Gabriel's (19-7, Jerry Anderson)   79-70   Uniontown St. John's (20-4, James "Lash" Nesser)
1971 A—Erie Cathedral Prep (22-3, Dick Fox)   **65-64**   **Allentown Central Catholic (14-13, Mike Koury)**
1971 B—Tamaqua Marian Catholic (25-4, Bob Fulton)   67-48   Pittsburgh St. Basil's (23-2, Bill "Red" Ryan)
1971 C—Herman St. Fidelis Seminary (20-4, Jim Meissner)   59-52   Wilkes-Barre St. Nicholas (22-4, Bob Schuler)
1972 A—Pittsburgh South Hills Catholic (20-5, Rick Keebler)   69-53   Allentown Central Catholic (23-3, Mike Koury)
1972 B—Bensalem Holy Ghost Prep (24-3, Tom Kaczor)   54-36   Pgh. South Side Catholic (24-5, Tom Maloney)
1972 C—Williamsport Bishop Neumann (22-4, Gary Koons)   70-64   Bradford Central Christian (22-4, Joe Vecellio)
1973 A—Scranton Prep (20-3, Jack Farrell)   48-46   Pittsburgh North Catholic (14-13, Don Graham)
1973 B—Scranton Bishop Hannan (17-5, Jerry Burke)   84-73   Elk County Christian (24-4, Jim Pfingstler)
1973 C—Bradford Central Christian (22-4, Joe Vecellio)   64-60   Pittston St. John's (11-14, Jim Kolmansberger)
1974 A—No tournament (lack of Class A teams)
1974 B—Bradford Central Christian (19-7, Joe Vecellio)   66-61   Braddock St. Thomas (21-3)
1974 C—McSherrystown Delone Catholic (13-12, Jim Livelsberger)   60-59   Pittsburgh South Side Catholic (22-5, Jim Dilla)

National Catholic Interscholastic Basketball Tournament At Loyola University, Chicago (IL)

NCIBT Champions		Runners-up
1924—Peoria (IL) Spalding Institute	21-7	Milwaukee (WI) Marquette Academy
1925—Chicago (IL) St. Mel	15-7	Milwaukee (WI) Marquette Academy
1926—Louisville (KY) St. Xavier	18-16	Rochester (NY) Aquinas Institute
1927—Joliet (IL) De La Salle	26-11	Philadelphia (PA) Roman Catholic
1928—Joliet (IL) De La Salle	32-11	St. Louis (MO) University Prep
1929—Chicago (IL) De La Salle Institute	25-16	Bay St. Louis (MS) St. Stanislaus
1930—Chicago (IL) De La Salle Institute	25-14	Jasper (IN) Academy
1931—Minneapolis (MN) De La Salle	23-21	Jasper (IN) Academy
1932—Chicago (IL) St. Patrick	22-20	Chicago (IL) St. Mel
1933—Indianapolis (IN) Cathedral	31-10	Chicago (IL) St. Rita of Cascia
1934—Joliet (IL) Catholic	30-17	Stockton (CA) St. Mary's
1935—Louisville (KY) St. Xavier	29-24	Chicago (IL) St. Mel
1936—Chicago (IL) De La Salle Institute	45-29	Anderson (IN) St. Mary
1937—Oak Park (IL) Fenwick	30-27	Joliet (IL) Catholic
1938—Louisville (KY) St. Xavier	31-22	Winnetka (IL) Loyola
1939—Fort Wayne (IN) Central Catholic	44-37	Chicago (IL) Leo
1940—Fort Wayne (IN) Central Catholic	35-33	Santa Fe (NM) St. Michael
1941—Chicago (IL) Leo	49-41(OT)	St. Francis (SD) Mission School

Pennsylvania Schools that participated in the NCIBT:

1924—None
1925—Pittston St. John's [lost to Bay St. Louis (MS) St. Stanislaus Academy, 39-13]
1926—None
1927—**Johnstown Central Catholic** [defeated Cedar Rapids (IA) St. Patrick's, 21-10; lost to Wichita (KS) Cathedral, 19-11]; **Philadelphia Roman Catholic** [defeated Peoria (IL) Spalding Institute, 28-10; Minneapolis (MN) De La Salle, 27-17; Decatur (IN) Catholic, 25-21; and Louisville (KY) St. Xavier, 22-16; lost to Joliet (IL) De La Salle in 3 OT championship game, 26-11]
1928—Philadelphia Roman Catholic [defeated Milwaukee (WI) Marquette, 30-23;]; Titusville St. Titus [lost to Chicago (IL) St. Philip's, 35-11]
1929—Philadelphia Northeast Catholic [lost to Peoria (IL) Spalding Institute, 23-13]; **Williamsport St. Joseph's** [lost to St. Louis (MO) McBride, 19-14]
1930—**Altoona Catholic** [lost to Decatur (IL) Catholic, 22-16]; Duquesne Prep [defeated Shawnee (OK) St Gregory, 35-16; lost to Union City (NJ) St. Michael, 41-33]
1931—**Duquesne Prep** [defeated Chicago (IL) DePaul, 24-15; lost to Indianapolis (IN) Cathedral, 25-24]
1932—**Scranton St. Thomas** [defeated Little Rock (AR) Catholic, 45-12; lost to Nashville (TN) Father Ryan, 35- 29]
1933—**DuBois St. Catherine's** [defeated DeWitt (IA) St. Joseph, 24-15; lost to Evansville (IN) Reitz Memorial,   22-18]
1934—**DuBois St. Catherine's** [lost to Indianapolis (IN) Cathedral, 23-16]; **Oil City St. Joseph's** [defeated Iowa City (IA) St. Mary's, 18-17; lost to Stockton (CA) St. Mary's, 23-11]; **Pittsburgh Central Catholic** [defeated Little Rock (AR) Catholic, 46-10; lost to Milwaukee (WI) St. John's, 34-30]
1935—**Bradford St. Bernard's** [defeated Mankato (MN) Loyola, 31-13; lost to St. Francis (SD) Mission School for Indians, 40-14]; **Oil City St. Joseph's** [lost to Anderson (IN) St. Mary's, 26-25]; Pittsburgh St. Joseph's [lost to Duluth (MN) Cathedral, 25-16]
1936—**Pittsburgh St. Joseph's** [lost to Dubuque (IA) Columbia Academy, 46-26]
1937—**Latrobe St. Vincent Prep** [lost to Joliet (IL) Catholic, 59-13; lost to Cumberland (MD) LaSalle, 34-17]; **Pittsburgh St. Joseph's** [lost to Chicago (IL) Loyola, 20-17; lost to St. Francis (WI) Pio Nono, 41-23]; **Philadelphia LaSalle College** [defeated Chicago (IL) Loyola, 31-27; lost to Huntington (WV) St. Joseph's in 3rd place consolation game, 37-27]
1938—**Ambridge St. Veronica's** [lost to Anderson (IN) St. Mary's, 31-29]
1939—**Philadelphia Southeast Catholic** [defeated Denver (CO) Holy Family, 30-24; lost to Fort Wayne (IN) Central Catholic, 46-37]; **Pittsburgh St. Basil's** [defeated Nashville (TN) Father Ryan, 60-41; defeated Cold Springs (MN) St. Boniface, 51-37; lost to Fort Wayne (IN) Central Catholic, 45-26]
1940—**Pittsburgh Central Catholic** [defeated Dubuque (IA) Loras Academy, 30-28; lost to Chicago (IL) Leo, 27-25]
1941—**Oil City St. Joseph's** [defeated LaCrosse (WI) Aquinas, 46-35; lost to Lynn (MA) St. Mary's, 39-37]; **Philadelphia Northeast Catholic** [lost to Chicago (IL) Leo, 57-23]

Bob Vilchinsky, Johnstown Central Catholic '53, became one of Gannon's early stars.

Ron Nathanic, Johnstown Central Catholic '51.

Johnston Central Catholic's great 1951 PCIAA state champs. Front, L to R: Kapusnak, Smith, Bresnicky, Ondrula, Osmar, Tracy, Furman, Stahr; Back: Nathanic, Janshego, Rusutek, Coach Majer, Pavlick, McKenzie, Vilchinsky.

National Catholic Invitational Basketball Tournament In Washington (DC

Champions	Stars
1954—New York City (NY) St. Ann's (29-1, Lou Carnesecca)	Don Lane
1955—New York City (NY) St. Ann's (Lou Carnesecca)	Tommy Kearns, York Larese
1956—Brooklyn (NY) St. Francis Prep (30-0, Frank "Chick" Keegan)	Sam Stith, Tom Stith
1957—New York City (NY) St. Ann's (29-3, Lou Carnesecca)	Willie Hall
1958—New York City (NY) Archbishop Molloy (33-0, f/k/a St. Ann's, Lou C.)	Willie Hall
1959—Washington (DC) Archbishop Carroll (32-2, Bob Dwyer)	"Monk" Malloy, Tom Hoover
1960—Washington (DC) Archbishop Carroll (34-0, Bob Dwyer)	John Thompson, George Leftwich
1961—Hyattsville (MD) DeMatha Catholic (27-1, Morgan Wootten)	John "Sleepy" Austin
1962—Hyattsville (MD) DeMatha Catholic (29-3, Morgan Wootten)	John "Sleepy" Austin
1963—Hyattsville (MD) DeMatha Catholic (36-4, Morgan Wootten)	Johnny Jones, Joe Kennedy
1964—No tournament	
1965—No tournament	
1966—Hyattsville (MD) DeMatha Catholic (28-1 Morgan Wootten)	Bob Petrini, Sid Catlett
1967—Hyattsville (MD) DeMatha Catholic (26-5 Morgan Wootten)	Sid Catlett, Aubrey Nash
1968—Hyattsville (MD) DeMatha Catholic (27-1, Morgan Wootten)	James Brown, Steve Garrett
1969—Hyattsville (MD) DeMatha Catholic (27-3, Morgan Wootten)	Don Willis, Ray Hite
1970—Washington (DC) St. Anthony's (John Thompson)	Alan Baker, Donald Washington
1971—Washington (DC) McKinley Tech (McKinley Armstrong)	James Monroe
1972—Washington (DC) St. Anthony's (John Thompson)	Merlin Wilson, Jonathan Smith
1973—Hyattsville (MD) DeMatha Catholic (30-1, Morgan Wooten)	Adrian Dantley, Bill Langloh
1974—Washington (DC) St John's (Joe Gallagher)	Pat Dosh
1975—Washington (DC) Dunbar (Joe Dean Davidson)	Stacy Robinson, Joe Thweatt
1976—Washington (DC) Dunbar (29-0, Joe Dean Davidson)	Craig Shelton, John Duren
1977—West Philadelphia (PA) (30-0, Joe Goldenberg)	Gene Banks
1978—West Philadelphia (PA) (33-1, Joe Goldenberg)	Clarence Tillman

Pittsburgh CC's legendary coach Joe Penzelek, here coaching against Prep in the 1956 PCIAA playoffs.

Pittsburgh Canevin Catholic.

Nat Hickey, one of basketball's early stars, became coach at Johnstown Central Catholic (1943).

Chicago Leo won the last NCIBT (1941).

Johnstown CC's John Stofa was the Cincinatti Bengals' first draft choice ever.

Pittsburgh North Catholic, 1959 PCIAA state champs. Front, L to R: Werner, Szykowny, Cegalis, Brown, Interieri; Back: Coach Graham, Dodaro, Sims, Rojik, Lofink, Hughes.

Allentown Central Catholic.

Leroy Leslie, Johnstown Central Catholic '48. He later starred at Notre Dame and was the Crushers' state championship coach.

Old Philadelphia Northeast Catholic.

Old Pittsburgh West End St. James.

Erie Parochial Grade School Basketball

Prepsters Father (later "Monsignor") Jim Sperry '33 and Ted (later "Monsignor Ted" Carter) '42 guided the 1942 St. Joseph's Orphanage team.

The phrase "Erie Parochial Grade School Basketball" evokes fond memories and big smiles. The Erie Diocese's Parochial League grade school basketball program, started in 1933 by Bishop John Mark Gannon through diocesan Director of Youth Activities and Cathedral Prep athletic director Father Walter Conway, has survived for over eight wonderful decades—most likely the longest continually surviving league of its kind in the nation. In days gone by, the Erie grade school Catholic league was a sacred ritual—a world of high-top Converse sneakers and center jumps at quirky gyms and tradition-rich schools, most of which no longer exist. The history of Cathedral Prep basketball would be incomplete without a strong mention of its main feeder program through the years.

The appeal of Parochial League basketball is difficult to describe, especially to non-Catholics. What made Parochial League basketball special in years gone by was the fact that everyone knew about everyone else—and not just their names, but their parents, their neighborhoods, their parishes, the playgrounds they frequented, their hoop reputations. Heady coaches bred heady players who became heady coaches themselves. Those who didn't became referees, or devoted fans, or fathered sons who also became "gym rats." Some other directors through the years include former Prep athletic director Monsignor Jim Gannon, Paul McFadden, former Prep coach Bill Flaherty, Bill Jones and currently Doug Chuzie, also the Villa Maria Academy head coach.

The best Parochial League teams were undersized, dedicated defensively and extremely well-coached. Adherence to discipline came easily, because the players experienced it every day from the nuns and priests who taught them. Show-offs or "butches" were as likely to earn a seat on the bench as much as a pat on the back. All, it seemed, could trace their basketball lineage back to fathers, uncles and older brothers who'd been schooled in the weave and the 2-1-2 zone defense at the league's ancient places, like St. Patrick's, St. Mary's, St. Peter's, St. Stanislaus, St. John's, St. Joseph's, Sacred Heart, St. Andrew's and even St. Joseph's Orphanage. The traditions at those schools imbued programs at newer ones, places closer to the city's edges or in the growing suburbs, such as St. George's, Our Lady of Peace, Blessed Sacrament, St. Luke's, St. James and Our Lady's Christian.

It wasn't only the Catholic league players who were close. From the kids to the parents to the coaches to the school-day teachers, everyone had a knowable past. They had encountered each other at playgrounds or Little League baseball, been in parish or CYO leagues together, and attended the same Catholic school classes that, especially in "Baby Boom" years, were often packed with over 100 kids. Some parents drank beer with coaches at neighborhood saloons, chatted about lineups and opponents and attended Mass with them.

There is a shared history, a shared vocabulary, shared memories. Everybody knew the stories about bandbox gyms, tile floors, the charm of St. Pat's Cauley Memorial Auditorium and the out-of-bounds brick wall and low ceiling at the Eastside Boys' Club where St. Stan's played. There was Joe [Sarvadi] Solony's record 43 points in 1950 for St. Andrew's against St. John's—a record broken just a week later by Eddie Grucza of St. Stan's who scored 45 against that same St. John's five. Discussions on the same will have persons soon telling a story or trying to come up with a name more obscure or a play more dramatic.

For anyone associated with Parochial League basketball, your parish was particularly significant. It was your ID. The question when you got to 9th grade at Cathedral Prep was, "Where you from?"—and it was not intended to elicit the name of a city neighborhood, suburban town or subdivision. The inquisitors wanted to know your parish. And hearing it, they immediately knew the priests, nuns, families, players and coaches who shaped you. They knew you. They knew about the Polish kids at Holy Trinity, St. Casimir's, St. Hedwig's and St. Stan's; the Irish kids at St. Ann's; the Slovak kids at Holy Family; the Italian kids at St. Michael's and St. Paul's; the Irish and Italian kids at St. Pat's; the German kids at St. Joe's and St. Mary's; the German and Polish kids at St. John's; the German and Italian kids at Sacred Heart; the German, Polish and Italian kids at Holy Rosary; and even about the orphans at St. Joe's Home or the "hoods" at Harborcreek Training School.

This author's first exposure to Catholic league basketball came as a young boy poring through the box scores in the sports pages of the weekly diocesan newspaper, the Lake Shore Visitor. We studied the box scores and the standings of the Class A and Class B divisions endlessly, as if they were sacred scrolls. We were mesmerized by the images of satin warmups and the unknowable secrets of exciting games in small, dark, far-away gymnasiums. As early as first grade we attended four o'clock games in St. George's gym and it felt like it was the pinnacle of American athletics. We saw the older

Mid-1950's action in the jam-packed Holy Family gym. Note Sister keeping the scorebook.

neighborhood kids—guys like Pat Lupo, Rene Hayes, Johnny DiBacco, Donny Felix, Billy Trambley, "Sonny" Sontheimer, Jimmy Trojan and others we considered saint-like gods— play right there. We were captured, hook-shot, line and sinker.

Local legends were made as teams battled for the Bishop Gannon Trophy, despite the fact it was just grade school basketball. Everyone knew about Fr. Joe Radziszewski's amazing championship run at St. Stan's in the 1940's (from 1944 through 1950 the Eagles of Father Joe were 110-5!); about the St. Pat's Shamrocks championship teams of the early-1940's, the early-1950's and the early-1960's, which included Erie's first two state titles; about some classic East-West-type championship playoff matchups between St. John's (22-3 in 1957, 30-4 in 1966) versus Sacred Heart (17-2 in 1957, 24-3 in 1966); and about all the Bill Garvey-coached champions at St. John's, a school that racked up no less than eight state crowns between 1969 and 1999.

Individuals reached icon status as well. An inadequate list of grade school luminaries includes stars like, from the West side of Erie: Jimmy Callista (Vincent), Joe Nolan (Tech), Don Laird, Paul Ashworth, Tom Bertges, Jack Crotty, Don Guerrein, Elvin "Bungo" Trucilla (Vincent), Sammy Williams (Vincent), Bill Cerrona, (Vincent), Joe Solony [Sarvadi], Chuck Bauder, Brian Jackman, Bill Rollinger, Toby Boggs (Vincent), Rick Scheppner, Jim Sitter, "Pudge" DiPlacido, Jim LeCorchick, Tom Boyd, "Dezzie" Long, Mark DiPlacido, Tim Gore, Chris Krug and the brothers Dentel, Wittman, Meuser, Wagner (Vincent), Barron (Prep & SV), and Elwell (Prep & SV) at **St. Andrew's**; Bill Habersack, Herbie Down (Academy), Bobby Pirrello (Vincent), Phil Hoydic, Jim Musone, Tom Doyle, Paul Petrianni, Bill Benko, Billy Guth, Bill "Schmoo" Martin, Jack Benson, Dan Heher (Tech), Rick Federici (Vincent), Bill Bensur, Tom Hesch, Ed Dalton, Gary Firch (Tech), Shawn Dombrowski, Jerry Cooley, Dan Nordin, Pat Menc (Tech), Tim Cacchione (Academy), Pete Sala (Vincent), Larry Raimondi, Brad Orlando (Vincent & McDowell), Jim Gemler, Chris Dudley, Greg Dufala, Steve Noonan, Raymond Blanks, Sean Meadows, Pete Petrianni and the brothers Engel, Weber, Alexa, Hintz (Vincent), Gianelli, Stadtmiller,

Cyterski, Nuara, Steiner, Marnella, Roach and Schumacher at **Blessed Sacrament**; and Charlie Horn, the Brabender twins (Vincent), Bob Barcio, Tom Coyne, Carl Carlotti, Jimmy Trost, Bill DiPlacido, Jack Flanagan, "Cards" Carideo, "Butchie" Roberts, Chuck Dillon, Don Wolf, Jimmy Lawless (Vincent), Alex Clement (Vincent), James Schneider (Vincent), Father Jim Fahey, Fred Delfino (Academy), Jim Murray, Benny Szumigala, Mickey Schriefer, Andre Heuer, Bill Coleman, Dan Cooney, Don Belton, "Spinner" Crotty (Tech), Gerry Mullen, John Marucci (Tech), Chris Dahlkemper, Rick Koehler, Mark Schumacher, Dick Mangold, Gary Suminski, Mike O'Brien, Al Zenner, Mike Manczka, Jawan Walker and the brothers Fuhrman, Karle, Marthaler, Hansen, Van Volkenburg, Wierbinski, Beck, Bengel, Achille, Dalton and Gaeta at **Sacred Heart**.

Also, Joey Barabas, Wendel Paulo, Donald Klemm, Carl Hutchison, the Droney brothers, Joe Luteran, Louie Distrula, Tom Zipperi, Ed Pamula, Ron Elekes, Bobby Baker, James Jewell and Marty Davis from **St. Joe's Home**; Ernie Spirito (Tech), Vince Cologrande (Vincent), the DeFazio cousins (Vincent), Roy Bernardini (Tech), Dominick Surace (Vincent), Johnny DeSarro (Vincent), Joe Cuzzola, Frank Vendetti (Vincent), Donny Calabrese (Tech),

Phil Ferrare, Lou Ensani, Rick Scalise, Eddie Mazza (Vincent), Dave Van Damia, Gene Placidi, Frank DiPlacido, Paul DeRaimo and the Jordano and Mifsud brothers at **St. Paul's**; George Geiger, Jack Krahe, George Carson (Academy), Danny Wenrick (Tech), Tom Schneider, Joe Bufalino, Barry Masterson, Denny Flanagan, Rick Weber (Tech), Marty DePalma, Russ Mosher, Sam DeLeo, Jim Schaaf, Joe Dolak, Bob Maxson (St. Mark's Seminary), Ricky Pointer and the brothers Flaherty, Sertz, Lanager, Shreve, Greene, Gibbs (Tech) and Mundy (Prep & Mercyhurst) at **St. Joseph's**; Billy Speros, Noah Pelkowski, G. T. Miller, Ryan Heidt and Dan Marz at **Villa Maria Elementary**; Rick Gette (Girard), Paul Simkovitch (Girard), John Schwab, John Pilewski (Girard), John Bowen, Billy Clark (Girard), Jimmy Bensur, Rob Rickard (Girard), Chuck Miller (Girard), Greg Featsent (Girard), Doug Chuzie (Girard), Jed Ryan and the Chesko (Girard), Maslar (Girard) and Straub brothers at **Girard St. John's**; and Mike Smith, Steve Blackman (McDowell), Mike Ford (McDowell), Dan Rettger (McDowell), Bill Bules, "Chip" Knight (McDowell), Dave Curtis, Dan Sculley, Larry Serafin, Tom Falconer, Paul Siegel (Fairview), Dan Quinn, Mark Atkinson, Joe Ianello, Matt Micholas (McDowell), Dale Williams, Mike Sertz, Corey Knight, Joe Fustine and the brothers Herbe (McDowell), Stebnisky (McDowell), Smrekar (Prep & McDowell), Hampy (McDowell), Agnello (McDowell) and Stablein (McDowell & Prep) at **OLP**.

Also, Greg Parsons, Chuck Lee, John Carrig, Jim Sperry (McDowell), Paul Greiner, Tim Fox, Mark Cieslak, Tim Pastore, Jerry Westhoff, Jeff Maries, Jeff Joint, Jeff Szumigale, Joe Nolan, Jim Roseto, Kevin Gallagher, Mark Zappia, Jim Hamilton, Ed Hinkel, Adam Braham, Alex Fatica, Brian Mahoney, Greg Podufal, Mike Kloecker, Connor Imboden and the brothers Dragoone, Hermann, Sweny, Hughes, Benoit, Bizjak, Jefferson, Fatica, Kubinski and Fessler at **OLC**; "Moe" Gross, Vinny "Flowers", Bernie Donatucci, Ray Fiorelli, Denny Cologrande (Tech) and the Ferrare (Vincent) and Garbin brothers (Prep & Vincent) at **St. Michael's**; Pat Lupo, John Vorsheck, Billy Trambley, "Sonny" Sontheimer (Academy), Jimmy Trojan (McDowell), Bob Smith, Bob Yamma (McDowell), Larry Szoszorek, Tom Karle, Mark Esser, Tim Brabender, Ed Clark, Chuck Longo, Tim Emling, Chris Filipkowski, Brian Carnicelli, Greg Clark, Si Thompson, Shawn O'Brien, John Stanek, Dean Heidt,

Note the score on the chalkboard at the moment: Holy Family 26, Harborcreek Training School 8 (1956).

Blessed Sacrament coaching legends Bob Achille, Gene Adams, Julio Achille.

Tony Ferrare, Jim Sitter, Jr., Ryan Infield, Randy Tecza, Pat Flaherty, Billy Scholz (Sr. and Jr.), Bobby Spoden, Matt Hess, Matt Viera, Joe Causgrove and the brothers Ferrick, Hayes, Felix, Addessi, Leone, Trombacco, Gilewicz, DiBacco, Shioleno, Rensel, Durkosky, Brabender, Sisinni, May, Sweeting (McDowell), Russo, Toohey, Anthony, Colpoys and the Lupo triplets at **St. George's**; and Jack Murphy, "Midget" Wright, Charlie Colvin, the Mead brothers, Jimmy Minton, Art Middleton, Vernon Toulon, Norm Zmyslinski, Bob Obert, Dan Collins, Charlie Augustine, Victor Bamberga, Bernie Farabaugh, Gary Gabutti, Jim Dwyer, Jim Marnella, Jim Reske, Jerry Fetzner, Tom Simmons, Dave Rinehardt, Nick Gervase, Denny Steele, Pat Quinn, John Hausman, Tim Boetger (Vincent), Brian Flanagan, Johnny Adiutori (Fairview), Billy Veihdeffer, Mike Sullivan, Tony Keim, Mark Behringer (Tech), Johnny Greulich, Dave Boetger (Tech), Tommy "Bird" Whalen (Tech), Mike Arrigo, Jerry Kaminsky, Dana Stewart, Brent Taylor, John Perrotti, Gary Ebach, Dan Fetzner, Matt Harris, the brothers Scibetta, Cox, Wilwohl and Barber, and John McCormick and all the McCormick brothers, cousins, uncles, sons, nephews and grandkids at **St. Peter's**.

From the East side of Erie: Chet Kupniewski, Art Hilinski, Carl Filipkowski, Tony Pol, Hank Glowacki, Jack Konkol, Dick Borowicz, Ed Witt, Ziggy Mazanowski, Ron Lukasewski (East), Eddie Grucza (Tech), Paul Modzelewski, Dave Wizikowski, Al Lubiejewski, Ken Kruszewski (Tech), Joe Kleiner and the brothers Wasielewski, Dombrowski, Tomczak, Kierzek and Robasky at **St. Stan's**; Dan Yurkovic (Tech), Bob Held, Mike Carey, Joe Peplinski, Jimmy Dailey, Joe Hassett, Ron Potocki, Dick Salamon, Stan Kupniewski, Jim Ireland, Jim Schaaf, and the brothers Brasington (East) and Wedzik (Tech) at **St. Ann's**; Don Fessler, Anthony Masi (Academy), Dick Yezzi (Academy), Mike Torrelli, Bob Izbicki, Ray Nicolia, George Feasler, Ron Costello, Hank Hokaj, Ed Davis, Joe Blaszczyk, Tom Desser, Billy Diefenbach, Don Rogowski, Dave Tomczak, Rich Matlak, Steve Sensor, Tom Kubinski, Harry Izbicki, Sr., Tony Janicki, Mike Madonia, Scott Tarasovitch, Billy Snider, Josh Schneidmiller, Eric Lewandowski, Joey Karpinski (Tech), Aaron DeCoursey and the brothers Shoemaker, Biondi (Prep & Academy),

Kulesza (Tech), Gianoni, Schonthaler, Lesniewski and Demski (Kanty Prep & Prep) at **Holy Rosary**; Bill Drayer, Teddy Morasky, Leo Bucheit, Eddie "Sonny" Grunzel (East), Frankie Ras, Sam Rothwell, Alton Burks, Roosevelt Walker, Tom Cason, Chuck Talbot and the DePaul and Tupek brothers at **Harborcreek Training School**; Don Gorski (Tech), Stan Baginski (East), Tom Yonko, Ron Homicz (East), Paul Krauza, Dan Bulishak, Stan Kisielewski (Tech), Jim Zielonka (Tech), Joe Luczynski (Tech) and John Waczo at **St. Casimir's**; Greg Beardsley, Jim Lipnicky, Pat Artise, Jeff Scrimenti, John Gray, Billy Wheeler, Greg O'Leary, Jim Triana, Brian Rizzo, Chad Tuttoilmondo, and the brothers Kirsch and Malesiewski (all North East) at **North East St. Gregory's**; Steve Potthoff, Joe Prugar, Mark Mele, Ryan Heath, Alex Macrino (Mercyhurst), Derek Brower and the brothers Knoll and Arrigo from **Mount Carmel**; and Bronislaus Baniszewski, the Cyterski brothers (Prep & Academy), Tom Walkiewicz, Tom Rys, Dave Kolakowski, Dave Sienicki, Bob Soliwoda, John Stano, Gary Gorniak, Rich Kujawinski, Dave Slomski, Tom Stachera, Kenny Duck and the Orzechowski brothers at **Holy Trinity**.

Also, John Somolani, Joe Regruth, Stan Walach (East), Bill Galla, Ron Rzepecki (East), Joe Lazorchak, Bobby Ward, Eddie Kuhar, Dave Erdely (Tech), James Yurcan (East), Kevin Buczynski (Villa), Deon Harvard (Vincent) and the brothers Satyshur (East), Palkovic and Barabas at **Holy Family**; Bill Razanoski, Chester Borowy (East), Len Jablonski (Tech) and Victor Glembocki at **St. Hedwig's**; Spiro Woolis (Tech), Chuck Detzel (East), Tom Becker (East), Esker Barnett (East), Jim Ehrman, the Donikowski brothers, "Tex" Reuter, Bob Borgia (Tech), Dave Whitby, Dave Farrell, the Mattis twins, Jim Kalista, Tim Amann, Francis Spearman (Academy), Stacey Hitt, Jay Killings, Sean Coleman and Tony McLaurin (Villa Maria) at **St. Mary's**; Dan Haley, Jimmy Phillips (Iroquois), Denny McLaughlin (Iroquois), Bob Spinelli, Dan Yurkovic, Jr. (Iroquois), Kevin Popowski (Iroquois), Joe Pacinelli (Iroquois), Don Holl, John Smith, Eugene Crosby, Brooks Marzka and the brothers Hornyak, Finegan, Repko, Causgrove, Strasser and Szewczykowski at **St. James**; John Fetzner, Dan Lynch, Bobby Kneib, Jon Boyer, Chuck Sanner (East), Mike Paluh, Jay Honard, Jamal Jones, Sean Coleman and the brothers Truitt and Izbicki at **Mount Calvary**; Jim Schwartz, Dave

Stingl (Academy), Mike Filutze, "Slater" Martin, Gerry Nowak, Tom Wisinski, Tom Laird, Mike Morrison, Denny Deiner, John Reynders, Ray Massing, Bob Tullio, Jeff Heintz, Mike Custer, Dan Nowak, Jim Canella, Rick Nierowski, Tim Harrington, Paul Brzozowski, Lance Trott, Ivan McBride (Mercyhurst), B. J. Bauman (McDowell), Jeff Cardot, Paul Samlock, Gregor Martin, R. J. Fiorelli, Graham Witherspoon, Mike Malloy, Steve White, Mark Chase, Nick Haller and the brothers Hanhauser, Steenberge, DeLuca, Webb, Leifield, Metzgar, Fessler, Hilinski, Shipley, Brabender, McCloskey, Dolak and Mikotowicz at **St. Luke's**; Fred Bartnicki, Joe Allgeier, Kevin Trapp, Ray Schlaufman, Jr. (Mercyhurst), Chris Kozik (Mercyhurst), John Yaple, Alex Borges (Mercyhurst) and the Pisano and Puskar brothers at **St. Boniface**; Joe Amoroso, Mike Cragg, Brian Quirk, Tom Miller, Bob Elchynski, Chris Zaphiris, Joe Buell, Kelly Cragg, Matt Kubich, Jeff Weis, Mike Downey, Mike Lukac, Sam Vanchieri, Adam Mennen, Jordan Joy, Craig Catalfu and the Cummings brothers (all Corry) at **Corry St. Thomas**; and Mike Tomczak, Jim Kaiser, Chuck Brower, Chip Lewis (East), Phil Sorenson, Dave Dombkowski, Bob Shopene and Rick Shopene (East) at **Spirit of Christ**.

Also, Thomas "Boody" Sullivan (in 1908), Chuck Kuhl, Ron Calabrese, "Red" Doyle, Ed Driscoll, Ed Razanauskas, Bill McCallion, Syl Mannarino, Lenny "Bomber" Vommaro, Johnny DeLuca, Jim White, Chuck Genck, Johnny Ruska, Art Ciotoli, Dick Dill, "Bugs" DeRaimo (Tech), Ben Drongosky, Ed Kopkowski, Tom Quirk, Maury Marchant, Rich Valahovic (Tech), Bill Serafini, Ken Brown, Bobby Alex, Don Gehrlein, Alex Stasko (Tech), Tim Maloney, Tom Calabrese, John Flanigan (Vincent), Dan Pakela, Jim Caldwell (East), Ray Davis, Don Gunter, Ed Zenewicz (East), Cliff Root (Vincent), Otto Borgia, Mike Rastatter (Tech), Herb Hoelter, "Bumpy" Callahan (Tech), Dave Damore (Tech), Dave Wilkinson (East), Nick Vicentini (Tech), Greg Grace (Vincent), Billy Krause (Vincent), Tim Watson (East), Stephon Fitzpatrick (Tech), Rick Niewierowski, Dan Williams, Shannon Pulliam (East), Brian Horn (Tech), Brian Booker, Luke Purvis, Craig Woodard (Mercyhurst) and the brothers Oldach (East & Prep), Mozdy, Eberlein, Messina, Callahan (Vincent), Wenrick, Cerami, Pry (Prep & Tech), Borowy, Perez and King at **St. Pat's**; and Tom Corapi, Bob Young (Academy), Al Stankiewicz, Dick Baniszewski, Joe St. George, Jim McCallion, Ron Chimenti, Charlie Fischer, Jerry Kruszewski, Mike Sullivan, Charlie Dippo, Tom Crocker, Mike Trott (Academy), Jimmy Olszewski, Dave Lichtinger, John Meister, Billy Hintz, Chuck Rosenthal, Bobby Hoffman (Academy), Phil Whittingham (McDowell), Dave Kierzek (Tech), Bruce Chrzanowski (Tech), Leo Bennett (Tech), Dave Kosobucki, Tom Smogorzewski, Barry Roach, Terry Colvin, Jeff Torrelli, Sonny Watson (Tech), Ed Gieza (Tech), Shawn Kendrick, Derrick Reid, Craig Fomich, Ramon Ellis, Julian Blanks, Joe Gabbard (McDowell), Greg Durr, the brothers Shade, Kleiner, Cardot, Fries, Kuhn (Academy), Hathaway (Academy & Prep), Hanson, Drabina, Messina (Academy), Fessler, Gambill, Hardner, Bukowski, Buettner, Wieczorek, Feeney, Bowers, Chojnacki, Cousart, Cuneo, Schroeck, Holland, Donoghue, Fuhrman, Stevenson, Tarasovitch, Sturm, Gredler, Kaczenski, Filipkowski, Viscuso, Bakka, Vahey, DiBello (Mercyhurst), Brewington (Academy), Hoffman (McDowell) and the whole entire Nies and Heberle families at **St. John's**.

Nearly all these boys listed in the above paragraphs went to Prep, except where noted or unknown. The Erie public schools obviously benefitted greatly from the Parochial League as well.

Some notably esteemed coaches include Claren Griffin and Monsignor Jim Sperry at **St. Joe's Home**; Charlie Colvin, Art Hilinski, Monsignor Jack Hagerty, Tom Simmons, Mark Behringer, Chris Hagerty, Ron Swanson, Owen McCormick, Matt Harris and John Bowen at **St. Peter's**; Bob Bowen and Pat Miller at **Girard St. John's**; Father Frank Kaltenbach, Nick Bruno, Bob Herbstritt, Dave Krepcho, Ron Sertz, Bill Bengel, Mike Arrigo and Jim Roddy at **Sacred Heart**; Gene Adams, John Crotty, Barry Roach, Jon Cacchione, brothers Dan Achille, Julio Achille and Bob Achille (16 years at BS, 342-127 record!), and brothers Mick Hintz and Chuck Hintz at **Blessed Sacrament**; Bill Stebnisky, Bruce Dreihorst, Mark Trigilio, "Chip" Knight, Jeff Baker, Guy Fustine and Mike Douds at **OLP**; Bob Horn at **Blessed Sacrament** and **OLP**; John Mundy, Bob Maxson and Dean Balkovic at **St. Joseph's**; "Bud" Elwell, Dick Schauble and Tom Comstock at **Villa Maria Elementary**; Jerry Porsch, Jim Sertz, Mark Eisert, Mark Fatica, Phil Agnello and Larry Piotrowicz at **OLC**; Bill Flaherty at **St. Joseph's** and **OLC**; Rupert Stadtmiller at **St. Mary's, St. Pat's** and **BS**; Joseph Costa, Father Tom Crowell, Jack Frew, Joe LeCorchick, Steve Wagner and Dave Armstrong at **St. Andrew's**; Carmen Catania, Father John Murray, Jim Bennetti, Joe Cuzzola, Bill Julio, Frank Scozzie and Bart Freitas at **St. Paul's**; Jerry Clark, Don Herbstritt, "Shorty" Bell, Bill Robinson, Dick Brabender, Don Rush, Frank Pluta, Paul Causgrove, Mike Colpoys, and Ben Noble at **St. George's**; and Rusty Felix at **St. George's** and **Spirit of Christ**.

Also esteemed coaching: Father Joe Radziszewski, John Stanczak and Rich Valahovic at **St. Stan's**; Father Lucien Malich, Father Coleman Lillig, Father Ted Weber and Jack Zollner at **St. Mary's**; Father Tom Geddes and Joe Peplinski at **St. Ann's**; Lou Cipalla, Sam Cipalla, Sister Mary Grace, Father Len Kuziora and Tom Connors at **Harborcreek Training School**; Ron Bules and Mike Krause at **Holy Family**; Father Anthony Nowakowski, Bob Ferretti, Kal Schonthaler, Tech Gianoni, Will O'Neil, Ken Wisniewski and Jeff Burger at **Holy Rosary**; Father Francis Zacharewicz, Tony Dombrowski and Ted Peggy at **Holy Trinity**; Joe Baressi, Jon Andrus, Randy Joy and Nick Waltier at **Corry St. Thomas**; Father Eugene Grohe, Dr. Bob O'Leary, Rick Maas and Jerry Hordych at **North East St. Gregory's**; John Nies, Joe Puskar, Ray Schlaufman and Ken Fugagli at **St. Boniface**; Frankie Bohun, Bob Merski and Mike Krause at **Holy Family**; Eddie Kuhar, Walt Seremet and Bob Repko at **St. James**; Bob Hanson, Paul Modzelewski, Tim Nick, Chris Knoll, Ed Pasko, Dave Williams and Paul DeRaimo at **Mount Carmel**; Jackie Harper, Harry Izbicki, Sr. and Walt Watrobsky at **Mount Calvary**; Jerry DeLuca at **Spirit of Christ**; Father Francis Tushim, A. Olsen, Father William Hastings, Eugene Stodolski, "Sparky" Reda, Morris Walker, Jack Dill, Dave Wenrick, Paul Pry, Mike Buchanan and John Purvis at **St. Pat's**; Father Ted Carter at **St. Joseph's, St. Pat's** and **St. Joseph's Home**; Steve Huefner, Ron Nietupski and Marcel Arribi at **St. Luke's**; Father Robert Schriefer, Tom Corapi, Pete Russo, Dr. Bill Garvey, Glenn Holland, Bob Hoffman, Dave Kosobucki, Stew Donoghue, Mel Witherspoon, and Joe Tarasovitch at **St. John's**; and Brian Flanagan at **St. Luke's** and **St. John's**.

Before the Parochial League was formed, there were other short-lived grade school leagues organized from time to time. One was the 1921-22 "Altar Boys League," a four-club circuit consisting of St. Andrew's, St. Peter's, St. Patrick's and the champion, St. Ann's. St. Ann's was led by future East High stars Ed

Brothers Bob and Dan Achille guiding the Blessed Sacrament Bulldogs.

Williams, "Bus" Downing and "Blubber" Sullivan and once defeated St. Peter's, 109-4! Other familiar names included future Prep hoopsters Walter McCallion, George Murphy, Harry Roland and Art Weindorf of St. Andrew's; Joe McGrath and (later) Father Dick Schumacher of St. Pete's; and Jim Mullen, "Buddy" Flanagan and (later) Father G. Carlton Ritchie from St. Pat's; also, Central High's "Buddy" North from St. Pat's.

A girls' Parochial League was formed in 1947 and lasts to this day. St. Patrick's and St. Mary's were the early powers, and St. John's posted several eras of domination in the early 1950's, late 1960's and the 1970's through 1984 under coach Marlene Smith. The Lassies won the 1978 state crown, finishing 19-0. St. Joseph's had a fantastic run under coaches "Pete" Holland and his son, Glenn Holland, winning every Class B title from 1963 through 1971. St. Joe's had a running battle with Class A St. John's from 1965-69, with the two alternating parochial playoff championships, then post-season city championship tournaments, each of those years. Holy Rosary was a Class B power in the mid-1970's and won the first girls' CYO state championship in 1975, noting that there is only one division in state play. The local Class A, B and C divisions were changed to the politically correct AAA, AA and A for both girls and boys in 1978.

North East St. Gregory's pulled in seven Class AA girls' crowns from 1982 to 1990, while St. Patrick's, Mount Calvary and St. Stanislaus had golden eras in AA and A action. St. Boniface, located just outside Erie in the village of Hammett, won every local AA title from 1994 to 1999, culminating with a 1999 state championship and local best-ever girls' record of 30-0. Mount Carmel and St.

James have dominated AA action in the new millennium.

St. Luke's became an incredible power, winning 13 local Class AAA titles from1983 through 2005. In six years under coach Randy Bowers (1988-94), the Crusaders racked up five Diocesan titles and had an overall mark of 170-18! OLP and St. George's have the lion's share of girls' Diocesan championships in recent years, mostly a product of changed demographics.

The girls' league has also produced many female luminaries over the years, most which went on to star at St. Benedict Academy ("Lassies"), Villa Maria Academy (first "Chicks", now "Victors") and Mercyhurst Prep School ("Lakers").

A short list of notables includes players like, from the West side of Erie: Mary Ann Roberts Fessler, Peggy

St. Benedict's Academy.

St. John's esteemed girls' coach Marlene Smith. She mentored the Lassies to the 1978 state crown.

Quinn Kelsey, Polly Speros, Denise Farver, Tammy Martinucci Purchase, Maria DiVecchio Gartrell and Emma Shimek at **Villa Maria Elementary**; Gerri Bressan Ruef, Kathy Lynch, Michelle Tomczak, Maria McGrorey Coccaro, Mary Ann Wilwohl Testa, Kathy Scibetta George, Amy Kissman Boldt, Renee Dahlkemper LaGue, Liza Behringer Eliason, Colleen Behringer Selleny, Brittany Wilwohl and Andrea McCormick at **St. Peter's**; Loretta Cargioli and Barb Santangelo at **St. Paul's**; Kathy Froess Malinowski, Judy Figaski, Mary "Magic" Kloecker Huber, Carol Kloecker Johnson, Mary Ann Baer Noel, Julianne Achille Rossi, Beth Arrowsmith, Amy Cermak Carlucci and Emily Polito Tojaga at **Sacred Heart**; Phyllis Traphagan Church Coe, Margaret Kinsinger, Carol Turek, Kathie Amann, Lisa Maxson Beery, Kristen Kephart Sinnott, Patty Driscoll, Terry Collins, and from St. Joe's golden championship years (1963-71): Patty McNamara, Patty McBride, Mary Kay McBride, Marguerite Timko Long, Virginia Knoll Steenberge, Julie Langer, the Smith sisters, the DePalma twins and the Holland sisters—Donna Zaksheske, Paula Wieczorek and Suzanne Bowers, all at **St. Joseph's**; Elaine Falandys, Kelly Erven Maslar, DeDe Onslow, Dana Butts Borczon, Janet Seyboldt Peters, Maureen Campbell Wegley, Chris Chiarelli Bernatowicz and Maria Sansone Guthartz at **St. Andrew's**; Joan Van Trapp, Stacy Shearer Corapi, Amy Kaus, Katie West Waddell, Peggy Ruland Maxwell, Angie Potthoff (of Penn State and WNBA fame) and Abbey Steudler at **Blessed Sacrament**.

Also, Karen Claunch, Amy Barickman Parini, Sharon Bruno, Carey Mastrian Vieira, Natalie Schroeck Kreidinger, Katie Dailey Dombkowski, Allison Braham, Sarah Grab Skelton, Anna Sweny and the Popovich sisters—Lisa Corsale, Erin Fontana and Julie Smith—at **OLC**; Tracy Soderberg, Olivia Schlosser, Cindy Marino, Lisa Landry Hadacky and Ainsley Ryan Showalter at **Girard St. John's**; Patty Baldwin Roach, Mary Ball, Linda Stickell DeHart, Cathy Bujnoski Thomas, Kelly Tofel Wallen, Kathy Sculley Tristani, Michelle Kuhar Shopene, Mary Beth Smrekar, Lisa Donikowski, Madi Miller, Kady Brink and the sisters Prischak, Ek, Herbe, Aronica, Fromnecht, Robbins, Shopene, Stoicovy, Steiner and Sanders at **OLP**; and Sister Patricia Lupc, Patti Strosser George, Carla Smith Torrelli, Mary Lou DiBacco Wilhelm, Marilyn Royer, Sue Finnegan Parsio, Kathy Dodsworth, Mary Ann DiCarlo Swanson, Dee Monocello Smith, Mary Ann Mehler Hauser, Susan Zimmer Rimpa, the Glass sisters, Sue Heidt

Koonmen, Paula Raydo Kubiak, Lisa Holtz Syrek, Suzy Sebastian, Lisa Fessler Thorne, Amy Galla Graves, the Potter sisters—Erica and Jessica, the DiSanza sisters, Allison Roberts, Beth Van Parys, Morgan Putnam, Mariah Elwell, Nicole Maxson, Abby Kenski, Molly Mraz and Sydney Johnston at **St. George's**.

Also, from the East side of Erie: Tillie Woznicki Miller and Patricia Sadowski at **St. Casimir's**; Joan Alamenciak Jersey, Jo Ann Lachowski Chrostowski, Wanda Drzewiecki Jurkiewicz, Ann Marie Dorobiala, Carol Kruszewski, Carol Raykowski, Cheryl Tomczak Majewski, Lisa Kruszewski, Pam Tomczak, Lori Druszewski, Kathy Czuwara and Stephanie Dombkowski at **St. Stan's**; the Dymski sisters—Christine Brzozowski and Anne Marie Pherigo, Dorothy "Dot" Plonski, the Grugin sisters—Joan, Pat and Sister Mary, Helen Zimmerman, Helen Wiederle, Patricia Cleaver Curry, the Rastatter sisters—Rosie and Madeline, Betty Brumboy, Cleta Trambley, Kathleen Barber Young, Caroline Mattis, Mary Schell Kuhar, Janet Respecki Benovic, Virginia Jendreck, Dorothy Buhl Mosher, Audrey Korn Riazzi, Sue Fava, Carol Kern and Annie Knoll at **St. Mary's**; Sister Audrey Steff and the Vladimiroff sisters—Sister Christine and Elaine Retzlaff at **St. Ann's**; Betty Burke Kaufmann, Cindy Maus Sage, Darice Miller, Cass Alberstadt Shimek, Carolyn Kuhl, Stacie Freeman Murzynski, Jill Serafini, Jenny Van Volkenburg Beightol, Teresa Szumigala, Katie Johnson Renkas, Eileen Uht Geffre, Katie Dobson, Jessica Gerono, Jennifer Wedzik, Dow Berarducci, Erin Kerner, Kirsten Olowinski, Kaylyn Maruca, Courey Schaetzle and the sisters Metzgar, Fessler, Cardot, Baumann and Brabender from **St. Luke's**; Audrey Truitt, Dina Lawson, Michelle Hamm, Diane Kane, Annie Murzynski Schodt and the Potocki sisters at **Mount Calvary**; Ruth Elchynski Mazurski, Julie Grippi Musbach, Jackie Cousins Saur, Sammy Courteau, Amy Hauser Sasso, Elysha Chrzanowski, Emily Kinecki and the Ewanick sisters, Kristi and Kelli, at **Mount Carmel**; Dollie Ulecki, Letty Chimenti, Chris Brower Krolczyk, Missy Renaud and Michelle Callahan at **St. Patrick's**; Sister Mary Lou Kownacki, Patricia Cieslak Parmarter, Sue Podgorny, Mary Matusiak Davis, Laurie Helminski Becker and Lisa Slomski at **Holy Trinity**; Laura Amendola and Darlene Korn Slupski at **Spirit of Christ**; Sandy White, Denise Pokash, Carol Dougherty, Chris Dobiszewski,

Amy Pinczewski, Dawn Tomczak Murawski, Becky Harrison and Julie Bardroff at **St. James**.

Also, Rita Cote Burick, Maria Conley, Amber Krumpe, Patty Runser Lacy, Katie Schlaufman, Lindsay Krumpe and Yvonne Wolski Shedlock at **St. Boniface**; Mary Ellen Donikowski DiMarco and Lola Rodriguez O'Sullivan at **St. Hedwig's**; Pat Lazorchak Kirk at **Holy Family**; Kelly Frisina, Missy Woodworth, Sally Burkhardt Burrows, Jill Roche, Jenny Russell, Cherie Varrassa, Jessica Higley, Julie Wieliczko, Chris Fenton, Chelsey Anderson Gerger and Bridget Minnick at **Corry St. Thomas**; Maria Puccio Semen, Cindy Koch, Stacie Triana Bowen, Wendy Marchini, Missy Drabic, Sheri Gallagher, Heidi Wilson Drapeau, Molly Martin, Carolyn O'Leary Mosier, Amy Malesiewski, Kathy O'Leary Zolman, Liz Langowski, Sarah Langowski Sheetz, Kelly Miller, Jackie Artise, Frankie Fetzner, Melissa Smith and the sisters Ciminnisi, and Trocki at **North East St. Gregory's**; Barbara "Bubbles" Schmitz LaPrice, Angeline Smith, Sister Carol "Pepper" Pregno, "Bitsy" Falconer, Marlene Smith, Mary Hoffman, Sue LeFaiver, Sue Berchtold Fitzgerald, Anne Spinks, Patty McCallion, the Clark sisters—Patty Lightner and Mary Nies, Tracy Bowers Stucke, Karen Vactor, Cheryl and Sandy Hanisek, Becky Hein, Ann Rzepecki, Karen Kantorowski Seggi, Mary Lynn Rote, Shelly Fetzner, Ann Tullio, Veronica Sansom, Kristy Artello, Jena DiBello, Lisa Kaczenski-Cope, Tina Fomich, Kayla McBride (of Notre Dame and WNBA fame) and Karlee McBride at **St. John's**; Frannie Horstman Jones, Joan Kinzig, Cathy Wilwohl, Helen Zysk Tkacik, Elizabeth Padovani, the Malizia sisters—Betsy Wickham and Rosie Kownacki, Amy Schneidmiller, Debbie Trott, Lisa Bruno, Debbie DelFreo Genovese, Jane Winarski London, the Camp sisters, Teresa Bruni Stankiewicz, Stephanie Hicks, Kristen Baginski and the Baginski twins at **Holy Rosary** and Helen Marz from Holy Rosary's 1975 state titlists, the first girls state champs in Pennsylvania.

Successful girls' coaches include "Pete" Holland, Glenn Holland, Joe Bricher, Jeff Nichols and Phil Miller at **St. Joseph's**; Sister Mary Magdalene and Delphine Rzepecki at **St. Mary's**; "Butch" Shearer and Steve Adams at **Blessed Sacrament**; Sister Nancy, Stacy Schwalbendorf and Joe Schember at **Sacred Heart**; Hank Andrae, Paul McFadden, Debbie Bentze and

"Little Villa's" only championship, 2012. Front, L to R: Coach Kelly Sawtelle, Raine Clark, Ashley Khouri, Taylor McMahon, Anna McGovern; Back: Aaleyah Lucas, Ana Hricz, Amelia Eagley, Emma Shimek, Juliza Fowler, Sara Vicary, Asst. Jay Shimek.

Joe Tssario at **St. Andrew's**; Linda Kean, Joe Dolak, "Bud" Wilwohl, and "Clutch" Tomczak at **St. Peter's**; Vi Shauberger, Paul Yoculan, Joe Chiera, Lisa Roberts, Amanda Ulrich, Lisa Beery, Eric Lytle and Andy Mraz at **St. George's**; Dick Tronoski, Dave Cyterski, Tom Laird, Jason Steiner, Bob Shopene and Tom Galleher at **OLP**; Bob Gausman, Dick Russell, Randy Bowers, Betsy Squeglia, Rick Gudowski and Bob Hvezda at **St. Luke's**; Tom Heberle, Mike Thompson, Dick Schauble, Mark Lucas, Kelly Sawtelle and Jay Shimek at **Villa Maria Elementary**; Sister Ann Louis, Emily Rubin and "Puck" Cardot at **OLC**; Mike Bluey, Mark Egan, John Soderberg and Tom Etzel at **Girard St. John's**; Joe Craig, Jim Triana, Pat Artise and Greg Beardsley at **North East St. Gregory's**; Lee Bailey, Frank Frisina, Bob Bailey, Steve "Skippo" Frisina and Dave Brown at **Corry St. Thomas**; Jim Przepyszny, Carl Krumpe and Ray Schlaufman (1999 state champs) at **St. Boniface**; Kay Christie, Bill Pepicello, Joe Pacinelli and Paul Plonski at **St. James**; Jane Farrell, Pat McCallion, Steve Kenski, and Pat Callahan at **St. Pat's**; Ed Adkins, Dennis Michalski, Ken Dixon and Bob Dunsmore at **Mount Calvary**; Mark Dombrowski, Paul Modzelewski, Patty Potter, Larry Courteau and Paul Przepierski at **Mount Carmel**; John Lenda, Katie Dailey and Angelia Merski at **Holy Family**; Bernie Slomski at **Holy Trinity** and **St. Stanislaus**; Patricia Bujalski at **St. Casimir's**; Steve Stull, Tim Trott, and Howard Hill at **Holy Rosary**, with Hill mentoring the 1975 state champs; and from **St. John's**, Sister Mary Daniel, Tony Spenik, Dan Sculley, Beth Squeglia, Pat Speice and Marlene Smith, who won a state title in 1978.

Powerful St. Patrick's is now gone. So is St. John's, Sacred Heart, St. Andrew's, St. Stan's, St. Casimir's, Holy Trinity, Mount Calvary, St. Michael's, St. Paul's, St. Hedwig's, St. Ann's, St. Mary's, Spirit of Christ, St. Joseph's, Holy Rosary, Girard St. John's, Corry St. Thomas, and St. Peter's (closed in 2016). Even the Orphanage is gone; and Harborcreek Training School is now Harborcreek Youth Services and for high school-aged students only. As many as 32 Erie area Catholic schools competed at one time or another in the Parochial League. By the 2014-15 season, the boys and girls Class AAA division consisted only of Blessed Sacrament, Our Lady's Christian; Our Lady of Peace, St. George's and St. Luke's. The AA division consisted of St. Peter's, St. James, Villa Maria Elementary, Holy Family, North East St. Gregory and a St. Boniface/Mount Carmel combine. By 2015-16, St, Greg's did not have a varsity boys' team and "Little Villa" could not present boys' or girls' varsity teams. Some of the schools that currently compete barely survive and student enrollments are a fraction of what they once were. St. Boniface and Mount Carmel are scheduled to close at the conclusion of the 2016-17 school year and several parishes in the Erie Diocese will be closing as well. The AAU and other traveling club teams seem to gather much attention nowadays. The importance and distinctiveness of the Parochial League has dimmed somewhat over the years, unfortunately, much like the role of the Roman Catholic Church itself in our aging lives.

ERIE PAROCHIAL LEAGUE GRADE SCHOOL BASKETBALL

Boys' Champions: MVPs (As selected by author):

Year — Champion	MVP(s)
1934—St. Joseph's Home (10-1)	Eckert, Monsman
1935—Harborcreek Training School (10-1)	Bill Drayer
1936—Harborcreek Training School (17-0)	Sam DePaul, Leo Bucheit
1937—St. Paul's (10-1)	Mike Spirito
1938—Harborcreek Training School (11-1)	Ted Morasky, Sonny Grunzel, Joe Tupek
1939—St. Patrick's (17-0)	Al Oldach
1940—St. Patrick's (14-1)	Ed Driscoll, Bill McCallion
1941—St. Patrick's (14-0)	Johnny DeLuca, Ray Oldach
1942—Sacred Heart (19-1)	Jim Carideo, Tom Coyne
1943—St. Patrick's (17-3)	Jim White
1944—St. Stanislaus (13-1)	Ray Tomczak, Hank Glowacki
1945—St. Stanislaus (20-1)	Art Hilinski
1946—St. Stanislaus (22-0)	Jack Konkol
1947 A—St. Stanislaus (14-2)	Len Tomczak
1947 B—St. Peter's (16-0)	Norm Zmyslinski
1948 A—St. Stanislaus (8-0)	Len Tomczak
1948 B—St. Ann's (1st half, 17-1), Sacred Heart (2nd half, 17-1)	Don Wolf (SH)
1949 A—St. Stanislaus (16-1)	Dan Tomczak, Rich Michalak
1949 B—St. Ann's* (13-0)	Jimmy Dailey, Al Wedzik
1950 A—St. Stanislaus (17-0)	Dan Tomczak
1950 B—Harborcreek Training School (14-0)	Larry Walter
1951 A—St. Patrick's (16-2)	Dick Dill, Paul DeRaimo
1951 B—St. Joseph's Home (14-1)	Louie Distrula, Tom Zipperi
1952 A—Holy Rosary (15-2)	George Feasler, Ron Costello
1952 B—Harborcreek Training School (16-5)	"Goose" Gossek
1953 A—St. Patrick's (14-3)	Ed Kopkowski
1953 B—St. Mary's (24-1)	Jim Ehrman, Esker Barnett
1954 A—St. Patrick's (15-1)	Bill Eberlein, Maury Marchant
1954 B—St. Joseph's Home (16-1)	Wygant, Breu
1955 A—St. Patrick's (14-3)	Rich Valahovic, Joe Messina
1955 B—St. Casimir's (18-2)	Stan Baginski
1956 A—St. Stanislaus (14-3)	Pat Tomczak
1956 B—Holy Family (19-0)	Bobby Ward, Eddie Kuhar Dave Erdely
1957 A—Sacred Heart (17-2)	Fred Delfino, Jim Murray
1957 B—Holy Trinity (16-3)	Tom Rys, Tom Rutkowski
1958 A—St. John's (17-2)	Ron Chimenti, Charlie Fischer
1958 B—Harborcreek Training School (18-2)	Scecco, Pruba
1959 A—St. John's (16-0)	Charlie Dippo, Mike Sullivan
1959 B—St. George's (17-1)	Pat Lupo
1960 A—St. Patrick's (#5 PA, 19-4)	Bobby Alex, Alex Stasko
1960 B—Holy Trinity (16-0)	Dave Sienicki, Bob Soliwoda
1961 A—St. Patrick's (#2 PA, 21-1)	Tim Maloney, Denny Cerami, Dave Wenrick
1961 B—St. James (21-2)	Dan Haley, Ron Hornyak
1962 A—St. Patrick's (#4 PA, 16-3)	Jimmy Flanagan, Jim Caldwell, Dan Pakela
1962 B—Harborcreek Training School (19-1)	Sam Rothwell, Alton Burks
1963 A—St. Patrick's (state champs, 20-2)	Ed Zenewicz, John Flanigan, Ray Davis, Don Gunter
1963 B—Holy Family (18-0)	Denny Satyshur, James Yurcan
1964 A—St. Patrick's (state champs, 20-1)	Paul Pry, Billy Callahan, Otto Borgia, Mike Rastatter
1964 B—Holy Family (16-0)	Denny Satyshur
1965 A—St. Patrick's (#4 PA, 18-3)	Billy Callahan, Gary Borowy
1965 B—Harborcreek Training School (11-1)	Tom Cason, Chuck Talbot
1966 A—Sacred Heart* (#2 PA, 24-3)	John Marucci, Tom Hansen
1966 B—St. Joseph's (18-1)	Rick Weber, Joe Greene, Luther Gibbs
1967 A—St. John's (25-4)	Willis Cardot, Randy Bowers, Dan Bukowski
1967 B—Our Lady's Christian (18-2)	Paul Greiner, Jim Sperry
1968 A—St. John's (26-1)	John Chojnacki, Jim Boback, Dave Schroeck
1968 B—Holy Family* (18-1)	Jeff Satyshur
1969 A—St. John's* (state champs, 30-1)	Bruce Chrzanowski, Dave Kierzek, Gary Wieczorek
1969 B—St. Peter's (16-2)	Tony Keim, Mark Behringer
1970 A—St. John's* (state champs, 32-1)	Bruce Chrzanowski, Dave Cousart, Leo Bennett
1970 B—Our Lady's Christian (22-3)	Mark Cieslak, Dan Sweny
1971 A—Sacred Heart * (state champs, 29-2)	Steve Wierbinski, Bengel twins
1971 B—Our Lady's Christian* (21-2)	Mark Hermann
1972 A—Blessed Sacrament* (state champs, 26-3)	Rick Federici, Mickey Hintz
1972 B—St. Peter's (30-3)	Tom Whalen, Jim McCormick, John Greulich
1973 A—Our Lady of Peace* (#5 PA, 29-4)	Dave Herbe, Dave Tobin
1973 B—Holy Rosary* (24-3)	Mark Demski
1974 A—Our Lady of Peace* (#3 PA, 23-2)	Dave Curtis, Dan Sculley
1974 B—Our Lady's Christian* (33-6)	Jeff Szumigale, Vic Benoit, Kevin Hughes
1975 A—St. George's* (#2 PA, 28-4)	Mike May, Tim Emling, Andy Sisinni
1975 B—Mount Carmel	
1975 C—N.E. St. Gregory's (14-0)	Ken Kirsch, John Gray
1976 A—St. Patrick's* (20-6)	Stephon Fitzpatrick, Dan Williams
1976 B—Our Lady's Christian	Joe Bizjak
1976 C—N.E. St. Gregory's* (13-2)	Billy Wheeler, Glenn Kirsch
1977 A—St. John's* (state champs, 29-0)	Joe Tarasovitch, Bob Nies
1977 B—Spirit of Christ* (19-1)	Chuck Brower
1977 C—St. Mary's (19-1)	Stacey Hitt
1978 AAA—Our Lady's Christian* (#2 PA, 24-3)	Jody Jefferson, Mark Zappia
1978 AA—Spirit of Christ*(18-5)	Phil Sorenson, Bob Shopene
1978 A—St. Joseph's (17-5)	Jim Schaaf, Terry Tighe
1979 AAA—Blessed Sacrament* (22-6)	Shawn Dombrowski, Len Cyterski
1979 AA—Girard St. John's* (24-2)	Greg Chesko, John Pilewski
1979 A—St. Joseph's (21-2)	Jim Schaaf, Joe Dolak
1980 AAA—St. John's* (state champs, 29-1)	Joe Fessler, Jim Stevenson, Sonny Watson
1980 AA—Girard St. John's (24-3)	John Bowen, Jimmy Bensur, Billy Clark
1980 A—Corry St. Thomas (14-3)	Joe Buell, Chris Zaphiris
1981 AAA—Blessed Sacrament* (#2 PA, 28-2)	Dan Gianelli, Jason Nuara, Jerry Cooley
1981 AA—Girard St. John's* (24-1)	Steve Maslar, Chuck Miller
1981 A—St. Joseph's (23-3)	Ricky Pointer, Jeff Tevis
1982 AAA—St. John's* (state champs, 31-1)	Tom Filipkowski, Ty Brewington, Bob Kaczenski
1982 AA—St. James	Jeff Strasser, Brian Lucas
1982 A—St. Joseph's*	Kevin Mundy, Keith Mundy
1983 AAA—St. John's* (#2 PA, 25-4)	Dean Gronostaj, Chris Viscuso, John Mundy
1983 AA—Holy Rosary* (22-1)	Eric Lewandowski, Rick Demski
1983 A—St. Joseph's	
1984 AAA—St. John's* (#6 PA, 24-4)	Doug Bakka, Charlie Britton, Jr.
1984 AA—Holy Rosary	Eric Lewandowski, Joey Karpinski
1984 A—Corry St. Thomas* (18-0)	Matt Kubich, Jeff Weis
1985 AAA—St. John's* (state champs, 26-1)	Steve Ziegler, Mike Heberle, Ed Gieza
1985 AA—Girard St. John's* (24-4)	Greg Maslar, Rob Rickard
1985 A—St. Mary's	
1986 AAA—Blessed Sacrament* (state champs, 29-2)	Dave Ashton, Eric Kuhn
1986 AA—St. Boniface	Kevin Trapp
1986 A—St. Patrick's	Joe King, Rob DiGello, Brian Booker
1987 AAA—St. John's* (#2 PA, 24-6)	Todd Filipkowski, Glenn Duck
1987 AA—Holy Rosary	Tim Colicchio, Josh Schneidmiller
1987 A—St. Patrick's	Craig Woodard, Gary King, Ace Perez
1988 AAA—St. George's* (#2 PA, 26-4)	Tony Ferrare, Jim Sitter, Pat Flaherty
1988 AA—Girard St. John's (18-6)	Doug Chuzie, Greg Featsent
1988 A—St. Patrick's*	Craig Woodard, Mike King, Ranfis Perez
1989 AAA—St. John's* (state champs, 31-0)	Rick Kaczenski, Derrick Reid, Shawn Kendrick
1989 AA—N. E. St. Gregory's (13-3)	Tim Malesiewski
1989 A—Mount Calvary (22-4)	Harry Izbicki, Jamal Jones, Sean Coleman
1990 AAA—St. George's* (#7 PA, 27-6)	Ryan Infield, Randy Tecza
1990 AA—Mount Calvary (21-4)	Justin Izbicki, Brian Baumann
1990 A—Holy Trinity	Kenny Duck
1991 AAA—St. John's (24-5)	Ramon Ellis, Craig Fomich
1991 AA—Girard St. John's* (state champs, 34-0)	Jed Ryan
1991 A—Holy Family (22-2)	Matt Babo, Mike Krause
1992 AAA—Blessed Sacrament (23-5)	Brad Orlando
1992 AA—St. James	Brian Szewczykowski, Nate Strasser, Brooks Marzka
1992 A—Holy Family (20-3)	Marc Turco, Dave Batkiewicz

1993 AAA—St. Luke's* (#2 PA, 33-3) — R. J. Fiorelli, Graham Witherspoon, Matt DiRaimo
1993 AA—St. Boniface — Ray Schlaufman, Chris Kozik
1993 A—Corry St. Thomas (14-3) — Jamie Cummings, Mike Downey
1994 AAA—Blessed Sacrament (26-3) — Jim Gemler, Chris Dudley, Steve Noonan
1994 AA—St. Boniface* (state champs) — Ray Schlaufman, Chris Kozik
1994 A—St. Joseph's
1995 AAA—Sacred Heart* (#6 PA) — Chris Kowalski
1995 AA—St. Boniface
1995 A—Corry St. Thomas (20-5) — Mike Lukac, Adam Mennen
1996 AAA—Our Lady of Peace — Dale Williams
1996 AA—N. E. St. Gregory's
1996 A—St. Joseph's
1997 AAA—St. Peter's (22-4) — Mark Kujawinski, Brian Kacprowicz
1997 AA—St. Boniface — John Yaple
1997 A—Mount Calvary
1998 AAA—St. Luke's* (#2 PA, 32-2) — Steve White, Mark Chase, Eric Presogna
1998 AA—St. Boniface (23-6) — John Yaple
1998 A—St. Stanislaus (17-2)
1999 AAA—St. John's* (state champs, 31-2) — Joe Gabbard, Sean Hoffman, Greg Durr
1999 AA—St. Boniface
1999 A—Holy Family (19-11) — Kevin Buczynski
2000 AAA—Our Lady's Christian — Alex Fatica, Brian Mahoney
2000 AA—N. E. St. Gregory's
2000 A—Holy Family — Kevin Buczynski
2001 AAA—Our Lady of Peace* (#8 PA, 22-10) — Corey Knight, Chris Miller
2001 AA—St. Peter's — Adam Kaiser
2001 A—Holy Family (20-2) — Deon Harvard
2002 AAA—Blessed Sacrament (27-4) — Mark Demski, Eric Schumacher
2002 AA—St. Peter's — Adam Kaiser
2002 A—Corry St. Thomas (22-7) — Craig Catalfu, Bobby Cummings
2003 AAA—Blessed Sacrament (27-4) — David Roach, Connor Connell
2003 AA—Mount Carmel — Josh Licata, Jeff Wisinski
2003 A—Holy Family (20-4)
2004 AAA—St. Peter's (30-3) — Brendan Barber, Mike Bukowski
2004 AA—Mount Carmel — Alex Macrino
2004 A—Holy Family — Deon Harvard
2005 AAA—Blessed Sacrament* (#5 PA, 30-5) — A. J. Schumacher, Jeff Roach, Ray Blanks
2005 AA—St. James
2005 A—Holy Family* — Deon Harvard
2006 AAA—
2006 AA—Mount Carmel — Mike Knoll
2007 AAA—Our Lady's Christian* (#2 PA, 31-2) — Connor Imboden, Greg Podufal, Steve Fatica
2007 AA—St. James
2008 AAA—St. George's* (#5, PA) — Conor Colpoys, Alex Geanous, Matt Hess
2008 AA—St. Peter's
2009 AAA—Blessed Sacrament — Chris Francis
2009 AA—St. Boniface (22-5) — Alex Borges
2010 AAA—St. George's* (29-3) — Joe Causgrove, Matt Viera, Matt Colpoys
2010 AA—St. Peter's (19-7) — Matt Harris
2010 A—Holy Family
2011 AAA—Our Lady of Peace (20-7) — Mike Douds, Joe Fustine
2011 AA—St. John/Holy Rosary (20-6) — Jake Tarasovitch
2012 AAA—Our Lady of Peace* (#4 PA, 20-12) — Jake Mays, Colin Ranus, Jeremy Hill
2012 AA—Mount Carmel
2013 AAA—Our Lady of Peace* (#4 PA, 24-8) — Mark Majewski, Joe Mischler, Franco Agnello
2013 AA—St. James
2014 AAA—St. George's* (#2 PA, 28-6) — Lupo triplets, Tommy Russo, Terry Roberts
2014 AA—St. James
2015 AAA—St. Luke's*(#4 PA, 22-8) — Jon Moore, Alex Miklinski, Codey Bengel
2015 AA—St. James
2016 AAA—Blessed Sacrament*(#4 PA, 28-8) — Jaelen Carson, Jaheim Howard
2016 AA—St. James
2017 AAA—Our Lady's Christian (#5 PA, 22-6) — Evan Rowane, Will Innes, Mike Lucarotti
2017 AA—St. James — Colby Yale

*Denotes Erie Diocesan champions, beginning in 1956.
BOLD denotes State Champions

Girls' Champions:

1948—St. Patrick's (6-1)
1949—St. Patrick's (5-0)
1950—St. Mary's (6-1)
1951—St. Casimir's (6-1)
1952—St. John's (9-0)
1953—St. John's (8-0)
1954—St. John's and St. Andrew's (both 8-1, co-champs)
1955—St. John's (10-0)
1956—St. John's (11-0)
1957—St. Casimir's (10-0)
1958—St. Mary's (11-2)
1959—St. John's (11-0)
1960—St. George's (11-0)
1961—St. Mary's (12-1)
1962—St. Andrew's (19-2)
1963 A—St. James (12-2)
1963 B—St. Joseph's (14-0)
1964 A—St. George's (16-0)
1964 B—St. Joseph's (13-1)
1965 A—St. John's* (21-3)
1965 B—St. Joseph's (12-2)
1966 A—St. John's (19-3)
1966 B—St. Joseph's* (14-0)
1967 A—St. John's* (18-1)
1967 B—St. Joseph's (14-2)
1968 A—St. John's (16-5)
1968 B—St. Joseph's* (17-0)
1969 A—St. John's* (20-4)
1969 B—St. Joseph's
1970 A—St. Luke's*
1970 B—St. Joseph's
1971 A—Sacred Heart
1971 B—St. Joseph's* (18-1)
1972 A—St. John's* (22-3)
1972 B—Holy Rosary
1973 A—St. John's* (15-0)
1973 B—St. Peter's (17-1)
1974 A—St. George's (16-3)
1974 B—Holy Rosary* (22-1)
1975 A—St. James
1975 B—Holy Rosary* (state champs, 33-1)
1976 A—St. John's* (#5 PA, 18-6)
1976 B—Holy Rosary
1976 C—Mount Calvary
1977 A—St. John's* (#2 PA, 24-1)
1977 B—St. Joseph's
1977 C—Holy Trinity
1978 AAA—St. John's* (state champs, 19-0)
1978 AA—Holy Rosary (16-1)
1978 A—St. Patrick's (12-2)
1979 AAA—Our Lady of Peace* (#3 PA)
1979 AA—St. Peter's
1979 A—Mount Calvary (16-3)
1980 AAA—St. John's* (#3 PA, 25-1)
1980 AA—St. Peter's* (20-3)
1980 A—St. Stanislaus
1981 AAA—St. Luke's* (#4 PA, 19-6)
1981 AA—St. Peter's
1981 A—St. Stanislaus* (27-2)
1982 AAA—Blessed Sacrament* (#2 PA, 28-4)
1982 AA—N. E. St. Gregory's (21-6)
1982 A—St. Stanislaus*
1983 AAA—St. Luke's* (#5 PA, 26-2)
1983 AA—N. E. St. Gregory's (25-1)
1983 A—Corry St. Thomas (13-5)
1984 AAA—St. John's* (#5 PA, 19-2)
1984 AA—St. Stanislaus
1984 A—St. Patrick's
1985 AAA—St. George's* (#2 PA)
1985 AA—N. E. St. Gregory's (19-5)
1985 A—St. Patrick's
1986 AAA—St. Luke's* (#3 PA, 27-1)
1986 AA—N. E. St. Gregory's (16-8)
1986 A—Farrell Monsignor Monti
1987 AAA—St. Luke's* (#2 PA, 30-1)
1987 AA—Holy Rosary
1987 A—St. Stanislaus (15-4)
1988 AAA—Blessed Sacrament
1988 AA—N. E. St. Gregory's (22-3)
1988 A—St. Joseph's
1989 AAA—St. Luke's* (#3 PA, 25-2)
1989 AA—N. E. St. Gregory's (20-6)
1989 A—St. Stanislaus (16-1)
1990 AAA—St. Luke's* (#4 PA, 29-2)
1990 AA—N. E. St. Gregory's
1990 A—Girard St. John's (20-3)
1991 AAA—St. Luke's* (#7 PA, 30-5)
1991 AA—Mount Carmel

1991 A—Holy Family (22-5)
1992 AAA—St. George's* (#5 PA)
1992 AA—St. Peter's (10-3)
1992 A—Holy Family (20-3)
1993 AAA—St. Luke's* (#6 PA, 31-2)
1993AA—Mount Carmel (21-6)
1993 A—Holy Trinity
1994 AAA—St. Luke's* (#3 PA, 29-2)
1994 AA—St. Boniface
1994 A—Corry St. Thomas (14-1)
1995 AAA—St. Luke's* (#6 PA)
1995 AA—St. Boniface
1996 AAA—St. Luke's* (#2 PA, 33-5)
1996 AA—St. Boniface
1996 A—Mount Calvary
1997 AAA—Our Lady's Christian
1997 AA—St. Boniface* (#6 PA, 17-3)
1997 A—St. Joseph's
1998 AAA—St. George's* (#2 PA, 27-8)
1998 AA—St. Boniface
1998 A—St. Stanislaus (13-2)
1999 AAA—St. Luke's
1999 AA—St. Boniface* (state champs, 30-0)
1999 A—Mount Calvary
2000 AAA—St. Luke's* (#6 PA, 22-6)
2000 AA—N. E. St. Gregory's (16-1)
2000 A—Corry St. Thomas (12-1)
2001 AAA—St. Luke's* (#2 PA)
2001 AA—N. E. St. Gregory's (16-1)
2001 A—Mount Calvary
2002 AAA—St. Luke's
2002 AA—St. James (25-3)
2002 A—Corry St. Thomas (11-6)
2003 AAA—St. John's
2003 AA—Mount Carmel
2004 AAA—St. John's
2004 AA—Mount Carmel*
2005 AAA—St. Luke's
2005 AA—
2006 AAA—
2006 AA—
2007 AAA—
2007 AA—Mount Carmel
2008 AAA—Our Lady of Peace* (#2 PA, 26-4)
2008 AA—
2009 AAA—Our Lady of Peace
2009 AA—Mount Carmel
2010 AAA—St. George's (22-9)
2010 AA—Mount Carmel
2011 AAA—St. George's* (#6 PA, 29-4)
2011 AA—St. James (14-1)
2012 AAA—Our Lady of Peace* (#2 PA, 36-4)
2012 AA—Villa Maria Elementary (14-12)
2013 AAA—Our Lady of Peace*(#3 PA, 31-4)
2013 AA—Mount Carmel (23-12)
2014 AAA—St. George's* (#4 PA, 27-7)
2014 AA—St. James (23-6)
2015 AAA—Our Lady of Peace* (#2 PA, 27-8)
2015 AA—St. James (21-7)
2016 AAA—Our Lady of Peace* (#2 PA, 30-7)
2016 AA—St. James
2017 AAA—Our Lady of Peace
2017 AA—St. James

Pennsylvania State CYO Basketball Tournaments

One of the most exciting events annually for winners of the Erie Parochial League is participation in post-season Diocesan and state Catholic tournaments. The boys' grade school state tourneys were originally sponsored by the Delta Sigma Phi fraternity of St. Francis College in Loretto (PA) and held at the college. The tournament originated in 1948 and was made state-wide first in 1960. Since that time the tournament has been instrumental in the promotion of fair play and good sportsmanship among Catholic youth in the Keystone State.

Beginning in 1960, invitations were extended

Rupert Stadtmiller coached St. Pat's to Erie's first state CYO championships in 1964 and 1965.

to each of the eight dioceses in Pennsylvania to send the winners of their own Diocesan titles to participate in the state championship bracket. Teams were responsible for their own transportation to Loretto, while Delta Sigma Phi paid for the room and board of the players and coaches. There was a $50 entrance fee per team, "due one week prior to the start of the tournament." The Eastern dioceses of Philadelphia, Scranton, Allentown and Harrisburg were always paired together, as were the Western dioceses of Erie, Pittsburgh, Greensburg and Altoona-Johnstown. Three games were guaranteed, including an East-West final, and losers also played for 3rd, 5th and 7th places. To win the state title was and is quite an accomplishment, for as late as 1988 there were 73 different Catholic grade school leagues, with 569 boys' teams and another 445 girls' teams across the state.

St. Patrick's School, having been winners of the Erie Class A title every year from 1960 through 1965, participated in the first six state tournaments. The undefeated Shamrocks of 1961, led by coach **Father Ted Carter** and players like **Tim Maloney** and **Dave Wenrick**, just missed, losing in a championship thriller. St. Pat's finally won crowns in 1963 and 1964 with **Rupert Stadtmiller** at the helm and with guys like **Paul Pry, "Bumpy" Callahan** and **Gary Borowy**.

The Erie Diocese later had an incredible string of five consecutive state titles, beginning with Farrell Our Lady of Fatima in 1968. The 1969 and 1970 state crowns were won by St. John's Knights under the coaching of **Dr. Bill Garvey** and the play of fellows like **Bruce Chrzanowski, Dave Kierzek** and **Leo Bennett**, all future Tech Memorial stars. In 1971, Sacred Heart won the state diadem with **Steve Wierbinski** and the **Bengel twins, Rick and Bob**. The Chargers were coached by **Ron Sertz**, who later became a coach and athletic

director at Cathedral Prep. Finally, in 1972, **Bob Horn's** Blessed Sacrament squad won the state championship. The Bulldogs were led by future Strong Vincent luminaries **Rick Federici** and **Mickey Hintz**.

Noting the success of the Loretto tournaments, the Pennsylvania State Catholic Youth Organization (CYO) Board of Athletic Directors initiated a parish high school boys' CYO tourney in 1973 and a girls' grade school tourney in 1975. The same format as the boys' grade school bracket was used, with pairings established to ensure an East-West final. Erie's Holy Rosary Tigers were honored as the first girls' state champions, finding success under the coaching of **Howard Hill** and the spectacular play of future St. Benedict's Academy star **Helen Marz**. In 1978 the undefeated St. John's Lassies, under esteemed coach **Marlene Smith**, easily won the crown with a balanced lineup. The only other girls' team from Erie County to win a state title was Hammett St. Boniface in 1999. The Braves were an amazing 30-0 that year with **Ray Schlaufman** coaching and his daughter **Katie Schlaufman** the big star.

The CYO Board of Directors took over the boys' grade school tournament in 1978, as the popularity of the championship series had outgrown the town of Loretto. There simply were not enough accomodations nearby for the teams and all of their fans. Since that time the tournaments are rotated among all eight dioceses for the boys' grade school, girls' grade school and boys' high school divisions. The first team from Erie to win the high school crown was St. John's under coach **Glenn Holland** in 1981 and the last to win was Our Lady of Peace under coach **Jack Holland** in 2010. Both teams finished 24-0. In between, Sacred Heart (1991), St. George's (1995), St. Jude's (1998) and Blessed Sacrament (2009) all

won the CYO state high school titles.

St. John's, now closed, won more state titles, eight to be exact, than any other grade school in Pennsylvania. **Coach Bill Garvey** won his third crown for the Knights in 1977; future Prep coach **Brian Flanagan** led St. John's to another title in 1980; and venerated coach **Glenn Holland** won the diadem in 1982. The Knights also won championships in 1985, 1989 and 1999, the last for any Erie team. St. John's benefitted from the excellent coaching of **Dave Kosobucki** ('85 & '89), **Stew Donoghue** ('89) and assistant **Joe Tarasovitch** in those years.

Other Erie County teams going all the way include Blessed Sacrament, winning its second crown in 1986 under the guidance of **Jon Cacchione**; Girard St. John's, which finished 34-0 with future Prep great **Jed Ryan** dominating play; and Hammett St. Boniface in 1994 with **Ray Schlaufman, Sr.** coaching and **Ray Schlaufman, Jr.** doing the scoring and rebounding. The last Erie Diocesan five to win a state title was Hermitage Notre Dame in 2006.

The Erie Diocese and the Prep-Villa Events Center hosted the 2016 Boys' Grade School State Tournament. Spectators from every corner of Pennsylvania raved about the beauty of the new Joann Mullen Gymnasium and the accomodations within. Smooth little guard **Hakim Byrd**, a name to remember, led St. Martin de Porres to the state title with a 53-41 championship game verdict over Monroeville St. Bernadette's. St. Martin's is located in North Philadelphia, about a block from where old Shibe Park/Connie Mack Stadium once stood and just another five blocks from where the old Baker Bowl (a/k/a the Cigar Box) used to be. Those ballparks were at one time the homes of the old Philadelphia Athletics and the Philadelphia Phillies.

The 1994 Blessed Sacrament Bulldogs, Class AAA Champs. Front, L to R: Julio Achille, Matt Magyar, Anthony DiSantis, Greg Rush, Turley, Chris Santabene; Middle: Matt Bengel, Andy Mehall, Mike Boetger, Ron DiSantis, Tim Cacchione, Steve Noonan, Craig Wilczynski; Back: Assst's Bob and Julio Achille, Nick Mehall, Andy Cook, Jacob Bishop, Greg Dufala, Chris Dudley, Kevin Brzezinksi, Paul Rennie, Jim Gemler, Coach Gene Adams.

Holy Family's 19-0 1956 Class B Champs. Included are stars in the top row: Eddie Kuhar, Dave Erdely, Joe Lazorchak, Bobby Ward and coach Frankie Bohun.

BOYS' STATE CHAMPIONS

(Erie Diocesan winners in **bold**)
1960—Pittsburgh St. Mary Magdalene
1961—Pittsburgh St. John's
1962—Johnstown St. Joseph's
1963—Erie St. Patrick's (20-2)
1964—Erie St. Patrick's (20-1)
1965—Coraopolis St. Malachy
1966—Greensburg St. Gertrude
1967—Coraopolis St. Malachy
1968—Farrell Our Lady of Fatima (28-1)
1969—Erie St. John's (30-1)
1970—Erie St. John's (32-1)
1971—Erie Sacred Heart (29-2)
1972—Erie Blessed Sacrament (26-3)
1973—Philadelphia St. Andrew's
1974—Greensburg Blessed Sacrament
1975—Pittsburgh St. Catherine's
1976—Pittsburgh St. Theresa
1977—Erie St. John's (29-0)
1978—Philadelphia St. Francis de Sales
1979—Philadelphia St. Anselm
1980—Erie St. John's (29-1)
1981—Philadelphia St. Bernard's
1982—Erie St. John's (31-1)
1983—Scranton St. Paul's
1984—Pittsburgh Resurrection
1985—Erie St. John's (31-0)
1986—Erie Blessed Sacrament (29-2)
1987—Scranton St. Paul's
1988—Scranton St. Paul's
1989—Erie St. John's (31-0)
1990—Pittsburgh St. Bartholomew
1991—Girard St. John's (34-0)
1992—Scranton St. Paul's
1993—Harrisburg St. Edward's
1994—Erie St. Boniface
1995—Wexford St. Alphonsus (26-0)
1998—Scranton Holy Rosary
1999—Erie St. John's (31-2)
2000—Scranton St. Paul's
2002—Scranton St. Mary of Mount Carmel
2003—Sharon St. Joseph's
2006—Hermitage Notre Dame (29-1)
2007—Scranton St. Paul's (32-1)
2008—Newton St. Andrew's
2009—Drexel Neumann Academy (21-C)
2010—Philadelphia Our Mother of Sorrows-
   St. Ignatius of Loyola (41-0)

2011—Newtown St. Andrew's (40-1)
2012—Pittsburgh Sister Thea Bowman
2013—West Chester St. Maximilian Kolbe (38-0)
2014—Glen Mills St. Thomas the Apostle
2015—Reading St. Peter the Apostle (23-0)
2016—Philadelphia St. Martin de Porres (41-1)
2017—Fairless Hills St. Frances Cabrini

GIRLS' STATE CHAMPIONS

(Erie Diocesan winners in **bold**)
1975—Erie Holy Rosary (33-1)
1976—Pittsburgh St. Cyril's
1977—Archbald St. Thomas Aquinas
1978—Erie St. John's (19-0)
1979—Pittsburgh St. Joseph's
1980—Pittsburgh Our Lady of Loretto
1981—Pittsburgh St. Bartholomew

1982—Camp Hill Good Sheperd
1983—Pittsburgh St. Bartholomew
1984—Pittsburgh Our Lady of Loretto
1985—Pittsburgh St. Bartholomew
1986—Pittsburgh St. Bartholomew
1987—Newtown Square St. Anastasia
1988—Pittsburgh St. Bartholomew
1991—Scranton St. Paul
1992—Morrisville St. John the Evangelist
1993—Norristown St. Theresa's of Avila
1994—West Lawn St. Ignatius
1996—Pottstown St. Patrick's
1998—Allentown St. Thomas More
1999—Erie St. Boniface (30-0)
2000—Newtown St. Andrew's
2001—Philadelphia Our Lady of Calvary
2002—Bethlehem Notre Dame
2003—Lancaster Sacred Heart (35-3)
2008—Hanover Annunciation BVM (39-2)
2009—West Chester St. Maximilian Kolbe (36-3)
2010—Pittsburgh St. Gabriel's
2011—Pittsburgh St. Gabriel's
2012—Philadelphia St. Alphonsus (38-2)
2013—Newtown Square St. Anastasia (36-5)
2014—Altoona St. Rose of Lima
2015—Newtown St. Andrew's (32-4)
2016—Wyoming Area Catholic (39-0)
2017—New Cumberland St. Theresa (32-5)

Prior Schools of All Cathedral Prep Players

(Years on Prep Varsity in parentheses) COLLEGE BASKETBALL PLAYED AT

Academy High "Lions"
1. Carl Maya (1931-32)
2. Robert Culhane (1934-35)
3. Jimmy Renz (1936-37)

Albion Junior High "Redskins"
1. Harrison Rogers (1930-31)
2. Leo Downey (1931-33)
3. Paul Downey (1941-42)

Ashtabula (OH) Junior High "Panthers"
1. Buckley Hubbard (1938-39)

The 1989 Mount Calvary Eagles. Front, L to R: Mike Bray, Lee Eighmy, Mike Brown, Brian Imler, Justin Izbicki, Jon Boyer; Back: K.J. Falk, Jim Rutkowski, Dave Negron, Don McCaleb, Randy Terrizzi, Jamal Jones, Harry Izbicki, Mike Burke.

Blessed Sacrament "Bulldogs", f/k/a "Astros"
1. Dave Engel (1960-62)
2. Fred Engel (1962-64)
3. Jack Benson (1968-69)
4. Jack "Jason" Weber (1971-73) PENN ST.-BEHREND
5. Bill Bensur (1975-77) WESTMINSTER
6. Tom Hesch (1975-77)
7. Andy Paris (1975-77)
8. John Alberstadt (1980-82)
9. Shawn Dombrowski (1981-83)
10. Mike Stadtmiller (1982-84) JOHN CARROLL
11. Jerry Cooley (1983-85)
12. Jason Steiner (1986-87)
13. John Steiner (1987-89)
14. Pat Marnella (1992-93)
15. Nick Bielak (1992-94) LOCK HAVEN
16. Matt Marnella (1993-95)
17. Jim Gemler (1995-98)
18. Steve Noonan (1996-98)
19. Joe Mifsud (1999-2000)
20. Julio Achille (1999-2001)
21. Mark Demski (2003-06) GANNON
22. Eric Schumacher (2004-05)
23. A. J. Schumacher (2008-09)
24. Damion Terry (2010-11)
25. Chris Francis (2010-13)
26. Taylor Mackowski (2013-15)
27. Trousie Thrower (2015-16)
28. Aaron McBride (2016-17)

Brockway Junior High "Rovers"
1. Richard Regotti (1945-46)

California (state of)
1. Chris Dunham (1995-97)

Central High "Fighting Colonels"
1. Harrison Clemens (1924-25)
2. Tom Doyle (1926-27)
3. Frank Richards (1927-28)
4. James "Jay" Lyons (1929-30)

Corry High "Beavers"
1. Brandon Ralph (1994-95)

Coudersport High "Falcons"
1. James White (1936-37)

Cumberland (MD) Bishop Walsh H. S. "Spartans"
1. Jared Ronai (1999-2001) UNC-ASHVILLE/ GEORGIA SOUTHWESTERN ST.

East High "Warriors"
1. Al Skonieczka (1927-28)
2. Ted Amann (1927-28)

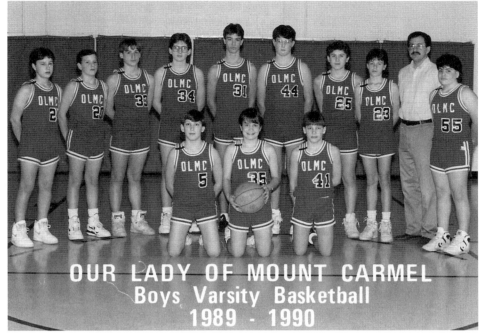

The 1990 OLMC Raiders. Front, L to R: Joe Silvaggi, n/a, Jeremy Patora; Back: Matt Fischer, Mike Klebes, Jason Stravinsky, John Colinear, Tana Kranz, Kevin Henry, Ken Krahe, Scott Hardner, Coach Tim Nick, Joe Perseo.

Emerson Elementary
1. Harry Roland (1924-25)

Erie Day School
1. David Hairston (1998-2000) PENN ST.-BEHREND
2. Jim MacKrell (2001-03)

Fairview/Garwood Middle School "Tigers"
1. John Donnelly (1988-91)
2. Cliff Dennett (1990-93) GANNON
3. Zach Meeder (1998-99)
4. Phil Stewart (2001-03)

France (country of)
1. Olivier Allinei (1986-88) ALLEGHENY

Girard Middle School "Yellowjackets"
1. Preston Bowen (1982-84) BALDWIN-WALLACE
2. Jeff Daisley (1998-2001) MERCYHURST
3. Mike Daisley (2001-03)

Girard St. John's "Panthers"
1. John Schwab (1980-82)
2. John Bowen (1982-84)

3. Claye Greene (1985-86)
4. Jed Ryan (1991-95) PENN
5. Ben Straub (1996-98)
6. Adam Straub (1996-99) ALLEGHENY

Gridley Junior High "Gremlins"
1. Walter McCallion (1924-25)
2. George Murphy (1924-25) CATHEDRAL
3. Francis "Irish" Carroll (1929-30)
4. Richard McCarthy (1931-32)
5. James Griffin (1934-37)
6. Fred Meiser (1935-36)
7. Bob Carrick (1935-37)
8. Chuck Britton (1968-69) CINCINNATI

Hamburg (NY) High "Bulldogs"
1. Bill Carey (1956-57) GANNON

Harborcreek "Huskies"
1. Jerry Blackwood (1947-49)
2. Mark Blazek (2004-08) HARTWICK
3. Keith Blazek (2007-09)
4. Adam Blazek (2008-11) GANNON
5. Dominic DiRaimo (2009-11)
6. Dan Blazek (2010-13)
7. Collin Irwin (2016-17)

Harborcreek Training School
1. Ted Morasky (1938-42)
2. Joseph Tupek (1938-39)

Harding "Dragons"
1. Alex Eaton (2004-05)

Holy Family "Knights"
1. Joe Regruth (1954-56)
2. Bill Galla (1956-58)
3. Joe Lazorchak (1958-59)
4. Eddie Kuhar (1958-60)
5. Bobby Ward (1958-60) GANNON
6. Joe Barabas (1970-71)
7. Deon Harvard (2005-06)

Holy Rosary "Tigers"
1. Joe Krotoszynski (1925-26)
2. Stanley Pickett (1931-34)
3. Lou Tullio (1933-35)
4. Joe Cecho (1936-37)
5. Harold Pfister (1936-38, 1939-40)
6. Wilfred Lohse (1938-40)

The 1964 St. John's Knights'. Front, L to R: Bill Hlopick, Bruce Kennedy, Rick Fessler, Vern Gambill, John Maleno, Bob Youngs, Gerry Fedor; Back: Fr. Fischer, Tom Vogt, Paul Gambill, Dave Wieczorek, Keith Hardner, Bill Dopierala, Coach Garvey.

FIRST IN 15 YEARS

St. George's won its first Parochial Basketball League championship in 15 years this past season, annexing the Class B crown with a 17 - 1 record. Front row, left to right, are B. DiTullio, D. McCarty, Rene Hays, J. Vorsheck. Second row, Dave Bagnoni, Pat Lupo, Dick Rebherb, captain Bill Nies, B. Detter and assistant coach Pat Hays. Head coach Don Herbstritt is standing.

The 1942 Orphanage high school squad. Coach Fr. Jim Sperry; Ted Carter, top row, second from right.

7. Bob Ferretti (1943-46)
8. Don Fessler (1947-48)
9. George Feasler (1954-56)
10. Ron Costello (1954-57)
11. Joe Blaszczyk (1958-60)
12. Rich Matlak (1959-61)
13. Mike Madonia (1974-75)
14. John Donikowski (1983-85)
15. Bill Snider (1983-85)
16. Rick Demski (1985-87) PENN ST.-BEHREND
17. Eric Lewandowski (1986-87)
18. Jim Camp (1986-88)
19. Tom Yonko (1987-88)
20. Josh Schneidmiller (1990-91)
21. Aaron DeCoursey (1998-2001)

Holy Trinity "Spartans"
1. Robert "Bob" Borczon (1942-44)
2. Len Cyterski (1948-51) GANNON
3. Charles Kaczmarek (1954-55)
4. Tom Walkiewicz (1956-58)
5. John Stano (1963-65) ALLIANCE
6. Marty Orzechowski (1971-73) ALLEGHENY
7. Felix Orzechowski (1980-82)
8. Kenny Duck (1992-94)

J. S. Wilson "Rams"
1. Rick Bordonaro (1974-76)
2. Nick Tarasovitch (2000-02)
3. Adam Upperman (2015-17)

Jamestown (NY) High "Red Raiders"
1. Booker Coleman (1991-94) WISCONSIN

Jefferson "Broncos"
1. Jake Narring (2014-16)

JoAnna Connell "Cougars"
1. Delton Williams (2009-13)

Kanty Prep "Eagles"
1. Stacey Hitt (1980-82) GANNON

Lawrence Park "Tigers"
1. James Opdyke (1935-36)

Luther Memorial "Lions"
1. Mark Tate (1989-92)
2. Joe Jones (2001-04) EDINBORO
3. Malik Moffett-Pullium (2011-12)

Madera (CA) High "Coyotes"
1. Jim Stroker (1932-33)

McDowell "Trojans"
1. Franco Agnello (2015-17)

Meadville "Bulldogs"
1. Dana Revel (2003-04)

Meadville Seton Catholic "Eagles"
1. Antonio Frisina (2013-15) ALLEGHENY

Memorial Junior High "Monarchs"
1. Bill Druckemiller (1962-64) DENISON

**Millcreek/ Intermediate/
McDowell High "Trojans"**
1. John Larson (1943-44)
2. Matt Hersch (1974-75)
3. Todd Stablein (1987-90) GANNON
4. Adam Montie (1996-98)
5. Brian Root (1996-98)
6. Preston Harris (2005-06) GANNON
7. Franco Agnello (2015-17)

Mohawk High "Warriors"
1. James Walrath (1931-32)

Mount Calvary "Eagles"
1. John Fetzner (1959-61)
2. Dan Lynch (1965-67)
3. Bob Kneib (1968-70)
4. Hank Bujalski (1976-78)
5. Harry Izbicki (1991-92)
6. Justin Izbicki (1993-95)

North East "Grapepickers"
1. William Lee (1931-32)
2. Paul Meyer (1936-38)
3. Srboljub Samailovic (2000-2001)
4. Dave Weber (2002-03)
5. Adam Malesiewski (2015-17)

Oil City Assumption
1. Joe Schossler (1954-56)

Oil City St. Joseph's "Irish"/"Hilltoppers"
1. Norman "Dick" Blissell (1926-30)

Oregon
1. Tyler Oedekoven (2016-17)

Osceola Mills "Mountaineers"
1. William "Bill" Laws (1935-37)

Our Lady of Mount Carmel "Raiders"
1. Jeff Kapsar (1983-84)
2. Mike Wernicki (1990-91) PITT
3. Derek Brower (2003-06)
4. Josh Licata (2005-07)
5. Jeff Wisinski (2005-07)
6. Mike Knoll (2008-11) PENN ST.-BEHREND

The 1966 St. John's Knights went 30-4, but lost out to Sacred Heart. Front, L to R: Kirk Hardner, Danny Bukowski, Bob Hoffman, Tom Heberle, Phil Whittingham, David Robinson; Back: Coach Garvey, Willis Cardot, Teddy Johnson, Larry Feeney, Dave Wieczorek, Chris Rupp, Tommy Nies, Fr. Fischer.

Our Lady of Peace "Crusaders"
1. Billy Bules (1970-72)
2. Dan Sculley (1975-78) BUCKNELL/GANNON
3. Mark Maruca (1978-79)
4. Mike Smith (1979-81)
5. Mark Atkinson (1982-84) BUCKNELL
6. Chris Keim (1983-85)
7. Joe Ianello (1984-86)
8. Kevin Misko (1986-87)
9. Todd Stablein (1987-90) GANNON
10. Brad Kons (1995-97)
11. Dale Williams (1998-2000)
12. Mike Sertz (2000-2002)
13. Cory Knight (2002-05) PFEIFFER/GANNON
14. Dave Galleher (2006-08)
15. Dominic Sansone (2009-11)
16. Nico Sisinni (2009-11)
17. Jeremy Lynch (2010-13) EDINBORO
18. Michael Douds (2013-15)
19. Joe Fustine (2013-15) GANNON
20. Mark Majewski (2014-17)
21. Jeremy Hill (2015-16)
22. Nate Serafin (2015-17)
23. Joe Mischler (2015-17)
24. Alex Douds (2016-17)

Our Lady's Christian "Raiders"
1. Tim Fox (1970-72) THIEL
2. Mark Cieslak (1972-74)
3. Jeff Maries (1973-74)
4. Jeff Joint (1975-76)
5. Kevin Hughes (1976-78)
6. Vic Benoit (1976-78)
7. Jeff Szumigale (1976-78) CLARION
8. Joe Nolan (1977-78)
9. Mark Fatica (1978-79)
10. Jim Roseto (1978-80)
11. Joe Bizjak (1978-80)
12. Doug Geiger (1978-80)
13. Chris Fatica (1979-81)
14. Mark Zappia (1980-82)
15. Jody Jefferson (1981-82)
16. Kevin Gallagher (1981-83)
17. Jeff Quirk (1983-85)
18. Vinnie DiNicola (1983-85)
19. Jon Jefferson (1984-85)
20. Ricky DiRienzo (1985-87)
21. Bill Parry (1985-87)
22. Pat Mastrian (1985-87)
23. Andy Mraz (1985-87)
24. Jim Hamilton (1988-91) NAVY
25. Mike Guelcher (1990-92)
26. Matt Bennett (1990-93)
27. Ed Hinkel (1998-2000)
28. Steve Kubinski (1999-2000)
29. Kevin Bogacki (1999-2000)
30. Andy Kubinski (1999-2002) MERCYHURST

The 1963 St. Joe's Rebels. Captain Bob Shreve (with ball), Coach Bill Flaherty, Father Ruhling.

31. Adam Braham (2000-01)
32. Derek Candela (2002-03)
33. Brian Mahoney (2003-05)
34. Alex Fatica (2003-04)
35. Mike Hubert (2004-06)
36. Steve Piotrowicz (2006-08) PENN ST.-BEHREND/GANNON
37. Andy Sweny (2007-09) GANNON
38. Ryan Dougan (2007-09)
39. Joe Sweny (2009-10)
40. Billy Fessler (2013-14)
41. Charlie Fessler (2014-15)
42. Peter Jefferys (2014-16)
43. Henry Fessler (2016-17)

Perry Elementary "Admirals"
1. Sheldon Zablotny (2009-13) NIAGARA CC/FLORIDA SOUTHERN

Pittsburgh St. Teresa of Avila "Titans"
1. Tom Burke (1969-71)

Roosevelt Junior High "Teddies"
1. Bob Bellomini (1941-42)
2. Caesar Montevecchio (1949-52)
3. Johnny Donatucci (1951-54)
4. Al Montevecchio (1953-55)

5. Dominic "Pete" Donatucci (1954-56)
6. Armand Grassi (1959-60)

Rouseville Elementary
1. John "Jack" Straub (1931-33)

Sacred Heart "Trotters"/"Chargers"
1. [Rev.] Eugene Coleman (1930-33)
2. Walter Coleman (1932-34)
3. Tom Clancey (1933-34)
4. Gene Carmosino (1934-35)
5. Edward Franz (1934-36)
6. Ed Pasqualicchio (1934-36)
7. Joseph "Bud" Healy (1934-36)
8. Andy Sanders (1935-36)
9. Robert "Bob" Formaini (1937-40)
10. Paul Clancey (1938-39)
11. John Roscher (1938-40)
12. Dick Rettger (1943-44)
13. Jim Trost (1943-44)
14. Jim Mahoney (1943-44)
15. Jim Carideo (1943-45)
16. Charlie Horn (1944-45)
17. Ron Carroll (1944-45)
18. Richard Roberts (1945-46)
19. Jim Fuhrman (1945-46)
20. Jack Earley (1945-46)
21. Bill DiPlacido (1945-48)
22. Jack Flanagan (1946-48)
23. Nick Bruno (1949-51)
24. Don Wolf (1949-52)
25. Charlie Maxwell (1950-52)
26. [Rev.] Jim "Red" Fahey (1951-53) VILLANOVA
27. Chuck Dillon (1952-54) GANNON
28. Ralph Hellman (1956-57)
29. Jim Rudy (1956-59)
30. Jim Murray (1959-60)
31. Don Belton (1965-67)
32. Dave Van Volkenburg (1966-68)
33. Gerry Mullen (1967-9)
34. Tom Hansen (1967-70) NOTRE DAME
35. Dick Mangold (1969-70)
36. Joe Cook (1969-71)
37. Tom Van Volkenburg (1970-72)
38. Don Wierbinski (1970-72)
39. Mike O'Brien (1971-73)
40. Mark Van Volkenburg (1972-74)
41. Rick Bengel (1972-75) HARVARD
42. Bob Bengel (1973-75)
43. Steve Wierbinski (1973-75)
44. John Hall (1974-75)

St. John's 1967 Parochial Champions. Front, L to R: Dave Anaya, Bob Bielinski, Dave Schroeck, Jimmy Boback, John Cousart, Kirk Hardner, Tom Schenk; Back: Fr. Fischer, Willis Cardot, David Robinson, Danny Bukowski, John Chojnacki, Mike Dill, Randy Bowers, Teddy Johnson, Coach Garvey.

St. Joseph's 1965 Rebels. Front, L to R: Dave Ruef, Jim Hammer, Marty DePalma, Denny Flanagan, Rick Weber, Joe Greene, Luther Gibbs, Angelo Natalie; Middle: Terry McAndrew, n/a, Mario Savelli, Ricky Gibbs, Bill Gillespie, Lenny Saunders, John Dolak; Back: Coach Flaherty, Fr. Ruhling, Msgr. Kleber.

45. Jim MacKrell (1974-75)
46. Dan Achille (1976-78) GANNON
47. Bob Van Volkenburg (1978-80)
48. John Achille (1979-81) WASHINGTON & JEFFERSON
49. Mark Hansen (1984-85)
50. Mike Manczka (1984-86)
51. Mark Dalton (1984-86)
52. Kevin Dalton (1985-87)
53. Joe Gaeta (1989-90)
54. Chris Kowalski (1997-98)
55. Jawan Walker (1998-99)
56. Tony DeMichele (2002-04)
57. Mike Arrigo (2003-04)
58. Earl Matson (2004-05)

St. Andrew's "Spartans"
1. Abe Louch (1933-35) CATHEDRAL
2. Jamie McCarthy (1936-37)
3. Bob Mangan (1936-37)
4. Lawrence Reilly (1936-37)
5. Edmund "Brub" Mehl (1937-41)
6. Tom Carrick (1938-39)
7. Jack Quinn (1938-39)
8. Jack Lalley (1939-40)
9. Tom Mangan (1942-43)
10. Carmen "Joe" Romeo (1944-45)
11. Dick Trombetta (1944-47) ALLIANCE
12. Don Laird (1945-48)
13. Jack Crotty (1947-50)
14. Jack Dalton (1948-50)
15. Don Guerrin (1948-50)
16. Jim Dentel (1949-50)
17. Joe Sarvadi (1952-54)
18. Chuck Wittman (1952-54) PRINCETON
19. Jim Keim (1954-56) JOHN CARROLL
20. Bob Timmons (1954-56)
21. Dave Mitchell (1955-57)
22. Ed Wittman (1956-58)
23. Chuck Bauder (1957-59)
24. Rick Scheppner (1960-62)
25. Jim Sitter (1960-62)
26. Paul Simon (1961-63)
27. John Behan (1964-66)
28. Chuck Meuser (1965-66)
29. John "Dezzie" Long (1970-71)
30. Kevin Barron (1972-74)
31. Matt Scheppner (1972-74)
32. Mark DiPlacido (1972-74)
33. Jay Simon (1973-74)
34. Kevin Elwell (1975-77) GANNON
35. Mark Fuhrman (1977-78)
36. Tim Gore (1977-80) MICHIGAN STATE
37. Tom Huff (1987-88)

38. Dominic Sansone (2009-11)

St. Ann's "Crusaders"/"Aces"
1. Tom Flatley (1929-30, 1931-32)
2. Willard Flatley (1929-32)
3. John O'Brien (1929-32)
4. Francis Fetzner (1931-32)
5. Robert "Bob" Dailey (1932-33)
6. Bob "Mickey" McLaughlin (1932-35) CATHEDRAL
7. Walter "Fudge" Kuziora (1934-38)
8. Tom Fuhrman (1936-1937, 1938-39)
9. Joe Flatley (1940-41)
10. John Burger (1944-45)
11. Mike Carey (1948-49)
12. Bob Held (1948-50)
13. Joe Peplinski (1950-52)
14. Jimmy Dailey (1951-53) DETROIT
15. Richard "Dick" Salamon (1951-53)
16. Al Wedzik (1952-53)
17. Dave Rouen (1955-56)

St. Boniface "Braves"
1. Fred Bartnicki (1971-73)
2. Kevin Trapp (1988-90)
3. Doug Lecker (1994-96)
4. John Yaple (1999-2002)

St. Casimir's "Royals"
1. Tom Yonko (1958-60)
2. Dan Bulishak (1960-62)

St. George's "Dragons"/ "Lancers"
1. Pat Lupo (1962-64)
2. Don Felix (1964-66)
3. Norb Barthelmes (1965-66)
4. Jeff Trombacco (1966-67)
5. Rusty Felix (1967-69)
6. Bob Smith (1969-70)
7. Larry Szoszorek (1970-72) PENN ST.-BEHREND
8. Mike Sisinni (1973-75) CLARION
9. Ed Clark (1975-76)
10. Tim Brabender (1975-77) DAYTON
11. Chuck Longo (1976-77)
12. Tim Emling (1977-79)
13. Mike May (1977-79)
14. Andy Sisinni (1978-80) DUQUESNE
15. Pete Russo (1979-81)
16. Jon Russo (1981-83)
17. Dean Heidt (1986-87)
18. Jim Toohey (1987-88) GANNON
19. Phil Kraus (1987-89)
20. [Rev.] Rich Toohey (1988-90)
21. Drew Hoffman (1989-90)
22. Jim Sitter (1990-92)
23. Keith Anthony (1991-94)
24. Kevin Anthony (1992-94)
25. Ryan Infield (1992-94)
26. Robbie Fugate (2002-03)
27. Billy Scholz (2002-04)
28. Matt Pluta (2004-06)
29. Bob Spoden (2007-09)
30. Joe Gnacinski (2009-11)
31. Shyquawn Pulliam (2009-10)
32. Conor Colpoys (2010-13)
33. Matt Hess (2010-13)
34. Alex Geanous (2011-12)
35. Joe Causgrove (2011-14)
36. Matt Viera (2012-14)
37. Matt Colpoys (2012-15) PENN ST.-BEHREND
38. Jaryn Simpson (2014-17)
39. Tommy Russo (2015-17)
40. Anthony Lupo (2016-17)

St. Hedwig's
1. Willy "Bill" Razanoski (1933-36)
2. Victor Glembocki (1954-56)

St. James "Panthers"
1. Dan Haley (1962-63)
2. Ron Hornyak (1963-65) PENN ST.-BEHREND
3. Tim Finegan (1965-67)

St. Joseph's 1975 JV's. Front: Mark DePalma; Kneeling: Mark Tevis, Tracy DeSanti, Rick Wienczkowski, Mark Rieger, Kurt Blum; Standing: Fr. Haupt, Terry Tighe, Jim Schaaf, Bob Maxson, Craig Allison, Rick Rumball, Mike DeSanti, Brian Franz, Coach Glenn Holland.

4.Dave Causgrove (1970-71)
5.Bob Repko (1970-72)
6.David Repko (1982-83)
7.Mike Szewczykowski (1985-87) ROCKFORD
8.John Smith (1987-89)
9.Joe Hellman (1987-88)
10.Mike Wernicki (1990-91) PITT
11.Brian Szewczykowski (1994-96) CLARION
12.Eric Hess (2008-09)

St. John's "Knights"
1.Bill Brown (1924-25)
2.Ralph Cochrane (1924-25)
3.[Rev.] Len Kuziora (1931-33)
4.Robert Culhane (1934-35)
5.Fred Yochim (1935-36)
6.Bill Nies (1935-36)
7.Fred Nies (1936-38)
8.Leo Davis (1937-38)
9.Harold Marshall (1939-40)
10.Richard Wolfram (1939-40)
11.Ray Quinlan (1939-40)
12.Jack Erb (1939-41)
13.Robert Nies (1940-42)
14.Johnny Flanigan (1940-43)
15.Donald Malmberg (1944-45)
16.Paul Murosky (1945-47)
17.Jim O'Brien (1947-49)
18.Al Stankiewicz (1956-59) GANNON
19.Steve Hanson (1957-58)
20.Bernie Nies (1958-60)
21.Bill Kleiner (1959-60)
22.Jim McCallion (1959-61) GANNON
23.John Cardot (1960-61)
24.Jerry Martin (1960-61)
25.Charlie Fischer (1960-62)
26.Ron Chimenti (1960-62)
27.Jerry Kruszewski (1960-62)
28.Dave Lichtinger (1962-65)
29.Mike Heberle (1963-64)
30.Jim Olszewski (1963-65)
31.John Meister (1963-65)
32.Mike McCoy (1965-66)
33.Rick Fessler (1965-68) ST. VINCENT'S/
    MERCYHURST
34.Chuck Goehring (1965-66)
35.Tommy Hathaway (1965-67)
36.Keith Hardner (1966-67)
37.Vern Gambill (1966-68)
38.Gary Bukowski (1967-68)
39.Chuck Rosenthal (1967-69) ALLEGHENY
40.Dave Wieczorek (1968-70) MERCYHURST
41.Willis "Puck" Cardot (1968-71) PITT/
    MERCYHURST
42.Kirk Hardner (1969-70)

St. Patrick's, 1940 Parochial League Champions, L to R: Coach A. Olsen, Driscoll, McCallion, Oldach, DeLuca, Ponti, Doyle.

43.Danny Bukowski (1969-71) MERCYHURST
44.Randy Bowers (1970-71)
45.Jim Feeney (1973-75)
46.Dave Cousart (1974-76)
47.Jim Heberle (1974-76)
48.Tom Smogorzewski (1975-76)
49.Barry Roach (1976-78)
50.Dave Kosobucki (1976-78)
51.Tim Nies (1977-79)
52.Bob Stevenson (1978-80)
53.Joe Tarasovitch (1979-81)
54.Jack Stevenson (1980-82)
55.Sonny Watson (1982-83)
56.Jim Stevenson (1982-84)
57.Joe Fessler (1982-84) MERCYHURST
58.Jeff Torrelli (1984-85)
59.Bob Kaczenski (1984-86)
60.Tom Filipkowski (1984-86) MERCYHURST
61.John Mundy (1986-87)
62.Steve Zeigler (1986-89)
63.Mike Heberle (1986-89)
64.Todd Filipkowski (1988-91) MERCYHURST
65.Rick Kaczenski (1990-91)
67.Derrick Reid (1990-93)
68.Courtney Mooney (1991-92)

69.Craig Fomich (1992-95)
70.Keith Nies (1992-96) MERCYHURST
71.John Trocki (1993-96) PITT-TITUSVILLE
72.Bob Vahey (1994-96)
73.Julian Blanks (1995-98) LA SALLE
74.Greg Durr (2001-03)
75.Merle Page (2006-07)
76.Noel Oduho (2008-10)
77.Ben Tate (2009-11)

St. Joseph's "Rebels"/"Patriots"
1.[Rev.] Frank Kaltenbach (1924-26)
2.Thomas Manning (1926-27)
3.Richard Sertz (1927-30)
4.Robert Applebee (1929-31)
5.James Smith (1929-31)
6.Bernard "Chub" Reiser (1932-33)
7.Joe LeCorchick (1932-34)
8.Frank "Bud" Raid (1932-34)
9.John Flanagan (1933-34)
10.George Jepson (1937-38)
11.Bob Young (1947-48)
12.Jack Krahe (1947-49)
13.George Palmer (1949-50)
14.Rob "Zeke" Szoszorek (1951-52)
15.Mike Flaherty (1960-63)
16.Tom Schneider (1961-63)
17.Chuck Shreve (1963-65)
18.Jim Schaaf (1981-83)
19.John Mundy (1986-87)

St. Joseph's Home "Orphans"
1.Patrick O'Neill (1927-28)
2.John Zelonish (1928-29)
3.Mike Figula (1928-30)
4.Henry Pluskota (1928-30)
5.Carl Spiesman (1934-35)
6.Joey Barabas (1936-37)
7.Joe Luteran (1946-48)

St. Luke's "Crusaders"
1.Steve Moore (1958-59)
2.Jim Schwartz (1960-61)
3.Fred "Rick" Hanhauser (1963-65)
4.Jim Murray (1964-65)
5.Jerry Nowak (1965-67)
6.Bill Giermak (1967-69)
7.Pat Steenberge (1967-69)
8.John Reynders (1969-71) ALLEGHENY
9.Ray Massing (1969-71)

The 1975 St. Joseph's Rebels. Front, L to R: Bill Nichols, Jim Zollner, Earl Matson, Tim Welch, Sam DeLeo, John Ott, Joe D'Aurora; Back: Fr. Haupt, Dan Reichert, Mark Franz, Tim McAndrew, Mark Schaaf, Don Wagner, Bobby Guenther, Coach Glenn Holland.

6.Harold Nash (1929-32)
7.Robert "Bob" Crotty (1931-33)
8.Robert Almeda (1932-33)
9.Bernie Quinn (1933-36)
10.Johnny Melvin (1937-38)
11.Dick Esser (1945-47)
12.Jim Mraz (1952-54)
13.Jim Ehrman (1955-57)
14.Dave Reuter (1958-60)
15.Dave Whitby (1960-62) DETROIT
16.Dave Farrell (1962-64)
17.Stacy Hitt (1980-82) GANNON

St. Michael's "Archangels"
1.Marino Phillips (1927-28)
2.Jim "Moe" Gross (1952-54)
3.Vinny "Flowers" Kwiatkowski (1954-56)
4.John Garbin (1957-58)

St. Patrick's "Shamrocks"
1.Lester Hahn (1924-26)
2.Kenny Sechrist (1924-27)
3.Maurice "Casey" Jones (1926-27)
4.James "Horse Cavanaugh (1926-27)
5.Todd Kress (1926-27)
6.Francis "Buddy" Flanagan (1926-29)
7.Don Hayes (1927-28)
8.Jim Mullen (1927-28)
9.Bill Holland (1929-31) EDINBORO
10.Harry "Bidge" Weindorff (1929-30, 1932-33)
11.John Scully (1929-31)
12.Richard "Red" McBride (1930-31)
13.Joe Sinnott (1931-32)
14.Joe Causgrove (1933-35)
15.Francis Hughes (1933-36)
16.Tom Meagher (1934-35)
17.John Wilson (1934-36)

St. Patrick's 1960 Parochial Champions. The Shamrocks were the first Erie grade school team to enter the CYO State Tournament. Front, L to R: Jim Henry, Tim Maloney, Rich Ohman, Tom Calabrese, Dan Brown, Denny Cerami; Back: Bobby Alex, Don Gehrlein, Jimmy "Killer" Kilgallon, Roger Amendola, Alex Stasko, Kenny Pruyn, Coach Fr. Ted Carter.

10.Dan Nowak (1971-72)
11.Tom Fessler (1971-73)
12.Mark Leifield (1973-74)
13.John Webb (1973-75) ALLEGHENY
14.Billy Fessler (1974-76)
15.Gary Metzgar (1977-79)
16.Tim Steenberge (1978-79)
17.Jeff Metzgar (1978-80)
18.Gary Miller (1980-82)
19.Jim Webb (1982-84) PENN ST.-BEHREND
20.Jeff Cardot (1987-1990)
21.Paul Samlock (1989-91)
22.Gregor Martin (1993-95)
23.Graham Witherspoon (1993-97) ROBERTS WESLEYAN
24.R.J. Fiorelli (1995-97) ST. JOHN FISHER
25.John Weber (1997-98)
26.Mike Malloy (1997-2000)
27.Jason Dolak (1998-2000) LA ROCHE
28.Mark Chase (1998-2002)
29.Casey McCloskey (2000-2003) ALLEGHENY

30.Steve White (2000-02)
31.Kyle Brabender (2001-02)
32.Adam Dolak (2002-04)
33.Nick Haller (2003-05) JOHN CARROLL/PENN ST.-BEHREND
34.T. J. Fessler (2005-07)
35.Tim Mikotowicz (2006-08)
36.Jordan Rydzewski (2008-10)
37.Joe Mikotowicz (2009-10)
38.Kyle Carmosino (2011-12)
39.Felix Manus-Schell (2013-14)

St. Mark's Seminary "Lions"
1.Mike McCoy (1965-66)

St. Mary's "Trojans"
1.Damon Daly (1925-26)
2.Robert Seus (1926-27)
3.Bill Kneib (1927-28)
4.Robert Schrenk (1928-31)
5.John Young (1928-31)

18.John "Jack" Goodill (1938-40)
19.Tim O'Hara (1939-40)
20.John McMahon (1939-40)
21.George Schickler (1939-42) GANNON
22.Joe Miller (1940-41)
23.Frank Mannarino (1940-41)
24.Ray Laughlin (1940-42)
25.Ed Driscoll (1940-43)
26.Richard "Red" Doyle (1940-44)
27.Sil Mannarino (1941-44)
28.Ray Oldakowski (Oldach) (1941-45)
29.Johnny DeLuca (1942-45) CANISIUS
30.Jim White (1943-47) GANNON
31.John "Jack" Doyle (1944-45)
32.Donald "Willie" Ester (1944-45)
33.Chuck Genck (1944-48) GANNON
34.Tom Eberlein (1949-51)

St. Patrick's third straight championship team (1941). Players include Mannarino (F, R); Seated: Oldach, Ponti, Razanauskus; Standing, R: DeLuca; Others: Mack, Duskus, Vommero.

The starting five for St. Patrick's 1961 champs, L to R: Dave Wenrick, Tim Maloney, Tom Calabrese, Denny Cerami, Jimmy Henry.

35. Al Hatkevich (1949-52)
36. Jim Lynch (1951-53)
37. Johnny Ruska (1952-54) CANISIUS
38. Richard "Dick" Dill (1953-55)
39. Don Vollbrecht (1955-56)
40. Ed Kopkowski (1955-57)
41. Tom Quirk (1955-57)
42. Bill Eberlein (1955-58)
43. Maury Marchant (1956-58)
44. Joe Messina (1957-59)
45. Rick Amendola (1957-60)
46. Bob Alex (1962-63)
47. Tim Maloney (1963-65) EDINBORO
48. Dave Wenrick (1963-65)
49. Denny Cerami (1963-65)
50. Dan Pakela (1964-66)
51. Jim Flanigan (1964-66)
52. Ray Davis (1965-67)
53. Don Gunter (1965-67)
54. Otto Borgia (1965-67)
55. Paul Pry (1966-68) LOUISVILLE
56. Gary Borowy (1967-69) PENN ST.-BEHREND
57. Mark Borowy (1970-72)
58. Tim Niewierowski (1973-75)
59. Dan DeDionisio (1975-77)
60. Mike King (1990-92)
61. Shawn Summerville (1992-93)

St. Paul's "Knights"
1. Jerry Mifsud (1965-68)
2. Joe Mifsud (1971-73)
3. Fran Mifsud (1975-77)
4. Joe Corella (1980-82)

St. Peter's Cathedral "Dukes"
1. Nelson "Fat" Schumacher (1924-26) CATHEDRAL
2. [Rev.] Richard Schumacher (1924-28) ST. VINCENT'S (PA)
3. Frank Richards (1925-26, 1927-28)
4. Joe McGrath (1925-28)
5. Frank Henry (1927-28)
6. Harry Liebel (1928-29)
7. Edward Mayer (1928-29)
8. Joe Earley (1928-31)
9. Robert Alexander (1930-32)
10. Bob Joyce (1931-33)
11. [Rev.] Jim Sperry (1932-33)
12. Bill Griskey (1932-35)
13. George Behringer (1934-35)
14. Harry Gannon (1934-36)
15. Robert Rooney (1935-36)
16. Michael Sullivan (1935-36)
17. Gerald Connell (1935-36)
18. Vincent McBride (1935-36)
19. Johnny Sunda (Pietrasanta) (1935-37)
20. John Latimer (1935-39)
21. John "Jack" Murphy (1936-38)
22. Joe McCafferty (1937-38, 1940-42)
23. Gerald Connell (1938-39)
24. Rodger Lamb (1938-41)
25. Bob Sensor (1939-40)
26. Richard Ankiel (1939-41)
27. Jim Miller (1940-41)
28. Bill Latimer (1940-41)
29. John "Hump" Sullivan (1940-41)
30. Ed Mead (1940-41)
31. Joe Weschler (1941-43)
32. Jimmy Mead (1943-44)
33. Charlie Colvin (1943-46)
34. Jerry Bechtold (1944-45)
35. Jim Minton (1944-45)
36. Garrett "Gary" Orr (1945-47)
37. John Harabedian (1946-48)
38. Art Middleton (1947-49) GANNON
39. Bob Fries (1948-49)
40. Norm Zmyslinski (1949-52)
41. Bob Hamm (1951-53)
42. Bernie Farabaugh (1953-55
43. Mike McCormick (1955-56)
44. Gary Gabutti (1957-58)

St. Pat's 1961 Parochial Champs. Front, L to R: Denny Cerami, Jimmy Henry, Dave Wenrick, Tim Maloney, Tom Calabrese; Back: "Bumpy" Callahan, Dave Callahan, Dan Pakela, Art Freitas, Jim "Truck" Caldwell, Coach Fr. Ted Carter, Jim Kopkowski, Jimmy "Killer" Kilgallon, Doug Frampton, Ray Davis.

45. John Aquino (1960-61)
46. Jim Marnella (1961-63) SLIPPERY ROCK
47. Jim Reszkowski (Reske) (1961-63)
48. Jerry Fetzner (1961-63)
49. Tom Simmons (1961-63)
50. Dave Hambly (1962-63)
51. Dick Scalise (1962-63)
52. Pat Quinn (1966-68)
53. Brian Flanagan (1968-70) LOYOLA (MD)
54. Jim Cox (1969-70)
55. Tony Keim (1971-73)
56. George Carrig (1972-74)
57. Pat Cox (1972-74)
58. Maurice Myers (1973-74)
59. Jim McCormick (1974-76)
60. Bob Kraus (1974-76)
61. Dwight Pace (1974-75)
62. Brian Denard (1974-75)
63. John Greulich (1974-76)
64. Jerry Kaminsky (1978-80)

65. Dana Stewart (1981-82)
66. John Perrotti (1982-84)
67. Chris Geisler (1984-85)
68. Mike Kujawinski (1988-90)
69. Mike McMahon (1994-96)
70. Greg Dufala (1996-97)
71. Chris Bates (1997-98)
72. Dan Fetzner (2000-02)
73. Bob Barber (2001-03)
74. Adam Kaiser (2004-06) PENN ST.-BEHREND
75. Brendan Barber (2005-08)
76. Mike Bukowski (2006-08)
77. Zach Hess (2007-09)
78. Pat Barber (2007-09)
79. Matt Harris (2010-14) MASSACHUSETTS-LOWELL
80. John "J.T." Bowen (2014-16)
81. Kenny Harden (2014-17)

The 1947 St. Peter's Cathedral squad. Seated, L to R: Rich McCormick, Bob Obert, Ozzie Lorei, Jack Palmisano, Norm Zmyslinski; Standing middle: Lou Scibetta, Pete Scibetta; Back: Coach Charlie Colvin, Jim Sanner, Bob Seyboldt, Mgr. Moskot, Herb Ellman, Bob Hamm, Father Weber.

St. Stanislaus "Eagles"
1. Joe Szczepanski (1924-25)
2. Joe Gorney (1924-27)
3. George Wozniak (1928-29)
4. James Ward (1930-31)
5. Charlie Grabowski (1934-35)
6. Frank Radziszewski (1936-37)
7. Cheslaus "Chet" Kupniewski (1942-43)
8. Ed Hyziewicz (Hunter) (1945-47) GANNON
9. Art Hilinski (1945-49)
10. Hank Glowacki (1946-48)
11. Jack Konkol (1947-50)
12. Len "Stretch" Szczypinski (1949-52)
13. Lenny Tomczak (1950-52)
14. Dan Tomczak (1952-54)
15. Bob "Clutch" Tomczak (1953-55)
16. Ziggy Mazanowski (1954-55)
17. Gene "Jiggs" Tomczak (1955-57)
18. Tom Konkol (1957-58)
19. Pat Tomczak (1957-60)
20. Paul Modzelewski (1959-60)
21. Al Lubiejewski (1960-62)
22. Ed Robasky (1961-62)
23. Eugene Tomczak (1990-93)

Seneca "Bobcats"
1. Jarret Pound (2012-13)

Sharon St. Joseph's
1. John Mehler (1928-29)
2. Hubert Davis (1928-29)

Spirit of Christ "Aces"
1. Jim Kaiser (1979-80)
2. Chuck Brower (1979-81) SIENA/MERCYHURST

Stone Mountain (GA) Stephenson High "Jaguars"
1. Anthony Easterling (2002-03)

Stoneboro (Lakeview) High "Sailors"
1. John Lyons (1928-29)

Strong Vincent High "Colonels"
1. Bob Carrick (1935-37)
2. Joe Weschler (1941-43)

Toledo (OH) Central Catholic "Leprechauns"
1. Dick Nolan (1949-51)

Villa Maria Elementary "Blue Wings"
1. Bill Speros (1987-88)
2. Noah Pelkowski (1998-2000)
3. G. T. Miller (2005-07)
4. Ryan Heidt (2005-07)
5. Dan Marz (2006-08)

Walnut Creek Middle School "Wildcats"
1. Jim Fetzner (1997-99) GROVE CITY
2. Marty Lindenberger (2004-05)
3. Phil Hampy (2008-10)
4. Jack Lindenberger (2012-15)
5. Carter Cross (2012-16)
6. Matt Falconer (2013-15)
7. Bruce Fagan (2014-17)

8. Marcus Lewkowicz (2016-17)
9. Ethan Rys (2016-17)

Wayne Middle School "Generals"
1. Anthony Pearson (2012-13)

West Philadelphia High "Speedboys"
1. Herbert "Joe" Perry (1928-30)

Westlake Middle School "Vikings"
1. Alex Greenawalt (2011-12)

Wilson Junior High/Middle School "Presidents"
1. Louis Pratt (1935-36)
2. Ralph Malina (1950-52)
3. Herb Foster (1957-59) SYRACUSE
4. Dave Paris (1959-60)
5. Doug Carter (1980-82)
6. Brian May (1985-87)
7. Jon Vincent (2002-03)
8. RaSean Thrower (2007-10)
9. Joel Nunez (2008-09)
10. Kimani Smith (2010-12)
11. Marlon Tyree (2012-14)
12. Jose Casiano (2014-16)
13. Dajon Heidelberg (2014-16)
14. Eddie Thompson (2015-16)

Yugoslavia (country of)
1. Sasha Pecarski (1988-89)
2. Dejan Milasinovic (2002-03)